Contemporary Authors ®

NEW REVISION SERIES

Explore your options!
Gale databases offered in
a variety of formats

DISKETTE/MAGNETIC TAPE

Many Gale databases are available on diskette or magnetic tape, allowing systemwide access to your most-used information sources through existing computer systems. Data can be delivered on a variety of mediums (DOS-formatted diskette, 9-track tape, 8mm data tape) and in industry-standard formats (comma-delimited, tagged, fixed-field). Retrieval software is also available with many of Gale's databases that allows you to search, display, print and download the data.

ONLINE

For your convenience, many Gale databases are available through popular online services, including DIALOG, NEXIS (Mead Data Central), Data-Star, Orbit, Questel, OCLC, I/Plus Direct, Prodigy, HOOVER and Telebase Systems.

CD-ROM

A variety of Gale titles are available on CD-ROM, offering maximum flexibility and powerful search software.

The information in this Gale
publication is also available in some
or all of the formats described here.
Your Gale Representative
will be happy to fill you in.

For information, call

GALE

Gale Research
1-800-877-GALE

ISSN 0275-7176

Contemporary

Authors®

**A Bio-Bibliographical Guide to
Current Writers in Fiction, General Nonfiction,
Poetry, Journalism, Drama, Motion Pictures,
Television, and Other Fields**

PAMELA S. DEAR
Editor

NEW REVISION SERIES
volume **49**

An ITP Information/Reference Group

I(T)P
Changing the Way the World Learns

NEW YORK • LONDON • BONN • BOSTON • DETROIT
MADRID • MELBOURNE • MEXICO CITY • PARIS
SINGAPORE • TOKYO • TORONTO • WASHINGTON
ALBANY NY • BELMONT CA • CINCINNATI OH

STAFF

Pamela S. Dear, *Editor, New Revision Series*

John D. Jorgenson, *Pre-Manuscript Coordinator*
Thomas Wiloch, *Sketchwriting Coordinator*
Deborah A. Stanley, *Post-Manuscript Coordinator*

Jeff Chapman, Kathleen Edgar, Christopher Giroux, Tom McMahon, Geri J. Speace,
Aarti Dhawan Stephens, and Janet Witalec, *Contributing Editors*

Brigham Narins, Polly A. Vedder, and Kathleen Wilson, *Associate Editors*

George H. Blair, Daniel Jones, and Ryan Reardon, *Assistant Editors*

Katherine Bailey, Suzanne Bezuk, Anne Blankenbaker, Bruce Boston, Gary Corseri,
Ken Cuthbertson, Stephen Desmond, Joan Goldsworthy, Lisa Harper, Anne Janette Johnson, Elizabeth Judd,
Anne Killheffer, Brett A. Lealand, Jim McWilliams, Robert Miltner, Julie Monahan, John Mort, Jean W. Ross,
Mary Katherine Wainwright, Michaela Swart Wilson, and Tim Winter-Damon, *Sketchwriters*

Barb Bigelow, Erika Dreifus, Conner Gorry, Laurie Collier Hillstrom, Doris Maxfield, Emily J. McMurray,
Nancy Rampson, Bryan Ryan, Pamela L. Shelton, and Kenneth R. Shepherd, *Copyeditors*

James P. Draper, *Managing Editor*

Victoria B. Cariappa, *Research Manager*

Barbara McNeil, *Research Specialist*

Michele P. Pica, Norma Sawaya, and Amy Terese Steel, *Research Associates*

Alicia Noel Biggers and Julia C. Daniel, *Research Assistants*

♾ ™ This book is printed on acid-free paper that meets the minimum requirements
of American National Standard for Information Sciences-
Permanence Paper for Printed Library Materials, ANSI Z39.48-1984.

Library of Congress Catalog Card Number 81-640179

ISBN 0-8103-9340-9
ISSN 0275-7176

Printed in the United States of America.

I(T)P™ Gale Research, an International Thomson Publishing Company.
ITP logo is a trademark under license.
10 9 8 7 6 5 4 3 2 1

Contents

Indexing note: All *Contemporary Authors New Revision Series* entries are indexed in the *Contemporary Authors* cumulative index, which is published separately and distributed with even-numbered *Contemporary Authors* original volumes and odd-numbered *Contemporary Authors New Revision Series* volumes.

As always, the most recent *Contemporary Authors* cumulative index continues to be the user's guide to the location of an individual author's listing.

Contemporary Authors
was named an
***"Outstanding
Reference Source"*** *by
the American Library
Association Reference
and Adult Services
Division after its 1962
inception.
In 1985 it was listed by
the same organization
as one of the
twenty-five most
distinguished reference
titles published in the
past twenty-five years.*

Preface

The *Contemporary Authors New Revision Series* (*CANR*) provides completely updated information on authors listed in earlier volumes of *Contemporary Authors* (*CA*). Entries for individual authors from *any* volume of *CA* may be included in a volume of the *New Revision Series*. *CANR* updates only those sketches requiring significant change.

Authors are included on the basis of specific criteria that indicate the need for significant revision. These criteria include bibliographical additions, changes in addresses or career, major awards, and personal information such as name changes or death dates. All listings in this volume have been revised or augmented in various ways. Some sketches have been extensively rewritten, and many include informative new sidelights. As always, a *CANR* listing entails no charge or obligation.

How to Get the Most out of *CA*: Use the Index

The key to locating an author's most recent entry is the *CA* cumulative index, which is published separately and distributed with even-numbered original volumes and odd-numbered revision volumes. It provides access to *all* entries in *CA* and *CANR*. Always consult the latest index to find an author's most recent entry.

For the convenience of users, the *CA* cumulative index also includes references to all entries in these Gale literary series: *Authors and Artists for Young Adults, Authors in the News, Bestsellers, Black Literature Criticism, Black Writers, Children's Literature Review, Concise Dictionary of American Literary Biography, Concise Dictionary of British Literary Biography, Contemporary Authors Autobiography Series, Contemporary Authors Bibliographical Series, Contemporary Literary Criticism, Dictionary of Literary Biography, DISCovering Authors, DISCovering Authors: British, Drama Criticism, Hispanic Literature Criticism, Hispanic Writers, Junior DISCovering Authors, Major Authors and Illustrators for Children and Young Adults, Major 20th-Century Writers, Native North American Literature, Poetry Criticism, Short Story Criticism, Something about the Author, Something about the Author Autobiography Series, Twentieth-Century Literary Criticism, World Literature Criticism,* and *Yesterday's Authors of Books for Children.*

A Sample Index Entry:

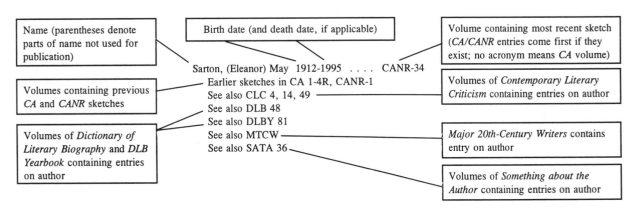

For the most recent *CA* information on Sarton, users should refer to Volume 34 of the *New Revision Series,* as designated by "CANR-34"; if that volume is unavailable, refer to CANR-1. And if CANR-1 is unavailable, refer to CA 1-4R, published in 1967, for Sarton's First Revision entry.

How Are Entries Compiled?

The editors make every effort to secure new information directly from the authors. Copies of all sketches in selected *CA* and *CANR* volumes previously published are routinely sent to listees at their last-known addresses, and returns from these authors are then assessed. For deceased writers, or those who fail to reply to requests for data, we consult other reliable biographical sources, such as those indexed in Gale's *Biography and Genealogy Master Index,* and bibliographical sources, such as *National Union Catalog, LC MARC,* and *British National Bibliography.* Further details come from published interviews, feature stories, and book reviews, and often the authors' publishers supply material.

* Indicates that a listing has been compiled from secondary sources believed to be reliable but has not been personally verified for this edition by the author sketched.

What Kinds of Information Does an Entry Provide?

Sketches in *CANR* contain the following biographical and bibliographical information:

- **Entry heading:** the most complete form of author's name, plus any pseudonyms or name variations used for writing

- **Personal information:** author's date and place of birth, family data, educational background, political and religious affiliations, and hobbies and leisure interests

- **Addresses:** author's home, office, or agent's addresses as available

- **Career summary:** name of employer, position, and dates held for each career post; resume of other vocational achievements; military service

- **Membership information:** professional, civic, and other association memberships and any official posts held

- **Awards and honors:** military and civic citations, major prizes and nominations, fellowships, grants, and honorary degrees

- **Writings:** a comprehensive, chronological list of titles, publishers, dates of original publication and revised editions, and production information for plays, television scripts, and screenplays

- **Adaptations:** a list of films, plays, and other media which have been adapted from the author's work

- **Work in progress:** current or planned projects, with dates of completion and/or publication, and expected publisher, when known

- **Sidelights:** a biographical portrait of the author's development; information about the critical reception of the author's works; revealing comments, often by the author, on personal interests, aspirations, motivations, and thoughts on writing

- **Biographical and critical sources:** a list of books and periodicals in which additional information on an author's life and/or writings appears

Related Titles in the *CA* Series

Contemporary Authors Autobiography Series complements *CA* original and revised volumes with specially commissioned autobiographical essays by important current authors, illustrated with personal photographs they provide. Common topics include their motivations for writing, the people and experiences that shaped their careers, the rewards they derive from their work, and their impressions of the current literary scene.

Contemporary Authors Bibliographical Series surveys writings by and about important American authors since World War II. Each volume concentrates on a specific genre and features approximately ten writers; entries list works written by and about the author and contain a bibliographical essay discussing the merits and deficiencies of major critical and scholarly studies in detail.

Available in Electronic Formats

CD-ROM. Full-text bio-bibliographic entries from the entire *CA* series, covering approximately 100,000 writers, are available on CD-ROM through lease and purchase plans. The disc combines entries from the *CA, CANR,* and *Contemporary Authors Permanent Series* (*CAP*) print series to provide the most recent author listing. It can be searched by name, title, subject/genre, and personal data, and by using boolean logic. The disc will be updated every six months. For more information, call 1-800-877-GALE.

Magnetic Tape. *CA* is available for licensing on magnetic tape in a fielded format. Either the complete database or a custom selection of entries may be ordered. The database is available for internal data processing and nonpublishing purposes only. For more information, call 1-800-877-GALE.

Online. The *Contemporary Authors* database is made available online to libraries and their patrons through online public access catalog (OPAC) vendors. Currently, *CA* is offered through Ameritech Library Services' Vista Online (formerly Dynix), and is expected to become available through CARL Systems and The Library Corporation. More OPAC vendor offerings will follow soon.

GaleNet. *CA* is available on a subscription basis through GaleNet, a new online information resource that features an easy-to-use end-user interface, the powerful search capabilities of the BRS/Search retrieval software, and ease of access through the World-Wide Web. For more information, call Melissa Kolehmainen at 1-800-877-GALE, ext. 1598.

Suggestions Are Welcome

The editors welcome comments and suggestions from users on any aspects of the *CA* series. If readers would like to recommend authors whose entries should appear in future volumes of the series, they are cordially invited to write: The Editors, *Contemporary Authors,* 835 Penobscot Bldg., Detroit, MI 48226-4094; call toll-free at 1-800-347-GALE; or fax to 1-313-961-6599.

CA Numbering System and Volume Update Chart

Occasionally questions arise about the *CA* numbering system and which volumes, if any, can be discarded. Despite numbers like "29-32R," "97-100" and "148," the entire *CA* series consists of only 124 physical volumes with the publication of *CA New Revision Series* Volume 49. The following charts note changes in the numbering system and cover design, and indicate which volumes are essential for the most complete, up-to-date coverage.

CA First Revision
- 1-4R through 41-44R (11 books)
  Cover: Brown with black and gold trim.
  There will be no further First Revision volumes because revised entries are now being handled exclusively through the more efficient *New Revision Series* mentioned below.

CA Original Volumes
- 45-48 through 97-100 (14 books)
  Cover: Brown with black and gold trim.
- 101 through 148 (48 books)
  Cover: Blue and black with orange bands.
  The same as previous *CA* original volumes but with a new, simplified numbering system and new cover design.

CA Permanent Series
- *CAP*-1 and *CAP*-2 (2 books)
  Cover: Brown with red and gold trim.
  There will be no further *Permanent Series* volumes because revised entries are now being handled exclusively through the more efficient *New Revision Series* mentioned below.

CA New Revision Series
- *CANR*-1 through *CANR*-49 (49 books)
  Cover: Blue and black with green bands.
  Includes only sketches requiring extensive changes; **sketches are taken from any previously published *CA*, *CAP*, or *CANR* volume.**

If You Have:	**You May Discard:**
CA First Revision Volumes 1-4R through 41-44R **and** *CA Permanent Series* Volumes 1 and 2	*CA* Original Volumes 1, 2, 3, 4 and Volumes 5-6 through 41-44
CA Original Volumes 45-48 through 97-100 **and** 101 through 148	**NONE:** These volumes will not be superseded by corresponding revised volumes. Individual entries from these and all other volumes appearing in the left column of this chart may be revised and included in the various volumes of the *New Revision Series*.
CA New Revision Series Volumes *CANR*-1 through *CANR*-49	**NONE:** The *New Revision Series* does not replace any single volume of *CA*. Instead, volumes of *CANR* include entries from many previous *CA* series volumes. All *New Revision Series* volumes must be retained for full coverage.

A Sampling of Authors and Media People
Featured in This Volume

Toni Cade Bambara

A respected civil rights activist and professor, Bambara is the author of novels including *The Salt Eaters* and editor of anthologies such as *Tales and Stories for Black Folks.*

John Barth

National Book Award winner Barth is known for intellectually challenging fiction such as *The Floating Opera, The Sot-Weed Factor,* and *Chimera.*

Michael Bond

British author Bond is the creator of the "Paddington" series of children's books, begun in 1958, as well as other children's series and a mystery series for adults.

Antonio Buero Vallejo

Spanish-born playwright and translator Buero Vallejo authored *Historia de una escalera,* described as comparable in its influence on Spanish society to the impact of Arthur Miller's *Death of a Salesman* on U.S. audiences.

J. P. Donleavy

An American-born Irish writer and playwright, Donleavy is best known for *The Ginger Man,* a novel later adapted into a play and deemed a modern classic.

Kazuo Ishiguro

Japanese-born Ishiguro is considered one of the foremost British authors of his generation for works including *A Pale View of Hills* and *The Remains of the Day.* He received the Order of the British Empire in 1995.

Emmanuel Le Roy Ladurie

One of the most celebrated historians of the Western world, Le Roy Ladurie is associated with the Annales school of thought. He is best-known for *Montaillou* and *Carnaval de Romans,* both historical examinations of small French towns.

Thomas McGuane

McGuane's novels, particularly the National Book Award nominee *Ninety-two in the Shade,* often draw comparisons to those of Ernest Hemingway for the authors' similar themes and locales.

James Merrill

Merrill twice received the National Book Award--in 1967 for *Nights and Days* and 1979 for *Mirabell: Books of Number*--and was awarded the 1976 Pulitzer Prize for the poetry collection *Divine Comedies.*

Bernard Slade Newbound

The author better known as Bernard Slade created the television show *The Partridge Family* before switching to plays. The film adaptation of his play *Same Time, Next Year* earned Slade an Academy Award nomination.

Bernard Pomerance

Pomerance's best-known work is the play *The Elephant Man,* based on the true story of Englishman John Merrick, for which the author received numerous awards including a Tony and an Obie.

Sonia Sanchez

An American poet and playwright, Sanchez's works include the poetry collections *We a BaddDDD People* and *Homegirls & Handgrenades* and the play *Uh Huh; But How Do It Free Us?*

George P. Shultz

Former U.S. Secretary of State Shultz has written several texts on labor relations and economics, including *The Dynamics of a Labor Market* and *Economic Policy beyond the Headlines.*

Kurt Vonnegut Jr.

A prolific fiction writer and playwright, Vonnegut explores the ways people wreak havoc on themselves and the world in novels such as *Slaughterhouse Five* and *Deadeye Dick.*

Alice Walker

Walker has written novels including the popular and highly lauded *The Color Purple* and *The Temple of My Familiar,* as well as poetry, children's works, and nonfiction.

Morris L. West

Australian novelist West depicts protagonists who represent the Catholic church in suspense novels such as *The Shoes of the Fisherman* and *The Clowns of God.*

Contemporary Authors®

NEW REVISION SERIES

*Indicates that a listing has been compiled from secondary sources believed to be reliable but has not been personally verified for this edition by the author sketched.

ABRAHAMS, Roger D(avid) 1933-

PERSONAL: Born June 12, 1933, in Philadelphia, PA; son of Robert David and Florence (Kohn) Abrahams; married third wife, Janet Anderson, March 13, 1977; children: (first marriage) Rodman David, Lisa. *Education:* Swarthmore College, B.A., 1955; Columbia University, M.A., 1958; University of Pennsylvania, Ph.D., 1961.

ADDRESSES: Home—1648 Chattin Road, Laverock, PA 19038. *Office*—University of Pennsylvania, Philadelphia, PA 19104-3325.

CAREER: University of Texas at Austin, instructor, 1960-63, assistant professor, 1963-66, associate professor, 1966-69, professor of English and anthropology, 1969-79, chairman of English department, 1974-79, associate director, Center for Intercultural Studies in Folklore and Oral History, 1968-69, director, African and Afro-American Research Institute, beginning 1969; Claremont Colleges, Claremont, CA, Alexander H. Kenan Professor of Humanities and Anthropology at Pitzer College and Scripps College, 1979-85; University of Pennsylvania, Philadelphia, professor of folklore and folklife, 1985—, Hum Rosen professor of folklore and folklife, 1989—. Visiting faculty member, Folklore Institute, Indiana University, 1967, 1975; Andersen Professor of American Studies, Carleton College, 1969; Walker-Ames Professor, University of Washington, 1992; Joseph Schick lecturer, Indiana State University, 1993—. Member of Social Science Research Council Committee on Afro-American Societies and Cultures, Texas Education Agency Consulting Committee on Confluence of Texas Cultures, and selection committee for the John Simon Guggenheim Foundation.

MEMBER: International Society for Folk Narrative Research, American Folklore Society (president, 1978-79), Phi Beta Kappa.

AWARDS, HONORS: Guggenheim fellow, 1965-66; National Institute of Mental Health fellow, 1968; American Folklore Society fellow, 1970; National Humanities Institute fellow, University of Chicago, 1976-77; lifetime achievement in scholarship and service to the profession, American Folklore Society, 1989; Finnish Scientific Academy folklore fellow, 1990—.

WRITINGS:

NONFICTION

Deep Down in the Jungle: Negro Narrative Folklore from the Streets of Philadelphia, Folklore Associates, 1964, revised edition, Aldine (Hawthorne, NY), 1970.

(With George W. Foss, Jr.) *Anglo-American Folksong Style,* Prentice-Hall, 1968.

Positively Black, Prentice-Hall (Englewood Cliffs, NJ), 1970.

Deep the Water, Shallow the Shore: Three Essays on Shantying in the West Indies (music transcribed by Linda Sobin), University of Texas Press (Austin, TX), 1974.

Talking Black, Newbury House (Rowley, MA), 1976.

Afro-American Folk Culture: An Annotated Bibliography, Institute for the Study of Human Issues (Philadelphia, PA), 1977.

Between the Living and the Dead: Riddles Which Tell Stories, Academia Scientarium Fennica, 1980.

The Man-of-Words in the West Indies, Johns Hopkins University Press (Baltimore, MD), 1983.

(Compiler) *African Folktales: Traditional Stories of the Black World,* Pantheon (New York City), 1983.

Singing the Master: The Emergence of African-American Culture in the Plantation South, Pantheon, 1992.

EDITOR

Jump Rope Rhymes: A Dictionary, University of Texas Press, 1969.

A Singer and Her Songs; Almeda Riddle's Book of Ballads,
Louisiana State University Press (Baton Rouge, LA),
1970.
(With Rudolph C. Troike) *Language and Cultural Diversity in American Education,* Prentice-Hall, 1972.
(With John F. Szwed) *Discovering Afro-America,* E. J.
Brill, 1975.
(With Lois Rankin) *Counting-Out Rhymes: A Dictionary,*
University of Texas Press, 1980.
(With Richard Bauman) *And Other Neighborly Names,*
University of Texas Press, 1981.
(With Szwed) *After Africa,* Yale University Press (New
Haven, CT), 1983.
*Afro-American Folktales: Stories from Black Traditions in
the New World,* Pantheon, 1985.
(With Goldstein and Hand) *By Land and by Sea,* Legacy
Books (Hatboro, PA), 1985.
The Folkways/Smithsonian Book of American Folksong,
HarperCollins (New York City), in press.

SIDELIGHTS: Roger D. Abrahams told *CA* that he is
"concerned with the impact of perceived traditions on the
creation of new nations out of the ashes of old empires. In
the United States, we have yet to answer some of the largest questions of cultural history as they bore in on us
today: things like what are the cultural implications of a
nation which has generated powerful forms of popular
culture over the first 220 years in which there is constant
imitation across cultural boundaries, whites dressing,
dancing, singing, acting the part of slaves and Indians? It
is such popular culture forms as minstrel hall songs and
dances, medicine shows, wild west shows, and the more
recent jazz, blues, rap, blue grass music, that have been exported throughout the world as being typically American.
This runs in counterpoint to the social problems associated with the populations out of which these forms
emerged. My latest work attempts to lay bare the history
of this exchange of expressive forms and styles."

BIOGRAPHICAL/CRITICAL SOURCES:

PERIODICALS

Los Angeles Times Book Review, September 11, 1983.
New York Times Book Review, November 20, 1983.
Times Literary Supplement, December 19, 1980.
Village Voice, August 6, 1985.
Washington Post Book World, September 4, 1983.

*　　　　*　　　　*

ADAMEC, Ludwig W(arren) 1924-

PERSONAL: Born March 10, 1924, in Vienna, Austria;
United States citizen; son of Ludwig and Emma (Kubitschek) Adamec; married Ena Vargas, June 9, 1962 (di-

vorced May 8, 1975), married Rahella Malikyar, November 27, 1987; children: Eric. *Education:* University of California, Los Angeles, California, B.A., 1960, M.A., 1961,
Ph.D., 1966.

ADDRESSES: Home—3931 East Whittier, Tucson, AZ
85711. *Office*—Department of Near Eastern Studies, University of Arizona, Tucson, AZ 85721.

CAREER: University of California, Los Angeles, CA,
postdoctoral fellow, 1966, lecturer in history, 1966-67;
University of Arizona, Tucson, AZ, assistant professor,
1967-69, associate professor, 1969-74, professor of Near
Eastern Studies, 1974—, director of Near Eastern Center,
1975-85. Research associate, University of Michigan,
summer, 1967, and University of California, Los Angeles,
1968; Fulbright professor in Iran, 1973-74; visiting professor and Fulbright consultant, University of Baluchistan,
Quetta, Pakistan, 1981-82. Member of board of governors,
American Research Center in Egypt, Center for Arabic
Study Abroad, American Research Institute in Turkey,
and American Research Institute in Yemen, 1974-81; vice
president, American Institute of Iranian Studies, 1979-81;
chief of Afghanistan Services, Voice of America, 1986-87;
steering committee of the International Institute for Asian
Studies, Stockholm, Sweden; board, Centre de Recherches
et d'Etudes Documentaires sur Afghanistan, Paris,
France.

MEMBER: Middle East Studies Association of North
America (fellow), Middle East Institute, American Association of University Professors.

AWARDS, HONORS: Fulbright-Hays award for research
in India and Afghanistan, 1964-65; Social Science Research Council grant, summer, 1968, 1975, and 1979;
Foundation for the Humanities grant, summer, 1978.

WRITINGS:

Afghanistan, 1900-1923: A Diplomatic History, University
of California Press (Berkeley, CA), 1967.
(Editor with George L. Gassmuck, and contributor) *Afghanistan: Some New Approaches,* Center for Near
Eastern and North African Studies, University of
Michigan (Ann Arbor), 1969.
(Editor) *Political and Historical Gazetteer of Afghanistan,*
Akademische Druck- und Verlagsanstalt (Graz, Austria), Volume 1: *Badakhshan and Northeastern Afghanistan,* 1972, Volume 2: *Farah and Southwestern
Afghanistan,* 1973, Volume 3: *Herat and Northwestern Afghanistan,* 1975, Volume 4: *Mazar-i-Sharif and
North-Central Afghanistan,* 1978, Volume 5: *Kandahar and South-Central Afghanistan,* 1979, Volume 6:
Kabul and Southwestern Afghanistan, 1985.

Afghanistan's Foreign Affairs in the 20th Century: Relations with Russia, Germany, and Britain, University of Arizona Press (Tucson), 1974.

(Editor) *Who's Who in Afghanistan,* Akademische Druck- und Verlagsanstalt, 1975.

Historical Gazetteer of Iran, Akademische Druck- und Verlagsanstalt, Volume 1: *Tehran and Northwestern Iran,* 1976, Volume 2: *Meshed and Northeastern Iran,* 1981, Volume 3: *Zahedan and Southeastern Iran,* 1987, Volume 4: *Ahvaz and Shiraz and Southwestern Iran,* 1988.

Supplement to the Who's Who of Afghanistan: Democratic Republic of Afghanistan, Akademische Druck- und Verlagsanstalt, 1979.

Biographical Dictionary of Contemporary Afghanistan, Akademische Druck- und Verlagsanstalt, 1987.

Historical Dictionary of Afghanistan, Scarecrow (Metuchen, NJ), 1991.

Also associate editor of *Afghanistan Journal,* 1974-76.

WORK IN PROGRESS: Historical Dictionary of Afghan Wars; a history of political development in Afghanistan, 1880-1987.

SIDELIGHTS: Ludwig W. Adamec has lived in Afghanistan, India, Iran, Europe, and the Arab Middle East. He is competent in German, French, Spanish, Persian, Arabic, and cognate languages.

*　　*　　*

ADLER, Bill
See ADLER, William

*　　*　　*

ADLER, William 1929-
(Bill Adler; Jay David, a pseudonym)

PERSONAL: Born May 14, 1929, in New York, NY; son of William J. (a display man) and Belle Adler; married Gloria Goodman, February 26, 1956; children: William, Diane. *Education:* Attended Brooklyn College (now Brooklyn College of the City University of New York), 1947-51.

ADDRESSES: Home—New York, NY.

CAREER: Full-time writer. Member of New York City Youth Board. *Military service:* U.S. Army, 1951-53.

MEMBER: Radio and Television Executives Society (former member of board of governors).

WRITINGS:

UNDER NAME BILL ADLER

(With Irving Settel) *Congratulations, It's Your Birthday!,* Citadel (New York City), 1959.

(With Settel) *Congratulations, You're a Grandparent!,* Citadel, 1959.

(With Settel) *Congratulations, You're Married!,* Citadel, 1959.

(With Bob Reisner) *Western on Wry,* Citadel, 1960.

(With Reisner) *What Goes on Here?,* Citadel, 1963.

(With Sayre Ross) *Pope Paul in the United States: His Mission for Peace on Earth,* Hawthorn (New York City), 1965.

(With Arnie Kogen) *What to Name Your Jewish Baby,* Dutton (New York City), 1966.

(With Ross) *Medicare and You,* New American Library (New York City), 1966.

Jewish Wit and Wisdom, Dell (New York City), 1969.

How to Be Funny in Your Own Lifetime, Playboy Press, 1973.

(With Jeffrey Feinman) *Mel Brooks: The Irreverent Funnyman,* Playboy Press, 1973.

(With Feinman) *Woody Allen: Clown Prince of American Humor,* Pinnacle Books (New York City), 1975.

The Kennedy Kids, Playboy Press, 1976.

A Quiz Book: Interesting Facts That Inform and Entertain, illustrations by Ed Malsberg, Grosset & Dunlap, 1977.

Bill Adler's Love Letters to Elvis, Grosset, 1978.

(With Gary Wagner) *The Second Time Is Better,* Playboy Press, 1979.

(With Wagner) *When I Fall in Love,* Playboy Press, 1979.

The Kennedy Children: Triumphs and Tragedies, F. Watts (New York City), 1980.

(With Bess Myerson) *The I [Love] New York Diet,* Morrow (New York City), 1982.

Inside Publishing, Bobbs-Merrill (New York City), 1982.

(With Phyllis George) *The I [Love] America Diet,* Morrow, 1983.

(With Suzy Chaffee) *The I [Love] NY Fitness Book,* Morrow, 1983.

Dear Grandma, illustrated by Bettye Beach, T. Nelson (Schooleys Mountain, NJ), 1985.

Bill Adler's Chance of a Lifetime, Warner, 1985.

(With Bill Adler, Jr.) *The Wit and Wisdom of Wall Street,* Dow Jones-Irwin (Homewood, IL), 1985.

Ronnie and Nancy: A Very Special Love Story, Crown (New York City), 1985.

The Cosby Wit: His Life and Humor, Quill, 1986.

Baseball Wit, Crown (New York City), 1986.

What Is a Cat?: For Everyone Who Has Ever Loved a Cat, illustrations by Douglas Florian, Morrow, 1987.

Fred Astaire: A Wonderful Life, Carroll & Graf (New York City), 1987.

Sinatra, the Man and the Myth: An Unauthorized Biography, New American Library, 1987.

The Generals: The New American Heroes, Avon (New York City), 1991.

(With Heather Harney) *The Anti-Cancer, Heart Attack, Stroke Diet,* T. Nelson, 1991.

Do You Remember the 50s?, Avon, 1992.

Do You Remember the 60s?, Avon, 1992.

(With Bruce Cassiday) *The World of Jay Leno: His Humor and His Life,* Carol Publishing, 1992.

(With Peggy Robin) *Outwitting Toddlers and Other Small Human Beings: Real Advice from Real Parents,* Lowell House, 1993.

The Letterman Wit: His Life and Humor, Carrol & Graf, 1994.

(With wife, Gloria Adler) *Marriage's Little Advice Book,* Morrow, 1994.

First, Kill all the Lawyers: Legal Proverbs, Epitaphs, Jokes, Anecdotes, Carol, 1994.

Outwitting the Neighbors, Simon & Schuster (New York City), 1994.

EDITOR, COMPILER; UNDER NAME BILL ADLER

Letters from Camp, Chilton (Radnor, PA), 1961.

Boys Are Very Funny People, Morrow, 1962.

Kids' Letters to President Kennedy, illustrated by Louis Darling, Morrow, 1962.

Love Letters to the Beatles, Putnam (New York City), 1964.

Dear President Johnson, illustrated by Charles M. Schulz, Morrow, 1964.

John F. Kennedy, *The Kennedy Wit,* Citadel, 1964.

John F. Kennedy and the Young People of America, McKay (New York City), 1965.

Love Letters to the Mets, Simon & Schuster, 1965.

Winston Churchill, *The Churchill Wit,* Coward, 1965.

Lyndon B. Johnson, *The Johnson Humor,* Simon & Schuster, 1965.

Kennedy, *More Kennedy Wit,* Citadel, 1965.

The Common Sense Wisdom of Three First Ladies, Citadel, 1966.

Dear Beatles, Wonder Books, 1966.

Dear Internal Revenue, Doubleday (New York City), 1966.

Dear 007, illustrated by Paul Bacon, Simon & Schuster, 1966.

Dear Senator Kennedy, Dodd, 1966.

Kids' Letters to the F.B.I., illustrated by Arnold Roth, Prentice-Hall, 1966.

Letters to Smokey Bear, Wonder Books, 1966.

More Letters from Camp, New American Library, 1966.

(With Ross) *The Pope John Album: His Life, His Family, His Career, His Words,* Hawthorn, 1966.

Presidential Wit from Washington to Johnson, Trident, 1966.

Adlai E. Stevenson, *The Stevenson Wit,* Doubleday, 1966.

Graffiti, Pyramid, 1967.

Letters from Vietnam, Dutton, 1967.

Letters to the Air Force on UFOs, Dell, 1967.

Love Letters to the Monkees, Popular Library, 1967.

Letters to the Editor, Doubleday, 1967.

Billy Graham and others, *My Favorite Funny Story,* Four Winds (Bristol, FL), 1967.

Washington—A Reader: The National Capitol as Seen through the Eyes of Thomas Jefferson and Others, Meredith, 1967.

(And author of introduction) *The Washington Wits,* Macmillan (New York City), 1967.

Graham, *The Wit and Wisdom of Billy Graham,* Random House (New York City), 1967.

(With Ross) *Astronaut Exercise Book,* New American Library, 1967.

Children's Letters to Santa Claus, Simon & Schuster, 1967.

Kennedy, *The Complete Kennedy Wit,* Citadel, 1967.

Prescription: Laughter—An Anthology of Medical Merriment, Harcourt (San Diego), 1968.

Funniest Stories for Grownups Only, Citadel, 1968.

A New Day: Robert F. Kennedy, New American Library, 1968.

Israel: A Reader, Chilton, 1968.

Fulton J. Sheen, *The Wit and Wisdom of Bishop Fulton J. Sheen,* Prentice-Hall, 1968.

Bridge Players Write the Funniest Letters to Charles H. Goren, Doubleday, 1968.

Dear Dating Computer, Bobbs-Merrill, 1968.

Dear Rabbi, Morrow, 1968.

Eugene J. McCarthy, *The McCarthy Wit,* Fawcett (New York City), 1969.

Richard M. Nixon, *The Wit and Humor of Richard Nixon,* Popular Library, 1969.

(With Catherine J. Greene) *The Wall Street Reader,* World Publishing, 1970.

Funny Letters from Famous People, illustrated by Al Kilgore, Four Winds, 1970.

Speaker's Complete Library of Wit and Humor, Parker Publishing (New York City), 1970.

Hip Kids' Letters from Camp, Morrow, 1971.

Kids' Letters to Spiro Agnew, Geis, 1971.

Letters to Wall Street, World Publishing, 1971.

(With Greene) *Profits in Real Estate: A Reader,* World Publishing, 1971.

Letters to the Obstetrician, St. Martin's (New York City), 1972.

Still More Letters from Camp, New American Library, 1973.

The Illustrated Book of World Records, Grosset, 1974.

Firsts, Facts, and Feats, Grosset, 1975.

World's Worst Riddles and Jokes, Grosset, 1976.

Again, More Letters from Camp, Manor (Staten Island), 1976.

Jimmy Carter, *The Wit and Wisdom of Jimmy Carter,* Citadel, 1977.

Dear Amy Carter, Playboy Press, 1977.

Kids' Letters to President Carter, Grosset, 1978.

Sports Question and Answer Book, Grosset, 1978.

The Runner's Liar's Diary, Grosset, 1979.

Dear Pastor, Thomas Nelson, 1980.

Dear Lord, illustrated by Bettye Beach, T. Nelson, 1982.

Please Save My World, illustrations by Candy Jernigan, Arbor House (New York City), 1984.

Motherhood, a Celebration, Carroll & Graf, 1987.

(With David Gallen) *Great Lawyer Stories: From Courthouse to Jailhouse, Tall Tales, Jokes, and Anecdotes,* Carol Publishing, 1992.

(With Robin) *The Wit and Wisdom of Abraham Lincoln,* Carol Publishing, 1993.

(Compiler with G. Adler) *The Joys of Having a Child: The Wisest, Wittiest, and Most Wonderful Things Ever Said about Having One,* Morrow, 1993.

Children's Letters to Santa Claus, Carol, 1993.

(With Robin) *Outwitting Toddlers and Other Small Human Beings: Real Advice from Real Parents,* illustrations by Loel Barr, Lowell House, 1993.

Children's Letters to Socks: Kids Write to America's "First Cat", Carol, 1994.

(With Adler, Jr.) *Ross Perot: An American Maverick Speaks Out,* Carol, 1994.

Kid's Letters from Camp, Carol, 1994.

CREATOR; UNDER NAME BILL ADLER

Thomas Chastain, *Who Killed the Robins Family?: And Where, and When, and How, and Why, Did They Die?,* Morrow, 1983.

Chastain, *The Revenge of the Robins Family,* Morrow, 1984.

Fran Tarkenton with Herb Resnicow, *Murder at the Super Bowl,* Morrow, 1986.

(Author of introductory note) Chastain and others, *Murder in Manhattan,* Morrow, 1986.

David R. Slavitt, *The Agent,* Doubleday, 1986.

Chastain, *The Picture-Perfect Murders,* photographs by Marjorie Dressler, Morrow, 1987.

Jon L. Breen and others, *Murder in Los Angeles,* Morrow, 1987.

The Adams Round Table, *A Body Is Found,* Wynwood, 1990.

Cassiday, *Murder Game: There's a $10,000 Reward for Solving the Murder; It Could Be Yours!* (novel), Carroll & Graf, 1991.

Cassiday, *Who Should Marry Melissa,* Carol, 1994.

UNDER PSEUDONYM JAY DAVID

The Young Fords, Award Books, 1975.

Autocize, Morrow, 1979.

The Meeting Book: Never Be Lonely Again, Cornerstone Press (St. Louis), 1979.

How to Play the Moonlighting Game, Facts on File (New York City), 1983.

Inside Joan Collins: A Biography, Carroll & Graf, 1988.

EDITOR; UNDER PSEUDONYM JAY DAVID

The Flying Saucer Reader, New American Library, 1967.

The Kennedy Reader, Bobbs-Merrill, 1967.

Growing Up Black, Morrow, 1968.

Letters from Israel: The Making of a Nation, 1948-1968, introduction by Leon Uris, Coward, 1968.

The Weight of the Evidence: The Warren Report and Its Critics, Meredith, 1968.

Growing Up Jewish, Morrow, 1969.

Flying Saucers Have Arrived!, World Publishing, 1970.

(With Mel Watkins) *To Be a Black Woman: Portraits in Fact and Fiction,* Morrow, 1971.

(With Greene) *Black Roots: An Anthology,* Lothrop (New York City), 1971.

(With Helise Harrington) *Growing Up African,* Morrow, 1971.

(With Elaine Crane) *Living Black in White America,* Morrow, 1971.

Black Joy, Cowles, 1971.

(With Crane) *The Black Soldier: From the American Revolution to Vietnam,* Morrow, 1971.

Black Defiance: Black Profiles in Courage, Morrow, 1972.

The American Indian: The First Victim, Morrow, 1972.

Growing Up Black: From Slave Days to the Present: Twenty-five African-Americans Reveal the Trials and Triumphs of Their Childhoods, Avon, 1992.

Also writer for the television programs *Candid Camera* and *Tex and Jinx.*

SIDELIGHTS: Although William Adler has published books on a variety of subjects, he probably is best known for his books reflecting the wit and humor of famous people. In most cases, Adler compiles a book by selecting and editing quotations and anecdotes of noteworthy individuals. Many critics feel that he shows his readers the human side of a celebrity—a side many people seldom have the opportunity to see. He usually accomplishes this goal through the use of humor. For example, a reviewer for *Time* writes that *The Stevenson Wit* "reminds readers that [Adlai] Stevenson was a singularly lighthearted and amusing man. There is, for example, his rallying call during the 1952 presidential campaign: 'Eggheads unite—you have nothing to lose but your yolks.' . . . Or the comment he made in 1960 when he was caught in a traffic jam at the Washington airport as Charles de Gaulle arrived: 'It seems my fate is always to be getting in the way of national heroes.' "

Other popular books edited by Adler are the collections of letters usually written to a well-known person or institution. Although humor is still a key factor in these books, serious problems are also explored by the authors. In a review of *Kids' Letters to President Carter* published in *Library Journal,* Ruth C. Mitchell explains that "Adler presents a selection of 335 preteenagers' letters written to President Carter during 1977, his first year in office. The letters are candid, friendly, full of unintentional chuckle-getters and insights. The kids offer advice on family and international problems, ask nosy questions. . . . But the book is more than just humorous. It reflects the interests and concerns of the children of this era . . . . Today's letter-writers seem more concerned with internal affairs: the lack of jobs and money, high taxes and prices, the energy crisis, women's rights, etc."

A number of critics have also recognized Adler's ability to handle the more serious topics confronted in these letters with understanding and sensitivity. Even in the political *Letters from Vietnam,* Adler shows us life through the eyes of others so that we may see the situation more clearly, understanding the various elements involved with the subjects under exploration. Orville Prescott writes in the *Saturday Review* that *Letters from Vietnam* is "an interesting and quietly moving book [which] . . . lets the men on the spot speak for themselves. They do so frankly, bitterly, eloquently. The result is unpretentious and almost casual, but a genuine contribution to the literature of war. . . . [The] different points of view make *Letters from Vietnam* provocative." And a writer for *Choice* explains that "accurately mirrored in these authentic, not written for publication, expressions of feeling and opinion is the national confusion about America's purposes in and justification for continued military involvement in what is essentially an Asiatic war. . . . [It is of value] especially because of its compiler's successful efforts to avoid one-sidedness on a most disputatious issue."

Having created a wealth of book ideas for himself to write, Adler began generating ideas in the 1980s for murder mysteries that were written by others. *Who Killed the Robins Family?: And Where, and When, and How, and Why, Did They Die?,* which was masterminded by Adler and written by Thomas Chastain, offered a $10,000 award to the reader who solved a series of crimes that led to the murder of the eight Robinses. Carolyn Banks, who reviewed this mystery novel for the *Washington Post Book World,* com-

ments: "In any case, this is obviously more gimmick than book, but it's a good gimmick. I'm even tempted to predict that *Who Killed the Robins Family?* will go on to replace the Parker Brothers' parlor game, 'Clue,' as the gag gift for mystery buffs at Christmastime." Of the sequel, *The Revenge of the Robins Family,* which again offered a cash reward for solving the murder mysteries, Cindy Lieberman writes in the *Los Angeles Times Book Review:* "This all reeks more of a marketing gimmick than an exercise in murder mystery writing, but mystery buffs and puzzle fans with the patience to wait nearly a year for solutions will certainly find it fun."

An agent and book packager as well as an author, Adler has written about the business side of books, notably in *Inside Publishing,* where he offered anecdotes and accounts of the publishing industry. Michele Slung criticizes *Inside Publishing* in the *Washington Post Book World,* noting that the book contributes to the widespread industry problems that it describes. She writes: "Full of conflicting advice, repetitious maxims, simplistic thinking and bulging at the seams with dropped names (from Buster Crabbe to William French Smith), it's practically a textbook example of what an unedited manuscript might read like." Meanwhile, Edwin McDowell, writing in the *New York Times,* finds at least one of Adler's anecdotes particularly illuminating. Adler recounts how Random House refused to publish *The Kennedy Wit,* a collection of public remarks made by the late President John F. Kennedy, when Kennedy's press secretary requested that the book not be published. More than 35 publishers rejected the manuscript before it was ultimately purchased by Citadel Press; Adler's *The Kennedy Wit* went on to enjoy more than six months on the *New York Times* best sellers list.

Adler is well known for his business sense: his books are timely and cover a wide range of topics. For instance, in the 1980s, he wrote a book about becoming a successful entrepreneur, titled *Bill Adler's Chance of a Lifetime.* Like *Who Killed the Robins Family?,* Adler offered a $25,000 prize to the reader who entered the best new business idea embodying the principles of *Chance of a Lifetime;* in order to enter participants paid a $1 processing fee. Allan Cox, reviewing this book for the *Los Angeles Times Book Review,* deems it a success: "Early on, the book is informative on the entrepreneurial spirit of the times and engrossing as Adler cites cases of people who have taken the plunge. The lessons to be drawn from their varying fates are valuable."

BIOGRAPHICAL/CRITICAL SOURCES:

PERIODICALS

Best Sellers, January 1, 1970.
Books, September, 1967.
Choice, November, 1967; June, 1969.

Globe & Mail (Toronto), September 1, 1984; December 20, 1986.

Harper's, December, 1964.

Library Journal, January 15, 1966; March 1, 1970; April 15, 1978.

Los Angeles Times, February 4, 1983.

Los Angeles Times Book Review, December 9, 1984; October 20, 1985; February 9, 1992.

New York Times, May 21, 1982.

New York Times Book Review, November 2, 1986, p. 33.

Publishers Weekly, January 21, 1983.

Saturday Review, April 29, 1967.

Show Business, March 28, 1970.

Time, February 4, 1966.

Times (London), December 10, 1964.

Village Voice Literary Supplement, July, 1988.

Washington Post Book World, September 5, 1982; August 30, 1983; September 28, 1985.*

* * *

ALDEN, Sue
See FRANCIS, Dorothy Brenner

* * *

ANGELL, Judie
See GABERMAN, Judie Angell

* * *

AR C'HALAN, Reun
See GALAND, Rene

* * *

ARRICK, Fran
See GABERMAN, Judie Angell

* * *

AVANZINI, John F. 1936-

PERSONAL: Born May 21, 1936, in Surinam; immigrated to United States; son of Christian M. and Rona Evilin Barrow (Zaal) Avanzini; married Patricia Ann Payne (Pastor of International Faith Center), February 18, 1955; children: Yvette, Tony, Sherri, John H., and David. *Education:* Received B.A. and M.A. from Baptist Bible College

of Sacramento, CA; received Ph.D. from Baptist Christian University. *Politics:* Conservative.

ADDRESSES: Office—P.O. Box 917001, Fort Worth, TX 76117-9001.

CAREER: Ordained Baptist minister; construction worker in Houston, TX, and Tampa, FL, 1955-62; pastor and president of Baptist Temple, Denver, CO, 1964-70; pastor of Harvest Temple, San Diego, CA, 1971-83; pastor of Assembly of God congregation, Joplin, MO, 1983-85; president of His Image Ministries, Inc., Fort Worth, TX, 1985-93; co-pastor and vice president of International Faith Center, 1992—.

WRITINGS:

The Wealth of the Wicked, His Image (Fort Worth, TX), 1986.

Faith Extenders, His Image, 1987.

Powerful Principles of Increase, Harrison House (Tulsa, OK), 1989.

30/60/Hundredfold, Harrison House, 1989.

Always Abounding, Harrison House, 1989.

Moving the Hand of God, Harrison House, 1990.

Rapid Debt-Reduction Strategies, HIS Publishing, 1990.

War on Debt, HIS Publishing, 1990.

The Victory Book, HIS Publishing, 1990.

Have a Good Report, HIS Publishing, 1991.

Financial Excellence, Harrison House, 1991.

John Avanzini Answers Your Questions, Harrison House, 1992.

It's Not Working, Brother John, Harrison House, 1992.

Stolen Property Returned, Harrison House, 1993.

The Debt Term-O-Nator, HIS Publishing, 1993.

The Wealth of the World, Harrison House, 1994.

God's Debt-Free Guarantee, Harrison House, 1994.

Things That Are Better Than Money, Harrison House, 1995.

Also author of *Bird's Roots, Weeds, and Good Ground; Paul's Thorn;* and *Financing the End Time Harvest.*

Many of Avanzini's works have been translated into Swedish, Russian, and Italian.

SIDELIGHTS: John F. Avanzini told *CA:* "The primary purpose of my writing is to teach Christians the principles of biblical economics, including how to get out of debt and stay out of debt."

* * *

AVICE, Claude (Pierre Marie) 1925-
(Pierre Barbet, David Maine, Olivier Sprigel)

PERSONAL: Born May 16, 1925, in Le Mans, France; son of Leon (a pharmacist) and Renee (Bardet) Avice;

married Marianne Brunswick (a pharmacist), July 23, 1952; children: Brigitte Avice Newman, Patrick, Olivier. *Education:* University of Paris, Docteur en pharmacie, 1954; Pasteur Institute, Garches. *Avocational interests:* Sculpture, tennis, model ships.

ADDRESSES: Home—4, square de l'Avenue du Bois, 75116 Paris, France, and Roseraies de St. Jean-Florian, 93 Traverse de Fontmerle, 06600 Antibes, France.

CAREER: Science fiction writer. Pharmacist in Paris, France, 1952-81. Director of laboratory for medical analysis, 1955-58. Diplomate in bacteriology, serology, parasitology and hematology.

MEMBER: Association Internationale des Critiques litteraires, World Science Fiction (member of the board, 1985), Societe francophone de Science-Fiction (vice-president, 1985), European Society of Science Fiction (co-ordinator, 1979), Science Fiction Writers of America (overseas director), Society of Doctors in Pharmacy (secretary), European Academy of Arts, Letters and Science (corresponding member).

AWARDS, HONORS: Gold medal from International Institute of Science Fiction (Poznan).

WRITINGS:

UNDER PSEUDONYM PIERRE BARBET

Vers un avenir perdu (title means "Towards a Lost Future"), Gallimard, 1962.

Babel 3,805, Gallimard, 1963.

Les Limiers de l'infini (title means "Bloodhounds of the Infinite"), Editions Fleuve Noir, 1966.

Les Cavernicoles de Wolf (title means "Cave Inhabitants of Wolf"), Editions Fleuve Noir, 1966.

L'Etoile du neant (title means "The Star of Nought"), Editions Fleuve Noir, 1967.

L'Enigme des quasars (title means "The Secret of Quasars"), Editions Fleuve Noir, 1967.

Hallali cosmique (title means "Cosmic Death"), Editions Fleuve Noir, 1967.

La Planete des cristophons (title means "Planet of Cristophons"), Editions Fleuve Noir, 1968.

Evolution magnetique (title means "Magnetic Evolution"), Editions Fleuve Noir, 1968.

Vikings de l'espace (title means "Space Vikings"), Editions Fleuve Noir, 1969.

Les Chimeres de Seginus (title means "The Chimeras of Seginus"), Editions Fleuve Noir, 1969.

L'Exile du temps (title means "Exile of Time"), Editions Fleuve Noir, 1969.

Etoiles en perdition (title means "Stars in Distress"), Editions Fleuve Noir, 1970.

Les Maitres des pulsars (title means "Masters of Pulsars"), Editions Fleuve Noir, 1970.

Les Grognards d'Eridan, Editions Fleuve Noir, 1970, translation by Stanley Hochman published as *The Napoleons of Eridanus,* DAW Books (New York City), 1976.

L'Agonie de la voie lactee (title means "The Agony of the Milky Way"), Editions Fleuve Noir, 1970.

Les Conquistadores d'Andromede (title means "The Conquistadors of Andromeda"), Editions Fleuve Noir, 1971.

Le Transmetteur de Ganymede (title means "Ganymede's Transmitter"), Editions Fleuve Noir, 1971.

Azraec de Virgo (title means "Azraec of Virgo"), Editions Fleuve Noir, 1971.

A quoi songent les psyborgs?, Editions Fleuve Noir, 1971, translation by Wendayne Ackerman published as *Games Psyborgs Play,* DAW Books, 1973.

L'Empire du Baphomet, Editions Fleuve Noir, 1972, translation by Bernand Kay published as *Baphomet's Meteor,* DAW Books, 1972.

Les Insurges de Laucor (title means "Insurgents of Laucor"), Editions Fleuve Noir, 1972.

La Planete empoisonnee (title means "Poisoned Planet"), Editions Fleuve Noir, 1972.

Tremplins d'etoiles (title means "Springboard of the Stars"), Editions Fleuve Noir, 1972.

La Planete enchantee, Editions Fleuve Noir, 1973, translation by C. J. Richards published as *Enchanted Planet,* DAW Books, 1975.

Liane de Noldaz, Editions Fleuve Noir, 1973, translation by Hochman published as *The Joan-of-Arc Replay,* DAW Books, 1978.

Les Bioniques d'Atria (title means "Bionics of Atria"), Editions Fleuve Noir, 1973.

Le Batard d'Orion (title means "The Bastard of Orion"), Editions Fleuve Noir, 1973.

Magiciens galactiques (title means "Galactic Magicians"), Editions Fleuve Noir, 1974.

L'Univers des Geons (title means "The Universe of Geons"), Editions Fleuve Noir, 1974.

Croisade stellaire (title means "Stellar Crusade"), Editions Fleuve Noir, 1974.

Les Mercenaires de Rychna (title means "The Mercenaries of Rychna"), Editions Fleuve Noir, 1974.

La Nymphe de l'espace (title means "Nymph of Space"), Editions Fleuve Noir, 1975.

Patrouilleur du neant (title means "Patrol of Nought"), Editions Fleuve Noir, 1976.

A Problem in Bionics, DAW Books, 1977.

Commandos sur commande, Editions Fleuve Noir, 1978.

Odyssee galactique, Editions Fleuve Noir, 1978.

Trafic stellaire, Editions Fleuve Noir, 1979.

Trafic de l'espace, Editions Fleuve Noir, 1979.

Periple galactique, Editions Fleuve Noir, 1980.

Cite des asteroides, Editions Fleuve Noir, 1980.

Stellar Crusaders, DAW Books, 1980.

Le Marechal rebelle, Editions Fleuve Noir, 1981.

Les Psychos de Logir, Editions Fleuve Noir, 1981.

Survivants de l'apocalypse, Editions Fleuve Noir, 1982.

Cites stellaires, Editions Fleuve Noir, 1982.

L'Empereur d'Eridan, Editions Fleuve Noir, 1982, translation by Hochman published as *The Emperor of Eridanus,* DAW Books, 1983.

Les charognards de S'nien, Editions Fleuve Noir, 1983.

Rome doit etre detruite, Editions Fleuve Noir, 1983.

Les colons d'Eridan, Editions Fleuve Noir, 1984.

Carthage sera detruite, Editions Fleuve Noir, 1984.

Eldorado stellaire, Editions Fleuve Noir, 1985.

Cite biotique, Editions Fleuve Noir, 1985.

Teleclones, Editions Fleuve Noir, 1985.

Putsch galactique, Editions Fleuve Noir, 1985.

Glaciation nucleaire, Editions Fleuve Noir, 1986.

Croisade des assassins, Editions Fleuve Noir, 1986.

Temps changeants, Editions Fleuve Noir, 1986.

Defense spatiale, Editions Fleuve Noir, 1987.

Captifs de Corvus, Editions Fleuve Noir, 1987.

Un Reich de 1000 ans, Editions Fleuve Noir, 1987.

Option zero, Editions Fleuve Noir, 1988.

Soleil de mort, Editions Fleuve Noir, 1990.

L'ere du Spatiopitheque, Editions Fleuve Noir, 1991.

UNDER PSEUDONYM DAVID MAINE

Les Disparus du club Chronos, Albin Michel, 1972.

Guerillero galactique (title means "Galactic Guerillas"), Albin Michel, 1976.

Renaissance planetaire, Albin Michel, 1980.

Invasion Cosmique, Albin Michel, 1982.

UNDER PSEUDONYM OLIVIER SPRIGEL

Crepuscule de futur, Librairie des Champs Elysees, 1975.

Venusine, Librairie des Champs Elysees, 1977.

Lendemains incertains, Librairie des Champs Elysees, 1978.

OTHER

Contributor to books, including *European Anthology,* edited by Donald A. Wollheim, Doubleday (New York City), 1976. Author (with others) of *La Grande Encyclopedie de la Science Fiction,* Del Drago (Italy). Under his own name, Avice has written several scientific publications, including *L'homme est-il seul dans l'Univers, L'antimatiere, La Bionique, Un peu de Futurologie, De la guerre du feu au spatiopitheque,* and *Qu'est-ce que la Science fiction?*

Contributor of science fiction short stories to anthologies and to French periodicals, including *Policier Mystere Magazine, Espionnage, Mystere, Fanzine Mercury, Anthologie OPTA,* and *Horizons du Fantastique.*

WORK IN PROGRESS: Three more science fiction works.

SIDELIGHTS: Claude Avice's works have been published in Brazil, Hungary, Poland, Portugal, Italy, Switzerland, Germany, Romania, Czechoslovakia, and the United States. Avice wrote *CA:* "As a young boy, I remember reading Jules Verne and Edgar Rice Burroughs with great passion, which, in my opinion, is what triggered my science fiction writing, after I wrote my thesis on bacteriology and hematology. The themes of biology permitted me to explore a wide variety of science fiction subjects like the clones or the evolution of a space civilization.

"The European legends also attracted me greatly in the field of the heroic fantasy: the Knights of Charlemagne, Huon de Bordeaux, the town of Ys and the forest of Broceliande. . . . I was, of course, very pleased to have 71 novels published in France and 15 novels translated in foreign countries, nevertheless, I believe that my most important contribution to literature was during my activity as coordinator of the European Society of Science Fiction when I had the possibility to introduce through the Iron Curtain the novels of western writers of science fiction prohibited at this epoch."

B

BAKER, Asa
See DRESSER, Davis

* * *

BAMBARA, Toni Cade 1939-
(Toni Cade)

PERSONAL: Surname originally Cade, name legally changed in 1970; born March 25, 1939, in New York, NY; daughter of Helen Brent Henderson Cade; children: Karma (daughter). *Education:* Queens College (now Queens College of the City University of New York), B.A., 1959; University of Florence, studied at Commedia dell'Arte, 1961; student at Ecole de Mime Etienne Decroux in Paris, 1961, New York, 1963; City College of the City University of New York, M.A., 1964; additional study in linguistics at New York University and New School for Social Research. Also attended Katherine Dunham Dance Studio, Syvilla Fort School of Dance, Clark Center of Performing Arts, 1958-69, and Studio Museum of Harlem Film Institute, 1970.

ADDRESSES: Home—5720 Wissahickon Ave., Apt. E12, Philadelphia, PA 19144.

CAREER: Free-lance writer and lecturer. Social investigator, New York State Department of Welfare, 1959-61; director of recreation in psychiatry department, Metropolitan Hospital, New York City, 1961-62; program director, Colony House Community Center, New York City, 1962-65; English instructor in Seek Program, City College of the City University of New York, New York City, 1965-69, and in New Careers Program of Newark, NJ, 1969; assistant professor, Livingston College, Rutgers University, New Brunswick, NJ, 1969-74; visiting professor of African-American studies, Stephens College, Co-

lumbia, MO, 1975; Atlanta University, visiting professor, 1977, research mentor and instructor, School of Social Work, 1977, 1979. Founder and director of Pamoja Writers Collective, 1976-85. Production artist-in-residence for Neighborhood Arts Center, 1975-79, Stephens College, 1976, and Spelman College, 1978-79. Production consultant, WHYY-TV, Philadelphia, PA. Has conducted numerous workshops on writing, self-publishing, and community organizing for community centers, museums, prisons, libraries, and universities. Has lectured and conducted literary readings at many institutions, including the Library of Congress, Smithsonian Institute, Afro-American Museum of History and Culture, and for numerous other organizations and universities. Humanities consultant to New Jersey Department of Corrections, 1974, Institute of Language Arts, New York Institute for Human Services Training, 1978, and Emory University, 1980. Art consultant to New York State Arts Council, 1974, Georgia State Arts Council, 1976, 1981, National Endowment for the Arts, 1980, and the Black Arts South Conference, 1981.

MEMBER: National Association of Third World Writers, Screen Writers Guild of America, African-American Film Society, Sisters in Support of South African Sisterhood.

AWARDS, HONORS: Peter Pauper Press Award, 1958; John Golden Award for Fiction from Queens College (now Queens College of the City University of New York), 1959; Theatre of Black Experience award, 1969; Rutgers University research fellowship, 1972; Black Child Development Institute service award, 1973; Black Rose Award from Encore, 1973; Black Community Award from Livingston College, Rutgers University, 1974; award from the National Association of Negro Business and Professional Women's Club League; George Washington Carver Distinguished African-American Lecturer Award from Simpson College; *Ebony's* Achievement in the Arts

Award; Black Arts Award from University of Missouri; American Book Award, 1981, for *The Salt Eaters;* Best Documentary of 1986 Award from Pennsylvania Association of Broadcasters and Documentary Award from National Black Programming Consortium, both 1986, for *The Bombing of Osage.*

WRITINGS:

Gorilla, My Love (short stories), Random House (New York City), 1972, reprinted, Vintage (New York City), 1992.

The Sea Birds Are Still Alive (short stories), Random House, 1977.

The Salt Eaters (novel), Random House, 1980, reprinted, Vintage, 1992.

(Author of preface) Cecelia Smith, *Cracks,* Select Press, 1980.

(Author of foreword) Cherrie Moraga and Gloria Anzaldua, editors, *This Bridge Called My Back: Radical Women of Color,* Persephone Press (Watertown, MA), 1981.

(Author of foreword) *The Sanctified Church: Collected Essays by Zora Neale Hurston,* Turtle Island (Berkeley, CA), 1982.

If Blessing Comes (novel), Random House, 1987.

Raymond's Run (juvenile; also see below), Creative Education (Mankato, MN), 1990.

SCREENPLAYS

Zora, produced by WGBH-TV, 1971.

The Johnson Girls, produced by National Educational Television, 1972.

Transactions, produced by School of Social Work, Atlanta University, 1979.

The Long Night, produced by American Broadcasting Co., 1981.

Epitaph for Willie, produced by K. Heran Productions, Inc., 1982.

Tar Baby (based on Toni Morrison's novel), produced by Sanger/Brooks Film Productions, 1984.

Raymond's Run, produced by Public Broadcasting System, 1985.

The Bombing of Osage, produced by WHYY-TV, 1986.

Cecil B. Moore: Master Tactician of Direct Action, produced by WHYY-TV, 1987.

EDITOR

(And contributor, under name Toni Cade) *The Black Woman: An Anthology,* New American Library (New York City), 1970.

(And contributor) *Tales and Stories for Black Folks,* Doubleday (New York City), 1971.

(With Leah Wise) *Southern Black Utterances Today,* Institute for Southern Studies (Durham, NC), 1975.

CONTRIBUTOR

Addison Gayle, Jr., editor, *Black Expression: Essays by and about Black Americans in the Creative Arts,* Weybright, 1969.

Jules Chametsky, editor, *Black and White in American Culture,* University of Massachusetts Press, 1970.

Ruth Miller, *Backgrounds to Blackamerican Literature,* Chandler Publishing, 1971.

Janet Sternburg, editor, *The Writer on Her Work,* Norton (New York City), 1980.

Paul H. Connolly, editor, *On Essays: A Reader for Writers,* Harper (New York City), 1981.

Florence Howe, editor, *Women Working,* Feminist Press (Old Westbury, NY), 1982.

Mari Evans, editor, *Black Women Writers (1950-1980): A Critical Evaluation,* Doubleday, 1984.

Baraka and Baraka, editors, *Confirmations,* Morrow (New York City), 1984.

Claudia Tate, editor, *The Black Writer at Work,* Howard University Press (Washington, DC), 1984.

OTHER

Contributor to *What's Happnin, Somethin Else,* and *Another Eye,* all readers published by Scott, Foresman, 1969-70. Contributor of articles and book and film reviews to *Massachusetts Review, Negro Digest, Liberator, Prairie Schooner, Redbook, Audience, Black Works, Umbra, Onyx,* and other periodicals. Guest editor of special issue of *Southern Exposure,* summer, 1976, devoted to new southern black writers and visual artists.

ADAPTATIONS: Three of Bambara's short stories, "Gorilla, My Love," "Medley," and "Witchbird," have been adapted for film.

SIDELIGHTS: Toni Cade Bambara is a well-known and respected civil rights activist, professor of English and of African-American studies, editor of anthologies of black literature, and author of short stories and novels. Throughout her career, Bambara has used her art to convey social and political messages about the welfare of the African-American community and of African-American women especially. According to Alice A. Deck in the *Dictionary of Literary Biography,* the author "is one of the best representatives of the group of Afro-American writers who, during the 1960s, became directly involved in the cultural and sociopolitical activities in urban communities across the country." However, Deck points out that "Bambara is one of the few who continued to work within the black urban communities (filming, lecturing, organizing, and reading from her works at rallies and conferences), producing imaginative reenactments of these experiences in her fiction. In addition, Bambara established herself over the years as an educator, teaching in colleges and independent community schools in various cities on the East Coast."

For Bambara, the duties of writer, social activist, teacher, and even student have all combined to influence her perspective. "It's a tremendous responsibility—responsibility and honor—to be a writer, an artist, a cultural worker . . . whatever you call this vocation," she explained in an interview in *Black Women Writers at Work*. "One's got to see what the factory worker sees, what the prisoner sees, what the welfare children see, what the scholar sees, got to see what the ruling-class mythmakers see as well, in order to tell the truth and not get trapped." Bambara has made it her objective to describe the urban black community without resorting to stereotype or simplification. A deep understanding of the complexities of African-American life informs all of her work.

Born Toni Cade in New York City in 1939, Bambara credits her mother with providing a nurturing environment for her budding creativity. Growing up in Harlem, Bedford-Stuyvesant, and Queens, and in Jersey City, New Jersey, she was encouraged to explore her imagination, to daydream, and to follow her inner motives. She published her first short story at the age of 20, a piece called "Sweet Town." The name "Bambara," which she later appended to her own, was discovered as part of a signature on a sketchbook she found in her great-grandmother's trunk.

Bambara received a bachelor's degree in theater arts and English from Queens College in 1959. In the following decade she served as a social worker and director of neighborhood programs in Harlem and Brooklyn, published short stories in periodicals, earned a master's degree and spent a year at the Commedia dell'Arte in Milan, Italy, and directed a theater program and various publications funded by the City College Seek program. This wide variety of experience inevitably found its way into her fiction and influenced her political sensibility as well.

Bambara's first book-length publication was *The Black Woman: An Anthology*, a collection of essays that was envisioned as a response to the so-called "experts" who had been conducting studies on the status of black American women. One of the first of its kind, the anthology provided an arena for black women's opinions not only on racism and sexism but also on a wealth of other equally important issues. She followed this work with *Tales and Stories for Black Folks*, a sourcebook intended to stimulate an interest in storytelling among young African-American students. The two anthologies and her first volume of fiction, *Gorilla, My Love*, were all published while she held a professorship at Livingston College, a division of Rutgers University.

Bambara's first two books of fiction, *Gorilla, My Love* and *The Sea Birds Are Still Alive*, are collections of her short stories. Susan Lardner remarks in the *New Yorker* that the stories in these two works, "describing the lives of black people in the North and the South, could be more exactly typed as vignettes and significant anecdotes, although a few of them are fairly long. . . . All are notable for their purposefulness, a more or less explicit inspirational angle, and a distinctive motion of the prose, which swings from colloquial narrative to precarious metaphorical heights and over to street talk, at which Bambara is unbeatable."

In a review of *Gorilla, My Love*, for example, a writer remarks in the *Saturday Review* that the stories "are among the best portraits of black life to have appeared in some time. [They are] written in a breezy, engaging style that owes a good deal to street dialect." A critic writing in *Newsweek* makes a similar observation, describing Bambara's second collection of short stories, *The Sea Birds Are Still Alive*, in this manner: "Bambara directs her vigorous sense and sensibility to black neighborhoods in big cities, with occasional trips to small Southern towns. . . . The stories start and stop like rapid-fire conversations conducted in a rhythmic, black-inflected, sweet-and-sour language." In fact, according to Anne Tyler in the *Washington Post Book World*, Bambara's particular style of narration is one of the most distinctive qualities of her writing. "What pulls us along is the language of [her] characters, which is startlingly beautiful without once striking a false note," declares Tyler. "Everything these people say, you feel, ordinary, real-life people are saying right now on any street corner. It's only that the rest of us didn't realize it was sheer poetry they were speaking."

In terms of plot, Bambara tends to avoid linear development in favor of presenting "situations that build like improvisations of a melody," according to a *Newsweek* reviewer. Commenting on *Gorilla, My Love*, Bell Gale Chevigny observes in the *Village Voice* that despite the "often sketchy" plots, the stories are always "lavish in their strokes—there are elaborate illustrations, soaring asides, aggressive sub-plots. They are never didactic, but they abound in far-out common sense, exotic home truths."

Numerous reviewers have also remarked on Bambara's sensitive portrayals of her characters and the handling of their situations, portrayals that are marked by an affectionate warmth and pride. Laura Marcus writes in the *Times Literary Supplement* that Bambara "presents black culture as embattled but unbowed. . . . Bambara depicts black communities in which ties of blood and friendship are fiercely defended." Deck expands on this idea, remarking that "the basic implication of all of Toni Cade Bambara's stories is that there is an undercurrent of caring for one's neighbors that sustains black Americans. In her view the presence of those individuals who intend to do harm to people is counterbalanced by as many if not more persons who have a genuine concern for other people."

C. D. B. Bryan admires this expression of the author's concern for other people, declaring in the *New York Times Book Review* that "Bambara tells me more about being black through her quiet, proud, silly, tender, hip, acute, loving stories than any amount of literary polemicizing could hope to do. She writes about love: a love for one's family, one's friends, one's race, one's neighborhood and it is the sort of love that comes with maturity and inner peace." According to Bryan, "all of [Bambara's] stories share the affection that their narrator feels for the subject, an affection that is sometimes terribly painful, at other times fiercely proud. But at all times it is an affection that is so genuinely genus *homo sapiens* that her stories are not only black stories."

In 1980, Bambara published her first novel, a generally well-received work entitled *The Salt Eaters.* Written in an almost dream-like style, *The Salt Eaters* explores the relationship between two women with totally different backgrounds and lifestyles brought together by a suicide attempt by one of the women. John Leonard, who describes the book as "extraordinary," writes in the *New York Times* that *The Salt Eaters* "is almost an incantation, poem-drunk, myth-happy, mud-caked, jazz-ridden, prodigal in meanings, a kite and a mask. It astonishes because Toni Cade Bambara is so adept at switching from politics to legend, from particularities of character to prehistorical song, from LaSalle Street to voodoo. It is as if she jived the very stones to groan."

In a *Times Literary Supplement* review, Carol Rumens states that *The Salt Eaters* "is a hymn to individual courage, a sombre message of hope that has confronted the late twentieth-century pathology of racist violence and is still able to articulate its faith in 'the dream'." And John Wideman notes in the *New York Times Book Review:* "In her highly acclaimed fiction and in lectures, [Bambara] emphasizes the necessity for black people to maintain their best traditions, to remain healthy and whole as they struggle for political power. *The Salt Eaters,* her first novel, eloquently summarizes and extends the abiding concerns of her previous work."

After serving as writer-in-residence at Spelman College during the 1970s, Bambara relocated to Philadelphia, where she has continued to write both fiction and film scripts. One of her best-known projects for film, *The Bombing of Osage,* explores a notorious incident in which the Philadelphia authorities used lethal force against a group of militant black citizens. The author's more recent books include another adult novel, *If Blessing Comes,* and a juvenile work, *Raymond's Run,* about a pair of siblings who like to run foot races. While never completely relin-quishing her fiction work, however, Bambara has become more and more involved with film. As she commented in *Black Women Writers at Work,* "I've always considered myself a film person. . . . There's not too much more I want to experiment with in terms of writing. It gives me pleasure, insight, keeps me centered, sane. But, oh, to get my hands on some movie equipment."

BIOGRAPHICAL/CRITICAL SOURCES:

BOOKS

Black Literature Criticism, Gale (Detroit), 1990.
Butler-Evans, Elliott, *Race, Gender, and Desire: Narrative Strategies in the Fiction of Toni Cade Bambara, Toni Morrison, and Alice Walker,* Temple University Press (Philadelphia), 1989.
Contemporary Literary Criticism, Volume 29, Gale, 1984.
Dictionary of Literary Biography, Volume 38: *Afro-American Writers after 1955: Dramatists and Prose Writers,* Gale, 1985.
Notable Black American Women, Gale, 1992.
Parker, Bell, and Beverly Guy-Sheftall, *Sturdy Black Bridges: Visions of Black Women in Literature,* Doubleday, 1979.
Prenshaw, Peggy Whitman, editor, *Women Writers of the Contemporary South,* University Press of Mississippi, 1984.
Tate, Claudia, editor, *Black Women Writers at Work,* Continuum (New York City), 1983.

PERIODICALS

Black World, July, 1973.
Books of the Times, June, 1980.
Chicago Tribune Book World, March 23, 1980.
Drum, spring, 1982.
First World, Volume 2, number 4, 1980.
Los Angeles Times Book Review, May 4, 1980.
Ms., July, 1977; July, 1980.
National Observer, May 9, 1977.
Newsweek, May 2, 1977.
New Yorker, May 5, 1980.
New York Times, October 11, 1972; October 15, 1972; April 4, 1980.
New York Times Book Review, February 21, 1971; May 2, 1971; November 7, 1971; October 15, 1972; December 3, 1972; March 27, 1977; June 1, 1980; November 1, 1981.
Saturday Review, November 18, 1972; December 2, 1972; April 12, 1980.
Sewanee Review, November 18, 1972; December 2, 1972.
Times Literary Supplement, September 27, 1985.
Village Voice, April 12, 1973.
Washington Post Book World, November 18, 1973; March 30, 1980.*

BARBET, Pierre
  See AVICE, Claude (Pierre Marie)

*   *   *

BARGAD, Warren 1940-

PERSONAL: Surname is pronounced "Bar-*gahd*"; born February 21, 1940, in Boston, MA; son of Gedalie (a cantor) and Kate (Wicnudel) Bargad; married Arlene S. Miller (a clinical social worker), January 28, 1962; children: Robert, Adena. *Education:* Hebrew College, B.J.Ed., 1959, M.H.L., 1965; attended Hebrew University of Jerusalem, 1959-60, 1966-67; Harvard University, B.A., 1962; Brandeis University, M.A., 1964, Ph.D., 1971.

ADDRESSES: Home—1424 Northwest 14th Ave., Gainesville, FL 32605. *Office*—Center for Jewish Studies, 441 Little Hall, University of Florida, Gainesville, FL 32611.

CAREER: Hebrew College, Brookline, MA, instructor in Hebrew literature, 1964-69; Hebrew Union College-Jewish Institute of Religion, Cincinnati, OH, assistant professor, 1969-72, associate professor of Hebrew literature, 1972-76; Spertus College of Judaica, Chicago, IL, professor of Hebrew literature, 1976-85, dean, 1979-85, vice president for administration, 1981-84; University of Florida, Gainesville, professor of modern Hebrew literature and director of Center for Jewish Studies, 1985—.

MEMBER: Modern Language Association of America, Association for Jewish Studies (member of board of directors, 1978-81, 1992-94).

AWARDS, HONORS: Lown exchange fellow in Israel, 1966-67; grants from American Philosophical Society, 1973, and Littauer Foundation, 1982; National Endowment for the Humanities, fellowship, 1984-85, travel grant, 1987.

WRITINGS:

Ideas in Fiction: The Works of Hayim Hazaz, Scholars Press (Chico, CA), 1982.
(Editor and translator, with Stanley F. Chyet) *Israeli Poetry: A Contemporary Anthology,* Indiana University Press (Bloomington), 1986.
"To Write the Lips of Sleepers": The Poetry of Amir Gilboa, Hebrew Union College Press (Cincinnati, OH), 1994.
From Agnon to Oz: Studies and Reviews in Modern Hebrew Literature, Scholars Press, 1995.

Member of editorial board of *Hebrew Annual Review,* 1976—, *Jewish Book Annual,* 1978—, and publications committee of the Jewish Publications Society.

WORK IN PROGRESS: Translation of several Israeli short stories (works by Gadi Taub and Shulamith Gilboa); a book-length collection of Ory Bernstein's poetry; a second volume of *Israeli Poetry* with Stanley F. Chyet; a comparative study of Israeli literature in the wakes of the Arab-Israeli wars (1948, '56, '67, '73, and '82).

SIDELIGHTS: Warren Bargad told *CA:* "My interest in Hebrew literature began in the 1950s at Hebrew College. I then spent a year at Hebrew University, from 1959 to 1960, and subsequently decided to make my career in this area. In 1966 I returned to Israel for my doctoral research on the works of Hayim Hazaz. Later trips in the 1970s, 1980s and 1990s involved research on contemporary Israeli fiction and poetry.

"Having collaborated on the translation of a large body of Israeli poetry, my co-author, Stanley Chyet, and I traveled to Israel in 1982 and met with the eleven poets we had chosen to appear in *Israeli Poetry: A Contemporary Anthology.* These poets included Amir Gilboa, Abba Kovner, Haim Gouri, Yehuda Amichai, Dan Pagis, Natan Zach, David Avidan, Dahlia Ravikovitch, Ory Bernstein, Meir Wieseltier, and Yona Wollach. Each poet was a distinct personality and each contributed greatly to the work of poetic translation. Meeting and working with these poets was the experience of a lifetime!

"Modern Hebrew literature offers many kinds of appeals and challenges. One of the challenges is keeping up with a still developing language while living in the United States. Another is keeping up with the amazing volume of fiction, poetry, and criticism produced annually in Israel. Much of the appeal of this literature derives from its being such a complex blend of old and new levels of language and styles, Middle Eastern, Jewish, and Israeli themes, and a variety of international literary traditions.

"The study of Hazaz's works was especially interesting because of the author's idiosyncratic mix of fiction and philosophy. Also fascinating is his attempt to recreate in Hebrew the speech patterns and milieus of both Russian Jewry and Yemenite Jews.

"*To Write the Lips of Sleepers* is a comprehensive study of Amir Gilboa's (1917-1984) fifty-year career as a poet. The study describes and interprets Gilboa's works at several stages of his life and defines his place in the canon of modern Hebrew poetry. His early works are composed mainly of romantic themes and a lyrical style; later he shifted his poetics—from figurative profusion in the forties, to ambivalence in his Holocaust works, to ambiguity in his modernist stage in the late sixties and seventies. These later poems reflect a highly idiosyncratic blend of romantic preoccupations and new modernist structures."

BARNET, Richard J. 1929-

PERSONAL: Born May 7, 1929, in Boston, MA; son of Carl J. and Margaret (Block) Barnet; married Ann Birnbaum, April 10, 1953; children: Juliana, Elisabeth, Michael. *Education:* Harvard University, B.A. (summa cum laude), 1952; LL.B. (cum laude), 1954.

ADDRESSES: Home—1716 Portal Dr. Washington, DC 20012. *Office*—1901 Q Street NW, Washington, DC 20009.

CAREER: Admitted to bar, 1954; American Law Institute, research fellow, 1957-58; Choate, Hall, and Stewart (law firm), Boston, MA, attorney, 1958-60; Russian Research Center, Harvard University, Cambridge, MA, research fellow, 1959-60; Arms Control and Disarmament Agency, Washington, DC, special assistant, 1961; Office of Political Research, U.S. Arms Control and Disarmament Agency, deputy director, 1962-63; Center for International Studies, Princeton University, Princeton, NJ, fellow, 1963; Institute for Policy Studies, Washington, DC, cofounder and senior fellow, 1963-77, 1990—. Visiting professor, Yale University, New Haven, CT, 1971; National University of Mexico, Mexico City, Mexico, 1973; University of Paris, Paris, France, 1982. Consultant to Department of Defense. *Military service:* U.S. Army, 1954-57, became first lieutenant.

MEMBER: World Peacemakers (president), Commission for National Security, Council on Foreign Relations, Committee of Compassion.

AWARDS, HONORS: Sidney Hillman Foundation Award, 1975, for *Global Reach: The Power of the Multinational Corporation;* University of Missouri School of Journalism Award, 1981.

WRITINGS:

Who Wants Disarmament?, Beacon (Boston, MA), 1960.
(Editor with Richard A. Falk) *Security in Disarmament,* Princeton University Press (Princeton, NJ), 1965.
(With Marcus G. Raskin) *After Twenty Years: The Decline of NATO and the Search for a New Policy in Europe,* Vintage (New York City), 1966.
Intervention and Revolution: The United States in the Third World, World Publishing, 1968.
The Economy of Death, Atheneum (New York City), 1969.
(With Raskin) *An American Manifesto: What's Wrong with America and What We Can Do About It,* New American Library (New York City), 1970.
Can the United States Promote Foreign Development?, Overseas Development Council (Washington, DC), 1971.
(With Ralph Stavins and Raskin) *Washington Plans an Aggressive War,* Vintage, 1971.

The Roots of War, Atheneum, 1972.
(With Ronald Mueller) *Global Reach: The Power of the Multinational Corporation,* Simon & Schuster (New York City), 1974.
The Giants: Russia and America, Simon & Schuster, 1977.
The Lean Years: Politics in the Age of Scarcity, Simon & Schuster, 1980.
Real Security: Restoring American Power in a Dangerous Decade, Simon & Schuster, 1981.
The Alliance: America, Europe, Japan: Makers of the Post-war World, Simon & Schuster, 1983, published in England as *Allies: America, Europe, and Japan since the War,* Cape (London), 1984.
The Rockets' Red Glare: When America Goes to War; The Presidents and the People, Simon & Schuster, 1990.
(With John Cavanagh) *Global Dreams: Imperial Corporations and the New World Order,* Simon & Schuster, 1994.

Contributor to *Harper's, New York Times Magazine, New Yorker, Science, Foreign Policy, New Republic, New York Review of Books,* and many scholarly publications.

SIDELIGHTS: Richard J. Barnet is, in the words of the *Washington Post*'s London correspondent Peter Osnos, "a rare creature among American authors, what the Europeans would call a 'writer on foreign affairs.' He is a blend of political scientist, historian, reporter and essayist who takes on major subjects, reads the literature copiously, travels a bit and then writes readable, often provocative surveys that are usually serialized in the *New Yorker*." Alan Tonelson, writing in the *New York Times Book Review,* further describes Barnet as "a well-known leftist critic of contemporary American foreign policy."

Reviewer Ronald Steele describes *Intervention and Revolution: The United States in the Third World* as a "brilliantly argued and devastatingly detailed study." "One of the great virtues of Barnet's splendid book," he elaborates, "is that it offers a devastating examination of the bureaucratic mentality that has led the United States on the path of intervention and counter-revolution." Tristram Coffin suggested that *Intervention and Revolution* "may well become one of those two or three [books] in a generation that move the mountain of history."

In *Global Reach: The Power of the Multinational Corporation,* Barnet and coauthor Ronald Mueller analyze multinational corporations on the "bold and original thesis," as David Fromkin describes it in the *New Republic,* "that the oligarchy of global corporations has developed a system that is in the nature of world government." The authors argue that large corporations are answerable to their stockholders, who invest for profit. Without adequate moral and legal controls, these companies have the capacity to shape economies and societies to their own ends.

Fromkin contends that the authors have not given the multinationals "enough credit for their positive achievements in such areas as the boosting of food production" and that they have "saddled themselves with the thesis that a world government already exists, in the form of a consortium of global corporations. They can't say that the world's economy needs a government because they've said that we already *have* such a government." Nicholas Faith, writing in the *Times Literary Supplement,* comments on the book's "verve and general readability," but he considers Barnet and Mueller "markedly radical" and *Global Reach* "an anti-imperialist work written from within the citadel. Hence an all-pervading assumption that, whatever the faults of the authors' native country, it is the one still setting pace, the one whose experience is the most valid, the most relevant in the future as in the past."

In the *Spectator,* Stuart Holland calls the book "an important and penetrative study . . . concerned essentially with power, whether that power is muscle over governments or the classic joint monopoly power to raise prices." Anthony Sampson also believes the book is important and, as he says in the *New York Times Review of Books,* "likely to have considerable influence, for it conveys the faults and abuses of the global corporations from inside, as well as outside. . . . The development of effective information and controls will not be easy, . . . but this book will certainly play a part in the new awareness."

Peter Osnos describes Barnet's 1977 book, *The Giants: Russia and America,* as "a laudable effort to explain Soviet-American relations, the focal political issue of our day, to the general reader. It is an intelligent essay, written cogently without heavy jargon or polemic. . . . Barnet's approach is valuable. It enables him to assess U.S.-Soviet dealings without really approving one side or the other, which is what few analysts can resist." Reviewing *The Giants* for the *New York Times,* Anthony Austin comments, "This book could not be more timely. . . . One does not have to agree with his conclusions to recognize him as a major social critic."

"*The Lean Years: Politics in the Age of Scarcity* announced the end of our Rome," Axel Madsen writes in *Saturday Review.* "Richard J. Barnet's hindsight is 20/20, but the powerful political vision he wishes were the possession of our leaders (in the largest sense) eludes him too. . . . *The Lean Years* is nevertheless a forceful summing up of where we are." In the *New Republic,* Stanley Hoffmann describes Barnet's book as "a survey of the politics of energy, minerals, food, and water, of the 'new international military order' that results from the 'increasingly sophisticated use of military systems for maintaining control over resources. . . .' To Barnet, the 'politics of scarcity' is . . . a deliberate creation of scarcity by the multinational corporations of the advanced countries, and particularly the

United States." Hoffmann reasons that the actions Barnet recommends would entail drastic social and political changes that "can hardly be achieved without revolution and violence, both domestic and international. Yet this is a reality from which Barnet shrinks, if only because his own view of the world suggests that in such battles the richer and stronger would win." Also critical of Barnet's failure to outline practical and enforceable methods of changing government structure, the *Nation*'s Richard Parker writes, "Barnet's contribution is to place the issue of planning squarely on the table. The essence of his neoliberalism is the assertion of democratic rights in the economic, as well as the political, realm and it is this that establishes his originality. *The Lean Years* offers us much; it could offer a great deal more." In the *New York Times Book Review,* Robert Lekachman finds that "Richard Barnet's cogent, frequently eloquent inspection of the economics and politics of [resources] adds comparatively little to the copious literature. . . . His major contribution is to organize coherently and evaluate intelligently the frequently conflicting claims of the experts."

Barnet's 1981 book, *Real Security: Restoring American Power in a Dangerous Decade,* is an expansion of an article published earlier in the *New Yorker.* The author's thesis here is in part that military power is insufficient to restore the United States to its former position of power in the world. "U. S. military power has been a wasting asset for a generation," he posits; among other mistakes, we have "confused stability with the status quo under the belief that our sheer power could stop the clock," disregarding other factors that have radically changed international politics. It is Walter Goodman's assessment in the *New York Times Book Review* that, "although Mr. Barnet's last chapter floats away on the kind of prose that participants in the arms debate . . . find irresistible, . . . his plea for an arms control agreement is compelling at a time . . . [of] so much drum beating, chest thumping, muscle flexing, knee jerking, and growling in the dark."

NATO, the North Atlantic Treaty Organization, is the subject of *The Alliance: America, Europe and Japan: Makers of the Postwar World,* a historical and political analysis of the alliance that was formed in 1948 primarily to assure the protection of its members against Soviet attack and that Barnet says has been "in 'disarray' of one sort or another from the day the NATO treaty was signed because the partners always had different expectations and different visions of what they were doing." In the *New York Times Book Review,* Daniel Yergin notes that the book "is not based on extensive primary research but is rather a synthesis" in which Barnet "combines lively narrative history with deft political analysis and vivid, psychologically acute portraits of the men who created and have led the alliance."

In a review from the other side of the Atlantic, Ian Nish writes in the *Times Literary Supplement* that "Mr. Barnet gives us a thoughtful and relevant study," though "he is strongest on Washington and does not explore the viewpoints of Europe and Japan with the same degree of thoroughness." In the *Spectator,* J. Enoch Powell declares that "Britain is not treated as an actor in the drama on the same plane as Japan, Germany, or France"—not because of Barnet's handling of his subject but for historical reasons of which his account "offers a handbook for those who want to understand how and why that has happened." Peter Osnos disagrees with Barnet's final point, that "American, European and Japanese outlooks on a variety of world problems are increasingly diverging" and "twilight is descending on the familiar postwar world." In the opinion of reviewer Sheldon E. Gordon of the *Globe and Mail* (Toronto), "Barnet describes the alliance's evolution in elaborate and often colorful detail. But he too often buries his analysis of the West's postwar relations in the welter of fact. He prescribes no antidote for the alliance's divisions, nor does he even assess their gravity."

The Rockets' Red Glare: When America Goes to War; The Presidents and the People is "a lucid and challenging account of how Americans fought on battlefields outside the United States during the last 150 years without constitutional sanction," says Herbert Mitgang in the *New York Times.* Mitgang deems this work of Barnet's a "generally well-conceived historical narrative," though "anachronisms occasionally creep in . . . because of his polemical tendencies." Writing for the *Los Angeles Times Book Review,* Alex Raskin observes, "As in his 1972 classic, *The Roots of War,* [Barnet] draws on his own experiences as an adviser in the Kennedy Administration to illustrate how the State Department's hermetic way of thinking has left it out of touch with geopolitical realities. . . . But unlike Barnet's previous books—urgent responses to crises of the present or recent past—*The Rockets' Red Glare* travels back to the founding of the republic to determine how the policy-makers came to be so far removed from the people."

In Tonelson's view, Barnet "provides ample evidence to document the gap" but fails to offer "the theoretical and philosophical discussion needed to figure out the proper role of public opinion in American foreign policy, let alone to support his grand conclusion that 'popular participation [in foreign policy] is becoming more necessary but also more possible.'" *Washington Post Book World* reviewer Staughton Lynd comments that "Barnet has no problem showing how often United States policymakers have disregarded the expressed will of the people" but, on the other hand, "argues persuasively that throughout the nation's history the people's will has set limits to how far presidents could go in unilateral warmaking."

BIOGRAPHICAL/CRITICAL SOURCES:

PERIODICALS

Atlantic Monthly, June, 1980, p. 92.
Chicago Tribune Book World, June 8, 1980, p. 4.
Globe and Mail (Toronto), August 4, 1984.
Los Angeles Times Book Review, February 2, 1990, pp. 2, 8, 13.
Nation, July 5, 1980, pp. 24-26.
New Republic, April 19, 1975, pp. 23-25; August 2, 1980, pp. 34-36.
New York Review of Books, November 6, 1980, p. 44.
New York Times, March 28, 1978; May 21, 1981; March 21, 1990.
New York Times Book Review, January 26, 1975, p. 2; June 8, 1980, pp. 13, 37; November 6, 1980, p. 44; May 17, 1981, p. 16; December 18, 1983, pp. 6, 17; February 4, 1990, p. 34; February 27, 1994, p. 16.
Saturday Review, June, 1980, pp. 73-75.
Spectator, October 4, 1975, p. 440; April 7, 1984, p. 24.
Times Literary Supplement, December 19, 1975, p. 1523; June 1, 1984, p. 604.
Washington Post Book World, November 20, 1977, p. E1-2; May 25, 1980, p. 7; May 31, 1981, pp. 1-2, 13; November 6, 1983, pp. 4-5; January 28, 1990, pp. 1, 13; February 27, 1994.

*　　*　　*

BARRON, Jerome A(ure) 1933-

PERSONAL: Born September 25, 1933, in Tewksbury, MA; son of Henry and Sadie (Shafmaster) Barron; married Myra Hymovich (a lawyer), June 18, 1961; children: Jonathan Nathaniel, David Jeremiah, Jennifer Leah. *Education:* Tufts University, A.B. (magna cum laude), 1955; Yale University, J.D., 1958; George Washington University, LL.M., 1960. *Politics:* Democrat. *Religion:* Jewish.

ADDRESSES: Home—3231 Ellicott St. N.W., Washington, DC 20008. *Office*—National Law Center, George Washington University, 720 20th St. N.W., Washington, DC 20052.

CAREER: Admitted to Massachusetts Bar, 1959, and District of Columbia Bar, 1960. U.S. Court of Claims, Washington, DC, law clerk, 1960-61; Cross, Murphy and Smith (law firm), Washington, DC, associate, 1961-62; University of North Dakota, Grand Forks, assistant professor of law, 1962-64; University of New Mexico, Albuquerque, visiting associate professor of law, 1964-65; George Washington University, Washington, DC, associate professor, 1965-68, professor of law, 1968-72; Syracuse University, Syracuse, NY, professor of law and dean of College of Law, 1972-73; George Washington University, professor of law, 1973-79, dean of National Center of Law, 1979–88, Lyle T. Alverson professor of law, 1987—. *Military service:* U.S. Army, 1958-59.

MEMBER: American Bar Association, Cosmos Club, Phi Beta Kappa.

AWARDS, HONORS: Frank Luther Mott research award from Kappa Tau Alpha, 1970, for *Mass Communication Law: Cases and Comment.*

WRITINGS:

(With Donald M. Gillmor) *Mass Communication Law: Cases and Comment,* West Publishing (St. Paul, MN), 1969, 5th edition, 1991.

Freedom of the Press for Whom?: The Right of Access to the Mass Media, Indiana University Press (Bloomington), 1973.

(With C. Thomas Dienes) *Constitutional Law, Principles and Policy: Cases and Materials,* Michie (Charlottesville, VA), 1975, 4th edition (with Dienes, Wayne McCormack, and Martin H. Redish), 1992.

(With others) *West's Review, Covering Multistate Subjects,* West Publishing, 1979.

(With Dienes) *Handbook of Free Speech and Free Press,* Little, Brown (Boston, MA), 1979.

Public Rights and the Private Press, Butterworth (Newton Upper Falls, MA), 1981.

(With Dienes) *Constitutional Law* ("Black Letter" series), West Publishing, 1983, 3rd edition, 1991.

(With Dienes) *Constitutional Law in a Nutshell,* West Publishing, 1986, 2nd edition, 1991.

(With Dienes) *First Amendment in a Nutshell,* West Publishing, 1993.

Contributor to *George Washington Law Review, Harvard Law Review, Northwestern University Law Review,* and *Texas Law Review.* Member of advisory board, *Media Law Reporter.*

*   *   *

BARTH, John (Simmons) 1930-

PERSONAL: Born May 27, 1930, in Cambridge, MD; son of John Jacob and Georgia (Simmons) Barth; married (Harriette) Anne Strickland, January 11, 1950 (divorced, 1969); married Shelly I. Rosenberg (a teacher), December 27, 1970; children: (first marriage) Christine Anne, John Strickland, Daniel Stephen. *Education:* Attended Juilliard School of Music; Johns Hopkins University, A.B., 1951, M.A., 1952.

ADDRESSES: Home—Baltimore, MD. *Office*—Writing Seminars, Johns Hopkins University, 3400 North Charles St., Baltimore, MD 21218. *Agent*—Wylie, Aitken, and Stone, 250 W. 57th St., New York, NY 10107.

CAREER: Pennsylvania State University, University Park, instructor, 1953-56, assistant professor, 1957-60, associate professor of English, 1960-65; State University of New York at Buffalo, professor of English, 1965-71, Edward H. Butler Professor of English, 1971-73; Johns Hopkins University, Baltimore, MD, Alumni Centennial Professor of English and Creative Writing, 1973-90, professor emeritus, 1990—.

MEMBER: American Academy and Institute of Arts and Letters, American Academy of Arts and Sciences.

AWARDS, HONORS: National Book Award nomination, 1956, for *The Floating Opera,* and 1968, for *Lost in the Funhouse: Fiction for Print, Tape, Live Voice;* Brandeis University Creative Arts Award, 1965; Rockefeller Foundation grant, 1965-66; National Institute of Arts and Letters grant, 1966, for *Giles, Goat-Boy; or, The Revised New Syllabus;* Litt.D., University of Maryland, 1969; National Book Award, 1973, for *Chimera.*

WRITINGS:

NOVELS

The Floating Opera, Appleton-Century-Crofts (Norwalk, CT), 1956, revised edition, Doubleday (New York City), 1967, reprinted with new foreword by the author, Doubleday-Anchor, 1988.

The End of the Road, Doubleday, 1958, revised edition, 1967, reprinted with new foreword by the author, Doubleday-Anchor, 1988.

The Sot-Weed Factor, Doubleday, 1960, revised edition, 1967, reprinted with new foreword by the author, Doubleday-Anchor, 1988.

Giles, Goat-Boy; or, The Revised New Syllabus, Doubleday, 1966, reprinted with new foreword by the author, Doubleday-Anchor, 1987.

Chimera (novella), Random House (New York City), 1972.

LETTERS, Putnam (New York City), 1979, reprinted with new foreword by the author, Dalkey Archive Press (Normal, IL), 1994.

Sabbatical: A Romance, Putnam, 1982, reprinted with new foreword by the author, Dalkey Archive Press, 1995.

Tidewater Tales: A Novel, Putnam, 1987.

The Last Voyage of Somebody the Sailor, Little, Brown (Boston), 1991.

Once Upon a Time: A Floating Opera, Little, Brown, 1994.

SHORT STORIES

Lost in the Funhouse: Fiction for Print, Tape, Live Voice,
    Doubleday, 1968, reprinted with new foreword by the
    author, Doubleday-Anchor, 1988.
On with the Story, Little, Brown, 1996.

NONFICTION

(Contributor) Quinn, editor, *The Sense of the 60s,* Free
    Press (New York City), 1968.
(Contributor) Weintraub and Young, editors, *Directions
    in Literary Criticism,* Pennsylvania State University
    Press (University Park), 1973.
*The Literature of Exhaustion, and The Literature of Re-
    plenishment* (essays), Lord John (Northridge, CA),
    1982.
The Friday Book: Essays and Other Nonfiction, Putnam
    (New York City), 1984.
*Don't Count on It: A Note on the Number of the 1001
    Nights,* Lord John, 1984.
*Further Fridays: Essays, Lectures, and Other Nonfiction,
    1984-1994,* Little, Brown, 1995.

OTHER

Contributor to numerous periodicals, including *Atlantic,
Esquire, Hopkins Review, Johns Hopkins Magazine,* and
Kenyon Review.

Barth's manuscripts are housed in the Library of Congress
and the libraries of Pennsylvania State and Johns Hopkins
Universities.

ADAPTATIONS: The End of the Road was adapted into
a 1970 film directed by Aram Avakian.

SIDELIGHTS: An eminent practitioner and theoretician
of postmodernist fiction, John Barth often defines himself
as a "concocter of comic novels," an inventor of universes
who is, above all, a lover of storytelling. For more than
forty years, the Maryland-born author has experimented
with a variety of fictional forms, drawing upon his vast experience with Western literary tradition. His short stories,
novellas, and novels concern themselves with the interaction of reader and text as well as the more fundamental
questions of personal identity and the innate absurdity of
human existence. Barth's complex and demanding fiction
has been the subject of numerous scholarly studies, but
general readers find, "in his fascinated commitment to the
art—and to the criticism—of storytelling, he has no
rival," declares William Pritchard in the *New York Times
Book Review. John Barth* author E. P. Walkiewicz names
the subject of his study a "writer who throughout his career has exhibited great versatility, technical virtuosity,
learning, and wit."

Introducing Barth as the "most cerebral of novelists,"
Curt Suplee goes on to state in the *Washington Post* that

Barth has reaped "a madcap eminence (and occasional
odium) for huge and bawdy intellectual fables, philosophical vaudeville, [and] rococo parodies of antique literary
forms." Barth's first novel, *The Floating Opera,* was sec-
ond-runner-up for the National Book Award in 1956; *Lost
in the Funhouse: Fiction for Print, Tape, Live Voice* was
nominated for the same award in 1968, and *Chimera* won
it in 1973. In addition, every year on his birthday the author hears from a nationwide fan club, The Society for the
Celebration of Barthomania. "Fortunately for the size of
one's ego, there are always at least as many critics telling
you to go back to [the] marsh and stick your head in it,"
Barth remarked to Suplee.

The unpredictable author's encyclopedic fictions have baf-
fled some critics, yet many reviewers recognize his genius
even when pronouncing his novels unreadable or tedious.
A review in the *Times Literary Supplement* rates *The Sot-
Weed Factor, Giles, Goat-Boy; or, The Revised New Syllabus,* and *Chimera* "easily the best worst in modern fiction." Their author, critics have found, is just as difficult
to assess. Efforts to place Barth in a literary category are
futile, Walkiewicz explains, due to "the formal complexity, verbal richness, and eclectic content" of his books.

Multiple puns, literary jokes and labyrinthine plots reminiscent of Vladimir Nabokov and Jorge Luis Borges secure Barth's standing with "the great sportsmen of contemporary fiction," to quote *City of Words: American Fiction, 1950-1970* author Tony Tanner. Frank D.
McConnell's study, *Four American Postwar Novelists: Bellow, Mailer, Barth, and Pynchon,* notes the difference between the pure sport of Nabokov's *Pale Fire* and Barth's
fiction, which combines lexical play with "the stuff of history, of change and the dynamic flux of ideas." The heroes
in Barth's "preposterous fictions" attempt to find "a
philosophical justification for life, search for values and a
basis for action in a relativistic cosmos, [and] concern
themselves with . . . the question of whether character
and external reality are stable or floating phenomena,"
Gerhard Joseph summarizes in *John Barth.* Furthermore,
indicates Walkiewicz, Barth consistently "has undermined the foundations of his own authority, and has toyed
with a profound skepticism that calls into question . . .
all systems of ethics and philosophy." In *The Contemporary Writer,* L. S. Dembo and Cyrena N. Pondrom affirm:
"It is appropriate that Barth should refuse to see himself
as a part of any intellectual tradition, including nihilism,
while remaining one of the best comic-absurdists of his
time." The books are not strictly novels of ideas, say critics, who point to an exuberant comic sexuality and a per-
vasive concern with aesthetics as dominating features of
Barth's work.

"Almost all commentators" saw Barth's first novel, *The
Floating Opera,* "as a philosophical work," Frank Gado

generalized in an interview with Barth published in *First Person: Conversations on Writers and Writing.* Barth admitted he was engrossed in certain problems, particularly suicide and nihilism (the view that all beliefs and values are relative and that life is meaningless). He planned to write a comic "philosophical minstrel show" informed by memories of a showboat he had seen as a child. "The plan grew . . . I decided to write three novels, all dealing with the problem of nihilism."

In *The Floating Opera,* narrator-protagonist Todd Andrews realizes that, if there are no absolutes, one's own version of reality amounts to only one of numerous other possibilities; even one's own identity is not certifiable in such a world. On the other hand, shifts in philosophical positions do nothing to alleviate the arbitrary nature and finality of biological facts such as Andrews' own potentially fatal heart condition. Finding no way to overcome such facts, and seeing no ultimate justification for any action, Andrews decides to commit suicide. *Dictionary of Literary Biography* contributor Arthur D. Casciato explains that "the story is 'fraught with curiosities, melodrama, spectacle, instruction, and entertainment.' Its digressive plot includes a grisly World War I foxhole scene in which Todd bayonets a German soldier, an adulterous *menage a trois,* and a hilariously complicated legal dispute complete with seventeen wills and 129 jars of human excrement."

The End of the Road, the second novel to treat nihilism according to Barth's plan, "would begin with the conclusion of the first as its premise but come to completely different conclusions—horrifying conclusions, where people who shouldn't die do die, where people are destroyed by their own and other people's ideas," the author explained to Gado. In *The Floating Opera,* main character Todd Andrews "reveals that he has only been able to move and act at all by adopting a series of masks," and he recognizes that the people in his life are equally inauthentic, notes Tanner. Protagonist Jacob Horner in *The End of the Road* promotes these views to Rennie, the wife of Joe Morgan, "a fanatical ideologue whose philosophical wrestling match" against Horner "ends disastrously," Joseph reports. Morgan, who has married Rennie because he can make her a disciple of his ethical system, deliberately introduces her to Horner "as an ethical experiment," to quote from the novel. Horner undermines Rennie's faith in her husband's authenticity, then sleeps with her. She conceives a child who may be either Morgan's or Horner's, then decides to have an abortion. Barth's all-pervasive humor dismisses "the ordinary moral and psychological implications" of these events, says Beverly Gross in the *Chicago Review.* But the novel "repudiates itself, or rather it repudiates what would seem to be its glib ability to deal with, and therefore dismiss, ugliness, pain,

and despair" when Rennie chokes to death on her own vomit during the abortion. "Rennie's hemorrhaging corpse cannot be transformed into comedy, nor does Barth try. This is the second stage of undercutting: having reduced everything to comedy," Barth exposes humor's inadequacy, maintains Gross.

The premise destroyed at the end of *The Sot-Weed Factor* is the radical innocence of seventeenth-century poet Ebenezer Cooke. At the outset of this mock-epic, Cooke determines to remain a virgin. He later finds that he must consummate his marriage to a whore in order to regain control of his estate in the morally and politically corrupt colony of Maryland. In *Forum-Service,* Leslie Fiedler notes that Barth "distorts the recognitions and reversals of popular literature, first in the direction of travesty and then of nightmare: brother and sister recognize each other on the verge of rape; Indian and white man find they possess a common father when they confess a common genital inadequacy; the tomahawked and drowned corpses in one chapter revive in the next. Yet . . . the parody remains utterly serious, the farce and melodrama evoke terror and pity, and the flagrant mockery of a happy ending constricts the heart. And all the while one laughs, at a pitch somewhere between hysteria and sheer delight." "The notion of any serious historical inquiry is undermined" in *The Sot-Weed Factor,* Tanner maintains. The book reminds us that American history is the result of "storytelling," one of "our attempts to name and control the world around us," McConnell concurs. For Heide Ziegler, *The Sot-Weed Factor* is, "a, or even the, decisive landmark in the development of postmodern fiction."

Barth indeed reinvents the universe, making it a University in *Giles, Goat-Boy; or, The Revised New Syllabus,* the novel that would prove to be his first commercial success. In a *Wisconsin Studies in Contemporary Literature* interview with John Enck, Barth said he set out to write a "comic Old Testament," or "souped-up Bible" after reviewers had alerted him to parallels between Ebenezer Cooke and the archetypical hero of world mythology. In preparation, Barth studied the works of comparative mythologists who had seen events and conditions recur in the life stories of many ritual heroes. These events include the archetypical descent into the underworld as a test to achieve immortality. Giles "was for better or worse the conscious and ironic orchestration" of this archetype, the author discloses in *Chimera.*

In *Giles, Goat-Boy; or, The Revised New Syllabus,* a "wildly rambunctious" novel, as *New York Times Book Review* contributor Guy Davenport describes it, George Giles, raised as the goat Billy Bockfuss, sets out to become the savior, or Grand Tutor, of his world. "The narrative requires Giles to work out a viable ethical position for himself and his potential tutees" and to descend into the belly of the computer that controls the University to either pass or fail, Robert Scholes sums up in the *New York Times Book Review.* Along the way, Barth supplies "sometimes sacrilegious imitations and distortions of . . . demigod heroes from Dionysius and Oedipus to Moses and Christ," McConnell notes. Tanner suggests that "it is perhaps another of Barth's ironies that it has taken over 700 pages to bring his hero to a realization that truth lies beyond terms."

If Barth debunks all orthodoxies and academic guideposts through Giles, as Scholes's study *The Fabulators* states, he also undercuts his own authority by enclosing the text in a frame of introductory publisher's and author's disclaimers, and several endnotes that question the testament's validity. Tanner comments: "We become aware of a writer going to perverse lengths . . . not only to demonstrate what he can invent—and that is prodigious—but to demonstrate how he can equivocate about, trivialize, and undermine his own inventions." The book's point, Gross speculates, is "to expose the fraudulence of [narrative] art."

"The Literature of Exhaustion," first printed in 1967 in the *Atlantic*, further increased Barth's fame. The seminal essay has been "reprinted, quoted, and 'explained' by any number of critics and teachers anxious to clarify and celebrate the fiction, not only of Barth, but of his contemporaries," McConnell reports. It was often misunderstood, claims Barth in a later essay, "The Literature of Replenishment." Perceived as a "death of the novel" treatise, it was actually a state-of-the-art message that proposed various keys to the novel's survival in the face of exhausted possibilities. The misread essay, Barth goes on, "was really about . . . the effective 'exhaustion' not of language or literature, but of the aesthetic of high modernism: that admirable, not-to-be-repudiated, but essentially completed 'program' " that had produced masterpieces of erudition and technique such as James Joyce's *Ulysses.* The next generation of high modernist authors had yet to produce a work that would be the next stage in the genre's history, and critics began to talk of the art form's death. But "a few people—like Beckett and the Argentinian, Borges, and Nabokov, for example—have been able to turn this ultimacy against itself in order to produce new work," Barth told Phyllis Meras of the *New York Times Book Review.* This view puts the novelist "in competition with the accumulated best of human history." One response to this problem, Barth later remarked to Gado, "is to ignore it." Barth instead focused on a number of ways to meet this challenge.

One way of meeting the challenge is "to write a novel about it," Barth's 1967 essay states. Fiction that aspires to become "part of the history of fiction," as Barth demonstrates in *The Friday Book: Essays and Other Nonfiction,*

"is almost always about itself," whatever else may be its concerns. Another way to go beyond the achievements of past novelists without repudiating their accomplishments is to parody them. "Far from disowning a received way of doing something difficult, [parody] is meant to show rather that it can be done easily and for sport," Richard Poirier explains in his study of postmodern fiction, *The Performing Self.* The writer can also move out of realism (which has been outdone by cinema and electronic media) into irrealism, to bring fiction up to date with "painting, music, and . . . the age," Joe David Bellamy notes in *The New Fiction: Interviews with Innovative American Writers.* Another way to extend the life of the novel is to seize upon one of the last resources of originality left to the modern artist, "the voice, the authorial instrument that shapes the retelling," in Joseph's words; or, as Paul Gray of *Time* puts it, "to exalt artifice and make the telling the subject of the tale." Such writing must be "comic about its own self-consciousness" to be interesting, Barth expressed to Bellamy in a *New American Review* interview. A writer can also revive an exhausted genre by going, Barth says, "back to the roots" of a tradition, or to the roots of storytelling itself, to discover unused possibilities or revive stories that may be reshaped to fit one's own purpose.

Barth's characters dramatize these solutions in *Lost in the Funhouse* and *Chimera,* two collections of shorter fiction that explore "the oral narrative tradition from which printed fiction evolved," according to his article, "Getting Oriented" in the *The Friday Book.* McConnell points out that "neither book is, finally, a 'collection.' Both are a series of tales which, in their order of telling and their explicit comments upon each other, are something like novels." When seen as novels, their plots become "what happens to the storyteller himself as he moves through the series" of related short stories and novellas.

The stories in *Lost in the Funhouse* depict characters lost in mazes of refracting and distorting mirrors and echo chambers. Their confusions express "the condition of disorientation" that Barth identifies in "Getting Oriented" as his own "fictionary stock in trade. Intellectual and spiritual disorientation is the family disease of all my main characters—a disease usually complicated by ontological disorientation, since knowing where you're at is often contingent upon knowing who you are." Puetz relates this concern to contemporary views on personality. "The novel of the sixties has celebrated . . . the second coming of Proteus, the archetypal shape-shifter. . . . If change itself is the defining feature of human existence, the argument goes, then why not . . . become a whole spectrum of varying selves?" This shape-shifting, Tanner feels, brings Barth to an "impasse" in which the author "can no longer get hold of any 'reality' at all; everything he touches turns into fictions," or the sound of his own voice. "To find an exit from a world of self-generated fictions . . . demands an intense effort," Puetz writes. "The feasibility and the formal implications of such an effort as much as the increasing worries about the exit from the maze of fiction prove to be the opening themes of . . . *Funhouse* and *Chimera.*"

Chimera contains three novellas, the retellings of three myths whose heroes, like Barth, are in the process of reorientation to discern their future: Bellerophon, who learns that one does not become a hero by merely imitating heroes; Dunyazade, who, after witnessing countless permutations of narrative and sexual expression while stationed at the foot of her sister Scheherazade's bed, must make her future out of whatever is left; and Perseus, whose walk into the future takes him past the scenes of his life so far, depicted on the walls of his temple, which is shaped like a nautilus shell. Unlike a closed circle, the temple spirals outward, allowing Perseus to move forward by retracing his own history. Barth explained in *Caliban* how the image further relates to his oeuvre: "When the chambered nautilus adds a new chamber to itself, that chamber is determined somewhat by its predecessors, but it's where the beast is living presently, and he's a larger animal for it." Each new room is a gnomon, "something you can add to an already existing figure to change its size without changing its basic shape." This structure replicates "the way I like to think about my past, present, and future work," he says; in other words, each new novel provides a way "to see what new changes I can ring around some old concerns without falling into complete self-parody." Though many reviewers see *Lost in the Funhouse* and *Chimera* as proof that Barth has been swallowed up by his own self-conscious obsession, others concur with McConnell that the author's attempt "to write himself out of a corner" generally succeeds. Subsequent books, they maintain, demonstrate Barth's ability to invent new work by recycling traditional literature, and his own.

LETTERS—larger and more complex than its predecessors, "brilliant, witty . . . and damn near unreadable as well," to quote Peter S. Prescott of *Newsweek*—rehearses Barth's literary past in letters he ostensibly receives from characters in previous novels. At the same time, scholars note, it carries the author beyond the "impasse" of predominantly aesthetic concerns into the world of public events. *LETTERS* sums up the decade of the seventies along with Barth's collected works, observes Frederick R. Karl in his *American Fictions, 1940-1980: A Comprehensive History and Critical Evaluation.* Because the book "put[s] the weight of the past on every present activity" and offers the War of 1812 as "the major clue to American history," Karl deems it "invaluable" as a cultural document despite complexities that bar a general readership. *LETTERS,* says Benjamin De Mott in an *Atlantic* review,

"is by turns a brain-buster, a marathon, an exasperation, a frustration, a provocation to earnest thought. Barth is preaching, wittily but with total conviction, on the limits of our kind, on the sanity of doubting that we know where, in our lives, fiction stops."

The Friday Book is "required reading for any serious student of Barth's canon," Weixlmann notes. Its contents constitute "a resume of my Stories" from *The Floating Opera* to *The Tidewater Tales,* "and an account of what I believe I have been up to in writing them," Barth says in the introduction to one of its pieces. The book begins with "Some Reasons Why I Tell the Stories I Tell . . . ," an essay that reveals the elements of his personal history that have become part of his unique aesthetic. His books "tend to come in pairs" because he was born an opposite-sex twin. "In myth, twins signified whatever dualisms a culture entertained: . . . good/evil, creation/destruction, what had they." For Western culture, he explains, they signify the divided or alienated self in search of the missing half. Thus he is a writer "in part because I no longer have my twin to be wordless with." And since twins share "a language before . . . and beyond speech," they acquire language primarily for "dealing with the outsiders," a factor that explains why Barth is "perhaps unnaturally conscious" of language, "forever at it, tinkering, foregrounding it." If being a twin underscored life's dualities, living in the landscape of tidewater Maryland where borders are always shifting blurred the distinctions between them. Barth remarks, "Your web-foot amphibious marsh-nurtured writer will likely by mere reflex regard many conventional boundaries and distinctions as arbitrary, fluid, negotiable: form versus content, realism versus irrealism, fact versus fiction, life versus art." The unimpeded flatness of the marshland, he claims, partly accounts for his drive to become distinguished at something.

As a young man with this goal in mind, Barth went to the Juilliard School of Music in New York to become a jazz arranger. Instead, he found himself a talented amateur among professionals, and "went home to think of some other way to become distinguished." As an undergraduate at Johns Hopkins University, he filed books in the Classics Department and the stacks of the Oriental seminary, and became enchanted with the tenth-century Sanskrit *Ocean of Story* and Richard Burton's annotated *Arabian Nights*—two reservoirs of frame-tale literature that were to inspire him throughout his career. The example of Scheherazade, whose tales told at night to her misogynist ruler prevented him from executing her in the morning, suggested to him several ways to survive twentieth-century pressures on the novel, and a justification for writing self-reflexive fiction. As he reasons in *The Friday Book,* "We tell stories and listen to them because we live stories and live in them. Narrative equals language equals life: To cease to narrate . . . is to die. . . . If this is true, then not only is all fiction fiction about fiction, but all fiction about fiction is in fact fiction about life."

Barth graduated with a commitment to become a writer and meanwhile earn a living by teaching. He has taught at Pennsylvania State University, the State University of New York at Buffalo, and at his alma mater. Partly due to these affiliations, Barth has been called an academic writer. Though he resisted this label at first, his mid-life orientation brought him to recognize, as he says in "Getting Oriented," that all of his novels are about education—or rather, "imperfect or misfired education." In *Harper's* he writes: "There is chalk dust on the sleeve of my soul. . . . I have never been away from classrooms for longer than a few months. . . . I believe I know my strengths and limitations as a teacher the way I know them as a writer: doubtful of my accomplishments in both *metiers,* I am not doubtful at all that they are my *metiers,* for good or ill." However, Barth remains an arranger at heart, as he says in *The Friday Book,* and his "chief pleasure is to take a received melody—an old narrative poem, a classical myth, a shopworn literary convention . . .— and, improvising like a jazzman within its constraints, re-orchestrating it to its present purpose."

With *Sabbatical: A Romance,* Barth "resume[s] a romance with realism," he intimates to Suplee. Shorter than previous novels and less obsessed with comments on his craft, the book stresses certain apocalyptic elements that Barth has carried from the beginning. "Todd Andrews in *The Floating Opera* (and again in *Letters*) wonders sentence by sentence whether his heart will carry him from subject to predicate; in 'Sabbatical,' set on Chesapeake Bay in 1980, the background question is whether the world will end before the novel does," Barth states in the *New York Times Book Review.* On their sabbatical, narrator-protagonists Fenwick Turner and Susan Seckler cruise to the Caribbean and return to the Chesapeake Bay. The possibly CIA-related death of Fenwick's twin brother is one of several mysteries they encounter along the way, and "the story fills up with the rough contemporary world," Michael Wood relates in the *New York Times Book Review.* In fact, the book "was occasioned" by the mysterious death of ex-CIA official John Paisley, whose corpse was found in Barth's "home waters" in 1978, as he told Suplee. Suplee notes, "This literal intrusion of the real world becomes a ditto in the novel: Barth simply reprints 20 pages of Paisley stories from *The Baltimore Sun.*"

Sabbatical nonetheless retains some familiar Barth trademarks, notes Charles Trueheart in the *Washington Post Book World.* It "is the record of its own composition" and "Fenn and Susan argue incessantly about the proper way to tell the story . . . and remind one another of the literary traditions into which their narrative falls." John W. Al-

dridge, also writing in the *Washington Post Book World,* approves Barth's new tack toward realism: "While to be sure the story does contain elements indicating that the familiar temporizing mind of John Barth is still hard at work, they are effectively subordinated to the strong realistic thrust of the narrative and so provide the book with an agreeable controlled complexity instead of burying it beneath the old fog-bank of endless equivocation."

By design, *Tidewater Tales* was to be "a sort of opposite-sex twin to *Sabbatical,*" featuring a married couple afloat on the same bay, whose situation, Barth reveals in *The Friday Book,* was to be "rather the reverse of Fenwick's and Susan's." Whereas Susan, in *Sabbatical,* wonders how she can bring children into the world at this late hour and aborts twins, Katharine Sagamore, in *Tidewater Tales,* happily carries and delivers twins, not fully knowing what to make of the fact that people still desire to procreate in a threatened world. Again, two lines of interest develop: one, a plot entangled with the problematical real world on the verge of apocalypse; and the other, related to stories from classical literature that parallel the Sagamore's voyage. *Globe & Mail* reviewer Douglas Hill praises the book's "dizzying . . . manipulations of literary forms and traditions." Aldridge concurs that it is "the richest, most ebullient and technically daring" of Barth's canon to date, "crowded" as it is "with grand virtuosic effects that seem to have nothing to do with the action except to interrupt it, . . . offered simply because they are such fun." The stories of Odysseus, Don Quixote, Scheherazade, Huck Finn, and more resurface here, their retelling facilitated by events in the realistic narrative. Some reviewers find the tales improved in the retelling while others, such as *New York Times Book Review* contributor William Pritchard, are less enamored. Pritchard qualifies his opinion by saying that "Barth gives ample food to please or displease everyone's taste." Moved by the book's "richness as a love story—marital, filial, domestic—and also its love of a place, of a country, even as place and country are scarred by human depredations," Pritchard leaves it to the reader to decide "whether the novel's ending—or its various coves and shallows sailed into along the way—give us something more rich and strange than a funhouse."

With *Tidewater* and *Sabbatical,* Barth seems to have "written the same novel twice," using materials already employed in previous works, notes *Los Angeles Times Book Review* contributor Richard Lehan, who wonders what kind of work can follow. Not surprisingly from an author fascinated by blurring the boundaries between past and present, reality and fiction, and one novel to the next, the author has continued to produce fictive tricks through stories in which the central character navigates sailing ships. *The Last Voyage of Somebody the Sailor* presents, as do its predecessors, an intensely self-absorbed hero who pilots his ship through the Chesapeake Bay as well as the familiar metaphoric waters of Sir Richard Burton's nineteenth-century translation of *A Thousand and One Nights. New York Times Book Review* correspondent Jonathan Raban cites Barth for his sensitive rendering of "the muddy, estuarine landscapes of Maryland's Eastern Shore in . . . fresh and glowing colors." Raban quickly adds, however: "Readers in search of authentic, original reality had better go elsewhere; they will not be happy in this ingenious multi-story fiction in which every floor turns out to be another false bottom."

Barth switched to the challenge of creating "book-end" works when he published *Once Upon a Time: A Floating Opera* in 1994. Purported to be the final work of a fictional character named John Barth, the novel is a meditation on autobiography, memoir, and narrative. "True to his lifelong fascination with twins and doubles, and his rage for symmetry and fictive order, both Mr. Barth's first and 'last' novels are floating operas, twinned mirror images of each other, reflecting the beginning and end," writes R. H. W. Dillard in the *New York Times Book Review.* "*Once Upon a Time* is an appropriately complicated texture of riffs and motifs, reflexive images and echoes from his other books. . . . *Once Upon a Time* is, then, its own complex and complete self, but it is also the satisfying last chapter and tying up of a much larger 12-volume work, the remarkable and altogether noteworthy opera and virtual voyages of John Barth." Dillard concludes of the work: "it is brilliantly conceived, elegantly written, bursting with life, profound in its understanding, bawdy and funny, and comic, in the wisest and best sense of the word."

Barth speculated to Israel Shenker for the *New York Times Book Review,* "Maybe when I'm 90 I'll be as grave as Sophocles at 90. More likely, Zeus willing, I'll be writing comedy in my 80's as Thomas Mann did, and die laughing." In any case, Barth has parlayed his talents into a permanent place in literary history; commentary proliferates in the wake of each new work, and criticism of his entire *oeuvre* shows no signs of abatement. According to Walkiewicz, "Barth's 'significance,' his place in the tradition remain, of course, matters very much under consideration or open to debate." Poirier explains why that place is not clear; he allows that Barth is "perhaps more intellectually attuned, . . . and surely more philosophically adroit than all but a few of the exclusively literary critics now writing in America or Europe." At the same time, however, Poirier goes on to observe, "admiration for [Barth's] thinking about literature must very often contend with the experience of reading [his] novels. . . . We sit in a favorite chair . . . and we open, let us say, *Giles, Goat-Boy.* Several days later we're probably no longer infatuated with repeated illustrations that literary and philo-

sophical structures are really put-ons, and that what we are doing is kind of silly."

"While there are those who, as always, are of the opinion that [Barth] has reduced the art of fiction to the chronicling 'of minstrel misery,' there are also many who are willing to affirm that he has added a number of 'minstrel masterpieces' . . . to the treasury," Walkiewicz notes. He adds that "if Barth has earned the high praise he . . . has received from some, . . . it is because he has given form and substance to a body of work that is traditional, contemporary, and trail-blazing, consistent and evolutionary, self-affirming and self-questioning, that acknowledges contradictions and contrarieties and enlists them in the service of art and humanity." Weixlmann comments: "Barth has, on various occasions, indicated that the true measure of his authorial success will not be taken for decades, even centuries; that his attempt, as a writer, is to rival Shakespeare and Cervantes rather than his contemporaries. In this context, Barth scholarship is in its infancy, despite the fact that much serious critical attention has already been focused on his work."

Indeed, Barth criticism has itself become the subject of several compendiums, including *Critical Essays on John Barth* by Joseph J. Waldmeir. In one essay collected by Waldmeir, Richard W. Noland concludes that Barth's "most interesting and important achievement . . . is the embodiment of philosophical ideas in a form both tragic and comic. . . . He considers each of the ways in which Western man has attempted to fill his life with value after the death of the old gods . . . only to find all of them inadequate." All inadequate, perhaps, except for storytelling, Josephine Hendin contends in *Harper's.* Her survey of Barth's early work distills Barth's message that "storytelling is life's means and only prize. And no one has written more glitteringly than John Barth of the worthlessness of the heart, or the great munificence of language in bestowing so much grandeur, so much richness, so many pearly epigrams on all us swine."

BIOGRAPHICAL/CRITICAL SOURCES:

BOOKS

Adams, Robert Martin, *After Joyce: Studies in Fiction after "Ulysses",* Oxford University Press (Oxford, England), 1977.

Allen, Mary, *The Necessary Blankness: Women in Major American Fiction of the Sixties,* University of Illinois Press (Urbana), 1976.

Authors in the News, Volumes 1 and 2, Gale (Detroit), 1976.

Baldwin, Kenneth H., and David K. Kirby, editors, *Individual and Community: Variations on a Theme in American Fiction,* Duke University Press (Durham, NC), 1975.

Barth, John, *The Floating Opera,* Appleton-Century-Crofts, 1956, revised edition, Doubleday, 1967, reprinted with a new foreword by the author, Doubleday-Anchor, 1988.

Barth, John, *The End of the Road,* Doubleday, 1958, revised edition, 1967, reprinted with a new foreword by the author, Doubleday-Anchor, 1988.

Barth, John, *The Sot-Weed Factor,* Doubleday, 1960, revised edition, 1967, reprinted with a new foreword by the author, Doubleday-Anchor, 1988.

Barth, John, *Lost in the Funhouse: Fiction for Print, Tape, Live Voice,* Doubleday, 1968, reprinted with new forward by the author, Doubleday-Anchor, 1988.

Barth, John, *Chimera,* Random House, 1972.

Barth, John, *LETTERS,* Putnam, 1979.

Barth, John, *The Friday Book: Essays and Other Nonfiction,* Putnam, 1984.

Bellamy, Joe David, *The New Fiction: Interviews with Innovative American Writers,* University of Illinois Press, 1974.

Bergonzi, Bernard, *The Situation of the Novel,* University of Pittsburgh Press (Pittsburgh), 1970.

Bowen, Zack R., *A Reader's Guide to John Barth,* Greenwood Press (Westport, CT), 1994.

Bryant, Jerry, *The Open Decision: The Contemporary American Novel and Its Intellectual Background,* Free Press, 1970.

Caramello, Charles, *Silverless Mirrors: Self and Postmodern American Fiction,* University Presses of Florida (Gainsville), 1983.

Contemporary Authors Bibliographical Series, Volume 1: *American Novelists,* Gale, 1986.

Contemporary Literary Criticism, Gale, Volume 1, 1973, Volume 2, 1974, Volume 3, 1975, Volume 5, 1976, Volume 7, 1977, Volume 9, 1978, Volume 10, 1979, Volume 14, 1980, Volume 27, 1984.

Dembo, L. S., and Cyrena N. Pondrom, editors, *The Contemporary Writer,* University of Wisconsin Press (Madison), 1972.

D'Haen, Theo, *Text to Reader: a Communicative Approach to Fowles, Barth, Cortazar, and Boon,* John Benjamins (Philadelphia), 1983.

Dictionary of Literary Biography, Volume 2: *American Novelists since World War II,* Gale, 1978.

Fogel, Stanley, *Understanding John Barth,* University of South Carolina Press (Columbia), 1990.

Gado, Frank, *First Person: Conversations on Writers and Writing,* Union College Press (Syracuse, NY), 1973.

Gardner, John, *On Moral Fiction,* Basic Books (New York City), 1978.

Harris, Charles B., *Contemporary American Novelists of the Absurd,* College and University Press, 1971.

Harris, Charles B., *Passionate Virtuosity: The Fiction of John Barth,* University of Illinois Press, 1983.

Hassan, Ihab, *The Dismemberment of Orpheus,* Oxford University Press, 1971.

Hauck, Richard Boyd, *A Cheerful Nihilism: Confidence and "The Absurd" in American Humorous Fiction,* Indiana University Press (Bloomington), 1971.

Hergt, Tobias, *Das Motiv der Hochschule im Romanwerk van Bernard Malamud und John Barth,* Peter Lang (New York City), 1979.

Hipkiss, Robert A., *The American Absurd: Pynchon, Vonnegut, and Barth,* Associated Faculty Press (Port Washington, NY), 1984.

Hyman, Stanley Edgar, *Standards: A Chronicle of Books for Our Time,* Horizon Press (New York City), 1966.

Joseph, Gerhard, *John Barth,* University of Minnesota Press (Minneapolis), 1970.

Karl, Frederick R., *American Fictions, 1940-1980: A Comprehensive History and Critical Evaluation,* Harper (New York City), 1983.

Kennard, Jean E., *Number and Nightmare,* Archon (Hamden, CT), 1975.

Klinkowitz, Jerome, *Literary Disruptions: The Making of a Post-Contemporary American Fiction,* University of Illinois Press, 1975.

Klinkowitz, Jerome, *Literary Subversions: New American Fiction and the Practice of Criticism,* Southern Illinois University Press (Carbondale), 1985.

Kostelanetz, Richard, editor, *American Writing Today,* Forum Books/Voice of America Editions, 1982.

Kostelanetz, Richard, editor, *On Contemporary Literature,* Avon (New York City), 1964.

Lehan, Richard, *A Dangerous Crossing,* Southern Illinois University Press, 1973.

Lindsay, Alan, *Death in the Funhouse: John Barth and Poststructural Aesthetics,* Peter Lang, 1995.

McConnell, Frank D., *Four Postwar American Novelists: Bellow, Mailer, Barth, and Pynchon,* University of Chicago Press (Chicago), 1976.

Morrell, David, *John Barth: An Introduction,* Pennsylvania State University Press, 1976.

Olderman, Raymond M., *Beyond the Waste Land: A Study of the American Novel in the Nineteen-Sixties,* Yale University Press (New Haven, CT), 1972.

Poirier, Richard, *The Performing Self,* Oxford University Press, 1971.

Porush, David, *The Soft Machine: Cybernetic Fiction,* Methuen (London), 1985.

Raban, Jonathan, *The Technique of Modern Fiction,* Edward Arnold (Baltimore, MD), 1966.

Scholes, Robert, *The Fabulators,* Oxford University Press, 1967.

Schulz, Max F., *Black Humor Fiction of the Sixties: A Pluralistic Definition of Man and His World,* Ohio University Press (Athens), 1973.

Schulz, Max F., *The Muses of John Barth: Tradition and Metafiction from Lost in the Funhouse to The Tidewater Tales,* Johns Hopkins University Press (Baltimore), 1990.

Stark, John O., *The Literature of Exhaustion: Borges, Nabokov, Barth,* Duke University Press, 1974.

Tanner, Tony, *City of Words: American Fiction, 1950-1970,* Harper, 1971.

Tharpe, Jac, *John Barth: The Comic Sublimity of Paradox,* Southern Illinois University Press, 1974.

Tilton, John W., *Cosmic Satire in the Contemporary Novel,* Bucknell University Press (Cranbury, NJ), 1977.

Tobin, Patricia Drechsel, *John Barth and the Anxiety of Continuance,* University of Pennsylvania Press, 1992.

Vidal, Gore, *Matters of Fact and Fiction: Essays, 1973-1976,* Random House (New York City), 1977.

Vine, Richard Allan, *John Barth: An Annotated Bibliography,* Scarecrow (Metuchen, NJ), 1977.

Waldmeir, Joseph J., editor, *Critical Essays on John Barth,* G. K. Hall (Boston), 1980.

Walkiewicz, E. P., *John Barth,* G. K. Hall, 1986.

Walsh, Thomas P. and Cameron Northouse, *John Barth, Jerzy Kosinski, and Thomas Pynchon: A Reference Guide,* G. K. Hall, 1977.

Weixlmann, Joseph, *John Barth: A Bibliography,* Garland Publishing (New York City), 1976.

Werner, Craig Hansen, *Paradoxical Resolutions: American Fiction since Joyce,* University of Illinois Press, 1982.

Ziegler, Heide, and Christopher Bigsby, editors, *The Radical Imagination and the Liberal Tradition: Interviews with English and American Novelists,* Junction, 1982.

PERIODICALS

America, September 17, 1966; November 26, 1966; October 7, 1972; November 18, 1972.

Amerikastudien, Volume XXV, number 2, 1980.

Antioch Review, spring, 1980; fall, 1982.

Atlantic, August, 1967, pp. 28-34; July, 1968; October, 1968; October, 1972; November, 1979; June, 1982; March, 1991, p. 133; June, 1994, p. 138.

Best Sellers, October 1, 1966; October 15, 1968; November 1, 1973; January, 1985, p. 390.

Booklist, November 15, 1966; November 15, 1972.

Books & Arts, October 26, 1979.

Books and Bookmen, April, 1967; November, 1968.

Book Week, September 26, 1965; August 7, 1966; November 18, 1984, p. 9.

Buffalo Courier Express Magazine, September 12, 1976.

Caliban, Volume XII, 1975.

Canadian Review of Contemporary Literature, June, 1982.

Chicago Review, winter-spring, 1959; November, 1968.

Chicago Tribune, August 21, 1960; September 15, 1968; June 7, 1987.

Chicago Tribune Book World, November 11, 1979; May 30, 1982; January 13, 1985.

Christian Century, September 21, 1966.

Commentary, October, 1966.

Commonweal, October 21, 1966; December 2, 1966.

Contemporary Literature, winter, 1971, pp. 60-73; winter, 1981, pp. 1-23; winter, 1985, pp. 460-81; winter, 1988, pp. 485-97.

Criticism, winter, 1970; spring, 1991, pp. 235-256.

Critique, fall, 1963; winter, 1965-66; Volume IX, number 1, 1966; Volume XIII, number 3, 1972, pp. 11-29, 31-43; Volume XVII, number 1, 1975, pp. 69-77; Volume XVIII, number 2, 1976, pp. 59-85; fall, 1991, p. 3.

Detroit News, September 17, 1972; September 30, 1979.

Encounter, June, 1967.

Esquire, October, 1979.

Falcon, spring, 1972.

Forum-Service, January 7, 1961.

Georgia Review, summer, 1974, pp. 290-306.

Globe & Mail (Toronto), September 3, 1966; January 26, 1985; July 4, 1987.

Guardian, October 13, 1961.

Harper's, September, 1972; September, 1973; November, 1986.

Harrisburg Patriot (Pennsylvania), March 30, 1965.

Horizon, January, 1963.

Hudson Review, autumn, 1967; spring, 1969; winter, 1972-73, pp. 703-14.

Illustrated London News, April 8, 1967.

Journal of Narrative Technique, winter, 1978, pp. 42-55; winter, 1981.

Kenyon Review, winter, 1961; May 1, 1987, p. 657.

Life, August 12, 1966; October 18, 1968; October 6, 1972.

Listener, March 30, 1967; October 3, 1968; September 18, 1969.

London Magazine, May, 1967; December, 1969.

Los Angeles Times Book Review, November 18, 1984, p. 3; June 28, 1987, p. 10.

Massachusetts Review, May, 1960.

Mississippi Quarterly, spring, 1979.

Modern Fiction Studies, winter, 1968-69; spring, 1973, pp. 69-78; autumn, 1974; summer, 1976; summer, 1979; winter, 1985, p. 763; winter, 1987, pp. 647-55; autumn, 1990, p. 405; summer, 1992, p. 427.

MOSAIC: A Journal for the Study of Literature and Ideas, Volume III, number 2, 1970; fall, 1974.

Nation, November 19, 1960; September 5, 1966; October 28, 1968, pp. 441-42; December 18, 1972, pp. 631-33; October 13, 1979.

National Observer, August 1, 1966; August 29, 1966; September 16, 1968; February 23, 1970; October 7, 1972.

National Review, December 3, 1968; October 13, 1972.

New American Review, April, 1972; September, 1985, p. 66.

New Leader, February 13, 1961; March 2, 1964; April 12, 1965.

New Republic, September 3, 1966; November 23, 1968, pp. 30, 34-35; December 1, 1979; August 10, 1987, pp. 35-37.

New Statesman, October 13, 1961; March 31, 1967; September 19, 1969; July 19, 1974.

Newsweek, August 8, 1966; December 19, 1966; September 30, 1968; February 16, 1970; October 9, 1972; January 1, 1973; October 1, 1979; May 24, 1982.

New Yorker, December 10, 1966; September 30, 1972; December 31, 1979; June 7, 1982.

New York Herald Tribune Book Review, July 20, 1958; September 26, 1965.

New York Review of Books, August 18, 1966; October 19, 1972; July 15, 1976; December 20, 1979; June 10, 1982.

New York Times, August 3, 1966; November 21, 1967; October 16, 1968; February 9, 1969; February 11, 1970; March 18, 1970; November 21, 1970; September 20, 1972; October 1, 1979; May 27, 1982; June 28, 1982.

New York Times Book Review, August 21, 1960; June 6, 1965; May 8, 1966; August 7, 1966; October 20, 1968; September 24, 1972; December 3, 1972; April 1, 1979; July 15, 1979; September 30, 1979; May 9, 1982; June 20, 1982; September 16, 1984; November 18, 1984, p. 16; January 5, 1986, p. 28; June 28, 1987, p. 7; February 3, 1991, p. 3; July 3, 1994, p. 13.

Novel: A Forum on Fiction, October 20, 1968; winter, 1971; September 24, 1972; December 3, 1972; July 15, 1979; September 30, 1979.

Observer, October 10, 1965; April 2, 1967; September 29, 1968; September 14, 1969; July 21, 1974; May 29, 1977; November 17, 1991, p. 65.

Partisan Review, winter, 1967; summer, 1968; spring, 1969, pp. 293-95, 297-99; summer, 1983.

Philadelphia Inquirer, February 22, 1976.

Playboy, March, 1967.

Prairie Schooner, summer, 1969; spring, 1992, p. 123.

Prism, spring, 1968.

Psychology Today, January, 1973.

Publishers Weekly, October 22, 1979; March 7, 1994, p. 52.

Punch, April 5, 1967; October 2, 1968.

Saturday Review, November 26, 1960; July 3, 1965; August 6, 1966; September 30, 1967; September 28, 1976, pp. 31-32; October 13, 1979.

South Atlantic Quarterly, summer, 1969.

Spectator, March 31, 1967; September 20, 1969; July 20, 1974, pp. 86-87; May 10, 1980; August 7, 1982; November 16, 1991, p. 50.

Studies in Short Fiction, fall, 1971, pp. 659-60; fall, 1973, pp. 373-80; fall, 1974, pp. 361-66; summer, 1975; summer, 1979, pp. 189-94.

Time, July 21, 1958; September 5, 1960; February 12, 1965; May 17, 1967; September 27, 1968; February 23, 1970; October 2, 1972; October 8, 1979; May 31, 1982; August 19, 1988, p. 901; November 15, 1991, p. 7.

Times Literary Supplement, October 27, 1961; March 30, 1967; October 10, 1968; September 18, 1969; July 26, 1974; May 30, 1980; July 23, 1982.

Tri-Quarterly, winter, 1967; winter, 1968; spring, 1975; fall, 1981.

Twentieth Century Literature, April, 1973, pp. 107-18; December, 1975; December, 1976.

Village Voice, October 6, 1966; September 17, 1979; November 19, 1979.

Virginia Quarterly Review, autumn, 1969; winter, 1972.

Voice Literary Supplement, May, 1982.

Washington Post, June 17, 1966; September 26, 1968; June 17, 1982; November 18, 1984, p. 9; June 7, 1987, pp. 1, 4.

Washington Post Book World, September 17, 1967; September 15, 1968; May 18, 1969; August 6, 1972; November 18, 1973; September 30, 1979; May 23, 1982; November 18, 1984; June 7, 1987.

Washington Post Potomac, September 3, 1967.

Wisconsin Studies in Contemporary Literature, winter-spring, 1965; autumn, 1966.

World Literature Today, spring, 1995, pp. 359-60.

Yale Review, spring, 1973.

*　　*　　*

BAUMOL, William J(ack) 1922-

PERSONAL: Born February 26, 1922, in New York, NY; son of Solomon (a bookbinder) and Lillian (Itzkowitz) Baumol; married Hilda Missel, December 27, 1941; children: Ellen Francis, Daniel Aaron. *Education:* City College (now City College of the City University of New York), B.S.S., 1942; London School of Economics and Political Science, Ph.D., 1949.

ADDRESSES: Home—P.O. Box 1502, Princeton, NJ 08542. *Office*—Department of Economics, Princeton University, Princeton, NJ 08540-1021.

CAREER: U.S. Department of Agriculture, Washington, DC, junior economist, 1942-43, 1946; University of London, London School of Economics and Political Science, London, England, assistant lecturer in economics, 1946-49; Princeton University, Princeton, NJ, assistant professor, 1949-52, associate professor, 1952-54, professor of economics, 1954-92, professor emeritus, 1992—, senior research economist, 1992—; New York University, New York City, professor of economics, 1972—, director of C. V. Starr Center for Applied Economics, 1972—. Member of board of trustees, Joint Council on Economic Education; member of board of directors, Theater Development Fund; member of advisory board, Fishman-Davidson Center for the Study of the Service Sector, Wharton School, University of Pennsylvania; founding member and member of advisory committee, World Resources Institute; chairperson and member, Economic Policy Council, State of New Jersey, 1967-75; member, National Academy of Sciences and Consultants in Industry Economics, Inc. Consultant to governments and industry. *Military service:* U.S. Army, 1943-46.

MEMBER: American Economic Association (vice-president, 1966-67; president, 1980; distinguished fellow, 1982), American Academy of Arts and Sciences, American Philosophical Society, Econometric Society (fellow; member of council, 1960-61), Association of Environmental and Resource Economists (president, 1979), Institute of Management Sciences, American Association of University Professors (past vice-president), Economic Association of Puerto Rico (distinguished member), Eastern Economic Association (president, 1978-79), Atlantic Economic Society (president, 1985-86).

AWARDS, HONORS: Guggenheim fellow, 1957-58; Ford faculty fellow, 1965-66; LL.D., Rider College, 1965; fellow, London School of Economics and Political Science, 1970; Dr. of Economics, Stockholm School of Economics, 1971; D.H.L., Knox College and University of Basel, both 1973; John R. Commons Award, Omicron Delta Epsilon, 1975; Townsend Harris Medal, Alumni Association of the City College of New York, 1975; Association of American Publishers, PSP Award, Professional and Scholarly Publishing Division, 1986, for *Superfairness: Applications and Theory,* and honorable mention in social sciences, 1989, for *Productivity and American Leadership: The Long Run;* Frank E. Seidman Distinguished Award in Political Economy, 1987; first Senior Scholar Award in the Arts and Sciences, New York University, 1992.

WRITINGS:

Welfare Economics and the Theory of the State, Harvard University Press (Cambridge, MA), 1951, 2nd edition, 1965.

Economic Dynamics, Macmillan (New York City), 1952, 3rd edition, 1970.

(With L. V. Chandler) *Economic Processes and Policies,* Harper (New York City), 1954.

Business Behavior, Value, and Growth, Macmillan, 1959, revised edition, Harcourt (San Diego, CA), 1967.

Economic Theory and Operations Analysis, Prentice-Hall (Englewood Cliffs, NJ), 1961, 3rd edition, 1972.

(Editor with Klaus Knorr) *What Price Economic Growth?,* Prentice-Hall, 1962.

The Stock Market and Economic Efficiency, Fordham University Press (Bronx, NY), 1965.

(With W. G. Bowen) *Performing Arts—the Economic Dilemma: A Study of Problems Common to Theater, Opera, Music, and Dance,* Twentieth Century Fund (New York City), 1966.

(Editor) E. M. Lerner and W. T. Carleton, *A Theory of Financial Analysis,* Harcourt, 1966.

(Editor) E. Shapiro, *Macroeconomic Analysis,* Harcourt, 1966.

(Editor with S. M. Goldfeld) *Precursors in Mathematical Economics: An Anthology,* London School of Economics (London), 1968.

Portfolio Theory: The Selection of Asset Combinations, McCaleb-Seiler, 1970.

(With M. Marcus) *Economics of Academic Libraries,* American Council on Education (Washington, DC), 1973.

(With W. E. Oates) *The Theory of Environmental Policy,* Prentice-Hall, 1975, 2nd edition, 1988.

(With Oates and S. A. B. Blackman) *Economics, Environmental Policy, and the Quality of Life,* Prentice-Hall, 1979.

(With A. S. Blinder) *Economics: Principles and Policy,* Harcourt, 1979, 6th edition, 1994.

(Editor) *Public and Private Enterprise in a Mixed Economy,* St. Martin's (New York City), 1980.

(With J. C. Panzar and R. D. Willig) *Contestable Markets and the Theory of Industry Structure,* Harcourt, 1980.

Superfairness: Applications and Theory, MIT Press (Cambridge, MA), 1986.

Microtheory: Applications and Origins, 1986.

(With L. Osberg and E. N. Wolff) *The Information Economy and the Implications of Unbalanced Growth,* 1989.

(With Blackman and Wolff) *Productivity and American Leadership: The Long View,* 1989.

(With Goldfeld, L. A. Gordon, and M. F. Koehn) *The Economics of Mutual Fund Markets: Competition vs. Regulation,* 1990.

(With Blackman) *Perfect Markets and Easy Virtue: Business Ethics and the Invisible Hand,* 1991.

Entrepreneurship, Management, and the Structure of Payoffs, 1993.

(With Gregory Sidak) *Toward Competition in Local Telephony,* 1994.

(Editor with R. R. Nelson and Wolff) *Convergence of Productivity: Cross-National Studies and Historical Evidence,* 1994.

Contributor of more than four hundred articles to periodicals. Member of editorial advisory board, *Supreme Court*

Economic Review; member of board of consultants, *Economia, Revista Quadrimestral* (Portugal).*

* * *

BEER, John B(ernard) 1926-

PERSONAL: Born March 31, 1926, in Watford, Hertfordshire, England; son of John Bateman (a civil servant) and Eva (Chilton) Beer; married Gillian Patricia Kempster Thomas (a university teacher), July 7, 1962; children: three sons. *Education:* St. John's College, Cambridge, B.A., 1950, M.A., 1955, Ph.D., 1957. *Avocational interests:* Travel, music, and walking in town and country.

ADDRESSES: 6 Belvoir Ter., Cambridge CB2 2AA, England, and Peterhouse, Cambridge University, Cambridge CB2 1RD, England.

CAREER: Cambridge University, St. John's College, Cambridge, England, research fellow, 1955-58; University of Manchester, England, lecturer in department of English, 1958-64; Cambridge University, fellow of Peterhouse, 1964-93, emeritus fellow, 1993—, university lecturer, 1964-78, reader, 1978-87, professor of English literature, 1987-93, emeritus professor, 1993—. Coleridge Bicentenary Lecturer at Christ's Hospital and Highgate, 1972; visiting professor, University of Virginia, 1975; visiting lecturer in India, 1978-79, 1993, in Korea, 1985, and in Hong Kong, 1993. *Military service:* Royal Air Force, 1946-48.

AWARDS, HONORS: British Academy fellow, 1994.

WRITINGS:

Coleridge, the Visionary, Chatto & Windus, 1959, Collier Books (New York City), 1962, reprinted, Greenwood Press (Westport, CT), 1978.
The Achievement of E. M. Forster, Chatto & Windus, 1962, Barnes & Noble (New York City), 1963.
(Editor) Samuel Taylor Coleridge, *Poems,* Dutton (New York City), 1963, reprinted, Dent, 1986, revised edition, 1993.
Milton, Lost and Regained, British Academy, 1964.
Blake's Humanism, Barnes & Noble, 1968.
Blake's Visionary Universe, Barnes & Noble, 1969.
(Editor and contributor) *Coleridge's Variety: Bicentenary Studies,* Macmillan (New York City), 1974.
Coleridge's Poetic Intelligence, Barnes & Noble, 1977.
Wordsworth and the Human Heart, Columbia University Press (New York City), 1978.
Wordsworth in Time, Faber, 1979.
(Editor with G. K. Das and contributor) *E. M. Forster, a Human Exploration: Centenary Essays,* New York University Press (New York City), 1979.

(Compiler with wife, Gillian Beer) *Heroes and Victims: Poems,* Macdonald Educational, 1979.
(Compiler with G. Beer) *Magic and Mystery: Poems,* Macdonald Educational, 1979.
(Compiler with G. Beer) *Taking a Closer Look: Poems,* Macdonald Educational, 1979.
(Compiler with G. Beer) *Telling a Story: Poems,* Macdonald Educational, 1979.
William Blake, 1757-1827, Profile Books (New York City), 1982.
(Compiler with G. Beer) *Delights and Warnings: A New Anthology of Poems,* Macdonald, 1984.
(Editor and contributor) *A Passage to India: Essays in Interpretation,* Barnes & Noble, 1986.

OTHER

Author of *Against Finality,* the inaugural lecture at Cambridge, 1993, and *Romantic Influences: Contemporary—Victorian—Modern,* 1994. General editor of *Coleridge's Writings,* 1990—. Also editor of *Aids to Reflection,* volume 9 of *The Collected Coleridge,* 1993, and of *Questioning Romanticism* [Baltimore], 1995. Contributor to numerous books, including *The English Mind,* edited by H. S. Davies and G. Watson, Cambridge University Press, 1964; *S. T. Coleridge,* edited by R. L. Brett, Bell, 1971; *Romanticism in Contemporary European Poetry,* edited by E. van Itterbeek, Louvain, 1983; *Modernita dei Romantici,* edited by L. M. C. Jones et. al., [Napoli, Italy], 1988; *Cambridge Guide to the Arts in Britain,* edited by B. Ford, 1989, 1990; *The Coleridge Connection: Essays presented to Thomas McFarland,* edited by R. Gravil and M. Lefebure, 1990; *Coleridge and the Armoury of the Human Mind,* edited by P. J. Kitson and T. N. Corns, 1991; *Tennyson: Seven Essays,* edited by Philip Collins, 1992; *Imagining Romanticism,* edited by P. Otto and D. Coleman, 1992; and *Historicizing Blake,* edited by S. Clark and D. Worrall, 1994. Contributor to *Encyclopaedia Britannica.* Contributor of articles to journals, including *Blake Newsletter, Cambridge Review, Charles Lamb Bulletin, Journal of English and Germanic Philology, Modern Language Review, New Statesman, Spectator, Review of English Studies, Times Higher Education Supplement, Times Literary Supplement,* and *The Wordsworth Circle.*

WORK IN PROGRESS: Research on nineteenth-century authors for a book on the idea of the unconscious; two further books on Coleridge and Wordsworth, *Coleridge's Play of Mind* and *Wordsworth and Coleridge: The Critical Dialogue;* and a new edition of the poems and writings of Arthur Hugh Clough.

SIDELIGHTS: John B. Beer once told *CA:* "In recent years I have been particularly interested in two related themes, which formed the topics of my twin books on Wordsworth. It is sometimes assumed that the unconscious was 'discovered' by Freud, but close study of Romantic and nineteenth-century literature shows that the phenomena which he was investigating had been a subject of deep interest for at least a century. Since analytic tools were not available, however, writers were forced to deal with it through their own art, concentrating on the creative powers of the psyche rather than on its functions of adaptation. Alongside this interest there persisted a belief in the power of the 'heart,' developed out of the eighteenth-century cult of sensibility and adopted as a counterweight to mechanistic interpretations of the world. To many modern readers the latter is simply embarrassing, but without an understanding of and allowance for it, we misread a good deal of nineteenth-century literature. The two books I am preparing will trace these topics, respectively, through a number of writers, including the early Romantics, Keats, De Quincey, Dickens, Ruskin, George Eliot, Forster and Lawrence. In several cases the same writer will figure strongly in both books.

"I am also interested in the interrelation of forms and energies as a theme both in the subject matter and in the creative work of the same period."

*   *   *

BEISTLE, Shirley
See CLIMO, Shirley

*   *   *

BENFORD, Gregory (Albert) 1941-
(Sterling Blake)

PERSONAL: Born January 30, 1941, in Mobile, AL; son of James Alton (a colonel in the U.S. Army) and Mary Eloise (a teacher; maiden name, Nelson) Benford; married Joan Abbe (an artist), August 26, 1967; children: Alyson Rhandra, Mark Gregory. *Education:* University of Oklahoma, B.S., 1963; University of California, San Diego, M.S., 1965, Ph.D., 1967.

ADDRESSES: Home—1105 Skyline Dr., Laguna Beach, CA 92651. *Office*—Department of Physics, University of California, Irvine, CA 92717.

CAREER: Lawrence Radiation Laboratory, Livermore, CA, fellow, 1967-69, research physicist, 1969-71, and consultant; University of California, Irvine, assistant professor, 1971-73, associate professor, 1973-79, professor of physics, 1979—. Visiting fellow at Cambridge University, 1976 and 1979. Consultant to Physics International Co. and National Aeronautics and Space Administration (NASA).

MEMBER: American Physical Society, Science Fiction Writers of America, Royal Astronomical Society, Social Science Exploration, Phi Beta Kappa.

AWARDS, HONORS: Woodrow Wilson fellowship, 1963-64; Nebula Award from Science Fiction Writers of America, 1975, for novella "If the Stars Are Gods," and 1981, for novel *Timescape;* British Science Fiction Association award, John W. Campbell Award from World Science Fiction Convention, and (Australian) Ditmar Award for International Novel, all 1981, for *Timescape.* Recipient of grants from National Science Foundation, 1972-76, Office of Naval Research, 1975 and 1982, Army Research Organization, 1977-82, Air Force Office of Scientific Research, 1982, and California Space Office, 1984-85.

WRITINGS:

SCIENCE FICTION NOVELS

Deeper Than the Darkness, Ace Books, 1970, revised edition published as *The Stars in Shroud,* Putnam (New York City), 1979.

Jupiter Project (for children), Thomas Nelson (Nashville, TN), 1975, 2nd edition, 1980.

(With Gordon Eklund) *If the Stars Are Gods* (based on the authors' novella of the same title), Putnam, 1977.

In the Ocean of Night, Dial (New York City), 1977.

(With Eklund) *Find the Changeling,* Dell (New York City), 1980.

(With William Rotsler) *Shiva Descending,* Avon (New York City), 1980.

Timescape, Simon & Schuster (New York City), 1980.

Against Infinity, Simon & Schuster, 1983.

Across the Sea of Suns, Simon & Schuster, 1984.

Time's Rub, Cheap Street (New Castle, VA), 1984.

Artifact, Tor (New York City), 1985.

Of Space-Time and the River, Cheap Street, 1985.

In Alien Flesh, Tor, 1986.

(With David Brin) *Heart of the Comet,* Bantam (New York City), 1986.

Great Sky River, Bantam (Toronto), 1987.

(With others) *Under the Wheel,* Baen, 1987.

We Could Do Worse, Abbenford Associates, 1988.

Tides of Light, Bantam (Toronto), 1989.

(With Arthur C. Clarke) *Beyond the Fall of Night,* Putnam, 1990.

Centigrade 233, Cheap Street, 1990.

(Under pseudonym Sterling Blake) *Chiller,* Bantam, 1993.

Furious Gulf, Bantam (New York City), 1994.

OTHER

(Editor with Martin H. Greenberg) *Hitler Victorious: Eleven Stories of the German Victory in World War II* (speculative fiction), Berkley Publishing, 1987.

(Editor with Greenberg and author of introduction) *What Might Have Been Volume 4: Alternate Americas* (anthology), Bantam, 1992.

Matter's End (science fiction short stories), illustrated by Judy J. King, Bantam, 1994 (first published in a limited edition by Cheap Street, 1991).

Also author with others of *Thread of Time,* published by Amereon. Contributor to anthologies, including *Again, Dangerous Visions,* edited by Harlan Ellison, Doubleday, 1972; *Universe 4,* Random House, 1974, *Universe 8,* Doubleday, 1978, and *Universe 9,* Doubleday, 1979, all edited by Terry Carr; and *New Dimensions, 5,* edited by Robert Silverberg, Harper, 1975. Also author of numerous research papers on astrophysics, plasma physics, and solid state physics. Contributor of articles and stories to magazines, including *Magazine of Fantasy and Science Fiction, Natural History, Omni,* and *Smithsonian.*

SIDELIGHTS: American astrophysicist and science fiction writer Gregory Benford "is one of the major talents to bring the science back into SF," says *Publishers Weekly* contributor Rosemary Herbert. In fact, Benford's achievements in the field of physics, writes Mark J. Lidman in the *Dictionary of Literary Biography Yearbook,* may overshadow his literary accomplishments. Benford holds a Ph.D. in theoretical physics and has done research on solid state physics, plasma physics, and high energy astrophysics, as well as astronomical research on the dynamics of pulsars, violent extragalactic events, and quasars. At the same time, his science fiction novels have earned him the respect of critics, fans, and his fellow writers, and "he has made no small achievement in writing since he took it up as a 'hobby' to distract himself from the pressures of studying for his doctorate in physics," Herbert relates.

As a scientist, Lidman feels, Benford is "acutely aware of modern society's fascination with technology, but his novels also stress the negative aspects of living in a technological age. His works about alien contact have an appeal that is widespread . . . , and his works which deal with science show us that we must learn to live intelligently in a technological world." The essayist states that Benford's novels "are characterized by thoughtful composition and scientific expertise, and his work experience lends authenticity to his perspective on science."

In an article on science fiction for the *Voice Literary Supplement,* Debra Rae Cohen lists Benford among the writers who "represent the idea of science as technology, of plot as problem solving. . . . SF has always been a forum for scientists to work out ideas that are unproven yet still right. . . . Gregory Benford [and others]. . . . test interdisciplinary limits [between fiction and science], not the limits of technology." For example, *Fantasy Review* contributor Gary K. Wolfe notes that *Artifact,* a thriller involving an archaeological find that has the potential to destroy the earth, combines "enough non-stop action and international intrigue . . . to satisfy the most jaded Robert Ludlum fan" together with "the familiar Benford elements—a very believable and at times satirical portrayal of academic politics, a fully-realized near-future world which is kept discretely in the background . . . , and a lot of real physics, carefully worked out and meticulously confined to a few plausible speculations." Like other reviewers, Wolfe observes that this attempt to crossbreed the science fiction novel and the international thriller yields "mixed results." Even so, maintains Gregory Feeley in a *Los Angeles Times* review, "It is the scientific side of *Artifact* that redeems the novel. . . . It is the subject matter and authority of the writer that intrigue, not the style of presentation." Writing in the *Washington Post Book World,* Feeley remarks, "As before, Benford effectively dramatizes the excitement and procedures of discovery, and his evocation of academic research, its protocols and rivalries, is impeccable."

Benford won the Nebula Award in 1981 and the praise of reviewers with the novel *Timescape.* "Its protagonists are physicists deeply and obsessively involved in the entangled arduous pursuit of (relatively) pure knowledge," John Clute reports in the *Times Literary Supplement.* Benford closes the gap between science and fiction in the novel by narrating the scientific activities of two groups of physicists; one group, living in 1998, is desperately trying to communicate to scientists in the 1960s the message that will prevent the destruction of the earth's ecosystem at the end of the century. The message consists of imaginary but plausible faster-than-light particles called tachyons sent in Morse code to a California physicist who is working with a substance which is "sensitive to tachyon bombardment," explains Clute. *Washington Post Book World* reviewer George R. R. Martin comments that Benford "makes research fully as intense and gripping as the events of any thriller, without compromising a whit, and manages the extremely difficult feat of conveying not only the meaning of his speculations in physics and cosmology, but the excitement as well. . . . [*Timescape*] is not only splendid science fiction, it is a thoroughly splendid novel."

Benford once told *CA:* "I am a resolutely amateur writer, preferring to follow my own interests rather than try to produce fiction for a living. And anyway, I'm a scientist by first choice and shall remain so. I began writing from the simple desire to tell a story (a motivation writers seem to forget as they age, and thus turn into earnest moralizers). It's taken me a long time to learn how. I've been labeled a 'hard SF' writer from the first, but in fact, I think the job of SF is to do it all—the scientific landscape, peopled with real persons, with 'style' and meaning ingrained, etc. I've slowly worked toward that goal, with many dead ends along the way. From this comes my habit of rewriting my older books and expanding early short stories into longer works (sometimes novels). Ideas come to me in a lapidary way, layering over the years. Yet, it's not the stirring moral message that moves me. I think writers are interesting when they juxtapose images or events, letting life come out of the stuff of the narrative. They get boring when they preach.

"To some extent, my novels reflect my learning various sub-categories of SF. *Deeper Than the Darkness* (later revised into *The Stars in Shroud*) was the galactic empire motif; *Jupiter Project,* the juvenile; *If the Stars Are Gods* and *In the Ocean of Night,* both the cosmic space novel. *Timescape* is rather different; it reflects my using my own experiences as a scientist. Yet short stories, where I labored so long, seem to me just as interesting as novels. I learned to write there. Nowadays, my novels begin as relatively brisk plotlines and then gather philosophical moss as they roll. If all this sounds vague and intuitive, it is: That's the way I work. So I cannot say precisely why I undertake certain themes. I like Graham Greene's division of novels into 'serious' and 'entertainments,' though I suspect the author himself cannot say with certainly which of his own are which.

"It seems to me my major concerns are the vast landscape of science, and the philosophical implications of that landscape on mortal, sensual human beings. What genuinely interests me is the strange, the undiscovered. But in the end it is how people see this that matters most."

BIOGRAPHICAL/CRITICAL SOURCES:

BOOKS

Bridges to Science Fiction, Southern Illinois University Press (Carbondale), 1981.
Carr, Terry, editor, *Universe 6,* Popular Library, 1976.
Dictionary of Literary Biography Yearbook, 1982, Gale (Detroit), 1983.
Platt, Charles, *Dream Makers: The Uncommon People Who Write Science Fiction; Interviews by Charles Platt,* Berkley Books (New York City), 1980.

PERIODICALS

Analog, November, 1985, p. 179; June, 1986; March, 1988, p. 178.
Booklist, March 15, 1985, p. 1010; October 15, 1987, p. 345; May 15, 1994, p. 1644.
Chicago Tribune Book World, March 23, 1986.
Christian Science Monitor, May 16, 1986; February 9, 1988, p. 20.
Fantasy Review, September, 1985, p. 17; February, 1986; July, 1986.
Foundation, winter, 1977-78.

Locus, April, 1991, p. 40; September, 1992, p. 13; October, 1992, p. 27; November, 1992, p. 53; August, 1994, p. 27.
Los Angeles Times, December 16, 1985; April 18, 1986.
Los Angeles Times Book Review, December 27, 1987, p. 11.
New York Times Book Review, January 27, 1977; March 27, 1977; November 25, 1984, p. 20; December 27, 1987, p. 11; August 14, 1994, p. 30.
Publishers Weekly, May 23, 1986; July 4, 1994, p. 56.
Science Fiction and Fantasy Book Review, September, 1983.
Science Fiction Chronicle, October, 1985, p. 42; June, 1986; July, 1986.
Science Fiction Review, August, 1984; August, 1985, p. 17; November, 1985, p. 23; February, 1986; May, 1986; June, 1986.
Times Literary Supplement, December 5, 1980.
Voice Literary Supplement, December, 1983.
Washington Post Book World, June 22, 1980; May 29, 1983; February 26, 1984; October 27, 1985, p. 6; March 23, 1986; October 25, 1988, p. 6.

*　　　*　　　*

BERKSON, Bill 1939-

PERSONAL: Born August 30, 1939, in New York, NY; son of Seymour (a journalist) and Eleanor (a publicist; maiden name, Lambert) Berkson; married; children: one son, one daughter. *Education:* Attended Brown University, 1957-59, Columbia University, 1959-60, New School for Social Research, 1959-61, and New York University Institute of Fine Arts, 1960-61.

ADDRESSES: Home—800 Chestnut St., San Francisco, CA 94133.

CAREER: Freelance art critic, 1962—. *Art News,* New York City, editorial associate, 1960-63; WNDT-TV, New York City, associate producer, *Art-New York* series, 1964-65; New School for Social Research, New York City, instructor in creative writing and literature, 1964-69; Yale University, New Haven, CT, visiting fellow, 1969-70; Big Sky Books, Bolinas, CA, editor and publisher, 1971-78; Bolinas-Stinson School District, Bolinas-Stinson, CA, teacher at Pine Gulch School, 1978-79; Poets in the Schools program, South Fork, Suffolk County, NY, coordinator and instructor, 1979-80; Southampton College of Long Island University, Long Island, NY, adjunct professor, 1980; California College of Arts and Crafts, Oakland, associate professor, 1983-84; San Francisco Art Institute, San Francisco, CA, professor and coordinator of public lectures, 1984—, interim dean, 1992, director, Letters and Science, 1994—.

Visiting fellow, Ezra Stiles College, Yale University, 1969-70; poet-teacher, Poets in the Schools program, Marin County, CA, 1974-84; visiting artist-scholar, American Academy in Rome, 1991; visiting lecturer or professor at numerous other institutions. Part-time writer, editor, and researcher, Museum of Modern Art, New York City, 1965-69; Bay Area correspondent, *Artforum,* 1985-91. Member of board of trustees, San Francisco Art institute, 1986-93; member of board of directors, Bay Area Consortium for the Visual Arts. Curator/organizer of numerous exhibitions and gallery showings. Has given numerous public readings and lectures throughout the U.S. and Italy.

MEMBER: International Art Critics Association, PEN West.

AWARDS, HONORS: Dylan Thomas Memorial Award for Poetry, New School for Social Research, 1959; Poets Foundation grant, 1968; Yaddo fellowship, 1968; Coordinating Council of Literary Magazines (CCLM), grants for publishing, 1972, 1974, 1976, and 1978, and honorable mention—editor's fellowship, 1979; National Endowment for the Arts, small press publishing grants, 1975 and 1977, and creative writing fellowship in poetry, 1979-80; Briarcombe fellowship, 1983; poetry award, Marin Arts Council, 1987; *Artspace* Award, 1991, for new writing in art criticism.

WRITINGS:

Saturday Night: Poems 1960-61, Tibor de Nagy, 1961.
(Editor) Frank O'Hara, *In Memory of My Feelings,* illustrated by thirty American artists, Museum of Modern Art (New York City), 1967.
Shining Leaves, Angel Hair, 1969.
(Editor with Irving Sandler) *Alex Katz,* Praeger (New York City), 1971.
(With Larry Fagin) *Two Serious Poems and One Other,* Big Sky (Southampton, NY), 1972.
Recent Visitors, Angel Hair, 1974.
Ants, Arif (Berkeley, CA), 1975.
100 Women, Simon & Schuster (New York City), 1975.
Enigma Variations, Big Sky, 1975.
Blue Is the Hero: Poems 1960-75, L Publications (Kensington, CA), 1976.
(With Ron Padgett, Fagin, and Michael Brownstein) *The World of Leon,* Big Sky, 1976.
(Editor with Joe LeSueur) *Homage to Frank O'Hara,* Creative Arts, 1980.
Start Over, Tombouctou (Bolinas, CA), 1983.
Red Devil, Smithereens Press, 1983.
Lush Life, Z Press (Calais, VT), 1984.
Ronald Blader: Early and Late (criticism), San Francisco Museum of Modern Art (San Francisco), 1990.

Editor and publisher, *Best and Company* (anthology), 1969; editor, with Frank O'Hara, of *Hymns of St. Bridget,* 1975. Contributor to *Biotherm,* by O'Hara, Arion (San Francisco), 1990; and *Wayne Thiebaud: Visions and Revisions,* Fine Art Museums of San Francisco (San Francisco), 1992; also contributor to exhibition catalogues. Also contributor to numerous anthologies. Editorial associate, *Portfolio and Artnews Annual,* 1960-63. Contributor of poetry and articles to numerous periodicals, including *Art International, Poetry, Paris Review, Yale Literary Magazine, Evergreen Review, Art and Literature,* and *Artspace.* Film editor, *Kulchur,* 1962-63; managing editor, *Location,* 1965; poetry editor, *Video and the Arts,* 1985-86; contributing editor, *Zyzzyva,* 1987-92; corresponding editor, *Art in America,* 1988—; coeditor of special issue, *Art Journal,* 1989. Berkson's poetry has been recorded on *Disconnected,* Giorno Poetry Systems, *The World Record,* St. Marks Poetry Project, 1980, and in the American Poetry Archive, San Francisco State University.

Berkson's poetry has been translated into Italian, French, German, Dutch, Romanian, and Hungarian.

BIOGRAPHICAL/CRITICAL SOURCES:

PERIODICALS

Poetry, August, 1962.
World, number 29, 1974.

*   *   *

BILLINGS, Charlene W(interer)   1941-

PERSONAL: Born January 11, 1941, in Manchester, NH; daughter of George E. (a power company employee) and Alice (a nurse; maiden name, Labbee) Winterer; married Barry A. Billings (an electrical engineer), December 16, 1961; children: Cheryl, Sharon. *Education:* University of New Hampshire, B.A. (cum laude), 1962; Rivier College, M.S., 1973.

ADDRESSES: Home—39 Coburn Ave., Nashua, NH 03063.

CAREER: Writer. Hopkinton High School, Hopkinton, NH, science teacher, 1962-63; University of New Hampshire, Durham, research assistant in biochemistry, 1963-64; manager of Coburn Designs (publisher of topographic map jigsaw puzzles), Nashua, NH.

MEMBER: American Society of Journalists and Authors, Society of Children's Book Writers, Phi Beta Kappa, Sigma Xi (honorary associate member), Phi Kappa Phi, Phi Sigma.

AWARDS, HONORS: "Outstanding Science Trade Book for Children" designations, National Association of Science Teachers, 1984, for *Microchip: Small Wonder,* 1986, for *Space Station: Bold New Step beyond Earth,* for *Fiber Optics: Bright New Way to Communicate,* for *Christa McAuliffe: Pioneer Space Teacher,* and 1989, for *Grace Hopper: Navy Admiral and Computer Pioneer;* selection as one of Dodd's best four children's books of 1986, Cooperative Children's Book Center, University of Wisconsin, for *Fiber Optics: Bright New Way to Communicate;* "Book for the Teenage" designations, New York Public Library, 1986, for *Christa McAuliffe: Pioneer Space Teacher,* 1989, for *Grace Hopper: Navy Admiral and Computer Pioneer,* 1991, for *Superconductivity: From Discovery to Breakthrough,* and 1992, for *Lasers: The New Technology of Light.*

WRITINGS:

CHILDREN'S BOOKS; NONFICTION

Spring Peepers Are Calling, illustrations by Susan Bonners, Dodd (New York City), 1978.
Salamanders, Dodd, 1981.
Scorpions, Dodd, 1983.
Microchip: Small Wonder, Dodd, 1984.
Space Station: Bold New Step beyond Earth, Dodd, 1986.
Fiber Optics: Bright New Way to Communicate, Dodd, 1986.
Christa McAuliffe: Pioneer Space Teacher, Enslow Publishers (Hillside, NJ), 1986.
Loon: Voice of the Wilderness (Junior Literary Guild selection), Dodd, 1988.
Grace Hopper: Navy Admiral and Computer Pioneer, Enslow Publishers, 1989.
Superconductivity: From Discovery to Breakthrough, Dutton (New York City), 1991.
Lasers: The New Technology of Light, Facts on File (New York City), 1992.
Pesticides: Necessary Risk, Enslow Publishers, 1993.
Supercomputers: Shaping the Future, Facts on File, 1995.

OTHER

Also contributor to *The Writer's Handbook,* 1994. Contributor to periodicals, including *Writer.*

SIDELIGHTS: Charlene W. Billings told *CA:* "Writing nonfiction books for children requires far more than just relating facts to young readers. The author must seek to transform facts into insights and knowledge that make the reader want to learn more. Well-written nonfiction books are as fundamental to children's reading as fine fiction. They must be accurate and should convey the excitement of discovery, as well as an understanding and appreciation of the natural and technical world we all share. Historical background offers young readers important perspectives about events that occurred before they were alive. Biogra-

phies provide valuable role models of inspiration, determination, and courage.

"In addition to writing, I manage Coburn Designs, a family publishing business that produces educational jigsaw puzzles from detailed topographic maps of America's national parks. The business carries on a tradition started in the 1760s by John Spilsbury, a London map maker, when he created the first jigsaw puzzle by dissecting a map of Europe into pieces to use as a tool to teach geography.

"I enjoy reading and writing about the wonders of nature, about advances in science, and about the people who help to shape our world. Topics for my books often introduce young readers to cutting-edge science—the possibilities of the latest discoveries as well as the responsibilities that accompany them."

BIOGRAPHICAL/CRITICAL SOURCES:

PERIODICALS

Appraisal: Children's Science Books, spring, 1980; winter, 1987; spring, 1987; summer, 1987; spring, 1991; winter, 1992; spring, 1993.
Catholic Library World, May, 1987.
Childhood Education, June, 1987.
Instructor, May, 1979.
Journal of Reading, March, 1985.
Science and Children, January, 1980; May, 1985.
Science Books and Films, September-October, 1985; November, 1986; January, 1987; February, 1987; May, 1987; May, 1989; January, 1990; August, 1991; April, 1993.
Voice of Youth Advocates, August, 1986; February, 1990; August, 1993.

*   *   *

BISHOP, Michael   1945-

PERSONAL: Born November 12, 1945, in Lincoln, NE; son of Lee Otis (in the U.S. Air Force) and Maxine (Mattison) Bishop; married Jeri Whitaker, June 7, 1969; children: Christopher James, Stephanie Noel. *Education:* University of Georgia, B.A., 1967, M.A., 1968. *Religion:* Methodist. *Avocational interests:* Archeology, anthropology, movies, music, detective fiction, and baseball.

ADDRESSES: Home—Box 646, Pine Mountain, GA 31822. *Agent*—Howard Morhaim, 179 Fifth Ave., New York, NY 10010.

CAREER: United States Air Force Academy Preparatory School, Colorado Springs, CO, teacher of English, 1968-72; University of Georgia, Athens, instructor in English, 1972-74; freelance writer, 1974—. *Military service:* U.S. Air Force, 1968-72; became captain.

MEMBER: Science Fiction Writers of America, Science Fiction Poetry Association, United Methodist Men's Club (president of local chapter).

AWARDS, HONORS: Phoenix Award, 1977; Clark Ashton Smith Award, 1978, and Rhysling Award, Science Fiction Poetry Association, 1979, both for the poem "For the Lady of a Physicist"; Nebula Award, Science Fiction Writers of America, 1981, for novelette *The Quickening;* Nebula Award, 1982, for novel *No Enemy but Time;* Locus Award, 1985, for novella "Her Habiline Husband," and 1986, for anthology *Light Years and Dark;* Mythopoeic Fantasy Award for best novel, 1988, for *Unicorn Mountain;* Townsend Fiction Prize nomination, 1988, for *Unicorn Mountain;* Nebula Award nomination, 1989, for *Apartheid, Superstrings, and Mordecai Thubana.*

WRITINGS:

NOVELS

A Funeral for the Eyes of Fire, Ballantine (New York City), 1975, revised edition published as *Eyes of Fire,* Pocket Books (New York City), 1980.
And Strange at Ecbatan the Trees, Harper (New York City), 1976, published as *Under the Shattered Moons,* DAW Books (New York City), 1977.
Stolen Faces, Harper, 1977.
A Little Knowledge, Berkley Publishing (New York City), 1977.
Transfigurations, Berkley Publishing, 1979.
(With Ian Watson) *Under Heaven's Bridge,* Gollancz (London), 1981, Ace Books (New York City), 1982.
No Enemy but Time (Science Fiction Book Club selection; Book of the Month Club alternate selection), Timescape (New York City), 1982.
Who Made Stevie Crye?, Arkham House (Sauk City, WI), 1984.
Ancient of Days, Arbor House (New York City), 1985.
The Secret Ascension: or, Philip K. Dick Is Dead, Alas, Tor Books (New York City), 1987.
Unicorn Mountain, Arbor House, 1988.
Apartheid, Superstrings and Mordecai Thubana (novella), limited edition, Axolotl Press, 1989.
Count Geiger's Blues, Tor Books, 1994.
Brittle Innings, Bantam, 1994.

STORY COLLECTIONS

Catacomb Years, Berkley Publishing, 1979.
Blooded on Arachne, Arkham House, 1982.
One Winter in Eden, Arkham House, 1984.
Close Encounters with the Deity, Peachtree Publishers, 1985.

Emphatically Not SF, Almost, Pulphouse Publishing, 1990.

EDITOR

(With Watson) *Changes* (anthology), Ace Books, 1982.
Light Years and Dark (anthology), Berkley Publishing, 1984.
Nebula Awards: SFWA's Choices for the Best Science Fiction and Fantasy, Volumes 23-25, Harcourt, 1989-91.

OTHER

Windows and Mirrors (poetry chapbook), Moravian Press, 1977.
(Author of introduction) Philip K. Dick, *Ubik,* G. K. Hall, 1979.

Work appears in many anthologies, including: *Best Science Fiction: 1973,* edited by Harry Harrison and Brian W. Aldiss, Putnam, 1974; *Emphasis,* edited by David Gerrold, Ballantine, 1974; *World's Best Science Fiction, 1974,* edited by Donald A. Wollheim, DAW Books, 1974; *World's Best Science Fiction, 1975,* edited by Wollheim, DAW Books, 1975; *Best American Short Stories, 1985,* edited by Gail Godwin and Shannon Ravenel, Houghton, 1985. Contributor of stories, poems, reviews and essays to *Omni, Analog, Galaxy, Isaac Asimov's Science Fiction Magazine, Interzone, Pulphouse, Amazing, Fantasy and Science Fiction, Locus, New York Review of Science Fiction, Science Fiction Age, Twilight Zone, Ellery Queen's Mystery Magazine, Alfred Hitchcock's Mystery Magazine, Washington Post Book World, New York Times, Atlanta Journal-Constitution, Mother Earth News, Libertarian Review, Playboy, Missouri Review, Georgia Review,* and other publications. Author of column "Pitching Pennies Against the Starboard Bulkhead," *Quantum.*

ADAPTATIONS: The short story "Seasons of Belief" was adapted for the syndicated television series *Tales from the Darkside;* film rights to *Brittle Innings* have been bought by Twentieth Century-Fox.

SIDELIGHTS: American science fiction writer Michael Bishop has earned a reputation as a "writer's writer." As Rob Latham writes in *Fantasy Review,* "of all the American SF writers to emerge since the early 1970s, probably the most consistently excellent—and consistently underrated—is Michael Bishop. His novels . . . have restlessly explored and relentlessly pushed forward the basic themes of the genre." Bishop's imaginative allegories often seem to be saying as much about contemporary American society and culture as they do about the distant worlds which serve as their backdrops. "Bishop," reviewer George Feeley of the *Washington Post Book World* points out, "is an unusually literate writer. . . . He is among the most interesting and resourceful writers of short fiction today, inside the sf field or beyond."

Bishop's first novel, *A Funeral for the Eyes of Fire,* tells of two brothers sent to an alien planet to subdue the natives. Instead they become entangled in the aliens' internal problems and are unable to perform their mission. A writer for *A Reader's Guide to Science Fiction* describes the book as "complex and involving, and though imperfectly structured. . . . An auspicious start." Bishop's next novel, *And Strange at Ecbatan the Trees,* is set in the distant future on a world where the inhabitants have been genetically engineered to display no emotions. While John Clute finds the book "somewhat less convincing" than was *Funeral,* he felt that Bishop nonetheless succeeded in creating a vivid and richly detailed alien landscape.

That intention is apparent in Bishop's novels *A Little Knowledge* and *Catacomb Years.* The two books grew out of a series of stories he wrote in the mid-1970s and are set on Earth in the late 21st Century in the domed city of NUAtlanta, which has retreated into religious exile as the rest of mankind has turned its attentions spaceward. The books deal with the impact of alien arrivals on the ruling religious theocracy and on the stability of their artificial world. Assessing *A Little Knowledge,* a writer for *A Reader's Guide to Science Fiction* observes that "the author's knowledge and understanding of religious thought and his powers of extrapolation provide the book's heart."

In *Transfigurations,* Bishop dealt again with serious themes. An expanded version of a novella entitled "Death and Designation Among the Asadi," *Transfigurations* deals with a genetically altered "neo-chimp" employed to communicate with a race of aliens. The plot has as much to do with America's attitudes toward race as it does with science fiction. The racial theme also resonates through Bishop's next novel, *No Enemy but Time,* which won the Nebula Award for 1982. The story chronicles the adventures of Joshua Kampa, a man who dreams of prehistoric Africa in surprisingly accurate detail. Enhanced by a newly-developed machine, Kampa's dreams become real, enabling him to explore the world of two million years ago as well as his own psyche. Reviewing the book for the *Washington Post Book World,* John Clute writes: "In the world of dreams, knowledge of the world and self-knowledge may be the same thing, but Bishop avoids any easy reduction of his complex, glowing, crystal-clear novel to a tale of self-delusion. In chapters that alternate the real past and the real present, *No Enemy but Time* gradually builds into a work of thrilling significance both as science fiction and as a study of character." Clute concludes that *No Enemy but Time* is a "strikingly intelligent new science fiction novel."

Ancient of Days is a further treatment of a character out of time and place. In this novel, Bishop relates the story of Adam, a descendant of the habiline species (the immediate precursor to mankind), who appears in a typical small town in the deep south in 1984, and then proceeds to marry and settle down. "Bishop's theme of evil inherent in humanity echoes William F. Golding," writes Bernard Goodman of *Fantasy Review.* "In some ways, *Ancient of Days* parallels Golding's *Lord of the Flies.*" Clute writes in the *Washington Post Book World* that *Ancient of Days* exhibits Bishop's recent tendency away from pure science fiction to a fiction "whose only speculative element lies in what might be called his anthropological point of view."

This same willingness to venture beyond the bounds of traditional science fiction is apparent in Bishop's writing during the late 1980s. *Close Encounters with the Deity* is a collection of intricate short stories with religious or metaphysical themes. Reviewer Fernando Quadros Gouvea of *Science Fiction Review* comments, "For those willing to do the work required, Bishop's work is a treat." Gregory Feeley of the *Washington Post Book World* agrees: "*Close Encounters with the Deity* is an excellent collection and should gain Bishop a wider audience."

The Secret Ascension: Philip K. Dick Is Dead, Alas, while working on one level as a tribute to the late science fiction writer Philip K. Dick, is also a futuristic drama about an America ruled by four-term president (or king) Richard Nixon. This future America "is reminiscent of Hitler's Germany," according to John Gregory Betancourt in the *Washington Post Book World.* Reviewer Don Dammassa of *Science Fiction Chronicle* terms the book "a stunningly effective novel, one in which Philip Dick would no doubt be proud of his existence as a character."

The critical reception for Bishop's *Count Geiger's Blues* suggests that he may have hit his stride as a writer of science fiction with crossover appeal in the literary mainstream. The book is set in a mythical southern state where a supercilious Fine Arts Editor at the local newspaper is transformed into a pop culture superhero after a chance encounter with illegally dumped nuclear waste. Reviewer Faren Miller of *Locus* magazine finds that this satirical novel "goes way beyond humor—well beyond, in its remarkable closing chapters. But they all build on what has gone before. In unleashing a startling talent for comedy and a wide-ranging knowledge of pop culture in both its absurdity and its splendor, Michael Bishop has written his best book yet—and perhaps the best summation of this mad last decade before the Millennium that the genre is likely to produce."

BIOGRAPHICAL/CRITICAL SOURCES:

BOOKS

Authors in the News, Volume 2, Gale, 1976.
Twentieth-Century Science Fiction Writers, St. Martin's, 1981.

PERIODICALS

Analog, May, 1979; June, 1979.

Atlanta Journal & Constitution, April 4, 1976.

Fantasy Review, June, 1985, p. 16; July/August, 1986, pp. 21-22.

Locus, April, 1992, p. 17.

Necrofile: The Review of Horror Fiction, fall, 1994.

New York Times Book Review, May 23, 1976; June 26, 1977.

Science Fiction Chronicle, February, 1985, p. 28; January, 1988, p. 48.

Science Fiction Review, August, 1977; summer, 1985, p. 37; winter, 1986, p. 41.

Times Literary Supplement, January 27, 1978.

Washington Post Book World, January 24, 1982; April 25, 1982; August 25, 1985; November 23, 1986, p. 8; November 29, 1987, p. 8; July 31, 1988, p. 8; December 31, 1989, p. 4.

—Sketch by Ken Cuthbertson

*   *   *

BLAIR, Shannon
See KAYE, Marilyn

*   *   *

BLAKE, Sterling
See BENFORD, Gregory (Albert)

*   *   *

BLEDSOE, Jerry 1941-

PERSONAL: Born July 14, 1941, in Danville, VA; son of Gurney F. (a builder) and Jean (Atkins) Bledsoe; married Linda Boyd, July 11, 1964; children: Erik.

ADDRESSES: Home—1421 Randolph Tabernacle Rd., Asheboro, NC 27203. *Office*—Down Home Press, P.O. Box 4126, Asheboro, NC 27204. *Agent*—Janklow & Nesbit, 598 Madison Ave., New York, NY 10022.

CAREER: Greensboro News & Record, Greensboro, NC, reporter and columnist, 1966-77, 1981-89; *Louisville Times,* Louisville, KY, feature writer, 1971; *Esquire,* New York City, contributing editor, 1972-75; *Charlotte Observer,* Charlotte, NC, columnist, 1977-81; Down Home Press, Asheboro, NC, publisher and editor, 1989—. *Military service:* U.S. Army, 1960-63.

AWARDS, HONORS: Ernie Pyle Memorial Award from Scripps-Howard Foundation, 1968-70; National Headliners Award, 1969; young newspaperman award from International Newspaper Promotion Association, 1971.

WRITINGS:

The World's Number One, Flat-Out, All Time Great Stock Car Racing Book, Doubleday (New York City), 1975.

You Can't Live on Radishes: Some Funny Things Happened on the Way Back to the Land, Grape Hill Press (Greensboro, NC), 1976.

Just Folks, Visitin' with Carolina People, Eastwoods Press (Charlotte, NC), 1980.

Where's Mark Twain When We Really Need Him?, Grape Hill Press, 1982.

Carolina Curiosities, Eastwoods Press, 1984, revised and expanded edition published as *North Carolina Curiosities,* Globe-Pequot (Old Saybrook, CT), 1990.

From Whalebone to Hot House: A Journey along North Carolina's Longest Highway, Globe-Pequot, 1986.

Bitter Blood: A True Story of Southern Family Pride, Madness and Multiple Murder, Dutton (New York City), 1988.

Country Cured: Reflections from the Heart, Longstreet Press (Atlanta, GA), 1989.

The Bare-Bottomed Skier: And Other Unlikely Tales, Down Home Press (Asheboro, NC), 1990.

Blood Games: A True Account of Family Murder, Dutton, 1991.

Blue Horizons: Faces and Places from a Bicycle Journey along the Blue Ridge Parkway, Down Home Press, 1993.

Before He Wakes: A True Story of Money, Marriage, Sex and Murder, Dutton, 1994.

WORK IN PROGRESS: A novel.

*   *   *

BLISS, Lee 1943-

PERSONAL: Born August 9, 1943, in Buffalo, NY; daughter of C. Perry (a university professor) and Louise (an ombudsman assistant; maiden name, Ramseyer) Bliss. *Education:* Stanford University, B.A., 1965; University of California, Berkeley, M.A., 1967, Ph.D., 1972.

ADDRESSES: Office—Department of English, University of California, Santa Barbara, CA 93106.

CAREER: Scripps College, Claremont, CA, assistant professor, 1972-73; University of California, Los Angeles, lecturer in English and humanities, 1974-75; University of California, Santa Barbara, visiting lecturer, 1975-76, assistant professor, 1977-82, associate professor, 1982-88, professor of English, 1988—. Visiting associate professor, Claremont Graduate School, 1986; Folger Shakespeare Library fellow, 1992-93.

MEMBER: Modern Language Association of America, Renaissance Society of America, Shakespeare Association of America, Malone Society.

WRITINGS:

The World's Perspective: John Webster and the Jacobean Drama, Rutgers University Press (New Brunswick, NJ), 1983.
Francis Beaumont, Twayne (Boston, MA), 1987.

Contributor to language and literature journals, including *Journal of English Literary History, Journal of English and Germanic Philology, Medieval and Renaissance Drama in England, Modern Language Review, Modern Language Quarterly, Renaissance Drama, Studies in English Literature,* and *Viator.*

WORK IN PROGRESS: An edition of Shakespeare's *Coriolanus.*

SIDELIGHTS: In *The World's Perspective: John Webster and the Jacobean Drama,* Lee Bliss discusses three plays by seventeenth-century dramatist John Webster within the context of the playwright's day. Bliss uses the work of such Webster contemporaries as William Shakespeare, George Chapman, and John Marston to delineate the social, philosophic, and artistic concerns of the Jacobean dramatists. Bliss also examines the resultant dramatic forms adopted during the period, focusing on Webster's use of tragicomedy and distancing—the detached observation of characters, manners, and morals. According to Lachlan Mackinnon's *Times Literary Supplement* review, Bliss errs in suggesting that such dramatic techniques originated with the Jacobean dramatists. "To complain is to carp, though," added the critic. "This is a profoundly stimulating and exciting book. It reads with great dash and is well buttressed with learning." Furthermore, Mackinnon concluded, the author "offers a useful and provocative way of thinking about [Webster] and more widely about the Jacobean drama."

Similarly complimentary was *Journal of English and Germanic Philology* contributor Robert Ornstein, who called Bliss "a very gifted critic." He found parts of the study "vivid, often elegant, and utterly convincing," although he deemed her judgments somewhat biased in others. Applauding the author on "a first-rate critical intelligence, a splendid command of the scholarship in her field, and an intimate knowledge of the plays of Shakespeare and his contemporaries," Ornstein declared that Bliss "is certain to be one of our foremost interpreters of Elizabethan and Jacobean drama."

BIOGRAPHICAL/CRITICAL SOURCES:

PERIODICALS

Choice, June, 1988, p. 1552.

Journal of English and Germanic Philology, July, 1984.
Renaissance Quarterly, spring, 1989, p. 142.
Times Literary Supplement, July 29, 1983; August 26, 1988, p. 935.

*   *   *

BLOCH, Barbara 1925-
(Phoebe Edwards)

PERSONAL: Born May 26, 1925, in New York, NY; daughter of Emil William (a stockbroker) and Dorothy (a bacteriologist and executive administrator; maiden name, Lowengrund) Bloch; married Joseph Bennet Sanders, August 3, 1944 (divorced January 4, 1961); married Theodore Simon Benjamin (a publisher), September 20, 1964; children: (first marriage) Elizabeth, Ellen; (stepchildren from second marriage) Phyllis, Jill. *Education:* Attended New York University and New School for Social Research; studied with American Symphony Orchestra League. *Politics:* Democrat. *Religion:* "Jewish/Humanist by affiliation."

ADDRESSES: Home and office—International Cookbook Services, 21 Dupont Ave., White Plains, NY 10605.

CAREER: Westchester Democratic County Committee, White Plains, NY, office manager, 1955-56; Westchester Symphony Orchestra, Scarsdale, NY, manager, 1957-62; P. K. Halstead Associates, Larchmont, NY, assistant to president, 1962-63; Active Employment Service, White Plains, office manager, 1963-65; International Cookbook Services, White Plains, president, 1978—; Benjamin Co. Inc., White Plains, cookbook editor, 1988—. Occasional lecturer and guest on television and radio shows. Consultant to cookbook publishers.

WRITINGS:

(Under pseudonym Phoebe Edwards) *Anyone Can Quilt,* Benjamin Co. (White Plains, NY), 1975.
The Meat Board Meat Book, introduction by Julia Child, McGraw (New York City), 1977.
Polly-O Cooking with Cheese, Polly-O Cheese Co., 1977.
If It Doesn't Pan Out: How to Cope with Cooking Disasters (Book-of-the-Month Cooking and Craft Club selection), Dembner (New York City), 1981.
Microwave Party Cooking, Peter Pauper (New York City), 1988.
A Little Jewish Cookbook, Appletree/Chronicle, 1989.
TCBY and More, Benjamin Co., 1989.
A Little New England Cookbook, Appletree/Chronicle, 1990.
A Little New York Cookbook, Appletree/Chronicle, 1990.
A Little Southern Cookbook, Appletree/Chronicle, 1990.
Goldstar Micro-Convection Cookbook, Benjamin Co., 1991.

AUTHOR OF "AMERICANIZED" EDITIONS OF FOREIGN COOKBOOKS

The Cuisine of Olympe, New Century (Piscataway, NJ), 1982.

Favorite Family Baking, Meredith Corp. (Des Moines, IA), 1982.

The Book of Baking, Meredith Corp., 1983.

Cakes and Pastries, Morrow (New York City), 1983.

Baking Easy and Elegant, H. P. Books (Tucson, AZ), 1984.

Best of Cold Foods, H. P. Books, 1985.

The Art of Cooking (Better Homes & Gardens Book Club selection), H. P. Books, 1986.

The Art of Baking (Better Homes & Gardens Book Club selection), H. P. Books, 1987.

Perfect Pasta, Gallo Ltd. (Spain), 1992.

Rocky Food, Page One Publishing (Sweden), 1994.

Also "Americanizer" of a cookbook series for Octopus, 1980, and for Marshall Cavendish, 1980, 1981, and 1982.

EDITOR

(And contributor) *The All Beef Cookbook,* Scribner (New York City), 1973.

(And contributor) Anne Borella, *In Glass Naturally,* Benjamin Co., 1974.

Microwave Miracles, Rutledge/Benjamin Co., 1974.

(And contributor) *Fresh Ideas with Mushrooms,* Benjamin Co., 1977.

Good Food Ideas Cheese Cookbook, Benjamin Co., 1977.

(And contributor) *Cook's Choice,* Benjamin Co., 1979.

Yesterday and Today: From the Kitchens of Stokely, Benjamin Co., 1980.

(And contributor) *The Sun Maid Cookbook,* Benjamin Co., 1980.

(And contributor) *Cooking with Jenn-Air,* Benjamin Co., 1980.

(And contributor) *The Any Oven Cookbook,* Benjamin Co., 1981.

(And contributor) *Ovenware of the Future Cookbook,* Benjamin Co., 1981.

Any Way You Make It, Benjamin Co., 1982.

(And contributor) *The Complete Chicken Cookbook,* Benjamin Co., 1984.

(And contributor) *Guilden's Makes Good Food Taste Great,* Benjamin Co., 1984.

(And contributor) *The Convenience of Canned, the Flavor of Fresh,* Benjamin Co., 1986.

(And contributor) *A Centennial Celebration,* Benjamin Co., 1988.

Salute to Great American Chefs, Benjamin Co., 1988.

A Little American Cookbook, Appletree (Ireland), 1988.

McCormick/Schilling New Spice Cookbook, Benjamin Co., 1994.

OTHER

Author of microwave cooking column in *House Beautiful,* 1984-87.

Some of Bloch's books have been published in foreign editions, including Japanese and Dutch.

SIDELIGHTS: Barbara Bloch once told *CA:* "Outside of my family and career, my main interests are classical music, liberal politics, gardening, young people, and a deep concern for the changing quality of life on our planet. My interest in travel did not develop until I could afford it, and my interest in food did not develop until my second marriage, when I found I had a husband who enjoyed eating good food.

"I became a full-time writer, editor, and teacher over twenty-five years ago when I decided I could not sit through another volunteer group meeting, or listen to the reading of the minutes of the previous meeting. It was also the time at which I concluded my four daughters no longer needed a full-time mother, a startling concept from which very few of us had been liberated at that time.

"In addition to writing and editing American cookbooks, I have added another specialty—that of Americanizing foreign cookbooks. In particular, both English and American publishers finally realize that, although we speak the same language over the dinner table, we do not speak the same language in the kitchen. It is a specialty that developed into a surprisingly successful business.

"I have been a guest on several radio and television programs, I lecture periodically, and I serve as a consultant to cookbook publishers. I have also taught cooking classes and love teaching, although I no longer have time to include it in my schedule.

"The number of poorly written cookbooks published every year distresses me. Too often, cookbooks are written by people who seem to be good cooks, but do not understand the demands of proper recipe writing—and evidently not all cookbook publishers are able to make proper judgment about the reliability of the recipes they publish. Cookbooks should be written carefully and clearly, and the recipes should be completely reliable—both food and time are too expensive to waste on improperly written recipes. However, in spite of the fact that I take the writing of a cookbook very seriously, my advice for most people who cook is 'relax.' People who make a fetish of food and cooking make me uncomfortable.

"I have always had an enormous urge to be creative. Having finally acknowledged that I could not act, paint, or make music, I have found a satisfying creative outlet in the combination of cooking and writing. But, as I get older,

I dream of a time when I'll be able to do more writing and less cooking!"

*   *   *

BLOOD, Matthew
See DRESSER, Davis

*   *   *

BLOOM, Lynn (Marie) Z(immerman) 1934-

PERSONAL: Born July 11, 1934, in Ann Arbor, MI; daughter of Oswald Theodore (a professor of chemical engineering) and Mildred (Kisling) Zimmerman; married Martin Bloom (a social psychologist), July 11, 1958; children: Bard, Laird. *Education:* University of Michigan, B.A., 1956, M.A., 1957, Ph.D., 1963. *Politics:* Liberal. *Avocational interests:* Cooking, swimming, travel.

ADDRESSES: Home—70 Southworth Dr., Ashford, CT 06278. *Office*—Department of English, U-25, University of Connecticut, Storrs, CT 06269.

CAREER: Western Reserve University (now Case Western Reserve University), Cleveland, OH, lecturer, 1962-63, instructor, 1963-65, associate in English, 1965-67; full-time writer, 1967-70; Butler University, Indianapolis, IN, assistant professor, 1970-73, associate professor of English, 1973-74; University of New Mexico, Albuquerque, associate professor of English, 1975-78, director of freshman English, 1976-78; College of William and Mary, Williamsburg, VA, associate professor of English, 1978-82, director of writing, 1979-81, co-director, Eastern Virginia Writing Project, 1979-81; Virginia Commonwealth University, Richmond, professor of English, 1982-90, chairperson of English department, 1982-83; University of Connecticut, Storrs, professor of English and Aetna Chair of Writing, 1988—. Part-time member of faculty, Washington University, 1974-77, and Carnegie-Mellon University, summer, 1978; faculty member, Northeastern University, Martha's Vineyard Summer Workshop, 1987, 1988, 1990, and 1991. Judge of various writing contests, 1973—; conductor of writer-anxiety workshops, 1978-85; consultant and evaluator of writing research and programs, 1978—; editorial consultant for various publishers, including Random House, St. Martin's, Harcourt, Heath, HarperCollins, Macmillan, G. K. Hall, Southern Illinois University Press, Indiana University Press, and Greenwood Press.

MEMBER: Modern Language Association of America, National Council of Teachers of English (chairperson of College Section Nominating Committee, 1981), Conference on College Composition and Communication (member of executive council, 1980-82), Council of Writing Program Administrators (member of board of directors, 1984-86; vice-president, 1987, 1988; president, 1989, 1990), American Studies Association, Phi Beta Kappa, Phi Kappa Phi, Alpha Lambda Delta, Omicron Delta Kappa.

AWARDS, HONORS: National fiction and nonfiction awards, *Mademoiselle* College Board Contest, 1955; Outstanding Educator Award, Butler University, 1972-73, 1973-74, and faculty fellowship, 1974; faculty research grants, University of New Mexico, 1976, 1977, 1978, and George Mason University, 1981; National Endowment for the Humanities grant, 1979-81, summer stipend, 1984, and fellowship for college teachers, 1986-87; National Project for College Assessment Program Evaluation fellow, 1985.

WRITINGS:

(Editor with Francis L. Utley and Arthur F. Kinney) *Bear, Man, and God: Seven Approaches to William Faulkner's "The Bear,"* Random House (New York City), 1964, revised edition published as *Bear, Man, and God: Eight Approaches to William Faulkner's "The Bear,"* Random House, 1971.

(Editor with Kinney and Kenneth W. Kuiper) *Symposium,* Houghton (Boston), 1969.

(Editor with Kinney and Kuiper) *Symposium on Love,* Houghton, 1970.

Doctor Spock: Biography of a Conservative Radical, Bobbs-Merrill (Indianapolis, IN), 1972.

(With Karen Coburn and Joan Pearlman) *The New Assertive Woman,* Delacorte (New York City), 1975.

(Editor and author of introduction) Natalie Crouter, *Forbidden Diary: A Record of Wartime Internment, 1941-1945,* B. Franklin, 1980.

(With Mary Louise Briscoe and Barbara Tobias) *American Autobiography, 1945-1980: A Bibliography,* University of Wisconsin Press (Madison), 1982.

Strategic Writing, Random House, 1983.

(Editor) *The Essay Connection: Readings for Writers,* Heath (Boston), 1984.

Fact and Artifact: Writing Nonfiction, Harcourt (New York City), 1985.

(Editor) *The Lexington Reader: Readings in Nonfiction,* Heath, 1987.

(Editor and author of introduction) Margaret Sams, *Forbidden Family: A Wartime Memoir of the Philippines, 1941-45,* University of Wisconsin Press, 1989.

(Editor with Edward M. White) *Inquiry,* Blair (Boston), 1993.

(Editor with Donald Daiker and White, and contributor) *Composition in the Twenty-First Century: Crisis and*

Change, Southern Illinois University Press (Carbondale), 1995.

Also contributor to various books, including *Classroom Practices in Teaching English, 1976-77: Responses to Sexism,* edited by Ouida Clapp, National Council of Teachers of English, 1977; *Women's Autobiographies: Essays in Criticism,* edited by Estelle Jelinek, Indiana University Press (Bloomington), 1980; *Writer's Craft, Teacher's Art,* edited by Mimi Schwartz, Heinemann (Portsmouth, NH), 1991; *Autobiography and Questions of Gender,* edited by Shirley Neuman, Frank Cass & Co. (London), 1991; *Writing and Publishing for Academic Authors,* edited by Joseph M. Moxley, University Press of America (Washington, DC), 1992; *American Women's Autobiography: Fea(s)ts of Memory,* edited by Margo Culley, University of Wisconsin Press, 1992; and *Southern Writers of the Second Renaissance: The Fiction,* edited by Joseph M. Flora and Robert Bain, Greenwood Press (Westport, CT), 1993. Also contributor of articles (several with husband, Martin Bloom), poetry, and book reviews, to periodicals, including *Women's Studies International Forum, Western Writers, Webster Review, Belles Lettres, Biography, Resources in Education,* and *St. Louis Post-Dispatch.* Manuscript reader for periodicals, including *PMLA,* 1976—, *College English,* 1986—, *College Composition and Communication,* 1986—, and *Rhetoric Review,* 1989—; member of editorial board, *Journal of English Teaching Techniques,* 1976-80, *Writing Program Administration,* 1981-83, *Journal of Advanced Composition,* 1983—, and *A/B: Auto/Biography Studies,* 1990—.

WORK IN PROGRESS: Songs of Ourselves: Reading, Researching, Writing Autobiography, for Prentice-Hall; an autobiography, parts of which have been published in *College English* and *A/B: Auto/Biography Studies.*

SIDELIGHTS: In *A/B: Auto/Biography Studies,* Lynn Z. Bloom described her writing procedure for *Doctor Spock: Biography of a Conservative Radical,* about the noted childrearing authority: "Fortunately for my research, Spock was as innocent of celebrity protocol as I was. After an hour's conversation I floated into the October sunshine, buoyed by the verbal agreement that we honored without ever again debating or even discussing it during the subsequent six-year process. Spock was planning to retire in the following May (1967), and was eager for someone to put in order a lifetime accumulation of primary sources—a treasure trove of professional papers, manuscripts and early editions of his books, editorial and parental commentary on *Baby and Child Care* (some ten thousand letters), royalty statements, tax returns, newspaper clippings beginning with his undergraduate days at Yale, his Olympic gold medal (Yale crew, 1929), and family photographs that would have made Cecil Beaton envious. He would let me have exclusive access to everything—no

strings. He would meet with me weekly for interviews, and I could interview his wife weekly at their house. He would write letters of introduction to anyone I needed to see, even—as it turned out—enemies. I could follow him around the hospital, attend his classes, and sit in on his one-on-one pediatric practicum with a second-year medical student—he'd lend me a white coat so I'd blend in. He could read my completed manuscript and supply corrections for errors of fact, but the interpretation would be my own. I'd get whatever royalties there were—and of course, I would change the world with my first book, just as Dr. Spock had done with his."

BIOGRAPHICAL/CRITICAL SOURCES:

BOOKS

Waldrep, Tom, editor, *Writers on Writing,* Random House, 1985.

PERIODICALS

A/B: Auto/Biography Studies, December, 1993.
College English, November, 1992.

*   *   *

BLOOMFIELD, Anthony (John Westgate) 1922-
(John Westgate)

PERSONAL: Born September 8, 1922, in London, England; son of William Henry and Edith (Tann) Bloomfield; married Anneliese Hubner, 1954; children: Timothy Walther. *Education:* Attended schools in England.

ADDRESSES: Home—22 Montpelier Court, Montpelier Road, Ealing, London W5 2QN, England.

CAREER: British Broadcasting Corp., London, England, senior editor, television news, 1955—. *Military service:* Royal Air Force, six years.

MEMBER: PEN.

WRITINGS:

NOVELS

Russian Roulette, Harcourt (San Diego, CA), 1955.
The Delinquents, Hogarth Press, 1958.
The Tempter, Scribner (New York City), 1961.
Throw, Scribner, 1965.
(Under name John Westgate) *Life for a Life,* Scribner, 1971.

Also author as John Westgate of *Reilly's Fire* (novel), 1980.

TELEPLAYS

Turn Off If You Know the Ending, British Broadcasting Corp. (BBC), 1966.

One Day It Could Be Different, BBC, 1966.

(Under name John Westgate) *Victor, Victor,* BBC, 1967.

(Under name John Westgate) *Inventory for the Summer,* BBC, 1967.

(Under name John Westgate) *Life for a Life,* BBC, 1967.

(Under name John Westgate) *Hands with the Magic Touch,* BBC, 1970.

(Under name John Westgate) *Beneath the Tide,* BBC, 1971.

OTHER

Contributor to *Encounter, Gallery, Ellery Queen, Alfred Hitchcock, Modern Reading, Writing Today, Books & Bookmen,* and other periodicals.

The author's works have been translated into French, Swedish, Romanian, and German.

SIDELIGHTS: Anthony Bloomfield is a British novelist and author of television plays. Bloomfield made his literary debut in 1956 with *Russian Roulette,* a novel that was met with some high praise. Anthony Boucher, writing in the *New York Times,* called *Russian Roulette* "something of an event." The reviewer continued: "As a curiously tenuous yet intense essay in personal relationship it may recall—to the literary addict—the best and subtlest novels of Georges Simenon; the rich-textured, allusive, sometimes dazzling prose may suggest William Sansome. Yet the total impression is that of a new, individual and highly welcome creator in the borderlands of crime."

Like several of Bloomfield's later novels, *Russian Roulette* is the story of a man who becomes obsessed with a member of the underworld; this identification leads the protagonist to psychological deterioration and ultimate downfall. In a later novel, *Throw,* Bloomfield's protagonist finds himself retaliating violently against the driver of the car that several years earlier had killed his young son. Although the novel received mixed reviews, Boucher described *Throw* in the *New York Times Book Review* as "a chillingly convincing picture of schizophrenic disintegration, plausible enough to serve as a case history."

In *Life for a Life,* Bloomfield again explores the themes of madness, evil, and complicity. When *Life for a Life's* hero, Larry Carpenter, rescues an underworld figure from drowning, the professional assassin promises Larry that he'll rub out anyone of Larry's choosing. Although Larry at first rejects the offer, his growing irritation with his wife, his mistress, and his co-workers makes the idea increasingly enticing. Some reviewers found Bloomfield's psychological thriller intriguing, while others dismissed it as pretentious. Martin Levin praised *Life for a Life* in the *New York Times Book Review* for its "concentrated texture" and wit. "Nightmare and reality," wrote Levin, "become interchangeable as the narrative pace accelerates—

and Mr. Bloomfield never loses control of a beautifully engineered thriller."

BIOGRAPHICAL/CRITICAL SOURCES:

PERIODICALS

Chicago Tribune, February 11, 1962.

New York Times, September 16, 1956.

New York Times Book Review, January 14, 1962; August 15, 1965; May 9, 1971.

Saturday Review, September 22, 1956.

Spectator, March 25, 1955.

Time, January 26, 1962.

Times Literary Supplement, April 29, 1955; March 17, 1961; May 6, 1965; July 9, 1971.

*   *   *

BLUTH, B(etty) J(ean)   1934-

PERSONAL: Born December 5, 1934, in Philadelphia, PA; daughter of Robert Thomas (a real estate agent) and Catherine (a model; maiden name, Boxman) Gowland; married Thomas Del Bluth, August 20, 1960 (deceased); children: Robert, Richard. *Education:* Bucknell University, B.A. (cum laude), 1957; Fordham University, M.A., 1960; University of California, Los Angeles, Ph.D., 1970.

ADDRESSES: Home—15 Rutledge Ct., Sterling, VA 20165. *Office*—National Aeronautics and Space Administration, Education Division, Code FE, 300 E St. S.W., Washington, DC 20546.

CAREER: Reading Laboratory, Philadelphia, PA, instructor, 1958-59; Rosary High School, San Diego, CA, teacher of history, civics, and English, 1959-60; Immaculate Heart College, Los Angeles, CA, instructor, 1960-63, assistant professor of sociology, 1963-65; California State University, Northridge, assistant professor, 1965-75, associate professor, 1975-79, professor of sociology, 1979-87, fellow at Institute for the Advancement of Teaching and Learning, 1974; National Aeronautics and Space Administration (NASA) Space Station Program Office, grantee in Washington, DC, 1983-87, aerospace technologist in Reston, VA, 1987-89, senior staff assistant to deputy director of Space Station Freedom Program and Operations, 1989-93, special technical assistant to director of Education Division, 1993—. Distinguished lecturer, American Institute of Aeronautics and Astronautics, 1972-83; Institute for the Advancement of Teaching and Learning, California State University, Northridge, fellow, 1974, associate fellow, 1976. Member of United Nations team on the relevance of space activities to economic and social development; member of Citizens Advisory Council on National Space Policy, and National Science and Technology

Council, 1994. Has presented numerous papers at annual meetings, conferences, and symposia; frequent public speaker and television interview subject. Consultant to businesses and religious groups, including Daughters of Mary and Joseph, 1969, Dominican Sisters, 1969, Immaculate Heart Community, 1971-73, Rico-Lion, Ltd., 1978, General Dynamics, 1982, and Comworld Productions, 1982.

MEMBER: International Academy of Astronautics, American Society of Astronautics (fellow), American Sociological Association, American Institute of Aeronautics and Astronautics, American Astronautical Society, Institute for the Social Science Study of Space (member of academic advisory board), Space Studies Institute, Air Force Association, L-5 Society (member of board of directors), Institute for the Advancement of Engineering (fellow), British Interplanetary Society, Phi Beta Kappa.

AWARDS, HONORS: Teaching award, Alpha Omega, 1966, 1974; Distinguished Teaching Award, California State University, Northridge, 1968; certificate of appreciation, American Astronautical Society, 1978, for *The SMD III and Spacelab Simulation: A Critical Look;* grants for "Update on Space Program," Rockwell International Corp., TRW, Inc., and Lockheed Corp., 1978-82; certificate of appreciation, Society of American Military Engineers, 1980, for presentation "Social and Psychological Aspects of Long Duration Space Flight"; special program award, Los Angeles section of American Institute of Aeronautics and Astronautics, 1980, for "An Evening with Kraft Ehricke"; Hypathia Cluster Award for excellence in furthering manned space flight, 1984; NASA Headquarters research grant, 1984-86; Award for Outstanding Achievement, International Academy of Astronautics, 1988; outstanding performance award, NASA, 1990, 1991, 1992, 1993, and 1994.

WRITINGS:

(Editor with Robert Chianese, James Kellenberger, and others) *Search for Identity Reader,* Xerox College Publishing, 1973.

(With John Irving, Sherry May, and Dick Smith) *Search for Community Reader,* Xerox College Publishing, 1977.

(Editor with S. R. McNeal) *Update on Space,* National Behavior Systems (Granada Hills, CA), Volume 1, 1981, Volume 2, 1982.

Parson's General Theory of Action: A Summary of the Basic Theory, National Behavior Systems, 1982.

Space Station Habitability Report, Boeing Aerospace Co. (Seattle), 1983.

Space Station/Nuclear Submarine Analog, Boeing Aerospace Co., 1983.

Crew System Interface Management Study, Boeing Aerospace Co., 1983.

Soviet Space Stations as Analogs, Boeing Aerospace Co., 1983, 2nd edition, National Aeronautics and Space Administration (NASA), 1986.

Space Station/Antarctic Analogs, NASA, 1984.

Human Performance in Space, Robert E. Krieger (Melbourne, FL), 1987.

(Principal investigator) Dennis F. Fielder, editor, *Soviet Space Station as Analogs: Mir,* NASA, Volume 2, 2nd edition, 1992, 3rd edition, 1993.

Contributor to numerous books, including *Remember the Future: The Apollo Legacy,* edited by Stan Kent, Univelt (San Diego, CA), 1979; *Space Humanization Series,* Volume 2, edited by Stephen Cheston, NASA, 1982; and *People in Space,* edited by James E. Katz, Transaction Books (New Brunswick, NJ), 1985. Contributor to periodicals, including *Teaching Sociology, Science,* and *Acta Astronautica.*

WORK IN PROGRESS: "Currently working on management 'lessons learned' of some great military leaders—Admiral Horatio Nelson (Royal Navy), Wellington, etc.—the 'threads that stay the same' regardless of times or technology."

SIDELIGHTS: B. J. Bluth once told *CA:* "Being involved with mankind's evolution into space is a distinctly exciting and challenging enterprise—worth a life. Unlike those at the departure of Columbus, we are able to appreciate the momentous changes as they come. By moving off-planet, in some ways humanity will probably grow and mature far beyond our present imagination, and in other ways we will need to draw on the wisdom of our predecessors. I hope to do what I can to know and outline the difference."

*   *   *

BOND, (Thomas) Michael   1926-

PERSONAL: Born January 13, 1926, in Newbury, Berkshire, England; son of Norman Robert and Frances Mary (Offer) Bond; married Brenda Mary Johnson, June 29, 1950 (divorced, 1981); married Susan Marfrey Rogers, 1981; children (first marriage) Karen Mary Jankel, Anthony Thomas. *Education:* Attended Presentation College, 1934-40. *Avocational interests:* Motoring, wine, theater, and gardening.

ADDRESSES: Office—c/o 94B Tachbrook St., London SWN 2NB, England. *Agent*—Harvey Unna & Stephen Durbridge Ltd., 24 Pottery Lane, Holland Park, London W11 4LZ, England.

CAREER: Writer. British Broadcasting Corp., London, England, television camera operator, 1954-66. Director,

Paddington Productions, Ltd. *Military service:* Royal Air Force, 1943-44, air crew; British Army, Middlesex Regiment, 1944-47.

AWARDS, HONORS: American Library Association Notable Book citation for *Tales of Olga Da Polga.*

WRITINGS:

"PADDINGTON" SERIES

A Bear Called Paddington (also see below), illustrations by Peggy Fortnum, Collins, 1958, Houghton (Boston, MA), 1960.

More about Paddington (also see below), illustrations by Fortnum, Collins, 1959, Houghton, 1962.

Paddington Helps Out (also see below), illustrations by Fortnum, Collins, 1960, Houghton, 1961.

Paddington Abroad, illustrations by Fortnum, Collins, 1961, Houghton, 1972.

Paddington at Large (also see below), illustrations by Fortnum, Collins, 1962, Houghton, 1963.

Paddington Marches On, Collins, 1964, illustrations by Fortnum, Houghton, 1965, Fontana (Huntington, NY), 1986.

Adventures of Paddington (also see below), Collins, 1965.

Paddington at Work (also see below), illustrations by Fortnum, Collins, 1966, Houghton, 1967.

Paddington Goes to Town, illustrations by Fortnum, Collins, 1968, Houghton, 1969, Fontana, 1986.

Paddington Takes the Air, illustrations by Fortnum, Collins, 1970, Houghton, 1971.

Paddington's 'Blue Peter' Story Book, illustrations by Ivor Wood, Collins, 1973, published as *Paddington Takes to T.V.,* Houghton, 1974.

Paddington on Top, illustrations by Fortnum, Collins, 1974, Houghton, 1975.

(With Albert Bradley) *Paddington on Stage* (play; adapted from Bond's *Adventures of Paddington*), illustrations by Fortnum, Collins, 1974, Samuel French (acting edition; New York City), 1976, Houghton, 1977.

Paddington Takes the Test, illustrations by Fortnum, Collins, 1979, Houghton, 1980.

Paddington: A Disappearing Trick and Other Stories (anthology; also see below), Collins, 1979.

Paddington for Christmas (also see below), Collins, 1979.

Paddington on Screen: The Second 'Blue Peter' Story Book, illustrations by Barry Macey, Collins, 1981, Houghton, 1982.

The Hilarious Adventures of Paddington (contains *A Bear Called Paddington, More about Paddington, Paddington at Large, Paddington at Work,* and *Paddington Helps Out;* issued as a boxed set), Dell (New York City), 1986.

Also author of fifty-six episodes of animated Paddington films and three half-hour Paddington specials for Home Box Office.

"PADDINGTON" PICTURE BOOKS

Paddington Bear, illustrations by Fred Banbery, Collins, 1972, Random House (New York City), 1973.

Paddington's Garden, illustrations by Banbery, Collins, 1972, Random House, 1973.

Paddington Goes Shopping, Collins, 1973.

Paddington at the Circus, illustrations by Banbery, Collins, 1973, Random House, 1974.

Paddington Goes Shopping, illustrations by Banbery, Collins, 1973, published as *Paddington's Lucky Day,* Random House, 1974.

Paddington at the Tower, illustrations by Banbery, Collins, 1975, Random House, 1978.

Paddington at the Seaside, illustrations by Banbery, Collins, 1975, Random House, 1976.

Paddington Takes a Bath, Collins, 1976.

Paddington Goes to the Sales, Collins, 1976.

Paddington's New Room, Collins, 1976.

Paddington at the Station, Collins, 1976.

Paddington Hits Out, Collins, 1977.

Paddington Does It Himself, Collins, 1977.

Paddington in the Kitchen, Collins, 1977.

Paddington Goes Out, Collins, 1980.

Paddington at Home, Collins, 1980.

Paddington and Aunt Lucy, illustrations by Barry Wilkinson, Collins, 1980.

Paddington in Touch, illustrations by Wilkinson, Collins, 1980.

Paddington Has Fun, Collins, 1982.

Paddington Works Hard, Collins, 1982.

Paddington's Storybook, illustrations by Fortnum, Collins, 1983, Houghton, 1984.

Paddington on the River, illustrations by Wilkinson, Collins, 1983.

Paddington Weighs In, illustrations by Wilkinson, Collins, 1983.

Great Big Paddington Bear Picture Book, Pan (London), 1984.

Paddington at the Zoo, illustrations by McKee, Collins, 1984, Putnam (New York City), 1985.

Paddington and the Knickerbocker Rainbow, illustrations by McKee, Collins, 1984, Putnam, 1985.

Paddington's Art Exhibition, illustrations by McKee, Collins, 1985, published as *Paddington's Painting Exhibition,* Putnam, 1986.

Paddington at the Fair, illustrations by McKee, Collins, 1985, Putnam, 1986.

Paddington at the Palace, illustrations by McKee, Putnam, 1986.

Paddington Minds the House, illustrations by McKee, Collins, 1986.

Paddington Spring Cleans, Collins, 1986.

Paddington Cleans Up, Putnam, 1986.

Paddington's Busy Day, illustrations by McKee, Collins, 1987.

Paddington and the Marmalade Maze, illustrations by McKee, Collins, 1987.

Paddington's Magical Christmas, illustrations by McKee, Collins, 1988.

Paddington Meets the Queen, HarperCollins (New York City), 1993.

Paddington Rides On!, HarperCollins, 1993.

Paddington's Magical Christmas, HarperCollins, 1993.

"PADDINGTON" LEARNING AND ACTIVITY BOOKS

The Great Big Paddington Book, illustrations by Banbery, Collins & World, 1976.

Paddington's Loose-End Book: An ABC of Things to Do, illustrations by Wood, Collins, 1976.

Paddington's Party Book, illustrations by Wood, Collins, 1976.

Fun and Games with Paddington, Collins & World, 1977.

Paddington's Birthday Party, Collins, 1977.

Paddington Carpenter, Collins, 1977.

Paddington Conjurer, Collins, 1977.

Paddington Cook, Collins, 1977.

Paddington Golfer, Collins, 1977.

Paddington's First Book, Collins, 1978.

Paddington's Picture Book, Collins, 1978.

Paddington's Play Book, Collins, 1978.

Paddington's Counting Book, Collins, 1978.

Paddington's Cartoon Book, illustrations by Wood, Collins, 1979.

(With daughter, Karen Bond) *Paddington at the Airport,* illustrations by Toni Goffe, Hutchinson (London), 1986.

(With Karen Bond) *Paddington Mails a Letter,* illustrations by Goffe, Macmillan (New York City), 1986 (published in England as *Paddington Bear Posts a Letter,* Hutchinson, 1986).

(With Karen Bond) *Paddington's Clock Book,* Hutchinson, 1986.

(With Karen Bond) *Paddington's London,* Hutchinson, 1986.

Paddington's ABC, HarperCollins, 1990.

Paddington's 123, HarperCollins, 1990.

Paddington's Colors, HarperCollins, 1990.

Paddington's Opposites, HarperCollins, 1990.

Paddington's First Word Book, HarperCollins, 1993.

Paddington's Things I Do, HarperCollins, 1994.

Paddington's Things I Feel, HarperCollins, 1994.

"PADDINGTON" POP-UP BOOKS

Paddington's Pop-Up Book, Collins, 1977.

Paddington and the Snowbear, Collins, 1981.

Paddington at the Launderette, Collins, 1981.

Paddington's Shopping Adventure, Collins, 1981.

Paddington's Birthday Treat, Collins, 1981.

SOUND RECORDINGS

A Bear Called Paddington, Caedmon (New York City), 1978.

Paddington: A Disappearing Trick and Other Stories, Caedmon, 1979.

Paddington for Christmas, Caedmon, 1979.

Paddington Turns Detective, Caedmon, 1979.

Also author of an audio version of *Paddington's Storybook.*

"THURSDAY" SERIES

Here Comes Thursday!, illustrations by Daphne Rowles, Harrap (London), 1966, Lothrop (New York City), 1967.

Thursday Rides Again, illustrations by Beryl Sanders, Harrap, 1968, Lothrop, 1969.

Thursday Ahoy!, illustrations by Leslie Wood, Harrap, 1969, Lothrop, 1970.

Thursday in Paris, illustrations by Wood, Harrap, 1971, Penguin, 1974.

"OLGA DA POLGA" SERIES

Tales of Olga Da Polga (omnibus volume), illustrations by Hans Helweg, Penguin, 1971, Macmillan, 1973.

Olga Meets Her Match, illustrations by Helweg, Penguin, 1973, Hastings House (New York City), 1975.

Olga Carries On, illustrations by Helweg, Penguin, 1976, Hastings House, 1977.

Olga Takes Charge, illustrations by Helweg, Penguin, 1982, Dell, 1983.

The Complete Adventures of Olga da Polga (omnibus volume), illustrations by Helweg, Delacorte (New York City), 1982.

First Big Olga da Polga Book, illustrations by Helweg, Longman (Harlow, England), 1983.

Second Big Olga da Polga Book, illustrations by Helweg, Longman, 1983.

Also author of *Eight Olga Readers,* 1975.

"OLGA DA POLGA" PICTURE BOOKS

Olga Counts Her Blessings, E.M.C., 1977.

Olga Makes a Friend, E.M.C., 1977.

Olga Makes a Wish, E.M.C., 1977.

Olga Makes Her Mark, E.M.C., 1977.

Olga Takes a Bite, E.M.C., 1977.

Olga's New Home, E.M.C., 1977.

Olga's Second House, E.M.C., 1977.
Olga's Special Day, E.M.C., 1977.

"PARSLEY" SERIES

Parsley's Tail, illustrations by Esor, BBC Publications (London), 1969.
Parsley's Good Deed, illustrations by Esor, BBC Publications, 1969.
Parsley's Last Stand, BBC Publications, 1970.
Parsley's Problem Present, BBC Publications, 1970.
Parsley's Parade [and] Parsley the Lion, Collins, 1972.
Parsley and the Herbs, edited by Sheila M. Lane and Marion Kemp, Ward, Lock (London), 1976.

Also author of *The Herbs* (thirteen-episode puppet series) and *The Adventures of Parsley* (thirty-two episode puppet series).

MYSTERIES FOR ADULTS

Monsieur Pamplemousse, Hodder, 1983, Beaufort (New York City), 1985.
Monsieur Pamplemousse and the Secret Mission, Hodder, 1984, Beaufort, 1986.
Monsieur Pamplemousse on the Spot, Hodder, 1986, Beaufort, 1987.
Monsieur Pamplemousse Takes the Cure, Hodder, 1987.
Monsieur Pamplemousse Aloft, Hodder, 1989.
Monsieur Pamplemousse Investigates, Hodder, 1990.
Monsieur Pamplemousse Rests His Case, Headline, 1991.
Monsieur Pamplemousse Stands Firm, Headline, 1992.
Monsieur Pamplemousse On Location, Headline, 1992.
Monsieur Pamplemousse Takes the Train, Headline, 1993.

OTHER

(Editor) *Michael Bond's Book of Bears,* Purnell (London), 1971.
The Day the Animals Went on Strike (picture book), illustrations by Jim Hodgson, American Heritage (New York City), 1972.
(Editor) *Michael Bond's Book of Mice,* Purnell, 1972.
(Translator with Barbara von Johnson) *The Motormalgamation,* Studio-Vista (Eastbourne, England), 1974.
Windmill, illustrations by Tony Cattaneo, Studio-Vista, 1975.
How to Make Flying Things (non-fiction), photographs by Peter Kibble, Studio-Vista, 1975.
Mr. Cram's Magic Bubbles, illustrations by Gioia Fiammenghi, Penguin (West Drayton, England), 1975.
Picnic on the River, Collins (London), 1980.
J. D. Polson and the Liberty Head Dime, illustrations by Roger Wade Walker, hand lettering by Leslie Lee, Mayflower (London), 1980.
J. D. Polson and the Dillogate Affair, illustrations by Walker, Hodder (London), 1981.

The Caravan Puppets, illustrations by Vanessa Julian-Ottie, Collins, 1983.
(With Paul Parnes) *Oliver the Greedy Elephant,* Methuen (London), 1985, Western Publishing (New York City), 1986.
The Pleasures of Paris (guidebook), photographs by the author, Pavilion (London), 1987.

Also author of radio and television plays for adults and children, including *Simon's Good Deed, Napoleon's Day Out, Open House,* and *Paddington* (various short- and full-length animated films), which have been shown in Great Britain, the United States, France, Germany, Scandinavia, Canada, South Africa, the Netherlands, Hong Kong, Italy, Ceylon, and many other countries. Contributor to British periodicals.

WORK IN PROGRESS: "Olga da Polga" for television; *Monsieur Pamplemousse Afloat;* an autobiography.

SIDELIGHTS: On Christmas Eve in 1957, Michael Bond stopped in a London store to find a present for his wife. "On one of the shelves I came across a small bear looking, I thought, very sorry for himself as he was the only one who hadn't been sold," Bond recalls in *Something about the Author Autobiography Series.* He continues, "I bought him and because we were living near Paddington station at the time, we christened him Paddington. He sat on a shelf of our one-roomed apartment for a while, and then one day when I was sitting in front of my typewriter staring at a blank sheet of paper wondering what to write, I idly tapped out the words 'Mr. and Mrs. Brown first met Paddington on a railway platform. In fact, that was how he came to have such an unusual name for a bear, for Paddington was the name of the station.' It was a simple act, and in terms of deathless prose, not exactly earth shattering, but it was to change my life considerably. . . . Without intending it, I had become a children's author."

Since then, Paddington has "become part of the folklore of childhood," writes Marcus Crouch in *The Nesbit Tradition: The Children's Novel in England 1945-70.* The now world-famous bear is recognized, despite a variety of illustrators, by his unkempt appearance, Wellington boots, and duffel coat. A foreigner from Peru, Paddington exhibits both innocence and a knack for trouble. "The humour of Paddington is largely visual; it is not what he is but what he does and how he does it that is funny," claims Crouch. In the *New York Times Book Review,* Ellen Lewis Buell cites the bear's "endearing combination of bearishness and boyishness" as one reason for his popularity. According to Pico Iyer in the *Village Voice,* "Paddington is a resolute little fellow of strong principles and few prejudices, full of resourcefulness and free of rancor: both the bear next door and something of a role model."

Despite the many accounts of Paddington's adventures, "One is immensely impressed by the way each collection of stories comes up so fresh and full of humorous and highly original situations," writes Eric Hudson in the *Children's Book Review.* Each additional book, praises a *Times Literary Supplement* contributor, gives "added substance and credibility . . . instead of flogging a good idea to death." And reports Iyer, "Through all the blandishments of multimedia fame—grasping toy-makers, television makeup men, translations into 20 tongues, and imitators neither sincere nor flattering—the little bear manages, as ever, to land on his paws with good nature intact."

Commenting on Paddington's appeal, Bond told *CA,* "When Paddington goes back home, it's the world that I remember from my childhood. In England, if you try to make a telephone call now, you find that the telephone box has been vandalized. Paddington lives in a world where that hasn't happened yet. So he's always on two levels."

In 1972, Bond started a Paddington picture book series, working with new illustrators and moving away from the popular original drawings by Peggy Fortnum. The transition was not a smooth one. Some reviewers agree with Katherine Heylman, who declares in the *School Library Journal* that "this is no substitute for the original Paddington." Zena Sutherland concurs in the *Bulletin of the Center for Children's Books,* writing that for her, the simplified language and action strip away much of the original charm of the stories, leaving "no opportunity to develop the small Peruvian bear as a character." Still, in the *Wilson Library Bulletin,* Barbara Dill finds that while the more recent Banbery illustrations create a different image for the bear, she feels that "this one is just as beguiling with a character all his own."

Bond defended the move away from the original Paddington in his interview with *CA.* "Looking at the original illustrations, you see that they vary in shape and size according to the story. When you come to something like film, or even a picture book, there's got to be continuity . . .I think dressing him in a duffel coat and a hat and Wellington boots gave him a signature," Bond said. "As long as he has at least one of those items, he's immediately recognizable."

Bond's other juvenile series also focus on very human animals. The "Thursday" series features mice as protagonists, with no supporting human characters. A *Times Literary Supplement* contributor praises them as "captivating creatures," and calls the books "far more ambitious" than the Paddington stories. Another creation, Olga da Polga the guinea-pig, contains "a touch of Bunter and Falstaff," comments a *Times Literary Supplement* reviewer. Olga is unlike the freewheeling Paddington, as she lives a shel-

tered life. Zena Sutherland writes in the *Bulletin of the Center for Children's Books,* "The humor is not so much in Olga's adventures, since she is hutchbound, but in her personality."

Bond enjoys his role as children's author. In *Something about the Author Autobiography Series,* he remarks: "One of the nice things about writing for children is their total acceptance of the fantastic. Give a child a stick and a patch of wet sand and it will draw the outline of a boat and accept it as such. I did learn though, that to make fantasy work you have to believe in it yourself. If an author doesn't believe in his inventions and his characters nobody else will. Paddington to me is, and always has been, very much alive."

In the early eighties, Bond moved to adult fiction with the tales of food inspector Monsieur Pamplemousse. While a human character, Pamplemousse does have canine assistance in his dog, Pommes Frites; the duo solve mysteries throughout France. Critics find the author's transition to adult fiction smooth and enjoyable. "Sympathetic characterisation, plenty of nice touches of verbal humour, and a delight in pursuing the absurd to the point where it merges in to the farcical, have all been translated intact and without incongruity into the adult sphere," says Reginald Hill in *Books and Bookmen.* Pamplemousse's adventures contain more humor than blood and mayhem. Writes Polly Morrice of *Monsieur Pamplemousse on the Spot* in the *New York Times Book Review,* "Like a successful souffle, this is light, fluffy, skillfully made, with no aftertaste or afterthoughts to disturb the reader." Sybil Steinberg, writing for *Publishers Weekly,* notes, "Pamplemousse and his faithful hound are an appealing pair and offer an evening of civilized entertainment."

Pommes Frites received particular praise in a review of *Monsieur Pamplemousse Rests His Case* by Pat Oswell in the *Washington Post Book World:* "The mournful hound is ingenious rescuer, agile cogitator, reliable judge of character, and fellow gourmet—a doggy Dr. Watson for one of crime's most entertaining sleuths."

For Bond, the birth of the culinary detective reflected a love of mystery as well as France. "I'm a great Georges Simenon fan; I like Maigret, and I wanted to write a book about a detective who was all that he wasn't," Bond recalled in the *CA* interview. "Maigret solved his cases by hard work and inspiration; I tend to write humorous books, and I wanted to write about a detective who usually solved his cases by accident."

Reflecting on his characters and life as a writer, Bond muses in the *Something about the Author Autobiography Series,* "Writing is a lonely occupation, but it's also a selfish one. When things get bad, as they do for everyone from time to time, writers are able to shut themselves away from it, peopling the world with their characters, making them behave the way they want them to behave, saying the things they want to hear. Sometimes they take over and stubbornly refuse to do what you tell them to do, but usually they are very good. Sometimes I am Paddington walking down Windsor Gardens en route to the Portobello Road to buy his morning supply of buns, but if I don't fancy that I can always be Monsieur Pamplemousse, sitting outside a cafe enjoying the sunshine over a baguette split down the middle and filled with ham, and a glass of red wine. I wouldn't wish for anything nicer."

Paddington's adventures have been published in nearly twenty countries, including Japan, Israel, South Africa, Iceland, Poland, Russia, Portugal, Holland, and Greece. The bear has been reproduced as a stuffed animal; there is a Paddington corner in the London Toy Museum.

BIOGRAPHICAL/CRITICAL SOURCES:

BOOKS

Blount, Margaret, *Animal Land,* Hutchinson, 1974.
Children's Literature Review, Volume 1, Gale (Detroit, MI), 1976.
Crouch, Marcus, *The Nesbit Tradition: The Children's Novel in England, 1945-70,* Benn (London), 1972.
Something about the Author Autobiography Series, Volume 3, Gale, 1986.

PERIODICALS

Armchair Detective, summer, 1991.
Booklist, December 1, 1990; September 15, 1991; December 15, 1991.
Books and Bookmen, February, 1985.
Books for Keeps, March, 1991; January, 1992.
Bulletin of the Center for Children's Books, November, 1973; February, 1974.
Children's Book Review, February, 1971.
Contemporary Review, November, 1971; January, 1984.
Los Angeles Times Book Review, June 9, 1985.
New Yorker, December 4, 1971; December 1, 1975.
New York Times Book Review, August 27, 1961; May 9, 1965; November 9, 1969; March 1, 1987.
Observer, March 10, 1985.
Publishers Weekly, July 29, 1988; June 23, 1989; July 28, 1989; October 12, 1990; September 6, 1991.
Saturday Review, November 9, 1968; April 17, 1971.
School Librarian, August, 1992.
School Library Journal, December, 1973; September, 1989; February, 1992; December, 1992.
Times Literary Supplement, November 24, 1966; November 12, 1970; October 22, 1971; November 3, 1972; December 6, 1974; October 1, 1976; September 30, 1983.
Village Voice, July 16, 1985.

Washington Post Book World, December 15, 1991.
Wilson Library Bulletin, January, 1974.

* * *

BORCHARDT, D(ietrich) H(ans) 1916-

PERSONAL: Born April 14, 1916, in Hanover, Germany; son of Max Noah (a physician) and Mina (Lewinski) Borchardt; married Janet Duff Sinclair, December 20, 1944 (deceased); married Pamela Rosemarie Trier, October 10, 1989; children: (first marriage) Sandra Helen, Ann Sinclair (deceased), Max William. *Education:* Victoria University of Wellington, M.A. (with honors), 1946; New Zealand Library School, diploma, 1947. *Avocational interests:* Gardening.

ADDRESSES: Home—57 Aylmer St., North Balwyn, Victoria 3104, Australia.

CAREER: Farm worker in Germany, Italy, and Spain, 1934-36, and in New Zealand, 1939-43; book dealer in Florence, Italy, 1936-39, and in Wellington, New Zealand, 1943-46; University of Otago, Dunedin, New Zealand, acquisitions librarian, 1947-50; University of Tasmania, Hobart, deputy librarian, 1950-53, librarian, 1953-64; La Trobe University, Bundoora, Victoria, Australia, chief librarian, 1965-81. United Nations Educational, Scientific, and Cultural Organization (UNESCO) library expert in Turkey, 1964-65; lecturer in bibliography at Graduate Library School, George Peabody College for Teachers (now George Peabody College for Teachers of Vanderbilt University), Nashville, TN, summers, 1968 and 1973.

MEMBER: Library Association of Australia (fellow; past president of university and college libraries section; member of board of examiners, 1962-64, 1966-69), New Zealand Library Association, Bibliographical Society of Australia and New Zealand, Society of Indexers.

AWARDS, HONORS: Carnegie grant to visit Europe and the United States, 1958; Queen Elizabeth II Jubilee Medal, 1977; H. C. L. Anderson Award, Library Association of Australia, 1979; Order of Australia, 1982; library named in his honor, La Trobe University; D.Soc.Sc., Melbourne Institute of Technology, 1987; D.Univ., La Trobe University, 1991.

WRITINGS:

(Compiler with B. Tilley, and author of introduction) *The Roy Bridges Collection in the University of Tasmania,* Cremorne, Stone, 1956.
Checklist of Royal Commissions, Select Committees of Parliament and Boards of Inquiry, Part 1: *Commonwealth of Australia, 1900-1950,* Cremorne, Stone, 1958, supplement published as *Commonwealth of*

Australia, 1950-1960, Wentworth Books, 1973, Part 2: *Tasmania, 1956-1959,* Cremorne, Stone, 1960, Part 3: *Victoria, 1856-1960,* Wentworth Books, 1970, Part 4: *New South Wales, 1856-1960,* La Trobe University Library (Bundoora, Victoria, Australia), 1975, Part 5: *Queensland, 1859-1960,* La Trobe University Library, 1978, Part 6: *Tasmania, Victoria, New South Wales, and Queensland, 1960-1980,* La Trobe University Library, 1986.

Australian Bibliography: A Guide to Printed Sources of Information, F. W. Cheshire (Harlow, Essex, England), 1963, 3rd edition, Pergamon Press (Oxford, England), 1976.

Senescence and Fertility (La Trobe University inaugural lectures), F. W. Cheshire, 1967.

How to Find Out in Philosophy and Psychology, Pergamon, 1968.

The Spread of Printing: Australia, Hertzberger, 1968, published as *Australia,* A. Schram (Tunbridge Wells, Kent, England), 1969.

(With J. I. Horacek) *Librarianship in Australia, New Zealand, and Oceania: A Brief Survey,* Pergamon, 1975, revised edition, 1986.

(Editor) *Seven Essays on Australian Subject Bibliography,* Australian Advisory Council on Bibliographical Services, 1977.

(Editor) *Australian Official Publications,* Longman Cheshire (Harlow, Essex, England), 1979.

(Editor) *Twelve Essays on Australian Subject Bibliography,* National Library of Australia, 1980.

(Compiler with J. D. Thawley) *Guide to the Availability of Theses Compiled for the Section of University Libraries and Other General Research Libraries,* K. G. Saur (London), 1981.

(Editor) *The Literature Related to Commonwealth Studies: Access, Dissemination, and Use; Papers and Proceedings of a Conference of Commonwealth University Librarians (South Pacific Region), Mysore, 17-20 March 1980,* La Trobe University Library, 1981.

A Bibliovision Splendid, La Trobe University, 1982.

(With Robert Stafford) *Devindex Australia: Index to Australian Literature on Social and Economic Development, 1975-1979,* Borchardt Library, La Trobe University, 1983.

(With R. D. Francis) *How to Find Out in Psychology: A Guide to the Literature and Methods of Research,* Pergamon, 1984.

Australians: A Guide to Sources, Fairfax, Syme, Weldon, and Associates, 1987.

Library Journals: How to Edit Them; Guidelines Prepared for the IFLA Round Table of Editors of Library Journals, International Federation of Library Associations and Institutions (The Hague), 1987.

(Editor with W. Kirsop) *The Book in Australia: Essays towards a Cultural and Social History,* Australian Reference Publications (Melbourne), 1988.

Checklist of Collective Bibliographies, Borchardt Library, La Trobe University, 1988.

Commissioners of Inquiry in Australia: A Brief Survey, La Trobe University Press (Melbourne), 1991.

Contributor of more than seventy-five articles and reviews to library journals. Editor, *Australia Academic and Research Libraries,* 1970-84, *Australian Historical Bibliography Bulletin,* 1982-86, and *Reference Australia: An Occasional Collection of Essays and Notes on Bibliographies, Geographical, and Statistical Sources,* 1987-90.

SIDELIGHTS: D. H. Borchardt once told *CA:* "I have always believed that it is useless to try and remember everything. Better by far, as Samuel Johnson already stressed, to know where to find out. That is what bibliography is all about—it is the veritable and only key to knowledge, and those who hold it are the true powerbrokers of our age."

Borchardt added: "Librarians must come to identify themselves with the notions of Universal Bibliographic Control and Universal Access to Publications—these are the foundations of our profession, are endorsed by IFLA, and represent the only safeguards for a true democracy."

*   *   *

BOREL, Jacques 1925-

PERSONAL: Born December 17, 1925, in Paris, France; son of Pierre (a civil servant) and Lucie (Dubee) Borel; married Christiane Idrac (a school principal), September 25, 1948; children: Denis, Anne, Helene, Claude, Claire. *Education:* Lycee Henri-IV, Paris, Baccalaureat, 1944, Licence, 1948; University of Paris, Sorbonne, Diplome d'etudes superieures, 1949.

ADDRESSES: Home—68 rue du Moulin, Lozere-sur-Yvette 91120 Essone, France.

CAREER: English teacher at Lycee Blaise-Pascal, Clermont-Ferrand, France, 1952-54, Lycee Paul Lapie, Courbevoie, France, 1954-56, and Lycee Rodin, Paris, France, 1956-67. Visiting professor at Middlebury College, Middlebury, VT, 1966, Portland State College (now University), Portland, OR, 1967, University of Hawaii, Honolulu, 1968, University of California, Irvine, 1969, University of California, Riverside, 1980, and New York University, New York City, 1983. French Embassy, Belgium, cultural attache, 1984-85.

AWARDS, HONORS: Prix Goncourt, 1965, for *L'Adoration;* Chevalier, Ordre des Arts et Lettres, 1971, Officier, 1986.

WRITINGS:

(Editor and author of notes) Paul Marie Verlaine, *Ouevres completes,* Club du Meilleur Livre, Volume I, 1959, Volume II, 1960.

(Editor and author of introduction) Verlaine, *Oeuvres poetiques completes,* Gallimard, 1962.

L'Adoration (novel), Gallimard (Paris, France), 1965, translation by Norman Denny published as *The Bond,* Doubleday, 1968.

(Translator from English) James Joyce, *Le Chat et le diable,* Gallimard (Paris, France), 1966.

(Editor and author of notes) Verlaine, *La Bonne Chanson, Romances sans paroles* [and] *Sagesse,* Librairie Generale Francaise, 1966.

(Translator from English and author of prefaces) Joyce, *Poemes: Chamber Music* [and] *Pomes penyeach,* bilingual edition, Gallimard (Paris, France), 1967.

Tata ou de l'education: Piece morale et didactique en 2 actes et 3 tableaux, Gallimard (Paris, France), 1967.

Le Retour (novel; sequel to *L'Adoration*), Gallimard (Paris, France), 1970.

Marcel Proust (essay), Seghers, 1972.

(Editor and author of introduction) Verlaine, *Oeuvres en prose completes,* Gallimard (Paris, France), 1972.

La Depossession, journal de Ligenere, Gallimard (Paris, France), 1973.

Commentaires: Rousseau, Stendhal, Proust, Gallimard (Paris, France), 1974.

Un Voyage ordinaire, La Table Ronde, 1975.

Poesie et nostalgie (essay), Berger-Levrault, 1979.

Histoire de mes vieux habits, Balland, 1979.

Petite Histoire de mes reves, Luneau-Ascot, 1981.

Hugo: Les Plus Belles Pages, Belfond, 1983.

Bonnard (essays), Beaux Arts, 1984.

L'Enfant Voyeur, Ulysse Fin de Siecle, 1987.

L'attente [and] *La Cloture,* Gallimard (Paris, France), 1989.

Commemorations, Le Temps Qu'il Fait, 1990.

Sur les murs du temps (poems), Le Temps Qu'il Fait (Cognac, France), 1990.

Author of preface for books, including *Romanciers au travail: Faulkner, Pasternak, Mauriac, E. M. Forster,* translation from the English by Jean Rene Major, Gallimard, 1967; and Frances Jammes, *De l'Angelus de l'aube a l'angelus du soir,* Gallimard, 1971. Contributor to books, including *Positions et oppositions sur le roman contemporain,* Editions Klincksieck, 1971; and *Paroles Ecrites,* Questions, 1986. Contributor of poems and essays to *Nouvelle Revue Francaise, Critique, Mercure de France, Cahiers du Sud, Figaro Litteraire, Botteghe Oscure, Europe, Cahiers du Chemin,* and other journals.

SIDELIGHTS: Winner of the Prix Goncourt in 1965, Jacques Borel's *L'Adoration* (published in English as *The Bond*) is a semi-autobiographical account of an only son and his relationship with his widowed mother. Commenting in the *Observer Review,* Claire Tomalin describes the book as "a huge, ironical slab of total recall . . . . Its piling up of detail is of the kind a patient might offer his analyst or a self-absorbed lover his very enraptured mistress . . . . Borel does, however, provide a perceptive comment of his own early in the story, in which he speaks of his consciousness at the age of 10, of himself as a figure from literature rather than life; his tantrums, runnings away, suicide attempt, erotic initiations—the implication, well sustained throughout, is that all were undergone to make raw material for the supreme experience of turning it into *la litterature.*"

Anna Balakian contends that *The Bond* owes much to traditional French literature. Writing in the *Saturday Review,* the critic remarks: "Since Jacques Borel has been in the avant-garde of literary criticism and a poet of original talent, one would have expected his first novel to be trailblazing and controversial. Instead [it] bows to literary tradition . . . . If Borel injects anything modern into the old formulas . . . it is the strict observance of the single perspective whereby he avoids analyzing anyone but himself." In short, concludes Mercier, in writing *The Bond* Borel has "substituted the journal for the confession box," and in the future he "might well turn to issuing installments of his journal instead of 'thinly disguised' autobiographies."

Paul A. Doyle notes in his *Best Sellers* review that "a curious unevenness possesses the book . . . . Too much space is given to trivial matters." Furthermore, says Doyle, "the hero is not at all likable, and it becomes difficult for the reader to identify with him or to show much sympathy." Vivian Mercier admits that the novel is an "egotistical work," but, unlike Doyle, she finds Borel's story "moving." In her *New York Times Book Review* article, she also characterizes *The Bond* as "a profoundly French book" with its focus on "the appalling strength of the 'bond' that joins [mother and son]," the leisurely pace of its narration, and the author's "Proustian fascination with his own portrait as well as his mother's."

BIOGRAPHICAL/CRITICAL SOURCES:

BOOKS

Beaujour, Michel, *Miroirs d'encre,* Editions du Seuil, 1980.

Brooks, Richard A., editor, *A Critical Bibliography of French Literature,* Volume VI, Syracuse University Press, 1980.

Knapp, Bettina, *French Novelists Speak Out,* Whitson, 1976.

Knapp, *Off-Stage Voices,* Whitson, 1975.

Simon, Pierre-Henri, *Parier pour l'homme,* Editions du
Seuil, 1973;

PERIODICALS

Best Sellers, August 1, 1968.
Books Abroad, May, 1974.
L'Express, May 25-31, 1970.
New York Times Book Review, September 8, 1968.
Observer Review, April 28, 1968.
Saturday Review, August 24, 1968.
Times Literary Supplement, July 7, 1973.*

*   *   *

BOSSE, Malcolm (Joseph, Jr.) 1933-

PERSONAL: Born May 6, 1933, in Detroit, MI; son of
Malcolm Clifford and Thelma (Malone) Bosse; married
Marie-Claude Aullas (a translator), July 4, 1969 (marriage
ended), married Laura Mack; children: (first marriage)
Malcolm-Scott, (second marriage) Mark Elliot. *Education:* Yale University, B.A., 1952; University of Michigan,
M.A., 1960; New York University, Ph.D., 1969. *Avocational interests:* Tai-Chi Chuan, yoga, Oriental mythology,
archaeology, myrmecology, Asian history, art (especially
sculpture), music (especially jazz), watching football on
television, classical ballet, Chinese cooking, jogging,
swimming.

ADDRESSES: Office—Department of English, City College of the City University of New York, New York, NY
10031.

CAREER: Barron's Financial Weekly, New York City,
editorial writer, 1950-52; free-lance writer, 1957-66; City
College of the City University of New York, New York
City, professor of English, 1969—; novelist, 1959—. Lecturer in India, Bangladesh, Burma, Thailand, Malaysia,
Singapore, Taiwan, China, Hong Kong, Japan, and Fiji Islands. Advisory board member of *Pequod* magazine. *Military service:* Served in U.S. Navy for six years; received
three Bronze Stars. Also served in U.S. Army and U.S.
Merchant Marines.

MEMBER: Modern Language Association of America,
PEN, Authors Guild, Society of Eighteenth Century
Studies and Scholars (England), Yale Club, Andiron
Club, Fulbright-Hays Alumni Association, Henry James
Associates (charter member), Phi Gamma Delta, Phi Beta
Kappa.

AWARDS, HONORS: Masefield Award from Yale University, 1949, for poetry and fiction; Hopwood Awards
from University of Michigan, 1956, for poetry and fiction;
University Scholar Award from New York University,
1969. Newberry Library Fellowship, 1970; certificate of
merit from Society of the Dictionary of International Biography, 1976, for distinguished service to the community; certificate of merit from Society of Who's Who in
America, 1977; creative writing fellowship from National
Endowment for the Arts, 1977-78; Fulbright-Hays lectureship grants for India, 1978 and 1979, and for Indonesia, 1987; special commendation from International Communication Agency, 1980, for work in India. *The Journey
of Tao Kim Nam* was selected by *Saturday Review of Literature* as one of the best novels of the year, 1960; Edgar
Allan Poe Award nominations for best first mystery of the
year, 1974, for *The Incident at Naha,* and best mystery of
the year, 1975, for *The Man Who Loved Zoos; The Seventy-nine Squares* was named notable book for 1979 by
American Library Association, selected as one of the best
books of the year by Library of Congress, 1980, received
nominations for Dorothy Canfield Fisher Award, 1981,
and for Dutch Children's Book Prize, 1984, received the
Preis der Leseratten for best children's book of the year
from German Television ZDF Schulerexpress, 1984, the
Prix du livre pour la jeunesse de la fondation de France,
1986, and the Prix Lecture-Jeunesse, 1987; *Cave beyond
Time* received awards from American Library Association Notable Book and National Council of Social Studies
Teachers, 1981, and nomination for Deutscher Jugendliteraturpreis, 1984; *Ganesh* received American Library Association Notable Book Award, 1982, Honor List of Book
Awards, Austrian Ministry of Education and Arts, 1982,
Deutscher Jugendliteraturpreis, 1983, was nominated for
American Book, Parent's Choice, and Omar awards, and
was named notable children's trade book in the field of social studies; *Deep Dream of the Rain Forest* was named
outstanding book for the middle-school reader, *Voice of
Youth Advocates,* 1994.

WRITINGS:

Journey of Tao Kim Nam, Doubleday (New York City),
1959.
The Incident at Naha, Simon & Schuster (New York
City), 1972.
The Man Who Loved Zoos, Putnam (New York City),
1974.
(Co-editor) *Foundations of the Novel* (also see below),
Garland Publishing (New York City), 1974.
(Co-editor) *The Flowering of the Novel,* Garland Publish-
ing, 1975, reissued with *Foundations of the Novel* as
The Novel in England: 1700-1775, Garland, 1977.
The Seventy-nine Squares (young adult), Crowell (New
York City), 1979.
Cave beyond Time (young adult), Crowell, 1980.
Ganesh (young adult), Crowell, 1981, reprinted under title
Ordinary Magic, Farrar, Straus and Giroux (New
York City).

The Barracuda Gang (young adult), Dutton (New York City), 1982.

The Warlord, Simon & Schuster, 1983.

Fire in Heaven, Simon & Schuster, 1986.

Captives of Time (young adult), Delacorte (New York City), 1987.

Strangers at the Gate, Simon & Schuster, 1989.

Mister Touch, Ticknor & Fields (New York City), 1991.

The Vast Memory of Love, Ticknor & Fields, 1992.

Deep Dream of the Rain Forest (young adult), Farrar, Straus and Giroux, 1993.

The Examination (young adult), Farrar, Straus and Giroux, 1994.

Co-editor of "Representative English Mid-Eighteenth Century Fiction, 1740-1775" series for Garland, 1975. Contributor of major critical essay to *Charles Johnstone's Chrysal: 1760-1765,* Garland Publishing. Also contributor of articles, short stories, and poems to periodicals, including *Literary Criterion, Remington Review, Voyages, California Quarterly, North American Review, Michigan Quarterly, Artesian, Massachusetts Review,* and *New York Times.* Work included in *Mississippi Valley Writers Collection.*

SIDELIGHTS: Malcolm Bosse is well known for his novels for both adults and young people. His works are often set in Asia and have been widely praised for the wealth of historical and cultural information the author uses to relate his characters' adventures. Taking place in a variety of times and cultures, Bosse's fiction commonly relates the encounters of people who embark on quests and experience personal growth and enhanced relationships.

Bosse's first novel met with critical success as did the endeavors that followed it. A witness to the plight of the Vietnamese, Bosse illustrates the politics and culture of that people in the *Journey of Tao Kim Nam.* The story of a Vietnamese farmer, the book records the many trials and perils he experiences as a refugee who leaves his home in the north in order to escape the communism of the Vietminh. "This novel," wrote a *Christian Century* reviewer, "comes very close to being a minor classic." It "is absorbing all the way," remarked Henry Cavendish of the *New York Times Book Review.*

The Incident at Naha, Bosse's second novel, was the author's first attempt at mystery writing. In this book, the war buddy of a Vietnam veteran is murdered, so the vet and his girlfriend set out to find the killer, uncovering an age-old racial conflict. Critically, the novel was recognized for its linking of separate elements such as Vietnam, drugs, Admiral Matthew Perry's trip to Japan in 1852, and racism.

Another mystery, *The Man Who Loved Zoos,* tells the story of a psychologically disturbed Vietnam veteran,

Warren Shore, who happens on a busload of dead tourists and rifles through their pockets, keeping whatever seems of value. Unaware of the import of what he has taken, Shore is hunted and killed by a ruthless government agent, Alexander Boyle, who has been assigned to find the thief. The crimes are solved by Shore's Aunt Victoria, a character who, according to the *New York Times Book Review,* proves elderly librarians make "immortal" and "indestructible" heroines. "Mr. Bosse," a critic stated in the *New Yorker,* "has put together a very strong plot, and his characterizations are too convincing to be discounted, and much too real to be easily forgotten."

After *The Man Who Loved Zoos,* Bosse produced his first novel for young adults, *The Seventy-nine Squares.* In this book, Eric Fisher, a fourteen-year-old vandal on probation for pelting rocks through his school's windows, discovers the meaning of life. The child of a couple more interested in social status than in him, Eric is just a lonely gang member until he meets Mr. Beck. Years earlier, Mr. Beck was convicted of killing his wife in a crime of passion, an act for which he served forty years in prison. Because he is dying of cancer, the eighty-two-year-old Beck is released from prison to live out his few remaining months in his garden. He instructs Eric, who befriended the old man after considerable hesitation, to divide the garden into seventy-nine squares and then to spend time in each plot studying the life there. In this way, Eric learns to "see."

This novel, heralded as a work that "shows the value of human commitment," was widely reviewed and praised by critics. As Anne G. Toensmeier of the *Interracial Books for Children Bulletin* noted: "The story is so compelling and the imagery so visual that the reader seems to see it all happening. This is only appropriate because the story is about learning to see." Other critics, such as Jack Forman of the *New York Times Book Review,* called the novel "a very moving, very private story." *The Seventy-nine Squares,* said *Best Seller's* Mary Columba, is "exquisite."

For his second young-adult novel, Bosse wrote the bildungsroman *Cave beyond Time.* With a "fascinating blend of fact and legend," the author, observed Patricia Anne Reilly of *Best Sellers,* created "a real winner." A disillusioned and bored fifteen-year-old orphan, Ben, is bitten by rattlesnakes while on an archaeological dig in Arizona. While unconscious, he dreams he is a nomad and a hunter in a prehistoric tribe, learning from various father figures and battling wild animals. "The extraordinarily vivid recreation of primitive life," commented A. A. Flowers in *Horn Book,* "makes a strong, often touching novel filled with absorbing detail, head-long action, and echoes of the past."

Ganesh, another novel for young adults, uses some of the insights Bosse gained as a lecturer in India for two years. "Ganesh," the name of the elephant-headed Hindu god of strength and wisdom, is the nickname of Jeffrey Moore, an American born and raised in India. While residing in that country, Jeffrey spends his fourteen years in a happy enough lifestyle, studying yoga and playing ball. Orphaned, he is sent to live with his understanding Aunt Betty in the American Midwest, where, because of his foreign mannerisms, he is not easily accepted by his peers. Jeffrey's place in the community, however, is secured when he battles the government, which is planning to route a highway over Aunt Betty's home, by using the peaceful resistance theories of the Satyagraha.

Again, Bosse's novel was applauded by reviewers. "*Ganesh* is not a book to be read by children looking only for light entertainment," maintained Bryna J. Fireside of the *New York Times Book Review.* "It is, rather, a shining little jewel to be savored and treasured by those who already know the merits of fine literature." Summing up the comments of many reviewers, Martha Cruse of the *Voice of Youth Advocates* exclaimed: "What a refreshing book!"

With the best-seller *The Warlord,* Bosse turned to a genre that has proven to be highly successful for him—historical fiction. Set in 1927 China, the novel traces the turbulent events of the Chinese Revolution. At its center is the fictional Philip Embree, a young missionary from the Yale Divinity School, who is kidnapped by Mongol bandits almost immediately upon his arrival in China and never returns to his original purpose. Instead he joins a rag-tag army led by General Tang-Shan-teh, the heroic, ruthless warlord who represents the old way of life in China. "*The Warlord* succeeds," wrote Christopher Lehmann-Haupt in the *New York Times* "because the invented characters who play the major roles are neither too specific nor too representative. . . . All of them are wonderfully alive and complicated."

Critics praised Bosse's ability to weave a dramatic tapestry from the harmony and conflict of every element of Chinese society. In *The Warlord,* Chinese philosophy and poetry are wrapped up in the most desperate of historical circumstances. Jean Zorn commented in the *New York Times Book Review,* "Not since *Shogun* has a Western novelist so succeeded in capturing the essence of Asia."

Bosse continued the Asian saga of *The Warlord* with the sequel, *Fire in Heaven.* The sequel carries *The Warlord*'s major characters through the events that shaped Asia in the 1930s and 1940s: the winning of India's independence, the victory of Mao Zedong's Red Army, and the Burma Campaign. Lehmann-Haupt wrote in a *New York Times* review, "The author's deep knowledge and love of the East is made manifest, and its history now and then comes

to breathtaking life." Some critics felt that the novel lacked the riveting narrative drama of *The Warlord.* Judy Bass observed in the *New York Times Book Review,* "Malcolm Bosse vividly evokes Asia's political tumult, but the narrative proceeds sluggishly because the characters often ruminate rather than act."

Captives of Time, also a work of historical fiction, is a novel for young adults set in medieval Europe. Anne and Niklas Valens are children who must travel across plague-ridden Europe to find their uncle after their parents are murdered. Together, Anne and her uncle create a design for a clock tower, a revolutionary invention. It is Anne's mission, after her uncle's death, to carry the plan to the city and help build the new clock.

Everyone from the aristocracy to the working class has some stake in seeing the project fail, and Anne's unusual abilities lead some to believe she is a witch. Anne emerges as a strong female character who perseveres with her vision of the future despite great danger and tragedy. In the *Los Angeles Times,* Carolyn Meyer praised Boss's accurate portrayal of the brutality and cruelty of the Middle Ages: Bosse "never condescends, never simplifies for his young adult readers. Bosse's characters are emotionally contemporary but historically anchored in a detailed panorama of Medieval Europe."

"A post-apocalyptic *Canterbury Tales*" is how *Publishers Weekly* summed up *Mister Touch,* a futuristic fantasy for adults. In this novel, a killer virus many hundreds of times more contagious than AIDS has virtually depopulated the earth. In New York City, savage gangs battle over territory and supplies; they must even fight to control the few remaining medical personnel. "Mister Touch," a gang leader and former Wall Street trader, leads his band of survivors on an epic trek to a new home in Arizona, and a new beginning for the human race. In the *New York Times Book Review,* Michael Bishop wrote, "Despite this grim scene, *Mister Touch* is a survival novel whose tone— despite absurd accidents, terrible natural catastrophes and unspeakable cruelty—remains life-affirming." Comparing the novel to Larry McMurtry's *Lonesome Dove,* another tale of migration and survival, Bishop concluded, "In both novels, the life-or-death nature of the episodes en route serve to reveal and strengthen the fundamental qualities of the principals, qualities that seem very familiar to us, even though they spring from a kind of life that is alien to our own."

Eighteenth-century London is the setting of *The Vast Memory of Love,* in which Bosse again fashioned drama out of the facts of history. The action revolves around the Earl of Sandwich, here portrayed as sexually and religiously obsessed, and the novelist Henry Fielding, the author of *Tom Jones.* Bosse tells a tale of kidnapping, rape, vengeance, and blackmail, with Fielding as the magistrate who must sort out the misdeeds. A *Publishers Weekly* reviewer concluded, "The sights and sounds of a city that spawned both filth and fashion . . . have never been more dashingly evoked."

Bosse returns to Asia for the setting of his next two young adult novels, *Deep Dream of the Rain Forest* and *The Examination*. Both works focus on young men. In *Deep Dream of the Rain Forest,* a fifteen-year-old boy becomes a part of a Bornean tribesman's quest to follow a dream that portends events of importance for him and his tribe. *The Examination* follows the journey of two brothers, Chen and Hong, in sixteenth-century China. When Chen, a scholar whose future promises prestige and prosperity, must travel to Beijing to take a civil-service exam, Hong accompanies him as his bodyguard. The brothers' love and respect for one another is deepened during the adventure, which includes secret missions, a pirate attack, and other events of intrigue. Both works were praised for their authentic descriptions of their Asian cultures as well as for their depictions of meaningful relationships.

Bosse told *CA:* "I consider any reader above ten or twelve years old (depending on the rate of maturation) to be an adult. I write for a young person as I would for someone my own age, leaving out perhaps the worst of my philosophical reflections or distortions, which, of course, is all for the best."

BIOGRAPHICAL/CRITICAL SOURCES:

PERIODICALS

Best Sellers, February, 1980; January, 1981.
Booklist, May 1, 1959; October 1, 1974; October 1, 1979; November 1, 1980; April 15, 1981.
Bulletin of the Center for Children's Books, January, 1980; December, 1980; July/August, 1981.
Chicago Sunday Tribune, April 5, 1959.
Childhood Education, April, 1980.
Children's Book Review Service, November, 1979; December, 1980; June, 1981.
China News, August 7, 1980.
Christian Century, April 8, 1959.
Daily Peoples View (Bangladesh), July 7, 1979.
English Journal, May, 1980.
Horn Book, February, 1981.
Interracial Books for Children Bulletin, Volume 11, Numbers 3 and 4, 1980.
Language Arts, September, 1981.
Los Angeles Times, January 23, 1988.
Los Angeles Times Book Review, May 12, 1991, p. 9.
Ms., August, 1980.
New Yorker, September 9, 1974.
New York Herald Tribune, April 12, 1959.
New York Times, May 12, 1983; January 23, 1986.

New York Times Book Review, March 22, 1959; August 25, 1974; December 9, 1979; August 9, 1981; June 5, 1983; February 9, 1986; August 20, 1989, pp. 20-21; May 19, 1991.
Observer, October 15, 1972; February 2, 1975.
Publishers Weekly, February 28, 1972; October 30, 1987, p. 72; January 3, 1985, p.41; February 22, 1991, p. 209; July 6, 1992; September 12, 1994, p. 92-93.
School Library Journal, September, 1979; November, 1980; May, 1981.
Times Literary Supplement, February 2, 1973.
Voice of Youth Advocates, June, 1980; December, 1980; June, 1981.
Washington Post Book World, August 18, 1974.*

—Sketch by Charity Anne Dorgan

*   *   *

BOWERING, Marilyn R(uthe) 1949-

PERSONAL: Born April 13, 1949, in Winnipeg, Manitoba, Canada; daughter of Herbert James (a carpenter) and Elnora (a purchasing agent; maiden name, Grist) Bowering. *Education:* Attended University of British Columbia, 1968-69; University of Victoria, B.A., 1971, M.A., 1973; also attended University of New Brunswick, 1975.

ADDRESSES: Home—3777 Jennifer Rd., Victoria, British Columbia, Canada V8P 3X1.

CAREER: Teacher in public schools at Masset, British Columbia, Canada, 1974-75; freelance writer and book reviewer, 1975-77; University of British Columbia, Vancouver, extension lecturer in poetry writing, 1977; Gregson/ Graham (marketing and communications firm), Victoria, British Columbia, editor and writer, 1978-80; University of Victoria, British Columbia, visiting lecturer, 1978-82, lecturer in creative writing, 1982-86, 1989, visiting associate professor of creative writing, 1993-94; Noel Collins and Blackwells, Edinburgh, Scotland, freelance editor, 1980-82; freelance writer in Seville, Spain, 1990-92; Banff Centre, Banff, Alberta, member of faculty, 1992, writer-in-electronic-residence, 1993-94.

MEMBER: Writers Union of Canada, League of Canadian Poets.

AWARDS, HONORS: Du Maurier Award for Poetry from Canada's National Magazine Awards, 1978, for "Rose Harbor Whaling Station"; National Magazine Award for Poetry, 1989; Long Poem prize, Malahat Review, 1994; recipient of various Canada Council Awards for poetry.

WRITINGS:

POETRY

The Liberation of Newfoundland, Fiddlehead Press (Retford, England), 1973.
One Who Became Lost, Fiddlehead Press, 1976.
The Killing Room, Sono Nis Press (Los Angeles), 1977.
Third/Child Zian, Sceptre Press (Bristol, England), 1978.
The Book of Glass, Sceptre Press, 1978.
Sleeping with Lambs, Press Porcepic, 1980.
Giving Back Diamonds, Press Porcepic, 1982.
The Sunday Before Winter, General Publishing, 1984.
Anyone Can See I Love You, Porcupine's Quill, 1987.
Grandfather Was a Soldier, Porcepic Books, 1987.
Calling All the World, Porcepic Books, 1989.
Love As It Is, Beach Holme, 1993.

NOVELS

The Visitors Have All Returned, Press Porcepic, 1979.
To All Appearances a Lady, Penguin Books (West Drayton, England), 1990.

OTHER

(Editor with David A. Day) *Many Voices: An Anthology of Contemporary Canadian Indian Poetry,* J. J. Douglas, 1977.
(Editor) *Guide to the Labor Code of British Columbia,* Government of British Columbia, 1980.

Work represented in anthologies, including *Whale Sound, North American Women Poets, New: West Coast, New Oxford Book of Canadian Verse, New Canadian Poets, Poets of the 80's,* and *Anything Is Possible.* Contributor to literary journals, including *Event, Toronto Life, Prism International, Malahat Review, Canadian Forum, New Poetry,* and *Signal Hill Broadsides.*

SIDELIGHTS: Marilyn R. Bowering's poems often have a surrealistic, dream-like quality. A Canadian poet and novelist, Bowering infuses her writings with mythological and symbolic imagery, and her work often depicts intense emotional experiences. In a review of her acclaimed collection *Giving Back Diamonds,* a contributor to *Canadian Literature* remarked that Bowering "writes with a kind of absolute pitch, her use of words spare, accurate, evocative. . . ."

In a review of an early work, *One Who Became Lost,* M. Travis Lane stated in *Fiddlehead* that "Bowering's poems are beautifully structured. . . . Poems that speak through dream imagery rather than through rationalized description and commentary are structurally nearer to painting or music than to prose, and we look for their structure in terms of themes and variations rather than terms of argument. Or again, we can understand them as we do a film by Bergman or Fellini, with the back of our mind, trusting our instincts—this *feels* right."

Doug Beardsly of the *Victoria Times* commented on another of Bowering's works, *The Visitors Have All Returned:* "As there are few stylists in our country, either in poetry or fiction, it's a real delight to come across Marilyn Bowering's first book of prose. . . . The author of several books of poems offers us a poetic prose, stripped bare, exposed, held up to the clear white light of the page. . . . Each paragraph seems chiselled, every important word chosen for its resonant qualities. What is left out is as significant as what's left in, and Michael Elcock's fine black-and-white photographs deepen the sense of mystery."

A later work, the novel *To All Appearances a Lady,* concerns Robert Lam, a half-Chinese, middle-aged bachelor who sets off to sea after the death of his 100-year-old stepmother, Lam Fan. The old woman's spirit joins him on board and begins revealing the details of Robert's mysterious ancestry, including the story of his mother, India Thackeray, an emigrant from Hong Kong who worked in a Vancouver opium factory and was marooned for several years in a leper colony. Robert's journey becomes one of self-realization and self-discovery.

To All Appearances a Lady garnered mixed critical reactions. Sybil Steinberg of *Publishers Weekly* described the book as a "strangely beautiful, haunting first novel," and *New York Times Book Review* contributor Edward Hower called the work "ambitious and often enjoyable." Other critics felt that the elaborate plot needlessly complicates the work. "[Bowering] must have spent months in the provincial archives," opined Sarah Harvey in the Toronto *Globe and Mail,* "savoring the delicious morsels of past lives and agonizing over which bits to use. It's a shame that she appears to have yielded to the temptation to use them all." Carolyn See of the *Los Angeles Times* concurred, writing, "The trouble is, with all this laudable research and history, the characters don't have room to breathe." "Marilyn Bowering does have a fascinating story to tell," Hower concluded, "If only she had told it more simply!" However, other critics thought the wealth of detail in Bowering's novel supported an impression of verisimilitude. Tom Adair of *Scotland on Sunday* commented: "Bowering writes at the edge of her talent: she is affirmative, clear, faithful to life's mysteries."

BIOGRAPHICAL/CRITICAL SOURCES:

BOOKS

Contemporary Literary Criticism, Volume 32, Gale, 1983.

PERIODICALS

Books in Canada, May, 1981, pp. 41-42; April, 1983, pp. 25-26.

Canadian Literature, winter, 1980, pp. 136-138; autumn, 1983, p. 96; autumn, 1989, p. 260.

Dalhousie Review, summer, 1977, p. 356; autumn, 1978, p. 567.

Fiddlehead, winter, 1977, pp. 156-160; summer, 1978, pp. 162-63.

Globe and Mail (Toronto), September 16, 1989.

Los Angeles Times, July 9, 1990.

New York Times Book Review, August 12, 1990, p.11.

Publishers Weekly, April 13, 1990, p. 55.

Scotland on Sunday, November 25, 1990.

Victoria Times, July 13, 1979.

Waves, volume 8, number 2, 1980; winter, 1983, pp. 88-92.

Windsor Star, November 12, 1977.

*   *   *

BRASCH, Walter Milton   1945-

PERSONAL: Born March 2, 1945, in San Diego, CA; son of Milton and Helen (Haskin) Brasch; married Ila Wales (a journalist-linguist), September 30, 1970 (divorced, March, 1977); married Vivian Fluck (a philosopher), June 14, 1980 (divorced, September, 1983); married Rosemary Renn (a labor specialist), December, 1983. *Education:* Attended University of California, 1962-64; San Diego State College (now University), A.B., 1966; Ball State University, M.A., 1969; Ohio University, Ph.D., 1974. *Politics:* Independent Democrat. *Religion:* Jewish. *Avocational interests:* Music (especially country, bluegrass, dixieland), theater, political public relations, popular culture, "and just about anything that happens to tickle my fancy at the moment."

ADDRESSES: Office—Department of Mass Communications, Bloomsburg University, Bloomsburg, PA 17815.

CAREER: Employed as sports editor, city editor, features writer, and investigative reporter for daily newspapers in California, Indiana, Iowa, and Ohio, 1965-72; MID Productions, Athens, OH, writer and executive director, 1972-74; freelance advertising-publicity writer and consultant, 1974—; Temple University, Philadelphia, PA, assistant professor of journalism and mass communications, 1974-76; Brasch & Brasch Publishers, Ontario, CA, editor-in-chief, 1976-80; Bloomsburg University, Bloomsburg, PA, assistant professor, 1980-82, associate professor, 1982-87, professor of journalism, 1987—, director of graduate program in communication, 1980-83. Member of Iowa Governor's Committee for the Employment of the Handicapped, 1971-73, and of Ohio Governor's Committee for the *Dictionary of American Regional English,* 1973-74; writer and producer for United Screen Artists, 1976-80; Commonwealth Speaker, Pennsylvania Humanities Council, 1981-85; editor-in-chief of *Spectrum* maga-

zine, 1986—; syndicated newspaper columnist, 1992—; member of U.S. Coast Guard Auxiliary.

MEMBER: Newspaper Guild, Writers Guild, American Dialect Society, Association for Education in Journalism, Society of Professional Journalists (state president, 1991—), Association of Pennsylvania State College and University Faculty (secretary, 1983-85), Phi Kappa Phi (president of Bloomsburg chapter, 1983-84), Pennsylvania Journalism Educators (founding coordinator, 1992-94), Kappa Tau Alpha, Pi Gamma Mu, Alpha Kappa Delta.

AWARDS, HONORS: Certificate of Outstanding Service, Alpha Phi Omega, 1966; Certificate of Appreciation, U.S. Department of Commerce, 1970; Certificate of Merit, Gordon Wiseman Conference on Interpersonal Communication, 1973; Creative Teaching Award, 1981, and Creative Arts Award, 1983, both from Bloomsburg University; *Scribendum Libros* award, Alpha Kappa Delta, 1985; also recipient of writing awards from Press Club of Southern California, Pacific Coast Press Club, and Society of Professional Journalists and of several research grants.

WRITINGS:

(With Ila Wales) *A Comprehensive Annotated Bibliography of American Black English,* Louisiana State University Press, 1974.

Black English and the Mass Media, University of Massachusetts Press, 1981, revised edition, University Press of America, 1984.

Columbia County Place Names, Columbia County Historical Society, 1982.

Cartoon Monickers: A History of American Animated Cartoons, Popular Press, 1983.

(With Dana Ulloth) *The Press and the State,* University Press of America, 1986.

ZIM, Associated University Presses, 1987.

Forerunners of Revolution: Muckrakers and the American Social Conscience, University Press of America, 1991.

With Just Cause: Unionization of the American Journalist, University Press of America, 1992.

Before the First Show, Iconoclast Press, 1994.

Joel Chandler Harris, Uncle Remus, and the American Social Conscience, Western Illinois University, 1994.

Betrayed: Death of an American Newspaper, Western Illinois University, 1994.

PLAYS

Answer Me Not in Mournful Numbers, first produced in Waterloo, IA, at Theatre Seventies, 1969.

Sand Creek, first produced at Theatre Seventies, 1972.

OTHER

Also author of multimedia shows, including *In the Beginning . . . (the Indian),* 1972, *A Language and Culture Hap-*

pening, 1972, *Songs of the Battle,* 1972, *Songs of the Civil War,* 1973, and *Sounds of Protest,* 1982. Author of television scripts. Contributor of over 250 articles to general-interest magazines and academic journals.

WORK IN PROGRESS: A collection of columns.

SIDELIGHTS: Walter Milton Brasch writes: "I'm a journalist, a writer who looks at society and tries to understand, then analyze and explain its many complex parts as they relate to each other to help the people better understand their own lives and what's both necessary and important to their lives. My writings—both academic and journalistic—can't be pigeonholed; the writings are about people; the process is journalism. I write about what I'm interested in, going from topic to topic, and issue to issue, as my needs and interests change. My syndicated newspaper column is usually humor/satire, but with the cutting edge of truth. The writing I do isn't usually what the 'Corporate Suits' ask for; I do not allow myself to be subjected to the whims of a large chunk of the industry who can pass judgment on what should be published solely on marketability but have never written anything other than business letters or reports. Thus I tend to be people- and issue-driven rather than market-driven. Equally importantly, I do not write the kind of 'academic' works that pass as scholarship yet are usually minuscule looks at unimportant things that only impress other 'scholars' who tend to judge people by how many pieces of data they can stuff into a set of statistical analyses. My writings, I hope, tend to be more universal, focusing upon the greater issues."

*   *   *

BRESSON, Robert   1901-

PERSONAL: Born September 25, 1901, in Bromont-Lamothe, France; son of Leon and Marie-Elisabeth (Clausels) Bresson; married Leida Van der Zee (deceased); married Marie-Madeleine van der Mersch. *Education:* Educated in France. *Religion:* Catholic.

ADDRESSES: Home—49 quai de Bourbon, 75004 Paris, France.

CAREER: Writer, director, and producer of motion pictures, 1933—. Worked as a painter in the early 1930s. *Military service:* Prisoner of German Army, 1941.

MEMBER: Society of French Film Directors (honorary president), Society of Film Producers (past honorary president).

AWARDS, HONORS: Grand Prix du Cinema Francais, 1943, for *Les Anges du peche;* Prix Louis Delluc and Grand Prix du Film d'Avant Garde, both 1950, and Grand Prix du Cinema Francais and International Grand

Prize of Venice Film Festival, both 1951, all for *Journal d'un cure de campagne;* award for best director, Cannes Film Festival, and best film award, French Film Academy, both 1957, both for *Un Condamne a mort s'est echappe;* Prix du Meilleur Film de l'Annee, 1959, for *Pickpocket;* Special Jury Prize, Cannes Film Festival, 1962, for *Proces de Jeanne d'Arc;* honorary mention, Venice Film Festival and Panama Festival, both 1966, both for *Au Hasard, Balthazar;* Grand Prize, Panama Festival, 1968, for *Mouchette;* decorated Officier, Legion d'Honneur, 1971; International Film Critics Award, Cannes Film Festival, 1974, for *Lancelot du lac;* Commandeur, Arts et Lettres, 1974; Silver Bear Award, Berlin Film Festival, 1977, for *Le Diable probablement;* Grand Prix National des Arts et des Lettres, 1978; Grand Prix de Creation, Cannes Film Festival, 1983, and Best Director Award, National Society of Film Critics, 1985, both for *L'Argent;* Prix Akira Kurosawa, San Francisco, 1988; Grand Croix, Ordre National du Merite, 1990. Lion D'Or, 1989, and Felix Europeen, 1994, both for body of work.

WRITINGS:

SCREENPLAYS; AND DIRECTOR OF FILMS

Affaires publiques (title means "Public Affairs"), Arc Films, 1934.

(With Jean Giraudoux) *Les Anges du peche* (title means "The Angels of Sin"), Synops/Roland Tual, 1943.

(With Jean Cocteau) *Les Dames du Bois de Boulogne,* Les Films Raoul Ploquin, 1945.

Journal d'un cure de campagne (released in the United States as *Diary of a Country Priest;* adapted from the novel by Georges Bernanos), UGC, 1951.

Un Condamne a mort s'est echappe (released in the United States as *A Condemned Man Escapes;* adapted from the account by Andre Devigny), Societe Nouvelle des Etablissements Gaumont/Nouvelles Editions des Films, 1956.

Pickpocket, Agnes Delahaie, 1959.

Proces de Jeanne d'Arc (released in the United States as *Trial of Joan of Arc*), Agnes Delahaie, 1962.

Au Hasard, Balthazar, Argos Films/Parc Film/Athos Film/Svensk Filmindustri/Svenska Filminstituet, 1966.

Mouchette (adapted from the novel by Bernanos), Parc Film/Argos Films, 1967.

Une Femme douce (title means "A Gentle Creature"; adapted from the short story "A Gentle Creature" by Fyodor Dostoyevski), Parc Film/Marianne Productions, 1969.

Quatre Nuits d'un reveur (released in the United States as *Four Nights of a Dreamer;* adapted from the novella *White Nights,* by Dostoyevski), Victoria Films/Albina Films/Films del'Orso, 1971.

L'Argent (title means "Money"), Marion's Films/FR3/ Eos Films SA, 1983.

OTHER

Also author of *Notes sur le cinematographe,* [France], 1975, translation by Jonathan Griffen published as *Notes on Cinematography,* Urizen Books (New York City), 1977; author of screenplay and director of *Lancelot du lac* (released in the United States as *Lancelot of the Lake;* adapted from the book *La Mort d'Arthur,* by Thomas Malory), 1974, and *Le Diable probablement* (released in the United States as *The Devil, Probably*), 1977.

SIDELIGHTS: Robert Bresson has achieved fame as one of the most unique filmmakers in contemporary cinema. Michael Wilmington of the *Los Angeles Times* noted that "though we have many magical and brilliant movie entertainers, we have only a handful of cinematic poets. Bresson heads that dwindling list." Wilmington described the director's films as "austere, rigorous, chaste, intense, utterly uncompromising." Bresson's techniques are distinguished by their steadfast opposition to such cinematic conventions as dramatic and technical virtuosity. He prefers to work with nonactors to eliminate the concept of "performances" in his films, and he insists on dictating every visual and aural element to further thwart any semblance of spontaneity. He seeks to present his images in a natural manner that subtly evokes the mysterious. This pursuit of the unknown has resulted in a style both deliberate and minimal. "Cinema is the art of showing nothing," Bresson explained to Charles Samuels in *Encountering Directors.* "I want to express things with a minimum of means, showing nothing that is not absolutely essential."

Bresson directed his first film, *Affaires publiques,* in 1934, and continued writing scripts and working on films through the late 1930s. In 1941, after the outbreak of World War II, Bresson was captured by the German army and held as a prisoner of war. Upon his release he returned to German-occupied France and resumed his work in the film industry.

With *Les Anges du peche* and *Les Dames du Bois de Boulogne,* Bresson's career began in earnest. *Les Anges du peche,* the first of Bresson's films to exhibit his exacting, stark touch, depicts romance and repression in a convent. *Les Dames du Bois de Boulogne* also presents issues dealing with women's suffering, though its real importance lies in its attention to the internalization of its characters' thoughts and emotions. In *Cinema Eye, Cinema Ear,* John Russell Taylor described the film as "a manifesto of Bresson's belief in the cinema as an interior art."

Despite critical acclaim, *Les Dames du Bois de Boulogne* lacked popular recognition, forcing Bresson to spend nearly five years securing funds for his next production. For *Diary of a Country Priest,* Bresson relentlessly rehearsed his largely unknown cast; the film produced another critical success for Bresson, and his spare and somber film of a young priest's gradual death garnered accolades from several quarters, including the Venice Film Festival.

Bresson based *A Condemned Man Escapes* on author Andre Devigny's account of his own incarceration. In this film, Bresson further developed his singular style to emphasize—in almost obsessive detail—the activities within a prison. Bresson encouraged one actor to repeat his dialogue three hundred times in order to obtain the properly reserved delivery.

Bresson followed *A Condemned Man Escapes* with *Pickpocket,* which he claimed was partially inspired by Dostoyevski's *Crime and Punishment.* Like its predecessors, *Pickpocket* revels in detail and monotonous emotion. Bresson meticulously examines the routines practiced by the film's protagonist and his fellow thieves; he focuses equally on the oppressive dreariness of the character's personal life. In *Sight and Sound,* Eric Rhode likened Bresson's approach to that of the documentary filmmaker, an observation echoed by Isabel Quigly in *Spectator.* While Rhode complained about Bresson's complete control over his film, Quigly perceived a broader purpose in Bresson's directing. "Bresson's technique is roughly documentary," Quigly noted, "down to that very stiltedness of dialogue and movement, and the film's most interesting moments are . . . those in which we see something new in action: the technical detail of thieving." Quigly found Bresson's depiction of the actual picking of pockets especially compelling: "This kind of thing is fascinating to watch," she declared, "and basically cinematic; it couldn't be shown in any other medium, and even its exaggerations of speed and slickness are cinematic."

In 1962 Bresson directed *Trial of Joan of Arc.* Relying almost exclusively on transcripts from the actual trial, Bresson managed to recreate the climate of religious, social, and political repression which claimed Joan of Arc as its victim. In *Sight and Sound,* Robert Vas hailed the "brilliance" of Bresson's stark presentation, commenting that "everything that is profane is only there to serve the sacred: the inner, spiritual drama." Vas's lone objection concerned Bresson's apparent unwillingness to explore Joan's internal struggle. "It seems that she is to be no more than another instrument put to the service of Bresson's vision," he asserted. "But Joan is no pickpocket. And this is exactly where this seemingly so Bressonian subject loses ground."

Bresson returned to the subjects of innocence and victimization in *Au Hasard, Balthazar,* a film centering on various characters' treatment of Balthazar, a donkey. The animal's owners change, and with each transition of ownership come varying degrees of affection and kindness directed toward the beast. Its first owner, a young girl, solemnly lavishes the donkey with love. A later owner, however, torments and mistreats the animal shamelessly. Finally, Balthazar becomes the possession of a thief, who uses him for transporting stolen goods. During a nighttime confrontation, the donkey is wounded, and the following morning, as numerous sheep graze in the morning sun, Balthazar stumbles among them and dies. Gilles Jacob, writing in *Sight and Sound*, labelled *Au Hasard, Balthazar* Bresson's greatest film. He admired Bresson's ability to fashion a Christian allegory from a donkey's experiences and declared that "only Bresson can make us sense the ineffable, see the invisible, touch the intangible."

Mouchette marks the first of several works in which Bresson depicts a suicide. The title character, a poor, withdrawn girl, suffers constant humiliation and harassment from her fellow villagers. After a night of degradation by an especially despicable man, Mouchette hurls herself into a ravine. The *New York Times*'s Roger Greenspan, while conceding that Mouchette's death touched a powerful chord, contended that Bresson's surprisingly sympathetic approach—based on Catholicism's consideration of suicide as a sin—reflected too much calculation in its attempt to portray the suicide as a transcendence, a triumph. Greenspan argued, "To be accepted into grace one must prepare. Mouchette does prepare. We know this intellectually . . . but we know too much in proportion to what we deeply feel, and the ultimate flight of the spirit loses some of its glory."

Bresson's 1969 film, *Une Femme douce*, which the filmmaker adapted from Dostoyevski's "A Gentle Creature," uses intermittent flashbacks to retrace the events leading to the suicide of a young woman. Bresson portrays her life in general as tedious and her marriage to a pawnbroker as stifling. By the film's end, viewers recognize the suicide as an escape from a hopeless and inconsequential life. The *New York Times*'s Greenspan described *Une Femme douce* as one of Bresson's greater films and noted the director's consistent use of death as an individual's sole recourse to futility and despair. He also found that "the corpse is the residue of something that has escaped, and for that escape we must be glad."

After *Une Femme douce*, Bresson completed two more literary adaptations, *Four Nights of a Dreamer* and *Lancelot of the Lake*. The former, from Dostoyevski's *White Nights*, concerns an aloof, lonely artist's companionship with an unhappy woman. For three successive evenings he listens to her tale of unrequited love. On the fourth evening, the woman is reunited with the man of her story, and the artist, who has fallen in love with her, is left with only

her memory. Thomas Malory's Arthurian legend provided the basis for *Lancelot of the Lake*. Unlike most films depicting medieval times, Bresson's work focuses on the effect a society's outmoded ethic—the code of chivalry and honor—has on its protectors and chief supporters. Many reviewers praised the film for its spare but faithful depiction of the times, but some considered it an oddity in the larger scope of Bresson's work. Vincent Canby of the *New York Times* declared that Bresson's "style is intact but the content is missing." He felt the film lacked "any urgent interior meaning" and suggested that its shortcomings may have stemmed from the obvious demands of visual detail. Still, he found the film consistent with Bresson's, as opposed to the genre's, style. "To the extent that *Lancelot of the Lake* has horses, costumes, and extras . . . , it may be called Robert Bresson's spectacle," Canby opined, "but it's unlike any conventional spectacle you've ever seen."

The Devil, Probably, Bresson's twelfth feature, returns to the director's earlier suicide theme and again uses the flashback technique. Wilmington, in the *Los Angeles Times,* described it as "the tale of a suicide about to happen." Bresson chronicles the descent of a young Adonis who engages in drug use and promiscuous sex while exploring religion and politics. Although Bresson portrays life's simple pleasures, such as fishing, as delightful activities, the young man's impression of civilization's overwhelming decay diminishes his enjoyment of such amusements. He sinks into overwhelming despair. Wilmington observed that "Bresson discloses such a catalogue of earthly horrors . . . that life itself seems sprung from its moorings, permanently out of joint." Canby noted in the *New York Times:* "The world he [Bresson] perceives still looks unlike that of any other director. Objects, people, places—everything is seen with a clarity so fine that his images achieve something beyond realism, as if clarity so intense could distort truth, at least as we have come to accept it."

The film's title comes from the response of a bus passenger who comments, in answer to the question of who is controlling the events of this chaotic world: "The devil, probably." Wilmington wrote that *The Devil, Probably* "is not an easy film, not a seductive entertainment. It is hard and pure: a withering vivisection of despair, futility, malaise, the deepest horrors of our time." Canby added that though *The Devil, Probably* seemed the work of a filmmaker "taking stock"—Bresson was seventy years old at the film's release—the director had become neither "sentimental" nor "gently autumnal." Canby asserted: "Time hasn't softened the Bresson esthetic."

Bresson's next film, *L'Argent*, earned him his first American box-office hit. In this film, which Canby described as "beautiful, astringent," Bresson "is at the top of his very idiosyncratic form." The film, whose title means "Money," deals with the corrupting influence of money and the ultimate destruction of an innocent young man falsely arrested for passing counterfeit bills. Canby concluded that *L'Argent* "is not an easy film. It's tough but it's also rewarding, and it's the kind of film that justifies film festivals." Paul Attanasio of the *Washington Post* observed that "Bresson tells his story with dazzling economy," adding that the film's "indictment of materialism" has an "intellectualized distance." "In Bresson's pessimistic universe," Attanasio added, "film alone is transcendent."

BIOGRAPHICAL/CRITICAL SOURCES:

BOOKS

Ayfre, Amedee, and others, *The Films of Robert Bresson,* Praeger (New York City), 1969.
Contemporary Literary Criticism, Volume 16, Gale (Detroit), 1981.
Samuels, Charles Thomas, *Encountering Directors,* Putnam (New York City), 1982.
Schrader, Paul, *Transcendental Style in Film: Ozu, Bresson, Dreyer,* University of California Press (Berkeley), 1972.
Semoule, Jean, *Bresson, ou, L'Acte pur des metamorphoses,* Flammarion (Paris), 1993.
Taylor, John Russell, *Cinema Eye, Cinema Ear: Some Key Filmmakers of the Sixties,* Hill & Wang (New York City), 1964.

PERIODICALS

Los Angeles Times, January 10, 1985.
Manchester Guardian, November 5, 1962.
New York Times, April 6, 1954; May 2, 1954; March 13, 1970; October 1, 1970; May 28, 1971; October 1, 1971; September 29, 1977; September 24, 1983; March 23, 1984.
Sight and Sound, July-September, 1953; autumn, 1960; winter, 1962-63; winter, 1966-67; spring, 1968; spring, 1970; winter, 1970-71; summer, 1974; winter, 1977-78.
Spectator, September 16, 1960.
Washington Post, January 4, 1985; February 22, 1985.*

*   *   *

BRIQUEBEC, John
   See ROWLAND-ENTWISTLE, (Arthur) Theodore (Henry)

BROCKWAY, George P(ond) 1915-

PERSONAL: Born October 11, 1915, in Portland, MA; son of Walter B. (an accountant) and Elizabeth E. (Priest) Brockway; married Lucile M. Hunt (an anthropologist), September 2, 1939; children: Susan, David H., Nancy, Carol, Sally, Douglas W., Laura, Andrew M. *Education:* Williams College, A.B. (cum laude), 1936; graduate study at Yale University, 1936-37. *Politics:* Democrat. *Religion:* None.

ADDRESSES: Home—63 Brevoort Rd., Chappaqua, NY 10514 (summer); 1615 Bayhouse, Ct., Sarasota, FL 34231 (winter).

CAREER: McGraw-Hill Book Co., New York City, trade salesman, 1937-42; W. W. Norton & Co., Inc., New York City, 1942-86, director, 1948-86, editor, 1949-84, vice-president, 1951-58, president, 1958-76, chair, 1976-84; Yale University Press, president of board of governors, 1982-86. *Military service:* U.S. Army, 1944-46; served in European theater.

MEMBER: Society of American Historians (honorary member), Publishers Lunch Club, Century Association, Phi Beta Kappa.

AWARDS, HONORS: Litt.D. from Williams College, 1982.

WRITINGS:

(Contributor) Chandler B. Grannis, editor, *What Happens in Book Publishing,* Columbia University Press (New York City), 1957.
(With wife, Lucile Brockway) *Greece: A Classical Tour with Extras,* Knopf (New York City), 1966.
Political Deals That Saved Andrew Johnson, Coalition of Publishers for Employment, 1977.
Economics: What Went Wrong, and Why, and Some Things to Do about It, Harper (New York City), 1985.
The End of Economic Man, 3rd edition, Norton (New York City), in press.
Economists Can Be Bad for Your Health, Norton, in press.

Also author of "The Dismal Science," a monthly column in *New Leader.* Contributor to economic journals and newspapers. Honorary editor of *Journal of Post Keynesian Economics.*

SIDELIGHTS: George P. Brockway believes, according to columnist Edwin M. Yoder, Jr., that economics should be regarded as a branch of ethics, rather than as a natural science. In his 1985 book, *Economics: What Went Wrong, and Why, and Some Things to Do about It,* the retired publisher observed that the economic policies of the 1980s (including deregulation of the banks and international high finance) have contributed to rising interest rates, corporate raiding, and abuse of the labor market. His alternatives, Yoder wrote in the *Washington Post,* include placing the Federal Reserve System under what Brockway calls "political control" and placing U.S. corporations under national regulation and taxation. A company's stock would be available only to people "with a direct and active interest in the company's institutional well-being" and "income distribution would move toward, if not all the way to, equality." Yoder's conclusion was that "*Economics* is a stimulating book, of special value to those who have not recently re-examined their rooted economic assumptions."

BIOGRAPHICAL/CRITICAL SOURCES:

PERIODICALS

Washington Post, April 5, 1985.

*   *   *

BROWN, Howard Mayer   1930-1993

PERSONAL: Born April 13, 1930, in Los Angeles, CA; died of a heart attack, February 20 (one source says February 21), 1993, in Venice, Italy; son of Alfred Ralph and Florence (Mayer) Brown. *Education:* Harvard University, B.A. (magna cum laude), 1951, M.A., 1954, Ph.D., 1959.

CAREER: Harvard University, Cambridge, MA, teaching fellow in music, 1954-58; Wellesley College, Wellesley, MA, instructor in music, 1958-60; University of Chicago, Chicago, IL, assistant professor, 1960-63, associate professor, 1963-67, professor of music and director of Collegium Musicum, 1967-72; King's College, London, England, King Edward Professor of Music, 1972-74; University of Chicago, Ferdinand Schevill Distinguished Service Professor of Music, 1976 onward. Director of the Camerata of the Boston Museum of Fine Arts, 1954-60; curator of musical instruments, Smithsonian Institution, Washington, DC, 1964-65.

MEMBER: International Musicological Society (President, 1978-80), American Musicological Society (Vice-president, 1982-87), Societe francaise de musicologie, Galpin Society, Music Teachers National Association, Phi Beta Kappa.

AWARDS, HONORS: Walter Naumburg travelling fellow, Harvard University, 1951-53, in Vienna, Austria; Huber fellow, Wellesley College, summer, 1959, in Paris, France; grants-in-aid, American Council of Learned Societies, 1961-62; Guggenheim fellow, 1963-64; American Association for the Advancement of Science fellow, beginning in 1979; Galileo Galilei Prize, University of Pisa, 1987.

WRITINGS:

Music in the French Secular Theater: 1400-1550, Harvard University Press (Cambridge, MA), 1963.
(Editor) *Theatrical Chansons in the Fifteenth and Early Sixteenth Centuries,* Harvard University Press, 1963.
Bibliography of Instrumental Music Printed before 1600, Harvard University Press, 1965.
(With Joan Lascelle) *Musical Iconography: A Manual for Cataloguing Musical Subjects in Western Art before 1800,* Harvard University Press, 1972.
Sixteenth-Century Instrumentation, American Institute of Musicology, 1973.
Embellishing Sixteenth-Century Music, Oxford University Press, 1976.
Music in the Renaissance, Prentice-Hall (Englewood Cliffs, NJ), 1976.
(Editor with Stanley Sadie) *Performance Practice: Music before 1600,* Macmillan (Basingstoke, NH), 1989.

Also author of *A Florentine Chansonnier from the Time of Lorenzo the Magnificent,* two volumes, 1983. Editor of "Italian Opera Librettos: 1640-1770" series, sixty volumes, Garland Publishing, 1976-79. Contributor of articles and reviews to professional journals.

OBITUARIES:

PERIODICALS

Chicago Tribune, February 23, 1993, section 3, p. 11.
New York Times, February 24, 1993, p. B6.*

*   *   *

BROWNE, Ray B(roadus)   1922-

PERSONAL: Born January 15, 1922, in Millport, AL; son of Garfield (a banker) and Anne Nola (Trull) Browne; married second wife, Alice Pat Matthews, August 1, 1965; children: (first marriage) Glenn, Kevin; (second marriage) Alicia. *Education:* University of Alabama, A.B., 1943; Columbia University, M.A., 1947; University of California, Los Angeles, Ph.D., 1956. *Politics:* Democrat.

ADDRESSES: Home—210 North Grove, Bowling Green, OH 43402. *Office*—Popular Culture Library, Bowling Green State University, Bowling Green, OH 43402.

CAREER: Instructor in English, University of Nebraska, Lincoln, 1947-50, and University of Maryland, College Park, 1956-60; Purdue University, Lafayette, IN, assistant professor, 1960-63, associate professor of American literature, 1963-67; Bowling Green State University, Bowling Green, OH, professor of popular culture, 1967—. University of Maryland, visiting professor, 1975-76; founder of the Popular Writers Hall of Fame and Museum. *Military service:* U.S. Army, Field Artillery, 1943-46; became sergeant.

MEMBER: Modern Language Association of America, Melville Society, Popular Culture Association (founder, 1970; secretary-treasurer), American Culture Association (founder, 1977; secretary-treasurer).

WRITINGS:

Folk Beliefs and Practices from Alabama, University of California Press, 1958.

Melville's Drive to Humanism, Purdue University Press, 1971.

Popular Abstracts, Bowling Green University, 1978.

Rituals and Ceremonies in Popular Culture, Bowling Green University, 1981.

Objects of Special Devotion: Fetishism in Popular Culture, Bowling Green University, 1982.

(With Marshall W. Fishwick) *The Hero in Transition,* Bowling Green University, 1983.

(With Gary Hoppenstand) *The Defective Detective in the Pulps,* Bowling Green University, 1983.

Heroes and Humanities: Detective Fiction and Culture, Bowling Green University, 1986.

The Spirit of Australia: The Crime Fiction of Arthur W. Upfield, Bowling Green University, 1988.

Against Academia: The History of the Popular Culture Association—American Culture Association and Popular Culture Movement 1967-1988, Bowling Green University, 1989.

The Many Tongues of Literacy, Bowling Green University, 1992.

EDITOR

The Burke-Paine Controversy: Text and Criticism, Harcourt, 1963.

(With William John Roscelli and Richard Loftus) *The Celtic Cross: Studies in Irish Culture and Literature,* Purdue University Studies, 1964.

John Williams, *The Indian Doctor: Frontier Pharmacology,* Indiana Historical Society, 1964.

(With Martin Light) *Critical Approaches to American Literature,* Crowell, 1965.

(With others) *New Voices in American Studies,* Purdue University Studies, 1966.

(With others) *Frontiers of American Culture,* Purdue University Studies, 1968.

Themes and Directions in American Literature, Purdue University Studies, 1969.

(With Ronald J. Ambrosetti) *Popular Culture and Curricula,* Bowling Green University, 1969, 2nd edition, 1970.

(With others) *Challenges in American Culture,* Bowling Green University, 1969.

Mark Twain's Quarrel with Heaven: "Captain Stormfield's Visit to Heaven" and Other Sketches, College and University Press, 1970.

(With Fishwick) *Icons of Popular Culture,* Bowling Green University, 1970, 2nd edition, 1972.

(With Russell Blaine Nye) *Crises on Campus,* Bowling Green University, 1970.

(With B. D. Owens) *Teach In: Viability of Change,* Bowling Green University, 1971.

(With David Madden) *The Popular Culture Explosion,* William C. Brown, 1972.

(With Fishwick and Michael Marsden) *Heroes of Popular Culture,* Bowling Green University, 1972.

Popular Culture and the Expanding Consciousness, Wiley, 1973.

Lincoln Lore: Lincoln in the Contemporary Popular Mind, Bowling Green University, 1975.

(And compiler) *A Night with the Hants and Other Alabama Folk Experiences,* Bowling Green University, 1976.

(With Larry N. Landrum and Pat Browne) *Dimensions of Detective Criticism,* Bowling Green University, 1976.

(With Fishwick) *Icons of America,* Bowling Green University, 1978.

The Alabama Folk Lyric: A Study in Origins and Media of Dissemination, Bowling Green University, 1979.

Forbidden Fruits: Taboos and Tabooism in Culture, Bowling Green University, 1984.

(With Glenn J. Browne) *Laws of Our Fathers: Popular Culture and the U.S. Constitution,* Bowling Green University, 1986.

(With Hoppenstand) *The Gothic World of Stephen King: Landscape of Nightmares,* Bowling Green University, 1987.

(With Fishwick) *The God Pumpers: Religion in the Electronic Age,* Bowling Green University, 1987.

(With Fishwick) *Symbiosis: Popular Culture and Other Fields,* Bowling Green University, 1988.

(With Fishwick and Kevin O. Browne) *Dominant Symbols in Popular Culture,* Bowling Green University, 1990.

(With Glenn J. Browne and Kevin O. Browne) *Contemporary Heroes and Heroines: A Biographical Guide to Heroic Figures of the Twentieth Century,* Gale, 1990.

(With Garyn G. Roberts and Hoppenstand) *Old Sleuth's Freaky Female Detectives,* Bowling Green University, 1990.

(With Pat Browne) *Digging into Popular Culture: Theories and Methodologies in Archeology, Anthropology, and Other Fields,* Bowling Green University, 1991.

(With Fishwick) *Rejuvenating the Humanities,* Bowling Green University, 1992.

Continuities in Popular Culture: The Present in the Past and the Past in the Present and Future, Bowling Green University, 1993.

Author of forward, *Hollywood as Historian: American Film in a Cultural Context,* edited by Peter C. Rollins, University Press of Kentucky, 1983. Editor of *Journal of Popular Culture,* 1967—, *Journal of American Culture,* 1977, and *Journal of Regional Cultures.*

*   *   *

BROWNING, (Zerilda) Sinclair   1946-

PERSONAL: Born November 17, in Long Beach, CA; daughter of George W. (an engineer) and Rowena M. (a relator and artist; maiden name, Morse) Sinclair; married Allyn D. Bates, September 2, 1966 (divorced August, 1974); married William D. Browning (a district court judge), December 17, 1974; children: (second marriage) Benjamin Sinclair. *Education:* University of Arizona, B.A., 1970; attended University of Guadalajara, 1970. *Politics:* Republican. *Religion:* "Metaphysicist."

ADDRESSES: Home—Tucson, AZ.

CAREER: Mountain Bell (telephone company), Tucson, AZ, clerk, 1966; Valley National Bank, Tucson, trainer of bank tellers, 1967-68; Southern Arizona Bank, Tucson, vault teller, 1968-70; real estate broker in Tucson, 1970—. Instructor in creative writing at Pima Community College. Vice-president of Pima Alcoholism Consortium, 1979, and Salvation Army Advisory Board, 1983-84; member of Pima County Air Pollution Control Hearing Board, Pima County Bar Auxiliary, and Arizona Right to Choose.

MEMBER: Authors Guild, Western Writers of America, Society of Southwestern Authors (vice-president, 1984-86), Arizona Authors Association, Arizona Federation of Republican Women.

WRITINGS:

Enju: The Life and Struggle of an Apache Chief from the Little Running Water, Northland Press (Flagstaff, AZ), 1982.
(With John Lyons) *Lyons on Horses,* Doubleday (New York City), 1991.
America's Best (biographical novel), AMC Publishing, 1995.

Also author of unpublished novel *Standard Messiah.* Past editor of *Tucson Realtors' Review.*

WORK IN PROGRESS: The Last Song Dogs and *The Sporting Club,* the first two books in the "Trade Ellis" mystery series.

SIDELIGHTS: Sinclair Browning once told *CA:* "I feel a real commitment to providing entertainment that is educational as well as 'just a good story.' I also try to consider the trees that are being destroyed in order to put my words in print and, because of that sacrifice, I try to tell stories, regardless of their time or setting, that have lessons that are applicable today.

"I'm lucky that money is not a problem. This gives me the freedom to create and write my own books, books that might not give me a six-figure income, but ones that I am proud to say I have written.

"Recently I have become involved in the metaphysical movement. While initially attracted to it because of the glamour, clairvoyance, psychometry, natural healing, and so on, I have also found many spiritual lessons there. Karma, the oneness of man, the God spark in us all, our continuing spiritual evolution are fascinating concepts. They are not only giving me a new way of looking at life, but the importance I place on them is gradually being seen in my work.

"A considerable part of the novel *America's Best* is family history. The Sullivan family in the novel is loosely structured after my husband's family. His father, like Tom Sullivan in the novel, was the chief engineer for the Benguet Consolidated Mines. He was asked to go to Corregidor by General MacArthur, was interned at Cabanatuan, and was killed aboard the *Arisan Maru.* My husband, his brother, and mother were all interned in Santo Tomas for three years.

"The writing of the book entailed extensive research. As luck would have it, a retired colonel in California heard that I was working on the book. He put me in touch with one of the remaining survivors of the *Arisan Maru.* I was invited to an annual Bataan Veterans convention in Las Cruces, New Mexico, in 1983. There I conducted personal interviews with men who were at the Bataan Death March, who were at Corregidor when it fell, and who were interned in Japanese prisoner of war camps.

"Personal letters and unpublished manuscripts were also researched. The most painful of those were the love letters written by my father-in-law and smuggled out of Cabanatuan into Santo Tomas. Forty years later the sentiments expressed in them are as moving as they were when they were written.

"I have tried to be true to the history and to the personalities of that era. I have also tried to be true to those who shared with me their stories and feelings about this chapter in their lives. For in the end, *America's Best* is not my story. It belongs to all of us."

BUERO VALLEJO, Antonio 1916-

PERSONAL: Surname listed in some sources as Buero-Vallejo; born September 29, 1916, in Guadalajara, Spain; son of Francisco Buero (a military engineer) and Cruz Vallejo; married Victoria Rodriguez (an actress), 1959; children: Carlos, Enrique. *Education:* San Fernando School of Fine Arts, Madrid, Spain, 1934-36. *Avocational interests:* Painting.

ADDRESSES: Home and office—Calle General Diaz Porlier 36, Madrid 28001, Spain.

CAREER: Playwright, 1949—. Lecturer at universities in the United States, 1966; speaker at Symposium on Spanish Theater, University of North Carolina at Chapel Hill, 1970.

MEMBER: International Committee of the Theatre of the Nations, Hispanic Society of America (corresponding member), American Association of Teachers of Spanish and Portuguese (honorary fellow), Society of Spanish and Spanish-American Studies (honorary fellow), Modern Language Association (honorary fellow), Deutscher Hispanistenverband (honorary fellow), Sociedad General de Autores de Espana, Real Academia Espanola, Ateneo de Madrid (honorary fellow), Circulo de Bellas Artes de Madrid (honorary fellow).

AWARDS, HONORS: Premio Lope de Vega, 1949, for *Historia de una escalera;* Premio Amigos de los Quintero, 1949, for *Las palabras en la arena;* Premio Maria Rolland, 1956, for *Hoy es fiesta,* 1958, for *Un sonador para un pueblo,* and, 1960, for *Las Meninas;* Premio Nacional de Teatro, 1957, for *Hoy es fiesta,* 1958, for *Las cartas boca abajo,* 1959, and for *Un sonador para un pueblo,* 1980; Premio March de Teatro, 1959, for *Hoy es fiesta;* Premio de la critica de Barcelona, 1960, for *Un sonador para un pueblo;* Premio Larra, 1962, for *El concierto de San Ovidio;* Premio Leopoldo Cano, 1966, 1970, 1972, 1974, and 1976; Medalla de Oro del Espectador y la critica, 1967, 1970, 1974, 1976, 1977, 1981, 1984, and 1986; Premio Mayte and Premio Foro Teatral, both 1974; Medalla de Oro "Gaceta illustrada," 1976; Officier des Palmes Academiques de France, 1980; Premio Ercilla and Medalla "Valle-Inclan" de la Asociacion de Escritores y Artistas, both 1985; Premio Pablo Iglesias and Premio Miguel de Cervantes, both 1986; Medalla de Oro e Hijo Predilecto de Guadalajara, 1987; Medalla de Oro al Merite en las Bellas Artes, 1994; Medalla de Oro de la Sociedad General de Autores de Espana, 1994.

WRITINGS:

PLAYS IN ENGLISH TRANSLATION

En la ardiente oscuridad: Drama en tres actos (title means "In the Burning Darkness: Three-Act Drama"; first produced in Madrid at Teatro Nacional Maria Guerrero, December 1, 1950; also see below), Alfil (Madrid), 1951, reprinted, Escelicer (Madrid), 1970, critical Spanish edition edited by Samuel A. Wofsy, Scribner (New York City), 1954, translation by Jerry Bembow as *In the Burning Darkness,* Utah State Theatre, 1975, translation by Marion Peter Holt of original Spanish version published as *In the Burning Darkness* in *Three Plays* (also see below).

La tejedora de suenos: Drama en tres actos, first produced in Madrid at Teatro Espanol, January 11, 1952; also see below), Alfil, 1952, translation by William I. Oliver published as *The Dreamweaver* in *Masterpieces of the Modern Spanish Theatre,* edited by Robert W. Corrigan, Collier Books (New York City), 1967.

Un sonador para un pueblo: Version libre de un episodio historico en dos partes (title means "A Dreamer for the People: A Version of a Historical Episode in Two Parts"; first produced at Teatro Espanol, December 18, 1958; also see below), Alfil, 1959, translation by Michael Thompson published as *A Dreamer for the People,* Aris & Phillips (London), 1994.

Las meninas: Fantasia velazquena en dos partes (title means "The Ladies-in-Waiting: Velazquen Fantasy in Two Parts"; first produced in Madrid at Teatro Espanol, December 9, 1960; first published in *Primer Acto,* January, 1961; also see below), Alfil, 1961, critical Spanish edition edited by Juan Rodriguez Castellano, Scribner, 1963, translation by Holt published as *Las meninas: A Fantasy,* Trinity University Press, 1987.

El concierto de San Ovidio: Parabola en tres actos (title means "The Concert at Saint Ovide: Three-Act Parable"; first produced in at Teatro Goya, November 16, 1962; first published in *Primer Acto,* December, 1962; also see below), Alfil, 1963, critical Spanish edition edited by Pedro N. Trakas, Scribner, 1965, translation by Farris Anderson of original Spanish version published as *The Concert at Saint Ovide,* Pennsylvania State University Press, 1967, Anderson's translation also published in *The Modern Spanish Stage: Four Plays,* edited by Holt, Hill & Wang (New York City), 1970.

El tragaluz: Experimento en dos partes (title means "The Skylight: Two-Part Experiment"; first produced in Madrid at Teatro Bellas Artes, October 7, 1967; first published in *Primer Acto,* November, 1967; also see below), Alfil, 1968, critical Spanish edition edited by Anthony M. Pasquariello and Patricia W. O'Connor, Scribner, 1977, translation by O'Connor of original Spanish version published as *The Basement Window* in *Plays of Protest from the Franco Era,* Sociedad General Espanola de la Libreria (Madrid), 1981, translation by Susana Nelson and John Koppenhauer published as *The Skylight* in *Modern International Drama,* 1992.

La doble historia del doctor Valmy: Relato escenico en dos partes (title means "The Double Case-History of Doctor Valmy: Story with Scenes, in Two Parts"; first produced in English translation in Chester, England, at Gateway Theatre, November 22, 1968; first produced in Spanish in Madrid at Teatro Benavente, January 29, 1976; first published in *Artes hispanicas/ Hispanic Arts* [bilingual; English translation by Anderson], 1967), edited and annotated by Alfonso M. Gil, Center for Curriculum Development (Philadelphia), 1970, critical Spanish edition edited by William Giuliano, Scribner, 1986.

El sueno de la razon: Fantasia en dos actos (title means "The Sleep of Reason: Two-Act Fantasy"; first produced in Madrid at Teatro de la Reina Victoria, February 6, 1970), Escelicer, 1970, critical Spanish edition edited by John C. Dowling, Center for Curriculum Development, 1971, translation by Holt published as *The Sleep of Reason* in *Three Plays* (also see below).

La fundacion (two parts; also see below), first produced in Madrid at Teatro Figaro, January 15, 1974, translation by Holt published as *The Foundation* in *Three Plays* (also see below).

La detonacion: Fantasia en dos partes (title means "The Detonation: Fantasy in Two Parts"; first produced at Teatro Bellas Artes, September 20, 1977), translation by David Johnston published as *The Shot,* Aris & Phillips, 1989.

Three Plays (contains *The Sleep of Reason, The Foundation,* and *In the Burning Darkness*), translation by Holt, Trinity University Press, 1985.

Jueces en la noche (title means "Judges in the Night"; first produced in Madrid at Teatro Lara, October 6, 1979), translation by John Koppenhauer published as *Judges in the Night* in *Modern International Drama,* 1989.

Lazaro en el laberinto: Fabula en dos partes, first produced in Madrid at Teatro Maravillas, December 18, 1986), translation by Hazel Cazorla published as *Lazarus in the Labyrinth* in *Plays of the New Democratic Spain (1975-1990),* Lanham (New York City), 1992.

Musica cercana: Fabula en dos partes (title means "The Music Window: Fable in Two Parts"; first produced at Teatro Maravillas, August 18, 1989), translation by Holt published as *The Music Window* in *Contemporary Spanish Plays,* [Pennsylvania], 1994.

PLAYS IN SPANISH

Las palabras en la arena: Tragedia en un acto (title means "Words in the Sand: Tragedy in One Act"; also see below), first produced at Teatro Espanol, December 19, 1949.

Historia de una escalera: Drama en tres actos (title means "Story of a Stairway: Three-Act Drama"; first produced at Teatro Espanol, October 14, 1949; also see below), Jose Janes (Barcelona), 1950, critical Spanish edition edited by Jose Sanchez, Scribner, 1955, critical Spanish edition edited by H. Lester and J. A. Zabalbeascoa Bilbao, University of London Press, 1963.

La senal que se espera: Comedia dramatica en tres actos (title means "The Expected Sign: Three-Act Dramatic Comedy"; first produced at Teatro de la Infanta Isabel, May 21, 1952), Alfil, 1952.

Casi un cuento de hadas: Una glosa de Perrault, en tres actos (title means "Almost a Fairy Tale: Three-Act Variation on Perrault"; first produced at Teatro Alcazar, January 10, 1953), Alfil, 1953, reprinted, Narcea, 1981.

El terror inmovil: Fragmentos de una tragedia irrepresentable (title means "Motionless Terror: Fragments of An Unrepresentable Tragedy"), Alfil, 1954.

Madrugada: Episodio dramatico en dos actos (title means "Daybreak: Two-Act Dramatic Episode"; first produced at Teatro Alcazar, December 9, 1953; also see below), Alfil, 1954, critical Spanish edition edited by Donald W. Bleznick and Martha T. Halsey, Blaisdell (Waltham, MA), 1969.

Irene o el tesoro: Fabula en tres actos (title means "Irene; or, The Treasure: Three-Act Fable"; first produced in Madrid at Teatro Nacional Maria Guerrero, December 14, 1954; also see below), Alfil, 1955.

Aventura en lo gris: Drama en dos actos unidos por un sueno increible (title means "Adventure in Grayness: Drama with Two Acts United by An Incredible Dream"; first published as *Aventura en lo gris: Dos actos grises, unidos por un sueno increible* [subtitle means "Two Gray Acts, United by an Incredible Dream"] in *Teatro: Revista internacional de la escena* [Madrid], January-March, 1954), Ediciones Puerta del Sol, 1955, revised version published as *Aventura en lo gris: Dos actos y un sueno* (subtitle means "Two Acts and A Dream"; first produced in Madrid at Teatro Recoletos, October 1, 1963), Alfil, 1964.

Hoy es fiesta: [Tragi]comedia en tres actos (title means "Today Is a Holiday: Three-Act [Tragi]comedy"; first produced in Madrid at Teatro Nacional Maria Guerrero, September 20, 1956; also see below), Alfil, 1957, reprinted, Alman, 1978, critical Spanish edition edited by J. E. Lyon, Harrap, 1964, Heath (Lexington, MA), 1966.

Las cartas boca abajo: Tragedia espanola en dos partes, y cuatro cuadros (title means "The Cards Face Down: Spanish Tragedy in Two Parts and Four Scenes"; first produced in Madrid at Teatro de la Reina Victoria, November 5, 1957; also see below), Alfil, 1958, critical Spanish edition edited by Felix G. Ilarraz, Prentice-Hall (New York City), 1967.

Llegada de los dioses (title means "The Gods' Arrival"; first produced at Teatro Lara, September 17, 1971; also see below), Aguilar, 1973.

Caiman (two parts; title means "Alligator"; also see below), first produced at Teatro de la Reina Victoria, September 10, 1981.

Dialogo secreto (two parts; title means "Secret Dialogue"; first produced in San Sebastian, Spain, at Teatro Victoria Eugenia, August 6, 1984), Espasa-Calpe, 1985.

Las trampas del azar (Dos tiempos de una cronica) (first produced in Segovia at Teatro Juan Bravo, September 23, 1994), published in *Sociedad General de Autores de Espana,* 1994.

OMNIBUS VOLUMES

Historia de una escalera [and] Las palabras en la arena, Alfil, 1952, reprinted, Escelicer, 1974.

Teatro, Losada (Buenos Aires), Volume I: *En la ardiente oscuridad, Madrugada, Hoy es fiesta, Las cartas boca abajo,* 1959, Volume II: *Historia de una escalera, La tejedora de suenos, Irene o el tesoro, Un sonador para un pueblo,* 1962.

Teatro selecto: Historia de una escalera, Las cartas boca abajo, Un sonador para un pueblo, Las meninas, El concierto de San Ovidio, edited by Luce Moreau-Arrabal, Escelicer, 1966.

Buero Vallejo: Antologia teatral (contains fragments of *Historia de una escalera, En la ardiente oscuridad,* and *Irene o el tesoro*), Coculsa (Madrid), 1966.

Dos dramas de Buero Vallejo: Aventura en lo gris [and] Las palabras en la arena, edited by Isabel Magana Schevill, Appleton-Century-Crofts, 1967.

En la ardiente oscuridad [and] Irene o el tesoro, Magisterio Espanol (Madrid), 1967.

Teatro: Hoy es fiesta, Las meninas, [and] El tragaluz (includes interviews and critical essays by others), Taurus (Madrid), 1968.

El tragaluz [and] El sueno de la razon, Espasa-Calpe (Madrid), 1970.

El concierto de San Ovidio [and] El tragaluz, edited by Ricardo Domenech, Castalia, 1971.

En la ardiente oscuridad [and] Un sonador para un pueblo, Espasa-Calpe, 1972.

Historia de una escalera [and] Llegada de los dioses, Salvat, 1973.

Historia de una escalera [and] Las meninas, prologue by Domenech, Espasa-Calpe, 1975.

La doble historia del Doctor Valmy [and] Mito, prologue by Francisco Garcia Pavon, Espasa-Calpe, 1976.

La tejedora de suenos [and] Llegada de los dioses, edited by Luis Iglesias Feijoo, Catedra, 1976.

La detonacion [and] Las palabras en la arena, Espasa-Calpe, 1979.

Jueces en la noche [and] Hoy es fiesta, prologue by Feijoo, Espasa-Calpe, 1981.

Caiman [and] Las cartas boca abajo, Espasa-Calpe, 1981.

Obra completa, Volume I: *Teatro,* Volume II: *Poesia, narrativa, ensayos y articulos,* Espasa-Calpe, 1994.

TRANSLATOR OF PLAYS

William Shakespeare, *Hamlet: Principe de Dinamarca* (first produced at Teatro Espanol, December 15, 1961), Alfil, 1962.

Bertolt Brecht, *Madre Coraje y sus hijos: Una cronica de la Guerra de los Treinta Anos* (first produced at Teatro Bellas Artes, October 6, 1966), Alfil, 1967.

Also translator of *Vildanden* by Henrik Ibsen, first produced as *El pato silvestre* at Teatro Nacional Maria Guerrero.

OTHER

(Author of prologue) Juan B. Devoto and Alberto Sabato, *Un responso para Lazaro,* Almafuerte (Buenos Aires), 1956.

Mito: Libro para una opera (title means "Myth: Book for an Opera"; first published in *Primer Acto,* November-December, 1968), Alfil, 1968.

Tres maestros ante el publico (biographical essays; title means "Three Masters before the Public"), Alianza, 1973.

Also author of screenplays and of sound recording *Me llamo Antonio Buero Vallejo* (title means "My Name Is Buero Vallejo"), Discos Aguilar (Madrid), 1964. Contributor to anthologies and to periodicals, including *Correo Literario, Primer Acto, Revista de Occidente, Pipirijaina, Cuadernos de Agora,* and *Estreno.*

ADAPTATIONS: Madrugada, Historia de una escalera, En la ardiente oscuridad and *Un sonador para un pueblo* were made into films.

SIDELIGHTS: From the production of his first drama in 1949, playwright Antonio Buero Vallejo sought creative means to defy censorship and challenge the repression of the dictatorship of Francisco Franco. "The 1949-1950 theatrical season represents a turning point in Spanish drama," writes Martha T. Halsey in *Antonio Buero Vallejo,* because of the "new direction" represented by Buero Vallejo's play *Historia de una escalera* ("Story of a Stairway"). This was one of the author's first produced plays, and its impact, according to Marion Peter Holt in *The Contemporary Spanish Theater (1949-1972),* was comparable to that of Arthur Miller's *Death of a Salesman,* which triumphed on the American stage during the same season. Not only were both plays popular and critical successes during their first theater runs, but they were also tragic portrayals of everyday existence in their respective societies.

The effect of Buero Vallejo's play on Spanish drama is described in an Arturo del Hoyo essay which Holt translates (it first appeared in the Spanish literary review *Insula* shortly after *Historia de una escalera* opened). "From the first moments of the performance," del Hoyo notes, "the spectator was aware that *Story of a Stairway,* with its sense of dramatic values, was what had been needed in our theater to help free itself from paralysis, from mediocrity. For since 1939 the Spanish theater had been living among the ruins of the past."

Spanish theater had been living "among the ruins" caused by the bloody Spanish civil war, which devastated the country from 1936 to 1939. Joelyn Ruple's *Antonio Buero Vallejo: The First Fifteen Years* gives a picture of the bleak state of postwar Spanish theater: "During the years immediately following the war the government used the theater and movies for propaganda. There were translations of works from other countries, presentations of the Spanish classics, and some works by contemporary writers, but works censored and in general of limited value." Strict censorship caused many writers to produce light, inoffensive works rather than risk government reprisals. "The early postwar years," Halsey explains, "had been characterized by a new type of escape theater, termed 'theater of evasion,' which renounced any purposeful interpretation of reality in favor of adventures of a strictly imaginative nature."

When Buero Vallejo (who had been studying painting) decided to become a playwright after the war, however, government censorship and the general evasiveness of Spanish plays of the period were not his most important concerns. He was an ex-prisoner, having been sentenced to death—later commuted to six years' imprisonment—for his activities with the Republican (Loyalist) army during the war. But, whereas many writers chose to flee Fascist rule, Buero Vallejo decided instead to remain in Spain and produce plays. While he chose not to overtly attack Spanish authorities in his works, his plays nevertheless subtly protested Spain's repressive society. He himself has characterized his work as part of a collective struggle for cultural rebirth.

Because of Buero Vallejo's technique of veiled criticism, Francis Donahue lists the playwright in *Books Abroad* as the leader of the Spanish "Theater of Commitment." This "Theater of Commitment," Donahue remarks, "is a nonpolitical, political theater, for it makes its impact by indirect means. . . . The antagonist in the Theater of Commitment is the Establishment. To point out specifically the nature of that antagonist . . . would mean the play would

remain unstaged. . . . The cause of the evil conditions remains unspecified, but implied: The Spanish Establishment." For his part, Buero Vallejo explained in Marie-Lise Gazarian Gautier's *Interviews with Spanish Writers* that he was trying to provide "a tragic perspective of human existence, as long as you understand that what I mean by 'tragic' is not something ominous or hopeless, but rather a riddle that can be solved. . . . It is expressed in concrete terms through specific subjects that are usually related to a critical vision of social problems in this world and our own personal reality."

Buero Vallejo's first published play, *En la ardiente oscuridad* ("In the Burning Darkness"), is a good example of his theater in general and shows how a playwright of the Theater of Commitment voices criticism in his or her work. According to Halsey the play "contains much of the thematics and symbolism . . . more fully developed in [Buero Vallejo's] later works." Holt concurs, noting, "A consideration of *In the Burning Darkness . . .* is fundamental to an understanding of the playwright's ideas and dramatic techniques."

Although Buero Vallejo may seem to avoid the issue of government oppression in, for example, *In the Burning Darkness,* his meaning is subtly revealed. The play tells the story of Ignacio's arrival at a school for the blind and how his anger at being blind disrupts the formerly tranquil life of the students. Ruple explains the social protest inherent in the play: "In [*In the Burning Darkness*] we find a philosophical or religious struggle within the protagonist as he pleads to society to look about and see the conditions under which it actually exists, to stop pretending that all is right with the world. . . . He . . . protests a lethargic society which refuses to recognize and reject a dictator." In *The Tragic Stages of Antonio Buero Vallejo,* Robert L. Nicholas agrees that this play, and many of Buero Vallejo's other works, can be viewed in terms of two levels: the surface story and its underlying philosophical truth. "As the play develops," he notes, "it becomes clear that physical blindness is symbolic of spiritual blindness and that a longing for truth, and not physical sight, is the real source of Ignacio's torment."

Many of Buero Vallejo's plays deal with a quest for the truth and the fate of those who look for it in a society blind to its own tragic reality. The seekers of truth in his plays are often "visionaries," according to Holt in his introduction to *Three Plays,* who look "beyond the present reality to a more enlightened future." Ignacio, the blind "troublemaker" of *In the Burning Darkness,* is one such visionary. In three later plays, Buero Vallejo chooses as protagonists figures from Spanish history—the painters Diego de Silva Velazquez and Francisco Jose de Goya, and the writer Mariano Jose de Larra. The three plays in which these historical characters appear—*Las meninas* ("The Ladies-in-

Waiting"), *El sueno de la razon* ("The Sleep of Reason"), and *La detonacion* ("The Detonation"), respectively—deal with, as Halsey comments in *Hispanic Journal,* "the role of the intellectual in a repressive society."

Las meninas takes its name from Velazquez's masterpiece, a ten foot by nine foot painting of five-year-old Princess Margarita and other members of Philip IV's royal household. The painting has fascinated art critics for centuries because the portrait of the princess also includes the shadowy images of Spain's king and queen in a background mirror. Buero Vallejo's play explores the political and social implications of the painting, and the painter, observes Nicholas, "is portrayed as the lonely intellectual who attacks all that is false and unjust in seventeenth-century Spanish society." According to Nicholas, *Las meninas* "is a . . . plea for justice. More than that, it is a call to responsibility for the intelligentsia. Buero [Vallejo] has pictorially revived a moment in history in order to address and indict his contemporaries. . . . *Las meninas* is a direct yet subtly conceived attack against censorship."

Nicholas, Halsey, and Ruple all note the importance of a scene in the play in which Pedro, a half-blind beggar, reacts to Velazquez's preliminary sketch for *Las meninas.* Ruple translates Pedro's words: "Yes, I think I understand. A serene picture, but containing all the sadness of Spain. Anyone who sees these creatures will understand how irredeemably condemned they are to suffer. They're living ghosts whose truth is death. Whoever sees them in the future will notice it with terror." By implication, Buero Vallejo suggests that under Franco's repression Spaniards of the twentieth century are also "irredeemably condemned . . . to suffer."

El sueno de la razon takes its name from a late eighteenth-century etching by Goya entitled *El sueno de la razon produce monstruos* ("The Sleep of Reason Produces Monsters"). The etching carries the caption: "Imagination abandoned by reason produces impossible monsters: united with her, she is the mother of the arts and the source of their wonders." The etching is a self-portrait of the artist asleep at his desk while evil-looking winged creatures hover about his head and a large catlike animal watches him with glowing eyes. The terror depicted in the etching is masterfully portrayed in Buero Vallejo's play, according to critics. Through a variety of techniques he captures the misery of the great artist left totally deaf by illness and under constant threat of harassment or death from the authorities. The playwright uses projections of the "Black Paintings"—strange dark scenes with which Goya covered the interior walls of his country house—to express his emotional turmoil.

Holt refers to a characteristic Buero Vallejo dramatic device introduced in *In the Burning Darkness* and later re-

fined in *The Sleep of Reason.* This technique, which the playwright calls *interiorizacion* ("interiorization"), appears in the earlier play in a scene that illustrates Ignacio's blindness for the audience. While Ignacio speaks of his horror at being blind, the stage lights begin to dim until the entire theater is completely dark. The darkness lasts through four or five lines of dialogue before the lights are turned on again.

In *The Sleep of Reason* Buero Vallejo forces the audience to experience Goya's deafness: in the latter's presence the actors mouth their lines of dialogue but make no sound. To simulate the artist's inner anguish, amplified heartbeats and the noise of flapping wings fill the theater, but only Goya reacts to them—they are not heard by the other characters. To heighten the drama, the projections of Goya's "Black Paintings" flash across the stage with ever increasing speed.

Holt comments: "The audience is drawn into the mind of a character or into a crucial dramatic situation with intensified personal identification, as the proscenium barrier is bridged and momentarily ceases to exist." Halsey refers to the techniques of interiorization as "psychic participation." She concludes that through interiorization in both *In the Burning Darkness* and in *The Sleep of Reason,* Buero Vallejo produces "a more authentic participation in the reality of the tragedy." According to Halsey the reality in both of these plays "is symbolic, for the blindness portrayed represents . . . man's lack of spiritual vision and the deafness, his alienation or estrangement from his fellow human beings."

The protagonist of Buero Vallejo's *La detonacion* ("The Detonation"), Mariano Jose de Larra, is a visionary similar to Ignacio, Velazquez, and Goya. Larra lived during the early 1800s, another period of political struggle in Spain characterized by strict censorship. Just as during Buero Vallejo's time, writers of Larra's era tried to avoid direct confrontation with the authorities by writing comedies. Larra refused to do so, preferring satirical essays in which he attacked almost every facet of society. In *Hispanic Journal* Halsey calls Larra an "author surrogate." She notes: "Larra stated that to write in Madrid was to weep. Buero [Vallejo] no doubt experienced the same sentiment during the Franco era and initial transition period" after the dictator's death.

In spite of tremendous obstacles, Buero Vallejo achieved success as a playwright from the very beginning of his career. *The Sleep of Reason,* after being acclaimed in Madrid, was subsequently produced in a number of European countries. In 1974, it became the first Buero Vallejo play to be produced professionally in the United States. In *The Contemporary Spanish Theater* Holt calls *The Sleep of Reason* "one of the most impressive achievements of

[Buero Vallejo's] career" and later adds: "With this play Buero [Vallejo] . . . sustained his right to be included among the major international writers of his day."

In a *Hispania* essay, Patricia W. O'Connor comments that because of Buero Vallejo's position as a highly respected playwright, Spanish censors have given him "relatively few problems" during his long career. However, almost all of his plays underwent at least a few *tachaduras,* or cuts, before they were allowed to be produced. *Aventura en lo gris* ("Adventure in Gray"), for example, although written in 1953, was not performed in Spain until 1963 and then only after extensive revision. *La doble historia del doctor Valmy* ("The Double Case-History of Doctor Valmy"), which deals with the torture of political prisoners, was not performed in Spain until 1976, after the death of Franco.

Even with the lifting of censorship in the post-Franco era, Buero Vallejo continues to deal with social issues in his plays, using his society as a setting for contemplations on the basic nature of the human condition. "Many people have said that my theater is tragic, but with an open window of hope," he commented in *Interviews with Spanish Writers.* "I always stress that I believe all writers with tragic bents have windows that are open to hope, although it may not be noticeable. In many of my plays, this so-called window is more or less apparent. In others, it isn't, and those plays appear closed, desperate, and without issue. I would hold, nevertheless, that even in those closed plays there is a window of hope. It doesn't matter that this does not seem to be the case: the play must call up that window in the audience. I think that the great tragedies were written to strengthen the hope of the public, not to weaken it, even though the text may seem to hold out no hope." Nicholas observes: "Buero [Vallejo] is no genius—he is not a Goya; he is just an honest, courageous playwright who tries to expose social injustice, and a good, humble man who seeks to understand human suffering. Each is an endless task."

Buero Vallejo told *CA:* "After three years of war and six long years in prison, I had fallen so far behind in my painting studies that I gave them up, and I set out to write for the theatre because, naturally, I had also loved the theatre since I was a child. Under Franco's strict censorship this undertaking proved even more difficult, but a set of favorable circumstances permitted me to continue onward. For me and for others, this censorship was a challenge, not just an obstacle, and I wasn't the only one to accept it. Poets, novelists, essayists, and other dramatists tried to convince the Spanish people (and themselves) that, although frequently very painful, a critical and reformative literature was possible in spite of all the environmental and administrative obstacles.

"In regards to the theatre, the official, unwritten watchwords were patriotism, escapism, moralism, and as much laughter as possible. Therefore, one had to do the opposite: tragedy which revealed instead of concealed the fact that one's destiny is a result of human and social factors instead of fate; a denunciation of injustices and frauds, a defense of liberty. And one had, at the same time, to produce serious experiences. Others will say to what extent each of us has attained these goals; perhaps they'll explain it tomorrow when the biases against this literature, which remain very strong, have been dismantled sociologically. I believe undeniably that, between all of us, something, and perhaps even a lot, has been gained. And because of this, our nation also had more support for resistance, hope, and clear thinking.

"The Greek tragedians, [William] Shakespeare, [Miguel de] Cervantes, [Pedro] Calderon [de la Barca], [Miguel de] Unamuno, [Henrik] Ibsen, [Luigi] Pirandello, [Bertolt] Brecht have been, among others, my teachers, and their imprint can be observed in my theatre. Although less frequently noted, but perhaps even more important in some of my works, is the presence of [H. G.] Wells and [Franz] Kafka. As a poet-friend of mind says about himself, I am also a 'child of well-known parents.' My originality, if I have any, is not based on denying them."

BIOGRAPHICAL/CRITICAL SOURCES:

BOOKS

Bejel, Emilio F., *Lo moral, lo social y lo metafisico en el teatro de Buero Vallejo,* Florida State University, 1970.

Buero Vallejo, Antonio, *Teatro: Hoy es fiesta, Las meninas* [and] *El tragaluz,* Taurus, 1968.

Buero Vallejo, *Three Plays,* edited and translated by Marion Peter Holt, Trinity University Press, 1985.

Contemporary Literary Criticism, Gale, Volume 15, 1980, Volume 46, 1988.

Corrigan, Robert W., *Masterpieces of the Modern Spanish Theatre,* Collier, 1967.

Cortina, Jose Ramon, *El arte dramatico de Antonio Buero Vallejo,* Gredos, 1969.

Cuevas Garcia, Cristobal, editor, *El teatro de Buero Vallejo: Texto y espectaculo,* Anthropos, 1990.

Domenech, Ricardo, *El teatro de Buero Vallejo,* Gredos, 1973.

Feijoo, Luis Iglesias, *La trayectoria dramatica de Antonio Buero Vallejo,* University of Santiago, 1982.

Forys, Marsha, *Antonio Buero Vallejo and Alfonso Sastre: An Annotated Bibliography,* Scarecrow, 1988.

Gazarian Gautier, Marie-Lise, *Interviews with Spanish Writers,* Dalkey Archive Press (Elmwood Park, IL), 1991.

Gerona Llamazares, Jose Luis, *Discapacidades y minusvalias en la obra teatral de Antonio Buero Vallejo,* Universidad Complutense (Madrid), 1991.

Halsey, Martha T., *Antonio Buero Vallejo,* Twayne, 1973.

Holt, Marion Peter, *The Modern Spanish Stage: Four Plays,* Hill & Wang, 1970.

Holt, *The Contemporary Spanish Theater (1949-1972),* Twayne, 1975.

Newman, Jean Cross, *Conciencia, culpa y trauma en el teatro de Antonio Buero Vallejo,* Albatros-Hispanofila (Valencia), 1992.

Nicholas, Robert L., *The Tragic Stages of Antonio Buero Vallejo,* Estudios de Hispanofila, 1972.

Paco, Mariano de, editor, *Estudios sobre Buero Vallejo,* Murcia Universidad, 1984.

Paco, editor, *Buero Vallejo (Cuarenta anos de teatro),* Caja Murcia (Murcia), 1988.

Paco, *De rebueriana,* Murcia Universidad, 1994.

Pajon Mecloy, Enrique, *El teatro de Antonio Buero Vallejo: Marginalidad e infinito,* Fundamentos (Madrid), 1991.

Rice, Mary, *Distancia e inmersion en el teatro de Buero Vallejo,* Peter Lang (New York City), 1992.

Ruggeri Marchetti, Magda, *Il teatro di Antonio Buero Vallejo o il processo verso la verita,* Bulzoni (Rome), 1981.

Ruple, Joelyn, *Antonio Buero Vallejo: The First Fifteen Years,* Eliseo Torres & Sons, 1971.

Verdu de Gregorio, Joaquin, *La luz y la oscuridad en el teatro de Buero Vallejo,* Ariel (Barcelona), 1979.

PERIODICALS

Books Abroad, summer, 1969.

Hispania, March, 1968; September, 1968; December, 1968; May, 1969; September, 1969; December, 1969; September, 1971; December, 1972; May, 1973; September, 1974; September, 1978.

Hispanic Journal, spring, 1984; fall, 1986.

Hispanofila, May, 1970.

Modern Drama, September, 1977.

Modern Language Journal, February, 1972; January, 1973; December, 1978; spring, 1984; fall, 1986.

Ottawa Hispanic Studies, Volume 19, 1994.

Revista de estudios hispanicos, November, 1969; May, 1978.

*   *   *

BULKA, Reuven P(inchas) 1944-

PERSONAL: Born June 6, 1944, in London, England; son of Jacob (a rabbi) and Ida (Alt) Bulka; married Naomi Jakobovits, September 9, 1967; children: Yocheveed Ruth, Shmuel Refael, Rena Dvorah, Efrayim Yechezkel (deceased), Eliezer Menachem, Binyomin David. *Educa-*tion: Rabbi Jacob Joseph Rabbinical Seminary, Rabbi, 1965; City University of New York, B.A., 1965; University of Ottawa, M.A., 1969, Ph.D., 1971.

ADDRESSES: Home—1747 Featherston Dr., Ottawa, Ontario, Canada K1H 6P4. *Office*—Congregation Machzikei Hadas, 2310 Virginia Dr., Ottawa, Ontario, Canada K1H 6S2.

CAREER: K'hal Adas Yeshurun, Bronx, NY, associate rabbi, 1965-67; Machzikei Hadas, Ottawa, Ontario, rabbi, 1967—. Member of board of advisers of Institute of Logotherapy. Rabbinical Council of America, member of executive committee, 1976-80. Founder of Center for the Study of Psychology and Judaism, 1976; Carleton University, lecturer, 1979, 1982, 1986, and 1988; chairperson and editor of Family and Marriage Committee, 1976-89; National Religious Affairs Committee of Canadian Jewish Congress, member of executive committee; chair of National Rabbinic Cabinet of State of Israel Bonds of Canada. CJOH-Radio, host of *Quest,* 1974-80, host and producer of *About Ourselves,* 1980-88; host of television series *In Good Faith,* 1988—; guest on various television and radio programs. Ottawa Talmud Torah Board, chair of Hebrew curriculum committee, 1972-74; Council of Adult Education of Ottawa, chair, 1973-76; Committee for Voluntary Probation Services for Ottawa, member, 1975-80; Ottawa Soviet Jewry Committee, co-chair, 1984-; Jews in Arab/Moslem Lands Committee, national chair, 1989—; Ottawa Jewish Community Council, member of executive committee; and member of Executive League for Human Rights.

MEMBER: American Psychological Association, Association of Health Clergy.

AWARDS, HONORS: J. I. Segal Award for Jewish Literature, J. I. Segal Foundation for Jewish Culture, 1981, for *As a Tree by the Waters;* Joseph Tanenbaum Book Award for Excellence in Literature, 1987; William C. Bier Award of Division 36, American Psychological Association, 1989.

WRITINGS:

The Wit and Wisdom of the Talmud, Peter Pauper, 1974.

(Editor with Joseph Fabry and William Sahakian) *Logotherapy in Action,* Jason Aronson (Northvale, NJ), 1979.

(Editor) *Mystics and Medics: A Comparison of Mystical and Psychotherapeutic Encounters,* Human Sciences Press (New York City), 1979.

Sex and the Talmud: Reflections on Human Relations, Peter Pauper, 1979.

The Quest for Ultimate Meaning: Principles and Applications of Logotherapy, Philosophical Library, 1979.

As a Tree by the Waters—Pirkey Avoth: Psychological and Philosophical Insights, Feldheim, 1980, revised editions published as *Chapters of the Sages: A Psychological Commentary on Pirkey Avoth,* Jason Aronson (Northvale, NJ), 1993, and *Pirkey Avoth: Psychological and Philosophical Insights,* Jason Aronson, 1994, all based on original Hebrew manuscript, *Mishnah Avot.*

(Editor) *Holocaust Aftermath: Continuing Impact on the Generations,* Human Sciences Press (New York City), 1981.

(Editor with Moshe Halevi Spero) *A Psychology-Judaism Reader,* Charles C. Thomas, 1983.

Torah Therapy: Reflections on the Weekly Sedra and Special Occasions, KTAV (Hoboken, NJ), 1983.

(Editor) *Dimensions of Orthodox Judaism,* KTAV (Hoboken, NJ), 1983.

Loneliness, Guidance Centre of University of Toronto, 1984.

The Coming Cataclysm: The Orthodox-Reform Rift and the Future of the Jewish People, Mosaic Press, 1984, second edition, 1986.

The Haggadah for Pesah, with Translation and Thematic Commentary, Pri Haaretz (Jerusalem), 1985.

Jewish Marriage: A Halakhic Ethic, KTAV (Hoboken, NJ), 1986.

The Jewish Pleasure Principle, Human Sciences Press (New York City), 1987.

Individual, Family, Community: Judeo-Psychological Perspectives, Mosaic Press, 1989.

What You Thought You Knew about Judaism: 341 Common Misconceptions about Jewish Life, Jason Aronson (Northvale, NJ), 1989.

Uncommon Sense for Common Problems, Lugus, 1990.

Jewish Divorce Ethics: The Right Way to Say Goodbye, Ivy League Press (Ogdensburg, NY), 1992.

Critical Psychological Issues: Judaic Perspectives, University Press of America (Lanham, MD), 1992.

More of What You Thought You Knew about Judaism: 354 Common Misconceptions about Jewish Life, Jason Aronson (Northvale, NJ), 1993.

More Torah Therapy: Further Reflections on the Weekly Sidrah and Special Occasions, KTAV (Hoboken, NJ), 1993.

Author of an opinion column in *Ottawa Citizen,* 1974-78, 1989—. Contributor to magazines, including *Jewish Digest, Midstream, Jewish Life,* and psychology journals. Founder and editor of *Journal of Psychology and Judaism,* 1976—; editor of *Family and Marriage Newsletter,* 1976-89; section editor of *Rabbinical Council of America Sermon Manual,* 1977-82; member of editorial boards of *International Forum for Logotherapy, Journal of Religion and Health, Pastoral Psychology,* and *Tradition;* member

of editorial advisory board of *Pastoral Counseling Encyclopedia.*

SIDELIGHTS: Reuven P. Bulka once told *CA:* "Logotherapy, best described as healing through meaning, is the psychological system of Viktor Frankl. It is a system of thought positing the primariness of the search for meaning as underlying human behavior. *The Quest for Ultimate Meaning: Principles and Applications of Logotherapy* is a wide-ranging study of this system of thought and how it relates to Judaism. *Torah Therapy: Reflections on the Weekly Sedra and Special Occasions* is essentially a book of psychological insights explaining incidents and episodes as well as chapters of the Bible.

"*The Coming Cataclysm: The Orthodox-Reform Rift and the Future of the Jewish People* is an essay on the potential disaster facing the Jewish community because of the split between the various trends, most pointedly between Orthodox and Reform. I attempt to show that the diverging policies of Orthodox and Reform concerning divorce and conversion are leading to a major split of the Jewish community into two separate entities, with the one having nothing to do with the other. The fall-out from such an eventuality is little short of disastrous for the future North American Jewish community.

"Writing forces me to put abstract ideas into intelligible form, in a way that others can understand. Writing is sharing. It is always exciting to write from differing vantage points, in my case primarily from psychological and religious (mainly Jewish) perspectives. When ideas meet and can shake hands, one feels a sense of fusion, a radiating of an integral truth about reality which whets the appetite for integration and harmony."*

*   *   *

BULLOUGH, Bonnie 1927-

PERSONAL: Born January 5, 1927, in Delta, UT; daughter of Ruth Uckerman; married Vern L. Bullough (a college professor), August 2, 1947; children: David (deceased), James, Steven, Susan, Robert. *Education:* University of Utah, R.N., 1947; Youngstown State University, B.S., 1957; University of California, Los Angeles, M.S. (nursing), 1962, M.A. (sociology), 1965, Ph.D., 1968, postdoctoral study, 1970-74.

ADDRESSES: Home—17434 Mayall St., Northridge, CA 91325. *Office*—Department of Nursing, University of Southern California, 1540 Alcazar St., Los Angeles, CA 90033.

CAREER: Santa Rosa General Hospital, Santa Rosa, CA, nurse, 1947-48; Salt Lake General Hospital, Salt Lake

City, UT, operating room head nurse, 1948-51; University of Chicago Clinics, Chicago, IL, operating room nurse, 1951-52; City of Chicago, Chicago, field nurse for health department, 1952-54; Youngstown State University, Youngstown, OH, part-time instructor in nursing, 1956-59; Northridge Hospital, Northridge, CA, part-time nurse, 1959-61; Cairo University, Higher Institute of Nursing, Cairo, Egypt, Fulbright lecturer in nursing, 1966-67; San Fernando Valley State College (now California State University, Northridge), part-time instructor in sociology, 1967-68; University of California, Los Angeles, assistant professor, 1968-72, associate professor of nursing, 1972-75; California State University, Long Beach, professor of nursing and coordinator of graduate nursing program, 1975-79; State University of New York at Buffalo, dean of School of Nursing, 1980-91, professor of nursing, 1991-93; University of Southern California, Los Angeles, 1993—. Certified family nurse practitioner, 1985, 1990, 1995 and certified pediatric nurse practitioner. Member of Planned Parenthood Medical Advisory Committee, 1980-86, and Council of Deans, New York State, 1980-91.

MEMBER: American Academy of Nursing, American Nurses Association, American Public Health Association, American College of Nurse Practitioners, American Society of Law and Medicine, American Sociological Association, American Humanist Association, Council of Primary Health Care Nurse Practitioners, National Association of Pediatric Nurse Associates and Practitioners, Society for the Scientific Study of Sexuality (fellow, 1983), New York State Coalition of Nurse Practitioners, California Coalition of Nurse Practitioners.

AWARDS, HONORS: Recipient of grants from National Center for Health Services, Research, and Development, 1970-72, and W. K. Kellogg Foundation, 1975-79; American Academy of Nursing fellow, 1978; Nurse Practitioner of the Year award for education and research, Syntex Laboratories, 1992; Kinsey Award (with Vern Bullough), 1995, for contributions to the scientific study of sexuality.

WRITINGS:

Social Psychological Barriers to Housing Desegregation, Center for Real Estate Research and Urban Economics, University of California, Berkeley, 1969.

(Contributor) Judith Lorber and Eliot Friedson, editors, *Medical Men and Their Work,* Aldine-Atherton (Hawthorne, NY), 1972.

(Editor and contributor) *The Law and the Expanding Nursing Role,* Appleton-Century-Crofts (New York City), 1975, 2nd edition, 1980.

(Editor) *The Management of Common Human Miseries: A Text for Primary Care Practitioners,* Springer Publishing (New York City), 1979.

Issues in Nursing: An Annotated Bibliography, Garland Publishing (New York City), 1985.

(With George Rosen) *Preventive Medicine in the United States, 1900-1990: Trends and Interpretations,* Science History Publications (Canton, MA), 1992.

Also author of *New Scholarship about Women and Nursing,* 1990. Contributor of chapters to other books. Also contributor of more than fifty-eight articles to professional journals, including *American Journal of Nursing, American Journal of Sociology, Journal of Sex Research,* and *Nursing Research.* Advisory board member and columnist for *Pediatric Nursing,* 1979-85. Referee for *Nursing Outlook, Western Journal of Nursing Research,* and *American Journal of Sociology.*

WITH HUSBAND, VERN BULLOUGH:

What Color Are Your Germs? (pamphlet), Committee to End Discrimination in Chicago Medical Institutions, 1954.

The Emergence of Modern Nursing, Macmillan (New York City), 1964, 2nd edition, 1969.

(Editors with others) *Issues in Nursing: An Annotated Bibliography,* Springer Publishing (New York City), 1966.

(Editors) *New Directions for Nurses,* Springer Publishing, 1971.

Poverty, Ethnic Identity, and Health Care, Appleton-Century-Crofts, 1972.

(Editors) *The Subordinate Sex: A History of Attitudes toward Women,* University of Illinois Press (Champaign), 1973.

Sin, Sickness, and Sanity: A History of Sexual Attitudes, New American Library (New York City), 1977.

(With Barret Elcano and Margaret Deacon) *A Bibliography of Prostitution,* Garland Publishing, 1977.

(Editors) *Expanding Horizons in Nursing,* Springer Publishing, 1977.

Prostitution: An Illustrated Social History, Crown (New York City), 1978.

The Care of the Sick: The Emergence of Modern Nursing, Prodist (New York City), 1978.

Nursing: An Historical Bibliography, Garland Publishing, 1981.

Health Care for the Other Americans, Appleton-Century-Crofts, 1982.

(Editors with Mary Claire Soukup) *Nursing Issues and Strategies for the Eighties,* Springer Publishing, 1983.

Women and Prostitution: A Social History, Prometheus (Buffalo), 1985.

Contraception: A Guide to Birth Control Methods, Prometheus, 1990.

Nursing in the Community, Mosby (St. Louis), 1990.

(Editors with Marietta P. Stanton) *Florence Nightingale and Her Era: A Collection of New Scholarship,* Garland Publishing, 1990.

Cross Dressing, Sex, and Gender, University of Pennsylvania Press (Philadelphia), 1993.

(Editors) *Nursing Issues for the Nineties and Beyond,* Springer Publishing, 1994.

(Editors) *Human Sexuality: An Encyclopedia,* Garland, 1994.

Sexual Attitudes: Myths and Realities, Prometheus, 1995.

SIDELIGHTS: Bonnie Bullough once wrote: "I consider this an exciting time to be involved in nursing. The role of the nurse is in a period of rapid change as nurses take on more responsibility in acute, long term, and primary care. This means that the education of nurses must necessarily be strengthened. Since social change of this proportion is always somewhat painful, the profession is also beset by many problems, and problems, if they are not overwhelming, can be interesting."

*   *   *

BURNFORD, S. D.
See BURNFORD, Sheila (Philip Cochrane Every)

*   *   *

BURNFORD, Sheila (Philip Cochrane Every) 1918-1984
(S. D. Burnford, Sheila Burnford Louisburgh)

PERSONAL: Born May 11, 1918, in Scotland; died of cancer, April 20, 1984, in Bucklers Hard, Hampshire, England; daughter of Wilfred George Cochrane and Ida Philip (Macmillan) Every; married David Burnford, 1941; children: Peronelle Philip, Elizabeth Jonquil, Juliet Sheila. *Education:* Privately educated in England, France, and Germany. *Religion:* Anglican. *Avocational interests:* Hunting, mycology, and astronomy.

CAREER: Writer.

MEMBER: Society of Authors (England), Canadian Authors Association, Authors Guild (United States).

AWARDS, HONORS: Canadian Book of the Year for Children medal, 1963, Aurianne Award, American Library Association, 1963, Lewis Carroll Shelf Award, 1971, William Allen White Award, Dorothy Canfield Fisher Award, Young People's *Choice Award,* Pacific Northwestern Libraries Association, and honorable mention, Hans Christian Andersen Awards, all for *The Incredible Journey;* "Books for the Teen Age" citation, New York Public Library, 1980-82, for *Bel Ria.*

WRITINGS:

FICTION FOR YOUNG ADULTS

The Incredible Journey, illustrated by Carl Burger, Little, Brown (Boston), 1961, revised edition, Hodder and Stoughton (London), 1961.

Mr. Noah and the Second Flood, illustrated by Michael Foreman, Praeger (New York City), 1973.

Bel Ria, Little, Brown, 1978, published in England as *Bel Ria: Dog of War,* Joseph (London), 1977.

NONFICTION FOR ADULTS

The Fields of Noon (autobiographical essays), Little, Brown, 1964.

Without Reserve, Little, Brown, 1969.

One Woman's Arctic, illustrated by Susan Ross, Hodder and Stoughton, 1972, Little, Brown, 1973.

OTHER

Contributor of essays to magazines and newspapers.

Some of Burnford's work has also been published under the names S. D. Burnford and Sheila Burnford Louisburgh.

ADAPTATIONS: The Incredible Journey was adapted as a motion picture by Walt Disney Studios.

SIDELIGHTS: Sheila Burnford's first book, *The Incredible Journey,* remains her most popular work and is considered a modern classic of children's literature. The story of three domestic pets—two dogs and a cat—who travel through the Canadian wilderness to return to their family, *The Incredible Journey* is often compared to Anna Sewell's *Black Beauty.*

Burnford's own trio of pets inspired *The Incredible Journey.* She once commented, "Communication between animals has always fascinated me, not just the instinctive means, but the day-to-day, individual and original communication that exists between animals of diversified species when they live harmoniously with common domestic background. There were endless examples of this with our animal trio, all members of it as different in their personalities as it is possible for animals to be, yet apparently able to receive the intent or communication of the others and act upon it."

"This is not merely a story for animal lovers. It is for all who enjoy the drama of a single purpose achieved with suffering but without complaint," Ruth Hill Viguers asserted in *Horn Book.* John Gillespie and Diana Lembo remarked in *Juniorplots: A Book Talk Manual for Teachers and Librarians,* "Through this story of three remarkable animals, the author has illustrated many admirable qualities: devotion to a cause, courage to face great difficulties, and the bonds of fidelity which can exist between animal and man."

BIOGRAPHICAL/CRITICAL SOURCES:

BOOKS

Arbuthnot, May Hill, and Zena Sutherland, *Children and Books,* Scott, Foresman, 1972, pp. 413-414.
Children's Literature Review, Volume 2, Gale (Detroit), 1976, pp. 19-20.
Egoff, Sheila, *The Republic of Childhood: A Critical Guide to Canadian Children's Literature in English,* 2nd edition, Oxford University Press, 1975, pp. 125-126.
Gillespie, John, and Diana Lembo, *Juniorplots: A Book Talk Manual for Teachers and Librarians,* Bowker, 1967, pp. 155, 157.

PERIODICALS

Atlantic, September, 1964.
Best Sellers, August 15, 1964; November 1, 1969.
Bulletin of the Center for Children's Books, March, 1962, p. 107; December, 1973, p. 59.
Canadian Forum, January, 1970.
Christian Science Monitor, December, 1961.
Horn Book, June, 1961, p. 253.
Junior Bookshelf, July, 1961, p. 161; June, 1973, p. 195.
Kirkus Reviews, July 15, 1973, p. 753.
Library Journal, August, 1964, June 1, 1973.
New York Times Book Review, December 16, 1973, p. 8.
Publisher's Weekly, August 27, 1973, p. 280; November 28, 1977.
Washington Post, May 1, 1984.

OBITUARIES:

PERIODICALS

Washington Post, May 1, 1984.*

*   *   *

BUSBY, F. M. 1921-

PERSONAL: Born March 11, 1921, in Indianapolis, IN; son of F. M., Sr. (a teacher) and Clara (a teacher; maiden name, Nye) Busby; married Elinor Doub, April 28, 1954; children: Michele B. Rowley. *Education:* Washington State University, B.Sc., 1946, B.Sc.E.E., 1947. *Politics:* "Eclectic; consider issues individually." *Religion:* "Much the same. . . ."

ADDRESSES: Home and office—2852 14th Ave. West, Seattle, WA 98119.

CAREER: Alaska Communication System: Headquarters, Seattle, WA, "trick chief" and project supervisor, 1947-53, telegraph engineer, 1953-70; writer, 1970—. *Military service:* National Guard, active duty, 1940-41. U.S. Army, 1943-45.

MEMBER: Science Fiction Writers of America (vice-president, 1974-76), Spectator Amateur Press Society.

WRITINGS:

SCIENCE FICTION

Cage a Man (Science Fiction Book Club selection; also see below), New American Library (New York City), 1974.
The Proud Enemy (also see below), Berkley Publishing (New York City), 1975.
Rissa Kerguelen (also see below), Putnam (New York City), 1976.
The Long View (also see below), Putnam, 1976.
All These Earths, Berkley Publishing, 1976.
Rissa Kerguelen (contains *Rissa Kerguelen* and *The Long View*), Berkley Publishing, 1977, published as *Young Rissa, Rissa and Tregare, [and] The Long View,* 1984.
Zelde M'tana, Dell (New York City), 1980.
The Demu Trilogy (includes *Cage a Man, The Proud Enemy,* and *End of the Line*), Pocket Books (New York City), 1980.
Star Rebel, Bantam (New York City), 1984.
The Alien Debt, Bantam, 1984.
Rebel's Quest, Bantam, 1985.
Rebels' Seed, Bantam, 1986.
Getting Home (story collection), Ace Books (New York City), 1987.
The Breeds of Man, Bantam, 1988.
Slow Freight, Bantam, 1991.
The Singularity Project, Tor Books (New York City), 1993.
Islands of Tomorrow, Avon (New York City), 1994.
Arrow from Earth, Avon, 1995.

OTHER

Contributor to numerous anthologies, including *New Dimensions 3,* edited by Robert Silverberg, New American Library, 1973; *1979 Annual World's Best Science Fiction,* edited by Donald A. Wollheim, DAW Books (New York City), 1979; and *Heroic Visions,* edited by Jessica Amanda Salmonson, Ace Books, 1983. Contributor of about forty stories to science fiction magazines.

WORK IN PROGRESS: The Triad Worlds and *The Parthogene Renalle,* science fiction novels; short stories.

SIDELIGHTS: F. M. Busby once told *CA:* "I 'played' with writing off-and-on for years before the chance came to take early retirement and try it in earnest. I like to deal with characters who are pushed hard by necessity and who generally manage to cope—but win or lose, they don't quit.

"Science fiction allows me to put characters into predicaments that could not exist in our own past and present; I like the challenge. It can also be fun to produce 'suspension of disbelief' by applying strict logic to a patently impossible premise. And of course, it always helps to keep the numbers straight."

C

CADE, Toni
   See BAMBARA, Toni Cade

*   *   *

CALLWOOD, June   1924-

PERSONAL: Born June 2, 1924, in Chatham, Ontario, Canada; daughter of Harold (a manufacturer) and Gladys (an office manager; maiden name, Lavoie) Callwood; married Trent Gardiner Frayne (a writer and columnist), May 13, 1944; children: Jill Callwood, Brant Homer, Jennifer Ann, Casey Robert (deceased, 1982). Education: Educated in Canada. Politics: Socialist democrat. Religion: "Don't know."

ADDRESSES: Home and office—21 Hillcroft Dr., Islington, Ontario, Canada M9B 4X4.

CAREER: Brantford Expositor, Brantford, Ontario, reporter, 1941-42; Globe and Mail, Toronto, Ontario, reporter, 1942-45, columnist, 1975-78, 1983-89; freelance writer, 1946—. Yorkville Digger House, founding affiliate, 1966-71; Nellie's Hostel for Women, co-founding president, 1974-78, director, 1986-92; Jessie's Center for Teenagers, founding president, 1982-83, director, 1983-85, 1986-89, president, 1987-89; Davenport-Perth Neighborhood Center, founding director, 1985-86, member of Family Services Resource Group, 1986—; Casey House Hospice, founding president, 1987-88, honorary director, 1988; Casey House Foundation, founding president, 1992-93, honorary director, 1993. Member of National Advisory Committee on the Battered Child, 1973; founding member of executive committee, Community Resources Consultants, 1975-78; co-chair, First National Conference on Human Rights, 1978; chair, Task Force on Teenaged Mothers, 1979-82; member of Assistive Devices Advisory Committee, Ontario Ministry of Health, 1981-86, chair of ADP Incontinence and Ostomy Sub-Committee, 1983-86; member of Metro Toronto Child Care Project Steering Committee, 1985-86; founder and chair, Hospice Steering Committee for AIDS Committee of Toronto, 1985-87. Panel member of Court of Opinions, 1959-67, and host of Human Sexuality, 1966, for Canadian Broadcasting Corp. (CBC) Radio; host of Generations, 1966, and In Touch, 1975-78, for CBC-TV; host of National Treasures, 1991-95, for Vision TV. Judge for numerous awards, including National Newspaper Awards, 1976-83, National Magazine Awards, 1977, and Governor-General's Literary Award, 1984-86; founding director, Toronto Arts Awards, 1984—. Gordon Fairweather Lecturer on Human Rights, University of Ottawa, 1984. Founding director, Ontario Film Development Corp., 1986.

MEMBER: Writers Union of Canada (founding member, 1973; chair, 1979-80; chair of Rights and Freedom Committee, 1986-87; life member, 1994), PEN Canada (founding member, 1984; secretary, 1985-87; vice president, 1987-88; president, 1989-90), Periodical Writers Association of Canada (founding member, 1976; vice president, 1977-78), Writers Development Trust (founding member, 1977; vice president, 1978; director, 1987—; Book and Periodical Council, vice president, 1994-95), Canadian Civil Liberties Association (founding vice president, 1965-88; honorary director, 1988), Amnesty International—Canada (council member, 1978—), Canadian Institute for the Administration of Justice (director, 1983-84), Canadian Council of Christians and Jews (director, 1978-88), Law Society of Upper Canada (bencher, 1987-91), Canadian Association for the Repeal of Abortion Laws (founding member, 1972; honorary director, 1982—), Coalition against Return of the Death Penalty, Learnxs Foundation (founding member, 1974; president, 1977-79), Justice for

Children (founding member, 1978; president, 1980), Bereaved Families of Ontario (honorary chair, 1983—), Women for Political Action (founding member, 1972), Feminists against Censorship (founding member, 1984—), Maggie's: Canadian Organization for the Rights of Prostitutes (founding member; president, 1986-93), Ian Adams Defense Fund (chair, 1980-81), Polish Journalists Aid Committee, Canadian Environmental Defence Fund (honorary director, 1985—), Canadian Native Arts Foundation (honorary director, 1985—), Canadian Magazines Awards Foundation (director, 1981-83), City of Toronto Children's Network, Toronto Arts Council (director, 1985—; chair of Literary Committee, 1985—), Toronto Memorial Society.

AWARDS, HONORS: "Woman of the Year," B'nai B'rith, 1969; award of merit from city of Toronto, 1974; member, Order of Canada, 1978; humanitarian award, Canadian Council of Christians and Jews, 1978; Ida Nudel Humanitarian Award, 1983; named to Canadian News Hall of Fame, 1984; Order of the Buffalo Hunt, Manitoba, 1984; Ontario Bicentennial Medal, 1984; award from Family Services Association, 1985; award from Planned Parenthood Federation of Canada, 1985; "Toronto Woman of Distinction," YWCA, 1986; officer, Order of Canada, 1986; certificate of appreciation from Metropolitan Community Church of Toronto, 1987; Quill Award, Windsor Press Club, 1987; humanitarian award, Ontario Psychological Association, 1987; Lifetime Achievement Award, Toronto Arts Foundation, 1990; Bob Edwards Award, 1991; Distinguished Canadian Award, University of Regina, 1993. Recipient of numerous honorary doctorate degrees, including Doctor of the University, University of Ottawa, 1987; Doctor of Sacred Letters, Trinity College, 1988; Doctor of Laws, Memorial University, Osgoode Hall Law School, and University of Toronto, all 1988, University of Western Ontario, 1993, and McMaster University, 1994; Doctor of Literature, Carelton University, 1988; Doctor of Letters, University of Alberta, 1988, University of Guelph, 1989, and University of New Brunswick, 1990; Doctor of Civil Law, Acadia University, 1993; and Doctor of Humane Letters, Mount St. Vincent University, 1993.

WRITINGS:

(With Marian Hillard) *A Woman Doctor Looks at Life and Love,* Doubleday (New York City), 1957.
Love, Hate, Fear, and Anger, Doubleday, 1964, revised edition published as *Emotions: What They Are and How They Affect Us,* 1986.
(With Charles W. Mayo) *Mayo: The Story of My Family and Career,* Doubleday, 1968.
(With Marvin Zuker) *Canadian Woman and the Law,* Copp Clark, 1971.

(With Barbara Walters) *How to Talk to Practically Anybody about Practically Anything,* Doubleday, 1973.
(With Judianne Densen-Gerber) *We Mainline Dreams,* Doubleday, 1974.
(With Zuker) *The Law Is Not for Women,* Pitman (Marshfield, MA), 1976.
(With Otto Preminger) *Otto Preminger Remembers,* Doubleday, 1977.
The Naughty Nineties: Canada's Illustrated Heritage, McClelland & Stewart (Toronto), 1978.
Portrait of Canada, Doubleday, 1981.
Emma: The True Story of Canada's Unlikely Spy, Stoddart, 1984.
Twelve Weeks in Spring, Lester & Orpen Dennys, 1986.
(With Bob White) *Hard Bargains: My Life on the Line,* McClelland & Stewart, 1987.
Jim: A Life with AIDS, Lester & Orpen Dennys, 1988.
The Sleepwalker, Lester & Orpen Dennys, 1990.
National Treasures, Stoddart, 1994.
No Easy Answer, Knopf (New York City), 1995.

Also author of television and radio scripts. Author of "The Informal . . . ," a column in *Globe and Mail,* 1975-78 and 1983-89. Contributor of nearly three hundred articles to magazines, including *Chatelaine* and *Maclean's.*

SIDELIGHTS: In *Emma: The True Story of Canada's Unlikely Spy,* Canadian writer and reformer June Callwood chronicles the life of Emma (Woikin) Sawula, a young Doukhobor woman from Saskatchewan convicted of spying for the Soviet Union and imprisoned in the late 1940s. Callwood's account details the controversial nature of Sawula's conviction, in particular the civil rights infractions that occurred at the time of her arrest and questioning. "More important than the circumstances of Emma's wrongdoing was the method of convicting her," observes William French in the Toronto *Globe and Mail,* "and . . . here Callwood, the noted civil libertarian, is at her best. Emma and . . . 12 [other] 'spies' . . . were scooped up, detained, interrogated and charged under conditions that, as Callwood notes, prevailed before King John signed the Magna Carta." French adds that Emma emerges in the book as "one of those tragic characters unwittingly caught up in the whirlpool of history, a victim perhaps of her naivete."

Twelve Weeks in Spring is the true story of Margaret Frazer, a terminally-ill retired school teacher whose wish to die at home was honored by friends and acquaintances—under Callwood's direction—who banded together to care for her. The book is both a detailed account of the group's coordinated response to Frazer's needs and, as Mary Lassance Parthun comments in the *Globe and Mail,* "a memorial to the dead Margaret Frazer and a tribute to friendship and the heights to which people can rise in a crisis."

More importantly though, the book is a statement of the group's commitment "to help Frazer . . . retain control over her life and death, in spite of the encroachments of society's definition of dying as a medical problem rather than an individual crisis or rite of passage." Parthun further states: "[Callwood] has been on the cutting edge of many attempts to adapt services to current needs. It is not surprising, then, that she has turned her energies to this particular problem of modern society—the sterile institutional death among strangers."

BIOGRAPHICAL/CRITICAL SOURCES:

PERIODICALS

Globe and Mail (Toronto), October 13, 1984; July 5, 1986; November 1, 1986; October 24, 1987.

*   *   *

CAMERON, Kenneth Walter 1908-

PERSONAL: Born October 12, 1908, in Martins Ferry, OH; son of Albert Ernest (an executive) and Zoe Shockley (Barker) Cameron. *Education:* West Virginia University, A.B., 1930, A.M., 1931; General Theological Seminary, S.T.B., 1935; Yale University, Ph.D., 1940. *Politics:* Republican.

ADDRESSES: Home—23-25 Wolcott St., Hartford, CT 06106. *Office*—Transcendental Books, Box A, Station A, Hartford, CT 06126.

CAREER: Berkeley Divinity School fellow, 1934-38; ordained Episcopal priest, 1935. North Carolina State College of Agriculture and Mechanic Arts (now North Carolina State University), Raleigh, instructor in English, 1938-43; Temple University, Philadelphia, PA, assistant professor of English, 1945-46; Trinity College, Hartford, CT, assistant professor, 1946-58, associate professor of English, 1958—. Manager of Transcendental Books, Hartford. Archivist and historiographer of Diocese of Connecticut, 1951—.

MEMBER: Modern Humanities Research Association of America, Modern Language Association of America, Melville Society, Thoreau Society, Emerson Society (executive secretary, 1955—).

WRITINGS:

(Editor and author of introduction) Ralph Waldo Emerson, *Nature* (1836 reprint), Scholar's Facsimiles Reprints, 1940.
(Editor) John Heywood, *Gentleness and Nobility,* Thistle Press, 1941.
Authorship and Sources of "Gentleness and Nobility," Thistle Press, 1941.

Background of John Heywood's "Witty and Wittless," Thistle Press, 1941.
John Heywood's "Play of the Wether," Thistle Press, 1941.
Ralph Waldo Emerson's Reading, Thistle Press, 1941, revised edition, Transcendental Books, 1962.
Emerson the Essayist: An Outline of His Philosophical Development through 1836, two volumes, Thistle Press, 1945.
(Editor) Emerson, *Indian Superstition,* Friends of the Dartmouth College Library, 1954, 2nd edition, 1963.
Genesis of Hawthorne's "The Ambitious Guest," Thistle Press, 1955.
The Genesis of Christ Church, Stratford, Connecticut, Christ Church, 1957.
Index of the Pamphlet Collection of the Diocese of Connecticut, The Historiographer, 1958.
Centennial History of Trinity Episcopal Church, Bridgeport, Connecticut, Trinity Episcopal Church, 1963.
The Catholic Revival in Episcopal Connecticut, 1850-1925, Trinity Episcopal Church, 1963.

PUBLISHED BY TRANSCENDENTAL BOOKS

The Presbury Family of Maryland and the Ohio Valley, 1950.
The Transcendental Workbook, 1957.
An Emerson Index; or, Names, Exempla, Sententiae, Symbols, Words, and Motifs on Selected Notebooks of Ralph Waldo Emerson, 1958.
The Transcendentalists and Minerva (also see below), three volumes, 1958.
Emerson and Thoreau as Readers (contains selected chapters from *The Transcendentalists and Minerva*), 1958, 2nd edition, 1972.
A Commentary on Emerson's Early Lectures, 1833-1836, with Index-Concordance, 1961.
Companion to Thoreau's Correspondence, 1964.
Emerson's Workshop: An Analysis of His Reading in Periodicals through 1836, 1964.
The Pardoner and His Pardons: Indulgences Circulating in England on the Eve of Reformation, 1965.
Transcendental Epilogue, 1965.
Thoreau's Harvard Years, 1966.
Transcendental Climate, 1967.
Hawthorne Index, 1968.
Transcendental Reading Patterns: Library Charging Lists, 1970.
Young Emerson's Transcendental Vision: An Exposition of His World View with an Analysis of the Structure, Backgrounds, and Meaning of Nature, 1971.
Emerson the Essayist: An Outline of His Philosophical Development through 1836 with Special Emphasis on the Sources and Interpretation of Nature, also Bibliographical Appendices, 1972.

Letter-book of the Reverend Henry Caner, S.P.G. Missionary in Colonial Connecticut and Massachusetts until the Revolution, 1972.

Longfellow's Reading in Libraries: The Charging Records of a Learned Poet Interpreted, 1973.

Response to Transcendental Concord, 1974.

Young Thoreau and the Classics, 1975.

Transcendental Apprenticeship, 1976.

Anglicanism in Early Connecticut and New England, 1977.

Young Reporter of Concord: A Checklist of F. B. Sanborn's Letters, 1978.

The Papers of Loyalist Samuel Peters, 1978.

Strictly Personal: A Teacher's Reminiscences, 1980.

Transcendentalists in Transition, 1980.

An Anglican Library in Colonial New England, 1980.

The Younger Doctor William Smith (1754-1820), 1980.

Samuel Seabury among His Contemporaries, 1981.

Parameters of American Romanticism and Transcendentalism, 1981.

The Episcopal Church in Connecticut and New England, 1981.

Correspondence of Franklin Benjamin Sanborn the Transcendentalist, 1982.

Abraham Jarvis: Connecticut's Second Anglican Bishop, 1982.

Seabury Traditions: The Reconstructed Journals of Connecticut's First Diocesan, two volumes, 1983.

Emerson's Transcendentalism and British Swedenborgism, 1984.

Transcendental Curriculum; or, Bronson Alcott's Library: To Which Is Added a Sheaf of Ungathered Letters, 1984.

Colonial Anglicanism in New England: A Guide, 1984.

Connecticut's First Diocesan: A Supplement to Seabury Traditions, 1985.

Hawthorne among Connecticut Congregationalists: The Odyssey of a Letter, 1985.

Studies in Emerson, Thoreau and the American Renaissance, 1987.

Emerson's Prose Poems: The Structure and Meaning of Nature (1836), 1988.

Toward a Thoreau Tertiary Bibliography, 1833-1899, 1988.

Firstlings of Emerson the Writer: A Study in Background and Sources, 1992.

Emerson's Apprenticeship: The College Notebooks Annotated with an Index, 1993.

Voices in Emerson's Sermons, Identified with Supplementary Annotations, 1994.

The Scholar's "Via Eminentiae": Emerson's Missionary Initiative at Phi Beta Kappa, 1994.

Emerson at Divinity School: His Address of 1838 and Its Significance, 1994.

EDITOR; PUBLISHED BY TRANSCENDENTAL BOOKS

Emerson, Thoreau, and Concord in Early Newspapers, 1957.

Thoreau's Literary Notebook in the Library of Congress, 1964.

Over Thoreau's Desk: New Correspondence 1838-1861, 1965.

Thoreau and His Harvard Classmates with Henry William's Memorials of the Class of 1837, 1965.

Poems of Jones Very, 1965.

Thoreau's Fact Book in the Harry Elkins Widener Collection in the Harvard College Library, three volumes, 1966.

The Works of Samuel Peters of Hebron, Connecticut, New England Historian, Satirist, Folklorist, Anti-patriot, and Anglican Clergyman, 1735-1826, with Historical Indexes, 1967.

Facsimiles of Early Episcopal Church Documents (1759-1789), 1970.

Phiothea or Plato against Epicurus: A Novel of the Transcendental Movement, 1975.

Whitman, Bryant, Melville and Holmes among Their Contemporaries, 1976.

The Church of England in Pre-Revolutionary Connecticut, 1976.

Samuel Hart, *Old Connecticut: Historical Papers,* 1976.

Romanticism and the American Renaissance, 1977.

The Episcopal Church of the American Renaissance, 1977.

Literary Comment in American Renaissance Newspapers, 1977.

Scholars' Companion to the American Renaissance, 1977.

Lowell, Whittier, Very and the Alcotts among Their Contemporaries, 1978.

Longfellow among His Contemporaries, 1978.

American Renaissance and Transcendentalism: Historical, Cultural, and Bibliographical Dimensions, 1978.

Samuel Seabury's Ungathered Imprints: Historical Perspectives, 1978.

Samuel Seabury (1729-1796): His Election, Consecration and Reception, 1978.

The New England Writers and the Press, 1980.

Ethos of Anglicanism in Colonial New England and New York, 1981.

Further Response to Transcendental Concord, 1982.

Anglican Church Music in America, 1763-1830, 1982.

The Vestry Lectures and a Rare Sermon by Ralph Waldo Emerson, 1983.

The Correspondence of Samuel Parker: Colonial Anglican Clergyman at Boston, 1984.

Anglican Apologetic in Colonial New England: Rare Tracts Defending the Polity, Theology and Liturgy of the Church of England before and during the Revolution, 1984.

The Correspondence of Loyalist Samuel Peters: An Inventory of Additions, 1985.

(And compiler of index) *Concord Literary Renaissance: Ungathered Memorabilia of Emerson, Thoreau, Hawthorne, Sanborn, the Alcotts, Margaret Fuller and Their Connections,* 1988.

Old Concord Massachusetts: A Notebook of Clippings from Nineteenth-Century Newspapers, 1988.

EDITOR OF BOOKS BY FRANKLIN BENJAMIN SANBORN; PUBLISHED BY TRANSCENDENTAL BOOKS

Lectures on Literature and Philosophy, 1975.

Transcendental and Literary New England, 1975.

Sixty Years of Concord: 1855-1915, 1976.

The Transcendental Eye, 1981.

Ungathered Poems and Transcendental Papers, 1981.

Table Talk, 1981.

Transcendental Horizons: Essays and Poetry by Franklin Benjamin Sanborn, 1984.

COMPILER; PUBLISHED BY TRANSCENDENTAL BOOKS

Early Anglicanism in Connecticut, 1962.

Index-Concordance to Emerson's Sermons, 1963.

Emerson among His Contemporaries: A Harvest of Estimates, Insights, and Anecdotes from the Victorian Literary World and an Index, 1967.

Research Keys to the American Renaissance: Scarce Indexes of "The Christian Examiner," "The North American Review," and "The New Jerusalem Magazine," for Students of American Literature, Culture, History, and New England Transcendentalism, 1967.

Connecticut Churchmanship: Records and Historical Papers Concerning the Anglican Church in Connecticut in the Eighteenth and Early Nineteenth Centuries, 1969.

The Massachusetts Lyceum during the American Renaissance: Materials for the Study of the Oral Tradition in American Letters, 1969.

Concord Harvest: Publications of the Concord School of Philosophy and Literature, 1970.

Contemporary Dimension—An American Renaissance Literary Notebook of Newspaper Clippings, [and] *Victorian Notebook: Literary Clippings from Nineteenth-Century American Newspapers,* 1970.

The Anglican Episcopate in Connecticut: A Sheaf of Biographical and Institutional Studies for Churchmen and Historians (1784-1899), 1970.

American Episcopal Clergy: Registers of Ordinations in the Episcopal Church in the United States, 1970.

Transcendental Log, 1973.

Anglican Climate in Connecticut: Historical Perspectives from Imprints of the Late Colonial and Early National Years, 1974.

Ammi Rogers and the Episcopal Church in Connecticut, 1790-1832: His Memoirs and Documents Illuminating

Historical, Religious, and Personal Backgrounds, 1974.

Episcopal Connecticut in Our Day: An Index to Illustrations in the "Connecticut Churchman," 1983.

American Authors in Pictures: The Major Nineteenth Century Writers and Their Backgrounds, 1983.

Vanished and Vanishing Episcopal Churches of Early Connecticut: A Pictorial Record, 1984.

An Index to the "Connecticut Churchman," 1906-1970, 1985.

The Emerson Tertiary Bibliography with Researcher's Index, 1986.

OTHER

Also author of *The Anglican Experience in Revolutionary Connecticut, New York and Areas Adjacent.* Editor of *Emerson Society Quarterly,* 1955-71, *American Transcendental Quarterly,* 1969-77, *American Renaissance Literary Report,* 1987—, and *Historiographer of the Episcopal Diocese of Connecticut.*

SIDELIGHTS: Kenneth Walter Cameron once told *CA:* "My Scottish background and love of books from childhood have encouraged me ever to break through the parameters of my ignorance, especially in the areas of history and literature. Five great teachers, during my formative years, gave indispensable direction. As I look back on a long career as professor and scholar, four 'blessings' stand out in my mind: the privilege of entering into the lives and works of a few authors, the sense of arriving at special competence in a few areas, the delight from association with a few productive and humane scholars and critics, and the hope (since so much has been passed on to me by others) that I may, perhaps, have been able to communicate some of my enthusiasm for ideas to my students."

*   *   *

CARLISLE, Rodney P. 1936-

PERSONAL: Born October 10, 1936, in Hempstead, NY; son of Prince Munroe (a journalist) and Gladys (Parker) Carlisle; married Anna Wilson, November 28, 1959; children: Nathan Kerry, Bonnie Lorca. *Education:* Harvard University, A.B., 1958; University of California, Berkeley, M.A., 1963, Ph.D., 1965. *Politics:* Democrat.

ADDRESSES: Home—Santa Fe, NM. *Office*—Department of History, Rutgers University, Camden, NJ 08102.

CAREER: Merritt College, Oakland, CA, instructor in history, 1964-66; Rutgers University, Camden, NJ, assistant professor and associate professor of history, 1966—, director of urban university department, 1969-71, chairman of department of history, 1973—, president of faculty senate, 1977-78. Visiting historian, U.S. Department of Energy, 1979-80; member of the board, Camden County Council of Economic Opportunity, 1967-71.

MEMBER: Historical Association (senior associate, 1981—).

AWARDS, HONORS: Hoover Scholar, 1979.

WRITINGS:

Prologue to Liberation: A History of Black People in America, Appleton, 1972.
The Roots of Black Nationalism, Kennikat (Port Washington, NY), 1975.
Hearst and the New Deal: The Progressive as Reactionary, edited by Frank Freidel, Garland (New York City), 1979.
Sovereignty for Sale: The Origins and Evolution of the Panamanian and Liberian Flags of Convenience, Naval Institute Press (Annapolis, MD), 1981.
The History of the Naval Ordnance Station at Indian Head, Maryland: One Hundred Years of Technical Achievement, Naval Ordnance Station (Indian Head, MD), 1990.
Powder and Propellants: Energetic Materials at Indian Head, Maryland, U.S. Navy (Washington, DC), 1990.

Contributor to *Labor History, Black World,* and other journals.

BIOGRAPHICAL/CRITICAL SOURCES:

PERIODICALS

Business History Review, spring, 1982, p. 181.
Choice, May, 1976, p. 423; December, 1981, p. 453.*

*   *   *

CARLSON, Dale (Bick) 1935-

PERSONAL: Born May 24, 1935, in New York, NY; daughter of Edgar M. (an orthopedic surgeon) and Estelle (Cohen) Bick (an interior designer); children: Daniel Bick, Hannah Bick. *Education:* Wellesley College, B.A., 1957.

ADDRESSES: Home and office—307 Neck Rd., Madison, CT 06443. *Agent*—Toni Mendez, Inc., 140 East 56th St., New York, NY 10022.

CAREER: Worked variously as bookseller, editor for various publishers including Doubleday and McGraw Hill, and teacher of creative writing. Parents League of New York, New York City, vice-president and editor-in-chief of *Parents League Bulletin,* 1968—; licensed wildlife rehabilitator, 1991—; International Wildlife Rehabilitation

Council, board of directors, 1993—; Bick Publishing House, founder and president, 1993—. Book reviewer for *New York Times;* guest lecturer in the United States and India; consultant to New York Board of Education.

MEMBER: Authors League of America, Authors Guild, International Wildlife Rehabilitation Council, Wind Over Wings.

AWARDS, HONORS: American Library Association Notable Book awards, 1972, for *The Mountain of Truth,* 1973, for *The Human Apes,* and 1974, for *Girls Are Equal Too;* Spring Festival honor book, for *Mountain of Truth;* Christopher Award, for *Where's Your Head?*

WRITINGS:

JUVENILE FICTION

Perkins the Brain, Doubleday (New York City), 1964.
The House of Perkins, Doubleday, 1965.
Miss Maloo, Doubleday, 1966.
(Editor) *The Brainstormers: Humorous Tales of Ingenious American Boys,* illustrated by Judith Gwyn Brown, Doubleday, 1966.
Frankenstein (juvenile adaptation of Mary Shelley's book), Golden Press (New York City), 1968.
The Electronic Teabowl, Golden Press, 1969.
Dracula (juvenile adaptation of Bram Stoker's book), Dell (New York City), 1970.
Warlord of the Genji, Atheneum (New York City), 1970.
The Beggar King of China, Atheneum, 1971.
Good Morning, Hannah (picture book), Atheneum, 1972.
Good Morning Danny (picture book), Atheneum, 1972.
Awful Marshall (picture book), World, 1972.
The Mountain of Truth, Atheneum, 1972.
The Human Apes, Atheneum, 1973.
Baby Needs Shoes, Atheneum, 1974.
Triple Boy, Atheneum, 1977.
The Plant People, Atheneum, 1977.
Wild Heart, Atheneum, 1977.
The Shining Pool, Atheneum, 1979.
Call Me Amanda, Dutton (New York City), 1981.
Charlie the Hero, Dutton, 1982.
The Frog People, Dutton, 1983.
Manners That Matter: For People under Twenty-one, Dutton, 1983.

JENNY DEAN SCIENCE FICTION MYSTERIES

The Secret of the Third Eye, illustrated by Suzanne Richardson, Grosset (New York City), 1983.
The Mystery of the Hidden Trap, illustrated by Richardson, Grosset, 1983.
The Mystery of the Shining Children, illustrated by Richardson, Grosset, 1983.
The Secret of the Invisible City, illustrated by Richardson, Grosset, 1984.

JAMES BUDD MYSTERIES

The Mystery of the Madman at Cornwall Crag, illustrated by Tom Lapadula, Golden Book, 1984.

The Mystery of Galaxy Games, illustrated by Lapadula, Golden Book, 1984.

The Secret of Operation Brain, illustrated by Lapadula, Golden Book, 1984.

The Mystery of the Lost Princess, illustrated by Lapadula, Golden Book, 1984.

JUVENILE NONFICTION

Girls Are Equal Too, Atheneum, 1974.

Where's Your Head?, Atheneum, 1977.

Loving Sex for Both Sexes, F. Watts (New York City), 1979.

Boys Have Feelings Too, Atheneum, 1980.

Also author of home activity workbooks for Dell Home Activity Series, 1969.

OTHER

Miss Mary's Husbands (novel), Dodd, Mead (New York City), 1988.

Basic Wildlife Rehabilitation Series (six volumes), Bick, 1994-95.

Basic Manuals for Friends of the Disabled (four volumes), Bick, 1995-96.

WORK IN PROGRESS: *Kashmir on Fire,* a novel.

SIDELIGHTS: Dale Carlson told *CA* that she was prompted to write children's books "because of all the pleasure my books gave me as a child. I continue to write books for children because of the pleasure my own children take in reading good books." Carlson has lived and traveled extensively in the Far East, India, China, Japan, Nepal, Indonesia, and teaches writing and literature in India at the Krishnamurti Foundation schools during part of each year.

BIOGRAPHICAL/CRITICAL SOURCES:

PERIODICALS

New York Times Book Review, May 20, 1990, p. 46.

*   *   *

CARROLL, Theodus (Catherine) 1928-

PERSONAL: Given name is pronounced "The-*odd*-us"; born September 26, 1928, in Pittsburgh, PA; daughter of Randolph and Eleanor (Scanlon) Foster; divorced; children: Michael, Randolph. *Education:* Attended Duquesne University, 1946-48, and Carnegie Institute of Technology (now Carnegie-Mellon University), summers, 1946-48.

CAREER: Avon Products, Darien, CT, district sales manager, 1959-65; CCM Inc., Stamford, CT, account representative, 1966-67; Fiorelli Films, Stamford, writer, sales representative, 1967; *Health Care Product News,* New Canaan, CT, writer, 1966-75; Health Care Publications, New York City, executive editor, 1968-75; Garrard Publishing Company, New Canaan, CT, senior editor, children's books, 1976—.

WRITINGS:

Evil Is a Quiet Word (novel), Warner Books (New York City), 1976.

First Under the Wire: The World's Fastest Horses, 1900-1950 (juvenile), Silver Burdett (Morristown, NJ), 1978.

The Mystery of the Body Clocks (juvenile), Silver Burdett, 1979.

The Lost Christmas Star (juvenile; based on a story by Elizabeth Yates), Garrard (Easton, MD), 1979.

SIDELIGHTS: Theodus Carroll told *CA:* "Adults need the security behind the horror story in the same way that children need the scary fairy tale—to give them a stable framework on which to hang their fears, and say—that couldn't happen to me."*

*   *   *

CASSELLS, Cyrus (Curtis III) 1957-

PERSONAL: Born May 16, 1957, in Dover, DE; son of Cyrus Curtis, Jr. (an aerospace engineer) and Mary (a tutor; maiden name, Williston) Cassells. *Education:* Stanford University, B.A., 1979.

ADDRESSES: *Home*—c/o Cassells, 2190 Belden Pl., Escondido, CA 92029. *Agent*—Bill Thompson, Briarwood Writers Alliance, 61 Briarwood Cir., Needham Heights, MA 02194.

CAREER: Poet. Sally Walters Agency, San Francisco, CA, clerical worker, 1980; Harcourt Brace Jovanovich, Inc., San Francisco, production assistant in media department, 1980-81; Sally Walters Agency, clerical worker and political researcher, 1982; Fine Arts Work Center, Provincetown, MA, creative writing fellow, 1982-83; College of the Holy Cross, Worcester, MA, lecturer and poet-in-residence, 1989-92; Emerson College, Boston, MA, lecturer, 1992. Creative writing fellow at Millay Colony, Austerlitz, NY, summer, 1983, and at Yaddo, Saratoga Springs, NY, fall, 1983; poet-in-residence, Northeastern University, Boston, MA, and Assumption College, Worcester, MA, both 1990. Fellowship and outreach coordinator, Massachusetts Artists Foundation, 1989.

Member of board of directors, Writers League of Boston, 1988-92.

MEMBER: International PEN, Poetry Society of America.

AWARDS, HONORS: Award from National Council of Teachers of English, 1974, for creative writing; awards from Scholastic Magazines, 1975, for poems *Vertigo, The Changeling, November,* and *Sleepwalking,* and story *The Magic Cat Bone;* prize from Academy of American Poets, Stanford University, 1979, for *The Women* and *Landscape with Traveler;* prize from National Poetry Series, 1981-82, and poetry award nomination from Bay Area Book Reviewers Association, 1982, both for *The Mud Actor;* fellowship invitation from Helen Wurlitzer Foundation of Taos, 1983; creative writing award, *Callaloo,* 1984; Peter I. B. Lavan Younger Poet Award, 1992; Lannan literary fellowship in poetry, 1993; "Best Books of 1994" citation, *Publishers Weekly,* 1994, for *Soul Make a Path through Shouting.*

WRITINGS:

The Mud Actor (poetry), Holt (New York City), 1982.
Soul Make a Path through Shouting (poetry), Copper Canyon Press (Port Townsend, WA), 1994.

Film critic, *Bay Windows,* Boston, 1991. Contributor of poetry to periodicals, including *Sequoia, Quilt, WPA, Shankpainter,* and *Callaloo.* Author of *Bayok,* a short film on Filipino-American dancer Gregory Silva, 1980.

WORK IN PROGRESS: The Troubadours Are Still in Rome, a volume of poetry; *Doctor Free,* a play about the Underground Railroad, set in Boston in 1851.

SIDELIGHTS: In his postscript to *The Mud Actor,* poet Cyrus Cassells explains that it was conceived "as a single work, with the three sections written simultaneously to create a poetic triptych, a book of identities that ultimately embraces the possibility of reincarnation." The first sequence examines the poet's child-self; the second is related by a French turn-of-the-century persona named Henri Lecroix; the final episode emerges when Cassells assumes the identity of a bombing victim in Hiroshima. A reviewer for the *Fresno Bee* described *The Mud Actor* as "a vital metaphor for man's necessity to confront history, his own life, himself." "It is a complex poem," added the critic, "moving in parts more than the whole, but it is an impressive piece, and richly rewarding to those who read it."

Other critics also reacted favorably. Andy Brumer, in the *San Francisco Chronicle,* called Cassells's third sequence, *The Memory of Hiroshima,* "a breathtaking piece." The reviewer further noted, "In a language as moving as it is clear, the poem is a reconciliation of our shameful past with the hope for a humane future." *San Francisco Review*

of Books critic Emily Leider admired Cassells's "ease and inventiveness with the language, a capacity to assume multiple identities, and an enveloping humanity."

Cassells, who speaks Spanish as a second language and has travelled extensively abroad, told *CA:* "My poetry is deeply rooted in my world travels and spiritual questing; it is characteristically panoramic, multicultural, and internationalist in spirit. I consider myself an African-American seeker, ambassador, and citizen of the world."

BIOGRAPHICAL/CRITICAL SOURCES:

PERIODICALS

Callaloo, February, 1984.
Fresno Bee, April 17, 1983.
Los Angeles Times, August 8, 1982.
Milwaukee Journal, July 11, 1982.
San Francisco Chronicle, November 30, 1982.
San Francisco Review of Books, January, 1983.

*   *   *

CHARLES, Donald
   See MEIGHAN, Donald Charles

*   *   *

CHILCOTE, Ronald H. 1935-

PERSONAL: Born February 20, 1935, in Cleveland, OH; son of Lee A. (a businessman) and Katherine (Hodell) Chilcote; married Frances Tubby, January 6, 1961; children: Stephen, Edward. *Education:* Dartmouth College, B.A., 1957; Stanford University, M.B.A., 1959, M.A., 1963, Ph.D., 1965; University of Lisbon, Diploma Superior, 1960; University of Madrid, Diploma Estudios Hispanicos, 1961.

ADDRESSES: Home—1940 San Remo Dr., Laguna Beach, CA 92651. *Office*—Department of Economics, University of California, Riverside, CA 92502.

CAREER: Stanford University, Stanford, CA, assistant director of Institute of Hispanic American and Luso-Brazilian Studies, 1961-63; University of California, Riverside, 1963—, began as assistant professor, currently professor of political science and economics.

MEMBER: International Political Science Association, Latin American Studies Association, American Political Science Association.

AWARDS, HONORS: University of California faculty fellowship, 1965; Haynes Foundation fellowship, 1966; Organization of American States grant, 1971; Social Science

Research Council grants, 1971 and 1974-75; Fulbright senior lectureship and grant (Brazil), 1983, 1984, 1991, and 1992.

WRITINGS:

The Press in Spain, Portugal, and Latin America: A Summary of Recent Developments, Institute of Hispanic American and Luso-Brazilian Studies, Stanford University (Stanford, CA), 1963.

Portuguese Africa, Prentice-Hall (Englewood Cliffs, NJ), 1967.

Spain's Iron and Steel Industry (monograph), Bureau of Business Research, University of Texas (Austin, TX), 1968.

Emerging Nationalism in Portuguese Africa: A Bibliography of Documentary Ephemera through 1965, Hoover Institution on War, Revolution, and Peace, 1969, new edition, 1972.

(Compiler) *Protest and Resistance in Angola and Brazil,* University of California Press (Berkeley, CA), 1972.

The Brazilian Communist Party: Conflict and Integration, 1922-1972, Oxford University Press, 1974.

(Editor with Joel C. Edelstein) *Latin America: The Struggle with Dependency and Beyond,* Schenkman (Cambridge, MA), 1974.

(Compiler) *Brazil and Its Radical Left: An Annotated Bibliography, 1922-1972,* Kraus International (Millwood, NY), 1981.

Theories of Comparative Politics: The Search for a Paradigm, Westview (Boulder, CO), 1981, revised edition, 1994.

(Editor) *Dependency and Marxism: Toward a Resolution of the Debate,* Westview, 1982.

O Partido Comunista Brasileiro, Edicoes Graal, 1982.

(Editor with Dale Johnson) *Theories of Development: Mode of Production or Dependency?,* Sage Publications (Beverly Hills, CA), 1983.

Theories of Development and Underdevelopment, Westview, 1984.

(Compiler with Sherry C. Lutjens) *Cuba, 1953-1978: A Bibliographical Guide to the Literature,* two volumes, Kraus International, 1986.

(With Joel C. Edelstein) *Latin America: Capitalist and Socialist Perspectives of Development and Underdevelopment,* Westview, 1986.

(Editor) *The Portuguese Revolution of 25 April 1974,* University of Coimbra, volume 1, 1987, volume 2, 1990.

Power and the Ruling Classes in Northeast Brazil: Juazeiro and Petrolina in Transition, Cambridge University Press, 1990.

(With others) *Transitions from Dictatorship to Democracy,* Taylor and Francis, 1990.

Amilcar Cabral, Revolutionary Theory and Practice, Lynne Rienner Publisher, 1991.

Contributor to several books, including *International Business Management,* edited by Ewing and Meissner, Wadsworth (Belmont, CA), 1964; *Southern Africa in Perspective,* edited by Potholm and Dale, Free Press (New York City), 1972; *Cities in the Third World,* edited by Abu-Lughod and Hay, Maaroufa Press, 1977; *Dialectics of Third World Development,* edited by Vogeler and Souza, Allanheld, Osmun, (Totowa, NJ), 1980; and *New Directions in Comparative Politics,* edited by Wiarda, Westview, 1985. Also editor of volume on "The Americas," *Worldmark Encyclopedia of Nations,* 1963; also contributor to encyclopedias and yearbooks. Contributor of about one hundred fifty articles and reviews to journals and newspapers, including *Latin American Research Review, Comparative Political Studies, Nation, New Republic, Journal of Modern African Studies, International Journal of Comparative Sociology,* and *Los Angeles Times.* Assistant editor of *Hispanic American Report,* 1961-63; managing editor of *Latin American Perspectives,* 1974—.

WORK IN PROGRESS: A synthesis on comparative political economy and a book on *State and Class in Portugal.*

*   *   *

CLARKE, Brenda (Margaret Lilian) 1926-
(Brenda Honeyman; Kate Sedley, a pseudonym)

PERSONAL: Born July 30, 1926, in Bristol, England; daughter of Edward (an insurance agent) and Lilian Rose (Brown) Honeyman; married Ronald John Clarke (a civil servant), March 5, 1955; children: Roger Stephen, Gwithian Margaret. *Education:* Cambridge University, school certificate, 1942. *Politics:* Socialist. *Religion:* Methodist. *Avocational interests:* Theater, reading, history, music.

ADDRESSES: Home—25 Torridge Rd., Keynsham, Bristol, Avon BS18 1QQ, England. *Agent*—David Grossman Literary Agency Ltd., 110/114 Clerkenwell Rd., London EC1M 5SA, England.

CAREER: British Civil Service, Ministry of Labour, Bristol, England, clerical officer, 1942-55; writer, 1968—. Section leader for British Red Cross, 1941-45.

MEMBER: Society of Authors, Wessex Writers' Association.

WRITINGS:

The Glass Island, Collins (London), 1978.
The Lofty Banners, Fawcett (New York City), 1980.
The Far Morning, Fawcett, 1982.
All through the Day, Hamlyn Paperbacks (London), 1983.
A Rose in May, Hutchinson (London), 1984.
Three Women, Hutchinson, 1985.
Winter Landscape, Century Hutchinson (London), 1986.

Under Heaven, Transworld Publishers (London), 1988.
Riches of the Heart, Pinnacle Books (New York City), 1989 (originally published in England as *An Equal Chance*).
Sisters and Lovers, Pinnacle Books, 1990.
Beyond the World, Transworld Publishers, 1991.
A Durable Fire, Transworld Publishers, 1993.

UNDER NAME BRENDA HONEYMAN

Richard by Grace of God, R. Hale (London), 1968.
The Kingmaker, R. Hale, 1969.
Richmond and Elizabeth, R. Hale, 1970, Pinnacle Books, 1973.
Harry the King, R. Hale, 1971, published as *The Warrior King,* Pinnacle Books, 1972.
Brother Bedford, R. Hale, 1972.
Good Duke Humphrey, R. Hale, 1973.
The King's Minions, R. Hale, 1974.
The Queen and Mortimer, R. Hale, 1974.
Edward the Warrior, R. Hale, 1975.
All the King's Sons, R. Hale, 1976.
The Golden Griffin, R. Hale, 1976.
At the King's Court, R. Hale, 1977.
A King's Tale, R. Hale, 1977.
Macbeth, King of Scots, R. Hale, 1977.
Emma, the Queen, R. Hale, 1978.
Harold of the English, R. Hale, 1979.

UNDER PSEUDONYM KATE SEDLEY

Death and the Chapman, St. Martin's (New York City), 1991.
The Plymouth Cloak, St. Martin's, 1992.
The Hanged Man, St. Martin's, 1993.
The Holy Innocents, Headline (London), 1994.

OTHER

Some of Clarke's books have been published in German, French, and Italian.

SIDELIGHTS: Brenda Clarke once told *CA:* "Acquiring an agent changed the course of my writing career. Instead of 'factional' novels about the Middle Ages and Saxon England, [my agent] persuaded me to turn my attention to romantic fiction."

She adds: "Several years ago, I felt the urge to return to my first love, historical fiction, but decided this time to combine it with one of my favourite forms of entertainment, the detective novel. The result has been a series of books, written under the pseudonym Kate Sedley, featuring Roger the Chapman, a lapsed Benedictine monk (which means he can read and write) now travelling late fifteenth-century England as a pedlar and solving various crimes as he goes. The background is the final years of the Wars of the Roses."

CLARKE, Lea
See ROWLAND-ENTWISTLE, (Arthur) Theodore (Henry)

*   *   *

CLIMO, Shirley   1928-
(Shirley Beistle)

PERSONAL: Born November 25, 1928, in Cleveland, OH; daughter of Morton J. (a paving contractor) and Aldarilla (a writer; maiden name, Shipley) Beistle; married George F. Climo (a corporate historian), June 17, 1950; children: Robert, Susan, Lisa. *Education:* Attended De-Pauw University, 1946-49. *Politics:* "Variable." *Religion:* Protestant.

ADDRESSES: Home—24821 Prospect Ave., Los Altos, CA 94022.

CAREER: WGAR-Radio, Cleveland, OH, scriptwriter for weekly juvenile series *Fairytale Theatre,* 1949-53; free-lance writer, 1976—. President of Morning Forum of Los Altos, 1971-73.

MEMBER: California Writers, Society of Children's Book Writers.

WRITINGS:

FOR CHILDREN

Piskies, Spriggans, and Other Magical Beings: Tales from the Droll-Teller, Retold by Shirley Climo, illustrated by Joyce Audy dos Santos, Crowell (New York City), 1981.
The Cobweb Christmas (picture book), illustrated by Joe Lasker, Crowell, 1982.
Gopher, Tanker, and the Admiral, illustrated by Eileen McKeating, Crowell, 1984.
Someone Saw a Spider, illustrated by Dirk Zimmer, Crowell, 1985.
A Month of Seven Days (historical novel), Crowell, 1987.
King of the Birds (picture book), illustrated by Ruth Heller, Harper (New York City), 1988.
T. J.'s Ghost, Crowell, 1988.
The Egyptian Cinderella (picture book), illustrated by Heller, Crowell, 1989.
City! San Francisco, photographs by George Ancona, Macmillan (New York City), 1990.
City! New York, photographs by Ancona, Macmillan, 1990.
City! Washington, D.C., photographs by Ancona, Macmillan, 1991.
The Match Between the Winds, illustrated by Roni Shepherd, Macmillan, 1991.
The Korean Cinderella (picture book), illustrated by Heller, HarperCollins (New York City), 1993.

Why Monkeys Live in Trees, illustrated by Karen Barbour, HarperCollins, 1993.

Stolen Thunder: A Norse Myth, illustrated by Alexander Koshkin, Clarion (New York City), 1994.

Atalanta's Race: A Greek Myth, illustrated by Koshkin, Clarion, 1995.

The Little Red Ant and the Great Big Crumb, illustrated by Francisco X. Mora, Clarion, 1995.

The Irish Cinderlad, HarperCollins, in press.

OTHER

(Contributor) Sylvia K. Burack, *Writing and Selling Fillers, Light Verse, and Short Humor,* Writer, Inc. (Boston, MA), 1982.

Also contributor to anthologies, including *Explorations,* Houghton (Burlington, MA), 1986; *Family Read-Aloud Christmas Treasury,* Little, Brown (Boston, MA), 1989; and *Teacher's Read-Aloud Anthology,* McGraw-Hill (New York City), 1993. Contributor to magazines, including *Cricket, Family Weekly, Ranger Rick, Seventeen,* and *Writer,* and to newspapers.

WORK IN PROGRESS: A Treasury of Princesses, A Treasury of Mermaids, and *The Persian Cinderella,* all planned for publication by HarperCollins.

SIDELIGHTS: Shirley Climo told *CA:* "To write children's books always seemed the most wonderful goal in the world to me—and the most natural. My earliest memory is rocking in a creaky wicker porch swing while my mother, a children's author, recited her stories. Long before I could read, I'd begun telling my own tales to anyone willing to listen.

"When I was sixteen, my first magazine story for children was published. Since then, when I wasn't scribbling grocery lists or PTA bulletins, I've completed eighteen books for children and have two more in the works. Although I've written picture books for the 'just-in-school' set, story collections for middle grades, nonfiction, and novels for preteens, I never stray far away from the favorite folktales of my childhood. Researching folklore fascinates me, and retelling it to entertain today's young people without losing yesterday's flavor is both a pleasure and a challenge.

"Folklorist Andrew Lang once said, 'Nobody can write a new fairytale; you can only mix up and dress the old stories and put characters into new dresses.' For me, playing dress-up is fun at any age."

BIOGRAPHICAL/CRITICAL SOURCES:

PERIODICALS

Booklist, November, 1980; May 1, 1993; May 1, 1994.

Bulletin of the Center for Children's Books, March, 1986; October, 1987; February, 1988, p. 114; October, 1989, p. 30; June, 1993, p. 311.

Chicago Tribune Book World, December 12, 1982.

Kirkus Reviews, March 15, 1989, pp. 460-461.

Los Angeles Times Book Review, March 27, 1988, p. 12.

New York Times Book Review, July 5, 1981; November 12, 1989, p. 50; October 31, 1993, p. 26.

School Library Journal, February, 1981; December, 1985, p. 87; December, 1987, p. 84; August, 1988, p. 79; November, 1989, p. 105; March, 1991; December, 1991; July, 1994.

Writer, June, 1978; December, 1979.

*   *   *

CLOUTIER, David 1951-

PERSONAL: Surname is pronounced "Clou-*tyay*"; born April 20, 1951, in Providence, RI; son of Maurice Roger and Adeleine Alice (Abbott) Cloutier; married Anne Frances Greene (a visual artist), June 11, 1972; children: Perrin Taleisin. *Education:* Attended Goddard College, 1970; Brown University, A.B. and M.A., 1974.

ADDRESSES: c/o M. Cloutier, 108 Lakeland Rd., Cranston, RI 02910.

CAREER: Rhode Island State Council on the Arts, Rhode Island Arts in Education Project, East Greenwich, poetry specialist and program consultant, 1970-75, Rhode Island Governor's School for Youth in the Arts, assistant in poetry, 1970, poetry instructor, 1971-74, coordinator of planning committee for school, 1974; Copper Beech Press, Providence, RI, editor and designer, 1975-82; Brown University, Providence, teaching associate in journalism, spring, 1981; Martin Community College, Williamston, NC, visiting artist in poetry, 1981-83. Community Council for the Arts, Kinston, NC, executive director, 1984-86. Editor and designer, Hellcoal Press, 1972-73; founder and editor, Bonewhistle Press, 1973-75; free-lance editor and designer; founder and editor, *A Carolina Literary Companion,* 1985-86.

WRITINGS:

Spirit Spirit: Shaman Songs, Incantations, Copper Beech Press (Providence, RI), 1973, revised and enlarged edition, 1980.

Northwest Coast Songs (pamphlet), Blue Cloud, 1974.

(Editor with Stephen Coon and contributor of translations) *The Ear of the Bull: Nine French Poets,* Bonewhistle Press, 1974.

Ghost Call (poems), Copper Beech Press, 1976.

Tracks of the Dead (chapbook of poems), Blue Cloud, 1976.

(Translator) *White Road: Selected Poems of Claude Este-*
ban, Charioteer Press, 1979.

My Grandfather's House: Tlingit Songs of Death and Sor-
row, Holmgangers, 1980.

Tongue and Thunder (poems), Copper Beech Press, 1980.

(Translator) *Transparent God: Poems of Claude Esteban,*
Kosmos (San Francisco), 1982.

Soft Lightnings (poems), Copper Beech, 1982.

(Translator) *The Beaches of Thule: Poems by Jean Laude,*
Kosmos (San Francisco), 1984.

News of Love: Poems of Itafiz, Unicorn Press (Greensboro,
NC), 1984.

The Waters at Uliassutai: Ten Songs of the Torgot Mon-
gols, Firefly, 1987.

By the Stream of Antique Song: Versions of Poems Mostly
Oral, Singular Speech (Canton, CT), 1988.

Also author of *Other Lights,* in press. Contributor of
poems and translations to numerous periodicals, including
*Chelsea, Shaman, Stinktree, Prism International, Cincin-
nati Poetry Review,* and *Akwesasne Notes.* Editor of special
oral poetry issue, *Contemporary Literature in Translation,*
Number 28, 1977-78.

WORK IN PROGRESS: Prose poems, and versions of
works of Ibn Arabi, the twelfth-century Arab poet and
philosopher.*

* * *

COATES, J(ohn) F(rancis) 1922-

PERSONAL: Born March 30, 1922, in London, England;
son of Joseph Edward (a chemist) and Ada Maria (a
chemist; maiden name, Finney) Coates; married Jane
Waymouth (a homemaker), July 23, 1954; children:
Henry, Julian. *Education:* Queen's College, Oxford, M.A.,
1946; attended Royal Naval College, Greenwich.

ADDRESSES: Home—Sabinal, Lucklands Rd., Bath,
BA1 4AU, England.

CAREER: Constructor, Royal Corps of Naval Construc-
tors, 1943, Chatham Dockyard, 1951-53, Naval Construction Research Establishment, Dunfermline, Scotland,
1953-57; naval architect in ship department, Ministry of
Defence, 1957-64, chief constructor in fleet maintenance,
1964-70, head of forward design in ship department,
1970-71; affiliated with Royal College of Defence Studies,
1971-74; superintendent of Naval Construction Research
Establishment, Dunfermline, 1974-77; deputy director of
ship design, Ministry of Defence, 1977-79; writer and researcher, 1979—.

MEMBER: Royal Institute of Naval Architects (fellow),
Society for Nautical Research, Nautical Archaeology Society.

AWARDS, HONORS: Officer of the Order of the British
Empire, 1955; Caird Medal, National Maritime Museum,
London, 1991.

WRITINGS:

(Editor with Sean McGrail) *The Greek Trireme of the*
Fifth Century B.C., Trustees of the National Maritime
Museum (London), 1984.

(With J. S. Morrison) *The Athenian Trireme: The History*
and Reconstruction of an Ancient Greek Warship,
Cambridge University Press (Cambridge, England),
1986.

(With Morrison) *Greek and Roman Oared Warships,* Oxford University Press (Oxford, England), 1995.

Also contributor to nautical journals and to *The Age of the*
Galley, edited by Morrison, [London], 1994.

SIDELIGHTS: J. F. Coates told *CA:* "Having retired after
a career as a professional naval architect and having always been interested in nautical research, I am using my
retirement to investigate the naval architecture of ancient
and medieval oared warships."

With the help of the Trireme Trust and the support of the
Greek Navy, Coates has been able to design and have built
an authentic reproduction of an ancient Athenian Trireme. The tentative launch date for the ship's sea trials
was set for the early part of 1987. Since the Greek Trireme
was unsinkable and left no archaeological evidence, the research that culminated in the book *The Athenian Trireme:*
The History and Reconstruction of an Ancient Greek War-
ship was far-ranging and rigorous. Critic Peter Jones
wrote in the London *Times:* "Probably the most exciting
part of the book is J. F. Coates's chapter on the fundamentals of design and reconstruction." Jones added that the
chapter was illustrated with the author's "superbly detailed line-drawings."

BIOGRAPHICAL/CRITICAL SOURCES:

PERIODICALS

Times (London), October 9, 1986.
Times Literary Supplement, May 15, 1987.

* * *

COLLINS, Pat(ricia) Lowery 1932-

PERSONAL: Born October 6, 1932, in Los Angeles, CA;
daughter of Joseph Michael (an accountant) and Margaret
(a radio scriptwriter; maiden name, Meyer) Lowery; married Wallace Collins (a network engineer), April 18, 1953;
children: Christopher, Kimberly (Mrs. David Jermain),
Colleen, Cathlin, Mathias. *Education:* Attended the University of California, Los Angeles, 1949, and Immaculate

Heart College, 1950; University of Southern California, A.B., 1953; further study at Choinard Art Institute (Los Angeles, CA), De Cordova Museum (Lincoln, MA), and Brandeis University. *Politics:* Republican. *Religion:* Roman Catholic.

ADDRESSES: Home and office—3 Wauketa Rd., Gloucester, MA 01930-1423.

CAREER: Writer, artist, and illustrator. Fellow-in-residence, Millay Colony of the Arts, 1990. Has artwork in public and private collections in the U.S. and Japan; does commissioned portraits. Past teacher of pastels, Somerset Art Association, Far Hills, NJ. Conducts workshops on writing, gives poetry readings, and visits schools.

MEMBER: Society of Children's Book Writers, Authors Guild, Authors League of America.

AWARDS, HONORS: First place winner, *American Health Magazine* short story contest, 1988; individual artist's fellowship in fiction, New Hampshire State Council on the Arts, 1991; selection as one of "Children's Books of the Year," Child Study Children's Book Committee, 1992, and selection as a Reading Rainbow book, 1994, both for *I Am an Artist;* selection as a "Book of the Year," Ohio Reading Circle, for *Don't Tease the Guppies.*

WRITINGS:

My Friend Andrew (juvenile), illustrated by Howard Berelson, Prentice-Hall (Englewood Cliffs, NJ), 1981.
The River Shares Its Secret (textbook), Houghton (Boston), 1981.
Tumble Tumble Tumbleweed (juvenile), illustrated by Charles Robinson, Albert Whitman (Niles, IL), 1982.
Taking Care of Tucker (juvenile), illustrated by Maxie Chambliss, Putnam (New York City), 1989.
Waiting for Baby Joe (juvenile), illustrated by Joan Whinham Dunn, Albert Whitman, 1990.
Tomorrow, Up and Away (juvenile), illustrated by Lynn Munsinger, Houghton, 1990.
I Am an Artist (juvenile), illustrated by Robin Brickman, Millbrook Press, 1992.
Don't Tease the Guppies (juvenile), illustrated by Marylin Hafner, Putnam, 1994.
(Illustrator) Isabel Joshlin Glaser, compiler, *Sports, Power, and Dreams of Glory* (poetry anthology), Atheneum (New York City), 1995.

Contributor to *Ten Times Round,* Ginn & Co., 1987; *Mystery Sneaker,* Ginn & Co., 1987; and *The 1994 Writer's Handbook.* Contributor to anthologies, including *Anthology of Writing by Women,* University of Chicago Press (Chicago), 1980. Contributor to periodicals, including *Writer, Northshore, Small Pond Review, WIND/Literary Journal, My Own Magazine, Parting Gifts,* and *Ad Hoc Monadnock.*

WORK IN PROGRESS: Poetry and short stories; *On the Air,* an adult novel; *Mika's Garden,* a young adult novel; *Between Two Rivers,* an author-illustrated picture book; other picture books.

SIDELIGHTS: Pat Lowery Collins told *CA:* "As a writer, I'm a poet first and believe that children's picture books are like good poetry in their simplicity and singular vision. Writing them hones my skills for all levels of poetry.

"My work takes other directions as well, into older juvenile fiction, adult fiction, and some nonfiction, and I always have work in progress in many areas. Having the space and time for close observation of the world and people in it is a necessary part of the creative process for me and what I had in mind when writing my book *I Am an Artist,* which advances the premise that art is more process that product. I will mull over an idea for minutes or months—even years—working it out in my head or on paper. When I'm finally ready to pull a story together, my best writing is done in the morning, and since I always read over and revise what I've written on the computer the day before, there is rarely anything that could be called a first draft.

"I'm also a visual artist and an illustrator. The major link between my painting and writing is my abiding interest in people—how they think, what they feel, their expressions, the things that touch their lives—which I may try to capture at one time with words and at another with paint, pencil, or pastel.

"Coming from a family of writers, I always understood that reading is an integral part of learning to be a writer and that the great writers of the past and present are the best teachers of how to use words well and how to craft compelling stories."

BIOGRAPHICAL/CRITICAL SOURCES:

PERIODICALS

Philadelphia Inquirer, May 8, 1994.
Publishers Weekly, December 23, 1988, p. 81.

* * *

COMPTON-HALL, (Patrick) Richard 1929-

PERSONAL: Born July 12, 1929, in Reigate, England; son of Richard William (a surveyor) and Gwynedd (Goode) Compton-Hall; married Gillian Slade-Baker, March 29, 1952 (deceased); married Eve Kilpatrick, December 27, 1962; children: Richard Mark, Simon Cunynghame (deceased). *Education:* Attended Naval Staff College, 1961-62, and Joint Services Staff College, 1966-67. *Poli-*

tics: "Old-fashioned socialist." *Religion:* Church of England.

ADDRESSES: Home—Upper Ffynnon Fair, Rhayader, Powys LD6 5LA, Wales.

CAREER: Royal Navy, career officer and submarine specialist, 1943-68, loaned to U.S. Navy as operations analysis officer for the submarine development group, 1958-60, retired as commander; John Lewis Partnership (department store and supermarket chain), London, England, director of services, 1968-71; full-time writer in France, 1971-75; Royal Navy Submarine Museum, Gosport, England, director and curator, 1975-94. Part-time technical translator for French government, 1977—. Lecturer/historian and submarine consultant, 1975—. Commentator for radio and television shows, including *Steel Boots, Iron Men,* Public TV, 1989, and *Sharks of Steel,* Discovery, 1992.

MEMBER: Society of Authors, Translators Association.

AWARDS, HONORS: Order of the British Empire, 1964.

WRITINGS:

Below Us Bootle (cassette recording of humorous submarine short stories), Royal Navy Submarine Museum (Gosport, England), 1980.
Submarines, Wayland (Sussex, England), 1982.
The Underwater War, 1939-1945, Sterling, 1982.
Submarine Boats, Conway Maritime Press (London, England), 1983.
The Submariner's World, Kenneth Mason Publications, 1983.
(Translator) *Naval Warfare Today and Tomorrow,* Basil Blackwell (Oxford, England), 1983.
Submarine Warfare, Ronstras & Ridgets, Sterling, 1985.
Lessons and Experiences of Submarine Warfare (published in Chinese), People's Liberation Army, 1987.
(With John Moore) *Submarine Warfare Today and Tomorrow,* Adler & Adler, 1987.
Submarine versus Submarine: The Tactics and Technology of Underwater Warfare, Orion (New York City), 1988.
Submarines and the War at Sea, 1914-18, Macmillan (London), 1991.

Radio and television writer. Frequent contributor to history and military journals.

SIDELIGHTS: Richard Compton-Hall once told *CA:* "My writing career arose from my having taken the first *conventional* submarine, *H.M.S. Grampus,* deep under the polar ice pack with some difficulty, damage, and a good deal of pleasurable excitement. The Navy required articles for journals and newspapers. The discovery that serious, even dangerous and highly classified operations and events can be treated as light comedy, and make a far greater impression than when treated heavily, led to a style that has since (apparently) become popular and much in demand.

"In particular I find a light approach evokes an important point to be made (one only!) in each book, article, or broadcast; and that one point is usually accepted, with this light treatment, by the people I am aiming at—politicians, senior naval officers, and the public alike. The most significant success in this direction is my plea in *The Underwater War* for much more effort and money to be spent on truly proving weapon systems in peacetime because otherwise they simply will not work in war, whatever highly prejudiced claims manufacturers and over-optimistic officers in all navies may make. In other words, my campaign in this respect is against 'wishful thinking,' particularly evident in the United States and Royal navies.

"My continuing campaign is against arrogance—in the church, business, trade unions, politics, and wherever; comedy, or at least light humor, is a splendid weapon."

*   *   *

CONSTANTELOS, Demetrios J.   1927-
(Dimitris Stachys)

PERSONAL: Born July 27, 1927, in Spilia, Messenia, Greece; naturalized U.S. citizen in 1958; son of John B. (a farmer) and Christine (Psilopoulos) Constantelos; married Stella Croussouloudis, August 15, 1954; children: Christine, John, Helen, Maria. *Education:* Holy Cross Greek Orthodox Theological School, Diploma in Theology, 1951, B.A., 1958; Princeton Theological Seminary, Th.M., 1959; Rutgers University, M.A., 1963, Ph.D., 1965.

ADDRESSES: Home—304 Forest Dr., Linwood, NJ 08221. *Office*—Arts and Humanities, Richard Stockton College of New Jersey, Pomona, NJ 08240.

CAREER: St. Demetrios Greek Orthodox Church, Perth Amboy, NJ, pastor, 1955-64; Dumbarton Oaks Research Library, Washington, D.C., junior fellow, 1964-65; Holy Cross Greek Orthodox Theological School, Brookline, MA, assistant professor, 1965-67, associate professor of history, 1967-71; Stockton State College (now Richard Stockton College of New Jersey), Pomona, NJ, professor of history and religious studies, 1971-86, Charles Cooper Townsend Distinguished Professor of History and Religious Studies, 1986—. Visiting lecturer in history, Boston College, 1967-68, and New York University, 1991. Member of U.S. National Committee for Byzantine Studies. Representative of Greek Orthodox Archdiocese of North and South America at national and international congresses.

MEMBER: American Historical Association, American Society of Church History, Mediaeval Academy of America, American Academy of Religion, Orthodox Theological Society of America (president, 1968-71).

AWARDS, HONORS: D.D. honoris causa, Holy Cross Greek Orthodox Theological Seminary/Hellenic College, 1991.

WRITINGS:

An Old Faith for Modern Man, Greek Orthodox Archdiocese (New York City), 1964.

The Greek Orthodox Church: History, Faith and Practice, Seabury (New York City), 1967.

Byzantine Philanthropy and Social Welfare, Rutgers University Press (New Brunswick, NJ), 1968, 2nd edition, 1991.

Marriage, Sexuality, and Celibacy: A Greek Orthodox Perspective, Light & Life Press (Winona Lake, IN), 1975.

Understanding the Greek Orthodox Church, Seabury, 1982, 2nd edition, Holy Cross Orthodox (Brookline, MA), 1990.

Byzantine Kleronomia, Damascus Publishing (Athens), 1990.

Poverty, Society and Philanthropy in the Late Medieval Greek World, Caratzas Publishing (New Rochelle, NY), 1992.

Ethnike Tautoteta Kai Threskeutike Idiaiteroteta, Damascus Publishing, 1993.

Christian Hellenism, Caratzas Publishing, 1995.

EDITOR

Encyclicals and Documents of the Greek Orthodox Archdiocese, Institute for Patristic Studies, 1975.

(With C. J. Efthymiou) *Greece: Today and Tomorrow,* Krikos, 1979.

Orthodox Theology and Diakonia: Trends and Prospects, Hellenic College Press (Brookline, MA), 1981.

OTHER

Contributor to numerous books, including *The Oxford Annotated Apocrypha,* edited by Bruce M. Metzger, Oxford University Press (Oxford, England), 1977; *Orthodox Synthesis: The Unity of Theological Thought,* edited by J. J. Allen, St. Vladimir's Seminary (Crestwood, NY), 1981; and *The Encyclopedia of Religion,* edited by Mircea Eliade, Macmillan (New York City), 1987. Contributor to *Dictionary of the Middle Ages,* edited by Joseph R. Strayer, Scribner (New York City), 1982—. Also contributor of more than forty studies, essays, articles, and reviews, some under pseudonym Dimitris Stachys, to theology, history, and popular publications in both the U.S. and Greece.

Some of Constantelos's books have been translated into Greek.

*   *   *

COTTINGHAM, John (Graham)   1943-

PERSONAL: Born July 12, 1943, in London, England; married in 1969; children: two. *Education:* St. John's College, Oxford, B.A. (with double first class honors), 1966, M.A., 1969, D.Phil., 1973.

ADDRESSES: Office—Department of Philosophy, University of Reading, Reading RG6 2AA, England.

CAREER: University of Washington, Seattle, lecturer in philosophy, 1967-68; Oxford University, Oxford, England, lecturer in philosophy at Exeter College, 1968-71; University of Reading, Reading, England, lecturer, 1971-87, reader, 1987-90, professor of philosophy, 1990—, department head, 1989- -. Scholar in residence, Randolph-Macon Woman's College, 1987. Consultant to Oxford University Press, Cambridge University Press, Basil Blackwell, Routledge, Collins, and other publishers.

MEMBER: British Society for the History of Philosophy (chair, 1992-95), Association for Legal and Social Philosophy.

AWARDS, HONORS: Fulbright scholar, 1987.

WRITINGS:

Descartes' Conversation with Burman, Oxford University Press (Oxford, England), 1976.

Rationalism: A Selective Critical Survey of Rationalist Thought from Plato to the Present Day, HarperCollins (New York City), 1984.

Descartes, Basil Blackwell (Oxford, England), 1986.

A History of Western Philosophy, Volume 4: *The Rationalists,* Oxford University Press, 1989.

The Olympian Vision: A Study of Descartes' "Discours de la methode," Lindau (Turin), 1991.

A Descartes Dictionary, Blackwell, 1991.

EDITOR

(And translator, with Robert Stoothoff and Dugald Murdoch; Volume 3 with A. Kenny) Rene Descartes, *The Philosophical Writings of Descartes,* three volumes, Cambridge University Press (Cambridge, England), 1985-91.

(And translator) Rene Descartes, *Descartes: Meditations on First Philosophy and Selections from the Objections and Replies,* Cambridge University Press, 1986.

The Cambridge Companion to Descartes, Cambridge University Press, 1993.

Reason, Will and Sensation: Studies in Cartesian Metaphysics, Oxford University Press, 1994.

OTHER

(Translator with Stoothoff and Murdoch) Rene Descartes, *Descartes: Selected Philosophical Writings,* Cambridge University Press, 1988.

Contributor to books, including *German Men of Letters,* Volume 6, edited by A. Natan and B. Keith-Smith, Wolff, 1972; *Philosophers Ancient and Modern,* Cambridge University Press, 1986; *Legal and Ethical Aspects of Medicine,* edited by M. Ockelton, Steiner Verlag (Wiesbaden), 1987; also to *Dictionary of Philosophy, Makers of Modern Culture, Oxford Companion to Mind,* and *Encyclopaedia of Philosophy.* Associate editor and contributor, *Croom Helm Encyclopaedia of Philosophy,* Croom Helm, 1987; reviews editor, *Cogito,* 1990—; member of editorial board, *UK Journal for the History of Philosophy,* 1990—; editor, *Ratio, An International Journal of Analytical Philosophy.* Contributor of approximately fifty articles and reviews to philosophy journals.

BIOGRAPHICAL/CRITICAL SOURCES:

PERIODICALS

Choice, April, 1994, p. 1307.
Times Educational Supplement, March 27, 1987, p. 29; February 17, 1989, p. B6.
Times Literary Supplement, March 29, 1985, p. 365; May 2, 1986; April 10, 1987, p. 80; April 28, 1989, p. 448.

*   *   *

CROLL, Carolyn 1945-

PERSONAL: Born May 20, 1945, in Sioux Falls, SD; daughter of Lionel and Evelyn A. (Rosen) Croll. *Education:* Philadelphia College of Art, B.F.A., 1967.

ADDRESSES: Home and office—1420 Locust St., No. 37E, Philadelphia, PA 19102.

CAREER: Freelance illustrator and writer. Has conducted workshops.

MEMBER: Philadelphia Children's Reading Round Table.

AWARDS, HONORS: World of Reading Readers Choice Award, Silver Burdett & Ginn, for *Too Many Babas;* selection as a "Pick of the Year," Federation of Children's Books Groups (U.K.), 1989, for *The Little Snowgirl;* First Lady Barbara Bush read *The Little Snowgirl* on the 1989 NBC-TV White House Christmas Special, and she selected *The Three Brothers* to be read by actor Gerald McRaney on *Mrs. Bush's Story Time,* a radio broadcast for the Children's Literacy Initiative; Drexel Citation, Drexel University College of Information Studies and

Free Library of Philadelphia, 1990, for special achievement in the field of children's books.

WRITINGS:

SELF-ILLUSTRATED CHILDREN'S BOOKS

Too Many Babas (Weekly Reader Book Club selection), Harper (New York City), 1979, full color edition, HarperCollins (New York City), 1994.
The Little Snowgirl, Putnam (New York City), 1989.
The Three Brothers, Putnam, 1991.
Redoute: The Man Who Painted Flowers, Putnam, 1996.

ILLUSTRATOR

Jane Flory, *Ramshackle Roost,* Houghton (Boston), 1972.
Flory, *We'll Have a Friend for Lunch,* Houghton, 1974.
Peter Limburg, *What's in the Names of Stars and Constellations,* Coward, 1976.
Flory, *The Unexpected Grandchildren,* Houghton, 1977.
Flory, *The Bear on the Doorstep,* Houghton, 1980.
Eleanor Coerr, *The Big Balloon Race,* Harper, 1981, full color edition, HarperCollins, 1992.
Nancy Smiler Levinson, *Clara and the Bookwagon,* Harper, 1988.
Melvin Berger, *Switch On, Switch Off,* Crowell (New York City), 1989.
Lynda DeWitt, *What Will the Weather Be?,* HarperCollins, 1992.
Lee Bennett Hopkins, *Questions,* HarperCollins, 1992.
Mary Packard, *The Story of Christmas* (Advent calendar), Workman Publishing (New York City), 1994.
Katharine Ross, *The Story of the Pilgrims,* Random House (New York City), in press.
Ann Rockwell, *Sweet Potato Pie,* Random House, in press.

OTHER

Contributor to *New York Times Book Review.*

Some of Croll's work has been published in foreign countries, including Norway, Sweden, Denmark, Iceland, South Africa, and Spain, and in South America.

ADAPTATIONS: The Little Snowgirl was produced as a videocassette by American School Publishers.

SIDELIGHTS: "I consider myself an artist, rather than a writer," Carolyn Croll once told *CA.* "I have come to writing through illustration, because I have the desire to make books for children and sometimes lack good material from other sources. I am very interested in history and the decorative arts, particularly European arts and history, and I love to travel. I've been to England, Scotland, France, Italy, Russia, Belgium, and the Netherlands. I collect folk art, hand-crafted toys, and original book illustrations. There are many creative people on both sides of my family, so I come by my interests quite naturally, I think."

*   *   *

CROSS, K(athryn) Patricia 1926-

PERSONAL: Born March 17, 1926, in Normal, IL; daughter of Clarence L. (a professor) and Katherine (Dague) Cross. *Education:* Illinois State University, B.S., 1948; University of Illinois, A.M., 1951, Ph.D., 1958.

ADDRESSES: Home—904 Oxford St., Berkeley, CA 94707. *Office*—3531 Tolman, University of California, Berkeley, CA 94720.

CAREER: Harvard Community High School, Harvard, IL, mathematics teacher, 1948-49; University of Illinois at Urbana-Champaign, research assistant in department of psychology, 1949-53, assistant dean of women, 1953-59; Cornell University, Ithaca, NY, dean of women, 1959-60, dean of students, 1960-63; Educational Testing Service, Princeton, NJ, director of college and university programs, 1963-66, and Berkeley, CA, director of college and university programs, 1966-69, senior research psychologist, 1969-76, distinguished research scientist, 1976-82; Harvard University, Cambridge, MA, professor of higher education, 1980-88, chair of department of administration, planning, and social policy, 1984-87; University of California, Berkeley, Elizabeth and Edward Conner Professor of Education, 1988—.

Research educator, Center for Research and Development in Higher Education, University of California, Berkeley, 1966-77; visiting professor, University of Nebraska, 1975-76; lecturer on higher education, University of California, Berkeley, 1977-80; Delta Sigma Epsilon national lecturer, 1981; visiting scholar, Miami-Dade Community College, fall, 1987. American Council on Education, commissioner or chair of several commissions, 1975-88; member of board of trustees, Antioch College, 1976-78, Council for the Advancement of Experiential Learning, 1982-85, and Bradford College, 1986-88; member of national advisory board, Kellogg Foundation Project, Center of Developmental Education, Appalachian State University, 1977—, and Oklahoma Board of Regents, 1985-88; member of board of directors and member of planning committee, National Center for Higher Education Management, 1980-83; chair of national planning board, Project for Enhancing State Role in Lifelong Learning, Education Commission of the States, 1980-83; member of research review board, Carnegie Foundation for the Advancement of Teaching, 1980-83; commissioner, New England Association of Schools and Colleges, Commission on Institutions of Higher Education,

1982-85, and American Association of Community and Junior Colleges study; member of board of directors, Council of Universities and Colleges, 1984-87; member of board of overseers, Regents College Degrees and Examinations, University of the State of New York.

Member of numerous government and private sector committees and councils, including Higher Education Colloquium, 1971—, National Commission on Future Academic Leadership, 1985—, and Higher Education Research Program of Pew Charitable Trusts, 1986-89. Participant in professional conferences, seminars, and meetings in the U.S. and abroad, 1979—. Fellow, National Policy Center on Education, Leisure, and Continuing Opportunities for Older Americans, 1982—. Consultant for numerous government and education organizations.

MEMBER: American Association of Higher Education (member of board of directors, 1972-75; vice president, 1973-74, 1987-88; president, 1974-75, 1988-89); National Academy of Education (vice chair, 1981-83).

AWARDS, HONORS: Foundation for Economic Education fellowship in industry, 1962; Best Books Award, Pi Lambda Theta, 1968, for *The Junior College Student: A Research Description;* Outstanding Books in Education Award, *School and Society,* 1971, for *Beyond the Open Door: New Students to Higher Education;* award for outstanding contribution to research, National Association of Student Personnel Administrators, 1972; Medallion of Honor, University of Illinois Mothers' Association, 1973; selected as one of forty-four leaders in American higher education, *Change* magazine poll, 1975; Borden Medal, American Council on Education, 1976, for *Accent on Learning: Improving Instruction and Reshaping the Curriculum;* Delbert Clark Award, 1979, for exceptional contributions to the advancement of adult education; Distinguished Alumni Award, Illinois State University, 1980; Regents Medal of Excellence, Board of Regents of University of the State of New York, 1984, for "outstanding contributions to the cause of human development and lifelong learning"; E. F. Lindquist Award, American Educational Research Association, 1986, for research on student development; Adult Educator of the Year, Coalition of Adult Education Organizers, 1987; National Person of the Year, National Council on Community Services and Continuing Education, 1988. LL.D., Illinois State University, 1970; L.H.D., Grand Valley State College, 1975, Hood College, 1979, Marymount Manhattan College, 1982, College of Saint Mary, 1985, DePaul University, 1986, and Thomas Jefferson University, 1987; Sc.D., Northeastern University, 1975, Loyola University of Chicago, 1980; Ped.D., Our Lady of the Lake University, 1977; Litt.D., State University of New York, 1988.

WRITINGS:

(With R. Linn and J. Davis) *A Guide to Research Design: Institutional Research Program for Higher Education,* Educational Testing Service (Princeton, NJ), 1965.

The Junior College Student: A Research Description, Educational Testing Service, 1968.

Beyond the Open Door: New Students to Higher Education, Jossey-Bass (San Francisco), 1971.

New Students and New Needs in Higher Education, Center for Research and Development in Higher Education, University of California, 1972.

(Editor with S. B. Gould, and contributor) *Explorations in Non-Traditional Studies,* Jossey-Bass, 1972.

The Integration of Learning and Earning: Cooperative Education and Non-Traditional Study, American Association for Higher Education (Washington, DC), 1973.

(With John R. Valley and others) *Planning Non-Traditional Programs: An Analysis of the Issues for Postsecondary Education,* Jossey-Bass, 1974.

Accent on Learning: Improving Instruction and Reshaping the Curriculum, Jossey-Bass, 1976.

The Missing Link: Connecting Adult Learners to Learning Resources (monograph), College Board (New York City), 1978.

Adults as Learners, Jossey-Bass, 1981.

(With Anne-Marie McCartan) *Adult Learning: State Policies and Institutional Practices,* Association for the Study of Higher Education (ASHE)/ERIC (Washington, DC), 1984.

(With McCartan) *Older Students, New Issues: State Responses to Adult Learning,* ASHE/ERIC, 1984.

(With Thomas A. Angelo) *Classroom Assessment Techniques: A Handbook for Faculty,* National Center for Research to Improve Postsecondary Teaching and Learning, University of Michigan (Ann Arbor), 1988, 2nd edition published as *Classroom Assessment Techniques: A Handbook for College Teachers,* Jossey-Bass, 1993.

Feedback in the Classroom: Making Assessment Matter (monograph), American Association for Higher Education, 1988.

(Author of foreword) Mardee S. Jenrette, *The Teaching-Learning Enterprise: Miami-Dade Community College's Blueprint for Change,* Anker Publishing, 1994.

Contributor to books, including *Trends in Postsecondary Education,* U.S. Government Printing Office (Washington, DC), 1970; *The Third Century: Twenty-six Prominent Americans Speculate on the Educational Future,* Change Magazine (New Rochelle, NY), 1977; and *Renewing the American Community College: Priorities and Strategies for Effective Leadership,* Jossey-Bass, 1985. Contributor to periodicals, including *Harvard Educational Review, Phi Delta Kappan, Community/Junior College Quarterly of Research and Practice, Journal of College Student Personnel, College Board Review,* and *Journal of Continuing Higher Education.* Editor, *Research Report,* 1966-73, and *Findings,* 1974-75; consulting editor, *Journal of Higher Education,* 1974—, and *Change: The Magazine of Higher Learning,* 1980—; member of editorial board, *Journal for Higher Education Management,* 1984—; member of advisory board, *Higher Education Abstracts,* 1984-88.

WORK IN PROGRESS: Research on higher and adult education; classroom research for the improvement of college teaching.

*   *   *

CULVER, Kathryn
See DRESSER, Davis

*   *   *

CUNLIFFE, Barrington Windsor 1939-
(Barry Cunliffe)

PERSONAL: Born December 10, 1939, in Portsmouth, England; son of George (a naval officer) and Beatrice (Mersh) Cunliffe. *Education:* St. John's College, Cambridge, B.A., 1961, M.A., 1963, Ph.D., 1966, Litt.D., 1976. *Avocational interests:* Travel (East Europe, Mediterranean, "especially France and Iberia"), food, Chinese pottery, mild self-indulgence.

ADDRESSES: Home—Oxford, England. *Office*—Institute of Archaeology, Oxford University, 36 Beaumont St., Oxford OX1 2PG, England. *Agent*—Curtis Brown Ltd., Haymarket House, 28-29 Haymarket, London SW1Y 4SP, England.

CAREER: University of Bristol, Bristol, England, lecturer in classics, 1963-66; University of Southampton, Southampton, England, professor of archaeology, 1966-72; Oxford University, Institute of Archaeology, Oxford, England, professor of European archaeology and fellow of Keble College, 1972—, O'Donnell lecturer in Celtic studies, 1983-84. Member, Ancient Monuments Board for England, 1976-84; commissioner of Historic Buildings and Monuments Commission for England, 1987-92, member of Ancient Monuments Advisory Committee, 1984—.

MEMBER: British Academy (fellow), Medieval Society, Prehistoric Society, Royal Archaeological Institute, Society of Antiquaries (fellow; vice president, 1982-86; president, 1994-95), Society for the Promotion of Roman Studies, *Antiquity* Trust.

AWARDS, HONORS: Order of the British Empire, fellow, 1979, commander, 1994; honorary D.Litt., Sussex, 1983, D.Sc., Bath, 1984.

WRITINGS:

UNDER NAME BARRY CUNLIFFE

Excavations at Richborough, Volume 5, Society of Antiquaries (London), 1968.

(Editor and contributor) *Roman Bath,* Society of Antiquaries, 1969.

Excavations at Fishbourne: 1961-1969, two volumes, Society of Antiquaries, 1971.

Fishbourne: A Roman Palace and Its Gardens, Johns Hopkins Press (Baltimore, MD), 1971.

Roman Bath Discovered, Routledge & Kegan Paul (London), 1971, 2nd edition, 1984.

Guide to the Roman Remains of Bath, Gerrard (Bath), 1971, published as *Roman Baths: A Guide to the Baths and Roman Museum,* Bath Archaeological Trust (Bath), 1980.

The Cradle of England, British Broadcasting Corp. (London), 1972.

The Making of the English, British Broadcasting Corp., 1973.

The Regni, Duckworth (London), 1974.

Iron Age Communities in Britain: An Account of England, Scotland, and Wales from the Seventh Century B.C. until the Roman Conquest, Routledge & Kegan Paul, 1974, 3rd edition, 1991.

Excavations at Porchester Castle, Hants, Society of Antiquaries, Volume 1: *1961-71: Roman,* 1975, Volume 2: *1961-71: Saxon,* 1976, Volume 3: *1961-71: Mediaeval—The Outer Bailey and Its Defenses,* 1977, Volume 4: *1973-79: Mediaeval—The Inner Bailey,* 1985.

Rome and the Barbarians, Walck, 1975.

(With Trevor Rowley) *Oppida: The Beginnings of Urbanisation in Barbarian Europe,* State Mutual Book and Periodical Service (New York City), 1976.

Hengistbury Head, Merrimack Book Service (Topsfield, MA), 1978.

Rome and Her Empire, McGraw (New York City), 1978, 2nd edition, 1994.

The Celtic World, McGraw, 1979, 2nd edition, designed by Emil M. Buhrer, St. Martin's Press (New York City), 1993.

Danebury: Anatomy of an Iron Age Hillfort, Batsford (London), 1983.

Danebury: An Iron Age Hillfort in Hampshire, Council for British Archaeology, Volumes 1 and 2, 1984, Volumes 4 and 5, 1991.

Heywood Sumner's Wessex, Gasson (Dorset), 1985.

(With Peter Davenport) *Temple of Sulis Minerva at Bath,* Volume I: *The Site,* Committee for Archaeology, Oxford University (Oxford), 1985.

The City of Bath, Sutton (Gloucester), 1986.

Hengistbury Head, Darcet, Volume I: *The Prehistoric & Roman Settlement, 3500 B.C.-A.D. 500,* Committee for Archaeology, Oxford University, 1987.

Mount Batten, Plymouth: A Prehistoric and Roman Port, Committee for Archaeology, Oxford University, 1988.

Greeks, Romans & Barbarians: Spheres of Interaction, Methuen (New York City), 1988.

Wessex to A.D. 1000, Longman (London), 1993.

EDITOR, UNDER NAME BARRY CUNLIFFE

Excavations in Bath, 1950-75, Committee for Rescue Archaeology in Avon, Gloucestershire and Somerset, 1979.

Coinage and Society in Britain and Gaul: Some Current Problems, Council for British Archaeology (London), 1981.

Antiquity and Man, Thames & Hudson (London), 1982.

(With David Miles) *Aspects of the Iron Age in Central Southern Britain,* Committee for Archaeology, Oxford University, 1984.

Origins: The Roots of European Civilisation, BBC Publications, 1987, Dorsey Press (Chicago, IL), 1988.

The Oxford Illustrated Prehistory of Europe, Oxford University Press (Oxford), 1994.

OTHER

Also author of television scripts for *Cradle of England* (six episodes), 1972, *Making of the English* (six episodes), 1973, *Pompeii,* 1974, and *Throne of Kings* (six episodes), 1975, for British Broadcasting Corp. (BBC-TV); author of scripts for BBC radio program *Origins.* Contributor to major excavation reports and archaeological journals, and contributor of reviews to *Nature, New Scientist,* and *Times Literary Supplement.* Editor of *Oxford Journal of Archaeology.*

WORK IN PROGRESS: Results of archaeological excavations in Great Britain; research on Europe during the thousand years before the Romans invaded it.

BIOGRAPHICAL/CRITICAL SOURCES:

PERIODICALS

Choice, May, 1987, p. 1450.

Times Literary Supplement, February 17, 1984; June 25, 1993, p. 32.

Tribune Books (Chicago), July 3, 1994, p. 4.

*   *   *

CUNLIFFE, Barry
  See CUNLIFFE, Barrington Windsor

D

DALES, Richard C(lark) 1926-

PERSONAL: Born April 17, 1926, in Akron, OH; son of Gerald Lee (a jeweler) and Lucile (Miller) Dales; married Nancy Gene Vogeler (a teacher), July 7, 1950; children: Susan Zoe, David Richard. *Education:* University of Rochester, B.A., 1949; University of Colorado, M.A., 1952, Ph.D., 1955.

ADDRESSES: Home—616 Chatham Pl., Flintridge, CA 91011. *Office*—Department of History, University of Southern California, Los Angeles, CA 90089-0034.

CAREER: North Dakota Agricultural College (now North Dakota State University), Fargo, instructor in history, 1954-55; Lewis and Clark College, Portland, OR, instructor, 1955-56, assistant professor, 1956-59, associate professor of history, 1959-63; University of Southern California, Los Angeles, associate professor, 1964-66, professor of history, 1966—, John R. Hubbard Professor of European History, 1992—, chairperson of department, 1969-72, acting chairperson of department of classics, 1975-76. Visiting associate professor, University of Southern California, 1962-63, and University of California, Santa Barbara, 1963-64. Member of Institute for Advanced Study, Princeton, NJ, 1966-67. *Military service:* U.S. Army, Corps of Engineers, 1946-47.

MEMBER: Royal Historical Society (fellow), Mediaeval Academy of America (fellow).

AWARDS, HONORS: Danforth fellow, 1957; American Council of Learned Societies fellow, 1960-61, grant, 1973; American Philosophical Society travel grant, 1967; University of Southern California Associates' Award, 1975, for creative scholarship and research.

WRITINGS:

(Editor) *Roberti Grosseteste Commentarius on VIII Libros Physicorum Aristotelis,* University Press of Colorado, 1963.

The Scientific Achievement of the Middle Ages, University of Pennsylvania Press (Philadelphia), 1973.

Marius on the Elements: An Edition with English Translation, University of California Press (Berkeley), 1976.

The Intellectual Life of Western Europe in the Middle Ages, University Press of America (Lanham, MD), 1979, 2nd edition, E. J. Brill (Long Island City, NY), 1990.

(Editor with Servus Gieben) Grosseteste, *Hexaemeron: Auctores Britannici Medii Aevi VI,* Oxford University Press (Oxford, England), 1982.

(Editor with Edward King) Grosseteste, *De cessatione legalirum: Auctores Britannici Medii Aevi VII,* Oxford University Press, 1986.

(Editor with King) Grosseteste, *De decem maudatis: Auctores Britannici Medii Aevi X,* Oxford University Press, 1987.

Medieval Discussions of the Eternity of the World, E. J. Brill, 1990.

Medieval Latin Texts on the Eternity of the World, E. J. Brill, 1991.

Contributor of about twenty articles to periodicals, including *Viator, Isis, Mediaeval Studies, Journal of the History of Ideas,* and *Speculum..*

WORK IN PROGRESS: The Problem of the Rational Soul in the Thirteenth Century.

DANIELS, Les(lie Noel III) 1943-

PERSONAL: Born October 27, 1943, in Danbury, CT; son of Leslie Noel, Jr. (a copywriter) and Eva (Ruppaner) Daniels. *Education:* Brown University, B.A., 1965, M.A., 1968.

ADDRESSES: Home—Box 814, Providence, RI 02901. *Agent*—Merrilee Heifetz, Writer's House, 21 West 26th St., New York City, NY 10010.

CAREER: Musician, composer, and writer. Formerly associated with the musical group "Soop."

WRITINGS:

Comix: A History of Comic Books in America, Outerbridge & Dienstfrey, 1971.
Living in Fear: A History of Horror in the Mass Media, Scribner (New York City), 1975, published in Britain as *Fear: A History of Horror in the Mass Media,* Paladin (London), 1977.
(Editor) *Dying of Fright: Masterpieces of the Macabre,* Scribner, 1976.
(Editor with Diane Thompson) *Thirteen Tales of Terror* (textbook), Scribner, 1976.
The Black Castle: A Novel of the Macabre, Scribner, 1978.
The Silver Skull: A Novel of Sorcery, Scribner, 1979.
Citizen Vampire (novel), Scribner, 1981.
Yellow Fog, Donald Grant (West Kingston, RI), 1986, expanded edition, Tor Books (New York City), 1988.
(Contributor) Dennis Etchison, editor, *Cutting Edge,* Doubleday (New York City), 1986.
No Blood Spilled (novel), Tor Books, 1991.
Marvel: Five Fabulous Decades of the World's Greatest Comics, introduction by Stan Lee, H. N. Abrams (New York City), 1991.

SIDELIGHTS: Les Daniels is a three-time nominee for the World Fantasy Award.

*   *   *

DAVID, Jay
See ADLER, William

*   *   *

DAVIDSON, Roger H(arry) 1936-

PERSONAL: Born July 31, 1936, in Washington, DC; son of Ross Wallace (a botanist) and Mildred (Younger) Davidson; married Nancy Dixon (acquisitions editor at Brookings Institution), September 29, 1961; children: Douglas Ross, Christopher Reed. *Education:* University of Colorado, B.A. (magna cum laude), 1958; Columbia University, Ph.D., 1963.

ADDRESSES: Home—3510 Edmunds St. NW, Washington, DC 20007. *Office*—1140B Tydings, University of Maryland, College Park, MD 20742.

CAREER: Fort Collins Coloradoan, Fort Collins, CO, municipal reporter, summers, 1957-59; Brookings Institution, Washington, DC, research assistant, 1960; Dartmouth College, Hanover, NH, assistant professor of government, 1962-68; University of California, Santa Barbara, associate professor, 1968-71, professor of political science, 1971-82; U.S. Library of Congress, Congressional Research Service, Washington, DC, senior specialist on American government, 1980-87; University of Maryland, College Park, professor of government and politics, 1987—. Staff associate, W. E. Upjohn Institute for Employment Research, Washington, DC, 1965-66; chair, Upper Valley Human Rights Council, Hanover, NH, 1967-68; scholar-in-residence, National Manpower Policy Task Force, 1970-71; professional staff member, Select Committee on Committees of U.S. House of Representatives, 1973-74, and of U.S. Senate, 1976-77; member, board of directors, Dirksen Congressional Center, Governance Institute.

MEMBER: American Political Science Association (joint committee member, Project 87-American Historical Association/American Political Science Association; chair, congressional fellowship committee, 1990, 1993), Legislative Studies Group (charter member; national chair, 1980-81), National Academy of Public Administration, Midwest Political Science Association, National Capitol Area Political Science Association (president, 1985-86), Western Political Science Association (member, board of directors, 1977-78), Phi Beta Kappa, Delta Sigma Rho.

AWARDS, HONORS: Woodrow Wilson National Foundation fellow, 1958; Gilder fellow, Columbia University, 1960; faculty fellow, Dartmouth College, 1965-66; Elliott-Winant Lectureship (United Kingdom), 1993.

WRITINGS:

(With D. M. Kovenock and M. K. O'Leary) *Congress in Crisis: Politics and Congressional Reform,* Wadsworth (Belmont, CA), 1966.
(With J. F. Bibby) *On Capitol Hill: Studies in Legislative Politics,* Holt (New York City), 1967, 2nd edition, 1972.
(With Sar A. Levitan) *Antipoverty Housekeeping: The Administration of the Economic Opportunity Act,* Institute of Labor and Industrial Relations, University of Michigan/Wayne State University (Ann Arbor, MI), 1968.

The Role of the Congressman, Pegasus (Vashon Island, WA), 1969.

The Politics of Comprehensive Manpower Legislation, Johns Hopkins University Press (Baltimore, MD), 1972.

(With Samuel C. Patterson and Randall B. Ripley) *A More Perfect Union: Introduction to American Government,* Dorsey (Chicago, IL), 1972, 3rd edition, 1985.

(With Walter J. Oleszek) *Congress against Itself,* Indiana University Press (Bloomington, IN), 1977.

(With Oleszek) *Congress and Its Members,* Congressional Quarterly Press (Washington, DC), 1981, 4th edition, 1994.

EDITOR

(With Oleszek) *Governing: Readings and Cases in American Politics,* Congressional Quarterly Press, 1987, 2nd edition, 1992.

(With Richard C. Sachs) *Understanding Congress: A Bicentennial Research Conference,* U.S. Government Printing Office (Washington, DC), 1989.

(With Uwe Thaysen and Robert Gerald Livingston) *The U.S. Congress and the German Bundestag: Comparisons of Democratic Processes,* Westview Press (Boulder CO), 1990.

(With Richard A. Baker), *First among Equals: Outstanding Senate Leaders of the Twentieth Century,* Congressional Quarterly (Washington, DC), 1991.

The Postreform Congress, St. Martin's Press (New York City), 1992.

(With Donald C. Bacon and Morton Keller), *The Encyclopedia of the United States Congress,* Simon & Schuster (New York City), 1995.

Contributor to *American Behavioral Scientist, American Journal of Political Science, Western Political Quarterly,* and other journals.

WORK IN PROGRESS: Continuing research into public opinion and attitudes toward legislative bodies, and into agenda and workload shifts in legislative bodies.

*   *   *

DAVIS, Don
    See DRESSER, Davis

*   *   *

DAVIS, Neil
    See DAVIS, T(homas) Neil

DAVIS, T. N.
    See DAVIS, T(homas) Neil

*   *   *

DAVIS, T(homas) Neil   1932-
    (Neil Davis, T. N. Davis)

PERSONAL: Born February 1, 1932, in Greeley, CO; son of Bon Valjean (a sociologist) and Bernice (a teacher; maiden name, Sappenfield) Davis; married Rosemarie McClatchey (a potter), June 10, 1951; children: Patricia Ann Davis Candler, Douglas Eugene, Deborah Jo Davis Van Stone. *Education:* Attended Iowa State College (now University), 1951-52; University of Alaska, B.S., 1955, Ph.D., 1961; California Institute of Technology, M.S., 1957. *Politics:* Independent. *Avocational interests:* Travel (including the U.S.S.R., Japan, Europe, and South America).

ADDRESSES: Home—375 Miller Hill Rd., Fairbanks, AK 99709; and 3802 Roche Harbor Rd., Friday Harbor, WA 98250. *Office*—Geophysical Institute, University of Alaska, Fairbanks, AK 99775.

CAREER: University of Alaska, Fairbanks, technician at Geophysical Institute, 1953-55, instructor, 1957-61, associate professor, 1961-65, professor of geophysics, 1965-81, professor emeritus, 1982—, assistant director of Geophysical Institute, 1965-70, deputy director of Geophysical Institute, 1971-77, acting director of Geophysical Institute and Division of Geosciences, 1976-77, acting manager of energy research, 1980-81, senior consultant to Geophysical Institute, 1982—. National Aeronautics and Space Administration, Goddard Space Flight Center, resident research associate of National Academy of Sciences, 1962-64, aerospace technologist in Fields and Plasmas Branch, 1964-65; Alaska Council on Science and Technology, member of council, 1978-83, chairman, 1979-81; member of National Earthquake Prediction Evaluation Council, 1980-82.

MEMBER: Arctic Institute of North America (fellow), American Association for the Advancement of Science (executive secretary of Arctic Division, 1979-81).

AWARDS, HONORS: Medal from Soviet Academy of Sciences, 1985; selection as one of Outstanding Academic Books, *Choice* magazine, 1992, for *The Aurora Watchers Handbook;* Distinguished Alumnus Award, University of Alaska, Fairbanks, 1994.

WRITINGS:

(Contributor under name T. N. Davis) W. N. Hess, editor, *Introduction to Space Science,* Gordon & Breach (New York City), 1965.

(Contributor under name T. N. Davis) B. M. McCormac, editor, *Aurora and Airglow,* Reinhold, 1967.

(Contributor under name T. N. Davis) L. O. Quan, editor, *Research in the Antarctic,* American Association for the Advancement of Science (Washington, DC), 1971.

(Under name Neil Davis) *Alaska Science Nuggets,* Geophysical Institute, University of Alaska (Fairbanks), 1982.

(Under name Neil Davis) *Energy-Alaska,* University of Alaska Press (Fairbanks), 1984.

(Under name Neil Davis) *The Aurora Watchers Handbook,* University of Alaska Press, 1992.

(Under name Neil Davis) *The College Hill Chronicles: How the University of Alaska Came of Age,* University of Alaska Foundation (Fairbanks), 1993.

(Under name Neil Davis) *Caught in the Sluice: Tales from Alaska's Gold Camps* (fiction), McRoy & Blackburn (Ester, AK), 1994.

Contributor to *Encyclopaedia Britannica.* Contributing editor of "Alaska Science Forum," a weekly column in fourteen newspapers in Alaska and northwestern Canada, 1976-82. Contributor to scientific journals and popular magazines.

The Aurora Watchers Handbook has been published in Japanese.

WORK IN PROGRESS: Permafrost, for University of Alaska Press.

SIDELIGHTS: T. Neil Davis once told *CA:* "I have been much influenced by James Michener and his philosophy, in part because a close family member had been a student of his many years ago in Greeley, Colorado. Some years ago, in an article in *Reader's Digest,* I believe, Michener said that it was not important what you did early in life, but when you got to be about forty-five, it was time to get serious. That statement influenced my decision to leave a research and teaching career at age forty-nine to direct my intellectual activities toward nonfiction writing aimed primarily at nonscientists. I believe that many members of the general public are quite interested in science and welcome writing that is understandable and informative about the world in which we all live."

*   *   *

DEBRETT, Hal
    See DRESSER, Davis

DeMARCO, Donald   1937-

PERSONAL: Born April 20, 1937, in Fall River, MA; married Mary Arendt; children: Jocelyn, Donald, Jr., Paul, Peter, Elizabeth. *Education:* Stonehill College, B.S., 1959, A.B., 1961; State College at Bridgewater (now Bridgewater State College) and Gregorian University, graduate study, 1961-62; St. John's University, Jamaica, N.Y., M.A., 1965, Ph.D., 1969. *Religion:* Roman Catholic.

ADDRESSES: Home—101 Silverspring Cir., Kitchener, Ontario, Canada N2M 4P3. *Office*—St. Jerome's College, University of Waterloo, Waterloo, Ontario, Canada N2L 3G3.

CAREER: Stonehill College, North Easton, MA, lecturer in music aesthetics, 1960-61; junior high school teacher of mathematics in Fall River, MA, 1962; high school teacher of mathematics and science in Dartmouth, MA, 1962-63; teacher of mathematics and sciences in private school in Fairhaven, MA, 1963-64; St. John's University, Jamaica, NY, 1965-70, began as instructor, became assistant professor of philosophy; University of Waterloo, St. Jerome's College, Waterloo, Ontario, assistant professor, 1970-75, associate professor of philosophy, 1975—. Scholar-in-residence, Holy Apostles' College, Cromwell, CT; visiting professor, St. Joseph's University College, Edmonton, Alberta, and Catholic Bible College of Canada, Canmore, Alberta; visiting scholar, St. Hyacinth College, Granby, MA, 1988-89 and 1992-94; teacher of medical ethics at St. Joseph's School of Nursing, Guelph, Ontario, 1972, and at St. Mary's School of Nursing, Kitchener, Ontario, 1972-75. Piano teacher in Fall River, 1962-64; has directed choirs and given piano recitals. Birthright of Kitchener-Waterloo, president of board of directors, 1971—, past member of international board; member of board of Federated Appeal of Kitchener-Waterloo, 1975—. Member of Anti-Euthanasia Task Force and Franciscan University of Steubenville. Advisor, Population Institute for Human Life International.

MEMBER: American Mauritian Association, Fellowship of Catholic Scholars, Society of Catholic Social Scientists.

WRITINGS:

The Peace Movement without Peer (booklet), Carmelite Nuns of Fort Worth, TX, 1973.
Abortion in Perspective: The Rose Palace or the Fiery Dragon?, Hiltz, 1974.
Sex and the Illusion of Freedom, Mission Press (Kenwood, CA), 1981.
Today's Family in Crisis, Marian Press, 1982.
The Anesthetic Society, Christendom College Press (Front Royal, VA), 1982.
The Shape of Love, Fidelity House, 1983.

In My Mother's Womb: The Catholic Church's Defense of Natural Life, Trinity Communications, 1987.

The Incarnation in a Divided World, Christendom College Press, 1987.

How to Survive as a Catholic in a Parochial World, St. Martin de Porres, 1988.

Hope for a World without Hope, St. Martin de Porres, 1991.

Biotechnology and the Assault on Parenthood, Ignatius (San Francisco), 1991.

Chambers of the Heart (poetry), St. Martin de Porres, 1992.

(Author of foreword) Jerome Lejeune, *The Concentration Can,* Ignatius, 1992.

Also author of *The Heart of Virtue,* 1994. Contributor to books, including *The Passion of Christ,* edited by Mykola Kolankiwsky, Niagara Falls Art Gallery and Museum, 1974; *New Perspectives on Human Abortion,* edited by Hilgers, Horan, and Mall, Altheia Books, 1981; and *The Politics of Prayer,* edited by Helen Hull Hitchcock, Ignatius, 1992. Contributor to anthologies, including *Human Life and Health Care Ethics,* edited by James Bopp, Jr., University Publications of America (Frederick, MD), 1985. Columnist and feature writer, *Toronto Catholic Register,* 1972—. Contributor of hundreds of articles and reviews to more than sixty professional journals, magazines, and newspapers, including *American Ecclesiastical Review, New Oxford Review, Communio, Human Life Review, Bread of Life, National Catholic Register,* and *Theologisches.* Associate editor, *Child and Family Quarterly;* advisory editor, *Fidelity* and *Social Justice Review.*

SIDELIGHTS: Donald DeMarco once told *CA:* "I write because I need to establish order, primarily in my own life, but also—and it is always difficult to know whether this is hubris or humility—to assist in establishing some degree of order in the world around me. Why order? Because we are saved when we can order our lives to the Transcendent, to that Supreme Cause of order whose original explosion of light brought order out of chaos. I also seek order because I do not find the prospect of being resorbed into chaos particularly attractive."

*   *   *

DeMOTT, Benjamin (Hailer)   1924-

PERSONAL: Born June 2, 1924, in Long Island, NY; son of D. Gerard and Janet (Sanders) DeMott; married Margaret Craig, June 22, 1946; children: Joel, Thomas, Benjamin, and one daughter. *Education:* Johns Hopkins University, George Washington University, B.A.; Harvard University, Ph.D.

ADDRESSES: Home—Box 356, Worthington, MA, 01098. *Agent*—Harold Ober, 425 Madison Ave., New York, NY 10017. *Office*—Department of English, Amherst College, Amherst, MA 01002.

CAREER: Journalist and freelance writer, Long Island, NY, Washington, DC, 1940-43, 1945-49; Amherst College, Amherst, MA, began as instructor, attained emeritus status, 1951. Massachusetts Institute of Technology, visiting professor of humanities; Marlboro College, council of advisors; Society of Magazine Writers, consultant. *Military service* U.S. Army, 1943-45; served in infantry.

AWARDS, HONORS: Guggenheim fellowship, 1963; Fulbright lecturer, England, 1965.

WRITINGS:

The Body's Cage (novel), Atlantic Monthly Press, 1959.
A Married Man (novel), Harcourt (New York City), 1968.
Close Imagining: An Introduction to Literature, St. Martin's (New York City), 1987.
The Imperial Middle: Why Americans Can't Think Straight About Class, Morrow (New York City), 1990.

ESSAYS

Hells and Benefits, Basic Books (New York City), 1962.
You Don't Say: Studies of Modern American Inhibitions, Harcourt, 1966.
Supergrow: Essays and Reports on Imagination in America, Dutton (New York City), 1969.
Surviving the Seventies, Dutton, 1971.

OTHER

Also author of *Scholarship for Society,* 1974, and *America in Literature,* 1977. Contributor to periodicals, including *Harper's, Kenyon Review, Nation, New Republic,* and *Saturday Evening Post.* Columnist, *Harper's,* 1962-64, 1982—; columnist, *Atlantic Monthly,* 1973-80, and contributing editor, 1977—. DeMott recorded discussions of poets' work in *Beyond Dailiness: Wordsworth and Hardy and Manchild,* and analyzed self-help books in another recording, *A Cultural Report on American Scenes Today,* all released by J. Norton Publishers.

SIDELIGHTS: A commentator on contemporary culture, Benjamin DeMott has tackled topics as diverse as academia, sex research, marital infidelity, and rock music in the United States. His written work, which includes essays, novels, and newspaper columns are cultural accounts that exhort the reader to re-examine various aspect of modern life.

DeMott has also published fiction, and his best-known novel, *A Married Man,* is the story of Gordon Flint, a respectable, middle-aged, family man who has an affair with a much younger co-worker. Although the story-line itself is stereotypical, as James McConkey pointed out in *Saturday Review,* the dilemma is made interesting because of the subjective reality of the narrator. In the *New York Times,* John Leonard said that DeMott "tells an old story, but tells it so superbly that it is made new." Wrote McConkey: "Told in the first person, Benjamin DeMott's brief novel owes something of its form and subject to those highly artful confessional narratives that [Andre] Gide and other French novelists have written, narratives which probe the weaknesses . . . of the narrators."

Besides fiction, DeMott has also written several volumes of essays. Among these works is *Supergrow: Essays and Reports on Imagination in America,* a work described by the *Washington Post*'s Thomas Grubisich as "an activist's manifesto for imagination." In this book, DeMott examines the American landscape in 1969 and concludes that "people should use their imaginations more." According to the author, there exists a conflict between a thinking, feeling individual and the compromises they need to make to survive in society. In *Saturday Review,* Robert Phillips praised *Supergrow:* "The quality of DeMott's imagination justifies his charging others with the non-usage of theirs. . . . When DeMott explodes a myth, as he does frequently, the detonation occurs within the civilized context of a beautifully developed essay."

In 1990 DeMott issued *The Imperial Middle: Why Americans Can't Think Straight About Class.* In this book, the author contends that the American myth of a classless society is dangerous because it perpetuates the existence of unequal opportunities. Rupert Wilkinson summarized DeMott's argument in the *Times Literary Supplement* as follows: "When Americans talk about class they do so in a way which trivializes it and removes it from considerations of public policy. In television and movie plots, a recurring delusion is that class is either a put-on or a veneer; people need not be deeply affected by it."

Critical opinion on DeMott's thesis varied. While Wilkinson asserted that DeMott's argument was plausible, he criticized the author for using sources selectively, writing that, "While citing academic studies which support its picture of covert class discrimination, [*The Imperial Middle*] . . . neglects almost everything which suggests that many middle-class Americans may be well aware of the importance of social class." And Alan Wolfe, writing in the *Washington Post Book World,* took exception to what he called the author's arrogance. Wolfe noted that the first sentence of *The Imperial Middle* "posits the existence of 'a nation in shackles, its thought, character, and public policy locked in distortion and lies.' DeMott is sure of himself in the way that only an amateur—his metier is literature, not sociology—can be."

Conversely, Barbara Ehrenreich wrote in the *New York Times Book Review* that *The Imperial Middle* "is not a hard-nosed, ax-grinding kind of book." It "is a work of cultural criticism, and if it is occasionally a bit elusive, it is also imaginative, challenging and a pleasure to read."

BIOGRAPHICAL/CRITICAL SOURCES:

BOOKS

DeMott, Benjamin, *Supergrow: Essays and Reports on Imagination in America,* Dutton, 1969.

PERIODICALS

Book World, November 17, 1968.
Harper's, September, 1969.
Los Angeles Times Book Review, December 2, 1990.
Nation, January 21, 1991.
New Republic, August 30, 1969, pp. 25-26; May 1, 1971.
Newsweek, September 9, 1968.
New York Review of Books, March 7, 1991.
New York Times, September 13, 1968; August 28, 1969.
New York Times Book Review, September 29, 1968; March 16, 1969; August 31, 1969; October 14, 1990, p. 9.
Saturday Review, October 12, 1968, pp. 37-38; September 20, 1969, pp. 39-40.
Times Literary Supplement, July 5, 1991, p. 11.
Tribune Books (Chicago), June 14, 1992, p. 8.
Washington Post, September 10, 1968; August 29, 1969.
Washington Post Book World, December 16, 1990, p. 3.*

*   *   *

De THOMASIS, Louis 1940-

PERSONAL: Born October 6, 1940, in Brooklyn, New York; son of Costantino (a businessman) and Anna De Thomasis. *Education:* University of Madrid, 1961; Georgetown University, B.S.F.S., 1963; graduate study at Providence College, 1973; Union Institute, Cincinnati, Ohio, Ph.D., 1982; postdoctoral study, Harvard University, 1986.

ADDRESSES: Office—Saint Mary's University of Minnesota, Winona, MN 55987.

CAREER: Metro-Graphics, Inc., Washington, DC, chief executive officer, 1964-68; entered Fratres Scholarum Christianarum (Christian Brothers; F.S.C.), 1968; teacher of comparative government and religious education at private school, Providence, RI, 1969-71; associate headmaster and chief operating officer of military academy, Oakdale, NY, 1971-73; Christian Brothers, Narragansett, RI, vicepresident for finance, 1973-76; president and chief executive officer of military academy, Oakdale, 1976-84; Saint Mary's University of Minnesota, Winona, MN, president and professor of interdisciplinary studies, 1984—.

Member of founding board of trustees of Religious Communities Trust, 1976-82; chair of finance committee of Christian Brothers of Narragansett, 1982-83; lecturer and presenter of workshops on general and financial management; financial investment and management consultant; consultant to Conference of Major Superiors of Men of the U.S.A. and U.S. Catholic Conference. Member of board of directors of Korean Cultural and Freedom Foundation, 1966; national director of finance of Young Democrats Club of America, 1966; chair of board of directors of Bright Day Travel, Inc., Moraga, CA, 1980—; chair of Christian Brothers Investment Services, 1985—; member of board of directors of Galaxy Fund, 1986—. Chair of board of directors of Martin de Porres School for Exceptional Children, 1975—; trustee of Manhattan College, 1977—, Saint Mary's University of Minnesota, Winona, 1978—, St. John's Military College High School, 1982—, and College of Santa Fe, 1985—; member of board of advisors of Seminary of the Immaculate Conception, Brooklyn, NY, and Rockville Centre Diocese Theologate, 1981-84; trustee of Ocean Tides Treatment Center for Juvenile Offenders, 1975—.

AWARDS, HONORS: Founders Certificate from Radio Free Asia, 1966; Christian Service Award from Franz W. Sichel Foundation, 1974; President's Medal for Christian Education from St. John's College High School, 1985; Bush fellow at Harvard University, 1986; Doctor of Laws, Honoris Causa, Illinois Benedictine College, 1989; Knighthood to the Equestrian Order of the Holy Sepulchre of Jerusalem, 1989; Leavey Foundation Award for excellence in private enterprise education, 1989.

WRITINGS:

The Finance of Education, Saint Mary's Press (Winona, MN), 1978.
Investing with Options, Saint Mary's Press, 1981.
Social Justice: A Christian Pragmatic Response in Today's World (monograph), Saint Mary's Press, 1982.
My Father's Business: Creating a New Future for the People of God, Christian Classics (Westminster, MD), 1984.
Business Ethics and Free Enterprise: The Challenges for Catholic Higher Education (monograph), Christian Brothers, 1986.

Also contributor to *Fund Raising Forum, Momentum, Christian Brothers,* and *Private School Quarterly.*

SIDELIGHTS: Louis De Thomasis told *CA:* "My writings attempt to integrate the complex and seemingly disparate worlds of faith and finance. The gap between the so-called spiritual and material worlds, the past separation of church from state, religion from politics, and business from spirituality are obsolete. I am convinced that with a proper understanding among clerics, lay, and religious,

the power of the financial world can be a beneficial and dynamic tool for guiding humanities future."

*   *   *

DiPALMA, Ray(mond)   1943-

PERSONAL: Born September 27, 1943, in New Kensington, PA. *Education:* Duquesne University, B.A., 1966; University of Iowa, M.F.A., 1968.

ADDRESSES: Home—226 West 21st St., Apt. 4-R, New York, NY 10011.

CAREER: Bowling Green University, Bowling Green, OH, instructor in English and creative writing, 1968-75; adjunct professor, Union Graduate School at Antioch College, 1976-77. Founder and editor, Doones Press and *Doones Magazine,* 1969.

WRITINGS:

Max, Body Press (Iowa City, IA), 1969.
(With Stephen Shrader) *Macaroons,* Doones Press (Bowling Green, OH), 1969.
Between the Shapes, Zeitgeist (East Lansing, MI), 1970.
Clinches, Abraxas Press (Madison, WI), 1970.
The Gallery Goers, Ithaca House (Ithaca, NY), 1971.
All Bowed Down, Burning Deck Press (Providence, RI), 1972.
Works in a Drawer, Blue Chair Press (Bowling Green, OH), 1972.
Borgia Circles, Sand Project Press (Southampton, NY), 1972.
(With Asa Benveniste and Tom Raworth) *Time Being,* Trigram Press (London), 1972.
(Editor) Merrill Gilfillan and others, *Shirt,* Doones Press, 1973.
Five Surfaces, Tottel's no. 12, 1974.
The Sargasso Transcries, 'X' Editions (Bowling Green, OH), 1974.
Max/ A Sequel, Burning Deck Press, 1974.
Soli, Ithaca House (Ithaca, NY), 1974.
Accidental Interludes, Turkey Press (Providence, RI), 1975.
Marquee, Asylum's Press (New York City), 1976.
10 Faces, Doones Press, 1976.
Outrageous Modesty, Doones Press, 1976.
The Black Notebook, Doones Press, 1977.
Matak, Doones Press, 1977.
Tzuuka, Doones Press, 1977.
Marquee: A Score, Asylum's Press, 1977.
Cuiva Sails, Sun & Moon Press (College Park, MD), 1978.
Observatory Gardens, Tuumba Press (Berkeley, CA), 1979.
Planh, Casement Books (New York City), 1979.
Genesis, Underwhich Editions (Toronto), 1980.

(With others) *Legend,* L—A—N—G—U—A—G—E/
Segue (New York City), 1980.

Labyrinth Radio, Case Books (New York City), 1981.

23 Works, Edition Vogelsang (Berlin), 1982.

17 Works, Edition Vogelsang, 1982.

Two Poems, Awede Press (Windsor, VT), 1982.

Chan, One of Ten (New York City), 1984. *January Zero,*
Coffee House Press (Minneapolis, MN), 1984.

Startle Luna, Sleight of Hand Press (New York City),
1984.

The Jukebox of Memnon, Potes & Poets Press (Elmwood,
CT), 1988.

Raik, Roof Books (New York City), 1989.

Night Copy, Stele (New York City), 1990.

(With Elizabeth DiPalma) *5 Ink Drawings/ 5 Poems,*
Stele, 1990.

Mock Fandango, Sun & Moon Press (Los Angeles, CA),
1991.

Metropolitan Corridor, Zasterle Press (Tenerife, Spain),
1992.

Numbers and Tempers, Sun & Moon Press, 1993.

27 Octobre 29 Octobre, Format americain (Paris), 1993.

(With Alexandre Delay) *Hotel des Ruines,* La Collection
Porterie/Editions Royaumont (Paris), 1993.

(With drawings by E. DiPalma) *Platinum Replica,* Stele,
1994.

Provocations, Potes & Poets Press, 1994.

Motion of the Cypher, Roof Books, 1995.

The Advance on Mesmer, Sun & Moon Press, 1996.

Also contributor to numerous anthologies, including *In
the American Tree,* National Poetry Foundation (Orono,
ME), 1986; *'Language' Poetries,* New Directions, 1987;
49+1 Nouveau Poetes Americains, Editions Royaumont,
1991; *The Other Side of the Century: A New American Poetry 1960-90,* Sun and Moon Press, 1994; and *Postmodern
American Poetry,* Norton (New York City), 1994. Contributor of poetry to numerous magazines, including
*Grand Street, Paris Review, American Poetry Review, O-
blek, To Magazine, Writing* (Vancouver), *Boundary 2, Exquisite Corpse, Open Letter* (Toronto), *Epoch, Action Poe-
tique* (Paris), *Tyuonyi, Avec, Partisan Review, New American Writing,* and *Poetry Review* (London).

Selections of DiPalma's writing have been translated into
French, Italian, German, Spanish, and Chinese.

*   *   *

DOERKSEN, Nan 1934-

PERSONAL: Born March 3, 1934, in Speedwell, Saskatchewan, Canada; daughter of Jacob A. (a pastor and
farmer) and Gertrude (Franzen) Enns; married Daniel
William Doerksen (a professor), June 27, 1959; children:

Daniel James, Alan Victor, Robert John. *Education:*
Grace Hospital School of Nursing, Winnipeg, Manitoba,
R.N., 1957; University of New Brunswick, B.A., 1978,
M.A., 1981. *Religion:* "Mennonite/Baptist." *Avocational
interests:* Travel (Britain and Europe), hiking.

ADDRESSES: Home—732 Fenety St., Fredericton, New
Brunswick, Canada E3B 4H2.

CAREER: King George Hospital, Winnipeg, Manitoba,
nurse, 1957-58; Department of Indian Health, Sandy
Lake, Ontario, nurse, 1958-59; Victorian Order of Nurses,
Winnipeg, nurse, 1959-60; volunteer worker, homemaker,
student, and writer, 1960—. Member of board of directors
of OPAL, Inc., 1979-86; chair of board of directors of
OPAL III-Fredericton Respite Services, Inc.; visiting author in "Writers in Schools Program," New Brunswick,
1994—.

WRITINGS:

JUVENILE

Bears for Breakfast, Kindred Press, 1983.
The First Family Car, Kindred Press, 1986.
Rats in the Sloop, Ragweed Press, 1986, 2nd edition, New
Ireland Press, 1993.

Also author of puppet scripts for social service agency.
Contributor of articles, stories, and poems to magazines
and newspapers, including *Decision, Canadian Baptist,*
and *Mennonite Mirror.*

WORK IN PROGRESS: A novel based on nursing experiences in northern Canada; a juvenile novel, *The Winter of
Change;* and "a collection of cross-generational adult
short stories, based on my family."

SIDELIGHTS: Nan Doerksen told *CA:* "Love of God,
family, and nature are probably the strongest motivational
forces in my life and writing. Much of my time in recent
years has been spent in volunteer work with senior citizens, the mentally handicapped (both adults and children), and international students.

"*Bears for Breakfast* is a series of adventure stories for
children of ages five to eight featuring one family. The stories grew out of experiences with my own children as well
as from working with children on a volunteer basis. The
stories emphasize such things as getting along with each
other in a family, appreciating nature, and learning to get
along with people who are different. *The First Family Car*
consists of pioneer adventures, based, to some extent, on
my own growing-up experience in northern Saskatchewan. Again, one family is featured. *Rats in the Sloop* is set
in 1819 in Fredericton, New Brunswick. In order to make
the story authentic in terms of setting and time I did a considerable amount of research in archives and history
books. The story is fictional, featuring two children who

have been recently orphaned and, according to their guardian's decree, are to be separated—Margaret to go to her aunt in Fredericton and Johnny to be sent to his uncle in England. However, the children make their own plans and the story evolves around that."

* * *

DOIG, Ivan 1939-

PERSONAL: Born June 27, 1939, in White Sulphur Springs, MT; son of Charles Campbell (a ranch worker) and Berneta (Ringer) Doig; married Carol Muller (a professor), April 17, 1965. *Education:* Northwestern University, B.S., 1961, M.S., 1962; University of Washington, Seattle, Ph.D., 1969. *Avocational interests:* Reading, hiking.

ADDRESSES: Home—17021 10th Ave. N.W., Seattle, WA 98177.

CAREER: Writer. Lindsay-Schaub Newspapers, Decatur, IL, editorial writer, 1963-64; Rotarian, Evanston, IL, assistant editor, 1964-66; freelance writer, 1969-78. *Military service:* U.S. Air Force Reserve, 1962-68; became sergeant.

MEMBER: Authors Guild, Authors League of America, PEN.

AWARDS, HONORS: National Book Award nomination and Christopher Award, both 1979, both for *This House of Sky: Landscapes of a Western Mind;* Pacific Northwest Booksellers Award for Literary Excellence, 1979, 1980, 1982, 1984, 1987, and 1993; National Endowment for the Arts fellowship, 1985; D.Lit., Montana State University, 1984, and Lewis and Clark College, 1987. Western Heritage Award for best western novel, 1985, for *English Creek;* Evans Biography Award, 1993, for *Heart Earth;* Western Literature Association Distinguished Achievement Award, 1989.

WRITINGS:

(With wife, Carol M. Doig) *News: A Consumer's Guide,* Prentice-Hall (Englewood Cliffs, NJ), 1972.
The Streets We Have Come Down (textbook), Hayden (Rochelle Park, NJ), 1975.
Utopian America: Dreams and Realities, Hayden, 1976.
Early Forestry Research, U.S. Forestry Service (Washington), 1976.
This House of Sky: Landscapes of a Western Mind (memoir), Harcourt (San Diego, CA), 1978.
Winter Brothers: A Season at the Edge of America (nonfiction), Harcourt, 1980.
The Sea Runners (novel), Atheneum (New York City), 1982.
(With Duncan Kelso) *Inside This House of Sky,* Atheneum, 1983.

English Creek (first novel in McCaskill family trilogy), Atheneum, 1984.
Dancing at the Rascal Fair (second novel in McCaskill family trilogy), Atheneum, 1987.
Ride with Me, Mariah Montana (final novel in McCaskill family trilogy), Atheneum, 1990.
Heart Earth, Atheneum, 1993.

Contributor to periodicals, including *Modern Maturity, New York Times, Los Angeles Times Book Review,* and *Writer's Digest.*

WORK IN PROGRESS: A novel "about a Depression-era family at work on the biggest earthen dam in the world, and their encounters with love, mystery, engineering, prostitution, and communism."

SIDELIGHTS: "Ivan Doig doesn't exactly own the Pacific Northwest," notes James Kaufmann in the *Los Angeles Times Book Review,* "but the loving and lively ways he describes it mark him as a regional writer in the absolute best sense of the word." Indeed, Doig has integrated his knowledge of this area of the United States into a number of well-known nonfiction books and novels, including *This House of Sky: Landscapes of a Western Mind, Winter Brothers: A Season on the Edge of America, Heart Earth,* and *English Creek, Dancing at the Rascal Fair,* and *Ride with Me, Mariah Montana,* Doig's fictional trilogy.

Of *This House of Sky*—a memoir that describes the harsh but rewarding life of the author's forebears, who settled in the mining towns of western Montana—*Washington Post* critic Curt Suplee says, "This is no country for tennis-shoe ecologists or Snail Darter evangels—in the uneasy lee of the great mountains, amid the heartless rocky sprawl, nature is not a friend, but an omnipotent and endlessly inventive adversary, and a daily measure of courage is needful as water." Remarking that the memoir format in general "is notorious for snaring even gifted writers in thickets of anecdotage and sentiment," *Time*'s Frank Trippet finds that Doig "avoids such traps. Exercising a talent at once robust and sensitive, he redeems the promise of [his] first fetching sentences." The author, Trippet concludes, "lifts what might have been marginally engaging reminiscence into an engrossing and moving recovery of an obscure human struggle. There is defeat and triumph here, grief and joy, nobility and meanness, all arising from commonplace events, episodes and locales."

Winter Brothers is a nonfiction work with an unusual premise: Doig recreated the journey of a nineteenth-century traveller named James Gilchrist Swan, who left a wife and children in antebellum Boston to explore the Pacific Northwest. Doig, who studied Swan's extensive diaries, intersperses passages of Swan's writing with his own comments on the trip he took with his wife. "Sometimes the exercise is forced; sometimes it pushes [the author] into overwriting," states Raymond A. Sokolov in the *New York Times Book Review.* "But the occasional patches of dullness or lushness should deter no one from devouring this gorgeous tribute to a man and a region unjustly neglected heretofore. The reader has the pleasure of encountering two contrasting styles and two angles of view, both infused with the fresh air and spirit of the Northwest."

Doig returns to the subject of his forebears with *Heart Earth,* a memoir inspired by a collection of his mother's letters and a "masterful companion to *This House of Sky,*" according to John Marshall of the *Seattle Post-Intelligencer.* Brad Knickerbocker of the *Christian Science Monitor* also has high praise for Doig's memoir, noting that though the book closes with the death of Berneta Doig when the author was six the "poignancy and sadness are not overwhelming, and one is left remembering the humor and family closeness (quarrels as well as affection), the strength of character and essential hopefulness that have come to be Doig trademarks." Novelist Michael Dorris, writing in the *Los Angeles Times,* praises Doig's lyricism, particularly as he describes his native Montana, but notes also that in the end *Heart Earth* is "a love story, the gift of a child to a parent who wouldn't stay forgotten."

Internal conflict among members of the McCaskill family and the coming-of-age of its younger son in 1939 form the basis for *English Creek,* a novel that "achieves a flawless weld of fact and fiction," according to Carol Van Strum in a *USA Today* article. As in his previous nonfiction, Doig describes the Pacific region of years past, evoking, as Van Strum says, "the sturdy, generous spirit of an era when survival—of child and adult—demanded quick wits, hard work and humor enough to fuel both." *English Creek* "is old-fashioned in the best sense of the word," notes *Christian Science Monitor* critic James Kaufmann. "Doig is concerned with telling a story that entertains, and he is also concerned with the novel's moral and ethical implications. He mounts no soapbox, however."

To *Newsday* reviewer Wendy Smith, Doig's novel "is neither nostalgic nor simple: It's too concrete and detailed in its evocation of the past, too tough-minded in its evaluation of human behavior for that. There are no truly evil characters, but there are weak ones, and Doig makes it clear that the West is cruel to those who can't stand up to its demands." Concluding that *English Creek* is "firmly anchored in the American West," Smith adds that the book "nonetheless resembles a 19th Century European novel in its leisurely pace, measured tone and focus on understanding rather than action. In supple, muscular prose as terse and yet redolent with meaning as the speech of Montana, [Doig] grapples with universal issues of character and morality."

The sequel to *English Creek, Dancing at the Rascal Fair,* occurs a generation earlier and features two Scotchmen, Rob Barclay and Angus McCaskell, who homestead in Montana. Richard Critchfield of the *Washington Post Book World* praises Doig's ability to interweave history and fiction and for his skills with dialogue, noting that "his people come alive when they talk" whether they are nineteenth Century Scotchmen speaking English with Biblical cadences or contemporary, rural Americans. Writing in the *Seattle Times,* Michael Dorris calls this "prequel" to *English Creek* a "fine work" in which "every word, every surprise, every resolution rings true."

In the conclusion of the trilogy, *Ride with Me, Mariah Montana,* Jick McCaskell, the adolescent protagonist of *English Creek,* is now a crusty, retired rancher who narrates the goings-on as he squires his daughter, Moriah, and her ex-husband around Montana to report on the state of the state for the *Missoula Montanian.* "Feeling the reins of present and future slip from his hands," writes Susan Dodd of the *Washington Post Book World,* "Jick has grown a little irritable, loss around him everywhere he looks." It's Jick's voice, Dodd suggests, "cranky, confused, honest, stubborn and lovelorn" that "orchestrates the journey" and "makes the whole novel sing." Even so, says Burr Snider in the *San Francisco Examiner,* "the real star of this book is Montana," and Doig "takes you right into its big troubled heart."

"I am Montana-born and now live within half a mile of Puget Sound," the author told *CA.* "Inevitably, or so it seems to me, my books are the result of those popular pulls of the Rocky Mountains and the Pacific. Whichever the setting, in both my fiction and nonfiction I try to work two stubborn substances, research and craft, into becoming the hardest alloy of all—a good story. And that to me is the ultimate 'region,' the true home, for a writer. Specific geographies, but galaxies of imaginative expression—we've seen them both exist in William Faulkner's postage-stamp size Yoknapatawpha County, and in Gabriel Garcia-Marquez' nowhere village of Macondo dreaming in its hundred years of solitude. It is my utter belief that writers of caliber can ground their work in specific land and lingo and yet be writing of that larger country: life."

BIOGRAPHICAL/CRITICAL SOURCES:

BOOKS

Bredahl, A. Carl. *New Ground: Western American Narrative and the Literary Canon,* University of North Carolina Press (Chapel Hill), 1989.

Doig, Ivan, *This House of Sky: Landscapes of a Western Mind,* Harcourt, 1978.

Doig, Ivan, *Winter Brothers: A Season at the Edge of America,* Harcourt, 1980.

Doig, Ivan, *Heart Earth,* Atheneum, 1993.

Martin, Russell, *Writers of the Purple Sage,* Viking (New York), 1984.

Morris, Gregory L., *Talking Up a Storm: Voices of the New West,* University of Nebraska Press (Lincoln, NE), 1994.

O'Connell, Nicholas, *At the Field's End: Interviews with 20 Pacific Northwest Writers,* Madrona Press (Austin, TX), 1987.

Simpson, Elizabeth, *Earthlight, Wordfire: The Work of Ivan Doig,* University of Idaho Press (Moscow, ID), 1992.

PERIODICALS

Aspen Times (CO), October 2-3, 1993.

Bloomsbury Review, July/August, 1991.

Boston Globe, October 10, 1982.

Bozeman Daily Chronicle (MT), September 12, 1993.

Chicago Tribune, September 17, 1978; December 10, 1987.

Christian Science Monitor, December 24, 1984; November 20, 1990; February 12, 1992; September 16, 1993.

Eugene (OR) Register-Guard, October 3, 1993.

Kirkus Reviews, July 1, 1993.

Los Angeles Times, September 13, 1978; October 20, 1980; August 29, 1993.

Los Angeles Times Book Review, December 9, 1984; October 18, 1987; February 12, 1992.

Montana: The Magazine of Western History, winter, 1985.

Newsday (NY), November 11, 1984.

New Yorker, January 21, 1985.

New York Times Book Review, January 7, 1979; January 11, 1981; October 3, 1982; November 1, 1987; September 5, 1993.

Northwestern Perspective, winter, 1992.

Ogden Standard-Examiner (UT), May 30, 1993.

Pacific Northwest Quarterly, October, 1987.

Publishers Weekly, September 18, 1987; July 5, 1993.

Salt Lake Tribune, August 15, 1993.

San Francisco Examiner, November 4, 1990.

Seattle Post-Intelligencer, October 1, 1978; September 30, 1993.

Seattle Times, September 13, 1987.

Time, September 11, 1978.

Tribune Books (Chicago), August 30, 1987; September 26, 1993.

USA Today, October 26, 1984.

Washington Post, December 11, 1978; January 6, 1981; November 28, 1987.

Washington Post Book World, October 17, 1982; October 18, 1987; September 30, 1990; January 19, 1992.

Western American Literature, winter, 1980; August, 1981; February, 1986.

Western Historical Quarterly, April, 1980.

DONALDS, Gordon
See SHIRREFFS, Gordon D(onald)

*   *   *

DONLEAVY, J(ames) P(atrick) 1926-

PERSONAL: Born April 23, 1926, in Brooklyn, NY; became Irish citizen, 1967; married Valerie Heron (divorced); married Mary Wilson Price, 1970 (divorced); children: (first marriage) Philip, Karen; (second marriage) Rebecca Wallis, Rory. *Education:* Attended Trinity College, Dublin.

ADDRESSES: Home and office—Levington Park, Mullingar, County Westmeath, Ireland.

CAREER: Writer and playwright. Founder with son Philip Donleavy and producer Robert Mitchell of De Alfonce Tennis Association for the Promotion of the Superlative Game of Eccentric Champions. *Military service:* U.S. Navy, served in World War II.

AWARDS, HONORS: Most Promising Playwright Award, *Evening Standard,* 1960, for *Fairy Tales of New York;* Brandeis University Creative Arts Award, 1961-62, for two plays, *The Ginger Man* and *Fairy Tales of New York;* citation from National Institute and American Academy of Arts and Letters, 1975; American Academy of Arts and Letters grantee, 1975; Worldfest Houston Gold Award, 1992; Cine Golden Eagle Award for writer and narrator, 1993.

WRITINGS:

FICTION

The Ginger Man (novel; also see below), Olympia Press (Paris), 1955, published with introduction by Arland Ussher, Spearman (London), 1956, Obolensky (New York City), 1958, complete and unexpurgated edition, Delacorte (New York City), 1965.

A Singular Man (novel), Little, Brown (Boston), 1963.

Meet My Maker the Mad Molecule (short stories; also see below), Little, Brown, 1964, reprinted, Penguin (New York City), 1981.

The Saddest Summer of Samuel S (novel; also see below), Delacorte/Seymour Lawrence (New York City), 1966.

The Beastly Beatitudes of Balthazar B (novel), Delacorte/Seymour Lawrence, 1968.

The Onion Eaters (novel), Delacorte, 1971, reprinted, Penguin/Eyre & Spottiswoode (Andover, England), 1986.

A Fairy Tale of New York (novel; also see below), Delacorte/Seymour Lawrence, 1973.

The Destinies of Darcy Dancer, Gentleman (novel), illustrations by Jim Campbell, Delacorte/Seymour Lawrence, 1977.

Schultz (novel), Delacorte/Seymour Lawrence, 1979.

Meet My Maker the Mad Molecule and The Saddest Summer of Samuel S, Dell (New York City), 1979.

Leila: Further in the Destinies of Darcy Dancer, Gentleman (novel; sequel to *The Destinies of Darcy Dancer, Gentleman*), Delacorte/Seymour Lawrence, 1983, published as limited edition with "A Special Message for the First Edition from J. P. Donleavy," Franklin Library, 1983, published in England as *Leila: Further in the Life and Destinies of Darcy Dancer, Gentleman,* Allen Lane (London), 1983.

Are You Listening Rabbi Loew (novel; sequel to *Schultz*), Viking (New York City), 1987.

That Darcy, That Dancer, That Gentleman (novel; sequel to *Leila*), Viking, 1990.

The Lady Who Liked Clean Rest Rooms (novella), Thornwillow Press, in press.

PLAYS

The Ginger Man (adaptation of his novel of same title; first produced at Fortune Theatre, London, September 15, 1959; produced at Gaiety Theatre, Dublin, October 26, 1959; produced on Broadway at Orpheum Theatre, November 21, 1963; contains introduction "What They Did in Dublin"; also see below), Random House (New York City), 1961, published in England as *What They Did in Dublin with The Ginger Man,* MacGibbon and Kee (London), 1961 (also see below).

Fairy Tales of New York (adaptation of his novel *A Fairy Tale of New York;* first produced at Comedy Theatre, London, January 24, 1961; also see below), Random House, 1961.

A Singular Man (first produced at Comedy Theatre, October 21, 1964; produced at Westport County [CT] Playhouse, September 4, 1967; also see below), Bodley Head (London), 1964.

The Plays of J. P. Donleavy (with a preface by the author; contains *What They Did in Dublin with The Ginger Man, The Ginger Man, Fairy Tales of New York, A Singular Man,* and *The Saddest Summer of Samuel S*), photographs of productions by Lewis Morley, Delacorte/Seymour Lawrence, 1973.

The Beastly Beatitudes of Balthazar B (adaptation of his novel of same title), first produced in London, 1981.

Also author of radio play, *Helen,* 1956.

OTHER

The Unexpurgated Code: A Complete Manual of Survival and Manners, illustrations by the author, Delacorte/Seymour Lawrence, 1975.

De Alfonce Tennis: The Superlative Game of Eccentric Champions, Its History, Accoutrements, Rules, Conduct, and Regimen, Dutton (New York City)/ Seymour Lawrence, 1984.

J. P. Donleavy's Ireland: In All Her Sins and in Some of Her Graces, Viking, 1986, published in England as *Ireland: In All Her Sins and in Some of Her Graces,* M. Joseph (London), 1986.

A Singular Country, Ryan (Peterborough, England), 1989, Norton (New York City), 1990.

The History of the Ginger Man, Houghton Mifflin (Boston), 1994.

Contributor of short fiction and essays to *Atlantic Monthly, Playboy, Queen, Saturday Evening Post,* and *Saturday Review.*

SIDELIGHTS: "If there is an archetypal post-World War II American writer-in-exile it may well be James Patrick Donleavy," writes William E. Grant in a *Dictionary of Literary Biography* essay. The son of Irish immigrant parents, J. P. Donleavy renounced the America of their dreams for an Ireland of his own, and became a citizen when Ireland granted tax-free status to its authors. Although literary success came several years after the publication of his stylistically innovative first novel, *The Ginger Man,* Donleavy is now internationally recognized for having written what many consider to be a modern classic. Referring to the "sense of exile and alienation that seems to haunt his life as well as his work," Grant observes that "even achieving the literary success he thought America would deny him has not lessened his alienation from his country, though it has enhanced the style in which he expresses his exile status." Donleavy now writes at his expansive two-hundred-year-old manor situated on nearly two hundred acres in County Westmeath. "He's a sort of born-again Irishman who enthusiastically embraces the life of a man of letters and leisure, adopting not only an Irish country estate but also the appropriate deportment and brogue," says Peter Ross in the *Detroit News.* "He also happens to be one of the funniest and most audacious writers around."

Donleavy's decision to emigrate, although precipitated by difficulty finding a publisher for his first novel, appears to have been the result of a slowly evolving dissatisfaction with what he refers to in his *Atlantic Monthly* essay, "An Expatriate Looks at America," as "a country corrosive of the spirit." Donleavy explains: "Each time I go to these United States I start anew trying to figure them out. After two weeks I decide that like anywhere, greed, lust and envy make them work. But in America it is big greed, big lust, big envy." Although Donleavy remembers his childhood in the Bronx as peaceful, New York City became an increasingly threatening presence, and the ubiquitous violence made him fearful of death there. He recalls in the *At-*

lantic Monthly that "something in one's bowels was saying no to this land. Where my childhood friends were growing up, just as their parents did, to be trapped trembling and terrified in a nightmare." Skeptical of America's treatment of its artists as well, Donleavy felt at the outset of his career that he stood little chance of achieving literary success in a land he describes in the *Atlantic Monthly* as a place "where your media mesmerized brain shuts off when the media does." He adds, "And if I stayed they would, without even trying, or knowing, kill me."

Donleavy was resolved to achieve recognition and relates in a *Paris Review* interview with Molly McKaughan: "I realized that the only way you could ever tackle the world was to write something that no one could hold off, a book that would go everywhere, into everyone's hands. And I decided then to write a novel which would shake the world. I shook my fist and said I would do it." That novel, *The Ginger Man,* is set in post-World War II Dublin and details the hedonistic existence of Sebastian Dangerfield who, according to Alfred Rushton in the Toronto *Globe and Mail,* gave "moral turpitude a new lease on life." While still a student, Donleavy began crafting the novel, but he returned to New York to complete and publish it. He indicates in the *Paris Review* that Scribners, to whom he first took the manuscript, thought it was one of the best ever brought to them; its content, however, prevented them from publishing it. Forty-five publishers rejected the novel because they "thought it was a dirty book—scatological, unreadable, obscene," Donleavy tells David Remnick in the *Washington Post.* "My life literally depended on getting this book into print, and when I couldn't, it just drove me out of America."

In the *Paris Review,* Donleavy recalls his reluctance to edit *The Ginger Man* into acceptability: "I had a sense that the book held itself together on the basis of these scatological parts. That its life was in these parts. And I was quite aware that cutting them would be severely damaging to it." Brendan Behan, the legendary Irish playwright and patriot with whom Donleavy became friends during his Dublin days, suggested sending the manuscript to the Olympia Press in Paris, where it eventually was accepted. Following its publication as part of an overtly pornographic series, however, a lengthy legal battle ensued in which Donleavy emerged as the owner of the publishing house. Despite "the potential for literary damage, publication by Olympia Press had the generally salutary effect of establishing the unexpurgated edition of *The Ginger Man* as an underground classic before complete editions became available," notes Grant. In order to ensure the novel's publication in England, though, and to get it recognized and reviewed, Donleavy agreed to certain cuts, stating in the *Paris Review:* "It was an act of pure practicality. If someone wanted to read the unexpurgated edi-

tion, they could buy it in Paris. I had published it as I had written it, so it wasn't wrong, then, to publish it to establish my reputation."

Although Donleavy's reputation had to endure both court battles and censors, his experience as a litigant proved invaluable in negotiating subsequent contracts with publishers. "He's very courtly, but he's a very sharp businessman," comments Donleavy's longtime publisher Seymour Lawrence, according to Samuel Allis in the *Washington Post.* "He does all of his negotiating and, unlike most authors, he understands copyrights. He drives a hard bargain, but he's the most professional author I've ever known." Donleavy's legal and business dealings have also given him a special sense of his profession. Money, says the author in the *Paris Review,* has a dramatic effect upon his writing: "In fact, I would say that money is everything in my profession. One's mind almost becomes a vast cash register. . . . To sit at a desk and think, and write, you must have peace, and to buy peace costs a fortune."

In 1994 Donleavy's *The History of the Ginger Man* was published. Not only does the book chronicle his effort to publish *The Ginger Man,* but it is Donleavy's autobiographical account of his struggles to become a writer while supporting his family. Many of the real-life people that enliven Donleavy's nonfiction book will seem familiar to his readers because Donleavy's friends and acquaintances made their debut appearances in fictional form in *The Ginger Man.* Even before the publication of *The History of the Ginger Man,* critics recognized the autobiographical aspects of Donleavy's best-known novel. Sally Eckhoff, writing in the *Voice Literary Supplement,* observes: "In Dangerfield, Donleavy created his prototypical diver into Irish society. Like his hero, the author has a history of Olympic pub-crawling—right down there under the rug with Flann O'Brien." Eckhoff also notes that Donleavy's writing exhibits a strong sense of setting. "Most of *The Ginger Man,*" writes Eckhoff, "takes place in Dublin—the world of dreams, populated by gullible shopkeepers, screaming kids, crooked priests, affectionate laundrywomen with time on their hands, and a pub on every corner with a weird name like 'The Bleeding Horse.' "

Critics were unsure at first how to categorize Donleavy and *The Ginger Man.* Grant observes that the critical establishment "debated whether Donleavy belonged with Britain's Angry Young Men, America's black humorists, or France's existentialists." In his *Doings and Undoings,* Norman Podhoretz calls *The Ginger Man* "fundamentally a book without hope." Similarly, in his *Radical Innocence: Studies in the Contemporary American Novel,* Ihab Hassan considers the novel to be "full of gusto, seething with life, but its energy may be the energy of negation, and its vitality has a nasty edge." The nihilism in *The Ginger Man* "refers us to the postwar, existential era," states Hassan.

"Traditional values are not in the process of dying, they have ceased entirely to operate, and their stark absence leaves men to shift for themselves as best they can." The "freshness" of the characterization of Sebastian Dangerfield was one of the most critically acclaimed aspects of the novel, notes Grant, who adds that some critics recognized that the character "existed almost totally outside any system of ideas." Eckhoff calls *The Ginger Man* "a hilarious, cruel, compassionate book."

Despite the commercial success of Donleavy's subsequent work, the critics generally consider his reputation to rest solely on *The Ginger Man*. "So far as most critics and reviewers are concerned, the later works have been but pale shadows of the first brilliant success, and the publication of each succeeding novel has seen a decline in critical attention," writes Grant. Some critics believe that Donleavy has run out of ideas, that he is refurbishing old material, reworking or resurrecting earlier work. For instance, in a *Harper's* review of *The Destinies of Darcy Dancer, Gentleman,* Michael Malone compares a Donleavy book to Guinness stout: "It's distinctive, it's carbonated, it's brimmed with what Hazlitt called 'gusto,' and those who like it can drink it forever. The ingredients never change." Donleavy pays attention to the critics only in a "fairly superficial way" because, as he says in the *Paris Review,* "A writer must always be aware that he has to be a supreme critic. . . . And only his judgement matters." Allis indicates, however, that Donleavy "displays something close to hostility toward academics and the people who review his books and plays," and that he discourages academic interest in his work because he says, "I never want [to] get that self-conscious of my literary position." Grant suggests that "though none individually rivals the first masterpiece, several of these later works deserve wider attention than they have had from the American reading public and critical establishment alike."

Critics point to several characteristics of *The Ginger Man* that surface in Donleavy's later work. Beneath the bawdy humor lies an inherent despondency, with licentiousness masking the more profound search for love; bizarre, eccentric characters, around whom his books revolve, tend to be alienated, victimized by life, and weakened by impending death. "The novels range from variations of the humorous—slapstick, scatological, sardonic—to the sentimental in an idiosyncratic style that conveys the pressure of time on language," writes Thomas LeClair in *Contemporary Literature.* "But such features of Donleavy's work are finally extensions of and returns to death, the test of man's mettle in landscapes made pale by death's presence."

An awareness of death figures significantly in Donleavy's work, and the question Donleavy's heroes "answer in their own, progressively inefficacious ways," writes LeClair in

Twentieth Century Literature, is, "How does a man weakened by an awareness of death survive in a world experienced as magical with malevolence?" LeClair observes that "to evade his consciousness of mortality, Sebastian Dangerfield . . . lives a hedonistic life in the present and dreams of relaxed ease for the future"; and the rich and reclusive George Smith of Donleavy's *A Singular Man,* who is absorbed with the idea of death and even builds his own mausoleum, "separates himself from the world in a parody of Howard Hughes' and John Paul Getty's attempts to avoid the disease of life." LeClair notes in *Critique: Studies in Modern Fiction* that "the heroes of *The Saddest Summer of Samuel S, The Beastly Beatitudes of Balthazar B,* and *The Onion Eaters* all attempt to overcome their fear of their own death or their sadness about the death of others through love."

According to Grant, the themes of love and loss are also important in much of Donleavy's work. *The Saddest Summer of Samuel S* is about an eminent literary figure in the United States who undergoes psychoanalysis in Vienna in order to live a more conventional life. Of this novel, Grant writes: "Longing for a love he has never had and cannot find because in spite of his need he cannot give, Samuel S is the victim of a life that cannot be lived over and a destiny that cannot be changed." The character, observes Grant, is withdrawn and "trapped in a life-in-death state of mind with neither belief nor passion to motivate him." Similarly, in *The Beastly Beatitudes of Balthazar B,* a novel that details the lonely life of a wealthy young man whose marriage collapses, the hero is "separated from those he loves . . . and seeks completion by loving others, a simple but impossible quest," says Shaun O'Connell in the *Nation.* Robert Scholes observes in the *Saturday Review* that although this "shy and gentle" character seeks love, "it proves elusive, even harder to keep than to find." And O'Connell sees in Donleavy "the joy of the artist who can embody his vision, however bleak, the self-certainty of the writer who can so eloquently move his hero to name his pain."

However, writing in the *Washington Post Book World* about Donleavy's *The Destinies of Darcy Dancer, Gentleman,* a novel in which a young aristocrat is thwarted in several of his attempts at love, Curt Suplee suggests that "Donleavy does not write novels so much as Oedipal fairy tales: semi-realistic fables in which the same patterns are obsessively reenacted. Invariably, a young man finds himself trapped in a society dominated by hostile father-figures and devoid of the uncritical comfort afforded by mothers. . . . Every time the young man attempts to assert his ego in this world, he fails or is beaten, and flees to succour—either to the manic medium of alcohol or the overt mother-surrogates who provide sex and self-esteem, for a while." O'Connell finds, though, that Donleavy's characters "press the possibilities of life with high style and win many tactical victories of great hilarity . . . before they are defeated," and he believes that "Donleavy's vision of sadness seems earned, won by a search of all the possible routes toward happiness."

Focusing on the bawdy humor in Donleavy's work, critics sometimes fault it for what they consider to be gratuitously lewd language and a reliance upon sexual slapstick. A *Times Literary Supplement* reviewer of *The Onion Eaters,* for instance, states that "the scenes of violence and the sexual encounters suggest an attitude to the human body and its functions, weaknesses and pleasures, which is anything but tender, compassionate, or celebratory." The novel is about a young and handsome character named Clayton Claw Clever Clementine, who in addition to being somewhat freakishly over-endowed sexually, has inherited an Irish manor and must confront what a *New Statesman* contributor refers to as a "bizarre collection of servants and . . . an ever-growing crew of sex-obsessed weirdies." Guy Davenport finds in the *National Review* that "Donleavy is uninterruptedly bawdy, yet his obscenity is so grand and so open, that it rises above giving offense into a realm of its own, unchallenged and wild."

Critics also recognize, however, that Donleavy's humor belies an inherent sadness. "Donleavy writes sad and lonely books," says R. Z. Sheppard in a *Time* review of *The Onion Eaters.* Sheppard finds that Donleavy's fictional worlds are "closed worlds, their boundaries no more distant than the most prominent erectile tissue. Alone, without context or meaning, the flesh is all." Sheppard suggests that the absence of meaning in the novel, as well as its "animal warmth, at once grotesque and touching," is perhaps Donleavy's way of asserting that "this warmth is the only thing about which we can be certain."

Writing in *Newsweek* about Donleavy's nonfiction book *The Unexpurgated Code: A Complete Manual of Survival and Manners,* Arthur Cooper describes Donleavy's humor: "Like Mel Brooks, he knows that bad taste is merely a joke that doesn't get a laugh. And like Brooks, Donleavy's demonic humor is utterly democratic, thrusting the needle into everyone regardless of race, creed, color, or ability to control one's bowels." Referring to the book as "a collection of bilious and often funny rules for living," Melvin Maddocks observes in *Time* that "between the lines, Donleavy's diatribes manage to say more." Maddocks believes that Donleavy's "visions of grace, chivalry and order" reveal the author as "an inverted romantic, profoundly sad beneath his disguise because he and the world are no better than they happen to be."

Similarly, in a *Midwest Quarterly* assessment of *The Unexpurgated Code,* Charles G. Masinton suggests that "Donleavy normally proceeds by means of instinct, inspiration,

and intuition—the tools of a romantic artist. He aims to produce belly laughs and . . . a sympathetic response to his chief characters; he does not set out to impose order and rationality on experience. And instead of elevated language (which he often parodies quite effectively), he records with great skill an earthy vernacular full of both comic and lyric possibilities." While Grant believes that Donleavy's "characteristic tone of pessimism, melancholia, alienation, and human failure . . . suggest Jonathan Swift's misanthropic humor," he also finds it reminiscent of Mark Twain's later work, "which combines pessimism and humor in an elegiac, melancholic, and misanthropic voice."

In the *Los Angeles Times Book Review,* David Hirson laments that while a unique blend of lyricism and farce still characterize Donleavy's later novels, his humor has begun to be derived almost exclusively from overkill. An example is *Are You Listening Rabbi Loew.* Despite its "dauntingly energetic prose," Hirson believes that the novel ultimately wears out the reader. Writes Hirson, "Funny though boorishness, bodily functions and excessive profanity can be, the effect, finally, is of a joke that takes too long in the telling, a numbingly protracted jape."

The style and language of Donleavy's fiction has attracted a great deal of critical attention over the years. Notes Thomas Lask, "critics keep citing his first book . . . some saying that nothing after it has equaled that first effort, and objecting to his language, which has a syntax of its own, without connectives or prepositions, shifting tense at will." Stylistically innovative, *The Ginger Man* employs not only a shifting point of view (from first to third person) so that Dangerfield becomes both observer and observed but, according to Grant, it "relies on rapidly moving, nearly staccato sentence fragments which capture brilliantly the chaotic and fragmented qualities of Dangerfield's world." In a *Times Literary Supplement* review of *That Darcy, That Dancer, That Gentleman* (the third volume in the trilogy that began with *The Destinies of Darcy Dancer, Gentleman*), Mark Sanderson observes that Donleavy's unusual use of language masks the thinness of the novel's plot. "The stylistic tics remain," writes Sanderson, "a fondness for the present continuous; hyphens reserved for double-barrelled surnames; each chapter rounded off by a homespun haiku; semi-colons and question marks entirely absent."

Donleavy explains that his use of language is "designed to reflect the way the mind works," says Lask in a *New York Times* review of *Schultz,* a novel about the exploits of an American producer of vulgar plays in London. In the *Paris Review,* Donleavy offers a more detailed explanation: "You're trying to get what you've written on your page into a reader's mind as quickly as possible, and to keep them seeing it. That is why I use the short, truncated telegraphic sentences. They are the most efficient use of language, and I think the brain puts words together the way I do."

Some critics think Donleavy has become a "prisoner of style," says Paul Abelman in the *Spectator,* that "he has never escaped from the prose techniques which he invented for his fine first novel." Abelman believes that "the style of the later books is not really that of *The Ginger Man* at all but simply one that employs superficial aspects of it and neglects the lyrical essence." Unlike *The Ginger Man,* says Abelman, the other books are "monster prose poems founded on the most plodding, leaden metrical foot known to the English language [the spondee—two stressed syllables regularly repeated]." Abelman, though, considers Donleavy "possibly the greatest lyrical humorist to emerge since the war," and adds that he "has that to his credit which few living writers can claim: a modern classic."

Although Donleavy indicates to Thomas Lask in the *New York Times* that he's as "delighted" with *The Ginger Man* as when he first wrote it, he feels that his subsequent books keep *The Ginger Man* alive. Commenting to Remnick that he does not feel *The Ginger Man* represents his "best work," Donleavy states, "When I pick it up and read it now critically as a piece of writing, in technical terms, it doesn't compare to later books." Acknowledging in the *Paris Review* that his subsequent writing has not provided the pleasure that *The Ginger Man* did, Donleavy says: "I don't think you ever have that again. When an author's recognized, all that leaves him, because that's what he's needed to force himself to go through the terrible agony of being unknown and being able to face the world and the fact that it's a giant, vast place where nearly every man is saying: Dear God, hear my tiny voice."

Another point of interest for critics of Donleavy's writing is the effect that leaving the United States for Ireland has had on the author. Grant believes that "Donleavy remains essentially the exile who once wrote of America, 'there it goes, a runaway horse, with no one in control.'" Donleavy recalls in his *Atlantic Monthly* essay, that "each time you arrive anew in America, you find how small you are and how dismally you impress against the giantness and power of this country where you are so obviously, and with millions like yourself, so totally fatally expendable." Grant notes that this vision is often expressed in Donleavy's portrayal of the United States as a nightmare. In *A Fairy Tale of New York,* for instance, the wife of the Brooklyn-born, Bronx-raised, and European-educated Cornelius Christian dies on their way to New York; and without money or friends, Christian is taken advantage of by everyone. "Affection, loathing, nostalgia and fear are the main components of the attitude he brings to bear upon his native place," writes Julian Moynahan in the

Washington Post Book World, adding that "hidden away in the book for those who can find it is a good deal of personal revelation, a good deal of alembicated and metamorphosed autobiography." As D. Keith Mano states in the *New York Times Book Review,* the book is "about social impotence and despair. Valleys of humiliation, sloughs of despond." The story focuses on the brutality of New York City; and Christian, who lacks the funds to move, sees emigration as the only answer to his liberation. "Yet Donleavy's thunderous, superb humor has the efficacy of grace," says Mano. "It heals and conquers and ratifies." And a *Times Literary Supplement* contributor, who remarks that "few writers know how to enjoy verbal promiscuity like . . . Donleavy," considers that "it is largely because of the confidence of the style, too, that you come out of the welter of failure and misery feeling good—nastiness is inevitably laced with hilarity and sentiment in his telling it."

Moving to Ireland changed his life "utterly," Donleavy says in the *Paris Review,* adding, "It also romanticized the United States for me so that it became a subject for me as a writer." However, in the *Atlantic Monthly,* Donleavy speaks about the indelibility of his American beginnings: "As far away as you may go, or as foreign as your life can ever become, there is something that always stays stained American in you." About living among the Irish, however, Donleavy remarks in a *Publishers Weekly* interview: "Literally, everywhere you go here, they're half nuts. It's very tough to discover real insanity, because the whole race is like that, and, indeed, this is the place to come if you're not right in the head."

John Kelly writes in the *Times Literary Supplement* that "during a disconsolate return to his native America," Donleavy discovered that "Ireland is a state of mind" and his recent *J. P. Donleavy's Ireland: In All Her Sins and Some of Her Graces* "attempts a description of that state of mind." Donleavy recreates his own first exposure to the postwar Dublin that, says Kelly, provided the "raw material" for "Donleavy's myth-making imagination." In a Toronto *Globe and Mail* review of the book, Rushton thinks that "Donleavy belongs to the people he describes, and acknowledges their kinship by giving them their full due." As Kevin E. Gallagher comments in the *Los Angeles Times Book Review,* it is "a love story that, I think never ends for anyone who cares, like this, about a place."

Although Donleavy's *The Ginger Man* remains the standard by which the entirety of his work is measured, his writing has generated the full spectrum of critical response. Ken Lawless in an *Antioch Review* of *The Destinies of Darcy Dancer, Gentleman,* for example, writes that "no literary artist working in English today is better than J. P. Donleavy, and few merit comparison with him." On the other hand, in the *New York Times Book Review,* Geoffrey

Wolff reacts to similar critical assessments of Donleavy's work with: "Nonsense. He is an Irish tenor who sets his blarney to short songs that are sometimes as soft as velvet or good stout, sometimes plangent, elliptical and coarse." However, Grant suggests that "at the very least, he represents the example of a writer who goes very much his own way, eschewing both the popular success of the best-sellers and the literary acclaim of the academic establishment. At best, a case can be made for a few of his novels as primary expressions within the black humorist tradition of modern literature. Certainly he is a foremost American exponent of the Kafkaesque vision of the modern world, and his better works strongly express that sense of universal absurdity at which we can only laugh."

"After all my years of struggle, it makes me realize that in my own way I have conquered America, totally silently, totally from underground and from within and that television or being interviewed doesn't matter," Donleavy relates in the *Paris Review*. In his *Saturday Review* essay, "The Author and His Image," Donleavy ponders the complexities of an author's image in its various aspects from obscurity through success, and concludes: "But you know no matter what you do the world will always finally turn its face away. Back into all its own troubled lives. . . . Forgetting what you wanted them to see. Silent with what you wanted them to say. And empty with what you wanted them to feel. Except somewhere you know there will be a voice. At least once asking. Hey what happened to that guy, did he die, you know the one, who wrote that book, can't remember his name but he was famous as hell. That was the author. And that was his image."

BIOGRAPHICAL/CRITICAL SOURCES:

BOOKS

Authors in the News, Volume 2, Gale (Detroit), 1976.

Contemporary Fiction in America and England, 1950-1970, Gale, 1976.

Contemporary Literary Criticism, Gale, Volume 1, 1973, Volume 4, 1975, Volume 6, 1976, Volume 10, 1979, Volume 45, 1987.

Dictionary of Literary Biography, Volume 6: *American Novelists since World War II,* Gale, 1980.

Donleavy, J. P., *The Ginger Man,* Olympia Press, 1955, published with introduction by Arland Ussher, Spearman, 1956, Obolensky, 1958, complete and unexpurgated edition, Delacorte, 1965.

Donleavy, J. P., *J. P. Donleavy's Ireland: In All Her Sins and in Some of Her Graces,* Viking, 1986.

Donleavy, J. P., *A Singular Country,* Ryan, 1989, Norton, 1990. Donleavy, J. P., *The History of the Ginger Man,* Houghton, 1994.

Hassan, Ihab, *Radical Innocence: Studies in the Contemporary American Novel,* Princeton University Press (Princeton, NJ), 1961.

Masinton, Charles G., *J. P. Donleavy: The Style of His Sadness and Humor,* Popular Press, 1975.

Podhoretz, Norman, *Doings and Undoings,* Farrar, Straus (New York City), 1964.

Sharma, R. K., *Isolation and Protest: A Case Study of J. P. Donleavy's Fiction,* Ajanta (New Delhi), 1983.

PERIODICALS

America, May 3, 1969; May 10, 1980.

Antioch Review, winter, 1978; winter, 1980, p. 122.

Architectural Digest, November, 1986.

Atlantic Monthly, December, 1968; December, 1976; December, 1977; June, 1979.

Books, November, 1987, p. 29.

Chicago Tribune, May 25, 1958; May 19, 1985.

Chicago Tribune Book World, October 28, 1979.

Commonweal, August 15, 1958; December 2, 1966; March 7, 1969; September 14, 1990, p. 518.

Contemporary Literature, Volume 12, number 3, 1971.

Critique: Studies in Modern Fiction, Volume 9, number 2, 1966; Volume 12, number 3, 1971; Volume 17, number 1, 1975.

Detroit News, October 2, 1983; June 9, 1985.

Economist, November 10, 1973.

Globe and Mail (Toronto), October 13, 1984; January 17, 1987; April 18, 1987.

Harper's, December, 1977.

Listener, May 11, 1978; December 13, 1984, p. 30; October 29, 1987, p. 32; November 2, 1989, p. 35; November 1, 1990, p. 34.

Los Angeles Times, October 28, 1983.

Los Angeles Times Book Review, October 7, 1979; May 5, 1985, p. 11; November 16, 1986, p. 11; November 13, 1988, p. 7.

Michigan Academician, winter, 1974; summer, 1976.

Midcontinent American Studies Journal, spring, 1967.

Midwest Quarterly, winter, 1977.

Nation, May 24, 1958; December 14, 1963; January 20, 1969.

National Review, October 18, 1971.

New Leader, December 19, 1977.

New Republic, December 14, 1963; March 1, 1969; July 24, 1971; December 15, 1979.

New Statesman, April 17, 1964; February 7, 1969; July 16, 1971; May 12, 1978; March 28, 1980, p. 483; October 14, 1983.

Newsweek, November 11, 1963; March 21, 1966; November 18, 1968; September 15, 1975.

New Yorker, October 25, 1958; May 16, 1964; October 15, 1966; October 8, 1973; December 19, 1977; July 16, 1990.

New York Herald Tribune Book Review, May 11, 1958.

New York Review of Books, January 2, 1969.

New York Times, May 11, 1958; November 16, 1979; April 17, 1987; October 12, 1988.

New York Times Book Review, November 24, 1963; November 7, 1965; December 5, 1965; March 20, 1966; December 29, 1968; September 5, 1971; September 23, 1973; November 6, 1977; October 7, 1979, p. 14; October 26, 1980; October 11, 1983; October 30, 1983; April 28, 1985, p. 24; November 27, 1988, p. 22; March 4, 1990, p. 38; December 2, 1990, p. 72.

Observer (London), October 28, 1984, p. 25; July 6, 1986, p. 24; November 8, 1987, p.28; November 4, 1990, p. 61.

Paris Review, fall, 1975.

Publishers Weekly, October 31, 1986.

Punch, October 21, 1987, p. 64.

Saturday Review, May 10, 1958; November 23, 1963; November 23, 1968; November 12, 1977; January 20, 1979.

Spectator, September 22, 1973; May 13, 1978; April 12, 1980; December 8, 1984, p. 33; July 19, 1986, p. 29; November 28, 1987, p. 36.

Studies in Contemporary Satire, Number 1, 1975.

Time, March 18, 1966; December 6, 1968; July 5, 1971; October 29, 1973; September 22, 1975; November 14, 1977; October 15, 1979.

Times (London), October 13, 1983; July 17, 1986, p. 15; October 29, 1987.

Times Literary Supplement, April 30, 1964; May 6, 1965; May 5, 1967; March 20, 1969; July 23, 1971; September 7, 1973; May 12, 1978; April 4, 1980, p. 382; October 28, 1983, p. 1185; November 16, 1984, p. 1302; December 19, 1986, p. 1433; February 1, 1991, p. 10.

Tribune Books (Chicago), January 25, 1987, p. 6; October 2, 1988, p. 7.

Twentieth Century Literature, January, 1968; July, 1972.

Village Voice, September 17, 1979.

Virginia Quarterly Review, spring, 1987, p. 56.

Voice Literary Supplement, October, 1988, p. 28.

Washington Post, October 30, 1979; February 24, 1985.

Washington Post Book World, September 30, 1973; November 13, 1977.

World Literature Today, summer, 1978; summer, 1980, p. 431; spring, 1984.

Yale Review, October, 1966.

*   *   *

DONOVAN, Josephine (Campbell) 1941-

PERSONAL: Born March 10, 1941, in Manila, Philippines (American citizen born abroad); daughter of William N. (a physician) and Josephine (Devigne) Donovan.

Education: Bryn Mawr College, A.B. (cum laude), 1962; University of Wisconsin (now University of Wisconsin—Madison), M.A., 1967, Ph.D, 1971.

ADDRESSES: Home—294 Dennett St., Portsmouth, NH 03801. *Office*—Dept. of English, 5752 Neville Hall, University of Maine, Orono, ME 04469-5752.

CAREER: University of Kentucky, Lexington, assistant professor in honors program, 1971-76; University of New Hampshire, Durham, coordinator of women's studies program, 1977-80; University of Tulsa, Tulsa, OK, visiting scholar, 1982; George Washington University, Washington, DC, visiting assistant professor, 1983-84; University of Maine, Orono, ME, professor of English, 1987—. Consultant to numerous university presses.

MEMBER: Modern Language Association of America, Women's Caucus for the Modern Languages, National Women's Studies Association.

AWARDS, HONORS: Outstanding academic book, *Choice* magazine, 1986, for *Feminist Theory: The Intellectual Traditions of American Feminism.*

WRITINGS:

(Editor and contributor) *Feminist Literary Criticism: Explorations in Theory,* University Press of Kentucky (Lexington, KY), 1975, revised edition, 1989.

Sarah Orne Jewett, Ungar (New York City), 1980.

New England Local Color Literature: A Women's Tradition, Ungar, 1983.

Feminist Theory: The Intellectual Traditions of American Feminism, Ungar, 1985, revised and expanded edition, 1992.

(Author of introduction, and editor with Charles G. Waugh and Martin H. Greenberg) Sarah Orne Jewett, *Best Stories of Sarah Orne Jewett,* illustrated by Peter Farrow, L. Tapley (Augusta, ME), 1988.

After the Fall: The Demeter-Persephone Myth in Wharton, Cather, and Glasgow, Pennsylvania State University Press (University Park, PA), 1989.

Gnosticism in Modern Literature: A Study of the Selected Works of Camus, Sartre, Hesse, and Kafka, Garland (New York City), 1990.

Uncle Tom's Cabin: Evil, Affliction, and Redemptive Love, Twayne (Boston, MA), 1991.

Also contributor to books, including *Images of Women in Fiction,* edited by Susan Koppelman-Cornillon, Bowling Green Popular Press, 1972; *American Women Writers: A Critical Reference Guide From Colonial Times to the Present,* edited by Luis Mainiero, Ungar, 1979; *Women and Language in Literature and Society,* edited by Ruth Borker, Nelly Furman, and Sally McConnell-Ginet, Praeger (New York City), 1980; *Feminist Literary Criticism,* National Humanities Center, 1981; *Critical Essays* on Sarah Orne Jewett, edited by Gwen L. Nagel, G. K. Hall (Boston, MA), 1984; *Feminist Issues in Literary Scholarship,* edited by Shari Benstock, Indiana University Press (Bloomington, IN), 1987; *Twentieth-Century Literary Theory: A Reader,* edited by K. M. Newton, St. Martin's Press (New York City), 1988; *A Feminist Critique of Language: A Reader,* edited by Deborah Cameron, Routledge (Boston, MA), 1990; *Writing the Woman Artist,* edited by Suzanne Jones, University of Pennsylvania Press (Philadelphia, PA), 1991; and *The (Other) American Traditions,* edited by Joyce Warren, Rutgers University Press (New Brunswick, NJ), 1993. Contributor of articles and reviews to literature journals, including *American Literature, Critical Inquiry, Massachusetts Review, Signs,* and *Tulsa Studies in Women's Literature.*

WORK IN PROGRESS: Women and the Rise of the Novel; articles on ecofeminism.

SIDELIGHTS: Josephine Donovan once told *CA:* "Feminist literary criticism assumes that there is a moral dimension to literature, that literature functions as part of the cultural propaganda of society, that it does affect people's lives, their ways of thinking, their behavior. In much of Western literature the moral being of women has been denied or repressed. Feminist literary criticism points this out and looks for works (often by women) in which women characters seek to achieve fullness of being. In this way it seeks to rewrite literary and cultural history."

*   *   *

DRESSER, Davis   1904-1977
(Asa Baker, Kathryn Culver, Don Davis, Peter Field, Brett Halliday, Anthony Scott, Anderson Wayne; Matthew Blood and Hal Debrett, joint pseudonyms)

PERSONAL: Born July 31, 1904, in Chicago, IL; died February 4, 1977; son of Justin and Mary Dresser; married Helen McCloy (a writer), 1946 (divorced, 1961); married Kathleen Rollins (a writer, sometimes under joint pseudonym Hal Debrett); married Mary Savage (a writer); children: (first marriage) Chloe. *Education:* Educated in Texas; Tri-State College, Angola, IN, Certificate of Civil Engineering.

CAREER: Worked as engineer and surveyor, as co-founder and owner of Torquil Publishing Company, and Halliday and McCloy Literary Agency, 1953-64, as founding editor of *Mike Shayne's Mystery Magazine,* and as writer of mystery and Western novels. *Military service:* U.S. Army; served in cavalry.

MEMBER: Mystery Writers of America (founding member), Western Writers of America, National Writers' Club.

AWARDS, HONORS: Edgar Allan Poe Award, Mystery Writers of America, for criticism, 1953.

WRITINGS:

UNDER PSEUDONYM ASA BAKER; JERRY BURKE MYSTERY SERIES

Mum's the Word for Murder, Dodd (New York), 1938.
The Kissed Corpse, Carlyle (New York), 1939.

UNDER JOINT PSEUDONYM MATTHEW BLOOD; MORGAN WAYNE MYSTERY SERIES

(With Ryerson Johnson) *The Avenger,* Fawcett (New York), 1952.
(With Johnson) *Death Is a Lovely Dame,* Fawcett, 1954.

UNDER PSEUDONYM KATHRYN CULVER; NOVELS

Love Is a Masquerade, Phoenix Press (New York), 1935.
Million Dollar Madness, Hillman-Curl (New York), 1937.
Too Smart for Love, Hillman-Curl, 1937.
Green Path to the Moon, Hillman-Curl, 1938.
Once to Every Woman, Godwin (New York), 1938.
Girl Alone, Grammercy (New York), 1939.

UNDER PSEUDONYM DON DAVIS; RIO KID WESTERN SERIES

Return of the Rio Kid, Morrow (New York), 1940.
Death on Treasure Trail, Hutchison (London), 1940, Morrow, 1941.
Rio Kid Justice, Morrow, 1941.
Two-Gun Rio Kid, Morrow, 1941.

UNDER JOINT PSEUDONYM HAL DEBRETT; MYSTERY NOVELS

(With wife, Kathleen Rollins) *Before I Wake,* Dodd, 1949.
(With Rollins) *A Lonely Way to Die,* Dodd, 1950.

AS DAVIS DRESSER; TWISTER MALONE WESTERN SERIES

Death Rides the Pecos, Morrow, 1940.
The Hangmen of Sleepy Valley, Morrow, 1940, published as *The Masked Riders of Sleepy Valley,* Ward Lock (London), 1941.
Lynch-Rope Law, Morrow, 1941.
Murder on the Mesa, Ward Lock, 1953.

AS DAVIS DRESSER UNLESS OTHERWISE NOTED; OTHER NOVELS

Let's Laugh at Love, Hillman-Curl, 1937.
Romance for Julie, Curl (New York), 1938.
Gunsmoke on the Mesa, Carlton (New York), 1941.
(Under pseudonym Anderson Wayne) *Charlie Dell,* Coward McCann (New York), 1952, published as *A Time to Remember,* Popular Library (New York), 1959.

UNDER PSEUDONYM PETER FIELD; POWDER VALLEY WESTERN SERIES

Guns from Powder Valley, Morrow, 1941.
Powder Valley Pay-off, Morrow, 1941.
Trail South from Powder Valley, Morrow, 1942.
Fight for Powder Valley!, Morrow, 1942.
Law Man of Powder Valley, Morrow, 1942.
Powder Valley Vengeance, Morrow, 1943.
Sheriff on the Spot, Jefferson House (New York), 1943.
Death Rides the Night, Jefferson House, 1944.
The Smoking Iron, Books, Inc. (New York), 1944.
Midnight Round-up, Jefferson House, 1944.
The Road to Laramie, Jefferson House, 1945.
The End of the Trail, Jefferson House, 1945.
Powder Valley Showdown, Jefferson House. 1946.

UNDER PSEUDONYM BRETT HALLIDAY; MIKE SHAYNE MYSTERY SERIES

Dividend on Death, Holt (New York), 1939.
The Private Practice of Michael Shayne, Holt, 1940.
The Uncomplaining Corpses, Holt, 1940.
Tickets for Death, Holt, 1941.
Bodies Are Where You Find Them, Holt, 1941.
Michael Shayne Takes Over (omnibus), Holt, 1941.
The Corpse Came Calling, Dodd, 1942.
Michael Shayne Investigates, Jarrolds (London), 1943, published as *Case of the Walking Corpse,* Quin (New York), 1943.
Murder Wears a Mummer's Mask, Dodd, 1943, published as *In a Deadly Vein,* 1943.
Blood on the Black Market, Dodd, 1943, published as *Heads You Lose,* 1943.
Michael Shayne's Long Chance, Dell (New York), 1944.
Murder and the Married Virgin, Dodd, 1944.
Michael Shayne Takes a Hand (omnibus), Jarrolds, 1944.
Dead Man's Diary [and] *Dinner at Dupre's,* Dell, 1945.
Murder Is My Business, Dodd, 1945.
Marked for Murder, Long, 1945.
Blood on Biscayne Bay, Ziff-Davis (Chicago), 1946.
Counterfeit Wife, Ziff-Davis, 1947.
Michael Shayne's Triple Mystery, Ziff-Davis, 1948.
Blood on the Stars, Dodd, 1948.
A Taste for Violence, Dodd, 1949.
Call for Mike Shayne, Dodd, 1949.
This Is It, Michael Shayne, Dodd, 1950.
Framed in Blood, Dodd, 1951.
When Dorinda Dances, Dodd, 1951.
What Really Happened, Dodd, 1952.
One Night With Nora, Dodd, 1953, published as *The Lady Came by Night,* Jarrolds, 1954.
She Woke to Darkness, Dodd, 1954.
Death Has Three Lives, Dodd, 1955.
Stranger in Town, Dodd, 1955.
The Blonde Cried Murder, Dodd, 1956.

Weep for a Blonde, Dodd, 1957.
Shoot the Works, Dodd, 1957.
Murder and the Wanton Bride, Dodd, 1958.
Fit to Kill, Dodd, 1958.
Date with a Dead Man, Dodd, 1959.
Target: Michael Shayne, Dodd, 1959.
Die like a Dog, Dodd, 1959.
Murder Takes No Holiday, Dodd, 1960.
Dolls Are Deadly, Dodd, 1960.
The Homicidal Virgin, Dodd, 1960.
Michael Shayne's Torrid Twelve, Dell, 1961.
Killer from the Keys, Dodd, 1961.
Murder in Haste, Dodd, 1961.
The Careless Corpse, Dodd, 1961.
Pay-off in Blood, Dodd, 1962.
Murder by Proxy, Dodd, 1962.
Never Kill a Client, Dodd, 1962.
Too Friendly, Too Dead, Dodd, 1963.
The Corpse That Never Was, Dodd, 1963.
The Body That Came Back, Dodd, 1963.
A Redhead for Mike Shayne, Dodd, 1964.
Shoot to Kill, Dodd, 1964.
A Taste of Cognac, Dell, 1964.
Michael Shayne's Fiftieth Case, Dodd, 1964.
Dangerous Dames, Dell, 1965.
Nice Fillies Finish Last, Dell, 1965.
The Violent World of Michael Shayne, Dell, 1965.
Armed . . . Dangerous, Dell, 1966.
Murder Spins the Wheels, Dell, 1966.
Mermaid on the Rocks, Dell, 1967.
Guilty as Hell, Dell, 1967.
Violence Is Golden, Dell, 1968.
So Lush, So Deadly, Dell, 1968.

UNDER PSEUDONYM ANTHONY SCOTT; NOVELS PUBLISHED BY GODWIN (NEW YORK)

Mardi Gras Madness, 1934.
Test of Virtue, 1934.
Ten Toes Up, 1935.
Virgin's Holiday, 1935.
Ladies of Chance, 1936.
Stolen Sins, 1936.
Satan Rides the Night, 1938.
Temptation, 1938.

EDITOR

(With wife, Helen McCloy) *20 Great Tales of Murder,* Random House (New York), 1951.
Big Time Mysteries, Dodd Mead (New York), 1958.
Murder in Miami, Dodd Mead, 1959.
Best Detective Stories of the Year, 16th and 17th Annual Collections, Dutton, 2 vols., Dutton (New York), 1961-62.

(With McCloy) *Murder, Murder, Murder: 10 Tales from 20 Great Tales of Murder,* Hillman Periodicals (New York), 1961.

Contributor of numerous stories to periodicals, under many pseudonyms, to mystery, Western and adventure "pulp" magazines.

SIDELIGHTS: In *Four and Twenty Bloodhounds,* edited by Anthony Boucher, Davis Dresser wrote of his recurring character, private eye, Michael Shayne: "I think the most important characteristic in his spectacular success as a private detective is his ability to drive straight forward to the heart of the matter, without deviating one iota for obstacles or confusing side issues. He has an absolutely logical mind which refuses to be sidetracked. He acts. On impulse sometimes, or on hunches; but always the impelling force is definite logic. In every instance he calculates the risk involved carefully, weighing the results that may be attained by a certain course of action against the probable lack of results if he chooses to move more cautiously." Dresser added that once Shayne is "convinced that a risk is worth taking, he moves forward and accepts the consequences as a part of his job. It is this driving urgency and lack of personal concern more than any other thing, I think, that serves to wind up most of Mike's most difficult cases so swiftly. In time, few of his cases consume more than one or two days. This sums up Michael Shayne as I know him."

Writing as Brett Halliday, Dresser's most popular series, the Mike Shayne books, sold millions of copies, were translated into seven foreign languages, and were adapted into motion pictures and television series. The novels published under Dresser's Brett Halliday byline after 1958 were ghost-written by other individuals.

BIOGRAPHICAL/CRITICAL SOURCES:

BOOKS

Boucher, Anthony, editor, *Four and Twenty Bloodhounds,* Simon & Schuster (New York), 1950.

PERIODICALS

Chicago Sun, July 2, 1948.
Los Angeles Times Book Review, July 4, 1982, pg. 8.
New York Herald Tribune Book Review, September 25, 1955.
New York Times, August 10, 1952; September 25, 1955.
New York Times Book Review, November 1, 1959; July 16, 1961.
San Francisco Chronicle, August 31, 1952; April 29, 1956; July 23, 1961.
Saturday Review of Literature, June 26, 1948.

OBITUARIES:

PERIODICALS

AB Bookman's Weekly, May 9, 1977.
New York Times, February 6, 1977.*

*　　　*　　　*

DUNNING, John H(arry) 1927-

PERSONAL: Born June 26, 1927, in Sandy, Bedfordshire, England; son of John Murray (a Baptist minister) and Anne Florence (Baker) Dunning; married Ida Teresa Bellamy, 1948 (divorced, 1975); married Christine Mary Brown, August 4, 1975; children: (first marriage) one son. *Education:* University College, London, B.S. (with first class honors), 1951; University of Southampton, Ph.D., 1957.

ADDRESSES: Office—Department of Economics, University of Reading, Whiteknights Park, Reading RG6 2AH, England.

CAREER: University of Southampton, Southampton, England, lecturer and senior lecturer in economics, 1952-64; University of Reading, Reading, England, Foundation Professor of Economics, 1964-74, head of department, 1964-87, Esmee Fairbairn Professor of International Investment and Business Studies, 1975-87, ICI Professor of International Business, 1987-92, professor emeritus of international business, 1992—. Visiting professor at University of Western Ontario and University of California, Berkeley, 1968-69, Boston University, 1976, Stockholm School of Economics, 1978, and University of Montreal, 1980; Walker Ames Professor of Economics at University of Washington, Seattle, 1981; Seth Boyden Distinguished Professor of International Management, 1987, and State of New Jersey Professor of International Business, 1989—, both Rutgers University. Chairman of Economists Advisory Group Ltd. Member of South East Economic Planning Council, 1965-69, and Chemical Economic Development Committee, 1970-77. Adviser to Committee on Invisible Exports; consultant to international agencies, national governments, and business enterprises, including United Nations, World Bank, and Department of Trade and Industry (United Kingdom).

MEMBER: Academy of International Business (fellow; president, 1986-88), International Trade and Finance Association (president, 1994), Royal Economic Society (member of council, 1969-73).

AWARDS, HONORS: D.Phil. from University of Uppsala, 1975, and from Universidad Autonoma de Madrid, 1990.

WRITINGS:

American Investment in British Manufacturing Industry, Allen & Unwin (London), 1958, Arno, 1976.

(With C. J. Thomas) *British Industry: Change and Development in the Twentieth Century,* Hutchinson (London), 1961.

Economic Planning and Town Expansion: A Case Study of Basingstoke, Workers Education Association, 1963.

(With P. G. Hall and others) *A New Town in Mid-Wales,* H.M.S.O. (London), 1966.

(With D. Lees and others) *The Economics of Advertising,* Hutchinson, 1967.

The Role of American Investment in the United Kingdom Economy, Political and Economic Planning, 1969.

Studies in International Investment, Allen & Unwin, 1970.

(With E. V. Morgan) *The City of London: An Economic Study,* Allen & Unwin, 1971.

(Editor) *The Multinational Enterprise,* Allen & Unwin, 1971.

Problems of the Small Firm in Raising External Finance, H.M.S.O., 1971.

Insurance and the Economy, Institute of Economic Affairs, (London) 1971.

(Editor) *Readings in International Investment,* Penguin (London), 1972.

(Editor) *Economic Analysis and the Multinational Enterprise,* Allen & Unwin, 1974.

(With R. D. Pearce) *Profitability and Performance of the World's Leading Companies,* Financial Times (London), 1975.

U.S. Industry in Britain, Wilton House (Aldershot, England), 1976.

(With T. Houston) *British Industry Abroad,* Financial Times, 1976.

United Kingdom Enterprises in Manufacturing Industry in LDC's and Their Effect on Trade Flows, United Nations Conference on Trade and Development, 1977.

(With G. Norman) *Factors Influencing the Location of Offices of Multinational Enterprises,* Location of Offices Bureau, 1979.

(With J. Stopford and K. Haverich) *The World Directory of Multinational Enterprises,* Macmillan (London), 1980.

International Production and the Multinational Enterprise, Allen & Unwin, 1981.

(With Pearce) *The World's Largest Industrial Enterprises,* Gower Press (Aldershot), 1981.

(With M. Burstall and A. Lake) *The Impact of Multinational Enterprises on National Scientific and Technological Capacity: The Pharmaceutical Industry,* Organization for Economic Cooperation and Development, 1981.

(With M. McQueen) *Transnational Corporations in the International Tourist Industry,* United Nations Center on Transnational Corporations, 1981.

(With John Black) *International Capital Movements,* Macmillan, 1982.

(Editor) *Multinational Enterprises, Economic Structure and International Competitiveness,* Wiley (Chichester, England), 1985.

Japanese Participation in British Industry, Croom Helm (Beckenham, England), 1986.

Decision-Making Structures in U.S. and Japanese Manufacturing Affiliates in the U.K.: Some Similarities and Contrasts, International Labour Office (London), 1986.

Explaining International Production, Unwin Hyman, 1988.

Multinational Technology and Competitiveness, Unwin Hyman, 1988.

Multinational Enterprises and the Global Economy, Addison Wesley (Wokingham, England), 1993.

The Globalisation of Business, Routledge & Kegan Paul (London), 1993.

(Editor) *The Theory of Transnational Corporations,* Routledge & Kegan Paul, 1993.

(General editor) *Co-operative Forms of Transnational Corporation Activity,* United Nations Transnational Corporations and Management Division (London), 1994.

OTHER

Contributor to books, including *Economic Integration in Europe,* Weidenfeld & Nicolson (London), 1969; *Foreign Investment: The Experience of Host Countries,* Praeger (New York City), 1970; *North American and Western European Policies,* Macmillan, 1970; *Recent Research on the Internationalisation of Business,* Almqvist & Wiksell (Stockholm), 1979; *Transnational Corporations and China's Open Door Policy,* Heath (Lexington, MA), 1988; *Transferimenti di Tecnologie e Finanziamenti ai Paesi in Via di Sviluppo,* Franco Angeli (Milan), 1989; *Services in World Economic Growth,* Mohr (Tubingen, Germany), 1989; *International Trade: Existing Problems and Prospective Solutions,* Taylor & Francis (London), 1989; *Multinationals and Europe 1992,* Routledge & Kegan Paul, 1990; *The Nature of the Transnational Firm,* Routledge & Kegan Paul, 1991; *Europe and America 1992: US-EC Economic Relations in the Single European Market,* Manchester University Press (Manchester), 1991; *Multinationals in the New Europe and Global Trade,* Springer-Verlag (New York City), 1992; *Comparative Work Practices of Multinational Firms,* Oxford University Press, 1993; and *The Globalisation of Professional Services,* Routledge & Kegan Paul, 1993.

Contributor to *Collier's Encyclopedia;* contributor of over 150 articles to business and economic journals. Founding editor of *Business Ratios;* member of editorial board of *Journal of International Business Studies, Journal of Business Research,* and *World Development.*

WORK IN PROGRESS: Research on "the theory of the international production and the interaction between multinational enterprises and patterns of economic development"; the implications of the globalization of international business for the domestic economic policy of advanced countries; the determinants of the competitiveness of firms and countries.

SIDELIGHTS: John H. Dunning once told *CA:* "I am one of the pioneers in the study of international direct investment and the multinational enterprise. I have maintained a lively interest in the subject since the mid-1950s. I am equally at home with theoretical issues as policy-oriented research, and am currently advising both the Organization for Economic Cooperation and Development (OECD) and the United Nations Center on Transnational Corporations on matters relating to multinational enterprise. I describe myself as a 'moderate' in my political attitude to multinational enterprises: I believe strongly that they can make an important contribution to economic development, particularly those of advanced developing countries, but that it is the responsibility of governments to manage their own affairs so that the net benefits of foreign direct investment can be maximized. I believe also that governments and multinational enterprises are learning to live with each other and that this augurs well for international economic relations in the 1990s."*

*　　　*　　　*

DURKIN, Barbara W(ernecke) 1944-

PERSONAL: Born January 13, 1944, in Baltimore, MD; daughter of Raymond Carl (an engineer) and Della (a baker; maiden name, Heinemann) Wernecke; married William John Durkin (an engineer and physicist), May 20, 1973; children: Matthew Richard, John Michael. *Education:* Essex Community College, Baltimore, MD, A.A., 1964; Towson State College (now University), B.S., 1966; attended Morgan State College (now University), 1968, and Johns Hopkins University, 1968-70. *Religion:* Lutheran.

ADDRESSES: *Home and office*—531 Phillips Rd., Webster, NY 14580.

CAREER: Currently owner of the Pizzazz Group, a writing/teaching/consulting business; Baltimore County Board of Education, Baltimore, MD, high school English teacher, 1966-75; worked as a teacher of creative writing and conducted workshops in writing.

MEMBER: International Women's Writing Guild, American Pen Women, American Society for Training & Development, National Association of Women Business Owners.

AWARDS, HONORS: *Oh, You Dundalk Girls, Can't You Dance the Polka?* was on the American Library Association's list of "Best of 1984" books for young adults.

WRITINGS:

Oh, You Dundalk Girls, Can't You Dance the Polka? (young adult novel), Morrow (New York City), 1984.
(Editor) *Visions & Viewpoints: Voices of the Genesee Valley,* self-published, 1993, 2nd edition, 1994.

Also author of short fiction, feature articles, and two resume manuals. Columnist for the Webster, NY, *Herald* and a contributor to *Writer's Digest's Fiction Writer's Market.*

SIDELIGHTS: Barbara Durkin told *CA:* "Owning a writing business leaves little time for my own writing, but the calling is always there—despite the lack of time, energy, and bright ideas I used to possess in abundance. That's why I continue to speak and teach about writing. I even teach teachers how to teach writing to their kids. The urge to communicate and to encourage others to do so never quits. For this I am profoundly grateful, because if it weren't for this job, I'd probably have to *work* for a living."

*　　　*　　　*

DYSON, R(obert) W(illiam) 1949-

PERSONAL: Born September 17, 1949, in Penzance, Cornwall, England; son of Robert Richard and Gwendoline Dyson; married Jane Mary Mantell, July, 1970 (divorced, 1976); married Valerie Margaret Tozer, November, 1976; children: (second marriage) Jessica Katharine. *Education:* University of Durham, B.A. (first class honors), 1977, M.A., 1978, Ph.D., 1980. *Avocational interests:* Music, literature, martial arts, fell walking.

ADDRESSES: *Home*—57 Grange Rd., Belmont, Durham, DH1 1AQ, England. *Office*—Department of Politics, University of Durham, Durham, England.

CAREER: University of Durham, Durham, England, fellow and lecturer in politics; tutor at Van Mildert College, 1978—.

WRITINGS:

(Editor and translator) Jonas of Orleans, *De Institutione Regia,* Exposition University Press, 1983.

(Editor and translator) Giles of Rome, *De Ecclesiastica Potestate of Aegidius Romanus,* Boydell & Brewer (Suffolk, England), 1986.

(Editor and translator) James of Viterbo, *On Christian Government,* Boydell & Brewer, 1995.

Also contributor of articles and reviews to British journals.

WORK IN PROGRESS: Editing and translating source material for the study of early fourteenth-century political controversy; research on ancient, medieval, and Renaissance political thought and institutions.

E

EAST, Michael
See WEST, Morris L(anglo)

* * *

EDELSTEIN, Scott 1954-

PERSONAL: Born October 17, 1954, in Pittsburgh, PA; son of Morris (in sales) and Estelle (an executive; maiden name, Rellis) Edelstein. *Education:* Oberlin College, B.A., 1978; University of Wisconsin—Milwaukee, M.A., 1984; graduate study at State University of New York at Buffalo.

ADDRESSES: Home—3800 Aldrich Ave. South, Minneapolis, MN 55409.

CAREER: University of Minnesota—Minneapolis, instructor, 1979-80, lecturer in English, 1979-83; *Artlines,* Taos, NM, staff writer and managing editor, 1983-84; *Taos News,* Taos, staff writer and acting arts editor, 1984; University of Akron, Akron, OH, lecturer in English, 1985-86. Adjunct instructor at Metropolitan State University, Hamline University, and lecturer at writers' conferences. Ghostwriter. Writing and publishing consultant.

WRITINGS:

(Editor) *Future Pastimes,* Sherbourne Press, 1977.
College: A User's Manual, Bantam (New York City), 1985.
The No-Experience-Necessary Writer's Course, Stein & Day (Briarcliff Manor, NY), 1987.
Surviving Freshman Composition, Lyle Stuart (Secaucus, NJ), 1988.
The Indispensable Writer's Guide, Harper (New York City), 1989.
Manuscript Submission, Writers Digest (Cincinnati, OH), 1989.

Putting Your Kids through College, Consumer Reports Books, 1989.
The Writer's Book of Checklists, Writers Digest, 1992.
The Truth about College, Lyle Stuart, 1992.
Thirty Steps to Becoming a Writer, Writers Digest, 1993.

Columnist for *Artist's* magazine, 1985—, and *Writer's Digest,* 1985—. Contributor to periodicals, including *Glamour, City Miner, Essence, Ellery Queen's Mystery Magazine, Single Parent,* and *Campus Life.*

SIDELIGHTS: Scott Edelstein once told *CA:* "I'm concerned with how writing, in all its forms, can best be taught. Most teachers and books focus entirely on writing as a craft, but the inspiration behind a written work is at least as important. My teaching, and some of my writing, is concerned with generating inspiration, with how a piece of writing gets started, with what sources spark creative impulses, and with what makes something worth writing in the first place."

* * *

EDWARDS, George Charles III 1947-

PERSONAL: Born January 3, 1947, in Rochester, NY; son of George Charles, Jr., and Mary Elizabeth Laing Edwards; married May 22, 1981; wife's name Carmella P.; children: Jeffrey Allen. *Education:* Stetson University, B.A. (magna cum laude), 1969; University of Wisconsin—Madison, M.A., 1970, Ph.D., 1973.

ADDRESSES: Home—2910 Coronado Dr., College Station, TX 77845. *Office*—Center for Presidential Studies, Texas A & M University, College Station, TX 77843-4348.

CAREER: Tulane University, New Orleans, LA, assistant professor of political science, 1973-78; Texas A & M University, College Station, associate professor, 1978-81, professor, 1981-90, distinguished professor of political science, 1990—, director of Center for Presidential Studies, 1991—. Visiting assistant professor at University of Wisconsin—Madison, summer, 1976; visiting professor of social sciences, United States Military Academy, 1985-88.

MEMBER: American Political Science Association (president of presidency research section, 1984-85), American Association of Public Opinion Research, Center for the Study of the Presidency, Midwest Political Science Association, Southern Political Science Association, Phi Beta Kappa, Pi Sigma Alpha, Phi Alpha Theta, Phi Kappa Phi, Pi Alpha Alpha.

AWARDS, HONORS: Woodrow Wilson fellow, 1969-70; decoration for distinguished civilian service, U.S. Army, 1988.

WRITINGS:

(Editor with William Gwyn, and contributor) *Perspectives on Public Policy-Making,* Tulane Studies in Political Science (New Orleans, LA), 1975.

(With Ira Sharkansky) *The Policy Predicament,* W. H. Freeman (New York City), 1978.

Presidential Influence in Congress, W. H. Freeman, 1980.

Implementing Public Policy, Congressional Quarterly (Washington, DC), 1980.

The Public Presidency, St. Martin's (New York City), 1983.

(Editor with Stephen Wayne, and contributor) *Studying the Presidency,* University of Tennessee Press (Knoxville), 1983.

(Editor) *Public Policy Implementation,* JAI Press (Greenwich, CT), 1984.

(With Stephen Wayne) *Presidential Leadership,* St. Martin's, 1985, 3rd edition, 1994.

(Editor with Steven A. Shull and Norman Thomas) *The Presidency and Public Policy Making,* University of Pittsburgh Press, 1985.

(Editor with Earl Walker) *National Security and the Constitution,* Johns Hopkins University Press (Baltimore, MD), 1988.

At the Margins, Yale University Press (New Haven, CT), 1988.

Presidential Approval, Johns Hopkins University Press, 1990.

(Editor with Bert A. Rockman and John H. Kessel) *Researching the Presidency,* University of Pittsburgh Press, 1993.

Also author, with Robert L. Lineberry and Martin P. Wattenberg, of *Government in America,* 4th edition, 1989, 6th edition, 1994, and also with Lineberry and Wattenberg, of *Government in America: Brief Edition,* 1993, 2nd edition, 1995. Contributor to numerous books, including

The Presidency: Studies in Policy-Making, edited by Shull and Lance T. LeLoup, King's Court (Brunswick, OH), 1979; *The American Presidency,* edited by Harry A. Bailey, Jr., and Jay M. Shafritz, Dorsey (Homewood, IL), 1988; and *The Clinton Presidency: First Appraisals,* edited by Colin Campbell and Rockman, Chatham House (Chatham, NJ), 1995. Contributor of articles and reviews to political science journals. Editor of newsletter of Presidency Research Group; member of editorial board of *American Journal of Political Science, American Review of Politics, American Politics Quarterly, Policy Studies Journal, Presidential Studies Quarterly,* and *Congress and the President.*

SIDELIGHTS: George Charles Edwards III once told *CA:* "Our libraries contain countless volumes that describe the life and times of presidents and the various roles they have played in the establishment of public policies. There is an equally large number of polemics reputing to place presidential administrations in the proper perspective. Despite all these contributions, we face a striking paradox: the single most important institution in American politics is the one we understand the least.

"My writings are concerned with bridging the gap between facts and polemics about the American presidency on the one hand, and understanding of it on the other. They focus on explaining why the public, Congress, the White House staff, and the bureaucracy behave in the ways they do toward the president and what difference the president's behavior makes. In other words, I am less interested in what a president did than in why he did it and what the consequences of his actions were. Why were certain decisions made? Why did the president succeed or fail to obtain the support of Congress or the public? Why were policies implemented as they were?

"Writing nonfiction that is both original and intellectually sound and at the same time appeals to an audience larger than a few dozen scholars poses a formidable challenge to an author. This is especially the case if one believes, as I do, that we should bring as much scientific rigor as possible to the examination of our topics. Anything smacking of statistics has a tendency to discourage many potential readers. Yet it is just this challenge, plus that of trying to understand the complex world of policymaking in America, that keeps me writing."

*   *   *

EDWARDS, Phoebe
See BLOCH, Barbara

ELLIS, Anyon
  See ROWLAND-ENTWISTLE, (Arthur)
Theodore (Henry)

*   *   *

ENDERLE, Judith (Ann) Ross 1941-
  (Jeffie Ross Gordon, a joint pseudonym)

PERSONAL: Surname is pronounced '*en*-der-lee'; born November 26, 1941, in Detroit, MI; daughter of Theodore P. (an engineer) and Ellenore (a teacher; maiden name, Tanner) Ross; married Dennis Joseph Enderle (business broker), August 18, 1962; children: Kevin Dennis, Brian Peter, Monica Ann. *Education:* University of Detroit, Certificate in Secretarial Business, 1962; also attended University of California, Los Angeles. *Avocational interests:* Reading, gardening, travelling.

ADDRESSES: Home—Malibu, CA. *Office*—11943 Montana Ave., Los Angeles, CA 90049. *Agent*—Ginger Knowlton, Curtis Brown Ltd., Ten Astor Pl., New York, NY 10003.

CAREER: Ford Motor Company, Wixom, MI, secretary, 1963-65; Santa Monica Emeritus College, Santa Monica, CA, teacher of writing for children, 1981-82. Writers Ink (an editorial service), partner; editor, *Totally Kids* magazine, published by Fox Broadcasting Company.

MEMBER: Society of Children's Book Writers and Illustrators, Southern California Council on Literature for Children and Young People, California Writers Club, Southern California Children's Booksellers Association.

AWARDS, HONORS: International Reading Association/Children's Book Council Children's Choice Book list, 1982, for *Good Junk,* and 1993 (with Stephanie Gordon Tessler), for *Two Badd Babies;* member of the year, 1990, Society of Children's Book Writers and Illustrators; Choice honorable mention, *L.A. Parents,* 1991, for *Six Sleepy Sheep;* several author's awards from *Highlights for Children.*

WRITINGS:

Good Junk, illustrations by Gail Gibbons, Elsevier-Nelson, 1981.
Cheer Me On!, Tempo Books, 1982.
Someone for Sara, Tempo Books, 1982.
Meet Super Duper Rick Martin, New American Library, 1985.
Adrienne and the Blob (fantasy), Silhouette, 1986.

ROMANCES; FOR YOUNG ADULTS

S.W.A.K., Sealed with a Kiss, Tempo Books, 1983.
Programmed for Love, Tempo Books, 1983.
When Wishes Come True, Tempo Books, 1983.

With Love, Lark, Dutton, 1983.
Sing a Song of Love, Tempo Books, 1984.
Will I See You Next Summer?, Tempo Books, 1984.
T.L.C., Tender Loving Care, Tempo Books, 1984.
Secrets, Silhouette, 1984.
Sixteen Sure Ways to Succeed with Sean, New American Library, 1984.
Ready, Set, Love, Tempo Books, 1985.
Kisses for Sale, Scholastic, 1985.
A Little Love Dust, New American Library, 1985.
Love and Kisses, Tempo Books, 1986.

"BAYSHORE MEDICAL CENTER" SERIES; WITH STEPHANIE GORDON TESSLER

Andrea Whitman: Pediatrics, Walker & Co., 1983.
Monica Ross: Maternity, Walker & Co., 1983.
Elizabeth Jones: Emergency, Walker & Co., 1984.
Gabriella Ortiz: Hot Line/Crisis Center, Walker & Co., 1984.

WITH TESSLER; FOR CHILDREN

(Under joint pseudonym Jeffie Ross Gordon) *Rutabaga Ruby* (poetry), Curriculum Associates, 1989.
(Under joint pseudonym Jeffie Ross Gordon) *Hide and Shriek* (a riddle book), Lerner Publications, 1991.
(Under joint pseudonym Jeffie Ross Gordon) *Rebus Treasury,* Boyds Mills Press, 1991.
(Under joint pseudonym Jeffie Ross Gordon) *Six Sleepy Sheep,* Boyds Mills Press, 1991.
Six Creepy Sheep, Boyds Mills Press, 1992.
(Under joint pseudonym Jeffie Ross Gordon) *Two Badd Babies,* illustrated by Chris L. Demarest, Boyds Mills Press, 1992.
(Under joint pseudonym Jeffie Ross Gordon) *Muriel and Ruth,* Boyds Mills Press, 1992.
A Pile of Pigs, Boyds Mills Press, 1993.
The Good for Something Dragon, Boyds Mills Press, 1993.
(Under joint pseudonym Jeffie Ross Gordon) *Rebus Treasury II,* Boyds Mills Press, 1993.
Six Snowy Sheep, Boyds Mills Press, 1994.

WITH TESSLER UNDER JOINT PSEUDONYM JEFFIE ROSS GORDON; FOR YOUNG ADULTS

Jacquelyn (historical romance), Scholastic, 1985.
A Touch of Genius (fantasy), Silhouette, 1986.
The Journal of Emily Rose (mystery), Silhouette, 1986.
A Touch of Magic (fantasy), Silhouette, 1987.
Nobody Knows Me, Silhouette, 1987.
Nora (historical romance), Scholastic, 1987.
Gimme a Z, Silhouette, 1988.

OTHER

Also author of *Let's Be Friends Again,* Dandelion Press, and (with Tessler) the "Read-a-Picture" series, Modern Publishing, 1989. Contributor to *The Writer's Digest*

Handbook of Short-Story Writing, 1986, and *Writing for Children and Teenagers,* by Lee Wyndham and Arnold Madison. Contributor to periodicals, including *Highlights for Children* and *Writer's Digest.*

Enderle's books have been translated into French, Italian, Spanish, German, Danish, Finnish, and Dutch.

WORK IN PROGRESS: What Would Mama Do, Kelly Beans, Francis the Earthquake Dog, Tough Times Birthday and *Secret of the Sarcophagus.*

SIDELIGHTS: Judith Ross Enderle, also known to young readers as Jeffie Ross Gordon, once told *CA:* "There's real joy in connecting words in a way that makes reading fun. It's so amazing what a writer can do with just twenty-six letters. In many of the books I write with Stephanie Gordon Tessler, we use alliteration, assonance, and onomatopoeia. Yet one cannot be an absolute judge of one's own work. The final judgment comes from the reader. Children chose *Two Badd Babies* as one of their favorites (1993 Children's Choice List). This is a book they memorize and recite with us in the classrooms. Why does this book work so well? It may be the repetition, alliteration, and onomatopoeia; it may be the internal rhyme; it may be the lively art by Chris L. Demarest. It is most likely the combination of all those things. A writer always hopes this kind of magic will repeat. If we can touch one reader, make someone smile, share the joy of language, that's success. Writing is draining, demanding, giving, and very, very satisfying."*

*   *   *

EPAFRODITO
See WAGNER, C(harles) Peter

*   *   *

ETTER, Dave   1928-

PERSONAL: Born March 18, 1928, in Huntington Park, CA; son of Harold Pearson and Judith (Goodenow) Etter; married Margaret Cochran, August 8, 1959; children: Emily Louise, George Goodenow. *Education:* University of Iowa, B.A., 1953. *Politics:* Democrat.

ADDRESSES: Home and office—414 Gates St., P. O. Box 413, Elburn, IL 60119.

CAREER: Before 1961, did odd jobs in Iowa, Indiana, Illinois, Massachusetts, and California; Northwestern University Press, Evanston, IL, editor, 1961-63; *Encyclopaedia Britannica,* Chicago, IL, editor and writer, 1964-73; Northern Illinois University Press, De Kalb, IL,

editor, 1974-80; freelance writer and editor, 1980—. *Military service:* U.S. Army, 1953-55.

AWARDS, HONORS: Bread Loaf Writers Conference fellow in poetry, 1967; Midland Poetry Award and Friends of Literature poetry award, both 1967, both for *Go Read the River;* Illinois Sesquicentennial Poetry Prize, 1968, for *The Last Train to Prophetstown;* Theodore Roethke Poetry Prize, 1971; Carl Sandburg Award, 1981, for *West of Chicago.*

WRITINGS:

POETRY

Go Read the River, University of Nebraska Press (Lincoln), 1966.
The Last Train to Prophetstown, University of Nebraska Press, 1968.
Strawberries, Juniper Press, 1970.
Voyages to the Inland Sea (also includes prose), University of Wisconsin Press (Madison, WI), 1971.
Crabtree's Woman, BkMk Press (Kansas City, MO), 1972.
Well You Needn't, Raindust Press, 1975.
Bright Mississippi, Juniper Press, 1975.
Central Standard Time: New and Selected Poems, BkMk Press, 1978.
Alliance, Illinois, Kylix Press (Ann Arbor, MI), 1978, 2nd edition, Spoon River Poetry Press (Peoria, IL), 1983.
Open to the Wind, Uzzano (Menomonie, WI), 1978.
Riding the Rock Island through Kansas, Wolfsong Press, 1979.
Cornfields, Spoon River Poetry Press, 1980.
West of Chicago, Spoon River Poetry Press, 1981.
Boondocks, Uzzano, 1982.
Home State, Spoon River Poetry Press, 1985.
Live at the Silver Dollar, Spoon River Poetry Press, 1986.
Selected Poems, Spoon River Poetry Press, 1987.
Midlanders, Spoon River Poetry Press, 1988.
Electric Avenue, Spoon River Poetry Press, 1988.
Carnival, Spoon River Poetry Press, 1990.
Sunflower County, Spoon River Poetry Press, 1994.

OTHER

Contributor to numerous books, including *Heartland: Poets of the Midwest,* edited by Lucien Stryk, Northern Illinois University Press (DeKalb), 1967; *Contemporary Poetry in America,* compiled by M. Williams, Random House (New York), 1973; *Beowulf to Beatles and Beyond: The Variations of Poetry,* edited by David R. Pichaske, Macmillan (New York), 1981; and *Inheriting the Land,* edited by Mark Vinz and Thom Tammaro, University of Minnesota Press (Minneapolis), 1993; also contributor to more than eighty other anthologies and textbooks. Contributor to more than two hundred periodicals, including

Prairie Schooner, TriQuarterly, New Letters, Saturday Review, Poetry, Nation, and *North American Review.*

ADAPTATIONS: Alliance, Illinois has been adapted for the stage by three different drama groups and has been seen by audiences throughout Illinois.

WORK IN PROGRESS: A book of poems.

SIDELIGHTS: "If there is a poet anywhere in the Midwest who picks up where [Carl] Sandburg, [Vachel] Lindsay and [Edgar Lee] Masters left off, it is Dave Etter," comments Norbert Blei in the *Chicago Tribune Book World,* adding that "Etter is to Midwestern poetry what Garrison Keillor is to 'A Prairie Home Companion.'" Blei notes in the *Milwaukee Journal:* "Whatever it is that characterized the Midwest—cows, crows, cicadas, hollyhocks, the back screen door banging real good—Etter has made a poem of it. . . . He knows the lay of the land and the junctions, loves the sleepy, smalltown life, and records it all as carefully as the village clerk."

Approximately two hundred monologues spoken by townspeople comprise Etter's *Alliance, Illinois,* which Joel A. Lipman labels a "brilliant, sustained work" in *Old Northwest.* Lipman remarks that the "apparent simplicity of Etter's subject matter and language disguises his talent and commitment to craft." Etter's poems "establish an instant unassuming, offhand bond" between the reader and the poet, says Lipman, who also considers the poetry "alive, humorous, and honest—excellent art that can be returned to for insight and pleasure." In *Chicago,* G. E. Murray of describes Etter's vision in *Alliance, Illinois* "indelible and immediate . . . one that names the names that truly know and echo the secrets of the heartland." Moreover, Murray believes that the work "displays a huge appetite for the life it creates and then generates into an unusual energy." In recording the "speech, presence, and circumstance" of the Midwest, writes Murray, Etter has created an art that "renders an exceptional spirit of place, one imbued with supremely ordinary people, their interconnectedness, their ruins, and abundances, their fertile but perilous land." For this achievement, Murray asserts, "Etter deserves praise and attention."

Dave Etter once told *CA:* "Most of my work so far has been about the small town and rural Midwest because that is all I know well, all I have a real feel for, all I really care about deeply. There is an endless wealth of poem material right in my hometown; I will never be forced to look elsewhere. It is not easy to say for sure what authors have influenced me the most but I would surely have to list Walt Whitman, Sherwood Anderson, Carl Sandburg, Langston Hughes, Mark Twain, George Ade, Thomas Hardy, William Faulkner, and Richard Bissell. I have always been considerably influenced by some of America's jazz greats, particularly Thelonious Monk, Dizzy Gillespie, Sonny Rollins, Horace Silver, and Miles Davis—they have shown me new rhythms, new ways to break the line, new structures."

BIOGRAPHICAL/CRITICAL SOURCES:

BOOKS

Blei, Norbert, *Door to Door,* Ellis Press (Peoria, IL), 1985.
Bray, Robert C., *Rediscoveries: Literature and Place in Illinois,* University of Illinois Press (Champaign), 1982.
Killoren, Robert, editor, *Late Harvest: Plains and Prairie Poets,* BkMk Press, 1977.

PERIODICALS

Chicago, December, 1980; January, 1984.
Chicagoland, November, 1968; March, 1969.
Chicago Tribune Book World, October 3, 1982.
Indiana Review, fall, 1985.
Midwest Quarterly, spring, 1987.
Milwaukee Journal, October 7, 1979.
New Letters, fall, 1984.
Old Northwest, fall, 1983.
Panorama, (Chicago Daily News), July 16, 1966.
Poetry, February, 1967; February, 1971; July, 1984.
San Francisco Review of Books, winter, 1983-84.

F

FARMER, William R(euben) 1921-

PERSONAL: Born February 1, 1921, in Needles, CA; son of William Reuben (a railroad section foreman) and Elsie (a nurse; maiden name, Vaughn) Farmer; married Nell Cochran (a real estate agent), November 24, 1946; children: Richard Cochran, William Vaughn, Donald Guy, Rebecca Nell. *Education:* Occidental College, A.B., 1942; Cambridge University, B.A., 1949, M.A., 1956, B.D., 1965; Union Theological Seminary, New York, NY, B.D., 1950, Th.D., 1952.

ADDRESSES: Home—4103 Emerson, Dallas, TX 75205. *Office*—University of Dallas, Box 684, 1845 E. Northgate Dr., Irving, TX 75062-4799.

CAREER: DePauw University, Greencastle, IN, visiting instructor in theology, 1952-54; Drew University, Madison, NJ, assistant professor of theology, 1955-59; Southern Methodist University, Dallas, TX, associate professor, 1959-64, professor, 1964-91, emeritus professor of New Testament, 1991—, chair of Gospels Research Group and resident fellow of Center for the Study of Religion in the Greco-Roman World, 1984—. Pastor of Methodist church in Coatesville, IN, 1952-55; chair of Southwest Seminar on Gospel Studies; co-chair of International Institute for the Renewal of Gospel Studies, 1980-87. Member of McMaster University Research Project on Normative Self-Definition in Judaism and Christianity; member of board of directors of Robert L. Lichten Foundation for Human Rights.

Visiting professor or lecturer at numerous institutions of higher learning, including Asian Center of Theological Studies; Cambridge University; Center for the Study of Democratic Institutions, Santa Barbara, CA; Emory University; Federated Theological Seminary of South Africa; Methodist Theological Seminary of Seoul, Korea; Oxford University; Pontifical Biblical Institute, Rome, Italy; Tokyo Union Theological Seminary; United Theological College, Bangalore, India; University of Basel; University of Bristol; University of Durban; University of Hamburg; University of London; University of Lund; University of Strasbourg; University of Uppsala; and Yonsei University. Chair of Dallas Citizens for a Free Flow of Information, 1972-74. *Military service:* U.S. Naval Reserve, active duty, 1942-46; became lieutenant senior grade.

MEMBER: American Society of Church History, Society of Biblical Literature and Exegesis (president of southwestern region, 1962, 1973), Society for New Testament Studies.

AWARDS, HONORS: Bollingen Foundation fellow in Palestine, 1955, 1957, 1959; Guggenheim fellow in Germany, 1964; Lilly Foundation grant, 1978.

WRITINGS:

Maccabees, Zealots, and Josephus: An Inquiry Into Jewish Nationalism in the Greco-Roman Period, Columbia University Press (New York City), 1956.

The Synoptic Problem: A Critical Analysis, Macmillan (New York City), 1964.

(Editor with C. F. D. Moule and R. R. Niebuhr, and contributor) *Christian History and Interpretation: Studies Presented to John Knox,* Cambridge University Press (New York City), 1967.

(Editor and author of introduction) *Flavius Josephus, The Great Roman-Jewish War: A.D. 66-70 (De Bello Margoliouth),* Peter Smith, 1970.

(Editor) *Synopticon: The Verbal Agreement between the Greek Texts of Matthew, Mark, and Luke Contextually Exhibited,* Cambridge University Press, 1969.

The Last Twelve Verses of Mark, Cambridge University Press, 1974.

(Author of introduction) Hans-Herbert Stoldt, *History and Criticism of the Marcan Hypothesis,* Mercer University Press, 1977.

Jesus and the Gospel: Tradition, Scripture, and Canon, Fortress (Philadelphia), 1982.

(Editor and contributor) *New Synoptic Studies: The Cambridge Gospel Conference and Beyond,* Mercer University Press (Macon, GA), 1983.

(With Denis Farkasfalvy) *The Formation of the New Testament Canon,* Paulist Press (Ramsey, NJ), 1983.

(Editor with Franz Neirynck and M. E. Boismard) *Papers from the Jerusalem Bible Conference,* Peeter's, 1987.

(Editor) David Barrett Peabody, *Mark as Composer,* Mercer University Press, 1987.

(With Roch Kereszty) *Peter and Paul and the Church of Rome: An Ecumenical Potential of a Forgotten Perspective,* Paulist Press, 1990.

The Gospel of Jesus: The Pastoral Relevance of the Synoptic Problem, Westminster Press (Philadelphia), 1994.

Also contributor to numerous books, including *Studies in the History and Text of the New Testament,* edited by Boyd L. Daniels and M. Jack Suggs, University of Utah Press (Salt Lake City), 1967; *Theological Perspectives in Stewardship,* General Board of the Laity Division of Stewardship and Finance, edited by Edwin M. Briggs, United Methodist Church, 1969; *Christianity, Judaism, and Other Greco-Roman Cults: Studies for Morton Smith, Part I: New Testament,* edited by Jacob Neusner, E. J. Brill (Long Island, NY), 1975; *The Relationships of the Gospels: An Interdisciplinary Dialogue,* edited by William O. Walker, Jr., Trinity University Press (San Antonio), 1978; *From Faith to Faith: Essays in Honor of Donald Miller,* edited by Dikran Y. Hadidian, Pickwick Press (Mill Valley, CA), 1979; *Texts and Testaments: Critical Essays on the Bible and Early Church Fathers,* edited by W. Eugene March, Trinity University Press, 1980; *Colloquy on New Testament Studies,* edited by Bruce C. Corley, Mercer University Press, 1983; *The New Testament Age: Essays in Honor of Bo Reicke,* Volume I, edited by William C. Weinrich, Mercer University Press, 1984; *Synoptic Studies: The Ampleforth Conferences of 1982 and 1983,* edited by C. M. Tuckett, J.S.O.T. Press, 1984; *Interpreters Dictionary of the Bible;* and *Encyclopedia Americana.* Contributor to periodicals. Series editor of *New Gospel Studies,* 1977—, *One Loaf, One Cup: Ecumenical Studies of 1 Cor 11 and Other Eucharistic Texts,* 1993, *A History and Critique of the Origin of the Marcan Hypothesis, 1835-66,* 1993, and *Arguments from Order in Synoptic Source Criticism,* 1993, all Mercer University Press. Editor-in-chief, *International Catholic Bible Commentary,* 1991—.

WORK IN PROGRESS: Christology in Crisis.

SIDELIGHTS: William R. Farmer once told *CA:* "A tremendous change has come into the world with the life and death of Jesus of Nazareth. All of my published writing represents, in one way or another, reflection upon and documentation of this change. Like that of my teacher, John Knox, much of my work is problem oriented and therefore sometimes takes on the character of a detective novel. I am an incurable historian and wish to guide my reader faithfully over the essential ground that has led me to my present conclusions on whatever matter I have been investigating.

"No doubt there is a mystical and practical dimension to my writing that reflects the fact I grew up on the fringes of the Great Mojave Desert, son of a Santa Fe Railroad section foreman. My understanding of power and *realpolitik* is doubtless influenced by military service and reflections upon the experience of war in the Pacific. Experience as pastor of a small Methodist church in Indiana has anchored my existence in a community of faith and served me well in academic life. I have not been hampered by too much learning from a proper 'European' education, but rather I have flourished as a child of the best that has come from the work of psychologist William James and philosopher John Dewey. My student days at Cambridge University have, however, left their mark on me, as have my many travels abroad."

*   *   *

FEUERSTEIN, Georg 1947-

PERSONAL: Surname is pronounced "*foy*-er-stine"; born May 27, 1947, in Wuerzburg, West Germany (now Germany); immigrated to England, 1966; immigrated to United States, 1981; son of Erwin (a jurist) and Dorothea (Gimperlein) Feuerstein; married Patricia Lamb (a book indexer and animal rights activist), February 14, 1985; children: (previous marriage) David, Daniel. *Education:* University of Durham, M.Litt., 1976; Greenwich University, Ph.D., 1993.

ADDRESSES: Home—P.O. Box 1386, Lower Lake, CA 95457.

CAREER: University of Durham, Durham, England, director of Yoga Research Centre, 1975-80; Dawn Horse Press, Clearlake, CA, editorial director, 1981-86; Integral Publishing, Lower Lake, CA, director, 1986—. Co-director of California Center for Jean Gebser Studies, 1986—, and of Healing Buddha Foundation, Sebastopol, CA, 1994—.

MEMBER: Authors Guild, American Academy of Religion, Indian Academy of Yoga.

WRITINGS:

Yoga: Sein Wesen und Werden (title means "Yoga: Its Essence and Development"), Schwab Verlag, 1969.

(With Jeanine Miller) *A Reappraisal of Yoga: Essays in Indian Philosophy,* Rider, 1969, published as *Yoga and Beyond: Essays in Indian Philosophy,* Schocken (New York City), 1972.

The Essence of Yoga: A Contribution to the Psychohistory of Indian Civilisation, Rider, 1974, Grove (New York City), 1976, revised edition published as *Wholeness or Transcendence? Ancient Lessons for the Emerging Global Civilization,* Larson, 1992.

Introduction to the Bhagavad-Gita: Its Philosophy and Cultural Setting, Rider, 1974, published as *The Bhagavad Gita: Its Philosophy and Cultural Setting,* Quest (Wheaton, IL), 1983.

Textbook of Yoga, Rider, 1975.

Yoga-Sutra: An Exercise in the Methodology of Textual Analysis, Arnold-Heinemann, 1979.

The Bhagavad-Gita: A Critical Rendering, Arnold-Heinemann, 1980.

The Yoga-Sutra of Patanjali: A New Translation and Commentary, Dawson, 1980.

The Philosophy of Classical Yoga, Manchester University Press (Dover, NH), 1980.

(With wife, Patricia Lamb Feuerstein) *Remembrance of the Divine Names of Da,* Dawn Horse (San Rafael, CA), 1982.

Yoga: The Technology of Ecstasy, Jeremy Tarcher, 1986.

Structures of Consciousness: The Genius of Jean Gebser; An Introduction and Critique, Integral Publishing (Pomfret Ctr., CT), 1987.

Jean Gebser: What Color is Your Consciousness?, Robert Briggs Associates, 1989.

Encyclopedic Dictionary of Yoga, Paragon House, 1990.

Scared Paths, Lawson, 1991.

Sacred Sexuality: Living the Vision of the Erotic Spirit, Jeremy Tarcher, 1991.

Holy Madness: The Shock Tactics and Radical Teachings of Crazy-Wise Adepts, Holy Fools, and Rascal Gurus, Paragon House, 1991.

Spirituality by the Numbers, Jeremy Tarcher, 1994.

The Mystery of Light: The Life and Teaching of Omraam Mikhael Aivanhov, Passage Press, 1994.

(With Subhash Kak and David Frawley) *In Search of the Cradle of Civilization,* Quest, 1995.

EDITOR AND AUTHOR OF INTRODUCTION

Da Free John, *Nirvanasara: Radical Transcendentalism and the Introduction of Advaitayana Buddhism,* Dawn Horse, 1982.

Da Free John, *Look at the Sunlight on the Water,* Dawn Horse, 1983.

Da Free John, *The Adept,* Dawn Horse, 1983.

Da Free John, *What Is the Conscious Process?,* Dawn Horse, 1983.

Da Free John, *Enlightenment and the Transformation of Man,* Dawn Horse, 1983.

(With Saniel Bonder) Da Free John, *The God in Every Body Book,* Dawn Horse, 1983.

John G. Bennett, *The Long Pilgrimage,* Dawn Horse, 1983.

Dwight Goddard, *Self-Realization of Noble Wisdom,* Dawn Horse, 1983.

Keith Dowman, *The Divine Madman,* Dawn Horse, 1983.

Da Free John, *The Transmission of Doubt,* Dawn Horse, 1984.

Da Free John, *Easy Death: Talks and Essays on the Inherent and Ultimate Transcendence of Death and Everything Else,* Dawn Horse, 1984.

Humor Suddenly Returns: Essays on the Spiritual Teaching of Master Da Free John, Dawn Horse, 1984.

T. S. Anantha Murthy, *Maharaj,* Dawn Horse, 1986.

Lee Sannella, *The Kundalini Experience: Psychosis or Transcendence?,* Integral Publishing, 1987.

Enlightened Sexuality: Essays on Body-Positive Spirituality, Crossing Press (Trumansburg, NY), 1989.

(With Stephan Bodian) *Living Yoga: A Comprehensive Guide for Daily Life,* Jeremy Tarcher/Perigree Books, 1993.

(With Trisha Lamb Feuerstein) *Voices on the Threshold of Tomorrow: 145 Views of the New Millennium,* Quest, 1993.

OTHER

Contributor to *The Encyclopedia of Religion,* yoga and philosophy journals, and various anthologies.

WORK IN PROGRESS: Shambhala Guide to Yoga and *Shambhala Encyclopedia of Yoga,* both by Shambhala Publications, expected in 1996; a volume containing English translations of Sanskrit texts on yoga and several books on psychospiritual healing.

SIDELIGHTS: "All of my work is concerned with the higher possibilities, and the ultimate transcendence, of human consciousness," Georg Feuerstein told *CA.* "Disenchanted with the Lutheran heritage of my childhood, I turned at an early age to the wisdom teachings of the East, notably the gnostic schools of yoga and vedanta, hoping that they would supply me with more convincing answers to the 'Big Questions' and a more viable outlook on life.

"Although I discovered many kindred spirits in the Sanskrit scriptures, which I learned to read in the original, my naturally critical bent of mind quickly sensitized me to the limitations of the traditional Eastern approaches. While allowing myself to be enriched by the vastly different life experience that I found crystallized in the ancient writings, I did not narrow my personal quest and scholarly research to Hindu and Buddhist wisdom but always consciously endeavored to integrate, on the levels of understanding and feeling, the two great halves of the human family—East and West.

"From the beginning of my career as an indologist, I liberally crossed the boundaries between academia and the public. Many of my published writings are attempts to communicate with a wider audience while fully respecting the exacting standards of sound scholarship. My maverick orientation proved useful, not only in fertilizing my chosen discipline—that of yoga research—but also in guiding many nonspecialists to a more judicious appreciation of the enormous complexities of Eastern religiophilosophical traditions and their vital significance for the spiritual renewal of contemporary humanity.

"I have arrived at the conclusion that the study of consciousness holds the key to understanding our confusing epoch and to creating a new global anthropology that takes the whole human being into account and without which we cannot master the contemporary civilization crisis. In particular my work is concerned with highlighting the uniquely human act of self-transcendence in its various forms—from living a harmonious life, practicing such timeless values as love, compassion and generosity, to realizing higher states of awareness that reveal the underlying unity of all things.

"In recent years, I have been especially interested in exploring—in theory and practice—psychospiritual healing as part of a self-transcending life. Specifically, I have been working closely with Lama Shakya Zangpo of the Healing Buddha Foundation, Sebastopol, California. According to the Medicine Buddha tradition of Tibetan Buddhism, suffering is a fundamental datum of ordinary human existence and while we can be cured of certain physical diseases or psychological maladjustments, we are ultimately healed only in the moment of our enlightenment. I have several books in progress that will address this profound insight into the human condition.

"I continue to learn and benefit from the wisdom of the East, and I also continue to appreciate the many efforts made by Western scientists and researchers to comprehend the dazzlingly complex and beautiful world in which we live. Together both streams of knowledge can provide us with a compass for navigating safely through our perplexing times.

"Throughout my scholarly work I have maintained, and attempted to demonstrate, that theory and praxis form a necessary unity. This conviction also informs my personal life and aspiration. The true power of knowledge lies in its capacity to transform us, to put us in touch with our higher possibilities, and give us the necessary means for living a meaningful, harmonious, and joyous life that includes others into its radiance and thus contributes to peace and happiness in the world."

FIELD, Peter
See DRESSER, Davis

*   *   *

FINCH, Robert (Duer Claydon)   1900-

PERSONAL: Born May 14, 1900, in Freeport, NY; son of Edward and Ada Finch. *Education:* University of Toronto, B.A., 1925; attended University of Paris, 1928.

ADDRESSES: Office—University of Toronto, Massey College, 4 Devonshire Pl., Toronto, Ontario, Canada M5S 2E1.

CAREER: Poet, literary critic, painter. University of Toronto, University College, Toronto, Ontario, lecturer, 1928-30, assistant professor, 1931-42, associate professor, 1942-51, professor, 1952-68, professor emeritus of French, 1970—, writer in residence, 1970-71. Member of board of trustees, Massey College, University of Toronto, and Leonard Foundation.

MEMBER: Societe Internationale d'Etudes Francaises, Royal Society of Canada (fellow).

AWARDS, HONORS: Jardine Memorial Prize, 1924, for poetry; Governor General's Awards, 1946, for *Poems,* and 1961, for *Acis in Oxford and Other Poems;* Lorne Pierce Gold Medal, 1968; LL.D., University of Toronto, 1973, and University of Winnipeg, 1984; D. Litt., York University, Toronto, 1976.

WRITINGS:

POETRY

Poems, Oxford University Press (New York City), 1946.
The Strength of the Hills, McClelland & Stewart (Toronto, Ontario), 1948.
Acis in Oxford and Other Poems, privately printed, 1959, University of Toronto Press, 1961.
Dover Beach Revisited and Other Poems, Macmillan (New York City), 1961.
Silverthorn Bush and Other Poems, Macmillan, 1966.
Variations and Theme, Porcupine's Quill (Erin, Ontario), 1980.
Has and Is, Porcupine's Quill, 1981.
Twelve for Christmas, Porcupine's Quill, 1982.
The Grand Duke of Moscow's Favorite Solo, Porcupine's Quill, 1983.
Double Tuning, Porcupine's Quill, 1984.
For the Back of a Likeness, Porcupine's Quill, 1986.
Sail-boat and Lake, Porcupine's Quill, 1990.
Miracle at the Jetty, Leeboard Press (Port Rowan, Ontario), 1991.
Impromptus, privately printed, 1994.

EDITOR

(With C. R. Parsons) *Chateaubriand, Rene,* University of Toronto Press (Toronto, Ontario), 1957.

(With Eugene Joliat) *French Individualist Poetry, 1686-1760: An Anthology,* University of Toronto Press, 1971.

(With Joliat) *Saint-Evremond, Sir Politick Would-Be,* Droz, 1978.

(With Joliat) Saint-Evremond, Les Opera, Droz, 1979.

OTHER

A Century Has Roots (masque), University of Toronto Press, 1953.

The Sixth Sense: Individualism in French Poetry, 1686-1760, University of Toronto Press, 1966.

Also contributor to *New Provinces: Poems of Several Authors,* Macmillan (Toronto), 1936; *Douglas Duncan: A Memorial Portrait,* edited by Alan Jarvis, University of Toronto Press, 1974; *The Enduring Word: A Centennial History of Wycliffe College,* edited by Arnold Edinborough, University of Toronto Press, 1978. Contributor to *Contemporary Verse* (Chicago), *Saturday Review, University of Toronto Quarterly,* and other periodicals. Work is represented in Canadian and international anthologies.

SIDELIGHTS: "At its best," writes L. A. MacKay in *Saturday Night,* Robert Finch's poetry "has a mannered dexterity, an ornate lucidity, and a studiously restrained tone that is capable alike of light grace and poignant though delicately phrased emotion." Writing in *Canadian Literature,* George Woodcock observes that Finch "writes with poise and self-consciousness. The Dionysic fury never leads him where his reason would not have him go, and his craftsmanship is controlled and accurate. Thus, one imagines, Flaubert might write if another incarnation made him a Canadian poet instead of a French novelist."

BIOGRAPHICAL/CRITICAL SOURCES:

BOOKS

Contemporary Literary Criticism, Volume 18, Gale, 1981.

PERIODICALS

Canadian Forum, December, 1967.
Canadian Literature, summer, 1962.
Comparative Literature, winter, 1968.
Saturday Night, May, 1949.

*   *   *

FISHER, Robert C(harles) 1930-

PERSONAL: Born March 3, 1930, in Burlington, IA; son of Ray Erwin (a tool designer) and Blanche Columbia (a teacher; maiden name, Brolin) Fisher. *Education:* Harvard University, A.B. (cum laude), 1955; graduate study at Columbia University, 1955-56, and Tokyo University, 1957-59. *Politics:* Independent. *Religion:* Protestant.

ADDRESSES: Home—New York, NY. *Office*—Simon & Schuster, 15th Fl., 15 Columbus Cir., New York, NY 10023.

CAREER: Fodor Guides, New York City, Far Eastern editor in Tokyo, Japan, 1959-64, associate editor in Litchfield, CT, 1964-66, executive editor in London, England, 1966-74, and New York City, 1974-77, executive vice-president, 1975-77, president, 1977-80; David McKay Co. (publisher), New York City, vice president, 1976-80; Fisher Travel Guides, New York City, president, 1980-88; Crown Insider's Travel Guides, New York City, general editor, 1988-89; Gault Millau Guides, editorial director, 1989-90; Simon & Schuster, New York City, consultant, 1990—. International Association for Medical Assistance to Travelers, member of board of directors, 1972—, vice president, 1985—. Founder and director, Kansas City (MO) Open Forum, 1949-50. Advisor to Prime Minister Takeo Miki of Japan, 1957-64; consultant to Central Research Institute (Tokyo), 1959-64. *Military service:* U.S. Army, 1952-54; became corporal; served in Korea.

MEMBER: International House of Japan, Society of American Travel Writers (director, 1978-80; vice president, 1981-83; president, 1983-84; president of Foundation, 1985-90), British Guild of Travel Writers (chairperson, 1970-71), Japan Society (New York), New York Travel Writers Association (president, 1979-81), Harvard Club (New York City), American Club of Japan.

AWARDS, HONORS: Scholarship recipient for study in Japan, 1956-59.

WRITINGS:

Klee, edited by Theodore Reff, Tudor (New York City), 1966.

Picasso, edited by Reff, Tudor, 1966.

(Editor) Ben F. Carruthers, *Bermuda 1983,* Fisher Travel Guides (New York City), 1982.

(Editor) Georgia I. Hesse, *California and the West, 1983-84,* Fisher Travel Guides, 1983.

Fisher's France, Fisher Travel Guides, 1983.

Crown Insiders' Guide to Japan, Crown (New York City), 1987.

(Editor) Michelle Da Silva Richmond and Florence Lemkowitz, *Crown Insiders' Guide to Mexico,* Crown, 1987.

(Editor) Patricia and Lester Brooks, *Crown Insiders' Guide to Britain,* Crown, 1987.

(Editor) *Insiders' Guide—France,* Crown, 1987.

(Editor) Barbara Hults, *Crown Insiders' Guide to Italy*, Crown, 1988.

(Editor with Colleen Dunn Bates) *The Best of Washington, D.C.*, revised edition, Prentice-Hall (Englewood Cliffs, NJ), 1990.

(Editor) *The Best of New Orleans*, Prentice-Hall, 1991.

EDITOR OF "FODOR'S MODERN GUIDE" SERIES

(With Eugene Fodor) *Fodor's Guide to Japan and East Asia*, McKay (New York City), 1962, revised edition published as *Fodor's Japan and East Asia*, McKay, 1979.

Fodor's India, Fodor's Modern Guides (Litchfield, CT), 1963, and numerous subsequent editions for McKay.

Fodor's U.S.A., Fodor's Modern Guides, eight volumes, 1966, revised edition published as *Fodor's U.S.A. 1980*, McKay, 1980.

Fodor's Guide to South America, Fodor's Modern Guides, 1966, revised edition published as *Fodor's South America 1980*, McKay, 1980.

(With Fodor and Barnett D. Laschever) *Rockies and Plains: Arizona, New Mexico, Colorado, Utah, Wyoming, Montana, North Dakota, South Dakota, Nebraska*, Fodor's Modern Guides, 1966, revised edition with Fodor and Stephen Birnbaum published as *Fodor's Rockies and Plains: Colorado, Nebraska, Utah, Wyoming, South Dakota, North Dakota, Montana*, McKay, 1974, revised edition with Leslie Brown published as *Fodor's Rockies and Plains*, McKay, 1978, revised edition published as *Fodor's Rockies and Plains 1980*, 1980.

(With Fodor and Laschever) *Pacific States: Southern California, Northern California, Nevada, Idaho, Oregon, Washington, Alaska*, Fodor's Modern Guides, 1966, 2nd revised edition, McKay, 1967.

(With Fodor and Laschever) *New England: Connecticut, Rhode Island, Massachusetts, Vermont, New Hampshire, Maine*, Fodor's Modern Guides, 1966, revised edition with Fodor and Birnbaum published as *Fodor's New England: Maine, New Hampshire, Vermont, Massachusetts, Connecticut, Rhode Island*, McKay, 1974, revised edition with Brown published as *Fodor's New England*, 1978, revised edition published as *Fodor's New England 1980*, 1980.

(With Fodor and Laschever) *South Central: Texas, Louisiana, Arkansas, Missouri, Kansas, Oklahoma*, Fodor's Modern Guides, 1966, 2nd revised edition, McKay, 1967.

(With Fodor and Laschever) *Southeast: Florida, South Carolina, Georgia, Alabama, Mississippi*, Fodor's Modern Guides, 1966, 2nd revised edition, McKay, 1967.

(With Fodor and Laschever) *Mid-Atlantic: Washington, D.C., Maryland, Delaware, Pennsylvania, Virginia,* *North Carolina, West Virginia, Kentucky*, Fodor's Modern Guides, 1966, revised edition with Fodor and Birnbaum published as *Fodor's Mid-Atlantic: Washington, D.C., Maryland, Delaware, Pennsylvania, Virginia, North Carolina, West Virginia, Kentucky*, McKay, 1974, revised edition published as *Fodor's Mid-Atlantic 1980*, 1980.

(With Fodor and Laschever) *Midwest: Illinois, Indiana, Ohio, Michigan, Wisconsin, Minnesota, Iowa*, Fodor's Modern Guides, 1966, revised edition with Fodor and Birnbaum published as *Fodor's Mid-West: Ohio, Illinois, Wisconsin, Indiana, Minnesota, Michigan, Iowa*, McKay, 1974.

(With Fodor and Laschever) *New York-New Jersey*, Fodor's Modern Guides, 1966, new edition with Fodor and Birnbaum published as *Fodor's New York and New Jersey*, McKay, 1974.

Fodor's Israel, McKay, 1967, and numerous subsequent editions.

Fodor's Spain, McKay, 1967, and numerous subsequent editions.

Fodor's Portugal, McKay, 1967, and numerous subsequent editions.

(With Fodor) *Fodor's Great Britain*, McKay, 1968, and numerous subsequent editions.

(With Fodor) *Fodor's Ireland*, Hodder & Stoughton (London), 1968, revised edition published as *Fodor's Ireland 1980*, McKay, 1980.

Fodor's Turkey, McKay, 1968, and numerous subsequent editions.

Fodor's Czechoslovakia, McKay, 1970, and numerous subsequent editions.

Fodor's Hungary, McKay, 1970, and numerous subsequent editions.

Fodor's Budget Europe, McKay, 1972, and numerous subsequent editions.

Fodor's Islamic Asia, McKay, 1973, and numerous subsequent editions.

Fodor's Tunisia, McKay, 1973, and numerous subsequent editions.

(With Fodor) *Fodor's Soviet Union*, McKay, 1974, revised edition, 1980.

Fodor's Paris, McKay, 1974.

Fodor's Vienna, McKay, 1974.

(With Fodor and Birnbaum) *Fodor's Far West: California, Oregon, Washington, Idaho, Nevada, Alaska*, McKay, 1974.

(With Fodor and Birnbaum) *Fodor's South-West: Texas, Oklahoma, Missouri, Kansas, Arizona, New Mexico*, McKay, 1974.

(With Fodor and Birnbaum) *Fodor's the South: Florida, Georgia, Alabama, Mississippi, Louisiana, Arkansas, North Carolina, South Carolina, Kentucky, Tennessee*, McKay, 1974.

Fodor's Japan, McKay, 1975.

Fodor's South-East Asia, McKay, 1975, revised edition published as *Fodor's Southeast Asia 1980,* 1980.

(With Eugene Fodor and Brown) *Fodor's Old West,* McKay, 1976.

(With Spencer Smith and Brown) *Fodor's Seaside America,* McKay, 1977.

Fodor's Cruises Everywhere, McKay, 1977.

Fodor's France 1977, Hodder & Stoughton, 1977, revised edition published as *Fodor's France 1979,* Hodder & Stoughton, 1979.

Fodor's Germany, West and East 1977, Hodder & Stoughton, 1977.

Fodor's Italy 1977, Hodder & Stoughton, 1977.

Fodor's Portugal 1977, Hodder & Stoughton, 1977.

Fodor's Scandinavia 1977, Hodder & Stoughton, 1977, revised edition published as *Fodor's Scandinavia 1980,* McKay, 1980.

Fodor's Morocco 1977, Hodder & Stoughton, 1977.

(With Rogers E. M. Whitaker and Brown) *Fodor's Railways of the World,* McKay, 1977.

(With Brown) *Fodor's Only-in-America Vacation Guide,* McKay, 1978.

(With Brown) *Fodor's Old South,* McKay, 1978.

(With Brown) *Fodor's Europe on a Budget 1978,* Hodder & Stoughton, 1978, revised edition published as *Fodor's Europe on a Budget 1979,* 1979.

(With Brown) *Fodor's Australia, New Zealand, and the South Pacific,* McKay, 1978, revised edition, 1980.

Fodor's People's Republic of China, McKay, 1979.

(With Brown) *Fodor's Outdoors America,* McKay, 1979.

(With Brown) Edmund Blair Bolles, *Fodor's Animal Parks of Africa,* McKay, 1979.

(With others) *Fodor's Sunbelt Leisure Guide,* McKay, 1979.

(With Brown) *Fodor's Bermuda 1979,* Hodder & Stoughton, 1979.

Fodor's Europe 1979, Hodder & Stoughton, 1979.

Fodor's London 1979, Hodder & Stoughton, 1979.

Fodor's Central America 1980, McKay, 1980.

Fodor's Mexico 1980, McKay, 1980.

Fodor's Hawaii 1980, McKay, 1980.

Fodor's Germany 1980, McKay, 1980.

Fodor's Europe 1980, McKay, 1980.

Fodor's Canada 1980, McKay, 1980.

Fodor's Austria 1980, McKay, 1980.

OTHER

Also author of *Guide to Japan,* 1981. Also editor of *Fodor's Iran, Fodor's Egypt,* and *Fodor's New York, City and State,* all McKay. Author of column, "Letter from London," in *World Travel.*

SIDELIGHTS: Robert C. Fisher once told *CA,* "I hope that the travel guide books I write and edit contain enough background material on the country's way of life, people, economics, and culture to make the visitor's stay one in which some sort of intelligent exchange is possible between him and the inhabitants."

BIOGRAPHICAL/CRITICAL SOURCES:

PERIODICALS

Los Angeles Times, September 27, 1987.
Washington Post, January 30, 1983, p. 14.*

*   *   *

FITTER, Richard Sidney Richmond   1913-

PERSONAL: Born March 1, 1913, in London, England; son of Sidney Harry (a produce broker) and Dorothy Isacke (Pound) Fitter; married Alice Mary (Maisie) Stewart Park (an editor), 1938; children: Jenny Elizabeth, Julian Richmond, Alastair Hugh. *Education:* Attended Eastbourne College; London School of Economics and Political Science, B.Sc., 1933. *Avocational interests:* Botanising, observing wild and human life, exploring new habitats, reading.

ADDRESSES: Home—Drifts, Chinnor Hill, Oxford OX9 4BS, England.

CAREER: Writer and naturalist. Member of research staff, Political and Economic Planning, 1936-40, Mass-Observation, 1940-42; member of operational research section, Coastal Command, 1942-45; editor of *London Naturalist,* 1942-46; secretary of Wildlife Conservation Special Committee, Hobhouse Committee on National Parks, 1945-46; assistant editor of *Countryman,* 1946-59; open air correspondent for *Observer,* 1958-66; director of intelligence unit, Council for Nature, 1959-63; editor of *Kingfisher,* 1965-72.

MEMBER: International Union for the Conservation of Nature (member of Survival Service Commission, 1963; chair of steering committee until 1988); World Wildlife Fund, United Kingdom (trustee, 1977-83); Fauna Preservation Society (honorary secretary, 1964-80; vice-chair, 1980-83; chair, 1983-88; vice president, 1988—); British Trust for Ornithology; Royal Society for the Protection of Birds; Berkshire, Buckinghamshire, and Oxfordshire Naturalists' Trust; Zoological Society of London (fellow); Athenaeum Club.

AWARDS, HONORS: Officier, Order of the Golden Ark, Netherlands, 1978.

WRITINGS:

The Starling Roosts of the London Area, London Naturalist, 1943.

(With E. R. Parrinder) *A Check-List of the Birds of the London Area,* London Naturalist, 1944.

London's Natural History: The New Naturalist, No. 3, a Survey of British Natural History, Collins (London), 1945.

Bird-Watching in London, Royal Society for the Protection of Birds (Sandy, England), 1948.

London's Birds, Collins, 1949.

(Editor) *British Birds in Colour,* Odhams, 1951.

Home Counties, Collins, 1951.

The Pocket Guide to British Birds, Collins, 1952, Dodd (New York), 1953, revised edition published as *Collins Pocket Guide to British Birds,* Collins, 1966, 3rd edition, 1970.

(With Job Edward Lousley) *The Natural History of the City,* Corporation of London (London), 1953.

Birds of Town and Village, Collins, 1953.

The Starling, School-Aid Department, Daily Mail, 1953.

(With Guy Charteris) *The Pocket Guide to Nests and Eggs,* Collins, 1954, revised edition published as *The Collins Pocket Guide to Nests and Eggs,* 1968.

(With David McClintock) *The Pocket Guide to Wild Flowers,* Collins, 1956.

Fontana Bird Guide, Collins, 1956.

Fontana Wild Flower Guide, Collins, 1957.

(Editor with H. N. Southern) Marie N. Stephens, *The Natural History of the Otter,* University Federation for Animal Welfare (London), 1957.

Your Book of Bird Watching (juvenile), Transatlantic, 1958.

The Ark in Our Midst: The Story of the Introduced Animals of Britain: Birds, Beasts, Reptiles, Amphibians, Fishes, Collins, 1959.

Six Great Naturalists: White, Linnaeus, Waterton, Audubon, Fabre, Huxley, Hamish Hamilton (London), 1959.

(Editor) *The Countryman Nature Book: An Anthology from the Countryman,* Brockhampton Press, 1960.

Your Book about Wild Flowers (juvenile), Faber (London), 1960.

Collins Guide to Bird-watching, Collins, 1963, 2nd edition, 1970.

Fitter's Rural Rides: The Observer Illustrated Map-Guide to the Countryside, Observer, 1963.

Wildlife in Britain, Gannon, 1963.

Wildlife and Death, Newman Neame, 1964.

British Wildlife: Rarities and Introductions, Kay, 1966.

(With wife, Maisie Fitter) *The Penguin Dictionary of British Natural History,* Penguin (New York City), 1967, revised edition, A. & C. Black (London), 1968.

Vanishing Wild Animals of the World, F. Watts (New York City), 1968.

(With Hermann Heinzel and J. L. F. Parslow) *The Birds of Britain and Europe with North Africa and the Mid-dle East,* Lippincott (Philadelphia, PA), 1972, 2nd edition, Collins, 1974, published as *The Collins Guide to the Birds of Britain and Europe; with North Africa and the Middle East,* Viking Penguin (New York City), 1984.

Finding Wild Flowers, Collins, 1972.

(Author of introduction) *BBONT: The First Ten Years, 1959-1969,* Berkshire, Buckinghamshire, and Oxfordshire Naturalists' Trust, 1973.

(Contributor) Alan Aldridge, *The Butterfly Ball and the Grasshopper's Feast,* J. Cape (London), 1973.

(With son, Alastair Fitter) *The Wild Flowers of Britain and Northern Europe,* Scribner (New York City), 1974.

(With Sir Peter Scott) *The Penitent Butchers,* Collins, 1978.

(With Marjorie Blamey) *Handguide to the Wild Flowers of Britain and Europe,* Collins, 1979.

Wild Flowers, Collins, 1980.

(With A. Fitter) *The Complete Guide to British Wildlife,* Collins, 1981.

(Editor with Eric Robinson) *John Clare's Birds,* Oxford University Press (New York City), 1982.

(With A. Fitter) *Collins Guide to the Countryside,* illustrated by John Wilkinson, Collins, 1984.

(With A. Fitter) *The Grasses, Sedges, Rushes and Fens of Britain and Northern Europe,* Collins, 1984.

Wildlife for Men: How and Why We Should Conserve Our Species, Collins, 1986.

(With R. Manuel) *Field Guide to the Freshwater Life of Britain and Northwest Europe,* Collins, 1986.

The Road to Extinction: Problems of Categorizing the Status of Taxa Threatened with Extinction, Island Press (Ft. Myers Beach, FL), 1987.

Also author of *The Wildlife of Thames Counties,* 1985, and, with A. Fritter, *Guide to the Countryside in Winter,* 1988; author of introduction to *The Gamekeeper at Home and the Amateur Poacher* by Richard Jefferies.*

*   *   *

FLORIAN, Douglas 1950-

PERSONAL: Born March 18, 1950, in New York, NY; son of Harold (an artist) and Edith Florian; married Marie Lallouz (a chef), November 3, 1985. *Education:* Queens College of the City University of New York, B.A., 1973; attended School of Visual Arts, 1976.

ADDRESSES: Home—147-42 Village Rd., Jamaica, NY 11435.

CAREER: Writer and freelance illustrator, 1971—.

AWARDS, HONORS: Reading Magic Award as one of year's ten best books, *Parenting* magazine, 1994, and

Books of Distinction finalist, *Hungry Mind Review,* both for *Bing Bang Boing;* Gold Medal, National Parenting Publications Awards, 1994, and Lee Bennett Hopkins Award for Poetry, 1995, both for *Beast Feast.*

WRITINGS:

SELF-ILLUSTRATED CHILDREN'S BOOKS

A Bird Can Fly, Greenwillow (New York City), 1980.
The City, Crowell (New York City), 1982.
People Working, Crowell, 1983.
Airplane Ride, Crowell, 1984.
Discovering Butterflies, Scribner (New York City), 1986.
Discovering Trees, Scribner, 1986.
Discovering Frogs, Scribner, 1987.
Discovering Seashells, Scribner, 1987.
A Winter Day, Greenwillow, 1987.
An Auto Mechanic, Greenwillow, 1991.
A Chef, Greenwillow, 1992.
A Painter, Greenwillow, 1993.
Monster Motel, Harcourt (San Diego), 1993.
A Fisher, Greenwillow, 1994.
Beast Feast, Harcourt, 1994.
Bing Bang Boing, Harcourt, 1994.

ILLUSTRATOR

(With Kristin Linklater) *Freeing the Natural Voice,* Dramabooks (New York City), 1976.
Dorothy O. Van Woerkom, *Tit for Tat,* Greenwillow, 1977.
Thomas M. Cook and Robert A. Russell, *Introduction to Management Science,* Prentice-Hall (Englewood Cliffs, NJ), 1977.

OTHER

Contributor of more than three hundred drawings to magazines and newspapers, including *Travel and Leisure, Across the Board, Nation,* and *New York Times.*

SIDELIGHTS: Douglas Florian told *CA:* "My early work, coming out of school, was as a political illustrator and cartoonist. I did many drawings for the *New York Times* and for the *New Yorker* magazine. I think this training made the jump into writing humorous poems easier. In both cases you're trying to combine two seemingly disparate elements into a logical conclusion. There's also an economy of means in cartooning and satire: no extra lines, no extra words. I'd rather understate than overstate. Although I consider myself more an artist than a writer, it's more fun to write light verse than to paint, where sometimes it takes five or six attempts to achieve what my mind's eye sees so beautifully."

FLYNN, Jackson
See SHIRREFFS, Gordon D(onald)

*   *   *

FONER, Eric   1943-

PERSONAL: Born February 7, 1943, in New York, NY; son of Jack Donald (a professor) and Liza (Kraitz) Foner; married Naomi Achs (an associate producer of Children's Television Workshop), June 20, 1965 (divorced, 1977); married Lynn Garafola (a writer on dance), May 1, 1980. *Education:* Columbia University, B.A., 1963, Ph.D., 1969; Oxford University, B.A., 1965.

ADDRESSES: Home—606 West 116th St., New York, NY 10027. *Office*—Department of History, Columbia University, New York, NY 10027.

CAREER: Columbia University, New York City, assistant professor of history 1969-73; City College of the City University of New York, New York City, associate professor of history, 1973-82; Columbia University, professor of history 1982-88, DeWitt Clinton Professor of History, 1988—.

MEMBER: American Historical Association, Organization of American Historians (president, 1993-94), Southern History Association, Phi Beta Kappa.

AWARDS, HONORS: American Council of Learned Societies fellowship, 1972-73; Guggenheim fellowship, 1975-76; National Book Award nomination for nonfiction, National Books Critics Circle nomination for general nonfiction, and *Los Angeles Times* Book Prize for history, all 1988, and Pulitzer Prize for history, 1989, all for *Reconstruction: America's Unfinished Revolution, 1863-1877.*

WRITINGS:

Free Soil, Free Labor, Free Men: The Ideology of the Republican Party before the Civil War, Oxford University Press (Oxford, England), 1970.
Nat Turner, Prentice-Hall (Englewood Cliffs, NJ), 1971.
Tom Paine and Revolutionary America, Oxford University Press, 1976.
Politics and Ideology in the Age of the Civil War, Oxford University Press, 1980.
Nothing but Freedom: Emancipation and its Legacy, Louisiana State University Press (Baton Rouge), 1983.
Reconstruction: America's Unfinished Revolution, 1863-1877, Harper (New York City), 1988.
A Short History of Reconstruction, 1863-1877, Harper, 1990.
(With Olivia Mahoney) *A House Divided: America in the Age of Lincoln,* Chicago Historical Society, 1990.

Freedom's Lawmakers: A Directory of Black Officeholders during Reconstruction, Oxford University Press, 1993.

EDITOR

America's Black Past: A Reader in Afro-American History, Harper, 1971.

Richard D. Brown, *Modernization: The Transformation of American Life, 1600-1865,* Hill & Wang (New York City), 1976.

James R. Green, *The World of the Worker and Labor in Twentieth Century America,* Hill & Wang, 1978.

Julie R. Jeffrey, *Frontier Women: The Trans-Mississippi West, 1840-1880,* Hill & Wang, 1979.

Harvard Sitkoff, *The Struggle for Black Equality, 1954-1980,* Hill & Wang, 1981.

Carl Kaestle, *Pillars of the Republican: Common Schools and American Society, 1970-1860,* Hill & Wang, 1983.

The New American History, Temple University Press (Philadelphia), 1990.

(With John A. Garraty) *The Reader's Companion to American History,* Houghton (Boston), 1991.

OTHER

Consulting editor of "American Century" series, Hill & Wang, 1985-1992, and "Critical Issues" series, Hill & Wang, 1993—. Contributor of articles and reviews to numerous periodicals, including *New York Times, New York Review of Books, Journal of American History, Journal of Negro History,* and *New York History.*

SIDELIGHTS: Eric Foner's widely praised *Reconstruction: America's Unfinished Revolution, 1863-1877* is a "long, brilliant and stylish book . . . of signal importance, not only to understanding one of the most controversial periods in American history but to comprehending the course of race relations in this country during the last century," according to critic Gary Nash in the *Los Angeles Times Book Review.* Nash added that *Reconstruction* "is the most comprehensive and convincing account of the effort to build a racially democratic and just society from the fiery ruins of slavery." Foner's book, which took nine years to complete, examines the economic, political, and social forces that subverted Reconstruction, and how its failure undermined the development of the nation and established a legacy of racism that remains even in contemporary times. In the *Nation,* Theodore Rosengarten declared that *Reconstruction* is "monumental in scope" and "a feat of research and synthesis that is not likely to be repeated for a generation."

In *Reconstruction,* Foner offers a revisionist view of the period that goes beyond mere criticism of Lincoln's ambivalences about the future of African-Americans and Andrew Johnson's political vision of "white supremacy in the South and his own re-election as president," wrote David Herbert Donald in the *New Republic.* Donald noted that "in a deliberate effort to overturn stereotypes, [Foner] offers an admiring picture of the freedman during the postwar years," later adding, "he has performed a real service in bringing blacks front and center in the Reconstruction drama, where they belong."

William S. McFeely observed in the *New York Times Book Review* that in his epilogue, Foner "asserts that Reconstruction had a direct bearing on the civil rights movement and suggests that the period speaks to the still-persisting denial of freedom to blacks that lingers in so many parts of society." McFeely concluded that with this book, "Foner becomes the pre-eminent historian of Reconstruction."

Foner's earlier works also drew praise from reviewers. In the words of David Donald, writing in the *New York Times Book Review,* Foner's book *Free Soil, Free Labor, Free Men: The Ideology of the Republican Party before the Civil War* "is a useful and fair-minded summary of what Republicanism meant in the 1850's, and it is especially valuable as a corrective to older historical stereotypes. . . ." Writing about *Politics and Ideology in the Age of the Civil War,* J. H. Silbey remarked in *American Historical Review:* "[Foner] is excellent at delineating the dominant ideologies and linking them to political events. . . . Foner also recognizes the early importance of intersectional political parties in resisting and containing sectional confrontation, but he emphasizes their demise in the face of popular sectional ideologies. . . . This is an important and invigorating work."

BIOGRAPHICAL/CRITICAL SOURCES:

PERIODICALS

American Historical Review, October, 1981.
Library Journal, July, 1970.
Los Angeles Times Book Review, October 16, 1988, p. 5.
Nation, May 28, 1988, pp. 748-754.
New Republic, November 22, 1980; August 1, 1988, pp. 41-44.
New York Review of Books, September 23, 1971; May 12, 1988, pp. 22-27.
New York Times, October 23, 1991.
New York Times Book Review, October 18, 1970; May 22, 1988, pp. 11-12.
Tribune Books (Chicago), February 4, 1990, p. 3.
Village Voice Literary Supplement, November, 1983.
Virginia Quarterly Review, autumn, 1970.
Washington Post Book World, May 15, 1988, p. 1.

FOWLER, Charles B(runer) 1931-

PERSONAL: Born May 12, 1931, in Peekskill, NY; son of Charles B. (a conductor) and Mabel (Ackerman) Fowler. *Education:* Crane School of Music, State University of New York at Potsdam, B.S.Mus.Ed., 1952; Northwestern University, M.M., 1957; Boston University, D.M.A., 1964. *Avocational interests:* Painting, theater, gardening, exercise, travel.

ADDRESSES: Home and office—320 Second St. S.E., Washington, DC 20003.

CAREER: Vocal music supervisor in elementary schools in Rochester, NY, 1952-56; Mansfield State College, Mansfield, PA, assistant professor of music, 1957-62; Northern Illinois University, DeKalb, associate professor of music, 1964-65; Music Educators National Conference, Washington, DC, editor of *Music Educators Journal,* 1965-71, director of publications, 1970-71; writer and consultant in the arts, 1971—. Manager of publications and editor-in-chief of *Parks and Recreation,* National Recreation and Parks Association, Washington, DC, 1973-75. Writer and consultant for opening of Walt Disney World, 1971; writer and creative consultant to the executive producer, Radio City Music Hall Productions, Inc., 1979-82; communications designer for opening events of Epcot Center, Walt Disney World, 1982.

MEMBER: Music Educators National Conference (life member), Music Critics Association, American Council for the Arts, Educational Press Association of America (member of board of directors of District of Columbia chapter, 1969-71), Kappa Delta Pi, Pi Kappa Lambda, Phi Mu Alpha Sinfonia (honorary life member).

AWARDS, HONORS: Danforth grants, 1962-63, 1963-64; certificate of excellence in educational journalism, Educational Press Association of America, 1970; William G. Anderson Award, 1985, for contributions to dance; Minerva Award (highest alumni award), State University of New York at Potsdam, College of Arts and Sciences; Distinguished Alumni Award, Boston University, 1990.

WRITINGS:

(With Robert W. Buggert) *The Search for Musical Understanding,* Wadsworth (Hartford), 1973.
The Arts Process, Pennsylvania State Department of Education, 1973.
Dance Is (booklet and slide/tape presentation), National Dance Association, 1978.
Careers in Entertainment (videotape), Walt Disney Productions, 1979.
(Editor and contributor) *An Arts in Education Source Book,* John D. Rockefeller III Fund, 1980.
Arts Education: A Promise (slide/tape presentation), John F. Kennedy Center, 1980.

Carmen Opera Box (multi-media teaching tool), Metropolitan Opera, 1980.
Porgy and Bess Opera Box (multi-media teaching tool), Metropolitan Opera, 1981.
First Flights: The Kennedy Center's Programs for Children and Youth (slide/tape presentation), John F. Kennedy Center, 1981.
Alaska 1984 (live and televised production), Radio City Music Hall Productions, 1981.
(Author of narration) *The Glory of Christmas: A Living Nativity,* Crystal Cathedral, 1981.
(Author of narration) *Encore: The Fiftieth Anniversary Show,* Radio City Music Hall, 1982.
The Message of Music (radio program), New York Philharmonic and National Public Radio, 1982.
Arts in Education/Education in Arts, National Endowment for the Arts, 1985.
A Mets Fan at the Met (children's story), Metropolitan Opera Guild, 1986.
Symposium '85 Report: Music Is Essential to Quality Education, Texas Music Educators Association, 1986.
(Editor) *Sing!* (secondary school textbook), Hinshaw, 1987.
(Author of script) *An Evening at the Kennedy Center,* United Way, 1987.
Can We Rescue the Arts for America's Children?, American Council for the Arts, 1988.
Music! Its Role and Importance in Our Lives, McGraw-Hill (New York City), 1994.

Also editor of *The Crane Symposium: Toward an Understanding of the Teaching and Learning of Musical Performance,* State University of New York at Potsdam. Author of two series for National Public Radio, *Alleluia!,* 1984, and *The 1984 Santa Fe Chamber Music Festival,* 1985. Contributor to *Encyclopedia of Education.* Contributor of more than two hundred and fifty articles to music and education journals. Education editor, *Musical America,* 1974-89; consulting editor, *Design for Arts Education,* 1980-85, and *Journal of Arts Management and Law,* 1986-89.

WORK IN PROGRESS: Strong Arts, Strong Schools, a book about arts education.

SIDELIGHTS: Charles B. Fowler once told *CA:* "While I probably would be categorized as a technical writer because much of my work is focused on arts education and music, I bring as much artfulness and craft to the task as my wits permit. Like most writers, I study writing by reading, and I enjoy giving life and veracity to an idea by casting it in the right clothes. I've found that making a living as an independent writer in the arts requires versatility. I've written books, articles, reports, pamphlets, flyers, scripts for radio, theater, and multi-media presentations, treatments for film and television—almost anything that comes along. The trick is to turn what could be mundane into something vibrant. To me, the challenge is to touch the reader's mind and heart—to find the essence and make it indelible."

*   *   *

FOX, J. N.
   See JANECZKO, Paul B(ryan)

*   *   *

FRANCIS, Dorothy Brenner   1926-
   (Sue Alden, Ellen Goforth, Pat Louis)

PERSONAL: Born November 30, 1926, in Lawrence, KS; daughter of Clayton (a district judge) and Cecile (Goforth) Brenner; married Richard M. Francis (a professional musician), August 30, 1950; children: Lynn Ann Francis Tank, Patricia Louise Francis Pocius. *Education:* University of Kansas, Mus.B., 1948. *Politics:* Republican. *Religion:* Methodist.

ADDRESSES: Home—1505 Brentwood Ter., Marshall-town, IA 50158.

CAREER: Band and vocal instructor in Orange, CA, 1948-50, Pleasant Hill, MO, 1950-51, Cache, OK, 1951-52, and Gilman, IA, 1961-62; former teacher of piano and trumpet and director of a Methodist junior high choir; correspondence teacher for Institute of Children's Literature, Redding Ridge, CT. Member of board of community chamber orchestra, Marshalltown, IA, 1967.

MEMBER: Society of Children's Book Writers, P.E.O. Sisterhood, Marshalltown Tuesday Music Club (former president), Mu Phi Epsilon.

WRITINGS:

Adventure at Riverton Zoo, Abingdon (Nashville, TN), 1966.
Mystery of the Forgotten Map, Follett, 1968.
Laugh at the Evil Eye, Messner (New York City), 1970.
Another Kind of Beauty, Criterion (Torrance, CA), 1970.
Hawaiian Interlude, Avalon (Hewlett, NY), 1970.
Studio Affair, Avalon, 1972.
Nurse on Assignment, Avalon, 1972.
A Blue Ribbon for Marni, Avalon, 1973.
Nurse under Fire, Avalon, 1973.
Nurse in the Caribbean, Avalon, 1973.
Murder in Hawaii, Scholastic (New York City), 1973.
Nurse of the Keys, Avalon, 1974.
Golden Girl, Scholastic, 1974.
Nurse of Spirit Lake, Avalon, 1975.
Keys to Love, Avalon, 1975.

The Flint Hills Foal, Abingdon, 1976.
Nurse at Playland Park, Avalon, 1976.
The Legacy of Merton Manor, Avalon, 1976.
Murder in the Balance, Avalon, 1976.
(Under pseudonym Sue Alden) *The Magnificent Challenge,* Avalon, 1976.
(Under pseudonym Sue Alden) *Nurse at St. John,* Avalon, 1977.
Two against the Arctic, Pyramid (St. Benwood, WV), 1977.
Piggy Bank Minds and Other Object Lessons for Children, Abingdon, 1977.
Run of the Sea Witch, Abingdon, 1978.
The Boy with the Blue Ears and Forty-nine Other Object Lessons for Children, Abingdon, 1979.
Shoplifting: The Crime Everybody Pays For, Lodestar (New York City), 1980, 3rd edition, 1982.
(Under pseudonym Ellen Goforth) *Path of Desire,* Silhouette (New York City), 1980.
New Boy in Town, Silhouette, 1981.
Special Girl, Silhouette, 1981.
(Under pseudonym Pat Louis) *Treasure of the Heart,* Harlequin (Tarrytown, NY), 1982.
A New Dawn, Silhouette, 1982.
Say Please, Silhouette, 1982.
Secret Place, Silhouette, 1982.
Captain Morgana Mason, Lodestar, 1982.
A Blink of the Mind, Dell (New York City), 1982.
The Ghost of Graydon Place, Scholastic, 1982.
Just Friends, Silhouette, 1983.
Vandalism: The Crime of Immaturity, Lodestar, 1983.
Promises and Turtle Shells, Abingdon, 1984.
Kiss Me Kit, Silhouette, 1984.
The Magic Circle, Silhouette, 1984.
The Warning, Scholastic, 1984.
Bid for Romance, Silhouette, 1985.
Follow Your Heart, Silhouette, 1986.
The Tomorrow Star, Weekly Reader Books, 1986.
Write On, Silhouette, 1986.
Stop Thief, Silhouette, 1986.
Computer Crime, Lodestar, 1987.
The Right Kind of Girl, Lodestar, 1987.
Vonnie and Monique, Silhouette, 1987.
Suicide, Lodestar, 1989.
Drift Bottles, Ballyhoo Books, 1990.
Metal Detecting for Treasure, Ballyhoo Books, 1992.

Contributor of articles, short stories and light verse to many publications including *New York Times, Ford Times, Western & Eastern Treasures, American Legion, The Writer* and *Writers Digest.*

Eighteen of Francis's books have been translated into foreign languages.

WORK IN PROGRESS: "An historical novel for middle grade readers set in the Florida Keys, in the 1930s."

SIDELIGHTS: Dorothy Brenner Francis told *CA,* "In all my books for children, I've tried to show different lifestyles which I hope will make the reader wonder and think and continue to read."

*   *   *

FRANCIS, Richard 1945-

PERSONAL: Born May 14, 1945, in Shawford, England; son of Leslie (a civil servant) and Marian (Rennie) Francis; married Jo Watson (a teacher), January 14, 1967; children: William Rennie, Helen Elizabeth. *Education:* Magdalene College, Cambridge, B.A. (with honors), 1967; attended Harvard University, 1970-72; University of Exeter, Ph.D., 1976. *Politics:* Supporter of British Labour Party. *Religion:* None. *Avocational interests:* Twentieth-century American poetry, music, travel, art collecting.

ADDRESSES: Home—9 Glenfield Rd., Heaton Chapel, Stockport SK4 2QP, England. *Office*—Department of American Studies, Victoria University of Manchester, Manchester, England. *Agent*—Peters, Fraser & Dunlop, 503-4, The Chambers, Chelsea Harbour, London SW10 0XF, England.

CAREER: Victoria University of Manchester, Manchester, England, lecturer in creative writing and American literature, 1972—. Lecturer at Al-Fateh University, 1976-77; visiting professor, University of Missouri—Columbia, 1987-88. Director, Password (poetry book distribution company).

WRITINGS:

NOVELS

Blackpool Vanishes (with poems), Faber (London), 1979.
Daggerman (with poems), Faber, 1980.
The Enormous Dwarf, Granada (London), 1982.
The Whispering Gallery, Deutsch (London) and Norton (New York City), 1984.
Swansong, Collins (London) and Atheneum (New York City), 1986.
The Land Where Lost Things Go, Carcanet (Manchester), 1990.
Taking Apart the Poco Poco, Fourth Estate (London) and Simon & Schuster (New York City), 1995.

OTHER

Contributor to *American Quarterly, Critical Quarterly, Studies in the American Renaissance* and *P.N. Review.*

WORK IN PROGRESS: A novel, as yet untitled, and an academic text, *The Law of Series,* for Cornell University Press.

SIDELIGHTS: Richard Francis told *CA:* "In all my published works, the central issue is the same—an attempt to explore the relationship between the transcendental and the everyday. In my earlier books this took the form of trying to reveal the implications of an alien presence in the 'normal' world. *Blackpool Vanishes,* my first novel, dealt with what you might call interterrestrial life, featuring beings who come not from another world but from overlooked little gaps in what we rather complacently think of as the continuum of reality. In *Daggerman,* the alien vision belongs to the deranged consciousness of a mass-murderer and is formulated into a religion of the 'third alternative.' *The Enormous Dwarf* is concerned with the problem of accommodating in the present an event which took place in the past and was so horrific that it challenges imaginative reconstruction.

"In my most recent work, the emphasis has changed slightly to an exploration of the effectiveness of our accounts of reality, the theme of news in *The Whispering Gallery,* of politics in *Swansong* (which deals with the Falklands War), and of literature itself in *The Land Where Lost Things Go,* which takes the form of a heavily autobiographical first draft of a children's novel by an aging and long out-of-print female writer. My new novel, *Taking Apart the Poco Poco,* follows the adventures of five members of a family (mother, father, daughter, son, and dog) as they proceed through what is ostensibly a routine day. Unknown to the others each of them goes through a series of strange, mysterious and often farcical experiences, but they all get home again in time for tea. What I'm interested in here is the way we narrate the story of our lives to ourselves, each creating our own epic of the ordinary.

"I think that my academic concern with the New England Transcendentalists has influenced my development as a novelist. I am just completing a book on their endeavor to find a bridging structure between the one and the many, our human experience and that total fabric of things which they refer to as God, or Nature. I call this connecting principle, which they never quite define, the law of series. It's not a solution I could endorse myself, but it reflects one of the deepest human needs, and it is a concern with that need which unites all the different genres and styles of writing I undertake."

BIOGRAPHICAL/CRITICAL SOURCES:

BOOKS

Aulich, James, *Framing the Falklands War: Nationhood, Culture and Identity,* Open University Press, 1990, pp. 124-127.

PERIODICALS

Guardian, April 5, 1979.

New York Times Book Review, July 13, 1980; December 2, 1984.

Sunday Times, August 10, 1987.

Times Literary Supplement, March 21, 1980; July 27, 1984; September 21, 1990.

*   *   *

FRANK, Katherine 1949-

PERSONAL: Born August 3, 1949, in Lake Forest, IL; daughter of Arthur and Isabel Voss. *Education:* University of Illinois at Chicago, B.A., 1972; University of Iowa, Ph.D., 1979. *Politics:* United States Democratic Party; British Labour Party.

ADDRESSES: Home—Staffordshire, England. *Agent*—Bruce Hunter, David Higham Associates Ltd., 5-8 Lower John St., Golden Sq., London W1R 4HA, England.

CAREER: University of Sierra Leone, Freetown, lecturer, 1980-83; Bayero University, Kano, Nigeria, senior lecturer, 1984—. Freelance journalist.

MEMBER: Modern Language Association of America, Women in Nigeria, Bronte Society.

WRITINGS:

A Voyager Out: The Life of Mary Kingsley, Houghton (Boston, MA), 1986.

A Chainless Soul: The Life of Emily Bronte, Houghton, 1990.

A Passage to Egypt: The Life of Lucie Duff Gordon, Houghton, 1994.

Contributor of articles and book reviews to periodicals, including *Miami Herald.*

SIDELIGHTS: Biographer Katherine Frank chronicles the life of nineteenth-century explorer Mary Kingsley in *A Voyager Out: The Life of Mary Kingsley.* After living the life of a homebound and dutiful daughter for the first thirty years of her life, Kingsley embarked on an exploration of Africa upon the death of her parents in 1892. She was "a most unlikely heroine," remarked Elinor Langer in the *New York Times Book Review,* and yet Kingsley's two major journeys to West Africa between 1893 and 1896 found the Victorian spinster paddling through swamps of the French Congo, climbing mountains, and living among Africans in tropical rain forests. Kingsley's exploits led her to write two books and brought her acclaim as a speaker in the select world of London's political and literary salons. But "she never fully fitted into life in England again, after that first trip [to Africa]," commented *Washington Post Book World* reviewer William Boyd.

Kingsley was one of the "great travelers of history [and] different from all the scientists, explorers and tourists," maintained Boyd, because the most important aspect of her explorations was that she "traveled to find herself." She died of typhoid at the age of thirty-seven, during Africa's Boer War, while nursing prisoners of war near Cape Town.

It is Kingsley's extraordinary life and the mysterious and alluring setting of Africa, Boyd noted, that Frank so aptly focuses on in *A Voyager Out.* "At its end," wrote Boyd, "one has come some way towards understanding the complexities of the unique person Mary Kingsley surely was." Although *Chicago Tribune* reporter Patrick Reardon claimed that Frank's "obvious affection and regard for her subject" is a minor drawback in that it "pushes Frank, unnecessarily, to explain away some of Kingsley's quirks," he conceded that "it animates Frank to tell the story of a complex and often hidden life with straight-forward strength and clarity."

Frank told *CA:* "I am a biographer, traveller and university teacher. For most of the 1980s, I lived, travelled and taught in West Africa, Jordan and Egypt. Though I am settled now in England, I spend a great deal of time in India and am currently working on a biography of Indira Gandhi. I am drawn to other cultures and interested in innovative biography which extends the boundaries of conventional nonfiction."

BIOGRAPHICAL/CRITICAL SOURCES:

PERIODICALS

Antioch Review, Volume 49, summer, 1991, p. 464.

Chicago Tribune, September 19, 1986.

Guardian Weekly, May 17, 1987, p. 23.

Listener, November 29, 1990, p. 34.

London Review of Books, April 2, 1987, p. 15; December 20, 1990, p. 16.

New York Times Book Review, November 30, 1986, p. 28; November 11, 1990, p. 13; August 14, 1994, p. 1.

Observer, March 1, 1987, p. 29; February 3, 1991, p. 54.

Publishers Weekly, July 25, 1986, p. 178; October 5, 1990, p. 83; January 1, 1992, p. 54; June 20, 1994, p. 88.

Punch, March 18, 1987, p. 63.

Spectator, April 11, 1987, p. 29; April 23, 1994, p. 38.

Times Educational Supplement, August 14, 1987, p. 16; March 27, 1992, p. 28.

Times Literary Supplement, May 6, 1994, p. 32.

Washington Post Book World, December 21, 1986; April 7, 1991, p. 12.

FRANKLAND, (Anthony) Noble 1922-

PERSONAL: Born July 4, 1922, in Ravenstonedale, England; son of Edward Percy and Maud (Metcalfe-Gibson) Frankland; married Diana Madeline Fovargue Tavernor, February 28, 1944 (died, 1981); married Sarah Katharine Davies, May 7, 1982; children: (first marriage) Roger, Linda. *Education:* Trinity College, Oxford, M.A., 1948, D.Phil., 1951.

ADDRESSES: Home—Thames House, Eynsham, Witney, Oxon 0X8 1DA, England.

CAREER: Air Ministry, London, England, Air Historical Branch, narrator, 1948-51, Cabinet Office, official military historian, 1951-60; Royal Institute of International Affairs, London, deputy director of studies, 1956-60; Imperial War Museum, London, director, 1960-82, H.M.S. Belfast director, 1978-82; Air Museum, Duxford, director, 1976-82. Lees Knowles Lecturer at Trinity College, Cambridge, 1963. Member of council of Morley College, 1962-66; trustee of Military Archives Center at King's College, University of London, 1963-82, and H.M.S. Belfast Trust, 1971-78 (vice-chair, 1972-78). Historical advisor to Thames T.V. series, *The World at War,* 1971-74. *Military service:* Royal Air Force, 1941-45, Bomber Command, 1943-45; awarded Distinguished Flying Cross, 1944.

AWARDS, HONORS: Rockefeller Foundation fellowship, 1953; created commander, Order of the British Empire, 1976; created companion, Order of the Bath, 1983.

WRITINGS:

(Editor with Vera King and Patricia Woodcock) *Documents on International Affairs,* Oxford University Press (New York City), Volume 1: *1955,* 1958, Volume 2: *1956,* 1959, Volume 3: *1957,* 1960.

Crown of Tragedy: Nicholas II, W. Kimber (London), 1960, published in the United States as *Imperial Tragedy: Nicholas II, Last of the Tsars,* Coward, 1961.

(With Charles Kingsley Webster) *The Strategic Air Offensive against Germany 1939-1945,* four volumes, H.M.S.O., 1961.

The Bombing Offensive against Germany: Outlines and Perspectives, Faber (Winchester, MA), 1965.

Bomber Offensive: The Devastation of Europe, Macdonald & Co. (London), 1969.

(Editor with Christopher Dowling) *Decisive Battles of the Twentieth Century: Land-Sea-Air,* McKay (New York City), 1976, published in England as *Decisive Battles of the Twentieth Century: Land, Sea, Air,* Sidgwick & Jackson (London), 1976.

Prince Henry: Duke of Gloucester, Weidenfeld & Nicolson (London), 1980.

Witness of a Century: The Life and Times of Prince Arthur Duke of Connaught, Shepheard-Walwyn (London), 1993.

Also editor with Dowling of the "Politics and Strategy of the Second World War" series, published by University of Delaware Press (East Brunswick, NJ), 1980; editor and contributor, *The Encyclopedia of Twentieth-Century Warfare,* Orion Books (New York City), 1989; contributor to *Manual of Air Force Law* and professional journals.

WORK IN PROGRESS: An autobiographical study of the study of history, including official military, cooperative international, and conventional history, history through museum exhibitions, television documentaries, and historical biography.

SIDELIGHTS: Noble Frankland told *CA:* "My object in writing is to illuminate the course of general history by the study of selected components of it. I seek to use these components as windows upon the wider scene. I do not believe that general history can be successfully addressed directly. Subjects such as the history of England, of Europe, of civilization cannot be approached by original research because they are too broad and research would take more than a lifetime. They can only be studied through secondary sources or, in other words, the research of others into their various components. As these others inevitably have different perspectives, different prejudices and different standards, they cannot form the basis of a viable historical synthesis. Such general works depend upon imaginative leaps of insight which, however interesting they may be, are not really the business of historians.

"The study of aspects of history, which can be approached by original research, offer the excitement of new knowledge and the results have the capacity of reflecting truths about, and insights into, wider and more general issues. Rather than writing about warfare in general, I have preferred to write about air warfare in particular and in the last ten years or so I have been experimenting with a biographical approach to general history. In this, the study of royalty has struck me as a particularly appropriate access and, contrary to much journalistic impression, I regard it as a serious as well as an entertaining form of historical understanding. In Britain at least, sovereigns and princes are often reflections of much more than their politically very limited positions. They are in many respects mirrors which can be held up to the events, trends and personages of which they are the witnesses.

"I concede that I am self-indulgent in the choice of my 'windows,' for I use only those which grip my interest without regard to what is thought to be fashionable and I have something of a horror of writing to the order of the commercial judgement of the big publishers. Though I am grateful for the royalties I receive, I do not, and never have, sought to make my living by my pen alone. If my books last reasonably well in the libraries, which they seem to do, I am more than content."*

*   *   *

FREDRICKSON, George M(arsh)   1934-

PERSONAL: Born July 16, 1934, in Bristol, CT; son of George (a merchant) and Gertrude (Marsh) Fredrickson; married Helene Osouf, October 16, 1956; children: Anne Hope, Laurel, Thomas, Caroline. *Education:* Harvard University, B.A., 1956, Ph.D., 1964; University of Oslo, graduate study, 1956-57.

ADDRESSES: Home—741 Esplanada Way, Stanford, CA 94305. *Office*—Department of History, Stanford University, Stanford, CA 94305.

CAREER: Harvard University, Cambridge, MA, instructor in history, 1963-66; Northwestern University, Evanston, IL, associate professor, 1966-71, professor of history, 1971-84, William Smith Mason professor of American history, 1979-84; Stanford University, Stanford, CA, Edgar E. Robinson professor of United States history, 1984—. Moscow University, Fulbright professor, 1983; Oxford University, Harmsworth professor of American history, 1988-89. *Military service:* U.S. Navy, 1957-60; became lieutenant junior grade.

MEMBER: American Academy of Arts and Sciences, American Antiquarian Society, American Historical Association, Organization of American Historians, Society of American Historians (fellow), Southern Historical Association.

AWARDS, HONORS: Guggenheim fellowship, 1967-68; Anisfield-Wolf Award in race relations, 1972, for *The Black Image in the White Mind: The Debate on Afro-American Character and Destiny;* National Endowment for the Humanities fellowship, 1973-74 and 1985-86; Center for Advanced Studies in the Behavioral Sciences fellowship, 1977-78; Ralph Waldo Emerson Award from Phi Beta Kappa, 1981, and Avery Craven prize from Organization of American Historians, 1982, both for *White Supremacy: A Comparative Study in American and South African History;* Ford senior fellowship, Dubois Institute, Harvard University, 1993.

WRITINGS:

The Inner Civil War: Northern Intellectuals and the Crisis of the Union, Harper (New York City), 1965, reprinted with a new preface, University of Illinois Press (Urbana, IL), 1993.

The Black Image in the White Mind: The Debate on Afro-American Character and Destiny, Harper, 1971.

(Contributor) Huggins, Kilson, and Fox, editors, *Key Issues in the Afro-American Experience,* Harcourt (New York City), 1971.

White Supremacy: A Comparative Study in American and South African History, Oxford University Press (New York City), 1981.

(With Robert A. Divine and others) *America: Past and Present,* Scott, Foresman (Glenview, IL), 1984, 4th edition, 1995.

The Arrogance of Race: Historical Perspectives on Slavery, Racism and Societal Inequality, Wesleyan University Press (Middletown, CT), 1988.

Black Liberation: A Comparative History of Black Ideologies in the United States and South Africa, Oxford University Press, 1995.

EDITOR

Albion Tourgee, *A Fool's Errand,* Torchbooks (New York City), 1966.

Hinton R. Halper, *The Impending Crisis of the South,* Harvard University Press (Cambridge, MA), 1968.

William Lloyd Garrison, Prentice-Hall (Englewood Cliffs, NJ), 1968.

A Nation Divided: Problems and Issues of the Civil War and Reconstruction, Burgess (Minneapolis, MN), 1975.

OTHER

Contributor to *American Historical Review, Dissent, Journal of American History, Journal of Southern History, New York Review of Books,* and other periodicals.

WORK IN PROGRESS: A book on the transformation of American society, 1865-1900; a book of essays on comparative history.

SIDELIGHTS: In *White Supremacy: A Comparative Study in American and South African History,* his history of race relations in the United States and South Africa, George M. Fredrickson systematically analyzes the similarities and differences between the two countries. Although *New York Times Book Review* critic David Brion Davis believes that such a comparison "evokes resistance," Robert Dawidoff of the *Los Angeles Times Book Review* suggests that "*White Supremacy* illustrates how clarifying and absorbing and how challenging comparative history can be. [Fredrickson] has written about white European domination of native and imported, slave and otherwise, unfree nonwhite people in South Africa and the United States." And, in doing so, says *Washington Post Book World* writer Jim Hoagland, Fredrickson "deftly picks apart the tangled threads of two brands of white power and traces them back to their sources."

In both countries, white supremacy began in the 1600s with the subjugation of natives who were not black and, in both cases, reactions to these native groups were preceded by "rehearsals" elsewhere on the part of the parent nations. "In England," explains C. Vann Woodward in the *New York Review of Books,* "the brutal subjugation of the 'Wild Irish' . . . was such a rehearsal. At the same time the Dutch commercially exploited the East Indies with the milder motives of trade, without the need for expropriation of the land or extermination of the natives. The English repeated their experience in colonizing America, treating the Indians as they had the 'Wild Irish.' The Dutch repeated theirs at the Cape of Good Hope." Neither the English nor the Dutch considered the indigenous populations their social or intellectual equals, and both groups found the natives unsuitable as sources of cheap labor or slaves.

Both societies solved their labor problems by importing slaves: Americans from West Africa, Cape colonists from East Africa, Madagascar, and the East Indies. Kathryn Marshall in *Commonweal* says, "Fredrickson points out that the institution of racial slavery was intimately linked to tensions within the white social order, with the dehumanization of blacks creating a basis for inter-class unity among whites," an important consideration when dealing with the chaos of a frontier society. Eventually both slave societies developed an ideology of what Fredrickson calls "*Herrenvolk* democracy"—or as Woodward explains it, "the equality of all white males—to justify white supremacy, and each developed its own style of patriarchalism."

Despite these and other similarities, there were also important differences in the way the countries developed. The descendants of the Dutch settlers, for instance, were primarily herdsmen, while the white Americans were farmers who wanted to clear, cultivate and claim title to the land. Responsive to the demands of its citizens, the American government committed itself to the spread of "civilization" and did little to protect helpless minorities. According to *New York Times Book Review* critic Davis, "these distinctive conditions of American settlement and expansion, when compared with those of South Africa, led at first to a more ruthless dispossession of the indigenes, to a more thoroughgoing commitment to Negro slavery and to a much earlier insistence on a rigid and impermeable color line." On the other hand, writes *Washington Post Book World* reviewer Hoagland, "South Africans will also have to register Fredrickson's conclusions that for all its imperfections and fitful halts, the United States has since the Civil War worked hard at eliminating the legalized 'dominative racism' while a new central government in South Africa has moved in exactly the opposite direction, with disastrous results."

Despite the temptation to moralize, Fredrickson restrains himself "and thereby fuels the reader's thinking on the issues he raises," *Los Angeles Times Book Review* critic

Dawidoff says. "Without saying what should or will happen, he does show what can happen here, because it did. He also suggests . . . that it might all have been different and therefore may yet be."

BIOGRAPHICAL/CRITICAL SOURCES:

PERIODICALS

Chicago Tribune Book World, April 5, 1981.
Commonweal, June 5, 1981.
Journal of American History, December, 1989, p. 894.
Journal of Southern History, August, 1990, p. 575.
Journal of the Society of Historians, spring, 1990, p. 648.
Los Angeles Times Book Review, March 29, 1981.
New York Review of Books, March 5, 1981.
New York Times Book Review, January 25, 1981; March 30, 1989, p. 29.
Review of American History, June, 1990, p. 256.
Times Literary Supplement, June 17, 1988, p. 667.
Washington Post Book World, March 1, 1981.

*   *   *

FRENCH, Simon 1957-

PERSONAL: Born November 26, 1957, in Sydney, Australia; son of Reginald (an electronics design draftsman) and Janette (a school librarian; maiden name, Frederick) French. *Education:* Mitchell College, Teacher's Diploma, 1979.

ADDRESSES: Home—1735 East Kurrajong Rd., East Kurrajong, New South Wales 2758, Australia.

CAREER: Infants' teacher at schools in New South Wales, Australia, 1980-84, 1988—; youth worker, 1984-87. Has also worked as a library clerical assistant, a fruit picker, and in preschool child care.

AWARDS, HONORS: Special mention from the Australian Children's Book of the Year Awards, 1976, for *Hey, Phantom Singlet;* commendation in Australian Children's Book Award competition, 1982, for *Cannily, Cannily;* Australian Children's Book of the Year, 1987, for *All We Know;* Family Award, 1991, Honour Book, Australian Children's Book Awards, 1992, and Children's Book of the Year, Bank St. School of Education (U.S.), 1993, all for *Change the Locks.*

WRITINGS:

FOR CHILDREN

Hey, Phantom Singlet (illustrated by Alex Nicholas), Angus & Robertson, 1975.
Cannily, Cannily, Angus & Robertson, 1981.
All We Know, Angus & Robertson, 1986.
Change the Locks, Scholastic, 1991.

WORK IN PROGRESS: A collection of short stories for ten- to fourteen-year-olds.

SIDELIGHTS: Simon French once told *CA:* "The suggestion to write a book came rather jokingly from my sixth-grade teacher. As I was someone who enjoyed reading books anyway, the suggestion didn't seem all that ludicrous; and so I set to work. After a few false starts, I became enthused about recording my day-to-day school life and so began putting together a no-holds-barred account of the high school I was attending. All the kids in my class found themselves depicted as characters in their own type of environment—rough and ready, merciless but honest. Almost the entire book was written at school—in notepads concealed inside textbooks, scribbled paragraphs at the back of exercise books. These devious methods worked incredibly well, except for the day my math teacher confiscated two whole chapters and I had to try to remember later what it was I had written.

"Thus, daily classroom humor and drama provided much live footage for the story that evolved. My suburban origins lent me a new cast of characters in addition to those at school, and chapter by chapter I pieced together the story of Matthew, whose dad is in jail, and whose mum has to work to support the family. Trying for publication was really an afterthought and of course did not prove easy. After quite a few rejections, I was lucky, and *Hey, Phantom Singlet* was published just before my seventeenth birthday. Shortly afterwards I finished high school. Being able to write away from the audience who had inspired me so much seemed very difficult for a while. With these sorts of upheavals, a second book was not an easy task.

"The politics in *Cannily, Cannily* are those of adult and peer pressure. The options open to Trevor—the child of two seasonal workers always on the move—are whether to bend to these attendant pressures and 'belong,' or to remain aloof and different, and so endure isolation and torment from the children of a conservative country town. Having been on the receiving end of peer politics, I looked at it as a significant set of experiences and ideas to put across.

"All it seems to take is a single strand of fiction to hold my ideas together, concerned as I am with reporting on real life. The challenge to me, of course, is to translate the realism and honesty to an audience, balancing the language and structure between the economical and the descriptive. My actual method of writing is not altogether studious or methodical; I do not sit down and write for an appointed time each day. Rather it is a single character or situation encountered at any time that causes me to sit with typewriter and paper, and write. I cannot offer any stunning or academic rationale as to how or why I write. My books have been written because I find it enjoyable

and because I perceive a need for the type of story that children can relate to their everyday existence. My writing is about coping, interacting, and sometimes personal hardship; but it is more so about succeeding and surviving—that is the essence of growing."

BIOGRAPHICAL/CRITICAL SOURCES:

PERIODICALS

Times Literary Supplement, November 20, 1981.

*   *   *

FREUNDLICH, August L(udwig) 1924-

PERSONAL: Surname is pronounced "*froind*-lick"; born May 9, 1924, in Frankfurt, Germany; son of Julius (a sales representative) and Evhi (Keller) Freundlich; married Lillian Grace Thomson, April 25, 1948; children: Mary, Jeffrey Paul, Heidi, Christopher Thomson. *Education:* Antioch College, B.A., 1949, M.A., 1950; New York University, Ph.D., 1960.

CAREER: Antioch Laboratory School, Yellow Springs, OH, art education specialist, 1949-50; University of Arkansas, Fayetteville, instructor in art education, 1950-53; State University of New York College at New Paltz, visiting professor of art, 1953-54; Eastern Michigan University, Ypsilanti, head of art department, 1954-58; George Peabody College for Teachers (now George Peabody College), Nashville, TN, chair of Arts Division and Sullivan Professor of Arts Education, 1958-64; University of Miami, Coral Gables, FL, chair of art department, 1964-69, director of Joe and Emily Lowe Art Gallery, 1964-69; Syracuse University, Syracuse, NY, professor and dean of School of Art, 1970-71, dean of College of Visual and Performing Arts, 1971-82, vice-president of Theatre Corp.; University of South Florida, Tampa, dean of College of Fine Arts, 1983-86, director of corporate and foundation relations, 1987-89, professor of art, 1989—. Vice-president of Southeast Music Conference, 1969; consultant and executive director of National Foundation for Advancement in the Arts, 1981-83; president of Richard A. Florsheim Art Fund, 1990—. Member of board of directors of Southeastern Museums Conference, 1967-69, Institute for Study of Art in Education, and Partners of Americas-Syracuse, Trinidad-Tobago, 1979-83; trustee of R. Florsheim Trust, Tennessee Fine Arts Center, 1962-64, Everson Museum, Syracuse, 1971, and Tampa Museum of Art. Work has been exhibited in galleries in New York, Nashville, and Woodstock, and in competitions in several states, including Ohio, Georgia, Kentucky, Michigan, New Jersey, and New Mexico. Judge of art competitions and lecturer on art and museum topics. Research consultant in higher education, Arts Education Americans. *Military service:* U.S. Marine Corps, 1942-46.

MEMBER: International Council of Fine Arts Deans, American Association of Museums, College Art Association of America, National Art Education Association (member of council, 1956-62), National Council of Arts Administrators, National College Arts Administrators (cofounder), Committee on Art Education (member of council, 1950-64), Committee to Rescue Italian Art (chair of South Florida Division, 1966-68), Western Arts Association (member of council, 1954-64; president, 1958-60), Southeastern College Art Association (president, 1969-70), Southeastern Art Museum Directors, Southeastern Museums Association, Southeastern Art Association, Florida Art Museum Directors, Florida Art Education Association, Florida Higher Education in Arts Council (cofounder), Florida Action Alliance (member of executive committee), New York State Art Education Association, New York State Association of Museums, New York State Art Deans, Tennessee Museum Directors.

AWARDS, HONORS: Samuel H. Kress Foundation grant, 1971; Founders Day Award, New York University, for scholarship.

WRITINGS:

William Gropper: Retrospective (monograph), George Ritchie (San Francisco), 1968.

Frank Kleinholz: The Outsider, University of Miami Press (Baltimore, MD), 1969.

Karl Schrag: A Catalogue Raisonne of the Graphic Works (monograph), Part 1: *1939-1970,* Syracuse University Press (Syracuse, NY), 1971, Part 2: *1971-1980,* College of Visual and Performing Arts, Syracuse University, 1980.

(Editor and translator) *Rembrandt: The Self Portrait,* University of Miami Press, 1971.

Richard Florsheim (monograph), A. S. Barnes (South Brunswick, NJ), 1976.

Federico Castellon: His Graphic Works, 1936-1971, College of Visual and Performing Arts, Syracuse University, 1978.

S. Rosenblum, Painter, Noboreme Press (Cincinnati), 1989.

Also author and editor of numerous exhibition catalogs. Contributor to periodicals, including *Museum News, National Art Education Association Journal, Motive, Arts, Western Arts Bulletin,* and *Christian Home.* Member of editorial board, *USA Today* and *Educational Perspectives.*

WORK IN PROGRESS: German Expressionist Art; Art of the Depression Years. *

G

GABERMAN, Judie Angell 1937-
(Judie Angell; Fran Arrick, and Maggie Twohill, pseudonyms)

PERSONAL: Born July 10, 1937, in New York, NY; daughter of David Gordon (an attorney) and Mildred (a teacher; maiden name, Rogoff) Angell; married Philip Gaberman (a pop and jazz music teacher and arranger), December 20, 1964; children: Mark David, Alexander. *Education:* Syracuse University, B.S., 1959. *Religion:* "Yes." *Avocational interests:* Singing, painting, cats, listening to music.

ADDRESSES: Home—South Salem, NY.

CAREER: Elementary school teacher in Brooklyn, NY, 1959-62; *TV Guide,* Radnor, PA, associate editor of New York City metropolitan edition, 1962-63; WNDT-TV (now WNET-TV), New York City, continuity writer, 1963-68; full-time writer, 1968—. Has also worked as a switchboard operator and a waitress.

AWARDS, HONORS: Ethical Culture School Book Award, 1977, for *In Summertime It's Tuffy,* and 1979, for *A Word from Our Sponsor; or, My Friend Alfred;* Best Books for Young Adults citation, American Library Association, 1978, for *Steffie Can't Come Out to Play,* 1980, for *Tunnel Vision,* 1983, for *God's Radar,* and 1985, for *One-Way to Ansonia.*

WRITINGS:

YOUNG ADULT NOVELS; UNDER NAME JUDIE ANGELL

In Summertime It's Tuffy, Bradbury Press (New York City), 1977.
Ronnie and Rosey, Bradbury Press, 1977.
Tina Gogo, Bradbury Press, 1978.
Secret Selves, Bradbury Press, 1979.

A Word from Our Sponsor; or, My Friend Alfred, Bradbury Press, 1979.
Dear Lola; or, How to Build Your Own Family: A Tale, Bradbury Press, 1980.
What's Best for You, Bradbury Press, 1981.
The Buffalo Nickel Blues Band, Bradbury Press, 1982.
First, the Good News, Bradbury Press, 1983.
Suds, a New Daytime Drama/Brought to You by Judie Angell, Bradbury Press, 1983.
A Home Is to Share—and Share—and Share—, Bradbury Press, 1984.
One-Way to Ansonia, Bradbury Press, 1985.
The Weird Disappearance of Jordan Hall, Orchard Books (New York City), 1987.
What's Best for You, Collier Books (New York City), 1990.
Don't Rent My Room!, Bantam Books (New York City), 1990.
Leave the Cooking to Me, Bantam Books, 1990.
Yours Truly, Orchard Books, 1993.

UNDER PSEUDONYM FRAN ARRICK

Steffie Can't Come Out to Play, Bradbury Press, 1978.
Tunnel Vision, Bradbury Press, 1980.
Chernowitz!, Bradbury Press, 1981.
God's Radar, Bradbury Press, 1983.
Nice Girl from Good Home, Bradbury Press, 1984.
Where'd You Get the Gun, Billy?, Bantam Books, 1991.
What You Don't Know Can Kill You, Bantam Books, 1992.

UNDER PSEUDONYM MAGGIE TWOHILL

Who Has the Lucky Duck in Class 4-B?, Bradbury Press, 1984.
Jeeter, Mason and the Magic Headset, Bradbury Press, 1985.
Bigmouth, Bradbury Press, 1986.

Valentine Frankenstein, Bradbury Press, 1991.
Superbowl Upset, Bradbury Press, 1991.

OTHER

Contributor of short stories to anthologies, including *Sixteen: Short Stories by Outstanding Writers for Young Adults,* edited by Donald R. Gallo.

ADAPTATIONS: Dear Lola; or, How to Build Your Own Family: A Tale was adapted as the videotape *The Beniker Gang* by Scholastic, 1984; *Ronnie and Rosey* was recorded on audiocassette as part of the Young Adult Cliffhangers Series by Listening Library, 1985.

SIDELIGHTS: Best known for her books under the name Judie Angell, Judie Angell Gaberman writes novels which blend serious emotions with humorous circumstances to explore both common and unique issues that young people face—in their families, with their peers, and with authority figures. Most of Angell's protagonists are experiencing transitions, and they tend to be clever and creative in meeting the challenges involved in moving toward adulthood.

Angell's first book, *In Summertime It's Tuffy,* is based on the author's fifteen summers away at camp as a camper, counselor-in-training, senior counselor, and dramatics counselor. The main character, eleven-year-old Betsy (whose summer nickname is Tuffy), and her friends were devised as "a composite of my friends and young charges during those years," the author explained. Amidst the typical camp activities, including swimming and arts and crafts, Tuffy befriends Iris, a new girl with creative talents and an interest in witchcraft. Iris, Tuffy eventually learns, has wealthy parents who send her to boarding school and summer camp while they travel the world. She is attempting to use black magic to force them to spend time with her. But the girls' more immediate problem is the heartless head counselor, Uncle Otto. Combining Tuffy's wit and Iris's voodoo, the two wage a war against him that lands them in hilarious straits.

In 1985, Angell published *One-Way to Ansonia,* a novel about a Jewish immigrant arriving in the United States in the late 1800s and inspired in part by the experiences of the author's maternal grandmother. Ten-year-old Rose Olshansky and her four brothers and sisters travel by boat from their Russian village to New York City's Lower East Side, in order to attend their father's wedding. When they arrive they learn that their stepmother has only been informed about the youngest child, Celia. The apartment is too small to accommodate the others, so Rose and her three older siblings find separate homes with neighbors, working to pay for their room and board. Although Celia attends school, Rose must work at a factory, where she sews twelve hours a day for pennies. At the age of four-

teen, she becomes determined to learn to read and write English and begins attending night school against her father's wishes. Walking to class one evening, she meets Hyman Rogoff, a young trade unionist who is attending a meeting in the same building. Later that night, the two walk home together, debating the value of union work versus the importance of education. Unlike most men in their community, who view women only as child-bearers and housekeepers, Hyman appreciates Rose's intellect, and the two become friends. When her father selects a husband for Rose whom she does not like, she quickly proposes to Hyman and convinces her father to permit them to marry. But soon after their first baby is born, Hyman contracts pneumonia and Rose's best friend is killed at a union rally. Sixteen-year-old Rose decides she has had enough of the ghetto. Promising to send for Hyman when she is settled, she takes the baby and her savings to Grand Central Station. Choosing her destination on the basis of what she can afford, she buys a one-way ticket to Ansonia, Connecticut, a town with hills and trees where she hopes to start a new life.

In the late 1970s Angell adopted the pseudonym Fran Arrick and began producing novels about controversial topics for older teens. By depicting realistic family and community scenarios, the author brings prominent social issues such as suicide, prostitution, and Acquired Immunodeficiency Syndrome (AIDS) into a personal context. *Tunnel Vision,* Arrick's 1980 work, begins with the death of Anthony, a bright, athletic, well-liked fifteen-year-old who hangs himself with his father's neckties and leaves no note. The novel explores the reactions of Anthony's friends and relations, revealing the events that led up to the suicide through flashbacks. In 1984 Arrick examined the impact of sudden unemployment on a well-off family in *Nice Girl from Good Home,* and her 1991 novel *Where'd You Get the Gun Billy?* uses a quiet town setting to present the problem of handgun violence when Billy, a high school student, shoots and kills his girlfriend, Lisa, and the entire community is deeply affected.

In contrast to the Arrick novels, which focus on harsh, serious topics for readers at the high school level, Angell's works under the pseudonym Maggie Twohill are lighter fare for middle-school children. Twohill's protagonists encounter difficult obstacles, such as a parent's remarriage or the loss of a friend. But these works also function on a level of pure entertainment as the characters become involved in unusual adventures.

While the novels written under the names Judie Angell, Fran Arrick, and Maggie Twohill differ in terms of characters' ages, subject matter, and reading audience, they are unified by the respect for young people that their author exhibits. Angell once reported that of all the rich childhood experience she brings to her writing, "Most important to me are the feelings I recall so well."

BIOGRAPHICAL/CRITICAL SOURCES:

BOOKS

Contemporary Literary Criticism, Volume 30, Gale (Detroit), 1984.
Gallo, Donald R., editor, *Speaking for Ourselves: Autobiographical Sketches by Notable Authors of Books for Young Adults,* National Council of Teachers of English, 1990, pp. 8-9.

PERIODICALS

Booklist, November 1, 1979, p. 442.
Bulletin of the Center for Children's Books, December, 1984; November, 1985; April, 1993.
Horn Book, March-April, 1986, pp. 205-206.
Publishers Weekly, December 22, 1989, p. 57.
School Library Journal, April, 1980, pp. 119-120; January, 1981, p. 56; August, 1982, p. 110; December, 1984, p. 88; September, 1985, p. 140; January, 1990, p. 120; March, 1991, p. 211; January, 1992, p. 117.
Voice of Youth Advocates, June, 1992, p. 91.
Washington Post Book World, August 14, 1977.

*   *   *

GALAND, Rene 1923-
(Reun ar C'halan)

PERSONAL: Born January 27, 1923, in Chateauneuf-du-Faou, France; came to United States in 1947, naturalized citizen, 1953; son of Pierre and Anna (Nedelec) Galand; married France Texier, December 23, 1959; children: Joel, Caroline. *Education:* Universite de Rennes, Licence es Lettres, 1944; Yale University, Ph.D., 1952.

ADDRESSES: Home—8 Leighton Rd., Wellesley, MA 02181.

CAREER: Yale University, New Haven, CT, instructor of French, 1949-51; Wellesley College, Wellesley, MA, assistant professor, 1951-57, associate professor, 1958-63, professor of French, 1964—, head of department, 1969-72; retired, 1993. *Military service:* French Army, 1944-46; became first lieutenant.

AWARDS, HONORS: Decorated Chevalier Ordre des Palmes Academiques by the Republic of France, 1971; Xavier de Langlais Prize, 1979.

WRITINGS:

L'Ame celtique de Renan, Yale University Press (New Haven, CT), 1959.
Baudelaire: Poetiques et poesie, Nizet, 1969.
Saint-John Perse, Twayne (Boston, MA), 1972.

Cameras, Corti, 1986.
Strategue de la lecture, Peter Lang (New York City), 1990.

UNDER NAME REUN AR C'HALAN; IN BRETON

Levr ar Blanedenn (poetry), Al Liamm, 1981.
Klemmgan Breizh (poetry), Al Liamm, 1985.
Lorc'h ar rouamed, Hor Yezh, 1989.

Also contributor to *Du a Gwyn,* Lolfa Press, 1982, and *Danevellou,* Hor Yezh, 1985. Contributor of articles, poems, and short stories to numerous Breton-language periodicals.

OTHER

Also contributor to books, including *Baudelaire as a Love Poet and Other Essays,* edited by Lois Boe Hyslop, Pennsylvania State University Press (University Park, PA), 1969, *Homosexualities and French Literature,* edited by George Stambolian and Elaine Marks, Cornell University Press (Ithaca, NY), 1979, *The Binding of Proteus: Perspectives on Myth and the Literary Process,* Bucknell University Press (Cranbury, NJ), 1980, *Critical Bibliography of French Literature,* Syracuse University Press (Syracuse, NY), 1980, and *The New Princeton Encyclopedia of Poetry and Poetics,* 1993. Contributor of articles and reviews to *World Literature Today,* 1979-93; also contributor to *Bulletin baudelairien, Collier's Year Book, French Review, PMLA, Romanic Review, Symposium, Yale French Studies, Revue de Litterature comparee,* and *Revue d'Histoire litteraire de la France.* Assistant editor of *French Review,* 1967-74.

*   *   *

GALVIN, Brendan 1938-

PERSONAL: Born October 20, 1938, in Everett, MA; son of James Russell (a letter carrier) and Rose (McLaughlin) Galvin; married Ellen Baer, August 1, 1968; children: Kim, Peter, Anne Maura. *Education:* Boston College, B.S., 1961; Northwestern University, M.A., 1964; University of Massachusetts at Amherst, M.F.A., 1967, Ph.D., 1970.

ADDRESSES: Home—P.O. Box 54, Durham, CT 06422; P.O. Box 383, Truro, MA 02666. *Office*—Department of English, Central Connecticut State University, Stanley St., New Britain, CT 06050.

CAREER: Northeastern University, Boston, MA, instructor in English, 1963-65; Slippery Rock State College, Slippery Rock, PA, assistant professor of English, 1968-69; Central Connecticut State University, New Britain, assistant professor, 1969-74, associate professor, 1974-80, professor of English, 1980—. Founder and director of Connecticut Writers Conference; visiting writer, Connecticut College, 1975-76; affiliated with Wesleyan-Suffield Writer-Reader Conference, 1977-78, Martha's Vineyard Poetry Seminar, 1986; Coal Royalty Visiting Chair in creative writing, University of Alabama, Tuscaloosa, spring, 1993.

AWARDS, HONORS: Fine Arts Work Center fellowship, 1971; National Endowment for the Arts creative writing fellowship, 1974, 1988; Artist Foundation fellowship, 1978; New England Film Festival, first prize, 1978, for *Massachusetts Story;* Connecticut Commission on the Arts fellowship, 1981, 1984; Guggenheim fellow, 1988; Sotheby Prize, Arvon Foundation, 1988; Levinson Prize, *Poetry* magazine, 1989; O. B. Hardison, Jr., Poetry Prize, Folger Shakespeare Library, 1991; Outstanding Academic Book, American Library Association, 1993, for *Saints in Their Ox-Hide Boat;* Chavity Randall Citation, International Poetry Forum, 1994.

WRITINGS:

POETRY

The Narrow Land, Northeastern University Press (Boston), 1971.
The Salt Farm, Fiddlehead, 1972.
No Time for Good Reasons, University of Pittsburgh Press (Pittsburgh, PA), 1974.
The Minutes No One Owns, University of Pittsburgh Press, 1977.
Atlantic Flyway, University of Georgia Press (Athens, GA), 1980.
Winter Oysters, University of Georgia Press, 1983.
A Birder's Dozen, Ampersand Press (Princeton, NJ), 1984.
Seals in the Inner Harbor, Carnegie-Mellon University Press (Pittsburgh, PA), 1985.
Raising Irish Walls (chapbook) Ampersand Press, 1989.
Wampanoag Traveler: Being, in Letters, the Life and Times of Loranzo Newcomb, American and Natural Historian, Louisiana State University Press (Baton Rouge, LA), 1989.
Great Blue: New and Selected Poems, University of Illinois Press (Champaign, IL), 1990.
Outer Life: The Poetry of Brendan Galvin, edited by Martha Christina, Ampersand Press, 1991.
Early Returns, Carnegie-Mellon University Press, 1992.
Saints in Their Ox-Hide Boat, Louisiana State University Press, 1992.
Islands (chapbook) Druid City Press (Tuscaloosa, AL), 1993.
Sky and Island Light, Louisiana State University Press, 1995.

OTHER

Massachusetts Story (documentary filmscript), produced by Gordon Massingham, 1978.
Today You Will Meet the Love of Your Life (poetry video), Connecticut Public TV, 1987-88.

Also author of short stories, reviews, and books on poetic theory. Contributor to numerous periodicals, including *American Review, Atlantic, Connecticut English Journal, Massachusetts Studies in English, Nation, New Republic, New Yorker, Paris Review, Ploughshares, Poetry, Sewanee Review,* and *Shenandoah.* Editor with George Garrett of *Poultry: A Magazine of Voice,* 1981—.

WORK IN PROGRESS: *Hotel Malabar,* a narrative poem.

SIDELIGHTS: Brendan Galvin told *CA:* "I began writing little stories on the kitchen floor when I was maybe nine or ten, using Disney characters in badly plotted one-pagers, and in high school received my first rejection when the faculty advisor to the student newspaper didn't believe I'd written the poems I submitted. I was a tackle on the football team, and I think he thought I took them from someone on the bus to school.

"Later, as a biology major at Boston College, I sometimes wrote at the back of a laboratory while my peers cut into a turtle's plastron to get at its terrified heart. Biology gave me a vocabulary I use in my poems without self-consciousness, so it's not unusual for me to use a word like meniscus.

"I was accepted at two dental schools, but decided on a master's degree in English, instead. At Northeastern University I took a poetry-writing course with Wallace Stevens scholar Samuel French Morse, who encouraged me to try for publication, and in the following year the *Atlantic* accepted two poems. I continued to write and publish at the University of Massachusetts, where I earned an MFA in Creative Writing and a Ph.D., with a dissertation on Theodore Roethke.

"Robert Frost, Theodore Roethke, Robert Lowell, James Dickey, Elizabeth Bishop, James Wright, Richard Wilbur, Galway Kinnel, and D. H. Lawrence are just a few of the poets I admire deeply and keep returning to in my reading. In addition I read a lot of fiction and history, natural history, and folklore.

"I continue to write about the natural world I live in at my home in the woods above a Cape Cod salt marsh. I accept the fact that my poems are 'underpeopled,' but am not perplexed by it. In many respects I'm a private person to whom the politics of literary reputation seem both a waste of time and an appalling example of our present-day lack of shame.

"Currently I am at work on my third book-length narrative poem, *Hotel Malabar,* about three federal agents investigating the possible Nazi connections of a ninety-year-old banana station director in Central America. The previous narratives were *Wampanoag Traveler,* told in the letters of an invented 18th century American natural historian, Loranzo Newcomb, and *Saints in Their Ox-Hide Boat,* about the discovery of America by 6th century Irish monks, led by St. Brendan the Navigator.

"Around the time I turned fifty, I walked into my study one afternoon and the autumn sun was falling through the skylight onto my open notebook. A pen was lying beside the notebook. Sounds like a scene from a bad movie, I know, but my first thought was, 'That's the most beautiful sight in the world!' I wonder how many people my age feel that way about the tools of their trade. That moment convinced me I'd chosen the right life, and I'm still deeply pleasured by feeling the poem grow under my fingertips. I believe the world exists so that writers can write about it."

Brendan Galvin's poetry is characterized by a sense of geographic place and personal heritage, and a keen interest in the landscapes, the fauna and flora, of the world about him. Some of his specific themes have included the country versus the city, the exploitation of workers, and the victimization of children. More generally, Galvin can be seen as a poet who celebrates the beauty of the natural world, making use of images from that world to explore human relationships: familial, interpersonal, social, and historical.

Writing in a precise yet lyrical free verse, influenced by his early work in metric forms, Galvin's voice interweaves the literary with the conversational, often borrowing from the local speech patterns of his native Cape Cod. He also makes use of scientific terminology, reflecting his lifelong interest in the natural sciences. His imagery tends to be realistic, firmly rooted in the direct experience of the senses, particularly the visual. Additional elements that make Galvin's poetry distinctive are its use of serio-comic effects and traditional narrative techniques.

Galvin's first book, *The Narrow Land,* deals with seasons along the Atlantic Coast. His second, *The Salt Farm,* broadens his range of topics, including poems about animals, the loss of loved ones, and the burning of an abandoned factory. In both books, Galvin's preference for the rural over the urban, the beauties of nature over the "the paranoia of supermarkets," is clearly expressed.

By the mid-seventies, Galvin had established his poetic reputation with publication in such major venues as *Harper's, Atlantic Monthly,* and *The New Yorker.* His third book, and first major collection, *No Time for Good Rea-*

sons, brought together forty-six poems, the best of ten years' work.

It received critical praise for its inventiveness, its organic use of language, and its sense of humor. In his next collection, *The Minutes No One Owns,* Galvin further developed his vision and deepened the texture of his language. Both of these books, as their titles indicate, are concerned with the passage of time, another of Galvin's recurrent themes.

Galvin's fifth collection, *Atlantic Flyway,* presents an example of why he has described his own work as underpeopled. Birds play a significant role in poems throughout this book, and human characters are often described in avian terms. Galvin also begins to explore his own heritage in *Atlantic Flyway,* including poems about a journey in search of his ancestral home, about his grandfather, and about the Irish potato famine.

Wampanoag Traveler: Being, in Letters, the Life and Times of Loranzo Newcomb, American and Natural Historian further demonstrates Galvin's interest in history and natural history, and as the author has stated, involved research in both fields. It also extends his narrative approach to poetry by creating an entire book-length story set in the eighteenth century. *Wampanoag Traveler* relates the tale of Loranzo Newcomb, who gathers seeds and other specimens in the New World for shipment to the Royal Society in England. It is told in fourteen sections, each an imaginary letter written by Newcomb, thirteen to the Society and a final letter addressed directly to the reader. Snakebites, hummingbirds, a trained alligator, and fiddler crabs are among the subjects covered, every one serving as a starting point for Newcomb's ponderings on a variety of themes, from unrequited love to the destruction of the environment. In the final letter, a discussion of apples, Galvin examines the question of history itself. Writing in *Poetry,* Ben Howard criticizes the book for its lack of thematic unity, and states: "Galvin's project is ambitious, but the power of the book lies less in its grand design than in its compelling local effects." Glyn Maxwell, in the *Times Literary Supplement,* attributes the success of the poem to "Newcomb's voice, the intelligence and humanity that Galvin breathes into this lonesome scientist."

Composed of sixty poems from eight previous collections, along with twenty new poems, *Great Blue: New and Selected Poems* provides a representative selection of Galvin's work. In the title poem of the book, a near-mystical parallel is drawn between the great blue heron and Galvin's mother, both of whom are seen as guardian spirits. Here one can also find poems about animals, folklore, nature, art, history, holiday rituals, Galvin's Irish ancestry, and other subjects. In *Shenandoah,* X. J. Kennedy praises the selection as "tightly-winnowed" and goes on to say that he is grateful for many of the poems "forthrightness, intensity and originality." Writing in *Prairie Schooner,* Philip Paradis describes *Great Blue* as "an outstanding collection by a major contemporary poet," and states that "Galvin's style with its lyricism, earthiness, penchant for irony, and realistic clear-sightedness suggests he is certainly acquainted with the wellsprings of Irish poetry."

In *Saints in Their Ox-Hide Boat,* Galvin returns to the book-length story format of *Wampanoag Traveler.* This tale centers on an actual historical character, his own namesake, the sixth-century Irish monk, Brendan the Navigator. Background for the poem relies heavily on the medieval *Voyage of St. Brendan,* which tells of a small fishing boat, manned by Brendan and other monks, that may well have sailed all the way to the New World. Galvin's version, however, is primarily a fictitious account, in which he creates personalities for Brendan and the other monks and adds adventures of his own. The premise of the book is that Brendan, as an old man, is dictating an account of his voyage to a young scribe in order to correct misconceptions about it. Phoebe-Lou Adams, in *Atlantic Monthly,* states: "Mr. Galvin's highly distinctive style blends legend, folktale, psychological reconstruction, and gritty commonplace into its own poetic coherence." Fred Chappel, in the *Georgia Review,* says: "This work is a true narrative poem even by my persnickety standards, and a fascinating story it is."

Galvin once wrote: "I grew up on Cape Cod and in a suburb of Boston, and these two poles have affected my work strongly, in that my poems are full of imagery from the sea, the land, austere and muted, of the outer Cape, and the urban blight that infects humans who come in contact with it, especially through their work, most of which is unfulfilling and worthless." Elsewhere, he has written "the true risk [in writing poetry] is presenting felt expressions of the way things are, statements that move the inner life of the hearer because they offer him a truth deeper than one he previously knew."

George Garrett notes in the *Dictionary of Literary Biography* that "whether he is being serious or funny, or, as is usual, a combination of both, it appears that Galvin is facing up to the desperate elements in nature as well as in social and private situations; he is working out crucial events with strokes both bold and delicate."

BIOGRAPHICAL/CRITICAL SOURCES:

BOOKS

Christina, Martha, editor, *Outer Life: The Poetry of Brendan Galvin,* Ampersand Press, 1991.
Contemporary Authors Autobiography Series, Volume 8, Gale, 1991.

Critical Survey of Poetry, Salem Press (Englewood Cliffs, NJ), 1982.
Dictionary of Literary Biography, Volume 5: *American Poets since World War II,* Gale, 1980.

PERIODICALS

American Book Review, January-February, 1982.
American Poetry Review, January-February, 1979.
Atlantic Monthly, June, 1992, p. 128.
Cimarron Review, April, 1993.
Georgia Review, fall, 1990; summer, 1992, pp. 376-79.
Hudson Review, spring, 1981.
New Review, May-June, 1992.
Northeast (the Hartford *Courant*), January 12, 1993.
Parnassus, Volume 17.2, 1993; Volume 18.1, 1993.
Pembroke Magazine, spring, 1988.
Pittsburgh Quarterly, winter, 1994.
Ploughshares, Volume IV, 1978.
Poetry, June, 1977; September, 1990, pp. 353-54; January, 1993, pp. 229-30.
Prairie Schooner, spring, 1993, pp. 168-73.
Publisher's Weekly, April 28, 1989, p. 72.
Shenandoah, winter, 1991, pp. 115-20.
Southern Humanities Review, winter, 1994, pp. 91-93.
Stand, spring, 1992, p. 30.
Tar River Poetry, fall, 1987; fall, 1992.
Texas Review, spring, 1988.
Three Rivers Poetry Journal, Volumes 19-20, 1982.
Times Literary Supplement (London), May 31, 1991, p. 11.
Washington Times, April 26, 1992.

*   *   *

GARROD, Rene J(eannette) 1954-

PERSONAL: Born May 26, 1954, in Tokyo, Japan (American citizen born abroad); daughter of Glen Charles (a school administrator) and Genevieve (a homemaker; maiden name, Eaton) Rathwick; married Delmar Garrod (a postal worker), April 6, 1974; children: Gabriel, Seth, Benjamin, Breanna. *Education:* Attended California State University, Fresno, 1972-75.

ADDRESSES: Home—East 2221 Diamond, Spokane, WA 99207.

CAREER: Homemaker, 1975-95; writer, 1983—.

MEMBER: Romance Writers of America; Novelists, Inc.; Published Authors Network (PAN).

WRITINGS:

HISTORICAL ROMANCE NOVELS

The Wild Rose, Avon (New York City), 1985.
Ecstasy's Bride, Zebra Books (New York City), 1987.
Wild Conquest, Zebra Books, 1987.
Silken Caress, Zebra Books, 1988.
Colorado Caress, Zebra Books, 1988.
Temptation's Wild Embrace, Zebra Books, 1990.
Passion's Endless Tide, Zebra Books, 1990.
Montana Magic, Zebra Books, 1991.
Wild Irish Embrace, Zebra Books, 1992.
Her Heart's Desire, Zebra Books, 1994.
Her Heart's Delight, Zebra Books, 1995.
The Crowded Heart, Zebra Books, 1996.

OTHER

Holiday Tradition (historical romance novella), Zebra Books, 1994.

Contributor to *Fiction Writers' Monthly.*

SIDELIGHTS: Rene J. Garrod once told *CA:* "The story of the publication of *The Wild Rose* reads like every writer's dream. I decided I wanted to write, read a few 'how-to' books, and eight months later had written a complete manuscript. The first publisher who saw it accepted it, and I am now a published novelist. My lifelong faith in fairy tales has been justified.

"This is not to say that writing a book is easy. A good book involves a lot of research, even more rewrites, respect for your readership, and the tenacity to see the project through to the end. It also involves a tremendous emotional commitment to your work.

"I entered the writing field innocently. It seemed an excellent way to combine a career with mothering. Since I have always been blessed (and cursed) with an overactive imagination, I believed I could write a novel. When I look back, the decision strikes me as terribly pompous, but I was blissfully naive and didn't realize it couldn't be done.

"Now I am thoroughly addicted to arranging words on paper in such a way as to create fanciful tales. I write to entertain, to give adults the same tales of adventure we all enjoyed as children."

*   *   *

GEARY, Roger 1950-

PERSONAL: Surname is pronounced "*Geer*-ee"; born September 10, 1950, in Hemel Hempstead, England; son of Lesley Ronald and Edith (Moles) Geary; married Sheila Margaret Grundy, August 14, 1976; children: An-

tony Dylan, Jessica. *Education:* University of Leeds, LL.B. (with honors), 1979; University of York, Ph.D., 1983; University of Wales, Post-Graduate Certificate in Education, 1985. *Politics:* Socialist. *Religion:* None.

ADDRESSES: *Home*—Riverside, Cheriton, Gower, West Glamorgan, Wales.

CAREER: West Glamorgan Institute of Higher Education, West Glamorgan, Wales, lecturer, 1983-86, senior lecturer, 1986-90, principal lecturer in law, 1990—.

MEMBER: Socio-Legal Studies Association, Society of Public Teachers of Law, British Association for Shooting and Conservation, Royal Society for the Protection of Birds, West Glamorgan Wildflowers Association.

WRITINGS:

Policing Industrial Disputes, 1893-1985, Cambridge University Press (New York City), 1985.
Solving Problems in Criminal Law, Cavendish (London), 1994.
Essential Criminal Law, Cavendish, 1994.

Also author of articles on criminal justice system and aspects of criminal law.

SIDELIGHTS: Roger Geary told *CA:* "In my academic writings I have attempted to apply a juristic rather than a scientific methodology—that is, the stating of a case rather than the disproving of a hypothesis. I have adopted this approach because I firmly believe that legal methodology—the testing and weighing of evidence, the concept of a 'balance of probabilities,' the ever-present possibility of the introduction of fresh evidence leading to an appeal—is actually a more appropriate means of conducting a social enquiry than the more formal and quantitative procedures usually advocated by social scientists."

*   *   *

GILLIATT, Penelope (Ann Douglass) 1932-1993

PERSONAL: Born March 25, 1932, in London, England; died following a long illness, May 9, 1993, in London, England; daughter of Cyril (a barrister) and Mary (Douglass) Conner; married Roger William Gilliatt (a professor), December, 1954 (divorced); married John Osborne (a playwright), May 25, 1963 (divorced), children: (second marriage) Nolan Kate. *Education:* Attended Bennington College, 1948. *Politics:* Socialist.

CAREER: Worked at Institute of Pacific Relations, New York City, and for magazines in London, England, including *Vogue,* where she became feature editor; *Observer,* London, England, film critic, 1961-64, drama critic, 1964-67; *New Yorker,* New York City, guest film critic, summer, 1967, regular film critic, six months a year, 1968-79.

AWARDS, HONORS: Prizes for best screenplay from National Society of Film Critics and New York Film Critics, both 1971, and from Writer's Guild of Britain, 1972, all for *Sunday Bloody Sunday;* American Academy of Arts and Letters award for literature, 1972.

WRITINGS:

One by One (novel), Atheneum (New York City), 1965.

A State of Change (novel), Secker & Warburg (London), 1967, Random House (New York City), 1968.

What's It Like Out? And Other Stories (short fiction; all except one selection previously published in *New Yorker*), Secker & Warburg, 1968, published as *Come Back If It Doesn't Get Better,* Random House, 1969.

Nobody's Business (short stories previously published in *New Yorker*), Viking (New York City), 1972.

Sunday Bloody Sunday (script of film released by United Artists, 1971), Viking, 1972.

Unholy Fools: Wits, Comics, Disturbers of the Peace (film criticism), Viking, 1973.

Jean Renoir: Essays, Conversations, Reviews, McGraw-Hill (New York City), 1975.

Jacques Tati, Woburn, 1976.

Splendid Lives (short stories), Secker & Warburg, 1977, Coward, McCann & Geoghegan, 1978.

The Cutting Edge (novel), Secker & Warburg, 1978, Coward, McCann & Geoghegan, 1979.

Three-Quarter Face: Reports & Reflections (film criticism), Coward, McCann & Geoghegan, 1980.

Quotations from Other Lives (short stories), Coward, McCann & Geoghegan, 1981.

They Sleep without Dreaming (stories), Dodd, Mead (New York City), 1985.

22 Stories, Dodd, Mead, 1986.

A Woman of Singular Occupation (novel) Scribner (New York City), 1988.

Lingo, Weidenfeld and Nicolson (London), 1990.

To Wit: Skin and Bones of Comedy (essays) Scribner, 1990, published in England as *To Wit: In Celebration of Comedy,* Weidenfeld and Nicolson, 1990.

Also author of *Mortal Matters,* 1983, and *Sunday Bloody Sunday: The Original Screenplay of the John Schlesinger Film, with "Making Sun,"* 1986. Short fiction anthologized in *Penguin Modern Stories,* 1971.

PLAYS

Property, produced Off-Broadway, 1980.

But When All's Said and Done, produced Off-Broadway, 1981.

OTHER

Also author of filmscripts for the British Broadcasting Company including *Living on the Box, The Flight Fund,* and *In the Likely Event of an Emergency,* and of the libretto for an opera, *Beach of Aurora;* contributor to periodicals, including *Vogue* (British), *Observer, New Yorker, Sunday Times* (London), *Transatlantic Review, New Statesman, Spectator, Sight and Sound, Encounter, Guardian, Partisan Review, Nation, Grand Street,* and *Harper's.*

SIDELIGHTS: Penelope Gilliatt is best known for the film criticism she wrote at the *New Yorker* from 1968 to 1979, alternating with Pauline Kael, and for the screenplay for the 1971 movie *Sunday Bloody Sunday,* for which she won top awards from the National Society of Film Critics, the New York Film Critics, and the Writer's Guild of Britain. In 1972 she won an American Academy of Arts and Letters award for literature.

Gilliatt was born in London, England, but grew up largely in the Northumberland area, which she wrote about for *Grand Street.* She lived in London during World War II and attended Queen's College there, before studying at Bennington College in Vermont in 1948. Prior to writing for the *New Yorker,* she worked at the Institute of Pacific Relations in New York City and for magazines in London, including *Vogue,* where she became feature editor, and the *Observer,* where she was film critic and then drama critic.

Gilliatt has been both praised and criticized for the verbal cleverness with which her characters define themselves and interact with each other in plots that often involve love triangles, the strains and dissolution of relationships, death and intimations thereof, and the alienation that seems inherent in contemporary life.

In *One by One,* Gilliatt's first novel, the marriage of Polly and Joe Talbot falls apart as a plague ravages London, killing Coker, a third main character, who is in a dependent relationship with Joe. *New York Time Book Review*'s Anthony Burgess found this a book "of great originality and whose particular flavor is . . . like a rarely consumed but classic dish." "*One By One,*" said a *Times Literary Supplement* reviewer, "does not quite gell into an effective novel. But the passion and intelligence which produced it are far too rare and ambitious for one to wish that it had been written in any other way or to forget the impression it leaves."

A State of Change, Gilliatt's second novel, also features a trio of primary characters. The expatriate Polish character who flees to Moscow, Kakia Grabowska, is romantically involved with two men, providing Gilliatt a vehicle through which to express her interest in the Soviet Union and the tensions in the post-World War II Communist world, in the view of Thomas O. Calhoun in the *Dictionary of Literary Biography.* Martin Shuttleworth, writing in *Punch,* found Gilliatt's observation of the world "precise" and "her epigrams . . . sometimes even profound, but," he continued, "*A State of Change* is chopped into innumerable different parts." *Listener* reviewer Hilary Corke judged it "extraordinarily rewarding, both as a highly subtle piece of construction, marvellously well written, and as an outstandingly sane exposition of a *human* point of view." As in *A State of Change,* politics played a role in *A Woman of Singular Occupation,* in which central character Catherine de Rochefauld is an English spy in Europe in 1939.

Critical response to *The Cutting Edge,* Gilliatt's third novel, reflected two differing views of Gilliatt's style. William Boyd, wrote in *New Statesman,* of a "looseness, an almost decadent lack of direction" in this story of a triangle formed by two brothers and the former wife of one of them. Ann Tyler, in the *New York Times Book Review,* considered ambiguity the novel's actual subject and Gilliatt's "nearly epigrammatic style" suitable to the brothers, demonstrating "the abstractedness of their lives in comparison to those of the characters around them."

Gilliatt's short stories, many of them published in the *New Yorker* before appearing as collections, have elicited praise for her style as well. In *Nobody's Business,* noted Joseph Kanon in *Saturday Review,* Gilliatt's writing exhibits an irony that "is fine-edged, rich, and funny—a species of literary humor rare in contemporary writing. She is a master of the revealing detail, the overheard snatch of restaurant conversation . . . [She has] an intuitive feel for the density of relationships, the almost impossible confusion and variety of life." In *British Book News,* Valerie Shaw compared Gilliatt's narrative techniques with those used in drama and found on this basis that "Purse," from another collection entitled *They Sleep without Dreaming,* demonstrated the author's "most valuable contribution to the twentieth-century British short story . . . her adventurous use of prose to convey the quirky rhythms of people's speech—as well as their silences."

Gilliatt's most critically acclaimed work was the screenplay for *Sunday Bloody Sunday,* a movie that starred Glenda Jackson, Murray Head, and Peter Finch. Calhoun called it "a brilliant portrayal of the character trio Gilliatt had been molding in prior novels and stories." In this trio, a homosexual Jewish doctor and a divorced professional woman share a lover, a young pop artist Calhoun described as representing "life lived on one's own terms." While the two older characters are trying to emulate this carefree attitude, they are, in fact, "becoming more immobile and solitary." In addition to winning awards from the National Society of Film Critics, the New York Film Critics, and the British Film Writers Guild, *Sunday Bloody Sunday* was nominated for an Oscar for best original script.

Along with film criticism and short stories, Gilliatt wrote profiles for the *New Yorker* on Graham Greene, John Cleese, and Jonathan Miller. Her other treatments of famous figures include *Jean Renoir: Essays, Conversations, Reviews* and *Jacques Tati.*

BIOGRAPHICAL/CRITICAL SOURCES:

BOOKS

Contemporary Literary Criticism, Gale, Volume 1, 1973; Volume 10, 1979; Volume 13, 1980; Volume 53, 1989.
Dictionary of Literary Biography, Volume 14: *British Novelists since 1960, Part 1: A-G,* Gale, 1983.

PERIODICALS

Book Week, July 18, 1965.
British Book News, May, 1986, p. 309.
Christian Science Monitor, February 11, 1991, p. 13.
Listener, May 25, 1967, p. 693.
New Statesman, April 30, 1965, p. 692; October 27, 1978.
New York Times Book Review, April 25, 1965; September 10, 1972, p. 4, 36; January 21, 1979, p. 14.
Observer, April 25, 1965.
Punch, May 17, 1967, p. 736.
Saturday Review, September 9, 1972, p. 73.
Spectator, April 30, 1965.
Times Literary Supplement, April 29, 1965, p. 324; March 23, 1990, p. 309.

OBITUARIES:

BOOKS

Who's Who, 145th edition, St. Martin's (New York City), 1993, p. 710.

PERIODICALS

Los Angeles Times, May 11, 1993, p. A20.
The New Yorker, May 24, 1993, p. 105.
New York Times, May 11, 1993, p. B6.
Times (London), May 12, 1993, p. 17.*

*　　　*　　　*

GLENN, Mel 1943-

PERSONAL: Born May 10, 1943, in Zurich, Switzerland (American citizen born abroad); son of Jacob B. (a physician) and Elizabeth (Hampel) Glenn; married Elyse Friedman (a teacher), September 20, 1970; children: Jonathan, Andrew. *Education:* New York University, A.B., 1964; Yeshiva University, M.S., 1967. *Religion:* Jewish.

ADDRESSES: Home—4288 Bedford Ave., New York, NY 11229. *Office*—Abraham Lincoln High School, Brooklyn, NY 11235.

CAREER: U.S. Peace Corps, Washington, DC, English teacher in Sierra Leone, 1964-66; Junior High School 240, New York City, English teacher, 1967-70; Abraham Lincoln High School, New York City, English teacher, 1970—.

MEMBER: Society of Children's Book Writers, Authors Guild.

AWARDS, HONORS: Best young adult books citation, American Library Association, 1982, and Honor Book plaque, Society of Children's Book Writers, both for *Class Dismissed!: High School Poems;* best books citation, *School Library Journal,* 1986, and Christopher Award, 1987, both for *Class Dismissed II: More High School Poems.*

WRITINGS:

Class Dismissed!: High School Poems, Clarion (Boston), 1982.
One Order to Go, Clarion, 1984.
Play-by-Play (for children), Clarion, 1986.
Class Dismissed II: More High School Poems, Clarion, 1986.
Back to Class, Clarion, 1989.
Squeeze Play (for children), Clarion, 1989.
My Friend's Got This Problem, Mr. Cundler, Clarion, 1991.
Who Killed Mr. Chippendale?, Viking Lodestar, in press.

SIDELIGHTS: Mel Glenn once told *CA:* "If I have one picture of my father, it is one of him sitting at the dining room table writing in English (and sometimes Yiddish) on yellow legal pads. If there is a gene on my chromosome that shouts 'writer,' it is one that he passed to me.

"My growing up in Brooklyn was fairly conventional. I adored the Brooklyn Dodgers and afternoons spent in the local park, shooting baskets until it was too dark to see the hoop.

"In college, I fit my classes around my schedule at the undergraduate newspaper. I covered games at the old Garden and wrote feature stories and columns. I thought at the time that I would become a journalist. That was the year before President Kennedy was assassinated.

"Following Kennedy's death, I joined the Peace Corps. Whether that desire came out of wanting to escape Brooklyn or to do something 'noble,' I don't know, but I became an English teacher in a small town in Sierre Leone, West Africa. I found out, between bouts of dysentery and rains that lasted for days, that I really loved teaching. I loved it all—the class discussions, marking reports that were written in fractured English. Most of all I loved the students I taught.

"When I came back to the States, I started teaching junior high and, three years later, I returned to Lincoln High, from which I had graduated in 1960. I have been there ever since.

"People sometimes ask how I came to be a writer. I think it was a natural outgrowth of my interest in writing and teaching. The idea for *Class Dismissed!* emerged, philosophically, from Edgar L. Masters's *Spoon River Anthology* and a New Year's resolution made in 1980. Another teacher had shown me his unpublished manuscript, and I said to myself that if he could write a book, so could I. I put myself on a strict schedule and wrote the book in six months. The source of the poems was the people around me. I have always prided myself on the fact that I am a good listener, and I was surrounded by hundreds of stories, some sad, some happy, some tragic—but all terribly real and poignant. Though styles and fashions may change, there are certain common denominators in being a teenager that connect all generations—the feeling of being alone, different, in love, in conflict with parents. No matter how old we grow, there will always be a part of us that is sixteen years old.

"I write about what I know. My second book, a novel, is set in a Brooklyn candy store, the old kind where you can get a real malted and an egg cream. The story concerns a young boy who is not sure about his future. I am certain that a large part of it is autobiographical, but in the larger sense, what writing isn't? You bring to your characters a sense of your own personal values and memories.

"In each of my books I have tried to do something different: first poetry, then a novel. My third book is a fictional account of a fourth grader as he learns about soccer. Again, the material was all around me. My son, Jonathan, was actively involved in a local soccer league and, between practices and games on cold Saturday mornings, I learned about this 'foreign' sport. As a writer, I tried to pay close attention to the language, characteristics, and social mores of nine-year-olds.

"I consider myself very lucky to be a writer. Most people are shocked when I tell them that *Class Dismissed!* was my very first submission to a publishing house. I'm also lucky to have had a wonderful editor at Clarion Books. Teaching is hectic; heck, living is hectic, but I hope I'll always make the time to write about the people I care about very much."

GOFORTH, Ellen
  See FRANCIS, Dorothy Brenner

*   *   *

GOLDMAN, Peter (Louis)   1933-

PERSONAL: Born February 8, 1933, in Philadelphia, PA; son of Walter S. (a salesperson) and Dorothy (Semple) Goldman; married Helen Dudar (a writer), July 16, 1961. *Education:* Williams College, B.A., 1954; Columbia University, M.S.J., 1955. *Religion:* Jewish.

ADDRESSES: Office—1650 Broadway, Suite 301, New York, NY 10019. *Agent*—The Robbins Office, 405 Park Ave., New York, NY 10022.

CAREER: St. Louis Globe-Democrat, St. Louis, MO, staff writer, 1955-62; *Newsweek,* New York City, associate editor, 1962-64, general editor, 1965-68, senior editor, 1969-88, contributing editor, 1988—.

MEMBER: Phi Beta Kappa.

AWARDS, HONORS: Nieman fellow, Harvard University, 1960-61; Sigma Delta Chi award for magazine reporting, 1963; National Headliners Award, 1963, for coverage of riot at University of Mississippi; New York Newspaper Guild's Page One Award, 1967, 1972, 1986, 1987, 1988, and 1989; Robert F. Kennedy Journalism Award, 1972; Silver Gavel Award, American Bar Association, 1972, for a report on criminal justice in America; National Magazine Award, 1982 and 1992; New York Bar Media Award, 1984; Deadline Club Award, 1992; has also received the American Legion Fourth Estate Award and an Overseas Press Club citation for excellence.

WRITINGS:

Civil Rights: The Challenge of the Fourteenth Amendment, Coward-McCann, 1965, revised edition, 1967.
Report from Black America, Simon & Schuster (New York City), 1970.
The Death and Life of Malcolm X, Harper (New York City), 1973, revised edition, University of Illinois Press (Champaign), 1979.
(With Tony Fuller, Richard Manning, Stryker McGuire, Wally McNamee, and Vern E. Smith) *Charlie Company: What Vietnam Did to Us,* Morrow (New York City), 1983.
(With Fuller) *The Quest for the Presidency 1984,* Bantam (New York City), 1985.
The End of the World That Was: Six Lives in the Atomic Age, Dutton (New York City), 1986.
(With Sylvester Monroe and others) *Brothers, Black and Poor: A True Story of Courage and Survival,* Morrow, 1988.

(With Tom Mathews and others) *The Quest for the Presidency 1988,* Simon & Schuster (New York City), 1989.
(With the staff of *Newsweek) Changing the Guard,* Times Books, 1993.
(With Thomas M. DeFrank, Mark Miller, Andrew Murr and Mathews) *Quest for the Presidency, 1992.* Texas A & M University Press (College Station, TX), 1994.

Also author with others of *Newsweek's* fiftieth anniversary commemorative issue, "American Dream," 1983. Also contributor to books, including *Black Leadership of the Twentieth Century,* edited by John Hope Franklin and August Meier, University of Illinois, 1982.

WORK IN PROGRESS: Road Warrior, an account of the work of political consultants.

SIDELIGHTS: Peter Goldman once told *CA:* "I am a career journalist, fulfilling an early boyhood ambition. I write about U.S. affairs, with subspecialties in national politics and the black American situation, and, as an avocation, about sports—particularly basketball."

Goldman's biography of political and religious leader Malcolm X, *The Death and Life of Malcolm X,* "owes its interest chiefly to the fact that it was written by a white man—which is surely a remarkable achievement in itself, since Malcolm X was vehemently anti-white," offers *Spectator* critic Dillibe Onyeama. Goldman and Malcolm X met often between 1962 and 1964, when Goldman was a reporter for the *St. Louis Globe-Democrat.* According to Orde Coombs in the *New York Times Book Review,* Goldman "does not pretend to have had Malcolm's ear or friendship, but he shows how Malcolm's vision of America altered [Goldman's] perception of the world and forced him to abandon the blinders he had worn when confronting the enormity of this country's racial antagonism." Coombs further finds *The Death and Life of Malcolm X* "a rich biography that pays little attention to Malcolm's early life, but elucidates in minute detail his last years, his death and subsequent sainthood. . . . In the final section of his book . . . Goldman, shiningly eloquent, accurately gauges the impact of Malcolm's life on a whole generation of black people." Expressing a somewhat different viewpoint, the *New York Times'* Christopher Lehmann-Haupt finds that Goldman's biography "is not an exciting book to read, but it is an eminently serviceable one. . . . By reading Mr. Goldman on the hopeful 1960's . . . we can begin to see more clearly what Malcolm meant to all of us, both black and white."

Turning to the subject of the Vietnam War, Goldman, with the aid of Tony Fuller and others, updated and expanded a 1981 *Newsweek* report based on several interviews with Vietnam veterans who had been members of the same army company. The resulting book, *Charlie*

Company: What Vietnam Did to Us, answers the question "What in hell happened in Vietnam?" writes *Los Angeles Times Book Review* critic Malcolm Boyd. "This book answers the question graphically, with soul-searching, vivid description and a needed sense of dimension." *Washington Post* reviewer Jonathan Yardley maintains that "none of the points [the book] makes about the horrors of the war or the callousness of our treatment of those who fought it will come as a surprise to anyone who has paid reasonably close attention to the subject; but by addressing that subject in terms of the individual stories of ordinary soldiers, it gives an intimacy to Vietnam and its legacy that makes much of the rest of the literature on that war seem trivial and evasive by comparison." Though Anatole Broyard in the *New York Times* suspects some exaggeration or distortion from those interviewed, he claims "a careful reader will find more truth in [*Charlie Company*] than most of us may care to take on. In fact, the story the book tells is so sad and so ugly that it might almost pass for a prize-winning piece of serious fiction."

BIOGRAPHICAL/CRITICAL SOURCES:

PERIODICALS

Atlantic Monthly, October, 1985.
Commonweal, September 6, 1985.
Los Angeles Times Book Review, April 10, 1983.
Newsweek, October 23, 1989, p. 10.
New York Times, January 8, 1973; April 2, 1983.
New York Times Book Review, January 28, 1973; May 1, 1983; August 18, 1985; December 10, 1989.
Spectator, July 13, 1974.
Times Literary Supplement, August 16, 1974.
Village Voice, August 20, 1985.
Washington Post, March 9, 1983.
Washington Post Book World, July 21, 1985; October 8, 1989.

*   *   *

GOMEZ-GIL, Alfredo 1936-

PERSONAL: Born November 1, 1936, in Alicante, Spain; son of Alfredo (a government employee) and Natividad (Gil-Escoto) Gomez-Torre; married Etsuko Asami, August 21, 1981; children: Natividad-Fumi, Aitana-Yuki. *Education:* School of Hermanos Maristas, B.A., 1953; University of Granada, additional study, 1956-58; University of Madrid, license, 1965, Ph.D., 1979. *Politics:* "Liberty inherent to justice; peace inherent to liberty."

ADDRESSES: Home—1265 Asylum Ave., Hartford, CT 06105. *Office*—Hartford College for Women, Hartford, CT 06105.

CAREER: Yale University, New Haven, CT, lecturer in Spanish language and literature, 1965-66; Hartford College for Women, Hartford, CT, assistant professor, 1968-72, associate professor, 1972-79, professor, 1979—; University of Hartford, West Hartford, CT, professor, 1991—. Visiting professor, Middlebury College, summer, 1969, and University of Beijing, People's Republic of China, 1982-83. *Military service:* Spanish Army, Infantry, summers, 1962-63; became sergeant.

MEMBER: Royal Yacht Club of Alicante (honorary member).

AWARDS, HONORS: Golden plaque of City of Murcia.

WRITINGS:

Escalas imprecisas (poems), [Barcelona], 1960.
Pesada arena (poems), Timon, 1962.
Brumas y cartones (poems), Timon, 1963.
El exconde Sucanor, Arcel, 1964.
Chispas y confetis, Orozco, 1966.
Por la distancia (poems), Agora, 1968.
Norte, Este, Oeste y Sur (poems), Oliveros, 1968.
Cerebros espanoles en USA, Plaza & Janes, 1971.
Introduccion a la esperanza (poems), El Toro de Granito, 1971.
Veinticuatro Poemas de Nieve, Cuadernos del Sur, 1971.
Desde al arca del Profeta (poems), Caja de Ahorros de la Diputacion Provincial, 1971.
Entre fetiches y Amuletos, Caffarena, Malaga, 1974.
Paisajes y formas de Schlotter a traves de un poeta, Ediciones de Arte, 1975.
La Vuelta de los Cerebros, Plaza & Janes, 1976.
La frente en el Suelo, Alicante, 1976.
The Vibrations of Silence (bilingual poetry), Ediciones Cultura Hispanica, 1978.
Concha Lagos bajo el dominio de la Literatura Comparada, Diputacion Provincial de Alicante, 1981.
(Translator) *Seleccion Poetica de Ai Qing,* Foreign Languages Press (Beijing), 1986.

Also author of *Tu, exiliado peregrino,* Alicante.

WORK IN PROGRESS: Anthology of Spanish Poetry; Dissection of the American Woman; Sobre la Marcha, a book of poems; *Antologia Poetica de la Dinastia Tang—Primer Periodo de Oro de la Literatura China; Antologia Poetica de la Dinastia Song—Periodo de Oro de la Literatura China.*

BIOGRAPHICAL/CRITICAL SOURCES:

BOOKS

Carenas, Francisco, editor, *Antologia Poetas Espanoles en USA,* Editorial Adonais, 1972.
Cela, Camilo Jose, editor, *Papeles de San Armadans,* Number 206, Mallorca, 1973.

Gili, Gustavo, editor, *Historia de la Literatura Espanola,* Valbuena Prat, 1968.

*　　*　　*

GONZALEZ, Gloria 1940-

PERSONAL: Born January 10, 1940, in New York, NY; daughter of Angel and Mary (Cabrera) Gonzalez; children: Arleen, Kelly, Troy. *Education:* Studied playwrighting at the New School with Harold Callen and Jean-Claude van Itallie, playwrighting and directing with Lee Strasberg, and acting with Anthony Mannino.

ADDRESSES: Home—9457 Las Vegas Blvd. S., #47, Las Vegas, NV 89123. *Agent*—Selma Luttinger, Robert Freedman Dramatic Agency, 1501 Broadway, New York, NY 10036; Charles Schlesinger, Brandt & Brandt Literary Dept., 1501 Broadway, New York, NY 10036.

CAREER: Investigative reporter for various New Jersey daily newspapers; copy editor for *New York Post;* playwright, novelist, television writer.

MEMBER: Dramatists Guild, Authors League of America, New York Newspaper Guild, Writer's Guild of America East.

AWARDS, HONORS: First prize, Jacksonville University College of Fine Arts national playwrighting contest, 1975, for *Curtains;* Theatre American Award and Altadena Playwrighting award, 1975, for *A Sanctuary in the City;* Stanley Drama Award finalist, 1975; Stanley Drama Award winner, 1982, for *Cafe con Leche;* Webster Groves Russell B. Sharp Annual Playwrighting Award, 1976, for *Lights;* first place, Teatro Unidad playwrighting competition, Ohio State University, 1984; award from Southeast Theatre Conference Competition for *A Former Gotham Gal.*

WRITINGS:

PLAYS

Chicken Little's Ass Is Falling (produced in New York City at Playbox Theatre, December, 1970), Studio Duplicating Service, 1970.
Let's Hear It for Miss America!, first produced in New York City, 1970.
Moving On! (one-act plays; includes *Moving On!,* first produced in New York City at Playbox Theatre, October, 1972; *Cuba: Economy Class!;* and *The New America*), Samuel French, 1971.
(With Edna Schappert) *Celebrate Me,* first produced in New York City at Playbox Theatre, April, 1971.
(With Schappert and Joseph Gath) *Tidings, Comfort and Joy,* produced in New York City at Playbox Theatre, November, 1971.

Love Is a Tuna Casserole, produced by New York Theatre Ensemble, September, 1971.
(Contributor) Frances Griffith and others, editors, *One-Act Plays for Our Times,* Popular Library, 1973.
Shadow of a Sovereign (one-act), Performance Publishing, 1973.
Waiting Room, produced in New York City at Theatre at Noon, January, 1974.
A Sanctuary in the City, produced in Altadena, CA, at Theatre Americana, March, 1975.
Curtains (produced in New York City at Hudson Guild Theatre, October, 1975), Dramatists Play Service, 1976.
(Contributor) Stanley Richards, editor, *Best Short Plays of 1976,* Dodd (New York City), 1976.
Lights, produced in St. Louis, at Webster Groves Theatre, 1976.
A Former Gotham Gal, produced in Los Angeles, at Actor's Alley, 1979.
Double Play, produced at Jacksonville University, 1981.
Father Gomez and St. Cecelia, produced in New York City at Repertorio Espanol, 1988.

Also author of *Checkmate of a Queen,* published by Performance Publishing, and of unpublished and unproduced plays, including *A Day in the Port Authority, Woola-Boola, Revolutionaries Don't Sit in the Orchestra, Black Thoughts on a Bright Monday,* and *The Puppet Trip.*

TELEVISION DRAMAS

Gaucho (also see below), first broadcast on Columbia Broadcasting System, Inc. (CBS-TV), June 2, 1970.

Also author of *A Christmas Fable, Thanksgiving Tale,* and *An Easter Story,* all for Showtime, and of episodes of *Kate & Allie* and *Comedy Zone,* both for CBS-TV.

YOUNG ADULT NOVELS

The Glad Man, Knopf (New York City), 1975.
Gaucho (based on the television drama), Knopf, 1977.
A Deadly Rhyme, Dell (New York City), 1986.

OTHER

Author of adult novel, *The Thirteenth Apostle,* published by St. Martin's Press. Author of short stories. Contributor to periodicals, including *New York Times, New York Daily News,* and *Dramatists Quarterly.*

SIDELIGHTS: Gloria Gonzalez told *CA:* "I never thought of writing as being a 'lonely profession.' I meet many more interesting people while sitting here alone by the amber glow of the computer screen than I do outside mingling with random humans. That's not to say that once in a while, sitting in a restaurant, waiting in line at Motor Vehicle, or strolling through a flea market, one might not overhear a snip of conversation, or spy an expression of such unbearable pain, that it forever stamps the soul till one exorcises it by committing it to paper. It is those chance encounters that propel one to become a writer in the first place."

BIOGRAPHICAL/CRITICAL SOURCES:

PERIODICALS

Horn Book, April, 1978.
Washington Post, February 13, 1980.

* * *

GORDON, Jeffie Ross
See ENDERLE, Judith (Ann) Ross and TESSLER, Stephanie Gordon

* * *

GORDON, Stewart
See SHIRREFFS, Gordon D(onald)

* * *

GOTTLIEB, (Anne Ruth) Vera 1945-

PERSONAL: Born September 4, 1945, in Cambridge, England. *Education:* University of Bristol, B.A. (with honors), 1967, M.Litt., 1978.

ADDRESSES: Home—London, England. *Office*—Goldsmith's College, University of London, London SE14, England.

CAREER: Royal Shakespeare Theatre Company, London, England, assistant to literary manager, 1967-69; Goldsmith's College, London, senior lecturer, 1969-89, professor of drama, 1989—. Director of plays, including *Waterloo Road,* produced in London, 1987, and *A Chekhov Quartet,* produced in London, Moscow, and Yalta, 1990.

MEMBER: Royal Society of Arts (fellow).

WRITINGS:

Experiments in English Teaching (essay), Edward Arnold, 1976.
Chekhov and the Vaudeville: A Study of Chekhov's One-Act Plays, Cambridge University Press, 1982.
Chekhov in Performance in Russia and Soviet Russia, Chadwyck-Healey, 1984.
(Coauthor) *Red Earth* (play), produced in London by Magna Carta Productions, 1985.
(Translator) Anton Chekhov, *A Chekhov Quartet,* Gordon & Breach, 1995.

Also contributor of articles to *New Theatre Quarterly* and anthologies.

WORK IN PROGRESS: Who Pays? Who Goes?: Anglo-Russian Perspectives on Contemporary Theatre.

SIDELIGHTS: In *Chekhov and the Vaudeville: A Study of Chekhov's One-Act Plays,* Vera Gottlieb relates Anton Chekhov's one-act plays to contemporary Russian vaudeville and to the playwright's later, serious drama. "Much of Chekhov's short dramatic work is farcical," noted Ronald Hingley in the *Times Higher Education Supplement,* in "sharp contrast with the elusive subtleties of the mature Chekhov." Yet, Hingley observed, "what may appear flippant, in the short plays, often has a far more serious underpinning. It is a merit of Vera Gottlieb's book that she draws attention to this feature." In conclusion, Hingley asserted, Gottlieb "makes an excellent case for [the short plays'] value as a corpus of lively and worthwhile writing."

BIOGRAPHICAL/CRITICAL SOURCES:

PERIODICALS

Times Higher Education Supplement, November 5, 1982.
Times Literary Supplement, December 31, 1982.

* * *

GRABO, Norman Stanley 1930-

PERSONAL: Born April 21, 1930, in Chicago, IL; son of Stanley Valentine and Effie (Nelson) Grabowski; married Carrol Joy Ferderber, 1958; children: Carolyn Deane, Scott David. *Education:* Elmhurst College, B.A., 1952; University of California, Los Angeles, M.A., 1955, Ph.D., 1958.

ADDRESSES: Home—1821 Nueces Dr., College Station, TX 77840. *Office*—Texas A&M University, College Station, TX 77843.

CAREER: Michigan State University, East Lansing, assistant professor of English, 1958-63; University of California, Berkeley, associate professor of English, 1963-77; Texas A&M University, College Station, distinguished professor of English, 1977—.

MEMBER: Modern Language Association, South Central Modern Language Association, Philological Association of the Pacific Coast, Society for Religion in Higher Education (fellow), Michigan Academy of Science, Arts and Letters.

AWARDS, HONORS: Fellow of Folger Shakespeare Library, 1959, Society of Religion in Higher Education, 1966-67, Guggenheim Foundation, 1970-71, National Endowment for the Humanities, 1980, and Frank L. Weil Foundation.

WRITINGS:

Edward Taylor, Twayne (New Haven, CT), 1961.

(Editor) Edward Taylor, *Christographia,* Yale University Press (New Haven, CT), 1962.

(Editor with R. B. Nye) *American Thought and Writing,* two volumes, Houghton (Boston, MA), 1965.

(Editor) Edward Taylor, *Treatise Concerning the Lord's Supper,* Michigan State University Press (East Lansing), 1966.

The Art of the Sermon in Early America (sound recording), Everett/Edwards (DeLand, FL), 1976.

The Coincidental Art of Charles Brockden Brown, University of North Carolina Press (Chapel Hill), 1981.

(Editor and author of introduction) *Edgar Huntly, or, Memoirs of a Sleep-walker,* Penguin (New York City), 1988.

Contributor to professional journals.*

*   *   *

GRAEBNER, Norman A. 1915-

PERSONAL: Born October 19, 1915, in Kingman, KS; son of Rudolph W. (a minister) and Helen (Brauer) Graebner; married Laura Baum, August 30, 1941. *Education:* Milwaukee State Teachers College (now University of Wisconsin—Milwaukee), B.S., 1939; University of Oklahoma, M.A., 1940; University of Chicago, Ph.D., 1949. *Religion:* Lutheran.

ADDRESSES: Home—250 Pantops Mountain Rd., Apt. 217, Charlottesville, VA 22901. *Office*—Department of History, University of Virginia, Charlottesville, VA 22903.

CAREER: Taught high school in Oklahoma; Oklahoma College for Women (now University of Science and Arts of Oklahoma), Chickasha, assistant professor, 1942-43, 1946-47; Iowa State University, Ames, 1948-56, began as assistant professor, became professor of history; University of Illinois at Urbana-Champaign, professor of history, 1956-67, chair of department, 1961-63; University of Virginia, Charlottesville, Edward R. Stettinius professor of modern American history, 1967-82, Randolph P. Compton emeritus professor of history and public affairs, 1982-86. Visiting associate professor, Stanford University, 1952-53; Commonwealth Fund lecturer, University of London, 1958; visiting professor, Stanford University, 1959 and 1972; Walter Lynwood Fleming Lecturer, Louisiana State University, 1962; Fulbright lecturer, University of Queensland, 1963, University of Sydney, 1983; Dis-

tinguished Visiting Professor, Pennsylvania State University, 1975-76; Harold Vyvyan Harmsworth professor, Oxford University, 1978-79; Pettyjohn Distinguished Lecturer, Washington State University, 1980; visiting professor, U.S. Military Academy, West Point, 1981-82; Phi Beta Kappa visiting scholar, 1981-82; Thomas Jefferson visiting scholar, Downing College, Cambridge University, 1985; National War College, distinguished visiting professor, 1994-95. Radio broadcaster from classroom, WILL, Champaign, 1958-59 and 1966, and of weekly program, *Background of the News,* WBBM, Chicago, IL, 1958-60. Has represented historical organizations on Joint Committee on Historians and Archivists and National Archives Advisory Council; former member of Advisory Committee for American Studies Abroad. *Military service:* U.S. Army, Ordnance Corps, 1943-46; became first lieutenant; received Commendation Ribbon for establishing first school for American soldiers in Japan, 1946.

MEMBER: Society for Historians of American Foreign Relations (vice president, 1970-71; president, 1971-72), Society of American Historians, American Historical Association, Organization of American Historians (executive board member), Southern Historical Association, Massachusetts Historical Society, Phi Beta Kappa (honorary member), Phi Alpha Theta, American Academy of Arts and Sciences.

AWARDS, HONORS: Outstanding teacher award, University of Illinois, 1962; Alumni Association Distinguished Professor Award, University of Virginia, 1980; Outstanding Civilian Service Medal, West Point, 1982; Thomas Jefferson Award, University of Virginia, 1985; awards from the Z Society, the IMP Society, and the Raven Society at the University of Virginia. Honorary D.Litt., Albright College, 1976, M.A., Oxford University, 1978, D.H.L., University of Pittsburgh and Valparaiso University, both 1981, and Eastern Illinois University, 1986, and D.Pegagogy, Marshall University, 1993.

WRITINGS:

Empire on the Pacific, Ronald, 1955, 2nd edition, 1983.

The New Isolationism: A Study in Politics and Foreign Policy since 1950, Ronald, 1956.

Cold War Diplomacy: American Foreign Policy, 1945-1960, Van Nostrand (New York City), 1962, 2nd edition, 1977.

(With Gilbert C. Fite and Philip L. White) *A History of the United States,* two volumes, McGraw (New York City), 1970.

(With Fite and White) *A History of the American People,* McGraw, 1970, 2nd edition, 1975.

(With Fite) *Recent United States History,* Ronald, 1972.

The Age of Global Power: The United States since 1939, Wiley (New York City), 1979.

America as a World Power: A Realist Appraisal from Wilson to Reagan, Scholarly Resources (Wilmington, DE), 1984.

Foundations of American Foreign Policy: A Realist Appraisal from Franklin to McKinley, Scholarly Resources, 1985.

EDITOR

The Enduring Lincoln, University of Illinois Press (Champaign), 1959.

Politics and the Crisis of 1860, University of Illinois Press, 1961.

An Uncertain Tradition: American Secretaries of State in the Twentieth Century, McGraw, 1961.

The Cold War: Ideological Conflict or Power Struggle?, Heath (Lexington, MA), 1963, 2nd edition, 1976.

Ideas and Diplomacy: Readings in the Intellectual Tradition of American Foreign Policy, Oxford University Press (New York City), 1964.

Manifest Destiny, Bobbs-Merrill (New York City), 1968.

Nationalism and Communism in Asia: The American Response, Heath, 1977.

Freedom in America: A 200-Year Perspective, Pennsylvania State University Press (University Park, PA), 1977.

American Diplomatic History before 1900, Harlan Davidson, 1978.

Traditions and Values: American Diplomacy, 1790-1865, University Press of America (Lanham, MD), 1985.

Traditions and Values: American Diplomacy, 1865-1945, University Press of America, 1985.

The National Security: Its Theory and Practice in the United States, 1945-1960, Oxford University Press, 1986.

OTHER

Also contributor to books, including *Lincoln for the Ages,* Doubleday (New York City), 1960; *Lincoln Images,* Augustana College Library (Rock Island, IL), 1960; *Why the North Won the Civil War,* Louisiana State University Press (Baton Rouge), 1960; *America's Ten Greatest Presidents,* Rand McNally (Chicago), 1961; *Contemporary Civilization,* Scott, Foresman (Glenview, IL), 1961; *The Unity of Western Europe,* Washington State University Press (Pullman, WA), 1964; and *Collier's Encyclopedia Yearbook, 1959-75.* Author of essays, chapters, and over 120 articles for periodicals. Contributing editor, *Current History.*

WORK IN PROGRESS: A general history of America's foreign relations; a brief history of the Cold War.

SIDELIGHTS: Norman A. Graebner once told *CA:* "My writings on U.S. foreign relations since the eighteenth century cover a wide variety of topics, but all advocate, as did the writings of the Founding Fathers, that national interests be precisely defined and never permitted to exceed the true intentions of government."

*   *   *

GRANT, Eva 1907-

PERSONAL: Born November 23, 1907, in New York, NY; daughter of Harry (owner of a women's clothing store) and Minnie (Cohen) Cohen; married Reuben Grant, February 5, 1927; children: Arleen, Judith. *Education:* Attended New York University, Bank Street College of Education, and New School for Social Research. *Religion:* Jewish.

ADDRESSES: Home—255 Kingsland Ter., South Orange, NJ 07079.

MEMBER: Society of Children's Book Writers of Laguna Beach (CA).

AWARDS, HONORS: First prize for narrative poem from Cooper Hill Writer's Conference, 1972, for "A Bit of Cheese"; Author Award from Newark College of Engineering, 1974, for *A Cow for Jaya.*

WRITINGS:

Timothy Slept On, Whitman Publishing (Racine, WI), 1964.

Cecil Kitten, Whitman Publishing, 1968.

A Cow for Jaya, Coward, 1973.

I Hate My Name, illustrated by Gretchen Mayo, Raintree (Milwaukee, WI), 1980.

Will I Ever Be Older?, illustrated by Susan Lexa, Raintree, 1981.

Also author of a series of kindergarten stories published by David C. Cook. Contributor to periodicals, including *Instructor, Highlights for Children, Young World, Humpty-Dumpty's Magazine,* scholastic magazines, and church publications.

WORK IN PROGRESS: "Now doing research on an easy-to-read book about a contemporary Chinese child."*

*   *   *

GRAY, Ralph D(ale) 1933-

PERSONAL: Born October 13, 1933, in Otwell, IN; son of Lee M. (a grocer) and Voris R. (Gray) Gray; married Janice R. Everett, September 2, 1956 (deceased); children: Karen, David, Sarah. *Education:* Hanover College, B.A., 1955; University of Durham, 1955-56; University of Delaware, M.A., 1958; University of Illinois, Ph.D., 1962. *Avocational interests:* All sports, travel, photography.

ADDRESSES: Home—1724 West 73rd Pl., Indianapolis, IN 46260. *Office*—Department of History, Indiana University-Purdue University at Indianapolis, 425 Agnes St., Indianapolis, IN 46202.

CAREER: Ohio State University, Columbus, instructor in history, 1961-64; Indiana University, Kokomo Campus, Kokomo (now Indiana University at Kokomo), assistant professor, 1964-67, associate professor of history, 1967-68; Indiana University-Purdue University at Indianapolis, associate professor, 1968-72, professor of history, 1972—. Special consultant to Monon Railroad, 1966, Cabot Corp., 1971, and Indiana Port Commission, 1990.

MEMBER: Society for Historians of the Early American Republic, American Historical Association, Organization of American Historians, Business History Conference, Indiana Historical Society, Indiana Oral History Roundtable (president, 1975-76), Marion County/Indianapolis Historical Society (director, 1981—).

AWARDS, HONORS: Fulbright scholar in England, 1955-56; Dickerson Award, University of Illinois, 1966, for *The National Waterway; A History of the Chesapeake and Delaware Canal, 1769-1965;* distinguished faculty service award, Indiana University-Purdue University at Indianapolis, 1978; McKean Cup, Antique Automobile Club of America, 1980, for *Alloys and Automobiles: The Life of Elwood Haynes;* Pinnell Award, Indiana University, 1990, for outstanding service.

WRITINGS:

The National Waterway: A History of the Chesapeake and Delaware Canal, 1769-1965, University of Illinois Press (Champaign, IL), 1967, 2nd edition, Army Corps of Engineers, 1988.

(Editor) *Gentlemen from Indiana: National Party Candidates, 1836-1940,* Indiana Historical Bureau, 1977.

Alloys and Automobiles: The Life of Elwood Haynes, Indiana Historical Society, 1979.

(Editor and author of introductions to sections) *The Hoosier State: Readings in Indiana History,* two volumes, Eerdmans (Grand Rapids), 1981.

(Editor and author of foreword) *Indianapolis: The First Century,* Indianapolis Historical Society, 1987.

(Editor and author of introductions to sections) *Indiana History: A Book of Readings,* Indiana University Press (Bloomington, IN), 1994.

(Co-editor with Michael A. Morrison) *New Perspectives on the Early Republic,* University of Illinois Press, 1994.

Also author of *Stellite: A History of the Stellite Company, 1912-1972,* 1974, and *Indiana's Favorite Sons,* 1988. Contributor to *Encyclopedia of World Biography,* McGraw

(New York City), 1973, *Dictionary of American Biography,* Supplement 5, 1977, *Encyclopedia of Southern History,* 1979, and *Biographical Directory of the Governors of the U.S.,* Meckler (Westport, CT), 1985. Contributor of articles and reviews to business history and regional history journals. Founder and editor, *Journal of the Early Republic,* 1981—.

WORK IN PROGRESS: Indiana's Public Ports: A History of the Indiana Port Commission, expected in 1995; coediting a Civil War diary tentatively titled *Soldier Boy from Indiana: The Civil War Diary of Samuel P. Herrington;* a study of the life and career of Meredith Nicholson, a Hoosier writer and diplomat, and of Carl M. Gray, an attorney and civic leader of Petersburg, IN.

SIDELIGHTS: Ralph D. Gray told *CA:* "My current work, after editing the *Journal of the Early Republic* for fourteen years (1980 to 1994), continues to focus largely upon Indiana and its remarkable group of politicians and writers, particularly those active around the turn of the century. Studying the life of Meredith Nicholson, both a best-selling author and a politician-diplomat later in life, as well as an informal historian of his beloved home state, has offered additional insight into all of the above topics. My newest research and writing project, delving into the life of one of Indiana's most prominent and successful trial lawyers, has the added attraction of [enabling me] to learn more about my own part of the state, that is, southern Indiana. It happens that Carl M. Gray (1895-1989) is a distant relative and he asked me, just shortly before his death, to explore his long career as an attorney that had stretched from his admission to the bar in 1917 into the final year of his life, fully seventy-two years later. This I have undertaken as a challenge, because of the lack of available public records, and as a way to share with others information about a remarkable legal career conducted from a small county-seat law office that impacted broadly throughout the state and even internationally. Perhaps I came to the study of Indiana's history and people naturally, having lived for a time in the home, also the office, of another author-editor-historian, my maternal grandmother, Beulah B. Gray, who then was editing a small-town newspaper (*The Otwell Star*) and filling its columns with reams of historical, genealogical, and human interest stories."

*   *   *

GREEN, Roger C(urtis) 1932-

PERSONAL: Born March 15, 1932, in Ridgewood, NJ; son of Robert Jefferson (a chain store manager) and Eleanor (Richards) Green; married Kaye Chandler Smith, December 20, 1958 (separated, 1969); children: Ian Rotui,

Nai Vivian (both adopted). *Education:* University of New Mexico, B.A., 1954, B.Sc., 1955; Harvard University, Ph.D., 1964.

ADDRESSES: Office—Department of Anthropology, University of Auckland, Private Bag 92019, Auckland, New Zealand; Research Associates (Pacifica), P.O. Box 60-054, Titirangi, Auckland 7, New Zealand.

CAREER: American Museum of Natural History, New York City, research associate in anthropology and leader of expeditions into Mangareva and Moorea, 1959-61; University of Auckland, Auckland, New Zealand, senior lecturer in anthropology and deputy dean of Faculty of Arts, 1961-67; B. P. Bishop Museum, Honolulu, HI, visiting associate anthropologist, 1965, anthropologist, 1967-73, research associate, 1973—, associate chair of department of anthropology, 1969-70; University of Auckland, professor of pre-history, 1973-92, head of department, 1980-84, professor emeritus, 1992—, board member, Foundation for Research, Science and Technology, 1993—. Visiting associate professor, University of Hawaii, 1965, 1967-70. Has conducted field research in Southwest United States, New Zealand, French Polynesia, Fiji, Samoa, Tonga, Hawaii, the Solomon Islands, and New Britain.

MEMBER: National Academy of Science, American Anthropological Association (fellow), Society for American Archaeology, Royal Society of New Zealand (fellow), Polynesian Society, New Zealand Archaeological Association (honorary member; president, 1964; member of editorial board), Phi Kappa Phi, Sigma Gamma Epsilon.

AWARDS, HONORS: Fulbright scholar (New Zealand), 1958-59; Captain James Cook fellowship, New Zealand, 1970-73; Elsdon Best Medal, Polynesian Society, 1973; Hector Medal, Royal Society of New Zealand, 1992.

WRITINGS:

A Review of the Prehistoric Sequence in the Auckland Province, University Bookstore (Dunedin, New Zealand), 1963, revised edition, 1970.

(Editor and contributor with J. M. Davidson) *Archaeology in Western Samoa,* Auckland Institute and Museum, Volume 1, 1969, Volume 2, 1974.

(Editor with Marion Kelly, and contributor) *Studies in Oceanic Culture History,* Bishop Museum Press (Honolulu), Volume 1, 1970, Volume 2, 1971, Volume 3, 1972.

(Contributor) Noel Barnard, editor, *Early Chinese Art and Its Possible Influence in the Pacific Islands,* Volume 3, Intercultural Arts Press, 1972.

(Contributor) G. Kuschel, editor, *Biogeography and Ecology in New Zealand,* W. Junk, 1975.

(Editor with M. M. Cresswell, and contributor) *Southeast Solomon Islands Cultural History: A Preliminary Survey,* Royal Society of New Zealand, 1976.

Makaha before 1880 A.D., Pacific Anthropological Records, Department of Anthropology, Bernice P. Bishop Museum, 1980.

(Contributor) J. Galipaud, editor, *Lapita et Peuplement Noumea,* Orstom, 1992.

(Editor with M. W. Graves, and contributor) *The Evolution and Organization of Prehistoric Society in Polynesia,* New Zealand Archaeological Association Monography, 1993.

Author of research reports. Contributor to symposia and encyclopedias. Contributor of more than 150 articles and reviews to anthropology journals, including *American Antiquity, Asian Perspectives, Man, Archaeology in Oceania, New Zealand Journal of Archaeology, Current Anthropology* and *New Zealand Archaeological Association Newsletter* (now *Archaeology in New Zealand*).

SIDELIGHTS: Roger C. Green once told *CA:* "If one is in research, one writes to communicate one's results and to enter into a kind of formally structured dialogue with one's colleagues on the subject in question. I write for these reasons and because I think there is something worth contributing to our growing history of man's past. Writing is the hardest part of my research programme and its only logical conclusion—so I keep at it despite the many other demands of a university museum and research career."

*　　*　　*

GRUBER, Gary R. 1940-

PERSONAL: Born November 19, 1940, in New York, NY; married; two children. *Education:* City College of the City University of New York, B.S. (with honors), 1962; Columbia University, M.A., 1964; Yeshiva University, Ph.D., 1969.

ADDRESSES: P.O. Box 657, Mill Valley, CA 94942.

CAREER: Author; developer and producer of research, learning, and testing programs. Cambridge University Press, New York City, chief editor in physics and mathematics, 1969; Hofstra University, Hempstead, Long Island, NY, assistant professor of physics and astronomy and director of astronomy and mathematical physics, 1969-73, senior research scientist, 1973-74; director of public affairs and the public understanding of science, New York Academy of Sciences, 1973-74; senior projects director, Center for the Study of Instruction, Harcourt, Brace, Jovanovich, Inc., 1976-77. Consultant to Prentice-Hall, John Wiley & Sons, and Oxford University Press, 1969—.

MEMBER: American Physical Society, American Association for the Advancement of Science, American Mathematical Society, American Astronomical Society, American Association of Physics Teachers, American Association of University Professors, National Association of Science Writers.

AWARDS, HONORS: Research fellowship, University of Glasgow, 1966-68; NASA fellow, 1966-69; National Science Foundation grant, 1971-72; grants received from American Telephone & Telegraph (AT&T), 3M Corporation, Mobil Oil, and various research foundations.

WRITINGS:

Physics, Monarch, 1971.

High School Equivalency Examination Test, Simon & Schuster (New York City), 1971, 3rd edition, 1976.

General Mathematical Ability, Simon & Schuster, 1971.

Correctness and Effectiveness of Expression, Simon & Schuster, 1971.

Reading Interpretation in the Natural Sciences and Literature, Simon & Schuster, 1971.

(With Edward C. Gruber) *Graduate Record Examination Aptitude Test: A Complete Review for the Verbal and Math Parts of the Test,* Simon & Schuster, 1971, 3rd edition, 1976.

(With E. C. Gruber) *Test of English as a Foreign Language,* Monarch, 1973, 6th edition, 1982.

Gruber's Preparation for the College-Level Examination Program, Monarch, 1973, 2nd edition, 1979.

Standard Written English Test, Simon & Schuster, 1974.

Gruber's Preparation for the American College Testing Programs for College Entrance, Simon & Schuster, 1974.

Gruber's Preparation for the Graduate Management Admissions Test, Simon & Schuster, 1975.

Gruber's Preparation for the Graduate Record Examination, Simon & Schuster, 1975.

Gruber's Preparation for the Professional and Administrative Career Program for the Federal Government, Simon & Schuster, 1976.

Gruber's Preparation for the Law School Admission Test, Simon & Schuster, 1976.

Gruber's Preparation for the New Medical College Admission Test, Contemporary Books (Chicago), 1977.

(With E. C. Gruber and Barry S. Willdorf) *Law School Admission Test,* Monarch, 1977, 2nd edition, 1979.

Gruber's Preparation for the Scholastic Aptitude Test, Contemporary Books, 1978.

Math Review for the Graduate Management Admission Test, Monarch, 1982.

Gruber's Shortcuts and Strategies for the Graduate Management Admission Test, Simon & Schuster, 1982.

Gruber's Shortcuts and Strategies for the Graduate Record Examination, Simon & Schuster, 1982.

Inside Strategies for the SAT, Educational Design, 1982.

The Gruber SAT Self-Instruction Course, Addison Wesley, 1984.

Gruber's Complete Preparation for the SAT, Harper (New York City), 1985.

Dr. Gruber's Essential Test-Taking Guide for Kids Grades 3-5, Morrow (New York City), 1986.

Dr. Gruber's Essential Test-Taking Guide for Kids Grades 6-9, Morrow, 1986.

Gruber's Super Diagnostic Test for the SAT, Barnes & Noble (New York City), 1988.

(With William N. Wingerd) *Understanding & Enjoying Adolescence,* Longman (New York City), 1988.

Gruber's Complete Preparation for the New SAT, Harper-Collins, 1994.

AUDIO TAPES

Add Up to 300 Points to Your SAT, Great American Audio, 1986.

How to Choose the Right College, Great American Audio, 1988.

Score High on Your ACT, Great American Audio, 1988.

VIDEO TAPES

Thinking Your Way to Better SAT Scores (with workbook), PBS Video (National Public Television), 1989.

Up Your Grades (with workbook), Cal Image Video, 1993.

Also author of *Increase Your Intelligence Everyday 1986 Calendar,* Landmark, 1986, *Math Basic Skills Calendar,* Hallmark, 1992, 1993, *Vocabulary Calendar,* Hallmark, 1992, 1993, *SAT Strategy Calendar,* Hallmark, 1992, 1993. Contributor of articles to journals, including *Foundations of Physics, Grolier's Encyclopedia, Physics Today,* and *Today's Catholic Teacher;* contributor of syndicated articles to newspapers and magazines, including *Washington Post, New York Times, San Francisco Chronicle, Dallas Morning News, Los Angeles Times, Detroit News, Seattle Post Intelligencer,* and *Sacramento Bee.*

WORK IN PROGRESS: An interactive learning and SAT software program for grades 9-12.

SIDELIGHTS: Recognized as an expert in the field of educational testing, Gary R. Gruber is the author of over twenty-five examination preparation manuals and of special examination review courses. His books have sold more than 5 million copies. Arville Finacom, writing in the *Daly City Record,* explains that "Gruber's activities today involve preparing high school and college students to confront and conquer the battery of aptitude tests challenging them on successive steps of the academic ladder."

In his book *Inside Strategies for the SAT,* Gruber writes that the Scholastic Aptitude Test, "which is supposed to measure verbal and math aptitude, is perhaps the most important exam anyone can take: This one test can determine a person's future career and his or her goals for a lifetime. The SAT is supposed to be an indicator of the intelligence and aptitude of the nation's young people, just as the Dow Jones Average is an indicator of the nation's economic health. . . . With colleges now increasing their standards, it is extremely important for a student to do well on this exam."

According to *Independent Journal*'s Mark Whittington, "Gruber gives the students an overview of the tests and teaches them strategies and shortcuts. But the key is practicing those techniques. The kids who improve the most are those who practice at home." However, Finacom believes that Gruber's strategies do more than just prepare students for a single test. He points out that "the skills Gruber teaches are those of critical thinking, analytical methods applicable easily to any number of problem solving situations in home or business as well as school. In effect, students who master Gruber's modes find themselves well prepared for the conditions and transactions they must approach objectively as they move through academic, career and personal futures."

Noting that average SAT scores have declined steadily over the past two decades, Gruber believes that the average scores would be even lower if the Educational Testing Service had not revised the exam over the years to make it simpler. As Gruber told the *Pacific Sun:* "Actually, I'll bet if you took a ten-year-old exam and used it instead of today's exam, the average score would be 300 instead of 400. . . . The verbal scores are low because kids don't read that much anymore. The math scores are declining because kids have been memorizing the math; then when they take the SAT and haven't had algebra or geometry for two years they're in trouble." Gruber continues: "The ironic thing is I think today's kids are as bright if not brighter than [their parents]. They're more alert, more aware of politics. The kids today seem to want to be entertained more than ever. . . . What kids don't realize—and here is the tragedy—is that work isn't necessarily tedious

. . . that the process can be enjoyable. The kids are missing out on the enjoyment of working."

Gruber once told *CA:* "I am out to bring out the potential of every student in this country. When I was in fifth grade I scored a 90 on an IQ test. I was so upset and my self-esteem became so low that [I] needed to prove that I could show myself that I was not what the IQ test indicated. I became so fascinated with test-taking and thinking that I developed my own strategies and thinking skills enough to increase my IQ to 150. This taught me a lesson. There are so many kids who have potential, and this potential does not come out unless a student is exposed to particular thinking skills. The tests can destroy a kid's self-image if the student doesn't learn how to think critically. I want to show all these kids how smart they really can be.

" 'Many a flower is born to blush unseen / and waste its sweetness on the desert air'—let's not let this happen to America's kids!"

BIOGRAPHICAL/CRITICAL SOURCES:

BOOKS

Gruber, Gary R., *Inside Strategies for the SAT,* Educational Design, 1982.

PERIODICALS

Chicago Tribune, September 29, 1981.
Curriculum Review, January, 1986, p.92.
Daly City Record, July 23, 1980.
Detroit News, October 3, 1982.
Houston Chronicle, October 3, 1982.
Independent Journal, March 21-22, 1981.
Library Journal, November 15, 1986, p. 92.
Los Angeles Times, November 29, 1981.
Oregonian, February 17, 1987.
Pacific Sun, August 21-27, 1981.
San Francisco Chronicle, February 21, 1981.
School Library Journal, October, 1992, p. 24.

H

HACKETT, John Winthrop 1910-

PERSONAL: Born November 5, 1910, in Perth, Australia; son of Sir John Winthrop (a journalist) and Deborah Vernon (Drake-Brockman) Hackett; married Margaret Frena, March 21, 1942; children: Bridget, Elizabeth, Susan. *Education:* New College, Oxford University, B.A., 1933, B.Litt., 1936, M.A., 1945; postgraduate study at Imperial Defence College, 1951. *Religion:* Anglican. *Avocational interests:* Fishing, wine, music.

ADDRESSES: Home—Coberley Mill, Cheltenham, Gloucestershire, GL53 9NH England. *Agent*—David Higham Associates, 35 Lower John St., London W1R 4HA, England.

CAREER: British Army, career officer, 1931-68, retiring as general; commissioned to 8th King's Royal Irish Hussars, 1931-36; served in Palestine, 1936; with Transjordan Frontier Force, 1937-40; served in Syria, 1941, secretary of commission of control for Syria and Lebanon, 1941; general staff officer with 9th Army, served in Western Desert, 1942, and Raiding Forces Middle East Land Forces, 1942-43; commander of Fourth Parachute Brigade, 1943; served in Italy, 1943 and 1946, and Arnhem, 1944; head of British Intelligence Organization in Vienna, 1946; commander of Transjordan Frontier Force, 1947; deputy quartermaster-general of British Army of the Rhine, 1952; commander of Twentieth Armoured Brigade, 1954; general officer commanding Seventh Armoured Division, 1956-58; commandant of Royal Military College of Science, 1958-61; colonel-commandant of Royal Electrical and Mechanical Engineers, 1961-66; commander-in-chief of Northern Ireland Command, 1961-63; deputy chief of Imperial General Staff, 1963-64; deputy chief of general staff of Ministry of Defence, 1964-66; commander-in-chief of British Army of the Rhine and commander of Northern Army Group in NATO, 1966-68. Instructor at Royal Naval College, Greenwich, England, 1943-44; Lees Knowles Lecturer at Cambridge University, 196..; Kermit Roosevelt Lecturer in the United States, 1967; University of London, London, England, principal of King's College, 1968-75, fellow, 1968; Harmon Memorial Lecturer at U.S. Air Force Academy, 1970; Basil Henriques Memorial Lecturer for National Association of Boys' Clubs, 1970; Visiting Professor in classics at Kings College, 1976—. Writer, 1975—.

MEMBER: Classical Association (president, 1970-71), English Association (president, 1973-74), Cavalry Club, Carlton Club, United Oxford and Cambridge University Club, White's Club.

AWARDS, HONORS: Member of Order of the British Empire, 1938; commander of order, 1953; companion of Order of Bath, 1962; knight commander, 1962, knight grand cross, 1967; deputy lieutenant for Gloucestershire, 1983; LL.D. from Queen's University, Belfast, University of Western Australia, 1963, and University of Exeter and Buckingham; fellow of St. George's College, University of Western Australia, 1965, Kings College, London, 1968, and New College, Oxford, 1973; Distinguished Service Order and bar; Military Cross; Colonel, Queen's Royal Irish Hussars; honorary colonel of Tenth Battalion and Tenth Volunteer Battalion Parachute Regiment; Oxford University Officers Training Corps; mentioned four times in despatches.

WRITINGS:

The Profession of Arms, Times Publishing, 1963; revised edition, Macmillan (New York City), 1983.

Reflections upon Epic Warfare, Classical Association (Newcastle), 1970.

Sweet Uses of Vicissitude, United Kingdom English Association, 1972.

I Was a Stranger, Chatto & Windus (London), 1977.

(With Norman Macrae and others) *The Third World War: August 1985,* Macmillan, 1979.

The Third World War: The Untold Story, Sidgwick and Jackson, 1982, Macmillan, 1982.

(Editor) *Warfare in the Ancient World,* Facts on File (New York City), 1989.

Contributor of articles and reviews to journals.

SIDELIGHTS: John Winthrop Hackett told *CA:* "I have been described as an academic who in a prolonged fit of absence of mind became a four-star general, and by someone else as an Indian at the White Man's camp fire. Perhaps there is an element of truth in both observations. Certainly the life I have led seems to have been marked by a restless quest for balance—between action and reflection, for instance, between form and content." Without doubt, Hackett is an anomaly, the warrior-philosopher who rose to the top of his profession as a military man, then retired to a position as visiting classics professor at King's College at the University of London. Much of his work reflects these seemingly divergent interests.

The Profession of Arms is a collection of lectures Hackett delivered in 1962 in which he explores what separates the profession of arms from other vocations: "The essential basis of the military life is the ordered application of force under an unlimited liability. It is the unlimited liability which sets the man who embraces this life apart. He will be (or should be) always a citizen. So long as he serves, he will never be a civilian." *Warfare in the Ancient World* is a collection of essays by historians, anthropologists, and sociologists about the theory and practice of war in ancient Greece and Rome, with emphasis on the Roman legions and their evolution. In *Spectator,* John Keegan called this book "a summary of the state of most recent scholarship on the single most important military institution the world has ever known."

The reading public, however, associates Hackett principally with two other books. In 1977, Hackett, already retired from the military, assembled a team of military and diplomatic experts. Gathered at his home, they envisioned a scenario that would lead to World War III in Europe. The result of their discussions was *The Third World War: August 1985,* which sold three million copies in ten languages worldwide. Later, Hackett expanded the book. He added details, strengthened the book's premises, and accounted for changes that had occurred in East-West relations. The new book was entitled *The Third World War: The Untold Story.*

Both books are set in a world in which the then-Soviet Union possesses enough military strength to go to war with the West. The countries of the North Atlantic Treaty Organization (NATO)—the Soviets targets—are unprepared. A three-week war ends in a shaky peace only after a nuclear exchange destroys the cities of Birmingham in England and Minsk in Russia. The West survives only because its political leaders begin to head the warnings of its military leaders.

Few critics treated either version of *The Third World War* as serious fiction. In the *Washington Post Book World,* Morton H. Halperin criticized the "implausibility" of the first book's scenario. Writing in the *Chicago Tribune Book World,* Jon Margolis called the expanded version "boring" and "unreadable," while Stanley Hoffmann, in the *New York Times Book Review,* found the book's technical descriptions "stultifying" and its characters "wooden." Other critics, however, approached the book less as a work of literary fiction and more as a military report. Ronald Lewin wrote in the (London) *Times:* "It is impossible to praise too highly the technical skill with which Sir John and his team of . . . advisers have digested an enormous mass of current information about weapons-systems and force-structures . . . and then constructed a clear, intelligible, and superficially convincing narrative." Finally, In the *Washington Post Book World,* Fred Haynes found the book's "wealth of detail" satisfying.

Hackett himself has summarized his intended purpose: Agreeing in 1979 that the first version was propaganda for NATO, Hackett told Judy Klemesrud of the *New York Times Book Review:* "I don't see anything wrong with that. My whole purpose is to tell a cautionary tale and that if we don't do better, there is an ogre just around the corner. That ogre is war by inadvertence."

BIOGRAPHICAL/CRITICAL SOURCES:

BOOKS

Hackett, John Winthrop, *The Profession of Arms,* Times Publishing, 1963; revised edition Macmillan (New York City), 1983.

PERIODICALS

Chicago Tribune Book World, November 7, 1982, sect. 7, p. 4.

Detroit News, December 19, 1982, p. 2K.

Los Angeles Times Book Review, September 19, 1982, p. 3.

New York Times, March 21, 1980, p. C24; September 22, 1982.

New York Times Book Review, May 5, 1979; May 27, 1979; November 28, 1982, pp. 7, 21.

Publishers Weekly, October 8, 1982, pp. 6-7.

Spectator, November 25, 1989, pp. 54-55.

Time, March 19, 1979, pp. K11-K13; September 13, 1982, p. 96.

Times (London), August 12, 1982.

Times Literary Supplement, September 3, 1982, p. 948; November 18, 1983, p. 1284; March 18, 1988, p. 313.
Washington Post Book World, April 29, 1979, pp. 1,3; October 24, 1982, p. 4.

*   *   *

HALIVNI, David
     See HALIVNI, David Weiss

*   *   *

HALIVNI, David Weiss 1928-
     (David Weiss, David Halivni)

PERSONAL: Born December 21, 1928, in Sighet, Romania; immigrated to the United States, 1947, naturalized citizen, 1952; son of Callel Wiederman and Fanny Weiss; married Tzipora Hager (a teacher), December 9, 1953; children: Baruch, Ephraim, Isaiah. *Education:* Brooklyn College (now of the City University of New York), B.A., 1953; New York University, M.A., 1956; Jewish Theological Seminary of America, M.H.L., 1957, D.H.L., 1958.

ADDRESSES: Home—435 Riverside Dr., New York, NY 10025. *Office*—Department of Religion, Columbia University, 626 Kent Hall, New York, NY 10027.

CAREER: Jewish Theological Seminary of America, New York, NY, instructor, 1957-62, assistant professor, 1962-68, associate professor, 1968-69, Morris Adler Professor of Rabbinics, 1969-85; Columbia University, New York, NY, professor of religion, 1986—. Visiting professor at Bar-Ilan University, 1966-67, 1974, and 1985-86, and Hebrew University, 1984. President of American Academy for Jewish Research; executive board member of the World Congress for Jewish Studies.

MEMBER: American Academy of Arts and Sciences.

AWARDS, HONORS: Grant from the Council for Research in the Humanities, 1964; Guggenheim fellow, 1970; Louis Ginzberg Fellowship for Research, Jewish Theological Seminary, 1970; fellowships from National Endowment for the Humanities, 1980, and Institute of Advanced Studies at Hebrew University of Jerusalem, 1981; Bialik Prize from city of Tel Aviv, Israel, 1984, for *Sources and Traditions: Critical Commentary on the Talmud;* Kenneth B. Smilen/*Present Tense* Literary Award, American Jewish Committee, 1986, for *Midrash, Mishnah, and Gemara: The Jewish Predilection for Justified Law;* D.H.L., Jewish Theological Seminary of America, 1987, and D. Phil., Haifa University, Israel, 1993.

WRITINGS:

Midrash, Mishnah, and Gemara: The Jewish Predilection for Justified Law, Harvard University Press (Cambridge, MA), 1986.
Peshat and Derash: Plain and Applied Meaning in Rabbinic Exegesis, Oxford University Press (New York), 1991.

UNDER NAME DAVID HALIVNI; IN HEBREW; TITLES IN TRANSLATION

Fragments of a Commentary on the Treatise Taanit, Mosaad Harav Kook (Jerusalem, Israel), 1959.
(Editor) Louis Ginzberg, *A Commentary on the Palestinian Talmud: A Study of the Development of the Halakah and Haggadah in Palestine and Babylonia,* Volume 4, Jewish Theological Seminary, 1961.
Sources and Traditions, Volume I: *A Source Critical Commentary on the Talmud,* Seder Nashim (Tel Aviv, Israel), 1968, Volume II: *From Joma to Hagiga,* Jewish Theological Seminary, 1973, Volume III: *Tractate Shabbath,* Jewish Theological Seminary, 1983, Volume IV: *Tractates Erubin and Pesahim,* Jewish Theological Seminary, 1983.

Contributor to books, including *Studies in Rabbinic Literature, Bible and Jewish History,* edited by Y. D. Gilath, C. Levine, and Z. M. Rabinowitz, Bar Ilan University Press, 1982. Contributor of articles in Hebrew and English to periodicals, including *Conservative Judaism, Tarbiz, Sinai, Judaism, Journal of Biblical Literature, Journal of American Academy of Religion, Journal of Jewish Studies, Harvard Theological Review,* and *Hadoar.*

SIDELIGHTS: David Weiss Halivni once told *CA:* "The purpose of all my books and most of my articles is to understand the rabbinic tradition, how it developed and how it became so influential. Through that tradition, I hope to understand the Jewish people, their history and their extraordinary survival.

"It is to the credit of the classical rabbis that the Jewish people, despite their inexpressible sufferings throughout the ages, remained believers in the ultimate justification of collective history and individual morality. The rabbis derived inspiration for these beliefs from a book which they interpreted, exposited, read into, and added to. The means and modes they employed always intrigued me, and after the Holocaust they became my personal redemption, a connection with eternity. For to understand the secret of rabbinic creativity is tantamount to the understanding of the secret of Jewish survival. On a higher level, as a religious person, I believe it is also (to use a rabbinic phrase) like becoming a partner in the divine creation."

BIOGRAPHICAL/CRITICAL SOURCES:

BOOKS

Haut, Irwin W., *The Talmud as Law and Literature,* Betshaar Press, 1982.

PERIODICALS

New York Times, September 19, 1977.

*   *   *

HALL-CLARKE, James
    See ROWLAND-ENTWISTLE, (Arthur) Theodore (Henry)

*   *   *

HALLIDAY, Brett
    See DRESSER, Davis

*   *   *

HAMILTON, Charles 1913-

PERSONAL: Born December 24, 1913, in Ludington, MI; son of Charles and Ethel Louise (Carr) Hamilton; married Diane Brooks (an autograph expert), March 21, 1962; children: Carolyn, Charles, Cynthia, Brooks. *Education:* University of California, Los Angeles, B.A., 1937, M.A., 1939. *Avocational interests:* Collecting old guns, swords, and books on snakes, birds, insects, and witchcraft.

ADDRESSES: Home—166 East 63rd St., New York, NY 10021. *Agent*—c/o Harcourt Brace Jovanovich, Inc., 1250 6th Ave., San Diego, CA 92101.

CAREER: Prentice-Hall, Inc., New York City, sales correspondent, 1940-41; William H. Wise & Co., New York City, office manager, 1941-42, 1946-47; Ben Sackheim, New York City, copywriter, 1948; Bibliotherapy, Inc., New York City, president, 1951-62; Charles Hamilton Autographs, Inc., New York City, president, 1953-85; Charles Hamilton Galleries, Inc. (first auction house in the world devoted exclusively to autographs), New York City, founder and president, 1963-85. Consultant on manuscripts and rare documents and expert witness on forgeries in both state and federal courts. Has appeared on numerous television programs, including *Dick Cavett, David Letterman, Nightline, Today Show,* and *Good Morning America. Military service:* U.S. Army Air Corps, 1942-45; became technical sergeant; awarded Bronze Star, Conspicuous Service Medal, five campaign medals, and six battle stars.

AWARDS, HONORS: Prize for best book on Abraham Lincoln, Civil War Round Table of New York, 1963, for

Lincoln in Photographs: An Album of Every Known Pose; Kentucky Colonel Award, 1980.

WRITINGS:

(Editor) *Cry of the Thunderbird: The American Indian's Own Story,* Macmillan (New York City), 1950.

Men of the Underworld: The Professional Criminal's Own Story, Macmillan, 1952, published as *Crime U.S.A.,* Macmillan (London), 1956.

(Editor) *Braddock's Defeat,* University of Oklahoma Press (Norman), 1959.

Collecting Autographs and Manuscripts, University of Oklahoma Press, 1961, revised and enlarged edition, Modoc Press (Santa Monica), 1993.

(With Lloyd Ostendorf) *Lincoln in Photographs: An Album of Every Known Pose,* University of Oklahoma Press, 1963, revised edition, Morningside House (Dayton), 1985.

The Robot That Helped to Make a President, privately printed, 1965.

Scribblers and Scoundrels, Paul Eriksson (Middlebury, VT), 1968.

(With wife, Diane Hamilton) *Big Name Hunting: A Beginner's Guide to Autograph Collecting,* Simon & Schuster (New York City), 1973.

The Book of Autographs, Simon & Schuster, 1978.

The Signature of America: A Fresh Look at Famous Handwriting, Harper (New York City), 1979.

Great Forgers and Famous Fakes: The Manuscript Forgers of America and How They Fooled the Experts, Crown (New York City), 1980.

Auction Madness, Everest House (New York City), 1981.

American Autographs: Signers of the Declaration of Independence, Revolutionary War Leaders, Presidents, 2 volumes, University of Oklahoma Press, 1983.

Leaders and Personalities of the Third Reich: Their Biographies, Portraits, and Autographs, R. James Bender (San Jose), 1984.

In Search of Shakespeare: A Reconnaissance into the Poet's Life and Handwriting, Harcourt (New York City), 1985.

(Editor) *The Illustrated Letter,* Universe Books (New York City), 1987.

(Author of preface) David Battan, *Handwriting Analysis: A Guide to Personality,* International Resources (Norwalk, CT), 1990.

(Author of foreword) Joe Nickell, *Pen, Ink, and Evidence: A Study of Writing and Writing Materials for the Penman, Collector, and Document Detective,* University Press of Kentucky (Lexington), 1990.

The Hitler Diaries: Fakes that Fooled the World, University Press of Kentucky, 1991.

(Editor) *William Shakespeare and John Fletcher: "Cardenio" or "The Second Maiden's Tragedy,"* Glenbridge Publishing (Lakewood, CO), 1993.

(Author of introduction) George Sanders, *Sanders' Price Guide to Autographs: Supplement to the Second Edition,* WorldComm, 1993.

Also author of privately printed pamphlets of poems and graphology. Also contributor to *Book of Lists,* Morrow, Volume 1, 1979, Volume 2, 1980, Volume 3, 1983, and Volume 4, 1993. Contributor to numerous periodicals, including more than fifty articles on autographs to *Hobbies.*

Hamilton's works have been translated into German, Czech, Italian, and Japanese, and have been transcribed into Braille and recorded by Talking Book Records.

WORK IN PROGRESS: William Shakespeare of the Cheshire Cheese; an autobiography; Sherlock Holmes; The Unknown Abraham Lincoln: French Light on His Character.

SIDELIGHTS: Charles Hamilton began his autograph collection as a boy, when he sent author Rudyard Kipling his week's allowance—ten cents—in exchange for his signature. Hamilton told Joyce Wadler in the *Washington Post* that "the signature brought me very close to [Kipling] . . . I touched the same thing he had touched. I've always been a hero worshiper." Since then, Hamilton, who coined the term "philography" (love of writing) for the hobby of autograph collecting, has become one of the country's best known and most controversial handwriting experts.

Before Hamilton actively entered the field of handwriting analysis, forgeries and thefts happened frequently in the manuscript-collecting business. To establish credibility for his autograph house, Charles Hamilton Galleries, Inc., Hamilton guaranteed the authenticity of each piece he sold. As a result of this policy, documents commanded record prices, and the gallery was soon grossing just under one million dollars per year. Through his gallery's example, Hamilton is credited with making autograph collecting a reputable and lucrative business.

Hamilton's ascent to the top in philography included some measure of controversy. Wadler notes that Hamilton is regarded as the "Bad Boy Without Equal" in the "genteel and scholarly world of collectible manuscripts." In one instance, Hamilton auctioned the signatures of assassinated president John F. Kennedy and his convicted assassin Lee Harvey Oswald on the same day. He has also sold the autographs of such notorious and infamous people as Adolf Hitler, "Son of Sam" mass murderer David Berkowitz, and Charles Manson. Though Hamilton once told *CA* that "I've been savagely criticized for selling Nazi documents and relics at auction and even been threatened by bombs and grenades," these tactics do not stop him because he

insists that "after investing four years of my life in fighting Hitler and his henchmen, I feel he 'owes me,' and I don't hesitate to make money out of the Nazis."

In 1985, Hamilton's business was "caught in a fiercely competitive crunch by the big auction houses," he told *CA.* He decided to close the gallery and turn instead to what he considers a far more exciting field—that of giving court testimony as an expert witness in criminal cases involving suspect or questioned documents. He reported to *CA* that as a forensic expert he "is as devastatingly accurate and flamboyant as in [my] previous career." Using his extensive knowledge of forgery, Hamilton has helped send over fifteen manuscript thieves and forgers to prison. Among the numerous cases in which he provided expertise have been the Lindbergh kidnapping (Hamilton served as consultant to New Jersey State Police for the ransom notes) and litigation involving artist Salvador Dali (Hamilton was retained by U.S. postal authorities regarding forged art works) and musician Skitch Henderson (Hamilton was retained by Internal Revenue Service about tax evasion).

In addition to his role as an expert witness, Hamilton writes books about philography "in the hope that I can set down for future generations the experiences of more than half a century as an autograph collector and dealer," he told *CA.* One of his books, *In Search of Shakespeare: A Reconnaissance into the Poet's Life and Handwriting,* draws upon Hamilton's many years of studying Elizabethan manuscripts and his fervent desire to locate documents written by Shakespeare. He argues in the book that he has identified several works, including the drama *Edmund Ironside,* as having been penned in Shakespeare's handwriting. *Washington Post Book World* reviewer Robert Giroux believes that Hamilton "presents page after page of plausible evidence," yet he admits that "though I would like to think that at least some of Hamilton's eight samples are Shakespeare's, I remain skeptical."

Hamilton told *CA* that, at the age of 69, he achieved a lifelong ambition when he realized he could identify Shakespeare's handwriting. He claims that he has since "turned up fifteen documents in the poet's script, as well as two complete manuscript plays entirely in the bard's hand." In Hamilton's *William Shakespeare and John Fletcher: "Cardenio" or "The Second Maiden's Tragedy,* he claims that his handwriting analysis proves that a document stored in the vaults of the British Museum since 1807 is in fact a play co-written by Shakespeare that had been presumed lost. In addition to his hunt for lost Shakespearean masterworks, Hamilton continues as an appraiser, annually examining and evaluating hundreds of private and public collections. He has appraised the family papers of Sigmund Freud, Albert Einstein, Franklin D. Roosevelt, Theodore Roosevelt, Duke Ellington, and John F. Kennedy, among others. He told *CA* that his appraisals have not been challenged in more than thirty years.

Reflecting on his lengthy career, Hamilton commented to Brad Danach in *People* on the reason that philography continues to hold his interest, stating that he loves "to play Peeping Tom at the keyhole of great events. When I see the blood splotches and the broken-off signatures on the proclamation Robespierre was writing when the bullet shattered his jaw, my heart jumps as if I'd heard the shot." He indicated to Danach that he won't stop collecting "until I've seen the order for Christ's execution—though I just might settle for Richard Nixon's letter of resignation."

BIOGRAPHICAL/CRITICAL SOURCES:

PERIODICALS

America, September 12, 1992, p. 146.
Americana, May-June, 1978.
American Weekly, May 19, 1963.
Esquire, October, 1979.
National Insider, September 12, 1965; November 14, 1965.
New York Herald Tribune, May 19, 1963.
New York Times Book Review, July 7, 1991, p. 3.
People, July 31, 1978.
Philatelic Review, January, 1980.
Saturday Evening Post, March, 1982.
Time, April 2, 1965; May 28, 1965.
Times Literary Supplement, November 14, 1986, p. 1273; August 5, 1994, p. 20.
Washington Post, June 15, 1983.
Washington Post Book World, November 24, 1985.
Wilson Library Bulletin, December, 1991, p. 126.*

*　　*　　*

HARDEN, Edgar F(rederick) 1932-

PERSONAL: Born February 10, 1932, in Scranton, PA; son of Clayton Edgar (an oil company executive) and Elizabeth (a homemaker; maiden name, Schraer) Harden; married Evelyn Adelaide Jasiulko (a professor), September 11, 1965; children: Edgar Frederick II. *Education:* Princeton University, A.B., 1953; Harvard University, A.M., 1958, Ph.D., 1960.

ADDRESSES: Home—455 Ailsa Ave., Port Moody, British Columbia, Canada V3H 1A2. *Office*—Department of English, Simon Fraser University, Burnaby, British Columbia, Canada V5A 1S6.

CAREER: Oberlin College, Oberlin, OH, instructor, 1960-62, assistant professor of English, 1962-66; Simon Fraser University, Burnaby, British Columbia, assistant professor, 1966-68, associate professor, 1968-77, professor

of English, 1977—. *Military service:* U.S. Army, Military Intelligence, 1954-56.

MEMBER: Victorian Studies Association of Western Canada, William Morris Society.

AWARDS, HONORS: Canada Council grants, 1967-68, 1974-75, 1980-81, fellowship, 1969-70; American Philosophical Society grant, 1977; Social Science and Humanities Research Council of Canada grants, 1981-82, 1993-96, fellowship, 1986-87; National Endowment for the Humanities grant, 1989-93.

WRITINGS:

The Emergence of Thackeray's Serial Fiction, University of Georgia Press (Athens), 1978.
Thackeray's "English Humourists" and "Four Georges," University of Delaware Press (East Brunswick, NJ), 1985.
A Critical Edition of Thackeray's "Henry Esmond," Garland Publishing (New York City), 1989.
Annotations for the Selected Works of W. M. Thackeray, two volumes, Garland Publishing, 1990.
The Letters and Private Papers of William Makepeace Thackeray, two volumes, Garland Publishing, 1994.
Thackeray's "Vanity Fair," Twayne (Boston), 1995.

Also contributor to *Thackeray: "Vanity Fair," a Casebook,* edited by Arthur Pollard, Macmillan (New York City), 1978, and to *Dictionary of Literary Biography.* Contributor of numerous articles to literature journals.

WORK IN PROGRESS: editing the selected correspondence of Thackeray; a critical study of Thackeray's artistic development from 1836 to 1848.

BIOGRAPHICAL/CRITICAL SOURCES:

PERIODICALS

Times Literary Supplement, March 14, 1980.

*　　*　　*

HARMAN, Mark 1951-

PERSONAL: Born March 6, 1951, in Dublin, Ireland; came to the United States in 1974, permanent resident, 1979; son of James Francis and Margaret Harman; married Anne Karen Menke; children: Eva, Keara. *Education:* National University of Ireland, M.A., 1974; Yale University, M.Phil., 1977, Ph.D., 1980.

ADDRESSES: Home—809 Martha Avenue, Lancaster, PA 17601.

CAREER: Dartmouth College, Hanover, NH, assistant professor of German, 1979-84; Oberlin College, Oberlin,

OH, visiting assistant professor of German, 1984-85; Franklin and Marshall College, Lancaster, PA, assistant professor of German, 1985-1990. Freelance writer, critic, translator, scholar, and teacher, 1990—.

MEMBER: Modern Language Association of America, American Association of Teachers of German, Kafka Society, American Conference on Irish Studies.

AWARDS, HONORS: Thomas MacDonagh 1916 Commemoration Scholarship in Modern Languages, 1969-72; Henry Hutchinson Stewart Prize in Modern Languages, National University of Ireland (Dublin), 1970; Browne Gold Medal in German and French, University College (Dublin), 1972; German Academic Exchange Scholarship, in Munich, 1972-73, and West Berlin, 1977-78; grant for research and translation, Swiss Arts Council (Zurich), 1986; grant for translation of Franz Kafka's *The Castle,* Austrian Ministry for Education and Art (Vienna), 1994.

WRITINGS:

(Editor and contributor of translations) *Robert Walser Rediscovered: Stories, Fairytale Plays, Critical Responses,* University Press of New England (Hanover, NH), 1985.
(Translator) *Hermann Hesse, Soul of the Age: Selected Letters of Hermann Hesse, 1891-1962,* edited by Theodore Ziolkowski, Farrar, Straus (New York City), 1991.
(Translator) Franz Kafka, *The Castle,* Schocken Books (New York City), in press.

Contributor to books, including *Heinrich von Kleist Studies,* edited by Alexej Ugrinsky, AMS Press (New York City), 1981; *Franz Kafka: His Craft and Thought,* edited by Roman Struc, Wilfrid Laurier Press, 1986; *Critical Survey of Short Fiction,* Magill/Salem, 1987; and *Traditions of Experiment from the Enlightenment to the Present,* University of Michigan Press (Ann Arbor), 1992. Contributor of essays, reviews, and translations to journals and newspapers, including *Sewanee Review, Georgia Review, Review of Contemporary Fiction, Translation Review, Los Angeles Times, Boston Globe, Philadelphia Inquirer, Washington Post,* and *Irish Times (Dublin).*

WORK IN PROGRESS: Essays on translating Franz Kafka's *The Castle,* on Kafka and Samuel Beckett, and on Robert Walser and Vincent Van Gogh.

SIDELIGHTS: Robert Walser Rediscovered: Stories, Fairytale Plays, Critical Responses, edited by Mark Harman, contains selections from Walser's prose, poetry, and plays, as well as critical responses to the Swiss author's works. Walser, whose work is said to have influenced author Franz Kafka, was largely overlooked during his lifetime and only recently has been recognized as a major writer of twentieth-century literature. Harman's book, as-

serted Agnes Cardinal in *Times Literary Supplement,* is "a valuable introduction to Walser" that contains careful translations of Walser's prose and a representative selection of his poetry.

Harman told *CA:* "In my translation of *The Castle* I have tried to capture Kafka's subtle sense of irony and humor, which is often overlooked. The stereotype of Kafka is of the apostle of angst. Yet, to my ear, there's scarcely a sentence in *The Castle* that hasn't an ironic or humorous undertow. Kafka himself liked to read his works aloud and his audience often burst into laughter. I had a similar experience with the translation. As I worked on the book, I read my translation aloud to a group of people in Lancaster, Pennsylvania. At first, they were reluctant to laugh because of Kafka's reputation as an exclusive purveyor of doom and gloom. However, they soon lightened up on realizing that deep-down *The Castle* is a comic novel.

"What I hear in conjuring up Kafka's voice in English is a strange blend of the old and the new: a combination of the concise language of a Jane Austen, echoes of the loftier reaches of nineteenth-century novelists such as Dickens, Hardy, George Eliot, and something of the colloquial fluency of a Beckett. The prose gets more Beckett-like as it goes along. The final chapter, in particular, marks a stylistic departure for Kafka, what with the shedding of punctuation, other than commas and occasional full stops.

"The only other existing translation of this classic of modern literature, by Edwin and Willa Muir, was first published in 1930 and is widely considered inadequate. It is based on an edition by Kafka's friend, Max Brod, which has long been regarded as slip-shod, and was superseded by a new German-language critical edition by Sir Malcolm Pasley, published in 1982.

"I should also mention that I had several Kafkaesque experiences while working on the translation. For instance, one day I received a letter from the publisher addressed to Franz Kafka, c/o Mark Harman. Inside was an unopened letter addressed to Franz Kafka, c/o Random House. It contained various incoherent proposals for book projects with the asking price given as two million dollars per word. That's certainly better than the going rate for literary translation!"

BIOGRAPHICAL/CRITICAL SOURCES:

PERIODICALS

New York Times, October 27, 1991.
Times Literary Supplement, January 10, 1986.

HARTMAN, Patience
See ZAWADSKY, Patience

*   *   *

HAURY, Emil W(alter) 1904-1992

PERSONAL: Born May 2, 1904, in Newton, KS; died of a heart ailment, December 5, 1992, in Tucson, AZ; son of Gustav A. (a professor) and Clara K. (Ruth) Haury; married Hulda E. Penner, June 7, 1928 (died, 1987); married Agnese N. Lindley, 1990; children: (first marriage) Allan Gene, Loren Richard. *Education:* Bethel College, Newton, KS, student, 1923-25; University of Arizona, A.B., 1927, M.A., 1928; Harvard University, Ph.D., 1934.

CAREER: University of Arizona, Tucson, instructor, 1928-29, research assistant, 1929-30, associate professor, 1937-38, head of department, 1937-64, professor of anthropology, 1938-70, Fred A. Riecker Distinguished Professor of Anthropology, 1970-80, professor emeritus, 1980-92. Gila Pueblo, Globe, AZ, assistant director, 1930-37. Director of Arizona State Museum, 1938-64. Faculty adviser at University of Bogota, 1958. Chairman of National Research Council's Division of Anthropology and Psychology, 1960-62; chairman of National Academy of Science's Section on Anthropology, 1960-63. Advisory Board on National Parks, Historic Sites, Buildings, and Monuments, member, 1964-70, chairman, 1968-70; National Council on the Humanities, member, 1966-68.

MEMBER: American Anthropological Association (vice-president, 1947; president, 1956), Society for American Archaeology (president, 1944), American Association for the Advancement of Science, American Academy of Arts and Sciences, National Academy of Sciences, American Philosophical Society, Tree-Ring Society, National Speleological Society (honorary life member), Phi Beta Kappa, Sigma Xi, Phi Kappa Phi.

AWARDS, HONORS: Viking Fund medal for anthropology, Wenner-Gren Foundation for Anthropological Research, 1950; University of Arizona Alumni Achievement Award, 1957; LL.D., University of New Mexico, 1959; University of Arizona Faculty Achievement Award, 1962; Salgo-Noren Foundation award, 1967, for excellence in teaching; conservation service award, 1976, U.S. Department of the Interior; Alfred Vincent Kidder Award, 1977; American Society for Conservation Archeology Award, 1980; Al Merito Award, Arizona Historical Society, 1981; Distinguished Scholar Award, Southwestern Anthropological Association, 1982; Distinguished Service Award, Society for American Archaeology, 1985.

WRITINGS:

(With Lyndon L. Hargrave) *Recently Dated Pueblo Ruins in Arizona,* Smithsonian Institution (Washington, DC), 1931.

Kivas of the Tusayan Ruin, Grand Canyon, Arizona, privately printed, 1931.

Roosevelt:9:6, a Hohokam Site of the Colonial Period, privately printed, 1932.

The Canyon Creek Ruin and the Cliff Dwellings of the Sierra Ancha, privately printed, 1934.

The Mogollon Culture of Southwestern New Mexico, privately printed, 1936.

Excavations in the Forestdale Valley, East-Central Arizona, University of Arizona (Tucson, AZ), 1941.

The Excavation of Los Muertos and Neighboring Ruins in the Slat River Valley, Southern Arizona: Based on the Work of the Hemenway Southwestern Archaeological Expedition of 1887-1888, Peabody Museum of Archaeology & Ethnology, Harvard University (Cambridge, MA), 1945, reprinted, Kraus Reprint (Millwood, NY), 1968.

(With E. B. Sayles) *An Early Pit House Village of the Mogollon Culture, Forestdale Valley, Arizona,* University of Arizona, 1947.

(With Kirk Bryan and others) *The Stratigraphy and Archaeology of Ventana Cave, Arizona,* University of Arizona Press, 1950, 2nd edition, 1975.

(Contributor) G. R. Willey, editor, *Prehistoric Settlement Patterns in the New World,* Wenner-Gren Foundation, 1956.

(Contributor) Thomas Weaver, editor, *Indians of Arizona: A Contemporary Perspective,* University of Arizona Press, 1974.

The Hohokam, Desert Farmers and Craftsmen: Excavations at Snaketown, 1964-1965, University of Arizona Press, 1976.

(With Isabel Truesdell Kelly and James E. Officer) *The Hodges Ruin: A Hohokam Community in the Tucson Basin,* edited by Gayle Harrison Hartmann, University of Arizona Press, 1978.

Mogollon Culture in the Forestdale Valley, East-Central Arizona, University of Arizona Press, 1985.

(Editor with David E. Doyel) *Emil W. Haury's Prehistory of the American Southwest,* University of Arizona Press, 1986.

Point of Pines, Arizona: A History of the University of Arizona Archaeological Field School, University of Arizona Press, 1989.

Contributor to scholarly journals.

SIDELIGHTS: Emil W. Haury once told *CA:* "A chance introduction to archaeology on the National Geographic Society project in the Valley of Mexico convinced me that archaeology was what I wanted to pursue. I perceive archaeology to be a humanistic subject employing scientific procedures wherever applicable in developing an understanding of how man saw himself, how he behaved, and especially how he adjusted his lifestyle to his natural setting."

During excavations in the 1930s and 1940s, Haury discovered the Mogollon Indian culture that flourished in Arizona some 3,000 years ago. He also made important contributions to knowledge of the Hohokam Indian culture.

OBITUARIES:

PERIODICALS

Los Angeles Times, December 12, 1992, p. A32.
New York Times, December 8, 1992, p. D22.*

*   *   *

HEATH-STUBBS, John (Francis Alexander) 1918-

PERSONAL: Born July 9, 1918, in London, England; son of Francis and Edith Louise Sara (a professional pianist; maiden name, Marr) Heath-Stubbs. *Education:* Queen's college, Oxford, B.A. (first class honors), 1943, M.A., 1972. *Politics:* Philosophical Tory. *Religion:* Church of England.

ADDRESSES: Home—22 Artesian Road, London W2 5AR, England. *Agent*—David Higham Associates, 5-8 Lower John St., London W1, England.

CAREER: Hall School, Hampstead, England, English master, 1944-1945; *Hutchinson's Illustrated Encyclopedia,* editorial assistant, 1945-46; Leeds University, Leeds, England, Gregory Fellow in Poetry, 1952-55; University of Alexandria, Alexandria, Egypt, visiting professor of English, 1960-61; part-time lecturer in English, College of St. Mark and St. John, Chelsea, London, 1963-72.

MEMBER: Royal Society of Literature (fellow)

AWARDS, HONORS: Arts Council of Great Britain Award, 1965, for *Selected Poems;* Queen's Gold Medal for Poetry, 1973; Oscar Williams/Jean Durwood Award, 1978; Cholmondeley Award, 1989; Commonwealth Poetry Prize, 1989; Howard Sargeant Award, 1989.

WRITINGS:

POETRY

Wounded Thammuz, Routledge & Kegan Paul (London), 1942.
Beauty and the Beast, Routledge & Kegan Paul, 1943.
The Divided Ways, Routledge & Kegan Paul, 1946.
The Charity of the Stars, Sloane, 1949.

The Swarming of the Bees, Eyre & Spottiswoode (Andover, England), 1950.
A Charm against the Toothache, Methuen (London), 1954.
The Triumph of the Muse and Other Poems, Oxford University Press, 1958.
The Blue-Fly in His Head, Oxford University Press (England), 1962.
Selected Poems, Oxford University Press, 1965.
Satires and Epigrams, Turrett Books (London), 1968.
Artorius, Book One, Burning Deck, 1970.
Artorius, Enitharmon (London), 1972.
(With Stephen Spender and F. T. Prince) *Penguin Modern Poets No. 20,* Penguin (West Drayton, England), 1972.
Four Poems in Measure, Helikon, 1973.
Indifferent Weather, Ian McKelvie, 1974.
A Parliament of Birds, Chatto & Windus (London), 1975.
The Watchman's Flute, Carcanet (Manchester, England), 1978.
The Mouse, the Bird, and the Sausage, drawings by David Gormley, Ceolfrith (Sunderland, England), 1978.
Birds Reconvened, Enitharmon, 1980.
This Is Your Poem, Pisces (Oxford), 1981.
Buzz Buzz: Ten Insect Poems, with a wood engraving by Richard Shirley Smith, Gruffyground Press (Avon, England), 1981.
Naming the Beasts, Carcanet, 1982.
The Immolation of Aleph, Carcanet, 1985.
Cats' Parnassus, illustrations by Emily Johns, Hearing Eye (England), 1987.
Collected Poems, 1943-1987, Carcanet, 1988.
Time Pieces, Hearing Eye, 1988.
A Partridge in a Pear Tree: Poems for the Twelve Days of Christmas, Hearing Eye, 1988.
A Ninefold of Charms, Hearing Eye, 1989.
Selected Poems, Carcanet, 1990.
Game of Love and Death, illustrated by Noel Connor, Dufour Editions, 1990.

TRANSLATIONS

Poems from Giacomo Leopardi, J. Lehmann (Gateshead, England), 1947.
Aphrodite's Garland, Crescendo Press, 1952.
(With Peter Avery) Hafiz of Shiraz, *Thirty Poems,* J. Murray (London), 1955.
(With Iris Origo) *Selected Prose and Poetry of Giacomo Leopardi,* Oxford University Press, 1966.
Alfred de Vigny, *The Horn/Le Cor,* Keepsake Press (Richmond, England), 1969.
(With Shafik H. Megally) *Dust and Carnations: Traditional Funeral Chants and Wedding Songs from Egypt,* TR Press (London), 1977.
(With Carol A. Whiteside) *The Poems of Anyte,* Greville (Warwick, England), 1979.

(With Avery) *The Ruba'iyat of Omar Khayyam,* Allen Lane, 1979.

CRITICISM

The Darkling Plain: A Study of the Later Fortunes of Romanticism in English Poetry from George Darley to W. B. Yeats, Eyre & Spottiswoode, 1950.

Charles Williams, Longmans, Green (for the British Council), 1955.

(Contributor) Bruce Alvin King, editor, *Dryden's Mind and Art,* Oliver & Boyd (Edinburgh), 1969.

The Ode, Clarendon Press (Oxford), 1969.

The Verse Satire, Clarendon Press, 1969.

The Pastoral, Clarendon Press, 1969.

EDITOR

Selected Poems of Shelley, Falcon Press (Wellingborough), 1947.

Selected Poems of Tennyson, Falcon Press, 1947.

Selected Poems of Swift, Falcon Press, 1947.

(With David Wright) *The Forsaken Garden: An Anthology of Poetry 1824-1909,* J. Lehmann, 1950.

William Bell, *Mountains Beneath the Horizon,* Faber, 1950.

Images of Tomorrow, SCM Press (London), 1953.

(With Wright) *The Faber Book of Twentieth-Century Verse,* Faber (London), 1954, third edition, 1975.

Selected Poems of Alexander Pope, Heinemann (London), 1964.

(With Martin Green) *Homage to George Barker on His 60th Birthday,* Brian & O'Keeffe, 1973.

Selected Poems of Thomas Gray, Carcanet, 1981.

Also editor with Phillips Salman of *Poems of Science,* 1984.

OTHER

Also author of *Helen in Egypt and Other Plays,* Oxford University Press, 1959; contributor to *Aquarius, Cairo Review of English Studies, Frontier, Modern Churchman's Journal, New English Review, New English Weekly, New Republic, Occult Observer, Poetry London, Poetry Quarterly, Spectator, Tablet, Time and Tide, Times Literary Supplement,* and other periodicals.

SIDELIGHTS: "John Heath-Stubbs," wrote John Press in *Rule and Energy,* "is a curiously anachronistic figure in post-war England: a neo-Romantic with a keen satirical wit, a scholar who frequents Soho, a Christian haunted by guilt, remorse, and a fear of damnation." Similarly, Robert Nye, writing in the London *Times,* called Heath-Stubbs "a scholar, an eccentric, and a teasing magus." Nye suggested that Heath-Stubbs's blindness sharpened his ear and allowed him to create poetry that is particularly well-suited to the speaking voice. Heath-Stubbs play-

fully wrote his own "Epitaph," in *A Charm against the Toothache,* and described himself this way: "Mr Heath-Stubbs as you must understand/ Came of a gentleman's family out of Staffordshire/ Of as good blood as any in England/ But he was wall-eyed and his legs too spare. . . . In his youth he would compose poems in prose and verse/ In a classical romantic manner which was pastoral."

Heath-Stubbs's poetry makes use of myth and history-as-myth. Thomas Blackburn, author of *The Price of an Eye,* pointed out that Heath-Stubbs takes care "to discipline his language by some ironic twist or dry, casual word, and so bring it to heel in the present day." Writing in the *Dictionary of Literary Biography,* A. T. Tolley called Heath-Stubbs's epic *Artorius,* "one of the few impressive poems in the heroic manner by a modern poet." The subject of the poem is King Arthur, and true to its epic form, *Artorius* includes an invocation to the muse, battles, a descent into the underworld, and a number of debates about the nature of poetry and of government. Tolley noted that "The vision of *Artorius* is traditional and conservative: 'Law is love in action' is a premise of the debate on government. . . . Heath-Stubbs clearly does not feel at home with the attitudes of the age in which he lives; and *Artorius* is not in the main line of the literature of the period. Indeed, it is a *tour de force* in its adaptation of a form that most would have regarded as outmoded."

At the same time, David Wright drew attention to the humor of Heath-Stubbs's poetry, especially his longer works. In the *Spectator* Wright observed, "Humor illumines his most ambitious poem *Artorius* (1972) which might be described as a potted Arthurian epic mounted on the same kind of elaborate scaffolding as Joyce's *Ulysses,* and like *Ulysses* pervaded and leavened by the author's comic vision and wide range of learning." Ironically, *Artorius* is, according to Wright, "more 'modern' than some ostensibly avant-garde or experimentalist efforts, because deeply rooted in tradition." Although Stephen Medcalf also praised Heath-Stubbs's "brilliant humour," he felt that his work is often compromised by a technical lack of order or narrative structure. In the *Times Literary Supplement,* Medcalf observed, "Even *Artorius,* though it is a kind of epic, does not tell the story of Arthur in a way that could be followed by anyone who did not already know it."

In his *Times Literary Supplement* review of *Birds Reconvened,* Tim Dooley praised Heath-Stubbs for his imaginative vocabulary and his technical abilities. "At sixty or so, John Heath-Stubbs is one poet," wrote Dooley, "who has gone on troubling about language and his new volume illustrates the riches that can be won by this kind of fastidiousness." Tolley concluded his essay by noting that Heath-Stubbs's career has been one of the most sustained and impressive among British poets of his generation: "He stands apart from the age in which he has written, bringing to it a criticism that derives from an erudite awareness of the legacy of past greatness, from which so much of his best work derives."

BIOGRAPHICAL/CRITICAL SOURCES:

BOOKS

Blackburn, Thomas, *The Price of an Eye*, Morrow (New York City), 1961.

Dictionary of Literary Biography, Volume 27, *Poets of Great Britain and Ireland, 1945-1960*, Gale (Detroit, MI), 1984.

Every, George, *Poetry and Personal Responsibility*, SCM Press, 1948.

Heath-Stubbs, John, *A Charm against the Toothache*, Methuen, 1954.

Hewison, Robert, *Under Siege: Literary Life in London, 1939-1945*, Weidenfeld & Nicolson (London), 1977.

Linden, Eddie S., editor, *In Honour of John Heath-Stubbs*, Linden (W. Sussex, England), 1978.

Press, John, *Rule and Energy*, Oxford University Press, 1963.

Stanford, Derek, *Inside the Forties*, Sidgwick & Jackson (London), 1977.

Van Domelen, John E., *John Heath-Stubbs: A Checklist*, Centaur (Congleton, England), 1988.

Wain, John, *Sprightly Running*, St. Martin's Press (New York City), 1962.

PERIODICALS

Encounter, March, 1989.

Listener, May 6, 1982; December 5, 1985; August 27, 1987.

New Statesman, November 9, 1973; May 7, 1982.

Observer, December 9, 1984.

Spectator, July 2, 1988.

Stand, spring, 1991; autumn, 1991.

Times (London), October 31, 1985; November 28, 1991.

Times Educational Supplement, April 23, 1982; August 24, 1984; February 10, 1989.

Times Literary Supplement, December 5, 1975; August 18, 1978; June 19, 1981; June 11, 1982; June 20, 1986; April 15, 1988; December 2-8, 1988; November 16, 1990.*

*   *   *

HEIM, Kathleen M(cEntee)   1948-

PERSONAL: Born in Chicago, IL; daughter of Frank Eugene (an electrician) and Margaret L. (a secretary; maiden name, de la Pena) McEntee; married Philip Gary Heim (an artist), March 20, 1972 (divorced, 1988); children:

Margaret Marie. *Education:* University of Illinois at Chicago Circle, B.A., 1969; Marquette University, M.A., 1970; University of Chicago, M.A., 1972; University of Wisconsin—Madison, Ph.D., 1980. *Politics:* Democrat. *Religion:* Roman Catholic. *Avocational interests:* Reading, vintage Thunderbirds (automobiles).

ADDRESSES: Office—125 D Boyd, Graduate School, Louisiana State University, Baton Rouge, LA 70803.

CAREER: Substitute teacher at public schools in Chicago, IL, 1969; mathematics teacher at St. Martin school in Kankakee, IL, 1970-71; Elmhurst College, Elmhurst, IL, reference librarian, 1971-73; Rosary College, River Forest, IL, director of public services at Rebecca Crown Library, 1972-76; Triton College, River Grove, IL, instructor in library technology, 1974-75; University of Wisconsin—Madison, E. B. Fred fellow, 1976, lecturer in library science, summers, 1976-77, winter, 1978; University of Illinois, Urbana-Champaign, assistant professor of library and information science, 1978-83; Louisiana State University, Baton Rouge, dean and professor of School of Library and Information Science, 1983-90, dean of graduate school, 1990—.

MEMBER: International Association for Social Science Information Service and Technology, American Library Association (chairperson of Status of Women in Librarianship committee, 1980-82; chairperson of Personnel Resources Advisory committee, 1984-87), Reference and Adult Service Division, Public Library Association, Association for Library and Information Science Education (president, 1987), Academy of Management, Women Library Workers, National Organization for Women, League of Women Voters, Illinois Library Association (chairperson of continuing education committee, 1980-81; chairperson of Equal Rights Amendment Task Force, 1980-82; treasurer, 1981-83), Louisiana Library Association, Baton Rouge Library Club, Beta Phi Mu.

WRITINGS:

Index to the Small Press Review, 1966-1974, Dustbooks (Paradise, CA), 1978.

(With Kathleen Weibel) *The Role of Women in Librarianship, 1876-1976: The Entry, Advancement, and Struggle for Equalization in One Profession*, Oryx (Phoenix, AZ), 1978.

(With Mary Mallory) *Directory of Library/Information Profession Women's Groups*, Committee on the Status of Women in Librarianship, American Library Association (Chicago), 1981.

(With Peggy Sullivan) *Opportunities in Library and Information Science*, foreword by Margaret Myers, VGM/Career Horizons (Lincolnwood, IL), 1982.

The Status of Women in Librarianship: Historical, Sociological and Economic Issues, Neal-Schuman (New York City), 1983.

(With Leigh S. Estabrook) *Career Patterns of Librarians: Final Report to the American Library Association,* American Library Association, 1983.

(With Katharine Phenix) *On Account of Sex: An Annotated Bibliography on the Status of Women in Librarianship, 1977-81,* American Library Association, 1984.

(Editor with William E. Moen) *Librarians for the New Millennium,* American Library Association, 1988.

(With Moen) *Occupational Entry,* American Library Association, 1989.

(With Phenix) *On Account of Sex: An Annotated Bibliography on the Status of Women in Librarianship, 1982-86,* American Library Association, 1989.

(Editor with Danny P. Wallace) *Adult Services: An Enduring Focus for Public Libraries,* American Library Association, 1990.

(With Margaret E. Monroe) *Partners for Lifelong Learning: Public Libraries & Adult Education,* Office of Library Programs, U.S. Department of Education (Washington, DC), 1991.

(With Myers) *Opportunities in Library and Information Service Careers,* foreword by Sullivan, VGM/Career Horizons, 1992.

Contributor to books, including *As Much to Learn as to Teach,* edited by Joel Lee and Beth Hamilton, Shoe String (Hamden, CT), 1979; *College Librarianship,* edited by William Miller and D. Stephen Rockwood, Scarecrow (Metuchen, NJ), 1981; *Women in Library Management: Theories, Skills, and Values,* edited by Darlene Weingand, Pierian (Ann Arbor, MI), 1982; *Advances in Librarianship,* Volume 12, edited by Wesley Simonton, Wiley (New York City), 1982; *The Service Imperative for Libraries,* edited by Gail Schlachter, Libraries Unlimited (Littleton, CO), 1982; *Library Literature 12: The Best of 1981,* edited by Weibel, Scarecrow, 1982; *Communicating Public Access to Government Information,* edited by Peter Hernon, Meckler (Westport, CT), 1983.

Editor of "Landmarks of References," a quarterly column in *Reference Services Review,* 1980-84, and "Current Issues in Reference and Adult Services," a column in *RQ,* 1982-86. Contributor to *ALA Yearbook* and *Bowker Annual of Library and Book Trade Information.* Contributor of more than fifty articles and reviews to journals in library and information science. Associate editor of *Serials Review,* 1979-80; assistant editor of *RQ,* 1981-82, editor, 1982-88; assistant column editor of *Serials Review,* 1975-79; book notices editor of *IASSIST Journal,* 1977—; chairperson of editorial advisory board of *RASD/RQ,* 1982-88; editor of *Library Trends,* autumn, 1979, winter,

1982; editor of *Public Libraries,* (official journal of the Public Libarary Association), 1989—.

BIOGRAPHICAL/CRITICAL SOURCES:

BOOKS

Riggs, D., and G. Sabine, editors, *Libraries in the 90's: What the Leaders Expect,* Oryx, 1988.

PERIODICALS

Serials Review, October/December, 1976.
Technicalities (interview), November, 1985.*

*   *   *

HEITZMANN, William Ray 1948-
(Wm. Ray Heitzmann; W. R. Tolland; William R. Vincent)

PERSONAL: Born February 12, 1948, in Hoboken, NJ; son of William Henry (a truck driver) and Mary Beatrice (a homemaker; maiden name, Tolland) Heitzmann; married Kathleen Esnes (a school librarian), June 20, 1970 (divorced); children: Richard Raymond, Mary Elizabeth. *Education:* Villanova University, B.S. (with honors), 1964; University of Chicago, M.A.T., 1966; attended Northwestern University, California State University at San Jose (now San Jose University); University of Delaware, Ph.D., 1974. *Politics:* Independent Republican. *Religion:* Roman Catholic.

ADDRESSES: Office—Department of Education and Human Services, Villanova University, Villanova, PA 19085.

CAREER: University of Chicago Laboratory School, Chicago, IL, middle school social studies teacher, 1964-65; DuSable High School, Chicago, IL, social studies teacher, 1965-66; North Chicago High School, North Chicago, IL, social studies teacher and basketball coach, 1966-67, and Highland Falls High School, Highland Falls, NY, 1967-69; Villanova University, Villanova, PA, instructor, 1969-74, assistant professor, 1974-77, associate professor of education and history, 1977—, recruiter of minority students and basketball players, coordinator of graduate teacher education, study skills lecturer. Member of adjunct faculty in the School of Allied Health Sciences at Thomas Jefferson University; basketball coach, Catholic Youth Organization, Villanova University Nite-Cats, Neuman College; women's flag football coach, Villanova University. Conducts and directs workshops; guest on radio programs in Texas, Pennsylvania, and New York. Heitzmann's Educational Learning Product Systems (HELPS), Havertown, PA, president. Consultant to Airco

Corp., U.S. Naval Institute, Office of Catholic Education, The Chubb Institute, and colleges and school districts.

MEMBER: North American Society of Oceanic Historians, American Association of University Professors, U.S. Naval Institute, National Council for the Social Studies (chair of committee of editors), National Marine Education Association, Oceanic Society, Community College Social Science Association, Naval Historical Association, Middle States Council for the Social Studies (member of executive committee, member of board of directors), Pennsylvania Council for the Social Studies (member of board of directors; vice president, 1977-78; president-elect, 1978-79; president, 1979-80), Philadelphia Council for the Social Studies (member of executive committee, 1974-78), Pennsylvania Association for Curriculum Development and Supervision, Delaware Valley Reading Association, Cousteau Society, Mystic Seaport Society, Philadelphia Writers' Organization, National Association of Basketball Coaches, Llanerch Optimist Club (member of board of directors, 1983—), Kappa Delta Pi, Phi Delta Kappa, Delta Tau Kappa.

AWARDS, HONORS: Outstanding Service Award, National Council for the Social Studies, 1980; also recipient of awards from Student Pennsylvania State Education Association, Weehawken School District, National Council for the Social Studies, and Pennsylvania Council for the Social Studies; Outstanding Alumnus Award, School of Education, University of Delaware, 1988; *MSCSS* Gold Medal, 1989, for research publications; writer in residence, The Ragdale Foundation.

WRITINGS:

NONFICTION; EDUCATIONAL

(Editor with Patricia Stetson) *The Psychology of Teaching and Learning,* MSS Education (New York), 1973.
(Editor with Charles Staropoli) *Student Teaching: Classroom Management and Professionalism,* MSS Education, 1974.
Educational Games and Simulations, National Education Association (Washington, DC), 1974, 2nd edition, 1983.
Fifty Political Cartoons for Teaching United States History, J. Weston Walch (Portland, ME), 1975.
America's Maritime Heritage and Energy Education (student workbooks), two volumes, Con-Stran Publications (Philadelphia), 1977.
Minicourses, National Education Association, 1977.
The Classroom Teacher and the Student Teacher, National Education Association, 1977.
The Newspaper in the Classroom, National Education Association, 1979.
Opportunities in Sports and Physical Education, National Textbook Co. (Lincolnwood, IL), 1980, 2nd edition,

1985, and 3rd edition, 1993, both published as *Opportunities in Sports and Athletics.*
Introduction to General Teaching Methods, Airco (Montvale, NJ), 1984.
Guide to Introduction to General Teaching Methods, Airco, 1985.
Note Taking Tips, Chubb Institute (Parsippany, NJ), 1989.
Test Taking Tips, Chubb Institute, 1989.

NONFICTION; OTHER

American Jewish Political Behavior: History and Analysis, R & E Research Associates (Palo Alto, CA), 1975.
Opportunities in Marine and Maritime Careers, National Textbook Co., 1979.
Political Cartoons, Scholastic Inc. (New York), 1980.
Opportunities in Sports Medicine, National Textbook Co., 1984.
Careers for Sports Nuts and Other Athletic Types, National Textbook Co., 1991.
Opportunities for Sports Medicine Careers, VGM Career Horizons (Lincolnwood, IL), 1992.
Opportunities in Sports and Athletics Careers, VGM Career Horizons, 1993.

Contributor to books, including *Affective Education: Innovations for Learning,* edited by Louis Thayer and Kent O. Beeler, University Associates, 1977. Contributor of articles and reviews to newspapers, scholarly journals, sports magazines (sometimes under pseudonyms William R. Vincent and W. R. Tolland), and popular magazines, including *Beachcomber, Career World, Catholic Standard and Times, Creative Teacher, Real World, Sea Heritage News,* and *Sea World.* Editorial board member of *The Social Studies,* and *Journal of Marine Education.* Contributing editor to *Sea History* and *Long Beach Island Magazine;* executive editor of *Social Studies;* book reviewer for *Community College Social Science Quarterly;* advertising manager of *MSCSS,* 1980-82.

SIDELIGHTS: William Ray Heitzmann once told *CA* that his interests include "a great desire to remind the American people of the nation's maritime tradition and to show that academic study (and cerebral activity) is intimately related to successful sports participation."

BIOGRAPHICAL/CRITICAL SOURCES:

PERIODICALS

Asbury Park Press, July 16, 1978.
Catholic Standard and Times, December 20, 1984.
County Press, January 30, 1985.
Delaware County Daily Times, April 23, 1985.
New York Daily News, February 18, 1979.
Philadelphia Bulletin, July 21, 1978.
Suburban and Wayne Times, August 30, 1979.

Temple Telegram, November 14, 1979.
Times Herald (Norristown, PA), February 11, 1985.
Voice of Youth Advocates, June, 1991, p. 123.*

*   *   *

HEITZMANN, Wm. Ray
See HEITZMANN, William Ray

*   *   *

HENNING, Charles N(athaniel) 1915-

PERSONAL: Born June 20, 1915, in Pittsburgh, PA; son of William P. and Eleanor (Hill) Henning; married Virginia Marie Doerr, June 30, 1945. *Education:* University of California, Los Angeles, B.A., 1938, M.A., 1940, Ph.D., 1953.

ADDRESSES: Home—12714 42nd Ave., N.E., Seattle, WA 98125. *Office*—School of Business Administration, University of Washington, Seattle, WA 98195.

CAREER: University of California, Los Angeles, lecturer in economics, 1941; U.S. Department of Commerce, Office of International Trade, Far Eastern Division, Washington, DC, economist, 1942-48; University of Washington, Seattle, assistant professor, 1948-53, associate professor, 1953-55, professor of finance and business economics, 1955-85, director of business administration faculty publications, 1961-1972, acting chairperson of finance, business economics and quantitative methods department, 1974, professor emeritus of finance and business and economics, 1985—. Educational adviser to the Pacific Coast Banking School. Member, U.S. Delegation, World Conference on Trade and Employment, Geneva, Switzerland, 1947; negotiator of some of tariff concessions incorporated in General Agreement on Tariffs and Trade (GATT). Member, various interdepartmental governmental committees on trade agreements, occupied areas, and international finance. Training advisor, in-service training program for Foreign Service officers, Department of Commerce, Washington, DC, 1948. Consultant to Operations Research Office, Johns Hopkins University, 1952-61, and Research Analysis Corporation, 1962—.

MEMBER: American Economic Association, American Finance Association, American Academy of Political and Social Science, Western Economic Association, Seattle World Affairs Council, World Trade Club of Seattle, Phi Beta Kappa, Beta Gamma Sigma, Omicron Delta Gamma (Artus), Alpha Kappa Psi, Pan Xenia.

WRITINGS:

International Finance, Harper (New York City), 1958.

(With James Crutchfield and William Pigott) *Money, Financial Institutions, and the Economy,* Prentice-Hall (Englewood Cliffs, NJ), 1965.
(With Pigott and Robert Haney Scott) *Financial Markets and the Economy,* Prentice-Hall, 1974, 5th edition, 1988.
(With Pigott and Scott) *International Financial Management,* McGraw (New York City), 1978.

Also contributor to books, including *Education in International Business,* edited by Stefan Robock and Lee Nehrt, Graduate School of Business Administration, Indiana University, 1964. Contributor to *Encyclopaedia Britannica* and to journals. Editor, *University of Washington Business Review,* 1954-71.

*   *   *

HENNING, Edward B(urk) 1922-1993

PERSONAL: Born October 23, 1922, in Cleveland, OH; died of complications following a stroke, April 18, 1993, in Cleveland Heights, OH; son of Harold Wagner and Marguerite (Burk) Henning; married Margaret Revacko (past assistant to director of Case Western Reserve University Press), December 31, 1942; children: Eric, Lisa, Geoffrey. *Education:* Attended Cleveland Institute of Art, 1946-49; Western Reserve University (now Case Western Reserve University), B.S. (magna cum laude), 1949, M.A., 1952; studied at Academie Julian, Paris, France, 1949-50. *Avocational interests:* Contemporary American and French literature and philosophy.

CAREER: Cleveland Museum of Art, Cleveland, OH, assistant curator of education, 1954-55, associate curator of education, 1955-58, assistant to director, 1958-70, curator of contemporary art, 1960-72, curator of modern art, 1972-79, chief curator of modern art, 1979-85. Case Western Reserve University, guest professor of art history; Cleveland Institute of Art, teacher of aesthetics. *Military service:* U.S. Army, 1942-46; served in European theater.

WRITINGS:

Paths of Abstract Art (museum catalogue), Cleveland Museum of Art (Cleveland, OH), 1960.
Fifty Years of Modern Art, 1916-1966 (museum catalogue), Cleveland Museum of Art, 1966.
The Spirit of Surrealism (museum catalogue), Cleveland Museum of Art, 1979.
The Art of Collecting Modern Art (museum catalogue), Cleveland Museum of Art, 1986.
Creativity in Art and Science, 1860-1960 (museum catalogue), Cleveland Museum of Modern Art, 1987.

Also author of other museum catalogues, including *Landscapes Interior and Exterior: Avery, Rothko and Schueler,*

1975. Contributor to periodicals, including *Dialectica, La Biennale di Venezia,* and *Art International.* Editorial assistant, *Journal of Aesthetics and Art Criticism,* 1955-63.

OBITUARIES:

PERIODICALS

New York Times, April 20, 1993, p. B7.*

*   *   *

HENRY, Sondra   1930-

PERSONAL: Born April 3, 1930, in Brooklyn, NY; daughter of Ben Parkoff and Gertrude Friedman; married Edward I. Henry (a physician), 1950; children: Scott, Patricia, Gordon. *Education:* Bennington College, A.B., 1950; Columbia University, J.D., 1953.

ADDRESSES: Home—22 Deepdale Dr., Great Neck, NY 11021.

CAREER: Practicing attorney, 1953—. Lecturer on women's history and Jewish history at Hofstra University, 1977-78, at Plainview Young Men's-Young Women's Hebrew Association, 1978-80, at Roslyn, NY, School District, 1981-86, at North Shore School District, 1983, at BOCES, In-Service for Teachers, Great Neck, NY, 1984, and at Hutton House, C. W. Post, 1985.

MEMBER: Authors Guild, Authors League of America, New York State Bar Association, Bar Association of Nassau County.

AWARDS, HONORS: Award from Court Counseling Service, 1975; award for service to children in family courts of New York from Jewish Board of Guardians.

WRITINGS:

WITH EMILY TAITZ

Written Out of History: A Hidden Legacy of Jewish Women Revealed Through Their Writings and Letters, Bloch Publishing (New York City), 1978, 4th edition, Biblio Press (New York City), 1990.
One Woman's Power: The Biography of Gloria Steinem, Dillon (Minneapolis, MN), 1987.
Israel: A Sacred Land, Dillon, 1988.
Everyone Wears His Name: A Biography of Levi Strauss, Dillon, 1990.
Betty Friedan: Fighter for Women's Rights, Enslow Publishers (Hillside, NJ), 1990.
Keeper of the Dream: A Biography of Coretta Scott King, Enslow Publishers, 1992.

WORK IN PROGRESS: Women of Achievement in Contemporary American Life.

HENRY, T. E.
See ROWLAND-ENTWISTLE, (Arthur) Theodore (Henry)

*   *   *

HIGGINS, Thomas J(oseph)   1899-

PERSONAL: Born April 20, 1899, in Philadelphia, PA; son of Thomas Joseph and Ellen (Slean) Higgins. *Education:* Woodstock College, A.B., 1921, A.M., 1922, Ph.D., 1931.

ADDRESSES: Home and office—Loyola College, 4501 North Charles St., Baltimore, MD 21210.

CAREER: Ordained Roman Catholic priest, member of Society of Jesus (Jesuits); Boston College High School, Boston, MA, instructor, 1922-25; St. Joseph's College, Philadelphia, PA, dean of men, 1929-31, dean, 1932-33, president, 1933-39; Loyola College, Baltimore, MD, professor of ethics, 1939—. Pastor at Church of Gesu, Philadelphia, 1933-39. Participant in International Congress of Philosophy, Brussels, Belgium, 1953. Judge, Archdiocesan Tribunal of Baltimore, 1970—.

MEMBER: Jesuit Philosophical Association of the United States and Canada (president, 1953), American Catholic Philosophical Association, Academy of Political Science, National Catholic Education Association, Canon Law Society of America.

WRITINGS:

Man as Man: The Science and Art of Ethics (college textbook), 1949, Bruce Publishing (Milwaukee), revised edition, 1958.
Perfection Is for You, Bruce Publishing, 1953.
Helps and Hindrances to Perfection, Bruce Publishing, 1955.
Dogma for the Layman, Bruce Publishing, 1961.
Ethical Theories in Conflict, Bruce Publishing, 1967.
Basic Ethics, Bruce Publishing, 1968.
Judicial Review Unmasked, Christopher, 1981.
Preaching the Sunday and Holy Day Scriptures, Sunday (Lake Worth, FL), 1986.

SIDELIGHTS: Thomas J. Higgins told *CA:* "From earliest youth I have wanted to write for publication. I asked the editor of a prominent weekly for advice. I was not able to put his advice to practice because I was too busy with other duties. One day toward the end of World War II I said to myself, 'I am going to write a book,' and pulled out paper and pencil and began to put my class notes into book form.

"To the aspiring writer I would say never give up. By plugging along, ignoring rejections, I published eight books. The book of sermons is the result of fifteen years of work and revision. When I am working on a book I start right in as soon as breakfast is over.

"As for the contemporary literary scene: I am happy we have passed beyond the Victorians but literature like the contemporary scene smells of sex, violence, and drugs. It is too bad when editors tell authors to put more sex into their work."

BIOGRAPHICAL/CRITICAL SOURCES:

PERIODICALS

America, August 15, 1953, pp. 481-82.
Catholic Review, November 17, 1961, p. 9; July 31, 1981.
Christian News, March 1, 1982.
Human Events, February 6, 1982, p. 18.
National Review, August 21, 1981, pp. 971-72.
Our Sunday Visitor, August 23, 1953.
Spiritual Life, March, 1957, pp. 60-63.
Theological Studies, December, 1972.*

*   *   *

HILDICK, E. W.
   See HILDICK, (Edmund) Wallace

*   *   *

HILDICK, (Edmund) Wallace 1925-
   (E. W. Hildick)

PERSONAL: Born December 29, 1925, in Bradford, England; married Doris Clayton (a teacher), 1950. *Education:* City of Leeds Training College, teacher's certificate, 1950.

ADDRESSES: Home—Monterey, St. Neot, Liskeard, Cornwall PL14 6NL, England. *Agent*—McIntosh & Otis, Inc., 310 Madison Ave., New York, NY 10017.

CAREER: Dewsbury Public Library, Yorkshire, England, junior assistant, 1941-42; clerk in a truck repair depot, Leeds, England, 1942-43; Admiralty Signals Establishment (Royal Navy), Sowerby Bridge, Yorkshire, and Haslemere, Surrey, England, laboratory assistant, 1943-46; Dewsbury Secondary Modern School, Yorkshire, England, teacher, 1950-54; full-time writer, 1954—. *Military service:* Royal Air Force, 1946-48.

MEMBER: Mystery Writers of America, Authors Guild, Society of Authors.

AWARDS, HONORS: Tom-Gallon Trust Award for short story, 1957; honor book citation, International Hans Christian Andersen Award, 1968, for *Louie's Lot;* Ameri-

can Ambassador Books booklist selection for children's literature, 1970, for *Manhattan Is Missing* and *Top Boy at Twisters Creek;* honor book citation, Austrian Children and Youth Book Prize Award, 1976, for *Lucky Les: The Adventures of a Cat of Five Tales;* Edgar Allan Poe special awards, Mystery Writers of America, 1979, for *The Case of the Secret Scribbler,* and 1995, for *Hester Bidgood, Investigatrix of Evill Deedes.*

WRITINGS:

NOVELS; FOR ADULTS

Bed and Work, Faber (London), 1962.
A Town on the Never, Faber, 1963.
Lunch with Ashurbanipal, Faber, 1965.
Bracknell's Law (mystery), Harper (New York City), 1975.
The Weirdown Experiment (mystery), Harper, 1976.
Vandals (mystery), Hamish Hamilton (London), 1977.
The Loop (mystery), Hamish Hamilton, 1977.

NONFICTION; FOR ADULTS

Word for Word: A Study of Authors' Alterations, with Exercises, Faber, 1965, abridged edition published as *Word for Word: The Rewriting of Fiction,* Norton (New York City), 1965.
Writing with Care: Two Hundred Problems in the Use of English, David White (New York City), 1967.
Thirteen Types of Narrative, Macmillan (London), 1968, C. N. Potter (New York City), 1970.
Children and Fiction: A Critical Study in Depth of the Artistic and Psychological Factors Involved in Writing Fiction for and about Children, Evans (London), 1970, World (New York City), 1971, revised edition, Evans, 1974.
(Under name E. W. Hildick) *Storypacks: A New Concept in English Teaching,* Evans, 1971.
Only the Best: Six Qualities of Excellence, C. N. Potter, 1973.

"JIM STARLING" JUVENILE SERIES, UNDER NAME E. W. HILDICK

Jim Starling, illustrations by Roger Payne, Chatto & Windus (London), 1958.
Jim Starling and the Agency, illustrations by Payne, Chatto & Windus, 1958.
Jim Starling and the Colonel, illustrations by Payne, Heinemann (London), 1960, Doubleday (Garden City, NY), 1968.
Jim Starling's Holiday, illustrations by Payne, Heinemann, 1960.
Jim Starling and the Spotted Dog, illustrations by Payne, Anthony Blond (London), 1963, revised edition, New English Library (London), 1971.

Jim Starling Goes to Town, illustrations by Payne, Anthony Blond, 1963.

Jim Starling Takes Over, illustrations by Payne, Anthony Blond, 1963, revised edition, New English Library, 1971.

"BIRDY JONES" JUVENILE SERIES, UNDER NAME E. W. HILDICK

Birdy Jones, illustrations by Richard Rose, Faber, 1963, Stackpole (Harrisburg, PA), 1969.

Birdy and the Group, illustrations by Rose, Macmillan, 1968, Stackpole, 1969.

Birdy Swings North, illustrations by Rose, Macmillan, 1969, Stackpole, 1971.

Birdy in Amsterdam, illustrations by Rose, Macmillan, 1970, Stackpole, 1971.

Birdy Jones and the New York Heads, Doubleday, 1974.

"LEMON KELLY" JUVENILE SERIES, UNDER NAME E. W. HILDICK

Meet Lemon Kelly, illustrations by Margery Gill, Cape (London), 1963, published as *Lemon Kelly,* illustrations by Arvis Stewart, Doubleday, 1968.

Lemon Kelly Digs Deep, illustrations by Gill, Cape, 1964.

Lemon Kelly and the Home-made Boy, illustrations by Iris Schweitzer, Dobson (London), 1968.

"LOUIE" JUVENILE SERIES, UNDER NAME E. W. HILDICK

Louie's Lot, Faber, 1965, David White, 1968.

Louie's S.O.S., illustrations by Schweitzer, Macmillan, 1968, Doubleday, 1970.

Louie's Snowstorm, illustrations by Schweitzer, Doubleday, 1974.

Louie's Ransom, Knopf (New York City), 1978.

"QUESTERS" JUVENILE SERIES, UNDER NAME E. W. HILDICK

The Questers, illustrations by Rose, Brockhampton Press (Leicester, England), 1966, illustrations by Ruth Chew, Hawthorn (New York City), 1970.

Calling Questers Four, illustrations by Rose, Brockhampton Press, 1967.

The Questers and the Whispering Spy, illustrations by Rose, Brockhampton Press, 1967.

"McGURK MYSTERY" JUVENILE SERIES, UNDER NAME E. W. HILDICK

The Nose Knows, illustrations by Unada Gliewe, Grosset (New York City), 1973, published in England with illustrations by Val Biro, Brockhampton, 1974.

Dolls in Danger, illustrations by Biro, Brockhampton, 1974, published as *Deadline for McGurk,* illustrations by Lisl Weil, Macmillan (New York City), 1975.

The Menaced Midget, illustrations by Biro, Brockhampton, 1975.

The Case of the Condemned Cat, illustrations by Weil, Macmillan, 1975, published in England with illustrations by Biro, Brockhampton, 1975.

The Case of the Nervous Newsboy, illustrations by Weil, Macmillan, 1976, published in England with illustrations by Biro, Hodder & Stoughton (London), 1976.

The Great Rabbit Robbery, illustrations by Biro, Hodder & Stoughton, 1976, published as *The Great Rabbit Rip-Off,* illustrations by Weil, Macmillan, 1977.

The Case of the Invisible Dog, illustrations by Weil, Macmillan, 1977, published in England with illustrations by Biro, Hodder & Stoughton, 1977.

The Case of the Secret Scribbler, illustrations by Weil, Macmillan, 1978, published in England with illustrations by Biro, Hodder & Stoughton, 1978.

The Case of the Phantom Frog, illustrations by Weil, Macmillan, 1979, published in England with illustrations by Biro, Hodder & Stoughton, 1979.

The Case of the Snowbound Spy, illustrations by Weil, Macmillan, 1980.

The Case of the Treetop Treasure, illustrations by Weil, Macmillan, 1980, published in England with illustrations by Biro, Hodder & Stoughton, 1980.

The Case of the Bashful Bank Robber, illustrations by Weil, Macmillan, 1981.

The Case of the Four Flying Fingers, illustrations by Weil, Macmillan, 1981.

The Case of the Felon's Fiddle, illustrations by Weil, Macmillan, 1982.

McGurk Gets Good and Mad, illustrations by Weil, Macmillan, 1982.

The Case of the Slingshot Sniper, illustrations by Weil, Macmillan, 1983.

The Case of the Vanishing Ventriloquist, illustrations by Kathy Parkinson, Macmillan, 1985.

The Case of the Muttering Mummy, illustrations by Blanche Sims, Macmillan, 1986.

The Case of the Wandering Weathervanes, illustrations by Denise Brunkus, Macmillan, 1988.

The Case of the Purloined Parrot, Macmillan, 1990.

The Case of the Dragon in Distress (fantasy), Macmillan, 1991.

The Case of the Weeping Witch (fantasy), Macmillan, 1992.

The Case of the Desperate Drummer, Macmillan, 1993.

The Case of the Fantastic Footprints, Macmillan, 1994.

The Case of the Absent Author, Macmillan, 1995.

The Case of the Wiggling Wig, Macmillan, 1996.

"GHOST SQUAD" JUVENILE SERIES, UNDER NAME E. W. HILDICK

The Ghost Squad Breaks Through, Dutton (New York City), 1984.

The Ghost Squad Flies Concorde, Dutton, 1985.

The Ghost Squad and the Halloween Conspiracy, Dutton, 1985.

The Ghost Squad and the Ghoul of Grunberg, Dutton, 1986.

The Ghost Squad and the Prowling Hermits, Dutton, 1987.

The Ghost Squad and the Menace of the Malevs, Dutton, 1988.

"FELICITY SNELL MYSTERIES" JUVENILE SERIES

The Purloined Corn-Popper, Benchmark (Tarrytown, NY), in press.

The Serial Sneak Thief, Benchmark, in press.

OTHER JUVENILES, UNDER NAME E. W. HILDICK

The Boy at the Window, illustrations by Ionicus, Chatto & Windus, 1960.

Mapper Mundy's Treasure Hunt, illustrations by John Cooper, Anthony Blond, 1963.

Lucky Les: The Adventures of a Cat of Five Tales, illustrations by Peter Barrett, Anthony Blond, 1967, revised edition, Brockhampton, 1974.

Here Comes Parren, illustrations by Michael Heath, Macmillan (London), 1968, illustrations by Robert Frankenberg, World, 1972.

Back with Parren, illustrations by Heath, Macmillan, 1968.

Those Daring Young Men in Their Jaunty Jalopies (based on an original story and screenplay by Jack Davies and Ken Annakin), Berkley (New York City), 1969, published in England as *Monte Carlo or Bust!,* Sphere Books (London), 1969.

Top Boy at Twisters Creek, illustrations by Oscar Liebman, David White, 1969.

Manhattan Is Missing, illustrations by Jan Palmer, Doubleday, 1969.

Ten Thousand Golden Cockerels, illustrations by Rose, Evans, 1970.

The Secret Winners, illustrations by Gustave Nebel, Crown (New York City), 1970.

The Dragon That Lived under Manhattan, illustrations by Harold Berson, Crown, 1970.

My Kid Sister, illustrations by Schweitzer, World, 1971.

The Prisoners of Gridling Gap, a Report: With Expert Comments from Doctor Ranulf Quitch, illustrations by Paul Sagsoorian, Doubleday, 1971.

The Secret Spenders (sequel to *The Secret Winners*), illustrations by Nebel, Crown, 1971.

The Doughnut Dropout, illustrations by Kiyo Komoda, Doubleday, 1972.

The Active-Enzyme, Lemon-Freshened, Junior High School Witch, illustrations by Schweitzer, Doubleday, 1973.

Kids Commune, illustrations by Liebman, David White, 1973.

Time Explorers, Inc., illustrations by Nancy Ohanian, Doubleday, 1976.

A Cat Called Amnesia, illustrations by Biro, David White, 1976.

The Top-Flight Fully-Automated Junior High School Girl Detective, illustrations by Schweitzer, Doubleday, 1977, published as *The Top-Flight Fully-Automated Girl Detective,* Deutsch (London), 1979.

The Memory Tap, Macmillan (London), 1989.

My Famous Father, Macmillan, 1990.

Hester Bidgood, Investigatrix of Evill Deedes, Macmillan (New York City), 1994.

TEXTBOOKS, UNDER NAME E. W. HILDICK

A Close Look at Newspapers, Faber, 1966.

A Close Look at Magazines and Comics, Faber, 1966.

A Close Look at Television and Sound Broadcasting, Faber, 1967.

A Close Look at Advertising, Faber, 1969.

Cokerheaton (storypack), illustrations by Payne, Evans, 1971.

Rushbrook (storypack), Evans, 1971.

OTHER

Contributor of articles, reviews, and stories to periodicals, including *Spectator,* London *Observer,* and *Times Literary Supplement. Kenyon Review,* visiting critic and associate editor, 1966-67; *Listener,* regular reviewer of adult fiction, 1968-69.

Many of Hildick's books have been published in translation in Germany, France, Italy, Portugal, Spain, Brazil, Japan, Poland, the former U.S.S.R., Yugoslavia, Sweden, Norway, Finland, Denmark, Iceland, Taiwan, and Holland.

WORK IN PROGRESS: The Hunting of Hester Bidgood, a sequel to *Hester Bidgood, Investigatrix of Evill Deedes.*

ADAPTATIONS: Jim Starling and *The Boy at the Window* were dramatized on British Broadcasting Corporation (BBC) Radio.

SIDELIGHTS: Wallace Hildick began to take a serious interest in writing when he was fourteen and has been "quite obsessively single-minded about the job ever since," he once commented. By the time he left school at the age of fifteen he was certain that he wanted to write fiction. He has written nearly one hundred books, primarily for children, since publishing his first book in 1958.

Hildick has called his childhood education in math and science "the best early training for a writer" because "it helps to give him mental toughness, tone, and agility, while keeping his talent fresh." He did not begin writing immediately after graduating, however. Like other developing writers, Hildick moved from job to job, working variously in clerical positions, communications, and education. He has revealed that teaching boys in their early teens taught him much about writing for children, because he had to learn to be clear, concrete, and concise to keep their attention.

It was not Hildick's original intent to write for children; when he became a full-time writer in 1954, he was writing adult fiction. His first children's novel, *Jim Starling,* was inspired when he learned of a shortage of juvenile books about the lives of working-class children. Hildick published two books featuring Starling in 1958, and thus was born the first of several children's series. During the 1960s Hildick and his wife, who had by then given up teaching to become his agent, had an opportunity to promote his juveniles in the United States, but many of his books seemed too British to American publishers. In response he began to write stories with American settings, of which *Top Boy at Twisters Creek* and *Manhattan Is Missing* were the first. Reviewing *The Top-Flight Fully-Automated Girl Detective* in the *Times Literary Supplement,* Jennifer Moody asserted that Hildick can successfully walk "the narrow path of acceptability on both sides of the Atlantic."

Hildick has also found success in the differing arenas of children's and adult literature; according to the author, the two kinds of writing complement each other. In Hildick's critical book *Children and Fiction,* Christopher Lehmann-Haupt recapped, he "dwells on what is wrong with children's books, and he is a model of good sense. He believes he knows what children look for. . . . He makes a persuasive case that in their affinities for literature children differ from adults only in the degree of experience they bring to books."

Most of Hildick's books are mysteries. *The Nose Knows* established the format and some of the characters for the McGurk tales, the longest of his juvenile mystery series. In these books young detectives (initially Wanda, Joey, and Willie, who has an unusually keen sense of smell) unravel various mysteries under the leadership of eleven-year-old ringleader Jack McGurk. Within the mystery *The Case of the Condemned Cat,* Hildick tells the story of the feline Whiskers, who is accused of killing a neighbor's dove but is shown to be innocent by the able detection of the children. "How they prove it is entertaining and clever," Donald J. Pattow commented in *Twentieth-Century Crime and Mystery Writers.* Though he found the central character "a bit too precocious," he pronounced the writing concise and the first-person narrative effective. In the *New York Times Book Review,* Joan Kahn gave kudos to another McGurk mystery, *The Case of the Bashful Bank Robber,* for having "plenty of humor and suspense." With the 1991 McGurk tale, *The Case of the Dragon in Distress,* Hildick brought the young detectives into the realm of fantasy.

Cats figure not only in the McGurk books but also in juvenile mysteries that do not fit into any of the series. In *Manhattan Is Missing,* a Siamese cat named Manhattan is kidnapped in the part of New York City he is named for and is recovered by a group of junior detectives whose activities provide the author with an opportunity to describe city sites. *A Cat Called Amnesia* is the tale of a lost but well-tended pet whose owners must be found within two days because cats are not allowed in the apartment of the Bleekers, the family to whom the cat has wandered. In what Patricia Craig described in the *Times Literary Supplement* as the "slight but expertly handled plot," the Bleeker children meet the challenge.

The title character of *Lucky Les: The Adventures of a Cat of Five Tales* is a cat who tempts fate and survives. Written in a format designed to make books appealing to children beguiled by video games, *Lucky Les* allows the reader to shape the story by choosing at various points among possible actions and then turning ahead to specified corresponding pages in the text. In this manner the story can be read several times with a different ending each time. Susan Chitty, writing for the *Times Literary Supplement,* disapproved of this construction, reasoning that although it might appeal to some, most readers would "probably find it both irritating and confusing."

Louie, for whom a short series of Hildick's juveniles is named, is a popular milk deliverer in an English town who hires a "lot" of helpers from young neighborhood applicants. These helpers accompany Louie on his rounds and in a series of adventures. In the inaugural book of the series, *Louie's Lot,* young Tim must prove himself superior among a large number of applicants for the one vacant position in Louie's lot. In the trial period after his acceptance, he has to figure out and overcome several mysterious attempts to discredit him. A *Times Literary Supplement* reviewer who praised *Louie's Lot* for its humor and pace also lauded Hildick for his "wonderfully free approach to the art of fiction" and labeled the book "positively seductive" reading. In later Louie books, the young helpers solve the mystery of strange objects that appear in the milk, help Louie on his Christmas Eve round, and figure in his trip to the United States, in which he is captured and held for ransom. Angela Huth raved of Hildick and *Louie's Snowstorm,* the Christmas Eve story, in the *Spectator,* "Here is a writer with the brightness of the poets: here is a book I swear the most reluctant child-reader would delight in."

Hildick also wrote several other short series for children. One features Jim Starling, who leads his friends in various adventures and challenges; in *Jim Starling and the Colonel* they try to prove to Colonel Splitt-Statham that modern young people can match the physical feats their elders once performed. The Birdy series, in which the main characters are older teens, includes *Birdy and the Group,* an account of the formation of a rock band featuring a pop whistler. The *Times Literary Supplement* reviewer found this book, notwithstanding its "hilarity and slapstick . . . touching as well as funny, with an edge of humanity missing from many more 'serious' stories." The Questers series centers on the activities of a group directed by young Peter Braine from his sickbed.

Hildick's fiction for adults is generally well received by critics, although he has been faulted for a formulaic approach to storytelling. In the mystery *Bracknell's Law,* Mrs. Bracknell discovers by reading her husband's diary that he is a serial killer. She then keeps a journal of events herself. A *Times Literary Supplement* critic described the book as "superb black comedy, wittily and elegantly told."

Hildick told *CA:* "One of the most rewarding aspects of working on a long series like the McGurk books, spanning over twenty years, is the way in which it begins to generate spontaneously strong natural independent offshoots. Thus, on one of their occasional time-traveling adventures, when the regular McGurk characters are transported to seventeenth-century New England, they go to the rescue of a young girl falsely accused of witchcraft (in *The Case of the Weeping Witch*). Hester Bidgood proved to be such a fascinating character in her own right that I was compelled to find out more about her and her times than the series plot required, with the result that *Hester Bidgood, Investigatrix of Evill Deedes* was created as a piece of historical fiction, totally independent of any Mc-Gurk connections, with a sequel of its own, *The Hunting of Hester Bidgood,* on the stocks.

"Similarly, the trend that has developed naturally over the years for the young McGurk detectives to seek further information in the local public library when following up various clues eventually gave rise to a growing insistence from that very background itself to be given more prominence. The final triggering-off occurred in *The Case of the Absent Author,* where the title character, a prolific bestselling adult mystery writer, disappears, leaving behind a hidden stash of unpublished manuscripts. Names had to be found for this fictitious author's works, of course, which is when, out of the blue, Felicity Snell leaped to life—straight off the tongue of one of the McGurk characters: 'And doesn't he write the Felicity Snell mysteries, too? . . . About this small-town librarian who's so much smarter at solving crimes than the regular police?' From that moment on, the new, casually hatched character began to grow at a furious rate, very soon demanding, with all the vigor and clamor of a young cuckoo, its own space and individual attention."

BIOGRAPHICAL/CRITICAL SOURCES:

BOOKS

Something about the Author Autobiography Series, Volume 6, Gale, 1988, pp. 161-77.
Reilly, John M., editor, *Twentieth-Century Crime and Mystery Writers,* St. Martin's, 1980.
Twentieth-Century Children's Writers, 3rd edition, St. James Press, 1989, pp. 449-51.

PERIODICALS

New York Review of Books, December 2, 1971, p. 25.
New York Times, December 20, 1971, p. 33.
New York Times Book Review, August 4, 1968, p. 20; April 30, 1978; April 26, 1981, p. 62.
Spectator, December 6, 1975, pp. 733-34.
Times Educational Supplement, December 22, 1989, p. 22; February 15, 1991, p. 29.
Times Literary Supplement, April 1, 1965, p. 249; December 9, 1965, p. 1142; November 24, 1966, p. 1074; May 25, 1967, p. 443; April 3, 1969, p. 363; October 30, 1970, p. 1259; December 11, 1970, pp. 1451-52; September 28, 1973, p. 1118; December 6, 1974; December 5, 1975, p. 1448; February 27, 1976, p. 212; July 15, 1977, p. 865; December 14, 1979, p. 124.
Voice of Youth Advocates, February, 1989, p. 285.

*   *   *

HILFIKER, David 1945-

PERSONAL: Surname is pronounced "*hil*-fick-er"; born February 12, 1945, in Buffalo, NY; son of Warren T. (a clergyman) and Carol (Koepf) Hilfiker; married Marja Kaikkonen (a teacher), June 21, 1969; children: Laurel, Karen, Kai. *Education:* Yale College (now University), B.A., 1967; University of Minnesota—Twin Cities, M.D., 1974. *Politics:* "Independent/Socialist." *Religion:* Ecumenical Christian. *Avocational interests:* "Individual spiritual journey as it relates to health, politics, and community"; running; cross-country skiing.

ADDRESSES: Home—2122 California St. N.W. #658, Washington, DC 20008-1803. *Office*—Joseph's House, 1750 Columbia Road N.W., Washington, DC 20009.

CAREER: Cook County Community Clinic, Grand Marais, MN, family practitioner, 1975-82; on sabbatical in Finland, 1982-83; Community of Hope Health Services, Washington, DC, physician to the indigent, 1983-92. Co-founder of Christ House (a medical recovery shelter for the homeless); founder of Joseph's House (a community for homeless men with AIDS); on sabbatical, 1993-94.

MEMBER: American Academy of Family Practice, Medical Society of the United States and Mexico (Washington, DC, chapter), Church of the Saviour.

AWARDS, HONORS: First place award in trade category from American Medical Writers Association, 1986; Christopher's Award, 1994, for *Not All of Us Are Saints.*

WRITINGS:

Healing the Wounds: A Physician Looks at His Work, Pantheon (New York City), 1985.
Not All of Us Are Saints, Hill & Wang (New York City), 1994.

Also contributor to *New England Journal of Medicine, Jama,* and *The Other Side.*

SIDELIGHTS: David Hilfiker began practicing medicine in a rural clinic in northern Minnesota after graduating from medical school in 1974 and completing his internship in 1975. Admittedly at odds with the demands for increased productivity in his work as well as the "unrealistic expectations" of his patients, wrote John G. Deaton in the *New York Times Book Review,* Hilfiker withdrew from his profession after seven years and went on retreat. He resumed doctoring one year later in Washington, D.C., administering health care to the indigent at a local clinic, at a recovery shelter for homeless men and women, and later, for homeless men with AIDS.

Healing the Wounds: A Physician Looks at His Work is an autobiographical account of Hilfiker's early experiences in medicine, which he wrote during a one-year sabbatical. Reviewing the book, Deaton observed that Hilfiker "is brutally honest" in revealing his personal anguish, conflicts, and mistakes. We "witness the pain that accompanies the discovery" of errors, continued Deaton, as well as the anguish of a failed attempt to save a life, or of telling a patient that he or she has cancer. In these instances "the book explores the stress and frustrations . . . of a sensitive physician," determined the reviewer, but *Healing the Wounds* is also "a medical odyssey from idealism to disenchantment and back."

Expressing a similar opinion in the *Washington Post,* Jonathan Yardley remarked that it is Hilfiker's purpose "to describe 'the conflicting pressures [doctors] face, which often seem to defy solution.' " From the standpoint of the lay person, assessed Yardley, "what is most useful about *Healing the Wounds* is its depiction, from the inside, of the stresses that make doctors behave the way they too often do." As Hilfiker points out, notes Yardley, physicians resort to "elaborate defense mechanisms in order to cope" with their patients' "utterly unrealistic" expectations of them as "ultimate healers, technological wizards, total authorities." The reviewer noted that Hilfiker has "by his own confession . . . fallen into some of the very traps he

deplores," which range from clinical detachment and callousness to condescension. Nonetheless, Yardley added, "he has earned our esteem" for both his convictions and this "thoughtful" book. Concurring, Deaton judged *Healing the Wounds* "triumphant," while a critique in *Newsweek* deemed it an "exceptionally interesting memoir . . . extraordinary."

Hilfiker told *CA:* "My motivation has been to find in my work and in my writings the source of our fullest life."

BIOGRAPHICAL/CRITICAL SOURCES:

PERIODICALS

Newsweek, December 30, 1985.
New York Times Book Review, November 3, 1985.
Washington Post, September 18, 1985.

*   *   *

HISCOCK, Bruce 1940-

PERSONAL: Born December 4, 1940, in San Diego, CA; son of Roy Burnett (a doctor) and Clara L. (a homemaker; maiden name, Hauser) Hiscock; married Mary Rebecca Habel (divorced, 1972); married Nancy A. Duffy (divorced, 1988); children: (first marriage) Julia Anne, Frederick William. *Education:* University of Michigan, B.S., 1962; Cornell University, Ph.D., 1966.

ADDRESSES: Home—354 Ballou Rd., Porter Corners, NY 12859.

CAREER: Dow Chemical Co., Midland, MI, research chemist, 1966-68; Utica College of Syracuse University, Utica, NY, assistant professor of chemistry, 1968-71; Cornell University, Ithaca, NY, laboratory director and equine drug tester at Saratoga Harness Track, 1972-80; Saratoga Springs City Schools, Saratoga Springs, NY, substitute teacher, 1980-90.

MEMBER: Adirondack Mountain Club, Nature Conservancy, John Burroughs Association, Audubon Society.

WRITINGS:

SELF-ILLUSTRATED JUVENILES PUBLISHED BY ATHENEUM (NEW YORK CITY)

Tundra: The Arctic Land, 1986.
The Big Rock, 1988.
The Big Tree, 1991.
The Big Storm, 1993.
When Will It Snow?, 1995.

ILLUSTRATOR; PUBLISHED BY ATHENEUM

Lorus J. Milne and Margery Milne, *Nature's Great Carbon Cycle,* 1983.
Pat Hughey, *Scavengers and Decomposers,* 1984.

James Jesperson and Jane Fitz-Randolph, *Rams, Roms, and Robots,* 1984.

Jesperson and Fitz-Randolph, *From Quarks to Quasars,* 1987.

L. J. Milne and M. Milne, *Radioactivity,* 1989.

Jesperson and Fitz-Randolph, *Exploring the Invisible Universe,* 1990.

Gail Haines, *Sugar Is Sweet,* 1992.

Jesperson and Fitz-Randolph, *Mummies, Dinosaurs, and Moon Rocks,* 1995.

OTHER

Contributor to magazines, including *American Artist* and *American Kennel Gazette.*

WORK IN PROGRESS: A how-to-draw book and a picture book about water.

SIDELIGHTS: Bruce Hiscock told *CA:* "I was never the kind of kid who read stacks of books every week. I was a good reader, but much of my own reading focused on finding out about things, like how to build a boat, or what plants I could eat if I had to survive in the woods. Mostly I loved to be active and doing projects, drawing, building, investigating the outdoors, fishing with my grandfather, and playing sports. As a young child I was raised on a steady diet of wonderful picture books. As I grew older, my mother and step-father often read aloud, usually funny, well-written short stories by Saki or Damon Runyon.

"I spent hours drawing pictures while growing up, but I only wrote when assignments were made by the teacher. As a chemistry major in college, I treasured the few literature courses I could squeeze in among the many science classes, but my writing was still pretty ordinary. When I began writing papers and a Ph.D. thesis based on my own research, writing really became exciting for me. Many years would pass before that excitement would take the form of a children's book.

"I began my career in children's books in my mid-thirties following a divorce. It took ten years of hard work and tons of reading to bring my skills up to a professional level. I didn't realize it at the time, but I had one of the most important qualities a writer can have, self-discipline. I love work, and when I begin a project, I can't wait to sit down at the computer or drawing board each morning. Late in the day I may go for a hike, or paddle my kayak, or work on the house, or see friends, but not until I have put in enough hours to be either satisfied or frustrated with my efforts.

"My writing, whether fiction or non-fiction, includes several interlocking parts. First there must be a story line, something real to engage the reader, even in a science book. Then there is information, usually at different levels.

Weather is the primary theme of *The Big Storm,* geography the underlying theme. I try to throw in some humor, at least enough to bring on a smile. Then I strive to make illustrations that will reflect the writing: beautiful, clean, full of details, but not too fussy. I want kids to feel they can enter the pictures. I work hard to maintain the balance between all of these things. I am not easily satisfied. I spend about two years on a picture book. One of the lessons of the artistic life is accepting yourself and your good effort as enough right now, knowing that five years from now, with practice, your work will be better. On most days I am simply grateful to be able to do the work I love."

BIOGRAPHICAL/CRITICAL SOURCES:

PERIODICALS

Washington Post Book World, November 9, 1986.

*　　*　　*

HOBFOLL, Stevan E(arl) 1951-

PERSONAL: Born September 25, 1951, in Chicago, IL; son of Edward P. (a butcher) and Anita (an artist and musician; maiden name, Grace) Hobfoll; married Ivonne Heras (a psychologist), May 28, 1977; children: Ari, Sheera, Jonathan. *Education:* Attended University of Illinois at Urbana-Champaign, 1969-71, 1972-73; attended Kings College, London, 1971-72; University of South Florida, M.S., 1975, Ph.D., 1977.

ADDRESSES: Office—Kent State University, Kent, OH 44242.

CAREER: Ben Gurion University, Beersheba, Israel, senior lecturer, 1980-83; Tel Aviv University, Tel Aviv, Israel, fellow professor in psychology, 1983-87; Kent State University, Kent, OH, director of Applied Psychology Center, 1987—.

MEMBER: American Psychological Association, Israeli Psychological Association.

WRITINGS:

Stress, Social Support, and Women, Hemisphere Publishing (Franklinville, NY), 1986.

The Ecology of Stress, Hemisphere Publishing, 1988.

(With wife, Ivonne Hobfoll) *Work Won't Love You Back: The Dual Career Couple's Survival Guide,* W. H. Freeman (New York City), 1994.

Editor of *Anxiety, Stress and Coping: An International Journal.*

SIDELIGHTS: Stevan E. Hobfoll told *CA:* "I have always been struck by how important it is to focus my work on issues of social concern, to make one's work relevant and meaningful. Academia generally frowns on this 'wet' approach to research, but it is the only path I can justify for myself."

*　　*　　*

HODGES, Donald Clark 1923-

PERSONAL: Born October 22, 1923, in Fort Worth, TX; son of Count Hal and Elinor (Clark) Hodges; married Gabrielle Baptiste, November 14, 1949 (divorced, 1963); married Margaret Helen Deutsch, January 3, 1963 (divorced, 1980); married Deborah Elizabeth Hepburn, June 21, 1980; children: (first marriage) Justin Blake, Peter Robin; (second marriage) MacIntyre Hardy, John Oliver, Ernest Van Every; (third marriage) Sojourner Truth. *Education:* Attended Swarthmore College, 1942-43; New York University, B.A. (summa cum laude), 1947; Columbia University, M.A., 1948, Ph.D., 1954.

ADDRESSES: Home—9601 Miccosukee Rd., MLC 50, Tallahassee, FL 32308. *Office*—Department of Philosophy, Florida State University, Tallahassee, FL 32306.

CAREER: Hobart and William Smith Colleges, Geneva, NY, instructor in philosophy, 1949-52; University of Missouri—Columbia, instructor, 1952-54, assistant professor, 1954-57, associate professor of philosophy, 1957-63, chair of humanities department; University of South Florida, Tampa, professor of philosophy, 1963-64; Florida State University, Tallahassee, professor of philosophy, 1964—, head of department, 1964-69, director of Center for Graduate and Postgraduate Studies in Social Philosophy, 1967-71, director of Latin American and Caribbean studies, 1987-93, affiliate professor of political science, 1988—. Visiting professor at University of Nebraska, 1963, University of Hawaii, 1965-66, and National Autonomous University of Mexico, 1982. Associate member, Institute for Social Philosophy, Pennsylvania State University.

MEMBER: American Philosophical Association, Society for the Philosophical Study of Dialectical Materialism (secretary-treasurer, 1963-73), Society for the Philosophical Study of Marxism (secretary-treasurer, 1973-87), Radical Philosophy Association.

WRITINGS:

(Editor with Kuang T. Fann) *Readings in U.S. Imperialism,* Sargent, 1971.

(Editor with Abu Shanab) *National Liberation Fronts,* Morrow (New York City), 1973.

(Editor and translator) *Philosophy of the Urban Guerilla: The Revolutionary Writings of Abraham Guillen,* Morrow, 1973.

Socialist Humanism: The Outcome of Classical European Morality, Warren Green (St. Louis), 1974.

The Latin American Revolution, Morrow, 1974.

Argentina 1943-1976: The National Revolution and Resistance, University of New Mexico Press (Albuquerque), 1976, 2nd edition, revised and enlarged, published as *Argentina, 1943-1987: The National Revolution and Resistance,* 1988.

The Legacy of Che Guevara, Thames & Hudson (London), 1977.

(With Abraham Guillen) *Revaloracion de la guerrilla urbana,* El Caballito, 1977.

(With Ross Gandy) *El destino de la revolucion Mexicana,* El Caballito, 1977, 3rd edition, enlarged and updated, 1987.

Marxismo y revolucion en el siglo XX, El Caballito, 1978.

(With Gandy) *Mexico 1910-1976: Reform or Revolution?,* Zed Press (Burbank), 1979, 2nd edition, enlarged and updated, published as *Mexico 1910-1982: Reform or Revolution?,* 1983.

The Bureaucratization of Socialism, University of Massachusetts (Amherst), 1981.

(With Gandy) *Todos los revolucionarios van al infierno,* Costa-Amic, 1983, 2nd edition, 1987.

Intellectual Foundations of the Nicaraguan Revolution, University of Texas (Austin), 1987.

Argentina's "Dirty War": An Intellectual Biography, University of Texas, 1991.

Sandino's Communism: Spiritual Politics for the Twenty-First Century, University of Texas, 1992.

Mexican Anarchism after the Revolution, University of Texas, 1995.

Work represented in numerous anthologies. Contributor of articles to numerous periodicals, including *Journal of Philosophy, Modern Schoolman, Archives of Criminal Psychodynamics, Science and Society, Inquiry,* and *Il Politico.* Consulting editor, *Indian Sociological Bulletin,* 1963—; member of editorial board, *Philosophy and Phenomenological Research,* 1969—; co-editor, *Social Theory and Practice,* 1971—, and *Latin American Perspectives,* 1978—.

WORK IN PROGRESS: America's Strange New Order: Capitalist Image and Socialist Reality.

SIDELIGHTS: Although Donald Hodges was born in Texas, he grew up in Argentina. He returned to the United States to attend college. His works have been published in West Germany and Mexico.

*　　*　　*

HOFSOMMER, Don(ovan) L(owell) 1938-

PERSONAL: Born April 10, 1938, in Fort Dodge, IA; son of Vernie G. and Helma J. (Schager) Hofsommer; married Sandra L. Rusch (a professor), June 13, 1964; children:

Kathryn Anne, Kristine Beret, Knute Lars. *Education:* University of Northern Iowa, B.A., 1960, M.A., 1966; Oklahoma State University, Ph.D., 1973. *Religion:* Presbyterian.

ADDRESSES: Home—1803 13th Avenue S.E., St. Cloud, MN 56304. *Office*—Department of History, St. Cloud University, St. Cloud, MN 56301.

CAREER: High school history teacher in Fairfield, IA, 1961-65; Lea College, Albert Lea, MN, instructor in history, 1966-70; Wayland College, Plainview, TX, associate professor of history and head of department, 1973-81; Southern Pacific Transportation Co., San Francisco, CA, special representative and historian, 1981-85; Burlington Northern, Inc., Seattle, WA, historical consultant, 1985-87; Augustana College, Center for Western Studies, Sioux Falls, SD, executive director, 1987-89; St. Cloud State University, St. Cloud, MN, professor of public history and director of department, 1989—. Guest professor in history, University of Montana, 1986-87. *Military service:* Iowa National Guard, 1960-66.

MEMBER: Organization of American Historians, Western History Association, Railway and Locomotive Historical Association, National Railway Historical Association, Lexington Group, State Historical Society of Iowa, Texas Historical Society, Phi Alpha Theta, Phi Delta Kappa.

AWARDS, HONORS: Award from American Association for State and Local History, 1976, for *Prairie Oasis;* Muriel H. Wright Heritage Endowment Award from Oklahoma Historical Society, 1979; Railroad History Award, book category, Railway and Locomotive Historical Society, for *The Southern Pacific, 1901-1985,* 1988; excellence in teaching award, St. Cloud State University, 1992.

WRITINGS:

Prairie Oasis: The Railroads, Steamboats, and Resorts of Iowa's Spirit Lake Country, Waukon & Mississippi Press, 1975.

(Compiler) *Railroads of the Trans-Mississippi West: A Selected Bibliography of Books,* Llano Estacado Museum, 1976.

Katy Northwest: The Story of a Branch Line Railroad, Pruett (Boulder), 1976.

(Editor) *Railroads in Oklahoma,* Oklahoma Historical Society, 1977.

(Editor) *Railroads in the West,* Sunflower University Press (Manhattan, KS), 1978.

The Southern Pacific, 1901-1985, Texas A & M University Press (College Station), 1986.

(With R. W. Hidy, M. E. Hidy, and R. V. Scott) *The Great Northern Railway: A History,* Harvard Business School (Boston), 1988.

The Quanah Route: A History of the Quanah, Acme & Pacific Railway, Texas A & M University Press, 1991.

Grand Trunk Corporation: Canadian National Railways in the United States, 1971-1992, Michigan State University Press (East Lansing), 1995.

Contributor of more than thirty articles to history and transportation journals and to newspapers. Editor of *Lexington Newsletter;* member of editorial board of *Railroad History, Journals of the West,* and *Annals of Iowa.*

WORK IN PROGRESS: The "Louie": A History of the Minneapolis and St. Louis Railway.

*   *   *

HOGROGIAN, Nonny 1932-

PERSONAL: Name is pronounced "*nonn*-ee ho-*groh*-gee-an"; born May 7, 1932, in New York, NY; daughter of Mugerdich (a photoengraver) and Rachel (Ansoorian) Hogrogian; married David Kherdian (a poet), March 17, 1971. *Education:* Hunter College (now Hunter College of the City University of New York), B.A., 1953; graduate study, New School for Social Research, 1957.

CAREER: Designer and office worker for William Morrow and Co., New York City; illustrator for Thomas Y. Crowell Co., Holt, Rinehart and Winston, and Charles Scribner's Sons, all New York City; illustrator and writer of children's books.

AWARDS, HONORS: Caldecott awards, 1966, for *Always Room for One More,* and 1972, for *One Fine Day;* New York Times Outstanding Books citation, 1971, for *About Wise Men and Simpletons;* Caldecott Honor Award, 1977, for *The Contest.*

WRITINGS:

SELF-ILLUSTRATED

One Fine Day, Macmillan (New York City), 1971.
Apples, Macmillan, 1972.
Billy Goat and His Well-Fed Friends, Harper (New York City), 1972.
The Hermit and Harry and Me, Little, Brown (Boston), 1972.
Handmade Secret Hiding Places, Overlook Press (New York City), 1975.
Carrot Cake, Greenwillow (New York City), 1977.
The Cat Who Loved to Sing, Knopf (New York City), 1988.

RETELLER AND ILLUSTRATOR

Rooster Brother (Armenian folk tale), Macmillan, 1974.
The Contest (Armenian folk tale), Greenwillow, 1976.

Jacob Ludwig Karl Grimm, *Cinderella,* Greenwillow, 1981.

Grimm, *The Devil with the Three Golden Hairs,* Knopf, 1983.

Grimm, *The Glass Mountain,* Knopf, 1985.

Noah's Ark, Knopf, 1986.

ILLUSTRATOR

Nicolete Meredith, *King of the Kerry Fair,* Crowell (New York City), 1960.

Henrietta Bancroft, *Down Come the Leaves,* Crowell, 1961.

Sorche Nic Leodhas (pseudonym of Leclaire G. Alger), *Gaelic Ghosts,* Holt (New York City), 1963.

Leodhas, *Ghosts Go Haunting,* Holt, 1965.

Aileen L. Fisher, *Arbor Day,* Crowell, 1965.

Leodhas, *Always Room for One More,* Holt, 1965.

Robert Burns, *Hand in Hand We'll Go: Ten Poems,* Crowell, 1965.

Barbara Schiller, reteller, *The Kitchen Knight,* Holt, 1965.

William Shakespeare, *Poems,* Crowell, 1966.

Virginia A. Tashjian, reteller, *Once There Was and Was Not,* Little, Brown, 1966.

Mary O'Neill, *The White Palace,* Crowell, 1966.

Julie Whitney, *Bears Are Sleeping,* Scribner (New York City), 1967.

Beatrice Schenk De Regniers, *The Day Everybody Cried,* Viking (New York City), 1967.

Isaac Bashevis Singer, *The Fearsome Inn,* translated by Elizabeth Shub, Scribner, 1967.

The Renowned History of Little Red Riding Hood, Crowell, 1967.

The Thirteen Days of Yule, Crowell, 1968.

Christian Morgenstern, *The Three Sparrows and Other Nursery Rhymes,* translated by Max Knight, Scribner, 1968.

The Story of Prince Ivan, the Firebird, and the Gray Wolf, translated from the Russian by Thomas P. Whitney, Scribner, 1968.

Theodore Fontane, *Sir Ribbeck of Ribbeck of Havelland,* translated from the German by Shub, Macmillan, 1969.

Virginia Hamilton, *The Time-Ago Tales of Jahdu,* Macmillan, 1969.

Esther Hautzig, *In School: Learning in Four Languages,* Macmillan, 1969.

Virginia Haviland, reteller, *Favorite Fairy Tales Told in Greece,* Little, Brown, 1970.

James Stephens, *Deirdre,* Macmillan, 1970.

Vasilisa the Beautiful, translated from the Russian by T. P. Whitney, Macmillan, 1970.

Rachel Hogrogian, *The Armenian Cookbook,* Atheneum (New York City), 1971.

Grimm, *About Wise Men and Simpletons,* translated by Shub, Macmillan, 1971.

Cheli Duran Ryan, *Paz,* Macmillan, 1971.

Tashjian, *Three Apples Fell from Heaven,* Little, Brown, 1971.

Kherdian, *Bird in Suet* (broadside), Giligia (Aurora, OR), 1971.

Kherdian, *Of Husbands and Wives* (broadside), privately printed, 1971.

Kherdian, *Hey Nonny* (broadside), privately printed, 1972.

One I Love, Two I Love, and Other Loving Mother Goose Rhymes, Dutton (New York City), 1972.

Kherdian, *Looking over Hills,* Giligia, 1972.

Kherdian, compiler, *Visions of America: By the Poets of Our Time,* Macmillan, 1973.

Kherdian, *Poem for Nonny* (broadside), Phineas Press, 1973.

Kherdian, *Onions from New Hampshire* (broadside), privately printed, 1973.

Kherdian, *In the Tradition* (broadside), University of Connecticut (Storrs), 1974.

Kherdian, *16:IV:73* (broadside), Arts Action Press, 1975.

Kherdian, editor, *Poems Here and Now* (broadside), Greenwillow, 1976.

Kherdian, compiler, *The Dog Writes on the Window with His Nose, and Other Poems,* Four Winds (Bristol, FL), 1977.

Kherdian, *Country Cat, City Cat,* Four Winds, 1978.

Leila Ward, *I Am Eyes, Ni Macho,* Greenwillow, 1978.

Kherdian, reteller (published anonymously), *The Pearl: Hymn of the Robe of Glory,* Two Rivers (Aurora, Oregon), 1979.

Kherdian, *I Remember Root River,* Overlook Press, 1981.

Kherdian, *The Farm: Book Two,* Two Rivers, 1981.

Pigs Never See the Stars, translated by Kherdian, Two Rivers, 1982.

A. L. Staveley, *Where Is Bernardino?,* Two Rivers, 1982.

Kherdian, *Right Now* (juvenile), Knopf, 1983.

Count Bobrinskoy, *Peacock from Heaven,* Two Rivers, 1983.

Kherdian, *The Animal* (juvenile), Knopf, 1984.

Kherdian, *Root River Run,* Carolrhoda Books (Minneapolis), 1984.

Kherdian, *Threads of Light,* Two Rivers, 1985.

George MacDonald, *The Day Boy and the Night Girl,* Knopf, 1988.

Kherdian, *A Song for Uncle Harry* (juvenile), Philomel, 1989.

Kherdian, *The Cat's Midsummer Jamboree* (juvenile), Putnam (New York City), 1990.

Kherdian, *The Great Fishing Contest* (juvenile), Philomel, 1991.

Rumer Godden, *Candy Floss,* Philomel, 1991.

Feathers and Tails: Animal Fables from Around the World (juvenile), retold by Kherdian, Philomel, 1992.

Kherdian, *Juna's Journey* (juvenile), Philomel, 1993.

Kherdian, *By Myself* (juvenile), Holt, 1993.

Kherdian, *Asking the River* (juvenile), Orchard (New York City), 1993.

Kherdian, *Toad and the Green Princess* (juvenile), Philomel, 1994.

OTHER

(Author of introduction) Walter Lester, *Housebuilding for Children,* Overlook Press, 1977.

SIDELIGHTS: Nonny Hogrogian is a writer, illustrator, and designer of children's books whose critically acclaimed works have been included in many exhibitions by the American Institute of Graphic Arts.

Growing up in an artistic family, Hogrogian began painting at the age of three or four and went on to study art at Hunter College. After graduation she worked in book-jacket design at William Morrow and free-lanced for a time. In 1958 she became a production assistant in children's books at Crowell, where she illustrated her first children's book, *King of the Kerry Fair.* Later, as art director at Holt, she illustrated Leclaire G. Alger's *Gaelic Ghosts.* Her work with Alger, who writes under the name Sorche Nic Leodhas, produced the 1966 Caldecott Medal winner *Always Room for One More.* Hogrogian won another Caldecott for her self-illustrated book *One Fine Day* in 1972, and received a 1977 Caldecott Honor Award for *The Contest,* a retelling of an Armenian folk tale. In 1971 Hogrogian married the poet David Kherdian, and the two have since collaborated extensively.

Hogrogian has garnered praise for her attention to detail, her ability to capture the personalities of sundry characters, and her skill in matching drawings to text. A *Booklist* reviewer noted that in *The Day Boy and the Night Girl* Hogrogian "reflect[s] the author's vision, quietly and precisely delineating the scenes and characters as the story unfolds." Assessing *Candy Floss, Booklist* concluded that Hogrogian could "paint enchantment." Despite such kudos, Hogrogian stated in *Something about the Author Autobiography Series,* "I am always dissatisfied with my work, always left with the feeling that I must try harder the next time."

BIOGRAPHICAL/CRITICAL SOURCES:

BOOKS

Alderson, Brian W., *Children's Book Review,* Five Owls Press, 1973.

Children's Literature Review, Volume 2, Gale (Detroit), 1976.

Something about the Author Autobiography Series, Volume 1, Gale, 1986, pp. 129-40.

PERIODICALS

Booklist, September 15, 1975, p. 165; April 1, 1988, p. 1348; November 1, 1991.

Bulletin of the Center for Children's Books, April, 1977; January, 1978; June, 1988, p. 207; February, 1993, pp. 180-81.

Horn Book, August, 1966; August, 1972; December, 1976; August, 1983, pp. 431-32; March/April, 1987, p. 201.

Junior Literary Guild, September, 1978.

Kirkus Reviews, August 15, 1992.

Publishers Weekly, October 26, 1984, p. 105; October 11, 1985, p. 65; August 3, 1992.

School Library Journal, March, 1983, p. 162; February, 1986, p. 74; January, 1987, p. 67; April, 1988, p. 80; December, 1991; October, 1992.*

*   *   *

HONAN, William H(olmes) 1930-

PERSONAL: Born May 11, 1930, in New York, NY; son of William Francis (a surgeon) and Annette (a journalist; maiden name, Neudecker) Honan; married Nancy Burton (an attorney), June 22, 1975; children: Bradley, Daniel, Edith. *Education:* Oberlin College, B.A., 1952; University of Virginia, M.A., 1955. *Religion:* Presbyterian.

ADDRESSES: Office—New York Times, 229 West 43rd St., New York, NY 10036. *Agent*—Roslyn Targ Literary Agency, 105 West 13th St., New York, NY 10011.

CAREER: Villager (weekly newspaper), New York City, editor, 1957-60; *New Yorker,* New York City, assistant editor, 1960-64; free-lance writer for national magazines, 1964-68; *Newsweek,* New York City, associate editor, 1969; *New York Times Magazine,* New York City, assistant editor, 1969-70, travel editor, 1970-72; *Saturday Review,* San Francisco, CA, managing editor, 1972-73; *New York Times,* travel editor, 1973-74, arts and leisure editor, 1974-82, culture editor, 1982-88, chief cultural correspondent, 1988-93, national higher education correspondent, 1994-95. *Military service:* U.S. Army, 1956-57.

WRITINGS:

Greenwich Village Guide, Bryan Publications, 1959.

Another LaGuardia (pamphlet), Citizen Press, 1960.

Ted Kennedy: Profile of a Survivor, Quadrangle, 1972.

Visions of Infamy: The Untold Story of How Journalist Hector C. Bywater Devised the Plans that Led to Pearl Harbor, St. Martin's (New York City), 1991.

Fire When Ready, Gridley (collection of naval writings), St. Martin's, 1993.

Contributor of articles on subjects ranging from local and national politics to visual and performing arts to periodicals, including *New Republic, American Heritage, Esquire, Saturday Review,* and *Reader's Digest.*

WORK IN PROGRESS: A book about the discovery of the Quedlinburg treasures.

SIDELIGHTS: Reviewing William H. Honan's 1972 biography, *Ted Kennedy: Profile of a Survivor,* for the *New York Times Book Review,* Martin F. Nolan declared that the book "vibrates with authenticity." Focusing particularly on the senator in episodes of crisis, "Honan succeeds in capturing a sense of Kennedy the man, not the mythic figure," wrote the critic. "Honan seems to regard Kennedy as a politician, not a repository for metaphor." Although differing with the author over the likelihood of a serious Kennedy presidential candidacy, Nolan determined that "perceptive interviews"—gathered largely from Honan's cross-country tour with the senator in late 1971—distinguish this campaign biography.

BIOGRAPHICAL/CRITICAL SOURCES:

PERIODICALS

New York Times Book Review, June 4, 1972; July 9, 1972. *Saturday Review,* May 13, 1972.

*   *   *

HONEYMAN, Brenda
    See CLARKE, Brenda (Margaret Lilian)

*   *   *

HOROWITZ, Michael M. 1933-

PERSONAL: Born November 2, 1933, in New York, NY; married Sylvia Gordon Huntley, 1955; children: Andrew Jesse, Stephanie Ruth, Daniel Benjamin. *Education:* Oberlin College, B.A. (with honors), 1955; Columbia University, M.A., 1956, Ph.D., 1959.

ADDRESSES: Home—22 Crestmont Rd., Binghamton, NY 13905. *Office*—Department of Anthropology, State University of New York, Binghamton, NY 13901.

CAREER: Kent State University, Kent, OH, assistant professor of anthropology, 1959-61; State University of New York at Binghamton, assistant professor, 1961-63, associate professor, 1963-69, professor of anthropology, 1969—, chair of department of anthropology, 1962-66, 1970-72. Visiting lecturer, University of Michigan, summer, 1964; Fulbright professor, University of Bergen, 1966-67; visiting professor, Haifa University, 1984. Field

researcher in Martinique, summers, 1956 and 1962, and 1957-58; New York State Department of Education educational team representative to Africa and Middle East, 1965; director, Republic of Niger project under National Science Foundation funding, 1967-72; president, Institute for Development Anthropology, 1976-90. Consultant on regional planning and rural development to the World Bank, the United Nations, and the U.S. Government, 1973—.

MEMBER: American Anthropological Association (fellow), Society for Applied Anthropology (fellow), Society for Medical Anthropology, Phi Beta Kappa, Sigma Xi.

AWARDS, HONORS: Woodrow Wilson fellow, 1955-56; American Anthropological Association fellow in ethnobotany, 1956, 1957; Social Science Research Council grants, 1957-58, 1962; National Science Foundation grant, 1967-72; Carnegie Corporation grant, 1968-69; grants from Agency for International Development, World Bank, and United Nations Development Programme, 1975—.

WRITINGS:

NONFICTION

Morne-Paysan: Peasant Village in Martinique, Holt (New York City), 1967.
Peoples and Culture of the Caribbean, Doubleday (New York City), 1971.
Manga of Niger, three volumes, Human Relations Area Files Press (New Haven, CT), 1972.
(Coauthor) *Anthropology of Rural Development in the Sahel,* Institute for Development Anthropology (Binghamton, NY), 1977.
The Sociology of Pastoralism and African Livestock Development, Agency for International Development, 1979.
(Coauthor) *Social and Institutional Aspects of Oman,* Institute for Development Anthropology, 1982.
Niger: A Social and Institutional Profile, Institute for Development Anthropology, 1983.
(With Muneera Salem-Murdock) *The Senegal River Basin Monitoring Activity: A Phase-One Synthesis,* Institute for Development Anthropology, 1990.

EDITOR

(With Thomas M. Painter) *Anthropology and Rural Development in West Africa,* Westview (Boulder, CO), 1986.
(With Peter D. Little and A. Endre Nyerges) *Lands at Risk in the Third World: Local-Level Perspectives,* Westview, 1987.
(With Salem-Murdock and Monica Sella) *Anthropology and Development in North Africa and the Middle East,* Westview, 1990.

OTHER

Also coauthor of *Problems and Prospects for Development in the Yemen Arab Republic,* Institute for Development Anthropology. Contributor to books, including *Urbanization and Work in Modernizing Societies,* edited by A. J. Field, Glengary Press, 1967; *Perspectives on Nomadism,* edited by N. Dyson-Hudson, E. J. Brill (Long Island, NY), 1972; and author of introduction to *Arabs and Nubians in New Halfa: A Study of Settlement and Irrigation,* University of Utah Press (Salt Lake City, UT), 1989. Contributor of more than thirty articles and reviews to professional journals in the United States and Europe.

WORK IN PROGRESS: Research on relationships between poverty, powerlessness, and environmental decline in Africa.

SIDELIGHTS: Michael M. Horowitz once told *CA:* "All of my work—teaching, administration, writing, and research—seeks to contribute, in humane and compassionate ways, to solutions to problems of social injustice throughout the world."*

*   *   *

HOSTETLER, Marian   1932-

PERSONAL: Born February 9, 1932, in Ohio, daughter of M. Harry (a grocer; in insurance; deceased) and Esther (Hostetler) Hostetler. *Education:* Goshen College, B.A., 1954; Goshen Biblical Seminary, graduate study, 1957-58; Indiana University, M.S., 1973. *Religion:* Mennonite. *Avocational interests:* Painting, reading.

ADDRESSES: Home—1910 Morton, Elkhart, IN 46516.

CAREER: Mennonite Board of Missions, Elkhart, IN, editorial assistant, 1958-60, teacher in Algeria, 1960-70; Concord Community Schools, Elkhart, elementary teacher, 1971-88; teacher of English in Somalia, 1988-89, and Djibouti, 1990-93; part-time work in local library (semi-retired), 1994—.

WRITINGS:

PUBLISHED BY HERALD PRESS (SCOTTDALE, PA)

African Adventure, 1976.
Foundation Series Curriculum, Grade 3, Quarter 2, 1977.
Journey to Jerusalem, 1978.
Fear in Algeria, 1979.
Secret in the City, 1980.
(Translator) Pierre Widmer, *Some People Are Throwing You into Confusion,* 1984.
Mystery at the Mall, 1985.
They Loved Their Enemies, 1988.
We Knew Paul, 1992.
We Knew Jesus, 1994.

African Adventure has been translated into Finnish, French, Spanish, Portugese, and German. Other of Hostetler's titles have been translated into Finnish, French and German.

WORK IN PROGRESS: Red Sea Rendezvous and *What Is Islam? Who Are the Muslims?*

SIDELIGHTS: Marian Hostetler told *CA:* "The years I spent in North Africa were important in giving me the occasion to begin writing as well as giving me useful background for my writing. On a 1985-86 sabbatical from teaching, I had a nine-month writing assignment in West Africa (Cote d'Ivoire, Benin, and Burkina Faso) with the Mennonite Board of Missions, Centre de Publications Evangeliques, and Africa Inter-Mennonite Mission. More recently, five years spent teaching English as a foreign language in eastern Africa (Somalia and Djibouti) were helpful in broadening my interests and knowledge."

*   *   *

HOUTS, Peter S.   1933-

PERSONAL: Born March 17, 1933, in Great Neck, NY; son of Thomas Cushing (a banker) and Charlotte (Stevens) Houts; married Mary Davidoff (an educator), June 19, 1960; children: Thomas, David. *Education:* Antioch College, B.A., 1955; Carnegie Institute of Technology, graduate study, 1955-57; University of Michigan, Ph.D., 1963.

ADDRESSES: Office—Department of Behavioral Science, College of Medicine, Pennsylvania State University, Hershey, PA 17033.

CAREER: Goucher College, Towson, MD, assistant professor of psychology, 1963-65; Stanford University Medical School, Palo Alto, CA, postdoctoral fellow in psychiatry, 1965-67; Pennsylvania State University, College of Medicine, Hershey, associate professor of behavioral science, 1967-95, professor of behavioral science and medicine, 1995—. Member of board of directors, Music at Gretna, Mt. Gretna, PA, 1990—. *Military service:* U.S. Army, 1957, U.S. Army Reserves, 1957-63.

MEMBER: American Psychological Association, American Society of Clinical Oncology, American Association for Cancer Education, Association of University Professors.

WRITINGS:

NONFICTION

(With Robert A. Scott) *Goal Planning in Mental Health Rehabilitation,* Mental Health Materials Center (New York), 1973.

(With Scott and Leaser) *Goal Planning with the Mentally Retarded,* Mental Health Materials Center, 1973.

(With Thomas S. Leaman) *Case Studies in Primary Medical Care: Social, Psychological, and Ethical Issues in Family Practice,* Pennsylvania State University, 1983.

(With Paul D. Cleary and Teh-wei Hu) *The Three Mile Island Crisis: Psychological, Social, and Economic Impacts on the Surrounding Population,* Pennsylvania State University Press (University Park, PA), 1988.

EDITOR

(With Michael Serber) *After the Turn On, What?: Learning Perspectives on Humanistic Groups,* Research Press (Champaign, IL), 1972.

American College of Physicians Home Care Guide for Cancer: How to Care for Family and Friends at Home, American College of Physicians (Philadelphia, PA), 1994.

Editor with other members of the Pennsylvania Department of Welfare staff of *The Pennsylvania Model Individualized Written Program Plan for Vocational Rehabilitation Facilities,* 1979; member of editorial board, *American Journal of Cancer Education,* 1989—,

BIOGRAPHICAL/CRITICAL SOURCES:

PERIODICALS

Times Literary Supplement, March 17-23, 1989, p. 272.

*   *   *

HUNTER, J(ames) Paul 1934-

PERSONAL: Born June 29, 1934, in Jamestown, NY; son of Paul Wesley (a clergyman) and Florence (Walmer) Hunter; married Kathryn Montgomery, July 1, 1971; children: Debra, Lisa, Paul III, Ellen, Anne. *Education:* Indiana Central College, A.B., 1955; Miami University, Oxford, OH, M.A., 1957; Rice University, Ph.D., 1963.

ADDRESSES: Home—1218 East Madison Pk., Chicago, IL 60615. *Office*—404 Wieboldt Hall, University of Chicago, Chicago, IL 60637.

CAREER: Instructor in English at University of Florida, Gainesville, 1957-59, and Williams College, Williamstown, MA, 1962-64; University of California, Riverside, assistant professor of English, 1964-66; Emory University, Atlanta, GA, associate professor, 1966-68, professor of English, 1968-80, department chairman, 1973-79; University of Rochester, Rochester, NY, dean of arts and sciences, 1981-86; University of Chicago, Chicago, IL, professor of English, 1987—, Chester D. Tripp Professor in the Humanities, 1990—.

MEMBER: Modern Language Association of America, American Society of Eighteenth-Century Studies (second vice-president, 1994).

AWARDS, HONORS: Guggenheim fellow, 1976-77; National Endowment for the Humanities fellow, 1986; National Humanities Center fellow, 1986; Lewis Gottschalk Prize, American Society of Eighteenth-Century Studies, for *Before Novels: The Cultural Contexts of Eighteenth-Century English Fiction,* 1991.

WRITINGS:

The Reluctant Pilgrim: Defoe's Emblematic Method and Quest for Form in "Robinson Crusoe," Johns Hopkins University Press (Baltimore), 1966.

Occasional Form: Henry Fielding and the Chains of Circumstance, Johns Hopkins University Press, 1975.

(With Martin C. Battestin) *Henry Fielding in His Time and Ours,* William Andrews Clark Memorial Library, University of California, Los Angeles, 1987.

Before Novels: The Cultural Contexts of Eighteenth-Century English Fiction, Norton (New York City), 1990.

EDITOR

Daniel Defoe, *Moll Flanders* (critical edition), Crowell (New York City), 1970.

(With Carl E. Bain & Jerome Beaty) *The Norton Introduction to Literature,* Norton, 1973, 6th edition, 1995.

The Norton Introduction to Poetry, Norton, 1973, 6th edition, 1995.

(With J. Douglas Canfield) *Rhetorics of Order/Ordering Rhetorics in English Neoclassical Literature,* University of Delaware Press (Newark), 1989.

(With Jerome Beaty) *New Worlds of Literature,* Norton, 1989, 2nd edition published as *New Worlds of Literature: Writings from America's Many Cultures,* 1994.

Daniel Defoe, *Moll Flanders,* Bedford, 1995.

Also editor of *The Plays of Edward Moore,* 1982. Contributor to *Critical Inquiry, Modern Philology, Eighteenth Century Studies, Philological Quarterly, Review of English Studies, Journal of English and Germanic Philology, Novel,* and *Scriblerian.*

WORK IN PROGRESS: A book on heroic couplets and their cultural contexts.

BIOGRAPHICAL/CRITICAL SOURCES:

PERIODICALS

Review of English Studies, February, 1993, p. 108.

HUXLEY, Anthony J(ulian) 1920-1992

PERSONAL: Born December 2, 1920, in Oxford, England; died December 26, 1992, in London, England; son of Julian (a biologist and writer) and Marie Juliette (Baillot) Huxley; married; wife's name Alyson; children: four daughters. *Education:* Attended Dauntsey's School, 1934-39; Trinity College, Cambridge, B.A., 1941, M.A., 1954. *Avocational interests:* Photography, gardening, looking for wild flowers, and conducting botanical tours.

CAREER: Royal Air Force, civilian scientific officer in operational research, 1941-47; British Overseas Airways Corp., economic researcher, 1947-49; *Amateur Gardening,* London, England, assistant editor, 1949-67, editor, 1967-71; free-lance writer, photographer, lecturer, and tour leader, 1971-92.

MEMBER: International Dendrology Society (chairman, 1979-82), Royal Horticultural Society (member of council, beginning 1979), Horticultural Club (London; president, 1975).

AWARDS, HONORS: Veith Memorial Medal, 1978, and Victoria Medal of Honour, 1980, both from Royal Horticultural Society.

WRITINGS:

Cacti and Succulents, Collingridge, 1953.
House Plants, Collingridge, 1954, revised edition, 1961.
Indoor Plants, edited by A. G. L. Hellyer, Collingridge, 1957.
Treasures of the Garden, Hanover House, 1959 (published in England as *Beauty in the Garden,* Rathbone Books, 1960).
Wild Flowers of the Countryside, illustrations by C. A. Tunnicliffe, Blandford, 1962.
Garden Terms Simplified, Collingridge, 1962, 2nd edition, David & Charles, 1971.
Flowers in Greece: An Outline of the Flora, Royal Horticultural Society, 1963, revised edition, 1972.
(With Oleg Polunin) *Flowers of the Mediterranean,* Chatto & Windus, 1965, Houghton (Boston, MA), 1966, revised edition, 1987.
Mountain Flowers in Colour, illustrations by Daphne Barry and Mary Grierson, Blandford, 1967, revised edition, 1986, published as *Mountain Flowers in Color,* Macmillan (New York City), 1968.
House Plants, Cacti and Succulents, Hamlyn, 1972.
Plant and Planet, Allen Lane, 1974, Viking (New York City), 1975, revised edition, Penguin (New York City), 1987.
(Adapter) Maggie Baylis, *House Plants for the Purple Thumb,* illustrations by E. D. Bills and the author, new edition, Pitman (Marshfield, MA), 1976.

(Adapter with Helena Radecka) John E. Bryan and Coralie Castle, *The Edible Ornamental Garden,* illustrations by Sara Raffetto, new edition, Pitman, 1976.
(With William Taylor) *Flowers of Greece and the Aegean,* Chatto & Windus, 1977.
(With Alyson Huxley) *Huxley's House of Plants,* Paddington, 1978.
An Illustrated History of Gardening, Paddington, 1978, Macmillan in association with Royal Horticultural Society, 1983.
(With Paul Davies and Jenne Davies) *Wild Orchids of Britain and Europe,* Chatto & Windus, 1983.
(With David Black) *Green Inheritance: The World Wildlife Fund Book of Plants,* Collins Harvill, 1984.

Also author of *The Painted Garden,* 1988.

EDITOR

(And translator) Marcel Belvianes, *Exotic Plants of the World,* Doubleday (New York City), 1957.
(And translator) Aloys Duperre, *Orchids of Europe,* Blandford, 1961.
(And contributor) *Standard Encyclopedia of the World's Mountains,* Putnam (New York City), 1962.
(And contributor) *Standard Encyclopedia of the World's Oceans and Islands,* Putnam, 1962.
(With R. Kay Gresswell and contributor) *Standard Encyclopedia of the World's Rivers and Lakes,* Weidenfeld & Nicolson, 1965, Putnam, 1966.
Garden Annuals and Bulbs in Color (also see below), Macmillan, 1971.
Alan R. Toogood, *Garden Perennials and Water Plants in Colour,* illustrations by Verner Hancke, Blandford, 1971, published as *Garden Perennials and Water Plants* (also see below), Macmillan, 1972.
Garden Flowers in Color, Macmillan, 1971, Volume I: *Garden Annuals and Bulbs in Color,* Volume II: *Garden Perennials and Water Plants.*
Denis Hardwicke and Toogood, *Evergreen Garden Trees and Shrubs in Colour,* illustrations by Hancke, Macmillan, 1973.
Hardwicke, *Deciduous Garden Trees and Shrubs in Colour,* Macmillan, 1973.
The Financial Times Book of Garden Design, David & Charles (North Pomfret, VT), 1975.
Eigel Kiaer and Hans Petersen, *Garden Planning and Planting,* illustrations by Hancke, Blandford, 1976.
The Encyclopedia of the Plant Kingdom, Hamlyn, 1977.
Success with House Plants, Reader's Digest Press (New York City), 1979.
The Penguin Dictionary of Gardening, Lane, 1981.
The Penguin Encyclopedia of Gardening, illustrations by Vana Haggerty, Allen Lane, 1981.
The Macmillan World Guide to House Plants, Macmillan, 1983.

Also editor of *Amateur Gardening Annual* for 1970 and 1971.

OTHER

Regular contributor to *Country Life* and *The Garden.*

SIDELIGHTS: Anthony J. Huxley comes from a family of distinguished scientists and writers. His great-grandfather, biologist and philosopher Thomas Henry Huxley, was one of the earliest and strongest proponents of Darwinism and the man who coined the term agnostic to reflect a position of suspended belief with respect to God. His uncle Aldous Huxley wrote the dystopian novel *Brave New World,* as well as a number of other widely read books. Huxley's father, Julian, was a biologist who earned the distinction of being Britain's "public scientist No. 1" because he made scientific information widely accessible through lectures, radio broadcasts, magazine articles, and books.

Anthony Huxley became well known in his own right as a significant contributor of published work on horticulture and botany. Although exposed to the natural world through his father, who was at one time secretary of the London Zoo, Anthony Huxley chose to study English literature at Trinity College of Cambridge. In 1949 he began an association with the periodical *Amateur Gardening* which lasted for more than twenty years. In 1971 he retired from his position as editor of the magazine and turned to writing full time. An avid traveler, Huxley occasionally used his experiences in such places as the Mediterranean to inform his work. The numerous books that he wrote and edited focus on a wide variety of plants—both those raised domestically and those suited to a natural habitat.

OBITUARIES:

PERIODICALS

Times (London), December 31, 1992, p. 19.*

*   *   *

HYINK, Bernard L(ynn) 1913-

PERSONAL: Born April 5, 1913, in Hawarden, IA; son of Bernard John and Inez (Lynn) Hyink; married June Rose Hinckley, August 7, 1938; children: Shirley June, Barbara Jean. *Education:* Antioch College, student, 1929-30; University of Redlands, A.B., 1935; University of California, Berkeley, A.M., 1936; University of Southern California, Ph.D., 1943. *Politics:* Republican.

ADDRESSES: Home—1206 East Melody Lane, Fullerton, CA 92631. *Office*—California State University, Fullerton, CA 92631.

CAREER: University of Redlands, Redlands, CA, assistant to president, 1937-41, professor of political science, 1942-48; U.S. Civil Service Commission, Washington, DC, assistant civil service examiner, 1942; National Institute for Public Affairs, Washington, DC, education counselor, 1949; University of Southern California, Los Angeles, dean of students, 1949-56, professor of political science, 1957-60; Orange Country State College (now California State University, Fullerton), professor of political science and vice-president of academic affairs, 1960-70; California State University, Sacramento, president, 1970-72; California State University, Fullerton, professor of political science, 1972—. Visiting professor, University of Tehran, 1956. Consultant to California State Constitutional Revision Commission, California Fulbright Commission, 1976—, and industry.

MEMBER: American Political Science Association, Western Political Science Association (past president), Phi Beta Kappa, Pi Kappa Delta, Pi Sigma Alpha, Kappa Sigma Sigma.

AWARDS, HONORS: D.Hum., University of Redlands.

WRITINGS:

American and California Government (monograph), Lucas Brothers (Columbia, MO), 1958.
(With Seyom Brown and Ernest W. Thacker) *Politics and Government in California,* Crowell (New York City), 1959, 12th edition, Harper & Row (New York City), 1989.
(With John Gaines) *Government in the Golden State,* Crowell, 1968.
(Co-author) *Issues in California Politics and Government,* Crowell, 1977.

Contributor to books, including *The Junior College,* edited by L. L. Medsker, McGraw (New York City), 1960. Also contributor to Collier's *Encyclopedia Yearbook,* and to professional publications.*

I-J

ISHIGURO, Kazuo 1954-

PERSONAL: Born November 8, 1954, in Nagasaki, Japan; resident of Great Britain since 1960; son of Shizuo (a scientist) and Shizuko (a homemaker; maiden name, Michida) Ishiguro; married Lorna Anne MacDougall, May 9, 1986. *Education:* University of Kent, B.A. (with honors), 1978; University of East Anglia, M.A. in Creative Writing, 1980.

ADDRESSES: Agent—Rogers, Coleridge & White, 20 Powis Mews, London W11 1JN, England

CAREER: Grouse beater for Queen Mother at Balmoral Castle, Aberdeen, Scotland, 1973; Renfrew Social Works Department, Renfrew, Scotland, community worker, 1976; West London Cyrenians Ltd., London, England, residential social worker, 1979-80, resettlement worker, 1981-83; writer 1983—.

AWARDS, HONORS: Winifred Holtby Award from Royal Society of Literature, 1983, for *A Pale View of Hills;* Whitbread Book of the Year Award, 1986, for *An Artist of the Floating World;* Booker Prize, 1989, for *The Remains of the Day;* Premio Scanno for Literature (Italy), 1995; Order of the British Empire (O.B.E.) for services to literature, 1995; honorary Litt.D., University of Kent, 1990, University of East Anglia, 1995.

WRITINGS:

A Pale View of Hills, Putnam (New York City), 1982.
An Artist of the Floating World, Putnam, 1986.
The Remains of the Day, Knopf (New York City), 1989.
The Unconsoled, Knopf, 1995.

Also contributor to *Introduction 7: Stories by New Writers,* Faber (London), 1981. Author of television film scripts, including *A Profile of Arthur J. Mason,* broadcast in 1984, and *The Gourmet,* broadcast in 1986. Contributor to literary journals, including *London Review of Books, Firebird, Bananas,* and *Harpers and Queen.*

ADAPTATIONS: The Remains of the Day was adapted into a feature film starring Anthony Hopkins and Emma Thompson by Merchant Ivory Productions in 1993.

WORK IN PROGRESS: A novel and a screenplay.

SIDELIGHTS: After three brief but highly respected novels, Japanese-born Kazuo Ishiguro emerged as one of the foremost British writers of his generation. Ishiguro's novels commonly deal with issues of memory, self-deception, and codes of etiquette, leading his characters to a re-evaluation or realization about the relative success or failure of their lives. His capture of the prestigious Booker Prize for his third novel, *The Remains of the Day,* confirms the critical acclaim his work has garnered.

Ishiguro's highly acclaimed first novel, *A Pale View of Hills,* is narrated by Etsuko, a middle-aged Japanese woman living in England. The suicide of her daughter, Keiko, awakens somber memories of the summer in the 1950s in war-ravaged Nagasaki when the child was born. Etsuko's thoughts and dreams turn particularly to Sachiko, a war widow whose unfortunate relationship with an American lover traumatizes her already troubled daughter, Mariko. Etsuko, too, will eventually embrace the West, and leave her Japanese husband to marry an English journalist. "Etsuko's memories, though they focus on her neighbor's sorrows and follies, clearly refer to herself as well," wrote Edith Milton in the *New York Times Book Review.* "The lives of the two women run parallel, and Etsuko, like Sachiko, has raised a deeply disturbed daughter; like her, she has turned away from the strangling role of traditional Japanese housewife toward the West, where she has discovered freedom of a sort, but also an odd lack of depth, commitment and continuity." Surrounded that summer by a new order that has shattered ancient ways, the two women chose the Western path of self-interest, compromising—to varying degrees—their delicate daughters. "In Etsuko's present life as much as in her past, she is circled by a chain of death which has its beginning in the war," suggested *New Statesman* reviewer James Campbell.

Reviewing *A Pale View of Hills* in the *Spectator,* Francis King found the novel "typically Japanese in its compression, its reticence and in its exclusion of all details not absolutely essential to its theme." While some reviewers agreed with *Times Literary Supplement* writer Paul Bailey—who stated "that at certain points I could have done with something as crude as a fact"—many felt that Ishiguro's delicate layering of themes and images grants the narrative great evocative power. "[It] is a beautiful and dense novel, gliding from level to level of consciousness," remarked Jonathan Spence, in *New Society.* "Ishiguro develops [his themes] with remarkable insight and skill," concurred Rosemary Roberts in the *Los Angeles Times Book Review.* "They are described in controlled prose that more often hints than explains or tells. The effect evokes mystery and an aura of menace." And King deemed the novel "a memorable and moving work, its elements of past and present, of Japan and England held together by a shimmering, all but invisible net of images linked to each other by filaments at once tenuous and immensely strong."

While Ishiguro's novel depicts the incineration of a culture and the disjointed lives of the displaced, it is not without optimism. Critics saw in the war survivors' tenacious struggle to resurrect some sort of life, however alien, great hope and human courage. "Sachiko and Etsuko become minor figures in a greater pattern of betrayal, infanticide and survival played out against the background of Nagasaki, itself the absolute emblem of our genius for destruction," Milton continued. "In this book, where what is stated is often less important than what is left unsaid, those blanked-out days around the bomb's explosion become the paradigm of modern life. They are the ultimate qualities which the novel celebrates: the brilliance of our negative invention, and our infinite talent for living beyond annihilation as if we had forgotten it." Reiterated Roberts: "There is nobility in determination to press on with life even against daunting odds. Ishiguro has brilliantly captured this phoenixlike spirit; high praise to him."

In *An Artist of the Floating World,* Ishiguro again explores Japan in transition. Set in a provincial Japanese town during 1949 and 1950, the story revolves around Masuji Ono, a painter who worked as an official artist and propagandist for the imperialist regime that propelled Japan into World War II. Knowing that his former ideals were errant does little to help Ono adjust to the bewildering Western-

ization that is going on all around him; nor does it quell his longings for the past, with its fervent patriotism, professional triumphs, and deep comradeship. "Ishiguro's insights . . . are finely balanced," wrote Anne Chisholm in the *Times Literary Supplement.* "He shows how the old Japanese virtues of veneration for the Sensei (the teacher), or loyalty to the group, could be distorted and exploited; he allows deep reservations to surface about the wholesale Americanization of Japan in the aftermath of humiliation and defeat. Without asking us to condone Ono's or Japan's terrible mistakes, he suggests with sympathy some reasons why the mistakes were made."

Admiring how "Ishiguro unravels the old man's thoughts and feelings with exceptional delicacy," Chisholm determined that the story "is not only pleasurable to read but instructive, without being in the least didactic." "The old man's longings for his past become a universal lament for lost worlds," added the critic, who judged *An Artist of the Floating World* a "fine new novel."

Of the first two novels, *A Pale View of Hills* and *An Artist of the Floating World,* Christopher Hitchens noted in the *Nation,* their form of "unmediated retrospective monologue." He cited their similar themes as well: "Each narrator has lived according to strict codes of etiquette and order; the ethos of actively and passively 'knowing one's place,' and adhering to protocol and precedent." Those same forms and themes shape the third novel, *The Remains of the Day,* which presents the narrative of Stevens, English butler to Lord Darlington of Darlington Hall. After more than thirty years of faithful service to the Lord, Stevens now finds himself in the employ of Mr. Farraday, a congenial American who has purchased the estate and kept Stevens on as part of the colorful trappings. Farraday urges Stevens to take a motoring holiday through Cornwall. Concurrently, Stevens has received a letter from Miss Kenton (now Mrs. Benn), the exemplary housekeeper who had left Darlington Hall some twenty years before. Mrs. Benn's letter hints at unhappiness in her marriage and suggests a willingness to return to service at Darlington. Short of staff in the downsized estate, the ever-dutiful Stevens justifies his absence with the utilitarian purpose of hiring the former housekeeper.

As the journey proceeds and Stevens rambles about in Farraday's old Ford (taking eight days to go about 100 miles), he reflects upon the people he meets, the countryside and, tellingly and ironically, his own life. At one point, Stevens proclaims the English landscape the most satisfying in the world precisely because of its lack of obvious drama or spectacle. This fondness to dampen the dramatic and spectacular and to fit in easily does, in fact, control his life. It is the reason he so thoroughly inhabits his role as butler.

Stevens thinks continually of those who were truly great—in his case, great butlers. For Stevens and his coterie of fellow butlers, professional prestige is firmly correlated with the moral worth of one's employer. Only through service to a great personage can one hope to make a contribution toward a better world. An unreliable witness to his own life, Stevens reveals more than he perceives. He ruminates with pride on the great, bustling days of Darlington Hall, when Lord Darlington had invited world movers and shakers to confer upon the Versailles Treaty. Darlington wanted better conditions for Germany, believing the other European powers had treated the defeated nation vengefully for a war in which they had shared the guilt. But the Lord proved a woeful amateur in the political arena of the 1930s, duped by Von Ribbentrop into making himself a useful tool and a rallying symbol for Nazi sympathizers.

As Stevens returns to the same memories again and again, the fog of self-deception lifts. One motoring mishap after another—a flat tire, overheated radiator—affords Stevens the time and perspective he has never had. Meeting the ordinary people who actually suffered during the war, Stevens has difficulty admitting to his long service at Darlington. He begins to doubt the Lord's—and his own—judgment.

The quiet tragedies of revelation continue as Stevens comes to realize what the perceptive reader has known all along: his proposed rendezvous with Mrs. Benn has more than a utilitarian purpose. She comprises, in fact, his last chance to seize happiness in life. Writing for the London *Observer,* Salman Rushdie noted: "Just below the understatement of the novel's surface is a turbulence as immense as it is slow." Mrs. Benn decides to return to her unhappy marriage, wondering poignantly what it might have been like had she and Stevens made a connection years ago when life was full of possibilities. On the pier at Weymouth, Stevens confesses to a stranger: "I can't even say that I made my own mistakes. . . . What dignity is there in that?"

The Remains of the Day met with highly favorable critical response. Galen Strawson, for example, praised the novel in the *Times Literary Supplement:* "*The Remains of the Day* is as strong as it is delicate, a very finely nuanced and at times humorous study of repression. . . . It is a strikingly original book, and beautifully made. . . . Stevens' . . . language creates a context which allows Kazuo Ishiguro to put a massive charge of pathos into a single unremarkable phrase." In the *Chicago Tribune,* Joseph Coates described the novel as "an ineffably sad and beautiful piece of work—a tragedy in the form of a comedy of manners." He continued: "Rarely has the device of an unreliable narrator worked such character revelation as it does here." Mark Kamine cited Ishiguro's technique

in the *New Leader:* "Usually the butler's feelings are hidden in painfully correct periphrasis, or refracted in dialogue spoken by other characters. . . . Few writers dare to say so little of what they mean as Ishiguro."

While many reviews of *The Remains of the Day* were favorable, this was not universally so. Writing for the *New Statesman,* Geoff Dyer wondered "if the whole idea of irony as a *narrative strategy* hasn't lost its usefulness." Dyer worried that Stevens' voice had been "*coaxed* in the interests of the larger ironic scheme of the novel." Comparing the novelist to Henry James, however, Hermione Lee defended Ishiguro's style in *New Republic:* "To accuse Ishiguro of costive, elegant minimalism is to miss the deep sadness, the boundless melancholy that opens out, like the 'deserts of vast eternity' his characters are reluctantly contemplating, under the immaculate surface."

In a profile by Susan Chira for the *New York Times Book Review,* Ishiguro stated: "What I'm interested in is not the actual fact that my characters have done things they later regret. . . . I'm interested in how they come to terms with it." Ishiguro continued: "On the one hand there is a need for honesty, on the other hand a need to deceive themselves—to preserve a sense of dignity, some sort of self-respect. What I want to suggest is that some sort of dignity and self-respect does come from that sort of honesty."

Ishiguro's fourth novel, *The Unconsoled,* was published six years after he won the Booker Prize for *Remains of the Day.* Winning the Booker Prize allowed Ishiguro "to break through the veil of expectations and constraints that both his success, and his readers' stubborn determination to take him absolutely literally, imposed," and "to try something wild and frightening that would prevent him from ever being taken as a realist again," according to Pico Iyer in a *Times Literary Supplement* review. Iyer noted that Ishiguro achieved this goal in *The Unconsoled:* "Even though every sentence and theme is recognizably [Ishiguro's], he has written a book that passes on the bewilderment it seeks to portray."

The Unconsoled details the journey of Ryder, a famous pianist, who finds himself in an unfamiliar town for a concert he does not remember arranging. Throughout the journey, Ryder "finds himself led, like a silent witness, through a never-ending sequence of unexplained mysteries, old wounds and vicious rivalries, none of which he (or we) can begin to understand. . . . Old friends from the past suddenly appear, and cause has no relation to effect. Time and space are weirdly exploded, so that the first night in town alone takes up 148 pages," wrote Iyer. "And, as in a dream, everything is so without context that one does not know whether to laugh or to weep."

Similar to the themes of his earlier books, Ishiguro again deals with codes of etiquette and order. "The book is in large part about assumptions and presumptions, about being put out and put upon—and about putting on a face of obliging acquiescence," stated Iyer. In one scene a hotel manager selfishly intent on making the pianist as comfortable as possible compels Ryder to change rooms, which in the end is an imposition rather than a kindness. *The Unconsoled* "present[s] us with . . . a whole society that wonders if it has missed the point and missed the boat, and comes to see that perhaps, at some critical juncture, it was too timid, too accommodating, too dutiful to stand up for its real needs," added Iyer. He concluded: "*The Unconsoled* is a humane and grieving book, as well as one of the strangest novels in memory."

BIOGRAPHICAL/CRITICAL SOURCES:

BOOKS

Contemporary Literary Criticism, Volume 27, Gale, 1984.

PERIODICALS

Chicago Tribune, October 1, 1989, p. 5.
Encounter, June-July, 1982.
Los Angeles Times, June 20, 1986.
Los Angeles Times Book Review, August 8, 1982; October 1, 1989; April 1, 1990; October 14, 1990.
Nation, June 11, 1990, p. 81.
New Leader, November 13, 1989, p. 21-22.
New Republic, January 22, 1990.
New Society, May 13, 1982.
New Statesman, February 19, 1982; May 26, 1989.
New Yorker, April 19, 1982.
New York Times Book Review, May 9, 1982; June 8, 1986; October 8, 1989.
Observer (London), May 21, 1989, p.53.
Publishers Weekly, July 3, 1995.
Spectator, February 27, 1982.
Times (London), February 18, 1982; February 28, 1983.
Times Literary Supplement, February 19, 1982; February 14, 1986; May 19, 1989; April 28, 1995.*

—Sketch by Gary Corseri

* * *

JANECZKO, Paul B(ryan) 1945-
(J. N. Fox; P. Wolny)

PERSONAL: Born July 27, 1945, in Passaic, NJ; son of Frank John and Verna (Smolak) Janeczko; married Nadine Edris; children: Emma. *Education:* St. Francis College, Biddeford, ME, A.B., 1967; John Carroll University, M.A., 1970. *Avocational interests:* Swimming, cooking vegetarian meals, biking, working with wood.

ADDRESSES: Home—Rural Route 1, Box 260, Marshall Pond Rd., Hebron, ME 04238.

CAREER: Poet and anthologist. High school English teacher in Parma, OH, 1968-72, and Topsfield, MA, 1972-77; Gray-New Gloucester High School, Gray, ME, teacher of language arts, 1977-90; visiting writer, 1990—.

MEMBER: National Council of Teachers of English, Educators for Social Responsibility, New England Association of Teachers of English, Maine Teachers of Language Arts, Maine Freeze Committee.

AWARDS, HONORS: Books for the Teen Age citations, New York Public Library, 1980 and 1981, for *Postcard Poems,* and 1982, for *Don't Forget to Fly: A Cycle of Modern Poems;* Best Book citations, *School Library Journal,* 1981, for *Don't Forget to Fly,* and 1983, for *Poetspeak: In Their Work, about Their Work;* Best Young Adult Book of the Year citations, American Library Association, 1981, for *Don't Forget to Fly,* 1983, for *Poetspeak,* 1984, for *Strings: A Gathering of Family Poems,* 1985, for *Pocket Poems: Selected for a Journey,* and 1987, for *Going Over to Your Place: Poems for Each Other;* English-Speaking Union Books-across-the-Sea Ambassador of Honor Book award, 1984, for *Poetspeak;* Children's Book of the Year citation, Child Study Association of America, 1985, for *Poetspeak.*

WRITINGS:

Loads of Codes and Secret Ciphers (nonfiction), Simon & Schuster (New York City), 1981.
Bridges to Cross (fiction), Macmillan (New York City), 1986.
Brickyard Summer (poetry), illustrations by Ken Rush, Orchard Books (New York City), 1989.
Stardust Hotel (children's poetry), illustrations by Dorothy Leech, Orchard Books, 1993.
(Under pseudonym J. N. Fox) *Young Indiana Jones and the Pirates' Loot,* Random House (New York City), 1994.
(Editor) *Wherever Home Begins: 100 Contemporary Poems,* Orchard Books, 1995.

POETRY ANTHOLOGIES

The Crystal Image, Dell (New York City), 1977.
Postcard Poems, Bradbury (New York City), 1979.
Don't Forget to Fly: A Cycle of Modern Poems, Bradbury, 1981.
Poetspeak: In Their Work, about Their Work, Bradbury, 1983.
Strings: A Gathering of Family Poems, Bradbury, 1984.
Pocket Poems: Selected for a Journey, Bradbury, 1985.
Going Over to Your Place: Poems for Each Other, Bradbury, 1987.
This Delicious Day: 65 Poems, Orchard Books, 1987.

The Music of What Happens: Poems That Tell Stories, Orchard Books, 1988.

The Place My Words Are Looking For: What Poets Say about and through Their Work, Bradbury, 1990.

Preposterous: Poems of Youth, Orchard Books, 1991.

Looking for Your Name: A Collection of Contemporary Poems, Orchard Books, 1993.

Poetry from A to Z: A Guide for Young Writers, Bradbury, 1994.

OTHER

Also contributor of articles to books, including *Censorship: A Guide for Teachers, Librarians, and Others Concerned with Intellectual Freedom,* edited by Lou Willett Stanek, Dell, 1976; *Young Adult Literature in the Seventies,* edited by Jana Varlejs, Scarecrow (Metuchen, NJ), 1978; and *Children's Literature Review,* Volume 3, Gale (Detroit, MI), 1978.

Author of "Back Pages," a review column in *Leaflet,* 1973-76. Contributor of numerous articles, stories, poems (sometimes under pseudonym P. Wolny), and reviews to newspapers, professional and popular magazines, including *Armchair Detective, New Hampshire Profiles, Modern Haiku, Dragonfly, Friend, Child Life,* and *Highlights for Children.* Guest editor of *Leaflet,* spring, 1977.

WORK IN PROGRESS: Editing a poetry anthology about conflict and writing his own poems.

SIDELIGHTS: Although Paul B. Janeczko has written his own volumes of poetry, fiction, and nonfiction for young adults, he is probably best known for his poetry anthologies. "Paul Janeczko is the best collector of poems working on behalf of young adults today," according to Beth and Ben Nehms in their *English Journal* review of *Strings: A Gathering of Family Poems.* Poems from internationally-known poets appear alongside those of up-and-coming writers in the more than twelve anthologies Janeczko has assembled. The books are distinctive because each provides multiple ways of understanding the experiences of young people through poetry while at the same time maintaining a distinct focus. Janeczko, who taught language arts for twenty-two years before becoming a full-time writer, is popular with young adults because he treats them with respect; the poems he selects are complex and challenging, and they never condescend to the reader.

Janeczko entered teaching after graduate school, he said in an interview with *Authors and Artists for Young Adults* (*AAYA*), because "I wanted to be the teacher I never had." His enthusiasm and joy in teaching soon led him into the two activities that have dominated his professional life: writing and collecting good poems. "The late 1960s was a hell of a time to be a teacher," he remembered. "Paperback books were the god of the classroom, so we were reading *The Outsiders, The Pigman,* and other young adult books. . . . I read them and taught them and said 'I could do this.' As it turned out I couldn't, but I was motivated to try. The other thing that got me interested in writing was that I started writing for teaching magazines like *English Journal* and I started experiencing the narcotic of seeing my name in print in a serious way. I've never looked back since then."

Janeczko began collecting poetry as a practical response to his needs as a teacher. He recalled in the *AAYA* interview being encouraged to "do his own thing" in the classroom, and one of the things he wished to do was to introduce his students to poetry. He combed the huge poetry anthology that was available to him for good poems, but insists that the book "just wasn't cutting it. This was the 'Age of Aquarius' and some really challenging people were writing. Poetry was going through a period of change and I wanted the kids to experience some of that new poetry. I've always felt that any kid will read if you give him or her the right stuff, and that applies to poetry as well. I felt like if kids found contemporary poetry to their liking then somewhere down the line they may, in fact, discover and enjoy some of the classics." Janeczko was soon bringing in some of the better poems he remembered from graduate school and copying poems out of the small magazines that publish contemporary poetry. The students responded enthusiastically, according to Janeczko, partly because they liked what they were reading, and partly because they were rebels and enjoyed exploring the cutting edge of poetry.

Janeczko's anthologies tend to center on an idea or a theme: *Postcard Poems,* his second book, contains poems short enough to fit on a postcard sent to a friend; *Strings: A Gathering of Family Poems* collects poems about family; *Pocket Poems: Selected for a Journey* is organized around the idea of being at home and then going out into the world and returning; and *Preposterous: Poems of Youth,* is primarily a book about boys, boys who are not quite men but feel the pull of manhood nonetheless. Despite their thematic coherence, each of the volumes contains a wide variety of poems. Janeczko told *AAYA,* "When I put a book together it's very similar to writing a novel in the structural sense. I hope the whole book tells a story, even though nobody is going to sit down and read one of my anthologies from cover to cover like they do a novel. But if they were to do that they would begin to find a sense of continuity in the book."

Many of the poems Janeczko includes in these anthologies explore challenging and potentially controversial subject matter, and his decision to include such poems indicates his refusal to make easy distinctions between adult and young adult poetry. Janeczko insists that one of his goals is to challenge young readers, to get them to stretch their minds. At the same time, he feels that there are important differences between poetry for adults and poetry for young adults. He contended in his *AAYA* interview, "I pick poems that deal with levels of experience that a teenager can understand."

Although each of Janeczko's anthologies has a different story to tell, the books are similar in that they all encourage the reader to think, to play with words, and possibly to write poetry themselves. One anthology that conveys this message is *Poetspeak: In Their Work, about Their Work,* which *English Journal* reviewer Dick Abrahamson called "a real find for teachers of poetry." In preparing this book, Janeczko asked all of his contributors to write a little note, no more than five hundred words, about one of the poems, about their writing process, or about anything else they wanted. The short essays encourage the young reader to dream, to imagine, to be a poet, for they remind the reader that poets are just people shaping their thoughts into words. Janeczko feels that this is an important message for kids to understand. He commented to *AAYA* that the message was best expressed by Al Young's poem "Don't Forget to Fly," the last poem in the collection of the same name. "I think for some kids 'Don't Forget to Fly' is a very important message, because they need to fly personally, creatively. As school budgets get cut and classes become more regimented it's going to be harder and harder for kids to fly. I do hope they get that message from my books, because I try to put in different ways of looking at life, and I'm hoping that there are going to be poems that connect with these kids."

BIOGRAPHICAL/CRITICAL SOURCES:

Authors and Artists for Young Adults, Volume 9, Gale, 1992.

PERIODICALS

Christian Science Monitor, November 2, 1990, p.11.
English Journal, September, 1982, pp. 87-88; January, 1984, p. 89; November, 1984, p. 24, 98; February, 1986, p. 105; February, 1989, pp. 84-85.
New York Times Book Review, April 27, 1980, p. 61; October 7, 1990, p. 30.
Publishers Weekly, June 27, 1986, p. 92.
Times Educational Supplement, November 11, 1988, p. 55.*

*　　　*　　　*

JANES, J(oseph) Robert 1935-

PERSONAL: Born May 23, 1935, in Toronto, Ontario, Canada; son of Henry F. (in public relations) and Phyllis (an artist; maiden name, Hipwell) Janes; married Gracia Joyce Lind (a social and environmental activist and project coordinator), May 16, 1958; children: Anne Janes Stewart, Peter, Catherine, Janes Damianoff, John. *Education:* University of Toronto, B.Sc., 1958, M.Sc., 1967; graduate study at McMaster University, Queen's University, Kingston, Ontario, and Brock University.

ADDRESSES: Home and office—P.O. Box 1590, Niagara-on-the-Lake, Ontario, Canada L0S 1J0.

CAREER: Mobil Oil of Canada, petroleum engineer in Alberta and Saskatchewan, 1958-59; Ontario Research Foundation, Toronto, research engineer in minerals beneficiation, 1959-64; high school geology, geography and mathematics teacher in Toronto, 1964-66; Ontario Research Foundation, field researcher in geology, 1966; Brock University, St. Catharines, Ontario, lecturer in geology, 1966-67; Ontario Science Centre, Toronto, earth scientist, 1967-68; Brock University, lecturer in geology, 1968-70; full time writer, 1970—. Consulting field geologist; lacrosse coach.

MEMBER: Association of Professional Engineers of Ontario, Crime Writers of Canada.

AWARDS, HONORS: Grants from J. P. Bickell Foundation, Canada Council, and Ontario Arts Council; thesis award from Canadian Institute of Mining and Metallurgy, 1958.

WRITINGS:

Geology and the New Global Tectonics (nonfiction), Macmillan (Canada), 1976.
The Great Canadian Outback (nonfiction), Douglas & McIntyre, 1978.
The Toy Shop (novel), General Publishing, 1981.
The Watcher (novel), General Publishing, 1982.
The Third Story (novel), General Publishing, 1983.
The Hiding Place (novel), Paperjacks, 1984.
(With J. D. Mollard) *Airphoto Interpretation and the Canadian Landscape* (nonfiction), Surveys and Mapping Branch, Department of Energy, Mines, and Resources, 1984.
The Alice Factor (novel), Stoddart, 1991.
Mayhem (novel), Constable, 1992, published as *Mirage,* D. I. Fine (New York City), 1992.
Carousel (novel), Constable, 1992.
Kaleidoscope (novel), Constable, 1993.
Salamander (novel), Constable, 1994.
Mannequin (novel), Constable, 1994.
Dollmaker (novel), Constable, 1995.
Stonekiller (novel), Constable, 1995.

FOR CHILDREN

Geology (television script), first broadcast by Metro Educational Television Authority, 1966.

Rocks, Minerals, and Fossils, Holt (Canada), 1973.
Earth Science, Holt (Canada), 1974.
The Tree-Fort War, Scholastic Inc., 1976.
(With C. Hopkins and J. D. Hoyes) *Searching for Structure,* Books One and Two, Holt (Canada), 1977.
Theft of Gold, Scholastic Inc., 1980.
Danger on the River, Clarke, Irwin, 1982.
Spies for Dinner, Collins of Canada, 1984.
Murder in the Market, Collins of Canada, 1985.

OTHER

Author of fifteen resource kits comprising teaching guides and slide sets for Holt (Canada), 1972. Contributor of articles and stories to Canadian magazines and newspapers, including *Canadian, Canadian Children's Annual, Toronto Globe and Mail,* and *Winnipeg Free Press.*

WORK IN PROGRESS: An adult novel, the eighth in the St.-Cyr/Kohler series of detective-mystery, psychological thrillers that began with *Mayhem.*

SIDELIGHTS: J. Robert Janes told *CA:* "For the past twenty-five years I've been a full-time writer, and on this tenuous living my wife and I raised four children. Generally I work all the time—that is to say, while I used to have hobbies and holidays, I have not had them in a very long time. Virtually everything I do is connected with my writing, the project I'm on, the one I'm about to begin, and those I want to do but can never seem to get the time for. I'm not complaining. This is simply the way it is. For others it will be vastly different.

"I write for kids and adults, both fiction and nonfiction, though in the last eight years I've concentrated almost totally on my adult fiction. While *The Alice Factor* is an international thriller about diamonds in the Second World War, *Carousel* and *Mayhem* (published in the U.S. under the title *Mirage*) and all the adult novels since are a series of detective-mystery, psychological thrillers set in occupied France in late 1942-43. My two detectives, one French from the Surete Nationale, one Bavarian from the Kripo of the Gestapo, are from opposite sides of the war. They are thrown together in the battle against common crime when officially-sanctioned crime was rampant. They get on because they have to and become friends in spite of it all. The novels are great fun with a fantastic background, and truly wonderful characters, because that's what it's all about. They have lots of suspense and pace. They're thrillers, really.

"Occasionally I'm asked why I gave up well-paying jobs for the constant stress of never knowing if and when I'd be paid and if it would be enough to meet the bills. There isn't any answer except that I've always wanted to write stories. This desire shows in my nonfiction too, but I have found that the writing of nonfiction is diametrically op-posed to that of fiction. It interferes so much I am no longer tempted to do it, though I sometimes ask, 'What if ?,' and may yet have to go back to it.

"I was the middle son of three boys and no doubt that helped because, being lonely and left to myself a lot, I used and developed my imagination. Mother was a very fine artist, very creative, a superb cook and the epitome of what the Great Depression and small-town Ontario could teach a person. That, too, helped so much, for she made me see things as an artist would. My father was once a reporter on the *Toronto Star and the Northern Miner,* though most of his working life was spent seven days a week at his firm of Public Relations Services Ltd., behind the King Edward Hotel. He didn't want me to write fiction but missed the series and *The Alice Factor.*

"I think story all the time and want only to work in that medium. In a sense, then, one crosses a threshold and wishes only to be totally involved in the work. It feeds itself and expands until the time is filled and there is no longer time enough for all one wants to do."

*   *   *

JEFFREY, David Lyle 1941-

PERSONAL: Born June 28, 1941, in Ottawa, Ontario, Canada; son of Lyle Elmo (a farmer) and Florence (Brown) Jeffrey; married Wilberta Johnson, June 17, 1961 (divorced, 1984); married Katherine Beth Brown, July 28, 1984; children: (first marriage) Bruce, Kirstin, Adrienne; (second marriage) Gideon, Joshua. *Education:* Wheaton College, Wheaton, IL, B.A., 1965; Princeton University, M.A., 1967, Ph.D., 1968.

ADDRESSES: Home—Windhover Farm, RR2, Spencerville, Ontario, Canada. *Office*—Department of English, University of Ottawa, Ottawa, Ontario, Canada K1N 6N5.

CAREER: Jef-flite of Canada (luggage manufacturers), Arnprior, Ontario, sales manager, 1960-61, general manager, 1961-63; University of Victoria, Victoria, British Columbia, assistant professor of English, 1968-69; University of Rochester, Rochester, NY, assistant professor, 1969-72, associate professor of medieval English, 1972-73; University of Victoria, associate professor of medieval English and chair of department of English, 1973-78; University of Ottawa, Ottawa, Ontario, professor of English, 1978—, chair of department, 1978-81. Visiting professor at University of British Columbia, Regent College, summers, 1970, 1973, and University of Hull, 1971-72.

MEMBER: Modern Language Association of America, Early English Text Society, Medieval Academy of America, Conference on Christianity and Literature, American Academy of Religion, Anglo-Norman Text Society, Association of Canadian University Teachers of English, Canadian Society of Biblical Studies, Institute for Advanced Christian Studies, Lambda Iota Tau.

AWARDS, HONORS: Awards from *Atlantic,* 1964, for short story "The Transfer," and 1965, for short stories "In Common Bond" and "New Hay," and for poems "To Marcel Proust" and "Nomad"; Woodrow Wilson fellow, 1965; Woodrow Wilson dissertation fellow, 1968; Canada Council humanities award, 1969, for research in Florence, Italy; Conference on Christianity and Literature annual book award, 1975, for *Franciscan Spirituality and the Early English Lyric;* Canadian Merit Award, 1978; Social Sciences and Humanities Research Council of Canada grant, 1983-86, for *A Dictionary of Biblical Tradition in English Literature;* IFACS research award, 1988-89; *Choice* outstanding academic book award, Conference on Christianity and Literature annual book award, and *Christianity Today* award for outstanding reference work, all for *A Dictionary of Biblical Tradition in English Literature,* 1993.

WRITINGS:

Modern Fictions and the Rebirth of Theology (monograph), State University of New York Press (Albany), 1973.

Franciscan Spirituality and the Early English Lyric, University of Nebraska Press (Lincoln), 1975.

(Editor) *By Things Seen: Reference and Recognition in Medieval Thought,* University of Ottawa Press, 1979.

(Editor and co-author) *Chaucer and Scriptural Tradition,* University of Ottawa Press, 1984.

Toward a Perfect Love: The Spiritual Counsel of Walter Hilton (study and translation), Multnomah (Portland), 1985.

Jack Hodgins: The Writer and His Work (monograph), ECW Press, 1987.

A Burning and a Shining Light: English Spirituality in the Age of Wesley, Eerdmans (Grand Rapids, MI), 1987, published as *English Spirituality in the Age of Wesley,* 1994.

The Law of Love: English Spirituality in the Age of Wyclif, Eerdmans, 1987.

(Co-author and editor with Brian Levy) *The Anglo-Norman Lyric,* Pontifical Institute of Medieval Studies, 1988.

(Editor and co-author) *A Dictionary of Biblical Tradition in English Literature,* Eerdmans, 1992.

People of the Book: Christian Identity and Literary Culture, Eerdmans, 1995.

Contributor to numerous books, including *Imagination and the Spirit,* edited by C. A. Huttar, Eerdmans, 1971;

Tolkien and the Critics II, edited by R. Zimbardo and Neil Issacs, Kentucky State University Press, 1981; *Fifteenth Century English Literature,* edited by R. F. Yaeger, Archon Press, 1982; *Mappings of the Biblical Terrain,* edited by Vincent Tollers and J. Maeir, Bucknell University Press (Cranbury, NJ), 1990; *The Idea of the University: 1789-1989,* edited by Kathleen Jaeger, Institute for Advanced Studies, 1990; *Best Essays in Theology,* edited by J. I. Packer, 1988; and *The Oxford Companion to the Bible,* edited by Bruce Metzger and M. Cougan, Oxford University Press (New York City), 1993. Contributor of articles and stories to professional journals, including *Journal of the American Academy of Religion, English Quarterly, Dalhousie Review, Shakespeare Studies, Journal of English and Germanic Philology, American Benedictine Review, Interpretation, University of Toronto Quarterly,* and *English Studies in Canada;* contributor of poetry to *Lit, Crux, Insignia, Green River Review, Wascana Review, Whetstone,* and *Northward Journal;* contributor of short story to *Antigonish Review.*

WORK IN PROGRESS: *Learning from Dissent,* a book about educational excellence on the margins; a volume of short stories.

SIDELIGHTS: "For me," David Lyle Jeffrey told *CA,* "writing is just another way of reading the book of the world, and remembering. There is an old European proverb which gives me comfort; it says: 'One can write straight with crooked lines.' William Everson quotes a Portuguese version which has it that even God writes in this way, suggesting, I suppose, that indirection is a signature of creative intention. The optative quality of the first version, however, is less than comforting by itself. It hints that one's prayer or ambition to 'write straight' may also be rather easily seduced—probably by too much 'sincerity' respecting these intimate personal frailties to which each of our 'readings' bears its crooked witness. Sometimes in the shelves of my books I seem to hear faintly hushed laughter, a rustling of leaves; their mocking whisper is *caveat lector! non est auctor!*

"In the volume of this book I thus confess myself a kind of literary bastard. Much of my own writing has been in scholarship and criticism, principally concerning the history of interpretation—reading of 'readings.' When a few years ago I was asked to participate in a writers' conference, addressing the subject of 'Scholarly Writing as Creative Writing,' the teasing prospect made me smile. The writers who asked me were no doubt indulging the tribal conviction that interpreters and all their works compose but orgies of plagiarism. In some respects, of course, I am bound to concede, and not only for my own sins. Yet I do so (almost) insincerely, for what seems to be true of interpretation—that none can quite pretend to be original—seems no less to hold true when one commits an act of poetry, or of story. It is always an old tale that creeps out, however much we try to tell it otherwise. But in admitting this too, I find a kind of comfort. In the telling again, even if to the wind and rain, old may become new, something transformed; or, as with that stony lady in *A Winter's Tale,* dead art may yet come back to life. They form an irresistible itinerary, these crooked lines, and one whose affection is for comfortable words can scarcely leave unconfessed that he gathers up their scattered analogues everywhere, tracing their image in crooked minims of his own execrable hand-writing—there, on the blotted page.

" 'Scrivened' isn't the same thing as 'shriven,' of course. But, recently, I find myself turning more and more to the crooked intricacies of poem and story, just when I want to be straight about where it is my guilty conscience—and gratitude—are really taking me. It's the optative in the old proverb—its intrigue of possibility—which make me laugh, and so cheers me. *Caveat, editor!*"

*   *   *

JONES, Harold   1904-1992

PERSONAL: Born February 22, 1904, in London, England; died June 10, 1992; son of William Edward and Ethel Jones; married Mollie Merry, July, 1933; children: Stephanie Angela, Gabrielle Pamela. *Education:* Attended St. Dunstans College, 1914-20, Goldsmith's College, London, 1920-21, and Camberwell School of Arts and Crafts, 1922-23; Royal College of Art, diploma, 1929.

ADDRESSES: Home—Doune Lodge, 27 Oxford Rd., Putney, London SW15 2LG, England. *Agent*—Laura Cecil, 17 Alwynevillas, London N1, England.

CAREER: Writer and illustrator. Bermondsey Central School for Boys, London, England, teacher, 1930-34; Ruskin School of Drawing, Ashmolean Museum, Oxford, England, teacher, 1937-40; Working Men's College, London, head of evening art school, 1937-40; Chelsea School of Art, London, teacher, 1945-58; Sunningdale School of Ballet, Sunningdale, England, teacher, 1945-46. Has held exhibitions at the Royal Academy, Leicester Gallery, National Book League, Piccadilly Gallery, and Green & Abbott. *Military service:* Royal Engineers, lithographic draftsman, 1939-45.

WRITINGS:

SELF-ILLUSTRATED

The Visit to the Farm, Faber, 1939.
The Enchanted Night, Faber, 1947.
The Childhood of Jesus, Gollancz, 1964.
There and Back Again, Atheneum (New York City), 1977.
Silver Bells and Cockle Shells, Oxford University Press (New York City), 1979.

Tales from Aesop, Julia Macrae Books, 1981.
A Happy Christmas, Andre Deutsch (New York City), 1983.
Tales to Tell, Julia Macrae Books, 1984.

ILLUSTRATOR

Cecil A. Joll, *Diseases of the Thyroid Gland,* Heinemann (Exeter, NH), 1932.
M. E. Atkinson, *August Adventure,* J. Cape, 1936.
Atkinson, *Mystery Manor,* Bodley Head, 1937.
Walter de la Mare, *This Year: Next Year,* Holt (New York City), 1937.
Atkinson, *The Compass Points North,* Bodley Head, 1938.
Atkinson, *Smuggler's Gap,* Bodley Head, 1939.
Atkinson, *Crusoe Island,* Bodley Head, 1947.
John Pudney, *Selected Poems,* Bodley Head, 1947.
Kathleen Lines, *Four to Fourteen,* Oxford University Press, 1950.
Lines, compiler, *Lavender's Blue,* Oxford University Press, 1954.
Lines, compiler, *Once in Royal David's City,* Oxford University Press, 1956.
Henry Fagen, *Nikya,* J. Cape, 1956.
Donald Suddaby, *Prisoners of Saturn,* Bodley Head, 1957.
Lines, compiler, *A Ring of Tales,* Oxford University Press, 1958.
William Blake, *Songs of Innocence,* Faber, 1958.
Elfrida Vipont, compiler, *Bless This Day,* Harcourt (New York City), 1958.
Lines, *Noah and the Ark,* Oxford University Press, 1961.
Songs from Shakespeare, Faber, 1961.
Charles Kingsley, *The Water Babies,* Watts (New York City), 1961.
Robert Browning, *The Pied Piper of Hamelin,* Oxford University Press, 1962.
Nathaniel Hawthorne, *The Complete Greek Stories of Nathaniel Hawthorne,* Gollancz, 1964.
Lewis Carroll, *The Hunting of the Snark* (limited edition), Whittington Press, 1975.
Oscar Wilde, *The Fairy Stories of Oscar Wilde,* Gollancz, 1976.
Paul Ries Collin, *Calling Bridge,* Oxford University Press, 1976.
Ruth Manning-Sanders, *The Town Mouse and the Country Mouse,* Angus Robertson, 1977.
The Silent Playmate: A Collection of Doll Stories, edited by Naomi Lewis, Macmillan (New York City), 1981.

Also designer of book jackets.

SIDELIGHTS: Harold Jones's work has been purchased by the Tate Gallery, the Victoria and Albert Museum, and the London County Council.

BIOGRAPHICAL/CRITICAL SOURCES:

BOOKS

William Feaver, *When We Were Young,* Thames & Hudson, 1977.

PERIODICALS

Arts Guardian, December 6, 1974.
Times (London), August 27, 1975.

OBITUARIES:

PERIODICALS

Junior Bookshelf, August, 1992, pp. 137-139.
Times (London), June 13, 1992, p. 21.*

*   *   *

JOSEPHSON, Elmer A.   1909-

PERSONAL: Born December 19, 1909, in Kansas City, MO; son of August (a machinist) and Wilhemine Christina (a homemaker; maiden name, Axene) Josephson; married Christine Crawford (an officer manager and author), January 1, 1961. *Education:* Attended Bethel Institute (now Bethel College and Seminary), St. Paul, MN, and Moody Bible Institute.

ADDRESSES: Office— P.O. Box 370, 900 W. 15th, Ottawa, KS 66067-0370.

CAREER: Ordained Baptist minister; Bible Light International, Ottawa, KS, founder, director, and publisher of *Bible Light Star,* 1956—. Director of Youth for Christ, Wichita, KS; director of tour groups to Israel.

WRITINGS:

God's Keys to Health and Happiness, Bible Light (Bronx), 1962, second edition, Revell (Tappan, NJ), 1977.
Israel: God's Key to World Redemption, Bible Light, 1974.
Key Bible Songs, Bible Light, 1977.
Key Tips to Reading Your Bible, Bible Light, 1980.
Bible Answers Concerning God the Father and Christ the Son, Bible Light, 1993.
Israel in the Revelation, Bible Light, 1994.

Also author of *Why Jews Reject Jesus* and *God's Key to Peace and Prosperity,* 1994.

WORK IN PROGRESS: Research on the Middle East and biblical subjects.

BIOGRAPHICAL/CRITICAL SOURCES:

PERIODICALS

Sunday School Times and Gospel Herald, July 1, 1981.

JUDD, Denis (O'Nan)   1938-

PERSONAL: Born October 28, 1938, in Byfield, England; son of Denis Allen (proprietor of a garage and bus business) and Joan (Shrimpton) Judd; married Dorothy Janet Woolf, July 10, 1964; children: Kate Emma, Luke Benedict, Benjamin Keir, Jacob Joseph. *Education:* Magdalen College, Oxford, B.A. (with second class honors), 1961; College of St. Mark and St. John, London, Postgraduate Certificate in Education, 1962; Birkbeck College, London, Ph.D., 1967. *Politics:* Socialist (Labour Party). *Religion:* Atheist. *Avocational interests:* Foreign holidays, the visual arts, theater ("especially the Royal Shakespeare Company"), cinema, sports, good food, family.

ADDRESSES: Home—20 Mount Pleasant Rd., London NW10 3EL, England. *Office*—Department of History and Philosophy, University of North London, London, NW5, England. *Agent*—David Higham Associates Ltd., 5-8 Lower John St., London W1R 4HA, England.

CAREER: University of North London, London, England, lecturer, 1964-68, senior lecturer, 1968-72, principal lecturer, 1972—, professor of history, 1990—, head of history, 1975—.

MEMBER: Historical Association, Royal Historical Society (fellow).

WRITINGS:

Balfour and the British Empire: A Study in Imperial Evolution, St. Martin's (New York), 1968.
The Victorian Empire: A Pictorial History, Praeger (New York), 1970.
Posters of World War Two, Wayland (East Sussex, England), 1972.
The British Raj (juvenile), Wayland, 1973.
Livingstone in Africa (juvenile), Wayland, 1973.
The Life and Times of George V, Weidenfeld & Nicolson (London), 1973.
The House of Windsor, Macdonald & Janes (London), 1973.
Someone Has Blundered: Calamities of the British Army in the Victorian Age, Arthur Baker, 1973.
Edward VII: A Pictorial Biography, Macdonald & Janes, 1975.
Palmerston, Weidenfeld & Nicolson, 1975.
The Crimean War, Hart-Davis (London), 1975.
The Royal Victorians: A Pictorial Biography, St. Martin's, 1975.
Eclipse of Kings: European Monarchies in the Twentieth Century, Macdonald & Janes, 1976.
The Adventures of Long John Silver, St. Martin's, 1977.
Radical Joe: A Life of Joseph Chamberlain, Hamish Hamilton (London), 1977.
The Boer War, Hart-Davis, 1977.

Return to Treasure Island, M. Joseph (London), 1978.

Prince Philip: Duke of Edinburgh, M. Joseph, 1980, Atheneum (New York), 1981.

Lord Reading: A Biography of Rufus Isaacs, Weidenfeld & Nicolson, 1982.

King George VI, M. Joseph, 1982, F. Watts (New York), 1983.

(With P. Slinn) *The Evolution of the Modern Commonwealth,* Macmillan (New York), 1982.

Alison Uttley: The Life of a Country Child, M. Joseph, 1986.

Further Tales of Little Grey Rabbit (juvenile), illustrated by Margaret Tempest, Collins (London), 1989.

(Author of preface) Peter Neville, *A Traveller's History of Ireland,* Interlink Publishing Group, 1993.

(Editor) Valerio Lintner, *A Traveller's History of Italy,* updated edition, Interlink Publishing Group, 1993.

Jawaharlal Nehru, University of Wales Press, 1993.

Also author of 'traveller's histories' of France, Spain, Paris, Japan, England, Russia, and Scotland. Contributor to periodicals, including *History, Times Literary Supplement, Journal of Imperial and Commonwealth History, History Today, Sunday Telegraph,* and *New Statesman and Society.*

SIDELIGHTS: Denis Judd has written extensively about the British royal family and about the personalities and events that have shaped modern England. His biography of Prince Philip details the life of a man whom a reviewer for *Punch* believes is "likely to remain something of a mystery." *Prince Philip: Duke of Edinburgh* follows the fortunes of the prince from his birth on the family dining room table as the son of Princess Alice of Battenberg and Prince Andrew of Greece, to his marriage to Elizabeth, future Queen of England, and beyond.

BIOGRAPHICAL/CRITICAL SOURCES:

PERIODICALS

Los Angeles Times, May 11, 1981.

New Statesman, May 5, 1982.

Punch, October 22, 1980.

Times (London), March 31, 1990.

Times Literary Supplement, November 13, 1970; November 2, 1973; January 18, 1974; December 5, 1975; January 30, 1976; May 13, 1977; July 2, 1982; December 31, 1982; January 7, 1983; December 5, 1986, p. 1378.

Washington Post Book World, June 7, 1981.

K

KACHRU, Braj B(ehari) 1932-

PERSONAL: Born May 15, 1932, in Srinagar, Kashmir, India; came to United States in 1963; son of Shyam Lal (an educator) and Tulsidevi (Tutu) Kachru; married Yamuna Keskar (a professor), January 22, 1965; children: Amita, Shamit. *Education:* Jammu and Kashmir University, B.A. (with honors), 1952; Allahabad University, M.A., 1955; University of Edinburgh, Ph.D., 1962. *Religion:* Hindu.

ADDRESSES: Home—2016 Cureton Dr., Urbana, IL 61801. *Office*—Department of Linguistics, University of Illinois at Urbana-Champaign, 707 S. Mathews Ave., Urbana, IL 61801.

CAREER: Lucknow University, Lucknow, India, assistant professor of English, in charge of linguistics program, 1962-63; University of Illinois at Urbana-Champaign, research associate, 1963-64, assistant professor, 1964-67, associate professor, 1967-70, professor of linguistics, 1970—, joint professorships of education, College of Education, 1980—, English, Division of English as an International Language, 1984—, comparative literature, 1986—, linguistics department, acting head, 1968, head, 1969-79, associate of Center for Advanced Study, 1971-72, 1979-80, and 1988, coordinator of Division of Applied Linguistics, 1976—, Division of English as a Second Language, acting director, 1984, director, 1985-91. Visiting professor, National University of Singapore, 1984. Visiting faculty member, Department of Education, Halifax, Nova Scotia, 1967, and East-West Center, Honolulu, HI, 1983; fellow, East-West Center, 1982, 1984, and 1985. Member of Language Committee, American Institute of Indian Studies, 1971-77; ; East-West Center, Honolulu, member of International Advisory Committee on English, 1978—, member, Working Committee on the Study of "Self Across Cultures", 1987—; member of board of trust-

ees, American Institute of Indian Studies, 1979-81 and 1987-89; chairperson, International Committee for South Asian Languages and Linguistics, 1980-85; International Corpus of English, Survey of English Usage, University College London, England, co-director, Component on Indian English, and member, International Advisory Board, both 1989—; Lecturer and keynote speaker at various seminars. Consultant to American Institute of Indian Studies, New Delhi, India, 1972, and to Ford Foundation, 1973-74.

MEMBER: International PEN, British Association of Applied Linguistics, Linguistic Society of India (life member), American Association for Applied Linguistics (member of program committee, 1978; vice-president and chair of program commission, 1983, president, 1984; chairperson, membership committee, 1984-85), American Oriental Society, Linguistic Society of America (member of Linguistic Institutes and Fellowships Committee, 1977-78; director of Linguistic Institute, 1978; member, Ad Hoc Committee on the LSA Professorship, 1984; Committee on Honorary Members, member, 1985-86, chairperson, 1987), National Council of Teachers of English, Teachers of English to Speakers of Other Languages (TESOL).

AWARDS, HONORS: British Council fellow 1958-60; grants from U.S. Department of Health, Education and Welfare's Institute of International Affairs, 1965-72, for *A Reference Grammar of Kashmiri,* and 1970-72, for *An Introduction to Spoken Kashmiri;* senior faculty research fellow of American Institute of Indian Studies, New Delhi, India, 1967-68, 1971-72, 1982, and 1988-89; Ford Foundation grant, 1978; fellow, The East-West Center, summer, 1982, fall, 1984, summer, 1985, and 1986; Arnold O. Beckman Research Award, University of Illinois at Urbana-Champaign, 1984, 1992, and 1994; joint first prize, Duke of Edinburgh English Language Book Competition, sponsored by English-speaking Union of the Commonwealth (presented by Prince Philip, Duke of Edinburgh, at Buckingham Palace), for *The Alchemy of English,* 1987; Jubilee Professor of Liberal Arts, University of Illinois, 1992; honored by the Association of Indians in America at 25th Anniversary Honour Banquet, 1992.

WRITINGS:

A Reference Grammar of Kashmiri, University of Illinois Press (Urbana, IL), 1969.

An Introduction to Spoken Kashmiri, two parts, University of Illinois Press, 1973.

Kashmiri Literature (monograph in series "History of Indian Literature"), Otto Harrassowitz (Weisbaden), 1981.

The Indianization of English: The English Language in India, Oxford University Press (New Delhi, India), 1983.

The Alchemy of English: The Spread, Functions and Forms of English in Non-Native Contexts, University of Illinois Press, 1986, 2nd U. S. edition, 1990.

EDITOR

(With wife, Yamuna Kachru) *Studies in Hindi Linguistics,* American Institute of Indian Studies (New Delhi), 1968.

(With Herbert W. Stahlke) *Current Trends in Stylistics,* Linguistic Research, Inc. (Edmonton, Canada), 1972.

(With R. B. Lees, S. Saporta, A. Pietrangeli, and Y. Malkiel) *Issues in Linguistics: Papers in Honor of Henry and Renee Kahane,* University of Illinois Press, 1973.

(And contributor with others) *Issues in Linguistics: Papers in Honor of Henry and Renee Kahane,* University of Illinois Press, 1973.

(With Edward Dimrock and Bh. Krishnamurti) *Dimensions of Sociolinguistics in South Asia: Papers in Memory of Gerald Kelley,* Oxford IBH Publications (New Delhi, India), 1992.

The Other Tongue: English across Cultures, University of Illinois Press, 1982, revised edition, 1992.

OTHER

Also contributor to books, including *In Memory of J. R. Firth,* edited by C. E. Bazell, J. C. Catford, M. A. K. Halliday, and R. H. Robins, Longman (London, England), 1966; *Language and Development: A Retrospective Survey of Ford Foundation Language Projects, 1952-1974,* edited by Melvin J. Fox, Ford Foundation, 1975; *Theory and Method in Lexicography: Western and Non-Western Perspective,* edited by Ladislav Zgusta, Hornbeam Press (Columbia, SC), 1980; *Literature and Language Teaching,* edited by R. Carter and C. Brumfit, Oxford University Press, 1986; *Discourse Across Cultures: Strategies in World Languages,* edited by Larry E. Smith, Prentice-Hall (New York City and London, England), 1987; *International Handbook of the Science of Language and Society,* Walter De Gruyter (Berlin, Germany, and New York City), 1988; *Learning, Keeping and Using Language,* edited by M. A. K. Halliday and others, John Benjamin, 1990; *Literary Relations East and West,* edited by J. Toyama and N. Ochner, University of Hawaii Press (Honolulu, HI), 1990; *Languages and Standards: Issues, Attitudes, Case Studies,* edited by M. L. Tickoo, SEAMEO Regional Language Center (Singapore), 1991; *English in Its Social Contexts: Essays in Historical Sociolinguistics,* edited by T. W. Machan and C. T. Scott, Oxford University Press, 1992; *Teaching English Pronunciation: A Book of Readings,* edited by Adam Brown, Routledge (London, England, and New York City), 1992; *Readings on Second Language Acquisition,* edited by D. Brown and S, Gonzo, Prentice-Hall, 1994; *Contact Linguistics: An International Handbook of Contemporary Research,* edited by H. Goebl, P. H. Stary, I. Stary, and W. Wolck, Walter De Gruyter, in press. Also author of introduction (with Henry Kahane and Charles Kisseberth) to *Studies Presented to Robert B. Lees by His Students,* Linguistic Research, Inc. (Edmonton), 1970; author of foreword to *University Administration in India and the USA,* by P. R. Mehendiratta, [New Delhi], 1984; and *Semantic Theories and Language Teaching,* by V. Prakasam and A. Abbi, Allied Publishers (New Delhi), 1986.

Also contributor to encyclopedias, histories and annuals, including *The Oxford Companion to the English Language* and *Oxford International Encyclopedia of Linguistics,* edited by William Bright, Oxford University Press, both 1992; *The Encyclopedia of Language and Linguistics,* Pergamon Press and Aberdeen University (Oxford, England), 1994; *Encyclopedia of Commonwealth Literature,* edited by E. Benson and G. D. Killian, Routledge, in press; and *Cambridge History of the English Language,* Volume V, Cambridge University Press, in press.

Editor of series "English in the International Context," Prentice-Hall International (London, England), 1984-89, "English in the Global Context," University of Illinois Press, 1989—; co-editor of series "Language in South Asian Society," Manohar Publications, New Delhi, India; associate editor, *The Oxford Companion to the English Language,* Oxford University Press, 1992.

Consultant to *Random House Dictionary of the English Language,* 1965-66 and 1987, and to *The International Dictionary of English Pronunciation.* Advisor to *English around the World: Sociolinguistic Perspectives,* Cambridge University Press, 1989. Evaluator of manuscripts for publishing houses, including Cambridge University Press, Harcourt Brace Javanovich, Harper and Row, Oxford University Press, and University of Illinois Press.

Contributor of articles and reviews to numerous language, education, and Oriental studies journals, including *Current Trends in Linguistics, English Around the World, English Language Forum, English Today,* and *Foundations of Language.*

Co-editor, *English World-Wide: A Journal of Varieties of English,* 1980-84, *Annual Review of Applied Linguistics,* 1980-88, and *World Englishes: Journal of English as an International and Intranational Language,* 1984—. Guest co-editor, *Journal of Asian Pacific Communication,* 1991, *Language and Identity,* special issue of *Journal of Asian Pacific Communication,* 1993, and *Twenty-five Years of Linguistics Research and Teaching at the University of Illinois,* special issue of *Studies in the Linguistic Sciences,* 1993.

Member of editorial board, *Studies in the Linguistic Sciences,* 1971—, *Papers in Linguistics,* 1972-83, *International Journal of the Sociology of Language,* 1974—, *Journal of South Asian Literatures,* 1980—, *Studies in Second Language Acquisition,* 1985-90, *IDEAL: Issues and Developments in English and Applied Linguistics,* 1986—, *IFE Studies in English Language* (Nigeria), 1987—, *Journal of Asian Pacific Communication,* 1989—, *South Asian Language Review,* 1991, and *Lingua Asia,* 1992—.

WORK IN PROGRESS: Continuing research on nonnative varieties of English, and on Kashmiri language and literature; sociolinguistics and bilingualism; book (with Henry Kahane), *Culture, Ideology and the Dictionary,* forthcoming from Max Niemeyer Verlag (Tubingen, Germany); contributor to book (edited by Baumgardner), *South Asian English: Structure, Use and Users,* forthcoming.

*   *   *

KAGAN, Jerome   1929-

PERSONAL: Born February 25, 1929, in Newark, NJ; son of Joseph (a businessman) and Myrtle (Liebermann) Kagan; married Cele Katzman, June 20, 1951; children: Janet. *Education:* Rutgers University, B.S., 1950; Yale University, Ph.D., 1954.

ADDRESSES: Home—210 Clifton St., Belmont, MA. *Office*—William James Hall, Harvard University, Cambridge, MA 02138.

CAREER: Fels Institute, Yellow Springs, OH, researcher in developmental psychology, 1957-64; Harvard University, Cambridge, MA, professor of human development, 1964—. Social Science Research Council, member of Committee on Learning and the Educational Process, 1966-70; National Institute of Child Health and Development, Advisory Committee on Training, 1966-68; National Academy of Sciences, Committee on Fellowship Evaluation, 1967 and 1974; President's Science Advisory Committee, Panel on Educational Research, 1969-72; National Institute of Education, Panel on Development, 1970-74; National Academy of Sciences, Committee on Brain Sciences, 1971-78. Member of board of directors, Foundation to Improve Television (Boston), 1969—, and of Foundations Fund for Research in Psychiatry, 1970-74. Consultant to Department of Pediatrics, Massachusetts General Hospital, 1965—. *Military service:* U.S. Army, 1955-57.

MEMBER: American Association for Advancement of Science, Society for Research in Child Development, American Psychological Association (member, board of scientific affairs, 1965-66; president, division of developmental psychology, 1966-67), American Academy of Arts and Sciences (fellow), National Institute of Medicine, National Academy of Sciences, Eastern Psychological Association (member, board of directors, 1973-75; president, 1974-75).

AWARDS, HONORS: Hofheimer Prize of American Psychiatric Association, 1963; Wilbur Lucius Cross Medal, Yale University.

WRITINGS:

(With H. Moss) *Birth to Maturity,* Wiley (New York City), 1962.

(With J. J. Conger and P. H. Mussen) *Child Development and Personality,* Harper (New York City), 1963, 6th edition, 1984.

(With Julius Segal) *Psychology: An Introduction,* Harcourt (San Diego), 1968, 8th edition, 1995.

(With others) *Change and Continuity in Infancy,* Wiley, 1971.

Personality Development, edited by Irving L. Janis, Harcourt, 1971.

Understanding Children: Behavior, Motives, and Thought, Harcourt, 1971.

(With R. Kearsley and P. Zelazo) *Infancy: Its Place in Human Development,* Harvard University Press (Cambridge), 1978.

Growth of the Child, Norton (New York City), 1978.

(With Cynthia Lang) *Psychology and Education: An Introduction,* Harcourt, 1978.

The Family, Norton, 1978.

(With O. S. Brim) *Constancy and Change in Human Development,* Harvard University Press, 1980.

The Second Year: The Emergence of Self-Awareness, Harvard University Press, 1981.

The Nature of the Child, Basic Books (New York City), 1984, revised edition, 1994.

Unstable Ideas: Temperament, Cognition, and Self, Harvard University Press, 1989.

(With Nancy Snidman, Doreen Arcus, and J. Steven Reznick) *Galen's Prophecy: Temperament in Human Nature,* Basic Books, 1994.

EDITOR

(With John C. Wright) *Basic Cognitive Processes in Children,* Child Development Publications, 1963, published with new introduction, University of Chicago Press (Chicago, IL), 1973.

(With Mussen) *Readings in Child Development and Personality,* Harper, 1965, 2nd edition, 1970.

Creativity and Learning, Houghton (Boston), 1967.

(With Marshall Haith and Catherine Caldwell) *Psychology: Adapted Readings,* Harcourt, 1971.

(With Nathan Bill Talbot and L. E. Eisenberg) *Behavioral Science in Pediatric Medicine,* W. B. Saunders (Philadelphia), 1971.

(With Robert Coles) *Twelve to Sixteen: Early Adolescence,* Norton, 1972.

(With Mussen) *Basic Contemporary Issues in Developmental Psychology,* Harper, 1975.

(With Sharon Lamb) *The Emergence of Morality in Young Children,* University of Chicago Press, 1987.

Contributor to books. Consulting editor, Harcourt, 1965—. Editorial consultant to *Child Development, Journal of Experimental Child Psychology, Journal of Consulting Psychology, Merrill-Palmer Quarterly, Psychological Bulletin,* and *Journal of Educational Psychology.*

SIDELIGHTS: Jerome Kagan, "one of today's most eminent child experts, enunciates the developing edge of consensus in his field," observes Daniel Goleman in the *New York Times Book Review.* According to Mark Caldwell in the *Voice Literary Supplement,* Kagan "has contributed mightily to the literature of child development, but never so originally as in *The Nature of the Child.*" Challenging the widely held theory that an individual's personality is determined entirely by experiences during infancy, "the book begins and ends with [Kagan's] assertion that currently influential accounts of childhood—whether Freudian, Eriksonian, or Piagetian—are too rigid," says Caldwell. "They all see growing up as an inviolable, continuous, ultimately mechanical process that builds an adult personality the way drops of water doggedly amass a stalagmite."

Caldwell finds that Kagan's "view of the child, while informed by a thorough knowledge of research, is refreshingly hesitant. He offers biology as a promising guideline, but warns that since we haven't found a fully workable theoretical construct for growth and development of the child, we shouldn't burden the models we have with too much emotion." Noting that the prevalent conception of

parental influence upon child development is "sentimental rather than scientific," Anatole Broyard indicates in his *New York Times* review of *The Nature of the Child,* "We are in the paradoxical position of trying to create our children while regarding them at the same time as self-determining." Considering it "inappropriate" to ask whether heredity or environment is more important in child development, Maya Pines suggests in the *Washington Post* that "they work together to create a human being." As Caldwell summarizes, "You can't take all the credit if your child grows up to be Eleanor Roosevelt, then again you don't have to take all the blame if she ends up in a Cheech and Chong movie." Broyard concludes that "while it's not for a layman to say whether . . . Kagan is right or wrong, he certainly stirs up interesting issues and brings a lot of experimental evidence to bear on them."

BIOGRAPHICAL/CRITICAL SOURCES:

PERIODICALS

American Science, July, 1989, p. 416.

American Sociological Review, October, 1963.

Antioch Review, spring, 1986, p. 244; winter, 1990, p. 109.

Choice, January, 1985, p. 745; November, 1988, p. 572; November, 1989, p. 562.

Contemporary Psychology, March, 1985, p. 245; February, 1986, p. 128; May, 1986, p. 413; September, 1989, p. 865.

Ethics, April, 1989, p. 644.

Harvard Educational Review, May, 1989, p. 260.

Kirkus Reviews, February 15, 1989, p. 271.

Library Journal, January, 1985, p. 51; March 1, 1985, p. 41; April 1, 1989, p. 102.

New Republic, November 5, 1984, p. 40.

New York Times, September 14, 1984.

New York Times Book Review, December 12, 1978; November 18, 1984; February 2, 1986; May 28, 1989, p. 16.

Phi Delta Kappan, June, 1985, p. 734.

Psychology Today, December, 1984, p. 70.

Readings, March, 1990, p. 4.

Review of Metaphysics, December, 1988, p. 393.

Science, April 19, 1963.

Science Books and Films, May, 1989, p. 269; September, 1989, p. 6.

SciTech Book News, September, 1988, p. 1; July 1989, p. 1.

Social Service Review, September, 1987, p. 544.

Times Educational Supplement, January 6, 1989, p. 25.

Voice Literary Supplement, November, 1984.

Washington Post, January 11, 1981.

KANET, Roger E(dward) 1936-

PERSONAL: Born September 1, 1936, in Cincinnati, OH; son of Robert George (a skilled worker) and Edith Mary (Weaver) Kanet; married Joan Alice Edwards (a registered nurse and hospital administrator), February 16, 1963; children: Suzanne Elise, Laurie Alice. *Education:* Berchmanskolleg, Pullach-bei-Muenchen, Germany, Ph.B., 1960; Xavier University, Cincinnati, A.B., 1961; Lehigh University, M.A., 1963; Princeton University, A.M., 1965, Ph.D., 1966. *Religion:* Roman Catholic.

ADDRESSES: Home—3805 Farhills Dr., Champaign, IL 61821-9304. *Office*—303 International Studies Bldg., University of Illinois, 910 South 5th St., Champaign, IL 61820.

CAREER: University of Kansas, Lawrence, assistant professor, 1966-69, associate professor of political science, 1969-74, director of undergraduate studies, 1969-70, associate chair, 1970-71; University of Illinois at Urbana-Champaign, visiting associate professor, 1973-74, associate professor, 1974-78, professor of political science, 1978—, director of graduate studies, 1975-78, head of political science department, 1984-87, associate vice-chancellor of academic affairs and director of international programs and studies, 1989—. Joint senior fellow, Research Institute on Communist Affairs and Russian Institute, Columbia University, 1972-73; associate, Center for Advanced Study, University of Illinois at Urbana-Champaign, 1981-82. Member of board of directors, Midwest University Consortium on International Activities, 1989—. International Committee for Soviet and East European Studies, member, and chair of program committee of First World Congress, 1974; member, University of Illinois at Urbana-Champaign Russian and East European Center, 1974—, Office of Arms Control, Disarmament and International Security, 1978—, African Studies Program, 1982—, and Council on Foreign Relations, 1991—. Kansas State Parents' Association for Hearing-Handicapped Children, co-founder, vice-president, 1969-70, president, 1970-71. Consultant, Institute for Public Policy Development, 1977-79.

MEMBER: International Studies Association, International Political Science Association (chair of American-Soviet relations section, 1990-92), Association of International Education Administration (member of journal editorial committee, 1993—), American Political Science Association, American Association for the Advancement of Slavic Studies (chair of bibliography and documentation committee, 1971-74), National Association of State Universities and Land Grant Colleges (member of international commission, 1992—), Midwest Political Science Association (member of program committee, 1983-84), Midwest Slavic Conference (program chair, 1980-81),

Central Slavic Conference (president, 1966-67; program chair, 1967), Kansas Political Science Association (program chair, 1970).

AWARDS, HONORS: American Council of Learned Societies grant, 1972-73, 1978; NATO Faculty Research Program grant, 1976; International Research and Exchanges Board grant, 1976; research award, U.S. Department of State, 1976; University of Illinois at Urbana-Champaign, College of Liberal Arts and Sciences and campus awards for excellence in undergraduate teaching, all 1981, department of political science award for excellence in undergraduate teaching, 1984, and Burlington Northern Faculty Achievement Award, 1989; international fellow, Federal Institute for East European and International Studies, Cologne, Germany, 1988; U.S. Institute for Peace award, 1991.

WRITINGS:

(Editor) *The Behavioral Revolution and Communist Studies: Applications of Behaviorally Oriented Political Research on the Soviet Union and Eastern Europe,* Free Press (New York), 1971.

(With others) *The Political and Legal Implications of the Development and Implementation of Remote Sensing Devices,* Center for Research, University of Kansas (Lawrence), 1971.

(Editor with Ivan Volgyes) *On the Road to Communism: Essays on Soviet Domestic and Foreign Politics,* University Press of Kansas, 1972.

(Editor) *The Soviet Union and the Developing Nations,* Johns Hopkins University Press (Baltimore), 1974.

(Compiler) *Soviet and East European Foreign Policies: A Bibliography of English and Russian Language Publications, 1967-71,* American Bibliographical Center-Clio Press (Santa Barbara, CA), 1974.

(Editor with Donna Bahry) *Soviet Economic and Political Relations with the Developing World,* Praeger (New York), 1975.

(Editor with Maurice D. Simon) *Background to Crisis: Policy and Politics in Gierek's Poland,* Westview (Boulder, CO), 1981.

(Editor) *Soviet Foreign Policy in the 1980s,* Praeger, 1982.

(Editor) *Soviet Foreign Policy and East-West Relations,* Pergamon (Elmsford, NY), 1982.

(Editor with Ray S. Cline and James Arnold Miller) *Asia in Soviet Global Strategy,* Westview, 1987.

(Editor with Cline and Miller) *Western Europe in Soviet Global Strategy,* Westview, 1987.

(Editor) *The Soviet Union, Eastern Europe and the Third World,* Cambridge University Press (Cambridge, England), 1987.

(Editor with Edward A. Kolodziej) *The Limits of Soviet Power in the Developing World,* Johns Hopkins University Press, 1988, published in England as *The Lim-*

its of Soviet Power in the Developing Nations: Thermidor in the Revolutionary Struggle, Macmillan (London), 1989.

(Editor with Kolodziej) *The Cold War as Cooperation: Superpower Cooperation in Regional Conflict Management,* Johns Hopkins University Press, 1991.

(Editor with Deborah Nutter Miner and Tamara J. Resler) *Soviet Foreign Policy in Transition,* Cambridge University Press, 1992.

(Editor with Kolodziej) *Coping with Conflict after the Cold War,* Johns Hopkins University Press, 1995.

Contributor to numerous books, including *From Underdevelopment to Affluence: Western, Soviet, and Chinese Views,* edited by Harry G. Shaffer and Jan S. Prybyla, Appleton, 1968; *Communist Systems in Comparative Perspective,* edited by Lenard J. Cohen and Jane P. Shapiro, Anchor (New York), 1974; *Soviet Politics in the Brezhnev Era,* edited by Donald R. Kelley, Praeger, 1980; *Polish Politics: Edge of the Abyss,* edited by Jack Bielasiak and Maurice D. Simon, Praeger, 1984; and *The USSR in the Third World,* edited by Carol Saivetz, Westview, 1989. Contributor to encyclopedias. General editor, publications from the First World Congress, 1974, and Second World Congress for Soviet and East European Studies, 1980. Contributor of more than two hundred articles and reviews to periodicals.*

*   *   *

KAYE, Marilyn 1949-
(Shannon Blair)

PERSONAL: Born July 19, 1949, in New Britain, CT; daughter of Harold Stanley and Annette (Rudman) Kaye. *Education:* Emory University, B.A., 1967, M.L.S., 1974; University of Chicago, Ph.D., 1983. *Politics:* Liberal Democrat. *Religion:* Jewish.

ADDRESSES: Home—Brooklyn, NY. *Office*—Division of Library and Information Science, St. John's University, Grand Central and Utopia Parkways, Jamaica, NY 11439. *Agent*—Amy Berkower, Writer's House, Inc., 21 West 26th St., New York, NY 10010.

CAREER: Library Quarterly, Chicago, IL, editorial assistant, 1977-79; University of South Carolina, Columbia, instructor in library science, 1980-82; St. John's University, Jamaica, NY, 1982—, began as instructor, became associate professor of library and information science, 1986—.

MEMBER: American Library Association (chairman of Notable Children's Books committee, 1981-82), Authors Guild, Beta Phi Mu.

WRITINGS:

JUVENILES

Will You Cross Me?, Harper (New York City), 1985.
Baby Fozzie Is Afraid of the Dark, Weekly Reader (Columbus, OH), 1986.
The Best Baby-Sitter in the World, Scholastic (New York City), 1987.
Miss Piggy and the Big Gorilla, Scholastic, 1988.
What a Teddy Bear Needs, Ladybird (London), 1989.
Gonzo the Great, Scholastic, 1989.
The Real Tooth Fairy, Harcourt (New York City), 1990.
Attitude, Fawcett (New York City), 1990.
The Atonement of Mindy Wise, Harcourt, 1991, (reprinted in paperback as *Mindy Wise*), Avon (New York City), 1993.
A Day with No Math, Harcourt, 1991.
Runaway, Harper, 1992.
Choose Me, Harper, 1992.
Real Heroes, Harcourt, 1993.
Dream Lover, Troll (Mahwah, NJ), 1995.

"OUT OF THIS WORLD" SERIES

Max on Earth, Simon & Schuster (New York City), 1986.
Max in Love, Simon & Schuster, 1986.
Max on Fire, Simon & Schuster, 1986.
Max Flips Out, Simon & Schuster, 1986.
Max Goes Bad, Penguin (London), 1989.
Max All Over, Penguin, 1989.

"SISTERS" SERIES; ALL PUBLISHED BY HARCOURT

Phoebe, 1987.
Daphne, 1987.
Cassie, 1987.
Lydia, 1987, also published in Germany as *Heisse Stories—Kalte Fusse,* Cora Verlag, 1992.
A Friend Like Phoebe, 1989.

"CAMP SUNNYSIDE FRIENDS" SERIES; ALL PUBLISHED BY AVON (New York City)

No Boys Allowed, 1989.
Cabin Six Plays Cupid, 1989.
Color War, 1989.
New Girl in Cabin Six, 1989.
Looking for Trouble, 1990.
Katie Steals the Show, 1990.
A Witch in Cabin Six, 1990.
Too Many Counselors, 1990.
The New and Improved Sarah, 1990.
Christmas Reunion, 1990.
Erin and the Movie Star, 1991.
The Problem with Parents, 1991.
The Tennis Trap, 1991.
Big Sister Blues, 1991.
Megan's Ghost, 1991.

Christmas Break, 1991.
Happily Ever After, 1992.
Camp Spaghetti, 1992.
Balancing Act, 1992.
School Daze, 1992.
The Spirit of Sunnyside, 1992.

"THREE OF A KIND" SERIES; ALL PUBLISHED BY HARPER

With Friends Like These, Who Needs Enemies?, 1990.
Home's a Nice Place to Visit, but I Wouldn't Want to Live There, 1990.
Will the Real Becka Morgan Please Stand Up?, 1991.
Two's Company, Four's a Crowd, 1991.
Cat Morgan, Working Girl, 1991.
101 Ways to Win Homecoming Queen, 1991.

"VIDEO HIGH" SERIES; ALL PUBLISHED BY KENSINGTON (New York City)

Modern Love, (New York City), 1994.
The High Life, 1994.
Date Is a Four Letter Word, 1994.
The Body Beautiful, 1994.
The Colors of the Heart, 1994.

UNDER PSEUDONYM SHANNON BLAIR; TEEN ROMANCES

Call Me Beautiful, Bantam (New York City), 1984.
Starstruck, Bantam, 1985.
Wrong Kind of Boy, Bantam, 1985.
Kiss and Tell, Bantam, 1985.

OTHER

Also editor (with Betsy Hearne) of *Celebrating Children's Books: Essays on Children's Literature in Honor of Zena Sutherland,* Lothrop (New York City), 1981; and *Top of the News* (journal of the Association of Library Service to Children and Young Adult Services), 1982-85. Contributor of articles and reviews to library journals and newspapers.

WORK IN PROGRESS: More "Video High" titles; a horror series; a young adult novel; an adult novel.

SIDELIGHTS: Marilyn Kaye told *CA:* "I began my writing career cautiously, unsure of what I was capable of doing. As a teacher of children's literature, I had read widely enough to believe I could possibly write an adequate teen romance. After four of these romances, however, I was curious as to the extent of my own abilities, and began to explore the possibilities of writing beyond the romance structure.

"Writing is enormously difficult for me. Each type of book I've attempted—comedy/fantasy, books for beginning readers, middle-grade fiction—has presented its own uniquely agonizing problems and challenges which I'm never quite sure I can meet. For me, writing is not a means of baring my soul or articulating personal angst. I want to tell stories, and as I write, I envision readers, and what they might want to hear. . . . Whenever I'm asked why I write children's books, I say that the child in me is close to surface, and she knows all the best stories."

*   *   *

KELEMAN, Stanley 1931-

PERSONAL: Born November 17, 1931, in Brooklyn, NY; son of Joe and Rose (Cohen) Keleman; married Gail Hughes; children: Katharine, Leah, Robert. *Education:* Attended Adelphi University, 1950; Chiropractic Institute of New York, D.C., 1954; attended Alfred Adler Institute, 1960-62. *Avocational interests:* Metal sculpting, public speaking.

ADDRESSES: Office—2045 Francisco St., Berkeley, CA 94709.

CAREER: Somatic psychologist, philosopher, and former bio-energetic trainer in private practice, Berkeley, CA, 1968—. Lecturer at colleges and associations.

WRITINGS:

Sexuality, Self, and Survival, Lodestar (New York City), 1970, 2nd edition published as *The Human Ground: Sexuality, Self, and Survival,* Science & Behavior Books (Palo Alto, CA), 1975.
Your Body Speaks Its Mind, Simon & Schuster (New York City), 1975.
Living Your Dying, Random House (New York City), 1976.
Somatic Reality, Center Press (Berkeley, CA), 1979.
In Defense of Heterosexuality, Center Press, 1982.
Emotional Anatomy, Center Press, 1985.
Embodying Experience: Forming a Personal Life, edited by Gene Hendrix, Center Press, 1986.
Patterns of Distress, Center Press, 1988.
Love: A Somatic View, Center Press, 1994.

*   *   *

KING, Edmund L(udwig) 1914-

PERSONAL: Born January 10, 1914, in St. Louis, MO; son of William F. B. Seifert and Lydia (Ludwig) Seifert King; stepson of Henry Grady King (a lumberman); married Willard Mae Fahrenkamp (a professor), January 29, 1951. *Education:* University of Texas, Main University (now University of Texas at Austin), A.B., 1933, M.A., 1934, Ph.D., 1949. *Politics:* Democrat. *Religion:* Episcopalian.

ADDRESSES: Home—171 Western Way, Princeton, NJ 08540-7207. *Office*—Department of Romance Languages, Princeton University, Princeton, NJ 08544.

CAREER: Mississippi State College (now University), Mississippi State, MS, assistant professor of Spanish, 1936-41; University of Texas, Main University (now University of Texas at Austin), instructor in English, 1946; Princeton University, Princeton, NJ, instructor, 1946-50, assistant professor, 1950-55, associate professor, 1955-66, professor of Spanish, 1966-75, Walter S. Carpenter, Jr. Professor of the Language, Literature, and Civilization of Spain, 1975-82, Walter S. Carpenter, Jr. Professor of the Language, Literature, and Civilization of Spain Emeritus, 1982—, chairman of department of romance languages, 1966-72. President of board of directors, International Institute in Spain, Madrid, 1977-82, resident director, 1982-83, treasurer, 1983-84. Editorial consultant, *American Heritage Larousse Spanish Dictionary,* 1986; *National Geographic Magazine* for Spanish projects. *Military service:* U.S. Army, 1941-45; became major; received Bronze Star Medal and Golden Cross of Merit (Poland).

MEMBER: Modern Language Association of America, Hispanic Society of America (corresponding member).

AWARDS, HONORS: Honorary director of International Institute in Spain.

WRITINGS:

Becquer: From Painter to Poet, Editorial Porrua S.A., 1953.
(Translator) Americo Castro, *The Structure of Spanish History,* Princeton University Press (Princeton, NJ), 1954.
(Editor) Gabriel Miro, *El Humo Dormido,* Dell (New York City), 1967.
(Editor and translator with S. Gilman) *An Idea of History: Selected Essays of Americo Castro,* Ohio State University Press (Columbus, OH), 1977.
(Editor and author of introduction) *Siguenza y el Mirador Azul y Prosas de "El Ibero," de Gabriel Miro,* Ediciones de la Torre, 1982.

Also editor of *Obra Completa de Gabriel Miro,* volumes 1 and 2, [Alicante, Spain]. Contributor to Romance language journals and to the *New Republic* and *Hudson Review.*

SIDELIGHTS: Edmund L. King once wrote: "Not a writer who makes a living as a professor, I am rather a professor who has been obliged to write. I abhor the slough of solemnity, obfuscation, mannerism, and cant into which many academic writers about literature have fallen, and feel quite filthy whenever I realize that I have slipped into it myself. My object in writing is to communicate to the reader what I know and understand about the matters more or less clearly identified in the titles of my books."*

*   *   *

KING, James   1942-

PERSONAL: Born June 14, 1942, in Springfield, MA; son of James Raymond and Alice (Gelinas) King; married Christine Dalton (a social worker), November 21, 1970; children: Alexander, Vanessa. *Education:* University of Toronto, B.A., 1967; Princeton University, M.A., 1969, Ph.D., 1970.

ADDRESSES: Home—69 Sydenham St., Dundas, Ontario, Canada L9H 2V1. *Office*—Department of English, McMaster University, Hamilton, Ontario, Canada L8S 4L9.

CAREER: McMaster University, Hamilton, Ontario, assistant professor, 1971-77, associate professor, 1977-83, professor of English, 1983—.

MEMBER: Royal Society of Canada (fellow).

AWARDS, HONORS: American Philosophical Society fellow, 1971; Canada Council fellow, 1972-78; Guggenheim fellow, 1980-81; Nuffield fellow, 1980; Arts Award, *Yorkshire Post,* 1988, for *Interior Landscapes: A Life of Paul Nash;* Killam research fellow, 1988-90.

WRITINGS:

(Editor with Charles Ryskamp) *The Letters and Prose Writings of William Cowper,* Oxford University Press (Oxford, England), Volume 1, 1979, Volume 2, 1981, Volume 3, 1982, Volume 4, 1984, Volume 5, 1986.
William Cowper: A Biography, Duke University Press (Durham, NC), 1986.
Interior Landscapes: A Life of Paul Nash, Weidenfeld & Nicolson (London), 1987.
(With Ryskamp) *Selected Letters of William Cowper,* Oxford University Press, 1989.
Virginia Woolf, Hamish Hamilton (London), 1994, Norton (New York), 1995.

Also author of *The Last Modern: A Life of Herbert Read* and *William Blake: His Life,* both published by St. Martin's (New York). Contributor to literature periodicals, including *Review of English Studies, English Studies,* and *Studies in Romanticism.*

WORK IN PROGRESS: A biography of American photographer and filmmaker Paul Strand.

BIOGRAPHICAL/CRITICAL SOURCES:

PERIODICALS

Times Literary Supplement, July 11, 1986.

KIRST, Michael W(eile) 1939-

PERSONAL: Born August 1, 1939, in West Reading, PA; son of Russell John and Marian Rick (Weile) Kirst; married Janet Lee Elliott, September 16, 1961; children: Michael E., Anne M. *Education:* Dartmouth College, A.B. (summa cum laude), 1961; Harvard University, M.P.A., 1963, Ph.D., 1964.

ADDRESSES: Home—131 Mimosa Way, Portola Valley, CA 94025. *Office*—School of Education, Stanford University, Stanford, CA 94305.

CAREER: U.S. Bureau of the Budget, Washington, DC, budget examiner, 1964; U.S. Office of Education, Washington, DC, program assistant to director of Division of Compensatory Education, 1965; National Advisory Council on Education of Disadvantaged Children, Washington, DC, associate director of President's Commission on White House Fellows, 1966; U.S. Office of Education, Bureau of Elementary and Secondary Education, director of program planning and evaluation, 1967; U.S. Senate, Washington, DC, staff director of subcommittee on manpower, employment, and poverty, 1968; Stanford University, School of Education, Stanford, CA, 1969—, currently professor of education and business administration, director of Joint Program in Educational Administration, 1969-72, member of board of directors of Stanford Center on Research in Teaching, 1971-72. Academy professor, National Academy of School Executives; director of Teacher Leadership Institute for Educational Policy Formulation, 1972; commissioner on California State Commission on Management and Evaluation of Education, 1972-75; vice-president of California State Board of Education. Has testified before U.S. Congress. Director, McCutchan Publishing Corp. Consultant to Merrill Palmer Institute, White House Domestic Policy Council, Ford Foundation, Education Commission of the States, State of Florida, U.S. Senate, and National Institute for Education.

MEMBER: American Educational Research Association (chairman of special interest group in politics, 1972-74), American Political Science Association, Dartmouth Club (San Francisco), Phi Beta Kappa, Phi Delta Kappa.

AWARDS, HONORS: Alfred P. Sloan Foundation fellow; Ford Foundation research grant, 1972, to study response of local districts to state school finance in California and to state finance reform; U.S. Office of Education grant for comparative political study of states that have approved substantial school finance reforms; formal citation from Governor Reubin Askew.

WRITINGS:

Government without Passing Laws, University of North Carolina Press (Chapel Hill, NC), 1969.
(Editor) *The Politics of Education at the Local, State, and Federal Level,* McCutchan (Berkeley, CA), 1970.
(With Joel Berke and others) *Federal Aid to Education: Who Governs, Who Benefits,* Heath (Lexington, MA), 1972.
(With Frederick Wirt) *The Political Web of American Schools,* Little, Brown (Boston, MA), 1972, published as *Political and Social Foundations of Education,* McCutchan, 1975.
(Editor) *State, School, and Politics,* Heath, 1972.
(With W. I. Garms) *Revising School Finance in Florida,* Office of the Governor of Florida, 1973.
Curriculum: A Key to Improving Academic Standards, College Entrance Examination Board, 1981.
(With Wirt) *Schools in Conflict: The Politics of Education,* McCutchan, 1982.
Who Controls Our Schools?: American Values in Conflict, Stanford Alumni Association (Stanford, CA), 1984.

Also author (with others) of *State School Finance Alternatives,* 1975. Contributor to *The Power of Competency Based Teachers,* edited by Benjamin Rosner, Allyn & Bacon (Boston, MA), 1973. Also contributor to *Review of Educational Research, Education and Urban Society, Education Digest,* and *Georgetown Law Review.* Member of editorial board of *Education and Urban Society,* 1973.

WORK IN PROGRESS: Guidelines for the Administration of Educational Television Projects in Developing Countries.

BIOGRAPHICAL/CRITICAL SOURCES:

PERIODICALS

American Political Science Review, March, 1970.
Educational Leadership, November, 1985.

L

LANGSTAFF, John (Meredith) 1920-

PERSONAL: Born December 24, 1920, in Brooklyn, NY; son of Bridgewater Meredith and E. Esther Knox (Boardman) Langstaff; married Diane Guggenheim (divorced); married Nancy Graydon Woodbridge, April 3, 1948; children: (first marriage) Carol; (second marriage) John Elliot, Peter Gerry, Deborah Graydon. *Education:* Attended Curtis Institute of Music, 1940-41; Juilliard School of Music, 1946-49; and Columbia University, 1949-51. *Avocational interests:* Camping, bee-keeping, hiking, morris dancing, modern art, and poetry.

ADDRESSES: Home—Carriage House, 83 Washington Avenue, Cambridge, MA 02140. *Office*—Revels, Inc., Box 290, Cambridge, MA 02138.

CAREER: Writer and musician. Director of music department, Potomac School, Washington, DC, 1953-68, and Shady Hill School, Cambridge, MA, 1969-72; instructor, Simmons College, Boston, 1970-86, Wheelock College, Boston, 1974-79, Massachusetts College of Art, Boston, 1977, University of Connecticut, Storrs, 1977-79, Boston College, 1979, and Lesley College, 1978—. Lecturer for Association of American Colleges; has given recitals in the United States and Europe; has appeared on radio and television programs, including a music series for British Broadcasting Corp. Recordings include *Hello World!* (with Little Orchestra Society and Mrs. Franklin D. Roosevelt), *Singing Games for Children, American Ballads and Folk Songs, Songs for Singing Children, Let's Make Music with John Langstaff, John Langstaff Sings, Recital of Purcell-Dowland Songs,* and *Contemporary Ballad Poetry. Military service:* U.S. Army, Infantry, c. 1940-45, became first lieutenant; received Purple Heart and Gold Star.

MEMBER: American Guild of Musical Artists, Actors Equity, International Folk Music Council, Country Dance Society of America (member of governing board), Folk Song Society (founder and director), Urban League, "Philosophers-Kings" Club, Washington, DC.

AWARDS, HONORS: Recognized by National Federation of Musicians, 1959, for presenting outstanding American music abroad; Hope S. Dean Memorial Award, Foundation for Children's Books, 1991.

WRITINGS:

FOR CHILDREN

Frog Went A-Courtin', illustrations by Feodor Rojankovsky, Harcourt (New York City), 1955.

Over in the Meadow, Harcourt, 1957.

On Christmas Day in the Morning!, Harcourt, 1959.

The Swapping Boy, Harcourt, 1960.

Ol' Dan Tucker, Harcourt, 1963.

(Compiler) *Hi! Ho! The Rattlin' Bog: And Other Folk Songs for Group Singing,* Harcourt, 1969.

(With wife, Nancy Langstaff) *Jim along, Josie: A Collection of Folk Songs and Singing Games for Young Children,* Harcourt, 1969.

The Golden Vanity, Harcourt, 1970.

Gather My Gold Together, Doubleday (Garden City, NY), 1971.

Saint George and the Dragon: A Mummer's Play, Atheneum (New York City), 1972.

The Two Magicians, Atheneum, 1973.

(Compiler) *Soldier, Soldier, Won't You Marry Me?,* Doubleday, 1973.

(With daughter, Carol Langstaff) *Shimmy, Shimmy, Coke-Ca-Pop! A Collection of City Children's Street Games and Rhymes,* Doubleday, 1973.

(Compiler) *The Season for Singing: American Christmas Songs and Carols,* Doubleday, 1974.

Oh, A-Hunting We Will Go!, illustrations by Nancy W. Parker, Atheneum, 1974, enlarged edition, 1991.

(Compiler) *Sweetly Sings the Donkey,* Atheneum, 1976.

Hot Cross Buns and Other Old Street Cries, Atheneum, 1978.

The Christmas Revels Songbook, David Godine (Boston), 1985.

Sally Go Round the Moon and Other Revels, Songs, and Singing Games for Young Children, Revels Publications (Cambridge, MA), 1986.

(Compiler and editor) *What a Morning! The Christmas Story in Black Spirituals,* illustrations by Ashley Bryan, Macmillan, 1987.

Climbing Jacob's Ladder: Heroes of the Bible in African-American Spirituals, illustrations by Bryan, Macmillan Child Group, 1991.

(Editor) *I Have a Song to Sing, O!: An Introduction to the Songs of Gilbert and Sullivan,* McElderry (New York City), 1994.

SIDELIGHTS: John Langstaff is best known for his efforts to teach young people about music and verse. A concert soloist, music teacher, and recording artist, he often lectures about the connections between songs and ballads and the folklore from the culture of the singers or balladeers.

In *Frog Went A-Courtin',* which received the 1956 Caldecott Medal for its fanciful illustrations by artist Feodor Rojankovsky, Langstaff retold a nursery ballad in a book designed for children. Ellen Lewis Buell, writing in the *New York Times Book Review,* describes the appeal of *Frog Went A-Courtin'* this way: "The tune is a simple one from the Southern Appalachians and the phrases and rhythms of the song have the hearty, old-fashioned flavor of that region." She notes that Langstaff provides a happy ending for the song rather than the traditional catastrophic one, and that this revision ought to please young readers.

In *What a Morning! The Christmas Story in Black Spirituals* Langstaff tells the Christmas story by interspersing illustrated Bible verses with five traditional black spirituals, arranged by John Andrew Ross, the music director of the National Center of Afro-American Artists. Together, the songs tell the story of the birth of Jesus from an African and Afro-American perspective. The songs selected by Langstaff range from a simple lullaby to a celebratory hymn to lyrics that connect the birth of Christ to that of infants born into troubled circumstances everywhere.

Langstaff's books appeal to the sense of folklore, music, and rhythm within his readers. For instance, *Shimmy Shimmy Coke-Ca-Pop! A Collection of City Children's Street Games and Rhymes,* which he wrote and compiled with his daughter, Carol, is a collection of action photographs, games, rhymes, and chants that are familiar to most school children. Writing of *Shimmy Shimmy Coke-Ca-Pop* in *Scientific American,* Philip and Phylis Morrison point out that these jingles and games recruit children into a special American subculture of their own. The Morrisons write: "Vigorous, as authentic as the rearing bike and the kicked can, the text and [Don MacSorley's] photographs are full of life and action, by no means prettified. The book is both a record and a guide to emulation." The collection, they say, is a "feast for eye and voice."

Langstaff is also known as the creator of the *Revels,* a series of performances that celebrate the changing of the seasons through drama, song, and dance; he has published some of these efforts in *The Christmas Revels Songbook* and *Sally Go Round the Moon and Other Revels, Songs and Singing Games for Young Children.* In *Horn Book* magazine, Susan Cooper calls the *Revels* "an answer to that submerged yearning for ritual, and for the marking of ancient landmarks in human life, which lies very deep in all of us and which very little in the American Way can satisfy."

First performed in 1957, the *Revels* are now seasonal events in several communities in the Northeast. Langstaff himself describes the significance of the *Revels* to Cooper in terms that apply equally to his whole life's work: "There's this need—the lack of opportunity in people's lives to have any communal celebration. . . . What we try to do is to fill this gap that people feel but don't quite understand. We do it in two ways, I think: By the nature of the *Revels* material, which comes from things in their own cultural backgrounds that they can no longer remember or pass on to their children, and by getting them to *participate.*"

BIOGRAPHICAL/CRITICAL SOURCES:

BOOKS

Children's Literature Review, Volume 3, Gale (Detroit), 1978.

Georgiou, Constantine, *Children and Their Literature,* Prentice-Hall (New York City), 1969.

PERIODICALS

Atlantic Monthly, June, 1955, p. 82.

Commonweal, November 21, 1969; November 23, 1973.

Horn Book, December, 1959; December, 1970; December, 1973; February, 1975; June, 1978; December, 1979; January, 1992; May, 1992.

New York Times Book Review, March 20, 1955, p. 26; November 9, 1969, p. 67; May 7, 1972; November 3, 1974; December 6, 1987, p. 80.

Observer, September 28, 1980.

Publishers Weekly, August 15, 1994, p. 96.

Saturday Review, May 14, 1955; December 19, 1959.

School Library Journal, January, 1992, p. 104.

Scientific American, December, 1973.

Times Literary Supplement, November 28, 1963; June 15, 1973; September 28, 1973; March 29, 1974; July 5, 1974.*

*   *   *

LARSON, Muriel 1924-

PERSONAL: Born February 9, 1924, in Orange, NJ; daughter of Eugene Louis and Helen (Fretz) Koller; children: Gay Maloney, Lori Rennie. *Education:* South River Bible Institute, diploma, 1957; Bob Jones University, additional study, 1967-69; Southern Baptist Center for Biblical Studies, M.R.E., 1988, D.R.E., 1989, Christian counselor certificate, 1989. *Politics:* Republican. *Religion:* Baptist. *Avocational interests:* Music (plays piano, organ, accordion, electronic keyboard, clarinet, and sings), gardening, reading, camping.

ADDRESSES: Home—10 Vanderbilt Circle, Greenville, SC 29609.

CAREER: Stenographer with printing company in Dunellen, NJ, 1955-57, and with Tennessee Valley Authority, Chattanooga, 1962-63; Bob Jones University, Greenville, SC, public relations writer, 1967-69; full-time writer, 1969—. Lecturer on creative writing and relationships. Has also worked as a counselor, choir director, substitute teacher, home missionary, children's evangelist, church organist, and instructor at writers' conferences; faculty advisor for Southern Baptist Center for Biblical Studies in writing.

WRITINGS:

Devotions for Women's Groups, Baker Book (Grand Rapids, MI), 1967.
How to Give a Devotion, Baker Book, 1967.
Devotionals for Children's Groups, Baker Book, 1969.
Living Miracles, Warner Press (Anderson, IN), 1973.
It Took a Miracle, Warner Press, 1974.
You Are What You Think, Bible Voice (Van Nuys, CA), 1974.
God's Fantastic Creation, Moody (Chicago), 1975.
The Bible Says Quiz Book, Moody, 1976.
Are You Real, God?, Bible Voice, 1976.
I Give Up, God, Bible Voice, 1978.
Joy Every Morning, Moody, 1979.
What Happens When Women Believe, Bible Voice, 1979.
Living by Faith, Aglow, 1984.
Praise Every Day, Huntington House (Shreveport, LA), 1984.
Ways Women Can Witness (Round Table Book Club book-of-the-month selection), Broadman (Nashville), 1984.
Me and My Pet Peeves, Broadman, 1988.
Petals of Praise, Moody, 1991.

Also author of a play, *Miracles,* and of gospel hymns and choruses. Contributor to books, including *God's Power to Triumph,* edited by James R. Adair, Moody, 1968; *Unhooked,* edited by Adair, Baker Book, 1971; *The Hairy Brown Angel,* edited by Grace Fox, Victor Books, 1977; *Escape from Darkness,* edited by Ted Miller and Adair, Victor Books, 1982; *Take Five to Grow,* Back to the Bible, 1982. Contributor of articles, stories, devotionals, and poems to *Moody Monthly, Home Life, Decision, Grit, Discipleship Journal, Reader's Digest,* and many other periodicals. Also prepares crossword puzzles for several publishers. Editor, *Reinhearter* (monthly church paper), Dallas, TX, 1966-67.

WORK IN PROGRESS: Whatever Became of Prince Charming and *Escape from Sodom.*

SIDELIGHTS: Muriel Larson once wrote *CA:* "I have always been interested in writing and started while in high school by writing for the school paper and preparing the social column for my town for a weekly paper.

"I began my career as a writer while a minister's wife. When I attended a national conference with my husband, a woman writer addressed us women and inspired me to start writing. The two stories I wrote on the way home from that conference were accepted eventually by two periodicals, and I was in business. Since then I have had more than five thousand first and reprint right writings accepted for publication by over three hundred periodicals, as well as my seventeen books, twenty gospel songs, and one play for radio.

"My main purpose in writing is to glorify God and point other people to Him, for I have found a wonderful life in serving and trusting the Lord. The purpose behind all my writings is to help others find the truth of God that leads to the abundant life He promised those who commit their way unto Him.

"The most important advice I give to aspiring writers at the conferences at which I teach is to keep trying. Persistence, perseverance, and self-discipline are necessary for success. Also, when you start submitting your work to editors, send two to four articles out to several places. Then if one is accepted, it encourages you to continue on. If you just send one out and it is rejected, you tend to lose heart and fall by the wayside."

*   *   *

LAWRENCE, J. T.
See ROWLAND-ENTWISTLE, (Arthur) Theodore (Henry)

LEES, Gene 1928-

PERSONAL: Born February 8, 1928, in Hamilton, Ontario, Canada; son of Harold (a musician, later a construction engineer) and Dorothy (Flatman) Lees; married Carmen Lister, 1951; married Micheline A. Ducreux, July, 1955; married Janet Suttle, 1971; children: (second marriage) Philippe. *Education:* Attended Ontario College of Art, Toronto, one year.

ADDRESSES: Home and office—P. O. Box 240, Ojai, CA 93024-0240.

CAREER: Reporter for *Hamilton Spectator, Toronto Telegram* and *Montreal Star,* 1948-55; *Louisville Times,* Louisville, KY, classical music critic and film and drama editor, 1955-58; *Down Beat* (jazz magazine), Chicago, IL, editor, 1959-61; *Hi Fi/Stereo Review,* New York City, contributing editor, 1962-65; columnist for *High Fidelity,* 1965-79; *Jazzletter,* Ojai, CA, founder and principal writer, 1981—. Lyricist, composer, and collaborator with other composers on songs; toured Latin America under the auspices of U.S. Department of State as manager of jazz sextet, 1962; thirty songs with his lyrics, among them "Waltz for Debby," "Song of the Jet," "Paris Is at Her Best in May," and "Someone to Light Up My Life," were released in a Richmond Organization portfolio, 1968. Radio and television writer and singer for the Canadian Broadcasting Corp. and various independent Canadian radio stations.

MEMBER: Society of Composers, Authors and Music Publishers of Canada.

AWARDS, HONORS: Reid fellowship, 1958-59; ASCAP-Deems Taylor Award, American Society of Composers, Authors, and Publishers, for articles in *High Fidelity,* 1978, for *Meet Me at Jim and Andy's,* 1989, and for *Waiting for Dizzy.*

WRITINGS:

And Sleep until Noon (novel), Simon & Schuster (New York City), 1966.

The Modern Rhyming Dictionary: How to Write Lyrics, Cherry Lane (Port Chester, NY), 1981.

Singers and the Song, Oxford University Press (New York City), 1987.

Meet Me at Jim and Andy's, Oxford University Press, 1988.

Oscar Peterson: The Will To Swing (biography), Lester & Orpen Dennys, 1988.

(With Henry Mancini) *Did They Mention the Music* (autobiography), Contemporary Books (Chicago), 1989.

Inventing Champagne: The Worlds of Lerner and Loewe (biography), St. Martin's Press (New York City), 1990.

Waiting for Dizzy, Oxford University Press, 1991.

(With photographer John Reeves) *Jazz Lives,* McClelland & Stewart (Toronto), 1992.

Cats of Any Color: Jazz Black and White, Oxford University Press, 1994.

Early Autumn: A Biography of Woody Herman, Oxford University Press, 1995.

Contributor of articles and short stories to the *New York Times, Los Angeles Times, Globe and Mail* (Toronto), *Saturday Review, American Film,* and other periodicals in the United States, Canada, and Europe.

WORK IN PROGRESS: Biographies of Glenn Miller and pianist Bill Evans.

SIDELIGHTS: A distinguished lyricist known for his words to "Quiet Nights of Quiet Stars" and other bossa nova songs, Gene Lees helped introduce the bossa nova in America and has translated the Portuguese lyrics of many Brazilian songs into English. His songs have been recorded by Frank Sinatra, Tony Bennett, and others, and he has collaborated with such composers as Charles Aznavour of France, Antonio Carlos Jobim of Brazil, and Lalo Schifrin of Argentina. In 1976, Lees collaborated with Roger Kellaway on the musical score for the film "The Mouse and His Child."

In 1983, Lees adapted to music the English version of a group of poems by Pope John Paul II, which Sarah Vaughan recorded in concert the following year. The resulting album—a suite of songs pleading for world peace—was released internationally under the title *The Planet Is Alive: Let It Live* and was well received critically. In 1984, Choice Records released an album of Lees singing his own songs, and in 1985, Stash Records released *Gene Lees Sings the Gene Lees Song Book,* a performance with orchestra of songs that Lees wrote with Jobim and other composers.

Also known as one of the finest jazz writers working today, Lees launched *Jazzletter* in 1980, and he has collected his essays from his newsletter into several published volumes. Interviewing Lees for a review of the first collection of *Jazzletter* essays, *Singers and the Song,* for the *New York Times Book Review,* Peter Keepnews wrote: "The singers closest to [Lees'] heart belong to a tradition he feels is fading, and he acknowledged that most of the essays have a nostalgic tone, as does the newsletter itself: 'It's not so much a news publication as a historical publication. And let's face it, most people in history are dead.'"

Lees wrote *CA* that *Jazzletter* has been a useful vehicle for his work: "Since I do not have to submit material to editors, I can determine for myself the importance of the subject matter, the nature of the treatment, and the length of it. I don't have to answer to anyone but my readers, an extremely distinguished group of musicians, professional people of all kinds, and scholars. They are brilliant people, and thus I am no longer in a position—as I was when I wrote for magazines—of having to write 'down' to the level of what an editor thinks his readers can understand. On the contrary, the very nature of my readership pushes me to seek my highest level of work."

BIOGRAPHICAL/CRITICAL SOURCES:

PERIODICALS

BMI (publication of Broadcast Music, Inc.), November, 1967.
Calendar, April 15, 1984.
Jazztimes, August 24, 1986.
Los Angeles Times Book Review, January 17, 1982.
New York Times Book Review, November 15, 1987.

*   *   *

LEMAY, J(oseph) A(lberic) Leo 1935-

PERSONAL: Born January 7, 1935, in Bristow, VA; son of Joseph Albert (a steelworker) and Valencia Lee (Winslow) Lemay; married Muriel Ann Clarke (a real estate broker), August 11, 1965; children: John, Lee, Kate. *Education:* University of Maryland, A.B., 1957, A.M., 1962; University of Pennsylvania, Ph.D., 1964. *Politics:* Republican. *Religion:* Unitarian Universalist.

ADDRESSES: Home—4828 Kennett Pike, Greenville, DE 19807. *Office*—Department of English, University of Delaware, Newark, DE 19716.

CAREER: George Washington University, Washington, DC, assistant professor of English, 1963-65; University of California, Los Angeles, assistant professor, 1965-70, associate professor, 1970-75, professor of English, 1975-77; University of Delaware, Newark, H. F. du Pont Winterthur Professor of English, 1977—. Center for Editions of American Authors, advisory committee member, 1974-76. *Military service:* U.S. Army, 1957-59.

MEMBER: Modern Language Association of America, American Humor Studies Association (president, 1981), American Antiquarian Society, Institute for Early American History and Culture (council member, 1978-81), Society for the Study of Southern Literature, Maryland Historical Society, Pennsylvania Historical Society, Virginia Historical Society.

AWARDS, HONORS: Guggenheim fellow, 1974-75; Institute for Advanced Study fellow, University of Delaware, 1980-81; senior fellowship, National Endowment for the Humanities, 1983-84, 1994-95; grants from American Philosophical Society and Colonial Williamsburg.

WRITINGS:

Ebenezer Kinnersley: Franklin's Friend, University of Pennsylvania Press (Philadelphia), 1964.
Men of Letters in Colonial Maryland, University of Tennessee Press (Knoxville), 1972.
A Calendar of American Poetry in Colonial Newspapers and Magazines through 1765, American Antiquarian Society (Worcester, MA), 1972.
"New England's Annoyances": America's First Folk Song, University of Delaware Press (Newark), 1985.
The Canon of Benjamin Franklin, 1722-1776: New Additions and Reconsiderations, University of Delaware Press, 1986.
The American Dream of Captain John Smith, University of Virginia Press (Charlottesville), 1991.
Did Pocahontas Save Captain John Smith?, University of Georgia Press (Athens), 1992.

EDITOR

The Oldest Revolutionary: Essays on Benjamin Franklin, University of Pennsylvania Press, 1976.
Essays in Early Virginia Literature Honoring Richard Beale Davis, Burt Franklin (New York City), 1977.
The Autobiography of Benjamin Franklin: A Genetic Text, University of Tennessee Press, 1981.
(With P. M. Zall) *Benjamin Franklin's Autobiography: A Norton Critical Edition,* Norton (New York City), 1986.
Deism, Masonry, and the Enlightenment: Essays Honoring Alfred Owen Aldridge, University of Delaware Press, 1987.
Benjamin Franklin: Writings, Literary Classics of the United States (New York City), 1987.
An Early American Reader, United States Information Agency (Washington, DC), 1988.
Robert Bolling Woos Anne Miller: Love and Courtship in Colonial Virginia, 1760, University Press of Virginia, 1990.
Reappraising Benjamin Franklin: A Bicentennial Perspective, University of Delaware Press, 1993.

Contributor to periodicals, including *American Literature, New England Quarterly,* and *Virginia Magazine of History and Biography.* Editorial board member, *American Literature,* 1976-79.

WORK IN PROGRESS: Benjamin Franklin: A Biography; The Accounts of Benjamin Franklin; and *Benjamin Franklin: A Chronological Documentary History.*

LEONHARDT, Fritz 1909-

PERSONAL: Born July 11, 1909, in Stuttgart, Germany; son of Gustav (an architect) and Lene (Schlecht) Leonhardt; married Liselotte Klein, September 6, 1936; children: Sabine, Monika, Haidemarie, Hansjeorg, Christine. *Education:* University of Stuttgart, Diplom-Ingenieur, 1931, doctorate in engineering, 1938; attended Purdue University, 1932-33.

ADDRESSES: Home—Lenzhalde 16, D-70192 Stuttgart, Germany.

CAREER: Bridge engineer for autobahns in Stuttgart, Cologne, and Berlin, Germany, 1934-42; Organisation Todt OT, Kivioeli, Estonia, and Munich, Germany, 1942-45; University of Stuttgart, Stuttgart, professor of engineering at Institute for Concrete Structures, 1958-74, president of the university, 1967-69; consulting engineer, 1938—.

MEMBER: Comite Euro-International du Beton (honorary member), International Association for Bridge and Structural Engineering, Federation Internationale de la Precontrainte, International Association for Shell and Spatial Structures, Verein Deutscher Ingenieure, Deutscher Architekten and Ingenieur Verband (honorary member), Deutscher Ausschuss fuer Stahlbeton, Deutsche Akademie fuer Staedtebau und Landesplanung, Verein Beratender Ingenieure, Architektenkammer (honorary member), Forschungsrat des Bundesministeriums Bauwesen, American Society of Civil Engineers (fellow), American Concrete Institute (honorary member), National Academy of Engineering (foreign associate), Swiss Academy of Engineering Sciences (corresponding member), Seventeenth Committee for Saving the Tower of Pisa.

AWARDS, HONORS: Ehrenmuenze (honor medal), 1953, and Grashof-Denkmuenze, 1973, both from Verein Deutscher Ingenieure; Paul-Bonatz-Preis from city of Stuttgart, 1959; Fritz-Schumacher-Preis from FVS, Hamburg, 1961; Goldene Ehrenmuenze (golden honor medal) from Austrian Association of Architects and Engineers, 1965; Verner-von-Siemens-Ring from W. V. Siemens Stiftung, 1965; Emil-Moersch-Denkmuenze from Deutscher Beton Verein, 1967; Belgian Medaille d'Or Gustave Magnel, 1968; Freyssinet Medal from Federation Internationale de la Precontrainte, 1974; distinguished service award from Oregon State University, 1974; named honorary member of Chamber of Architects of Baden-Wuerttemberg, 1974; Gold Medal from Institution of Structural Engineers of London, 1975; Distinguished Service Medal of Baden-Wuerttemberg, 1976; Gold Medal from Associazione Italiana Cemente Armato e Precompresso, 1977; Grosses Verdienstkreuz des Verdienstordens (great order of merit) from government of West Germany, 1980; International Award for Structural Engineering from International Association for Bridge and Structural Engineering, 1981; Gold Medal for Merits from city of Vienna, Austria, 1982; named honorary member of Academy of Sciences of Heidelberg, 1982; honorary doctorates from Technical University of Braunschweig, 1972, Technical University of Denmark, 1974, Purdue University, 1980, and University of Liege, 1980; First DAI-Preis, 1995, des Deutschen Architekten und Ingenieur Verbandes, Berlin.

WRITINGS:

Die Gestaltung der Bruecken (title means "Design of Bridges"), Volk und Reich Verlag, 1937.

Die vereinfachte Traegerrostberechnung (title means "Simplified Analysis of Girder Grids"), J. Hoffmann, 1940.

Spannbeton fuer die Praxis, Wilhelm Ernst, 1955, translation published as *Prestressed Concrete: Design and Construction,* Wilhelm Ernst, 1964.

Vorspannung mit konzentrierten Spanngliedern (title means "Prestressing with Concentrated Tendons"), Wilhelm Ernst, 1956.

Moersch, Bruecken aus Stahlbeton und Spannbeton, 6th edition, Konrad Wittwer, 1958.

Studenten-Unruhen (title means "Students Unrest"), Seewald, 1968.

Vorlesungen ueber Massivbau (title means "Lectures on Concrete Structures"), Volumes I-VI, Springer Verlag, 1973-86.

Ingenieurbau (title means "Civil and Structural Engineering"), Carl Habel, 1974.

Der Bauingenieur und seine Aufgaben (title means "The Civil Engineer and His Tasks"), Deutsche Verlags-Anstalt, 1981.

Bruecken: Aesthetik und Gestaltung/Bridges: Aesthetics and Design (parallel text in German and English), Deutsche Verlags-Anstalt, 1982, MIT Press, 1984.

Ponts/Puentes (title means "Bridges"), Presses Polytechniques Romandes, 1986.

Also co-author with E. Heinle of a book on towers for Deutsche Verlags-Anstalt. Contributor of numerous articles to architectural and structural journals.

Some of Leonhardt's works have been translated into French, Spanish, English and Italian.

SIDELIGHTS: Since 1938, Fritz Leonhardt has worked as a consulting engineer, specializing in bridge design and other difficult structures. He is one of the first successful designers of long-span bridges that utilize prestressed concrete and stay cables. Leonhardt designed the first high-rise concrete tower, the Stuttgart Television Tower, in 1953, and he has since been responsible for several other similar structures, as well as bridges in Brazil, Argentina, Venezuela, Austria, Switzerland, Pakistan, India, Japan, and the United States. The engineer also designed the German Pavilion for Montreal's Expo '67 and contributed designs of structures for the Olympic Games held in Munich, Germany in 1972.

Leonhardt told *CA:* "With all that we build, we impress our fellow people—individuals and society—consciously or subconsciously. Bad aesthetic qualities like ugly slum areas or jammed high-rise buildings can cause depression or aggression leading to crime. For all that we design, we must keep in mind the psychic requirements of human beings—the users. They should feel well and comfortable. This aesthetic in all fields of building is an important feature. We must be aware of this responsibility."

*   *   *

LE ROY LADURIE, Emmanuel (Bernard) 1929-

PERSONAL: Born July 19, 1929, in Moutiers, France; son of Jacques (an agriculturalist and government minister) and Leontine (Dauger) Le Roy Ladurie; married Madeleine Pupponi (a physician), July 9, 1955; children: Francois, Anne. *Education:* Ecole Normale Superieure, Paris, agrege d'histoire, 1953, docteur des lettres, 1956. *Politics:* "Centre-Gauche." *Religion:* Catholic.

ADDRESSES: Home—88 rue d'Alleray, 75015 Paris, France. *Office*—College de France, 11 place Marcelin-Berthelot, 75005 Paris, France. Bibliotheque Nationale, 58 rue Richelieu, 75084 Paris Cedex 02, France.

CAREER: Lycee de Montpellier, Montpellier, France, teacher, 1953-57; Centre National de la Recherche Scientifique, Paris, France, researcher, 1957-60; Faculte des Lettres de Montpellier, Montpellier, assistant professor, 1960-63; Ecole Pratique des Hautes Etudes, Paris, master assistant professor, 1963-65, director of studies, 1965-69; Faculte des Lettres de Paris, lecturer, 1969; Sorbonne, Universite de Paris, Paris, lecturer, 1970-71; Universite de Paris-VII, Paris, professor of geography and social sciences, 1970-73; College de France, Paris, professor of history of modern civilization, 1973—. Bibliotheque Nationale, Paris, general administrator, 1987—.

AWARDS, HONORS: Named chevalier of the French Legion of Honor; received honorary doctorate from the University of Geneva; received silver medal from the Centre National de la Recherche Scientifique, 1966. Also received honorary degrees from the University of Michigan, Geneva, Leeds, Hull, and Leicester.

WRITINGS:

NONFICTION; IN ENGLISH TRANSLATION

Les Paysans de Languedoc, Mouton, 1966, translation with introduction by John Day published as *The Peas-*
ants of Languedoc, consulting editor, George Huppert, University of Illinois Press (Champaign), 1974.

Histoire du climat depuis l'an mil, Flammarion (Paris), 1967, translation by Barbara Bray, with revisions and updated material, published as *Times of Feast, Times of Famine: A History of Climate since the Year 1000,* Doubleday (New York City), 1971.

(With Joseph Goy) *Les Fluctuations de produits de la dime: Conjoncture decimale et dominiale de la fin du moyen age au XVIIIe siecle,* Mouton/DeGruyter (Berlin), 1972, translation by Susan Burke published as *Tithe and Agrarian History from the Fourteenth to the Nineteenth Centuries: An Essay in Comparative History,* Cambridge University Press, 1982.

Le Territoire de l'historien (essays), Gallimard (Paris), Volume I, 1973, Volume II, 1978, translation of Volume I by Ben and Sian Reynolds published as *The Territory of the Historian,* University of Chicago Press, 1979, translation of Volume II by B. Reynolds and S. Reynolds published as *The Mind and Method of the Historian,* University of Chicago Press, 1981.

Montaillou: Village occitan de 1294 a 1324, Gallimard, 1975, translation by Barbara Bray published in the United States as *Montaillou: The Promised Land of Error,* Braziller (New York City), 1978, in England as *Montaillou: Cathars and Catholics in a French Village, 1294-1324,* Scolar, 1978.

(With Michael Morineau) *Histoire economique et sociale de la France,* Volume I: *De 1450 a 1660,* Volume II: *Paysannerie et croissance,* 1976, translation by Alan Sheridan published in the United States as *The French Peasantry, 1450-1660,* University of California Press (Berkeley), 1987.

Le Carnaval de Romans: De la Chandeleur au mercredi des Cendres, 1579-1580, Gallimard, 1979, translation by Mary Feeney published in the United States as *Carnival in Romans,* Braziller, 1979, in England as *Carnival: A People's Uprising at Romans, 1579-1580,* Scolar, 1980.

L'Argent, l'amour, et la mort en Pays d'Oc, Seuil (Paris), 1980, translation by Alan Sheridan published as *Love, Death, and Money in the Pays d'Oc,* Braziller, 1982.

La Sorciere de Jasmin, Seuil, 1984, translation by Brian Pearce published as *Jasmin's Witch,* Braziller, 1987.

L'Etat royal: De Louis XI a Henri IV, 1460-1610, Hachette (Paris), 1987, translation by Juliet Vale published as *The Royal French State: 1460-1610,* Blackwell (Oxford, UK), 1994.

IN FRENCH

Histoire de Languedoc, Presses Universitaires de France (Paris), 1962.

Le Climat des XIe et XVIe siecles: Series comparees, Armand Colin, 1965.

(With Jean Paul De Saive and J. P. Goupert) *Medecins, climat, et epidemies a la fin du 18e siecle,* Mouton/DeGruyter, 1972.

(With Hugues Neveux and Jean Jacquart) *L'Age classique des paysans, 1340-1789,* Seuil, 1975.

Aix-en-Provence, L'Arc [Versailles, France], 1976.

Paris-Montpellier, Gallimard, 1982.

(With Orest Ranum) *Pierre Prion, scribe: Memoires d'un ecrivain de campagne au XVIIIe siecle,* Gallimard, 1985.

L'Ancien Regime: De Louis XIII a Louis XV, 1610-1770, Hachette, 1991.

Also author of *Introduction cartographique a une ecologie quantitative de la France traditionnelle, XVIIe-XIXe siecles,* 1966, and *Parmi les historiens,* 1983. Co-author of *Inventaire des campagnes,* 1980, and *L'Histoire urbaine de la France,* volume 3, 1981.

SIDELIGHTS: One of the most celebrated historians of the Western world, Emmanuel Le Roy Ladurie is associated with the Annales school of thought. The Annales group, or Annalistes, derive their name from the journal *Annales,* which was established in 1929 by French historians who wanted to change the focus of historical analysis and to break away from the traditional view of the history of events. They felt that concentrating on major political actions and powerful people provided too little information about the way most people lived at any given time; instead, they wanted to analyze history in terms of quantitative, material data, and to focus on ordinary communities.

Le Roy Ladurie's collection of essays *Le Territoire de l'historien,* the first volume of which was originally published in 1973, reflects the Annaliste attitudes embraced by the author during the 1960s and early 1970s. As in other of his early writings, Le Roy Ladurie stresses the use of computerized information and statistical analysis of everything from weather patterns and crop production to disease and the distribution of taxes. The message of these essays is "harsh and clear," Lawrence Stone of the *New York Review of Books* explained in response to the 1979 translation of Volume I of *Le Territoire de l'historien:* "Narrative history, the history of events, political history, and biography are dead. The methodology of history must now be strictly quantitative; . . . it must concern itself with long-term shifts in the material bases of life; it must focus on the masses, not the elite. . . . It will be true 'scientific history,' based at bottom on the relationship of population to food supply."

Some of the conclusions of this approach were considered untenable by reviewers like Stone. For instance, one outcome of *Le Territoire de l'historien* is the idea of "l'histoire immobile," which holds that from 1300 until the eco-

nomic upswing of the eighteenth century, European history did not change. Stone deemed this conclusion "nonsense" and "a gross oversimplification" that ignored five centuries of significant ideological, moral, and social developments. The critic also explained that *Le Territoire de l'historien,* as a collection of Le Roy Ladurie's early essays and articles, reflected an outdated Annaliste approach and represented "neither the current central interests and methods of the new historians, nor those of the author himself." Rather, Stone remarked, Le Roy Ladurie's more recent works reflected "a wholly different intellectual universe . . . . Gone are the computers, the graphs, and the statistical tables. Gone too is the obsession with long-term structures." In later works Le Roy Ladurie turned to individual communities, their attitudes, values, customs, and beliefs.

Montaillou and *Carnaval de Romans,* Le Roy Ladurie's best-known books, are products of their author's shift in concentration. In these books Le Roy Ladurie retains his original Annaliste focus on the ordinary masses and still includes economic information in his analyses, yet he balances quantitative measures with sociological ones. These two works, according to a *New Republic* article by Eugen Weber, represent Le Roy Ladurie "at his storytelling best, squeezing life and local color out of dusty documents." In *Montaillou,* for instance, the author reconstructs the fourteenth-century lives of the villagers of Montaillou, a small town in southern France. The analysis consists of two parts: the first the author calls "the ecology of Montaillou" and in it deals with the material aspects of the village and its inhabitants; in the second part, "an archaeology of Montaillou," Le Roy Ladurie writes about the attitudes, practices, mores and perceptions of the villagers. The result is, according to *New York Review of Books* critic Keith Thomas, "a wholly successful demonstration of the historian's capacity to bring together almost every dimension of human experience into a single satisfying whole."

A bestseller in France, *Montaillou* appealed to both scholars and the general public. Critics cited the licentious character of the village as a major reason for the book's popularity. They noted that the villagers, most of them followers of the Cathar or Albigensian heresy, lived by the motto "since everything is forbidden, everything is allowed." Unaffected by religious qualms, the villagers led promiscuous lives. The network of Church spies and closet heretics, who manipulated people with threats of exposure to the Inquisition, only encouraged the exchange of sexual favors.

Prurient appeal aside, *Montaillou*'s critical and public acclaim was largely due to the author's methodology and style. Thomas hailed Le Roy Ladurie's work as "witty and sophisticated, fertile and inventive, [bubbling] over with ideas and comparisons, though sometimes with a faint touch of slickness." Stone noted *Montaillou*'s "sheer brilliance in the use of a unique document to reconstruct in fascinating detail a previously totally unknown world." The document Stone cited is a verbatim account of interrogations conducted by Inquisitor Jacques Fournier, then bishop of Pamiers, later Pope Benedict XII. In Fournier's attempt to eradicate heresy, he questioned twenty-five Montaillou villagers and recorded their comments in their own words. The result is an extensive account of the villagers' values, lifestyles, and conceptions of the world. Fournier's ledgers are so thorough and detailed, noted Stone, that they "enabled Le Roy Ladurie to bring the Middle Ages to life in a way that has probably never been achieved before by any historian."

In *Carnaval de Romans* Le Roy Ladurie again approaches his historical subject, this time a small southeastern French town in the sixteenth century, with a view to both the socio-economic situations and the mental attitudes of its inhabitants. In addition, the author takes advantage of semiotics, or the interpretation of symbols, in order to read festival rituals in terms of the political, economic, and social preoccupations of the town of Romans. Moreover, as William H. McNeill noted in the *Chicago Tribune Book World,* "by focusing on the microcosm of a small town, [Le Roy] Ladurie illuminates the complex conflicts of the age: noble vs. commoner . . . rich vs. poor within the town itself, and most massive of all, peasant vs. everyone else in society."

These conflicts, as *Carnaval de Romans* reveals, came to a head in 1580 during the Mardi Gras (Shrove Tuesday) festivities in Romans. Every year the town divided itself into "kingdoms" of common folk and elites for the pre-Lenten Carnival rituals. In the Romans Carnival of 1580 the artisans' "kingdom" chose the master draper, Paumier, as its festival king. Paumier also happened to be the leader of a coalition of craftsmen and peasants who objected to what they considered an unjust tax burden. According to Le Roy Ladurie, the coincidence of Paumier's political and festival leaderships drew attention to the disputes between Paumier's supporters and the tax-exempt nobles of Romans. As a result, Paumier's followers' actions during Carnival took on more than ritual significance. Indeed, the nobles became convinced that a violent revolt was imminent. To prevent an attack, Judge Guerin, the legal and festival leader of the nobles, seized the city gates and had Paumier shot. The judge then tried and executed more than 1000 villagers.

According to Stone, the main interest of *Carnaval*'s story "lies in the interplay of real social conflicts, described with acuity and learning at the beginning and end of the book, and the symbolism of the carnival parades, feasts, and masquerades, which forms the core." But the symbolism, and Le Roy Ladurie's interpretations of its meaning, drew

a mixed reaction from reviewers, including Stone. Critics observed that the author seemed biased in his portrayal of Judge Guerin as an evil villain in the midst of a clear-cut class war. Stone, for instance, found the Guerin described by Le Roy Ladurie "too evil to be convincing," especially in light of "evidence that there was a real threat of radical violence from Paumier and his friends [and] the even greater threat that they might open the city gates to their peasant allies prowling outside." Stone also remarked: "Once overenthusiastic in his acceptance of computerized 'scientific' history, Le Roy Ladurie is now overenthusiastic in his acceptance of folklore and semiotics. As a result, some of his ingenious interpretations of the symbolic meaning of the events of the carnival seem a little farfetched."

Even so, Stone deemed *Carnaval de Romans* "a dazzling psychodrama," asserting: "Whether the data has been correctly interpreted is another matter, but maybe one that, in the last resort, does not matter too much." What does matter, Stone contended, is "the fascination of the story and the author's dexterous interweaving of a brilliant analysis of social conflicts on the one hand with a more dubious but intriguing interpretation of the parades, masquerades, and feasts of carnival time on the other."

Like *Montaillou* and *Carnaval de Romans, Jasmin's Witch,* which was first published in 1984 and translated into English in 1987, relied heavily upon folklore and the everyday life of villagers in a small community in southern France. In *Jasmin's Witch* Le Roy Ladurie bases his investigation of the phenomenon of witchcraft on an obscure poem written in the Gascon dialect during the 1840s by a barber whose pen name was Jasmin. The poem had been transmitted orally for several generations before Jasmin committed it to paper. It told the story of Francouneto, a beautiful young woman who lived in the small community of Roquefort. When Francouneto spurned a soldier to marry another man, the soldier hired a sorcerer to spread the rumor that any man who married Francouneto would die. Alarmed because two former suitors had broken limbs while courting Francouneto, the community began to accuse her of other suspicious activities, including causing hailstorms and interfering with the villagers' sexual potency and fertility. Eventually, Francouneto herself began to wonder whether she might be a witch. Then her true love married her and survived, thereby proving that the curse was a wicked plot and convincing the villagers to surrender their belief in witches.

One of the most important aspects of this work, according to Jeffrey B. Russell, writing in the *Los Angeles Times Book Review,* is its potential to spur other historians to explore seemingly unpromising events and unearth new kinds of historical material. "With the Annaliste's nose for a good story behind the story," wrote Russell, "[Le Roy]

Ladurie visited the region around Agen to see whether there was any historical basis for Jasmin's poem. Here the book is at its best. Using his understanding of religion, folklore, and language, he works back to a historical Francouneto who lived not in the 1500s as in Jasmin's poem but about 1660-1690." Russell suggested that *Jasmin's Witch* is "most successful as a work in historical detection," and for that reason he likened it to Umberto Eco's *Name of the Rose.*

Calling Le Roy Ladurie an "original" as well as "entertaining" writer, Laurence Wylie, who reviewed *Jasmin's Witch* for the *Washington Post Book World,* also praised him for his unsurpassed knowledge of the history of southwestern France. However, Wylie complained about the effort required to digest the various materials with which Le Roy Ladurie makes his case. "Le Roy Ladurie's style is not obscure," noted Wylie, "on the contrary it is almost conversational. But he expects his reader to follow and retain all the details and to arrive with him at a conclusion. He seems to ignore our need for clarification, but that is apparently the habit of most French intellectuals today." Nonetheless, Wylie was impressed by the author's "brilliant archival and anthropological research," which he said was most clearly evident in the second half of *Jasmin's Witch.* Concluded Wylie: "Le Roy Ladurie is the Sherlock Holmes of the scholarly world."

BIOGRAPHICAL/CRITICAL SOURCES:

PERIODICALS

Chicago Tribune Book World, November 4, 1979.
Guardian Weekly, March 22, 1987.
Los Angeles Times Book Review, October 18, 1981; July 26, 1987, p. 13.
New Republic, July 27, 1987, pp. 38-41.
New Statesman, June 13, 1980.
New Yorker, February 1, 1982.
New York Review of Books, October 12, 1978; November 8, 1979; February 28, 1985, p. 32.
New York Times Book Review, August 6, 1978; September 2, 1979; November 4, 1979; November 25, 1979; November 9, 1980; December 12, 1982.
Time, August 21, 1978; January 7, 1980.
Times Literary Supplement, February 16, 1973; March 6, 1981; May 28, 1982; July 2, 1982; February 24, 1984; July 3, 1987, p. 725.
Village Voice, November 30, 1982.
Washington Post Book World, January 12, 1975; August 20, 1978; December 3, 1978; September 2, 1979; November 4, 1979; September 27, 1981; December 19, 1982; August 30, 1987, pp. 10-12.*

LIBERMAN, Robert Paul 1937-

PERSONAL: Born August 16, 1937, in Newark, NJ; married, 1961 (divorced); married second wife, Janet Brown, 1973; children: five. *Education:* Dartmouth College, A.B. (summa cum laude), 1959, diploma in medicine (with honors), 1960; University of California, San Francisco, M.S., 1961; Johns Hopkins University, M.D., 1963; postgraduate study at Harvard University, 1966-68.

ADDRESSES: Home—528 Lake Sherwood Dr., Thousand Oaks, CA 91361. *Office*—Community and Rehabilitative Psychiatry Section (116AR), West Los Angeles Veterans Affairs Medical Center, 11301 Wiltshire Blvd., Los Angeles, CA 90073; Camarillo State Hospital, Research Center, Box 6022, Camarillo, CA 93011-6022.

CAREER: Bronx Municipal Hospital, Bronx, NY, intern, 1963-64; Massachusetts Mental Health Center, Boston, resident in psychiatry, 1964-68; Washington School of Psychiatry, Washington, DC, faculty member of group psychotherapy training program, 1968-70; University of California, Los Angeles, assistant clinical professor, 1970-72, associate clinical professor of psychiatry, 1972-73, associate research psychiatrist, 1973-76, research psychiatrist, 1976-77, professor of psychiatry in residence, 1977—, director of clinical research program at Camarillo-Neuropsychiatric Institute Research Center, 1973—; Mental Health Clinical Research Center for Schizophrenia and Psychiatric Rehabilitation, West Los Angeles Veterans Affairs Medical Center, principal investigator and director, 1977—. Private practice of psychiatry in Boston, MA, 1967-68, in Reston, VA, 1968-70, and in Thousand Oaks, CA, 1977—. Adjunct lecturer at Antioch College West-University without Walls, 1971-74; lecturer at University of California, Santa Barbara, 1971-74, and California Lutheran College, 1973-74; honorary professor at University of San Marcos, Lima, Peru, 1984, Einstein College of Medicine, 1986, and University of Kansas, 1992.

Psychiatrist for National Institute of Mental Health career development program, 1964-70; senior psychiatrist at Boston State Hospital Drug Addiction Center, 1965-66; psychiatrist at Faulkner Hospital, 1966-67, Fairfax Hospital, 1968-70, and Ventura County General Hospital, 1970—. Ventura County Mental Health Department, staff psychiatrist, 1970-75, deputy program leader and director of Oxnard Regional Community Health Center, 1973-74. Member of medical staff at University of California, Los Angeles Hospital, 1971—, and Woodview-Calabasas Hospital, 1977-81. Research psychiatrist at Saint Elizabeth's Hospital, 1968-70. California Department of Mental Hygiene, Camarillo State Hospital, research specialist IV, 1970-72, research specialist V, 1972-73, director of laboratory of behavior modification and clinical research unit. Surgeon for U.S. Public Health Service, 1964-68; medical officer for U.S. Department of Health, Education and Welfare, 1968-70. Chief of Rehabilitation Medicine Service, Brentwood Veterans Administration Medical Center, 1980-92; project director, Research and Training Center for the Rehabilitation of the Mentally Ill, 1980-85. Member of junior staff advisory committee to director of National Institute of Mental Health, 1966-70; member of research and evaluation sub-committee, California Conference of Local Mental Health Program Directors, 1971-75; member of training and education sub-committee, Ventura Sub-Region Criminal Justice Planning Board, 1972-74 member of research advisory committee, California Department of Mental Health, 1985-89.

Diplomate of National Board of Medical Examiners, 1964; licensed to practice medicine in Massachusetts, Virginia, District of Columbia, and California, 1965; diplomate in psychiatry of American Board of Psychiatry and Neurology, 1969; community college instructor credential from California Community Colleges, 1973. Consultant in psychiatry at Valleyhead Hospital, 1965-66, Washingtonian Hospital for Substance Abuse, 1965-66, Professional Counseling Services and St. Paul's Rehabilitation Institute for the Blind, both 1966-68, and Prince William County Mental Health Clinic, 1968-69; consultant in group psychotherapy, New Hampshire Department of Mental Health, 1967-68; honorary researcher and consultant, Institute of Psychiatry and Bethlehem-Maudsley Hospitals, London, 1975-76; consultant to Mental Health and Behavioral Sciences Education Division of Sepulveda Veterans Administration Medical Center, 1975-80, Atascadero State Hospital, 1975-80, California Department of Corrections, 1976-80, Children's Behavioral Sciences, 1977-81, and Charter Pacific Hospital, 1984-86.

MEMBER: American Psychiatric Association, Association for the Advancement of Behavior Therapy (member of executive committee, 1970-72; member of board of directors, 1973-77), Association for Clinical Psychosocial Research (member of board of directors, 1986—), Physicians for Social Responsibility (member of executive committee), Phi Beta Kappa.

AWARDS, HONORS: Harry Solomon Award, Massachusetts Mental Health Center, 1966; Hospital Physician Essay Award, 1967; National Institute of Mental Health research grants, 1967-68, 1972-75, 1973-75, 1977-95, 1986-96; Citizen of the Year Award, City of Oxnard, 1972; California Department of Health grant, 1972-75; California Council on Criminal Justice grant, 1972-73; physicians' recognition award in continuing medical education, American Medical Association, 1973-76; National Institute on Drug Abuse research grants, 1974-77, 1975-77; National Institute of Health, general research support grant, 1975-76; international senior fellow at Institute of Psychiatry, London, 1975-76; Joint Spanish-

U.S.A. Cultural Committee grant, 1980-83; National Institute of Handicapped Research grant, 1980-85; first prize, International Rehabilitation Film Festival, 1984; Social Security Administration research grant, 1984-88; American Psychiatric Association, co-recipient of Manfred Guttmacher Award in forensic psychiatry, 1985, Samuel Hibbs Award, 1988, for innovations in the treatment of chronic mental illness; Arnold Van Ameringen Award for Psychiatric Rehabilitation, 1990, recipient with Camarillo-UCLA Research Center of Award for Exemplary State-University Collaboration, 1991; Silvano Arieti Award, Association for the Advancement of Psychoanalysis, 1986; Howard Davis Memorial Award, Knowledge Transfer Society, 1989; International Exchange of Experts in Rehabilitation fellowship to China, 1991; Arthur Noyes Award for Research in Schizophrenia, Pennsylvania Consortium of Medical Schools, 1992; Award for Exemplary Psychiatric Rehabilitation, World Association of Psychosocial Rehabilitation—U.S.A. branch, 1993; certificate of outstanding achievement, Hospital and Community Psychiatry Institute of American Psychiatric Association, 1993; Lawrence Kolb Award, Middletown (NY) Psychiatric Center, 1994.

WRITINGS:

A Guide to Behavioral Analysis and Therapy, Pergamon (New York City), 1972.

(With L. W. King, W. J. DeRisi, and M. J. McCann) *Personal Effectiveness: Guiding People to Assert Their Feelings and Improve Their Social Skills,* Research Press (Champaign, IL), 1975.

(With E. J. Callahan) *Innovative Treatment Methods for Narcotic Addiction,* National Institute for Drug Abuse (Rockville, MD), 1976.

(Editor) *Psychiatric Clinics of North America,* Volume 1: *Behavior Therapy in Psychiatry,* W. B. Saunders (Philadelphia), 1978.

(With others) *Handbook of Marital Therapy: An Educational Approach to Treating Troubled Relationships,* Plenum (New York City), 1980.

(With T. G. Kuehnel and C. C. Phipps) *Resource Book for Community Support Programs,* Office of Publications, University of California, Los Angeles, 1985.

(With others) *Psychiatric Rehabilitation of Chronic Mental Patients,* American Psychiatric Press (Washington, DC), 1988.

(With DeRisi and K. Mueser) *Social Skills Training for Psychiatric Patients,* Pergamon, 1989.

(Editor and contributor) *Handbook of Psychiatric Rehabilitation,* Macmillan, (New York City), 1992.

(With others) *Integrated Psychological Therapy for Schizophrenic Patients,* Hogrefe & Huber (Toronto), 1994.

(Editor with P. W. Corrigan) *Behavior Therapy in Psychiatric Care,* Springer Publishing (New York City), 1994.

(Editor with J. Yager) *Stress in Psychiatry,* Springer Publishing, 1994.

Also author of *Resource Book for Psychiatric Rehabilitation.* Also editor of *Effective Psychiatric Rehabilitation,* a special issue of *New Directions in Mental Health Services,* Jossey-Bass (San Francisco), 1992. Contributor to more than one hundred books, including *Family Therapy: Theory and Technique,* edited by G. D. Erickson and T. P. Hogan, Brooks/Cole (Monterey, CA), 1972; *Controversy in Psychiatry,* edited by J. P. Brady and H. K. Brodie, W. P. Saunders, 1978; *The Chronically Mentally Ill: Research and Services,* edited by M. Mirabi, SP Medical and Scientific Books (New York City), 1984; *Schizophrenia Concepts, Vulnerability and Intervention,* edited by E. R. Straube and K. Hahlweg, Springer-Verlag (Berlin), 1989; and *Foundations of Psychotherapy: Theory, Research and Practice,* edited by B. Bongar and L. E. Buetler, Oxford University Press (New York City), 1994. Contributor to numerous encyclopedias, annuals, and *Proceedings* of professional organizations.

Contributor of more than one hundred articles and reviews to medical journals, including *Journal of Psychiatric Research, American Journal of Psychiatry, British Journal of Psychiatry, Journal of Clinical Psychopharmacology, Behavior Therapist, Japanese Journal of Social Psychiatry,* and *Psychiatry Research.* Member of editorial board, *Journal of Applied Behavior Analysis,* 1972-78, *Journal of Marriage and Family Counseling,* 1974-78, *Journal of Behavior Therapy and Experimental Psychiatry,* 1975—, *Behavior Therapy,* 1979-85, *Assessment and Intervention in Developmental Disabilities,* 1980-84, *Gesellschaft zur Forderung Kognitives un Psychosoziales Therapie Kouz,* 1988—, and *International Review of Psychiatry,* 1988—; associate editor, *Journal of Applied Behavior Analysis,* 1976-78, and *Schizophrenia Bulletin,* 1981-89.

Also author of films, including *Reinforcing Social Interaction in a Group of Chronic Schizophrenics,* 1970, *Reinforcement Therapy in a Day Hospital,* 1971, *Assertive Training,* 1972, *Contingency Contracting in Families,* 1972, *Personal Effectiveness: Training Skills in a Group,* 1974, *Kids Are People Too: How to Use Social Reinforcement with Children,* 1974, *Treatment and Rehabilitation of the Chronic Mental Patient,* 1984, *Introducing Behavioral Family Management,* 1985, *Living on the Edge,* 1985, and *What is Schizophrenia?,* 1986; also author of video-assisted modules for training social and independent living skills, including *Basic Conversation Skills, Job Finding, Social Problem-Solving, Grooming and Self-Care Skills, Recreation for Leisure, Medication Management,* and *Symptom Management,* Psychiatric Rehabilitation Consultants; co-author of three cassette tapes, *Principles and Practice of Behavior Therapy,* Audio Digest Foundation, 1978.

Some of Liberman's work has been translated into Spanish, German, French, Finnish, Dutch, Swedish, Hungarian, Japanese, Korean, Chinese, Norwegian, Russian, Italian, Bulgarian, Polish, and Czechoslovakian.

WORK IN PROGRESS: Prevention of chronic schizophrenia; ongoing research on schizophrenia, social skills, training, community mental health, and rehabilitation of the chronic mental patient.

SIDELIGHTS: Robert Paul Liberman told *CA:* "As a scientist-practitioner in psychiatry, I realized early in my career that if I wanted the results of my research to be actually utilized and make an impact on the field, I would have to disseminate my work widely. While the printed page is still a time-honored way of disseminating information, knowledge and technology transfer to other people and settings much better when they can be readily adapted to local conditions, are 'user friendly,' and do not require great time, effort, and money to implement. Thus, during the past ten years, my research group and I have concentrated on designing, writing, producing, validating through research and field tests, and widely disseminating video-assisted packages or 'modules' for use by the full range of mental health and rehabilitation practitioners (of all disciplines) in hospital and community facilities. These modules have been well-received by thousands of professionals.

"It gives me great satisfaction to know that the work done by our small group of scientist-practitioners in Southern California at institutions affiliated with the UCLA School of Medicine has had such far-reaching impact on the lives of thousands of mentally-ill persons and their professional caregivers."

*   *   *

LIGOTTI, Thomas (Robert) 1953-

PERSONAL: Born July 9, 1953, in Detroit, MI; son of Gasper C. (deceased) and Dolores (Mazzola) Ligotti. *Education:* Attended Macomb County Community College, 1971-73; Wayne State University, B.A., 1977.

ADDRESSES: Home—23065 Gary Lane, St. Clair Shores, MI 48080. *Office*—Gale Research Co., 835 Penobscot Bldg., Detroit, MI 48226.

CAREER: Comprehensive Educational Training Act, Oak Park, MI, teaching assistant, 1977-79; Gale Research Co., Detroit, MI, editorial assistant, 1979, assistant editor, 1980-81, senior assistant editor, 1981-82, associate editor, 1982—.

AWARDS, HONORS: Award for best author of horror/weird fiction from Small Press Writers and Artists Organization (SPWAO), 1982, for story "The Chymist"; Rhysling Award nomination from Science Fiction Poetry Association, 1986, for "One Thousand Painful Variations Performed Upon Divers Creatures Undergoing the Treatment of Dr. Moreau, Humanist"; World Fantasy Award nomination, 1990, for "The Last Feast of Harlequin," and 1992, for *Grimscribe: His Lives and Works.*

WRITINGS:

Twentieth-Century Literary Criticism, Gale (Detroit), 1979—, Volume 2 (editorial assistant), Volumes 3 and 4 (assistant editor), Volumes 5 and 6 (senior assistant editor), Volumes 7-60 (associate editor).
Songs of a Dead Dreamer, with introduction by Ramsey Campbell, Silver Scarab Press (Albuquerque), 1986, revised edition, Carrol & Graf (New York City), 1989.
Grimscribe: His Lives and Works, Carrol & Graf, 1991.
Noctuary, Carrol & Graf, 1994.
The Agonizing Resurrection of Victor Frankenstein and Other Gothic Tales, Silver Salamander Press (Woodinvale, WA), 1994.

Contributor of stories to anthologies and to periodicals. Contributing editor of *Grimoire,* 1982-85.

WORK IN PROGRESS: Another collection of horror stories.

SIDELIGHTS: Thomas Ligotti's horror fiction has been critically praised for its richly evocative prose style and its ability to suggest the nightmarish essence of existence itself. Ligotti's stories often focus on those anomalous moments in which a character's perception of his world is shaken and he is forced to confront a frightening and essentially chaotic universe. As Steven J. Mariconda writes in *Necrofile: The Review of Horror Fiction,* "At his best Ligotti is resoundingly successful in convincing us that everywhere behind the common facade of life are other, sinister realms of entity more 'real' than that through which we so blithely move." In his introduction to the collection *Songs of a Dead Dreamer,* Ramsey Campbell calls Ligotti "one of the few original voices in contemporary horror fiction."

Reviewers of *Songs of a Dead Dreamer,* Ligotti's first collection of stories, point out the author's penchant for suggestion and the absence of detailed, graphic accounts of violence in his stories. Stefan Dziemianowicz, writing in *Dagon,* considers "The Frolic" a good example of "the subtle ways in which [Ligotti] brings the certainty of a familiar world into question." "The Frolic" opens with Dr. David Munck, a prison psychologist, telling his wife of a new prisoner referred to as John Doe. Doe has been im-

prisoned for what he calls "frolicking" with children before murdering them. Doe claims that this frolicking takes place, Munck tells his wife, in a "a place that sounded like the back alleys of some cosmic slum, an inner dimensional dead end [with] a moonlit corridor where mirrors scream and laugh, dark peaks of some kind that won't remain still, [and] a stairway that's 'broken' in a very strange way." Munck explains this place as Doe's demented description of some abandoned building or ghetto neighborhood but it eventually becomes painfully clear that it is far more than a delusion; Doe is able to enter a netherworld beyond normal dimensions. "By the end of the story," Dziemianowicz writes, "[Munck] must confront the fact that his self-assurance has blinded him to many uncertainties, and that in a world where nothing is absolutely certain, the reality of what John Doe says can be doubted, but it can't be ruled out conclusively."

Michael Morrison writes in *Fantasy Review* that the stories "Dream of a Mannikin or, The Third Person" and "Drink to Me Only with Labyrinthine Eyes" are particularly successful because they "tickle our subconscious with intimations of 'demonic powers lurking just beyond the threshold of sensory perception.' " Ligotti describes a character in "Alice's Last Adventure"—a story in which an elderly authoress is haunted by one of her own troublesome characters—as a "conjurer of stylish nightmares." Morrison adds that this description is equally apt for Ligotti.

Like Morrison, critic Neal Wilgus, writing in *Science Fiction Review,* is generally positive about the stories in *Songs of a Dead Dreamer.* Wilgus, however, contends that Ligotti's plots are rather weak, but a weakness more than compensated for by "a unique and arresting style." He writes, "all of the stories are well done and many are excellent." Writing in *Haunted Library Newsletter,* Rosemary Pardoe, too, praises the collection's tales for their uniquely eerie effect. She states, "Ligotti's supernatural fiction invariably features characters who struggle on the edge of a strange and sometimes hideously beautiful madness."

Like its predecessor, Ligotti's second book, *Grimscribe: His Lives and Works,* has had a generally positive critical reception. This second book presents thirteen new stories in the guise of a novel. Douglas Winter, in a review in the *Washington Post Book World,* describes the book: "Its eponymous narrator is a living library of voices—the damned, the demonic, the dreamer, among others—all interwoven in a compelling celebration of the first-person. It is a hypnotic narration; each story is a singular experience, yet each turns on the other, creating what Ligotti rightly calls a 'wheel of terror'."

Among the stories in this collection are "The Mystics of Muelenburg," in which the residents of a town cease to expend the necessary psychic energy to keep reality alive and ultimately suffer the dissolution of their world, "The Cocoons," the comic story of a demented psychiatrist and his two patients, one of whom is breeding inhuman monsters, and "The Last Feast of Harlequin," the tale of an anthropologist whose investigation of a small town's "Fool's Feast" leads him to uncover an ancient cult. Speaking of "The Last Feast of Harlequin," S. T. Joshi in *Studies in Weird Fiction* claims that the story "may perhaps be the very best homage to [horror writer H. P.] Lovecraft ever written." *Grimscribe,* according to Mariconda, "achieves near-classic status."

Noctuary, Ligotti's third book, contains not only short fiction, but also nineteen prose poems and an introductory essay in which Ligotti discusses his concept of weird fiction. In this essay Ligotti emphasizes his belief that the experience of the weird is a fundamental and inescapable fact of life. "Like all such facts," he writes, "it eventually finds its way into forms of artistic expression. One of those forms has been termed, of all things, weird fiction."

Noctuary is, according to Edward Bryant in *Locus,* "a challenging and rewarding experience for the adventurous and eclectic reader." Ligotti, Bryant writes, "suggests something of a sharper H. P. Lovecraft (with perhaps a strong dash of Clark Ashton Smith and a real undercurrent of Mr. Poe) retooled for the last half of this twentieth century. I frankly feel that Ligotti is a far more exacting stylist than [Lovecraft], even when his dense style flirts with the prolix and embraces the darkly adjectival."

Reviewing the collection for the *New York Review of Science Fiction,* Dziemianowicz defines how Ligotti approaches horror fiction: "In his literary universe, the occurrence of the inexplicable forces a harsh reassessment of the criteria by which the natural and supernatural, the real and the unreal, the normal and the uncanny are distinguished from one another." Similarly, Joshi, writing in *Necrofile: The Review of Horror Fiction,* claims that Ligotti "shows that what we take to be 'real' is itself a sort of mad dream."

Dreams play a prominent role in "Mrs. Rinaldi's Angel," the fourth story in *Noctuary.* The tale tells of a young boy plagued by terrible nightmares who is cured by Mrs. Rinaldi, only to develop instead a hearty appetite for "the absurd and horrible, even the perfectly evil" to take the place of his dreams. In this story Ligotti, according to Dziemianowicz, "proffers dreams as parasitical 'maggots of the mind and soul' that feed vampirically on our personalities and experiences." In "The Prodigy of Dreams," a story Joshi believes "comes very close to realising Ligotti's goal of presenting the real world as the quintessence of nightmare," mundane events stir within a sensitive

scholar a trembling awareness of the underlying chaos of the world.

Ligotti's interest in presenting a dreamlike or nightmarish world is evident in many of his stories. When asked by Shawn Ramsey in *Deathrealm* about his goal as a writer of horror fiction, Ligotti responded: "I suppose my ultimate aspiration as a horror writer would be to compose tales that on the surface would seem to be utter phantasmagoric nonsense, yet would convey all those incredible sensations and meanings that overwhelm us in our dreams."

Horror enthusiasts have praised Ligotti for his elegant prose and his ability to suggest subtle, sometimes philosophical terrors. "For nearly a decade," Winter notes, "while lesser talents have stocked the bookracks with a relentless supply of carbon-copy chills, Ligotti has labored, unheralded and virtually unknown, to create a canon of short stories so idiosyncratic as to defy almost any description save demented." According to Joshi, Ligotti "remains the most refreshing voice in weird fiction, the one writer who can never be mistaken for someone else."

Ligotti once explained his fiction as an attempt to "reflect—however imperfectly—my attachment to a type of horror tale that is no longer practiced to any significant extent. Some of its most obvious traits are: an idiosyncratic prose style, characters who are abnormal in striking ways, an intensely dreamlike atmosphere created primarily by means of visual images, and an ultimately dark view of human existence."

BIOGRAPHICAL/CRITICAL SOURCES:

BOOKS

Contemporary Literary Criticism, Volume 44, Gale, 1987.
Ligotti, Thomas, *Songs of a Dead Dreamer,* with introduction by Ramsey Campbell, Silver Scarab Press, 1986, revised edition, Carrol & Graf, 1989.
Short Story Criticism, Volume 16, Gale, 1994.

PERIODICALS

Aboriginal Science Fiction, November-December, 1990, p. 29.
Bloomsbury Review, June, 1992, pp. 16-17.
Crypt of Cthulhu, June 15, 1986, pp. 57-58.
Dagon, September/December, 1988, pp. 3-82.
Deathrealm, Number 8, spring, 1989.
Fangoria, May, 1994.
Fantasy Review, June, 1986, pp. 23-24.
Haunted Library Newsletter, November, 1986.
Horror Show, spring, 1987, pp. 32-33.
Interzone, January, 1992, p. 64.
Kirkus Reviews, April 15, 1990, p. 524.
Locus, February, 1992; March, 1994, pp. 31-32.

Los Angeles Times Book Review, December 23, 1990, p. 6.
Mystery Scene, June, 1990, p. 115.
Necrofile: The Review of Horror Fiction, spring, 1992, pp. 1-3; spring, 1994, pp. 11-13.
New York Review of Science Fiction, April, 1994, pp. 4-6.
Science Fiction & Fantasy Book Review Annual, 1991, pp. 109-118.
Science Fiction Review, August, 1986, pp. 44-45.
Studies in Weird Fiction, Number 7, spring, 1990, pp. 37-39; Number 9, spring, 1991, pp. 27-31; Number 12, spring, 1993, pp. 30-36.
Teke-Li!: Journal of Terror, winter-spring, 1992, pp. 18-41.
Washington Post Book World, September 30, 1990, p. 10; February 16, 1992, p. 9.
Weird Tales, winter, 1991-92, pp. 3-130.
Wilson Library Bulletin, March, 1994, pp. 102-103.

*   *   *

LIND, William S(turgiss) 1947-

PERSONAL: Born July 9, 1947, in Cleveland, OH; son of David L. (a commercial artist) and Dorothea (Sturgiss) Lind. *Education:* Dartmouth College, A.B., 1969; Princeton University, M.A., 1971. *Politics:* Conservative. *Religion:* Episcopalian.

ADDRESSES: Office—National Empowerment Television, 717 Second St. N.E., Washington, DC 20002.

CAREER: U.S. Senate, Washington, DC, legislative aide to Senator Robert Taft, Jr., 1973-77, and to Senator Gary Hart, 1977-87. Free Congress Research and Education Foundation, Washington, DC, research scholar at Institute of Government and Politics, 1983-86; director of Institute for Cultural Conservatism, 1986—. National Empowerment Television, host of "Modern War." Associate publisher of *The New Electric Railway Journal,* 1988—.

WRITINGS:

Maneuver Warfare Handbook, Westview (Boulder, CO), 1985.
(With Gary Hart) *America Can Win: The Case for Military Reform,* Adler & Adler, 1986.
(Editor with William H. Marshner) *Cultural Conservatism: Toward a New National Agenda,* Free Congress Foundation (Washington, DC), 1987.

Also contributor to military journals, including *Marine Corps Gazette, Military Review,* and *Air University Review.*

WORK IN PROGRESS: Retroculture.

SIDELIGHTS: In *America Can Win: The Case for Military Reform,* William S. Lind and former Colorado Sena-

tor Gary Hart offer a wide-ranging discussion of the defects they see in the U.S. military and make proposals for change. Lind has been a defense adviser to Hart for several years, and the two men have been in the forefront of the 1980s movement to reform the military.

Suggesting that U.S. battle plans are based on an outmoded doctrine of attrition, in which the enemy is slowly beaten into submission at a high cost in lives and money, Lind and Hart propose that the military adopt what the authors call "maneuver warfare," which emphasizes fast-moving, imaginative battlefield tactics designed to throw the enemy off balance and win wars quickly with less bloodshed. They point to the Israel Defense Forces, which have used such an approach to hold their opponents at bay for decades. Lind and Hart also propose a massive reduction in the number of officers in the middle and upper ranks (majors through generals), many of whom, they charge, serve no useful purpose and are professional bureaucrats rather than leaders of a fighting force. Surveying America's navy, the authors criticize aircraft carriers as vulnerable to attack, proposing instead an emphasis on submarines and the creation of a new, smaller ship that could be quickly reconfigured to carry out different assignments.

Reactions to *America Can Win* were mixed. Many reviewers, such as *Washington Post Book World* contributor Benjamin F. Schemmer, gave Lind and Hart high marks for raising an important issue although he questions some of the book's specifics. The authors "make a substantive, constructive case for military reform," Schemmer noted, though "in places, they overstate their case or slice the onion only one peel deep." But as the reviewer observed, "the book is a lot more honest than reassurances we hear from the Pentagon that the only problem with America's defense is Congress' failure to fund it at the levels Caspar Weinberger and Ronald Reagan would have us buy."

BIOGRAPHICAL/CRITICAL SOURCES:

PERIODICALS

Christian Science Monitor, October 3, 1986.
Los Angeles Times Book Review, April 20, 1986.
New York Times Book Review, June 8, 1986.
Washington Post Book World, May 4, 1986.

*   *   *

LIPSON, Charles 1948-

PERSONAL: Born February 1, 1948, in Clarksdale, MS; son of Harry M., Jr. (a merchant) and Dorothy (Kohn) Lipson; married Susan Bloom (a psychiatric social worker), March 26, 1946; children: Michael Henry, Jonathan Sandler. *Education:* Yale University, B.A. (magna cum laude), 1970; Harvard University, M.A., 1974, Ph.D., 1976. *Religion:* Jewish.

ADDRESSES: Home—5809 S. Blackstone Ave., Chicago, IL 60637. *Office*—Department of Political Science, University of Chicago, 5828 South University Ave., Chicago, IL 60637.

CAREER: Harvard University, Cambridge, MA, research associate at Harvard Center for International Affairs, 1976-77; University of Chicago, Chicago, IL, assistant professor, 1977-84, associate professor of political science, 1984—, director of graduate studies, Department of Political Science, 1989-92, director of program on interdependent political economy, 1983-87, director of program on international politics, economics, and security, 1987—, chair of Committee on International Relations, 1991—, member of Council of the University Senate, 1991—, member of executive committee of Center for the Study of Industrial Societies, member of standing committees for Council for Advanced Studies in Peace and Cooperation, Council on Latin American Studies, and Center for the Study of Banks. Visiting scholar at Harvard Center for International Affairs, 1979-80; visiting fellow at London School of Economics, Centre for International Studies, 1988-89; principal investigator, Chicago/Pew Project to Integrate the Study of Economics and National Security, 1987-92; consultant to John D. and Catherine T. MacArthur Foundation, Program in International Peace and Security, 1988-89; member of British-American Conference for the Successor Generation, 1987—; speaker, United States Information Service, 1989—; academic advisor to teachers for East Europe, Civic Education Project, Yale University, 1991—.

MEMBER: International Institute for Strategic Studies (London), International Research Committee on Politics and Business, International Studies Association, Royal Institute for International Affairs (London), American Political Science Association (secretary, 1990-91), American Society for International Law, The Chicago Committee (sponsored by Chicago Council on Foreign Relations), Chicago Council on Foreign Relations, Chicago Area Hillel-Jewish Federation College Age Youth Services (member of governing commission), Hillel Foundation (University of Chicago campus organization for Jewish students; chair of board of directors and executive committee), K. A. M. Isaiah Israel Congregation (board of directors).

AWARDS, HONORS: Chase Prize from Harvard University, 1977; Rockefeller Foundation fellow, 1979-81; fellow of German Marshall Fund, 1983-84; MacArthur Foundation grant, 1985-92; University of Chicago Faculty Achievement Award from Burlington Northern Foundation, 1986; Ford Foundation, awarded principal investiga-

tor status, Scholarly Exchange Project with the Graduate Institute of International Studies, Geneva, 1987-91; Pew Charitable Trusts, awarded principal investigator status, Project on Economics and National Security, 1987-92.

WRITINGS:

Standing Guard: Protecting Foreign Capital in the Nineteenth and Twentieth Centuries, University of California Press (Berkeley and Los Angeles), 1985.

Contributor to books, including *Debt and the Less Developed Countries,* edited by Jonathan David Aronson, Westview (Boulder, CO), 1979; *International Debt in Historical Perspective,* edited by Barry Eichengreen and Peter Lindert, M. I. T. Press (Cambridge, MA), 1989; *Power, Economic Relations and Security: The United States and Japan in Focus,* edited by Henry Bienen, Westview, 1992; *Neorealism and Neoliberalism: The Contemporary Debate,* edited by David Baldwin, Columbia University Press (New York City), 1993; *The Oxford Companion to Politics of the World,* Oxford University Press (New York City), 1993; *Collective Security beyond the Cold War,* edited by George Downs, University of Michigan Press (Ann Arbor, MI), 1994; *International Law Anthology,* edited by Anthony D'Amato, Anderson (Cincinnati, OH), 1994; *Regional Security Regimes: Israel and Its Neighbors,* edited by Ephraim Inbar, SUNY (Albany, NY), 1995; and *American-Israeli Relations and the "New World Order",* edited by Gabriel Sheffer, in press.

Also contributor of articles and reviews to magazines, newspapers, and scholarly journals, including *American Journal of International Law, American Political Science Review, Boston Globe, Chicago Sun-Times, International Organization, Journal of Politics, Nation, Political Science Quarterly,* and *World Politics.* Also associate editor *Economics and Politics,* 1987-90; member of board of editors, 1984-90, member of executive committee of the board, 1987-90, of *International Organization.* Consultant and contributor to *Encyclopaedia Britannica,* 1987—.

WORK IN PROGRESS: Hard Bargains: The Logic and Limits of International Agreements; contributions to *International Political Economy: A Reader,* edited by Tsuneo Akaha and Kendall Stiles, Harper and Row (New York City); *The International Political Economy and the Developing Countries,* edited by Stephen Haggard, Edward Unger (Cheltenham, England); *The International Political Economy of Monetary Relations,* edited by Benjamin J. Cohen, Edward Unger; *International Political Economy and International Institutions,* edited by Oran R. Young, E. Elgar (Brookfield, VT and England).

SIDELIGHTS: Charles Lipson told *CA:* "I am currently working on a variety of fundamental issues in international relations, especially the problem of sustaining international agreements. I am also studying the protection of property rights and contracts internationally. Much of this work combines theory and historical interpretation."

Critic Deepak Lal wrote in the *Times Literary Supplement* that "Charles Lipson's useful *Standing Guard* provides a survey of the changing political risks which have attended foreign lending during the last century and a half." These risks include a withering of public support of private property rights in the face of nationalization for the "general good," the nationalism that accompanied decolonization and led to the formation of what are now numerous Third World nations, and, more recently, the involvement and increasing competition of multinational corporations. These developments do not lead Lipson to anticipate a comfortable return to the standards which once insured the safety of capital investments abroad.

BIOGRAPHICAL/CRITICAL SOURCES:

PERIODICALS

Times Literary Supplement, May 2, 1986.

*   *   *

LISTER, Raymond (George) 1919-

PERSONAL: Born March 28, 1919, in Cambridge, England; son of Horace (an engineer) and Ellen (Arnold) Lister; married Pamela Brutnell, June 6, 1947; children: Rory Brian George, Delia Fionnuala. *Education:* Attended Cambridge schools until the age of fifteen. *Avocational interests:* Book collecting, mountaineering in the fens.

ADDRESSES: Home—9 Sylvester Rd., Cambridge CB3 9AF, England.

CAREER: George Lister & Sons Ltd. (architectural metal-workers), Cambridge, England, director, 1939-94; Golden Head Press Ltd., Cambridge, managing director and editor, 1952-72; Wolfson College, Cambridge University, honorary senior member, 1971-75, fellow, 1975-86, emeritus fellow, 1986—; syndic of Fitzwilliam Museum, 1980-89. Miniature painter, with work exhibited occasionally at one-man shows in Federation of British Artists Galleries, London.

MEMBER: Royal Society of Arts, Royal Society of Miniature Painters, Sculptors and Engravers (treasurer, beginning 1958; president, 1970-80), Federation of British Artists (governor, 1972-80), Private Libraries Association (president, 1971-72), Liveryman of Worshipful Company of Blacksmiths (prime warden, 1989-90), Sette of Odd Volumes (president, 1960, 1981).

WRITINGS:

Decorative Wrought Ironwork in Great Britain, G. Bell (London), 1957, 2nd edition, David & Charles (Newton Abbot), 1970.

(Translator from the French) V. I. Stepanov, *Alphabet of Movements of the Human Body,* Golden Head Press (Cambridge), 1958.

Decorative Cast Ironwork in Great Britain, G. Bell, 1960.

The Craftsman Engineer, G. Bell, 1960.

Private Telegraph Companies of Great Britain and Their Stamps, Golden Head Press, 1961.

Great Craftsmen, G. Bell, 1962.

Edward Calvert, G. Bell, 1962.

The Miniature Defined (booklet), Golden Head Press, 1963.

How to Identify Old Maps and Globes, Archon Books (Hamden, CT), 1965.

Beulah to Byzantium: A Study of Parallels in the Works of W. B. Yeats, William Blake, Samuel Palmer and Edward Calvert, Dolmen Press (Portlaoise), 1965.

College Stamps of Oxford and Cambridge, Golden Head Press, 1966.

The Craftsman in Metal, G. Bell, 1966.

Victorian Narrative Paintings, C. N. Potter (New York City), 1966.

Great Works of Craftsmanship, G. Bell, 1967.

William Blake: An Introduction to the Man and to His Work, G. Bell, 1968.

Samuel Palmer and His Etchings, Watson-Guptill (New York City), 1969.

Hammer and Hand: An Essay on the Ironwork of Cambridge (booklet), privately printed, 1969.

Antique Maps and Their Cartographers, Archon Books, 1970.

British Romantic Art, G. Bell, 1973.

Samuel Palmer: A Biography, Faber & Faber (Winchester, MA), 1975.

(Editor) *The Letters of Samuel Palmer,* two volumes, Oxford University Press (New York City), 1975.

Infernal Methods: A Study of William Blake's Art Techniques, G. Bell, 1975.

Samuel Palmer: A Vision Recaptured, Victoria and Albert Museum (London), 1978.

George Richmond: A Biography, R. V. Garton (London), 1981.

Prints and Printmaking, Methuen (London), 1984.

The Paintings of Samuel Palmer, Cambridge University Press (New York City), 1985.

The Paintings of William Blake, Cambridge University Press, 1986.

Samuel Palmer: His Life and Art, Cambridge University Press, 1987.

A Catalogue Raisonne of the Works of Samuel Palmer, Cambridge University Press, 1987.

(Translator from the French) A. Michel Saint-Leon, *Stenochoreography,* Deighton, Bell (Cambridge), 1992.

With My Own Wings: The Memoirs of Raymond Lister, Oleander Press (Cambridge), 1994.

Also author of *Apollo's Bird,* 1975, *For Love of Leda,* 1977, and *Great Images of British Printmaking,* 1978.

Author of numerous pamphlets. Contributor to *Times Literary Supplement, Connoisseur, Apollo, Journal of Royal Society of Arts, Irish Book, Blake Studies,* and *Blake Newsletter.*

BIOGRAPHICAL/CRITICAL SOURCES:

BOOKS

Cammell, C. R., and others, *Raymond Lister: Five Essays,* Golden Head Press, 1963.
Lissim, Simon, *The Art of Raymond Lister,* Gray, 1958.

*   *   *

LIU, Aimee E. 1953-

PERSONAL: Born April 19, 1953, in Connecticut; daughter of Maurice T. and Jane H. (Clark) Liu. *Education:* Yale University, B.A., 1975.

ADDRESSES: Home—Los Angeles, CA. *Agent*—Arthur Pine Agency, 250 West 57th Street, New York, NY 10019.

CAREER: Wilhelmina Agency, New York City, fashion model, 1969-75; United Airlines, New York City, flight attendant, 1975-78; writer, 1979—.

WRITINGS:

Solitaire (autobiographical narrative), Harper & Row (New York City), 1979.
(With Art Ulene and Steve Shelov) *Bringing Out the Best in Your Baby,* Macmillan (New York City), 1986.
(With Stan J. Katz) *False Love and Other Romantic Illusions,* Ticknor & Fields (New York City), 1988.
(With Katz) *Success Trap,* Ticknor & Fields, 1990.
(With Katz) *The Codependency Conspiracy,* Warner Books (New York City), 1991.
(With the American Academy of Pediatrics) *The Academy Book of Childcare,* Bantam (New York City), 1991.
Face (novel), Warner Books, 1994.

Author of *Fisherman's Revenge* (one-act play), first produced in New York City at Fort Tryon Park, August 19, 1979.

Contributor of articles in *Aim Plus, Cabletime, Cosmopolitan, Entrepreneur, Feeling Great, Footwear News, Glamour, Lear's, New Woman,* and *Self.*

SIDELIGHTS: Solitaire is the narrative of Aimee E. Liu's own affliction with and recovery from anorexia nervosa, a disorder that usually strikes young middle- to upper-class women between the ages of thirteen and thirty. Obsessed with fears of being overweight, they literally starve themselves by refusing to eat, taking excessive doses of laxatives, inducing vomiting, and exercising to the point of exhaustion. Still believing they are fat despite their emaciation, victims of the disease sometimes continue this behavior until they are hospitalized or even die.

Liu once told *CA:* "Many of my readers and friends have expressed amazement that I could have exposed such a personal side of my life as I did in *Solitaire.* Their reaction amazed me. The notion that I am so special, so precious that I must not open myself up for scrutiny irks me. We are all the same animal, we human beings. We all share the same feelings, appetites, needs. We differ in our modes of expression, in the traps we create for ourselves and the escape mechanisms we use to free ourselves, but basically we understand each other, or can when we learn the common language."

In 1994 Liu published her first novel, *Face,* a story of an Amerasian photographer named Maibelle Chung, who comes to terms with her own mixed-race identity and the secrets of her family's past. Although only one-quarter Chinese, Maibelle feels a strong affinity for Chinatown, which she photographs. More recently, Liu wrote *CA:* "The question that guided the evolution of my story from this moment on was, *Why?* Why does my character care so much about Chinatown if she is only one quarter Chinese? Why does she choose photography as a career? Why is she alone? As I moved through the answers to these questions, my novel gradually unfolded. It expanded into three generations of Maibelle's family history and took as central themes issues of biracial identity and intermarriage between Chinese and Caucasians."

BIOGRAPHICAL/CRITICAL SOURCES:

PERIODICALS

New York Times Book Review, July 29, 1979.
Washington Post, July 27, 1979; July 31, 1979.

*   *   *

LIVINGSTONE, Marco (Eduardo) 1952-

PERSONAL: Born March 17, 1952, in Detroit, MI; son of Leon (a professor) and Alicia (Arce) Livingstone. *Education:* Attended State University of New York at Buffalo,

1969-70; University of Toronto, B.A., 1974; Courtauld Institute of Art, London, M.A., 1976.

ADDRESSES: Home and office—36 St. George's Ave., London N7 0HD, England.

CAREER: Freelance journalist for Canadian and British popular music magazines and weekly newspapers, 1970-74; Walker Art Gallery, Liverpool, England, assistant keeper of British art, 1976-82; Museum of Modern Art, Oxford, England, deputy director, 1982-86; Macmillan Publishers, London, England, twentieth-century art editor of *The Dictionary of Art,* 1986-87, deputy editor, 1987-91; advisor to Art Life, Ltd., Tokyo, 1989—.

MEMBER: Society of Authors, Association Internationale des Critiques d'Art.

AWARDS, HONORS: Award from Arts Council of Great Britain, 1979.

WRITINGS:

Allen Jones: Retrospective of Paintings, 1957-1978, Walker Art Gallery (Liverpool), 1979.

Sheer Magic by Allen Jones, Congreve (New York City), 1979.

David Hockney, Holt (New York City), 1981, revised edition, Thames & Hudson (London), 1987.

Patrick Caulfield: Paintings, 1963-1981, Walker Art Gallery, 1981.

Peter Phillips retroVISION: Paintings, 1960-1982, Walker Art Gallery, 1982.

Anish Kapoor: Feeling into Form, Walker Art Gallery, 1983.

Duane Michals: photographs/sequences/texts 1958-1984, Museum of Modern Art (Oxford), 1984.

Stephen Buckley: Many Angles, Museum of Modern Art, 1985.

R. B. Kitaj, Rizzoli (New York City), 1985, revised edition, Thames & Hudson, 1992.

Arthur Tress: Talisman, Thames & Hudson, 1986.

David Hockney: Faces, Thames & Hudson, 1987.

Stephen Farthing: Mute Accomplices, Museum of Modern Art, 1987.

Michael Sandle: Sculpture & Drawings, 1957-88, Whitechapel Art Gallery (London), 1988.

David Hockney: Etchings and Lithographs, Thames & Hudson, 1988.

Pop Art: A Continuing History, Abrams (New York City), 1990.

Jim Dine, Isetan Museum (Tokyo), 1990.

Pop Muses: Images of Women by Roy Lichtenstein and Andy Warhol, Isetan Museum (Tokyo), 1991.

Objects for the Ideal Home: The Legacy of Pop Art, Serpentine Gallery (London), 1991.

Pop Art, Rizzoli, 1991.

Patrick Caulfield: Paintings 1963-1992, Serpentine Gallery, 1992.

Tim Head, Whitechapel Art Gallery, 1992.

Tom Wesselmann: A Retrospective Survey 1959-1992, Isetan Museum, 1993.

Duane Hanson, Montreal Museum of Fine Arts, 1994.

David Hockney in California, Takashimaya Art Gallery (Tokyo), 1994.

Jim Dine: Flowers and Plants, Abrams, 1994.

Duane Hanson, Art Life (Tokyo), 1995.

Contributor to books, including *Andy Warhol: A Retrospective,* edited by Kynaston McShine, Museum of Modern Art, 1989, and *Tilson,* Thames & Hudson, 1993. Also author of introductions to books.

WORK IN PROGRESS: Hockney's California, Thames & Hudson.

SIDELIGHTS: A renowned art scholar, Marco Livingstone has specialized in writing about the British Pop Art movement. Writing of Livingstone's *David Hockney* in the *Times Literary Supplement,* Frances Spalding drew attention to the author's balanced treatment of an artist who has recently gained an enormous popular reputation. She wrote: "[Livingstone's] impartiality is impressive and must have involved skilful diplomacy, for in a monograph on a living artist the author is necessarily dependent on his subject's goodwill. Outspoken criticism is combined with keen appreciation and a ready grasp of the art-historical allusions culled by Hockney from various periods and cultures." Livingstone has garnered praise for his ability to explain artists and their work in a way that's meaningful for a lay audience, as well as for art historians and artists themselves.

BIOGRAPHICAL/CRITICAL SOURCES:

PERIODICALS

Times Literary Supplement, July 24, 1981.

*   *   *

LIVO, Norma J. 1929-

PERSONAL: Born July 31, 1929, in Tarentum, PA; daughter of David J. (a chemist) and Della (a teacher; maiden name, Kline) Jackson; married George O. Livo (a geophysicist), 1951; children: Lauren, Keith, Kim, Robert. *Education:* University of Pittsburgh, B.S., 1962, M.Ed., 1963, Ed.D., 1969; postdoctoral study at University of Utah, 1969, 1971, and 1973, and University of Colorado, 1976 and 1980.

ADDRESSES: Home—11960 W. 22nd Place, Lakewood, CO 80215.

CAREER: Gulf Research Laboratory, Harmarville, PA, geophysical assistant, 1950-52; University of Pittsburgh, Pittsburgh, PA, demonstration teacher at Falk Laboratory School, 1962-67, lecturer in elementary education, 1965-67; University of Colorado at Denver, assistant professor, 1968-71, associate professor, 1971-77, professor of education, 1977-92. Visiting professor of reading at University of Denver, 1968; visiting professor of education at Oklahoma State University, 1972; visiting professor of storytelling at Lesley College, 1979-81.

MEMBER: International Reading Association (state president), National Storytelling Association, Society of Children's Book Writers, Colorado Author's League, Denver Women's Press Club.

AWARDS, HONORS: Meritorious Professional Achievement, University of Pittsburgh, 1981; Outstanding Service Award for Project Wild, Colorado Division of Wildlife, 1985; Award for Excellence in Research and Creative Endeavor, University of Colorado at Denver, 1987; winner of American Newspapers Publishers Association Outstanding Achievement Award for Newspapers in Education, 1990; honored at the 24th Annual Virginia Westerberg Children's Literature Conference, sponsored by the Colorado Language Arts Society, University of Colorado at Boulder, and the Boulder Public Library, 1993; Governor's Award for Excellence in the Arts, 1995.

WRITINGS:

Free Rein, Allyn Bacon (Boston, MA), 1978.
(With Sandra A. Rietz) *Storytelling: Process and Practice,* Libraries Unlimited (Littleton, CO), 1986.
(With Rietz) *Storytelling Activities,* Libraries Unlimited, 1987.
(Editor and contributor) *Joining In,* Yellow Moon Press (Brighton, MA), 1988.
Hmong Textile Designs, Stemmer House (Owings Mills, MD), 1990.
(With Dia Cha) *Hmong Folkstories,* Libraries Unlimited, 1991.
(With Rietz) *Storytelling Folklore Sourcebook,* Libraries Unlimited, 1991.
(With Glen McGlathery) *Who's Endangered on Noah's Ark?,* Libraries Unlimited, 1992.
Who's Afraid. . . ..? Facing Children's Fears with Folktales, Libraries Unlimited, 1994.
(With daughter, Lauren J. Livo, and McGlathery) *Of Bugs and Beasts,* Libraries Unlimited, 1995.

Also author of media productions *Mining in Colorado,* University of Colorado at Denver, 1988; and *The Hmong, Hmong at Peace and War, Hmong Folkstories,* Colorado Endowment for the Humanities, 1989. Contributor to journals. Columnist for *Rocky Mountain News.*

SIDELIGHTS: Norma J. Livo told *CA:* "When asked by a fellow professor, as he riffled through *Storytelling: Process and Practice,* 'How long did it take you to write this?' I was able to answer, 'Oh, over one hundred years. Add Sandie's age to mine and that's what you get.' Of course my answer is fact. It took both of us all of our lives to get to the point of sharing our passion and beliefs about storytelling.

"Why storytelling? Storytelling and listening to stories stimulates interest, emotional and language development, and the imagination. As W. R. S. Ralston expressed it, 'One touch of storytelling may in some instances make the whole world kin.'"

*   *   *

LONDON, Mel 1923-

PERSONAL: Born August 21, 1923, in New York, NY; son of Harry and Faye (Feldman) London; married Sheryl Adams (a writer and filmmaker), June 2, 1946. *Education:* Attended City College (now of the City University of New York), 1941-42, and Columbia University, 1942-43.

ADDRESSES: Home—170 Second Ave., New York, NY 10003.

CAREER: Worked at American Forces Network in Germany, 1944-47; radio and television director, producer, and writer, 1948-56; worked at On Film, Inc., 1956-60; Wilding International, New York City, president, 1960-65; David Wolper Associates, Hollywood, CA, vice-president, 1965-66; Vision Associates, New York City, partner and filmmaker, 1966-79; Symbiosis, Inc., New York City, owner and filmmaker, 1979—; New York University, New York City, adjunct assistant professor of film, 1987—. Seminar leader; visiting scholar, Dalton School, New York City; lecturer at New York University, Northwestern University, and Memphis State University. *Military service:* U.S. Army, Signal Corps, 1943-47; became second lieutenant.

MEMBER: Directors Guild of America, American Film Institute.

AWARDS, HONORS: Academy Award nomination from Motion Picture Academy of Arts and Sciences, 1963, for documentary film *To Live Again;* Tastemaker Award, 1980, for *The Fish-Lovers' Cookbook;* James Beard Book Award, single category cookbook, 1994, for *A Seafood Celebration;* eighteen Golden Eagle Awards from Council on International Nontheatrical Events, for various films; four blue ribbons from American Film Festival.

WRITINGS:

Getting into Film, Ballantine (New York City), 1977.

Bread Winners, Rodale Press (Emmaus, PA), 1979.

(With wife, Sheryl London) *The Fish-Lovers' Cookbook,* Rodale Press, 1980.

Easy Going (travel), Rodale Press, 1981.

Second Spring (nonfiction), Rodale Press, 1982.

(With S. London) *Sheryl and Mel London's Creative Cooking with Grains and Pasta,* Rodale Press, 1982.

Bread Winners Too: Second Rising, edited by Charles Gerras, Rodale Press, 1983.

The Bread Winners' Cookbook, Simon & Schuster (New York City), 1983.

Making It in Film, Simon & Schuster, 1985.

(With S. London) *The Herb and Spice Cookbook: A Seasoning Celebration,* Rodale Press, 1986.

The Second Spring of Your Life, Continuum (New York City), 1990.

Getting Into Video, Ballantine, 1990.

(With S. London) *Fresh Fruit Desserts: Classic and Contemporary,* Prentice-Hall (Englewood Cliffs, NJ), 1990.

(With S. London) *The Versatile Grain and the Elegant Bean,* Simon & Schuster, 1992.

(With S. London) *A Seafood Celebration,* Simon & Schuster, 1993.

Also author of movie and television scripts. Contributor to magazines, including *Simply Seafood Magazine.*

SIDELIGHTS: Mel London told *CA:* "Though I had written television scripts, radio shows, and, eventually, motion picture documentary scripts, the idea of a book was frightening, even one that dealt with my primary profession, that of a filmmaker. Where television scripts were a 'sprint,' the book form represented the 'long distance run,' and even if I had one in me, did I have more?

"The first book, then, was the 'one book that everyone has in him.' I found that I like the long distance run—so *Getting into Film* was followed by a bestseller on bread baking. And now . . . the seventeenth book was published last year, ten of them co-authored with my wife, Sheryl.

"Through it all, I have wanted, and managed, to stay with film. The two as a double effort make a full, and sometimes difficult, life. My best advice to a young writer would be not to write the complete book before trying to sell it to a publisher. An outline, chapter details, and a sample chapter are really all that anyone is going to go through."

London once told *CA:* "If writing a book is a long distance run, then writing a novel must certainly be a marathon event." Following the advice of two publishers who suggested that he try to write a novel, London wrote *CA* that he has started the research for his first novel.

BIOGRAPHICAL/CRITICAL SOURCES:

BOOKS

Kranz, Stewart, *Science and Technology in the Arts,* Van Nostrand, 1974.

PERIODICALS

New York Times, September 28, 1980; April, 19, 1992.

*　　　*　　　*

LONDON, Perry　1931-1992

PERSONAL: Born June 18, 1931, in Omaha, NE; died of cancer, June 19, 1992, in New Brunswick, NJ; married; children: four. *Education:* Yeshiva University, B.A. (cum laude), 1952; Columbia University, M.A., 1953, diploma in clinical psychology, 1956, Ph.D., 1956.

CAREER: Walter Reed Army Medical Center, Washington, DC, intern in clinical psychology, 1954-55; Madigan Army Hospital, Tacoma, WA, clinical psychologist, 1956-59; University of Illinois, Urbana, assistant professor, 1959-62, associate professor of psychology, 1962-63; University of Southern California, Los Angeles, associate professor, 1963-66, professor of psychology, beginning 1967, professor of psychiatry at College of Medicine, beginning 1967, director of Psychological Research and Service Center, 1963-66. Pacific Lutheran College, associate in psychology, 1957-59; Stanford University, visiting associate professor, 1962-63; Fuller Theological Seminary, visiting scholar, winter, 1966; speaker at colloquia and workshops. National Science Foundation visiting lecturer at West Virginia State College, 1961, Fullerton Junior College, 1964, Sonoma State College, 1965, and Santa Clara University, 1967. *Military service:* U.S. Army, Medical Service Corps, 1954-59; became first lieutenant.

MEMBER: International Society of Clinical and Experimental Hypnosis, American Psychological Association (fellow; member of executive committee, 1971), American Association for the Advancement of Science (fellow), New York Academy of Science.

AWARDS, HONORS: Research scientist development fellow, National Institute of Mental Health, 1966-71; grant from Wenner-Gren Foundation for Anthropological Research, to study sources of altruistic social autonomy, 1966; U.S. Public Health Service grants, 1960-65, 1966-68, 1968-71, 1969-72, 1971-74, 1971-72; U.S. Office of Education grant to study influence of hypnosis and instructions on retention of meaningful material, 1967-68.

WRITINGS:

The Children's Hypnotic Susceptibility Scale, Consulting Psychologists Press, 1963.

The Modes and Morals of Psychotherapy, Holt (New York City), 1964.

(Editor with D. L. Rosenhan, and contributor) *Foundations of Abnormal Psychology,* Holt (New York City), 1967.

(Editor with Rosenhan, and contributor) *Theory and Research in Abnormal Psychology,* Holt (New York City), 1969.

Beginning Psychology, Dorsey Press (Homewood, IL), 1975, revised edition, 1978.

Contributor to books, including *Dress, Adornment, and the Social Order,* edited by M. E. Roach and J. B. Eicher, Wiley, 1965; *Changing Perspectives in Mental Illness,* edited by S. C. Plog and R. B. Egerton, Holt, 1969; and *Behavior Modification: The Human Effort,* edited by R. Bradfield, Dimensions Press, 1970. Also author of technical reports. Contributor to proceedings and yearbooks. Contributor of about seventy-five articles and reviews to journals, including *Journal of Personality and Social Psychology, International Journal of Psychiatry, American Psychologist,* and *Educational and Psychological Measurement.* Advisory editor, *International Journal of Clinical and Experimental Hypnosis,* 1971; advisory editor, Holt, Rinehart & Winston, Inc.

OBITUARIES:

PERIODICALS

Chicago Tribune, June 22, 1992, section 1, p. 12.
New York Times, June 22, 1992, p. D10.*

*   *   *

LOUIS, Pat
   See FRANCIS, Dorothy Brenner

*   *   *

LOUISBURGH, Sheila Burnford
   See BURNFORD, Sheila (Philip Cochrane Every)

*   *   *

LOW, Joseph   1911-

PERSONAL: Born August 11, 1911, in Coraopolis, PA; son of John Routh and Stella (Rent) Low; married Ruth Hull, October 21, 1940; children: Damaris, Jennifer. *Education:* Attended University of Illinois, 1930-32; attended Art Students League, New York City, studied with George Grosz, 1935. *Avocational interests:* Sailing.

ADDRESSES: Home—RFD 278, Chilmark, MA 02535.

CAREER: Printmaker, graphic artist, children's author and illustrator. Began art career in 1933 by typesetting and printing his own work; free-lance designer in New York City, 1941; Indiana University at Bloomington, instructor in design and graphic art, 1942-45, also established the university's Corydon Press; worked for advertising agencies and editorial offices in Morristown, NJ, 1946-54; Eden Hill Press, Newton, CT, founding owner, 1959—. Work represented in permanent collections at Boston Museum of Fine Arts, Library of Congress, State Department, Princeton University, Dartmouth College, University of Kentucky, Williams College, University of Illinois, Wesleyan University, Virginia Museum of Fine Arts, San Francisco Public Library, Boston Atheneum, Harvard College Library, Pratt Institute, University of Oklahoma, Newberry Library, Metropolitan Museum of Art, Ohio State University, Bodleian Library, and Oxford University. *Exhibitions:* Princeton University, Dartmouth College, University of Illinois, Philadelphia Museum of Art, Brandeis University, Williams College, Grinnell College, Carnegie Institute of Technology, Herron Art Institute, University of Kentucky, and many others.

AWARDS, HONORS: "Best Illustrated Children's Book of the Year" citation, *New York Times,* 1953, for *Mother Goose Riddle Rhymes,* and 1976, for *Little Though I Be;* Children's Spring Book Festival Award, *New York Herald Tribune,* 1954, for *Egyptian Adventures,* and 1962, for *Adam's Book of Odd Creatures;* New Jersey Institute of Technology award, 1968, for *Hear Your Heart* and *Shrimps; Trust Reba* and *The Land of the Taffeta Dawn* exhibited in the American Institute of Graphic Arts Children's Book Show, 1973-74; "Fifty Books of the Year" citation, American Institute of Graphic Arts, 1974, and Children's Book Showcase selection, 1975, both for *The Mouse and the Song;* Children's Book Showcase selection, 1976, for *Boo to a Goose,* and 1977, for *Meat Pies and Sausages;* Caldecott Honor Book, 1981, for *Mice Twice.*

WRITINGS:

SELF-ILLUSTRATED WITH WIFE, RUTH LOW

Mother Goose Riddle Rhymes, Harcourt (San Diego), 1953.

Adam's Book of Odd Creatures, Atheneum (New York City), 1962.

Smiling Duke, Houghton (Boston), 1963.

There Was a Wise Crow, Follett (Chicago), 1969.

Trust Reba, McGraw (New York City), 1974.

Boo to a Goose, Atheneum, 1975.

Five Men under One Umbrella, and Other Ready-to-Read Riddles, Macmillan (New York City), 1975.

Little Though I Be, McGraw, 1976.

What If. . .? 14 Encounters—Some Frightful, Some Frivolous—That Might Happen to Anyone, Atheneum, 1976.

A Mad Wet Hen and Other Riddles, Morrow (New York City), 1977.

The Christmas Grump, Atheneum, 1977.

Benny Rabbit and the Owl, Greenwillow (New York City), 1978.

My Dog, Your Dog, Macmillan, 1978.

The Devil Himself, McGraw, 1978.

Mice Twice, Atheneum, 1980.

Don't Drag Your Feet, Atheneum, 1983.

Beastly Riddles, Macmillan, 1983.

ILLUSTRATOR

Wright, Wendell William, and Helene Laird, *Rainbow Dictionary,* World Publishing, 1947, reprinted as *The Rainbow Dictionary for Young Readers,* Collins & World, 1972.

Rugoff, Milton Allan, editor, *Harvest of World Folk Tales,* Viking (New York City), 1949.

Coolidge, Olivia E., *Egyptian Adventures,* Houghton, 1954.

Osborne, Maurice Macado, *Rudi and the Mayor of Naples,* Houghton, 1958.

Schlein, Miriam, *The Big Cheese,* W. R. Scott (New York City), 1958.

de la Mare, Walter, *Jack and the Beanstalk,* Knopf (New York City), 1959.

Jordan, Helene Jamieson, *How a Seed Grows,* Crowell (New York City), 1960.

Mincieli, Rose Laura, *Pulcinella; or, Punch's Merry Pranks,* Knopf, 1960.

Mincieli, Rose Laura, *The Wren-Boy's Rhyme,* Eden Hill Press (Newton, CT), 1961.

Burland, Brian, *St. Nicholas and the Tub,* Holiday House (New York City), 1964.

Goldin, Augusta R., *Spider Silk,* Crowell, 1964.

Swift, Jonathan, *Directions to Servants,* Pantheon (New York City), 1964.

Bulla, Clyde Robert, *More Stories from Favorite Operas,* Crowell, 1965.

Bro, Marguerite Harmon, *How the Mouse Deer Became King,* Doubleday (New York City), 1966.

De La Iglesia, Maria Elena, *The Cat and the Mouse, and Other Spanish Tales,* Pantheon, 1966.

Frankenberg, Lloyd, editor, *Poems of Robert Burns,* Crowell, 1967.

Hawes, Judy, *Shrimps,* Crowell, 1967.

Kohn, Bernice, *Telephones,* Coward (Branford, CT), 1967.

Walker, Barbara K., and Mine Suemer, *Stargazer to the Sultan,* Parents' Magazine Press (New York City), 1967.

Zimelman, Nathan, *To Sing a Song as Big as Ireland,* Follett, 1967.

Hieatt, Constance B., *The Knight of the Lion,* Crowell, 1968.

Liss, Howard, *Friction,* Coward, 1968.

Showers, Paul, *Hear Your Heart,* Crowell, 1968.

Tresselt, Alvin R., *The Legend of the Willow Plate,* Parents' Magazine Press, 1968.

Aldan, Daisy, editor, *Poems from India,* Crowell, 1969.

Cullen, Countee, *The Lost Zoo,* Follett, 1969.

Fenton, Sophia Harvati, *Greece,* Holt (New York City), 1969.

Mendoza, George, *A Beastly Alphabet,* Grosset (New York City), 1969.

Mendoza, George, *Flowers and Grasses and Weeds,* Funk (New York City), 1969.

The Compleat Gamester (limited edition), Barre (New York City), 1969.

Twain, Mark, *The Notorious Jumping Frog and Other Stories,* edited by Edward Wagenknecht, Heritage Press (Baltimore), 1970.

Livingston, Myra Cohn, editor, *Speak Roughly to Your Little Boy: A Collection of Parodies and Burlesques,* Harcourt, 1971.

Colum, Padraic, *The White Sparrow,* McGraw, 1972.

Kalina, Sigmund, *Your Bones Are Alive,* Lothrop (New York City), 1972.

Belting, Natalia Maree, *The Land of the Taffeta Dawn,* Dutton (New York City), 1973.

Hoberman, Mary Ann, *The Raucous Auk: A Menagerie of Poems,* Viking, 1973.

Longfellow, Henry Wadsworth, *Paul Revere's Ride,* Windmill Books (New York City), 1973.

Erickson, Russell E., *The Snow of Ohreeganu,* Lothrop, 1974.

Roach, Marilynne K., *The Mouse and the Song,* Parent's Magazine Press, 1974.

Branley, Franklyn Mansfield, *Roots Are Food Finders,* Crowell, 1975.

Van Woerkom, Dorothy O., *Meat Pies and Sausages,* Greenwillow, 1976.

Livingston, *A Lolligag of Limericks,* Atheneum, 1978.

Griffith, Helen V., *Alex and the Cat,* Greenwillow, 1982.

Livingston, compiler, *A Learical Lexicon,* Atheneum, 1985.

SIDELIGHTS: Critically acclaimed for what a *Publishers Weekly* reviewer once described as "deceptively effortless portraits in muted tones," Joseph Low has received numerous citations for his illustration work. As a youth, although Low was very interested in books and their illustrations, his classroom studies in art did little to encourage him in his own drawing. Instead, as he described in *Third Book of Junior Authors,* Low relied on finding "voices here and there in the art of the past, and among a few of the moderns, speaking a visual language I could recognize as my own."

Low's venture into picture books began by providing illustrations for books by other authors, before producing both text and illustrations for his first book, *Mother Goose Riddle Rhymes*, in 1953. Low's collaborator for the book was his wife Ruth, whom he had married in 1940. A *Saturday Review* critic described the Lows' *Mother Goose Riddle Rhymes* as "a perfect book for a rainy day to be shared with boys and girls of almost any age," while a *New York Times* reviewer praised the pictures as "beautifully drawn, reproduced in fresh colors."

Low has also been critically praised for the animated style of illustration in his other books. Primarily pen and ink with color washes, Low's pictures often feature animal subjects such as horses, dogs, and mice. Regarding the central mouse character in *The Christmas Grump*, a reviewer in *Bulletin of the Center for Children's Books* noted that "Low's frisky, scrabbly pictures have flair and humor," while another reviewer for the same journal cited *My Dog, Your Dog* for illustrations of "lively line and bright, sometimes off-register colors."

One of Low's best-received books was *Mice Twice*, published in 1980, for which he was a runner-up for the prestigious Caldecott Medal, bestowed annually for the highest achievement in children's books. In her review of the book, Diane Roback in *Publishers Weekly* praised Low's imaginative prose and found that the "illustrations are the artist's gleeful best." A *Horn Book Magazine* reviewer observed that the book "has a wry, sly bunch of anthropomorphic animals outsmarting each other [in a] story [which] seems more spoken than written."

BIOGRAPHICAL/CRITICAL SOURCES:

BOOKS

De Montreville, Doris, and Donna Hill, editors, *Third Book of Junior Authors*, H. W. Wilson (Bronx), 1972, pp. 183-184.
Kingman, Lee, editor, *Illustrators of Children's Books: 1957-1966*, Horn Book, 1968.
Klemin, Diana, *The Illustrated Book*, Bramhall House, 1970.

PERIODICALS

Bulletin of the Center for Children's Books, December, 1977; September, 1978.
Horn Book Magazine, September/October 1986, p. 615; November/December 1986, p. 713.
New York Times, November 1, 1953.
Publishers Weekly, April 30, 1982, p. 59; May 30, 1986, p. 72.
Saturday Review, November 14, 1953.*

LOWE, John (Evelyn) 1928-

PERSONAL: Born April 23, 1928, in London, England; son of Arthur and Evelyn Lowe; married, 1956 (divorced, 1981). *Education:* New College, Oxford, M.A., 1952.

ADDRESSES: Office—Paillole Basse, Cours, 47360 Prayssas, France.

CAREER: Victoria and Albert Museum, London, England, assistant keeper in department of woodwork, 1953-56; Rank Organisation, Pinewood Studios, Iver Heath, Buckinghamshire, England, deputy story editor, 1956-57; Victoria and Albert Museum, London, assistant keeper in department of ceramics, 1957-61, assistant to the director, 1961-64; Birmingham Museum and Art Gallery, Birmingham, England, director, 1964-69; Weald and Downland Open Air Museum, Singleton, Sussex, England, director, 1969-74; West Dean College, Chichester, England, principal, 1973-78; Doshisha University, Kyoto, Japan, visiting professor of British cultural studies, 1979-81; literary editor of *Kansai Time Out*, 1983-88. *Military service:* British Army, Royal Army Education Corps, 1947-49; became sergeant.

MEMBER: Royal College of Art (honorary fellow), Royal Society of Arts (fellow), Society of Antiquaries (fellow).

WRITINGS:

The Furniture of Thomas Chippendale, [Munich], 1955.
Cream Coloured Earthenware, H.M.S.O., 1957.
Japanese Crafts, J. Murray, 1983.
Into Japan, J. Murray, 1986.
Corsica: A Traveller's Guide, J. Murray, 1988.
A Surrealist Life—Edward James, Collins, 1991.

Also author of *A Short Guide to the Kyoto Museum of Archaeology*. Founding editor of "Furniture Series" published by Faber. Contributor to *Oxford Junior Encyclopaedia* and *Encyclopaedia Britannica*.

WORK IN PROGRESS: The Companion Guide to Japan and *The Warden—A Portrait of John Sparrow*.

SIDELIGHTS: John Lowe told *CA:* "Each of my books is different. As a writer, I believe that the author should say what he has to say in his books and after that retire into silence."

*   *   *

LOWE, Richard G. 1942-

PERSONAL: Surname rhymes with "snow"; born July 5, 1942, in Eunice, LA; son of Grady B. and Iris (McManus) Lowe; married Cheron Fontenot, July 22, 1962 (died May

3, 1989); married Kathy Mothersbaugh, June 2, 1992; children: (first marriage) Kevin, Christopher, Mark. *Education:* University of Southwestern Louisiana, B.A., 1964; Harvard University, A.M., 1965; University of Virginia, Ph.D., 1968.

ADDRESSES: Office—Department of History, University of North Texas, Denton, TX 76203.

CAREER: University of North Texas, Denton, assistant professor, 1968-72, associate professor, 1972-77, professor of history, 1977-94, Regents professor, 1994—, varsity soccer coach, 1980-94.

MEMBER: Society of Civil War Historians, Southern Historical Association, Virginia Historical Society, Texas State Historical Association.

WRITINGS:

(With Randolph B. Campbell) *Wealth and Power in Antebellum Texas,* Texas A & M University Press, 1977.
(With Campbell) *Planters and Plain Folk: Agriculture in Antebellum Texas,* Southern Methodist University Press (Dallas, TX), 1987.
Republicans and Reconstruction in Virginia, 1856-1870, University Press of Virginia (Charlottesville, VA), 1991.

Contributor to history journals, including *Civil War History, Journal of American History, Journal of Southern History, Southwestern Historical Quarterly, Virginia Magazine of History and Biography,* and *William and Mary Quarterly.* Editor of journal, *Military History of the West,* 1989—; co-editor, H-CIVWAR mailing list on Internet, 1994—.

WORK IN PROGRESS: Quantitative and Traditional History of Walker's Texas Division, C. S. A.; The Texas Overland Expedition, 1863.

*   *   *

LUTZ, John (Thomas) 1939-

PERSONAL: Born September 11, 1939, in Dallas, TX; son of John Peter and Jane (Gundelfinger) Lutz; married Barbara Jean Bradley, March 25, 1958; children: Steven, Jennifer, Wendy. *Education:* Attended Meramec Community College, 1965. *Politics:* "Reasonable."

ADDRESSES: Home and office—880 Providence Ave., Webster Groves, MO 63119. *Agent*—Dominick Abel Literary Agency Inc., 146 West 82nd St., New York, NY 10024.

CAREER: Writer. Has worked in construction, as a civilian police employee, and as a truck driver.

MEMBER: Mystery Writers of America, Private Eye Writers of America.

AWARDS, HONORS: Mystery Writers of America scroll, 1981, for short story "Until You Are Dead"; Shamus Award, Private Eye Writers of America, 1982, 1989; Edgar Allan Poe Award, Mystery Writers of America, 1986, for short story "Ride the Lightning."

WRITINGS:

MYSTERY NOVELS

The Truth of the Matter, Pocket Books (New York City), 1971.
Buyer Beware, Putnam (New York City), 1976.
Bonegrinder, Putnam, 1976.
Lazarus Man, Morrow (New York City), 1979.
Jericho Man, Morrow, 1980.
The Shadow Man, Morrow, 1981.
(With Bill Pronzini) *The Eye,* Mysterious Press (New York City), 1984.
Nightlines, St. Martin's (New York City), 1985.
The Right to Sing the Blues, St. Martin's, 1986.
Tropical Heat, Holt (New York City), 1986.
Ride the Lightning, St. Martin's, 1987.
Scorcher, Holt, 1987.
Dancer's Debt, St. Martin's, 1988.
Shadowtown, Mysterious Press, 1988.
Time Exposure, St. Martin's, 1989.
Kiss, Holt, 1990.
Flame, Holt, 1990.
Diamond Eyes, St. Martin's, 1990.
SWF Seeks Same, St. Martin's, 1990.
Bloodfire, Holt, 1991.
Hot, Holt, 1992.
Dancing with the Dead, St. Martin's, 1992.
Spark, Holt, 1993.
Thicker Than Blood, St. Martin's, 1993.
Torch, Holt, 1994.

STORY COLLECTIONS

Better Mousetraps, St. Martin's, 1988.
Shadows Everywhere, Mystery Scene Press, 1994.

OTHER

Also contributor to anthologies, including *Ellery Queen's Mystery Bay,* edited by Ellery Queen, World Publishing, 1972; *Best Detective Stories,* edited by E. Hoch, Dutton, 1976; *Alfred Hitchcock's Tales to Make Your Blood Run Cold,* edited by Eleanor Sullivan, Dial, 1978; *Ellery Queen's Circumstantial Evidence,* edited by Queen, Dial, 1980; *Arbor House Treasury of Mystery and Suspense,* edited by Martin Greenberg, Malzberg, and Pronzini, Arbor House, 1981; *Arbor House Treasury of Horror and the Supernatural,* Arbor House, 1981; *Creature,* edited by Pronzini, Arbor House, 1981. Contributor of about 200 stories to magazines.

ADAPTATIONS: Lutz's novel *SWF Seeks Same* was filmed as *Single White Female.*

WORK IN PROGRESS: Short stories; a novel; a screenplay.

SIDELIGHTS: John Lutz once told *CA:* "It would be difficult for me to say exactly what motivated me to begin writing; it's possible that the original motivation is gone, much as a match that starts a forest fire is consumed in the early moments of the fire. I continue writing for selfish reasons. I thoroughly enjoy it."

*   *   *

LYNNE, Becky
    See ZAWADSKY, Patience

M

MACLEAN, Norman (Fitzroy) 1902-1990

PERSONAL: Born December 23, 1902, in Clarinda, IA; died August 2, 1990, in Chicago, IL; son of John Norman (a minister) and Clara Evelyn (Davidson) Maclean; married Jessie Burns, September 24, 1931 (deceased); children: Jean Snyder, John Norman. *Education:* Dartmouth College, A.B., 1924; University of Chicago, Ph.D., 1940.

CAREER: Dartmouth College, Hanover, NH, instructor in English, 1924-26; worked in logging camps and U.S. Forest Service in Montana and Idaho, 1926-28; University of Chicago, Chicago, IL, instructor, 1930-41, assistant professor, 1941-44, associate professor, 1944-54, professor of English, 1954-73, William Rainey Harper Professor of English, 1963-73, professor emeritus, 1973-90, dean of students, 1941-46, chairman of Committee on General Studies, 1956-64. Member of board of directors of Southeast Chicago Commission. Acting director of Institute for Military Studies, 1943-45.

MEMBER: Modern Language Association of America, Beta Theta Pi, Quadrangle Club.

AWARDS, HONORS: Prize for excellence in undergraduate teaching from University of Chicago, 1932, 1940, and 1973; D.L., Montana State University, 1980; National Book Critics Circle Award, 1992, for *Young Men and Fire; Young Men and Fire* named one of nine best books of 1992 by the *New York Times Book Review.*

WRITINGS:

(Editor with R. S. Crane and others, and contributor) *Critics and Criticism: Ancient and Modern,* University of Chicago Press (Chicago), 1952.
A River Runs through It and Other Stories, University of Chicago Press, 1976; title story published separately, with photographs by Joel Snyder, as *A River Runs through It,* 1983, new edition with wood engravings by Barry Moser, 1989.
Young Men and Fire, University of Chicago Press, 1992.

Also author, with Everett C. Olson, of *A Manual of Instruction in Military Maps and Aerial Photographs,* 1943. Contributor of articles and stories to magazines.

ADAPTATIONS: A River Runs through It was produced as a film in 1992, and as an audiotape by Recorded Books, 1993; *Young Men and Fire* was produced as an audiotape by NorthWord Audio Productions, 1993; the novella *USFS 1919: The Ranger, the Cook, and a Hole in the Sky* was filmed for television as "The Ranger, the Cook, and a Hole in the Sky," 1995.

SIDELIGHTS: From his childhood until his old age, Norman Maclean's life was devoted to two passions: nature and literature. When he was more than seventy years old, he fused the two interests by starting to write fiction based on his experiences in the Montana wilderness. The title piece of his first published book of fiction, *A River Runs through It and Other Stories,* focused on fly-fishing in the Big Blackfoot River. His second work, *Young Men and Fire,* examined an infamous forest fire that in 1949 killed a dozen young firefighters. Both books were enjoyed by the general public and acclaimed by critics, who praised Maclean's work for succeeding on two levels. His fiction is realistic, accurate, and detailed in its descriptions; at the same time, it offers insight into the metaphysical implications of man's interactions with nature.

Maclean's family moved to western Montana from Iowa when the author was six years old. Maclean's father, who was a very strong influence in his son's life, was a Scottish-born, Presbyterian minister. He taught his two sons at home, reading from the Bible and classic literature and giving them thought-provoking writing assignments. Lessons were conducted in the mornings, while in the afternoons the boys were left free to explore the nearby wilderness. When Maclean was ten years old, this educational system was disrupted by the local truant officer, who insisted that the boys attend their local district school.

For the rest of his life, Maclean would follow the pattern established during those early years, alternating between the rugged, outdoor life and the world of formal education. As a teenager, he worked for the United States Forest Service; then, in his early twenties, he went east to Dartmouth College. He remained there for two years after his graduation, working as a teacher of English. In 1926 he left that post, returning west to work for two years as a logger and forest ranger in Montana and Idaho. He seriously considered devoting his life to the Forest Service, but chose instead an academic career. A primary motivation for doing so was his belief that teaching would give him the best of both his worlds. Summers would be free to spend in the log cabin he and his father had built in 1922 on Montana's Seeley Lake, while the rest of the year could be given over to teaching the literature he loved.

In 1930, Maclean began work as an instructor at the University of Chicago, where he was awarded a Ph.D. in 1940. His career there was distinguished; over the years, he won three awards for excellence in his profession, and his classes—even though they were known to be extremely difficult—were always popular with students. His reputation was that of a teacher who was devoted to both his subject and his students, one who minced no words when critiquing their writing assignments. He was said to be enthusiastic in his praise and scathing in his disapproval.

After retiring from the university in 1973, Maclean decided to work on his writing—not as a hobby, but for many hours a day, seven days a week, thereby foregoing the abundant leisure time usually associated with retirement. This attitude was in keeping with his belief that life should be a constant process of learning, renewal, and self-improvement. He had already published a military manual and some literary criticism, but his focus now was to be fiction. For stylistic inspiration, he looked to some of his favorite writers, including William Wordsworth, Robert Browning, Gerard Manley Hopkins, Mark Twain, Robert Frost, Ernest Hemingway, and Charlie Russell. For his subject matter, Maclean reviewed his life and singled out those periods that still stood out as momentous to him. He once told *CA:* "All the reasons why I started to write stories about Montana are not clear to me, but an important one has to be connected with a lifetime of trying to make companion pieces of my love and knowledge of the woods and of my love and knowledge of literature and writing."

Maclean's first two published pieces concerned his academic years; both of them were published in the *University of Chicago Magazine.* " 'This Quarter I Am Taking McKeon': A Few Remarks on the Art of Teaching" was a memoir of some of his teaching experiences and his thoughts on the profession. " 'Billiards Is a Good Game': Gamesmanship and America's First Nobel Prize Scientist" recalled his first year at the University of Chicago and the relationship he established at that time with the great scientist Albert Michelson, whose measurements of the speed of light paved the way for Einstein to create his theory of relativity.

In 1976 *A River Runs through It and Other Stories* was published. It consisted of two novellas—the title piece and *USFS 1919: The Ranger, the Cook, and a Hole in the Sky*—and one short story, "Logging and Pimping and 'Your Pal, Jim'." The collection had been rejected by all the established fiction publishing houses to which Maclean had submitted it, and appeared in print only after those in charge of the University of Chicago Press decided to bring it out under their imprint. This was an unprecedented move; the University of Chicago Press had never published anything but nonfiction. The decision was a good one, however. *A River Runs through It and Other Stories* was a serious contender for the Pulitzer Prize, a resounding critical success, and a popular bestseller that went into one printing after another.

USFS 1919 was based on Maclean's experience with the Forest Service, and what he learned about life and art at that time. "Logging and Pimping and 'Your Pal, Jim' " was a character sketch of a seemingly superhuman lumberjack who worked as a pimp during the off-season. John Cawelti, a reviewer for *New Republic,* found Maclean's stories to "have that magical balance of the particular and the universal that good literature is all about and that so many attempts at Western fiction miss completely. . . . He writes brilliantly about work and sport. His pages describing logging, packing, mule-skinning, trail-cutting and fishing are full of precise images which convey as rich a sense of the spiritual form of these activities together that bear comparison with such classics as [Andy] Adams' *Log of a Cowboy.*"

While all of the pieces in *A River Runs through It and Other Stories* have been praised, the title novella clearly stands out as Maclean's most acclaimed work. In it, the author reflects on his years of fishing with his father and brother on the Big Blackfoot River. He explains in his opening sentence that in his family, there was no clear distinction between religion and fly fishing, and throughout the story, the river is presented as a sacred place. Maclean's brother, Paul, is a truly great fisherman; therefore, he is a holy man despite his chronic drinking, gambling, and fighting. When Paul's body is found dumped in an alley in town, the father and brother are left to brood over his life, his mysterious death, and his skill with a fishing rod.

Commenting on the obviously autobiographical nature of the work, Wallace Stegner stated in an essay published in the book *Norman Maclean* that "one suspects he hasn't even bothered to alter names. The only thing that has happened to young Maclean's experience is that it has been recollected in tranquillity, seen in perspective, understood, and fully felt. . . . *A River Runs through It* is a story rooted in actuality, in known people and remembered events. But it is a long way from a limited realism. It is full of love and wonder and loss, it has the same alternations of sunshine and shadow that a mountain stream has, and its meaning can be heard a long way from its banks. It is an invitation to memory and the pondering of our lives."

"Remarkable in many ways, [Maclean's] novella deserves recognition as (I believe) a classic in western American literature," enthused Harold P. Simonson in *Western American Literature*. "As for the analogy between religion and fly fishing, Maclean hooks it, plays and fights it, and finally lands it with masterful form. In short, the analogy works artistically. . . . I find it difficult to restrain my admiration; I find Maclean in this story equal to anything in Hemingway and a good deal more courageous, theologically." Wendell Berry also pointed out the similarities between *A River Runs through It* and Hemingway's work—specifically, the story "Big Two-Hearted River." In an essay published in *Norman Maclean,* Berry concluded that Maclean's novella is "not so neat or self-contained as Hemingway's [story] but just as fine, on its own terms, and far more moving."

"I know of no other 20th-Century American work that is at all like [*A River Runs through It*]," stated Alfred Kazin in the Chicago *Tribune Books*. "It is remarkably well written and altogether beautiful in the power of its feeling. . . . The book is in fact all feeling, and not a little shattering in the intensity of its restraint. . . . There are passages here of physical rapture in the presence of unsullied primitive America that are as beautiful as anything in Thoreau and Hemingway." Although Maclean enjoyed reviews such as these, he also indicated that a bigger thrill came from reading letters from fishermen who gave their approval to his book.

The author's research for his second book went on for decades, and in his view, *Young Men and Fire* was never completed. His working manuscript was published posthumously, however, and like *A River Runs through It, Young Men and Fire* garnered strong reviews. The book was Maclean's attempt to make sense out of the Mann Gulch fire that burned a huge section of Montana land in 1949. The blaze, started by lightning, appeared to be nothing out of the ordinary when the U.S. Forest Service sent fifteen "smokejumpers" or parachutists to extinguish it. As the young, inexperienced crew took up their firefighting positions, however, the modest fire inexplicably blew up into an inferno that left twelve men dead. The families of those who perished questioned the conduct of the crew's leader, Wag Dodge, who had saved himself by lighting an "escape fire" ahead of the main blaze and lying in its embers while the larger fire passed over him. Dodge claimed that he had ordered the other men to join him, but due to panic or their inability to hear him, they had continued in their fatal race with the main fire.

Maclean had been fascinated by the fire for many years and visited the site many times. In the first part of *Young Men and Fire,* he describes the event as one who was there, and according to Christopher Lehman-Haupt, reviewer for the *New York Times,* he did a masterful job of it: "He evokes the hell of the conflagration with details of rolling rocks and exploding trees and tiny dust devils of flame that suddenly rise up into apocalyptic whirlwinds." When Maclean shifts his focus to the investigation following the fire and his own years of careful research, "remarkably, the drama . . . heightens," reports Lehman-Haupt.

James R. Kincaid explains in the *New York Times Book Review* that *Young Men and Fire* is "not simply or even mainly [about] the Mann Gulch fire but Maclean's search to get at the truth of that fire, at the truth of his own artistry and his own morality, at the truth of tragic form. By the time we are a third of the way through the book, the Mann Gulch fire has cooled and Maclean is trying to encircle a different kind of enemy. The major story now is his attempt to mold this tragedy and to confront his own life and approaching death. He does so by telling other and related stories, examining documents, conducting interviews, learning new science and new art, and returning obsessively to the site where the young men lost the race with the monster. . . . This great book takes us to that ancient reef blocking us from the summit and then whirls and looks straight into the heart of the fire. It is that valiant honesty that allows it to stand against the fire and hold its own even as the flames advance over it."

BIOGRAPHICAL/CRITICAL SOURCES:

BOOKS

Contemporary Literary Criticism, Volume 78, Gale (Detroit), 1994.
McFarland, Ron, and Hugh Nichols, editors, *Norman Maclean,* Confluence Press, 1988.
Short Story Criticism, Volume 13, Gale, 1993.

PERIODICALS

America, October 9, 1976.
Audubon, November-December 1992, pp. 126, 128.

Los Angeles Times Book Review, September 6, 1992, p. 4.
New Republic, May 1, 1976, pp. 24-26.
Newsweek, August 30, 1976; October 12, 1992, p. 87.
New York Review of Books, May 27, 1976.
New York Times, August 10, 1992, p. C18.
New York Times Book Review, September 19, 1976; August 16, 1992, pp. 1, 27-28.
Rocky Mountain Review of Language and Literature, winter, 1980, pp. 34-45.
Sewanee Review, winter, 1977, pp. ii, iv, vi, vii, x.
Smithsonian, September, 1992, pp. 121-22, 124-34.
Times Literary Supplement, August 10, 1990, p. 841; January 8, 1993, p. 4.
Tribune Books (Chicago), August 6, 1989, pp. 1, 9.
TriQuarterly, spring, 1984.
Village Voice, March 29, 1976.
Western American Literature, winter, 1977, pp. 358-59; August, 1982, pp. 149-55; August, 1990, pp. 145-56.

OBITUARIES:

PERIODICALS

Chicago Tribune, August 3, 1990.
Los Angeles Times, August 4, 1990.
New York Times, August 3, 1990.
Times (London), August 8, 1990.*

—Sketch by Joan Goldsworthy

*   *   *

MAINE, David
See AVICE, Claude (Pierre Marie)

*   *   *

MARTIN, David 1915-
(Spinifex)

PERSONAL: Born December 22, 1915, in Budapest, Hungary; emigrated to Australia, 1949; son of Leo and Hedwig (Rosner) Detsinyi; married Elizabeth Richenda Powell, 1941; children: one son. *Education:* Educated in Germany. *Politics:* "I call myself an 'international nationalist.'"

ADDRESSES: Home—28 Wood St., Beechworth, Victoria 3747, Australia. *Agent*—Curtis Brown Ltd., 86 Williams St., Sydney, New South Wales 2021, Australia.

CAREER: Worked in European service for British Broadcasting Corp. (BBC), as foreign correspondent for *London Daily Express,* and as literary editor for *Reynolds News,* all in London, England, 1938-47; foreign correspondent in India, 1948-49; writer, 1949—. *Military service:* International Brigade, 1937-38; served in Spain.

MEMBER: Australian Society of Authors (council member, 1973—), Australian Literature Board.

AWARDS, HONORS: Australia Council senior fellowship, 1973-76.

WRITINGS:

NOVELS

Tiger Bay, Martin & Reid, 1946.
The Stones of Bombay, Wingate, 1950.
The Young Wife (also see below), Macmillan (London), 1962.
The Hero of the Town, Morrow, 1965, published in England as *The Hero of Too,* Cassell, 1965.
The Littlest Neutral, Crown, 1966, published in England as *The King Between,* Cassell, 1966.
Where a Man Belongs, Cassell, 1969.

CHILDREN'S FICTION

Hughie, St. Martin's, 1971.
Gary, Cassell, 1972.
Frank and Francesca, Thomas Nelson, 1972.
The Chinese Boy, Hodder & Stoughton, 1973.
The Cabby's Daughter, Hodder & Stoughton, 1974.
(With wife, Elizabeth Richenda Martin) *Katie,* Hodder & Stoughton, 1974.
Mister P and His Remarkable Flight, Hodder & Stoughton, 1975.
The Devilfish Mystery of the Flying Mum, Thomas Nelson, 1977.
The Mermaid Attack, Outback Press, 1978.
The Man in the Red Turban, Hutchinson, 1978.
Peppino Says Goodbye, Rigby, 1980.
Peppino Changes His Luck, Rigby, 1981.
Peppino in the Tobacco War, Rigby, 1981.
The Girl Who Didn't Know Kelly, Hutchinson, 1984.
Fox on My Door, Collins Dove, 1987.
Clowning Sim, Collins Dove, 1988.

POETRY

Battlefields and Girls, Macmillan, 1942.
(With Hubert Nicholson and John Manifold) *Trident,* Fore, 1944.
(Editor) *Rhyme and Reason: Thirty-four Poems,* Fore, 1944.
From Life: Selected Poems, Current, 1953.
(Under pseudonym Spinifex) *Rob the Robber: His Life and Vindication,* J. Waters, 1954.
Poems, 1938-1958, Edwards & Shaw, 1958.
Spiegel the Cat: A Story-Poem Based on a Tale by Gottfried Keller, F. W. Cheshire, 1961, C. N. Potter, 1971.
The Gift: Poems, 1959-1965, Jacaranda, 1966.

The Idealist, Jacaranda, 1968.
I Rhyme My Time (juvenile), Jacaranda, 1980.

OTHER

The Shepherd and the Hunter (three-act play; first produced in London, 1945), Wingate, 1946.
The Shoes Men Walk In (short stories), Pilot Press, 1946.
(With F. E. Emery) *Psychological Effects of the "Western" Film: A Study in Television Viewing* (nonfiction), University of Melbourne, 1957.
Television Tension Programmes: A Study Based on a Content Analysis of Western, Crime, and Adventure Programmes Televised by Melbourne Stations, 1960-61 (nonfiction), Australian Broadcasting Control Board, 1963.
The Young Wife (play; adaptation of his novel of the same title), first produced in Melbourne, 1966.
On the Road to Sydney (travel), Thomas Nelson, 1970.
Foreigners, Rigby, 1981.
Armed/Neutrality for Australia, Dove Communications, 1984.

Also author of *I'll Take Australia.*

SIDELIGHTS: David Martin once told *CA:* "I was described by the *Times Literary Supplement* as 'Australia's outstanding literary acquisition from post-war immigration.' I am one of my adopted country's most prolific writers. Having first won a reputation as a poet (though my mother language is German), I also became a novelist. My most widely read work of fiction is *The Young Wife,* which tells of a Greek migrant woman in Melbourne. I have also written 'young' novels. They, too, deal mainly with the insider-outsider theme, often using Australia's colorful background."

*   *   *

MARTIN, Valerie 1948-

PERSONAL: Born March 14, 1948, in Sedalia, MO; daughter of John Roger Metcalf (a sea captain) and Valerie (Fleischer) Metcalf; married Robert M. Martin (an artist), December 10, 1970 (divorced, 1984); married James Ellsworth Watson, March 30, 1985; children (first marriage): Adrienne. *Education:* University of New Orleans, B.A., 1970; University of Massachusetts, M.F.A., 1974.

ADDRESSES: Agent—Jed Mattes, International Creative Management, 40 West 57th St., New York, NY 10019.

CAREER: University of New Mexico, Las Cruces, visiting lecturer in creative writing, 1978-79; University of New Orleans, New Orleans, LA, assistant professor of English, 1980-84, 1985-86; University of Alabama, Tuscaloosa, writer in residence, 1984-85; Holyoke College,

South Hadley, MA, lecturer in creative writing, beginning 1986; University of Massachusetts—Amherst, currently assistant professor of English.

MEMBER: Authors Guild, Authors League of America.

AWARDS, HONORS: Louisiana Division of the Arts grant, 1982.

WRITINGS:

Set in Motion (novel), Farrar, Straus (New York City), 1978.
Alexandra (novel), Farrar, Straus, 1979.
A Recent Martyr (novel), Houghton (Boston), 1987.
The Consolation of Nature, and Other Stories, Vintage (New York City), 1988.
Mary Reilly (novel), Doubleday (New York City), 1990.
The Great Divorce, Doubleday, 1994.

SIDELIGHTS: Valerie Martin writes stories which, Michiko Kakutani of the *New York Times* believes, "recall those by Edgar Allan Poe. It's not just the gothic subject matter or the tightly designed plots. It's [Martin's] ability to take that material and communicate extreme states of mind—to make it yield startling psychological truths that resonate in the mind." Susan Slocum Hinerfeld of the *Los Angeles Times Book Review* describes Martin's work as "neo-Gothic hyperbole of the New Orleans School. This is the literature of excess, swerving toward violence and despair. It's not easy to control such iridescent prose, such ardent imaginings." Martin's novels include *A Recent Martyr, The Great Divorce* and *Mary Reilly,* a version of Robert Louis Stevenson's *Dr. Jekyll and Mr. Hyde* told from the point of view of the doctor's housemaid. Her collection *The Consolation of Nature and Other Stories* has also received critical attention.

A Recent Martyr, set in a plague-ridden New Orleans of the near future, depicts the sadomasochistic love affair between Emma Miller, who is unhappily married, and Pascal Toussaint. When Toussaint becomes obsessed with Claire, a postulant nun who works with Emma caring for the dying within the quarantine zone, their tangled relationship plays itself out amid the misery and fear of the suffering city. Geoffrey Stokes, writing in the *Village Voice,* claims that "Martin can flat-out write. . . . In prose of liquid clarity, [she] applies pressure to her characters—a touch here, a prod there, a contusive thump in an out-of-the-way alley—and lets it flow, equally and undiminished, through every corner of their souls, every page of her remarkable book." Carolyn Banks, writing in the *New York Times Book Review,* finds that "there is much in *A Recent Martyr* that, in another author's hands, might be overwrought. . . . We are told these things, however, in Emma's voice, always steady, clear, elegant and direct."

A woman narrates *Mary Reilly* as well, the story of Dr. Jekyll and Mr. Hyde retold by the doctor's housemaid. Mary Reilly writes in her journal of the increasingly strange state of affairs around the Jekyll home, especially after the doctor supposedly hires an assistant named Edward Hyde. *Newsweek*'s David Gates praises the author's memorable characters, especially "the utterly convincing Mary, with a housemaid's eye (rooms, to her, are furnished with things to be cleaned), a servant girl's rigorous sense of place—and a sufferer's hard-won dignity." In the *Los Angeles Times Book Review,* Judith Freeman also reflects on Mary as "a character of great kindness and goodness. Her perceptions of human nature ring with simple truth."

Abused by a drunken father, Mary tries hard to please the kindly Dr. Jekyll. "When Master is gay and kind to me," she writes in the journal she keeps, "then all the sadness I feel lifts as suddenly as a bird. . . . When he tells me he trusts me and shows he trusts me more than anyone else in this house, my heart leaps." The novel, writes Elizabeth Castor in the *Washington Post,* is "part psychological novel, part social history, part eerie horror tale . . . dark and moving and powerful—a fitting complement to the 19th-century original." Ellen Pall, writing in the *Chicago Tribune,* considers it "curiously lacking in . . . resonance for our time; despite the politically intriguing female-underclass point of view it adopts, it seems finally not to be about very much." But John Crowley's glowing review in the *New York Times Book Review* is more typical. Crowley states that "*Mary Reilly* is an achievement—creativity skating exhilaratingly on thin ice." He concludes: "I think Valerie Martin's treatment of [Robert Louis Stevenson's] story actually succeeds in ways Stevenson himself could not have brought off and might well have admired."

In the novel *The Great Divorce,* Martin weaves three stories concerning the relationship between humans and animals. One story tells of Ellen Clayton, a veterinarian for a New Orleans zoo, whose husband is leaving her for a younger woman at the same time the zoo is suffering from a viral outbreak. The second story concerns Camille, the zoo's keeper of big cats, who imagines herself as a leopard to escape from her intolerable private life. The third story tells of Elizabeth Schlaeger, nicknamed the catwoman of St. Francisville, a 19th century woman who savagely murdered her husband. "In all three of its tales," writes Emily Mitchell in *Time,* "*The Great Divorce* evocatively humanizes the wild nature that is just beneath the surface of us all." Francine Prose, writing in the *Los Angeles Times Book Review,* calls *The Great Divorce* an "intellectually ambitious and readable new book" that "provides the immediate pleasures of a literary page-turner, but also has a more lasting influence."

Animals also play a prominent role in the stories gathered together in *The Consolation of Nature and Other Stories.* In this ironically-titled collection, Martin spins tales of unease. "One comes away from these stories," explains Marianne Gingher in the *Washington Post Book World,* "feeling ambivalent about nature's role in human solace. Innocent lovers drown, a sea creature murderously castrates a fisherman, a hungry cat absurdly traps its face in a salmon can and dies, an enormous rat seizes a man by the throat." As Kakutani notes, Martin displays "a preoccupation with the dark underside of life, a taste for disturbing, even macabre imagery, and a tendency to use that imagery to delineate turning points in people's lives." Although Hinerfeld claims that "what [the book] lacks—entirely—is humor," Gingher finds *The Consolation of Nature* to be "a curious, spooky, distinctive book."

BIOGRAPHICAL/CRITICAL SOURCES:

PERIODICALS

Belles Lettres, July, 1988, p. 13; fall, 1991, p. 30.

Detroit Free Press, January 21, 1990.

Entertainment Weekly, April 8, 1994, p. 53.

Glamour, February, 1990.

Los Angeles Times Book Review, July 12, 1987, p. 4; February 7, 1988, p. 7; January 21, 1990, pp. 1, 10; March 27, 1994, p. 2.

New Statesman and Society, August 5, 1994, p. 37.

Newsweek, July 24, 1978, p. 82; March 12, 1990, p. 90.

New Yorker, July 30, 1979, pp. 88-89.

New York Times, June 23, 1978, p. C23; June 21, 1979; January 13, 1988; January 26, 1990, p. B4; February 18, 1994, p. C28.

New York Times Book Review, August 5, 1979, p. 10; June 7, 1987; February 4, 1990, p. 7; March 13, 1994, p. 7.

Observer (London), July 21, 1991, p. 54.

Publishers Weekly, April 10, 1978, p. 68; May 21, 1979, pp. 56-57; February 9, 1990, pp. 41-42; January 3, 1994, p. 70.

Sewanee Review, October, 1978, p. 609.

Southern Review, autumn, 1978, p. 849; spring, 1988, p. 445.

Time, February 19, 1990, p. 84; March 28, 1994, p. 67.

Times Literary Supplement, February 8, 1980, p. 146; October 28, 1988; June 1, 1990, p. 586.

Tribune Books (Chicago), February 4, 1990, p. 5.

Village Voice, June 30, 1987, p. 55.

Voice Literary Supplement, October, 1987.

Washington Post, January 17, 1990, p. D2; March 4, 1990.

Washington Post Book World, March 6, 1988, p. 9.

Women's Review of Books, July, 1990, p. 34.

MARTY, Martin E(mil) 1928-

PERSONAL: Born February 5, 1928, in West Point, NE; son of Emil A. (a teacher) and Anne Louise (Wuerde- mann) Marty; married Elsa Schumacher, June 21, 1952 (deceased); married Harriet Lindeman, August 23, 1982; children: (first marriage) Joel, John, Peter, Micah. *Educa- tion:* Attended Concordia University and Washington University; Concordia Seminary, A.B., 1949, M.Div., 1952; Lutheran School of Theology at Chicago, S.T.M., 1954; University of Chicago, Ph.D., 1956. *Politics:* Demo- crat. *Religion:* Lutheran.

ADDRESSES: Home—239 Scottswood, Riverside, IL 60546.

CAREER: Ordained Lutheran minister; minister at Christ Lutheran Church, Washington, DC, Pilgrim Lutheran Church, Bethesda, MD, Grace Lutheran Church, River Forest, IL, and Lutheran Church of the Holy Spirit, Elk Grove Village, IL, 1950-63; University of Chicago, Divin- ity School, Chicago, IL, member of faculty, 1963—, Fair- fax M. Cone Distinguished Service Professor, 1978—, as- sociate dean of divinity school, 1970-75. Consultant on re- ligious history, *Encyclopaedia Britannica;* founding president and George B. Caldwell senior scholar-in- residence at the Park Ridge Center for the Study of Health, Faith, and Ethics.

MEMBER: American Society of Church History (presi- dent, 1971), American Catholic Historical Association (president, 1981), American Academy of Religion (presi- dent, 1987).

AWARDS, HONORS: Brotherhood Award, 1960, for *The New Shape of American Religion;* National Book Award for philosophy and religion, 1971, for *Righteous Empire: The Protestant Experience in America;* Christopher Award, 1985, for *Pilgrims in Their Own Land: Five Hun- dred Years of Religion in America;* 54 honorary degrees; American Academy of Arts and Sciences fellow, Ameri- can Philosophical Society, elected member.

WRITINGS:

A Short History of Christianity, Meridian, 1959, 2nd re- vised edition, Fortress Press (Philadelphia, PA), 1987.
The New Shape of American Religion, Harper (New York City), 1959, reprinted, Greenwood Press, 1978.
The Improper Opinion, Westminster, 1961.
The Infidel: Freethought and American Religion, Meridi- an-World, 1961.
Baptism, Fortress, 1962, reprinted, 1977.
The Hidden Discipline, Concordia, 1963.
Second Chance for American Protestants, Harper, 1963.
Babylon by Choice, Friendship Press, 1964.

Church Unity and Church Mission, W. B. Eerdmans (Grand Rapids, MI), 1964.
Varieties of Unbelief, Holt, 1964.
Youth Considers "Do-It-Yourself" Religion, Nelson, 1965.
The Search for a Usable Future, Harper, 1969.
The Modern Schism: Three Paths to the Secular, Harper, 1969.
Righteous Empire: The Protestant Experience in America, Dial, 1970, 2nd revised edition published as *Protes- tantism in the United States,* Scribner, 1986.
Protestantism, Holt, 1972.
The Fire We Can Light: The Role of Religion in a Sud- denly Different World, Doubleday, 1973.
The Lutheran People, Cathedral Publishers, 1973.
You Are Promise, Argus Communications, 1974.
What a Catholic Believes as Seen by a Non-Catholic, Thomas More Press, 1974.
The Pro and Con Book of Religious America: A Bicenten- nial Argument, Word Books, 1975.
Lutheranism: A Restatement in Question and Answer Form, Cathedral Publishers, 1975.
A Nation of Behavers, University of Chicago Press, 1976.
Good News in the Early Church, Collins, 1976.
Religion, Awakening and Revolution, Consortium, 1977.
The Lord's Supper, Fortress, 1980.
Religious Crises in Modern America, Baylor, 1980.
Friendship, Argus Communications, 1980.
By Way of Response, Abingdon, 1981.
The Public Church: Mainline, Evangelical, Catholic, Crossroad Publishing, 1981.
A Cry of Absence: Reflections for the Winter of the Heart, Harper (San Francisco, CA), 1983, revised edition, 1993.
Health and Medicine in the Lutheran Tradition: Being Well, Crossroad Publishing, 1983.
Being Good and Doing Good, Fortress, 1984.
Christian Churches in the United States, 1800-1983, Wins- ton Press, 1984, 2nd edition, 1987.
Christianity in the New World, Winston Press, 1984.
Pilgrims in Their Own Land: Five Hundred Years of Reli- gion in America, Little, Brown, 1984.
The Word: People Participating in Preaching, Fortress, 1984.
Modern American Religion, University of Chicago Press, Volume 1: *The Irony of It All, 1893-1919,* 1986, Vol- ume 2: *The Noise of Conflict, 1919-1941,* 1990, Vol- ume 3: *Under God, Indivisible, 1941-1960,* 1996.
Invitation to Discipleship, Augsburg, 1986.
Religion and Republic: The American Circumstance, Bea- con Press (Boston, MA), 1987.
A Short History of American Catholicism, Thomas More Press, 1995.

CO-AUTHOR

The Outbursts That Await Us, Macmillan, 1963.

The Religious Press in America, Holt, 1963.

Pen-Ultimates, Holt, 1963.

(With Stuart E. Rosenberg and Andrew Greeley) *What Do We Believe?: The Stance of Religion in America,* Meredith, 1968.

(With Douglas W. Johnson and Jackson W. Carrol) *Religion in America, 1950 to the Present,* Harper, 1979.

(With Kenneth L. Vaux) *Health/Medicine and the Faith Traditions: An Inquiry into Religion and Medicine,* Fortress, 1982.

(With Joan D. Chittister) *Faith and Ferment: An Interdisciplinary Study of Christian Beliefs and Practices,* Liturgical Press, 1983.

(With R. Scott Appleby) *The Glory and the Power: The Fundamentalist Challenge to the Modern World,* Beacon Press (Boston, MA), 1992.

(With son, Micah Marty) *Places along the Way: Meditations on the Journey of Faith,* Augsburg Fortress (Minneapolis, MN), 1994.

(With Micah Marty) *Our Hopes for Years to Come,* Augsburg Fortress, 1995.

EDITOR

New Directions in Biblical Thought, Association, 1960.

No Ground beneath Us, Methodist Student Movement, 1964.

(With Kyle Haselden) *What's Ahead for the Churches?,* Sheed & Ward, 1964.

(With Robert Lee) *Religion and Social Conflict,* Oxford University Press, 1964.

The Death and Birth of the Parish, Concordia, 1964.

(Co-editor) *New Theology,* Numbers 1-10, Macmillan, 1964-73.

(With Dean G. Peerman) *Handbook of Christian Theologians,* World, 1965, Abingdon, 1980.

Our Faiths, Cathedral Publishers, 1975.

Martin Luther, *The Place of Trust: Martin Luther on the Sermon on the Mount,* Harper, 1983.

(With Frederick E. Greenspahn) *Pushing the Faith: Proselytism and Civility in a Pluralistic World,* Crossroad (New York), 1988.

(With R. Scott Appleby) *The Fundamentalism Project,* University of Chicago Press (Chicago, IL), Volume 1: *Fundamentalisms Observed,* 1991, Volume 2: *Fundamentalisms and Society: Reclaiming the Sciences, the Family, and Education,* 1993, Volume 3: *Fundamentalisms and the State: Remaking Polities, Economies, and Militance,* 1993, Volume 4: *Accounting for Fundamentalisms: The Dynamic Character of Movements,* 1994, Volume 5: *Fundamentalisms Comprehended,* 1995.

(With Jerald Brauer) *The Unrelieved Paradox: Studies in the Faith of Franz Bibfeldt,* W. B. Eerdmans (Grand Rapids, MI), 1994.

EDITOR AND AUTHOR OF INTRODUCTION

(With Peter Berger) *The Place of Bonhoeffer: Problems and Possibilities in His Thought,* Association, 1962.

(And author of afterword) *Where the Spirit Leads: American Denominations Today,* John Knox, 1980.

William James, *The Varieties of Religious Experience: A Study in Human Nature,* Penguin Books, 1982.

Civil Religion, Church and State, K. G. Saur (Munich), 1992.

Missions and Ecumenical Expressions, K. G. Saur, 1992.

Protestantism and Regionalism, K. G. Saur, 1992.

Varieties of Protestantism, K. G. Saur, 1992.

The Writing of American Religious History, K. G. Saur, 1992.

Protestantism and Social Christianity, K. G. Saur, 1992.

New and Intense Movements, K. G. Saur, 1992.

Theological Themes in the American Protestant World, K. G. Saur, 1992.

Trends in American Religion and the Protestant World, K. G. Saur, 1992.

Ethnic and Non-Protestant Themes, K. G. Saur, 1993.

Fundamentalism and Evangelicalism, K. G. Saur, 1993.

Varieties of Religious Expression, K. G. Saur, 1993.

Women and Women's Issues, K. G. Saur, 1993.

Native American Religion and Black Protestantism, K. G. Saur, 1993.

OTHER

Co-editor of *Church History, American Society of Church History,* and *Ecumenical Studies in History,* John Knox Press. Author and editor of *Context* (fortnightly newsletter), 1969—; editor of *Making the Rounds,* journal of the Park Ridge Center for the Study of Health, Faith, and Ethics. General editor of Harper "Forum" series, Lippincott "Promise of Theology" series, and University of Chicago "History of Religion in America" series. Senior editor for *Christian Century,* 1956—; contributing editor to *Christian Ministry,* and former contributing editor to the *Cresset, Dialog, American Lutheran,* and *Paddock* suburban newspapers; former art editor of *Response.* Contributor to numerous books, and of religious articles to encyclopedias.

WORK IN PROGRESS: The remaining volume of *Modern American Religion,* a projected four-volume work.

SIDELIGHTS: "People who go to the roots of their spiritual traditions and wrestle with the mysteries they find there are the sort of people [Martin E.] Marty likes," write Peter Hewitt and William Griffin in *Publishers Weekly.* That description might well fit Marty himself. Ordained a pastor within the conservative Missouri synod of the Lutheran church and active as such for two decades, Marty is nonetheless liberal enough to be in the vanguard of the Christian ecumenical movement and to act as a senior editor of the progressive Protestant magazine *Christian Century.* While juggling these two careers, along with those of professor and scholar, Marty has also found time to write or edit over fifty books on religious subjects ranging from Christian perspectives on health to the natures of friendship and grieving.

Marty's foremost field of expertise is religious history. His 1970 publication *Righteous Empire: The Protestant Experience in America* not only chronicles the course of Protestant religions in this country, but illustrates their influence on the course of national events as well. During the first hundred years of the nation's history, explains Marty, the overwhelming preponderance of white, English-speaking Protestants created a virtual "empire" of values and beliefs. As the Civil War approached, however, Protestantism became divided over slavery and related issues. Waves of Catholic and Jewish immigrants pouring into the country after the war further diluted Protestantism's strength. Marty discusses the confused period that American Protestantism entered at that time and its eventual entry into its present stage, which, in his view, is characterized by a new search for unity rooted in spirituality.

Righteous Empire is "a notable contribution to an understanding of American Protestantism and American society," asserts *Christian Century* reviewer Winthrop S. Hudson. Walter Arnold comments in *Saturday Review,* "That Dr. Marty has written such a book at all [considering Protestantism's many forms and its long history in the United States], especially one so filled with lore and keys to understanding, is a tribute to his learning, industry and courage." Among histories of this sort, *Righteous Empire* "stands out from the others by the evenness of its grasp upon sources and issues across the centuries and across the denominations," maintains *New York Times Book Review* contributor Jaroslav Pelikan.

It is from the vantage point of the historian that Marty looks toward the years to come in *The Search for a Usable Future.* The book was published in 1969, at the end of one of the most tumultuous decades of the century, when conventional morals and religions were challenged as never before. Marty's book probes the reasons for this phenomenon, examines the "new" theologies of the day, and suggests the direction that Christianity might take in order to meet the needs of a changing people, while remaining true to its precepts. "We know of no one better qualified to do what Martin Marty has done in this book," points out Robert L. Short in the *New York Times Book Review,* adding: "As a historian of the modern church, he possesses an encyclopedic knowledge of the vast cultural changes

that have occurred in the past decade; as a theologian of no mean insight, he knows how to put this information together into a significant whole and project it toward the future; as an editor of one of America's most influential Protestant publications, the *Christian Century,* he knows how to express his conclusions with clarity, verve and wit." *Commonweal* contributor Philip Deasy states, "Written in a prose of unfailing readability, *The Search for a Usable Future* provides all the delight of following a first-rate mind in action. [It is] a rare—and inspiring—intellectual treat."

One of Marty's most comprehensive writing projects has been his 500-page work *Pilgrims in Their Own Land: Five Hundred Years of Religion in America.* The author presents his history through portraits of individual figures in American history—"pilgrims who marked out new paths and pioneered new ways," explains *Christian Century* reviewer Robert T. Handy. Critics in numerous publications praise Marty's scope and his engaging style, naming his book an important contribution to religious history as well as an absorbing read. As Michael Kammen reports in the *New York Times Book Review, Pilgrims in Their Own Land* is "page for page, . . . the most engaging one-volume history of American religion we now have. It incorporates more information than I would have thought possible, yet it does so with no sacrifice of readability. When Mr. Marty's prose is not lucidly descriptive, it ranges from eloquent to chatty. Perhaps because of its biographical emphasis, the book has vigorous narrative drive. Despite some rather abrupt transitions, it draws the reader along with compelling force." "It reads like a book one would not mind curling up with on a winter's evening, . . . " Catherine L. Albanese similarly describes in the *Yale Review,* concluding that "Marty has given Americans probably the first significant and comprehensive work in the genre [of public history] by an American religious historian."

With the publication of *The Irony of It All, 1893-1919* in 1986, Marty gave the public a first taste of his projected four-volume work, *Modern American Religion.* In a *CA* interview with Walter W. Ross, Marty explained that his goal in undertaking this project was "to describe the contours of twentieth-century American religion, a task which has never been done before." Some critics have observed how closely religion and politics are linked in Marty's work. Discussing the second volume of *Modern American Religion, The Noise of Conflict, 1919-1941,* in the *New York Times Book Review,* David M. Kennedy observes that Marty distinguishes himself from other social critics by insisting that the religious dimensions of America's diversity have had serious political consequences. Kennedy summarizes Marty's thesis: "And the apparently arcane arguments that at times convulsed pulpit and pew, synod and minyan and presbytery, Mr. Marty insists, were not 'mere tempests in denominational teapots.' Eventually, these value-laden and deadly serious debates broke out of the confined precincts of sectarian squabbling and took on 'geopolitical significance.' Thus public issues—including immigration restriction, labor relations, prohibition, birth control, pacifism or responses to the Great Depression—were, Mr. Marty ecumenically claims, 'based in religious beliefs and passions.' " Although James H. Moorhead contends in Chicago *Tribune Books* that there are few surprises in *The Noise of Conflict,* he notes that the story is told "with a verve seldom equalled," adding that "*The Noise of Conflict* bears the usual hallmarks of a Marty book: a smoothly flowing narrative, passages studded with suggestive insight inviting further research, and apt quotations that capture the gist of complicated issues."

The numerous writings and other career-related activities that take up the majority of Marty's time led a *Publishers Weekly* writer to describe him as a "whirlwind whose productivity astonishes." And in a letter to *CA* discussing these varied activities, Marty once remarked, "I like to think of myself as being in what Paul Tillich called 'boundary situations,' believing people have a perspective that best illumines the human situation if they are not wholly captive of a single situation. So my career has brought together at all times at least two vocations: minister and editor, professor and editor, administrator and professor and editor—and all the time, writer." Aside from his professional activities, Marty also stressed that "family has to be mentioned as a major interest; our house has always been open to others than our own four sons. We brought into the family a brother-sister foster pair, have taken in small boys from Uganda as grade-school 'foreign students,' I now have a step-daughter, and the like. We try to covenant with several other families in a pattern we call 'collegial families,' an echo of the extended family." Marty's family has now expanded; he has eight grandchildren.

Although Marty once conceived of *Modern American Religion* as the culmination of his scholarly career, he recently told *CA* that two events "came along to complicate my life." In 1987 he was asked by the American Academy of Arts and Sciences to direct the six-year Fundamentalism Project. Around that time, he was also asked to found the Park Ridge Center for the Study of Health, Faith, and Ethics, which he says has "become one of the nation's major medical ethics centers." "Medical ethics is not my field," Marty continues. "I contribute as an historian, story-teller, humanist, and theologian of sorts." When considering the relation of religion to healing and the relation of healing to extreme militancy, Marty adds: "Some-

one said, 'Marty only gets interested in religion when it heals someone or kills someone.' That is a hyperbolic statement, but it is a reminder to me of the potency, volatility, danger, and promise whenever anyone deals with the sacred, as I like to do."

For a previously published interview, see *Contemporary Authors New Revision Series,* Volume 21, pp. 274-78.

BIOGRAPHICAL/CRITICAL SOURCES:

BOOKS

Dolan, Jay P., and James P. Wind, editors, *New Dimensions in American Religious History: Essays in Honor of Martin E. Marty,* W. B. Eerdmans (Grand Rapids, MI), 1993.

PERIODICALS

Best Sellers, January 1, 1971.
Charlotte Observer, January 21, 1995.
Chicago Tribune, March 3, 1995.
Christian Century, February 17, 1971; May 20, 1981; July 29, 1981; August 26, 1981; September 7, 1983; September 16, 1984.
Commentary, May, 1969.
Commonweal, March 28, 1969; February 22, 1985; November 29, 1985; March 13, 1987; May 17, 1991.
Library Journal, October 7, 1976.
Los Angeles Times Book Review, June 24, 1984; April 19, 1987; December 27, 1992.
New York Review of Books, October 28, 1976.
New York Times Book Review, May 25, 1969; March 14, 1971; November 11, 1973; January 21, 1977; April 19, 1981; June 17, 1984; January 4, 1987; June 16, 1991; January 26, 1992; May 31, 1992.
Publishers Weekly, February 20, 1981.
Saturday Review, January 4, 1969; May 10, 1969; February 6, 1971.
Times Literary Supplement, March 2, 1973.
Tribune Books (Chicago), June 23, 1991.
Voice Literary Supplement, February, 1993.
Washington Post Book World, July 1, 1984.
Yale Review, summer, 1969; winter, 1985.*

*　　　*　　　*

MATARAZZO, James M. 1941-

PERSONAL: Born January 4, 1941, in Stoneham, MA; son of Angelo Michael (a candy-maker) and Anna (Finamore) Matarazzo; married Alice Marie Keohane, September 3, 1966; children: James M. Jr., Susan Eileen. *Education:* Boston College, B.S., 1963, M.A., 1972; Simmons College, M.S., 1965; University of Pittsburgh, Ph.D., 1978.

ADDRESSES: Home—146 Cottage Park Rd., Winthrop, MA 02152. *Office*—Graduate School of Library and Information Science, Simmons College, 300 The Fenway, Boston, MA 02115.

CAREER: Massachusetts Institute of Technology, Cambridge, assistant science librarian, 1965-67, documents librarian, 1967-68, serials librarian, documents librarian, and head of technical reports, 1968-69; Simmons College, Graduate School of Library and Information Science, Boston, MA, lecturer, 1968, instructor, 1969-70, assistant professor, 1971-73, associate professor, 1973-80, professor of library science, 1980—, acting assistant director, 1974-75, assistant dean, 1975-79, associate dean, 1979-88, dean, 1994—. Library consultant to corporations, including Arthur B. Little Inc., Conoco Chemicals Co., IBM, Dean Witter Reynolds, and Monitor Company.

MEMBER: American Library Association (member of committee on accreditation, 1979-82, member of council, 1979-87, member of committee on program evaluation and support, 1982-86, 1989-90), Association of College and University Librarians (New England Chapter), Special Libraries Association (president, Boston chapter, 1979-81, member of executive board, 1983-85, named fellow, 1988), Commonwealth of Massachusetts Board of Library Commissioners, Massachusetts Library Association.

AWARDS, HONORS: Marian and Jasper Whiting Foundation fellowship, 1976; University of Pittsburgh Graduate School of Libraries and Information Science teaching fellowship, 1976; Special Library Association's Professional Award, for study of management decision-making process in the closure of several corporate libraries; Special Libraries Association, 1988 Annual Conference, President's Award for efforts as chair of the President's Task Force on the Value of the Information Professional.

WRITINGS:

Library Problems in Science and Technology, Bowker (New York City), 1971.

Closing the Corporate Library: Case Studies in the Decision-Making Process (doctoral dissertation) Special Libraries Association, 1981.

President's Task Force on the Value of the Information Professional, Special Libraries Association, 1987.

Corporate Library Excellence, Special Libraries Association (Washington, DC), 1990.

(With Laurence Prusak and Michael R. Gauthier) *Valuing Corporate Libraries: A Survey of Senior Managers,* Special Libraries Association, 1990.

Also author, with Laurence Prusak, of *Information Management and Japanese Success,* Special Libraries Association.

EDITOR

(With James M. Kyed) *Scientific, Technical, and Engineering Societies: Publications in Print, 1974-75,* Bowker, 1974.

The Serials Librarian: Acquisitions Case Studies, Faxon, 1975.

(With Kyed) *Scientific, Medical, and Engineering Societies: Publications in Print, 1976-77,* Bowker, 1977.

(With Kyed) *Scientific, Engineering and Medical Societies: Publications in Print, 1979-80,* Bowker, 1979.

(With Kyed) *Scientific, Engineering and Medical Societies: Publications in Print, 1980-81,* Bowker, 1981.

(With Miriam A. Drake) *Information for Management: A Handbook,* Special Libraries Association, 1994.

OTHER

Also contributor to books, including (with James G. Williams and Ian I. Mitroff) *Library Resource Sharing,* edited by Allen Kent and Thomas J. Galvin, Dekker (New York City), 1977; *Library Education and Resistance to Technology,* U.S. Office of Education, 1980; *The Information Profession: Facing the Challenges,* Special Libraries Association, 1987; *Recruiting, Educating and Training Catalog Librarians,* edited by Sheila S. Intner and Janet Swan Hill, Greenwood Press (Westport, CT), 1989. Contributor of over one hundred articles, reports and reviews to library journals.

WORK IN PROGRESS: Research on corporate libraries and the reasons for their excellence, and on the value of Special Libraries, both for Special Libraries Association.

*   *   *

MATEJKO, Alexander J. 1924-

PERSONAL: Born July 21, 1924, in Warsaw, Poland; son of Peter (an engineer) and Maria (a lawyer; maiden name, Wroblewska) Matejko; married Joanna Grzeskowiak (a historian), April 4, 1952; children: Agnieszka. *Education:* Jagiellonian University, M.A. (economics) and M.A. (sociology), 1949; University of Michigan, graduate study, 1957-59; University of Warsaw, Ph.D., 1960, docent in sociology, 1962. *Politics:* "Christian democrat." *Religion:* Roman Catholic.

ADDRESSES: Home—7623 119th St., Edmonton, Alberta T6G 1W4, Canada. *Office*—Department of Sociology, University of Alberta, Edmonton, Alberta, Canada T6G 2H4.

CAREER: University of Warsaw, Warsaw, Poland, associate professor of sociology, 1959-68; University of Alberta, Edmonton, professor of sociology, 1970-92. Visiting professor, University of Leningrad, 1962, University of

Moscow, 1962-63, University of North Carolina, 1966, University of Zambia, 1968-69, Carleton University, 1974-75, St. Anthony College, Oxford University, 1975-76, University of Goteburg, 1979, Centre National de la Recherche Scientifique, Paris, 1983, Verwaltungsschule Speyer, 1986, Institute for Graduate Studies, Vienna, 1986-87, and University of Berger, 1989-90. Affiliated with Canadian Executive Service Organisation in Poland at Westpomeranian Business School and Polish-American Business School, 1993, and with Polish chambers of commerce, 1994. Guest lecturer at numerous universities and institutions in Europe, United States, and Canada.

MEMBER: International Sociological Association, Amnesty International, Canadian Sociology and Anthropology Association, American Sociological Association, Polish Sociological Association.

WRITINGS:

Socjologia zakladu pracy (title means "Sociology of the Workplace"), Wiedza Powszechna (Warsaw), 1961, 2nd edition, 1969.

Socjologia przemyslu w Stanach Zjednoczonych Ameryki (title means "Industrial Sociology in the U.S."), PWN (Warsaw), 1962.

Kultura pracy zbiorowej (title means "Culture of Work"), Wydawnictwo Zwiazkowe (Warsaw), 1962.

Praca i kolezenstwo (title means "Work and Companionship"), Wiedza Powszechna, 1962.

Postawy zawodowe dziennikarzy na tle systemu spolecznego redakcji (title means "Professional Attitudes of Journalists within the Social System of a Newsroom"), KOOP (Krakow), 1963.

Spoleczne warunki pracy tworczej (title means "Social Conditions of Creative Work"), PWN, 1963.

Hutnik na tle jego srodowiska pracy (title means "The Steelworker and His Work Environment"), Slaski Instytut Naukowy (Katowice, Poland), 1964.

(Editor) *Czlowiek i technika wspolczesna* (title means "Man and Modern Technology"), Wydawnictwo Zwiazkowe, 1964.

System spoleczny zespolu naukowego (title means "Social System of Scientific Teams"), PWN, 1965.

Spoleczne warunki pracy tworczej (title means "Social Conditions of Creativity"), PWN, 1965.

(Editor) *Kierowanie kadrami pracowniczymi* (title means "Human Resources Management"), PWE (Warsaw), 1966.

Nastin sociologie prace (title means "Outline of Sociology of Work"), Nakladatelstvi Prace (Prague), 1967.

System spoleczny instytutu (title means "Social System of Research Institutes"), PWN, 1967.

Socjologia pracy (title means "Sociology of Work"), PWE, 1968.

System spoleczny katedry (title means "Social System of College Departments"), PWN, 1969.

Wiez i konflikt w zakladzie pracy (title means "Integration and Conflict at the Workplace"), KIW (Warsaw), 1969.

Socjologia kierownictwa (title means "Sociology of Management"), PWE, 1969.

Uslovia tworczeskogo truda (title means "Conditions of Creative Work"), Mir (Moscow), 1970.

Sociology of Work and Leisure, European Centre for Leisure and Education (Prague), 1972.

Social Change and Stratification in Eastern Europe: An Interpretive Analysis of Poland and Her Neighbours, Praeger (New York), 1974.

Social Dimensions of Industrialism, Sadhna Prakashan (Meerut, India), 1974.

The Social Technology of Applied Research, Sadhna Prakashan, 1975.

The Upgrading of Zambians, Sadhna Prakashan, 1976.

Overcoming Alienation in Work, Sadhna Prakashan, 1976.

The Polish Blue Collar Worker, North American Study Center of Polish Affairs, 1977.

Beyond Bureaucracy?: A Sociotechnical Approach to the Dialectics of Complex Organizations, Verlag fuer Gesellschaftsarchitektur (Cologne), 1984.

(Editor with A. Jain) *Marx and Marxism,* Praeger, 1984.

The Self-Defeating Organization: A Critique of Bureaucracy, Praeger, 1986.

In Search of New Organizational Paradigms, Praeger, 1986.

Comparative Work Systems: Ideologies and Reality in Eastern Europe, Praeger, 1986.

Organizational Culture: The West German Case, Institute for Advanced Studies (Vienna), 1986.

Entering the Postindustrial Society: The Canadian Case, Institute for Advanced Studies, 1986.

(With Jain) *A Critique of Marxist and Non-Marxist Thought,* Praeger, 1986.

The Sociotechnical Perspective on Trust at Work, Hochschule fuer Verwaltungwissenschaften (Speyer, Germany), 1988.

A Christian Approach to Work and Industry, Edwin Mellen (Lewiston, NY), 1989.

Upgrading Industrial Relations and Work Organization: A Sociotechnical Approach, 2 volumes, Institute of Public Administration and Organization Theory, University of Bergen (Bergen, Norway), 1990.

Various Approaches to Complex Organizations, Institute of Public Administration and Organization Theory, University of Bergen, 1991.

Socjotechnika zarzadzania (title means "Sociotechnics of Management"), Westpomeranian Business School (Szczecin, Poland), 1994.

Contributor to numerous books, including *Education in Europe,* edited by M. A. Mattijssen and C. E. Veroort, Mouton (Hawthorne, NY), 1969; *From Prairies to Cities,* edited by Benedykt Heydenkorn, Canadian Polish Research Institute, 1975; *Quality of Working Life and the Kibbutz Experience,* edited by Albert B. Cherns, Norwood (Norwood, PA), 1980; *Central and East European Ethnicity in Canada: Adaptation and Presentation,* edited by T. Yedlin, Central and East European Studies Association of Alberta (Edmonton), 1985; and *Dilemmas of Effective Social Action,* edited by J. Kubin, Polish Sociological Association (Warsaw), 1990. Contributor to proceedings of international conferences and professional meetings. Contributor to periodicals. Co-editor, *Przeglad Zagadnien Socjalnych,* 1950-51; member of editorial board, *International Journal of Contemporary Sociology,* 1971—, *Canadian Slavonic Papers,* 1971-73, *Sociologia Internationalis,* 1979—, *Materials on Sociotechnics,* 1984—, *Journal of Interdisciplinary Studies,* 1990—, and *Guru Nanak Journal of Sociology,* 1991—.

WORK IN PROGRESS: All in Polish—*Management as a Game* (collection of cases in the managerial decision-making in postcommunist Poland); *Between Gestures and Deeds: The Transformations of Polist Mentalist and Her Economic Impact;* his life history.

SIDELIGHTS: Alexander J. Matejko, who is fluent in Polish, Russian, Czech, and German, and knows French, told *CA:* "Since the dramatic experience of the Nazi occupation (1939-45) and the exposure to the Stalinist rule (1939-40; 1945-56), I have become much interested in the theory and practice of trust relationships. First I took the cooperative studies at the Jagiellonian University (Poland), and I became an organisational instructor in the work cooperatives. I also studied them in Bohemia, Moravia, and Slovakia. When the state socialist rule in Poland led to the actual suppression of the free cooperative movement I switched to sociology, and in 1957, I was actually the first scholar who managed to obtain the U.S. scholarship to study at the University of Michigan. After returning to Poland, I was quite successful in disseminating my knowledge gained in the U.S.—even if I was under the constant surveyance of the communist secret police. My Roman-Catholic faith together with my commitment to cooperation inspired me to study and teach a version of management which would be morally sound and inspiring to genuine human growth.

"After retiring from university teaching, I devoted myself to the volunteer services in the field of management training in the postcommunist part of Europe as well as in other parts of the world. I am trying to implement practically what I learned and created theoretically. I hope that I am giving a positive personal example and a useful professional service."

McCLENDON, James William, Jr.   1924-

PERSONAL: Born March 6, 1924, in Shreveport, LA; son of James William and Mary (Drake) McClendon; married Marie Miles, 1949 (divorced, 1982); married Nancey Murphy (a teacher), 1983; children: (first marriage) James William III, Thomas Vernon. *Education:* University of Texas, B.A. (with high honors), 1947; Southwestern Baptist Theological Seminary, B.D., 1950, Th.D., 1953; Princeton Theological Seminary, Th.M., 1952; postdoctoral study at University of California, 1959-62, and Oxford University, 1962-63.

ADDRESSES: Home—Altadena, CA. *Office*—Fuller Theological Seminary, Pasadena, CA 91182.

CAREER: Minister, Southern Baptist Convention; pastor in Austin, TX, 1946-47, and Keatchie, LA, 1948-50; Princeton University, Princeton, NJ, chaplain to Baptist students, 1950-51; interim pastor in Sydney, Australia, 1952; pastor in Ring-gold, LA, 1953-54; Golden Gate Baptist Seminary, Mill Valley, CA, assistant professor, 1954-57, associate professor, 1958-64, professor of theology, 1964-66; University of San Francisco, San Francisco, CA, associate professor of theology, 1966-69; Graduate Theological Union, Church Divinity School, Berkeley, CA, professor of theology, 1971-90; Fuller Theological Seminary, Pasadena, CA, Distinguished Scholar-in-Residence, 1990—. Visiting professor of religion, Stanford University, 1967, Temple University, 1969, and University of Notre Dame, 1976-77; Jeffrey Lecturer in Religion, Goucher College, 1970-71. Member of National Faith and Order Colloquium, National Council of Churches. Trustee, Institute for Ecumenical and Cultural Research. *Military service:* U.S. Naval Reserve, 1943-46; became lieutenant junior grade.

MEMBER: American Philosophical Association, American Academy of Religion, Pacific Coast Theological Society, United Nations Association of Marin County (president, 1967-69), Phi Beta Kappa.

WRITINGS:

Pacemakers of Christian Thought, Broadman (Nashville, TN), 1962.
Biography as Theology, Abingdon (Nashville, TN), 1974, Trinity Press International (Philadelphia, PA, and London, England), 1990.
(With J. M. Smith) *Understanding Religious Convictions,* University of Notre Dame Press (Notre Dame and London), 1975, published as *Convictions: Defusing Religious Relativism,* Trinity Press International, 1994.
(Editor with A. Stever) *Is God GOD?,* Abingdon, 1981.

Doctrine: Systematic Theology, Abingdon, Volume I: *Ethics: Systematic Theology Volume I*, 1986, Volume II: *Ethics: Systematic Theology Volume II, 1994.*

Also contributor to books, including *What Can You Believe*, edited by W. Junker, Broadman (Nashville, TN), 1966; *American Philosophy and the Future*, edited by Michael Novak, Scribner (New York City), 1968; *The Weight of Glory: A Vision and Practice for Christian Faith: The Future of Liberal Theology; Essays for Peter Baelz*, edited by D. W. Hardy and P. H. Sedgwick, T & T Clark (Edinburgh, Scotland), 1991; *Ethics, Religion, and the Good Society: New Directions in a Pluralistic World*, edited by Joseph Runzo, Westminster/John Knox (Louisville, KY), 1992; *Mennonites and Baptists: A Continuing Conversation*, edited by Paul Toews, Kindred Press (Winnipeg, Canada, and Hillsboro, NC), 1993; *Ties That Bind: Life Together in the Baptist Vision*, edited by Gary Furr and Curtis Freeman, Smyth and Helwys (Macon, GA), 1994.

Contributor to religious journals, including *Baptist Student, Brethren in Christ History and Life, Concilium, Faith and Philosophy, Harvard Theological Review, Journal of Ecumenical Studies, Journal of Religious Ethics, Mennonite Quarterly Review, Modern Theology, Perspectives in Religious Studies, Religious Studies Review, Review and Expositor, Theology Today*, and other publications.

WORK IN PROGRESS: Final book of three-volume *Doctrine: Systematic Theology*, Volume III: *Vision*, forthcoming from Abingdon.

*　　　*　　　*

McDARRAH, Fred W(illiam) 1926-

PERSONAL: Born November 5, 1926, in Brooklyn, NY; son of Howard Arthur and Elizabeth (Swahn) McDarrah; married Gloria Schoffel, November 5, 1960; children: Timothy Swann, Patrick James. *Education:* New York University, B.A., 1954.

ADDRESSES: Home—505 La Guardia Pl., New York, NY 10012. *Office*—36 Cooper Square, New York, NY 10003.

CAREER: Writer and photojournalist. Worked for advertising and publishing firms during 1950s; *Village Voice*, New York City, staff photographer, 1958-71, picture editor, 1971—. *Exhibitions:* Photographs have been displayed at galleries and museums, including Soho Photo Gallery, New York City, 1973, Whitney Museum, New York City, 1974 and 1976-77, Dallas Museum of Art, 1974, Wadsworth Athenaeum, San Francisco Museum of Art, 1975, Sidney Janis Gallery, 1976, Alfred Stieglitz

Gallery, New York City, 1976, Empire State Museum, Albany, NY, 1978, Overseas Press Club, New York City, 1978, Ashawagh Hall, East Hampton, NY, 1979, Cameravision, Los Angeles, CA, 1981, International Ausstellung, Cologne, Germany, 1981, Lightworks Gallery, Syracuse University, Syracuse, NY, 1981, Cape Cod Gallery, Provincetown, MA, 1982, Galleria di Franca Mancini, Pesaro, Italy, 1983, Musee du Quebec, 1987, Reinhold-Brown Gallery, New York City, 1988, Anita Shapolsky Gallery, New York City, 1988, Center of Photography, Woodstock, NY, 1989, Images Gallery, Cincinnati, OH, 1989, Hartnett Gallery, University of Rochester, Rochester, NY, 1989, G. Ray Hawkins Gallery, Los Angeles, CA 1989, Museum of Art/Science/Industry, Bridgeport, CT, 1989, New York City Gallery, Queens Museum, 1989, Read Gallery, Antioch College, Antioch, OH, 1989, Foundation Cartier, Jouy-en-Josas, Paris, France, 1990, Frumkin/Adams Gallery, New York City, 1990, Musee d'Art Contemporain, Montreal, 1990, Musee d'Art Moderne de la Ville de Paris, France, 1990, Pollack-Krasner Museum, East Hampton, NY, 1990, Marty Carey Pictures Gallery, Woodstock, NY, 1992, Bibliotheque Municipale, Belort, France, 1992, Galerie Contrejour-Odile Deboc, Belfort, France, 1992, Galerie Gilles Ringuet, Belfort, France, 1992, Susan Cooper Fine Art, Woodstock, NY, 1994, Galleria La Pescheria, Cesena, Italy, 1994, New York Public Library, New York City, 1994, New York University, New York City, 1994, Tribes Gallery, New York City, 1994, 292 Gallery, New York City, 1994; additional exhibitions, including Jack Kerouac Travelling Writers, Saint-Malo (France) International Festival, 1991, Jack Kerouac Visions of the Road, Les Rencontres D'Arles, Arles, France, 1991, and Images of Greenwich Village, New York Camera Club, New York City, 1992. *Military service:* U.S. Army, paratrooper, 1944-47; became staff sergeant.

MEMBER: American Society of Magazine Photographers, Authors Guild, American Society of Picture Professionals, National Press Photographers Association, New York Press Club, New York Press Photographer's Association.

AWARDS, HONORS: Awards from New York Press Association, 1964, 1965, 1967, 1968, 1970, all for spot news photography, 1965 and 1967, both for feature photography, and 1969 and 1970, both for picture stories; first place awards from National Newspaper Association, 1966, for best pictorial series, and 1971, for spot news photography; Page One Award from New York Newspaper Guild, 1971 and 1980, both for best spot news photography; John Simon Guggenheim Memorial Foundation Award in photography, 1972; second place for Edward Steichen Memorial Award in newspaper photography, 1976.

WRITINGS:

(With wife, Gloria Schoffel McDarrah) *The Artist's World in Pictures,* Dutton (New York City), 1961, Shapolsky Books, 1988.

Greenwich Village, Corinth Books (Chevy Chase, MD), 1963.

New York, New York: A Photographic Tour of Manhattan Island from Battery Park to Spuyten Duyvil, Corinth Books, 1964.

(With G. S. McDarrah) *Museums in New York,* Dutton, 1967, 5th edition, St. Martin's Press (New York City), 1990.

(Editor) *Photography Market Place,* R. R. Bowker (New York City), 1975, revised edition, 1977.

(Editor) *Stock Photo and Assignment Source Book: Where to Find Photographs Instantly,* R. R. Bowker, 1977, 2nd edition, Photographic Arts Center (New York City), 1984.

(Compiler) *Kerouac and Friends: A Beat Generation Album,* Morrow (New York City), 1984.

(With son, Patrick J. McDarrah) *Guide to Greenwich Village,* a cappella books, 1992.

(With G. S. McDarrah) *Frommer's Atlantic City and Cape May,* 5th edition (the McDarrahs were not associated with earlier editions), Prentice Hall (Englewood Cliffs, NJ), 1993.

(With son, Timothy S. McDarrah) *Gay Pride: Photographs from Stonewall to Today* (photo documentary celebrating Gay Pride, 1965-95), a cappella books, 1994.

(With G. S. McDarrah) *Frommer's Virginia Guide,* 2nd edition (the McDarrahs were not associated with earlier editions), Prentice Hall, 1994.

CATALOGUE CREDITS

Art of U.S.A. Now, two volumes, C. J. Boucher (Switzerland), 1962.

Sculpture in Environment, New York City Parks Department (New York City), 1967.

James J. Young, editor, *Bring Us Together: 3D Living Room Dialogues,* Friendship Press, 1970.

Guide for Ecumenical Discussion, Paulist Press (Ramsey, NJ), 1970.

Summer Catalogue, New School, 1973.

The Beat Book (portfolio), Unspeakable Visions (California, PA), 1974.

Poets of the Cities (catalogue), Dutton, 1974.

The Beat Diary (portfolio), Unspeakable Visions, 1977.

Big Sky Anthology (portfolio), Big Sky Publishers (Southampton, NY), 1978.

The Beat Journey (portfolio), Unspeakable Visions, 1978.

How'm I Doing? The Wit and Wisdom of Ed Koch, Lion Books (New York City), 1981.

Beat Angels (portfolio), Unspeakable Visions, 1982.

Provincetown 1959-Photographs, Provincetown Arts, 1989.

Moving through Here (portfolio), Citadel Press (Secaucus, NJ), 1990.

New York 1960: Architecture and Urbanism between WW II and the Bicentennial, Monacelli Press, 1995.

OTHER

Book critic, *Infinity* magazine, 1972-73; book reviewer, *Photo District News,* 1985-88, and *The Picture Professional,* 1989—. Also contributor of book reviews and articles for periodicals, including *Bolex Reporter Cue Magazine, Book Views Magazine, Culture Hero, The Family Handyman, Invitation to Photography (Popular Photography), New York Times Book Review, Saga Magazine, Village Voice, Village Voice Literary Supplement,* and *Village Voice Photography Supplement.* Also editor of *Executive Desk Diary* for *Saturday Review,* 1962-64.

Several of Fred W. McDarrah's books have been translated and published in foreign-language editions.

BIOGRAPHICAL/CRITICAL SOURCES:

PERIODICALS

Archives of American Art Journal, July, 1971.
Arrival Magazine, fall, 1987.
Camera 35, November, 1972; September, 1981.
Cue, March 5, 1960; March 31, 1975.
Darkroom Photography, Volume 3, number 2, 1980.
East Hampton Star, October 4, 1990.
El Diaro/La Prensa, March 6, 1985.
Family Weekly, October 2, 1960.
Herald Tribune, May 1, 1960.
Images Inc., Volume 4, number 2, 1989; Volume 4, number 3, 1989.
Invitation to Photography, spring, 1976.
Newsday, July 27, 1975; September 21, 1990.
New York Magazine, June 26, 1989.
New York Post, July 23, 1989.
New York Times Magazine, April 17, 1960.
Our Town, July 15, 1979; July 29, 1979.
Photo Methods, February, 1975.
Popular Photography, March, 1976; November, 1985.
35MM Photography, winter, 1977.
Time, February 15, 1960.
SOHO Weekly News, February 13, 1975.
Village Voice, May 14, 1970; August 29, 1974.

*   *   *

McGUANE, Thomas (Francis III) 1939-

PERSONAL: Born December 11, 1939, in Wyandotte, MI; son of Thomas Francis (a manufacturer) and Alice

(Torphy) McGuane; married Portia Rebecca Crockett, September 8, 1962 (divorced, 1975); married Margot Kidder (an actress), August, 1976 (divorced May, 1977); married Laurie Buffett, September 19, 1977; children: (first marriage) Thomas Francis IV; (second marriage) Maggie; (third marriage) Anne Buffett, Heather (stepdaughter). *Education:* Attended University of Michigan and Olivet College; Michigan State University, B.A., 1962; Yale University, M.F.A., 1965; additional study at Stanford University, 1966-67.

ADDRESSES: Home—Box 25, McLeod, MT 59052. *Agent*—Amanda Urban, International Creative Management, 40 West 57th St., New York, New York, 10019.

CAREER: Full-time writer.

AWARDS, HONORS: Wallace Stegner fellowship, Stanford University, 1966-67; Richard and Hinda Rosenthal Foundation Award in fiction from American Academy, 1971, for *The Bushwacked Piano;* National Book Award fiction nomination, 1974, for *Ninety-two in the Shade;* honorary doctorate degrees from Montana State University, 1993, and Rocky Mountain College, 1995; Montana Governor's Award for the Arts.

WRITINGS:

NOVELS

The Sporting Club, Simon & Schuster (New York City), 1969.
The Bushwacked Piano (also see below), Simon & Schuster, 1971.
Ninety-two in the Shade (also see below), Farrar, Straus (New York City), 1973.
Panama, Farrar, Straus, 1977.
Nobody's Angel (also see below), Random House (New York City), 1982.
Something to Be Desired, Random House, 1984.
Keep the Change (also see below), Houghton (Boston, MA), 1989.
Nothing but Blue Skies, Houghton, 1992.
Three Complete Novels: Keep the Change, Nobody's Angel, and The Bushwacked Piano, Wings Books (New York City), 1993.

SCREENPLAYS

Rancho Deluxe, United Artists, 1975.
(Also director) *Ninety-two in the Shade* (adapted from his novel of the same title), United Artists, 1975.
Missouri Breaks (produced by United Artists, 1976), Ballantine, 1976.
(With Bud Shrake) *Tom Horn,* Warner Brothers, 1980.

Also author (with Jim Harrison) of *Cold Feet.*

OTHER

An Outside Chance: Essays on Sport, Farrar, Straus, 1980, reprinted as *An Outside Chance: Classic & New Essays on Sports,* Houghton, 1990.
In the Crazies: Book and Portfolio (signed limited edition), Winn Books, 1984.
To Skin a Cat (short stories), Dutton, 1986.
Silent Seasons: Twenty-one Fishing Stories, Clark City Press (Livingston, MT), 1988.

Special contributor to *Sports Illustrated,* 1969-73.

ADAPTATIONS: The Sporting Club was adapted by Lorenzo Semple, Jr., for a full-length film released by Avco Embassy Pictures in 1971.

WORK IN PROGRESS: A novel.

SIDELIGHTS: Thomas McGuane has been described in the *New York Times Book Review* as a "highly self-conscious literary grandson of Ernest Hemingway." McGuane's fiction—some of which shares locales and sensibilities with that of Hemingway—brings an ironic twist to the plight of the modern American male. "Thomas McGuane likes dogs, horses, Indians, golf, the road, hawks, rocks, peppery food and outdoor sex," writes Beverly Lowry in the *New York Times Book Review*. "For characters he has a soft spot for loony old men, hateful, dead or vanished fathers, hot-blooded, sharp-tongued women, struggling protagonists with high-stakes, dangerous male friends. . . . Much more than the *things* of fiction, however, Mr. McGuane is concerned with irony, voice, lingo, dialogue that cries to be read aloud, descriptive passages that are never coy or sloppy. Which is to say that although facts and not literature itself form the backdrop against which he performs, what he's really after is language—fully extended and at serious play." In novels, screenplays and short fiction, McGuane has combined a fascination with language and an affection for macho heroes who—with humor or pathos—retreat from the banality of their middle class backgrounds toward more authentic and self-aware lives.

McGuane's first three novels established his reputation as a flamboyant stylist and satirist. *The Sporting Club, The Bushwacked Piano* and *Ninety-two in the Shade* juxtapose the ugly materialism of modern America against the beauty and power of the natural world. According to *Detroit* magazine writer Gregory Skwira, this trio of books perfectly captures "the hip disillusionment and general disorientation of the late 1960s." Although his early work had earned him high praise from the literary establishment, McGuane temporarily abandoned the novel in the early 1970s for work in the film industry. The personal chaos he experienced during that time is reflected in such later novels as *Panama, Something to Be Desired,* and

Nothing but Blue Skies. In these books, emotional depth and honesty take precedence over stylistic flamboyance, and many critics regard them as McGuane's finest.

McGuane grew up in an Irish family where storytelling was a natural art. When he announced his intention to become a writer, however, his parents disapproved of his ambition, calling it hopelessly impractical. To counter their skepticism, McGuane devoted himself almost exclusively to his artistic efforts. While his university classmates enjoyed traditional college parties and diversions, McGuane wrote, read voraciously, studied the novel, or engaged in esoteric discussions with fellow students and contemporary novelists Jim Harrison and William Hjortsberg. McGuane's sober disposition earned him the nickname "The White Knight." His singlemindedness paid off: *The Sporting Club* was published when he was nearly thirty, *The Bushwacked Piano* and *Ninety-two in the Shade* followed in quick succession.

The plots of these three novels are very different, but they are closely linked in style, theme, and tone. Each is written in what R. T. Smith calls in *American Book Review* "amphetamine-paced, acetylene-bright prose." "All present a picture of an America which has evolved into a 'declining snivelization' (from *Bushwacked*), a chrome-plated, chaotic landscape which threatens to lead right-thinking men to extremes of despair or utter frivolity," explains Larry McCaffrey in *Fiction International.* "Each of them presents main characters . . . who have recognized the defiled state of affairs around them, and who are desperately seeking out a set of values which allows them, as Skelton [the protagonist of *Ninety-two in the Shade*] puts it, 'to find a way of going on.' " In McCaffrey's estimation, the most remarkable thing about McGuane's writing is that he is "able to take the elements of this degraded condition and fashion from them shocking, energetic, and often beautiful works of prose—works which both mirror and comment upon our culture and . . . in their eloquence, transcend it."

McGuane's intense approach to his art was altered forever in 1972. Driving at 120 miles per hour on a trip from Montana to Key West, he lost control of his car and was involved in a serious accident. He walked away from it physically unharmed, but so profoundly shaken that he was unable to speak for some time thereafter. After this brush with death, his relentless concentration on writing seemed misguided to him. McCaffrey quotes McGuane in the *Dictionary of Literary Biography Yearbook:* "After the accident, I finally realized I could stop pedaling so intensely, get off the bike and walk around the neighborhood. . . . It was getting unthinkable to spend another year sequestered like that, writing, and I just dropped out." McGuane was also finding it increasingly difficult to support his family on a novelist's income; while his books had received

critical acclaim, none had been best-sellers. Accordingly, when movie producer Elliot Kastner asked him if he would be interested in a film project, McGuane eagerly accepted. Over the next few years he wrote several screenplays, and directed the screen version of *Ninety-two in the Shade.*

Changes were not limited to the author's work; his personal life was undergoing a transformation as well. Together with the other members of "Club Mandible"—a loosely-structured group of friends including singer Jimmy Buffett—McGuane began to enjoy a hedonistic lifestyle. He explained to Thomas Carney in *Esquire:* "I had paid my dues. . . . Enough was enough. In 1962 I had changed from a sociopath to a bookworm and now I just changed back. Buffett was in the same shape. We both heard voices telling us to do something." Accordingly, writes Carney, "McGuane the straight arrow who had spent years telling his friends how to live their lives while he lived his like a hermit became McGuane the boogie chieftain, rarely out of full dance regalia. The White Knight began staying out all night, enjoying drugs and drink in quantities. And women other than his wife."

McGuane's name began appearing in tabloids when he became romantically involved with actress Elizabeth Ashley during the shooting of his first film, *Rancho Deluxe.* While still linked with Ashley, McGuane began an affair with Margot Kidder, while both actresses were working on *Ninety-two in the Shade.* When McGuane and his first wife, Becky, divorced, Becky married the male lead of *Ninety-two in the Shade,* Peter Fonda. Tom McGuane subsequently married Margot Kidder, already the mother of his second child. McGuane and Kidder divorced several months later. The unexpected deaths of his father and sister compounded the confusion in McGuane's life. He told Skwira that the media depiction of his activities at that time was "overblown," but admitted, "I had a lot of fun drinking and punching people out for a short period of time."

The turmoil of that interval was clearly reflected in *Panama,* McGuane's first novel in four years. It is a first-person description of the disintegrating life of rock star Chester Hunnicutt Pomeroy, an overnight sensation who is burning out on his excessive lifestyle. In McCaffrey's words, *Panama* "in many ways appears to be a kind of heightened, surreal portrayal of McGuane's own suffering, self-delusion, and eventual self-understanding—a book which moves beyond his earlier novels' satiric and ironic stances." The book drew strong reactions, both favorable and unfavorable. Many reviewers who had unreservedly praised McGuane's earlier work received *Panama* coldly, with some implying that the author's screenwriting stint had ruined him as a novelist. In a *Washington Post Book World* essay, Jonathan Yardley dismisses *Pan-*

ama as "a drearily self-indulgent little book, a contemplation of the price of celebrity that was, in point of fact, merely an exploitation of the author's new notoriety." Richard Elman complains in the *New York Times Book Review* that *Panama* "is all written up in a blowsy, first-person prose that goes in all directions and winds up being, basically, a kvetch." He states that McGuane, "who was once upon a time wacky and droll [and who] is now sloppy and doleful," suffers from an inability to recognize "good" versus "bad" writing. "Everything of craft that must be done right is done wrong. . . . This book isn't written; it is hallucinated. The reader is asked to do the writer's work of imagining."

Other reviewers applaud *Panama* as the novel that finally joins McGuane's stylistic brilliance with an emotional intensity lacking in his earlier efforts. Susan Lardner suggests in a *New Yorker* review that McGuane's work as a director perhaps enriched the subsequent novel: "Maybe as a result of the experience, he has added to his store of apprehensions some dismal views of fame and the idea that life is a circus performance. . . . Whatever risk McGuane may have sensed in attempting a fourth novel with a simultaneous plunge into first person narration, the feat proves successful. The audience is left dazzled by the ingenuity of his turn, somewhat aghast at the swagger, hungry for more." Writing in the *Washington Post Book World,* Philip Caputo calls it McGuane's "most relentlessly honest novel. . . . Although *Panama* is as well written as its predecessors, its first-person point of view endows it with a greater directness; and the book not only gives us a look at the void, it takes us down into it . . . . *Panama* also contains some of the finest writing McGuane has done so far." *Village Voice* contributor Gary L. Fisketjon notes: "*Panama* is more ambitious if less slick than the earlier novels, which were restrained and protected by the net of a hot-wired style and a consummate mockery; the humor here is not as harsh, and the objectivity is informed more by empathy than disdain. . . . Moving beyond satire, McGuane has achieved something difficult and strange, a wonderfully written novel that balances suffering and understanding." And in a Toronto *Globe & Mail* essay, Thad McIlroy deems *Panama* "one of the best books to have been published in the United States in the last 20 years. It's minimal, mad, disjointed at times, and consistently brilliant, terrifying and exhilarating. McGuane's use of language, and his ever-precise ear for dialogue, raise the novel out of the actual and into the universal, the realm of our finest literature."

McGuane's life stabilized considerably after his 1977 marriage to Laurie Buffett, sister of his friend Jimmy Buffett. He told *CA:* "Laurie and I share everything. She deserves a lot of credit for my sanity and happiness." Living on his Montana ranch, the author perfected his riding and roping techniques and became a serious rodeo competitor. He commented to Carney in *Esquire,* "I've come to the point where art is no longer as important as life. Dropping six or seven good colts in the spring is just as satisfying as literature." McGuane's new down-to-earth attitude carried over to his prose style, as he explained to a *Detroit* magazine interviewer: "I'm trying to remove the tour de force or superficially flashy side of my writing. I'm trying to write a cleaner, plainer kind of American English. . . . I feel I have considerably better balance than I have ever had in my life and I don't care to show off; I just want to get the job done." Christopher Lehmann-Haupt refers favorably to McGuane's new direction in his *New York Times* review of the novel *Nobody's Angel:* "Both the author's affection for his characters and the strength of his narrative seem to matter even more to him than his compulsion to be stylistically *original.*"

While *Nobody's Angel* echoes the dark tone of *Panama,* McGuane's next novel marks the first time that one of his restless protagonists finds fulfillment. *Something to Be Desired* revolves around Lucien Taylor and his two loves, Emily and Suzanne. When Emily, the more seductive and mysterious of the two, drops Lucien to marry a doctor, Lucien marries the virtuous Suzanne. The newlyweds go to work in Central America, where Lucien finds himself unable to forget Emily. When he hears she has murdered her husband, he deserts his wife and child to bail her out. He moves to Emily's ranch and becomes her lover, but she soon jumps bail, leaving him the ranch. Lucien converts it into a resort and finds happiness in a reconciliation with his family. Ronald Varney comments in the *Wall Street Journal* that "the somewhat bizarre plot twists of Mr. McGuane's story occasionally seem implausible. . . . And yet Mr. McGuane manages to pull this story off rather well, giving it, as in his other novels, such a compressed dramatic style that the reader is constantly entertained and diverted." *New York Times Book Review* critic Robert Roper names McGuane's sixth novel "his best, a remarkable work of honest colors and fresh phrasings that deliver strong, earned emotional effects."

With his 1989 novel *Keep the Change,* McGuane "expanded his emotional territory and deepened his literary and human concerns," to quote *New York Times Book Review* contributor Beverly Lowry. The story centers on Joe Starling, a struggling artist who travels to Montana to take possession of a cattle ranch he is not even sure he wants. During a season of ranching on the family farm, Joe confronts the peculiar characters who have their own ambitions for the land as well as the changing landscape of his hometown of Deadrock. In her review of the work, Lowry concludes: "I don't know of another writer who can walk Thomas McGuane's literary high wire. His vaunted dialogue has not been overpraised; authenticity for him is only the beginning. He can describe the sky, a bird, a rock, the dawn, with such grace that you want to go see for yourself; then he can zip to a scene so funny that it makes you laugh out loud. . . . It's encouraging to see a good writer getting better."

Mid-life crisis is the subject of McGuane's eighth novel, *Nothing but Blue Skies*. The protagonist, Frank Copenhaver, suddenly finds himself separated from his wife and in dire financial straits due to his own wacky behavior. Noting that Frank is "a fully fleshed, believable character," *Bloomsbury Review* correspondent Gregory McNamee adds that the book is "a well-considered study of a man confronting midlife crisis and, in the end, overcoming it by sheer force of will." *Time* magazine reviewer John Skow writes of the work: "McGuane, whose recent novels have seemed a touch broody, enjoys himself with this one. The fine barrelhouse prose of *The Bushwacked Piano* and *Ninety-Two in the Shade* is working again. He waves his arms, he hoots and hollers and thrashes out a rowdy parody of the male psyche under the stress of having to defend itself in the supermarket."

McGuane's work has drawn comparisons to many famous authors, including William Faulkner, Albert Camus, Thomas Pynchon, F. Scott Fitzgerald, and most especially to Hemingway. Both McGuane and Hemingway portray virile heroes and anti-heroes vibrantly aware of their own masculinity; each author explores themes of men pitted against themselves and other men; each passionately loves game fishing and the outdoors. Discussing *Ninety-two in the Shade*, Thomas R. Edwards of the *New York Times Book Review* claims: "Clearly this is Hemingway country. Not just the he-man pleasures of McGuane's men but even the locales of the novels . . . recapitulate Hemingway's western-hemisphere life and works." McCaffrey concurs in a *Fiction International* piece: "If [the set of value-systems of McGuane's protagonists] sounds very familiar to Hemingway's notion of a 'code' devised to help one face up to an empty universe, it should; certainly McGuane's emphasis on male aggressions, his ritualized scenes involving fishing, . . . and even the locales (Key West, the upper Rockies, up in Michigan) suggest something of Papa's influence, though with a distinctly contemporary, darkly humorous flavor."

When asked by Carter in *Fiction International* about the numerous Hemingway comparisons, McGuane replied: "I admire him, of course, and share a lot of similar interests, but I really don't write like him. . . . We have totally different styles. His world view was considerably more austere than mine. His insistence on his metaphysical closed system was fanatical. And he was a fanatic. But it gave him at his best moments a very beautiful prose style. And anyone who says otherwise is either stupid or is a lying sack of snake shit. We have few enough treasures in this

twerp-ridden Republic to have to argue over Ernest Hemingway's greatness." To John Dorschner of the *Miami Herald* he speculated, "I can only agree that [my life and Hemingway's] appear to be similar, but that's all. What might be more pertinent is to think how my father was influenced by Hemingway. Places like the Keys and northern Michigan, those were places I was taken by my father."

Discussing his writing habits with Skwira in *Detroit* magazine, McGuane noted, "I find it to my advantage to show up for work in an extremely regular, quite uninterrupted way." He averages eight to ten hours of work a day, six or seven days a week. He credits his temperate lifestyle with giving him a keener awareness of his craft, admitting that in earlier years "I really didn't quite know how I was achieving the effects I was achieving in literature. . . . But I know exactly how [*Something to Be Desired*] was written: long hours and a sore a—, in a state of clarity. And at the end, I remembered how I did all of it. With that behind me, as I sit down to start again, I start with a sort of optimism, with some expectation of achieving a certain level of results. . . . The thing that's most exciting to me now is that I feel that, barring illness, I think I'm looking at a long stretch of time where I can concentrate longer and harder on what I do best, more so than I've ever done before. And feeling that in itself produces kind of a glow."

BIOGRAPHICAL/CRITICAL SOURCES:

BOOKS

Authors in the News, Volume 2, Gale (Detroit), 1976.

Contemporary Literary Criticism, Gale, Volume 3, 1975; Volume 7, 1977; Volume 18, 1981; Volume 45, 1987.

Dictionary of Literary Biography, Volume 2: *American Novelists since World War II*, Gale, 1978.

Dictionary of Literary Biography Yearbook: 1980, Gale, 1981.

Klinkowitz, Jerome, *The New American Novel of Manners: The Fiction of Richard Yates, Dan Wakefield, and Thomas McGuane*, University of Georgia Press (Athens, GA), 1986.

Wallace, Jon, *The Politics of Style: Language as Theme in the Fiction of Berger, McGuane, and McPherson*, Hollowbrook, 1992.

Westrum, Dexter, *Thomas McGuane*, Twayne, 1991.

PERIODICALS

America, May 15, 1971.

American Book Review, May-June, 1983.

Atlantic, September, 1973.

Bloomsbury Review, July-August, 1993.

Book World, May 2, 1971.

Chicago Tribune, November 5, 1978; April 12, 1985; November 3, 1986.

Chicago Tribune Books, October 14, 1990.
Chicago Tribune Book World, February 15, 1981.
Commonweal, October 26, 1973.
Crawdaddy, February, 1979.
Critique: Studies in Modern Fiction, August, 1975.
Detroit (Sunday supplement to *Detroit Free Press*), January 27, 1985.
Detroit News, April 25, 1982; November 18, 1984.
Detroit News Magazine, August 17, 1980.
Esquire, June 6, 1978.
Feature, February, 1979.
Fiction International, fall/winter, 1975.
Globe & Mail (Toronto), January 26, 1985; April 4, 1987.
Hudson Review, winter, 1973-74.
Los Angeles Times Book Review, September 17, 1989.
Miami Herald, October 13, 1974.
Nation, January 31, 1981; March 20, 1982.
New Mexico Humanities Review, fall, 1983.
New Republic, August 18, 1979.
Newsweek, April 19, 1971; July 23, 1973.
New Statesman, July 26, 1974.
New Yorker, September 11, 1971; June 23, 1973; April 19, 1979.
New York Review of Books, December 13, 1973.
New York Times, November 21, 1978; May 23, 1980; March 4, 1982; December 10, 1984; October 11, 1986; September 14, 1989.
New York Times Book Review, March 14, 1971; July 29, 1973; November 19, 1978; October 19, 1980; February 8, 1981; March 7, 1982; December 16, 1984; September 24, 1989; September 13, 1992.
Observer, (London), January 24, 1993.
Partisan Review, fall, 1972.
People, September 17, 1979; November 3, 1980.
Prairie Schooner, summer, 1993.
Rapport, January, 1993.
Saturday Review, March 27, 1971.
Spectator, July 13, 1974.
Time, August 6, 1973; June 30, 1980; November 2, 1992.
Times Literary Supplement, May 24, 1985; January 29, 1993.
Village Voice, September 15, 1975; December 11, 1978.
Virginia Quarterly Review, spring, 1981.
Wall Street Journal, December 24, 1984.
Washington Post, December 30, 1980; October 2, 1986.
Washington Post Book World, November 19, 1978; February 28, 1982; December 16, 1984.

*   *   *

McKISSACK, Fredrick L(emuel) 1939-

PERSONAL: Born August 12, 1939, in Nashville, TN; son of Lewis Winter (an architect) and Bessye (Fizer) McKissack; married Patricia Carwell (a writer), December 12, 1964; children: Fredrick Lemuel, Jr., Robert and John (twins). *Education:* Tennessee Agricultural and Industrial State University (now Tennessee State University), B.S., 1964. *Politics:* Independent. *Religion:* African Methodist Episcopal. *Avocational interests:* Collecting antique model ships, gardening, spending time with pet cat, Kit.

ADDRESSES: Home—5900 Pershing Ave., St. Louis, MO 63112. *Office*—225 South Meramec Ave., #206, Clayton, MO 63115.

CAREER: Worked as a civil engineer for city and federal governments, 1964-74; owner of general contracting company in St. Louis, MO, 1974-82; writer, 1982—; co-owner with wife, Patricia, of All-Writing Services. *Military service:* U.S. Marine Corps, 1957-60.

MEMBER: National Writers Guild, Society of Children's Book Writers.

AWARDS, HONORS: C. S. Lewis Silver Medal award, Christian Educators Association, 1985, for *Abram, Abram, Where Are We Going?;* Jane Addams Children's Book Award, Women's International League for Peace and Freedom, and Coretta Scott King Award, both 1990, both for *A Long Hard Journey: The Story of the Pullman Porter;* Coretta Scott King Honor Award, 1993, for *Sojourner Truth: Ain't I a Woman?;* Children's Award, Tennessee Book Selection Volunteer Committee.

WRITINGS:

FOR CHILDREN; WITH WIFE, PATRICIA C. McKISSACK

Look What You've Done Now, Moses, illustrated by Joe Boddy, Chariot Books (Elgin, IL), 1984.
Abram, Abram, Where Are We Going?, illustrated by Boddy, Chariot Books, 1984.
Lights Out, Christopher, illustrated by Bartholomew, Augsburg (Minneapolis), 1984.
Cinderella, illustrated by Tom Dunnington, Childrens Press (Chicago), 1985.
Country Mouse and City Mouse, illustrated by Anne Sikorski, Childrens Press, 1985.
The Little Red Hen, illustrated by Dennis Hockerman, Childrens Press, 1985.
The Three Bears, illustrated by Virginia Bala, Childrens Press, 1985.
The Ugly Little Duck, illustrated by Peggy Perry Anderson, Childrens Press, 1986.
When Do You Talk to God? Prayers for Small Children, illustrated by Gary Gumble, Augsburg, 1986.
King Midas and His Gold, illustrated by Dunnington, Childrens Press, 1986.
Frederick Douglass: The Black Lion, Childrens Press, 1987.

A Real Winner, illustrated by Quentin Thompson and Ken Jones, Milliken (St. Louis), 1987.

The King's New Clothes, illustrated by Gwen Connelly, Childrens Press, 1987.

Tall Phil and Small Bill, illustrated by Kathy Mitter, Milliken, 1987.

Three Billy Goats Gruff, illustrated by Dunnington, Childrens Press, 1987.

My Bible ABC Book, illustrated by Reed Merrill, Augsburg, 1987.

The Civil Rights Movement in America from 1865 to the Present, Childrens Press, 1987, 2nd edition, 1991.

All Paths Lead to Bethlehem, illustrated by Kathryn E. Shoemaker, Augsburg, 1987.

Messy Bessey, illustrated by Richard Hackney, Childrens Press, 1987.

The Big Bug Book of Counting, illustrated by Bartholomew, Milliken, 1987.

The Big Bug Book of Things to Do, illustrated by Bartholomew, Milliken, 1987.

The Big Bug Book of Opposites, illustrated by Bartholomew, Milliken, 1987.

The Big Bug Book of Places to Go, illustrated by Bartholomew, Milliken, 1987.

The Big Bug Book of the Alphabet, illustrated by Bartholomew, Milliken, 1987.

Bugs!, illustrated by Clovis Martin, Childrens Press, 1988.

The Children's ABC Christmas, illustrated by Kathy Rogers, Augsburg, 1988.

Constance Stumbles, illustrated by Dunnington, Childrens Press, 1988.

A Troll in a Hole, illustrated by Bartholomew, Milliken, 1988.

Oh, Happy, Happy Day! A Child's Easter in Story, Song, and Prayer, illustrated by Elizabeth Swisher, Augsburg, 1989.

God Made Something Wonderful, illustrated by Ching, Augsburg, 1989.

Messy Bessey's Closet, illustrated by Hackney, Children Press, 1989.

No Need for Alarm, Milliken, 1990.

James Weldon Johnson: "Lift Every Voice and Sing," Childrens Press, 1990.

A Long Hard Journey: The Story of the Pullman Porter, Walker & Co. (New York), 1990.

Taking a Stand against Racism and Racial Discrimination, F. Watts (New York), 1990.

W. E. B. DuBois, F. Watts, 1990.

The Story of Booker T. Washington, Childrens Press, 1991.

Messy Bessey's Garden, illustrated by Hackney, Childrens Press, 1991.

African Americans, Milliken, 1991.

Sojourner Truth: Ain't I a Woman?, Scholastic Inc. (New York), 1992.

From Heaven Above, Augsburg, 1992.

Mary McLeod Bethune, Childrens Press, 1992.

The Royal Kingdoms of Ghana, Mali, and Songhay: Life in Medieval Africa, Holt (New York), 1993.

Tennessee Trailblazers, March Media, 1993.

African-American Scientists, Millbrook Press (Brookfield, CT), 1994.

African-American Inventors, Millbrook Press, 1994.

Lorraine Hansberry: Dramatist and Activist, Delacorte (New York), 1994.

Christmas in the Big House, Christmas in the Quarters, illustrated by John Thompson, Scholastic Inc., 1994.

"GREAT AFRICAN AMERICANS" JUVENILE SERIES; WITH P. McKISSACK

Carter G. Woodson: The Father of Black History, illustrated by Ned Ostendorf, Enslow (Hillside, NJ), 1991.

Frederick Douglass: Leader against Slavery, illustrated by Ostendorf, Enslow, 1991.

George Washington Carver: The Peanut Scientist, illustrated by Ostendorf, Enslow, 1991.

Ida B. Wells-Barnett: A Voice against Violence, illustrated by Ostendorf, Enslow, 1991.

Louis Armstrong: Jazz Musician, illustrated by Ostendorf, Enslow, 1991.

Martin Luther King, Jr.: Man of Peace, illustrated by Ostendorf, Enslow, 1991.

Mary Church Terrell: Leader for Equality, illustrated by Ostendorf, Enslow, 1991.

Mary McLeod Bethune: A Great Teacher, illustrated by Ostendorf, Enslow, 1991.

Marian Anderson: A Great Singer, illustrated by Ostendorf, Enslow, 1991.

Ralph J. Bunche: Peacemaker, illustrated by Ostendorf, Enslow, 1991.

Jesse Owens: Olympic Star, illustrated by Michael David Biegel, Enslow, 1992.

Langston Hughes: Great American Poet, illustrated by Biegel, Enslow, 1992.

Sojourner Truth: A Voice for Freedom, illustrated by Michael Bryant, Enslow, 1992.

Zora Neale Hurston: Writer and Storyteller, illustrated by Bryant, Enslow, 1992.

Satchel Paige: The Best Arm in Baseball, illustrated by Biegel, Enslow, 1992.

Madam C. J. Walker: Self-Made Millionaire, illustrated by Bryant, Enslow, 1992.

Booker T. Washington: Leader and Educator, illustrated by Bryant, Enslow, 1992.

Paul Robeson: A Voice to Remember, illustrated by Biegel, Enslow, 1992.

OTHER

Also contributor with P. McKissack to *The World in 1492,* edited by Jean Fritz, Henry Holt, 1992. Also author, with P. McKissack, of "Start Up" series for beginning readers, four volumes, Childrens Press, 1985; editor with P. McKissack of "Reading Well" series for Milliken.

Some of McKissack's books have been published in Spanish.

SIDELIGHTS: Fredrick L. McKissack once told *CA:* "A lot of people wonder how a general contractor can become a writer. The two occupations are not that far removed. I render the service for which I am paid, but writing is much more satisfying than construction work because of the wonderful children I have met. It's an enjoyable experience, and it's also one I've come to love."*

*   *   *

McMULLIN, Ernan 1924-

PERSONAL: Born October 13, 1924, in Donegal, Ireland; son of Vincent (a lawyer) and Carmel (a doctor; maiden name, Farrell) McMullin. *Education:* Maynooth College, Ireland, B.Sc., 1945, B.D., 1948; Attended Institute of Advanced Studies, Dublin, Ireland, 1949-50; University of Louvain, Ph.D., 1954.

ADDRESSES: Home—P.O. Box 1066, Notre Dame, IN 46556. *Office*—Reilly Center for Science, Technology, and Values, 309 O'Shaughnessy, University of Notre Dame, Notre Dame, IN 46556.

CAREER: Ordained Roman Catholic priest, 1949. University of Notre Dame, Notre Dame, IN, 1954—, began as instructor, became professor of logic and philosophy of science, 1967-94, John Cardinal O'Hara Chair of Philosophy, 1984-94, professor emeritus, 1994—, chairman of department of philosophy, 1965-72, director of Reilly Center for Science, Technology, and Values. Research fellow, Yale University, 1957-59, 1973-74, Cambridge University, 1968-69, and University of Pittsburgh, 1979; visiting professor, Georgetown University, summer, 1963, Center for the Philosophy of Science, University of Minnesota, 1964-65, College of Science, University of Cape Town, summers, 1972 and 1973, University of California, Los Angeles, 1977, Princeton University, spring, 1991, and Yale University, spring, 1992; Phi Beta Kappa National Lecturer, 1986-87; Romanell/Phi Beta Kappa Professorship of Philosophy, 1993-94.

International Congress for Logic and Methodology, U.S. delegate, 1967, 1977, chair of U.S. delegation, 1983, 1987; International Congress of Philosophy, president of Philosophy of Science Division, Vienna, 1968, Varna, 1973; U.S. National Committee on the International Union of the History and Philosophy of Science, chair, 1982-84, 1986-88; National Science Foundation, member of advisory panel on the philosophy of science, 1963-65, 1982, chair of history and philosophy of science fellowship panel, 1966, and of oversight committee, 1981; International Federation of Philosophical Societies, member of Congress Commission, 1979-80; member of Galileo Working Group of Vatican Observatory, 1982-92.

MEMBER: International Academy of the History of Science (fellow), American Philosophical Association (member of Western Division executive council, 1977-81; president of Western Division, 1983-84), American Academy of Arts and Sciences (fellow), Society of Christian Philosophers (member of executive committee, 1982-87), Council for Philosophical Studies (member of executive committee, 1970-75), American Association for the Advancement of Science (fellow; chairman of section on the history and philosophy of science, 1977-78), American Catholic Philosophical Association (president, 1966-67), Philosophy of Science Association (member of executive council, 1970-73; president, 1980-82), History of Science Society (member of executive council, 1988-91), Metaphysical Society of America (member of executive council, 1968-70; president, 1973-74), Society for Religion in Higher Education (fellow), Sigma Xi.

AWARDS, HONORS: Fellowships or research grants from Yale University, 1957-59, Cambridge University, 1968-69, 1973-74, 1983, and 1987, and University of Pittsburgh, 1979; D.H.L., Loyola University, Chicago, 1969; faculty award, University of Notre Dame, 1973, for distinguished service, and 1990, for contribution to graduate education; Aquinas Medal, American Catholic Philosophical Association, 1981; Centennial Medal, John Carroll University, 1985; honorary doctorate in letters, National University of Ireland, 1990.

WRITINGS:

(Editor and author of introduction) *The Concept of Matter,* University of Notre Dame Press (Notre Dame, IN), 1963, revised edition published as *The Concept of Matter in Modern Philosophy,* 1978.

(Editor and author of introduction and bibliography) *Galileo: Man of Science* (includes "Bibliografia Galileiana") Basic Books (New York City), 1967, reprinted without "Bibliografia Galileiana," Scholars' Bookshelf, 1988.

(Author of introduction) J. Roslansky, editor, *The Uniqueness of Man,* North-Holland (Amsterdam), 1968.

(Editor and author of introduction) *Death and Decision,* Westview (Boulder, CO), 1978.

Newton on Matter and Activity, University of Notre Dame Press, 1978.

(Editor and author of introduction) *Evolution and Creation,* University of Notre Dame Press, 1985.

(Editor and author of introduction) *Construction and Constraint: The Shaping of Scientific Rationality,* University of Notre Dame Press, 1988.

(Editor with James T. Cushing) *The Philosophical Consequences of Quantum Theory: Reflections on Bell's Theorem,* University of Notre Dame Press, 1989.

(Editor and author of introduction) *The Social Dimensions of Science,* University of Notre Dame Press, 1992.

The Inference That Makes Science, Marquette University Press (Milwaukee), 1992.

Contributor to numerous books, including *The Concept of Order,* edited by P. Kuntz, University of Washington Press (Seattle), 1968; *New Perspectives on Galileo,* edited by R. Butts and J. Pitt, D. Reidel (Dordrecht, The Netherlands), 1978; *Hegel and the Sciences,* edited by R. D. Cohen and M. Wartofsky, D. Reidel, 1983; *The Nature of Metaphysical Knowledge,* edited by G. McLean and H. Meynell, University Press of America (Lanham, MD), 1988; and *World Changes: Thomas Kuhn and the Nature of Science,* edited by P. Horwich, MIT Press (Cambridge, MA), 1993. Contributor to encyclopedias and dictionaries, and to *Proceedings* of professional organizations and international conferences and meetings. Editor, "Fundamentals of Logic" series, Prentice-Hall (Englewood Cliffs, NJ), 1963-66. Contributor to numerous periodicals, including *New Blackfriars, Boston Studies in the Philosophy of Science, Theological Studies, American Philosophical Quarterly, Philosophy of Science, American Historical Review,* and *Review of Metaphysics.*

Editor and author of introduction of *Issues in Computer Diagnosis,* a special issue of *Journal of Medicine and Philosophy,* 1983; member of editorial board, *Studies in the History and Philosophy of Science,* 1970-75, 1983—, University of Notre Dame Press, 1974-78, *Philosophy of Science,* 1975-81, *Isis,* 1976-80, *Journal of Medicine and Philosophy,* 1977-93, *Nature and System,* 1978—, *Faith and Reason,* 1983-88, *Astronomy Quarterly,* 1985—, *British Journal for the Philosophy of Science,* 1988—, *International Studies in the Philosophy of Science,* 1989—, and *Perspectives on Science,* 1992—; editorial consultant, *American Philosophical Quarterly,* 1964-73, *New Scholasticism,* 1964-80, and *Philosophy Research Archives,* 1978—.

WORK IN PROGRESS: Studies of seventeenth-century theories of rationality and realism in science, and the relations of science and religion.

BIOGRAPHICAL/CRITICAL SOURCES:

PERIODICALS

Choice, July, 1986, p.1688; June, 1987, p. 1518; January, 1993, p. 818.

Commonweal, March 13, 1987, p. 153.

*   *   *

McQUAID, Kim   1947-

PERSONAL: Born November 2, 1947, in Norwalk, CT; son of Francis Walter (an antiquarian bookseller) and Margaret Fitzgerald (a motel operator and hairdresser; maiden name, Phelan) McQuaid. *Education:* Antioch College, B.A., 1970; graduate study at University of British Columbia, 1970-71; Northwestern University, M.A., 1973, Ph.D., 1975.

ADDRESSES: Home—Modockawando Farm, North Edgecomb, ME 04556. *Office*—Department of History, Lake Erie College, Painesville, OH 44077.

CAREER: Worked as arts and crafts teacher and social worker, 1965-69, as illustrator, 1969, and as antiquarian bookseller, 1974-75; Antioch College, Yellow Springs, OH, instructor in history, 1975; Northwestern University, Evanston, IL, part-time instructor in history, 1976-77; Lake Erie College, Painesville, OH, assistant professor, 1977-84, associate professor, 1984-91, professor of history, 1991—. University College, Dublin, Mary Ball Washington visiting professor of U.S. history, 1985-86; Claremont Graduate School, visiting associate professor of U.S. history, 1989-90.

MEMBER: Economic History Association, Business History Conference, American Historical Association.

AWARDS, HONORS: Woodrow Wilson fellowship, 1970.

WRITINGS:

(Contributor) Paul Uselding, editor, *Research in Economic History: An Annual Compilation of Research,* Volume 1, JAI Press, 1976.

(With Edward Berkowitz) *Creating the Welfare State: The Political Economy of Twentieth-Century Reform,* Praeger, 1980, 2nd revised and expanded edition, 1988.

Big Business and Presidential Power, Morrow, 1982.

A Response to Industrialism, Garland, 1986.

The Anxious Years: America in the Vietnam-Watergate Era, Basic Books, 1989.

Uneasy Partners: Big Business in American Politics, 1945-90, Johns Hopkins, 1994.

Contributor to history, business, economics, geography, and law journals.

SIDELIGHTS: Kim McQuaid told *CA:* "Writing, to me, is a way to cheat death; and a way to converse with futures

I shall never see. Knowing my individual fate, I yet attempt to transcend it as any artist does: by adding something to the sum of human wisdom.

"Too often today, writers, like other Americans, surrender to trendy end-of-millennium pessimisms which stop creativity before it begins, and which lead analysts to put old whine in new bottles. For all the wails, laments, and gnashings of teeth, however, we live in one of the most exciting times in human history; one rich with both accomplishments and possibilities. Future generations yet-unborn will, I believe, marvel at the mean-spirited and frightened futilitarianism now so evident among the various intellectual elites of our Celebrity-, Credentials-, and Crisis-driven culture. They will see us, perhaps, as human insects undergoing a collective metamorphosis: one during which our old faiths have turned brittle, and during which the forms of our new faiths are not yet clear. In fifty to one hundred years, the vast majority of our current fixations on the micropolitics of the jockeying for economic, social, and political power will be as mostly-irrelevant to people charting the directions of their time as the minutiae of the age of William McKinley or Queen Victoria is to us.

"What the future will remember, instead, are a host of far-reaching science- and technology-driven innovations, among which nuclear power and thermonuclear weaponry, computer technologies and information networking, space exploration, the inevitably-contentious definition of precise environmental-ecological trade-offs, biomedical advances and genetic engineering, and the occupational, social, and political advances of women and the globalization of the world's economy will figure very prominently indeed.

"Presently, comparatively little of the most valuable and cogent analysis of such key, central, and resonating matters is being produced by academic historians, perhaps because academe's still-largely-feudal methods of intellectual organization and training are notably out-of-step with the emergent directions of our times. . . . In an era in human affairs when established social, economic, and political ways-of-thought and methods-of-action are undergoing a process of thorough and sometimes-wrenching change, the Professorate has to do better than much of it is yet even currently attempting.

"History, after all, is a wonderfully synthetic discipline. It can (and sometimes even does) deal with vast reaches of the tragedy, farce, poetry, beauty, purity, and ugliness of humanity. To make it boring, therefore, approximates the criminal; and to write it badly requires dullness of truly-awesome dimensions."

MEAD, Sidney Moko 1927-

PERSONAL: Born January 8, 1927, in Wairoa, New Zealand; son of Sidney Montague (a contractor) and Paranihia Mead; married June Te Rina (a teacher), October 22, 1950. *Education:* University of Auckland, B.A., 1964, M.A., 1965; University of Southern Illinois, Ph.D., 1968. *Politics:* Any pro-Maori party. *Religion:* Anglican.

ADDRESSES: Home—10 Spiers St., Karori, Wellington N.2, New Zealand. *Office*—Te Whare Wananga o Awanuiarangi, Apanui Education Centre, Private Bag, Whakatane, New Zealand.

CAREER: Art and craft specialist, 1947-51; head teacher at schools in New Zealand, 1951-70; University of Auckland, Auckland, New Zealand, lecturer in Maori studies, 1970-71; McMaster University, Hamilton, Ontario, associate professor of anthropology, 1971-72 and 1973-77; Victoria University of Wellington, Wellington, New Zealand, professor of Maori, 1977-91. Chairman of Ngati Awa Trust Board, 1990; chairman of Establishment Committee of Te Whare Wananga o Awanuiarangi, 1990—.

MEMBER: Pacific Arts Association (past president).

AWARDS, HONORS: Canadian Commonwealth research fellowship for University of British Columbia, Vancouver, Canada, 1972-73; Elsdon Best Memorial Medal, 1983; Pacific Arts Association Frigate Bird Award, 1984; Fellow of the Royal Society of New Zealand, 1991.

WRITINGS:

Taniko Weaving, A. H. & A. W. Reed (Wellington, New Zealand), 1952.

We Speak Maori, A. H. & A. W. Reed, 1959.

(Editor with Bruce Biggs and Patrick Hohepa) *Selected Readings in Maori,* A. H. & A. W. Reed, 1959, 2nd edition with illustrations by Mead, 1967.

The Art of Taniko Weaving: A Study of Its Context, Technique, Style, and Developments, A. H. & A. W. Reed, 1968.

Traditional Maori Clothing: A Study of Technological and Functional Change, A. H. & A. W. Reed, 1969.

(Translator into modern text with G. C. Petersen) *Portraits of the New Zealand Maori Painted in 1844 by George French Angas,* A. H. & A. W. Reed, 1972.

Material Culture and Art in the Star Harbour Region, Eastern Solomons (monograph), Royal Ontario Museum, 1973.

(With L. Birks, H. Birks, and E. Shaw) *The Lapita Pottery Style of Fiji and Its Associations,* Polynesian Society, 1975.

Exploring the Visual Art of Oceania, University Press of Hawaii (Honolulu), 1979.

(Editor) *Te Maori: Maori Art from New Zealand Collections,* Abrams (New York City), 1984.

Magnificent Te Maori: Te Maori Whakahirahira, Heine-mann (Auckland, New Zealand), 1986.

Te Toi Whakairo: The Art of Maori Carving, Reed Meth-uen, 1986.

IN MAORI

Ko Te Tahae Nei ko Tawhaki (title means "This Fellow Tawhaki,") A. H. & A. W. Reed, 1960.

(Editor with Biggs) *He Kohikohinga Aronui* (title means "A Collection of Valuable Texts,") A. H. & A. W. Reed, 1964.

Nga Taonga Tuki Iho a Ngati Awa: The Writings of Hami-ora Tumutara Te Tihi-o-whenua Pio, 1885-87, A. H. & A. W. Reed, 1981.

OTHER

Also author of *The Costume Styles of Classical Maori in New Zealand,* 1969; *Ngati Awa Me Ona Karangaranga-tanga,* Research Report No. 3 and *Te Kaupapa o Te Rau-patu i Te Rohe o Ngati Awa: The Ethnography of the Ngati Awa Experience of RAupatu,* Research Report No. 4, *Te Roopu Whakaemi Korero o Ngati Awa, Te Runanga o Ngati Awa,* Whakatane, 1994.

SIDELIGHTS: Sidney Moko Mead wrote *CA:* "I am con-cerned with Maori rights in New Zealand, with the cul-tural renaissance that is happening, with the Treaty of Wailangi and other issues of pressing moment, but my main contribution to our people is through knowledge and the power of the written word."

Mead retired as Professor of Maori at Victorian Univer-sity of Wellington in 1991 and is now involved in estab-lishing a tribally based Whare Wananga or Tribal College of Higher Education in Whakatane. The college is now in its third year of operation. Over the last ten years he has been involved in preparing the cause of his tribal group, Ngati Awa, to take before the Waitangi Tribunal of New Zealand. The culmination of years of research are the ac-tual hearings which began July 4, 1994. Increased involve-ment with tribal affairs is reflected by the fact that he is known more widely as Hirini Moko than as Sidney Mead.

*   *   *

MEIGHAN, Donald Charles 1929-
(Donald Charles)

PERSONAL: Born March 15, 1929, in San Francisco, CA; son of Charles (a writer) and Lucille (Mellin) Meig-han; married Shirley Blakeslee (an artist), March 4, 1950; children: Kathleen, Matthew, Timothy. *Education:* At-tended University of California, Berkeley, 1945-47, and Art League School, 1950-54.

ADDRESSES: Home—412 North Ninth St., Murphys-boro, IL 62966.

CAREER: San Francisco Chronicle, San Francisco, CA, feature writer and artist, 1948-50; Flair Merchandising Agency (advertising agency), creative director, 1956-65; freelance illustrator and writer, 1965—. Also worked as a truck driver, longshoreman, and ranch hand. *Military service:* U.S. Army, 1947-50; editor of weekly newspaper.

MEMBER: Authors Guild, Authors League of America, Art Institute of Chicago.

AWARDS, HONORS: Gold medal from National Point of Purchase Advertising Institute, 1960, for "Old Time Train" construction; awards of merit from San Francisco Advertising Club, 1961, Graphic Arts Council of Chi-cago, 1965, and Artists Guild of Chicago, 1979, all for il-lustrations; silver medal from Printworld, 1976; honors from Children's Reading Round, 1982, 1983, 1985, 1987, 1989, 1991, 1993.

WRITINGS:

SELF-ILLUSTRATED; UNDER NAME DONALD CHARLES

Busy Beaver's Day, Children's Press (Chicago, IL), 1972.

Count on Calico Cat, Children's Press, 1974.

Letters from Calico Cat, Children's Press, 1974.

Calico Cat Looks Around, Children's Press, 1975.

Calico Cat's Rainbow, Children's Press, 1975.

Fat, Fat Calico Cat, Children's Press, 1977, Spanish trans-lation published as *Gordito, gordon Gato Galano,* Children's Press, 1991.

Calico Cat Meets Bookworm, Children's Press, 1978.

Time to Rhyme with Calico Cat, Children's Press, 1978, Spanish translation published as *Mira las formas con Gato Galano,* Children's Press, 1991.

The Jolly Pancake, Children's Press, 1979.

Shaggy Dog's Animal Alphabet, Children's Press, 1979.

Shaggy Dog's Tall Tale, Children's Press, 1980.

Calico Cat at School, Children's Press, 1981.

Calico Cat at the Zoo, Children's Press, 1981.

Calico Cat's Exercise Book, Children's Press, 1982, Span-ish translation published as *El libro de ejercicios de Gato Galano,* Children's Press, 1991.

Shaggy Dog's Halloween, Children's Press, 1984.

Calico Cat's Year, Children's Press, 1984, Spanish transla-tion published as *El ano de Gato Galano,* Children's Press, 1991.

Shaggy Dog's Christmas, Children's Press, 1985.

Shaggy Dog's Birthday, Children's Press, 1986.

Paddy Pig's Poems, Simon & Schuster (New York City), 1989.

Pickles & Pepper, Simon & Schuster, 1990.

Calico Cat's Sunny Smile, Children's Press, 1990.

Gato Galano mira los colores, Children's Press, 1991.

Chancay and the Secret of Fire, Putnam (New York City), 1992.

Ugly Bug, Dial (New York City), 1994.

ILLUSTRATOR; UNDER NAME DONALD CHARLES

D. L. Hubbard, *The Dragon Comes to Admela: Another Book about Admela and Its Royal Family,* Reilly & Lee, 1967.

Hubbard, *Dragons, Dragons: A Story,* Reilly & Lee, 1967.

Derlyne Gibson, *How Far Can It Go?,* Reilly & Lee, 1970.

Virginia Poulet, *Blue Bug and the Bullies,* Children's Press, 1971.

Gibson, *How Big Can It Grow?,* Reilly & Lee, 1971.

Illa Podendorf, *Tools for Observing,* Children's Press, 1971.

Poulet, *Blue Bug's Safety Book,* Children's Press, 1973.

Poulet, *Blue Bug's Vegetable Garden,* Children's Press, 1973.

Margaret Hillert, *The Little Cookie,* Follet, 1980.

WORK IN PROGRESS: "I stockpile manuscripts for four or five years before rewriting and developing appropriate illustrations. Currently, I have about twenty picture stories waiting for that critical second look."

SIDELIGHTS: Donald Charles Meighan wrote *CA:* "In school, I showed an early proclivity for art, and received encouragement from a succession of wonderful teachers. There was never any doubt in my mind that I wanted to be a book illustrator. In addition to art work, I wrote for school publications, and composed poems and stories for my own amusement.

"Although I started late in the children's book field, it seems as though everything I've done has prepared me for what I'm doing now. I have no problem searching for ideas. They flow so easily that I can dream up far more work than I can ever produce. The real challenge is not what to do, but how to do it. Many people think that the creative person starts with nothing, like God, and assembles something full-blown out of the cosmos. Actually, we are more like sculptors confronted with blocks of stone: we must painstakingly remove the unneeded material in order to expose the masterpieces that lie within.

"Most of the books early in my career had a rather didactic bent and were intended for school libraries. I've now done more trade books, and I have a whole closet full of nonsense and whimsy waiting for me to give it pictorial life. I have some strong beliefs about the content of children's books. It may sound trite to say that I believe in entertainment, information, and enlightenment, but my prejudices may also define my beliefs: I detest mannered or 'precious' writing and illustration which I feel is condescending and therefore demeaning to the child. 'Sophisticated' children's books should be published as adult picture books since they are really for the amusement of adults and generally baffle children.

"I've stubbornly clung to the more American tradition of story lines which amuse and entertain with fanciful characters (rather than realistic creatures in costume), and with a positive point-of-view buried in the plot. Unfortunately, many publishers currently yield to the broader market demands for 'politically correct' themes and overblown artwork, relying more on sales figures and less on their own creative judgments.

"Writing and illustrating children's books is not the most lucrative thing I've ever done, but it's rewarding in more important ways. When I get a letter from a reader, I remember when I was small, and how the distress of the moment was so often set aside by the magic of a book. I hope I can continue to repay that debt to the authors and illustrators who preceded me."

*　　*　　*

MELADY, John 1938-

PERSONAL: Surname is pronounced "Muh-*lay*-dee"; born September 12, 1938, in Seaforth, Ontario, Canada; son of Maurice (a farmer) and Mary (a homemaker; maiden name, Flynn) Melady; married Mary Lemaire (a teacher), August 25, 1962; children: Paul, Mark, Tim. *Education:* University of Western Ontario, B.A., 1962; University of Toronto, M.Ed., 1973. *Religion:* Roman Catholic. *Avocational interests:* International travel, photography, golf and downhill skiing.

ADDRESSES: R.R. 3, Brighton, Ontario K0K 1H0, Canada.

CAREER: Construction worker in Cobourg, Ontario, 1958-59; elementary schoolteacher in Prescott, Ontario, 1959-60; high school teacher of English in Trenton, Ontario, 1962-69; Hastings County Board of Education, secondary school vice principal, 1969-94. Presents workshops at elementary and high schools, colleges and universities; guest on radio and television programs across Canada.

MEMBER: Writers' Union of Canada, Royal Canadian Military Institute, Officers' Mess Canadian Forces Base Trenton, Wackworth Ontario Golf Club.

AWARDS, HONORS: Writing awards from Province of Ontario for three of seven published books.

WRITINGS:

Explosion, Mika, 1980.

Escape from Canada!, Macmillan (Toronto), 1981.

Korea: Canada's Forgotten War, Macmillan, 1983.

Cross of Valour (juvenile), Scholastic Inc. (New York City), 1985.

The Little Princes (children), Scholastic Inc., 1988.

Overtime, Overdue: The Bill Barilko Story (sports), City Print, 1988.

Pilots, McClelland & Stewart (Toronto), 1989.

Columnist for the *Catholic Register,* 1980-87, and *OSSTF Forum,* 1979-84. Contributor of articles to newspapers and magazines.

WORK IN PROGRESS: A juvenile book on heroes for young people; research for a book on Japanese prisoner of war camps in the Second World War; assisting in preparation of a television documentary about German prisoners of war in Canada.

SIDELIGHTS: John Melady told *CA:* "The books I have written so far were done because they filled a void in Canadian history. For example, I had been out of university for some time before I even knew we had incarcerated German prisoners of war here. The book resulting from this was *Escape from Canada!* It has been a great success, both in hardback and paperback.

"I wrote my book on Korea because Canada had a sizable contingent of troops in that war, and no one knew it. My research took me to Korea, where I walked the battlefields where our soldiers fought, prayed at their graves in Pusan, and enjoyed the same recreational outlets as they did in Japan. The book was both a Book-of-the-Month Club and Literary Guild choice. It is still selling.

"My book *Pilots* was written because I have always been interested in planes, and the men and women who fly them. As part of my research here, I was able to fly in the cockpit of several commercial airliners. As well, I flew with the Brazilian Air Force aerobatic team, and as a rear seat observer in the Canadian Air force fighter pilot, the F-18. Being given the chance to take the stick and roll the plane over, and to experience after-burner takeoff were thrills I will not soon forget.

"To me, researching nonfiction is almost as pleasant as writing it. Gathering the information involves travel, meeting interesting people, and seeing the world through the eyes of others. I have traveled on all the continents except Antarctica, but I hope my writing will take me there eventually.

"I also do a great deal of book reviewing because doing so helps me to keep up to date with what is current, not only in Canada, but in Britain, the United States, and elsewhere."

MELCHER, Daniel 1912-1985

PERSONAL: Born July 10, 1912, in Newton Center, MA; drowned following an epileptic seizure, July 29, 1985, in Charlottesville, VA; son of Frederic Gershom (president, R. R. Bowker Co. and editor of *Publishers Weekly*) and Marguerite (a writer, playwright, and poet; maiden name, Fellows) Melcher; married Peggy Zimmerman, March 3, 1937 (died March, 1967); married Margaret Saul, October 3, 1967; children: Frederic G. II. *Education:* Harvard University, A.B., 1934.

CAREER: Allen & Unwin, London, England, publicity assistant, 1934; student of publishing methods in London and Leipzig, Germany, 1935; Henry Holt & Co., New York City, editorial and sales work, 1936; Oxford University Press, New York City, direct mail and advertising manager, 1937-39; Alliance Book Corporation, New York City, production manager, 1939-40; Viking Press, New York City, children's book promotion, 1940-42; U.S. Treasury Department, War Bond Division, Education Section, Washington, DC, national director, 1942-45; National Committee on Atomic Information, Washington, DC, director, 1946; R. R. Bowker Company, New York City, promotion manager, 1947-58, publisher of *Library Journal,* 1947-68, vice president, 1959-63, president, 1963-68, chairman of the board, 1968-69; publishing consultant, with assignments, among others, from American Book Publishers' Council and American Library Association; Institutes for the Achievement of Human Potential, Philadelphia, PA, member of board of directors, 1970; Gale Research Company, Detroit, MI, chairman of the board, 1971-73. Succeeded his father as donor of the Newbery and Caldecott Medals, awarded annually by the Children's Services Division of the American Library Association to the most distinguished children's books of the year; sponsor of Frederic G. Melcher Award awarded annually by the Unitarian-Universalist Association for the most distinguished contribution to the literature of liberal religion.

WRITINGS:

Young Mr. Stone, Book Publisher (juvenile career book), Dodd (New York City), 1939, special printing, Court Book Co., 1941.

(With Nancy Larrick) *The Printing and Promotion Handbook: How to Plan, Produce, and Use Printing, Advertising, and Direct Mail,* McGraw (New York City), 1949, 3rd edition, 1966.

So You Want to Get into Book Publishing: The Jobs, the Pay, and How to Start (pamphlet), Publishers Weekly, 1956, revised edition, 1967.

(With wife, Margaret Saul Melcher) *Melcher on Acquisition,* American Library Association (Chicago), 1971.

(Contributor) Sigfred Taubert, editor, *Book Trade of the World*, Volume II: *Americas, Australia, New Zealand*, Bowker (New York City), 1976.

Contributor to *Encyclopedia of Library and Information Science*, edited by Allen Kent, Dekker, 1977. Contributor to *Library Journal, Pocket Book Magazine, Publishers Weekly, Bookseller* (London), and *American Libraries.*

SIDELIGHTS: It is hard even for older people in the world of books to remember that *Books in Print* has not always existed, or for younger users to imagine that libraries, book shops, or publishing firms could ever get along without it. It was not until 1949, however, that *Books in Print* first appeared, the product of Daniel Melcher's publishing imagination and mechanical ingenuity (he was the inventor of both the camera and mounting equipment that made the speedy, economical production of *BIP* possible.) Innovative until his death in 1985 at the age of 73, Melcher once told *CA* that among his favorite mottos was the following: "If you have always done it that way, it is probably wrong."

Melcher seldom did things the wrong way. During his career at the R. R. Bowker Co., he also created *Subject Guide to Books in Print, Paperbound Books in Print, American Book Publishing Record, Forthcoming Books, School Library Journal,* the *Bowker Annual,* and *Libros en Venta.* In preparation for work on the latter, a "books-in-print" of the Spanish speaking world, he liked to play Spanish tapes while shaving, driving, working in his shop, and so on. "A real break-through," he once told *CA,* "came from hearing in Spanish mostly things I already knew well in English . . . ranging from 'The Lord's Prayer' to the poetry of Robert Frost."

Melcher's colleague Nancy Larrick Crosby once described the experience of working with him. "Quiet, somewhat retiring in a large group," she wrote, "Dan Melcher has a knack of forging deeply loyal friendships in some quarters while raising antagonism in others. . . . Anyone who has worked with Melcher is soon aware that his mind simply operates in a higher gear than anyone else's, a fact he has never fully accepted," she explained. It was also a fact that sometimes lead to tensions and misunderstandings on the job. "But," Larrick continued, "as one devoted friend of 25 years' standing put it, 'Dan apologizes so beautifully that it's worth the price.' " Melcher's rejoinder, according to Larrick, was: " 'Maybe I've had more practice than anyone.' "

Melcher's sharp-focus approach to problems and his wide grasp of publishing technology and economics perhaps contributed to his resignation from Bowker after the firm was acquired by Xerox. In a typically direct statement that was widely quoted by delighted conglomerate-watchers, Melcher explained his resignation in a front-page *New York Times* interview: "It was a communications problem. The planning group within the Xerox Education Division has no background in education or publishing, and I had no background in oil, plastics, chemicals or business machine sales, and we just weren't on the same wavelength."

All was not mechanics and economics in Melcher's world, however. As Larrick pointed out: "Each of the Melcher miracles [was] basic to a great dream of universal education and world understanding. . . . He [did] these things as a poet sharpens his pencil before writing a sonnet. The big objective [was] that more books [would] be read by more people."

A logical aspect of this objective was a concern for the ability—or inability—to read, and it was an interest in dyslexia that caused him to familiarize himself with work on brain function that was being carried out by Glenn Doman and Carl Delacato and their associates at the Institutes for the Achievement of Human Potential in Philadelphia.

Melcher once described for *CA* the reasons for his fascination with the work of this group: "Out of their thirty years' work, and thousands of case histories," he explained, "emerges what I find to be convincing evidence that a child—any child—can and will learn to read as early as he learns to talk, granted equal opportunity. The two processes are, after all, neurologically equivalent. Understanding words in print in no way asks more of the brain than understanding words of speech. (Sensing the difference between two words in print may actually be easier than sensing the difference between two human faces.)

"All infants have an inborn 'rage to learn,' blunted though it may be by years of 'don't,' 'not now,' 'can't you see mother is busy,' 'do be quiet,' and 'why don't you go and play with your toys. Consider the vast relief to child, mother, and teacher alike if a child, unutterably bored with his 'toys,' could, at will, replace the all-too-exhaustible resources of toys or teacher with the inexhaustible resources of the printed page.

"Consider the gain to all if a child could be introduced to 'Look, Jane, look,' at an age when he was still excited over discovering the very existence of language—instead of four years later when the let down from TV to reading primer is almost enough to put him off reading for life."

Having succeeded his father as donor of the Newbery and Caldecott Medals for children's books, Melcher made a point of ensuring a child's continuing interest in reading. In a 1982 foreword to *Newbery and Caldecott Medal and Honor Books: An Annotated Bibliography,* Melcher expanded upon his life-long interest: "Concern is being voiced about whether textbooks and teachers can long compete against 'more interesting' latter-day teaching technologies—audio and visual, tape and disk, data processing and word processing. Real readers, on the other hand, wonder who would willingly work with words on cathode ray tubes if they could have them on paper.

"Might books and reading be made obsolete, too, by later developments in communication?" he continued. "Don't you believe it! Textbooks and teachers may be on trial . . . but books as such never had it better.

"Each year sees us writing more books, printing more books, and moving more books . . . There have been changes in the ways we set the type and get the ink onto the paper—but the 'page' survives and thrives." Melcher added: "We must be doing something right."

BIOGRAPHICAL/CRITICAL SOURCES:

BOOKS

Newbery and Caldecott Medal and Honor Books: An Annotated Bibliography, G. K. Hall & Co., 1982.

PERIODICALS

Bulletin of Bibliography, May-August, 1966.
New York Times, December 20, 1967; January 31, 1969.
Publishers Weekly, June 10, 1968.
Technicalities, September 1982, p. 4.

OBITUARIES:

PERIODICALS

Library Journal, September 1, 1985.
New York Times, July 31, 1985.
Publishers Weekly, August 9, 1985, p. 22; August 21, 1985.
School Library Journal, September, 1985, pp. 2, 10, 12.*

*   *   *

MELLINS, Thomas   1957-

PERSONAL: Born April 6, 1957, in New York, NY; son of Harry Z. (a physician) and Judith (an archivist; maiden name, Weiss) Mellins. *Education:* Columbia University, B.A., 1979; City University of New York, M.A., 1981.

ADDRESSES: Home—155 West 68th St., Apt. 931, New York, NY 10023.

CAREER: Institute for Architecture and Urban Studies, New York City, assistant editor of Oppositions Books, 1981-83; architectural historian and writer, 1983—. Lecturer at universities and museums; exhibitor in art shows.

AWARDS, HONORS: National Book award nomination, 1987, and American Institute of Architects (New York

Chapter) special citation, 1994, both for *New York 1930: Architecture and Urbanism between the Two World Wars.*

WRITINGS:

(With Robert A. M. Stern and Gregory Gilmartin) *New York 1930: Architecture and Urbanism between the Two World Wars,* Rizzoli International, 1987.
(With Stern and David Fishman) *New York 1960: Architecture and Urbanism between the Second World War and the Bicentennial,* Monacelli Press, 1995.

Scriptwriter and associate producer for eight-part television series *Pride of Place: Building the American Dream,* Public Broadcasting System (PBS), 1986; author of exhibition catalogue essays including "The Fall and Rise of New York," Queens Museum, 1987, and "42nd Street: Glorious Past, Fabulous Future," The Urban Center, 1988; also author of "Housing America," *Architectural Record,* centennial issue, July 1991.

BIOGRAPHICAL/CRITICAL SOURCES:

PERIODICALS

Chicago Tribune, May 21, 1987.
Elle Decor, December 1994/January 1995.
Los Angeles Times, July 5, 1987.
New Republic, February 1, 1988.
Newsweek, December 21, 1987.
New York, September 12, 1994.
New York Times Book Review, May 31, 1987.
Philadelphia Inquirer, June 4, 1987.

*   *   *

MERKL, Peter H(ans)   1932-

PERSONAL: Born January 29, 1932, in Munich, Germany; became U.S citizen, 1963; son of Robert Joseph (a businessman) and Berta (Mitterer) Merkl; married Elisa M. Cruz (a writer), August 28, 1954; children: Jacqueline Susan, John Peter. *Education:* Attended University of Munich, 1951-52, 1953-54; University of Minnesota, M.A., 1953; University of California, Berkeley, Ph.D, 1959.

ADDRESSES: Home—6543 Camino Venturoso, Goleta, CA 93117. *Office*—Department of Political Science, University of California, Santa Barbara, CA 93106.

CAREER: University of California, Santa Barbara, assistant professor, 1958-68, professor of political science, 1968-93, acting chair of department, 1972-73, professor emeritus, 1993—. Visiting professor, University of Augsburg, 1983, University of Istanbul, 1987, University of Bogazici, 1987, University of Bosphorus, 1987, University of Gottingen, 1990, University of Berlin, 1991; visiting scholar, University of Bologna, 1994, Sophia University, 1994.

MEMBER: International Political Science Association, International Sociological Association (secretary, research committee on comparative sociology, 1986-92), American Political Science Association, Conference Group on German Politics (board member, 1969-84, president, 1984-86).

AWARDS, HONORS: Bavarian State scholarship for the gifted, 1951, 1953; Jordan fellow, University of California, Berkeley, 1954; Haynes Foundation fellow, 1960; Social Science Research Council grant, 1962; University of California faculty fellow, 1963; Rockefeller Foundation grant, 1964; National Endowment for the Humanities grant, 1967, 1970, and 1980-84; Ford Foundation fellow, 1970; Ford Foundation and National Institute for Mental Health grant, 1974-76; DAAD; Deutscher Akademischer Anstaushcdienst (German Academic Exchange Service) grant, 1974, 1977; Biomedical Sciences grant, 1978; Volkswagen Foundation grant, 1979-82; Japan Society for the Promotion of Science grant, 1980-84, 1994; Toyota Foundation grant, 1980-84; Institute for Global Conflict and Cooperation grant, 1985-87; Federal Order of Merit, West German Government, 1986; Ford Foundation grant, 1988.

WRITINGS:

The Origin of the West German Republic, Oxford University Press (New York City), 1963, German translation published as *Die Entstehung der Bundesrepublik,* Kohlhammer-Verlag (Stuttgart), 1965.

Germany: Yesterday and Tomorrow, Oxford University Press, 1965.

(With Otey Scruggs) *Rassenfrage und Rechtsradikalismus in den USA,* Colloquium Verlag (Berlin), 1966.

Political Continuity and Change, Harper (New York City), 1967, revised edition, 1977.

Modern Comparative Politics, Holt, 1970, revised edition, Dryden, 1977, Spanish translation published as *Teorias politicas comparadas,* Editorial Roble (Mexico), 1973.

German Foreign Policies, West and East: On the Threshold of a New European Era, Clio Press (Santa Barbara, CA), 1974.

Political Violence under the Swastika: 581 Early Nazis, Princeton University Press (Princeton, NJ), 1975.

(With Dieter Raabe) *Politische Soziologie der USA: Die konservative Demokratie,* Akademische Verlagsgesellschaft (Wiesbaden), 1977.

The Making of a Stormtrooper, Princeton University Press, 1980.

(With Herman Pritchett, William Ebenstein, Henry Turner, and Dean Mann) *American Democracy in World Perspective,* 5th edition, Harper, 1980.

German Unification in the European Context, Pennsylvania State University Press (University Park, PA), 1993.

The Federal Republic at Forty-Five, Macmillan (New York City), 1995.

EDITOR

Western European Party Systems: Trends and Prospects, Free Press/Macmillan, 1980.

(With others) *Who Were the Fascists?: Social Roots of European Fascism,* Norwegian University Press (Oslo), 1980.

West German Foreign Policy: Dilemmas and Directions, Chicago Council on Foreign Relations, 1982.

(With Ninian Smart) *Religion and Politics in the Modern World,* New York University Press, 1983.

New Local Centers in Centralized States, University Press of America, 1985.

Political Violence and Terror: Motifs and Motivations, University of California Press, 1986.

(With Kay Lawson) *When Parties Fail—Emerging Alternative Organizations,* Princeton University Press, 1988.

The Federal Republic at Forty, New York University Press, 1989.

(With G. Smith and W. E. Paterson) *Developments in West German Politics,* Macmillan (London), 1989.

(With G. Smith, W. E. Paterson, and Stephen Padgett) *Developments in German Politics,* Macmillan (London), 1992.

(With Leonard Weinberg) *Encounters with the Radical Right: Western and Eastern Europe, Israel, and the U.S.,* Westview (Boulder, CO), 1993.

(With H. Fukui) *The Politics of Economic Change in Japan and West Germany,* Macmillan (London), 1993.

OTHER

Contributor of chapters and articles to books and journals in the United States and Germany, including *American Political Science Review* and *World Politics.*

WORK IN PROGRESS: Small Town in Bavaria; The Political Management of Economic Change in Postwar Japan and Germany, volume 2; *The Revival of Rightwing Extremism in the Nineties in Europe;* comparative studies of political violence and terrorism and the impact of single issue movements and protest on party systems; terrorism in Germany; German unification.

SIDELIGHTS: Peter H. Merkl told *CA* that he believes social scientists "have a special obligation to contribute to the understanding of our generation, both of itself and among other groups, nations, and civilizations."

BIOGRAPHICAL/CRITICAL SOURCES:

PERIODICALS

American Political Science Review, June, 1994.
Foreign Affairs, November/December, 1993.
New York Review of Books, October 26, 1967; January 13, 1994.

*　　　*　　　*

MERRILL, James (Ingram)   1926-1995

PERSONAL: Born March 3, 1926, in New York, NY; died of a heart attack February 6, 1995, in Tucson, AZ; son of Charles Edward (a stockbroker) and Hellen (Ingram) Merrill. *Education:* Amherst College, B.A., 1947.

ADDRESSES: Home—107 Water St., Stonington, CT 06378.

CAREER: Poet, novelist, and playwright. *Military service:* U.S. Army, 1944-45.

MEMBER: National Institute of Arts and Letters.

AWARDS, HONORS: Oscar Blumenthal Prize, 1947; Poetry magazine's Levinson Prize, 1949, and Harriet Monroe Memorial Prize, 1951; Morton Dauwen Zabel Memorial Prize, 1965, for "From the Cupola"; National Book Award in poetry, 1967, for *Nights and Days,* and 1979, for *Mirabell: Books of Number;* D.Litt., Amherst College, 1968; Bollingen Prize in Poetry, 1973; Pulitzer Prize, 1976, for *Divine Comedies; Scripts for the Pageant* was nominated for a National Book Critics Circle award, 1980.

WRITINGS:

POETRY

Jim's Book: A Collection of Poems and Short Stories, privately printed, 1942.
The Black Swan, Icarus (Athens), 1946.
First Poems, Knopf (New York City), 1951.
Short Stories, Banyan Press (Pawlet, VT), 1954.
The Country of a Thousand Years of Peace, Knopf, 1959, revised edition, Atheneum (New York City), 1970.
Selected Poems, Chatto & Windus (London), 1961.
Water Street, Atheneum, 1962.
Nights and Days, Atheneum, 1966.
The Fire Screen, Atheneum, 1969.
Braving the Elements, Atheneum, 1972.
Two Poems: From the Cupola and the Summer People, Chatto & Windus, 1972.
Yannina, Phoenix Book Shop (New York City), 1973.

The Yellow Pages: 59 Poems, Temple Bar Bookshop (Cambridge, MA), 1974.
Divine Comedies (includes "The Book of Ephraim"; also see below), Atheneum, 1976.
Metamorphosis of 741, Banyan Press (Chicago), 1977.
Mirabell: Books of Number (published as "Mirabell's Books of Number" in *The Changing Light at Sandover;* also see below), Atheneum, 1978.
Scripts for the Pageant (also see below), Atheneum, 1980.
The Changing Light at Sandover (contains "The Book of Ephraim," "Mirabell's Books of Number," "Scripts for the Pageant," and a new coda), Atheneum, 1982.
From the First Nine: Poems 1946-1976, Atheneum, 1982.
From the Cutting-Room Floor, University of Nebraska Press (Lincoln, NE), 1983.
Late Settings, Atheneum, 1985.
The Inner Room, Knopf, 1988.
Selected Poems, 1946-1985, Knopf, 1992.
A Scattering of Salts, Knopf, 1995.

NOVELS

The Seraglio, Knopf, 1957, reprinted, Atheneum, 1987.
The (Diblos) Notebook, Atheneum, 1965, reprinted, Dalkey Archive Press, 1994.

NONFICTION

Recitative: Prose, North Point Press (San Francisco), 1986.
A Different Person: A Memoir, Knopf, 1993.

PLAYS

The Immortal Husband, produced in New York, 1955, published in *Playbook,* New Directions (New York City), 1956.
The Bait, produced in New York, 1953, published in *Artists Theatre,* Grove (New York City), 1960.
The Image Maker: A Play in One Act, Sea Cliff Press (New York City), 1986.

CONTRIBUTOR TO ANTHOLOGIES

Poetry for Pleasure, edited by I. M. Parson, Doubleday (New York City), 1960.
Contemporary American Poetry, edited by Donald Hall, Penguin (New York City), 1962.
New Poets of England and America, edited by Hall, Meridian (New York City), 1962.
Poet's Choice, edited by Paul Engle and J. T. Langland, Dial (New York City), 1962.
Modern Poets, edited by J. M. Brinnin and Bill Read, McGraw (New York City), 1963.
Poems on Poetry, edited by Robert Wallace and J. G. Taaffe, Dutton (New York City), 1965.
Poems of Our Moment, edited by John Hollander, Pegasus (Indianapolis), 1968.

New Yorker Book of Poems, Viking (New York City), 1970.

OTHER

Contributor to *Hudson Review, Poetry,* and other periodicals. Some of Merrill's poetry has been translated into Greek.

SIDELIGHTS: The late James Merrill was recognized as one of the master poets of his generation. Merrill's work was praised for its elegance of style, its moral sensibilities, and its transformation of autobiographical moments into deep and complex poetry. Through a long and productive career, Merrill wrote plays, prose, and fiction, but the bulk of his artistic expression can be found in his poetry. His work won almost every important literary citation from the Pulitzer Prize to the Bollingen Prize and the National Book Award, and he was, according to *New York Times Book Review* essayist Peter Stitt, "one of the most cunning, elusive, thoughtful, challenging and rewarding poets writing." *New York Times* columnist Michiko Kakutani commended Merrill for his "mastery of various verse forms and conventions, his exquisite command of irony and wit . . . his achievement of a wholly distinctive voice—a voice that is cooly elusive as melting sherbet, poised and elaborate as a finely-wrought antique clock." *Washington Post Book World* contributor Joel Conarroe called Merrill "an extravagantly gifted artist . . . America's leading poet."

Since he began publishing poetry in 1951, Merrill has been recognized as a virtual master of poetic forms. He once explained in the *New York Review of Books* how he took "instinctively . . . to quatrains, to octaves and sestets, when I began to write poems." His earliest works reflect the gentility of his upperclass upbringing as well as his eloquence and wit. But for all their technical virtuosity, his early verses are largely static works, more concerned with objects than people. It was not until his themes became more dramatic and personal that he began to win serious attention and literary acclaim. Merrill received his first National Book Award in 1967 for *Nights and Days,* his second in 1979 for *Mirabell: Books of Number.* In the interim he won both the Bollingen Prize in Poetry and the Pulitzer Prize, the latter for a book of occult poetry called *Divine Comedies.*

Known in popular circles as "the Ouija poet"—one who composed with assistance from the spirit world—Merrill was always most popular with scholarly audiences. As Brigitte Weeks noted in the *New York Times Book Review,* "Mr. Merrill's artistic distinction is for the most part acknowledged, particularly in the academy, where he has already become part of the permanent canon. With his technical virtuosity and his metaphysical broodings, he is, like Wallace Stevens, an ideal seminar poet whose complex work lends itself to exhaustive explication."

Born into a fabulously wealthy New York family, James Merrill was privately educated in schools that placed a good deal of emphasis on poetry. His interest in language was also fired by his governess—a Prussian/English widow called Mademoiselle who was fluent in both German and French. She taught young James that English was merely one way of expressing things, while his parents encouraged his early efforts at verse. His first book of poems was privately printed by his father—co-founder of the famous stockbrokerage known as Merrill Lynch—during James's senior year at Lawrenceville.

When Merrill was twelve, his parents divorced, his governess was discharged, and he was sent to boarding school. The diary he kept during a subsequent vacation to Silver Springs, Florida, included what, in retrospect, would prove to be a revealing entry: "Silver Springs—heavenly colors and swell fish." Years later, in the *New York Review of Books,* Merrill explained how that statement reflected his feelings of loss and foreshadowed a major theme in his poetry. " 'Heavenly colors and swell fish.' What is that phrase but an attempt to bring my parents together, to remarry on the page their characteristic inflections—the ladylike gush and the regular-guy terseness? In reality my parents have tones more personal and complex than these, but the time is still far off when I can dream of echoing them. To do so, I see in retrospect, will involve a search for magical places real or invented, like Silver Springs or Sandover [an imaginary setting in his mystical trilogy *The Changing Light at Sandover*] . . . . By then, too, surrogate parents will enter the scene, figures more articulate than Mademoiselle but not unlike her, either, in the safe ease and mystery of their influence: Proust and Elizabeth Bishop; Maria [an old Athenian friend] and Auden in the Sandover books. The unities of home and world, and world and page, will be observed through the very act of transition from one to the other."

Such fusion of autobiography and archetype would become a hallmark of Merrill's verse, according to Andrew V. Ettin who wrote in *Perspective,* "The transformation of the natural, autobiographical, narrative events and tone into the magical, universal, sonorous, eternal is one of the principal characteristics of Merrill's poetry, perhaps the main source of its splendid and moving qualities." *Dictionary of Literary Biography* contributor William Spiegelman credited Merrill with discovering "what most lyric poets . . . have yet to find: a context for a life, a pattern for presenting autobiography in lyric verse through the mediation of myth and fable."

Influenced not only by events, but also by the act of writing, Merrill, "with increasing awareness, courage and delight, has been developing an autobiography: 'developing' as from a photographic negative which becomes increasingly clear," David Kalstone explained in the *Times Liter-*

ary Supplement. "He has not led the kind of outwardly dramatic life which would make external changes the centre of his poetry. Instead, poetry itself has been one of the changes, something which continually happens to him, and Merrill's subject proves to be the subject of the great Romantics: the constant revisions of the self that come through writing verse. Each book seems more specious because of the one which has come before."

While Merrill's verse abounds with details from daily life, Joseph Parisi noted in *Poetry* that it "never reeks of ego." Or, as Helen Vendler put it in the *New York Times Book Review,* the best of Merrill's poems "are autobiographical without being 'confessional': they show none of that urgency to reveal the untellable or unspeakable that we associate with the poetry we call 'confessional'. . . . It is as though a curtain had been drawn aside, and we are permitted a glimpse of . . . a life that goes on unconscious of us, with the narrator so perfectly an actor in his own drama that his presence as narrator is rendered transparent, invisible."

One of the ways Merrill achieved this stance was through the manipulation of meter and rhyme. "His mastery of forms, whether old or new, keeps his self-revelatory poems (and some of them are painful) from the worst lapses of recent poets of the confessional school," X. J. Kennedy observed in the *Atlantic Monthly.* "Merrill never sprawls, never flails about, never strikes postures. Intuitively he knows that, as Yeats once pointed out, in poetry, 'all that is personal soon rots; it must be packed in ice or salt.' "

Because they both wrote mystical poems, Yeats and Merrill have often been compared. Like Yeats, whose wife was a medium, Merrill believed he received inspiration from the world beyond. His *Divine Comedies* features an affable ghost named Ephraim who instructs the poet, while Yeats's "A Vision" features the spirit Leo Africanus in a similar role. Critics have found other influences at work in Merrill's poems as well, drawing parallels between his writing and the work of Dante (whose *Divine Comedy* was the inspiration for Merrill's title), W. H. Auden (who, like Merrill, believed that poems are constructed of words, not emotions), and Marcel Proust (who was also dismissed as a mere aesthete early in his career).

In a *Times Literary Supplement* review, David Kalstone further explained how Proust's vision colors Merrill's world. "When he turned to narrative and social comedy, it was always with the sense—Proust's sense—that the world discerned is not quite real, that in its flashing action he might catch glimpses of patterns activated by charged moments of his life." Spiegelman believed that as "an heir to Proust, Merrill achieves a scope in poetry comparable to that of the major novelists: his great themes are the recovery of time (in spite of loss) through willed or auto-

matic memory, and the alternating erosions and bequests of erotic experience. He focuses on what is taken, what abides, in love and time, and considers how to handle them."

In Merrill's early poems these concerns seldom surface. The verse of *First Poems* and *The Country of a Thousand Years of Peace and Other Poems* sometimes struck reviewers as needlessly obscure, devoid of human passion, and removed from actual life. In his *Babel to Byzantium,* James Dickey wrote that to read such poems is "to enter a realm of connoisseurish aesthetic contemplation, where there are no things more serious than gardens (usually formal), dolls, swans, statues, works of art, operas, delightful places in Europe, the ancient gods in tasteful and thought-provoking array, more statues, many birds and public parks, and, always, 'the lovers,' wandering through it all as if they surely lived." Writing of this kind, continued Dickey, "has enough of [Henry] James's insistence upon manners and decorum to evoke a limited admiration for the taste, wit, and eloquence that such an attitude makes possible, and also enough to drive you mad over the needless artificiality, prim finickiness, and determined inconsequence of it all."

In 1959, when Merrill began spending six months of each year in Athens, his poetry took on some of the warmth and intimacy of the old Greek culture. And, as the poems became more personal, they also became more accessible, although their appeal was still limited, as Ian Hamilton explained. "Even though (with Water Street in 1962) he had toughened and colloquialized his verse line and eliminated much of the wan artifice that marked his very early work, there was still—in his usual persona—a delicate strain of yearning otherworldliness, a delicate discomfiture which was neither neurotic nor ideological. His was a poetry of, and for, the few—the few kindred spirits," Hamilton wrote in the *Washington Post Book World.*

With each step he took away from rigid formalism, Merrill gained critical ground. Unwilling to restrict his choice and assembly of language, he nevertheless progressed toward a more conversational verse reminiscent of the structure of prose. "The flashes and glimpses of 'plot' in some of the lyrics—especially the longer poems—reminded Merrill's readers that he wanted more than the usual proportion of dailiness and detail in his lyrics, while preserving a language far from the plainness of journalistic poetry, a language full of arabesques, fancifulness, play of wit, and oblique metaphor," wrote Helen Vendler in the *New York Review of Books.* In fact, Merrill tried his hand at both plays and novels and considered writing his epic poem "The Book of Ephraim" as a prose narrative. He abandoned the idea, for reasons that he explains in the poem: "The more I struggled to be plain, the more / Mannerism hobbled me. What for? / Since it had never truly fit, why wear / The shoe of prose? In verse the feet went bare."

It was "The Book of Ephraim"—which appeared in *Divine Comedies*—that prompted many critics to reevaluate the poet. Among them was Harold Bloom, who wrote in the *New Republic:* "James Merrill . . . has convinced many discerning readers of a greatness, or something like it, in his first six volumes of verse, but until this year I remained a stubborn holdout. The publication of *Divine Comedies* . . . converts me, absolutely if belatedly, to Merrill. . . . The book's eight shorter poems surpass nearly all the earlier Merrill, but its apocalypse (a lesser word won't do) is a 100-page verse-tale, 'The Book of Ephraim,' an occult splendor in which Merrill rivals Yeats' 'A Vision,' . . . and even some aspects of Proust."

William Spiegelman described *Divine Comedies* as "Merrill's supreme fiction, a self-mythologizing within an epic program," he observed in the *Dictionary of Literary Biography*. "At last Merrill's masters combine with graceful fluency in a confection entirely his own: the reader finds Proust's social world, his analysis of the human heart and the artist's growth; Dante's encyclopedia of a vast universal organization; and Yeats's spiritualism, for which the hints in the earlier volumes gave only small promise. Added to these are the offhand humor of Lord Byron and W. H. Auden, a Neoplatonic theory of reincarnation, a self-reflexiveness about the process of composition, and a virtual handbook of poetic technique. 'The Book of Ephraim,' the volume's long poem, is chapter one of Merrill's central statement."

The two volumes that followed—*Mirabell: Books of Number* and *Scripts for the Pageant*—continue the narrative that "The Book of Ephraim" begins. Together these three poems form a trilogy that was published with a new coda in *The Changing Light at Sandover.* This unprecedented 560-page epic records the Ouija board sessions that Merrill and David Jackson, his lifelong companion, conducted with spirits from the other world.

Appropriately, Merrill organized each section of the trilogy to reflect a different component of their homemade Ouija board. The twenty-six sections of "The Book of Ephraim" correspond to the board's A to Z alphabet, the ten sections of *Mirabell: Books of Number* correspond to the board's numbering from 0 to 9, and the three sections of *Scripts for the Pageant* ("Yes," "&," and "No") correspond to the board's Yes & No. The progression of poems also represents a kind of celestial hierarchy, with each book representing communication with a higher order of spirits than the one before. Humans in the poem are identified by their initials—DJ and JM; spirits speak in all capitals. By the time Merrill transcribed the lessons of the archangels in book three, he offered nothing less than a

model of the universe. "Were such information conveyed to us by a carnival 'spiritual adviser,' we could dismiss it as mere nonsense," observed Fred Moramarco in the *Los Angeles Times Book Review,* "but as it comes from a poet of Merrill's extraordinary poetic and intellectual gifts, we sit up and take notice."

In the first book, Merrill's guide is Ephraim, "a Greek Jew / Born AD 8 at XANTHOS," later identified as "Our Familiar Spirit." Over a period of twenty years and in a variety of settings, Ephraim alerts DJ and JM to certain cosmic truths, including the fact that "on Earth / We're each the REPRESENTATIVE of a PATRON" who guides our souls through the nine stages of being until we become patrons for other souls. Witty, refined, full of gossip, Ephraim is "a clear cousin to Merrill's poetic voice," Kalstone said in the *Times Literary Supplement.*

Other spirits also appear in the poem, many of them family members or old friends who have died: Merrill's mother and father, the young poet Hans Lodeizen (whose death Merrill addressed in *The Country of a Thousand Years of Peace*), the Athenian Maria Mitsotaki (a green-thumbed gardener who died of cancer), as well as literary figures such as W. H. Auden and Plato. They form a community, according to Ephraim, "WITHIN SIGHT OF & ALL CONNECTED TO EACH OTHER DEAD OR ALIVE NOW DO YOU UNDERSTAND WHAT HEAVEN IS IT IS THE SURROUND OF THE LIVING." As Helen Vendler explained in the *New York Review of Books,* "The host receives his visible and invisible guests, convinced that . . . the poet's paradise is nothing other than all those beings whom he has known and has imagined." For this reason, Vendler maintained that "The Book of Ephraim" is "centrally a hymn to history and a meditation on memory—personal history and personal memory, which are, for this poet at least, the muse's materials."

Aware of the incredulity his spiritualism would provoke, Merrill addressed this issue early in book one: "The question / Of who or what we took Ephraim to be / And of what truths (if any) we considered / Him spokesman, had arisen from the start." Indeed, Vendler said, "for rationalists reading the poem, Merrill includes a good deal of self-protective irony, even incorporating in the tale a visit to his ex-shrink, who proclaims the evocation of Ephraim and the other Ouija 'guests' from the other world a *folie a deux* [mutual madness] between Merrill and his friend David Jackson."

In a *Poetry* review, Joseph Parisi suggested that Merrill used "his own doubt and hesitation to undercut and simultaneously to underscore his seriousness in recounting . . . his fabulous . . . message. Anticipating the incredulity of 'sophisticated' and even cynical readers, the poet portrays his own apparent skepticism at these tales from the spirit world to preempt and disarm the attacks, while making the reader feel he is learning the quasi-occult truths . . . along with the poet."

As the experience proceeded, Merrill's skepticism declined. And while the reader's may not, Judith Moffett suggested in the *American Poetry Review* that disbelief is not the issue: "Surely any literary work ought to be judged not on its matter but on the way the matter is presented and treated . . . The critical question, then, should be not Is this the story he ought to have told? but How well has he told this story?" Moffett, as well as numerous other critics, believed Merrill has told it very well: " 'The Book of Ephraim' is a genuinely great poem—a phrase no one should use lightly—and very possibly the most impressive poetic endeavor in English in this century."

In book two, Ephraim is overshadowed by a band of bat-like creatures who "SPEAK FROM WITHIN THE ATOM," demanding "POEMS OF SCIENCE" from JM. These are the fallen angels whose task is now to mind the machinery put in motion by God Biology, whose enemy is Chaos. Their request appears on the board: "FIND US BETTER PHRASES FOR THESE HISTORIES WE POUR FORTH / HOPING AGAINST HOPE THAT MAN WILL LOVE HIS MIND & LANGUAGE." As poet, Merrill serves as a vehicle for divine revelation, and, by tapping his "word bank," the bats can combat Chaos. They explain: "THE SCRIBE SHALL / SUPPLANT RELIGION, & THE ENTIRE APPARATUS / DEVELOP THE WAY TO PARADISE." At another point, Merrill learns that he was chosen to receive this vision in part because of his homosexuality: he will devote his energies not to children, but to art.

God Biology's chief messenger is a spirit initially identified as 741, who Merrill names Mirabell. Mirabell warns of the two major threats to man's existence: overpopulation and nuclear power. In passages that almost all critics consider elitist, Mirabell explains that there are only two million enlightened souls in the world. The rest are inferior animal souls who reproduce prolifically and into whose hands atomic weaponry now threatens to fall. Too little given to reason and restraint, these souls allow Chaos to gain ground.

While acknowledging that "one can see the intricate rationale of such statements in the context of Mirabell's general themes," Joseph Parisi maintains that readers "may be uncomfortable with the elitism which is implicit, and ultimately counterproductive, if indeed the poem pretends to enlighten and to teach. . . . For all the charm of Mirabell's small circle of friends, some may be put off by their blithe air of superiority, as others may be by the High Tea (not to mention Camp) atmosphere of the Heavenly get-

togethers." Stephen Spender agreed, pointing out in the *New York Review of Books* that "this reader sometimes feels that Merrill's heaven is a tea party to which he is not likely to be invited because he will not understand the 'in' jokes." Remarked Moffett: "By portraying intelligent poetic and musical gays as the evolutionary *creme de la creme,* Merrill makes himself vulnerable to charges of narcissism; the same could be said of passages in which heaven lavishes praise upon its spokesmen." But, "to be fair," concluded Edmund White, "I should point out that the fault lies not in Merrill, but in his bats; they are the ones who portray the hierarchical system. He is merely their scribe."

One of the duties of the bats, Merrill explained in the *Kenyon Review,* is to prepare David and he for "a seminar with the angels—whose 25 lessons are in fact the marrow of the third volume." While the poet here confronts essential questions about the mystery of creation, the structure of the universe, and the fate of man, some critics find the final message of *Scripts for the Pageant* in its organizing principle, "Yes & No." Charles Molesworth explained in the *New Republic* that, "taken serially, these three words form irreducible language acts, namely assertion, qualification, and denial. Taken all together, they form the essence of equivocation, which can be seen as either the fullest sort of language act or the very subversion of language." By characterizing his acceptance of the spirits' wisdom in terms of "Yes & No," Merrill "transforms the poem into a hymn celebrating, among other things, 'resistance' as 'Nature's gift to man,' " Mary Jo Salter wrote in the *Atlantic Monthly.* As the myth is reappraised and corrected by the characters who are themselves a part of it, Salter believed that " 'Yes & No' becomes an answer to every question: not an equivocation of authorial (or divine) responsibility, but an acknowledgement that 'fact is fable,' that the question of man's future, if any, is one he must answer for himself."

By the time *Scripts for the Pageant* ends, Merrill has made clear his vision of the self as a story that unfolds over time. During one lesson, the angels discuss two previous races of creatures who were destroyed. Afterwards, Merrill, to use Molesworth's words, "advances a set of parallels between the account of the two earlier races and his own childhood, as he was preceded by two siblings and his parents divorced while he was still a child. Autobiography and creation myth: by hinting they're the same Merrill deals with a key modernist, and a key American theme."

Molesworth concluded in the early 1980s: "Five years ago, Merrill hoped to be measured by Auden and Stevens; now his work asks comparison with that of Yeats and Blake, if not Milton and Dante. But the clearest analogue may be that of Byron, who, desiring a scale both intimate and grand, yet wanting a hero, decided to fill the role himself."

Merrill was one of the rare artists who, by virtue of his Merrill Lynch fortune, never needed to concern himself with making a living. His gratitude for that is reflected in his creation of the Ingram Merrill Foundation, a permanent endowment created for writers and painters. Merrill died of a heart attack in February of 1995 while vacationing in Tucson. He continued to write poetry and prose until his death and even published a memoir, *A Different Person,* in 1993. Many critics who eulogized Merrill accented the complexity of his style and world-view, but *New York Times Book Review* correspondent Carolyn Kizer commended the poet for another gift entirely. "Mr. Merrill is a great love poet," the critic concluded. "There have been so many breathtaking feats of prestidigitation before our busy eyes that this may have escaped our notice. But it's true. Most of his poems breathe with love. And that is another and even greater gift he has given us."

BIOGRAPHICAL/CRITICAL SOURCES:

BOOKS

Bloom, Harold, editor, *James Merrill,* Chelsea House (New York City), 1985.

Contemporary Literary Criticism, Gale (Detroit), Volume 2, 1974, Volume 3, 1975, Volume 6, 1976, Volume 8, 1978, Volume 13, 1980, Volume 18, 1981, Volume 34, 1988.

Dickey, James, *Babel to Byzantium,* Farrar, Straus, 1968.

Dictionary of Literary Biography, Volume 5: *American Poets since World War II,* Gale, 1980.

Dictionary of Literary Biography Yearbook 1985, Gale, 1986.

Kalstone, David, *Five Temperaments: Elizabeth Bishop, Robert Lowell, James Merrill, Adrienne Rich, John Ashbery,* Oxford University Press (New York City), 1977.

Lehman, David and Charles Berger, editors, *James Merrill: Essays in Criticism,* Cornell University Press (Ithaca, NY), 1982.

Yenser, Stephen, *The Consuming Myth: The Work of James Merrill,* Harvard University Press (Cambridge, MA), 1987.

PERIODICALS

American Poetry Review, September-October, 1979.
Atlantic Monthly, March, 1973; October, 1980.
Chicago Tribune Book World, December 17, 1978; April 24, 1983.
Los Angeles Times Book Review, February 13, 1983.
New Leader, December 4, 1978.
New Republic, June 5, 1976; November 20, 1976; July 26, 1980.

Newsweek, February 28, 1983.
New York Review of Books, May 6, 1971; September 20, 1973; March 18, 1976; December 21, 1978; May 3, 1979; February 21, 1982.
New York Times, January 29, 1983; May 29, 1985; September 15, 1993.
New York Times Book Review, September 24, 1972; March 21, 1976; April 4, 1976; April 29, 1979; June 15, 1980; March 13, 1983; November 12, 1984; September 1, 1985; December 12, 1993; May 22, 1995.
Partisan Review, winter, 1967.
Perspective, spring, 1967.
Poetry, June, 1973; October, 1976; December, 1979.
Publishers Weekly, February 27, 1995, p. 98.
Saturday Review, December 2, 1972.
Shenandoah, summer, 1976; fall, 1976.
Time, April 26, 1976; June 25, 1979.
Times Literary Supplement, September 29, 1972; October 28, 1977; January 18, 1980; May 22, 1987; December 2, 1988.
Village Voice, December 21, 1993.
Village Voice Literary Supplement, March, 1983.
Washington Post Book World, July 6, 1980; March 27, 1983; July 28, 1985; December 14, 1986.
Yale Review, winter, 1971; spring, 1975.

OBITUARIES:

PERIODICALS

New York Times, February 7, 1995.*

*   *   *

MEVES, Christa   1925-

PERSONAL: Born March 4, 1925, in Neumuenster, Germany; daughter of Carl and Else (Rohweder) Mittelstaedt; married Harald Meves (a doctor), December 18, 1946; children: two daughters. *Education:* Received degrees from University of Breslau, 1943, University of Kiel, 1948, University of Hamburg, 1949, and Psychotherapeutic Institute of Hannover and Goettingen, 1955. *Religion:* Catholic.

ADDRESSES: Home—Albertstrasse 14, 29525 Uelzen 1, Germany.

CAREER: Child psychotherapist in private practice, Uelzen, Germany, 1960—.

AWARDS, HONORS: Wilhelm Boelsche medal; Prix Amade; gold medal of Herderbuecherei; Niedersaechsischer Verdienstorden first class; Konrad-Adenauer prize; Bundesverdienstkreuz first class.

WRITINGS:

Die Schulnoete unserer Kinder: Wie Eltern ihnen vorbeugen und abhelfen koennen, Furche-Verlag, 1969, 17th edition, Guetersloher Verlagshaus Mohn, 1981, revised edition (with Dieter Guenter) *Neue Schulnoete,* Verlag Herder, 1990.

Mut zum Erziehen: Erfahrungen aus der psychagogischen Praxis, Furche-Verlag, 1970, reprinted as *Mut zum Erziehen: Seelische Gusundheit; Wie koennen wir sie unseren Kindern vermitteln?,* Gueterslohe Verlagshaus, 1976, revised edition, Verlag Herder, 1990.

Erziehen lernen aus tiefenpsychologischer Sicht (title means "Learning to Educate"), Bayrischer Schulbuch-Verlag, 1971, revised edition, 1973, reprinted as *Erziehen lernen aus tiefenpsychologischer Sicht: Ein Kursbuch fuer Ellern und Erzieher,* Herder-Verlag, 1985.

Verhaltensstoerungen bei Kindern (title means "Disorders in the Behavior of Children"), Piper-Verlag, 1971, revised edition, 1991.

Wunschtraum und Wirklichkeit (title means "Illusion and Reality"), Herder-Verlag, 1972.

Die Bibel antwortet uns in Bildern: Tiefenpsychologische Textdeutungen im Hinblick auf Lebensfragen heute, Herder-Verlag, 1973, translation by Hal Taussig published as *The Bible Answers Us with Pictures,* Westminster Press, 1977.

Ehe-Alphabet (title means "Alphabet of Marriage"; also see below), Herder-Verlag, 1973.

Ich will leben: Briefe an Martina; Probleme des Jugendalters (title means "I Want to Live!"), Verlag Weisses Kreuz, 1974.

Wer passt zu mir? Der Lebenspartner—Wahl oder Qual? (title means "Who Is Suited to Me?"), Verlag Weisses Kreuz, 1974.

Ninive darf nicht untergehen: Verantwortung fuer die Zukunft (title means "Ninive Must Not Die!"), Verlag Weisses Kreuz, 1977, revised edition published as *Europa darf nicht untergehen* (title means "Europe Must Not Die!").

Antrieb—Charakter—Erziehung: Werden wir ein Volk von Neurotikern? (title means "Shall We Become a Nation of Neurotics?"), Fromm-Verlag, 1977, 3rd revised edition, 1984.

Ich habe ein Problem: Lebensfragen junger Menschen, Verlag Weisses Kreuz, 1978, 5th edition, 1984.

(With Jutta Schmidt) *Anima-Verletzte Maedchenseele: Die Frau zwischen Verfremdung und Entfaltung,* Verlag Weisses Kreuz, 1979.

Kleines ABC fuer Seelenhelfer: Grundregeln fuer die Begegnung mit Ratsuchenden und Patienten, Herder-Verlag, 1980, 6th revised edition published as *ABC der Lebeusberatung,* Brunnen Verlag, 1992.

Unsere Kinder wachsen heran: Wie wir ihnen halfen koennen, Herder-Verlag, 1981, revised edition, 1985.

Das grosse Fragezeichen: Merkwuerdige Erlebnisse von Astrid, Andreas, Monika, Peter, Maria, Thomas und Alexander, Verlag Weisses Kreuz, 1981.

Das Geringste gilt: Ansprachen und Aufsaetze, Verlag Weisses Kreuz, 1981.

Problemkinder brauchen Hilfe: ABC der Verhaltensstoerungen fuer Eltern (also see below), Herder-Verlag, 1981.

Das Grosseltern-ABC: Was man wissen mus, um mit Kindern und Enkeln glueclich zu werden (also see below), Herder-Verlag, 1983.

Was unsere Liebe vermag: Eine Lebenskunde, Herder-Verlag, 1983, reprinted as *Was unsere Liebe vermag: Hilfe fuer bedraengte Eltern,* Herder-Verlag, 1984.

Der Mensch hinter seiner Maske: Aufsaetze zu seelischen Grundphaenomenen (title means "Men after Their Masks"), Verlag Weisses Kreuz, 1985.

Lebensrat von A-Z: Ehepartner, Kinder, Grosseltern (contains *Ehe-Alphabet, Grosseltern-ABC,* and *Problemkinder brauchen Hilfe*), Herder-Verlag, 1985, 5th edition, 1991.

Nusschalen im Ozean: Von der Hoffnung, ans Ufer zu kommen, Verlag Weisses Kreuz, 1985.

Ohne Familie geht es nicht: Ihr Sinn und ihre Gestaltung, Verlag Weisses Kreuz, 1985.

Aus Vorgeschichten lernen: Vom Massenelend vermeidbarer seelischer Erkrankungen, Herder-Verlag, 1985.

Plaedoyer fuer das Schamgefuehl: Und weilere aktuelle Beitraege, Verlag Weisses Kreuz, 1985.

Kraft, aus der Du leben kannst: Geburtstagsbriefe an die Enkel, Herder-Verlag, 1986, 4th edition, 1990.

Ermutigung zur Freude, Verlag Herder, 1987, 2nd edition, 1988.

Wurzeln des Glucks, Verlag Herder, 1987.

Positiv gesehen, Verlag Herder, 1987, 3rd edition, 1991.

Es geht um unsere Kinder, Brunnen Verlag, 1988, 2nd edition, 1989.

Der alte Glaube und die neue Zeit, Verlag Herder, 1988, 3rd edition, 1990.

Ein neues Vaterbild, Christiana Verlag, 1989.

Im Schutzmantel geborgen, Verlag Herder, 1989.

Glucklich ist, wer anders lebt, Verlag Herder, 1989.

Eltern-ABC, Verlag Herder, 1990.

Zeitloses Mab in maBloser Zeit, Verlag Herder, 1991.

Die Bibel hilft heilen, Verlag Herder, 1992.

Kurswechsel, Verlag Herder, 1992.

KindegmaBe Sexualerziehung, Verlag WeiBes Kreuz, 1992.

Wenn ihr werdet wie die Kinder, Verlag Herder, 1993.

Wahrheit befreit, Christiana Verlag, 1993, 2nd edition, 1994.

Alte Narben—neue Note, Verlag Herder, 1994.

(With A. Dillon) *Hochsommer*, Christiana Verlag, 1994.

Contributor of numerous articles to journals. Co-editor of weekly magazine, *Rheinischer Merkur* (title means "Rhenanian Gazette").

WORK IN PROGRESS: Verlog Wepes Kreut, a revised edition of *Unsere Kinder wachsen heran: Wie wir ihnen halfen koennen.*

SIDELIGHTS: Christa Meves told *CA:* "In the early 1960s, I proposed a new theory regarding the development of disorders in children's behavior, based on scientific experiments. In collaboration with Konrad Lorenz and Joachim Illies, both scientists at different Max Planck Institutes, I concluded that children being cared for under extremely unnatural circumstances would develop severe and irreversible psychic disorders, subsequently handicapping their adult lives. The results would be neurotic depression, manifested in eating disorders, drug addiction and/or criminal behavior.

"In view of the limited literature dealing with the psychic development of infants being nursed (breast-feeding six months at least!) and raised in non-traditional environments, I wrote my first book outlining my specific scientific theory, *Verhaltensstoerungen bei Kindern* ('Disorders in the Behavior of Children'). My next work dealt with conclusions drawn from my theories which were applicable to the practical education of children, *Erziehen lernen aus tiefenpsychologischer Sicht* ('Learning How to Educate from the Point of Depth-Psychology'). In subsequent years, I published numerous books as well as articles in various journals and magazines.

"The educational climate in West Germany during the late '60s and early '70s reflected a strong tendency towards a Marxist ideology, with a reluctant hostility towards 'old fashioned' family values in general. Despite this, or perhaps as a result of it, an increasing number of parents and teachers began to subscribe to my theories. During this same period, I also began publishing ten- and twenty-year projections of long term psychic disorders (also in sexual behavior) likely to result from abandonment of the traditional family values in nursing and raising infants.

"Psychic disorders have taken on epidemic proportions in almost all western industrialized nations, exactly as I had projected years ago. Despite this adverse development, no change has been forthcoming in the basic educational process, nor has there been a significant social shift back to traditional family values. Since this may, as well, reflect an increasing loss of faith, my most recent books and articles have delved deeper into theological as well as philosophical ramifications."

MICKIEWICZ, Ellen Propper 1938-

PERSONAL: Surname is pronounced Mits-*keh*-vich; born November 6, 1938, in Hartford, CT; daughter of George K. and Rebecca (Adler) Propper; married Denis Mickiewicz (a professor), June 2, 1963; children: Cyril. *Education:* Wellesley College, B.A., 1960; Yale University, M.A., 1961, Ph.D., 1965.

ADDRESSES: Home—205 Tadley Cr., Chapel Hill, NC 27514. *Office*—Department of Public Policy Studies, Duke University, Durham, NC 27708-0241.

CAREER: Yale University, New Haven, CT, lecturer in political science, 1965-67; Michigan State University, East Lansing, assistant professor, 1967-69, associate professor, 1969-73, professor of political science, 1973-80, associate professor in Computer Institute for Social Science Research, 1972-73, academic administrative intern in Office of Provost, 1976-77; Emory University, Atlanta, GA, dean of Graduate School of Arts and Sciences, 1980-85, professor of political science, 1980-88, director of international media and communications program, 1986-93; Duke University, Durham, NC, James R. Shepley Professor of public policy studies, 1994—, director of DeWitt Wallace Center for Communications and Journalism, Terry Sanford Institute of Public Policy, 1994—. Kathryn W. Davis Visiting Professor, Wellesley College, 1978; associate, Harvard University Russian Research Center, 1978; fellow, Carter Center, 1986—; director, Commission on Radio and Television Policy, 1990—. Founder and first chairman of the board of directors, Opera Guild of Greater Lansing.

MEMBER: International Studies Association (vice-president for North America, 1983—), American Political Science Association, American Association for the Advancement of Slavic Studies (vice-president and president-elect, 1986-87, president, 1987-88).

AWARDS, HONORS: Guggenheim fellowship, 1973-74; Sigma Xi grant, 1973-74; Ford Foundation grant, 1979-80; Markle Foundation grants, 1984-86; Rockefeller Foundation grant, 1986-87; W. Alton Jones Foundation grant, 1987-88.

WRITINGS:

Soviet Political Schools, Yale University Press (New Haven, CT), 1967.
(Editor and contributor) *Handbook of Soviet Social Science Data,* Free Press (New York City), 1973.
Media and the Russian Public, Praeger (New York City), 1981.
(Co-editor) *Soviet Calculus of Nuclear War,* Heath (Lexington, MA), 1986.
(Co-editor) *International Security and Arms Control,* Praeger, 1986.

Split Signals: Television and Politics in the Soviet Union, Oxford University Press (New York City), 1987.

(Co-author) *Television and Elections,* Aspen Center-Carter Center, Emory University (Atlanta), 1992.

(Co-author) *Television/Radio News and Minorities,* Aspen Center-Carter Center, Emory University, 1994.

Also contributor to books, including *Communication in International Politics,* University of Illinois Press, 1972. Contributor to Grolier's *Encyclopedia International,* 1969 and 1979. Contributor of articles and reviews to newspapers and journals, including *Corriere della sera, Journal of Communication, New York Times, Public Opinion Quarterly,* and *Slavic Review.* Editor of *Soviet Union,* 1980—.

*   *   *

MILLER, J(ames) P(inckney)   1919-

PERSONAL: Born December 18, 1919, in San Antonio, TX; son of Rolland James (a builder) and Rose Jetta (Smith) Miller; married Ayers Elizabeth Fite, May 16, 1942 (divorced, 1947); married Juanita Marie Currie, November 29, 1948 (divorced, 1962); married Julianne Renee Nicolaus, November 20, 1965; children: (first marriage) James Pinckney, Jr.; (second marriage) John R., Montgomery A.; (third marriage) Lia Marie, Anthony Milo, Sophie Jetta. *Education:* Rice Institute (now Rice University), B.A., 1941; studied drama at Yale University, 1946-47, and at American Theatre Wing, 1951-53. *Politics:* Democrat.

ADDRESSES: Home—Stockton, NJ.

CAREER: Worked as a professional boxer under the name Tex Frontier; began writing career by publishing poetry in small literary magazines; writer, *Philco TV Playhouse,* c. 1953-59; screenwriter and novelist, 1959—. President, Kingwood Enterprises, New York City, 1965—; has taught courses in creative writing. Chairman, New Jersey Motion Picture Commission, 1980-81. *Military service:* U.S. Navy, 1941-46; served in Pacific theater; became lieutenant; received Presidential Unit Citation and Purple Heart.

MEMBER: Dramatists Guild, PEN, Academy of Motion Picture Arts and Sciences, Authors Guild, Authors League of America, Writers Guild of America—West.

AWARDS, HONORS: Emmy Award for outstanding achievement in drama, Academy of Television Arts and Sciences, 1969, for teleplay *The People Next Door;* Mystery Writers of America awards, 1974, for *Your Money or Your Wife,* and Edgar Allan Poe Award, 1977, for television adaptation of the book *Helter Skelter;* Emmy Award

nomination for outstanding writing in a special program, Academy of Television Arts and Sciences, 1976, for *The Lindbergh Kidnapping Case,* Emmy Award nomination (with Cynthia Whitcomb), Academy of Television Arts and Sciences, 1989, for teleplay *I Know My First Name Is Steven.*

WRITINGS:

NOVELS

The Race for Home, Dial (New York City), 1968.
Liv, Dial, 1973.
The Skook, Warner Books (New York City), 1984.

FOR TELEVISION

The Rabbit Trap, Columbia Broadcasting System (CBS; also see below), 1954.
Days of Wine and Roses, CBS (also see below), 1958, Dramatists Play Service (New York City), 1973.
The People Next Door, CBS, 1968, Dramatists Play Service, 1969, Dell (New York City), 1970.
Your Money or Your Wife, CBS, 1972.
Helter Skelter (adaptation of the novel by Vincent Bugliosi, Jr.), CBS, 1976.
The Lindbergh Kidnapping Case, NBC, 1976.
Gauguin the Savage, CBS, 1980.
(With Cynthia Whitcomb) *I Know My First Name Is Steven,* National Broadcasting Company (NBC), 1989.

Also author of *Hide and Seek, Old Tasslefoot,* and *The Pardon-Me Boy,* all for CBS, and *The Preppie Killing* and *The Unwanted.*

FILM

The Rabbit Trap, United Artists, 1959.
(With Edward Anhalt) *The Young Savages,* United Artists, 1961.
Days of Wine and Roses, Warner Bros., 1962.
Behold a Pale Horse, Columbia, 1964.
The People Next Door, AVCO-Embassy, 1970.

OTHER

Author of plays *Is There Anybody There?* and *The Coleridge Clubs.* Contributor of short stories and poetry to periodicals.

ADAPTATIONS: Days of Wine and Roses was adapted as a novel by David Westheimer, Bantam Books (New York City), 1963.

SIDELIGHTS: Playwright and novelist J. P. Miller is best known as the author of the television play *Days of Wine and Roses.* Since it first aired on the *Philco TV Playhouse* in 1958, this dramatic portrayal of alcoholism has become an American drama classic; Miller went on to adapt his successful work into a motion picture in 1962 and wrote a modern adaptation of the 1950's drama for Broadway in the late 1980's.

Miller grew up on the Gulf Coast of Texas. After serving in the Navy during World War II, he enrolled in the Yale Drama School, determined to make it as a writer. He found a market for his work due to a demand for scripts generated by the new medium of live television during the 1950s. "I wrote my first successful script . . . an episode of 'Man Against Crime' for which I got $750," Miller told Rex Polier of the *Philadelphia Bulletin.* "I wrote all my plays for Fred Coe and *Philco TV Playhouse,* for which I got $1,300 per script, including 'Days of Wine and Roses.' "

When the golden age of television began its decline at the end of the decade, Miller made the switch to films; his screenplay adaptation of his teleplay, *Rabbit Trap,* in 1959 was quickly followed by the 1962 movie version of *Days of Wine and Roses,* which starred Jack Lemmon and Lee Remick. An emotion-filled exploration of alcoholism and its impact on people and their relationships, *Days* grew out of Miller's personal experience. "I was a big boozer myself at one time and went to a lot of AA meetings," Miller confided to Leslie Cross in the *Milwaukee Journal.*

As a successful screenwriter, Miller soon found himself uncomfortable with the Hollywood lifestyle. "It victimized me," he told Cross. "I'm a natural-born hedonist, and here I was inundated with big houses, swimming pools, starlets, 12-year-old scotch. It wasn't worth it." Miller turned his attention away from scripts and began writing novels. "When you write a book it's yours," he explained to Cross. "A script writer is a second banana to some director. You don't know what's going to happen to your story. I've been lucky in casting and so on, but after a while the situation just didn't appeal to me."

Miller's first novel, 1968's *The Race for Home,* was followed, in 1973, by *Liv,* a study of criminal psychology and prison reform. Inspired after learning about the brainwashing techniques used on American prisoners during the Korean War, Miller became intrigued about whether such methods could be used in more positive ways—to reform criminals. Miller's protagonist, a female psychologist named Liv, attempts to test such methods on a convict, with interesting results.

Miller explored a more imaginary genre with his next novel, *The Skook,* published in 1984. In it, a middle-aged builder is interrupted during one of his usual drinking and fishing trips to the Delaware River by a demon biker gang who wants to use him for a sacrifice. Escaping, he falls into a mysterious underground cave and is confronted by a character he created in the stories he once told his children. The "Skook", as described by *Globe & Mail* reviewer H. J. Kirchhoff, is "a dachshund-sized creature with short, bowed legs, wings, horns and a long curly tail." The novel's plot twists between elements of horror and everyday-life machinations in a yarn that Kirchhoff called "first and foremost a human story" and "not just another 'critter' book." Observing that the book could not "easily be categorised as fantasy, horror or realistic adventure," Kim Newman wrote in *New Statesman* that Miller's book is "essentially about the Hemingwayesque need to opt out of placid, job-of-work normality into a world of danger and adventure."

Despite his successes as a novelist, Miller has returned periodically to writing for television. A decade after the initial television success of *Days of Wine and Roses,* he won an Emmy Award for *The People Next Door,* which aired on a CBS revival of *Playhouse 90* in 1968. The drama, which starred David Greene, Eli Wallach, Deborah Winters, and Cloris Leachman, portrayed the relationships between two suburban families and explored the "generation gap" within each family, dealing in depth with the subject of drug-use.

The 1989 television drama *I Know My First Name Is Steven,* which Miller co-wrote with Cynthia Whitcomb, was based on the real-life abduction, in 1972, of seven-year-old Steven Gregory from Merced, California. It recounts Steven's seven-year psychological ordeal by captor Ken Parnell, who also sexually molested the boy until he escaped with another kidnapped youngster. Howard Rosenberg in the *Los Angeles Times* termed the drama "utterly grim and unrelenting" in its depiction of "a boy who had become psychologically dependent on the very man who abused him and stole him from his parents."

Miller once told *CA:* "Most of my reading, except for research, is in the poets. [I] like to believe all my writing has poetry in it." He echoed this sentiment in his interview with television critic Rex Polier: "I'm really a closet poet. The thing I enjoy most is to . . . write poetry which I know will never be published and never read by anybody but me."

BIOGRAPHICAL/CRITICAL SOURCES:

PERIODICALS

Globe & Mail (Toronto), October 6, 1984.
Los Angeles Times, May 22, 1989.
Milwaukee Journal, April 29, 1973.
New Statesman, July 18, 1986, p. 29.
New York Times, June 12, 1987.
Philadelphia Bulletin, April 1, 1976.*

MOIR, Alfred 1924-

PERSONAL: Surname is pronounced Moy-er; born April 14, 1924, in Minneapolis, MN; son of William Wilmerding (a physician) and Blanche (Kummer) Moir. *Education:* Harvard University, A.B., 1948, M.A., 1949, Ph.D., 1953; University of Rome, graduate study, 1950-52.

ADDRESSES: Home—51 Seaview Dr., Santa Barbara, CA 93108. *Office*—Department of History of Art and Architecture, University of California, Santa Barbara, CA 93106.

CAREER: Harvard University, Harvard College, Cambridge, MA, proctor, 1949-50; Tulane University, Newcomb College, New Orleans, instructor, 1952-54, assistant professor, 1954-59, associate professor of art history, 1959-63; University of California, Santa Barbara, associate professor, 1963-65, professor of art history, 1965-91, professor emeritus, 1991—, chairman of department, 1963-69, director of Education Abroad Program in Italy, 1978-80, adjunct curator of drawings, University Museum, 1985-93. Consultant, Isaac Delgado Museum of Art, New Orleans, 1954-57. Art historian in residence, American Academy in Rome, 1969-70, and 1980. *Military service:* U.S. Army, 1943-46; became master sergeant.

MEMBER: College Art Association, Society of Architectural Historians, Mediaeval Academy of America, Renaissance Society of America, Southern California Art Historians, Society of Fellows, American Academy in Rome, Italian Art Society, Ateneo Veneto.

AWARDS, HONORS: Fulbright fellow in Italy, 1950-51; honorary alumnus, Tulane University; named outstanding alumnus, the Blake School, Minneapolis, 1993.

WRITINGS:

The Italian Followers of Caravaggio, Harvard University Press (Cambridge, MA), 1967.

(Editor) *Seventeenth-Century Italian Drawings from the Collection of Janos Scholz,* University of California, 1973.

Caravaggio and His Copyists, College Art Association of America, 1975.

European Drawings in the Santa Barbara Museum of Art, [Santa Barbara, CA], 1976.

(Editor) *Regional Styles of Drawing in Italy,* [Santa Barbara], 1977.

Caravaggio, Abrams (New York City), 1982.

(Editor and contributor) *Old Master Drawings from the Feitelson Collection,* University of Washington Press (Seattle), 1983.

Van Dyck's Antwerp, Museum Plantin Moretus and Stedelijk Prentenkabinett (Antwerp), 1991.

Van Dyck, Abrams, 1994.

Contributor to books, including *Art in Italy, 1600-1700,* Detroit Institute of Arts (Detroit), 1965; editor of *Old Master Drawings from the Collection of John and Alice Steiner,* 1986. Contributor to art journals.

*   *   *

MOORE, Raymond S. 1915-

PERSONAL: Born September 24, 1915, in Glendale, CA; son of Charles David and Dorothy (Holcomb) Moore; married Dorothy Nelson, June 12, 1938; children: Dennis Raymond, Dorothy Kathleen (Mrs. Bruce D. Kordenbrock), Mari Toki-zaki-Lim (foster daughter). *Education:* Pacific Union College, A.B., 1938; University of Southern California, M.Ed., 1946, Ed.D., 1947. *Politics:* Independent. *Religion:* Seventh-Day Adventist.

ADDRESSES: Home—36211 South East Sunset View, Washougal, WA 98671. *Office*—Hewitt Research Foundation, P.O. Box 9, Washougal, WA 98671.

CAREER: Teacher at public schools in California, 1938-40, principal, 1940-41, superintendent, 1945-46; Pacific Union College, Angwin, CA, director of graduate studies and chairman, department of education and psychology, 1947-51; Nihon San-iku Gakuin College, Chiba-ken, Japan, president, 1951-56; Philippine Union College, Manila, president and graduate dean, 1956-57; Emmanuel Missionary College (now Andrews University), Berrien Springs, MI, chairman of department of education and psychology, 1957-60; Loma Linda University, Loma Linda, CA, vice president, 1960-62; Southwestern Union College, Keene, TX, president and professor, 1962-64; U.S. Office of Education, Washington, DC, graduate program officer, 1964-67; Hewitt Research Foundation, Washougal, WA, 1964-87; Moore Foundation, chairman, and chief executive officer, 1987—. Director of Seventh-Day Adventist church school system in Japan, 1951-56; coordinator of work-study committee, White House Conference on Children and Youth, 1960; executive vice president, Cedar Springs Foundation, 1964-69; director, Smithsonian Conference on Intercultural Education, 1967; executive director, Center for Advanced International Studies, Chicago, IL, 1967-69; co-director, First World Conference on Intercultural Education, 1968. Visiting professor, Southern Illinois University at Carbondale, 1967-68; adjunct professor, Andrews University, Berrien Springs, MI, 1970-83; lecturer, Western Michigan University, 1972-78, and Indiana University, 1978—; faculty member, University of Nevada National College of Juvenile and Court Judges, 1982—. Expert witness in more than forty trials in the United States and Canada. Consultant on higher education to numerous institutions, including the White House, U.S. Department of Education, and Japan Ministry of Education. *Military service:* U.S. Army, 1941-46; became major.

MEMBER: American Men of Science, Phi Delta Kappa.

AWARDS, HONORS: Commendation from Japanese imperial family, 1952, for work in distributive education and work-study programs; Philippines congressional commendation and presidential citation, 1957; citation from White House Conference on Children and Youth, 1960, for planning and coordination of work-study committees; commendation from International Academy for Preventive Medicine, 1975-76, for research in early childhood education; Phi Delta Kappa commendation, 1976, for distinguished service and leadership in education.

WRITINGS:

Science Discovers God, Fukuinsha, 1953, revised edition, 1978.

Michibiki, Review & Herald (Washington, DC), 1956.

China Doctor, Harper (New York), 1961, revised edition, Pacific Press Publishing Association (Mountain View, CA), 1969.

A Guide to Higher Education Consortiums: 1965-66, U.S. Government Printing Office, 1967.

Consortiums in American Higher Education: 1965-66, U.S. Government Printing Office, 1967.

(With wife, Dorothy N. Moore) *Better Late Than Early,* Reader's Digest Press (New York), 1975.

Adventist Education at the Crossroads, Pacific Press Publishing Association, 1976.

Balanced Education, Pacific Union College, 1976.

(With D. N. Moore and others) *School Can Wait,* Brigham Young University Press (Provo, UT), 1979.

(With D. N. Moore) *Exploring Early Childhood* (correspondence course), Home Study Institute, 1979.

(With D. N. Moore) *Home-Grown Kids* (sequel to *School Can Wait*), Word, Inc. (Irving, TX), 1981.

(With D. N. Moore, Penny Estes Wheeler, and others) *Homespun Schools: Teaching Children at Home—What Parents Are Doing and How They Are Doing It,* Word, Inc., 1982.

(With D. N. Moore, son Dennis R. Moore, daughter Kathleen Kordenbrock, and Jolene Oswald) *Homestyle Teaching: A Handbook for Parents and Teachers,* Word, Inc., 1984.

The Abaddon Conspiracy, Bethany House (Minneapolis, MN), 1985.

(With D. N. Moore) *Home Made Health,* Word, Inc., 1986.

(With D. N. Moore, D. R. Moore, and Kordenbrock) *Home Built Discipline,* Thomas Nelson (Nashville, TN), 1987.

Minding Your Own Business, Thomas Nelson, 1990.

The Successful Homeschool Family Handbook, Thomas Nelson, 1994.

Contributor to books, including *Religious Education,* edited by Marvin J. Taylor, Abingdon, 1961; *Emerging Strategies in Early Childhood Education,* edited by J. Wesley Little and Arthur J. Brigham, MSS Information Corporation, 1973; (with D. R. Moore and Moon) *Issues in Urban Education,* University Press of America, 1978; *Education Today,* edited by Wayne L. Wolf, Ginn & Company, 1979; and *Parents and Children,* Victor Books, 1986. Contributor to numerous journals, including *Education Record, School and Society, National Education Association Journal,* and *Journal of Teacher Education;* to professional journals in Japan, Philippines, Germany, and Australia; and to religious periodicals.

JUVENILE

(With D. N. Moore) *Guess Who Took the Battered-Up Bike: A Story of Kindness,* illustrated by Julie Downing, Thomas Nelson, 1985.

(With D. N. Moore) *Oh No! Miss Dent's Coming to Dinner,* illustrated by Downing, Thomas Nelson, 1985.

(With D. N. Moore) *Quit? Not Me! A Story of Dependability,* illustrated by Downing, Thomas Nelson, 1985.

WORK IN PROGRESS: A book on simple solutions to major problems in American education; articles on early childhood education; a book and tapes on parenthood education; inspirational books.

SIDELIGHTS: Raymond S. Moore once told *CA:* "I write because I believe this is the route of optimum influence. Sound writing also requires one to dig up essential facts and thus become better informed. My philosophy is that we should do less accommodating of trends that are tending to erode our society and face up to fundamental concepts that will rebuild our society." In 1964 he led a scientific expedition to Mt. Ararat in northeastern Turkey, which was jointly sponsored by the governments of the United States and Turkey. His first book, *Science Discovers God,* has been translated into Korean, Indonesian, and Turkish. Moore speaks some Japanese and Spanish.

Moore and his wife, Dorothy, are known as pioneers of the modern home school movement, an alternative education movement purported to have over a million students. Moore's research has been accepted by many American, Canadian, and overseas universities of Western and Oriental nations, and the Moore Foundation has more than three hundred research associates.

MOORHOUSE, Geoffrey 1931-

PERSONAL: Born November 29, 1931, in Bolton, Lancashire, England; son of William and Gladys (Hoyle) Heald (later Moorhouse); stepson of Richard Moorhouse; married Janet Murray, May 12, 1956 (divorced); married Barbara Jane Woodward, September 23, 1974 (divorced); married Marilyn Isobel Edwards, July 7, 1983; children: (first marriage) Ngaire Jane, Andrew Murray, Michael John, Brigid Anne (died 1981). *Education:* Attended Bury Grammar School, Lancashire, eight years. *Avocational interests:* "Music, walking in the hill country, looking at buildings, watching cricket and football."

ADDRESSES: Home—Park House, Gayle, near Hawes, North Yorkshire, England. *Agent*—Hilary Rubinstein, A. P. Watt & Son, 26-28 Bedford Row, London WC1R 4HL, England.

CAREER: Bolton Evening News, Bolton, Lancashire, England, reporter, 1952-54; *Auckland Star,* Auckland, New Zealand, sub-editor, 1954-57; *News Chronicle,* Manchester, England, sub-editor, 1957-58; *Manchester Guardian,* Manchester, deputy features editor, 1958-63; *Guardian,* London, England, chief features writer, 1963-70; freelance writer, 1970—. *Military service:* Royal Navy, 1950-52.

MEMBER: Royal Geographical Society (fellow), Royal Society of Literature (fellow), Lancashire County Cricket Club.

AWARDS, HONORS: Thomas Cook Travel Book Award, 1984, for *To the Frontier: A Journey to the Khyber Pass;* Cricket Society Award for *The Best-Loved Game: One Summer of English Cricket.*

WRITINGS:

The Other England, Penguin (London), 1964.
The Press, Ward, Lock (London), 1964.
Against All Reason, Stein & Day (Briarcliff Manor, NY), 1969.
Calcutta, Harcourt (London), 1971.
The Missionaries, Lippincott (London), 1973.
The Fearful Void, Lippincott, 1974.
The Diplomats, J. Cape (London), 1977.
The Boat and the Town, Little, Brown (Boston), 1979.
The Best Loved Game: One Summer of English Cricket, Hodder & Stoughton (London), 1979.
Prague, Time-Life Books (Alexandria, VA), 1980.
India Britannica, Harper (New York), 1983.
Lord's, Hodder & Stoughton, 1983.
To the Frontier: A Journey to the Khyber Pass, Hodder & Stoughton, 1984, Holt (New York), 1985.
Imperial City: The Rise and Rise of New York, Henry Holt (New York), 1988.
At the George (essays), Hodder & Stoughton, 1989.

Apples in the Snow: A Journey to Samarkand, Hodder & Stoughton, 1990.
On the Other Side: A Journey through Soviet Central Asia, Henry Holt, 1991.
Hell's Foundations, Henry Holt, 1992.
Om: An Indian Pilgrimage, Rupa (Calcutta), 1993.

SIDELIGHTS: British author Geoffrey Moorhouse is best known for his innovative travel writings. An editor and writer affiliated with various English newspapers for nearly two decades, he began publishing book-length accounts of his world travels in the 1960s. His research for *Against All Reason,* an investigation into monastic life, was "broad and unprecedented," according to a *New Yorker* reviewer. Results of the inquiry into what Catholic and Protestant monks and nuns think and hope were deemed "fascinating and touching, for the struggle of the human to reach the divine is painful, not invariably successful, but—for some, at any rate—inescapably alluring."

The Fearful Void describes Moorhouse's solitary crossing of the Sahara desert—2,000 miles by the most deadly route possible. Paul Theroux wrote of the account: "This man of fairly ordinary physical gifts . . . decided to put his fear to test and cross the Sahara by camel." Moorhouse "was near death by dehydration—the most painful death imaginable—several times; again and again, he wanted to abandon the whole enterprise and simply go home. . . . He is ingenuous enough to record how every setback and loss of temper reduced him almost to despair." Moorhouse did not reach his original objective of Luxor; "but while he is at pains to point out how ordinary he is and how he failed," Theroux noted, "his book is about achievement."

The Boat and the Town was the product of a year the author spent working as a deep-sea fisherman out of Gloucester, Massachusetts. Reviewing it in the *Sunday Telegraph,* Ronald Blythe commented, "His qualities as a writer derive partly from the hard-eyed look he gives to actuality, that direct intention of his to get all that is happening down on paper, and partly from a recognition that both facts and imagination are needed if one is dealing with another man's world. His books are a kind of documentary-plus . . . something more complex than good reporting."

Moorhouse has written several books about the subcontinent of South Asia. Reviewing one of them, *India Britannica,* for the *Washington Post Book World,* Valerie Fitzgerald suggested that "those familiar with Moorhouse's *Calcutta* will know that he has done more than produce just another coffee-table tome. It is, in fact, a compressed but thoroughly enlightened account of the British Raj, written with style and judgment . . . a miracle of considered choice, apt quotation and illuminating incident." Christopher Hicks, writing in *Newsday,* found the book "notable for its deep and exact sense of justice" and called it "a well-judged evocation of past days for our day."

In 1984's *To the Frontier: A Journey to the Khyber Pass,* Moorhouse recounts his trip across Pakistan in 1983. *Washington Post Book World* contributor John Kenneth Galbraith asserted that despite Moorhouse's care with details, his "eye for people and scene," and "a good ear for speech," his report is "an unduly casual introduction to the country, fragmentary and accidental." Philip Glazebrook commented in the *New York Times Book Review* that *To the Frontier* is, "on the whole, rapid, enjoyable journalism" but marred by its writer's confusion of purpose and lack of reflection. In the *Los Angeles Times,* however, Sharon Dirlam noted the author's "unflappable optimism" and "boundless curiosity" in the face of difficult traveling conditions. And Gene Lyons, writing for *Newsweek,* dubbed the travel writer "a diverting companion" and his book "a model of its kind."

Moorhouse moved from the stark drama of Pakistan to an urban stage in *Imperial City: The Rise and Rise of New York,* a collection of his observations on New York City. Wendy Smith wrote in the *Washington Post Book World,* "Perhaps only a foreigner could write about America's most controversial city with such lucid affection." In the *Times Literary Supplement,* reviewer David Hirson lauded Moorhouse for his "blessedly realistic" treatment, "an amalgam of personal reflections and historical research . . . as toughly critical as it is celebratory." Though Hirson faulted Moorhouse for sometimes being "panoramic at the expense of direction and balance," he acknowledged that the topic of New York City tempts writers generally to "err on the side of trying to do too much" and concluded by pronouncing Moorhouse's *Imperial City* "responsible, engaging, and humane."

Moorhouse again focused on his travels to Asia in *Apples in the Snow: A Journey to Samarkand,* published in 1990, and *On the Other Side: A Journey through Soviet Central Asia,* published in 1992. According to John Ure in the *Times Literary Supplement,* the former is less a travel narrative than a "series of set-piece essays about the various cities of the [Soviet] plains," blended with historical background on the places where Moorhouse was taken by his official escorts. Ure accorded the author "an honourable place" among the distinguished writers about this part of the world for doing best "the hardest thing of all: he writes with feeling and compassion about the soul of Mother Russia." Of *On the Other Side,* John Maxwell Hamilton of the *New York Times Book Review* credited Moorhouse for his ability to "summon up novelty even for those who may think they know a place well." Dirlam, however, believed that the author should have "departed from the

apolitical style of the National Geographic Society (which sponsored his trip) long enough to ask more probing questions of the locals" and thus get at the discontent that later erupted in strikes and ethnic rioting in the region.

"Sensitive and vibrant . . . social history of uncanny force" were Paul West's words in the *New York Times Book Review* for *Hell's Foundations,* Moorhouse's 1992 study of the mill town of Bury, Lancashire, after nearly 2,000 of the Lancashire Fusiliers died in the ill-conceived attack on Gallipoli, Turkey, in World War I. "Mr. Moorhouse's analysis of myths and mores in postwar Bury," West declared, "develops into a startling, luminous and humane study of how propaganda—elegiac and mesmeric—goes to work on the cannon fodder of the future."

Moorhouse's 1993 book *Om: An Indian Pilgrimage* chronicles his journey of enlightenment through southern India. Named for the sacred Hindu incantation, *Om* offers insights into the mystical nature of the Indian nation and further solidifies its author's reputation as a skilled travel writer.

BIOGRAPHICAL/CRITICAL SOURCES:

PERIODICALS

Chicago Tribune, October 18, 1988.
Los Angeles Times, August 11, 1985.
Los Angeles Times Book Review, April 28, 1991.
Newsday, August 7, 1983.
New Statesman, April 25, 1969.
Newsweek, June 3, 1985, p. 75.
New Yorker, July 5, 1969.
New York Times, February 18, 1972; July 26, 1983.
New York Times Book Review, June 16, 1985; June 9, 1991; June 28, 1992, p. 13; October 18, 1992, p. 52; July 18, 1993, p. 24.
Observer (London), July 18, 1993, p. 58; September 26, 1993, p. 19; September 11, 1994, p. 25.
Sunday Telegraph (London), March 25, 1979.
Times (London), May 12, 1983; October 20, 1983; April 7, 1988.
Times Literary Supplement, April 15, 1983; June 3, 1988; February 1, 1991; May 8, 1992.
Washington Post Book World, March 26, 1974; August 14, 1983, p. 4; March 24, 1985; September 11, 1988.*

* * *

MORGAN, Edmund S(ears) 1916-

PERSONAL: Born January 17, 1916, in Minneapolis, MN; son of Edmund Morris (a professor of law) and Elsie (maiden name, Smith) Morgan; married Helen Mayer (a historian), June 7, 1939; married Marie Caskey, June 22,

1983; children: (first marriage) Penelope, Pamela. *Education:* Harvard University, A.B., 1937, Ph.D., 1942; London School of Economics, University of London, graduate study, 1937-38.

ADDRESSES: Home—244 Livingston St., New Haven, CT 06511. *Office*—Department of History, Yale University, New Haven, CT 06520.

CAREER: Massachusetts Institute of Technology, Cambridge, instrument maker in Radiation Laboratory, 1942-45; University of Chicago, Chicago, IL, instructor in social sciences, 1945-46; Brown University, Providence, RI, assistant professor, 1946-49, associate professor, 1949-51, professor of history, 1951-55; Yale University, New Haven, CT, professor of history, 1955-65, Sterling Professor of History, 1965-86, professor emeritus, 1986—. Johnson Research Professor, University of Wisconsin, 1968-69. Member of council, Institute of Early American History and Culture, 1953-56, 1958-60, and 1970-72; trustee of Smith College, 1984-89.

MEMBER: Society of American Historians, American Antiquarian Society, Organization of American Historians (president, 1971-72), American Philosophical Society, American Academy of Arts and Sciences, Connecticut Academy of Arts and Sciences, Massachusetts Historical Society, Colonial Society of Massachusetts, British Academy, Royal Historical Society.

AWARDS, HONORS: Research fellow, Huntington Library, 1952-53; William Clyde DeWane Medal, 1971; Douglass Adair Memorial Award, 1972; Bruce Catton Award, 1992; honorary degrees from Rutgers University, Brown University, Colgate University, Washington College, William and Mary, University of New Haven, and Williams College.

WRITINGS:

The Puritan Family: Religion and Domestic Relations in Seventeenth-Century New England, Boston Public Library (Boston, MA), 1944, new edition, Harper (New York), 1966.
Virginians at Home: Family Life in the Eighteenth Century, Colonial Williamsburg (Williamsburg, VA), 1952.
(With wife, Helen M. Morgan) *The Stamp Act Crisis: Prologue to Revolution,* University of North Carolina Press (Chapel Hill), 1953, revised edition, Collier (New York), 1963, third edition, University of North Carolina Press, 1994.
The Birth of the Republic, 1763-89, University of Chicago Press (Chicago, IL), 1956, third edition, 1992.
The Puritan Dilemma: The Story of John Winthrop, Little, Brown (Boston), 1958.

The American Revolution: A Review of Changing Interpretations, Service Center for Teachers of History (Washington, D.C.), 1958.
The Gentle Puritan: A Life of Ezra Stiles, 1727-1795, Yale University Press (New Haven, CT), 1962, reissued, Norton (New York), 1984.
(With others) *The National Experience: A History of the United States,* Harcourt (New York), 1963.
Visible Saints: The History of a Puritan Idea, New York University Press (New York), 1963.
(With others) *The Emergence of the American,* Educational Services, 1965.
Roger Williams: The Church and the State, Harcourt (New York), 1967.
So What about History?, Atheneum (New York), 1969.
American Slavery, American Freedom: The Ordeal of Colonial Virginia, Norton, 1975.
The Challenge of the American Revolution, Norton, 1976.
The Meaning of Independence: John Adams, George Washington, and Thomas Jefferson, University Press of Virginia (Charlottesville), 1976.
The Genius of George Washington, Norton, 1980.
Inventing the People: The Rise of Popular Sovereignty in England and America, Norton, 1988.

EDITOR

Prologue to the Revolution: Sources and Documents on the Stamp Act Crisis, 1764-1766, University of North Carolina Press, 1959.
The Founding of Massachusetts: Historians and the Sources, Bobbs-Merrill (Indianapolis, IN), 1964.
The American Revolution: Two Centuries of Interpretation, Prentice-Hall (Englewood Cliffs, NJ), 1965.
Puritan Political Ideas, 1558-1794, Bobbs-Merrill, 1965.
The Diary of Michael Wigglesworth, 1653-1657: The Conscience of a Puritan, Harper, 1965.

OTHER

Contributor to *The Mirror of the Indian,* Associates of the John Carter Brown Library, 1958. Author of introduction to *Paul Revere's Three Accounts of His Famous Ride,* Massachusetts Historical Society, 1961, 2nd edition, 1968. Also contributor of articles and reviews to historical journals. Member of editorial board, *New England Quarterly.*

SIDELIGHTS: Described by Michael Kammen in the *Washington Post Book World* as "one of the most distinguished historians of the United States," Edmund S. Morgan is the author of over fifteen books that have challenged traditional assumptions about the forces that shaped early American history, including the lives and beliefs of the Puritans and the impetus for the Revolutionary War. With works such as *The Stamp Act Crisis: Prologue to Revolution, The Puritan Dilemma: The Story of John Winthrop,* and *Inventing the People: The Rise of Popular*

Sovereignty in England and America, Morgan has earned a reputation as an historian of people as well as of ideas, and as a writer of wide appeal.

Much of Morgan's acclaim has resulted from not only his ideas, but also his attention to the lives of human beings. In an essay for the *Dictionary of Literary Biography,* William D. Liddle explained that "Morgan's writings generally exhibit an affinity for people, a preoccupation with the details of their daily lives, and a concern for even the most mundane events and experiences when they touch upon things human. Attracted to the concrete and averse to abstractions, Morgan traces the history of ideas in their specific settings." In the opinion of Pauline Maier in the *New York Times Book Review,* he is "a man with a rare gift for telling the story of the past simply and elegantly without sacrificing its abundant complexity." Morgan has been able to reach wide audiences "by writing in language distinguished by simplicity, precision, grace, and wry humor. To achieve clarity and resonance he assumes that his audience is brighter than he is but completely ignorant of his subject and therefore dependent on the information he makes available. With Morgan, this is a formula for writing remarkable history," Liddle asserted. Because of this, Morgan's work appeals to audiences as diverse as Harvard scholars and the junior high school students who have read his *So What about History?*

Morgan's ideas have sparked lively debates for more than forty years. "The intellectual history of the American Revolutionary era was rewritten by scholars who followed the path marked out by Edmund S. Morgan," Liddle noted. For Liddle, Morgan's achievement is singular because the historian has never made such an influence his goal. "There is no 'Morgan thesis' on the American Revolution or on any other subject, and there is no 'Morgan school' either," Liddle added. "As he never became a disciple, so he never sought disciples."

Morgan's influence has been particularly strong in the study of the early Puritans, the subject of the historian's first book, *The Puritan Family: Essays on Religion and Domestic Relations in Seventeenth-Century New England,* published in 1944, and of many that followed. "Rarely have the Puritans emerged from modern scholarship as more human figures than in these writings," Liddle claimed. Liddle called *The Puritan Dilemma: The Story of John Winthrop,* first published in 1958, "a beautifully written volume," later adding: "Perhaps the book's most conspicuous and characteristic feature is the human touch with which its author treats complex beliefs and ideas."

Morgan returned to America's earlier history in his 1962 biography, *The Gentle Puritan: A Life of Ezra Stiles, 1727-1795,* a work that illuminates the man whose writings Morgan had often used as source material for his own. For historians, Maier wrote, the book is "the inside favorite" among Morgan's works. In 1963, he published *Visible Saints: The History of a Puritan Idea,* which explained Puritan thought in the light of their policies toward church membership.

Morgan's writings on the Revolutionary War are considered integral to an understanding of the early United States. Among those books considered most important is *The Stamp Act Crisis: Prologue to Revolution,* written with Morgan's first wife, Helen M. Morgan, and published in 1953. Using a method that Liddle noted "has been described as seeking 'historical objectivity through cumulative partiality,'" Morgan looks at what had not previously been considered a significant British/colonist conflict in the instigation of the American Revolution, the Stamp Act, and reveals its importance through the eyes of six of its major figures. In this respect, Morgan's methods are considered revolutionary as well.

American Slavery, American Freedom: The Ordeal of Colonial Virginia is, in Liddle's opinion, "arguably Morgan's most important book; it is unquestionably his most controversial work." The book argues that it was the practice of owning slaves that spurred Virginians to want to be free of the British, in turn paving the way for revolution. "When Virginians became remarkably eloquent about the threat of 'slavery' and the danger to their 'liberties' in new British measures of the 1760s and 1770s, Morgan saw in their rhetoric a vital link between the very real freedom they enjoyed, the bondage they imposed on others, and 'a conglomeration of republican ideas' from which the ideology of Revolution was drawn," Liddle explained. Maier admired the "hilarious comparison of Indians with the barbarous Englishmen of 17th century Virginia," and wrote that the book "will delight anyone with a taste for the human comedy and good writing."

In *The Genius of George Washington,* published in 1980, Morgan's analysis of the first president is backed up by excerpts from his subject's own letters. According to the *Atlantic Monthly,* Morgan's thesis is that Washington's true acumen lay in his "superb understanding of power," a side of the first president that had not previously been widely explored, and one that is reinforced by Washington's personal correspondence.

Morgan's *Inventing the People: The Rise of Popular Sovereignty in England and America* received a great deal of attention from critics and colleagues alike. Morgan's study of what he describes as the "political fictions" behind the notion of government by representation, *Inventing the People* argues that it was James Madison's fear of diversity leading to division that led him to "invent" the "fiction" of the "one people" upon which the U.S. Constitution is based. Samuel H. Beer commented in the *New Republic* that the problem was one of size: "On the one hand, as Morgan observes, the country was already so far united that its government had to be conducted [in Morgan's words], 'in terms of a whole continent.' On the other hand, because of the weakness of the federal authority under the Articles of Confederation, the forces of localism dominated at the center as well as the periphery. How to overcome localism, [Morgan] says, was 'the central problem' confronting the aspiration for self-government." According to Kammen, the power of the book is that it explores the roots of "American notions concerning governmental power: where it actually lies, where we prefer to *believe* it ultimately resides and how the relationship between those two—fact and fiction—shapes our perception of political representation." As such, *Inventing the People* provoked a wide range of responses.

Reactions to the ideas advanced in *Inventing the People* were mixed. In the *New York Review of Books*, Keith Thomas contended that Morgan neglects to consider several other historical examples (including the French Revolution) of the developments of the same 'fictions' that Morgan considers peculiar to the birth of the United States. However, Thomas wrote that when Morgan leaves off what the critic sees as the author's dependence on the work of other historians, he "puts forward original arguments of his own. In a series of brilliant chapters he probes the myths that sustained eighteenth-century American notions of liberty, and he reveals in each case the huge gulf between the high-sounding platitudes and the brutal realities of political life." Kammen called *Inventing the People* "a creative synthesis of considerable significance." Despite concerns that the historian may have overstated the extent to which colonists were devoted to the idea of equality at the time of the Revolution, Kammen assessed that Morgan has "made a penetrating contribution to our understanding of the origins of American political culture."

BIOGRAPHICAL/CRITICAL SOURCES:

BOOKS

Dictionary of Literary Biography, Volume 17: *Twentieth-Century American Historians,*, Gale, 1983.

PERIODICALS

Atlantic Monthly, May, 1981, p. 81.
Los Angeles Times Book Review, March 13, 1988, p. 4.
New England Quarterly, June, 1994, p. 202.
New Republic, August 1, 1988, p. 49.
New York Review of Books, November 24, 1988, p. 43.
New York Times, June 28, 1965.
New York Times Book Review, July 3, 1988, p. 10.
Spectator, December 24, 1988, p 70.
Washington Post Book World, April 24, 1988, p. 7.

Yale Review, winter, 1969.*

—*Sketch by Heather Aronson*

* * *

MORRIS, Julian
See WEST, Morris L(anglo)

* * *

MORRISON, Dorothy Nafus

PERSONAL: Born in Nashua, IA; daughter of Roy A. (a merchant) and Edwinna (a teacher of Latin and German; maiden name, Bolton) Nafus; married Carl V. Morrison (a psychiatrist), April 25, 1936 (deceased, 1980); married Robert C. Hunter (an attorney), 1981 (deceased, 1993); children: (first marriage) James, Anne (Mrs. John Feighner), David, John. *Education:* Attended University of Northern Iowa; University of Iowa, B.A.

ADDRESSES: Home—17000 Southwest Nafus Lane, Beaverton, OR 97007.

CAREER: Music teacher in public schools in Iowa; teacher of stringed instruments in public schools in Beaverton, OR, 1954-66; writer, 1965—.

WRITINGS:

JUVENILE FICTION

The Mystery of the Last Concert, Westminster (Philadelphia), 1971.
Whisper Goodbye, Atheneum (New York City), 1985.
Somebody's Horse, Atheneum, 1986.
Whisper Again, Atheneum, 1987.
Vanishing Act, Atheneum, 1989.

NONFICTION

(With husband, Carl V. Morrison) *Can I Help How I Feel?,* Atheneum, 1976.
Ladies Were Not Expected: Abigail Scott Duniway and Women's Rights, Atheneum, 1977.
The Eagle and the Fort: The Story of John McLoughlin, Atheneum, 1978.
Chief Sarah: Sarah Winnemucca's Fight for Indian Rights, Atheneum, 1980.
Under a Strong Wind: The Adventures of Jessie Benton Fremont, Atheneum, 1983.
Oregon, Macmillan (New York City), 1991.

OTHER

Contributor to books, including *Writing to Inspire,* edited by William Gentz, Writer's Digest (Cincinnati), 1982.

Morrison's books have been translated into German and Danish.

WORK IN PROGRESS: An adult biography.

SIDELIGHTS: Dorothy Nafus Morrison once told *CA:* "I started writing when I was eight years old, with a 'novel' laid in a West I had never seen. Years later, when I moved to this area, I felt I had at last come to the place where I belonged.

"In several of my books I tried to picture the rich history of this area by writing biographies of its important citizens. I wrote about the fur trade, the Oregon trail, the heroic efforts to promote migration to the West, the growth of women's rights, the fight for Indian rights, and the gold rush. These were exciting events, which happened to real people. In exploring them I visited the places where they occurred, and made extensive use of primary sources, such as letters and journals. Rather than invent scenes or dialogue, I quoted brief passages from my subjects' own writings.

"When I moved into fiction, I continued to write about the Northwest. I have laid two novels in the Columbia Gorge, one concerned with the problems which a high dam can cause when it floods a town, the other hinging on Indian petroglyphs. A third book takes place on a Wyoming ranch, and another is about the Oregon Coast.

"One of the bonuses of writing is the focus it gives for travel. Besides doing research in Oregon, I have spent time on a Wyoming ranch, in the Mother Lode country of California, around Pyramid Lake in Nevada, in many parts of the state of Washington, and the fur country of Canada, especially that around Thunder Bay. I hope my books will stir young readers to greater understanding of the country in which they live, and of the people who helped it grow."

BIOGRAPHICAL/CRITICAL SOURCES:

PERIODICALS

School Library Journal, November, 1977; September, 1979; November, 1980; November, 1983; May, 1985.

N

NASH, Ronald H. 1936-

PERSONAL: Born May 27, 1936, in Cleveland, OH; son of Herman and Violet (Pankratz) Nash; married Betty Jane Perry, June 8, 1957; children: Jeffrey Alan, Jennifer Anne. *Education:* Barrington College, A.B., 1958; Brown University, M.A., 1960; Syracuse University, Ph.D., 1964. *Politics:* Republican. *Religion:* Baptist.

ADDRESSES: Office—Reformed Theological Seminary, P.O. Box 945120, Maitland, FL 32794.

CAREER: Barrington College, Barrington, RI, instructor in philosophy, 1958-60; Houghton College, Houghton, NY, instructor in philosophy, 1960-62; Syracuse University, Syracuse, NY, instructor in philosophy, 1963-64; Western Kentucky University, Bowling Green, began as associate professor, became professor of philosophy, 1964-91; Reformed Theological Seminary, Orlando, FL, professor of philosophy, 1991—. Served two terms as advisor to U.S. Commission on Civil Rights; served five years as baptist minister in churches in Penn Yan, NY, and Fall River, MA; has lectured in Great Britain, Russia, and the Ukraine.

WRITINGS:

Dooyeweerd and the Amsterdam Philosophy, Zondervan (Grand Rapids, MI), 1962.
The New Evangelicalism, Zondervan, 1963.
The Light of the Mind: St. Augustine's Theory of Knowledge, University of Kentucky Press, 1969.
Freedom, Justice, and the State, University Press of America (Lanham, MD), 1980.
The Concept of God, Zondervan, 1983.
Evangelicals in America, Abingdon, 1987.
Faith and Reason, Zondervan, 1988.
The Closing of the American Heart, Probe, 1990.

Social Justice and the Christian Church, University Press of America, 1992.
The Gospel and the Greeks, Probe, 1992.
The Word of God and the Mind of Man, Zondervan, 1992.
Christian Faith and Historical Understanding, Probe, 1992.
Beyond Liberation Theology, Baker, 1992.
Great Divides, NavPress (Colorado Springs, CO), 1993.
Is Jesus the Only Savior, Zondervan, 1994.
Choosing a College, Summit (New York City), 1995.

EDITOR

The Philosophy of Gordon H. Clark: A Festschrift, Presbyterian & Reformed, 1968.
Ideas of History, Dutton (New York City), 1969.
The Case for Biblical Christianity, Eerdmans (Grand Rapids, MI), 1969.
Liberation Theology, Mott, 1984.
Process Theology, Baker, 1987.
Evangelical Renewal in the Mainline Churches, Crossway (Westchester, IL), 1987.

Contributor of numerous articles to periodicals. Also contributing editor to *The Freeman.*

*   *   *

NELSON, Geoffrey K(enneth) 1923-

PERSONAL: Born August 8, 1923, in Dereham, Norfolk, England; son of William John (a malthouse fireman) and Florence (Pitcher) Nelson; married Irene Griggs, July 31, 1955; children: Elizabeth, Christopher, Rosemary, David. *Education:* University of Liverpool, certificate in social science, 1950; Shoreditch College of Education, teacher's certificate, 1954; University of London, B.Sc., 1958, M.Sc., 1961, Ph.D., 1967.

ADDRESSES: Home—32 Clun Rd., Birmingham B31 1NU, England. *Office*—School of Sociology, University of Central England, Birmingham, England.

CAREER: Westwood School, March, Cambridgeshire, England, teacher, 1956-62; Bournville College, Birmingham, England, assistant lecturer in sociology, 1962-64; Birmingham Polytechnic, Birmingham, England, lecturer, 1964-69, senior lecturer, 1969-75, principal lecturer in sociology, 1975-88; University of Central England, Birmingham, honorary research fellow, 1988—. Part-time tutor, Wolsey Hall, Oxford, 1961—. Visiting lecturer, department of theology, University of Birmingham. Honorary fellow, Institute for the Study of Worship and Religious Architecture, University of Birmingham, 1969-80; sociological advisor, Parliamentary group on video violence and children, 1980-84. Has been employed in social work, agriculture, and civil service. *Military service:* Home Guard, 1940-45.

MEMBER: British Sociological Association, American Sociological Association, Society for the Scientific Study of Religion, British Association for the Advancement of Science (secretary of sociology section, 1968-80), University of London Convocation (chair of West Midland branch, 1967-82), Worcestershire Nature Conservation Trust.

WRITINGS:

Spiritualism and Society, Schocken and Routledge, 1969.
(With Rosemary A. Clews) *Mobility and Religious Commitment,* University of Birmingham, 1971.
(Contributor) A. Bryman, editor, *Religion in the Birmingham Area,* University of Birmingham, 1975.
History of Modern Spiritualism, Spiritualists' National Union, 1976.
Cults, New Religions and Religious Creativity, Routledge & Kegan Paul (London), 1987.
To Be a Farmer's Boy, Alan Sutton (Gloucester), 1991.
Countrywomen on the Land, Alan Sutton, 1992.
Seen and Not Heard, Alan Sutton, 1993.
Over the Farmyard Gate, Alan Sutton, 1995.

POETRY

Butterfly's Eye, G. K. Nelson, 1980.
A Poet's Reading, G. K. Nelson, 1980.
Caught in the Net, Envoi Poets (Dyfed), 1994.

Also author, with C. Hill and others, of *Video: Violence and Children* (a report of the Parliamentary Group Video Enquiry), 1984. Contributor to sociology journals and religion journals, including *British Journal of Sociology, Sociological Review, Journal for the Scientific Study of Religion, Review of Religious Research, Social Compass, Sociology and Social Research,* and *Reviewing Sociology;* contributor of articles on local history, religion, and natural history to newspapers and popular magazines, including *New Knowledge and Man, Myth,* and *Magic;* contributor of poetry to numerous magazines.

WORK IN PROGRESS: Study of influence of psychic and mystical factors on the rise of religion; east anglian country life; poetry.

SIDELIGHTS: Geoffrey K. Nelson told *CA:* "After a life devoted to teaching research and scholarship in sociology, which has been interspersed by the writing of poetry, I have broadened my literary work to include rural social history and wildlife. Those familiar with my work will detect a consistent attempt to synthesize poetry, mysticism, and science in the understanding of life and will consequently appreciate my interest in the psychic and mystical influences on religion."

BIOGRAPHICAL/CRITICAL SOURCES:

BOOKS

Yinger, J. Milton, *The Scientific Study of Religion,* Macmillan, 1970.

PERIODICALS

Times Literary Supplement, June 26, 1969.

*   *   *

NEWBOUND, Bernard Slade 1930-
(Bernard Slade)

PERSONAL: Born May 2, 1930, in St. Catharines, Ontario, Canada; came to United States, 1963; son of Fred (a mechanic) and Bessie (maiden name, Walbourne) Newbound; married Jill Foster Hancock (an actress), July 25, 1953; children: Laurel, Christopher. *Education:* Educated in England and Wales. *Religion:* "None." *Avocational interests:* Tennis.

ADDRESSES: Home—11500 San Vicente Blvd. Apt. 204, Los Angeles, CA 90049; and Flat 3, 4 Egerton Place, London, S.W.3, England. *Agent*—Jack Hutto, 405 West 23rd St., New York, NY 10011.

CAREER: Writer. Worked as an actor in more than two hundred stage productions in Ontario, 1949-57; television writer for Columbia Pictures, Los Angeles, CA, 1957-74.

MEMBER: Writers Guild of America (West), Dramatists Guild of America, Academy of Motion Picture Arts and Sciences, Society of Authors and Artists (France).

AWARDS, HONORS: Drama Desk Award, American Academy of Humor Award, and nomination for Antoinette Perry (Tony) Award from American Theatre Wing, all 1975, all for *Same Time, Next Year;* Academy Award nomination for best screenplay, Academy of Motion Picture Arts and Sciences, 1978, for *Same Time, Next Year.*

WRITINGS:

PLAYS; ALL UNDER NAME BERNARD SLADE

Simon Gets Married (three-act comedy), first produced in Toronto, Ontario, at Crest Theatre, December 8, 1960.

A Very Close Family (three-act drama), first produced in Winnipeg, Manitoba, at Manitoba Theatre Centre, May 10, 1963.

Same Time, Next Year (two-act comedy; first produced in Boston at Colonial Theatre, February, 1975; produced in New York City at Brooks Atkinson Theatre, March 13, 1975), Delacorte (New York), 1975.

Tribute (two-act comedy-drama; first produced in Boston at Colonial Theatre, April 6, 1978; produced in New York City at Brooks Atkinson Theatre, June 1, 1978), Samuel French (New York), 1978.

Fling! (two-act comedy), Samuel French, 1979.

Romantic Comedy (three-act comedy; first produced in New York City at Ethel Barrymore Theatre, November 8, 1979), Samuel French, 1980.

Special Occasions (two-act drama; first produced in New York City at Music Box Theatre, February 7, 1982), Samuel French, 1982.

Fatal Attraction (two-act thriller; first produced in Toronto, Ontario, at St. Lawrence Center Theatre, November 8, 1984), Samuel French, 1986.

An Act of the Imagination (two-act mystery; first produced as *Sweet William* in Guildford, England, September 15, 1987), Samuel French, 1988.

Return Engagements (comedy; first produced in Westport, CT, at Westport Summer Theatre, 1988), Samuel French, 1989.

You Say Tomatoes (two-act comedy; first producesd at Vineyard Playhouse, Martha's Vineyard), Samuel French, 1994.

I Remember You (two-act comedy; first produced at Madach Theatre, Budapest, Hungary), Samuel French, 1995.

Same Time, Another Year (sequel to *Same Time, Next Year*), Samuel French, 1995.

Also author of *Every Time I See You* (musical version of *Same Time, Next Year*), first produced at Madach Theatre, Budapest, Hungary, 1991.

SCREENPLAYS

Stand Up and Be Counted, Columbia, 1972.
Same Time, Next Year, Universal, 1978.
Tribute, Twentieth Century-Fox, 1980.
Romantic Comedy, MGM, 1983.

Also author of teleplays for Canadian Broadcasting Corp., including *The Prizewinner*, 1957, and *Men Don't Make Passes, Innocent Deception, The Gimmick, Do Jerry Parker, The Most Beautiful Girl in the World, The Big Coin Sound, The Reluctant Angels, A Very Close Family, Blue Is for Boys,* and *The Oddball.* Creator of eight television series and author of more than one hundred television scripts for numerous series, including *Love on a Rooftop, The Flying Nun, The Partridge Family,* and *Bewitched.*

SIDELIGHTS: Bernard Slade Newbound, better known as Bernard Slade, has come a long way since *The Partridge Family.* The popular sitcom's creator (who also originated *Bridget Loves Bernie, Love on a Rooftop,* and *The Flying Nun* and was a writer for *Bewitched*) left television behind for the stage and screen, where he found even greater success. "Ironically," he told Toronto *Globe and Mail* writer Stephen Godfrey, "I went into television to make money, and it was the labor of love [the play] *Same Time Next Year* that made me rich." The Canadian-born playwright's gentle comedy was a critical and commercial hit upon its Broadway debut in 1975. In fact, it was one of Broadway's longest-running comedies. After winning a Drama Desk Award and an Antoinette Perry (Tony) Award nomination, the play was made into a popular movie starring Alan Alda and Ellen Burstyn—and Slade's screenplay was nominated for an Academy Award. Slade is also the author of the scripts for the 1981 movie *Tribute* and the 1983 film *Romantic Comedy,* each adapted from the author's original Broadway plays.

Though *Tribute* is a play about death, and *Romantic Comedy* and *Same Time, Next Year* explore serious themes, humor is an important element in all three works. Slade told *CA:* "I was strongly influenced by the romantic comedies of Philip Barry, John Van Druten, S. N. Behrman, and Noel Coward. I try to write plays that combine comedy with situations and characters that touch the audience emotionally. I deal in the area of comedy because I find listening to two thousand people roaring their heads off enormously satisfying. Besides, nobody has ever convinced me that *life* isn't a comedy."

Same Time, Next Year marked a pinnacle for the author, whose earlier plays (*Simon Gets Married* and *A Very Close Family*) received little attention outside of Canada, and whose succeeding efforts haven't quite matched the critical and popular acclaim earned by this tale of a longterm, once-yearly, extramarital affair. Along with tracing the changes in the lives of the protagonists through the twenty-six years of their relationship, the play traces the changes America itself undergoes in that same tumultuous time span from the 1950s to the 1970s. For many critics, the combination of these two elements creates a depth that is an important part of the play's appeal. As Chris Johnson explains in the *Dictionary of Literary Biography:* "The slick, sometimes risque comedy offers two human portraits and some pointed comment on the political, social, and economic events which have shaped their lives." Despite its uniquely American backdrop, *Same Time, Next Year* has proved to have global appeal: the play has been produced in cities all over the world, including London, Paris, Madrid, Stockholm, Copenhagen, Athens, Moscow, Rome, Rio de Janeiro, Caracas, Germany, and Chile, and has been translated into a great many languages.

While a critical success in its stage version, the filmed story fared less well in some reviews. In Gene Siskel's opinion, what he terms Slade's "gag writing" works well for the stage, but translates poorly to the screen. In his *Chicago Tribune* review, Siskel concludes that *Same Time, Next Year* is "merely harmless, lightweight entertainment."

Slade's *Tribute,* which opened on Broadway in 1978, "pays homage to all the unknown soldiers of *Variety's* obituary pages," Ronald Bryden writes in Canada's *Maclean's* magazine. *Tribute* is the story of the terminally ill Scottie Templeton, an entertaining, witty press agent beloved by nearly everyone in his life—except his son, Jud. Templeton's need to heal his relationship with Jud before he succumbs to leukemia serves as the play's focal point.

Later made into a movie starring Jack Lemmon (who recreated his Broadway role), *Tribute* was a financial success. "The play was so successful during its out-of-town run," Tony Schwartz notes in the *New York Times,* "that its backers had the rare good fortune of having been completely paid off" by *Tribute's* opening night on Broadway. Yet critical acclaim eluded the drama. John Simon in *New York* magazine that "I am not sure about how good a play *Tribute* is; what I know is that it is extremely clever and likable. . . . You have the happy feeling that the many very genuine witticisms in it are not, as usual, made at the expense of other people. . . . Only a nice man could have written [it]." Johnson deems it "More ambitious than [Slade's] earlier plays," but adds that it fails in its "attempts to balance comedy and drama."

Slade's *Romantic Comedy* fared similarly. The play traces the long relationship of a man and a woman, both playwrights, whose dramatic collaboration threatens to become romantic despite their untimely meeting on the man's wedding day. "I intended this play as a sort of valentine to those old romantic comedies about the obstacles to consummation," Slade told Schwartz. Theater-goers accepted Slade's valentine, and *Romantic Comedy* was a hit on Broadway, in London's West End, and in Paris.

But the play earned a lukewarm reception from theater critics. John Simon sees *Romantic Comedy* as being only half a success. In a review for *New York* magazine, he writes that it "almost makes up in comedy what it lacks in romance," but asserts that the play suffers in the development of the latter. Simon attributes some of that failing to characters that have been stereotyped rather than convincingly brought to life. Walter Kerr suggests in the *New York Times* that the characters Slade created belong in two different plays.

In a largely negative review for the *Chicago Tribune* of the play's screen version (starring Dudley Moore and Mary Steenburgen), Siskel points out "one of Slade's dramatic points" with which the critic finds favor: "that some people are destined to be friends and always just miss being more," a point the critic finds "bittersweet." London *Times* columnist Anthony Masters makes a similar claim in his review of the play's London run: "Somewhere in the couple's developing understanding through a dozen hits and flops, and their inability to get it together emotionally, is a genuinely touching play."

Slade's reworking of *Same Time, Next Year* for 1982's *Special Occasions* failed to draw the audiences of his earlier efforts. Though Rosalind Carne termed it an "unusual and, in many ways, endearing comedy" in her *Plays and Players* review, this story of a divorced couple meeting for the shared events of their separate lives closed after a brief run on Broadway. For Masters, the play is an improvement over Slade's previous material, despite what the critic sees as its contrived format and its tendency toward gloss at the expense of depth. For Johnson, it is "in many respects the best of Slade's later plays." Johnson describes Slade's development of the postdivorce relationship between the play's only characters as having been created with "considerable sensitivity and warmth." *Special Occasions* has, nevertheless, been produced the world over, including a seven-year run in Hungary.

Slade turned to darker writing for his next dramatic effort, the murder mystery *Fatal Attraction.* According to Godfrey, the play "is a thriller about a fading Hollywood star who comes back east to Nantucket and becomes involved in a series of murders," and it represents the author's sole attempt at the genre. "No matter what its fate," he explains, "Slade doubts he will write another thriller."

So far, the playwright has remained true to his word. In 1986, however, Slade did return to another genre: along with other well-known playwrights like Beth Henley and Wendy Wasserstein, he contributed a television script to the Public Broadcasting Service (PBS-TV) comedy series *Trying Times.* But Slade's return to television was only brief. His ensuing efforts include a work entitled *Return Engagements*—a comedy in the genre Slade returns to again and again: the play.

Slade told *CA:* "Each play creates totally different problems. That's what's so fascinating—and so frustrating—about playwriting. Even after you've acquired a certain expertise, there's no formula for the texture, the chemistry, or whatever it is, that makes a play work." According to Schwartz, reviews arguing that a Slade play doesn't work have been known to upset the playwright, but he isn't bothered by suggestions that his dramas lack depth. "I'm an entertainer," Slade told Schwartz. "My plays aren't meant to be life-changing."

BIOGRAPHICAL/CRITICAL SOURCES:

BOOKS

Contemporary Authors Autobiography Series, Volume 9, Gale, 1989.
Contemporary Literary Criticism, Volume 46, Gale, 1988.
Dictionary of Literary Biography, Volume 53: *Canadian Writers since 1960, First Series,* Gale, 1986.

PERIODICALS

Canadian, July 26, 1975.
Chicago Tribune, February 9, 1979, p. 15; October 14, 1980; October 7, 1983.
Esquire, December, 1975.
Globe and Mail (Toronto), November 10, 1984.
Los Angeles Times, April 20, 1975.
MacLean's, July 1975; May 15, 1978, p. 80.
Newsday, April 13, 1975.
New York, June 12, 1978; June 19, 1978, p. 74; November 26, 1979, p. 90.
New York Post, April 19, 1975; June 2, 1978.
New York Times, April 13, 1975; May 28, 1978; June 2, 1978; June 3, 1978; June 11, 1978; November 22, 1978; April 13, 1979; October 8, 1979, p. C15; November 4, 1979, p. D23; November 9, 1979, p. C3; May 9, 1980, p. C9; December 14, 1980; February 8, 1982; October 7, 1983; October 7, 1985; December 14, 1986.
Plays and Players, February, 1984, p. 32.
Times (London), February 3, 1983; December 22, 1983; November 1, 1985; November 28, 1985.
Washington Post, February 13, 1981, p. C6; October 12, 1983.*

—*Sketch by Heather Aronson*

*   *   *

NOEL, Thomas Jacob 1945-

PERSONAL: Born May 6, 1945, in Cambridge, MA; son of Dix Webster (a professor of law) and Louise (a psychiatrist; maiden name, Jacob) Noel; married Violet Sumiko Kamiya (a visiting nurse coordinator), August 25, 1973. *Education:* University of Denver, B.A., 1966, M.A., 1969; University of Colorado, Ph.D., 1978. *Politics:* Democrat. *Religion:* Roman Catholic.

ADDRESSES: Home—1245 Newport St., Denver, CO 80220. *Office*—Department of History, Campus Box 182, P.O. Box 173364, University of Colorado, Denver, CO 80217-3364.

CAREER: University of California, Riverside, librarian, 1969-70; Colorado Historical Society, Denver, artifacts technician, 1970-72; University of Colorado, Denver, instructor, 1972-79, assistant professor, 1979-82, associate professor, 1982-90, professor of history, 1990—, director of Colorado Studies Center, 1981—, chair of history department, 1991—. Part-time instructor at Arapahoe Community College, Colorado Women's College, Regis University, Metro State, and University of Denver. Tour guide for Smithsonian Institution Travel Associates. Member of board of directors of Historic Denver, Inc., 1982-85; Denver landmark commissioner, 1984—; Denver Public Library Friends Foundation board member, 1984—.

MEMBER: Colorado Authors League, Colorado Historical Society, Western History Association, Westerners (Denver Posse), Friends of the Denver Public Library (member of board, 1984—).

AWARDS, HONORS: Hafen Prize from Colorado Historical Society, 1975, for article "The Multi-Functional Frontier Saloon"; Top Hand Award from Colorado Authors League and Pursuit of Excellence Prize from University of Colorado, both 1981, for *Denver: Rocky Mountain Gold;* plaque from Downtown Denver, Inc., 1981, for books, tours, and classes; Colorado Authors League Award, 1981, for article "A Chat with Louis L'Amour," and 1984, for article "The Most Hated and Feared Man in America: Big Bill Haywood," in *Colorado Heritage;* Noel Park dedicated, 1984, in Larimer Square, Denver; Colorado Preservation Alliance award for *Denver: The City Beautiful and Its Architects,* and other contributions to historic preservation; American Association of State and Local History award of merit, 1991, for research, writing, and interpretation of Denver's history; National Endowment for the Humanities grant, 1993, for research and writing of *Buildings of the U.S.: Colorado.*

WRITINGS:

Richthofen's Montclair: A Pioneer Denver Suburb, Pruett (Boulder, CO), 1978.
Denver: Rocky Mountain Gold, Continental Heritage (Tulsa, OK), 1980.
Denver's Larimer Street: Main Street, Skid Row, and Urban Renaissance, Historic Denver, 1981.
The City and the Saloon: Denver, 1853-1916, University of Nebraska Press (Lincoln, NE), 1982.
(With Fay Metcalf and Duane Smith) *A Colorado History,* Pruett, 1983.

Denver: Emergence of a Great City (television script), Denver Public Library, 1984.

The WPA Guide to 1930s Colorado, University Press of Kansas (Lawrence, KS), 1987.

(With Barbara Norgren) *Denver: The City Beautiful and Its Architects,* Historic Denver, 1987.

Colorado Catholicism, University Press of Colorado, 1989.

(With Steve Leonard) *Denver: Mining Camp to Metropolis,* University Press of Colorado, 1990.

The Denver Athletic Club, 1884-1984, Denver Athletic Club, 1993.

(With Paul Mahoney and Dick Stevens) *Historical Atlas of Colorado,* University of Oklahoma Press (Norman, OK), 1994.

Colorado: A Liquid History, Fulcrum, 1995.

Colorado: The Highest State, University Press of Colorado, 1995.

Buildings of the U.S.: Colorado, Oxford University Press (New York City), 1995.

Also columnist for *Denver Post,* 1990—. Contributor to books including newspapers.

SIDELIGHTS: Thomas J. Noel told *CA:* "I specialize in walking tours of Denver neighborhoods, cemeteries, churches, saloons, parks, and businesses as well as excursions to Colorado railroad and mining towns. There is a need for historical awareness, for a sense of place in turnstile towns such as Denver. Colorado history, with its venerable Indian and Spanish roots, is fascinating. And the twentieth-century drama of those who stayed and tried to keep communities going after the gold and silver busts remains largely untold.

"In my books and articles I have tried to focus on Colorado people and places that have been underappreciated, such as Denver's immigrant groups and the Hispanic villages of the Upper Rio Grande Valley."

*   *   *

NORRIE, Ian 1927-

PERSONAL: Born August 3, 1927, in Southborough, England; son of James Shepherd (a chemist) and Elsie (Tapley) Norrie; married Mavis Kathleen Matthews (a teacher), April 2, 1955; children: two daughters. *Politics:* "Pragmatist." *Religion:* None.

ADDRESSES: Home—75 Crescent West, Hadley Wood, Barnet, Herts. EN4 0EQ, England. *Office*—High Hill Bookshops Ltd., 6-7 High St., Hampstead, London N.W. 3, EN4 0EQ, England.

CAREER: High Hill Bookshops, London, England, manager, 1956-64, managing director, 1964-88; High Hill Press, director, 1968-91.

MEMBER: Society of Bookmen (chair, 1971-73), Garrick Club.

WRITINGS:

NOVELS

Hackles Rise and Fall, Dobson (Durham, England), 1962.

Quentin and the Bogomils, Dobson, 1966.

Plum's Grand Tour, Macdonald & Co. (London), 1978.

NONFICTION

(With Frank Arthur Mumby) *Publishing and Bookselling,* J. Cape (London), 1974.

Hampstead, Highgate Village, and Kenwood: A Short Guide, with Suggested Walks, photos by Philip Greenall, drawings by Ronald Saxby, High Hill Press (London), 1977, revised edition, 1983.

Hampstead: London Hill Town, High Hill Press, 1981.

Publishing and Bookselling in the Twentieth Century, Bell & Hyman (London), 1982, corrected edition with new preface, 1984.

Sabbatical: Doing Europe for Pleasure, High Hill Press, 1983.

A Celebration of London, photos by Dorothy Bohm, Deutsch (London), 1984, reprinted as *Walks around London,* 1986.

Sixty Precarious Years, National Book League (London), 1985.

A Hampstead Memoir, High Hill Press, 1989.

Next Time Round in Provence, drawing by Michael Floyd, Aurum Press, 1993.

Barnet in Old Photographs, Allan Sutton (Gloucester, England), 1993.

Next Time Round in the Dordoene, drawings by Michael Floyd, Aurum, in press.

EDITOR

The Book of Hampstead, drawings by Moy Keightley, High Hill Press, 1960, 2nd revised edition, photos by Christopher Oxford, Colin Penn, L. H. Reader, and Edwin Smith, 1968.

The Book of the City, photos by Smith and Ronald Saxby, High Hill Press, 1961.

The Heathside Book of Hampstead and Highgate, photos by Smith and Saxby, High Hill Press, 1962.

The Book of Westminster, photos by Smith and Saxby, High Hill Press, 1964.

Writers and Hampstead, High Hill Press, 1987.

Also a guest editor of *A Celebration of Books,* National Book League, 1975.

OTHER

Contributor to *The Bookseller, Publishing News,* and *Hampstead and Highgate Express.*

BIOGRAPHICAL/CRITICAL SOURCES:

PERIODICALS

Times (London), December 5, 1985.

O

OBOJSKI, Robert 1929-

PERSONAL: Surname is pronounced "O-boy-ski"; born October 19, 1929, in Cleveland, OH; son of Thomas (a machinist) and Sophia (Sliwa) Obojski; married Danuta Galka (a librarian), March 6, 1965. *Education:* Western Reserve University (now Case Western Reserve University), A.B., 1951, A.M., 1952, Ph.D., 1955. *Politics:* Democrat. *Religion:* Polish National Catholic.

ADDRESSES: Home—58 Orchard Farm Rd., Port Washington, NY 11050.

CAREER: Detroit Institute of Technology, Detroit, MI, assistant professor, 1955-57, professor of English, 1957-60; Coin World Weekly, Sidney, OH, feature editor, 1961-62; Western Kentucky State University, Bowling Green, professor of English, 1963-64; Alliance College, Cambridge Springs, PA, professor of English, 1964-69; Sterling Publishing Co., Inc., New York City, numismatic editor, 1969-70; freelance writer, 1970—.

MEMBER: American Numismatic Association, Society for American Baseball Research.

WRITINGS:

Prodigy at the Piano: The Amazing Story of Sugarchile Robinson, Tower Press (New York City), 1962.
Poland in Pictures, Sterling (New York City), 1969, revised edition, 1994.
Ships and Explorers on Coins, Sterling, 1970.
(With Burton Hobson) *Illustrated Encyclopedia of World Coins,* Doubleday (New York City), 1970, 2nd edition, 1983.
Bush League: A History of Minor League Baseball (alternate Sports Illustrated Book Club selection), Macmillan (New York City), 1975.
The Rise of Japanese Baseball Power, Chilton (Radnor, PA), 1975.

All-Star Baseball since 1933, Stein & Day (Briarcliff Manor, NY), 1980.
Coin Collector's Price Guide, Sterling, 1986, revised edition, 1995.
Stamp Collector's Price Guide, Sterling, 1986.
Great Moments of the Playoffs and World Series, Sterling, 1988.
Strange Baseball, Sterling, 1988.
Baseball Bloopers and Other Curious Incidents, Sterling, 1989, new edition, 1991.
Baseball Memorabilia, Sterling, 1991.
(With Bill Clayton) *Boxing Memorabilia,* Sterling, 1992.

EDITOR

Burton Hobson, *Stamp Collector's Handbook,* Sterling, 1980.
Hobson, *Coin Collector's Handbook,* Sterling, 1980.
Hobson, *Stamp Collecting as a Hobby,* Sterling, 1982, revised edition, 1986.
Hobson, *Coin Collecting as a Hobby,* Sterling, 1982, revised edition, 1986.
Hobson, *Getting Started in Stamp Collecting,* Sterling, 1982.
Hobson and Fred Reinfeld, *Catalogue of the World's Most Popular Coins,* Sterling, 1983, 12th edition, 1986.

OTHER

Also contributor to stamp and coin magazines. Contributing editor to *Guinness Book of World Records, Guinness Sports Record Book, Collectors Editions Quarterly, Sports Collectors Digest,* and *Global Stamps News.*

WORK IN PROGRESS: Confederate State Currency, Dover (New York City), scheduled for 1995.

SIDELIGHTS: Robert Obojski once told *CA:* "I wrote my first 'published' work for my junior high school mimeographed monthly, graduated to the senior high school type-set bi-weekly, wrote for the Western Reserve University weekly *Tribune* for four years, and then contributed a great deal of material gratis to various newspapers. After writing for hobby publications (mostly on baseball, stamps, and coins) for a number of years (and usually for very modest rates), I was finally invited by New York publishers to write and edit books.

"Evolving as a professional writer usually takes a great deal of time. I've seen too many young people who feel they're ready almost immediately to start writing for the major magazines and to produce books without going through the necessary apprenticeship process."

"I've been writing for print now for fifty-one years. After all these years, I have no thoughts of retiring and really feel that I've just begun to hit my stride. Finally, there's no question in my mind that no one can become a successful writer unless he's had an innate desire to become an avid reader. One of my idols, Will Durant, who with his wife Ariel, wrote the magnificent multi-volume *The Story of Civilization,* once said: 'As a writer of history, I am compelled to spend most of my time reading.' We must also remember that William Shakespeare, perhaps the greatest of all writers in the English language, read widely throughout his entire life."

"From a personal standpoint, I've always alternated between writing books and writing articles for periodicals. Many of those periodical articles have been incorporated into my books."

*   *   *

OLIVA, Leo E. 1937-

PERSONAL: Born November 5, 1937, in Woodston, KS; son of E. I. (a farmer) and Lela (Miller) Oliva; married Marlene Causey, August 31, 1958 (divorced, 1975); married Bonita M. Pabst, February 14, 1976; children: (first marriage) Eric, Stephanie, Rex. *Education:* Fort Hays State University, A.B., 1959; University of Denver, M.A., 1960, Ph.D., 1964. *Avocational interests:* reading Western and Indian literature; Rafting western rivers; hiking and biking; visiting the Grand Canyon, historic sites in Kansas and the West, and museums.

ADDRESSES: Home—R.R. 1, Box 31, Woodston, KS 67675.

CAREER: Texas Wesleyan College, Fort Worth, assistant professor of history, 1962-64; Fort Hays State University, Hays, Kansas, assistant professor, 1964-67, associate professor, 1967-69, professor of history, 1969-78, acting chair of department, 1966-67, chair of department, 1967-75; self-employed, 1978—, as farmer, freelance writer, and

owner-operator of Type "O" (typesetting business), Heritage Tours, and Western Books (publisher). Visiting professor of history, Fort Hays State University, 1982—. Consultant to Fort Leavenworth Museum, 1975-76, Kansas Committee for the Humanities projects, 1980-94, Kansas Heritage Center, Dodge City, 1986—, public television station KOOD, Bunker Hill, KS (for series on Kansas history), 1988-90, National Park Service Planning Team for the Santa Fe National Historical Trail survey, 1988-89, *Cobblestone Magazine* (for issue on Santa Fe Trail), 1989-90, Classic Big Barn, Inc. (for restoration of Historic Thomas Barn and development of draft-horse museum), 1989—, Smithsonian Institution (for proposed television series on American Trails), 1990, (for tours of the Santa Fe Trail), 1994, FOF Productions, Washington, DC (for educational film on the Santa Fe Trail), 1990-92, Kansas Department of Travel and Tourism planning team for celebration of 175th anniversary of the opening of the Santa Fe Trail, 1994; presenter of over 100 programs to local historical societies, libraries, museums, schools, and service organizations; tour guide for bus trips on the Santa Fe Trail.

MEMBER: American Association for State and Local History, National Farmers Union (life member), Western History Association (charter member), Coronado Trail Association (charter member), Santa Fe Trail Association (charter member; member of board, bylaws committee), Kansas Anthropological Association, Kansas History Teachers Association (executive board member, 1970-73; vice-president, 1975-76; president, 1976-77), Kansas State Historical Society (board of directors member, 1969—), Kansas Corral of the Westerners (founding member; sheriff, 1972; representative, 1974, 1977; Trail Boss, 1980-81; secretary-treasurer, 1982-88), Rooks County Historical Society, Fort Larned Historical Society, Fort Larned Old Guard (member, board of directors), Friends of Historic Fort Hays, Classic Big Barn, Inc. (founding member; secretary, 1989-92; treasurer, 1992—).

WRITINGS:

Soldiers on the Santa Fe Trail, University of Oklahoma Press (Norman, OK), 1967.
Fort Hays: Frontier Army Post, 1865-1889, Kansas State Historical Society (Topeka, KS), 1980.
Fort Larned on the Santa Fe Trail, Kansas State Historical Society, 1982.
Ash Rock and the Stone Church: The History of a Kansas Rural Community, Sons and Daughters of Ash Rock and Western Books (Woodston, KS), 1983.
Fort Scott on the Indian Frontier, Kansas State Historical Society, 1984.
Woodston: The Story of a Kansas Country Town, Western Books, 1985.

Santa Fe Trail Trivia, Western Books, 1985, enlarged edition with wife, Bonita M. Oliva, 1987, 3rd edition, 1989.

(Editor) *Adventures on the Santa Fe Trail,* Kansas Historical Society, 1988.

Fort Union and the Frontier Army in the Southwest, National Park Service, 1993.

OTHER

Author of *Stockton Heritage in Wood, Stone, and Brick: The Town and Its Historic Structures,* 1985. Contributor to books, including *Brand Book of the Westerners,* Denver Posse, 1960; *The United States Army in Peacetime: Essays in Honor of the Bicentennial,* edited by Robin Higham and Carol Brandt, Military Affairs (Manhattan, KS), 1975; *Kansas and the West: Bicentennial Essays in Honor of Nyle H. Miller,* Kansas State Historical Society, 1975; and *Comparative Histories of the Heartland: State and Region in the American Midwest,* edited by James H. Madison, Indiana University Press (Bloomington, IN), 1988.

Contributor of numerous articles to journals and other periodicals, including *American West, Gone West, Journal of the West, Kansas Historical Quarterly, Kansas Quarterly, Military, The Trail Guide,* and *Western American Literature;* contributor of over 200 book reviews to numerous journals, including *American Indian Quarterly, Journal of the West, Kansas History, Library Journal, Military Affairs, Overland Journal, Wagon Tracks, Western Historical Quarterly,* and *Wichita Eagle-Beacon.* Author of over 30 scholarly papers presented at conferences. Editor and publisher of newsletters, *Wagon Tracks* (Santa Fe Trail Association quarterly), 1986—, *Big Barn Bulletin,* 1990—; member of editorial board, *Kansas Corral of the Westerners.*

WORK IN PROGRESS: A revised edition of *Soldiers on the Santa Fe Trail;* a series on forts of Kansas for Kansas State Historical Society; historical research on western subjects, including the soldiers of Smoky Hill Trail, the Indian in American literature since 1890, historic churches of Kansas, General George A. Custer, and the location of the 1867 Medicine Lodge Peace Treaty negotiations.

*   *   *

OLSON, Richard Paul 1934-

PERSONAL: Born July 19, 1934, in Rapid City, SD; son of Ole (a minister) and Hazel (a county auditor; maiden name, Doty) Olson; married Mary Ann Edland, June 3, 1957; children: Julie, Lisa, Laurie. *Education:* Sioux Falls College, B.A. (with honors), 1956; Andover Newton

Theological School, B.D., 1959, S.T.M. (with honors), 1960; Boston University, Ph.D., 1972.

ADDRESSES: Home—Overland Park, KS. *Office*—Prairie Baptist Church, 7416 Roe Ave., Prairie Village, KS 66208.

CAREER: Ordained American Baptist minister in 1959; minister in Parker, SD, 1960-63, and in Beaver Dam, WI, 1963-67; associate minister in Lexington, MA, 1967-71; First Baptist Church, Racine, WI, senior pastor, 1971-80; First Baptist Church, Boulder, CO, pastor, 1980-86; Prairie Baptist Church, Prairie Village, KS, senior pastor, 1986—. Professor at Sioux Falls College, 1961-62; teacher at Beaver Dam Vocational Technical School, 1965-67; field education supervisor at Harvard Divinity School, 1970-71; lecturer at College of Racine, 1972-74, and Holy Redeemer College, 1973-74; counselor at Addiction Center of Racine, 1973-80; president of Downtown Cooperative Parish of Racine, 1974, 1979; member of advisory committee on desegregation of Racine Unified School District, 1974-76, and of Funeral and Memorial Society of Racine and Kenosha, 1974-76; adjunct professor of Christian ethics and homiletics, Central Baptist Theological Seminary, 1987—.

MEMBER: American Association of Pastoral Counselors (fellow), Ministers Council of American Baptist Churches.

AWARDS, HONORS: Ministry with Families in Flux was named one of the ten most important books of 1990 by the Academy of Paris Clergy.

WRITINGS:

A Job or a Vocation, Thomas Nelson (Nashville, TN), 1973.

Mid-Life: A Time to Discover, a Time to Decide, Judson (Valley Forge, PA), 1980.

Changing Male Roles in Today's World, Judson, 1982.

(With Wayne G. Johnson) *Each Day a Gift,* Morrow (New York City), 1982.

(With Carole Della Pia-Terry) *Ministry with Remarried Persons,* Judson, 1984.

(With Pia-Terry) *Help for Remarried Couples and Families,* Judson, 1984.

(With Joe H. Leonard, Jr.) *Ministry with Families in Flux,* Westminster/John Knox (Philadelphia, PA), 1990.

The Practical Dreamer and Other Stories to Tell at Christmas, Upper Room (Nashville, TN), 1990.

Contributor to *Directions 80, Christian Home, Baptist Leader, Adult Class, High Call,* and *Foundations.*

WORK IN PROGRESS: How to Aid Your Child's Vocational Discovery (working title; with Helen Froyd), for United Church Press, publication expected in 1995; *The*

Church and the Once in Future Family (with Joe H. Leonard, Jr.); *The Middle Third of Life;* and another book of Christmas stories.

SIDELIGHTS: Richard Olson told *CA:* "My writings arise out of the persons, needs, [and] issues I encounter as a minister of the gospel. It is my hope that in turn these writings contribute to other people and other ministries."

* * *

ORDWAY, Frederick I(ra) III 1927-

PERSONAL: Born April 4, 1927, in New York, NY; son of Frederick Ira, Jr. and Frances Antoinette (Wright) Ordway; married Maria Victoria Arenas, April 13, 1950; children: Frederick Ira IV, Albert James, Aliette Marisol. *Education:* Harvard University, S.B., 1949; graduate study, Sorbonne, University of Paris, 1950-51, 1953-54, Alexander Hamilton Business Institute, 1952-58, Air University, 1952-63, and Industrial College of the Armed Forces, 1953-63; summer graduate study, University of Algiers, 1950, University of Barcelona, 1953, and University of Innsbruck, 1954. *Avocational interests:* Tennis, skiing, collecting rare books and prints, international travel.

ADDRESSES: Home—2401 North Taylor St., Arlington, VA 22207; and 3423 Lookout Dr., S.E., Huntsville, AL 35801. *Office*—U.S. Department of Energy, Forrestal Building, 4A 107, 1000 Independence Ave. S.W., Washington, DC 20585.

CAREER: Field and laboratory worker in Venezuela for Mene Grande Oil Co., San Tome, and Orinoco Mining Co., Ciudad Bolivar, 1949-50; Reaction Motors, Inc., Lake Denmark, NJ, assistant engineer, 1951-53; Republic Aviation Corp., Guided Missiles Division, Hicksville, NY, member of Engineering Division staff, 1954-55; General Astronautics Research Corp., Huntsville, AL, and Washington, DC, president, 1955-59; National Research and Development Corp., Atlanta, GA, vice-president, 1957-59; Army Ballistic Missile Agency and Army Ordnance Missile Command, Redstone Arsenal, Huntsville, AL, special assistant to director of Advanced Research Projects Agency-National Aeronautics and Space Administration (ARPA-NASA) projects office (became Saturn projects office), 1959-60; NASA George C. Marshall Space Flight Center, Huntsville, chief of space information systems branch, 1960-64; General Astronautics Research Corp., Washington, DC, president, 1964-66; University of Alabama, School of Graduate Studies and Research, Huntsville, professor of science and technology applications, 1966-73; National Science Foundation, Science and Technology Policy Office, Washington, DC, consultant, 1974-75; U.S. Energy Research and Develop-

ment Administration, Washington, DC, special assistant to administrator, 1975-77; U.S. Department of Energy, Office of Policy and Evaluation, Washington, DC, special advisor to the International Energy Development Program, 1977-81, director of special projects office, 1981—.

Contributor to and co-curator of touring retrospective exhibition of Ordway's rare book, print, and paintings collection "Blueprint for Space," which opened at the U.S. Space and Rocket Center, Huntsville, AL, June, 1991. Only American observer at First International Astronautical Congress, Paris, 1950, and delegate to numerous subsequent congresses, 1951-93. Lecturer on rocketry, high altitude research, and space flight in North America, South America, Europe, Australia, and New Zealand. Has appeared on television and radio shows and in documentary films as space flight and energy expert. Consultant to Smithsonian Institution's National Air and Space Museum; General Research Corp., Washington, DC, and McLean, VA, Exsa Co., Bogota, Colombia, and Andex Co., Bogota, 1974-75; *American College Dictionary, Encyclopaedia Britannica,* and *Random House Unabridged Dictionary of the English Language;* Metro-Goldwyn-Mayer production of movie *2001: A Space Odyssey,* 1965-66, and Paramount Picture Corp. production of *The Adventurers,* 1968-69. *Military service:* U.S. Naval Reserve, discharged in 1945; later transferred to U.S. Air Force Reserve, attached to Headquarters, Office of the Assistant Chief of Staff Intelligence in the Pentagon.

MEMBER: International Academy of Astronautics (committee chair), American Association for the Advancement of Science (fellow), American Institute of Aeronautics and Astronautics (associate fellow; member of history committee, 1970—, and international affairs committee, 1980-91; former director of Alabama section), National Space Society (director), Space Association of Australia, British Interplanetary Society (fellow), Agrupacion Astronautica Espanola, Explorers Club, Literary Society of Washington, DC (past member of executive committee), Cosmos Club (Washington, DC; officer; committee chair; member of board of management; vice-president, 1988-90), Harvard Club (New York).

AWARDS, HONORS: Recipient with Wernher von Braun of diplome d'honneur, Commission Francaise de Bibliographie d'Histoire et d'Art, 1969; American Institute of Aeronautics and Astronautics, Pendray Award, 1974, for major contributions to astronautical literature, and Hermann Oberth Award, 1977, for outstanding contributions to space flight; National Science Foundation grants for study and lecturing in Antarctica, U.S.S.R, and New Zealand; special diploma, Tsiolkowsky State Museum of the History of Cosmonautics, Kaluga, U.S.S.R, 1988; honorary doctor of science degree, University of Alabama, 1992; special resolution, Alabama Space Science Exhibit Commission, 1992, for contributions to the U.S. Space and Rocket Center.

WRITINGS:

(With Carsbie C. Adams) *Space Flight,* McGraw (New York City), 1958.

(With Ronald C. Wakeford) *International Missile and Spacecraft Guide,* McGraw, 1960.

Annotated Bibliography of Space Science and Technology, Arfor, 1962.

(With James Patrick Gardner and Mitchell R. Sharpe, Jr.) *Basic Astronautics: An Introduction to Space Science, Engineering and Medicine* (college text), Prentice-Hall (Englewood Cliffs, NJ), 1962.

(With Adams and Wernher von Braun) *Careers in Astronautics and Rocketry,* McGraw, 1962.

(With Gardner, Sharpe, and Wakeford) *Applied Astronautics: An Introduction to Space Flight* (college text), Prentice-Hall, 1963.

(With Wakeford) *Conquering the Sun's Empire,* Dutton (New York City), 1963.

Life in Other Solar Systems, Dutton, 1964.

(With Roger A. MacGowan) *Intelligence in the Universe,* Prentice-Hall, 1966.

(With von Braun) *History of Rocketry and Space Travel,* Crowell (New York City), 1966, 2nd edition, 1975.

L'Histoire mondiale de l'astronautique, Larousse (New York City), 1968.

(With Sharpe and Adams) *Dividends from Space,* Crowell, 1972.

Pictorial Guide to Planet Earth, Crowell, 1975.

(With von Braun) *The Rockets' Red Glare,* Doubleday (New York City), 1976.

(With von Braun) *New Worlds: Discoveries from Our Solar System,* Doubleday, 1979.

(With Sharpe) *The Rocket Team,* Crowell, 1979.

(With von Braun and Dave Dooling) *Space Travel: A History,* Harper (New York City), 1985.

(With Ernst Stuhlinger) *Wernher von Braun: Aufbruch in den Weltraum Die Biographie,* Bechtle Verlag (Esslingen, Germany), English-language edition by the authors published as *Wernher von Braun: Crusader for Space,* Volume 1: *An Illustrated Memoir,* Volume 2: *A Biographical Memoir,* Robert E. Krieger (Melbourne, FL), 1994.

EDITOR

Advances in Space Science, Volume 1, Academic Press (New York City), 1959, Volume 2, 1960, published annually as *Advances in Space Science and Technology,* Volumes 3-11, Academic Press, 1961-72.

Introduction to Astrodynamics, Academic Press, 1960.

(With Stuhlinger, George C. Bucher, and Jerry C. McCall) *From Peenemunde to Outer Space,* National

Aeronautics and Space Administration—Marshall, 1962.

(With Stuhlinger, McCall, and Bucher, and contributor) *Astronautical Engineering and Science,* McGraw, 1963.

Lunar and Planetary Surface Conditions, Academic Press, 1965.

History of Rocketry and Astronautics, Volume 9, Univelt (San Diego), 1989.

(With Randy Liebermann) *Blueprint for Space: Science Fiction to Science Fact,* Smithsonian Institution Press (Washington, DC), 1992.

OTHER

Also author of technical and research reports. Contributor to books, including *Handbook of Astronautical Engineering,* McGraw, 1961; *Medical and Biological Problems of Space Flight,* Academic Press, 1963; *Between Sputnik and the Shuttle: New Perspectives on American Astronautics,* edited by Frederick C. Durant III, Univelt, 1981; *Macroengineering and the Future: A Management Perspective,* edited by Frank P. Davidson and C. Lawrence Meador, Westview (Boulder, CO), 1982; and *Science Fiction and Space Futures: Past and Present,* edited by Eugene M. Emme, American Astronautical Society, 1982. Editor of *History of Rocketry and Astronautics Proceedings of the Ninth, Tenth, and Eleventh History Symposia of the International Academy of Astronautics, Lisbon, Portugal, 1975, Anaheim, California, U.S.A., 1976, Prague, Czechoslovakia, 1977,* Univelt, 1989. Contributor to *Encyclopedia Americana, Encyclopaedia Britannica, Compton's Encyclopedia, World Book Encyclopedia, Encyclopaedia Universalis,* and *Grolier's Encyclopedia.* Member of editorial board for 1959 and 1960 editions of *Proceedings* of International Astronautical Congress. Advisor to Time-Life Books' "Voyage Through the Universe" series and ICSU's "Universe and Its Origin."

Contributor of more than three hundred reviews and articles to professional and technical journals, including *Sky and Telescope, Rocket, Aviation Week, Spaceflight, Journal of the British Interplanetary Society, Aeronautics and Astronautics,* and *Science Digest.* Former editor of *Journal of Astronautics;* guest editor, *Acta Aeronautica,* October, 1987; former research and development editor of *GSE Magazine of Missile and Space Support Engineering;* member of board of consultants, *Space Journal;* former member of editorial board of *Space Business Daily, Space Journal, Missiles and Rockets,* and *Ciencia Aeronautica.*

Creator, with von Braun, of "Antares Space Filmstrips" (a series of five), Doubleday Multi-Media, 1971. Co-developer of space-related puzzles and games for Springbok and Parker. Creator of "Chesley Bonestell's Vision of Space" (cassette/slide set), for Japanese exhibition of

Bonestell's work, 1983. Finley Holiday Film Corp. has released the video, laser disc, and slide/cassette portions of "Blueprint for Space" which accompany touring exhibition of the same title that Ordway helped develop.

The U.S. Space and Rocket Center archives houses Ordway's library of ancient books, rare prints, and documents relating to the history of rocketry and space travel.

SIDELIGHTS: Drawing on his first-hand knowledge of astronautics and his close association with rocket pioneer Wernher von Braun, Frederick I. Ordway III has produced a body of writings that serves both as an introduction to space science and technology and as a history of the space program. *The Rocket Team,* co-authored with Mitchell R. Sharpe, chronicles the work of von Braun and other scientists and engineers from Germany—where they developed the V-1 and V-2 missiles used by the Nazis against England—to the United States, where they achieved their original goal: putting a man on the moon.

This group of scientists, "the team," first met in the early 1930s as members of the Society for Space Travel, a German research organization interested in the then-experimental science of rocketry. The German army soon funded their research for its possible military applications. "Through extensive research [the authors] have traced the German development programs," notes Charles Duelfer in the *Washington Post Book World,* "highlighting the bureaucratic conflicts and revealing how, ultimately, the emergent weapons were militarily ineffective." Even so, as Ordway and Sharpe reveal, the British viewed the rockets as a serious threat and actively prepared against them. After World War II, von Braun and many of his colleagues were brought to the United States to work at developing rockets for the American military and later to launch the space program. With the National Aeronautics and Space Administration (NASA), "the team" realized their dreams in the Saturn-5 rocket shot to the moon.

Ordway told Joseph Barbato in a *Publishers Weekly* interview how he and Sharpe came to pen *The Rocket Team:* "Von Braun told me he might never write an autobiography of 'the team'—he always thought in terms of the team, that group of engineers who worked with him in Germany and then [in the United States]. One day, he said, 'Why don't you start talking to all of our people, and maybe some day we'll make a book out of it.'" Ordway and Sharpe interviewed some two hundred German scientists working in America, scientists still working in Germany, former intelligence agents, and others involved with the German or American rocket programs.

The Rocket Team, Henry S. F. Cooper, Jr., comments in the *New York Times Book Review,* "is full of fascinating characters, who are allowed to describe one another and the episodes in which they were involved." Duelfer points

out that "the authors have reconstructed events on a personal level. . . . They have recreated events in a human context and laced their narrative with individual anecdotes." This approach, according to Cooper, allows the authors to "overcome the tedium that often accompanies accounts of the development of military or aerospace hardware; they are . . . telling a story, and they tell it very well, letting the facts cascade in an understated, well-controlled manner."

As a drawback to the book, Cooper finds that "the authors do not supply much judgment or analysis of motives; whatever examination or introspection there is the characters supply themselves." Cooper also believes that "although the facts are adequately—often compellingly—laid out in this book, the story has yet to be put into larger perspective." Duelfer, however, concludes that "the authors have made a commendable contribution in detailing this portion of important but frequently overlooked history. Moreover, they have presented it in a manner that focuses our attention on the past but at the same time encourages us to examine the future."

Blueprint for Space: Science Fiction to Science Fact, edited by Ordway and Randy Liebermann, is a collection of illustrated essays by twenty-three contributors, including astronauts, scientists, and science fiction writers. The essays provide an overview of space travel in myth, fiction, and science as well as descriptions of pioneers in the field, an overview of the U.S. Apollo project, and an optimistic look toward the future.

BIOGRAPHICAL/CRITICAL SOURCES:

PERIODICALS

Atlanta Journal and Constitution, November 15, 1979.
Christian Science Monitor, May 9, 1963.
Journal of American History, December, 1980.
Natural History, December, 1963; November, 1965.
Newsworld, September 1, 1979.
New Technical Books, March, 1993, p. 334.
New York Herald Tribune Book Review, May 12, 1963.
New York Times Book Review, July 29, 1979.
Observer (London), September 23, 1979.
Portland Press Herald (ME), October 8, 1979.
Publishers Weekly, April 16, 1979; June 4, 1979; January 18, 1992.
Saturday Review, July 20, 1963.
School Library Journal, November, 1992.
Technology and Culture, April, 1993, p. 461.
Times Literary Supplement, December 28, 1969.
Washington Post Book World, September 9, 1979.*

OWEN, Edmund
  See TELLER, Neville

P

PARK, Edwards 1917-

PERSONAL: Born September 21, 1917, in Boston, MA; son of Charles Edwards (a minister) and Mary (Turner) Park; married E. Jean Speirs, June 27, 1944; children: Alexander, Nicholas, Felicity Anne. *Education:* Yale University, A.B., 1939. *Politics:* Independent.

ADDRESSES: Home and office—17 Pinkney St., Annapolis, MD 21401.

CAREER: Freelance writer in Melbourne, Australia, 1946-51; *Boston Globe,* Boston, MA, feature writer, 1951-55; *National Geographic,* Washington, DC, deputy head of Book Service, 1955-69; *Smithsonian,* Washington, DC, member of board of editors, 1969-82; writer, 1982—. Leader of creative writing workshops for Smithsonian Associates. Lecturer. *Military service:* U.S. Army Air Forces, 1942-45; became captain; received Air Medals, Distinguished Flying Cross, and Purple Heart.

WRITINGS:

Nanette (nonfiction), Norton (New York City), 1977.
Treasures of the Smithsonian, Smithsonian Institution (Washington, DC), 1983.
(With Peggy Thomson) *The Pilot and the Lion Club: Odd Tales from the Smithsonian,* Smithsonian Institution, 1986.
A New View from the Castle, Smithsonian Institution, 1987.
Fighters: The World's Great Aces and Their Planes, Thomasson-Grant (Charlottesville, VA), 1990.
Aviation Pioneers, U.S. Postal Service, 1992.
Washington, DC: Our Nation's Capitol, HarperCollins (New York City), 1994.
The Art of William S. Phillips: The Glory of Flight, Greenwich Workshop, 1994.

Angels Twenty (memoir), University of Queensland (Australia), 1994.
Over America (television program), KCTS, 1995.

Columnist for *Smithsonian* and *Air and Space Smithsonian.* Contributor to magazines.

WORK IN PROGRESS: Memoir of living in Australia, a sequel to *Angels Twenty;* historical novel based on Civil War.

*   *   *

PARKER, (William George) Derek 1932-

PERSONAL: Born May 27, 1932, in Looe, Cornwall, England; son of George Nevin (an agriculturist) and Ivy Vashti (Blatchford) Parker; married Julia Louise Lethbridge (a consultant astrologer and author), July 27, 1957. *Education:* Attended schools in England until age seventeen. *Politics:* Social Democrat. *Religion:* Agnostic.

ADDRESSES: Home—41 Elsham Rd., London W14 8HB, England; and Severalls, Foxton, Cambridgeshire SG8 6RP, England. *Agent*—David Higham Associates Ltd., 5 Lower John St., Golden Sq., London W1R 4HA, England.

CAREER: Cornishman, Penzance, Cornwall, England, reporter, 1949-54; *Western Morning News,* Plymouth, Devonshire, England, drama critic, 1955-57; TWW-TV, Cardiff, Wales, interviewer and newscaster, 1957-58; former host, *The Paperback Programme,* BBC World Service; freelance writer and broadcaster, 1958—. Has appeared on British radio and television; lecturer.

MEMBER: Radiowriters' Association (chairman, 1973-76), Society of Authors (chairman of management committee), Royal Academy of Dancing (member of grand council), Royal Literary Fund (registrar).

WRITINGS:

The Fall of Phaethon (poems), Zebra Press, 1954.

(With Paul Casimir) *Company of Two* (poems), Zebra Press, 1955.

Byron and His World, Vanguard, 1968.

(Editor with John Lehmann) *Selected Letters of Edith Sitwell,* Macmillan (New York City), 1970.

Astrology in the Modern World, Taplinger (New York City), 1970.

The Question of Astrology: A Personal Inquiry, Eyre & Spottiswoode (Andover), 1970.

The West Country, Hastings, 1973.

(Editor) *Sacheverell Sitwell: A Symposium,* Bertram Rota, 1975.

John Donne and His World, Thames & Hudson (London), 1975.

Familiar to All: William Lilly and Astrology in the Seventeenth Century, J. Cape (London), 1975.

Radio: The Great Years, David & Charles (Abbot, Devonshire), 1977.

The Complete Zodiac Name Book, Transatlantic, 1977.

The West Country and the Sea, Longman (Harlow, Essex), 1980.

(Editor) *An Anthology of Erotic Verse,* Constable (London), 1981.

(Editor with William Blatchford) *Grande Horizontal,* Stein & Day (New York City), 1983, published in England as *The Memoirs of Cora Pearl,* Granada, 1983.

(Editor) *Love Confessed,* Constable, 1983.

God of the Dance: Vaslav Nijinsky, Thorsons (Wellingborough), 1988.

(With John Chandler) *Wiltshire Churches: An Illustrated History,* A. Sutton Publishing, 1993.

How to Write Erotic Literature, A. & C. Black, in press.

PUBLISHED ANONYMOUSLY

Eros in the Country, Headline (London), 1988.

Eros in Town, Headline, 1989.

Eros on the Grand Tour, Headline, 1989.

Eros in the New World, Headline, 1989.

Eros in the Far East, Headline, 1990.

Eros in High Places, Headline, 1991.

Eros in Society, Headline, 1991.

Tales of Eros, Headline, 1992.

Eros Off the Rails, Headline, 1992.

Eros at Play, Headline, 1993.

Eros Strikes Gold, Headline, 1993.

Eros in Springtime, Headline, 1993.

Eros in Summer, Headline, 1994.

WITH WIFE, JULIA PARKER

The Compleat Astrologer, McGraw (New York City), 1971, reprinted as *The New Compleat Astrologer,* Crown (New York City), 1984.

The Compleat Lover, McGraw, 1972.

The Natural History of the Chorus Girl, Bobbs-Merrill (Indianapolis), 1975.

The Immortals, McGraw, 1976.

The Story and the Song, Elm Tree, 1979.

How Do You Know Who You Are?, Thames & Hudson, 1980.

Do It Yourself Health, Thames & Hudson, 1982.

A History of Astrology, Deutsch, 1983.

Dreaming, Remembering, Interpreting, Benefitting, Crown, 1985.

The Traveller's Guide to the Nile Valley, J. Cape, 1986.

The Traveller's Guide to Cyprus, J. Cape, 1988.

Parker's Astrology, Dorling Kindersley, 1991.

The Sun and Moon Signs Library (one title for each of the twelve signs of the zodiac), Dorling Kindersley, 1992.

The Power of Magic, Simon & Schuster, 1993.

OTHER

Contributor to several books and to *Times, Listener* and other periodicals. Editor, *Poetry Review,* 1965-70, and *Author,* 1986—.

BIOGRAPHICAL/CRITICAL SOURCES:

PERIODICALS

Times Literary Supplement, January 23, 1969; December 12, 1975; October 24, 1980.

*　　*　　*

PARKER, Nancy Winslow 1930-

PERSONAL: Born October 18, 1930, in Maplewood, NJ; daughter of Winslow Aurelius (a textile executive) and Beatrice McCelland (Gaunt) Parker. *Education:* Mills College, B.A., 1952; additional study at Art Students League, 1956, 1957, and School of Visual Arts, 1966-67. *Avocational interests:* Carpentry, tennis, gardening, genealogy.

ADDRESSES: Home—51 East 74th St., New York, NY 10021.

CAREER: National Broadcasting Co., Inc. (NBC), New York City, sales promoter, 1956-60; New York Soccer Club, New York City, sports promoter, 1961-63; Radio Corp. of America (RCA), New York City, sales promoter, 1964-67; Appleton-Century-Crofts, Inc. (publisher), New York City, art director, 1968-70; Holt, Rinehart & Winston, Inc. (publisher), New York City, graphic designer, 1970-72; freelance writer and illustrator of children's books, 1972—.

MEMBER: Authors Guild, Authors League of America, Mills College Club of New York.

AWARDS, HONORS: Jane Tinkham Broughton fellowship in writing for children, Bread Loaf Writers Conference, 1975; Notable Children's Book in the field of social studies, 1975, for *Warm as Wool, Cool as Cotton: The Story of Natural Fibers,* and 1976, for *The Goat in the Rug;* citation as "best of the season" in children's books, *Saturday Review,* 1976, for *The Goat in the Rug;* citation as "year's best children's book," *Philadelphia Inquirer,* 1976, for *Willy Bear;* Christopher Award, 1976, for *Willy Bear,* and 1981, for *My Mom Travels a Lot;* selection as a notable book, American Library Association, 1980, for *Poofy Loves Company;* selection as one of the ten best illustrated books, *New York Times,* 1981, for *My Mom Travels a Lot;* honorable mention, New York Academy of Science, 1981, and placement on Sequoyah Children's Book Award Masterlist, Oklahoma Library Association, 1983-84, both for *The President's Car;* New York Public Library list of children's books, 1983, for *The Christmas Camal,* and 1985, for *The United Nations from A to Z;* Library of Congress' Books for Children, 1986, for *Paul Revere's Ride,* and 1988, for *Bugs;* Association of Booksellers for Children Choice Award, 1988, for *Bugs.*

WRITINGS:

SELF-ILLUSTRATED CHILDREN'S BOOKS

The Man with the Take-Apart Head, Dodd (New York City), 1974.
The Party at the Old Farm, Atheneum (New York City), 1975.
Mrs. Wilson Wanders Off, Dodd, 1976.
Love from Uncle Clyde (Junior Literary Guild selection), Dodd, 1977.
The Crocodile under Louis Finneberg's Bed, Dodd, 1978.
The President's Cabinet (nonfiction; Junior Literary Guild selection), Parents Magazine Press (New York City), 1978, revised edition, HarperCollins (New York and London), 1991.
The Ordeal of Byron B. Blackbear, Dodd, 1979.
Puddums, the Cathcarts' Orange Cat, Atheneum, 1980.
Poofy Loves Company (Junior Literary Guild selection), Dodd, 1980.
The Spotted Dog, Dodd, 1980.
The President's Car (nonfiction), Crowell, 1981.
Cooper, the McNallys' Big Black Dog, Dodd, 1981.
Love from Aunt Betty, Dodd, 1983.
Christmas Camel, Dodd, 1983.
The United Nations from A to Z, Dodd, 1985.
(Co-author) *Bugs,* Greenwillow (New York City), 1987.
(Co-author) *Frogs, Toads, Lizards, and Salamanders,* Greenwillow, 1990.
Working Frog, Greenwillow, 1992.
U. S. Currency, HarperCollins, 1995.

ILLUSTRATOR

John Langstaff, *Oh, A-Hunting We Will Go!* (songbook; Junior Literary Guild selection), Atheneum, 1974.
Carter Hauck, *Warm as Wool, Cool as Cotton: The Story of Natural Fibers,* Seabury (New York City), 1975.
Blood and Link, *The Goat in the Rug,* Parents Magazine Press, 1976.
Kantrowitz, *Willy Bear* (Book-of-the-Month Club selection), Parents Magazine Press, 1976.
Langstaff, *Sweetly Sings the Donkey* (songbook), Atheneum, 1976.
Lawler, *The Substitute,* Parents Magazine Press, 1977.
Langstaff, *Hot Cross Buns and Other Old Street Cries* (songbook), Atheneum, 1978.
Yolen, *No Bath Tonight* (Junior Literary Guild selection), Crowell (New York City), 1978.
Bauer, *My Mom Travels a Lot,* Warne (New York City), 1981.
Henry Wadsworth Longfellow, *Paul Revere's Ride,* Greenwillow, 1985.
Rice, *Aren't You Coming Too?,* Greenwillow, 1988.
Field, *General Store,* Greenwillow, 1988.
Rice, *Peter's Pockets,* Greenwillow, 1989.
Nietzel, *The Jacket I Wear in the Snow,* Greenwillow, 1989.
Rice, *At Grammy's House,* Greenwillow, 1990.
Guy, *Black Crow,* Greenwillow, 1991.
Lillie, *When the Rooster Crowed,* Greenwillow, 1991.
Whittier, *Barbara Frietchie,* Greenwillow, 1991.
Nietzel, *The Dress I'll Wear to the Party,* Greenwillow, 1992.
T. B. Read, *Sheridan's Ride,* Greenwillow, 1993.
Pomeranz, *Here Comes Henny,* Greenwillow, 1994.
Nietzel, *The Bag I'm Taking to Grandma's,* Greenwillow, 1995.

WORK IN PROGRESS: Making wood constructions combining oils, wood carving, and electric lights.

SIDELIGHTS: Nancy Winslow Parker is an award-winning children's book author and illustrator whose works, Dulcy Brainard writes in *Publishers Weekly,* "are marked by a fresh simplicity and an observant, ironic sense of humor that is particularly apparent in the unexpected ways her pictures expand on the text."

Parker often finds inspiration for her books in real-life situations. *Poofy Loves Company,* for example, is based on an actual incident in which Parker's overly-friendly dog ambushed a visiting youngster, messing up her clothes and stealing her cookie. In the *Junior Literary Guild* Parker recalls that the story "took about fifteen minutes to write, the whole thing coming at once in a delicious outburst of creativity."

Animals, especially dogs, often figure into Parker's stories. In *Love from Uncle Clyde,* a boy named Charlie receives a three-thousand-pound hippopotamus as a Christmas present from his uncle. These same characters appear again in *The Christmas Camel,* in which Uncle Clyde sends Charlie a magical camel who takes the boy to Bethlehem on Christmas Eve.

Parker's nonfiction books have also achieved success. The award-winning *Bugs,* written with Joan R. Wright, examines the physical structure and habitats of several types of common insects. Patti Hagan, writing in the *New York Times Book Review,* claims that the book's "color illustrations, with precise anatomical tags, are a fine tool for introducing children" to the insects portrayed.

In addition to the books she has written, Parker has illustrated the works of other children's authors as well, including the Christopher Award-winning *Willy Bear* by Mildred Kantrowitz and *My Mom Travels a Lot* by Caroline Feller Bauer. Both of these works focus on children adjusting to new and sometimes frightening situations in their lives. *In Willy Bear* a youngster uses his teddy bear to act out his fear of going to school, and in *My Mom Travels a Lot,* a young girl reacts to her hectic mother's lack of time for her.

Parker once told *CA:* "I cannot remember when I have not been interested in children's literature. As a writer, [I find] the field has limitless potential for fantasy and the joy of creation. As an illustrator, [I believe] the opportunity to let yourself go in wild interpretation is an artist's dream come true."

BIOGRAPHICAL/CRITICAL SOURCES:

PERIODICALS

Booklist, May 1, 1991, p. 1710; June 15, 1992, p. 1851.
Junior Literary Guild, March, 1980, p. 8.
Kirkus Reviews, April 1, 1992, p. 470.
Library Talk, November, 1991, p. 28.
New York Times Book Review, February 7, 1988, p. 29.
Publishers Weekly, February 22, 1985, pp. 161-162; May 4, 1992, p. 56.
Quill & Quire, July, 1992, p. 50.
Reading Teacher, September, 1993, p. 51.
School Library Journal, July, 1991, p. 84; August, 1992, p. 146.

* * *

PARKINSON, Claire L(ucille) 1948-

PERSONAL: Born March 21, 1948, in Bay Shore, NY; daughter of C. V. (a business consultant) and Virginia (Hafner) Parkinson. *Education:* Wellesley College, B.A. (with high honors), 1970; Ohio State University, M.A., 1974, Ph.D., 1977. *Politics:* Independent.

ADDRESSES: Home—8345 Canning Ter., Greenbelt, MD 20770. *Office*—Code 971, Goddard Space Flight Center, National Aeronautics and Space Administration, Greenbelt, MD 20771.

CAREER: National Center for Atmospheric Research, Boulder, CO, research assistant, 1976-78; National Aeronautics and Space Administration (NASA), Goddard Space Flight Center, Greenbelt, MD, scientist, 1978—.

MEMBER: International Glaciological Society, American Meteorological Society, Oceanography Society, American Polar Society, Phi Beta Kappa, Sigma Xi.

AWARDS, HONORS: Exceptional Performance Award, Goddard Space Flight Center, 1979; Group Achievement Award, NASA, 1982, for co-authorship of *Antarctic Sea Ice, 1973-1976: Satellite Passive-Microwave Observations;* Goddard Laboratory for Atmospheric Sciences award, 1983, for paper "On the Development and Cause of the Weddell Polynya in a Sea Ice Simulation," and 1988, for leadership in the publication of *Arctic Sea Ice, 1973-1976: Satellite Passive-Microwave Observations;* award from Goddard Laboratory for Hydrospheric Processes, 1993, for co-editorship of *Atlas of Satellite Observations Related to Global Change.*

WRITINGS:

(With others) *Antarctic Sea Ice, 1973-1976: Satellite Passive-Microwave Observations,* National Aeronautics and Space Administration (Greenbelt, MD), 1983.
Breakthroughs: A Chronology of Great Achievements in Science and Mathematics, G. K. Hall (Boston), 1985.
(With Warren M. Washington) *An Introduction to Three-Dimensional Climate Modeling,* University Science Books (Mill Valley, CA), 1986.
(With others) *Arctic Sea Ice, 1973-1976: Satellite Passive-Microwave Observations,* National Aeronautics and Space Administration, 1987.
(With others) *Arctic and Antarctic Sea Ice, 1978-1987: Satellite Passive-Microwave Observations and Analysis,* National Aeronautics and Space Administration, 1992.
(Editor with Robert J. Gurney and James L. Foster) *Atlas of Satellite Observations Related to Global Change,* Cambridge University Press (New York City), 1993.

Associate editor, *Annals of Glaciology,* 1989. Contributor to science and mathematics journals. Associate editor, *IEEE Geoscience and Remote Sensing Society Newsletter,* 1982-84; scientific editor, *Journal of Glaciology,* 1990-92.

WORK IN PROGRESS: Research on the validity of various conservation laws and on the impact of notational advances on the development of mathematics and chemistry; a workbook on understanding satellite images.

SIDELIGHTS: Claire L. Parkinson once told *CA:* "Predominantly interested in theoretical mathematics as a student in the 1960s, I was deeply affected by the civil rights movement, the Vietnam war, and some college courses in biblical history. Partly as a result, I turned from mathematics to science and the history of science, always hoping to return to math eventually.

"I participated in research expeditions to Antarctica in 1973-74 and to the sea ice of the Bering Sea in 1981. However, my main work as a scientist has been desk-based, developing computer models of polar sea ice and analyzing satellite imagery in the context of global climate, while my main intellectual inclination remains mathematics, and much of my non-salaried time is devoted to probing the processes of scientific development, from both a historical and a personal viewpoint.

"I wrote *Breakthroughs* after unsuccessfully seeking a book like it as an aid in understanding the progression of scientific development. The book presents a chronology of scientific developments from 1200 to 1930, providing readers with concise statements of what happened, year by year, in the history of science, with indications of hundreds of interconnections amongst events."

*   *   *

PARKINSON, Kathryn N. 1954-
(Kathy Parkinson)

PERSONAL: Born December 2, 1954, in Los Gatos, CA; daughter of William Evan (a doctor) and Joan (a housewife; maiden name, Peterson) Nunn; married Thomas W. Parkinson (a consultant), July 15, 1978; children: John Thomas, Sarah Joan, Emily Kathryn. *Education:* University of California, Davis, B.S., 1976; University of California, Los Angeles, M.A., 1979.

ADDRESSES: Home and office—83 Bow Rd., Belmont, MA 02178.

CAREER: Freelance illustrator, teacher, and designer, 1980—.

MEMBER: Society of Children's Book Writers, Massachusetts Society of Children's Book Writers, Cambridge Illustrators Group.

WRITINGS:

(Under name Kathy Parkinson, self-illustrated) *The Enormous Turnip* (juvenile), Albert Whitman, 1985.

ILLUSTRATOR

Sandra Guzzo, *Fox and Heggie,* Albert Whitman (Niles, IL), 1983.

E. W. Hildick, *The Case of the Vanishing Ventriloquist,* Macmillan (New York City), 1985.

The Farmer in the Dell, Albert Whitman, 1988.

Abby Levine, *Too Much Mush,* Albert Whitman, 1989.

Maribeth Boelts, *Dry Days, Wet Nights,* Albert Whitman, 1994.

WORK IN PROGRESS: Books for children.

SIDELIGHTS: Kathryn N. Parkinson told *CA:* "Primarily I am an illustrator. It was my interest in folk tales that led me to illustrate *The Enormous Turnip.* Although at present writing is secondary to my illustration work, I hope to write more as time goes on.

"In my illustration I try to capture the feeling and the action of the moment being illustrated. My style tends to be loose so as to give the work a fresh, lively quality.

"Secondarily, I enjoy my work because of the involvement with color. Using watercolors and acrylics for the illustration and a rich array of fabric paints for the fabrics is very challenging and tremendously satisfying when I am a success at it!

"Finally, I enjoy the people contact through this work and my teaching at the elementary level. It is a real pleasure to see kids trying new techniques and getting results. Their varied solutions to creative problems are a pleasure to see."

*   *   *

PARKINSON, Kathy
See PARKINSON, Kathryn N.

*   *   *

PEARSALL, Derek (Albert) 1931-

PERSONAL: Born August 28, 1931, in Birmingham, England. *Education:* University of Birmingham, B.A., 1951, M.A., 1952.

ADDRESSES: Office—Department of English, Harvard University, Cambridge, MA 02138.

CAREER: University of London, King's College, London, England, assistant lecturer, 1959-61, lecturer in English, 1961-65; University of York, Kings Manor, England, lecturer, 1965-68, senior lecturer, 1968-71, reader, 1971-76, professor of English, 1976-87, co-director of Centre for Medieval Studies, 1978-87; Harvard University, Cambridge, MA, Gurney Professor of English, 1987—. Visiting professor at University of Toronto, 1963-64, University of Minnesota, spring, 1974, University of Connecticut, autumn, 1981-84, and Harvard University, 1985-87; Lamont Distinguished Visiting Professor at Union College, NY, 1990; University of California at Los Angeles, visiting professor in Department of English, 1991, Distinguished Visiting Professor in Center for Medieval and Renaissance Studies, 1991; lecturer at universities in the United States, Canada, Europe, England, and Australia.

MEMBER: American Academy of Arts and Sciences (fellow), Early English Text Society (member of council), Medieval Academy of America (fellow), New Chaucer Society (president, 1988).

WRITINGS:

Gower and Lydgate: Writers and Their Work, edited by Geoffrey Bullough, Longmans, Green (London), 1969.

(With Elizabeth Salter) *Landscapes and Seasons of the Medieval World,* Elek, 1973.

Old English and Middle English Poetry, Routledge & Kegan Paul (London), 1976.

(Co-author of introduction) *The Auchinleck Manuscript,* Scholar Press, 1977.

Piers Plowman: An Edition of the C-Text, Edward Arnold (Baltimore, MD), 1978.

The Canterbury Tales: A Critical Study, Allen & Unwin (London), 1985.

An Annotated Critical Bibliography of Langland, Harvester Wheatsheaf (London), 1990.

EDITOR

The Floure and the Leafe and The Assembly of Ladies, Thomas Nelson (Nashville, TN), 1962, reprinted, 1980.

(With Salter) *Piers Plowman: Selections from the C-Text,* Edward Arnold 1967.

(With R. A. Waldron) *Medieval Literature and Civilization: Studies in Memory of G. N. Garmonsway,* Athlone Press (London), 1969.

(With A. S. G. Edwards) *Middle English Prose: Essays on Bibliographical Problems,* Garland Publishing (New York City), 1981.

Manuscripts and Readers in Fifteenth-Century England: The Literary Implications of Manuscript Study, D. S. Brewer (Cambridge), 1983.

Geoffrey Chaucer, *The Nun's Priest's Tale* (variorum edition), University Press, 1983.

(With Nicolette Zeeman) Salter, *Fourteenth-Century English Poetry: Contexts and Readings,* Clarendon Press (Oxford, England), 1984.

Manuscripts and Texts: Editorial Problems in Later Middle English Literature, D. S. Brewer, 1987.

(With Jeremy Griffiths) *Book Production and Publishing in Britain, 1375-1475,* Cambridge University Press, 1989.

The Floure and the Leafe, The Assembly of Ladies, The Isle of Ladies, Medieval Institute Publications, Western Michigan University (Kalamazoo, MI), 1990.

Studies in the Vernon Manuscript, D. S. Brewer, 1990.

(With Kathleen Scott) *Introduction to Piers Plowman: A Facsimile of Bodleian Library, Oxford, MS Douce 104,* D. S. Brewer, 1992.

OTHER

Contributor to books. Contributor of articles and reviews to literature journals. Chairman of advisory committee of *Index of Middle English Prose;* member of advisory board of *Modern Language Review* and *Yearbook of English Studies.*

WORK IN PROGRESS: John Lydgate: A Documentary Biography, Variorum Press; *Chaucer to Spenser: An Anthology,* Blackwell (Oxford, England); *The Chaucer Portraits,* D. S. Brewer.

SIDELIGHTS: In *Old English and Middle English Poetry,* Derek Pearsall surveys medieval English poetry. It is the first book in a six-volume History of English Poetry projected by Routledge & Kegan Paul. To write such a survey, *Times Literary Supplement* reviewer T. A. Shippey observes, "demands an implausible blend of knowledge, tact and boldness. All these qualities are shown to great advantage by Derek Pearsall."

Shippey notes that one of the book's greatest strengths is "its grasp of the different functions of poetry in premodern times." He also admires "the sense of abundance" that Pearsall evokes by elaborating not just on standard anthology pieces, but on others that never "quite made the grade." "No one is going to come away from this book without a note of something new to look up," the reviewer concludes. "Old English and Middle English Poetry does not aim at provoking total agreement . . . but it will educate the most learned on some points and stimulate the most ignorant on others."

BIOGRAPHICAL/CRITICAL SOURCES:

PERIODICALS

Times Literary Supplement, September 2, 1977.

* * *

PEITCHINIS, Stephen G(abriel) 1925-

PERSONAL: Surname is pronounced "*Pay*-chin-is"; born October 12, 1925, in Macedonia, Greece; became Canadian citizen; married Jacquelyn A. Elliott (a psychologist), September 12, 1952. *Education:* University of Western Ontario, B.A. (honors), 1954, M.A., 1955; London School of Economics and Political Science, Ph.D., 1960.

ADDRESSES: Home—#13, 1901 Varsity Estates Drive N.W., Calgary, Alberta, Canada. *Office*—Department of Economics, University of Calgary, Calgary, Alberta T2N 1N4, Canada.

CAREER: University of Western Ontario, London, instructor in economics and political science, 1955-58, assistant professor, 1960-63, associate professor of labor and public finance, 1963-68; University of Calgary, Calgary, Alberta, professor of economics, 1968-73; dean of faculty of business, 1973-76; head of department of economics, 1985-92; professor emeritus of economics, 1992—. Human Resources Research Council of Alberta, associate director, 1969-70; Council of Ministers of Education of Canada, director of research, 1970-71; Federal Department of Industry and Commerce, Ottawa, consultant, 1978-81; conciliation commissioner.

WRITINGS:

The Economics of Labour, McGraw (Canada), 1965.
Canadian Labour Economics, McGraw, 1970.
Labour-Management Relations in the Railway Industry, Queen's Printer, 1971.
The Canadian Labour Market, Oxford University Press, 1975.
The Effect of Technological Changes on Educational and Skill Requirements of Industry, Department of Industry, Trade, and Commerce (Ottawa, Canada), 1978.
Economic Implications of Computers and Telecommunications Technology, Department of Communications (Ottawa, Canada), 1980.
Computer Technology and Employment: Retrospect and Prospect, St. Martin's, 1983.
Issues in Management-Labour Relations in the 1990s, St. Martin's, 1985.
Women at Work: Discrimination and Response, McClelland & Stewart (Toronto, Ontario), 1989.

Contributor to journals in Canada, the United States, and Australia.

WORK IN PROGRESS: The Economic Implications of an Aging Population, and *Jobless Growth and Home Security.*

*   *   *

PEREZ-FIRMAT, Gustavo (Francisco) 1949-

PERSONAL: Born March 7, 1949, in Havana, Cuba; immigrated to the United States, 1960, naturalized citizen, 1973; son of Gustavo Perez (in sales) and Luz-Maria Fir-

mat (a secretary); married Rosa Perelmuter (a professor), August 10, 1973 (divorced 1990); married Mary Anne Adamson, 1991; children: (first marriage) David, Miriam. *Education:* University of Miami, B.A., 1972, M.A., 1973; University of Michigan, Ph.D., 1979.

ADDRESSES: Home—1114 Tallyho Trail, Chapel Hill, NC 27516. *Office*—Department of Romance Languages, Duke University, Durham, NC 27706.

CAREER: Duke University, Durham, NC, instructor, 1978-79, assistant professor, 1979-83, associate professor, 1983-87, professor of romance languages, 1987—, chairman, 1988-89. Visiting professor of Spanish at Middlebury College, 1983.

MEMBER: American Association of Teachers of Spanish and Portuguese, Modern Language Association of America, South Atlantic Modern Language Association.

AWARDS, HONORS: American Council of Learned Societies fellow, 1981; Mellon Foundation fellow, 1981-82; John Simon Guggenheim Memorial Foundation fellow, 1985; National Endowment for the Humanities senior fellow, 1985-86.

WRITINGS:

Idle Fictions: The Hispanic Vanguard Novel, 1926-1934, Duke University Press (Durham, NC), 1982, expanded edition, 1993.
Literature and Liminality: Festive Readings in the Hispanic Tradition, Duke University Press, 1986.
Carolina Cuban: Poems, Bilingual Review Press (Tempe, AZ), 1987.
The Cuban Condition: Translation and Identity in Modern Cuban Literature, Cambridge University Press (New York City), 1988.
Cuban Literature, Cambridge University Press, 1989.
Equivocaiones, Editorial Betania (Madrid, Spain), 1989.
(Editor and author of introduction) *Do the Americas Have a Common Literature?* Duke University Press, 1990.
Life on the Hyphen: The Cuban-American Way, University of Texas Press (Austin, TX), 1994.
Bilingual Blues, Bilingual Review Press, 1995.
Next Year in Cuba, Doubleday (New York City), 1995.

Contributor to journals, including *Bilingual Review, Caribbean Review, Comparative Literature Studies, Diacritics, Hispania, Hispanic Review, Linden Lane, Modern Language Notes,* and *Proceedings of the Modern Language Association.* Member of editorial board, *Critica Hispanica,* 1982—, *Cuban Literary Monographs,* 1983—, *Latin American Literary Review,* 1985—, and *Anales de la literatura espanola contemporanea,* 1985—, *Cuban Studies,* 1990—, *Revista de estudios colombianos,* 1991—, and *Americas Review,* 1993—.

WORK IN PROGRESS: A novel.

SIDELIGHTS: In his first book, *Idle Fictions,* Gustavo Perez-Firmat examines a lost genre of Hispanic literature—the "vanguard novel" that flourished between 1926 and 1934. As reviewer Carolyn Richmond notes in *Hispania,* the vanguard novel, "by its very nature, eludes all attempts at categorization." Thus it has come to be defined mainly negatively, in terms of what it lacks: "lifelike characters," "a believable fictional world," and "a structured plot," according to James H. Abbott in a *World Literature Today* review. Perez-Firmat divides his treatment of the genre into sections on the literary criticism of the period and on the novels themselves, including works by Pedro Salinas and Jaime Torres Bodet. Praising Perez-Firmat's "brilliant" analyses of vanguard novels, Richmond calls *Idle Fictions* "a kind of organic, many-faceted exploration of the relationship between criticism and fiction" and judged it "superbly written."

Perez-Firmat told *CA:* "I was born in Havana, but I was made in the USA. Hence I write in Spanish—my mother tongue, in English—my other tongue, and in diverse combinations of the two. My writings, critical and creative (but is there a difference?), take turns at reflecting upon, complaining about, and rejoicing in this ambivalent cultural and linguistic positioning."

BIOGRAPHICAL/CRITICAL SOURCES:

PERIODICALS

Hispania, May, 1984.
Modern Fiction Studies, winter, 1983.
World Literature Today, autumn, 1983.

*   *   *

PERLMUTTER, Nathan 1923-1987

PERSONAL: Born March 2, 1923, in New York, NY; died of lung cancer, July 12, 1987, in New York, NY; son of Hyman (a tailor) and Bella (Finkelstein) Perlmutter; married Ruth Ann Osofsky, April 2, 1943; children: Nina Perlmutter Mohit, Dean. *Education:* Attended Georgetown University, 1942-43, and Villanova College (now University), 1943-44; New York University, LL.B., 1949. *Politics:* "Variable." *Religion:* Jewish. *Avocational interests:* "Horses, when they're racing, birds not in cages, flowers and trees anywhere, anytime."

CAREER: Anti-Defamation League of B'nai B'rith, assistant director, Denver, CO, 1949-52, regional director, Detroit, MI, 1952-53, assistant director of Community Service Division, New York City, 1953-56, regional director, Miami, FL, 1956-64, director, New York City, 1964-65; American Jewish Committee, New York City, associate national director, 1965-69; Brandeis University, Waltham, MA, vice president for development, 1969-73; Anti-Defamation League of B'nai B'rith, New York City, assistant national director, 1973-79, national director, 1979-87. *Military service:* U.S. Marine Corps, 1943-46; became second lieutenant.

MEMBER: International League for the Rights of Man, American Civil Liberties Union, National Association of Intergroup Relations Officials.

AWARDS, HONORS: Nomination for 13th Annual Book Award for Best Political Book of 1982, *Washington Monthly,* for *The Real Anti-Semitism in America;* Presidential Medal of Freedom, 1987, for public service.

WRITINGS:

How to Win Money at the Races, Crowell-Collier (New York City), 1964, revised edition, Collier Books (New York City), 1979.
A Bias of Reflections: Confessions of an Incipient Old Jew, Arlington House (New York City), 1972.
(With wife, Ruth Ann Perlmutter) *The Real Anti-Semitism in America,* Arbor House (New York City), 1982.

Contributor of articles to numerous periodicals, including *Frontier, Nation, Progressive, New Leader, Commentary, National Jewish Monthly,* and *Florida Historical Quarterly.*

BIOGRAPHICAL/CRITICAL SOURCES:

PERIODICALS

Commentary, October, 1982, p. 64.
Jewish Floridian, May 22, 1964.
Miami Herald, April 22, 1964.
Miami News, March 22, 1964.
New Leader, October 4, 1982, pp. 16-17.
New York Times Book Review, October 3, 1982, pp. 15, 33.
Washington Post, June 24, 1987.

OBITUARIES:

PERIODICALS

Chicago Tribune, July 14, 1987.
Los Angeles Times, July 14, 1987.
Newsweek, July 27, 1987.
New York Times, July 14, 1987.
Time, July 27, 1987.
Washington Post, July 14, 1987.*

PERLOFF, Marjorie G(abrielle) 1931-

PERSONAL: Born September 28, 1931, in Vienna, Austria; naturalized U. S. citizen in 1945; daughter of Maximilian (a lawyer) and Ilse (an economist; maiden name, Schueller) Mintz; married Joseph K. Perloff (a physician), July 31, 1953; children: Nancy, Carey. *Education:* Attended Oberlin College, 1949-52; Barnard College, A.B., 1953; Catholic University of America, M.A., 1956, Ph.D., 1965. *Religion:* Jewish. *Avocational interests:* Travel, France, visual arts, visiting museums, photography.

ADDRESSES: Home—1467 Amalfi Dr., Pacific Palisades, CA 90272. *Office*—Department of English, Stanford University, Stanford, CA 94305.

CAREER: Catholic University of America, Washington, DC, assistant professor, 1965-68, associate professor of English, 1968-71; University of Maryland, College Park, associate professor, 1971-73, professor of English, beginning 1973; University of Southern California, Los Angeles, Florence R. Scott Professor of English and Comparative Literature, 1977-86; Stanford University, Stanford, CA, professor of English and comparative literature, 1986—, Sadie D. Patek Professor of Humanities, 1990—. Phi Beta Kappa visiting scholar, 1994-95.

MEMBER: Modern Language Association of America (member of executive council, 1977-81), American Association of University Professors, American Comparative Literature Association (president, 1993-95), Modern Humanities Research Association, Northeast Modern Language Association, South Atlantic Modern Language Association, Phi Beta Kappa.

AWARDS, HONORS: Guggenheim fellow, 1981-82; National Endowment for the Humanities senior fellow, 1985-86.

WRITINGS:

Rhyme and Meaning in the Poetry of Yeats, Mouton (Hawthorne, NY), 1970.
The Poetic Art of Robert Lowell, Cornell University Press (Ithaca, NY), 1973.
Frank O'Hara: Poet among Painters, Braziller (New York City), 1977.
The Poetics of Indeterminacy: Rimbaud to Cage, Princeton University Press (Princeton, NJ), 1981.
The Dance of the Intellect: Studies in the Poetry of the Pound Tradition, Cambridge University Press (New York City), 1985.
The Futurist Movement: Avant Garde, Avant Guerre and the Language of Rupture, University of Chicago Press (Chicago), 1986.
(Editor with others) *The Columbia Literary History of the United States,* Columbia University Press (New York City), 1987.

(Editor and author of introduction) *Postmodern Genres,* University of Oklahoma Press (Norman), 1989.
Poetic License: Essays in Modernist and Postmodernist Poetics, Northwestern University Press (Evanston), 1990.
Radical Artifice: Writing Poetry in the Age of Media, University of Chicago Press, 1992.
(Editor with Charles Junkerman, and author of introduction) *John Cage: Composed in America,* University of Chicago Press, 1994.
Towards a Wittgensteinian Poetics, University of Chicago Press, 1995.

Contributor to numerous books, including *Poetry Dimension,* edited by Dannie Abse, No. 2, Haworth Press (New York City), 1975; *George Oppen: Man and Poet,* Poetry Foundation, 1981; *Pound among the Poets,* University of Chicago Press, 1985; and *Robert Lowell: Essays on the Poetry,* Cambridge University Press, 1986. Contributor of more than one hundred fifty articles and one hundred reviews to journals.

SIDELIGHTS: Writing in the *Times Literary Supplement,* A. Walton Litz describes Marjorie G. Perloff's *The Dance of the Intellect: Studies in the Poetry of the Pound Tradition* as "a collection of occasional essays, but they are held together by a single point of view." The reviewer comments on Perloff's appreciation of the various aspects of the Pound poetic and asserts "the strongest essays are those where her comprehensive understanding of modern painting and sculpture come into play."

Perloff told *CA:* "My special pleasure, in the last few years, has been to write about contemporary poets who are also intellectuals—poet-theorists we might call them, like Susan Howe, Lyn Hejinian, Steve McCaffery, and Charles Bernstein. I think that despite all the doom-and-gloom talk about the terrible state of poetry, wonderful work is being done. That work points us back to some of the great avant-gardists of the century from Ezra Pound to John Cage. I consider myself a revisionist, and I've been writing parts of a revisionist literary history of our century. And what a century! Modernism, for a time in bad repute because of its associations with elitism and proto-Fascism, is once again being seen as the great period it was—but a complicated period, there being so many different Modernisms.

"At the moment, I'm writing a book about Wittgenstein's role as a poet and as the philosopher that poets, artists, film makers, and dramatists have turned to. Wittgenstein is endlessly fascinating in his contradictions and his genuine uniqueness. His brand of 'modernism,' which relates to writers like Gertrude Stein and Samuel Beckett, is one we don't yet fully understand. And I suppose that part of my attraction to Wittgenstein has to do with a return to my Viennese roots. I'm also writing about the Austrian writers Ingeborg Bachmann and Thomas Bernhard. This 'return to Vienna' is new for me but it relates, I think, to my other interests."

BIOGRAPHICAL/CRITICAL SOURCES:

PERIODICALS

Times Literary Supplement, October 10, 1986.

*   *   *

PERRET, Gene (Richard) 1937-

PERSONAL: Surname is pronounced *"purr*-it"; born April 3, 1937, in Philadelphia, PA; son of Joseph H. (a longshoreman) and Mary (a homemaker; maiden name, Martin) Perret; married Joanne Bonavitacola (a nurse), October 11, 1958; children: Joseph, Theresa Perret Martin, Carole Perret Maurer, Linda. *Education:* Attended Drexel Institute of Technology, 1956-60. *Avocational interests:* Tennis, guitar.

ADDRESSES: Home and office—2439 Kirsten Lee Drive, Westlake Village, CA 91361. *Agent*—Don Clark, 800 Wilshire Blvd., Los Angeles, CA 90017.

CAREER: General Electric Co., Philadelphia, PA, electrical drafting apprentice, 1956-59, electrical draftsman, 1959-63, designer, 1963-65, electrical engineer, 1965-69, drafting supervisor, 1969. Comedy writer for Mickey Shaughnessy, 1959-60, Slappy White, 1959-65, Phyllis Diller, 1964—, and Bob Hope, 1969—; scriptwriter for television shows including *The Jim Nabors Show,* 1969-70, *Rowan & Martin's Laugh-In,* 1971, *The New Bill Cosby Show,* 1972, *The Helen Reddy Show,* 1972, and *The Carol Burnett Show,* 1973-78; producer and head writer of television shows including *Welcome Back, Kotter,* 1979, *Three's Company,* 1980, *The Tim Conway Show,* 1980-81, and *Mama's Family,* 1982-83; head writer for Bob Hope specials, 1989—.

MEMBER: American Society of Journalists and Authors, National Writers Club, Authors Guild, Writers Guild.

AWARDS, HONORS: Emmy Awards for best writing of a single program in a variety or music series, National Academy of Television Arts and Sciences, 1974, 1975, and 1978, and Writers Guild Award for best television variety show script, 1974, all for *The Carol Burnett Show;* named to Upper Darby Hall of Fame, Rotary Club (Upper Darby, PA), 1978; named outstanding new performer in the field of humor, International Platform Association, 1983; Civilian Desert Shield/Desert Storm Medal, U.S. Department of Defense, 1992, for entertaining troops in Saudi Arabia.

WRITINGS:

Hit or Miss Management: The World's First Organic, Natural, Holistic, Environmentally Sound Management Technique, illustrated by Jeffrey Lieppman, Houghton (Boston), 1980.

How to Write and Sell (Your Sense of) Humor, Writer's Digest (Cincinnati), 1982, published as *Comedy Writing Step by Step: How to Write and Sell Your Sense of Humor,* Samuel French (Los Angeles), 1990.

How to Hold Your Audiences with Humor: A Guide to More Effective Speaking, Writer's Digest, 1984.

Using Humor for Effective Business Speaking, Sterling Publishing (New York), 1989.

Gene Perret's Funny Business: Speaker's Treasury of Business Humor for All Occasions, Prentice-Hall (Englewood Cliffs, NJ), 1990.

Comedy Writing Workbook, Sterling Publishing, 1990.

Funny Comebacks to Rude Remarks (juvenile joke collection), Sterling Publishing, 1990.

The Laugh-a-Minute Joke Book (juvenile joke collection), Sterling Publishing, 1991.

Super Funny School Jokes (juvenile joke collection), Sterling Publishing, 1991.

(With daughter, Terry Perret Martin) *Great One-Liners,* illustrated by Myron Miller, Sterling Publishing, 1992.

Shift Your Writing Career into High Gear, Writer's Digest, 1993.

I Love My Boss and 969 Other Business Jokes, Sterling Publishing, 1993.

(With daughter, Linda Perret) *Bigshots, Pipsqueaks, and Windbags: Jokes, Stories, and One-Liners about People, Power, and Politics,* Prentice-Hall, 1993.

Successful Stand-Up Comedy: Advice from a Comedy Writer, Samuel French, 1994.

(With Martin) *Classic One-Liners,* illustrated by Miller, Sterling Publishing, 1994.

(With Martin) *On the 8th Day God Laughed,* Hannibal Books, 1995.

Author of a monthly humor column, "Wit Stop," in *Arizona Highways.* Founder and publisher of *Round Table,* a newsletter for speakers and comedy writers. Contributor to periodicals, including *Writer's Digest* and *Toastmaster.*

WORK IN PROGRESS: If Bob Hope Calls, Tell Him I'm Not Home, "recollections of twenty-five years writing comedy for the beloved entertainer"; *Make Me Laugh or Else,* "a novel about a comedy writer with the worst assignment in the world"; *Tales from the Script,* "wacky stories of TV comedy writers"; *Clean Underwear* and *Be Cool, Don't Drool in School,* 2 volumes of humorous poetry for school children; and *Hilarious One-Liners,* collection of one-line jokes written with Martin.

SIDELIGHTS: "A good joke is a series of words that ends in a paycheck," claims comic writer Gene Perret, who has penned material for such noted comedians as Phyllis Diller, Bill Cosby, and Bob Hope. The author of monologues, television scripts, and joke books for young audiences, Perret has also compiled several works on the comedy writing process. In his 1990 book, *Comedy Writing Step by Step: How to Write and Sell Your Sense of Humor* (previously published as *How to Write and Sell [Your Sense of] Humor*), Perret opens his world of comic writing to any and all who have a sense of humor and can put pen to paper. "*Everybody* does jokes," observes Perret; improving those jokes depends only on practice. The book offers methods of sharpening one's comic skills and includes strategies for developing jokes, routines, and full skits. In a second instructional work, *How to Hold Your Audiences with Humor: A Guide to More Effective Speaking,* Perret presents his belief that speakers should use humor to capture an audience's attention and to help convey a message. Loaded with advice, both books communicate Perret's interest in sharing the art he loves. "I've written some good jokes in some bad places and some bad jokes in some good places," notes Perret, "but I've been delighted with every minute of it."

Gene Perret once told *CA:* "We've all been told that writing is a lonely profession. Comedy writing for beginners is especially so. Outside of New York and Los Angeles, there aren't any clubs or associations that an aspiring humorist can turn to. That's why I founded *Round Table,* a newsletter that's devoted to education and communication among humor writers. It's at least a monthly contact with others interested in the same profession.

"Humor has long been thought an unapproachable occupation, and many who are in the business keep the myth alive. I disagree. We have certainly learned and improved our technique through experience—why can't we pass some of that knowledge on to the next generation? Creating humor is so much fun that it should be enjoyed by more than the few who write for television or films. It can be a pleasant and useful hobby, a profitable source of part-time income, or a well-paying profession.

"I'm proud of the fact that as a television head writer and producer I've introduced many new talents into the Writers Guild. One gentleman wrote me a letter after reading an article of mine in *Writer's Digest.* I coached him for several months on a writing career, then when Bob Hope needed a lot of material for a special show, I recommended my protege, Bob Mills. He then became a full-time writer for Hope. (In fact, he made the historic trip to Red China with Hope while I had to stay home and work on *The Carol Burnett Show.*) I enjoy the enthusiasm of young writers and would like to actively teach comedy writing

or author a correspondence course for beginning humorists.

"Since I'm active in working with young writers, people ask me if comedy writing can be taught. A large part of any writing is learning the disciplines and the logistics. These can be taught, and a writer with promise can develop that much more quickly. If we only taught piano to those who would become concert performers, the world would miss out on a lot of music."

About comedians finding their own "voice," Perret once told *CA:* "It takes a long time. People like Jack Benny and Bob Hope and George Burns put in that time. They struggled; they found out the things that they *couldn't do,* and did the things they *could* do. I was amazed, in working with the good television performers, that there are many, many things they can't do. And yet, it never shows because they protect themselves against those things. They've learned to go with their strengths. It's almost the same way it is with a good tennis player or a good golfer; they play with their strengths, and they keep other people from exploiting their weaknesses. That's really what comics do. There was a good book on radio comedians that I read, and I discovered that people like Benny, Hope, and Burns kept constantly changing, changing, changing—experimenting—until they found what they were good at. Then they went with it. That's how you develop a good, strong comedy characterization."

Perret also mentioned to *CA* the benefits of studying the work of other comedy writers and comedians: "I think you find out what you do best, and you use that. You also find out what you do weakly and cover it. I tend to get very literal in my comedy; my jokes tend to get more philosophical, along the Will Rogers line, as opposed to the zany or the bizarre. And knowing this, I have to force myself sometimes in writing a routine to stop and say, OK, now it's time to do something outlandish. By doing that I give a different coloration, a different shading, to my material. I think you have to study people who do what you do, and if not take their approach totally, at least use it to shade your own strengths and give more depth to them."

BIOGRAPHICAL/CRITICAL SOURCES:

PERIODICALS

Booklist, February 1, 1993, p. 966.
Chicago Tribune, June 3, 1984.
Los Angeles Times Book Review, June 17, 1984.

PFAFF, William (Wendle III) 1928-

PERSONAL: Born December 29, 1928, in Council Bluffs, IA; son of William Wendle, Jr. (in business) and Adele (Keeline) Pfaff; married Carolyn Frances Cleary, May 1, 1964; children: Nicholas James William, Alexandra Frances Astley. *Education:* University of Notre Dame, B.A., 1949. *Politics:* Independent. *Religion:* Roman Catholic.

ADDRESSES: Home and office—72 Avenue Victor Hugo, 75116 Paris, France. *Agent*—Harold Ober Associates, Inc., 425 Madison Ave., New York, NY 10017.

CAREER: Commonweal, New York City, associate editor, 1949-55; American Broadcasting Co., News and Public Affairs, New York City, writer, 1955-57; Free Europe Committee, Inc., New York City, executive, 1957-61; Hudson Institute, Inc., Croton-on-Hudson, NY, senior member, 1961-78; Hudson Research Europe Ltd., Paris, France, deputy director, 1971-78; writer. *Military service:* U.S. Army, 1951-52.

AWARDS, HONORS: Rockefeller Foundation grant in international studies as senior fellow, Russian Institute, Columbia University, 1962-63; Best American Essays, 1987; nonfiction finalist, National Book Awards, 1989, and City of Geneva's Prix Jean-Jacques Rousseau (for French translation of book), both 1989, for *Barbarian Sentiments: How the American Century Ends;* LL.D., University of Notre Dame, 1990.

WRITINGS:

(With Edmund Stillman) *The New Politics: America and the End of the Postwar World,* Coward (New York City), 1961.
(With Stillman) *The Politics of Hysteria: The Sources of Twentieth-Century Conflict,* Harper (New York City), 1964.
(With Stillman) *Power and Impotence: The Failure of America's Foreign Policy,* Random House (New York City), 1966.
(With Frank E. Armbruster, Raymond Gastil, Herman Kahn, and Stillman) *Can We Win in Vietnam?,* Praeger (New York City), 1968.
Condemned to Freedom, Random House, 1971.
Barbarian Sentiments: How the American Century Ends, Hill & Wang (New York City), 1989.
The Wrath of Nations: Civilization and the Furies of Nationalism, Simon & Schuster (New York City), 1993.

OTHER

Contributor to books. Contributor to *Foreign Affairs, Harper's,* and other periodicals. Political commentator, *New Yorker,* 1972-92; columnist, *International Herald Tribune,* 1978—, and the *Los Angeles Times* syndicate, 1986—.

Pfaff's *Barbarian Sentiments: How the American Century Ends* has been translated into French, German, and Spanish.

BIOGRAPHICAL/CRITICAL SOURCES:

PERIODICALS

Salmagundi, spring-summer, 1986.

*　　*　　*

POCOCK, Thomas Allcot Guy 1925-
(Tom Pocock)

PERSONAL: Born August 18, 1925, in London, England; son of Guy Noel (a writer) and Dorothy (Bowers) Pocock; married Penelope Casson, April 26, 1969; children: Laura Jane, Hannah Lucy. *Education:* Attended Westminster School and Cheltenham College, England. *Religion:* Church of England.

ADDRESSES: Home—22 Lawrence St., London SW3 5NF, England.

CAREER: Leader, London, England, war correspondent, 1945, feature writer, 1945-48; *Daily Mail,* London, naval and military correspondent and special writer, 1949-52; *Times,* London, naval correspondent, 1952-55; *Daily Express,* London, Middle East correspondent and feature writer, 1955-57; *Elizabethan,* London, co-editor, 1957-59; Evening Standard Co. Ltd., London, *Evening Standard,* defense and war correspondent, 1960-74, travel editor, 1974-82, *London Standard,* special writer, 1982-1988. *Military Service:* Served in Royal Navy, 1943-44.

MEMBER: Chelsea Society (member of council, 1965—), Garrick Club, Chelsea Arts Club, Norfolk Club.

WRITINGS:

UNDER NAME TOM POCOCK

Nelson and His World, Thames & Hudson (London, England), 1968.
Chelsea Reach: The Brutal Friendship of Whistler and Walter Greaves, Hodder & Stoughton (London, England), 1970.
London Walks, Thames & Hudson, 1973.
Fighting General, Collins (London, England), 1973.
Remember Nelson, Collins, 1977.
The Young Nelson in the Americas, Collins, 1980.
1945: The Dawn Came Up Like Thunder, Collins, 1983.
East and West of Suez: The Retreat from Empire, Bodley Head (London, England), 1986.
Horatio Nelson, Bodley Head, 1987.
Alan Moorehead, Bodley Head, 1990.
Sailor King, Sinclair-Stevenson, 1991.

Rider Haggard and the Lost Empire, Weidenfeld and Nicolson (London, England), 1993.

Author of documentary film scripts for public service groups; contributor to magazines.

WORK IN PROGRESS: Norfolk, A History.

SIDELIGHTS: Thomas Allcot Guy Pocock once commented to *CA:* "I am a journalistic rather than an academic historian, and have used my long experience as a newspaper correspondent (including covering wars in Algeria, Malaya, Arabia, Borneo, Cyprus, Aden, India, and Vietnam, as well as the end of World War II) to recreate the physical and emotional background to historical events. I have visited all the scenes of Lord Nelson's activities around the world, using the knowledge gained to give depth to material gathered through documentary research."

Critics praise Pocock for his ability to recreate the atmosphere of a particular historical period. In the London *Observer,* Vernon Bogdanor writes that Pocock "brilliantly evokes the sights and sounds of Britain and Europe" in his *1945: The Dawn Came Up Like Thunder.* Bogdanor thinks that "Pocock conveys beautifully the sense of wonder which that land of riches, luxury and power across the Atlantic inspired in those days." In a review of *East and West of Suez: The Retreat from Empire,* which chronicles Britain's diminishing colonialism, *Times Literary Supplement*'s John Luxmoore points out: "There are, in Pocock's colourful and unpretentious account, traces of make-believe which aptly convey the flavour of these events." Although A. J. Stockwell suggests in *British Book News* that the "immediacy of his original despatches" is not completely recaptured, he feels that what is "successfully conveyed by [Pocock's] chilling accounts . . . is the dread risk run by journalists committed to bringing us world news."

BIOGRAPHICAL/CRITICAL SOURCES:

PERIODICALS

British Book News, October, 1980; October, 1986.
Observer (London), October 9, 1983.
Times Literary Supplement, October 23, 1970; December 19, 1980; December 19, 1986.

*   *   *

POCOCK, Tom
     See POCOCK, Thomas Allcot Guy

POLK, Noel E(arl)   1943-

PERSONAL: Born February 23, 1943, in Picayune, MS; son of Earl E. (a merchant) and Ayeleen (a librarian; maiden name, Hamilton) Polk; married Patricia Parrott, January 27, 1967 (divorced, September, 1990); children: Jennifer, Scott. *Education:* Mississippi College, B.A., 1965, M.A., 1966; University of South Carolina—Columbia, Ph.D., 1970.

ADDRESSES: Home—707 Adeline St., Hattiesburg, MS 39401. *Office*—Department of English, University of Southern Mississippi, Hattiesburg, MS 39406.

CAREER: University of Texas at Arlington, assistant professor of English, 1970-74; University of South Carolina at Columbia, visiting associate research professor and bibliographer in Southern Studies Program, 1974-76; independent researcher, 1976-77; University of Southern Mississippi, Hattiesburg, assistant professor, 1977-79, associate professor, 1979-83, professor of English, 1983—. Founding member, past president, and member of board of governors of Mississippi Institute of Arts and Letters.

MEMBER: Modern Language Association of America, South Atlantic Modern Language Association, South Central Modern Language Association, Mississippi Historical Society.

AWARDS, HONORS: Grants from National Endowment for the Humanities, 1979-81, 1986-89, 1991, 1994-95; Professeur Associe at University of Strasbourg, 1981-82.

WRITINGS:

(Editor) *Faulkner's "Marionettes,"* University Press of Virginia (Charlottesville, VA), 1977.
(Editor with James R. Scafidel) *An Anthology of Mississippi Writers,* University Press of Mississippi (Jackson, MS), 1979.
The Literary Manuscripts of Harold Frederic: A Catalogue, Garland Publishing (New York City), 1979.
Faulkner's "Requiem for a Nun": A Critical Study, Indiana University Press (Bloomington, IN), 1981.
(Editor) *Faulkner's "Sanctuary": The Original Text,* Random House (New York City), 1981.
(Editor) William Faulkner, *The Sound and the Fury,* Random House, 1984.
An Editorial Handbook for "The Sound and the Fury," Garland Publishing, 1985.
(Editor) *Faulkner: Novels, 1930-1935,* Library of America, 1985.
(Editor) William Faulkner, *"Absalom, Absalom!": The Corrected Text,* Random House, 1986.
(Editor) *Faulkner: Novels, 1936-1940,* Library of America, 1988.
(Editor) *Faulkner: Novels, 1942-1954,* Library of America, 1994.

Eudora Welty: A Bibliography of Her Work, University Press of Mississippi, 1994.

Also textual editor of "William Faulkner Computer Concordance," University Microfilms, 1978—.

WORK IN PROGRESS: Children of the Dark House: William Faulkner, 1927-1936.

SIDELIGHTS: According to *Times Literary Supplement* reviewer Peter Kemp, Noel Polk's *Faulkner's "Requiem for a Nun": A Critical Study* represents an attempt to disprove the generally accepted claim that this work is one of Faulkner's more simple-minded achievements, an inferior and simplistic novel. Polk regards *Requiem for a Nun* as a major work. Kemp commends Polk's "alert perusal of the text," which "supplies much that is valuably thought-provoking."

BIOGRAPHICAL/CRITICAL SOURCES:

PERIODICALS

Times Literary Supplement, January 22, 1982.

*   *   *

POLNER, Murray   1928-

PERSONAL: Surname is pronounced *Pole*-ner; born May 15, 1928, in Brooklyn, NY; son of Alex (a salesman) and Rebecka (Meyerson) Polner; married Louise Greenwald (a teacher) June 16, 1950; children: Beth, Alex, Robert. *Education:* City College (now City College of the City University of New York), B.S.S., 1950; University of Pennsylvania, M.A., 1951; Columbia University, graduate study, 1951-53, 1955-57, certificate of Russian Institute, 1967; Union Graduate School, Ph.D., 1972. *Politics:* Liberal. *Religion:* Judaism.

ADDRESSES: Home—50-10 Concord Ave., Great Neck, NY 11020. *Agent*—Philip Spitzer Literary Agency Inc., 50 Talmadge Farm Lane, East Hampton, NY 11937.

CAREER: Thomas Jefferson High School, Brooklyn, NY, social studies teacher, 1956-66; Suffolk County Community College, Selden, NY associate professor of history, 1966-69; Board of Education, Brooklyn, NY, member, then executive assistant to the New York City Public Schools chancellor, 1969-72; *Present Tense,* New York City, editor in chief, 1972-1990. Visiting lecturer in history and political science, at various institutions, including Brooklyn College (now Brooklyn College of the City University of New York), Queens College (now Queens College of the City University of New York), Adelphi University, University of Maine at Orono, and St. Dunstan University, Canada, 1965-76; Lakeville Press, Inc., president,

1980-89. *Military Service:* U.S. Naval Reserve, 1947-52. U.S. Army, 1953-55.

MEMBER: PEN American Center, American Society of Journalists and Authors, Jewish Peace Fellowship (vice president, 1975—), Fellowship of Reconciliation.

WRITINGS:

Enriching Social Studies, Prentice-Hall (Englewood Cliffs, NJ), 1961.
(With Arthur Barron) *Where Shall We Take the Kids?,* Doubleday (New York City), 1961.
(With Barron) *The Questions Children Ask,* Macmillan (New York City), 1964.
No Victory Parades: The Return of the Vietnam Veteran, Holt (New York City), 1971.
Rabbi: The American Experience, Holt, 1977.
(With David Bresnick and Seymour P. Lachman) *Black, White, Red and Green,* Longman (New York City), 1978.
Branch Rickey: A Biography, Atheneum (New York City), 1982.
Peace and Justice, New Society Publishers (Philadelphia, PA), 1994.

Also contributor to *America and the Asian Revolutions,* edited by Robert Jay Lifton, Aldine, 1970; *Crisis: Student Dissent in the Public Schools,* edited by Irving G. Hedrick and Reginald L. Jones, Houghton, 1971; *Abnormal Psychology and Modern Life,* edited by William Broen and James C. Coleman, 4th edition, Scott, Foresman, 1972. Contributor to *New York Times Book Review, New York Times, Commonweal, Nation, Washington Monthly, Washington Post,* and other journals and newspapers.

EDITOR

Reflections of a Russian Statesman, University of Michigan Press (Ann Arbor, MI), 1965.
"The Conquest of the United States by Spain" and Other Essays by William Graham Sumner, Regnery, 1965.
When Can I Come Home: A Debate on Amnesty for Antiwar Prisoners, Exiles and Others, Doubleday (New York City), 1972.
The Disarmament Catalog, Pilgrim Press (New York City), 1982.
American Jewish Biographies, Facts on File (New York City), 1982.
Jewish Profiles: Great Jewish Personalities & Institutions of the Twentieth Century, J. Aronson (New York City), 1991.
(Co-editor) *The Challenge of Shalom: The Jewish Tradition of Peace and Justice,* New Society Publishers, 1994.

Also editor of *Shalom: Jewish Peace Letter,* and co-editor, *P.S.: The Intelligent Guide to Jewish Affairs.*

WORK IN PROGRESS: Biography of Daniel and Philip Berrigan for Basic Books.

*　　*　　*

POMERANCE, Bernard 1940-

PERSONAL: Born in 1940 in Brooklyn, NY. *Education:* Attended University of Chicago.

ADDRESSES: Office—c/o Faber & Faber Ltd., 3 Queen Sq., London, WC1N 3AU, England.

CAREER: Playwright. Co-founder of Foco Novo theatre group, London.

AWARDS, HONORS: Antoinette Perry (Tony) Award, New York Drama Critics Circle Award, Drama Desk Award, and Obie Award, all 1979, all for *The Elephant Man.*

WRITINGS:

PLAYS

High in Vietnam Hot Damn (first produced by Foco Novo Theatre Group, London, 1971), published in *Gambit 6,* 1972.

Hospital (first produced by Foco Novo Theatre Group, London, 1971), published in *Gambit 6,* 1972.

Thanksgiving before Detroit (first produced by Foco Novo Theatre Group, London, 1971), published in *Gambit 6,* 1972.

Foco Novo, produced by Foco Novo Theatre Group, London, 1972.

Someone Else Is Still Someone, produced by Foco Novo Theatre Group, London, 1974.

A Man's a Man (adaptation of a play by Brecht), produced in London, 1975.

The Elephant Man (first produced at Hampstead Theatre, London; produced Off-Broadway at Theater of St. Peter's Church, January 14, 1979; produced on Broadway at Booth Theater, April 19, 1979), Grove (New York City), 1979.

Quantrill in Lawrence (first produced in London, 1980), Faber (London), 1981.

Melons, first produced at Pit Theatre, London, 1985; produced in New Haven, CT, 1987.

POETRY

We Need to Dream All This Again: An Account of Crazy Horse, Custer, and the Battle for the Black Hills, Penguin (New York City), 1987.

Contributor of poetry to *Harper's Magazine.*

SIDELIGHTS: When Bernard Pomerance left his native New York city to settle in London in the early 1970s, his ambition was to be a novelist. Before long, however, he realized that drama was his forte. Pomerance became involved with the left-wing fringe theatre groups that were flourishing in London at the time. Teaming up with director Roland Rees, he founded the Foco Novo Theatre Group, which has subsequently produced all of his plays, including *High in Vietnam Hot Damn* and *Someone Else Is Still Someone.* The play that first brought Pomerance to the attention of the general public was *The Elephant Man,* which had a long and successful run at the Hampstead Theatre before being brought to New York City in January of 1979, where it met with widespread critical acclaim.

Pomerance's award-winning play is based on the true story of Englishman John Merrick (1836-1890). Merrick was afflicted with a disease (scientists now believe it was neurofibromatosis, a genetic disorder) that grotesquely deformed him. His head was thirty-six inches in circumference, hideous growths covered his body, and his hips were so deformed that he could barely walk. He earned a living as a sideshow freak before he was befriended by Frederick Treves, a prominent surgeon. In addition to providing Merrick with a home at London Hospital, Treves sought to introduce the young man to Victorian society. Under Treve's guidance, Merrick became a figure in London society, visited by members of the Royal Family and aristocrats. Pomerance first learned of Merrick while he was visiting the medical museum at London Hospital, where Merrick's bones are on display. A book written by Treves, *The Elephant Man and Other Reminiscences,* and a study of Merrick by Ashley Montagu provided the source material for Pomerance's play.

One of the problems in staging *The Elephant Man* is how to convey the sense of Merrick's hideously misshapen body, In a prefatory note to *The Elephant Man,* Pomerance wrote: "Any attempt to reproduce his (Merrick's) appearance and his voice naturalistically—if it were possible—would seem to me not only counterproductive, but the more remarkably successful it was, the more distracting it would be." Instead of relying on make-up and padding to suggest Merrick's deformity, Pomerance uses a clever theatrical device. Early in the play, Treves brings Merrick to London Hospital to lecture about him. In the course of the lecture the audience views enlarged photographs of the real Merrick. "The pictures are so horrifying, so explicit in their detail, that we transfer the image to the actor beside the screen, even though he is simply contorting his body," Martin Gottfried observed in the *Saturday Review.* Other critics as well found that they had no difficulty in believing that the actor on the stage was horribly deformed. Many paid tribute to the talent of Philip Anglim, who played the part of Merrick in the New York production. Through his twisted motions and muffled speech, Anglim convinced the audience that the man he was playing was so repulsive that people would shriek and run away from him in terror.

However deformed his body, Merrick is portrayed in the play as an intelligent and sensitive man. His innocence often causes him to challenge the ideas and assumptions presented to him by his more worldly benefactors. According to Richard Eder in the *New York Times,* Pomerance "has made Merrick not an abstraction, but a most individual exemplar of Natural Man. His deformities are external; they stand for the deformities, social and moral, that twist the lives of those who crowd about him; but his spirit is clear, vulnerable and acute." As the play progresses, Merrick's pure and questioning spirit is subdued. The drama, Eder explained, is a "haunting parable about natural man trading his frail beauty and innocence for the protection and prison of society."

The two other principal characters in the play are Treves and Madge Kendal. Treves, *New Yorker* contributor Edith Oliver pointed out, is portrayed as "a complex man, responsible, encouraging, and sympathetic, but a Victorian whose spontaneous kindness seems to conflict with his squeamishness about sex and his utter trust in rules and standards." The kindly physician teaches Merrick how to conform to society, but he tragically comes to realize that this educational process has had many detrimental effects on both the physical and mental health of his patient.

Initially, Treves has difficulty finding anyone who would care for the horribly deformed Merrick. He resorts to hiring an actress, Madge Kendal, to visit Merrick in the hopes that she can use her acting skills to hide her repulsion. Merrick and Kendal become close friends. He is able to express his deepest feelings to her, and in a moving scene she reaches out to this sexually repressed man by undressing to the waist for him. Both characters benefit from their relationship. Carole Shelly, the actress who played Kendal in the New York production, asserted that Kendal is "a woman who has crippled herself by not trusting others. It's through her experience with Merrick that she opens herself to goodness again. It comes full circle at the end. She has given him the ability to laugh at his pain and she herself comes out richer, having known the elephant man."

Several critics observed that the driving tension of *The Elephant Man* fell off in the second act. John Simon, writing in *New York* magazine, described the first act as "terse, thoughtful, theatrical in the best sense, and devoid of spurious rhetoric—a lesson from Brecht well learned, with an added touch of humanity often lacing in the master." However, he felt that the second act suffers from "some insufficiently developed marginalia . . . , some less than revelatory speechifying . . . , some top-heavy irony with a few minor characters reduced to overconvenient contrivances. Above all, too many, and conflicting, layers of symbolism." Eder offered an explanation as to why the second act is the weaker half of the play: "In part it is inevitable: the opening up of the Elephant Man is more exciting than his decline. And furthermore many of the themes that are dramatized at the beginning remain to be expounded at the end. They are expounded very well indeed, but some of the play's immediacy flags a bit."

In viewing *The Elephant Man* as a whole, however, reviewers were generous with their praise. Gottfried commented that its flaws "do not fatally mar the play, for what counts most is its overwhelming humanity; its tragedy and compassion; its soaring poetry; the theatrical beauty it makes of the contrast between innocence, deformity, and the stark Victorian staging." "*The Elephant Man,*" Stanley Kauffmann maintained in the *New Republic,* "is the best new American play since 1972," while T. E. Kalem, writing in *Time,* declared that the drama is "lofted on poetic wings and nests in the human heart."

Despite the stunning success of *The Elephant Man,* Bernard Pomerance remains a mysterious figure. He fled back to England shortly after *The Elephant Man* opened in New York City. In a rare interview, he talked with Michael Owen of the *New York Times* about his conception of drama. "The most important element in theater is the audience's imagination," he remarked. "What is in them, is in me. It goes back to the function of memory. My function is—I don't know the proper word—is to remind them that this too is true, though our consciousness may deny it. I don't mean to tell them something they do not already know. I'm not bringing hot news. My interest in the audience is to remind them of a common thing and, if only temporarily, they do then become a unity, a community."

Pomerance's play *Melons* was produced in London in the 1985-1986 season. Writing a report on the London theater scene for the *New York Times,* Benedict Nightingale said that this play was "recognizably the fruit of the same moral imagination, it too is about a noble savage oppressed and exploited by a civilization with less claim to true virtue than himself." *Melons* is set on a New Mexico Pueblo Indian reservation in 1906, where an old Apache warrior leader named Caracol (called John Lame Deer by the white men) is living in seclusion. Caracol is confronted by a former enemy, ex-cavalry officer Stolsky, who is now working for an oil company that wishes to survey the Indian's land, an assignment that needs Caracol's cooperation.

Irving Wardle, reviewing *Melons* for the London *Times,* felt that the play's confusing structure diminished its appeal. "Instead of proceeding in a straight line toward an inescapable tragic outcome," he wrote, "the action undergoes labyrinthian contortions, as Caracol embarks on prolonged speeches evoking the massacre of his family and his reunion with them, events loop into flashbacks and double-flashbacks." Nightingale agreed, suggesting that the play might have worked better as a "ruminative monologue" for the central character alone. Both reviewers, however, had high praise for actor Ben Kingsley in the role of Caracol/John Lame Deer. In 1987, *Melons* was given its American premiere by the Yale Repertory Theater. Despite strong performances in all the major roles, *New York Times* reviewer Mel Gussow reported that the play was "thoughtful drama, but its portent has to be mined from beneath the verbiage." As had reviewers of the London performance, Gussow was jarred by the bloody conclusion of the play, in which Caracol ritualistically beheads two geologists.

In 1987, Pomerance also published *We Need to Dream All This Again: An Account of Crazy Horse, Custer, and the Battle for the Black Hills.* This book-length narrative poem recreates the events surrounding the 1876 Battle of the Little Big Horn. Martin Kirby in the *New York Times Book Review* called Pomerance's verse "prosy" and described the narrative as "mixing pathos and satire." Kirby felt that Pomerance was unsuccessful in the devices he used in an attempt to revitalize what has become a cliche Indian/White confrontation. He objected particularly to the use of "arch, smirking metaphors derived from current popular culture. 'Crazy Horse goes not left or right, but—imagine Dr. J. driving on Bill Russell—takes it straight to Red Cloud.' " Kirby concluded his review by flatly stating, "The book simply does not work."

BIOGRAPHICAL/CRITICAL SOURCES:

BOOKS

Contemporary Literary Criticism, Volume 13, Gale (Detroit), 1980.

Graham, Peter W., and Fritz H. Oehlschlaeger, *Articulating the Elephant Man: Joseph Merrick and His Interpreters,* Johns Hopkins University Press (Baltimore, MD), 1992.

Pomerance, Bernard, *The Elephant Man,* Grove (New York City), 1979.

PERIODICALS

Chicago Tribune, June 6, 1979.
Drama, winter, 1972; autumn, 1974; winter, 1977-1978.
Harper's, April, 1987, p. 31.
Library Journal, May 15, 1987, p. 98.
New Republic, February 17, 1979; May 12, 1979.
Newsweek, February 5, 1979, p. 67.
New York, May 7, 1979.
New Yorker, January 29, 1979; April 30, 1979, p. 45-46.

New York Times, January 15, 1979; February 4, 1979; April 15, 1979; April 20, 1979, p. 7; April 21, 1979; May 1, 1979; June 3, 1979; August 14, 1979; January 26, 1986; November 14, 1987.
New York Times Book Review, August 23, 1987, p. 17.
Publishers Weekly, April 3, 1987, p. 66.
Saturday Review, March 17, 1979, p. 60.
Time, January 29, 1979, p. 64.
Times (London), December 20, 1985.
Variety, November 11, 1987, p. 97.
Washington Post, May 20, 1979.
Western American Literature, winter, 1988, p. 358.

*   *   *

POOLE, Peggy 1925-
(Terry Roche)

PERSONAL: Born March 8, 1925, in Canterbury, Kent, England; daughter of Reginald and Barbara (Tate) Thornton; married Reginald Poole (an executive), August, 1949 (died in 1994); children: Catherine, Barbara, Elizabeth. *Education:* Attended Benenden School in England.

ADDRESSES: Home—36 Hilbre Court, West Kirby, Wirral, Merseyside L48 3JU, England.

CAREER: Worked in the Bodleian Library, Oxford, England, 1946-47; secretary for physicians in London, 1947-49; British Broadcasting Corp. (BBC), Radio Merseyside, editor and presenter of *First Heard* poetry program, 1976-88; BBC North, poetry adviser to *Write Now,* 1988—. Adjudicator for various national poetry contests. *Military service:* Women's Royal Naval Service, 1943-45.

MEMBER: Poetry Society, Society of Women Writers and Journalists, Jabberwocky, Windows Management Group, Merseyside Arts Association.

WRITINGS:

POEMS

Never a Put up Job (poetry), Quentin Nelson, 1970.
Cherry Stones and Other Poems, Headland (Penzance, England), 1983.
No Wilderness in Them, Windows (Liverpool), 1984.
Midnight Walk and Other Poems, Envoi (Newport, England), 1986.
Hesitations, Brentham Press (London), 1990.
Trusting the Rainbow, Brentham Press, 1994.

UNDER PSEUDONYM TERRY ROCHE

Brum (for children), illustrated by Beryl Sanders, Dobson (Brancepeth Castle, England), 1978.
Shadows on the Sand (for children), Dobson, 1979.
Your Turn to Put the Light Out (for teenaged readers), Dobson, 1980.

Also author of *Spring of Wild Heather,* 1989.

OTHER

(Coeditor) *Windfall* (anthology), Kettleshill Press, 1994.
Sydney the Airport Sparrow (for children), EPD Singapore, 1995.
Clarissa the Station Cat (for children), EPD Singapore, 1995.

Work has appeared in anthologies, including *All Made of Fantasy,* 1980. Contributor of poems to books, including *Criminal Records,* Viking Penguin, 1994; *Stand-Up Poetry,* Leicester University Press; *Christian Poetry,* Collins; and *Poet's England: Kent,* Brentham Press. Poetry also broadcast on BBC Radio 4. Contributor of short stories, poems, and articles to *Guardian, Liverpool Daily Post, Loving, She, Woman's Weekly, Acumen, The Countryman, Country Quest, New Poetry, Orbis, Outposts, Poetry Nottingham,* and *Smoke.* Columnist, *Deesider,* 1974-75.

SIDELIGHTS: Peggy Poole told *CA:* "In my children's books, fact mixes with fiction. Six successive holidays on the canals resulted in *Brum,* while *Shadows on the Sand* is set in Merseyside. The best part, for me as author, is when the fictional characters take over the story; the controversial ending in *Your Turn to Put the Light Out* was 'dictated' to me in the night. The two 'transport' books of 1995 were triggered by personal experiences at Manchester Airport and British Railway's Liverpool Line Street.

"For sixteen years I co-organised Jabberwocky, a monthly evening of poetry old and new, published and unpublished. Jabberwocky also produced four poetry collections and enjoyed readings from national poets including Stephen Spender, Ted Hughes, Seamus Heaney, Thom Gunn, and Douglas Dunn.

"Reading other poets' work on radio every week is a responsibility I never underestimate, and I never cease to relish the fact that radio can seduce and surprise people into enjoying poetry.

"Living on the shores of the Dee estuary with Wales across the water means my work is increasingly influenced by the sea, and the title poem of *Trusting the Rainbow* is a long allegory of a modern Noah. Art is another spur, and I have written poems on the work of Sir Stanley Spencer, Lucien Frend, Sir John Everett Millais, John Constable, and many others."

*   *   *

PORQUERAS-MAYO, Alberto 1930-

PERSONAL: Born January 13, 1930, in Lerida, Spain; immigrated to United States, c. 1958, naturalized citizen, 1973; son of Jose Maria (a physician) and Pilar (Mayo) Porqueras; children: Maria Teresa, Nicole, Meritxell. *Education:* Attended University of Barcelona, 1947-50; University of Madrid, Licenciatura (master's degree), 1952, Ph.D., 1954; University of Bonn, postdoctoral study, 1954-55. *Religion:* Roman Catholic.

ADDRESSES: Office—4080 Foreign Language Building, 707 South Matthews, University of Illinois, Urbana, IL 61801.

CAREER: University of Madrid, Madrid, Spain, assistant professor of Spanish literature, 1953-54; University of Hamburg, Hamburg, Germany, lecturer in Spanish language and literature, 1955-58; Emory University, Atlanta, GA, assistant professor of Spanish, 1958-60; University of Missouri—Columbia, associate professor, 1960-64, professor of Spanish, 1964-68; University of Illinois at Urbana-Champaign, professor of Spanish literature, 1968—, associate member of Center for Advanced Studies, 1970-71, 1981-82, and 1988-89. International University of Santander, instructor in Spanish, summers, 1952, 1953, and 1957; University of Bonn, codirector of seminar of Catalan dialectology, summer, 1955; visiting professor at Western Reserve University (now Case Western Reserve University), summers, 1959 and 1963, University of Colorado, summer, 1961, University of Mainz, 1985-86, Universidad Autonoma, Barcelona, 1989, University of Genova, 1989, University of Palermo, 1993, University of Barcelona, 1993-94, and University of Lleida, 1994.

MEMBER: International Association of Hispanists, International Association of Catalan, American Comparative Literature Association, Asociacion Europea de Profesores de Espanol, North American Catalan Association (honorary president).

AWARDS, HONORS: Scholarship to study literary criticism in Germany, High Council of Scientific Research in Madrid, 1954-55; Menendez Pelayo Prize for research in literature, 1955; nominated Miembro Correspondiente of Instituto de Estudios Ilerdenses, 1964, in recognition of research on Lope de Vega and Lerida; American Philosophical Society grants for research in Spain, 1966-67 and 1976; research grant, Comite Conjunto Hispano-norteamericano, 1988-89.

WRITINGS:

El prologo como genero literario: Su estudio en el Siglo de Oro (title means "The Prologue as Literary Genre: Its Study in the Golden Age"), Consejo Superior de Investigaciones Cientificas, 1957.
El problema de la verdad poetica en el Siglo de Oro (monograph; title means "The Problem of Poetic Truth in the Golden Age"), Ateneo, 1961.

(With F. Sanchez Escribano) *Preceptiva dramatica espanola del Renacimiento y Barroco* (title means "Spanish Dramatic Theory in Renaissance and Baroque"), Gredos, 1965, 2nd edition, 1972.

El prologo en el Renacimiento espanol (title means "The Prologue in Spanish Renaissance"), Consejo Superior de Investigaciones Cientificas, 1965.

El prologo en el Manierismo y Barroco espanoles (title means "The Prologue in Spanish Mannerism and Baroque"), Consejo Superior de Investigationes Cientificas, 1968.

(With J. L. Laurenti) *Ensayo bibliografico del prologo en la literatura* (title means "Bibliographic Essay on the Prologues in Literature"), Consejo Superior de Investigaciones Cientificas, 1971.

Temas y formas de la literatura espanola (title means "Themes and Forms in Spanish Literature"), Gredos, 1972.

(Author of introduction) Calderon, *La vida es sueno* [and] *El alcalde de Zalamea*, Espasa-Calpe, 1977.

(With Laurenti) *The Spanish Golden Age (1472-1700): A Catalog of Rare Books Held in the Library of the University of Illinois and in Selected North American Libraries*, G. K. Hall (Boston), 1979.

(With Laurenti), *Estudios bibliograficos de la Edad de Oro. Fondos raros y colecciones en la Universidad de Illinois*, preface by Jose Simon Diaz, Puvill, 1984.

La teoria poetica en el Renacimiento y Manierismo espanoles, Puvill Libros (Barcelona, Spain), 1986.

La teoria poetica en el Manierismo y Barroco espanoles, Puvill, 1989.

(With Laurenti) *Nuevos estudios bibliograficos de la Edad de Oro. (Mas fondos y colecciones de la Universidad de Illinois) Nuevos estudios bibliograficos de la Edad de Oro. Mas fondos raros y colecciones de la Universidad de Illinois*, Publicaciones y Promociones Universitarias, 1994.

EDITOR

Alfonso de Carvallo, *El cisne de Apolo* (title means "The Swan of Apollo"), two volumes, Consejo Superior de Investigaciones Cientificas, 1958.

(With C. Rojas) *Filologia y critica hispanica: Homenaje al Prof. F. Sanchez Escribano* (title means "Spanish Philology and Criticism: Homage to Prof. F. Sanchez Escribano"), Alcala, 1969.

Pedro Calderon, *El principe constante*, Espasa-Calpe, 1975.

(With Jaume Marti i Olivella and Carme Rey i Grange) *Antologia de la narrativa catalana dels 70*, Publicacions de L'Abadia de Montserrat, 1980, translation published as *The New Catalan Short Story: An Anthology*, University Press of America (Lanham, MD), 1983.

(With J. C. Mundi and F. Mundi) *Estudios sobre Calderon y el teatro Edad de Oro, homenaje a Kurt y Roswitha Reichenberger*, Promociones y Publicaciones Universitarias (Barcelona), 1989.

Contributor of articles and reviews to *Atlantida, Boletin de Filologia Espanola, Bulletin Hispanique, Estudios Clasicos, Hispanic Review, Revista de Filologia Espanola, Revista Hispanica Moderna, Revista de Literatura, Romance Notes, Romanische Forschungen, Segismundo,* and many other journals.

WORK IN PROGRESS: Two books; several articles and book reviews.

BIOGRAPHICAL/CRITICAL SOURCES:

BOOKS

Laurenti, Joseph L., and Vern G. Williamsen, editors, *Varia hispanica, homenaje a Alberto Porqueras-Mayo,* Reichenberger (Kassel, Germany), 1989.

*   *   *

PORTER, Bernard (John) 1941-

PERSONAL: Born February 5, 1941, in Essex, England; son of Cyril George (a teacher) and Ruth (a teacher; maiden name, Rabbett) Porter; married Deirdre O'Hara (a state registered nurse), July 29, 1972; children: Zoe Caroline, Benedict Campion, Kate. *Education:* Corpus Christi College, Cambridge, B.A., 1963, M.A. and Ph.D., both 1967. *Religion:* "Agnostic, with Methodist upbringing." *Avocational interests:* Art, architecture, classical music (especially nineteenth-century romantic music), cricket, science fiction.

ADDRESSES: Home—20 Lansdowne Gardens, Jesmond, Newcastle-upon-Tyne, NE2 1HE, England. *Office*—Department of History, University of Newcastle, Newcastle, NE1 7RU, England.

CAREER: Cambridge University, Cambridge, England, research fellow at Corpus Christi College, 1966-68; University of Hull, Hull, England, lecturer, 1968-78, senior lecturer, 1978-87, reader in history, 1987-92; University of Newcastle, Newcastle, England, professor of modern history, 1992—.

MEMBER: Association of University Teachers, Historical Association, Royal Historical Society (fellow).

WRITINGS:

Critics of Empire: British Radical Attitudes to Colonialism in Africa, 1896-1914, Macmillan (New York City), 1968.

The Lion's Share: A Short History of British Imperialism, 1850-1970, Longman (New York City), 1976, 2nd edition published as *The Lion's Share: A Short History of British Imperialism, 1850-1983,* 1984.

The Refugee Question in Mid-Victorian Politics, Cambridge University Press (New York City), 1979.

Britain, Europe, and the World, 1850-1982, Allen & Unwin (Winchester, MA), 1983, 2nd edition published as *Britain, Europe, and the World, 1850-1986,* 1987.

The Origins of the Vigilant State: The London Metropolitan Police Special Branch before the First World War, Weidenfeld (London), 1987.

Plots and Paranoia: A History of Political Espionage in Britain, 1790-1988, Unwin Hyman (London), 1989.

Britannia's Burden: The Political Evolution of Modern Britain, 1857-1990, Edward Arnold (London), 1994.

OTHER

Contributor to books, including *The South African War,* edited by Peter Warwick, Longman, 1980; *Edwardian England,* edited by Donald Read, Croom Helm (London), 1982; *Fabian Essays in Socialist Thought,* edited by B. Pimlott, Heinemann (London), 1984. Contributor of articles to professional journals, including *Journal of Imperial and Commonwealth History, Immigrants and Minorities, Victorian Studies, Historical Journal, History Today, Times Higher Education Supplement, Intelligence and National Security, Bulletin of the Society for the Study of Labour History,* and *Encyclopedia International.* Editor, *Journal of Imperial and Commonwealth History,* 1979-82.

*   *   *

POWLING, Chris 1943-

PERSONAL: Born February 16, 1943, in London, England; son of Leonard (in sales) and Queenie (Richings) Powling; married Janet Smith (a bookseller and promoter), August 27, 1966; children: Katie, Ellie. *Education:* St. Catherine's College, Oxford, M.A., 1965; King's College, London, Postgraduate Certificate in Education, 1966; Royal Academy of Music, L.R.A.M., 1968; Institute of Education, London, Advanced Diploma in Education, 1970; University of Sussex, M.A., 1984. *Politics:* Liberal socialist. *Religion:* Agnostic.

ADDRESSES: Home—Old Chapel, Easton, near Winchester, Hampshire, England. *Office*—King Alfred's College, Winchester, Hampshire, England. *Agent*—Murray Pollinger, 4 Garrick St., London W.C.2, England.

CAREER: Schoolteacher in London, England, 1966-75, head teacher, 1975-85; King Alfred's College, Winchester, England, senior lecturer in English, 1985—.

WRITINGS:

FOR CHILDREN

Daredevils or Scaredycats, Abelard (London, England), 1979.

Mog and the Rectifier, Abelard, 1980.

The Mustang Machine, Abelard, 1981.

Uncle Neptune, Abelard, 1982.

Roald Dahl (nonfiction), Hamish Hamilton (London, England), 1983.

The Conker as Hard as a Diamond, Kestrel (London, England), 1984.

Stuntkid, Abelard, 1985.

The Phantom Carwash, Heinemann (London, England), 1986.

Flyaway Frankie, Blackie & Son (Glascow), 1987.

Fingers Crossed, Blackie/Knight, 1987.

Hiccup Harry, A & C Black (London, England), 1988.

Hoppity-Gap, Hamish Hamilton, 1988.

Ziggy and the Ice Ogre, Heinemann, 1988.

Bella's Dragon, Blackie, 1988.

Harry's Party, A & C Black, 1989.

The Golden Years of Mother Goose, Walker, 1989.

A Spook at the Superstore, Heinemann, 1990.

What It's Like to Be. . . ., Grinn, 1990.

Elf 61, Hamish Hamilton, 1990.

Dracula in Sunlight, Blackie, 1990.

Harry with Spots On, A & C Black, 1990.

Butterfingers, Blackie, 1991.

Where the Quarry Bends, HarperCollins, 1992.

Wesley at the Water Park, Blackie, 1992.

Harry Moves House, A & C Black, 1993.

A Razzle Dazzle Rainbow, Viking-Kestrel, 1993.

It's That Dragon Again, Hamish Hamilton, 1993.

(Editor) *The Kingfisher Book of Scary Stories,* Kingfisher, 1994.

Famous with Smoky Joe, Heinemann, 1995.

OTHER

(Editor) *The Best of Books for Keeps,* Bodley Head (London, England), 1994.

WORK IN PROGRESS: Books for children.

SIDELIGHTS: Chris Powling once told *CA:* "I've always been fascinated by books. Though I didn't grow up in an especially literary home, my parents had the good sense to turn me loose on the local library at a very early age and then to stand well back. Since then I've managed to sneak books into almost every corner of my life—as a parent, teacher, critic, and occasional broadcaster. Once in awhile I've been known to pass a whole day without opening a book—but usually I suffer acute withdrawal symptoms.

"So why do I write *children's* books? For the standard reasons, I suppose: a liking for the sheer liveliness of kids; a preference for fiction that tells stories; a hunch, common to most children's authors, that my own childhood comes into the category of 'unfinished business.' Yet my target reader is by no means the nose-in-a-book type of youngster that I was myself. I concentrate on plot and pace and try to keep my prose very close to the vocabulary and rhythms of everyday speech. That way, with luck, I may lure into reading kids who tend to look elsewhere for their fun. It's my firm belief that all fiction, however sophisticated, has its roots in the natural narrative of jokes and gossip and that we neglect at our peril the universal tendency to comment on experience by turning it into some form of story. What begins as fun ends as a celebration of feeling."

Powling added: "It's not that I have any highfalutin designs on my readership. But if I can give kids sufficient relish for the words on the page to keep them turning over, then that's good enough for me."

*   *   *

POWNALL, David   1938-

PERSONAL: Born May 19, 1938, in Liverpool, England; married Glenys Elsie Jones, 1961 (divorced), partner of Mary Ellen Ray, 1972, married Alex Sutton, 1993; children: three sons. *Education:* University of Keele, B.A. (Hons.) in English and History, 1960.

ADDRESSES: Home—Guildford, England. *Agent*—Andrew Hewson, John Johnson Ltd., 45-47 Clerkenwell Green, London EC1R OHT, England.

CAREER: Novelist and playwright. Ford Motor Company of England, Dagenham, England, personnel officer, 1960-63; Anglo-American, Zambia, personnel officer, 1963-69; Century Theatre touring group, resident writer, 1970-72; Duke's Playhouse, Lancaster, England, resident playwright, 1972-75; Paines Plough Theatre, London, founder and resident writer, 1975-80.

AWARDS, HONORS: Royal Society of Literature, fellow, 1976; Edinburgh Festival Fringe Award 1976, for *Music to Murder By,* and 1977, for *Richard III, Part II;* BBC Giles Cooper Award, for *Beef,* 1981; Arts Council of Great Britain John Whiting Award for *Beef,* 1982; Giles Cooper Award for *Ploughboy Monday,* 1985; Sony Silver Award for Original Radio Drama for *Kitty Wilkinson,* 1994; Sony Gold Award for Original Radio Drama for *Elgar's Third,* 1995.

WRITINGS:

NOVELS

The Raining Tree War, Faber (London), 1974.
African Horse, Faber, 1975.

The Dream of Chief Crazy Horse (also see below), Faber, 1975.
God Perkins, Faber, 1977.
Light on a Honeycomb, Faber, 1978.
Beloved Latitudes, Gollancz (London), 1981.
The White Cutter, Viking (New York City), 1989.
The Gardener, Gollancz, 1990.
Stagg and His Mother, Gollancz, 1991.
The Sphinx and the Sybarites, Sinclair-Stevenson, 1994.

PLAYS

As We Lie, produced at Nkana-Kitwe Arts Society, 1969.
How Does the Cuckoo Learn to Fly?, produced on tour, 1970.
How to Grow a Guerrilla, produced in Preston, Lancashire, England, 1971.
All the World Should Be Taxed, produced in Lancaster, England, 1971.
The Last of the Wizards (for children), produced in London, 1972.
Gaunt, produced in Lancaster, 1973.
Lions and Lambs, produced on Lancashire tour, 1973.
The Dream of Chief Crazy Horse (for children) produced at Fleetwood, Lancashire, 1973.
Beauty and the Beast, music by Stephen Boxer, produced in Lancaster, 1973.
The Human Cartoon Show, produced in Lancaster, 1974.
Crates on Barrels, produced on Lancashire tour, 1974.
The Pro, produced in London, 1975.
Lile Jimmy Williamson, produced in Lancaster, 1975.
Buck Ruxton, produced in Lancaster, 1975.
Ladybird, Ladybird, produced in Edinburgh, 1976.
A Tale of Two Town Halls, produced in Lancaster, 1976.
Music to Murder By, (produced in Canterbury, England, 1976), Faber, 1978.
Motorcar/Richard III, Part II, music by Boxer, (produced in Edinburgh and London, 1977), Faber, 1979.
Seconds at the Fight for Madrid, produced in Bristol, England, 1978.
Livingston and Sechele, produced at Edinburgh Festival, 1978.
An Audience Called Edouard (produced at Greenwich Theatre, London, 1978), Faber, 1979.
Barricade, produced in Warwick, England, 1979.
Later, produced in London, 1979.
Beef (produced in London, 1981), published in *Best Radio Plays of 1981,* Methuen (London), 1982.
The Hot Hello, produced in Edinburgh, 1981.
(Adapter) *Pride and Prejudice* (based on the novel by Jane Austen), produced by Cambridge Theatre Company, 1983.
Crates on Barrels, produced by Royal Shakespeare Company, 1983.
Master Class (produced in London, 1983), Faber, 1983.

Ploughboy Monday, broadcast 1985, published in *Best Radio Plays of 1985,* Metheun, 1986.

The Viewing, produced in London, 1987.

Black Star, produced in Bolton, Lancashire, 1987.

The Edge, produced in London, 1987.

King John's Jewel, produced in Birmingham, England, 1987.

Rousseau's Tale, produced in London, 1991.

My Father's House, produced in Birmingham, 1991.

Nijinsky: Death of a Faun, produced in Edinburgh, 1991.

Dinner Dance, produced in Leicester, 1991.

Elgar's Rondo, produced in Stratford and London, 1993.

Also author of radio plays, including *Free Ferry,* 1972; *Free House,* 1973; *A Place in the Country,* 1974; *An Old New Year,* 1974; *Fences,* 1976; *Under the Wool,* 1976; *Back Stop,* 1977; *Butterfingers,* 1981; *The Mist People,* 1981; *Flos,* 1982; *Beloved Latitudes,* based on his novel, 1986; *The Bridge at Orbigo,* 1987; *A Matter of Style,* 1988; *Plato Not NATO,* 1990; *The Glossomaniacs,* 1990; *Bringing Up Nero,* 1991; *Dreams and Censorship,* 1992; *Kitty Wilkinson,* 1994; and *Elgar's Third,* 1994. Author of plays for television, including *High Tides,* 1976; *Mackerel Sky,* 1976; *Return Fare,* 1978; *Follow the River Down,* 1979; *Room for an Inward Light,* 1980; *The Sack Judies,* 1981; *Love's Labour* (Maybury series), 1983; *The Great White Mountain* (Mountain Men series), 1987; and *Something to Remember You By,* 1991.

OTHER

(With Jack Hill) *An Eagle Each: Poems of the Lakes and Elsewhere* (verse), Arena (Carlisle, Cumbria), 1972.

(Contributor) *Introduction 5,* Faber, 1973.

My Organic Uncle, and Other Stories (short stories), Faber, 1976.

Another Country (verse), Peterloo (Liskeard, Cornwall), 1978.

Between Ribble and Lune: Scenes from the North-West (travel and biography; photographs by Arthur Thompson), Gollancz, 1980.

(Editor with Gareth Pownall) *The Fisherman's Bedside Book,* Windward (London), 1980.

The Bunch from Bananas (for children), Gollancz, 1980, Macmillan (New York City), 1981.

SIDELIGHTS: Farce, satire, and comedy characterize the works of David Pownall. Three of his novels—*The Raining Tree War, African Horse,* and *Beloved Latitudes*—and several of his plays are set in Africa, where Pownall lived for six years during the 1960s. According to Peter Ackroyd of the *Spectator,* Pownall's first novel, *The Raining Tree War,* is a "funny" book "which turned Africa's 'Liberation' into the material of farce at the same time as it brought the native breed into a new and sympathetic light." With characters like Maud Mamuntu, Tarzan Cool-Guy, and French aviator "Bwana Arse," Pownall "is not satirizing the black races themselves," Ackroyd remarked, "but rather the Western idea of them." In the *Observer,* Godfrey Smith wrote: "Pownall has done for emergent nationalism in his first novel what Joseph Heller did for war in *Catch-22:* he has rendered it somehow tolerable by making it ridiculous."

Pownall's second novel, *African Horse,* is set in the imaginary country of Zonkendawo, and is "Swiftian in its sharpness," as H. B. Mallalieu observed in the *Stand.* The book describes, Mallalieu said, "the atmosphere in an emergent black nation as self-seeking, as ridiculous, as incompetent as its former rulers." Around the hero Hurl Halfcock's search for identity amid sexual, political, and alcoholic adventures, emerges a comic version of Africa. "In spite of the craziness, the goonery, the cruelty even," Mallalieu remarked, "a compassion comes through." Ackroyd concluded: "*African Horse* is the only novel to bring this puzzling life into the light without pomposity or the slow, grinding tedium of 'serious' novels."

With *God Perkins* the setting shifts to England in a farce about a struggling theatre company. The story revolves around the intrigues of the members of the Dramacart who contend for the influential manager's support. Ackroyd observed: "No comic novel is complete without its great set-scenes, when a whole dizzy edifice of coincidence and farce is suddenly made transparent—like water turning into ice, just for a second. Pownall contrives these moments with great care, skating easily over the fine boundary which divides old-fashioned English farce from old-fashioned English satire." A particularly effective scene, John Mellors of the *Listener* reported, is the frustrated writer's attempt to commit suicide. "He climbs to a mountain tarn, puts on the leotard he had worn when 'forced to join the morning session of eurythmics and voice training,' and thrusts stones inside the garment until he bulges at every limb and looks like 'a human cairn.'" Wrote Peter Prince in the *Times Literary Supplement:* "Fans of freewheeling farce should certainly feel they have been taken a full fifteen rounds by *God Perkins.*"

Light on a Honeycomb seems to proceed on the assumption that "all the world's mad except me and thee," according to Eric Korn in the *Times Literary Supplement.* The chief industry of Rougerossbergh is its insane asylum, where "doom-inspired Dr. Zander" encounters both the certified and uncertified mad. In the town reside Sir Alphonse Bourge, who contrives plans for spray-on carpets and tidal power; the Class War Action syndicate, composed of squatters, pot-heads, union reporters, sociology students, and Marxist actors; a tycoon who, in love with the land, has sex with a trench; murderous bouncers from the Paradise Ballroom; and a yoga center operator who dreams of establishing a Western Europeanization Centre in Delhi. "Insanity impregnates the town like the smell from a brewery," Korn remarked.

The novel's extravagance seemed to confuse reviewers, who, according to Malcolm Page's essay in the *Dictionary of Literary Biography*, for the most part responded to it negatively. Korn noted that the reader is "punch-drunk" from the feeling that anything can happen in this novel. Of *Light on a Honeycomb*, Mellors wrote: "The book suffers from both verbal and conceptual anarchy, mainly because of the author's over-inventiveness. Before one idea can take root it is replaced by another. The result is fantasy run wild and a plot that defies precis."

Pownall returned to Africa in his next novel, *Beloved Latitudes*, which is set in a prison that has only two occupants. The first prisoner, a charismatic man and one-time president of an unnamed African nation, is dictating his memoirs to the other prisoner, a white man who was his former minister. Both are to be executed by the new dictator, an intellectual about to return from United States exile. In the *Dictionary of Literary Biography*, Page described the novel as a "savage, intelligent comedy," and pointed out that the leaders represent two very different types of leadership in contemporary Africa. In the London *Times*, Stuart Evans praised *Beloved Latitudes* as a "splendid and mordantly ironic novel." "What is most impressive," wrote Evans, "is the consistently sharp but compassionate satire aimed at political, social, familial and individual targets. The ending is powerful and fantastic in the true sense of the word."

The White Cutter takes as its subject the itinerant masons (known as "white cutters") who built the great cathedrals of Europe. The novel is set in thirteenth-century England, where a talented young stonemason named Hedric has murdered his less-talented mason father and is writing this autobiographical tale as a final act of expiation. In the *New York Times Book Review*, Patricia Hampl described the novel as fundamentally recreating a world in which architecture serves as metaphor for an emerging Western consciousness. Thus, she suggested that the book be read "not as a novel but as a meditation on the interior strivings that have brought Western civilization to its future." Gregory Frost, reviewing the novel for the *Washington Post Book World*, suggested that it could be read in a variety of ways. "*The White Cutter*," he observed, "is a book rich and pleasurable on many levels—as a mystery, medieval adventure story, and a tale of artistic and architectural growth."

The Sphinx and the Sybarites, Pownall's tenth novel, is a "dense, complex and powerful novel, based on the history of the Greek city of Sybaris in South Italy and its conflicts with the neighboring town of Kroton," according to the *Times Literary Supplement*'s Mary Beard. The novel is narrated by Kallias, a Greek diviner from the sixth cen-

tury B.C., who is hired by Telys, the tyrannical ruler of the opulent town of Sybaris, to uncover how long the city's extravagant wealth will last. The seer Kallias takes his work seriously and does not allow the pressures of Telys to hurry his work. As Kallias seeks to learn the fate of the city, he encounters many challenges and struggles including political manipulation, religious doubts, and war. He learns first hand just how corrupt and evil Greek's celebrated philosophers could be. A party given by his friend, the ambitious philosopher Pythagoras, turns into a nightmare for Kallias when he is sexually assaulted by Pythagoras and other guests. Throughout Kallias's search to learn the future, the town of Sybaris comes into conflict with the neighboring town of Kroton and, in the end, is destroyed by the physical strength of Kroton's less wealthy inhabitants.

While noting that only Greek and Italian history specialists of sixth century B.C. will understand the many details of the story, Beard found *The Sphinx and the Sybarites* "challenges that sense of respectful awe that marks most modern discussions of the these early Greek philosophers." She added: "Woven into the narrative is a devastatingly subversive view of the 'Greek enlightenment', directed at the usual part-progressive, part-complacent, part-romantic account of the development of rationality, philosophy and scepticism in the classical world. . . . Pownall focuses on the dreadful personal consequences of revolutionary intellectual change." A *Kirkus Reviews* contributor praised *The Sphinx and the Sybarites:* "Eloquent testimony that ideas skillfully presented in vividly evoked settings and situations can be as exciting as nonstop derring-do. A riveting and provocative read."

Pownall has also written plays throughout his career. *Master Class*, one of his better-known plays, is the imagined result of a meeting in which Soviet Marshal Josef Stalin and his cultural commissar, Zhdanov, force the famous Russian composers Sergey Prokofiev and Dmitry Shostakovich to compose a "folk cantata" that will glorify the party line. The story, according to Pownall, was inspired by an actual meeting called by Stalin in 1948 to purge Russian music of its so-called perversions. In a *New York Times* article, Dena Kleiman quoted the playwright himself on *Master Class:* "'I use music to make Stalin reevaluate himself as a man,' said Mr. Pownall. 'He is forced to show who he is. To give his humanity some existence. He remains an abomination, but a complex, strange and even more frightening creature.'" Irving Wadle wrote in the London *Times* that "*Master Class*, however, is not so much a character study of Stalin as an examination of artistic practice under a political tyranny. Most obviously, it converts that sober theme into delicious comedy, as the two artists writhingly attempt to preserve the atmosphere of a comradely discussion while abjectly falling into line."

Master Class "is a feat of imagination that rewards an audience's alertness with [Pownall's] own brand of disturbing and mordant insight," observed the London *Times* contributor Anthony Masters. In *Contemporary Dramatists* Page commented: "Though some critics have argued that Pownall trivialized the issues, *Master Class* poses important questions about art and politics, elitism and social purpose, and the distance between modern music and the general public."

BIOGRAPHICAL/CRITICAL SOURCES:

BOOKS

Contemporary Dramatists, 5th edition, St. James Press (London), 1993.
Contemporary Literary Criticism, Volume 10, Gale (Detroit), 1979.
Dictionary of Literary Biography, Volume 14: *British Novelists since 1960,* Gale, 1983.

PERIODICALS

Atlantic Monthly, April, 1989, p. 100.
Guardian, January 29, 1975, p. 8; March 16, 1977, p. 8.
Listener, March 17, 1977; June 15, 1978; September 4, 1980; July 2, 1981; October 27, 1989.
New Statesman, May 29, 1981.
New York Times, December 13, 1985; June 1, 1986; June 6, 1986.
New York Times Book Review, February 26, 1989, p. 20.
Observer, June 30, 1974; July 27, 1975; September 19, 1976; March 27, 1977; June 26, 1977; January 1, 1978; July 27, 1980; December 7, 1980; May 31, 1981; February 8, 1987; September 4, 1988.
Radio Times, December 8-14, 1979. pp. 22-23.
Spectator, July 6, 1974; July 26, 1975; October 2, 1976; March 12, 1977; June 17, 1978; June 2, 1990, p. 31.
Time, December 9, 1985, p. 94.
Times (London), January 29, 1983; January 20, 1984; February 4, 1987; March 13, 1987; May 28, 1987; August 14, 1991, p. 11; November 5, 1991, p. 21.
Times Educational Supplement, July 23, 1982.
Times Literary Supplement, August 2, 1974; July 25, 1975; September 24, 1976; March 11, 1977; June 30, 1978; August 1, 1980, p. 864; July 3, 1981; June 18, 1993, p. 23.
Washington Post Book World, February 12, 1989.*

*   *   *

POYNTER, Dan(iel Frank) 1938-

PERSONAL: Born September 17, 1938, in New York, NY; son of William Frank (a sales engineer) and Josephine (a newspaper columnist; maiden name, Thompson)

Poynter. *Education:* Attended City College of San Francisco, 1956-57, University of the Pacific, 1957-59, and University of San Francisco, 1958-59; Chico State College (now California State University, Chico), B.A., 1960; graduate study at San Francisco Law School, 1961-62. *Avocational interests:* Skydiving, aviation, traveling.

ADDRESSES: Home and office—P. O. Box 2206, Santa Barbara, CA 93118-2206.

CAREER: Paladin Sport Parachutes, Oakland, CA, manager, 1962-64; Tri-State Parachute Company, Flemington, NJ, general manager, 1964-65; Parachutes Incorporated, Orange, MA, marketing manager and research and development director, 1965-66; Strong Enterprises, Inc., North Quincy, MA, parachute design specialist, 1967-73; Para Publishing (formerly Parachuting Publications), owner, North Quincy, 1969-74, Santa Barbara, CA, 1974—. Federally licensed master parachute rigger with all ratings, back, seat, and chest; expert parachutist with highest class license and 1200 jumps; parachuting instructor and examiner. Licensed pilot, single engine land planes and gliders; hang gliding flight examiner. *Military service:* California National Guard, 1956-59; U.S. Army Reserve, 1959-64.

MEMBER: Commission Internationale de Vol Libre of the Federation Aeronautique Internationale (U.S. delegate; past president; honorary lifetime president), International Frisbee Association, American Institute of Aeronautics and Astronautics (senior member; technical committee), Association of American Publishers, Aviation/Space Writers Association, Committee of Small Magazine Editors and Publishers (past member of the board of directors; Santa Barbara chapter president, 1979-82), Experimental Aircraft Association, Museum of Parachuting and Air Safety (past director), National Aeronautics Association (past delegate), Parachute Equipment Industry Association (past secretary; past president; chair of technical committee), Publishers Marketing Association (member of the board; past vice president), Soaring Society of America, Society of Automotive Engineers (chair of technical committee), Survival and Flight Equipment Association, United States Hang Gliding Association (life member; past member of the board; chief of U.S. team delegation), United States Parachute Association (life member; member of the board, 1966-79; secretary; chair of the board; chief of U.S. team delegation), Book Publicists of Southern California, Northeast Sport Parachute Council (past secretary; past president), Northern California Parachute Council (past secretary), Calistoga Skydivers (past secretary).

AWARDS, HONORS: Gold Parachutists Wings, United States Parachute Association, 1972, for 1000 freefall sport parachute skydives; Diplome d'Honneur, Federation

Aeronautique Internationale, 1979, for contributions to the sport of hang gliding; achievement award, United States Parachuting Association, 1981, for contributions to the association and the sport of parachuting; Paul Tissandier Diploma, Federation Aeronautique Internationale, 1984; Benjamin Franklin Person of the Year Award, Publishers Marketing Association, 1991, for many years of helping people market their books; Certificate of Membership-30, United States Parachute Association, 1992, for 30 years of continuous membership; membership in National Forensic Center elevated to fellow, 1993; meritorious achievement award and certificate, Central Atlantic Sport Parachute Association, for parachute equipment advances and twenty years of membership; Bronze Otto Lillienthal Medal, U.S. Hang Gliding Association.

WRITINGS:

(Editor) *The Parachute Songbook,* Northeast Sport Parachute Council, 1967.

I-E Course for Parachuting Instructor/Examiner Candidates, Parachuting Publications (North Quincy, MA), 1971, 3rd edition published as *Parachuting I-E Course: A Program of Study to Prepare the Expert Parachutist for the U.S.P.A. Instructor/Examiner Written Examination,* 1978, 5th edition, 1994.

The Parachute Manual: A Technical Treatise on the Parachute, Parachuting Publications, 1972, 3rd edition published as *The Parachute Manual: A Treatise on Aerodynamic Decelerators,* Para Publishing (Santa Barbara, CA), 1984, 4th edition, 1991.

Hang Gliding: The Basic Book of Skysurfing, D. F. Poynter, 1973, 10th edition published as *Hang Gliding: The Basic Handbook of Ultralight Flying,* Para Publishing, 1981.

Manned Kiting: The Basic Handbook of Tow-Launched Hang Gliding, D. F. Poynter, 1974.

Hang Gliding Manual and Log: A Basic Text for the Novice, Parachuting Publications, 1976.

Parachuting Manual and Log: A Text for the Novice, Parachuting Publications, 1976, 7th edition, 1984.

Parachute Rigging Course: A Course Study for the FAA Senior Rigger Certificate, Parachuting Publications, 1977, revised edition, Para Publishing, 1981, 3rd edition, 1994.

(With Martin Hunt and David Hunn) *Hang Gliding,* Arco, 1977.

Parachuting: The Skydiver's Handbook, Parachuting Publications, 1978, 6th edition, 1992.

(With Mark Danna) *Frisbee Player's Handbook,* Parachuting Publications, 1978.

The Self-Publishing Manual: How to Write, Print, and Sell Your Own Book, Parachuting Publications, 1979, 8th edition, Para Press, 1995.

Publishing Short-Run Books: How to Paste Up and Reproduce Books Instantly Using Your Copy Shop, Parachuting Publications, 1980, 5th edition, 1988.

Toobee Player's Handbook: The Amazing Flying Can, Para Publishing, 1981.

Book Fairs: An Exhibiting Guide for Publishers, Para Publishing, 1981, 4th edition, 1986.

Business Letters for Publishers: Creative Correspondence Outlines, Para Publishing, 1981, 4th edition, 1990.

Word Processors and Information Processing: A Basic Manual on What They Are and How to Buy, Para Publishing, 1982.

Computer Selection Guide: Choosing the Right Hardware and Software—Business—Professional—Personal, Para Publishing, 1983.

Parachuting Manual for Square/Tandem Equipment, Para Publishing, 1985, 7th edition, 1993.

(With Mindy Bingham) *Is There a Book Inside You?: A Step-By-Step Plan for Writing Your Own Book,* Para Publishing, 1985, 3rd edition, 1992.

OTHER

Contributor to the *Encyclopedia Americana.* Contributor to *Frisbee World, Hang Glider Weekly, Parachutist, Publishers Weekly, Skydiver, Small Press,* and *Success in Self-Publishing.* Founder/editor of *Spotter,* 1965-74; founder/editor of *Para-Newsbriefs;* editor of *Publishing Poynters,* 1986—. Author of column, "Parachuting Poynters," in *Parachutist* magazine, 1963—.

WORK IN PROGRESS: Books on parachutes and publishing.

SIDELIGHTS: Dan Poynter told *CA:* "My writing career began with magazine articles. The articles helped me to develop a writing style, bank materials for a later book, and establish a readership. The first book, *The Parachute Manual,* required eight years to research and draft. Since no publisher would be interested in such an obscure subject, it was self-published.

"This unique fifty-dollar treatise sells at the rate of one thousand copies per year and was revised in 1977, 1984 and 1991. In 1973, the sport of hang gliding was being reborn. Unable to find a book on the subject, I wrote *Hang Gliding.* So far, it has been through the press ten times for 130,000 [copies] in print, and there are two printings of a German edition. After *Hang Gliding* my book output accelerated to as many as two per year while all the other books were being revised as they came up for reprinting. All books were self-published except for the four translations and the sale of *Word Processors* to Prentice-Hall. Noting my successes in publishing, many people asked for the secrets. To comply with their demands, I wrote *The Self-Publishing Manual* in 1979; it was self-published, of course; the 8th edition was published in 1995; there are

95,000 copies in print. Several other books on various aspects of publishing followed.

"My publishing success should be attributed to my marketing insight rather than to any particular literary ability. For years I wrote about aviation sports and served on the boards of the national and international sport aviation organizations. More recently, I've been applying all I have learned to book promotion. Publishing and book promotion are exciting and fun. Book marketing is stimulating—and easy, if you don't do it the traditional New York way.

"I enjoy publishing and marketing my written wares. The information I provide is useful and enjoyed by others while it provides a good living for me."

Dan Poynter is the grandnephew of novelists Kathleen Norris and Frank Norris, and of poet Stephen Vincent Benet. He holds a patent on a type of parachute pack. In 1994, he went on a skydiving expedition to the North Pole.

BIOGRAPHICAL/CRITICAL SOURCES:

PERIODICALS

ABA Booklist, December, 1979; January, 1984.
American Libraries, September, 1983.
Choice, December, 1978; January, 1980.
Library Journal, August 12, 1975; February 14, 1978; March 17, 1978; May 15, 1982.
New York Times Book Review, February 18, 1978.
Publishers Weekly, February 28, 1978; August 21, 1978.
Santa Barbara News and Review, January 12, 1983.
Santa Barbara News-Press, March 17, 1982.
Small Press Review, May, 1979; November, 1980; January, 1982.
West Coast Review of Books, July, 1982.
Western Publisher, October, 1980; January, 1981; February-March, 1982.
Writer's Digest, December, 1980; May, 1981.

*   *   *

PRICE, Beverley Joan   1931-
(Beverley Randell)

PERSONAL: Born in 1931 in Wellington, New Zealand; daughter of William Harding and Gwendolyn Louise (Ryall) Randell; married Hugh Price (a book publisher), October 17, 1959; children: Susan. *Education:* Victoria University of Wellington, B.A., 1952; Wellington Teachers College, Diploma of Teaching, 1953.

ADDRESSES: Home and office—24 Glasgow St., Kelburn, Wellington, New Zealand 6005.

CAREER: Freelance writer and editor. Teacher of junior classes at schools in Wellington, Raumati, and Marlborough, New Zealand, 1953-59, and London, England, 1957-58; Price Milburn & Co. Ltd., Wellington, editor, 1962-84.

MEMBER: International PEN, New Zealand Women Writers Society, Australian Society of Authors.

WRITINGS:

JUVENILE; UNDER NAME BEVERLEY RANDELL

Tiny Tales, sixteen volumes, Wheaton, 1965.
PM Commonwealth Readers, sixteen volumes, A. H. & A. W. Reed, 1965.
John, the Mouse Who Learned to Read, Collins, 1966, reprinted, Penguin (London), 1986.
Methuen Number Story Caption Books, sixteen volumes, Methuen, 1967.
Methuen Caption Books, Volumes I-IV: *Blue Set,* Volumes V-VIII: *Green Set,* Volumes IX-XII: *Orange Set,* Volumes XIII-XVI: *Purple Set,* Volumes XVII-XX: *Red Set,* Volumes XXI-XXIV: *Yellow Set,* Methuen, 1967, 2nd edition, 1974.
Bowmar Primary Reading Series: Supplementary to All Basic Reading Series, sixty volumes, Bowmar, 1969.
Instant Readers, sixteen volumes, Price Milburn (Wellington, NZ), 1969-70.
Listening Skillbuilders, twenty-four volumes, Price Milburn, 1971.
Mark and Meg Books, five volumes, Methuen, 1971.
Guide to the Ready to Read Series, and Supporting Books, Price Milburn, 1972.
PM Story Books, one hundred volumes, Price Milburn, 1972-76.
First Phonics, twenty-four volumes, Methuen, 1973.
PM Creative Workbooks, nine volumes, Price Milburn, 1973.
(With Robin Robilliard) *Country Readers,* eighteen volumes, Price Milburn, 1974, also published as *Country Books,* four volumes, Methuen, 1974.
(With Clive Harper) *Animal Books,* sixteen volumes, Thomas Nelson, 1978.
Readalongs, eighteen volumes, Price Milburn and Methuen, 1979-81.
Phonic Blends, twenty-four volumes, Methuen, 1979.
Singing Games, Price Milburn, 1981.
Joining-In Books, sixteen volumes, Nelson, 1984.
Rhyme and Rhythm Books, four volumes, Heinemann, 1985.
Look and Listen, twenty-four volumes, Heinemann, 1985.
New PM Story Books, sixty-two volumes, Nelson Price Milburn, 1994.

EDITOR; UNDER NAME BEVERLEY RANDELL

Red Car Books, Price Milburn, 1967, revised edition, 1974.

Instant Readers, Price Milburn, 1969-70.
PM Town Readers, Price Milburn, 1971.
Dinghy Stories, Methuen, 1973.
PM Everyday Stories, Price Milburn, 1973-80.
PM Science Concept Books, Price Milburn, 1974.
PM People at Work, Price Milburn, 1974.
PM Seagulls, Price Milburn, 1980.
PM Early Days, Price Milburn, 1982.

OTHER

(Under name Beverley Randell) *A Crowded Thorndon Cottage,* Gondwanaland Press, 1992.

Contributor to *Reading Is Everybody's Business,* International Reading Association (Wellington, New Zealand), 1972. Randell's books have been translated into several languages, including Italian, Greek, Chinese, Japanese, Welsh, and Australian Aboriginal languages.

SIDELIGHTS: Beverley Joan Price, better known as Beverley Randell, once wrote: "In 1972 I traveled to England to lecture on reading at teachers' centers, and I have several times lectured in Australia, particularly in 1980. My interest is in understanding how children learn to read, and writing (and editing) the sorts of books that can help them. The school books I dislike most are those that are narrow and restricting—mere reading exercises (often 'based on linguistic principles'). But I like those that strike a spark—that are sensible and worth reading."

R

RANDELL, Beverley
   See PRICE, Beverley Joan

*　　　*　　　*

REINHARZ, Jehuda 1944-

PERSONAL: Born August 1, 1944, in Haifa, Palestine (now Israel); came to the United States, 1961, naturalized, 1966; son of Fred and Anita (Weigler) Reinharz; married Shulamit Rothschild (a professor of sociology). *Education:* Columbia University, B.S., 1967; Jewish Theological Seminary in America, B.R.E., 1967; Harvard University, M.A., 1968; Brandeis University, Ph.D., 1972.

ADDRESSES: Office—Office of the President, Brandeis University, 415 South St., Waltham, MA 02254.

CAREER: Hebrew College, Brookline, MA, instructor in Jewish history, 1969-70; Brandeis University, Hiatt Institute, Jerusalem, Israel, instructor in Jewish history, 1970; University of Michigan, Ann Arbor, assistant professor, 1972-76, associate professor, 1976-80, professor of history, 1981-82, staff member of Center for Near Eastern and North African studies, 1972-82; Brandeis University, Waltham, MA, Richard Koret Professor of Modern Jewish History, 1982—, provost and senior vice president for academic affairs, 1992-94, president, 1994—. Tauber Institute for the Study of European Jewry and the Jacob and Libby Goodman Institute for the Study of Zionism and Israel, director, 1984-94. Member of Presidential Advisory Committee to the President, State of Israel.

MEMBER: Association for Jewish Studies (member of board of governors, 1974-94), Leo Baeck Institute, World Union of Jewish Studies, American Historical Association, American Friends of the Hebrew University (member of academic advisory board, 1977—), International Council of Yad Vashem, National Foundation for Jewish Culture (member of academic advisory council, 1986-1994), American Section of the International Association of Historical Societies for the Study of Jewish History (member of executive committee, 1986—), Yad Chaim Weizmann (member of board of directors, 1990—), United States Holocaust Memorial Council (member of academic committee, 1990—), Institute for Polish Jewish Studies (member of advisory board, 1991—), International Committee for the Promotion of Jewish Studies in Eastern Europe (member of board of governors, 1992—), World Union of Jewish Studies (member of council, 1993—), Atran Foundation (member of board, 1993—), United Israel Appeal/Jewish Agency (member of board of governors, 1994—) American Jewish Joint Distribution Committee (member of board of directors and executive committee, 1994—).

AWARDS, HONORS: Woodrow Wilson fellowship for research in Germany and Israel, 1970-71, 1973, and 1975-76; American Council of Learned Societies fellowship, 1974; Leo Baeck Institute fellow, 1975-76, 1982; National Endowment for the Humanities grant, 1979-80, 1987-88; Kenneth B. Smilen Literary Award in biography, 1985; *Present Tense*/Joel H. Cavior Literary Award, 1985, and National Jewish Book Award, 1986, both for *Chaim Weizmann: The Making of a Zionist Leader;* Lady Davis fellow, Hebrew University, 1987-88; Shazar Prize in history (Israel), 1988; President of Israel Prize, Israeli Knesset, 1990; Royal Historical Society fellow (England), 1992; American Academy for Jewish Research fellow, 1993; "Honor Book," National Jewish Book Award, 1994, for *Chaim Weizmann: The Making of a Statesman.*

WRITINGS:

Fatherland or Promised Land?: The Dilemma of the German Jew, 1893-1914, University of Michigan Press (Ann Arbor), 1975.

(Editor) *The Letters and Papers of Chaim Weizmann,* Volume 9: *1918-1920,* Israel Universities Press and Rutgers University Press, 1977.

(Editor with Paul R. Mendes Flohr) *The Jew in the Modern World,* Oxford University Press (New York City), 1980.

(Editor) *Dokumente zur Geschichte des deutschen Zionismus 1882-1933,* J. C. B. Mohr, 1981.

(Editor with Daniel Swetschinski) *Mystics, Philosophers and Politicians,* Duke University Press (Durham, NC), 1982.

(Editor with Itamar Rabinovich) *Israel in the Middle East, 1948-1983,* Oxford University Press, 1984.

Chaim Weizmann: The Making of a Zionist Leader, Oxford University Press, 1985.

(Editor with Walter Schatzberg) *The Jewish Response to German Culture: From the Enlightenment to World War II,* University Press of New England (Hanover, NH), 1985.

(Editor) *Living with Anti-Semitism,* University Press of New England, 1987.

Hashomer Hazair in Germany, 1928-1939, Sifriat Poalim, 1987.

(Editor with Yisrael Gutman, Ezra Mendelsohn and Chone Shmeruk) *The Jews of Poland between Two World Wars,* University Press of New England, 1989.

Chaim Weizmann: The Making of a Statesman, Oxford University Press, 1993.

(Editor with Anita Shaprira) *Essential Papers on Zionism,* New York University Press (New York City), 1995.

Contributor to books, including *Zionism,* edited by Geoffrey Wigoder, Keter Publishing House, 1973; *Texts and Studies: Essays in Honor of Nahum N. Glatzer,* edited by Michael A. Fishbane and Paul R. Flohr, Brill, 1975; and *Leo Baeck Institute Year Book,* 1977. Guest editor (with George Mosse), *The Impact of Western Nationalisms,* special issue of *Journal of Contemporary History,* September, 1991.

WORK IN PROGRESS: With Ben Halpern, *The Emergence of the Jewish State 1880-1948;* co-editing *Zionism and Religion, The Letters and Papers of Manya Wilbushevitz Shohat, Zionist Leadership,* and *Jewish Nationalism.*

SIDELIGHTS: Jehuda Reinharz, president of Brandeis University and a professor of modern Jewish history, has won acclaim for his biography of Israel's first president, entitled *Chaim Weizmann: The Making of a Zionist Leader.* Writes *New York Times Book Review* contributor Chaim Raphael, "It was high time for something like an official biography to be written, if only to give the author, with access to a vast quantity of archives and unofficial sources, a chance to pinpoint the magic that singled Weizmann out among the European Zionists of the time." John Gross, writing in the *New York Times,* deems the biography "admirable," and "easily the most authoritative so far."

In a subsequent work, *Chaim Weizmann: The Making of a Statesman,* Reinharz follows his subject from the beginning of the First World War through some of Weizmann's greatest triumphs, including the Balfour Declaration, the founding of the Hebrew University of Jerusalem, and the British Mandate for Palestine.

BIOGRAPHICAL/CRITICAL SOURCES:

PERIODICALS

Anglo Jewish Press, September, 1985.
Globe & Mail (Toronto), August 22, 1987.
New York Times, May 7, 1985.
New York Times Book Review, June 30, 1985.
Times Literary Supplement, September 26, 1986.
Washington Post Book World, June 23, 1985.

*   *   *

REINKE, William A(ndrew)   1928-

PERSONAL: Born August 10, 1928, in Cleveland, OH; son of William Adolph (a manufacturer's agent) and Agnes (Stranberg) Reinke; married Charlene Pelton, January 30, 1960 (marriage ended in divorce); children: Cheryl, Deborah, Cara, William. *Education:* Kenyon College, B.A., 1949; University of Pennsylvania, M.B.A., 1950; Western Reserve University (now Case Western Reserve University), Ph.D., 1961. *Religion:* Protestant.

ADDRESSES: Home—9 Airway Circle, Baltimore, MD 21286. *Office*—School of Public Health, Johns Hopkins University, 615 North Wolfe St., Baltimore, MD 21205.

CAREER: Western Reserve University (now Case Western Reserve University), Cleveland, OH, instructor in mathematics, 1959-61; Corning Glass Works, Corning, NY, senior researcher in mathematics, 1961-63; University of Maryland, School of Medicine, Baltimore, assistant professor of preventive medicine, 1963-64; Johns Hopkins University, School of Public Health, Baltimore, MD, associate professor, 1965-68, professor of international health, 1968—, assistant dean, 1974-76, associate dean, 1976-77. Consultant to World Health Organization. *Military service:* U.S. Army, 1953-55; became sergeant.

MEMBER: American Public Health Association, Institute of Management Sciences, American Statistical Association, Phi Beta Kappa.

WRITINGS:

Statistics for Decision Making, National Foremen's Institute, 1963.

The Planning of Health Services, School of Hygiene and Public Health, Johns Hopkins University (Baltimore), 1969.

(Editor) *Health Planning: Qualitative Aspects and Quantitative Techniques,* Johns Hopkins University, 1972.

(With F. Grundy) *Health Practice Research and Formalized Managerial Methods,* World Health Organization, 1973.

The Functional Analysis of Health Needs and Services, Asia Publishing House (New York City), 1976.

Health Planning for Effective Management, Oxford University Press (New York Press), 1988.

Analytical Techniques for Improved Management Decisions, Johns Hopkins University, 1994.

Contributor to journals.

*   *   *

REISS, Albert J(ohn), Jr. 1922-

PERSONAL: Born December 9, 1922, in Cascade, WI; son of Albert John and Erma Amanda (Schueler) Reiss; married Emma Lucille Hutto, June, 1953 (divorced August, 1986); children: Peter C., Paul Wetherington, Amy. *Education:* Marquette University, Ph.B., 1944; University of Chicago, M.A., 1948, Ph.D., 1949.

ADDRESSES: Home—P.O. Box 208265, New Haven, CT 06520-8265. *Office*—Department of Sociology, Yale University, 140 Prospect St., New Haven, CT 06520.

CAREER: Illinois Board of Public Welfare Commissioners, Springfield, social research analyst, 1946-47; University of Chicago, Chicago, IL, instructor, 1947-49, assistant professor of sociology and administrative secretary of department, 1949-52, assistant director of Chicago Community Inventory, 1947-52, and acting director, 1951-52; Vanderbilt University, Nashville, TN, associate professor, 1952-54, professor of sociology, 1954-58, chairman of department of sociology and anthropology, 1952-58; University of Iowa, Iowa City, professor of sociology, 1958-60, chairman of department of sociology and anthropology, 1959-60, director of Iowa Urban Community Research Center, 1959-60; University of Wisconsin-Madison, professor of sociology and director of Wisconsin Survey Research Laboratory, 1960-61; University of Michigan, Ann Arbor, professor of sociology, 1961-70, chairman of de-

partment, 1964-70, director of Center for Research on Social Organization, 1961-70, lecturer in law, 1968-70; Yale University, New Haven, CT, professor of sociology, 1970-77, William Graham Sumner Professor of Sociology, 1977-93, professor emeritus, 1993—, chairman of department, 1972-78, 1985-89, lecturer in law, 1972-93, professor of sociology in Institution for Social and Policy Studies, 1970—; Harvard University, Cambridge, MA, adjunct professor of sociology, school of public health, 1994—, co-director of the program on human development and criminal behavior, 1994-95.

Visiting professor, University of Denver Law School, summers, 1970-72; visiting fellow, Cambridge University, 1974; George W. Beto Chair in Criminal Justice, Sam Houston State University, summer, 1985. Member of Mental Health Small Grants Committee, National Institutes of Health, 1960-63; member of advisory panel for sociology and social psychology, National Science Foundation, 1963-65; member of behavioral sciences panel to Wooldridge Committee, Executive Office of the President, Office of Science and Technology, 1964; consultant to President's Commission on Law Enforcement and Administration of Justice, 1966-67, and National Advisory Commission on Civil Disorders, 1967-68.

Member of National Advisory Committee for Juvenile Justice and Delinquency Prevention, 1975-78; chairman of advisory committee, Juvenile Justice and Delinquency Prevention in the state of Connecticut, 1976-79; member of Connecticut Justice Commission, 1977-79; member of advisory board, Police Decision Making Project, Center for Research in Criminal Justice, University of Illinois, 1978-79; member of advisory panel and technical committee, National Crime Survey Re-design Project, 1979-81; member of Governor's Task Force on Jail and Prison Overcrowding, state of Connecticut, 1980-81; member of Panel on Research on Criminal Careers, National Research Council, 1983-86; member of law and social sciences advisory panel, National Science Foundation, 1983-87; member of advisory board, Program Evaluation and Methodology Division, U.S. General Accounting Office, 1985—. *Military service:* U.S. Army Air Forces, 1943-44.

MEMBER: International Society of Criminology (member of executive council, 1983-85, 1985-89; president of scientific commission, 1985-89, president, 1990-95), International Sociological Association, American Society of Criminology (fellow; executive counselor, 1979-82; president, 1983-84), American Sociological Association (fellow; member of council, 1962-65; member of executive committee, 1963-65), American Association for the Advancement of Science (fellow), Society for the Study of Social Problems (member of council, 1965-67; vice-president, 1966-67; president, 1969), American Statistical

Association (fellow), Law and Society Association, Sociological Research Association, Eastern Sociological Association, Ohio Valley Sociological Association (president, 1966).

AWARDS, HONORS: Bicentennial Medal, Columbia University, 1954; M.A. (privatim), Yale University, 1970; Bruce Smith Sr. Award, Academy of Criminal Justice Sciences, 1981; Edwin H. Sutherland Award, American Society of Criminology, 1981; LL.D. (honoris causa), John Jay College of Criminal Justice of the City University of New York, 1981; fellow, Western Society of Criminology, 1982, American Academy of Arts and Sciences, 1983, and American Statistical Association, 1983; docteur honoris causa, University of Montreal, 1985; distinguished professional achievement alumni award, Lakeland College, 1990; Beccaria Gold Medal, Neue Kriminologishe Gesellschaft, 1990.

WRITINGS:

(With Otis Dudley Duncan) *Social Characteristics of Urban and Rural Communities,* John Wiley & Sons (New York City), 1956.

Occupations with Social Status, The Free Press of Glencoe (New York City), 1961.

(With Rosemary Sarri and Robert Vintner) *Treating Youthful Offenders in the Community,* Correctional Research Associates (Washington, DC), 1966.

The Police and the Public, Yale University Press (New Haven, CT), 1971.

Methodological Studies in Crime Classification, Yale University Press, 1972.

Deterrence and Incapacitation: Estimating the Effects of Criminal Sanctions on Crime Rates, National Academy of Sciences (Washington, DC), 1978.

(With Albert D. Biderman) *Data Sources on White-Collar Law Breaking,* National Institute of Justice (Washington, DC), 1981.

Policing a City's Central District: The Oakland Story, National Institute of Justice, 1985.

Private Employment of Public Police, National Institute of Justice (Washington, DC), 1988.

EDITOR

Selected Readings in Social Pathology, University of Chicago Bookstore, 1947.

(With Paul K. Hatt) *Reader in Urban Sociology,* Free Press (Glencoe, IL), 1951, revised edition published as *Cities and Society; A Reader in Urban Sociology,* 1957.

(With Elizabeth Wirth Marvick) *Community Life and Social Policy: Selected Papers by Louis Wirth,* University of Chicago Press (Chicago, IL), 1956.

(And author of introduction) *Louis Wirth on Cities and Social Life,* University of Chicago Press, 1964.

(And author of introduction) *Schools in a Changing Society,* Free Press, 1965.

(With Johannes Knutsson and Eckhart Kuhlhorn, and contributor) *Police and the Social Order: Contemporary Research Perspectives,* National Swedish Council for Crime Prevention (Stockholm), 1979.

(With Stephen E. Fienberg, and contributor) *Indicators of Crime and Criminal Justice: Quantitative Studies,* Bureau of Justice Statistics (Washington, DC), 1980.

(With Michael H. Tonry, and contributor) *Communities and Crime,* University of Chicago Press, 1986.

(With Jeffrey A. Roth) *Understanding and Preventing Violence,* National Academy Press (Washington, DC), 1993.

(With Tonry) *Beyond the Law: Crime in Complex Organizations,* University of Chicago Press, 1993.

(With Roth) *Biobehavioral Influences,* National Academy Press, 1994.

(With Roth) *Social Influences,* National Academy Press, 1994.

(With Roth) *Consequences and Control,* National Academy Press, 1994.

OTHER

Contributor to many books. Author of several reports and surveys. Also author of numerous book reviews in books and journals. Contributor to sociology, law, and education periodicals, including *American Journal of Sociology, Stanford Law Review, Journal of Human Relations, Social Forces, Law and Contemporary Problems,* and *Journal of Criminal Law and Criminology.* Editor, "Arnold and Caroline Rose" monograph series, American Sociological Association, 1968-71; editor with Harold Wilensky, "Introduction to Modern Society" series, 1968-74. Associate editor, *American Journal of Sociology,* 1950-52, 1961-64, *Sociological Quarterly,* 1960-62, *Social Problems,* 1961-64, *Sociological Methods and Research,* 1971-73, and *Social Forces,* 1974-77. Book review editor, *Journal of Marriage and Family Living,* 1949-52; sociology editor, *Encyclopedia of the Social Sciences,* 1961-67; advisory editor, *Encyclopaedia Britannica,* 1969—, *American Journal of Sociology,* 1979-81, *Law and Society Review,* 1982-83, and *Howard Journal of Criminal Justice,* 1983—; member of editorial board, *Journal of Conflict Resolution,* 1972-75, *Current Sociology,* 1973-76, *Victimology: An International Journal,* 1976-79, *Sociometry,* 1977-79, *Criminology,* 1978-81, *Crime and Justice: An Annual Review of Research,* 1978-85, and *Journal of Quantitative Criminology,* 1984—.

RICH, Elaine Sommers 1926-

PERSONAL: Born February 8, 1926, in Plevna, IN; daughter of Monroe and Effie (Horner) Sommers; married Ronald L. Rich (a chemistry professor), June 14, 1953; children: Jonathan, Andrew, Miriam, Mark. *Education:* Goshen College, B.A., 1947; Michigan State University, M.A., 1950. *Religion:* Mennonite.

ADDRESSES: Home—112 South Spring St., Bluffton, OH 45817.

CAREER: Goshen College, Goshen, IN, instructor in speech and English, 1947-49, 1950-53; Bethel College, North Newton, KS, instructor in speech, 1953-66; International Christian University, Tokyo, Japan, lecturer, 1971-78; Bluffton College, Bluffton, OH, advisor to international students, 1979-89; University of Findlay, Findlay, OH, adjunct professor of English, 1990—.

MEMBER: American Association of University Women, Women's International League for Peace and Freedom, Amnesty International.

WRITINGS:

(Editor) *Breaking Bread Together,* Herald, 1958.
Hannah Elizabeth, Harper (New York City), 1964.
Tomorrow, Tomorrow, Tomorrow, Herald, 1966.
Am I This Countryside? (poems), Pinchpenny Press, 1981.
Mennonite Women, 1683-1983: A Story of God's Faithfulness, Herald, 1983.
Spiritual Elegance: A Biography of Pauline Krehbiel Raid, Bluffton College (Bluffton, OH), 1987.
Prayers for Everyday, Faith & Life (Newton, KS), 1990.
(Editor) *Walking Together in Faith,* Central District Conference, 1993.

Author of *The Bridge Love Built* and of an unpublished play, *Tough Dove.* Contributor to books, including *They Met God,* edited by J. C. Wenger, Herald, 1964; *A Farthing in Her Hand,* edited by Helen Alderfer, Herald, 1964; and *Prayers of Women,* edited by Lisa Sergio, Harper, 1965. Author of fortnightly column, "Thinking with . . . " in *Mennonite Weekly Review,* 1973—. Contributor to periodicals, including *Poet* and *Japan Christian Quarterly.*

WORK IN PROGRESS: A novel about an 83-year-old woman in a retirement home.

SIDELIGHTS: Elaine Sommers Rich told *CA:* "C. S. Lewis once said that some of the books he wanted to read did not exist. Therefore he had to write them. I feel that way about my own writing.

"I believe that Jesus Christ is Lord of history. He works in a wonder-inspiring way. (The Pennsylvania Dutch have a saying, 'It wonders me.') Some tremendous things happen, happen quietly without making big headlines in the world's newspapers. That's exciting to me. Inner growth is exciting. Genuine goodness is exciting, and I'd rather try to portray growth and goodness than to try to write about 'cops 'n robbers and military victories. *Hannah Elizabeth* tells of how a girl came to glimpse deeply the meaning of her own faith. *Tomorrow, Tomorrow, Tomorrow* shows a tiny seed of love that grew into a tree: improved treatment of the mentally ill. *The Bridge Love Built,* unfortunately never published, tells about a boy who came to understand that he belonged to two cultures, not just one, as most people do."

Rich later told *CA:* "For twenty years I had the privilege of living intimately with our own four children and their many friends, who were in and out of our home in North Newton, Kansas, and on the campus of the International Christian University in Tokyo. I have great respect for the intellect and spiritual sensitivity of these children and of my adult readers.

"I also have great hope for the future. Human beings can learn to use nuclear energy constructively rather than destructively. We could well be on the threshold of a great time in history, a time of worldwide peace when every human being has the good things of life, from food and music to the rights enumerated in the *Universal Declaration of Human Rights.* I hope these values come through in what I write."

She adds: "Among contemporary writers I most admire Elizabeth Yates and Aleksandr Solzhenitsyn. I like Yates' inner independence and integrity. Throughout her long productive lifetime she has stood aloof from literary fads and fashions in her choice and treatment of subjects. Solzhenitsyn has attempted to tell the truth. Difficult! He has demonstrated the power of one lone voice telling the truth. I also like Chaim Potok's earlier works and James A. Michener's autobiography.

"From the preceding generation I like Virginia Woolf for her treatment of psychological time, Pearl Buck for her recognition that it is great but difficult to have been born female, and Willa Cather for her classical style and portrayal of the dignity and beauty inherent in everyday life.

"I also like *haiku* by Japanese masters (Basho, Issa). I like Selma Lagerlof, Sigrid Undset, Sarah Orne Jewett, Christina Rossetti, Robert Browning, Blake, Keats, Gerard Manley Hopkins, and Walt Whitman."

*   *   *

RICHARDS, Martin P(aul) M(eredith) 1940-

PERSONAL: Born January 26, 1940, in Cambridge, England; son of Paul Westmacott (a botanist) and Anne (a botanist; maiden name, Hotham) Richards. *Education:* Trinity College, Cambridge, B.A., 1962, M.A. and Ph.D., both 1965.

ADDRESSES: Home—57 Selwyn Rd., Cambridge, CB3 9EA, England. *Office*—Centre for Family Research, Cambridge University, Cambridge, CB2 3RF, England.

CAREER: Princeton University, Princeton, NJ, visiting fellow in biology, 1966-67; Harvard University, Cambridge, MA, visiting fellow at Center for Cognitive Studies, 1967; Cambridge University, Cambridge, England, research worker, 1967—, lecturer in social psychology, 1970—, reader in human development, 1989—.

MEMBER: International Society for the Study of Behavioral Development, Society for Research in Child Development, Society for Reproductive Psychology.

AWARDS, HONORS: Postdoctoral fellowships from Science Research Council, 1965-67, Trinity College, Cambridge University, 1965-69, and Mental Health Research Fund, 1969-70; Windegard visiting professor, University of Guelph, 1987; honorary visiting professor, City University, London, 1992-94.

WRITINGS:

EDITOR

(With Kenneth Richardson and David Spears) *Race, Culture and Intelligence,* Penguin (New York City), 1972.

The Integration of a Child into a Social World, Cambridge University Press (New York City), 1974.

(With Tim Chard) *Benefits and Hazards of the New Obstetrics,* Heinemann Medical (London, England), 1977.

(With F. S. W. Brimblecombe and N. R. C. Roberton) *Separation and Special Care Nurseries,* Heinemann Medical, 1978.

(With J. A. Davis and Roberton) *Parent-Infant Attachment in Premature Infants,* Croom Helm (Kent, England), 1983.

(With P. Light) *Children of Social Worlds,* Polity Press/ Harvard University Press (Cambridge, MA), 1986.

(With J. Garcia and R. Kilpatrick) *The Politics of Maternity Care,* Oxford University Press (New York City), 1989.

(With T. Chard) *Obstetrics for the 1990s: Current Controversies,* MacKeith Press/Cambridge University Press, 1992.

OTHER

Infancy: The World of the Newborn, Harper (New York City), 1980.

(With J. Burgoyne and R. Ormrod) *Divorce Matters,* Penguin, 1987.

(With J. Reibstein) *Sexual Arrangements: Marriage and Affairs,* Heinemann, 1992, Scribner (New York City), 1993.

Also contributor to scientific and popular journals. Member of editorial board of *Early Human Development, Birth, Journal of Infant and Reproductive Psychology,* and *International Journal of Law and the Family Birth.*

WORK IN PROGRESS: With T. Marteau, *The Benefits and Hazards of the New Genetics* for Cambridge University Press.

SIDELIGHTS: Martin P. M. Richards told *CA:* "I have strong interests in conservation and natural history and chair the Bardzey Island Trust which has responsibility for the most beautiful of the Welsh islands."

*   *   *

RICHIE, Donald (Steiner) 1924-

PERSONAL: Born April 17, 1924, in Lima, OH; son of Kent Hayes and Ona (Steiner) Richie; married Mary Evans (a writer), November, 1961 (divorced, 1965). *Education:* Attended Antioch College, 1942; attended U.S. Maritime Academy, 1943; Columbia University, B.S., 1953.

ADDRESSES: Home—Yanaka 1, 1-18 (304), Taito-ku, Tokyo 110, Japan.

CAREER: Pacific Stars and Stripes, Tokyo, film critic, 1947-49; *Saturday Review of Literature,* New York City, arts critic, 1950-51; *Japan Times,* Tokyo, film critic, 1953-69, literary critic, 1972—; *Nation,* New York City, arts critic, 1959-61; New York Museum of Modern Art, New York City, curator of film, 1968-73; *Newsweek,* New York City, arts critic, 1973-76. Lecturer in American literature, Waseda University, Tokyo, 1954-59; advisor to UniJapan Film, 1963—; Toyoda Chair, University of Michigan, 1993. Designer and presenter of several film retrospectives, including Yanagimachi retrospective, Toronto, 1990, and Ozu retrospective, Sydney, Australia, 1994. Director of experimental films. *Wartime service:* U.S. Maritime Service, 1942-45.

AWARDS, HONORS: Citation from Japanese government, 1963, 1970; citation from U.S. National Society of Film Critics, 1970; Kawakita Memorial Foundation Award, 1983; Presidential Citation, New York University, 1989; Novikoff Award, San Francisco Film Festival, 1990; Tokyo Metropolitan Government Cultural Award, 1993; John D. Rockefeller III Award, 1994.

WRITINGS:

Where Are the Victors? (novel), C. E. Tuttle, 1956, new edition, 1986.

(With Joseph L. Anderson) *The Japanese Film: Art and Industry,* Grove, 1959, expanded edition, Princeton University Press, 1982.

The Japanese Movie: An Illustrated History, Kodansha (England), 1965, revised edition, 1982.

The Films of Akira Kurosawa, University of California Press, 1965, revised edition, 1995.

Companions of the Holiday (novel), Weatherhill (Tokyo), 1968, new edition, Tuttle, 1977.

(Editor) Akira Kurosawa, *Rashomon: A Film,* Grove, 1969.

George Stevens: An American Romantic, Museum of Modern Art, 1970.

The Inland Sea, Weatherhill, 1971, new edition, Kodansha (Tokyo), 1993.

Japanese Cinema, Doubleday, 1971.

Three Modern Kyogen, C. E. Tuttle, 1972.

Ozu: The Man and His Films, University of California Press, 1974.

(With Mana Maeda) *Ji: Signs and Symbols of Japan,* Kodansha, 1975.

(Editor) Yasujiro Ozu, *Tokyo Story,* translated by Richie and Eric Klestadt, Knopf (New York), 1977.

The Japanese Tatoo, photographs by Ian Buruma, Weatherhill, 1980.

Zen Inklings: Some Stories, Fables, Parables, Sermons and Prints with Notes and Commentaries, Weatherhill, 1982.

A Taste of Japan: Food Fact and Fable; What the People Eat; Customs and Etiquette, Kodansha, 1985.

Viewing Film, Kenkyusha (Tokyo), 1986.

Introducing Tokyo, Kodansha, 1987.

Lateral View (collected essays), Stone Bridge Press (Berkeley, CA), 1987, new edition, 1992.

Different People: Pictures of Some Japanese, Kodansha, 1987.

Tokyo Nights, Harrap (London), 1988, new edition, C. E. Tuttle, 1994.

Japanese Cinema: An Introduction, Oxford University Press (New York City), 1990.

The Honorable Visitors, C. E. Tuttle, 1994.

Also editor of film scenarios: *Ikiru,* translated by Akiro Kurosawa, 1968, new edition, Knopf, 1977, and *Seven Samurai,* translated by Kurosawa, 1970, new edition, Faber (London), 1992. Editor, *International House of Japan Bulletin,* 1981—.

SIDELIGHTS: Donald Richie told *CA:* "Living as I do in Japan, for nearly fifty years now, I write mainly about this country and its people. It has become my subject, one which I seek to describe, understand, maybe even to illuminate. The experience of attempting to encompass an entire culture has given me, I think, a deeper insight than I might otherwise have had into all other cultures.

"I came to the word through the picture—having spent much of my early years in movie theaters. It was through motion pictures that I first began to learn about life. Movies taught me to look around and consequently to begin to understand. When I came to Japan it was film that became a paradigm for the country. And just as I had learned to see through the movies into the reality of early small town American life, so I now learned to decipher the language of Japanese film and reconstruct the realities of Japanese life. Having seen these I could then describe them."

BIOGRAPHICAL/CRITICAL SOURCES:

BOOKS

Contemporary Authors Autobiography Series, Volume 20, Gale (Detroit), 1994.

PERIODICALS

Communicator, December, 1988.
Daily Yomiuri, April, 1990; May 13, 1993.
Hawaii Herald, December 16, 1983.
International Herald-Tribune, August 7, 1982.
Japan Times, April 25, 1991.
Okura Lantern, spring, 1994.
St. Andrews Review, Volume 1, number 2, 1971.
Times Literary Supplement, July 3, 1987.
Tokyo Journal, March, 1992.

*　　*　　*

RIENSTRA, Ellen Walker 1940-

PERSONAL: Born December 27, 1940, in Beaumont, TX; daughter of John H. (in business) and Esther (Hooks) Walker; married John D. Rienstra, Jr. (an attorney), August 4, 1962 (died September 23, 1994); children: John Daniel, Judith Marian, William Allen. *Education:* Lamar University, B.A., 1962, M.A., 1980.

ADDRESSES: Home and office— 6150 Clifton, Beaumont, TX 77708. *Agent—*Maureen Walters, Curtis Brown Ltd., 10 Astor Pl., New York, NY 10003.

CAREER: Writer. Violinist with Beaumont Civic Opera Orchestra, 1964-83, Beaumont Symphony Orchestra, 1965-83, Beaumont Interfaith Choir Orchestra, 1966-81, Lake Charles Symphony Orchestra and Rapides Symphony Orchestra, 1973-83, and Lamar University Violin Ensemble, 1981-83. Member of board of directors of Beaumont Symphony Orchestra, 1965, Beaumont Civic Opera, 1968-70, Young Audiences of Beaumont, 1971-72, and Southeast Texas Youth Symphony, 1983-84. Coordinator of Golden Triangle Writers Conference, 1986; researcher for John Jay French House Historic Restoration; public speaker.

MEMBER: Authors Guild, Texas Folklore Society, Texas Gulf Historical Society, Southeast Texas Genealogical and Historical Society, Beaumont Heritage Society (member of board of directors, 1972-73), Golden Triangle Writers Club (conference coordinator, 1986).

WRITINGS:

(Contributor) Francis E. Abernethy, editor, *Tales from the Big Thicket,* University of Texas Press (Austin), 1966.
(With Judith Linsley) *Folk Music in Texas: Frontier to 1900,* Beaumont Heritage Society, 1980.
(With Linsley) *Beaumont: A Chronicle of Promise,* Windsor Publications (Woodland Hills, CA), 1982.
(With Callie Coe Wilson) *A Pride of Kin: A Frank Wardlaw Book,* Texas A & M University Press, 1985.

Also author, with Linsley, of 3 book-length works of historical and contemporary fiction. Co-author of six historical articles for new edition of *The Handbook of Texas.* Contributor to history journals and local magazines and newspapers. Co-editor of *Texas Gulf Historical and Biographical Record,* 1986-89.

WORK IN PROGRESS: Editing a group of letters from the Texas revolutionary period; fiction.

SIDELIGHTS: Ellen Walker Rienstra told *CA:* "I became a writer for the usual reason—the desire to communicate. Writing happens to be the main way I've chosen to express myself. The idea which emerges strongest of all in my writing is my strong sense of place. It seems to pervade everything I do. This sense of place includes everything from the North American continent to my own back yard. I am an American, a Southerner, a Texan, an East Texan, and a Beaumonter, by turns or all at once, with all the attendant geographical characteristics, traditions, and ways of life implicit in what I do and the way I think. I write from, and about, my place in the universe. The most surprising thing is that my sense of place comes through in my writing, whether I intended it to be that way or not.

"Beaumont, Texas, my hometown, is a unique little community because it lies at the conjunction of numerous natural resources that have made a rich life for its inhabitants, from the time of the earliest Indian tribes until the present: first the water (the Neches River, the Gulf of Mexico, the heavy rainfall); the blackland prairies, for raising cattle and rice; the East Texas Piney Woods, first for game and later for timber; and last, the oil, which, with the advent of the Spindletop Oil Field in 1901, changed the course of the world's future. In spite of, or perhaps because of, this wealth of resources, Beaumont has had more than its share of problems, not the least of which is attitudinal, but

it's still a good place to live. More than that, it's my home. I'm a product of its unique blend of geography and traditions.

"*A Pride of Kin* is a very personal family memoir, written in alternating essays by myself and a cousin, Callie Coe Wilson, to portray the unique family heritage bequeathed us by our common (no pun intended) ancestors, the Hooks clan of Hardin County, in East Texas. This book portrays the family whose way of life was the spiritual seed-bed of my very deepest-rooted, most basic ideals and beliefs. Callie and I were fortunate that Texas A & M University Press chose *A Pride of Kin* as one of three books to launch its Frank Wardlaw series, named for one of Texas' famed men of letters.

"I spent most of my young adulthood communicating in a different form: music. For many years, I was semiprofessional free-lance violinist, playing symphonies, operas, and popular gigs, weddings, Bar-Mitzvahs, and any other occasion that called for a fiddle player. Now that my children are grown, I've turned back to my original love, writing, and am now, in middle age, launching myself in this new direction. No one, including myself, knows where, or how far, it's going to lead."

*   *   *

RILEY, Lee
    See VARE, Ethlie Ann

*   *   *

RINGER, Alexander L(othar) 1921-

PERSONAL: Born February 3, 1921, in Berlin, Germany; naturalized U.S. citizen; son of Abe (pronounced Ah-bay; a banker) and Anna (Prager) Ringer; married Claude Pouderoux, January 24, 1947; children: Miriam, Deborah. *Education:* College Francais, Berlin, Germany, abitur, 1938; attended Hollaender Conservatory of Music, 1936-38, and Amsterdam Muzieklyceum, 1940-42; University of Amsterdam, B.A., 1947; New School for Social Research, M.A., 1949; Columbia University, Ph.D., 1955. *Religion:* Jewish.

ADDRESSES: Home—11 Stanford Pl., Champaign, IL 61820. *Office*—2136 Music Building, University of Illinois, 1114 West Nevada St., Urbana, IL 61801.

CAREER: American Joint Distribution Committee, New York City, field representative in charge of World War II displaced persons in Germany and the Netherlands, 1945-47; City College (now City College of the City University of New York), New York City, instructor,

1948-51, lecturer in music, 1951-52; University of Pennsylvania, Philadelphia, assistant professor of music, 1952-55; University of California, Berkeley, assistant professor of music, 1955-56; University of Oklahoma, Norman, associate professor of music, 1956-58; University of Illinois at Urbana-Champaign, associate professor, 1958-63, professor of musicology, 1963-91, chairman of Division of Musicology, 1963-69, professor emeritus, 1991—. Fulbright visiting professor, Hebrew University, 1962-63, 1966-67; visiting professor, University of Heidelberg, 1983-84; has lectured at universities in Zurich, Marburg, Frankfurt, and Berlin, and at University of Amsterdam, University of Utrecht, University of Tehran, Kiel University, Weizmann Institute of Science, University of California, University of Colorado, University of Tel Aviv, University of North Carolina, Yale University, and Coe College. Cantor, organist, and choral director in synagogues in the United States and the Netherlands, 1941-58. Project director, Kodaly Fellowship Program, National Endowment for the Arts, 1968-73. Worked with Israel Kodaly Program, 1985-1993. Artistic advisor, Jerusalem Music Centre (Israel), 1991-93.

MEMBER: International Musicological Society, American Society for Jewish Music, American Professors for Peace in the Middle East (member of executive board and council, 1968—; chairman of Midwest Region, 1977-78), Institute of Advanced Musical Studies, Kings College, University of London (corresponding member), International Kodaly Society (honorary member), Federated Jewish Charities (member of board of directors of local branch, 1965—), Pi Kappa Lambda, Philomathean Society (honorary member).

AWARDS, HONORS: Distinguished service award from Philadelphia Jewish Music Council, 1955; grants from American Council of Learned Societies, Smithsonian Institution, Ford Foundation, National Endowment for the Arts, University of Oklahoma, and University of Illinois.

WRITINGS:

(Editor) Edward Pierce, *For Hunting,* Theodore Presser, 1958.

(Editor and author of introduction) *Yearbook of the International Folk Music Council,* University of Illinois Press (Champaign-Urbana), Volume 1, 1970, Volume 2, 1971.

An Experimental Program in the Development of Musical Literacy among Musically Gifted Children in the Upper Elementary Grades (monograph), U.S. Department of Health, Education, and Welfare (Washington, DC), 1970.

Arnold Schoenberg and the Prophetic Image in Music, J. Arnold Schoenberg Institute, 1979.

Arnold Schoenberg and the Politics of Jewish Survival, J. Arnold Schoenberg Institute, 1979.

Schoenberg, Weill and Epic Theater, J. Arnold Schoenberg Institute, 1980.

Arnold Schoenberg: The Composer as Jew, Oxford University Press (New York City), 1990.

(Editor and author of introduction) *The Early Romantic Era: Between Revolutions, 1789 and 1848,* Prentice-Hall (Englewood Cliffs, NJ), 1990.

Musik als Geschichte, Laaber Verlag (Laaber), 1993.

Beethoven: Interpretationen seiner Werke, two volumes, Laaber Verlag, 1994.

Author of program notes. Contributor of chapters and essays to numerous books, including *The Creative World of Beethoven,* edited by P. H. Lang, Norton (New York City), 1971; *Music in the Classic Era,* edited by Allan W. Atlas, Pendragon, 1985; *Wagner in Retrospect,* edited by Leroy R. Shaw, Nancy R. Cirillo, and Marion S. Miller, Rodolpi, 1987. Contributor to honorary volumes, yearbooks, and symposia, and to *Encyclopaedia Britannica, Encyclopedia of Music and Musicians, Encyclopedia of Religion, Grove's Dictionary of Music,* and *Dictionary of Twentieth-Century Music.* Contributor of over one hundred articles and reviews to periodicals, including *Saturday Review, Musical Quarterly, Music and Letters, Journal of Higher Education, Comparative Literature Studies, Journal of the Arnold Schoenberg Institute, Current Musicology, Studia Musicologica, Journal of the History of Ideas, Die Musik Forschung, Forum Musicologicum, Analecta Musicologica,* and *Studies in Medieval Culture.* Member of editorial board, *Musica Judaica.*

WORK IN PROGRESS: A Language of Feeling: Studies in Nineteenth-Century Music, Arnold Schoenberg und seine Zeit, and *Music Through Education: Report on an American Kodaly Experiment;* co-editing *The Collected Writings of Arnold Schoenberg.*

*   *   *

ROCHE, Terry
See POOLE, Peggy

*   *   *

ROCHER, Guy   1924-

PERSONAL: Born April 20, 1924, in Berthierville, Quebec, Canada; son of Barthelemy (a civil engineer) and Jeanne (Magnan) Rocher; married Suzanne Cloutier, 1949 (divorced, 1981); married Claire-Emmanuelle Depocas, 1986; children: (first marriage) Genevieve, Anne-Marie, Isabelle, Claire. *Education:* University of Montreal, B.A., 1943, Laval University, M.A., 1950; Harvard University, graduate study, 1950-52, Ph.D., 1958.

ADDRESSES: Home—5610 Ave. Decelles, Apt. 16, Montreal, Quebec, Canada H3T 1W5. *Office*—Law Faculty, University of Montreal, Montreal, Quebec, Canada H3C 3J7.

CAREER: Laval University, Quebec City, Quebec, assistant professor, 1952-57, associate professor of sociology, 1957-60, director of School of Social Service, 1958-60; University of Montreal, Montreal, Quebec, professor of sociology, 1960—, director of department, 1960-65, assistant dean, Faculty of Social Sciences, 1962-67, affiliated with Center for Research into Public Law, Faculty of Law, 1979—. Member of Royal Commission of Inquiry on Education in Province of Quebec, 1961-65; governor of Canadian College of Workers, 1963-66; president of commission of inquiry on the New French University at Montreal, 1965; member of Canadian Broadcast Board, 1966-68; vice-president of Arts Council of Canada, 1969-74; deputy minister of cultural development, Quebec Government, 1976-79; president of administrative council of Radio-Quebec, 1979-81; deputy minister for social development, Quebec Government, 1981-83.

MEMBER: International Young Catholic Students (Canada; president, 1945-48), International Association of French-speaking Sociologists (treasurer, 1958-59), Canadian Association of Sociology (president, 1961-62), French-Canadian Association of Sociologists and Anthropologists (president, 1967-69), American Sociological Association, Canadian Economic Association, French-Canadian Association for the Advancement of Science.

AWARDS, HONORS: Carnegie Foundation fellow at Harvard University, 1951-52; research grants from Royal Society of Canada, 1957-58, Arts Council of Canada, 1965-66, 1968-69, and Social Science Research Council, 1988-95; Companion of the Order of Canada, 1971, for contribution to Canadian education; Chevalier de l'Ordre national du Quebec, 1991.

WRITINGS:

(With P. H. Chombard de Lauwe and others) *Famille et habitation,* Centre National de la Recherche Scientifique (Paris), 1960.
(With others) *Rapport de la commission royale d'enquete sur l'enseignement,* Queen's Printer, Volume 1, 1963, Volume 2, 1964, Volume 3, 1964, Volume 4, 1966, Volume 5, 1966.
Introduction a la sociologie generale, three volumes, Editions H.M.H., 1968-69, translation by Peta Sheriff published as *A General Introduction to Sociology: A Theoretical Perspective,* St. Martin's (New York City), 1972.

(With Pierre W. Belanger) *Ecole et societe au Quebec,* Editions H.M.H., 1971, new edition, 1975.
Talcott Parsons et la sociologie americaine, Presses Universitaires de France, 1972, translation by Barbara and Stephen Mennell, with an introduction by Stephen Mennell, published as *Talcott Parsons and American Sociology,* Nelson (London), 1974, Barnes & Noble (New York City), 1975.
Le Quebec en mutation, Editions H.M.H., 1973.
(With others) *Ecole de demain,* Editions Delachaux, 1976.
(With Leon Bernier and Belanger) *Generation, maturation et conjoncture: Une Etude des changements d'attitude dans le Quebec des annees 1970,* Faculte des Sciences de l'Education, Universite Laval and Department de Sociologie, Universite de Montreal, 1980.
(With others) *Continuite et rupture: Les Sciences sociales au Quebec,* Les Presses de Universite de Montreal, 1984.
(With Gerard Daigle) *Le Quebec en jeu,* Les Presses de l'Universite de Montreal, 1992.
(With Rene Cote) *Entre droit et technique,* Les Editions Theuris, 1994.

Contributor to professional journals, committee reports, and to *Montreal Star.* Contributor to books, including *Le Nouveau defi des valeurs,* Editions H.M.H., 1969; *Perspectives on Revolution and Evolution,* Duke University Press, 1979; *Les hommes, leurs espaces et leurs aspirations,* L'Harmattan (Paris), 1994; and *Etudes juridiques en l'honneur de Jean Beetz,* Editions Theuris (Montreal), 1994. Managing editor, *Service Social,* 1958-60; member of editorial board, *Recherches sociographiques, Sociologie et societes, Quebec-Science, Maintenant,* and *Cahiers de recherches sociologiques.*

Introduction a la sociologie generale has been translated into Spanish, Portuguese, Italian, and Persian; *Talcott Parsons et la sociologie americaine* has been translated into Italian, Dutch, and Japanese.

WORK IN PROGRESS: A book on the sociology of law; research on the legal and ethical dimensions of technological change.

* * *

ROJAS, Carlos 1928-

PERSONAL: Surname is pronounced "Ro-has"; born August 12, 1928, in Barcelona, Spain; son of Carlos Pinilla and Luisa (Vila) Rojas; married Eunice Mitcham, March, 1966. *Education:* University of Madrid, Ph.D., 1955. *Politics:* "A liberal and a pacifist."

ADDRESSES: Home—1378 Harvard Rd., Atlanta, GA 30306. *Office*—Department of Romance Languages,

Emory University, Atlanta, GA 30322. *Agent*—Ramon Serrano, Copernico, 85, Barcelona 6, Spain.

CAREER: Rollins College, Winter Park, FL, assistant professor of Spanish, 1957-60; Emory University, Atlanta, GA, assistant professor, 1960-63, associate professor, 1963-67, professor of Spanish, 1967-80, Charles Howard Candler Professor, 1980—.

AWARDS, HONORS: Premio Ciudad de Barcelona, 1959, for *El Asesino de Cesar;* Premio Nacional de Literatura, 1968, for *Auto de fe;* Premio Planeta, 1974, for *Azana;* Premio Eugenio Nadal, 1979, for *El Ingenioso Hidalgo y Poeta Federico Garcia Lorca asciende a los infiernos.*

WRITINGS:

NOVELS

De Barro y de Esperanza, Editorial L. de Caralt, 1957.
El Futuro ha comenzado, Editorial A.H.R., 1958.
El Asesino de Cesar, Editorial Planeta, 1959.
Las Llaves del infierno, Editorial L. de Caralt, 1962.
La Ternura del hombre invisible, Editorial Plaza-Janes, 1963.
Adolfo Hitler esta en mi casa, Ediciones Rondas, 1965.
Dialogos para otra Espana, Ediciones Ariel, 1966.
Auto de fe, Ediciones Guadarrama, 1968.
Luis III, el Minotauro, Ediciones Cuentatras, 1970.
Por que perdimos la guerra, Ediciones Nauta, 1970.
Aguelarre, Ediciones Nauta, 1970.
Diez Figuras ante la Guerra Civil, Ediciones Nauta, 1973.
Azana, Editorial Planeta, 1974.
El Valle de los Caidos, Ediciones Destino, 1978.
La Guerra en Cataluna, Plaza-Janes, 1979.
El Ingenioso Hidalgo y Poeta Federico Garcia Lorca asciende a los infiernos, Ediciones Destino, 1980.
La Barcelona de Picasso, Plaza-Janes, 1981.
El Sueno de Sarajevo, Ediciones Destino, 1982.
El Mundo mitico y magico de Picasso, Editorial Planeta, 1984.
El Mundo mitico y magico de Salvador Dali, Plaza-Janes, 1985.

TRANSLATOR INTO SPANISH

Paul Valery, *Le Cimitiere Marin,* Instituto Castellonese de Cultura, 1955.
Aldous Huxley, *Point Counterpoint, Those Barren Leaves* [and] *Eyeless in Gaza,* Editorial Planeta, 1958.
John Dos Passos, *Manhattan Transfer,* Editorial Planeta, 1958.

Also author of introductions to Spanish editions of the complete works of Huxley and Dos Passos, published by Editorial Planeta, 1958.

EDITOR

De Cela a Castillo-Navarro, Prentice-Hall, 1965.
(With Thomas R. Hart) *La Espana moderna vista y sentida por los Espanoles,* Prentice-Hall, 1966.
Maestros Americanos, Editorial Planeta, 1967.

OTHER

Contributor to *Encyclopedia Espana.* Contributor of short stories, in English, to *Archon* and *Stylus.*

SIDELIGHTS: Carlos Rojas told *CA:* "I am interested in fiction, history, literary and artistic criticism because I believe in words as the best means to an end which is always freedom." In addition to Spanish, Rojas speaks English, French, Italian, and Catalan.

BIOGRAPHICAL/CRITICAL SOURCES:

BOOKS

Prat, Angel Valbuena, *Historia de la literatura Espanola,* Gustavo Gili, 1968.
Schwartz, Kessel, *Studies on Twentieth-Century Spanish American Literature,* University Press of America, 1983.
Vilar, Sergio, *Arte y libertad,* Las Americas, 1963.

*   *   *

ROOP, Connie
    See ROOP, Constance Betzer

*   *   *

ROOP, Constance Betzer   1951-
(Connie Roop)

PERSONAL: Born June 18, 1951, in Elkhorn, WI; daughter of Robert Sterling (a funeral director) and Marjorie (a homemaker; maiden name, Gray) Betzer; married Peter G. Roop (an educator and author), August 4, 1973; children: Sterling Gray, Heidi Anne. *Education:* Lawrence University, B.A., 1973; attended University of Wisconsin—Madison and Colorado School of Mines, 1974; Boston College, M.S.T., 1980. *Politics:* Independent. *Religion:* Christian.

ADDRESSES: Home and office—2601 North Union St., Appleton, WI 54911.

CAREER: Appleton Area School District, Appleton, WI, science teacher, 1973—; science teacher at school in Kington, England, 1976-77. Educational consultant for D. C. Heath, 1985-87; writer and consultant for Harcourt, Brace, and Jovanovich, 1987, 1990. Workshop coordinator at Duquesne University and University of Wisconsin—Madison; member of Lawrence University Educational Advisory Committee.

MEMBER: American Association of University Women (chairperson of international relations), National Education Association, American Field Service, Society of Children's Book Writers, National Science Teachers Association, Wisconsin Society of Science Teachers, Wisconsin Earth Science Teachers Association, Wisconsin Regional Writers, Friends of the Appleton Library.

AWARDS, HONORS: Children's Choice Awards from International Reading Association and Children's Book Council, 1985, for *Out to Lunch!* and *Space Out!; Keep the Lights Burning, Abbie* was named Children's Book of the Year and Irma Simonton Black Honor Book by the Bank Street College of Education, 1986, an "outstanding trade book in the language arts" by the National Council of Teachers of English, and was chosen as a 1987 feature book for Public Broadcasting System's "Reading Rainbow" program; named Woman Leader in Education for State of Wisconsin, American Association of University Women, 1988; *Seasons of the Cranes* was named a National Science Teacher Association Notable Trade Book, 1989; Library of Congress Book of the Year, International Reading Association Teachers Choice, and American Library Association Young Adult Editor's Choice book, all 1990, all for *I, Columbus;* Kohl Education Foundation Award for exemplary teaching, 1990; National Council for the Social Sciences Notable Trade Book, 1992, for *Ahyoka and the Talking Leaves* and 1993, for *Off the Map: The Journals of Lewis and Clark.*

WRITINGS:

CHILDREN'S BOOKS; UNDER NAME CONNIE ROOP; WITH HUSBAND, PETER ROOP

Space Out!, Lerner Publications (Minneapolis), 1984.
Go Hog Wild!, Lerner Publications, 1984.
Out to Lunch!, Lerner Publications, 1984.
Keep the Lights Burning, Abbie, Carolrhoda (Minneapolis), 1985.
Buttons for General Washington, Carolrhoda, 1986.
Stick Out Your Tongue!, Lerner Publications, 1986.
Going Buggy!, Lerner Publications, 1986.
Let's Celebrate!, Lerner Publications, 1986.
The Extinction of the Dinosaurs, Greenhaven Press (St. Paul, MN), 1987.
Mysteries of the Solar System, Greenhaven Press, 1987.
Poltergeists, Greenhaven Press, 1987.
We Sought Refuge Here, Appleton Schools, 1987.
Seasons of the Cranes, Walker & Co. (New York City), 1989.
I, Columbus, Walker & Co., 1990.
One Earth, A Multitude of Creatures, Walker & Co., 1992.

Ahyoka and the Talking Leaves, Lothrop (New York City), 1992.
Off the Map: The Journals of Lewis and Clark, Walker & Co., 1993.
Capturing Nature: The Art and Writings of Audubon, Walker & Co., 1993.
Goodbye for Today, Puffin Books (New York City), 1995.
Mary Jemison, Puffin Books, 1995.
The Pilgrims' Voices, Walker & Co., 1995.
Small Deer and the Buffalo Jump, Northland Press, 1996.
David Farragut, Lothrop, 1996.

"DISCOVERING NONFICTION" SERIES, WITH PETER ROOP

Discovering Sea Creatures, Perfection Learning, 1992.
Discovering The Solar System, Perfection Learning, 1992.
Discovering Flowering Plants, Perfection Learning, 1992.
Discovering Insects and Spiders, Perfection Learning, 1992.
Discovering Dinosaurs, Perfection Learning, 1992.

OTHER

Contributor, with Peter Roop, to *Writers in the Classroom,* Christopher-Gordon, 1991, and *Writers Express,* Write Source, 1994. Contributor, with Peter Roop, to periodicals, including *Learning and Appraisal, Educational Psychology, Science Scope,* and *Learning.*

WORK IN PROGRESS: With Peter Roop, *San Francisco Earthquake,* Lothrop.

SIDELIGHTS: "I am an avid reader," Constance Betzer Roop told *CA.* "My serious interest in children's books developed while pursuing a master's degree in science teaching. I began to read many of the books assigned to my husband, Peter, in his Master's of Children's Literature Program as a change from science journals. Based on this reading, I developed a fiction book list to supplement the science curriculum in my junior high school life science classes. These scientifically accurate and exciting books provided my entry into the world of writing for children and young adults.

"I began to write articles for educational journals and to review books for *Appraisal.* Peter and I then collaborated on a series of six joke and riddle books, followed by two historical novels for young readers. We've been writing together ever since.

"Peter and I feature real young heroes and heroines in our books. It is people, including children, who make history. We hope young people can learn from and gain inspiration from courageous children of the past like Abbie Burgess, John Durragh, Ahyoka, and David Farragut, who are featured in our books.

"Traveling through books and visiting the places we write about are both critical to our writing. These voyages have inspired us to make primary sources accessible to young readers. students are encouraged to keep journals. Journals kept in the past can be an authentic glimpse into the thoughts and actions of historical events plus a terrific model for young journalists today.

"I am frequently asked to present educational and writing workshops. I believe it is important for young authors to see hear and ask questions of a 'real, live' author. It is extremely rewarding when students ask insightful questions and share their love for our books.

"Peter and I are committed to children. Writing the best possible books for young readers is our goal. We hope to open more vistas and distant horizons to inquiring, curious minds. We hope our books help young people discover the joy of learning we possess."

*　　　*　　　*

ROSEN, Haiim B(aruch) 1922-
(Heinz Erich Rosenrauch)

PERSONAL: Original name, Heinz Erich Rosenrauch; name legally changed in 1949; born March 4, 1922, in Vienna, Austria; immigrated to Israel, 1938; son of Georg and Olga (Gerstl) Rosenrauch; married Hannah Steinitz, 1953; children: Adi Jonathan. *Education:* Hebrew University, M.A., 1943, Ph.D., 1948; Ecole des Hautes Etudes, postdoctoral study, 1951-52. *Religion:* Jewish.

ADDRESSES: Home—13 Bruria St., Jerusalem 93184, Israel. *Office*—Hebrew University, Mount Scopus, Jerusalem 91905, Israel.

CAREER: Teacher of Latin and Hebrew grammar in high schools, 1943-49; Hebrew University, Jerusalem, Israel, beginning 1949, associate professor, 1961-68, professor of general and Indo-European linguistics, beginning 1968, now professor emeritus; Tel Aviv University, Tel Aviv, Israel, professor of classics and Hebrew philology, beginning 1968, now professor emeritus. Visiting professor at College of Jewish Studies, University of Chicago, 1958-59; associate of Columbia University, 1958-61; visiting professor of Hebrew linguistics at Sorbonne, University of Paris, 1965-66 and 1971-72, Ecole des Hautes Etudes (Paris), 1972, 1978-79, and 1985, and College de France (Paris), 1976 and 1991. *Military service:* Haganah, 1942-49; became officer.

MEMBER: Comite International Permanent des Linguistes (representative of Israel), Israel National Academy of Sciences and Humanities, Groupe d'Etudes Linguistiques Chamito-Semitiques, Linguistic Society of America, Societe Asiatique, Societas Linguistica Europaea (vice president, 1978), Indogermanische Gesellschaft, Societe

des Etudes Grecques, Societe de Linguistique de Paris, Linguistic Circle of New York.

AWARDS, HONORS: Israel State Prize in the Humanities, 1977; Alexander von Humboldt Research Award, 1992.

WRITINGS:

(Under name Heinz Erich Rosenrauch) *Elementa Linguae Latinae, I-II,* Omanut, 1947, 3rd edition, 1962.
Ha-ivrit shelanu (title means "Our Hebrew Language"), Am Oved, 1955.
(Translator with wife, Hannah Rosen) Aristotle, *Politics III-IV,* Politeia, 1957-59.
Ivrit Tova (title means "Good Hebrew"), Kiryat-Sefer (Reseda, CA), 1958.
Eine Laut- und Formenlehre des herodotischen Sprachform, Winter, 1962.
A Textbook of Israeli Hebrew, University of Chicago Press, 1962, 2nd edition, 1976.
(Translator with H. Rosen) Aristotle, *Metaphysics VII-IX,* Politeia, 1967.
Contemporary Hebrew, Mouton (Hawthorne, NY), 1977.
(Editor) *Herodoti Historiae,* Volume 1, Teubner (Leipzig), 1987.

Also author of *L'hebreu et ses rapports avec le monde classique,* Geuthner (Paris). Contributor to professional journals.

SIDELIGHTS: Haiim B. Rosen's fields of research include general linguistics, Indo-European linguistics (with special attention to classical Greek), and Hebrew and Semitic (with special attention to Israeli Hebrew). "The laying of the foundation for the linguistic analysis of Israeli Hebrew," he once told *CA,* "is generally attributed to me; at any rate, I am considered to have coined the term 'Israeli Hebrew.' "

*　　　*　　　*

ROSEN, Michael J(oel) 1954-

PERSONAL: Born September 20, 1954, in Columbus, OH; son of Marvin and Nona Rosen. *Education:* Attended Kent State University, 1972-73; Ohio State University, B.S., 1976, graduate study, 1976-77; attended St. George's School of Medicine, Grenada, 1978; Columbia University, M.F.A., 1981.

ADDRESSES: Home—1623 Clifton Ave., Columbus, OH 43203. *Office*—Thurber House, 77 Jefferson Ave., Columbus, OH 43215. *Agent*—Gouverneur and Co., 10 Bleecker St., New York, NY 10012.

CAREER: Ohio State University, Columbus, instructor, 1978-84, lecturer, 1983 and 1985; free-lance illustrator and designer, 1981—; Thurber House, Columbus, OH, literary director, 1983—. Youth services director, program coordinator, and administrator of children's services for Leo Yassenoff Jewish Center, 1973-78; assistant at Bread Loaf Writers' Conference, 1977- 79; design consultant to Jefferson Center for Learning and the Arts, 1982—; has taught in the Ohio Art Council Poetry-in-the-Schools Program and Greater Columbus Arts Council Artist-in-the-Schools Program; has conducted over 300 young authors' conferences, in-service days, writing workshops, guest author days, and residencies (for elementary, middle school, and high school students and teachers), as well as giving readings from his works. Member of board of directors, Share Our Strength, Washington, DC (national organization fighting hunger and homelessness).

MEMBER: International PEN (American Center), Poetry Society of America, Academy of American Poets, Associated Writing Programs.

AWARDS, HONORS: Fellow of Ohio Arts Council, 1981, 1985, 1987; Ingram Merrill fellow (in poetry), 1982-83 and 1989; National Endowment for the Arts, fellow, 1984; Gustav Davidson Award from Poetry Society of America, 1984, for "The Map of Emotions"; Ohioana Library Award in poetry and Ohio Poetry Day Award, both 1985, for *A Drink at the Mirage;* grant from Jefferson Center for Learning and the Arts, 1988 and 1989; National Jewish Book award, 1993, and Living the Dream Award, 1994, both for *Elijah's Angel: A Story for Chanukah and Christmas.*

WRITINGS:

A Drink at the Mirage (poetry), Princeton University Press (Princeton, NJ), 1985.

50 Odd Jobs: A Wild and Whacky Rhyming Guide to One-of-a-Kind Careers (children's picture book of poetry) self-illustrated, Willowisp Press, 1988.

The Kid's Book of Fishing (juvenile), self-illustrated, Workman Publishing (New York City), 1991.

60 Fish (juvenile), Workman, 1991.

Elijah's Angel: A Story for Chanukah and Christmas (juvenile), illustrated by Aminah Brenda Lynn Robinson, Harcourt (New York City), 1992.

Kids' Best Dog Book, Workman Publishing, 1993.

All Eyes on the Pond (juvenile poetry), illustrated by Tom Leonard, Hyperion Books for Children (Westport, CT), 1994.

The Greatest Fable (juvenile poetry), Harcourt, 1994.

Bonesy and Isabel (picture book), illustrated by James Ransome, Harcourt, 1995.

A School for Pompey Walker, illustrated by Robinson, Harcourt, 1995.

Purr . . .Children's Book Illustrators Brag about Their Cats, Harcourt, in press.

EDITOR

Collecting Himself: James Thurber on Writing and Writers, Humor, and Himself, Hamish Hamilton (London, England), 1989, paperback edition, HarperCollins (New York City), 1991.

(And author of foreword and afterword) *The Company of Dogs: 21 Stories by Contemporary Masters,* Doubleday (New York City), 1990.

Home (writings and drawings by contemporary children's authors), HarperCollins, 1992.

(And author of preface) *The Company of Cats: 20 Stories of Family Cats,* Doubleday, 1992.

(And author of foreword) *The Company of Animals: 20 Stories of Animal Encounters,* Doubleday, 1993.

(And author of preface) *Speak! Children's Book Illustrators Brag about Their Dogs* (juvenile), Harcourt, 1993.

(And author of introduction) *People Have More Fun Than Anybody: A James Thurber Centennial Collection,* Harcourt, 1994.

Dog People: Portraits of Canine Companionship, Artisan, 1995.

OTHER

Work represented in anthologies, including *Literature: Options for Reading and Writing,* edited by Donald Daiker, Harper & Row, 1984; *A Place of Sense: Eight Essays in Search of the Midwest,* edited by Michael Martone, University of Iowa Press (Iowa City, IA), 1988; *The Direction of Poetry,* edited by Robert Richman, Houghton (Burlington, MA), 1988; and *Louder Than Words,* edited by William Shore, Vintage (St. Paul, MN), 1990; *The Best Poems of 1994,* edited by David Lehman, Knopf (New York City), 1995. Contributor of poetry, fiction, reviews and articles to periodicals, including *Atlantic Monthly, Bloomsbury Review, Boston Review, Confrontation, Epoch, High Plains Literary Review, Indiana Review, Kenyon Review, Nation, New Criterion, New York Times Book Review, New Yorker, Paris Review, Poet & Critic, Prairie Schooner, Salmagundi, Shenandoah, Southwest Review,* and *Yale Review.* Associate poetry editor, 1987-89, poetry editor, 1990—, *High Plains Literary Review.* Contributor of illustrations to magazines, including *Gourmet* and *New Yorker.* Columnist for *Canine Press.*

WORK IN PROGRESS: The poetry collections *Telling Things, Traveling in Notions,* and *Pilgrim Signs and Other Poems;* the novel *Unfamiliar Trees;* several children's books, including *A Pup and His Puppets, The Real For-Real Magician,* and *The Good Night Zoo;* several completed books await publication—*Bubbe's Wishbones* (juvenile) is scheduled for fall, 1996, Blue Sky Books, a division of Scholastic, *The Walkers of Hawthorn Park* (juvenile), Harcourt, and an anthology edited and illustrated by Rosen, *Food Fight: Poets Join the Fight Against Hunger* with *Poems to Their Favorite Foods* (proceeds to benefit the homeless, for Share Our Strength), Harcourt, scheduled for fall, 1996 publication.

SIDELIGHTS: Michael J. Rosen told *CA:* "In the last few years, I've been engaged by ways in which an individual can contribute to significant social issues beyond the financial and political channels—that is, beyond donations and activism. I am, of course, grateful to those individuals who have the resources and strengths to perform those valuable roles. But beyond those, I've been looking for other kinds of confidence and moral commitment. My anthologies *The Company of Dogs* and *Home,* the first to benefit animal welfare agencies and the latter to benefit homeless shelters and perishable food programs, created ways that individuals could contribute their talent and their good names to urgent problems. Such collections of well-known authors provide volumes that garner not only funds but genuine media attention. It has been an enormous honor to precipitate such collections and a concomitant reward to know that these generated funds offer such lasting benefits. Rather than imagine this a unique design, I hope that such collective philanthropy becomes a perennial enterprise in publishing."

A number of Rosen's books benefit charities. Profits from *The Company of Dogs: 21 Stories by Contemporary Masters, The Company of Cats: 20 Stories of Family Cats, The Company of Animals: 20 Stories of Animal Encounters, Dog People: Portraits of Canine Companionship, Speak! Children's Book Illustrators Brag about Their Dogs,* and *Purr . . .Children's Book Illustrators Brag about Their Cats* are donated to benefit The Company of Animals Fund, which Rosen established in 1990 to offer grants to animal welfare agencies nationwide. Profits from *Home* and *Food Fight: Poets Join the Fight Against Hunger with Poems to Their Favorite Foods* Rosen said, "benefit the homeless, [and were] conceived and edited on behalf of Share Our Strength."

*　　　*　　　*

ROSENRAUCH, Heinz Erich
　　See ROSEN, Haiim B(aruch)

*　　　*　　　*

ROWLAND-ENTWISTLE, (Arthur) Theodore (Henry) 1925-
　　(John Briquebec, Lea Clarke, Anyon Ellis, James Hall-Clarke, T. E. Henry, J. T. Lawrence)

PERSONAL: Born July 30, 1925, in Clayton-le-Moors, Lancashire, England; son of Arthur (an author and jour-

nalist) and Sylvia Morton (a teacher; maiden name, Clarke) Rowland-Entwistle; married Jean Isobel Esther Cooke (a writer and editor; died, 1994), March 18, 1968. *Education:* Open University, B.A., 1977. *Religion:* Church of England.

ADDRESSES: Home—West Dene, Stonestile Lane, Hastings, East Sussex TN35 4PE, England. *Agent*—Rupert Crew Ltd., King's Mews, Gray's Inn Rd., London WC1N 2JA England.

CAREER: Daily Mail, Manchester and London, England, sub-editor, 1944-55; *TV Times,* London, chief sub-editor, 1955-56, production editor, 1956-60, assistant editor, 1961; *World Book Encyclopaedia,* London, senior editor, 1962-67; director, Leander Associates Ltd. (editorial consultants), 1967-69; director, First Features Ltd. (a newspaper features agency), 1972-79.

MEMBER: Royal Geographical Society (fellow), Zoological Society of London (fellow).

WRITINGS:

NONFICTION

Teach Yourself the Violin, English University Press, 1967, published as *Violin,* McKay, 1974.
Insect Life: The World You Never See, Rand McNally (Chicago), 1976.
Natural Wonders of the World, Octopus (London), 1980.
(With wife, Jean Cooke) *Factfile,* W. H. Smith (New York City), 1989.
(With Cooke) *The World Almanac Infopedia,* World Almanac (New York City), 1990.

JUVENILE

(Under pseudonym John Briquebec) *Winston Churchill,* McGraw (New York City), 1972.
Napoleon, Hart-Davis (London), 1973.
Facts and Records Book of Animals, Purnell (Milwaukee), 1975.
The Restless Earth, Purnell, 1977.
Exploring Animal Homes, illustrations by Graham Allen and others, F. Watts (New York City), 1978.
Exploring Animal Journeys, illustrations by Allen and others, Ward, Lock (London), 1978.
Let's Look at Wild Animals, edited by Jennifer Justice, illustrations by Mike Atkinson, Ward, Lock, 1978.
Habits and Habitats: Insects, World, 1979.
(Editor) *Pictorial Encyclopedia of Nature,* Purnell, 1980.
The Illustrated Atlas of the Bible Lands, Longman (London), 1981.
Ancient World, Galley Press, 1981.
(Under pseudonym John Briquebec) *Animals and Man,* Purnell, 1982.

(Under pseudonym Anyon Ellis) *Wild Animals,* illustrations by Bernard Robinson and Wendy Meadway, Granada (London), 1982.

(Under pseudonym John Briquebec) *Trees,* illustrated by David Salariya, Granada, 1982.

(Under pseudonym J. T. Lawrence) *Fossils,* Granada, 1982.

(Under pseudonym James Hall-Clarke), *Fishes,* Granada, 1983.

Insects, Granada, 1983.

(Under pseudonym T. E. Henry) *The Seashore,* Granada, 1983.

Heraldry, Granada, 1984.

Houses, Wayland (Brighton, England), 1985.

World of Speed, Christensen, 1985.

Confucius, Wayland, 1986.

Stamps, Wayland, 1986.

Nebuchadnezzar, Wayland, 1986.

Rivers and Lakes, Wayland, 1986.

Focus on Rubber, Wayland, 1986.

Great British Architects, F. Watts, 1986.

Great British Investors, F. Watts, 1986.

Great British Kings and Queens, F. Watts, 1986.

Great British Reformers, F. Watts, 1986.

Focus on Coal, Wayland, 1987.

The Royal Marines, Wayland, 1987.

The Secret Service, Wayland, 1987.

The Special Air Service, Wayland, 1987.

Jungles and Rainforests, Wayland, 1987.

Flags, Wayland, 1987.

Guns, Wayland, 1988.

Thomas Edison, Cherrytree Books, 1988.

Wilbur and Orville Wright, Cherrytree Books, 1988.

A Three-Dimensional Atlas of the World, Simon & Schuster (New York City), 1988.

Focus on Silk, Wayland, 1989.

(Under pseudonym John Briquebec) *Historical Atlas: Ancient World,* Kingfisher, 1990.

The First Empires, F. Watts, 1990.

Prehistoric Life, Belitha Press, 1990.

Prehistory, Belitha Press, 1990.

Weather and Climate, Belitha Press, 1991.

"FUNFAX HISTORY OF BRITAIN" SERIES

Invaders, Henderson Publishing, 1993.

Middle Ages, Henderson Publishing, 1993.

Tudor Times, Henderson Publishing, 1993.

Cavaliers and Roundheads, Henderson Publishing, 1993.

Revolution and Change, Henderson Publishing, 1993.

The Victorians, Henderson Publishing, 1993.

JUVENILE; WITH WIFE, JEAN COOKE

Animal Worlds, illustrations by Bernard Robinson and others, Sampson Low, 1974.

Famous Composers, David & Charles (London), 1974.

Famous Explorers, David & Charles, 1974.

Famous Kings and Emperors, David & Charles, 1976.

(Also with Ann Kramer) *World of History,* Hamlyn (London), 1977.

(Editors) *The Junior Encyclopedia of General Knowledge,* Octopus, 1978.

(Editors) *Purnell's Concise Encyclopedia of the Arts,* Purnell, 1979.

(Editors) *Purnell's Pictorial Encyclopedia,* Purnell, 1979.

(Editors) *Purnell's Pictorial Encyclopedia of Nature,* Purnell, 1980.

(Under pseudonym Lea Clarke) *The Beaver Book of Sporting Rules,* Hamlyn, 1980.

(Also with Kramer) *History Factfinder,* Ward, Lock, 1981.

Rainbow Fact Book of British History, W. H. Smith, 1984.

OTHER

Contributor to books, including *Everyman's Factfinder,* edited by Michael W. Dempsey Dent, 1982; *Quest for the Past,* edited by Kramer and Lindy Newton, Reader's Digest Association, 1984; *The Giant Book of Facts,* Octopus, 1987; *Facts and Fallacies,* Reader's Digest, 1988, and *How Is It Done,* Reader's Digest, 1990. Contributor of articles and consultant to encyclopedias, including *New Junior World Encyclopedia, Apollo Encyclopedia, Modern Century Illustrated Encyclopedia, Encyclopedia of Wild Life, Encyclopedia of Africa, Encyclopedia of Inventions, Concise Encyclopedia of Geography, Concise Encyclopedia of History, Rainbow Encyclopedia, St. Michael Encyclopedia of Natural History, Pictorial Encyclopedia of History,* and *Young Student's Encyclopedia.* Contributor of articles and consultant to atlases, including *St. Michael Atlas of World Geography, My First Picture Atlas,* and *Encyclopedic Atlas of the World.* Editor of *Hastings Talking Newspaper for the Blind,* 1981—. Contributor of articles to periodicals.

SIDELIGHTS: Theodore Rowland-Entwistle told *CA:* "Apart from my unpublished poetry, I am a non-creative writer; I produce reference material for young people and nonspecialist adults. Consequently, my main objectives are accuracy and clarity. I would recommend the discipline of sub-editing for a national newspaper as training for any writer, but don't stick at it too long. I was fortunate to be able to collaborate with my wife, Jean Cooke, on most of my work, until her untimely death from cancer in 1994."

*   *   *

RUESCHEMEYER, Marilyn 1938-

PERSONAL: Born June 3, 1938, in New York, NY; daughter of Julius and Bela (Wax) Schattner; married

Dietrich Rueschemeyer (a professor), June 14, 1964; children Julia, Simone. *Education:* Queens College, B.A., 1959; University of Toronto, M.A., 1965; Brandeis University, Ph.D., 1978.

ADDRESSES: Office—Department of Liberal Arts, Rhode Island School of Design, 2 College St., Providence, RI 02903.

CAREER: Rhode Island School of Design, Providence, assistant professor, 1980-87, associate professor, 1987-93, professor of sociology, 1994—, head of department of history, philosophy and social sciences, 1985-88, 1994—; Harvard University, Cambridge, MA, research associate at Center for European Studies, 1985-92, fellow of Russian Research Center, 1986—. Senior associate of St. Antony's College, Oxford, 1979 and 1982; adjunct associate professor at Brown University, 1987—; visiting fellow, Hebrew University of Jerusalem, Israel, 1990; visiting fellow, Stockholm Institute of Soviet and Eastern European Economics, 1992. Member of board of directors of New Music Ensemble and Brandeis Alumni Council.

MEMBER: American Sociological Association (co-chair for Committee on International Sociology; East European liaison to Committee on World Sociology, 1985—), Research Commission on Women in Politics in Eastern Europe, International Research and Exchanges Board (United States Coordinator, 1991-92), Association of the United States (member of executive committee).

AWARDS, HONORS: Exchange visitor of National Academy of Sciences in East Germany, 1981; grants from International Research and Exchanges Board, 1984, 1986, 1991, and 1992; research grant, American Council of Learned Societies, 1987-88; invited guest, Wissenschaftszentrusn Berlin, 1994.

WRITINGS:

Professional Work and Marriage: An East-West Comparison, St. Martin's (New York City), 1981.
(With Igor Golomshtek and Janet Kennedy) *Soviet Emigre Artists Life and Work in the United States and the U.S.S.R.,* M. E. Sharpe (New York City), 1985.
(Editor with Christine Lemke) *The Quality of Life in the German Democratic Republic Changes and Developments in a State Socialist Society,* M. E. Sharpe, 1989.
(Editor with David Childs and Thomas Baylis) *East Germany in Comparative Perspective,* Routledge & Kegan Paul (London), 1989.
(Editor and contributor) *Women in the Politics of Post-Communist Eastern Europe,* M. E. Sharpe, 1994.

Contributor to scholarly journals. Editor, *German Democratic Republic Newsletter,* 1985-86.

SIDELIGHTS: Marilyn Rueschemeyer has conducted sociological research in East and West Germany, Canada, the Soviet Union, Israel, and the United States. Her book *Professional Work and Marriage* was hailed by *Times Literary Supplement* reviewer Jennifer Uglow as "a vivid excursion into the 'concrete experience' of individual professionals, their wives and husbands in America and Eastern Europe." Rueschemeyer's book consists of seventy lengthy interviews that compare East-West attitudes and contrast dual-career and single-career families. The author revealed that attitudinal differences were not as great as one might expect. As Uglow noted, "Dual-career families in both societies are burdened by traditional role expectations, especially with regard to child care."

BIOGRAPHICAL/CRITICAL SOURCES:

PERIODICALS

Times Literary Supplement, February 5, 1982.

*   *   *

RUGOFF, Milton   1913-

PERSONAL: Surname is pronounced "*Rue*-goff "; born March 6, 1913, in New York, NY; son of David and Jennie (maiden name, Joseph) Rugoff; married Helen Birkenbaum, January 31, 1937; children: Kathy. *Education:* Columbia University, B.A., 1933, M.A., 1934, Ph.D., 1940.

ADDRESSES: Home—18 Ox Ridge Rd., Elmsford, NY 10523. *Office*—Chanticleer Press, 424 Madison Ave., New York, NY 10017.

CAREER: Alfred A. Knopf, Inc. (publishers), New York City, associate editor, 1943-47; *The Magazine '47,* New York City, associate editor, 1947-48; Chanticleer Press, New York City, editor and vice-president, 1948-83. *Military service:* U.S. Army, 1943-46.

MEMBER: PEN American Center, Authors Guild, Hakluyt Society.

AWARDS, HONORS: American Book Award nomination, 1982, for *The Beechers: An American Family in the Nineteenth Century.*

WRITINGS:

Donne's Imagery: A Study in Creative Sources, [New York City], 1939, reprinted, Russell, 1961.
Marco Polo's Adventures in China, American Heritage Press (New York City), 1962.
Prudery and Passion: Sexuality in Victorian America, Putnam (New York City), 1971.
The Beechers: An American Family in the Nineteenth Century, Harper & Row (New York City), 1981.

America's Gilded Age: Intimate Portraits from an Era of Extravagance and Change, 1850-1890, Holt (New York City), 1989.

Also author of *The Private Lives of Animals.*

EDITOR

A Harvest of World Folk Tales, Viking (New York City), 1949, reissued as *Penguin Book of World Folk Tales,* 1977.

The Great Travelers, two volumes, Simon & Schuster (New York City), 1960.

Travels of Marco Polo, New American Library (New York City), 1962, reprinted, 1982.

Bligh's Mutiny on the H.M.S. Bounty, New American Library, 1962.

The Britannica Encyclopedia of American Art, Simon & Schuster, 1973, reprinted as *Encyclopedia of American Art,* Dutton (New York City), 1981.

The Wild Places: A Photographic Celebration of Unspoiled America, Harper, 1973.

SIDELIGHTS: Milton Rugoff has remained especially interested in the fields of biography, folklore, social history, and art; each of his books fills a gap found in these subject areas. *A Harvest of World Folk Tales* includes about two hundred folk tales collected from nineteen different areas of the world. The stories "offer rich stuff for speculation when we are in a philosophic mood," Marvin Lowenthal points out. *The Great Travelers* is a collection of firsthand narratives of wayfarers, wanderers, and explorers in all parts of the world, from 450 B.C. to the present. According to Martin Levin in the *New York Herald Tribune Book Review,* it is a "stunning collection" of photographs, prints, and skillful editing, making it "a beautifully orchestrated symposium."

Nominated for an American Book Award in 1982, Rugoff's *The Beechers: An American Family in the Nineteenth Century,* which Rugoff described for *CA* as "[an] intimate 650-page portrait of Lyman Beecher [and] his eleven children, almost all of them famous, including novelist Harriet Beecher Stowe, preacher Henry Ward Beecher, educator Catharine Beecher [and] feminist Isabella Beecher," has earned the favor of many reviewers. Along with others, *Newsweek* writer Walter Clemons applauds Rugoff's choice of the family as the subject of study: "This explosion of talent, energy and eccentricity deserves a group biography, and Milton Rugoff's is unfailingly interesting." Richard Eder remarks in the *New York Times* that "the life of the book is the chronicling of dozens of Beechers and their friends and connections."

For many critics, however, the success of *The Beechers* is due as much to its evocation of a time as of a family. "Milton Rugoff's lively and readable biographical account," Martha Saxton writes in the *New York Times Book Review,* "not only squeezes a great deal of fascinating material about the influential, verbal and unbalanced family into a relatively short space, but also illuminates a central strand of American social history: how notions of goodness changed throughout the course of the 19th century." James R. Mellow makes a similar claim in the *Chicago Tribune Book World:* "Few books give one, as Rugoff's does in its personal histories of the various Beechers, such a sharp sense of the vital, even visceral, importance of religion in 19th Century American life."

Among Rugoff's accomplishments in the writing of *The Beechers,* according to Dan McCall in the *Washington Post Book World,* is the intelligence of his narration: "The stories are often sensational, but not once does [Rugoff] sensationalize them; his head is clear, and he knows there are no easy answers. He has conceived his task as something at once simple and immensely demanding: to *see* the Beechers, to *hear* them, all, and to put us in their presence. The very calmness of his voice makes us eager to listen to him. We need him; he does not explain what someone has said, he places it for us, he gives utterance its context."

Rugoff continued his exploration of nineteenth-century America and Americans in *America's Gilded Age: Intimate Portraits from an Era of Extravagance and Change, 1850-1890,* a book Richard C. Skidmore characterizes in the *New York Times Book Review* as "a pop history of personality, a digest of scandalous and extreme behavior that illuminates a time of high passions and low scruples."

Rugoff told *CA:* "I am increasingly fascinated by the lives of interesting people. That accounts for my books on the great travelers and explorers, on Marco Polo and Captain Bligh, on individuals who exemplify the tremendous effect of Victorian morality in America, and, most of all, the members of one of the most extraordinary and distinguished families in 19th century America, the Beechers. I am most proud of the reviews of this book that said it read like a novel."

BIOGRAPHICAL/CRITICAL SOURCES:

PERIODICALS

Chicago Tribune Book World, September 6, 1981, Sec. 7, p. 1.

Milwaukee Journal, November 11, 1973.

Newsweek, August 24, 1981, p. 69.

New York Herald Tribune Book Review, December 14, 1949.

New York Times, August 23, 1981, p. 21; August 28, 1981; February 3, 1982.

New York Times Book Review, December 4, 1960; September 20, 1981, p. 9; July 9, 1989, p. 19.

Washington Post, April 12, 1989.

Washington Post Book World, September 20, 1981, p. 1.*

*   *   *

RYAN, Alan 1940-

PERSONAL: Born May 9, 1940; son of John William (an accountant) and Ivy (Tickle) Ryan; married wife, Joanna Frances (a psychologist), July 28, 1962 (divorced). *Education:* Attended Christ's Hospital, Horsham, 1952-59; Balliol College, Oxford, B.A., 1962. *Politics:* Labour. *Religion:* None. *Avocational interests:* Dinghy sailing, long train journeys.

CAREER: University of Keele, Keele, England, lecturer in politics, 1963-66; University of Essex, Colchester, England, lecturer in politics, 1966-69; New College, Oxford University, Oxford, England, fellow and tutor in politics, 1969-78, reader, 1978-87; Princeton University, Princeton, NJ, professor of politics, 1988—. Visiting professor in politics at City University of New York, 1967-68, University of Texas, 1972, University of California, 1977, and the Witwaterstand, 1978. Visiting Fellow, Australian National University, 1974, 1979; de Carle Lecturer, University of Ontago, 1983; Mellon Fellow, Institute for Advanced Study, Princeton University, 1991-92.

WRITINGS:

John Stuart Mill, Pantheon, 1970, second edition, 1987, also published as *The Philosophy of John Stuart Mill.*
A Philosophy of Social Science, Pantheon, 1971.
(Editor) *The Idea of Freedom: Essays in Honour of Isaiah Berlin,* Oxford University Press (Oxford, England), 1979.
Property and Political Theory, B. Blackwell (Oxford), 1984.
Property, Open University Press, 1987, University of Minnesota Press (Minneapolis), 1987.
(Editor) *The Blackwell Encyclopedia of Political Thought,* B. Blackwell, 1987.
(Editor) *Utilitarianism and Other Essays: J. S. Mill and Jeremy Bentham,* Penguin (New York City), 1987.
(Editor with G. A. J. Rogers) *Perspectives on Thomas Hobbes,* Clarendon Press (Oxford), 1988.
Bertrand Russell: A Political Life, Penguin Books (London), 1988, Hill and Wang (New York City), 1988.
(Editor) *Justice* (Oxford readings in politics and government), Oxford University Press (New York City), 1993.

Also author of *J. S. Mill,* 1975.

SIDELIGHTS: Distinguished Oxford scholar Alan Ryan, who became professor of politics at Princeton University in 1988, is an accomplished editor and commentator on philosophy and politics. Ryan stirred critics with his book *Property and Political Theory* and attracted more critical attention with his work *Bertrand Russell: A Political Life.*

Calling *Property and Political Theory* an "eminently readable and reasonable book," critic Harold Perkin, writing in the *Times Literary Supplement,* praises the book as a "very good value, since it is really two books, or rather a book and a pamphlet." In the first part of the book, Ryan analyzes the views of great philosophers—including Locke, Rousseau, Kant, Godwin, Bentham, Hegel, Mill, and Marx—on the concept of property and examines its relationship to their own political philosophies. In the seventh and final chapter Ryan poses the provocative question, "Why Are There So Few Socialists?" or, as Perkin puts it, the author attempts "to explain why Marx and Mill were wrong, and how both the intellectuals and the working classes came to lose interest in the question of ownership of the means of production and switched instead to the question of distribution of its proceeds." While Perkin quarrels with what he sees as Ryan's "static" view of property in the book's conclusion, he does praise his study of the major philosophers, calling it "as good an introduction to their work as can be found in so short a space and can be confidently recommended."

Ryan turned his analytical powers to the long life and many achievements of Bertrand Russell, the radical English philosopher, in his book *Bertrand Russell: A Political Life.* "Despite Ryan's disclaimer that he has not written a biography," writes critic Oliver Conant in the *Voice Literary Supplement, Bertrand Russell* covers various aspects of Russell's life, from the early influences that shaped his political views to his vocal protests against World War I, the war in Vietnam, and nuclear proliferation. Conant points out that while Ryan obviously admires Russell, he retains a critical eye in his work. "Russell's faults—his tendency to demonize his opponents, his polemical excesses and recklessness, his arrogance, what Ryan tellingly calls the 'curious thinness' in his argumentative style—are kept in plain view," Conant explains.

Writing in the *Times Literary Supplement,* reviewer John Campbell commends Ryan's unique approach to chronicling the life of the multi-dimensional Russell. "His format is in fact a clever device for allowing him to write freely about the public Russell, whom most of us are interested in, leaving out on the one hand the mathematics and most of the philosophy and on the other all Russell's tortuous emotional and marital entanglements," writes Campbell. "Having thus cleared his ground, he has written an enjoyably lucid, shrewd and critically admiring assessment of the old goat's extraordinary mixture of clearsighted and cock-eyed ideas." Joining in on the critical praise that welcomed Ryan's book, Walter Goodman comments in the *New York Times:* "In concentrating on the public figure, Alan Ryan makes a pertinent contribution to Russelliana."

Distinguished economist and statesman John Kenneth Galbraith, however, claims in the *Washington Post Book World* that Ryan reached a bit too far beyond his writing ability with *Bertrand Russell.* "The sheer volume, especially of the nonacademic writing, is a problem for Professor Ryan. There is simply too much to summarize, but he tries, and the reader is left at times with a feeling of the sketchiness of the comment as well as with a far greater number of textual references than anyone could possibly keep in mind." But Galbraith goes on to say, "Yet there is redemption. In nearly all this account one is struck by Bertrand Russell's prescience." Galbraith praises Ryan's depiction of Russell's uncanny ability to be ahead of his time: in promoting positive encouragement rather than punishment in education; in opposing World War I at a time when such opposition was considered treasonous; and on recognizing the terrible threat posed by the nuclear arms race. Galbraith also complains about Ryan's awkwardness in presenting the contradictory philosopher's changing views, but he concludes, "These problems apart, this is a very good book."

In a lengthy discussion of Ryan's *Bertrand Russell* in the *New York Review of Books,* Stuart Hampshire calls the book "very pleasantly written and enjoyable." Hampshire draws attention to Ryan's account of Russell's involvement in the Cuban missile crisis, "in which Khrushchev and Kennedy, replying to telegrams from Russell urging a compromise, presented their arguments to the world 'through the sitting-room of a ninety-year-old philosopher.' " Hampshire notes that Ryan "then states the moral that the whole book skillfully conveys: the significance today of Russell's sustained efforts to provoke thought on public issues, and particularly on the issues of war and peace; Russell's involvement and participation, in spite of all the hostility and derision that he aroused." In fact, says Hampshire, this refusal to simply and quietly "assent" to the injustices going on around him is Russell's strongest legacy, which makes Ryan's book "relevant to the political dilemmas facing us now."

BIOGRAPHICAL/CRITICAL SOURCES:

PERIODICALS

New York Review of Books, March 20, 1980, p. 31; February 2, 1989, p. 7.
New York Times, December 29, 1988.
Times Literary Supplement, January 18, 1985, p. 59; July 1, 1988, p. 723.
Voice Literary Supplement, November, 1988, p. 3.
Washington Post Book World, October 30, 1988, p. 1.*

S

SAMS, Eric 1926-

PERSONAL: Born May 3, 1926, in London, England; son of Henry Sydney (in Royal Navy) and Violet (Hill) Sams; married Enid Tidmarsh (a music teacher), June 30, 1952; children: Richard, Jeremy. *Education:* Corpus Christi College, Cambridge, B.A., 1950, Ph.D., 1970. *Politics:* Social Democrat. *Religion:* None. *Avocational interests:* Chess.

ADDRESSES: Home—32 Arundel Ave., Sanderstead, Surrey CR2 8BB, England.

CAREER: Department of Employment, London, England, principal officer, 1950-78; writer, 1978—. Visiting professor at McMaster University, 1976-77. *Military service:* British Army, Intelligence Corps, 1944-47.

MEMBER: Institute of Germanic Studies, Schubert Institute, Civil Service Club, Society of Authors, Oxford and Cambridge Music Society, Peter Warlock Society.

AWARDS, HONORS: Award from Leverhulme Trust, 1983, for editing *Edmund Ironside;* named honorary member of Guildhall School of Music, 1983.

WRITINGS:

The Songs of Hugo Wolf, Methuen (London), 1961, revised and enlarged edition, Eulenburg, 1983.
The Songs of Robert Schumann, Methuen, 1969, revised edition, Eulenburg, 1975.
Brahms Songs, BBC Publications (London), 1972.
(Contributor) Alan Walker, editor, *Schumann: The Man and His Music,* Barrie & Jenkins (London), 1972, revised edition, 1976.
(With Maurice Brown) *Schubert,* Macmillan (New York City), 1982.

(Editor) *Shakespeare's Lost Play "Edmund Ironside,"* St. Martin's (New York City), 1985, revised edition, Wildwood House, 1986.
The Real Shakespeare, 1564-94, Yale University Press (New Haven, CT), 1995.

Contributor to *Early Romantic Masters* and *Late Romantic Masters,* both Macmillan, 1985. Contributor to *The New Grove Dictionary of Music and Musicians.* Contributor to music and literary journals and to other periodicals.

Brahms Songs was translated into French.

WORK IN PROGRESS: Editing William Shakespeare's *Edward III,* publication expected by Yale University Press; *The Songs of Johannes Brahms,* publication by Faber; a sequel to *The Real Shakespeare,* expected date of publication 1999.

SIDELIGHTS: Eric Sams told *CA:* "My work involves semantic analysis in the areas of nineteenth-century European song and other music, historical cipher and shorthand, and Shakespeare attribution studies. Their common factor is the cumulative study of motifs, symbols, images, and ideas in general considered both as elements of aesthetic expression and as data in problem solving."

*   *   *

SANCHEZ, Sonia 1934-

PERSONAL: Born Wilsonia Benita Driver, September 9, 1934, in Birmingham, AL; daughter of Wilson L. and Lena (Jones) Driver; married albert Sanchez (divorced); children: Anita, Morani Neusi, Mungu Neusi. *Education:* Hunter College (now Hunter College of the City University of New York), B.A., 1955; post-graduate study, New York University. *Politics:* "Peace, freedom, and justice."

ADDRESSES: *Home*—407 W. Chelten Ave., Philadelphia, PA 19144. *Office*—Department of English, Temple University, Philadelphia, PA 19141.

CAREER: Staff member, Downtown Community School, New York City, 1965-67; San Francisco State College (now University), San Francisco, instructor, 1966-68; University of Pittsburgh, Pittsburgh, PA, assistant professor, 1969-70; Rutgers University, New Brunswick, NJ, assistant professor, 1970-71; Manhattan Community College of the City University of New York, New York City, assistant professor of Black literature and creative writing, 1971-73; City College of the City University of New York, New York City, teacher of creative writing, 1972; Amherst College, Amherst, MA, associate professor, 1972-75; University of Pennsylvania, Philadelphia, PA, 1976-77; Temple University, Philadelphia, associate professor, 1977, Laura H. Carnell Professor of English, 1979—, faculty fellow in provost's office, 1986-87, presidential fellow, 1987-90. Adjunct professor, Haverford College, Haverford, PA, 1984-86; Distinguished Minority Faculty Fellow, University of Delaware, Newark, DE, 1987; Distinguished Poet-in-Residence, Spelman College, Atlanta, GA, 1989; Zale Writer in Residence, Newcomb College, Tulane University, New Orleans, LA, 1992. Member, Literature Panel of the Pennsylvania Council on the Arts, Literary Arts Task Force of the National African American Museum Project, and Poetry in the Schools Project.

MEMBER: Poetry Society of America, American Studies Association, Academy of American Poets, PEN, National Association for the Advancement of Colored People (lifetime membership).

AWARDS, HONORS: PEN Writing Award, 1969; National Institute of the Arts and Letters grant, 1970; honorary Ph.D., Wilberforce University, 1972; National Endowment for the Arts Award, 1978-79; Honorary Citizen of Atlanta, 1982; Tribute to Black Women Award, Black Students of Smith College, 1982; Lucretia Mott Award, 1984; American Book Award from Before Columbus Foundation, 1985, for *Homegirls & Handgrenades;* International Womens Award from Mayor's Commission for Women, Philadelphia, 1987; Welcome Award from Museum of Afro American History, Boston, 1990; Women Pioneers Hall of Fame citation from Young Women's Christian Association, 1992; Oni Award from International Black Women's Congress, 1992; Roots Award from PAN-African Studies Community Education Program, 1993; PEN fellowship in the arts, 1993-94; Legacy Award from Jomandi Productions, 1994.

WRITINGS:

Homecoming (poetry), Broadside Press (Highland Park, MI), 1969.

We a BaddDDD People (poetry), with foreword by Dudley Randall, Broadside Press, 1970.

It's a New Day: Poems for Young Brothas and Sistuhs (juvenile), Broadside Press, 1971.

(Editor) *Three Hundred and Sixty Degrees of Blackness Comin' at You* (poetry), 5X Publishing Co. (New York City), 1971.

A Sun Lady for All Seasons Reads Her Poetry (record album), Folkways, 1971.

Ima Talken bout the Nation of Islam, TruthDel, 1972.

Love Poems, Third Press (New York City), 1973.

A Blues Book for Blue Black Magical Women (poetry), Broadside Press, 1973.

The Adventures of Fat Head, Small Head, and Square Head (juvenile), Third Press, 1973.

(Editor and contributor) *We Be Word Sorcerers: 25 Stories by Black Americans,* Bantam (New York City), 1973.

I've Been a Woman: New and Selected Poems, Black Scholar Press (San Francisco), 1978.

A Sound Investment and Other Stories (juvenile), Third World Press (Chicago), 1979.

Crisis in Culture—Two Speeches by Sonia Sanchez, Black Liberation Press (New York City), 1983.

Homegirls & Handgrenades (poems), Thunder's Mouth Press (New York City), 1984.

Under a Soprano Sky (poems), Africa World Press (Trenton, NJ), 1987.

Wounded in the House of a Friend, Beacon Press (Boston, MA), 1995.

Does Your House Have Lions, Beacon Press, 1995.

PLAYS

The Bronx Is Next, first produced in New York at Theatre Black, October 3, 1970 (included in *Cavalcade: Negro American Writing from 1760 to the Present,* edited by Arthur Davis and Saunders Redding, Houghton, 1971).

Sister Son/ji, first produced with *Cop and Blow* and *Players Inn* by Neil Harris and *Gettin' It Together* by Richard Wesley as *Black Visions,* Off-Broadway at New York Shakespeare Festival Public Theatre, 1972 (included in *New Plays from the Black Theatre,* edited by Ed Bullins, Bantam, 1969).

Dirty Hearts, published in *Breakout: In Search of New Theatrical Environments,* Swallow Press (Chicago), 1973.

Uh Huh; But How Do It Free Us?, first produced in Chicago at Northwestern University Theater, 1975 (included in *The New Lafayette Theatre Presents: Plays with Aesthetic Comments by Six Black Playwrights, Ed Bullins, J.E. Gaines, Clay Gross, Oyamo, Sonia Sanchez, Richard Wesley,* edited by Bullins, Anchor Press, 1974).

Malcolm Man/Don't Live Here No More, first produced in Philadelphia at ASCOM Community Center, 1979.
I'm Black When I'm Singing, I'm Blue When I Ain't, first produced in Atlanta, Georgia at OIC Theatre, April 23, 1982.
Black Cats Back and Uneasy Landings, first produced in Philadelphia at Freedom Theatre, 1995.

OTHER

Contributor to anthologies, including *Black Fire: An Anthology of Afro-American Writing,* edited by Le Roi Jones and Ray Neal, Morrow (New York City), 1968; *We Speak as Liberators: Young Black Poets,* edited by Orde Coombs, Dodd (New York City), 1971; *Understanding the New Black Poetry: Black Speech and Black Music as Poetic References,* edited by Stephen Henderson, Morrow, 1973; *Giant Talk: An Anthology of Third World Writings,* edited by Quincy Troupe and Rainer Schulte, Random House (New York City), 1975; *Understanding Poetry,* edited by Brooks and Warren, Holt (New York City), 1976; *Confirmation: An Anthology of African-American Women,* edited by Amiri and Amina Baraka, Morrow, 1983; *Every Shut Eye Ain't Asleep: An Anthology of Poetry by African Americans since 1945,* edited by Michael S. Harper and Anthony Walton, Little, Brown (Toronto), 1994; and *Celebrating America: A Collection of Poems and Images of the American Spirit,* edited by Laura Whipple, Philomel Books (New York City), 1994.

Poems also included in *Night Comes Softly, Black Arts, To Gwen With Love, New Black Voices, Blackspirits, The New Black Poetry, A Rock Against the Wind, America: A Prophecy, Nommo, Black Culture,* and *Natural Process.* Author of column for *American Poetry Review,* 1977-78, for *Philadelphia Daily News,* 1982-83. Contributor of poems to *Minnesota Review, Black World,* and other periodicals. Contributor of plays to *Scripts, Black Theatre, Drama Review,* and other theater journals. Contributor of articles to journals, including *Journal of African Civilizations.*

SIDELIGHTS: Sonia Sanchez is often named among the strongest voices in black nationalism, the cultural revolution of the 1960s in which many black Americans sought a new identity distinct from the values of the white establishment. C. W. E. Bigsby comments in *The Second Black Renaissance: Essays in Black Literature* that "the distinguishing characteristic of her work is a language which catches the nuance of the spoken word, the rhythms of the street, and of a music which is partly jazz and partly a lyricism which underlies ordinary conversation." Her emphasis on poetry as a spoken art, or performance, connects Sanchez to the traditions of her African ancestors, an oral tradition preserved in earlier slave narratives and forms of music indigenous to the black experience in America. In addition to her poetry, for which she has won many prizes,

Sanchez has contributed equally well-known plays, short stories, and children's books to the body of black American literature. *Belles Lettres* contributor Kamili Anderson cites the poet's work for its "precision and insightfulness" and commends Sanchez for her "substantial and finely honed literary talents."

In *Southern Women Writers: The New Generation,* Joanne Veal Gabbin notes that much of Sanchez's work reveals her Southern roots, even though she lived in New York City from late childhood onward. "Throughout her poetry . . . Sanchez demonstrates the complexity of her Southern imagination," the critic writes. "Though she spent a relatively short period of her life in the South, her way of looking at the world is generously soaked in the values she learned during her childhood in Birmingham, Alabama. The importance of the family and love relationships, her fascination with the past and her ancestry, her search for identity amid the chaos and deracination of the North, her communion with nature, her exploration of the folk culture, her response to an evangelical religious experience, and her embracing of a militancy nurtured in fear and rage are Southern attitudes that inform her poetry. . . . Her early Southern experience watered her sensibility—the greening of her mind—and nourished her purpose as a poet: to create positive values for her community."

Born Wilsonia Benita Driver in Birmingham, Sanchez faced many difficulties as a youngster. Her mother died when she was only a year old, and for a time Sanchez and her sister were cared for by their paternal grandmother, Elizabeth "Mama" Driver. This beloved grandparent is the "Dear Mama" of Sanchez's poem by the same name in *Under a Soprano Sky.* Mama Driver died when Sanchez was five, and the frail youngster endured a period of family instability, including abuse and neglect by a stepmother and frequent moves from one relative's house to another's. When Sanchez was nine her father married a third time and took his family north to New York City. Gabbin writes: "In the small apartment she shared with her sister, her father, and his third wife, [Sanchez] felt hemmed in. Her tiny bedroom, whose window faced a redbrick wall, further mocked her sense of loss, now far from the greener open space of the South."

Sanchez began writing out of this sense of isolation, and also because writing was a way to express herself without the annoying stuttering that had developed in her youth. Alienated from her family and her peers, she found little solace in her studies toward a bachelor's degree at Hunter College. It was only after she enrolled in graduate courses at New York University that she found the encouragement she needed from other writers. She in turn organized a writers' workshop in Greenwich Village that attracted young black poets such as Amiri Baraka (Le Roi Jones) and Larry Neal. At the time Sanchez was also politically active, having joined the Congress of Racial Equality and the Reform Democrats club. Her marriage to a Puerto Rican immigrant named Albert Sanchez gave her a new surname; her budding poetic sensibility provided the rest of the name by which she has become known.

Sanchez reached adulthood in Harlem, which only thirty years before had been the cradle of the first literary "renaissance" in the United States to celebrate the works of black writers. Political science and poetry were the subjects of her studies at Hunter College and New York University during the 1950s. In the next decade Sanchez began to combine these interests into one activity, "the creat[ion] of social ideals," as she wrote for a section about her writings in *Black Women Writers (1950-1980): A Critical Evaluation,* edited by Mari Evans. For Sanchez, writing and performing poetry is a means of constructive political activism to the extent that it draws her people together to affirm pride in their heritage and build the confidence needed to accomplish political goals. Yet the terms of "black rhetoric," or words by themselves, are not enough, she says often in poems and interviews. Biographers cite her record of service as an educator, activist, and supporter of black institutions as proof of her commitment to this belief. Writing in the *Dictionary of Literary Biography,* Kalamu ya Salaam introduces Sanchez as "one of the few creative artists who have significantly influenced the course of black American literature and culture."

Before Sanchez became recognized as a part of the growing black arts movement of the 1960s, she worked in the Civil Rights movement in New York City. At that time, she, like many educated black people who enjoyed economic stability, held integrationist ideals. But after hearing Malcolm X say that blacks would never be fully accepted as part of mainstream America despite their professional or economic achievements, she chose to base her identity on her racial heritage. David Williams reports that the title of her first book, *Homecoming,* announces this return to a sense of self grounded in the realities of her urban neighborhood after having viewed it for a time from the outside through the lens of white cultural values. In the title poem, "Sanchez presents the act of returning home as a rejection of fantasy and an acceptance of involvement," notes Williams in *Black Women Writers (1950-1980).* For the same reasons, Sanchez did not seek a major publisher for the book. She preferred Dudley Randall's Broadside Press, a publisher dedicated to the works of black authors, that was to see many of her books into print. Reacting to the poems in *Homecoming,* Johari Amini's review in *Black World* warns that they "hurt (but doesn't anything that cleans good) and [the] lines are blowgun dartsharp with a wisdom ancient as Kilimanjaro." Haki Madhubuti's essay in *Black Women Writers*

(1950-1980) comments on this same effect, first remarking that Sanchez "is forever questioning Black people's commitment to struggle," saying again later that she is "forever disturbing the dust in our acculturated lives."

One aspect of her stand against acculturation is a poetic language that does not conform to the dictates of standard English. Madhubuti writes, "More than any other poet, [Sanchez] has been responsible for legitimizing the use of urban Black English in written form. . . . She has taken Black speech and put it in the context of world literature." Salaam elaborates, "In her work from the 1960s she restructured traditional English grammar to suit her interest in black speech patterns"—a technique most apparent, he feels, in *We a BaddDDD People.* In one poem cited by Madhubuti which he says is "concerned with Black-on-Black damage," Sanchez predicts that genuine "RE VO LU TION" might come about "if mothas programmed / sistuhs to / good feelings bout they blk / men / and i / mean if blk / fathas proved / they man / hood by fighten the enemy. . . ." These reviewers explain that by inserting extra letters in some words and extra space between lines, words, and syllables within a poem, Sanchez provides dramatic accents and other clues that indicate how the poem is to be said aloud.

The sound of the poems when read aloud has always been important to Sanchez. Her first readings established her reputation as a poet whose energetic performances had a powerful effect on her listeners. She has visited Cuba, China, the West Indies, Europe, and more than five hundred campuses in the United States to give readings, for which she is still in demand. Of her popularity, Salaam relates, "Sanchez developed techniques for reading her poetry that were unique in their use of traditional chants and near-screams drawn out to an almost earsplitting level. The sound elements, which give a musical quality to the intellectual statements in the poetry, are akin to Western African languages; Sanchez has tried to recapture a style of delivery that she felt had been muted by the experience of slavery. In her successful experimentation with such techniques, she joined . . . others in being innovative enough to bring black poetry to black people at a level that was accessible to the masses as well as enjoyable for them."

Sanchez is also known as an innovator in the field of education. During the 1960s, she taught in San Francisco's Downtown Community School and became a crusader and curriculum developer for black studies programs in American colleges and universities. Materials on black literature and history had been absent from the schools she had attended, and she has worked to see that other young people are not similarly disenfranchised. Sanchez was, in fact, the first college professor ever to offer a full-fledged seminar on literature by black American women—she accomplished this while teaching at Amherst College in Massachusetts. Since then Sanchez has remained in the academic arena, striving to shape and encourage the next generation. She wrote two books for her children (*The Adventures of Fat Head, Small Head, and Square Head,* and *A Sound Investment and Other Stories*) for reasons she expressed to interviewer Claudia Tate in *Black Women Writers at Work:* "I do think that it's important to leave a legacy of my books for my children to read and understand; to leave a legacy of the history of black people who have moved toward revolution and freedom; to leave a legacy of not being afraid to tell the truth. . . . We must pass this on to our children, rather than a legacy of fear and victimization."

Because she takes action against oppression wherever she sees it, she has had to contend with not only college administrators, but also the FBI, and sometimes fellow members of political organizations. Reviewers note that while her early books speak more directly to widespread social oppression, the plays she wrote during the 1970s give more attention to the poet's interpersonal battles. For example, *Uh Huh; But How Do It Free Us?* portrays a black woman involved in the movement against white oppression who also resists subjection to her abusive husband. This kind of resistance, writes Salaam, was not welcomed by the leaders of the black power movement at that time.

Sanchez joined the Nation of Islam in 1972 but resigned after three years of membership. She had joined because she wanted her children to see an "organization that was trying to deal with the concepts of nationhood, morality, small businesses, schools. . . . And these things were very important to me," she told Tate. As Sanchez sees it, her contribution to the Nation was her open fight against the inferior status it assigned to women in relation to men. Believing that cultural survival requires the work of women and children no less than the efforts of men, Sanchez felt compelled to speak up rather than to give up the influence she could exert through public readings of her poetry. "It especially was important for women in the Nation to see that," stated Sanchez, who also told Tate that she has had to battle the "so-called sexism" of many people outside the Nation as well.

Thus Sanchez became a voice in what Stephen E. Henderson calls "a revolution within the Revolution" that grew as black women in general began to reassess their position as "the victims not only of racial injustice but of a sexual arrogance tantamount to dual colonialism—one from without, the other from within, the Black community," he writes in his introduction to Evans's book. This consciousness surfaces in works that treat politics in the context of personal relationships. Sanchez told Tate, "If we're not careful, the animosity between black men and women will

destroy us." To avoid this fate, she believes, women must refuse to adopt the posture of victims and "move on" out of damaging relationships with men, since, in her words recorded in the interview, "If you cannot remove yourself from the oppression of a man, how in the hell are you going to remove yourself from the oppression of a country?"

Consequently, *A Blues Book for Blue Black Magical Women,* written during her membership in the Nation, examines the experience of being female in a society that "does not prepare young black women, or women period, to be women," as she told Tate. One section tells about her political involvements before and after she committed herself to the establishment of ethnic pride. In this book, as in her plays and stories, "Sanchez uses many of the particulars of her own life as illustrations of a general condition," writes Salaam. He offers that Sanchez "remains the fiery, poetic advocate of revolutionary change, but she also gives full voice to the individual human being struggling to survive sanely and to find joy and love in life." *Love Poems* contains many of the haiku Sanchez wrote during a particularly stressful period of her life in which she was beset by the problems of relocation, illness and poverty. The poems in these two books are no less political for their being more personal, according to reviewers. "The haiku in her hands is the ultimate in activist poetry, as abrupt and as final as a fist," comments Williams. In Salaam's opinion, "No other poet of the 1960s and 1970s managed so masterfully to chronicle both their public and personal development with poetry of such thorough-going honesty and relevant and revelatory depth."

Madhubuti says of the poet: "Much of her work is autobiographical, but not in the limiting sense that it is only about Sonia Sanchez." For example, in her well-known story "After Saturday Night Comes Sunday," a woman on the verge of madness finds strength to break out of a painful liaison with a drug abuser without herself becoming trapped in self-pity or alcoholism. "It's not just a personal story," the poet, who has survived two divorces, told Tate. "It might be a personal experience, but the whole world comes into it." Readers of all backgrounds can appreciate writings concerned with black identity and survival, she declares in *Black Women Writers at Work,* mentioning that her works have been translated into European languages and remarking that "you don't have to whitewash yourself to be universal." At another point in the interview, she explained why she deliberately pushes her writing beyond autobiography: "We must move past always focusing on the 'personal self' because there's a larger self. There's a 'self' of black people. And many of us will have to make a sacrifice in our lives to ensure that our bigger self continues." In her statement for *Black Women Writers (1950-1980),* she presents her own life as an example of the price that must be paid to contribute to social change: "I see myself helping to bring forth the truth about the world. I cannot tell the truth about anything unless I confess to being a student. . . . My first lesson was that one's ego always compromised how something was viewed. I had to wash my ego in the needs/aspiration of my people. Selflessness is key for conveying the need to end greed and oppression. I try to achieve this state as I write."

Speaking in *Black Women Writers (1950-1980)* of the creative tension between protest and affirmation in her writing, Sanchez declared: "I still believe that the age for which we write is the age evolving out of the dregs of the twentieth century into a more humane age. Therefore I recognize that my writing must serve a dual purpose. It must be a clarion call to the values of change while it also speaks to the beauty of a nonexploitative age." Throughout her poems, Sanchez emphasizes the importance of strong family relationships, and exposes the dangers of substance abuse among people who hope to be the vital agents of change, relates Richard K. Barksdale in *Modern Black Poets: A Collection of Critical Essays.* Her message, as he notes, is that the desired revolution will not come about through "violence, anger, or rage;" rather, "political astuteness and moral power" among black people are needed to build the new world. Commenting on the content of the poems as it has broadened over the years, Madhubuti observes that Sanchez "remains an intense and meticulous poet who has not compromised craft or skill for message."

From the "revolution within the Revolution," Sanchez has pulled a particular feminine sensibility that informs her work. Kamili Anderson claims that from her earliest years as a poet onward, "Sanchez was a leading spokes-sister for the women's side of things. . . . It was often she who, even as a female follower of the Honorable Elijah Muhammad and the Nation of Islam, was the strongest feminist poetic voice in a cultural movement with strong sexist leanings." Sanchez has continued to develop a more private, introspective womanist poetry in works such as *Under a Soprano Sky,* a book that contains moving love poems to those people who inspired her and those family members who nurtured her. Gabbin states that in Sanchez's poems, "one senses a power that is feminine, and consciously so. It comes from her understanding of her connections with the universe, her connections with her ancestors, and her strong matrilineal ties with a universe that has given to its kind not only the responsibility but, indeed, the power to bear the children and nurture seed. Her power comes from a faith in continuity; seeds grow into flowers and produce their own seeds. Sanchez clearly presents the life cycle and cherishes it."

"[Sanchez's] work has matured; she's a much better writer now than she was ten years ago. She has continued to grow, but her will has not changed," states critic Sherley Anne Williams, who told Tate that black women poets as a group have kept their commitment to social revolution strong, while others seem to be letting it die out. In the same book, Sanchez attributes this waning, in part, to the rewards that have been given to black writers who focus on themes other than revolution. "The greatness of Sonia Sanchez," believes Salaam, "is that she is an inspiration." Madhubuti shares this view, concluding, "Sanchez has been an inspiration to a generation of young poets. . . . Her concreteness and consistency over these many years is noteworthy. She has not bought refuge from day-to-day struggles by becoming a writer in the Western tradition. . . . Somehow, one feels deep inside that in a real fight, this is the type of black woman you would want at your side."

BIOGRAPHICAL/CRITICAL SOURCES:

BOOKS

Bankier, Joanna, and Deirdre Lashgari, editors, *Women Poets of the World,* Macmillan (New York City), 1983.

Bell, Bernard W., *The Folk Roots of Contemporary Afro-American Poetry,* Broadside Press, 1974.

Bigsby, C. W. E., editor, *The Second Black Renaissance: Essays in Black Literature,* Greenwood Press (Westport, CT), 1980.

Black Literature Criticism, Gale, 1992, p. 1647-70.

Contemporary Literary Criticism, Volume 5, Gale, 1976.

Dictionary of Literary Biography, Volume 46: *Afro-American Poets since 1955,* Gale, 1985.

Dictionary of Literary Biography Documentary Series, Volume 8, Gale, 1991, pp. 226-53.

Evans, Mari, editor, *Black Women Writers (1950-1980): A Critical Evaluation,* with introduction by Stephen E. Henderson, Doubleday-Anchor (New York City), 1984.

Gibson, Donald B., editor, *Modern Black Poets: A Collection of Critical Essays,* Prentice-Hall (New York City), 1973.

Hartigan, Karelisa V., editor, *The Many Forms of Drama,* University Press of America (Lanham, MD), 1985.

Inge, Tonette Bond, editor, *Southern Women Writers: The New Generation,* University of Alabama Press, 1990, pp. 180-203.

Poetry Criticism, Volume 9, Gale, 1994, pp. 202-46.

Randall, Dudley, *Broadside Memories: Poets I Have Known,* Broadside Press, 1975.

Redmond, Eugene B., *Drumvoices: The Mission of Afro-American Poetry, A Critical History,* Anchor, 1976.

Sanchez, Sonia, *We a BaddDDD People,* Broadside Press, 1970.

Tate, Claudia, editor, *Black Women Writers At Work*, Continuum, 1983.

PERIODICALS

Belles Lettres, winter, 1989, p. 14.
Black Creation, fall, 1973.
Black Scholar, May, 1979; January, 1980; March, 1981.
Black World, August, 1970; April, 1971; September, 1971; April, 1972; March, 1975.
Book World, January 27, 1974.
CLA Journal, September, 1971.
Ebony, March, 1974.
Essence, July, 1979.
Indian Journal of American Studies, July, 1983.
Negro Digest, December, 1969.
New Republic, February 22, 1975.
Newsweek, April 17, 1972.
Phylon, June, 1975.
Poetry, October, 1973.
Poetry Review, April, 1985.
Publishers Weekly, October 1, 1973; July 15, 1974.
Time, May 1, 1972.

*   *   *

SAUVAIN, Philip Arthur 1933-

PERSONAL: Born March 28, 1933, in Burton on Trent, Staffordshire, England; son of Alan (an education officer) and Norah (a teacher; maiden name, Humphreys) Sauvain; married June Maureen Spenceley (a teacher), July 27, 1963; children: Richard Philip, Rachel Anne. *Education:* Cambridge University, M.A. (with honors), 1956; University of London, postgraduate certificate in education, 1957.

ADDRESSES: Home and office—70 Finborough Rd., Stowmarket, Suffolk 1P14 1PU, England.

CAREER: Writer, 1974—. Steyning Grammar School, Sussex, England, head of geography department, 1957-61; Penistone Grammar School, Sheffield, England, head of geography department, 1961-63; James Graham College, Leeds, England, senior lecturer in geography, 1963-68; Charlotte Mason College of Education, Ambleside, England, head of environmental studies department, 1968-74. Member of committee of Educational Writers' Group, 1978.

MEMBER: Incorporated Society of Authors, Playwrights, and Composers.

AWARDS, HONORS: Honorary senior scholar of Emmanuel College, Cambridge, 1956; Runner-up, Times Educational Supplement Information Book Award, 1975, for *Looking around in Town and Country.*

WRITINGS:

PUBLISHED BY HULTON EDUCATIONAL PUBLICATIONS (CHELTENHAM, GLOUCESTERSHIRE), EXCEPT AS INDICATED

A Map Reading Companion, 1961.
A Geographical Field Study Companion, 1964.
Lively History, Volume 1: *Lord and Peasant: Old Stone Age to 1485 A.D.*, 1970, Volume 2: *Town and Country: 1485-1789*, 1971, Volume 3: *Empire, City and Industry: 1789-1901*, 1973, Volume 4: *Conflict, Science and Society: The Twentieth Century*, 1973.
Practical Geography, Volume 1: *Pictures and Plans*, 1970, Volume 2: *Facts, Maps, and Places*, 1970, Volume 3: *Man and Environment*, 1971, Volume 4: *Advanced Techniques and Statistics*, 1972.
The First Men on the Moon, 1972.
The Great Wall of China, 1972.
Looking around in Town and Country, F. Watts (New York City), 1975.
Looking Back, F. Watts, 1975.
Junior Guide to Arundel Castle, F. Watts, 1978.
Certificate Mapwork, 1979.
Macmillan Local Studies Kit, Macmillan (New York City) 1979.
First Elements of Geography: The British Isles, 1980.
(With Michael Carrier) *Topics for Discussion and Language Practice: Books I and II*, 1980.
The World about Us: Science Discussion Pictures, Macmillan, Pack 1, 1981, Pack 2, 1983.
Britain's Living Heritage, Batsford (London), 1982.
Theatre, Bell & Hyman (London), 1983.
Modern World History 1919 Onwards, 1983.
The Modern World since 1917, Blackwell Scientific Publications, 1983.
British Social and Economic History, Blackwell Scientific Publications, 1985.
European and World History 1815-1919, 1985.
France and the French, Blackwell Scientific Publications, 1985.
How History Began, Piper (Boston), 1985.
Castles and Crusaders, Piper, 1986.
Communications, Schuster Young Books, 1992.

"ENVIRONMENTAL STUDIES" SERIES; PUBLISHED BY HULTON EDUCATIONAL PUBLICATIONS

Exploring at Home, 1966.
Exploring Britain, 1966.
Exploring the World, 1967.

"DISCOVERY" SERIES; PUBLISHED BY MACMILLAN

About the Weather, 1970.
Along a Road, 1970.
In a Garden, 1970.
Near Your Home, 1970.

Where You Live, 1970.
Where You Go to School, 1970.

*"BREAKAWAY" SERIES; PUBLISHED BY HULTON
EDUCATIONAL PUBLICATIONS*

Finding a Job and Settling Down, 1973.
People with Problems, 1973.
Keeping the Peace, 1974.
Living in Towns, 1974.
Vanishing World, 1974.
World of Adventure, 1974.
Enjoying Ourselves, 1976.
Where the Money Goes, 1976.

*"EXPLORING THE WORLD OF MAN" SERIES; PUBLISHED BY
HULTON EDUCATIONAL PUBLICATIONS*

Man the Builder, 1973.
Man the Farmer, 1973.
Man the Traveller, 1973.
Man the Manufacturer, 1974.
Man the Pleasure Lover, 1974.
Man the Warrior, 1974.
Man the Discoverer, 1975.
Man the Citizen, 1976.
Man the Artist, 1977.
Man the Thinker, 1977.

"FIRST LOOK" SERIES; PUBLISHED BY F. WATTS

Maps and How to Read Them, 1973.
Winds, 1975.
Dinosaurs, 1976.
Discoveries and Inventions before the Age of Steam, 1977.
Rain, 1978.
Snow and Ice, 1978.

*"ENVIRONMENT BOOK" SERIES; PUBLISHED BY
MACMILLAN*

By Land, Sea, and Air, 1974.
On a Farm, 1974.
On a Holiday, 1974.
Under Your Feet, 1974.
Back in the Past, 1978.
Dial 999, 1978.
In Town, 1978.
Made in Britain, 1978.

*"IMAGINING THE PAST" SERIES; PUBLISHED BY
MACMILLAN*

A Castle, 1976.
A Medieval Town, 1976.
An Abbey, 1976.
A Tudor Mansion, 1976.
Prehistoric Britain, 1976.
Roman Britain, 1976.
A Georgian Town, 1980.

An Eighteenth-Century Village, 1980.
A Regency Coaching Inn, 1980.
A Victorian Factory Town, 1980.
Stuart Britain, 1980.
The Victorian Seaside, 1980.

*"LOOKING AROUND" CARDS SERIES; PUBLISHED BY F.
WATTS*

Houses and Towns, 1978.
Villages and Farms, 1978.
Hills and Coasts, 1979.
Valleys and Routeways, 1979.

"STORY OF BRITAIN" SERIES; PUBLISHED BY MACMILLAN

Britain in the Middle Ages, 1980.
Early Britain, 1980.
From Nelson to the Present, 1980.
Tudors, Stuarts, and Georgians, 1980.

*"HISTORY OF BRITAIN" SERIES; PUBLISHED BY
MACMILLAN*

Before 1066, 1982.
Henry VII to George III, 1982.
Modern Times, 1982.
The Middle Ages, 1982.

*"NEW GEOGRAPHIES" SERIES; PUBLISHED BY HULTON
EDUCATIONAL PUBLICATIONS*

Europe, 1983.
North America and the USSR, 1983.
Teacher's Handbook, 1983.
The British Isles, 1983.
The Developing World, 1983.

*"JUNIOR GEOGRAPHY" SERIES; PUBLISHED BY
MACMILLAN*

About the World, 1983.
At Home and Around, 1983.
How We Live, 1983.
In Britain Now, 1983.

*"NEW HISTORIES" SERIES; PUBLISHED BY HULTON
EDUCATIONAL PUBLICATIONS*

Crown and Parliament, 1984.
Serf and Crusader, 1984.
Tribes and Tribunes, 1984.
Forge and Factory, 1985.
Teachers' Handbook, 1985.
War and Peace, 1985.

*"WHAT TO LOOK FOR" SERIES; PUBLISHED BY LONGMAN
(WATFORD)*

At the Country House, 1986.
At the Castle, 1986.
At the Cathedral, 1986.
At the Roman Fort and Villa, 1986.

PUBLISHED BY STANLEY THORNES (CHELTENHAM, GLOUCESTERSHIRE)

British Economic and Social History, Book I: *1700-1870,* 1987, Book II: *1850 to the Present Day,* 1987.
Skills for Geography, 1989.
The Modern World: 1914-1980, 1989.
The Era of the Second World War, 1993.

"EXPLORING ENERGY" SERIES; PUBLISHED BY MACMILLAN EDUCATION

Carrying Energy, 1987.
Oil and Natural Gas, 1987.
Wind and Water Power, 1987.
Wood and Coal, 1987.

"SKILLS FOR HISTORY" SERIES; PUBLISHED BY STANLEY THORNES

British and European History, 1988.
British Economic and Social History, 1988.
Modern World History, 1988.
(With Nigel Shepley and Stuart Archer) *Standard Grade History,* 1990.

"WORLD OF WORK" SERIES; PUBLISHED BY MACMILLAN EDUCATION

Airport, 1989.
Mine, 1989.
Ship, 1989.

"HOW WE BUILD" SERIES; PUBLISHED BY MACMILLAN CHILDREN'S BOOKS

Roads, 1989.
Skyscrapers, 1989.
Tunnels, 1989.

"EXPLORING THE PAST" SERIES; PUBLISHED BY STANLEY THORNES

Old World, 1991.
Changing World, 1992.
Expanding World, 1993.

PUBLISHED BY WAYLAND (SUSSEX)

Holidays and Pastimes, 1991.
Work, 1991.
El Alamein (part of the "Great Battle and Sieges" series), 1992.
Hastings (part of the "Great Battle and Sieges" series), 1992.

"THE WAY IT WORKS" SERIES; PUBLISHED BY HEINEMANN CHILDREN'S REFERENCE (EXETER, NH)

Air, 1992.
Motion, 1992.
Water, 1992.

"HISTORY DETECTIVE" SERIES; PUBLISHED BY ZOE BOOKS

In Ancient Greece, illustrated by Graham Humphreys, 1992.
Over 1,600 Years Ago: In the Roman Empire, illustrated by Harry Clow, 1992.
Over 450 Years Ago: In the New World, illustrated by Richard Hook, 1993.
Over 3,000 Years Ago: In Ancient Egypt, illustrated by Eric Rowe, 1993.

PUBLISHED BY ZOE BOOKS

Midway (part of the "Great Battles and Sieges" series), 1993.
Robert Scott in the Antarctic, illustrated by Gibbons and Fred Anderson, 1993.
Waterloo (part of the "Great Battles and Sieges" series), 1993.

"TARGET GEOGRAPHY" SERIES; PUBLISHED BY WARD LOCK EDUCATIONAL (LONDON)

Big Book, 1994.
Near and Far, 1994.
Look Around, 1994.
Using the Land, 1994.
Maps and Places, 1994.
At Home and Abroad, 1994.
Around the World, 1994.
At Home and in Britain, 1994.
About Our World, 1994.
Our Earth, 1994.
Teacher's Guide: KS1/KS2, 1995.

OTHER

Contributor of articles to periodicals, including *Times Educational Supplement, Teachers World, Child Education, Pictorial Education,* and *British Heritage.* Edited *Collins School Database* diaries for older children, 1988-93.

WORK IN PROGRESS: History coursebooks for older students.

SIDELIGHTS: Philip Arthur Sauvain's book *Looking around in Town and Country* is filled with information for young readers. The author explores towns, coasts, railways, and other locations. He describes buildings along the way and explains the purposes of objects encountered. Designed as a pictorial guide to the environment of the British Isles, the book offers several indexes for young readers of varied levels of understanding. Sauvain drew on his experience as a teacher of environmental studies when preparing the work.

Sauvain followed *Looking around in Town and Country* with *Looking Back,* a pictorial encyclopedia to British history that highlights the key events, personalities, and facets of everyday life in the past. The author used his own color transparencies to show children the many buildings, relics, and monuments still seen today in all parts of Britain.

Sauvain told *CA:* "I always find it helpful to envisage the final layout of words and pictures at the time of writing the text. For some time now I have been photographing many of the characteristic features that illustrate the history and geography of the British Isles and Western Europe. My color transparencies and monochrome prints illustrate most of the books I have written. Indeed, some of my work, such as a set of science-discussion pictures for five- to seven-year-olds, has been largely photographic.

"I first started to write in response to a challenge from an old acquaintance who said, 'Why not write a book for schools?' It was also something of a family tradition. My father and my maternal grandfather (G. A. Humphreys) had both written school textbooks in the 1930s, and my great-grandfather Aime Sauvain wrote a French textbook, *Presque mot a mot,* in 1887.

"Writing and preparing materials for use by children in schools is one of the essential, but least glamorous, branches of authorship. It imposes certain constraints that many general writers might find particularly irksome, such as restricted vocabulary and writing within strict word limits to the page.

"I shall always remember the day my first book appeared in November, 1961, because I drove into the back of a vehicle half an hour after receiving my complimentary copies through the post!"

BIOGRAPHICAL/CRITICAL SOURCES:

PERIODICALS

Educational Development Centre Review, January, 1972.
Geographical Journal, March, 1965.
Growing Point, September, 1975; November, 1977; September, 1978; February, 1979.
Learning for Living, May, 1974.
School Librarian, November, 1992, pp. 153; February, 1993, pp. 34.
School Library Journal, January, 1993, pp. 110+; February, 1993, p. 104; March, 1993, p. 203; July, 1993, p. 95; August, 1993, p. 182; March, 1994, p. 23.
Secondary Teacher, summer, 1977.
Teacher, June 8, 1973; August 23, 1974; October 25, 1974.
Teachers World, June 3, 1966; January 6, 1967; June 18, 1976.
Times Educational Supplement, July 24, 1970; June 8, 1973.*

SAVARY, Louis M(ichael) 1936-

PERSONAL: First syllable of surname rhymes with "pave"; born January 17, 1936, in Scranton, PA; son of Louis Michael and Margaret (Nagy) Savary; married Patricia H. Berne, 1992. *Education:* Fordham University, A.B., 1960; Woodstock College, Ph.L., 1961, S.T.L., 1968; Catholic University of America, M.A., 1963, Ph.D., 1965, S.T.D., 1970.

ADDRESSES: Home and office—3404 Ellenwood Ln., Tampa, FL 33618.

CAREER: Ordained Roman Catholic priest, 1967, member of Society of Jesus (Jesuits), 1954; left Jesuits, 1984; Collins Associates, New York City, writer and senior editor, 1967-74; affiliated with Just for You Books, Brielle, NJ, 1974-80; affiliated with Inner Development Associates (specialists in interpersonal and spiritual growth), Washington, DC, and Tampa, FL, 1980—. Currently senior training analyst with Education Systems for the Future, Columbia, MD. Adjunct member of faculty of St. Joseph College, West Hartford, CT, Chestnut Hill College, Philadelphia, PA, and Notre Dame College, Belmont, CA. Former adjunct member of faculty of Loyola University, New Orleans, LA, and Pacific School of Religion, Berkeley, CA.

MEMBER: American Personnel and Guidance Association, American Society of Composers, American Statistical Association, American Teilhard Association, Authors and Publishers (ASCAP), Institute for Consciousness and Music, Mathematical Association of America.

AWARDS, HONORS: Christopher Book Award, 1970, for *Listen to Love.*

WRITINGS:

His World and His Work, Paulist Press (Ramsey, NJ), 1967.
The Kingdom of Downtown: Finding Teenagers in Their Music, Paulist Press, 1967.
(Co-author) *Christian Awareness,* four volumes, Christian Brothers Publications, 1968.
(Co-author) *Listen to Love,* Regina Press, 1968.
(Co-author) *Patterns of Promise,* St. Mary's College Press (Winona, MN), 1968.
(Co-author) *Living with Christ,* with teacher's guides, four volumes, St. Mary's College Press, 1968-69.
(With Adrianne Blue) *Faces of Freedom,* St. Mary's College Press, 1969.
(With Blue) *Horizons of Hope,* St. Mary's College Press, 1969.
(With Maureen P. Collins) *Ritual and Life,* St. Mary's College Press, 1970.
(With Collins) *Shaping of a Self,* St. Mary's College Press, 1970.

(Co-author) *Teaching Your Child about God,* St. Mary's College Press, 1970.

(With Thomas J. O'Connor) *Finding Each Other,* Paulist/Newman (Ramsey, NJ), 1971.

(With O'Connor) *Finding God,* Paulist/Newman, 1971.

Getting High Naturally, Association Press, 1971.

Love and Hate in America Today, Association Press, 1971.

Popular Song and Youth Today, Association Press, 1971.

Touch with Love, Association Press, 1971.

Cycles, three volumes, Regina Press (Savannah, GA), 1971-73.

One Life Together: A Celebration of Love in Marriage, Regina Press, 1972.

A Time for Salvation, Regina Press, 1972.

Jesus: The Face of Man, Harper (New York City), 1972.

(With Marianne S. Andersen) *Passages: A Guide for Pilgrims of the Mind,* Harper, 1972.

(With Helen L. Bonny) *Music and Your Mind: Listening with a New Consciousness,* Harper, 1973, Station Hill Press (Barrytown, NY), 1991.

Psychological Themes in the Golden Epistle of William of Saint Thierry, University of Salzburg (Salzburg, Germany), 1973.

Integrating Values: Theory and Exercises for Clarifying and Integrating Religious Values, Pflaum/Standard (Fairfield, NJ), 1974.

Creativity and Children: Stimulating Imaginative Responses to Music, ICM Press, 1974.

(With Shirley Linde) *The Sleep Book,* Harper, 1974.

(With Muriel James) *The Power at the Bottom of the Well: Transactional Analysis and Religious Experience,* Harper, 1974.

(With Bonny) *ASC and Music Experience: A Guide for Facilitators and Leaders,* ICM Press, 1974.

(With James) *The Heart of Friendship,* Harper, 1975.

(With Mary Paolini and George Lane) *Interpersonal Communication: A Worktext for Self-Understanding and Growth in Personal Relations,* Loyola University Press (Chicago, IL), 1975.

Who Has Seen the Wind?: The Holy Spirit in the Church and the World, Regina Press, 1975.

(With Paolini and William E. Frankhauser) *The Storyteller's Bible,* Regina, 1978.

(With Margaret Ehlen-Miller) *Mindways: A Guide for Exploring Your Mind,* Harper, 1978.

(With wife, Patricia H. Berne) *Prayerways: For Those Who Feel Discouraged or Distraught, Frightened or Frustrated, Angry or Anxious, Powerless or Purposeless, Over-Extended or Under-Appreciated, Burned Out or Just Plain Worn Out,* Harper, 1980.

(With Theresa O'Callaghan Scheihing) *Our Treasured Heritage: Teaching Christian Meditation to Children,* Crossroad (New York City), 1981.

(With Berne) *Building Self-Esteem in Children,* Continuum (New York City), 1981.

(With Berne) *What Will the Neighbors Say?,* Continuum, 1982.

(With Berne and Strephon K. Williams) *Dreams and Spiritual Growth: A Christian Approach to Dreamwork,* Paulist Press, 1984.

(With Stephen Halpern) *Sound Health: The Music and Sounds That Make Us Whole,* Harper, 1985.

Welcome to the Wonderful World of the Somatron: A Manual for Its Uses, Somasonics, 1987.

(With Berne) *Kything: The Art of Spiritual Presence,* Paulist Press, 1988.

(With Berne) *Dream Symbol Work,* Paulist Press, 1991.

JUVENILE

The Life of Jesus for Children, Regina Press, 1979.

The Friends of Jesus for Children, Regina Press, 1979.

The Miracles of Jesus for Children, Regina Press, 1979.

The Prayers of Jesus for Children, Regina Press, 1980.

The Holy Spirit for Children, Regina Press, 1980.

The Rosary for Children, Regina Press, 1981.

The Stations of the Cross for Children, Regina Press, 1981.

The Mission of Catherine Laboure: The Miraculous Medal, Regina Press, 1981.

The Seasons of the Church Year for Children, Regina Press, 1982.

My First Prayer Book, Regina Press, 1982.

My First Book of Saints, Regina Press, 1982.

The Life of Mary for Children, Regina Press, 1982.

GHOSTWRITER

Mary Conway Kohler, *Young People Learning to Care: Making a Difference through Youth Participation,* Seaburg, 1983.

Robert Fritz, *The Path of Least Resistance: Principles for Creating What You Want to Create,* DMA, 1984, Ballantine (New York City), 1986.

Hyler Bracey and others, *Managing from the Heart,* Delacorte (New York City), 1991.

Richard Rohr, *Enneagram II,* Crossroad, 1995.

Rohr, *A Preacher Looks at Luke's Gospel,* Crossroad, 1995.

Charles Smith, *The Merlin Factor,* Merlin Press (San Jose, CA), 1995.

Douglas A. Wilson, *Managing by Values,* Values Press, 1995.

EDITOR

(With O'Connor) *The Heart Has Its Seasons,* Regina Press, 1971.

(With Paul Carrico) *Contemporary Film and the New Generation,* Association Press, 1971.

(With M. P. Collins) *Peace, War and Youth,* Association Press, 1971.

(With Thomas P. Collins) *A People of Compassion: The Concerns of Edward Kennedy,* Regina Press, 1972.

(With Paolini) *Moments with God: A Book of Prayers for Children,* Regina Press, 1975.

FILMSTRIPS

Images of Christ, Thomas S. Klise, 1971.

Images of Revelation, Thomas S. Klise, 1971.

Images of Love, Thomas S. Klise, 1971.

Images of the Future, Thomas S. Klise, 1971.

Images of the New Man, Thomas S. Klise, 1972.

A Time to Grow, Sisters of the Good Shepherd, 1972.

Social Studies, W. H. Sadlier (New York City), 1972-73.

A Call to Consecration, Sisters of the Good Shepherd, 1973.

Religious Awareness, (series), Thomas S. Klise, 1973.

CASSETTES

Self-Actualization I, National Catholic Reporter (Kansas City, MO), 1975.

Self-Actualization II, National Catholic Reporter, 1975.

Biblical Meditations with Music I, National Catholic Reporter, 1975.

Biblical Meditations with Music II, National Catholic Reporter, 1975.

Meditations with Music: Cycle B, National Catholic Reporter, 1976.

Meditations with Music: Cycle C, National Catholic Reporter, 1976.

The Inner Me, National Catholic Reporter, 1977.

Carrying Out Life Decisions, National Catholic Reporter, 1977.

The Lord's Prayer: Integrating Eastern and Western Prayer (four cassettes), National Catholic Reporter, 1977.

You Are Called (twenty cassettes), National Catholic Reporter, 1978.

Psalms of Reconciliation, National Catholic Reporter, 1978.

Life at the Heart of the World, National Catholic Reporter, 1979.

Spiritual Growth through Dreams (six cassettes), National Catholic Reporter, 1979.

Prayers of Power: Mantra Chanting, National Catholic Reporter, 1979.

Body/Mind/Spirit Prayers: Twenty Ways to Stay Spiritually Alive (four cassettes), National Catholic Reporter, 1980.

Spirituality of Teilhard de Chardin (four cassettes), National Catholic Reporter, 1980.

Gift of Life, National Catholic Reporter, 1980.

The Joyful Mysteries, National Catholic Reporter, 1981.

The Sorrowful Mysteries, National Catholic Reporter, 1981.

The Glorious Mysteries, National Catholic Reporter, 1982.

Healing through Mary, National Catholic Reporter, 1982.

Praying with the Right Brain, (four cassettes), National Catholic Reporter, 1983.

Affirmations for Personal Power (two cassettes), National Catholic Reporter, 1986.

Healing and Wholeness: Meditations with Music (three cassettes), National Catholic Reporter, 1986.

Hail, Mary!, National Catholic Reporter, 1987.

The Life of Mary: Meditations with Music (three cassettes), National Catholic Reporter, 1987.

INSTRUCTIONAL MODULES

(With Peter Esseff and Mary Esseff) *The Future of Christianity in Lebanon,* Educational Systems for the Future, 1986.

(With P. Esseff and M. Esseff) *The Management of Training,* Educational Systems for the Future, 1986.

(With P. Esseff and M. Esseff) *Interactive Teaching Skills,* revised edition, Educational Systems for the Future, 1987.

(With P. Esseff and M. Esseff) *Advanced Interactive Teaching Skills,* Educational Systems for the Future, 1987.

(With P. Esseff and M. Esseff) *Master Instructor Training,* Educational Systems for the Future, 1987.

(With P. Esseff and M. Esseff) *How to Develop and Instruct People-to-People Machine Demonstrations,* Educational Systems for the Future, 1987.

(With P. Esseff and M. Esseff) *How to Develop and Instruct People-to-People Role Plays,* Educational Systems for the Future, 1987.

(With P. Esseff and M. Esseff) *How to Develop and Instruct People-to-Paper Case Studies,* Educational Systems for the Future, 1987.

(With P. Esseff and M. Esseff) *Instructional Development Learning System: Pro Trainer I* (seven instruction modules), Educational Systems for the Future, 1987.

Orientation for New General Motors Salaried Employees (eight instructional modules), General Motors Education and Training, 1987.

OTHER

(Co-author) *Religious Awareness Teaching Program,* six volumes with teaching guide, St. Mary's Press, 1970.

Author of two recordings for the Institute for Consciousness and Music, *Creative Listening: Music and Imagination Experiences for Children,* and, with M. Trinitas Bochini, *A New Way to Music: Altered States of Consciousness and Music.* Also author of four booklets for Just For You Books, including *Getting to Know You: A Funbook for Families,* 1974, and *Side by Side: Another Funbook for*

Couples, 1975. Contributor to *Religious Book Guide, Review for Religious Praying,* and *Sisters Today.*

SIDELIGHTS: Louis M. Savary told *CA:* "I see myself as a specialist in interpersonal and spiritual growth, a 'technician of the sacred,' sharing practical ways of expanding consciousness and developing the whole person. My vision is to introduce people to powerful psychological techniques and spiritual practices in order to help society evolve through the inner transformation of individuals and relationships."

*   *   *

SCHECHTER, Ruth Lisa   1927-

PERSONAL: Born January 2, 1927, in Boston, MA; married; husband's name, Jerry. *Education:* Attended New York University, 1960-62, and New School for Social Research, 1962-64.

ADDRESSES: Home—9 Van Cortlandt Place, Croton-on-Hudson, NY 10520. *Office—Croton Review,* P.O. Box 277, Croton-on-Hudson, NY 10520.

CAREER: Holds New York Board of Education certification as teacher of creative writing; certified poetry therapist. Poetry therapist at Alfred Adler Mental Hygiene Clinic, 1968, and Odyssey Institute, New York City, 1971-78; poet-in-residence, Mundelein College, 1969; counsellor and poetry therapist, Odyssey House, New York City, 1971-77. Teacher of poetry workshops in universities, adult education groups, and privately for special writing students. Has given poetry readings at New York public libraries, colleges and universities, including Colgate University, Syracuse University, Marymount College, Hunter College, the City University of New York, University of Connecticut, Marist College, South Dakota State University, and University of Maine. Chair of poetry/literature program, Bronx Council of the Arts, 1969; director, Croton Council on the Arts, 1977; editor and founder, *Croton Review.*

MEMBER: PEN, Poetry Society of America, American Poetry Therapists, National Association for Poetry Therapy, National Writers Union.

AWARDS, HONORS: MacDowell Colony fellowships, 1963, 1970; Cecil Hemley Award, Poetry Society of America, 1975; National Endowment for the Arts grant recipient for the *Croton Review;* "Woman of the Year" tribute, Croton-Cortlandt Women's Center, 1980.

WRITINGS:

POETRY

Near the Wall of Lion Shadows, Salt Mound Press, 1969, 2nd edition, 1970.

Movable Parts (narrative poem), Folder Editions (Forest Hills, NJ), 1970.
Suddenly Thunder, Barlenmir House (New York City), 1972.
Offshore, Barlenmir House, 1974.
(With Paul Kaufman) *Double Exposure,* Barlenmir House, 1978.
Moving Closer, Catalyst Press, 1979.
Clockworks, Barlenmir House, 1979.
Speedway, Chantry Press (Midland Park, NJ), 1983.
Chords and Other Poems, Chantry Press, 1986.
Many Rooms in a Winter Night, Croton Review, 1989.

OTHER

Alan, Carlos, Theresa (two-act play), produced Off Broadway, 1969.

Also author of *Poetry Therapy: A Therapeutic, Healing Tool* (monograph), 1983. A long-play recording of Schechter reading her poems with commentary was produced at Lamont Poetry Library of Harvard University, 1969. Work included in poetry anthologies, including *Rising Tides,* Washington Square Press, *From the Belly of the Shark,* Random House, *The Writing on the Wall,* Doubleday, *We Mainline Dreams,* Doubleday, *For Neruda: For Chile,* Beacon Press, *70 on the 70's,* and *Soncatcher.* Contributor of poetry to periodicals, including *American Dialog, Beloit Poetry Journal, Chicago Tribune, Forum, International Quarterly, New York Quarterly, Occidental Review, Prairie Schooner, Rising Tides, Southwest Review,* and *Up from Under.*

SIDELIGHTS: Ruth Lisa Schechter once told *CA:* "A bird flies, a fish swims and a writer writes—a natural and inevitable compulsion to express thoughts and feelings in words, despite the low remuneration offered for daily living, the adoration of the long dead writer, the acceptance and rejection which is merged with the writer's lifestyle. As e. e. cummings said: 'Does this sound dismal? It isn't. It's the most wonderful life on earth. Or so I feel.'

"For me, the making of a poem creates some order in its demands for definitions that change relative to love, life, birth, death and loneliness . . . those large, universal emotions in which we are all involved, no matter what age, color or creed. The craft of poetry is a constant challenge and never dull . . . an adventure much like mountain climbing, an act of curiosity, skill and exhilaration akin to the joy of being and staying alive. With it, quite naturally, is the pain of struggling with a poem that refuses to get born at a particular time.

"I've been influenced by other writers, American, Indian, Japanese, Chinese and European. Amongst many have been and still are: Seferis, Neruda, Bogan, Millay, Dickinson, Muir, Levertov, Sexton, Lorca, Ginsberg, Whitman,

Rich. Their perceptivity, passion and originality, fidelity to 'the word' and respect for their craft have inspired and encouraged me.

"The current literary scene is not too different for poets than other former scenes, except for the changes in language and more government grant support for some writers. Publishing has changed. It is an industry of mergers and corporation structure and the 'big sale' is not necessarily equated with literary quality. Few editors have the time to form the kind of relationship that Perkins had with Thomas Wolfe. Our libraries are still not stocked with enough books of poetry that are representative of the active and energetic contemporary poetry scene. On the positive side, more people are writing poetry and more women are participating as teachers, authors and poets.

"The tools of the trade remain revision, craft, and language, essential to poetry and similar to learning the scales in music or the handling of color in visual arts. To aspiring writers, I can only emphasize the need to read and write more. The muse must be fed."

In a review of *Clockworks* published in *World Literature Today*, D. Aldan quoted from Schechter's foreword to her work: "While I bent over like a watchmaker repairing parts and pieces of *Clockworks*, tree after tree grew elsewhere." Aldan concluded his praise of Schechter's work by writing, "Indeed, like a watchmaker whose intense attention to details is essential, Schechter's sure control of her craft helps create an entity when line, sound and rhythms combine to tell correctly—our time."

BIOGRAPHICAL/CRITICAL SOURCES:

PERIODICALS

World Literature Today, summer, 1980.*

*   *   *

SCHECTER, Jerrold L. 1932-

PERSONAL: Born November 27, 1932, in New York, NY; son of Edward and Miriam (maiden name, Goshen) Schecter; married Leona Protas (a literary agent and writer), June 12, 1954; children: Evelind, Steven, Kate, Doveen, Barnett. *Education:* University of Wisconsin, B.S., 1954; Oxford University, summer, 1954; Harvard University, graduate study, 1963-64. *Politics:* Democrat. *Religion:* Jewish.

ADDRESSES: Home and office—3748 Huntington St. N.W., Washington, DC 20015. *Agent*—Leona Schecter, 3748 Huntington St. N.W., Washington, DC 20015.

CAREER: Wall Street Journal, New York City, staff correspondent, 1957-58; *Time,* New York City, contributing

editor, 1958-60; Time News Service, staff correspondent for China-Southeast Asia Bureau, Hong Kong, 1960-63; Harvard University, Nieman fellow, 1963-64; Time-Life, bureau chief in Tokyo, Japan, 1964-68, bureau chief in Moscow, Soviet Union, 1968-70; *Time,* New York City, White House correspondent in Washington, DC, 1970-73, diplomatic editor, 1973-77; associate White House press secretary and spokesman for the National Security Council, 1977-80; Occidental Petroleum Company, Public Affairs, vice president, 1980-82; *Esquire,* Washington editor and foreign affairs columnist, 1982-84; Schecter Communications Corp., Washington, DC, chairman, 1983—. *We/Mbl* (independent Soviet-American weekly newspaper), editor-at-large, and *Izvestia,* founding editor, 1990-94. *Military service:* Officers Candidate School, Newport, RI; U.S. Naval Reserve Officer, active duty in Japan and Korea, 1953-57; became lieutenant.

AWARDS, HONORS: The Palace File: The Remarkable Story of the Secret Letters from Nixon and Ford to the President of South Vietnam and the American Promises That Were Never Kept was named a *New York Times* best book of the year, 1987.

WRITINGS:

The New Face of Buddha: Buddhism and Political Power in Southeast Asia, Coward McCann (New York City), 1967.

(Author of introduction) *Khrushchev Remembers: The Last Testament,* Little, Brown (Boston), 1974.

(With wife, Leona Schecter, and children) *An American Family in Moscow,* Little, Brown, 1975.

(With Nguyen Tien Hung) *The Palace File, The Remarkable Story of the Secret Letters from Nixon and Ford to the President of South Vietnam and the American Promises That Were Never Kept,* Harper (New York City), 1986.

(With Leona Schecter, and children) *Back in the U.S.S.R., An American Family Returns to Moscow,* Scribner (New York City), 1988.

Back in the U.S.S.R. (television documentary), Public Broadcasting System (PBS-TV), 1988.

(Editor and translator) *Kruschev Remembers the Glasnost Tapes,* Little, Brown, 1990.

(With Peter Deriabin) *The Spy Who Saved the World: How a Soviet Colonel Changed the Course of the Cold War,* Scribner, 1992.

(With Pavel A. Sudoplatov, Anatoli Sudoplatov and Leona Schecter) *Special Tasks, The Memoirs of an Unwanted Witness—A Soviet Spymaster,* Little, Brown, 1994.

Contributor to periodicals, including *Connoisseur Magazine, New York Times Magazine* and *Washington Post.*

BIOGRAPHICAL/CRITICAL SOURCES:

PERIODICALS

New York Times Book Review, May 21, 1967.
Time, June 16, 1967.
Virginia Quarterly Review, autumn, 1967.

*   *   *

SCHELLING, Thomas Crombie 1921-

PERSONAL: Born April 14, 1921, in Oakland, CA; son of John M. and Zelda M. (Ayres) Schelling; married Corinne T. Saposs, September 13, 1947; children: Andrew, Thomas, Daniel, Robert. *Education:* University of California, Berkeley, B.A., 1944; Harvard University, Ph.D., 1951.

ADDRESSES: Home—Lexington, MA 02173. *Office*—John F. Kennedy School of Government, Harvard University, 79 Boylston Street, Cambridge, MA 02138.

CAREER: Economic Cooperation Administration Mission to Denmark, economist, 1948-49; Office of the Special Representative, Paris, France, economist, 1949-50; associate economic adviser to the special assistant to the President, The White House, Washington, DC, 1950-51; Office of the Director for Mutual Security, Washington, DC, officer-in-charge, European program affairs, c. 1951; Yale University, New Haven, CT, professor of economics, 1953-58; RAND Corporation, Santa Monica, CA, economist, 1958-59; Harvard University, Cambridge, MA, professor of economics, 1958—, faculty member of the J.F.K. School of Government, 1969—, Lucius N. Littauer professor of political economy, 1974—.

MEMBER: Institute for Strategic Studies, American Economic Association, National Academy of Sciences, American Academy of Arts and Sciences (fellow).

AWARDS, HONORS: Frank E. Seidman Award in political economy, 1977.

WRITINGS:

National Income Behavior, McGraw (New York City), 1951.
International Economics, Allyn and Bacon (Newton, MA), 1958.
The Strategy of Conflict, Harvard University Press (Cambridge, MA), 1960.
(With Morton H. Halperin) *Strategy and Arms Control,* Twentieth Century Fund (New York City), 1961.
Arms and Influence, Yale University Press (New Haven, CT), 1966.
Micromotives and Macrobehavior, Norton (New York City), 1978.
Choice and Consequence, Harvard University Press, 1984.

Bargaining, Communication, and Limited War, Irvington Publishers (New York City), 1993.

EDITOR

Incentives for Environmental Protection, MIT Press (Cambridge, MA), 1983.
(With Armand Clesse) *The Western Community and the Gorbachev Challenge,* Nomos (Baden-Baden, West Germany), 1989.

Member of board of editors of several publications, including *American Economic Review,* 1957-59; *Journal of Conflict Resolutions,* 1958—; *Quarterly Journal of Economics, The Review of Economics and Statistics,* and *World Politics.* Contributor to *Current History, Econometrica, Foreign Affairs, World Politics,* and other journals.

BIOGRAPHICAL/CRITICAL SOURCES:

PERIODICALS

Commonweal, November 30, 1984.
Los Angeles Times Book Review, May 27, 1984.
New Republic, August 27, 1984.
New York Times Book Review, February 16, 1969; November 30, 1980; July 1, 1984, p. 10.*

*   *   *

SCHLINK, Basilea
See SCHLINK, Klara

*   *   *

SCHLINK, Klara 1904-
(Basilea Schlink, M. Basilea Schlink, Mother Basilea Schlink)

PERSONAL: Born October 21, 1904, in Darmstadt, Germany; daughter of a college professor. *Education:* University of Hamburg, Ph.D., 1934.

ADDRESSES: Home—Evangelical Sisterhood of Mary, P.O. Box 13 01 29, D-6100 Darmstadt 13, Germany; and (American branch), Evangelical Sisterhood of Mary, 9849 North 40th St., Phoenix, AZ 85028.

CAREER: Evangelical Sisterhood of Mary, Darmstadt, West Germany (now Germany), co-founder and leader, 1947—; name in religion, Mother Basilea. Founder of Little Canaan centers, now in over twenty countries; a Brotherhood was also established. Former national president of the women's section, German Student Christian Movement.

WRITINGS:

*ORIGINALLY PUBLISHED BY EVANGELISCHE
MARIENSCHWESTERNSCHAFT (EVANGELICAL SISTERHOOD
OF MARY; DARMSTADT-EBERSTADT, GERMANY)*

Lass mein Lieben Dich begleiten: Die Passion Jesu—ein Ruf an uns, 1956, translation published as *Behold His Love,* Lakeland Paperbacks, 1973.

Busse, glueckseliges Leben: Die taegliche Umkehr als befreiende Loesung und Quelle bestaendiger Freude, 1959, translation published as *Repentance: The Joy-Filled Life,* Zondervan (Grand Rapids, MI), 1968.

Krankentrostbuechlein: Antworten auf Fragen und Noete des Kranken, 1960, translation published as *The Blessings of Illness,* Lakeland Paperbacks, 1973.

Maria, der Weg der Mutter des Herrn: Das Zeugnis der heiligen Schrift ueber ihr Leben in der Nachfolge Jesu, 1960, translation published as *Mary, the Mother of Jesus,* Lakeland Paperbacks, 1986.

Die Ihn lieben: Liebe zu Jesus als lebensgestaltende Macht, 1961, translation published as *Those Who Love Him,* Zondervan, 1969.

Heiliges Land-heute: Staetten des Lebens und Leidens Jesu, 1962, translation published as *The Holy Land Today,* Faith Press, 1963.

Realitaeten: Gottes Wirken heute erlebt, 1962, translation published as *Realities: The Miracles of God Experienced Today,* Zondervan, 1966, new edition published as *Realities of Faith,* Bethany Fellowship, 1983.

Der niemand traurig sehen kann: Ein Wort des Zuspruchs fuer jeden Tag des Jahres, 1965, translation published as *Father of Comfort,* Marshall, Morgan & Scott, 1971.

Wo der Geist weht: Wesen und Wirken des Heiligen Geistes damals und heute, 1967, translation published as *Ruled by the Spirit,* Bethany Fellowship, 1970.

Er redet noch: Gottes Gebot—Gottes Angebot fuer jeden Tag, 1968, translation published as *More Precious than Gold,* Creation House (Wheaton, IL), 1978.

Alles fuer Einen: Vom Groessten Schatz jedes Christenlebens—der Liebe zu Jesus, 1969, translation published as *My All for Him,* Marshall, Morgan & Scott, 1971.

Wir bergen uns in Deine Hand: Trost, Staerkung und Bereitung fuer Notzeiten, 1969, translation published as *Hidden in His Hands,* Creation House, 1979.

So wird man anders: Seelsorgerliche Hilfe fuer den konkreten Fall, 1971, translation published as *You Will Never Be the Same,* Bethany Fellowship, 1972.

Reiche der Engel und Daemonen: Aktuelle Wirklichkeit fuer unsere Zeit, 1972, translation published as *The Unseen World of Angels and Demons,* Lakeland Paperbacks, 1985.

Hoelle-Himmel-Wirklichkeiten, 1974, translation published as *What Comes after Death?: The Reality of Heaven and Hell,* Lakeland Paperbacks, 1976.

Wie ich Gott erlebte: Sein Weg mit mir durch sieben Jahrzehnte, 1975, translation published as *I Found the Key to the Heart of God: My Personal Story,* Bethany Fellowship, 1975, published in England as *A Foretaste of Heaven.*

Ich will hier bei Dir stehen: Jesu Lieben und Leiden damals und heute, 1975, translation published as *Let Me Stand at Your Side,* 1975.

Patmos—da der Himmel offen war: Die Offenbarung des Johannes wird lebendig in den Geschehnissen unserer Zeit, 1976, translation published as *Patmos: When the Heavens Opened,* Creation House, 1976.

Jesu kleine Getreue: Fuer 8-12 jaehrige Kinder, 1977, translation published as *What Made Them So Brave?* (juvenile), 1978.

Wo liegt die Wahrheit?: Ist Mohammeds Allah der Gott der Bibel?, 1982, translation published as *Allah or the God of the Bible: What Is the Truth?,* Lakeland Paperbacks, 1984.

Zum Gewinn ward mir das Leid, 1983, translation published as *The Hidden Treasure in Suffering,* Lakeland Paperbacks, 1985.

*IN GERMAN; PUBLISHED BY EVANGELISCHE
MARIENSCHWESTERNSCHAFT*

Dem Ueberwinder die Krone: Ein Ratgeber in Sorgen, Leiden, Anfechtungen und Schwierigkeiten mit Mitmenschen, 1949.

Macht des Gebets: Eine Hinfuehrung zu Bitte, Dank, Anbetung und immerwaehrendem Gebet, 1950.

Kommte, es ist alles bereit: Das grosse Angebot im Heiligen Mahl, 1954.

Gebetsleben: Ein Wegweiser zum persoenlichen Gebet—praktische Anleitung und Gebete, 1955.

Trostbuechlein: Fuer Bekuemmerte, 1957.

Vatergebete: Zur Anregung fuer das persoenliche Gebet, 1957.

Wege durch die Nacht zur Heiligen Dreieinigkeit, 1957.

Geduldbuechlein: Fuer Wartezeiten, 1958.

Ich will euch troesten: Trostbuechlein fuer Trauernde, 1959.

Weihnachtsbuechlein: Gespraeche an der Krippe, 1959.

Morgen—und Abendgebete, 1960.

Wider die Verzagtheit: Glaubenshilfe fuer dunkle Stunden, 1961.

Zielklar ist Gott am Werk: Der Weg von zwei frueh heimgegangenen Marienschwestern, 1963.

Sinai heute: Staetten der Gottesoffenbarung zwischen Nil und Moseberg, 1966.

Wenn einer nicht lieben kann: Schluessel zu versoehntem Leben, 1971.

OTHER

Schlink's works have been published under several name variations, including Basilea Schlink, M. Basilea Schlink, and Mother Basilea Schlink. Also author of numerous booklets in German, some translated into English; author of pamphlets, leaflets, tracts, and posters. Also composer of numerous religious songs, some of which have been published in songbooks: *Wellsprings of Joy; Songs and Prayers of Victory; O None Can Be Loved as Is Jesus; The King Draws Near;* and *My Father, I Trust You.* Recordings of her songs include *Jesus, O Joy Eternal; Jesus, Jesus, We Love You, Lord; Glory beyond Compare; In Praise of Our Heavenly Father;* and *Lift Up Your Voices with Joy.*

Schlink's books have been published in sixty languages, including Twi, Swahili, Amharic, Afrikaans, Tahi, and Mandarin Chinese.

SIDELIGHTS: Mother Basilea (Klara Schlink's religous name) dreamed of establishing a religious community where love for Jesus Christ is a way of life after her birthplace, Darmstadt, Germany, was leveled by an air raid in 1944. Following World War II, Mother Basilea founded the Evangelical Sisterhood of Mary within the framework of the German Protestant State Church. The ministry grew, and the Land of Canaan and a Brotherhood were established. The Sisters and Brothers of Canaan convey Mother Basilea's testimony and religious faith by means of radio programs and films which have been broadcast worldwide.

BIOGRAPHICAL/CRITICAL SOURCES:

BOOKS

Schlink, Basilea, *Wie ich Gott erlebte: Sein Weg mit mir durch sieben Jahrzehnte,* Evangelische Marienschwesternschaft, 1975, translation published as *I Found the Key to the Heart of God: My Personal Story,* Bethany Fellowship, 1975, published in England as *A Foretaste of Heaven.*

PERIODICALS

Bookstore Journal, June, 1976.
Christian Life, April, 1976; August, 1977.*

*   *   *

SCHLINK, M. Basilea
    See SCHLINK, Klara

*   *   *

SCHLINK, Mother Basilea
    See SCHLINK, Klara

SCHWARTZ, Alvin   1927-1992

PERSONAL: Born April 25, 1927, in Brooklyn, NY; died of lymphoma, March 14, 1992, in Princeton, NJ; son of Harry (a taxi-driver) and Gussie (Younger) Schwartz; married Barbara Carmer (a learning consultant), August 7, 1954; children: John, Peter, Nancy, Elizabeth. *Education:* Attended City College (now of the City University of New York), 1944-45; Colby College, A.B., 1949; Northwestern University, M.S., 1951. *Politics:* Independent.

CAREER: Newspaper reporter, 1951-55; writer for nonprofit and commercial organizations, 1955-59; Opinion Research Corp., Princeton, NJ, director of communications, 1959-64; freelance writer and author of books for adults and children, 1963-92. Adjunct professor of English, Rutgers University, 1962-78. Trustee, Joint Free Library of Princeton, 1972-74. Member of national council, Boy Scouts of America, 1972-74. *Military service:* U.S. Navy, 1945-46.

MEMBER: Authors League of America, Authors Guild.

AWARDS, HONORS: New Jersey Institute of Technology awards, 1966, for *The Night Workers,* 1968, for *The Rainy Day Book,* 1969, for *University: The Students, Faculty, and Campus Life at One University,* 1972, for *A Twister of Twists, A Tangler of Tongues,* 1977, for *Kickle Snifters and Other Fearsome Critters Collected from American Folklore,* 1980, for *When I Grew Up Long Ago: Family Living, Going to School, Games and Parties, Cures and Deaths, a Comet, a War, Falling in Love, and Other Things I Remember; Older People Talk about the Days When They Were Young,* 1981, for *Chin Music: Tall Talk and Other Talk,* and 1987, for *Ten Copycats in a Boat and Other Riddles* and *Tales of Trickery from the Land of Spoof.*

American Library Association notable book citations, 1967, for *Museum: The Story of America's Treasure Houses,* 1982, for *The Cat's Elbow and Other Secret Languages,* 1983, for *Unriddling: All Sorts of Riddles to Puzzle Your Guessery,* and 1984, for *In a Dark, Dark Room and Other Scary Stories; New York Times* Outstanding Book citations, 1972, for *A Twister of Twists, A Tangler of Tongues,* and 1973, for *Tomfoolery: Trickery and Foolery with Words;* National Council of Teachers of English citation, 1972, for *A Twister of Twists, a Tangler of Tongues,* 1975, for *Whoppers: Tall Tales and Other Lies Collected from American Folklore;* American Library Association and National Endowment for the Humanities bicentennial book, 1972, for *The Unions: What They Are, How They Came to Be, How They Affect Each of Us,* and 1973, for *Central City/Spread City: The Metropolitan Regions Where More and More of Us Spend Our Lives;* "Notable Children's Trade Book in the Field of Social Studies" citations, National Council for the Social Studies and the Children's Book Council, 1973, for *Central City/Spread City,* 1974, for *Cross Your Fingers, Spit in Your Hat: Superstitions and Other Beliefs,* 1975 for *Whoppers,* 1979, for *Chin Music,* and 1980, for *Flapdoodle: Pure Nonsense from American Folklore;* "Book of the Year" citations, Child Study Association of America, 1973, for *Witcracks: Jokes and Jests from American Folklore,* 1974, for *Central City/Spread City* and *Cross Your Fingers, Spit in Your Hat,* 1975, for *Whoppers,* and 1979, for *Tales of Trickery from the Land of Spoof, There Is a Carrot in My Ear and Other Noodle Tales, In a Dark, Dark Room,* and *Ten Copycats in a Boat and Other Riddles;* "Children's Choice" citations, International Reading Association and Children's Book Council, 1975, for *Cross Your Fingers, Spit in Your Hat,* 1976, for *Whoppers,* 1977, for *Kickle Snifters and Other Fearsome Critters,* and 1981, for *Ten Copycats in a Boat and Other Riddles; Kickle Snifters and Other Fearsome Critters* was named one of *School Library Journal's* Best Books of the Year, 1976.

Witcracks was chosen one of New York Public Library's Books for the Teen Age, 1980, and *Cross Your Fingers, Spit in Your Hat,* in 1980, 1981, and 1982; *In a Dark, Dark Room and Other Scary Stories* was selected as a Notable Children's Book by the Association for Library Service to Children, 1984; Ohio Buckeye Children's Book Award, State Library of Ohio, and Colorado Children's Book Award, both 1986, and Arizona Young Readers Award, Arizona State University, 1987, all for *Scary Stories to Tell in the Dark;* Ohio Buckeye Children's Book Award, Washington Library Media Association, Virginia Children's Book Award, New Jersey Library Association, all 1986, all for *In a Dark, Dark Room and Other Scary Stories;* honored for body of work by Rutgers University School of Communications, Information and Library Studies, 1986.

WRITINGS:

FOR CHILDREN

A Parent's Guide to Children's Play and Recreation, Collier (New York City), 1963.

How to Fly a Kite, Catch a Fish, Grow a Flower, and Other Activities for You and Your Child, Macmillan (New York City), 1965.

America's Exciting Cities: A Guide for Parents and Children, Crowell (New York City), 1966.

The Night Workers, illustrated with photographs by Ulli Steltzer, Dutton (New York City), 1966.

What Do You Think?: An Introduction to Public Opinion, How It Forms, Functions, and Affects Our Lives, Dutton, 1966.

The City and Its People: The Story of One City's Government, Dutton, 1967.

Museum: The Story of America's Treasure Houses, Dutton, 1967.

The People's Choice: The Story of Candidates, Campaigns, and Elections, Dutton, 1967.

To Be a Father: Stories, Letters, Essays, Poems, Comments, and Proverbs on the Delights and Despairs of Fatherhood, Crown (New York City), 1968.

Old Cities and New Towns: The Changing Face of the Nation, Dutton, 1968.

The Rainy Day Book, Simon & Schuster (New York City), 1968.

University: The Students, Faculty, and Campus Life at One University, Viking (New York City), 1969.

Going Camping: A Complete Guide for the Uncertain Beginner in Family Camping, Macmillan, 1969, revised edition published as *Going Camping: A Complete Guide for the Family Camper,* 1972.

(Compiler) *A Twister of Twists, a Tangler of Tongues,* illustrated by Glen Rounds, Lippincott (Philadelphia), 1972.

Hobbies: An Introduction to Crafts, Collections, Nature Study, and Other Life-Long Pursuits, illustrated by Barbara Carmer Schwartz, Simon & Schuster, 1972.

The Unions: What They Are, How They Came to Be, How They Affect Each of Us, Viking, 1972.

(Compiler and reteller) *Witcracks: Jokes and Jests from American Folklore,* Lippincott, 1973.

(Compiler and reteller) *Tomfoolery: Trickery and Foolery with Words,* Lippincott, 1973.

Central City/Spread City: The Metropolitan Regions Where More and More of Us Spend Our Lives, Macmillan, 1973.

(Compiler and reteller) *Cross Your Fingers, Spit in Your Hat: Superstitions and Other Beliefs,* illustrated by Rounds, Lippincott, 1974.

(Reteller) *Whoppers: Tall Tales and Other Lies Collected from American Folklore,* illustrated by Rounds, Lippincott, 1975.

Kickle Snifters and Other Fearsome Critters Collected from American Folklore, illustrated by Rounds, Lippincott, 1976.

Stores, illustrated with photographs by Samuel Nocella, Jr., Macmillan, 1977.

(Editor and compiler) *When I Grew Up Long Ago: Family Living, Going to School, Games and Parties, Cures and Deaths, a Comet, a War, Falling in Love, and Other Things I Remember; Older People Talk about the Days When They Were Young,* illustrated by Harold Berson, Lippincott, 1978.

(Compiler) *Chin Music: Tall Talk and Other Talk,* illustrated by John O'Brien, Lippincott, 1979.

Flapdoodle: Pure Nonsense from American Folklore, Lippincott, 1980.

(Compiler) *Ten Copycats in a Boat and Other Riddles,* illustrated by Marc Simont, Harper (New York City), 1980.

(Reteller) *Scary Stories to Tell in the Dark,* Lippincott, 1981.

(Compiler) *The Cat's Elbow and Other Secret Languages,* illustrated by Stephen Gammell, Farrar, Straus (New York City), 1982.

Busy Buzzing Bumblebees and Other Tongue Twisters, illustrated by Kathie Abrams, Harper, 1982.

There Is a Carrot in My Ear and Other Noodle Tales, illustrated by Karen Ann Weinhaus, Harper, 1982.

(Compiler) *Unriddling: All Sorts of Riddles to Puzzle Your Guessery,* illustrated by Susan Truesdell, Lippincott, 1983.

(Reteller) *In a Dark, Dark Room and Other Scary Stories,* illustrated by Dirk Zimmer, Harper, 1984.

(Compiler) *More Scary Stories to Tell in the Dark,* illustrated by Gammell, Lippincott, 1984.

(Reteller) *Fat Man in a Fur Coat and Other Bear Stories,* illustrated by David Christiana, Farrar, Straus, 1984.

(Compiler) *Tales of Trickery from the Land of Spoof,* Farrar, Straus, 1985.

(Reteller) *All of Our Noses Are Here and Other Noodle Tales,* illustrated by Weinhaus, Harper, 1985.

Telling Fortunes: Love Magic, Dream Signs and Other Ways to Learn the Future, illustrated by Tracey Cameron, Harper, 1987.

(Reteller) *Gold and Silver, Silver and Gold: Tales of Hidden Treasure,* illustrated by Christiana, Farrar, Straus, 1988.

I Saw You in the Bathtub and Other Folk Rhymes, illustrated by Syd Hoff, Harper, 1989.

Ghosts!: Ghostly Tales from Folklore, illustrated by Victoria Chess, Harper, 1991.

Scary Stories, No. 3: More Tales to Chill Your Bones, illustrated by Gammell, Harper, 1991.

And the Green Grass Grew All Around: Folk Poetry from Everyone, illustrated by Truesdell, HarperCollins (New York City), 1992.

Stories to Tell a Cat, illustrated by Catherine Huerta, HarperCollins, 1992.

OTHER

Evaluating Your Public Relations (pamphlet), National Public Relations Council of Health and Welfare Services, 1965.

No Such Mirrors (novel), Writers' Cooperative (Montreal), 1972.

Contributor to numerous periodicals, including *Redbook, Coronet, Parade, Parents', Public Opinion Quarterly, Journal of Marketing, New York Times,* and *New York Herald Tribune.*

ADAPTATIONS:

Tongue Twisters (cassette), Caedmon, 1974.

Scary Stories to Tell in the Dark (record or cassette), Caedmon, 1986.

More Scary Stories to Tell in the Dark (cassette, with teacher's guide), Listening Library, 1986.

In a Dark, Dark Room (cassette), Harper, 1986.

SIDELIGHTS: Alvin Schwartz, the author of many best-selling books for children, was noted for his appealing use of folklore, his humor, a sense of absurdity, and also for some frightening characters in his books. Schwartz, who knew early in life that he wanted to write, studied journalism in college and worked as a newspaper reporter and professional writer during the 1950s. In the 1960s he became a freelance writer and went on to publish more than fifty books. Many of his most popular books are compilations of folk tales, ghost stories, tongue-twisters, jokes, riddles, and superstitions, but he also wrote nonfiction about such institutions as fatherhood, workers' unions, stores, museums, universities, and the government. Although much of Schwartz's work is funny and lighthearted, the witches, ghosts, and zombies in books such as *In a Dark, Dark Room and Other Scary Stories, Ghosts: Ghostly Tales from Folklore,* and *Scary Stories, No. 3: More Tales to Chill Your Bones,* were considered by some parents and teachers to be too frightening for youthful readers. Polls, however, have shown Schwartz to be a favorite among students.

"If the current generation grows up with a knowledge of traditional humor, it may well be because of Alvin Schwartz's many volumes of humorous American folklore," comments a reviewer in the *Horn Book Magazine.* Humor plays an important role in many of Schwartz's books; William Cole, writing for the *New York Times Book Review,* says, "We can do with a little laughter. Thus a hearty welcome to Alvin Schwartz's [*Tomfoolery: Trickery and Foolery with Words*], a collection of verbal tricks from American folklore that can be as successful with adults as with children." Cole praises the author's sense of the absurd, and continues, "[With] this collection, his notes, sources and bibliography Mr. Schwartz has elevated foolishness to a form of art."

In an article written for *Horn Book Magazine,* Schwartz explained why he used his particular brand of humor: "I first became interested in folklore when most of us do, in childhood. But at that time I had no idea that the games, sayings, songs, rhymes, taunts, and jokes I knew; the things I wrote on walls; the superstitions I relied on; the tales I heard and learned; the customs we practiced at home; or the ways we had of doing things were all folklore. I also did not realize that much of this lore gave my life structure and continuity, that these games, songs, jokes, tales, and customs were often very old, that ordinary people like me had created them, and that all this had survived simply and remarkably because one person had told another."

Schwartz stressed the need for tradition and continuity in modern society. He commented in the *Horn Book* article that "as our technology has advanced, we have come to rely increasingly on other people for goods, services, and entertainment and less on ourselves and on those we know. The extended family and the traditions it preserved have disappeared. . . . As a result of such changes, we have to a serious extent become alienated from our traditions and have lost a sense of place and a sense of self. If this perception is correct, we have altered the fabric of our society, and we are changing from something we were to something we have not yet become."

BIOGRAPHICAL/CRITICAL SOURCES:

BOOKS

Authors of Books for Young People, 3rd edition, Scarecrow (Metuchen, NJ), 1990.
Children's Literature Review, Volume 3, Gale (Detroit), 1978.

PERIODICALS

Horn Book Magazine, June, 1977; August, 1977; February, 1984.
New York Times Book Review, May 6, 1973; January 17, 1982.

OBITUARIES:

PERIODICALS

Chicago Tribune, March 16, 1992, section 1, p. 13; April 22, 1992, section 2, p. 6.
Los Angeles Tribune, March 17, 1992, p. A18.
Washington Post, March 18, 1992, p. C7.

*   *   *

SCOTT, Anthony
  See DRESSER, Davis

*   *   *

SEDLEY, Kate
  See CLARKE, Brenda (Margaret Lilian)

*   *   *

SHAPCOTT, Thomas W(illiam) 1935-

PERSONAL: Born March 21, 1935, in Ipswich, Australia; son of Harold (an accountant) and Dorothy (Gillespie)

Shapcott; married Margaret Hodge (a teacher), April 18, 1960; married Judith Rodriguez, October 13, 1982; children: (first marriage) Katherine, Alison, Richard, Isabel. *Education:* University of Queensland, B.A., 1969.

ADDRESSES: Home—18 Churchill Street, Mount Albert, Victoria 3127, Australia.

CAREER: H. S. Shapcott (public accountant), Ipswich, Australia, clerk, 1951-63; Shapcott & Shapcott (accountants), Ipswich, partner, 1963-72; Public Accountant and sole trader in Ipswich, 1972-78. Secretary, Ipswich Fire Brigade, 1970—. Literature Board of Australia Council, deputy chairman, 1973-76, director, 1983-90. Executive director, National Book Council, 1992—.

AWARDS, HONORS: Grace Leven Prize for poetry, 1961, for *Time on Fire;* Sir Thomas White Memorial Prize for poetry, 1967, for *A Taste of Salt Water;* Sydney Myer Charity Trust Award, 1967, for *A Taste of Salt Water,* and 1969, for *Inwards to the Sun;* Churchill fellowship to the United States and England, 1972; gold wreath, Struga Poetry Festival, Yugoslavia, 1989; Christopher Brennan Award for Poetry, 1994; Officer in the Order of Australia, 1989; D.Litt., Macquarie University, 1989.

WRITINGS:

POEMS

Time on Fire, Jacaranda Press, 1961.
Twelve Bagatelles, Australian Letters, 1962.
The Mankind Thing, Jacaranda Press, 1964.
Sonnets 1960/1963, B. Donaghey, 1964.
A Taste of Salt Water, Angus & Robertson (London), 1967.
Inwards to the Sun, University of Queensland Press (St. Lucia, Queensland, Australia), 1969.
Fingers at Air: Experimental Poems, privately printed, 1969.
Begin with Walking, University of Queensland Press, 1969.
Interim Report, privately printed, 1972.
Shabbytown Calendar, University of Queensland Press, 1976.
Seventh Avenue Poems, Angus & Robertson, 1976.
Selected Poems, University of Queensland Press, 1978.
Turning Full Circle: Prose Poems, New Poetry (Sydney), 1978.
Stump and Grape and Bobble-nut, Bullion Publications, 1981.
Welcome!, University of Queensland Press, 1983.
Travel Dice, University of Queensland Press, 1987.
Selected Poems, 1956-88, University of Queensland Press, 1989.
In the Beginning, National Library of Australia (Canberra), 1990.

The City of Home, University of Queensland Press, 1995.

EDITOR

(With Rodney Hall) *New Impulses in Australian Poetry,* University of Queensland Press, 1969.

Australian Poetry Now, Sun Books, 1970.

Poets on Record, 14 volumes, University of Queensland Press, 1970-74.

Contemporary American and Australian Poetry, University of Queensland Press, 1976.

Consolidation: The Second Poets Anthology, University of Queensland Press, 1982.

Contemporary Australian Poetry (Macedonian edition), Skopje (Macedonia), 1989.

Pamphlet Poets Series 2, 6 volumes, National Library of Australia, 1991.

NOVELS

The Birthday Gift, University of Queensland Press, 1982.

White Stag of Exile, Allen Lane (London), 1984.

Holiday of the Ikon, Puffin Books (Harmondsworth, England), 1984.

Hotel Bellevue, Chatto & Windus (London), 1986.

The Search for Galina, Chatto & Windus, 1989.

(With Steve Spears) *Mr. Edmund,* McPhee Gribble, 1990.

(With A. R. Simpson) *His Master's Ghost,* McPhee Gribble, 1990.

Mona's Gift, Penguin (Sydney), 1993.

OTHER

Focus On Charles Blackman (art monograph), University of Queensland Press, 1967.

The Seven Deadly Sins (opera libretto), privately printed, 1970.

The Literature Board: A Brief History, University of Queensland Press, 1988.

Limestone and Lemon Wine (stories), Black Swan (London), 1988.

(With Robin Burridge) *The Art of Charles Blackman,* A. Deutsh (London), 1989.

Biting the Bullet: A Literary Memoir, Simon & Schuster (Brookvale, New South Wales, Australia), 1990.

What You Own (stories), Angus & Robertson, 1991.

Also author of *Those Who Are Compelled,* 1980.

SIDELIGHTS: Thomas W. Shapcott has steadily developed a reputation as not only a formidable poet, but as a novelist and a leading editor in Australian literature. Shapcott's poetry has evolved from using traditional forms to a looser, more experimental style. His themes range from the artist's search for self-definition to the contrast between the poet's inner perceptions and the external world.

Time on Fire, Shapcott's first published collection of poetry, won the young poet the Grace Leven Prize. "Shapcott's best passages are those in which his finely attentive response to the natural scene develops inwardly: the pressure of the scene and the pressure of his own preoccupations fuse in a meaningful vision," David Moody writes in a *Meanjin* review of the book.

Shapcott's poems about the natural world continued to develop in *The Mankind Thing.* In the poem "Two and Half Acres," Carl Harrison-Ford notes in *Meanjin,* "the natural cycles of nature foster an awareness of form and of variety within it that obviously relates to [Shapcott's] aims in poetry. Shapcott sums this up succinctly yet unobtrusively: My fingers catch / at bark, twig, seed. There's no captivity / to hold them in. The act escapes from me. / Matter is form to hold such mystery."

A Taste of Salt Water won Shapcott two major Australian poetry awards and a wider critical attention. Divided into five sections, the book includes "sonnets and lyrics, a New Testament sequence, poems with various urban themes, elegies celebrating the deaths of people and things and a very polished poem entitled 'Macquarie as Father' " observes Robert Ward in the *Australian Book Review.* Calling Shapcott "a mature and intelligent poetic talent," Ward praises his controlled use of language, its vividness and capacity, saying "He can surprise one by saying 'Let me sing / even the buzz of flies defines the spring' " Joining in the praise for *A Taste of Salt Water,* James Tulip calls the book "a series of adroit, sensitive ventures into a variety of subjects." In his review for *Southerly,* Tulip speaks of Shapcott's religious approach to myths, his fresh look at historical poetry and "strongest of all in my view, poems dealing with closely observed personal relations." Tulip goes on to admire Shapcott's verse as having "character . . . a tone, an honesty, a registering of personal engagement with the facts of normal living." But Tulip was not without complaints about the collection. He found that Shapcott's "lightness of tone often becomes a mildness of tone, and his attitudes soft and self-indulgent."

The frankly experimental work *Fingers at Air* found Shapcott poet breaking away from his traditional inclinations and working in more abstract forms. "Take the first sequence 'Dance, Dance'. . . .," writes S. E. Lee in *Southerly.* "It runs I think for 12 pages . . . and employs a recurring line design that one commonly observes on old-fashioned tiled floors. . . . The spaces inside and outside the diamond are gradually filled with cryptic words and chunks of sentences taken out of context until at the end we have a cluttered page." *Begin with Walking* continues Shapcott's abstract poetic experiments, this time introducing more American-influenced work, including poems with only one word per line. Some poems written on a visit to New York City were collected in *Seventh Avenue*

Poems. Shapcott furthered the effects of free-form American styles on Australian writers by editing the anthology *Contemporary American and Australian Poetry,* published in 1976.

Shapcott's attempts at abstraction had value, despite some failures, Harrison-Ford states in a *Meanjin* analysis of the poet's work. "The many poems published since *Fingers at Air* suggest that those naked experiments proved fruitful," Harrison-Ford argues. "The privately produced *Interim Report* (1972) includes many of those poems and displays a style that is new and characteristic."

Following through on his poetic breakthroughs, Shapcott published *Shabbytown Calendar.* Called an "intricate and mature volume" by Christopher Pollnitz in *Southerly,* it "traces all twelve months, allotting three poems to each. Two poems deal with persons, places, flora and weathers loosely appropriate to the season, the third is a 'fugue' dedicated to the month." For Pollnitz, "The overriding concern of the *Calendar* is with time, with ways of mummifying, recapturing, regenerating, transcending or being reconciled to time." Pollnitz concludes that Shapcott "may have found a hint" for his poetic innovations in "contemporary American poetry." But Shapcott's work was also an important "discovery and achievement" for "contemporary Australian poetry." Kevin Hart, reviewing *Shabbytown Calendar* in *Southern Review,* finds a number of "inconsequential sketches" in the book. But there is also evidence of "a strong imaginative mind meditating on central human concerns." Hart contends that "*Shabbytown Calendar* must be seen as a flawed but persuasive attempt at a verse-novel."

Shapcott turned his talents to the novel form in 1983 with publication of *The Birthday Gift.* Following the lives of twins, Ben and Benno, Shapcott switches the point of view from their Queensland childhood in the 1940s to scenes from their young adulthood in the 1950s. These "jagged time fragments" make the novel "difficult to follow," Annette James writes in *Library Journal,* although she admits that the book contains "rich and sensitive prose." Tulip, writing about *The Birthday Gift* in *Southerly,* finds that it "lacks fictional freedom; it is one step from being a journal, an autobiography, a confession." But Tulip also sees the novel as proof of Shapcott's position as "a central reflecting intelligence of his generation."

In *White Stag of Exile* Shapcott tells the story of Karoly Pulszky, a 19th century Hungarian art historian who immigrated to Australia when political turmoil drove him from his homeland. Shapcott tells the story in a disjointed manner, using letters and other documents to assemble a biography of Pulszky. In a review for *New Statesman,* Roger Lewis claims that *White Stag of Exile* "is hardly a novel at all" but more a "scrapbook of letters, journals and

reports." Although Lewis concludes that it is an "odd book," one "that lingers uneasily in the limbo between fact and fantasy," Roger Manvell, writing in *British Book News,* calls *White Stag* "absorbing" and "a notable combination of research and invention."

A return to the past plays a role in Shapcott's novel *Hotel Bellevue* as well. In this book, Boyd Kennedy leaves a broken marriage to return to his grandmother's house in Brisbane. Confronting his past, he becomes involved in preventing the destruction of the historic hotel of the book's title. "A sense of the inevitable" motivates Shapcott's characters, Anthony Sattin notes in a *Times Literary Supplement* review, but that sense "works against the impact of the neatly constructed narrative." Sattin finds, however, that like most of Shapcott's work, the book is "a vigorous and energetic piece of writing" and contains "some serious and sensitive meditations on the past, and the price still to pay for it." Critic Margaret Walters, writing in the *Observer,* explains that *Hotel Bellevue* "explores the ambiguities of memory—the need to preserve the past, but the need, as well, to recognise how it traps and destroys us." Ultimately, Walters concludes that the novel "doesn't have the symbolic resonance Shapcott clearly intends, and the book's interesting but disparate strands never quite cohere."

In his short story collection *Limestone and Lemon Wine* Shapcott invents the town of Limestone, set in the Australian countryside, to explore "those elements of life which can emerge particularly vividly in a small town," as Mansel Stimpson writes in the *Times Literary Supplement.* The collection's longest story, "Water and Blood," reveals once again the author's interest in the relationships between the past and present. It covers a hundred years of family history while focusing on an adopted girl's obsession with her origins. "Built up from disparate sections," Stimpson writes, "[the story] shows Shapcott's skill at holding things together." Commenting on his ability to present stories in an unobtrusive style, Stimpson concludes that Shapcott's "is an art which conceals art, and is the more enjoyable for it."

Shapcott once told *CA:* "I am deeply interested in the development of poetry in Australia and in its wider relevance in English speaking contexts. My own development has been from lyrical celebratory beginnings, through increasing awareness of social process to (most recently) a sense of regional mythology within a world in flux. I do not see myself as a regional poet, though; rather, as one man rediscovering himself through others."

BIOGRAPHICAL/CRITICAL SOURCES:

BOOKS

Contemporary Literary Criticism, Volume 38, Gale, 1986.

PERIODICALS

Apollo, September, 1990, p. 211.

Australian, October 9, 1993.

Australian Book Review, October, 1967, p. 197; March, 1970, pp. 127-128; September, 1991, p. 18; September, 1993, pp. 17-18.

Australian Literary Studies, October, 1990.

Australian Magazine, February 25, 1989.

British Book News, December, 1984, p. 750.

Canberra Times, August 19, 1988.

Illustrated London News, March, 1988, p. 79.

London Magazine, September, 1986.

Magpies, March, 1991, p. 30.

Meanjin, December, 1961, pp. 503-505; September, 1972, pp. 300-307; April, 1979, pp. 56-68.

New Statesman, August 3, 1984, p. 27.

Observer, July 29, 1984, p. 20; September 14, 1986, p. 27; February 14, 1988, p. 27; June 25, 1989 p. 45.

Overland, June, 1988.

Poetry, January, 1978, p. 225.

San Francisco Review of Books, winter, 1983, p. 11.

Southerly, Volume 25, number 2, 1965, pp. 131-137; Volume 28, number 1, 1968, pp. 71-73; Volume 30, number 4, 1970, pp. 306-311; Volume 31, number 1, 1971, pp. 72-73; Volume 33, number 2, 1973, p. 239; Volume 36, number 4, 1976, pp. 464-470; Volume 43, number 1, 1983, pp. 113-118.

Southern Review, March, 1977, pp. 79-80.

Times Literary Supplement, November 7, 1986, p. 1255; November 27, 1987, p. 1327; February 26, 1988, p. 215.

World Literature Today, autumn, 1979, p. 743; winter, 1984, p. 170; summer, 1984, p. 471; autumn, 1988, p. 725.

*   *   *

SHARP, Ronald A(lan)   1945-

PERSONAL: Born October 19, 1945, in Cleveland, OH; son of Jack Trier (an advertising executive) and Florence (a housewife; maiden name, Tenenbaum) Sharp; married Inese Brutans (a teacher), June 22, 1968; children: Andrew Janis, James Michael. *Education:* Kalamazoo College, B.A., 1967; University of Michigan, M.A., 1968; University of Virginia, Ph.D. (with distinction), 1974. *Religion:* Jewish.

ADDRESSES: Home—11671 Kenyon Rd., Mount Vernon, OH 43050. *Office*—Department of English, Kenyon College, Gambier, OH 43022.

CAREER: Western Michigan University, Kalamazoo, instructor in English, 1968-70; Kenyon College, Gambier, OH, instructor in English, 1970-72, assistant professor, 1974-78, associate professor, 1978-85, professor, 1985-90, John Crowe Ransom Professor of English, 1990—. Visiting professor of English, Concordia University, summer, 1978. Co-director, Keats Bicentennial Conference, Harvard University, 1995.

MEMBER: Modern Language Association of America, Wordsworth-Coleridge Association, Keats-Shelley Association.

AWARDS, HONORS: Fellowship from Ford Foundation, 1971, Danforth Foundation, 1972, English-Speaking Union, 1973, Saltz and Seay (both University of Virginia), 1973-74, Mellon Foundation, 1980, National Humanities Center, 1981-82 (declined), 1986-87, National Endowment for the Humanities, 1981-82, 1984, 1985, 1986-87, 1994, and American Council of Learned Societies, 1986-87 (declined); grants from Kenyon Faculty Development, 1983, 1988, 1989, 1992, 1994, National Endowment for the Humanities Chairman's Grant, 1987; National Endowment for the Humanities (in conjunction with the Wenner-Gren Foundation), 1990, National Endowment for the Humanities, 1995; award for editorial excellence from Ohioana Association, 1980, for editing the *Kenyon Review.*

WRITINGS:

(Author of preface) Thomas Daniel Young, editor, *The New Criticism and After,* University Press of Virginia (Charlottesville, VA), 1976.

Keats, Skepticism, and the Religion of Beauty, University of Georgia Press (Athens, GA), 1979.

(Translator) *Three Short Plays of Federico Garcia Lorca: Original Translations from the Spanish of "Teatro Breve,"* Modern International Drama, 1979.

Friendship and Literature: Spirit and Form, Duke University Press (Durham, NC), 1986.

(With Eudora Welty) *The Norton Book of Friendship,* Norton (New York City), 1991.

(With Nathan A. Scott, Jr.) *Reading George Steiner,* Johns Hopkins University Press (Baltimore, MD), 1994.

Also author of scripts for program *Soundings* on National Public Radio. Contributor to *Cauldron, College Composition and Communication, ELN, The Explicator, Keats-Shelley Journal, Modern Philology, New Literary History, Papers on Language and Literature, Paris Review, Reading Horizons, American Literature,* and *Kenyon Review.* Founding co-editor of the new series *Kenyon Review,* 1978-82.

WORK IN PROGRESS: A book on John Keats and friendship, publication expected in 1996; research on the fate of pastoral in contemporary American poetry, and on gift exchange.

SIDELIGHTS: Ronald A. Sharp's *Friendship and Literature: Spirit and Form* is an analysis of friendship, its expression, and its role in literature and in real life. In what a *Virginia Quarterly Review* writer characterized as a "splendidly human" and "refreshingly modern consideration" of the concept of friendship, Sharp explores such topics as the choosing of friends, the growth and decline of friendships, gender's role in friendship, and friendships that develop in different stages of one's life. Sharp also examines the custom of gift-giving, explaining that "my concern is not so much with the actual giving of gifts by one friend to another—though that too is of interest—as with the richness of gift-giving as a metaphor for friendship." Containing literary references from works as early as those of Homer and Cicero to those of present-day writers, *Friendship and Literature* also features an essay on William Shakespeare's *Merchant of Venice,* a work chosen specifically, Sharp relates, "because it is widely known and because it deals as directly and profoundly with the questions I address throughout the book as any work I know." Summarizing *Friendship and Literature* in the *Kenyon Review,* Patricia Hampl writes that Sharp has endowed his study with "the winning grace of a genuine search conducted by a writer galvanized by the ideas he is attempting to synthesize." An *Encounter* critic lauds Sharp for having written "an elegant and idiosyncratic book. . . . This work is a delicate plea on behalf of civilised forms." Mary Dryden remarks in the *Los Angeles Times Book Review* that Sharp "addresses himself to the concept of friendship . . . with an admirable degree of panache."

The Norton Book of Friendship, a collaborative effort between Sharp and Eudora Welty, is a 600-page compilation of writings on the subject of friendship, with quoted material from such diverse sources as Aristotle, Lord Byron, Albert Camus, Raymond Carver, Anton Chekhov, Emily Dickinson, T. S. Eliot, F. Scott Fitzgerald, Gustav Flaubert, Nadine Gordimer, Ernest Hemingway, Horace, Samuel Johnson, John Keats, Ursula K. LeGuin, Groucho Marx, Marianne Moore, Wolfgang Mozart, Boris Pasternak, the "demon poet" Li Po, V. S. Pritchett, Sappho, William Shakespeare, and W. B. Yeats. While noting that the book "has a real sleeper of a title," *Chicago Tribune* reviewer Joseph Coates praises its "exhilarating tendency to keep us reading till dawn's early light, pursuing the elusive mystery of our own humanity." Coates also finds that "the arrangement of the pieces—essays, poems, letters, short stories, histories and memoirs and excerpts therefrom, farewells and frequent clusters of 'affinities' that overlap all the other categories—keeps us going by sheer appeals to our curiosity about what comes next." George Myers, Jr., in the *Columbus Dispatch* notes that each selection "gleams with generosity and 'congeniality'." He credits the book's strengths and synergisms as

springing from the authors' varied backgrounds: while Welty "has long been regarded as one of America's most beloved storytellers," Sharp has "long [been] interested in what makes friendships tick and stick." Similarly, Donna Seaman comments in *Booklist* that "Welty delights" not only in her friendship and partnership with Sharp, but in "the ways in which their different approaches to the topic enriched the collection." Pearl A. McHaney, writing in the *Atlanta Journal-Constitution,* described the collection as "a marvelous book" in which Sharp and Welty "have built a 'sweet disorder' out of the literature of friendship."

BIOGRAPHICAL/CRITICAL SOURCES:

PERIODICALS

Arts Journal, February, 1987, p. 14.
Atlanta Journal-Constitution, January 19, 1992.
Booklist, October 15, 1991.
Boston Globe, December 29, 1978.
Chicago Tribune, October 24, 1978; November 15, 1991, Section 14, p. 7.
Christian Science Monitor, February 14, 1979.
Cleveland Plain Dealer, March 29, 1992, p. 11-H.
Columbus Dispatch, January 5, 1992, p. 1F.
Encounter, November, 1986, p. 48.
Kenyon Review, winter, 1987.
Los Angeles Times Book Review, September 7, 1986.
New York Times, January 12, 1977.
Playboy, September, 1986, p. 20.
Virginia Quarterly Review, winter, 1987.

*   *   *

SHEA, George 1940-

PERSONAL: Born June 12, 1940, in New York, NY; son of George Vincent, Sr. and Mary Agnes (Foley) Shea; married Anique Taylor, May 28, 1980 (divorced October, 1982); children: Madeleine Todd. *Education:* Attended College of the Holy Cross, 1957-58; Fordham University, B.A., 1963; graduate study at New York University, 1966-67. *Politics:* Independent. *Religion:* "None."

ADDRESSES: Office—Random House Children's Division, 225 Park Avenue South, New York, NY 10003.

CAREER: Writer, 1976—. Substitute nursery school teacher in New York City, 1968-70; Raw Guts and American Know-How, New York City, improvisational comedy actor, 1969-71; Paul Bunyan Playhouse, Bemidji, MN, actor, 1973; National Public Radio, Minneapolis, MN, radio comedy actor, 1973-76; East/West Network, New York City, staff writer, 1985-87. Improvisational comedy actor at Dudley Riggs Brave New Workshop, 1973-74.

MEMBER: Motion Picture Screen Cartoonists Union.

WRITINGS:

JUVENILE

Alligators, EMC Corp. (Cockeysville, MD), 1977.
Bats, EMC Corp., 1977.
Spiders, EMC Corp., 1977.
Wolves, EMC Corp., 1977.
I Died Here, Childrens Press (Chicago), 1979.
Nightmare Nina, Bowmar/Noble (Los Angeles), 1979.
Big Bad Ernie, Bowmar/Noble, 1979.
Cheap Skates, Scholastic Book Services (New York City), 1980.
Jody, Scholastic Book Services, 1980.
Whales, EMC Corp., 1981.
Big Cats, EMC Corp., 1981.
Bears, EMC Corp., 1981.
Snakes, EMC Corp., 1981.
Dolphins, EMC Corp., 1981.
Silly Quizzes, Scholastic Book Services, 1981.
Strike Two, Children's Press, 1981.
(With Anique Taylor) *What to Do When You're Bored,* Simon & Schuster (New York City), 1982.
Manage Your Own Baseball Team: Make the Playoffs! Blues vs. Sharks, Wanderer Books (New York City), 1983.
Coach Your Own Football Team: Make It to the Superbowl! Panthers vs. Grizzlies, Wanderer Books, 1983.
ESP McGee to the Rescue, Avon (New York City), 1984.
Amazing Rescues, illustrated by Marshall H. Peck III, Random House (New York City), 1992.
The Boy Who Knew Too Much, Random House, 1993.
The Silent Hero, Random House, 1994.

Also author of *How Many Nerds Does It Take to Screw in a Lightbulb?, Danger in Eagle Park,* and *The Great Talking Contest,* all Scholastic Book Services, and other fiction and educational books for children. Contributor to children's magazines, including *Sprint* and *Scholastic Science Monthly.*

PLAYS

Mad Dog (one-act comedy), produced at Playwrights Horizons, 1976.
Until the Last Christian Has Been Eaten (series of one-acts), produced at Playwrights Horizons, October, 1977.
Bless Me, Father, for I Have Sinned (three-act comedy), produced Off-Broadway at Phoenix Theatre, November, 1980.

OTHER

(With Vincent Sardi) *Sardi's Bar Guide,* Ballantine (New York City), 1988.

Also author of television scripts *Who Killed Susie Smith?* (juvenile documentary), televised by American Broadcasting Company; *The Animal Snatchers* (juvenile), televised by National Broadcasting Company; *Flakes* (comedy pilot), released by Videotape Network and Universal Pictures Television; and *The ABC's of Love and Sex* (comedy special), released by Home Box Office. Writer for radio programs *Hour Times* and *All Things Considered;* animator for *Teenage Mutant Ninja Turtles, Mario Brothers,* and other shows; writer for advertising and promotional films and other audiovisual productions. Contributing editor of *Attenzione,* 1980-82.

WORK IN PROGRESS: A children's book about the Wright Brothers; a theatre piece; a collaboration with Martha Stevens about the westward movement.*

*   *   *

SHERWIN, Byron L(ee) 1946-

PERSONAL: Born February 18, 1946, in New York, NY; son of Sidney (an attorney) and Jean (an accountant; maiden name, Rabinowitz) Sherwin; married Judith Rita Schwartz (an attorney), December 24, 1972; children: Jason Samuel. *Education:* Columbia University, B.S., 1966; Jewish Theological Seminary, B.H.L., 1966, M.H.L., 1968, Rabbi, 1970; New York University, M.A., 1969; University of Chicago, Ph.D., 1978. *Politics:* Republican. *Avocational interests:* Cooking.

ADDRESSES: Home—6702 North Sheridan Rd., Chicago, IL 60626. *Office*—Spertus College of Judaica, 618 South Michigan Ave., Chicago, IL 60605.

CAREER: Spertus College of Judaica, Chicago, IL, assistant professor of Jewish religious thought, 1970-74, associate professor of Jewish philosophy and mysticism, 1974-78, professor of Jewish theology and mysticism, 1978—; vice president for academic affairs, 1984—. Visiting professor at Mundelein College, 1974-82. Director of holocaust studies project for National Endowment for the Humanities, 1976-78.

MEMBER: Rabbinical Assembly of America, American Academy of Religion, American Association of University Professors, Religious Education Association, Society for Business Ethics.

WRITINGS:

(With Samuel H. Dresner) *Judaism: The Way of Sanctification,* United Synagogue (New York City), 1978.
Abraham Joshua Heschel, John Knox (Atlanta), 1979.
(Editor with Susan G. Ament) *Encountering the Holocaust: An Interdisciplinary Survey,* Impact Press (Chicago), 1979.

Garden of the Generations, Spertus College Press (Chicago), 1981.

Jerzy Kosinski: Literary Alarmclock, Cabala Press (Chicago), 1982.

Mystical Theology and Social Dissent: The Life and Works of Judah Loew of Prague, Fairleigh Dickinson University Press (East Brunswick, NJ), 1982.

The Golem Legend: Origins and Implications, University Press of America (Lanham, MD), 1985.

Contexts and Content: Higher Jewish Education in the United States, Spertus College Press, 1987.

Thank God: Prayers of Jesus and Christians Together, Litergy Training Publications, 1989.

In Partnership with God: Contemporary Jewish Law and Ethics, Syacuse University Press, 1990.

(With Harold Kasimow) *No Religion Is an Island,* Orbis, 1991.

Toward a Jewish Theology, Edwin Mellen (Lewiston, NY), 1992.

(With Seymour J. Cohen) *How to Be a Jew: Ethical Teaching of Judaism,* Jason Aronson (New York City), 1992.

(In Polish) *The Spiritual Heritage of Polish Jews,* [Warsaw], 1995.

WORK IN PROGRESS: A book on the meaning of life.

SIDELIGHTS: Byron L. Sherwin told *CA:* "My writing and research are motivated by a desire to discover who I am by investigating where I have come from—my historical and spiritual roots.

"*Jerzy Kosinski: Literary Alarmclock*—is an attempt to extract a comprehensive philosophy of life from his work. It also includes a biographical chapter. The subtitle, 'Literary Alarmclock,' indicates the notion that through his literary works Kosinski is trying to wake up his readers both to the precarious and to the marvelous nature of human existence. My work on Kosinski grew out of a longtime personal and academic involvement with the holocaust and with its implications for contemporary existence, as well as out of a friendship with Kosinski.

"Judah Loew of Prague was a leading Jewish mystic and communal leader of the sixteenth century. He lived in Bohemia, Moravia, and Poland. In legend he is known as the creator of the golem, an artificial human being. My book *Mystical Theology and Social Dissent: The Life and Works of Judah Loew of Prague* is the first attempt to give a comprehensive and systematic presentation of his life, thoughts, and ideas.

"*The Golem Legend: Origins and Implications* deals with the history of the legend of the golem, the creation of artificial life—particularly artificial life through magical means. It also considers the legal and moral implications of the golem legend and discusses issues such as bioengineering, gene-splicing, and artificial intelligence.

"*How to Be a Jew: Ethical Teachings of Judaism* does not express my own personal views. The book's approach is conceptual and historical. The first two chapters feature the nature of Jewish religious ethics and the nature of Jewish ethical literature, particularly that of the medieval period. The bulk of the work discusses fifteen values and issues in Jewish ethics, with excerpts from classical Jewish ethical literature—which again are derived mostly from the medieval period. These values include love, parenting, charity, repentance, and sexual ethics."

BIOGRAPHICAL/CRITICAL SOURCES:

PERIODICALS

American Literature, October, 1982.
Choice, June, 1980; November, 1982.
London Review of Books, January 20, 1983.
Religious Studies Review, October, 1980; January, 1981.
Times Literary Supplement, November 18, 1983.
World Literature Today, autumn, 1982.

*   *   *

SHIRREFFS, Gordon D(onald) 1914- (Gordon Donalds, Jackson Flynn, Stewart Gordon)

PERSONAL: Born January 15, 1914, in Chicago, IL; son of George and Rose (maiden name, Warden) Shirreffs; married Alice Johanna Gutwein, February 8, 1941; children: Carole Alice, Brian Allen. *Education:* Attended Northwestern University, 1946-49; Armed Forces Information School, Carlisle Barracks, PA, graduate, 1948; California State University, Northridge, B.A., 1967, M.A., 1973. *Avocational interests:* Arms collecting, model making, marksmanship (pistol, rifle, and bow), fishing, hunting, travel, Southwest legends, and sea lore.

ADDRESSES: Home and office—17427 San Jose St., Granada Hills, CA 91344. *Agent*—Hank Stine, Forrest J. Ackerman Agency, 2495 Glendower Avenue, Hollywood, CA 90027.

CAREER: Union Tank Car Co., Chicago, IL, clerk, 1935-40, 1946; Brown & Bigelow, Chicago, salesman, 1946-47; Shirreffs Gadgets and Toys, Chicago, owner, 1948-52; professional writer, 1952—. *Military service:* U.S. Army, 1940-45, 1948; became captain.

MEMBER: Authors Guild, Authors League of America, Veterans of Foreign Wars, Disabled American Veterans, National Rifle Association, Western Writers of America.

AWARDS, HONORS: Commonwealth Club of California Silver Medal Award, 1962, for *The Gray Sea Raiders.*

WRITINGS:

The Road to Victory (historical nonfiction), Yale Press, 1946.

Rio Bravo, Gold Medal Books (New York City), 1956.

Code of the Gun, Crest Books (New York City), 1956.

(Under pseudonym Gordon Donalds) *Arizona Justice,* Avalon, 1956.

Range Rebel, Pyramid Books, 1956.

Fort Vengeance, Popular Library, 1957.

(Under pseudonym Stewart Gordon) *Gunswift,* Avalon, 1957.

Bugles on the Prairie, Gold Medal Books, 1957.

Massacre Creek, Popular Library, 1957.

Son of the Thunder People, Westminster (Philadelphia, PA), 1957.

(Under pseudonym Gordon Donalds) *Top Gun,* Avalon, 1957.

Shadow Valley, Popular Library, 1958.

Ambush on the Mesa, Gold Medal Books, 1958.

Swiftwagon, Westminster, 1958.

Last Train from Gun Hill, Signet Books (New York City), 1958.

The Brave Rifles, Gold Medal Books, 1959.

The Lonely Gun, Avon (New York City), 1959.

Roanoke Raiders, Westminster, 1959.

Fort Suicide, Avon, 1959.

Trail's End, Avalon, 1959.

Shadow of a Gunman, Ace Books (New York City), 1959.

Renegade Lawman, Avon, 1959.

Apache Butte, Ace Books, 1960.

They Met Danger, Whitman, 1960.

The Mosquito Fleet, Chilton (Radnor, PA), 1961.

The Rebel Trumpet, Westminster, 1961.

The Proud Gun, Avon, 1961.

Hangin's Pards, Ace Books, 1961.

Ride a Lone Trail, Ace Books, 1961.

The Gray Sea Raiders, Chilton, 1961.

Powder Boy of the Monitor, Westminster, 1961.

The Valiant Bugles, Signet Books, 1962.

Tumbleweed Trigger, Ace Books, 1962.

The Haunted Treasure of the Espectros, Chilton, 1962.

Voice of the Gun (also see below), Ace Books, 1962.

Rio Desperado (also see below), Ace Books, 1962.

Action Front!, Westminster, 1962.

The Border Guidon, Signet Books, 1962.

Mystery of Lost Canyon, Chilton, 1963.

Slaughter at Broken Bow, Avon, 1963.

The Cold Seas Beyond, Westminster, 1963.

The Secret of the Spanish Desert, Chilton, 1964.

Quicktrigger (also see below), Ace Books, 1964.

Too Tough to Die, Avon, 1964.

The Nevada Gun, World Distributors, 1964.

The Hostile Beaches, Westminster, 1964.

The Hidden Rider of Dark Mountain, Ace Books, 1964.

Blood Justice, Signet Books, 1964.

Gunslingers Three, World Distributors, 1964.

Judas Gun, Gold Medal Books, 1964.

Last Man Alive, Avon, 1964.

Now He Is Legend, Gold Medal Books, 1965.

The Lone Rifle, Signet Books, 1965.

The Enemy Seas, Westminster, 1965.

Barranca, Signet Books, 1965.

The Bolo Battalion, Westminster, 1966.

Southwest Drifter, Gold Medal Books, 1967.

Torpedoes Away, Westminster, 1967.

The Godless Breed, Gold Medal Books, 1968.

Five Graves to Boothill, Avon, 1968, revised edition, 1970.

The Killer Sea, Westminster, 1968.

Mystery of the Lost Cliffdwelling, Prentice-Hall (Englewood Cliffs, NJ), 1968.

Showdown in Sonora, Gold Medal Books, 1969.

Jack of Spades, Dell Books (New York City), 1970.

The Manhunter, Gold Medal Books, 1970.

Brasada, Dell Books, 1972.

Bowman's Kid, Gold Medal Books, 1973.

Mystery of the Haunted Mine, School Book Service, 1973.

(Under pseudonym Jackson Flynn) *Shootout,* Universal Publishing, 1974.

Renegade's Trail, Gold Medal Books, 1974.

The Apache Hunter, Gold Medal Books, 1976.

The Marauders, Gold Medal Books, 1977.

Legend of the Damned, Gold Medal Books, 1977.

Rio Diablo, Ace Books, 1977.

Captain Cutlass, Gold Medal Books, 1978.

Three from the West (contains *Rio Desperado, Quicktrigger,* and *Voice of the Gun*), Ace Books, 1978.

Calgaich the Swordsman, Playboy Press, 1980.

The Untamed Breed, Gold Medal Books, 1981.

Bold Legend, Gold Medal Books, 1982.

Glorieta Pass, Gold Medal Books, 1984.

The Ghost Dancers, Gold Medal Books, 1986.

Hell's Forty Acres (first novel in Dave Hunter/Ash Mawson series), Gold Medal Books, 1987.

Maximilian's Gold (second novel in Dave Hunter/Ash Mawson series), Gold Medal Books, 1988.

The Walking Sands (third novel in Dave Hunter/Ash Mawson series), Gold Medal Books, 1990.

The Devil's Dance Floor (fourth novel in Dave Hunter/Ash Mawson series), Gold Medal Books, 1994.

Also author of *Silent Reckoning.* Contributor of over 150 short stories and novelettes to periodicals.

ADAPTATIONS: Massacre Creek was filmed as *Galvanized Yankee* for the television series *Playhouse 90; Rio Bravo* was filmed as *Oregon Passage* by Allied Artists, *Silent Reckoning* as *The Lonesome Trail* by Lippert Productions, *Judas Gun* as *A Long Ride from Hell* by B.R.C. Productions, and *Blood Justice* by Jacques Bar Productions.

WORK IN PROGRESS: A continuation of the Dave Hunter/Ash Mawson Series.

SIDELIGHTS: Gordon D. Shirreffs's western novels have been published in Norway, Sweden, Denmark, Finland, Germany, France, Italy, Spain, England, Canada, and Australia. He told *CA:* "As a writer of the historical/saga type of novel, I like to walk the ground and view the scenes depicted in the novel. Some such areas which I covered thoroughly in a search for authenticity have been Sonora, Chihuahua, Durango, and Baja California in Mexico; Scotland, England, and Rome for a fourth-century novel *Calgaich the Swordsman;* four thousand miles by automobile through Utah, Wyoming, Colorado, West Texas, and New Mexico for background material essential to my 'Southwestern Saga' novels *The Untamed Breed, Bold Legend, Glorieta Pass,* and *The Ghost Dancers.* I like to feel that when I write of an area I have been there and know it well. I research many autobiographies, journals and contemporary accounts of the times involved in each novel. I believe that the land itself, the flora and fauna, are background characters in the novel. The weapons used, food and drink, types of housing, customs, etc., are thoroughly researched to give a full three-dimensional effect to the novel. I realize now, after thirty-four years as a full-time professional writer, that no story or novel is just quite what I wanted it to be, and that research is never quite complete. However, this serves to good purpose—it makes one strive just a little harder on the work in progress to achieve that will-o-the-wisp goal."*

*　　　*　　　*

SHULTZ, George P(ratt) 1920-

PERSONAL: Born December 13, 1920, in New York, NY; son of Birl E. (founder and director of New York Stock Exchange Institute) and Margaret Lennox (Pratt) Shultz; married Helena Maria O'Brien (a military nurse), February 16, 1946; children: Margaret Ann, Kathleen Pratt Shultz Jorgensen, Peter Milton, Barbara Lennox Shultz White, Alexander George. *Education:* Princeton University, B.A. (cum laude), 1942; Massachusetts Institute of Technology, Ph.D., 1949. *Religion:* Episcopalian.

ADDRESSES: Office—Hoover Institution, Stanford University, Stanford, CA 94305-6010.

CAREER: Massachusetts Institute of Technology, Cambridge, MA, instructor, 1948-49, assistant professor, 1949-55, associate professor of industrial relations, 1955-57; University of Chicago, Chicago, IL, professor of industrial relations, 1957-68, dean of Graduate Business School, 1962-68; Executive Office of the President, Washington, DC, U.S. secretary of labor, 1969-70, director of Office of Management and the Budget, 1970-72, U.S. secretary of the treasury and assistant to the president, 1972-74; Bechtel Corp., San Francisco, CA, executive vice-president, 1974-75, president and member of board of directors, 1975-82; Executive Office of the President, Washington, DC, U.S. secretary of state, 1982-89; Bechtel Corp., San Francisco, director, 1989—. Hoover Institution, Stanford University, Stanford, CA, Distinguished Fellow, 1989—. Fellow, Center for Advanced Study in the Behavioral Sciences, Palo Alto, CA, 1968; professor, Stanford University, 1974—; Sperry & Hutchinson Lecturer, Tulane University; member of board of visitors, U.S. Naval Academy.

Senior staff economist, President's Council of Economic Advisers, 1955-56; member of steering committee, Study of Collective Bargaining in the Basic Steel Industry, 1960; director, Public Interest in National Labor Policy, 1961; co-chair, Automation Fund Committee, 1962-68; member of research advisory board, Committee for Economic Development, 1965-57; chair, U.S. Department of Labor Task Force on U.S. Employment Service, 1965-68; member, National Manpower Policy Task Force, 1966-68, and President Nixon's Cost of Living Council and National Commission on Productivity; chair, Council on Economic Policy, 1972-74, and East-West Trade Policy committee, 1973-74; member, U.S. board of governors of International Monetary Fund, International Bank for Reconstruction and Development, Inter-American Development Bank, and Asian Development Bank, 1972-74; member, Foreign Intelligence Advisory Board, 1974—, and Treasury Advisory Committee on Reform of the International Monetary System, 1975—; U.S. representative to General Agreement on Trade and Tariffs (GATT), 1973; member, President's Economic Advisory Board, 1981-82.

Member, Illinois governor's committee on unemployment, 1961-62, and committee on job vacancies, 1963-64; member of board of directors, National Opinion Research Center, 1962-69, Borg-Warner Corp, 1964-69, J. I. Case Corp., 1964-68, General American Transportation Corporation, 1966-69, Stein, Roe & Farnham Stock Fund and Balanced Fund, 1966-69, Morgan Guaranty Trust Co., 1974-81, Sears Roebuck & Co., 1975-80, Alfred P. Sloan Foundation, 1974-80, SRI International, 1979—, Council on Foreign Relations, 1980—, and Dillon, Read & Co., Inc., 1981—; director, General Motors Corporation, 1981-82, 1989—, and G.M. Corporate Advisor's Council, 1989—; director, Boeing Corp., Tandem Computers Inc., and Chevron Corp. Member of arbitration panels. Guest on television programs, including *Issues and Answers. Military service:* U.S. Marine Corps Reserve, active duty, 1942-45; served in Pacific theater; became captain.

MEMBER: American Economic Association, Industrial Relations Research Association (member of executive board, 1963-66; president, 1968), National Academy of Arbitrators, American Association of University Professors.

AWARDS, HONORS: LL.D. from University of Notre Dame, 1969, Loyola University, Chicago, 1972, and University of Pennsylvania, 1973; Sc.D. from University of Rochester and Princeton University, both 1973, Carnegie-Mellon University, 1975, and Baruch College, 1979; Jefferson Award, American Institute for Public Service, 1986, for greatest public service performed by an elected or appointed official; Common Wealth Award, Bank of Delaware, 1989, for distinguished service in government.

WRITINGS:

Pressures on Wage Decisions: A Case Study in the Shoe Industry, Wiley (New York City), 1951.

(With Charles Andrew Myers) *The Dynamics of a Labor Market: A Study of the Impact of Employment Changes on Labor Mobility, Job Satisfaction, and Company and Union Policies,* Prentice-Hall (Englewood Cliffs, NJ), 1951.

(Editor, with John R. Coleman) *Labor Problems: Cases and Readings,* McGraw (New York City), 1953.

(Editor, with Thomas Whisler) *Management Organization and the Computer,* Free Press (New York City), 1960.

(Editor and author of introduction, with Robert Z. Aliber) *Guidelines, Informal Controls, and the Market Place: Policy Choices in a Full Employment Economy,* University of Chicago Press (Chicago), 1966.

(With Arnold R. Weber) *Strategies for the Displaced Worker: Confronting Economic Change,* Harper (New York City), 1966.

(With Albert Rees) *Workers and Wages in an Urban Labor Market,* University of Chicago Press, 1970.

Leaders and Followers in an Age of Ambiguity, New York University Press (New York City), 1975.

(With Kenneth W. Dam) *Economic Policy beyond the Headlines,* Stanford Alumni Association, 1977.

The U.S. and Central America: Implementing the National Bipartisan Commission Report: Report to the President from the Secretary of State, U.S. Department of State (Washington, DC), 1986.

U.S. Policy and the Dynamism of the Pacific; Sharing the Challenges of Success, East-West Center (Honolulu), Pacific Forum, and the Pacific and Asian Affairs Council, 1988.

Turmoil and Triumph: My Years as Secretary of State, Scribner (New York City), 1993.

WORK IN PROGRESS: Another nonfiction book for Scribner, to appear in conjunction with a Public Broadcasting Service program on statecraft.

SIDELIGHTS: When George P. Shultz was sworn in under President Ronald Reagan as the United States's six-

tieth secretary of state, he was the only man ever to have held four cabinet-level posts. After serving Presidents Eisenhower and Kennedy as a consultant, Shultz had entered government service at the cabinet level in 1968, when he was tapped by President Richard Nixon to serve as secretary of labor. During the Nixon years, Shultz would go on to become the first director of the Office of Management and Budget, and then the secretary of the treasury and assistant to the president. This experience, combined with his tenure as a professor of industrial economics and his role in the private sector with the Bechtel Corporation, enabled Shultz to bring a unique understanding of arbitration, politics, and economics to the role of secretary of state under Reagan. His skill at performing the duties of this office earned him the respect of many Washington critics and politicians and, as reported in *Time,* prompted former Secretary of State Henry Kissinger to write in his memoirs, "I met no one in public life for whom I developed greater respect and affection. . . . If I could choose one American to whom I would entrust the nation's fate, it would be George Shultz."

During his early academic career, Shultz focused on labor relations and employment problems. His second published book, *The Dynamics of a Labor Market: A Study of the Impact of Employment Changes on Labor Mobility, Job Satisfaction, and Company and Union Policies,* written with Charles Myers, became a popular text for college courses. In the book, Shultz and Myers argued that outsiders, such as mediators, government agents, and arbitrators, often cause more problems than they solve in labor disputes because they do not understand the issues as well as the parties involved. Notwithstanding that statement, Shultz did act as an arbitrator of labor-management disputes during his academic career, and earned the respect of many businesspeople and union leaders for his skill in doing so.

His experience as a mediator served Shultz well during his eighteen-month tenure as secretary of labor. During this time Shultz dealt with strikes by East Coast longshoremen, workers at General Electric, and postal workers. Shultz's appointment of Elizabeth Duncan Koontz to his high command in the department of labor marked the first major appointment of an African-American in the Nixon administration. It foreshadowed his civil rights concerns, evident in his battle against Jim Crow barriers to jobs, which A. H. Raskin referred to in a *New York Times Magazine* article as Shultz's "biggest concentration point in the Labor Department." This concern led to Shultz's backing of the "Philadelphia Plan," which Raskin describes as a "formula that set numerical goals for bringing blacks and other minorities into jobs on federally financed construction" projects.

Shultz's appointment as the director of the powerful Office of Management and Budget (O.M.B.) and assistant to the president was "greeted with enthusiasm by Federal officials responsible for national economic policy," according to *New York Times* correspondent Eileen Shanahan, because it placed a "man with comprehensive knowledge of economics in a newly created dual position." Raskin called the formation of the O.M.B. "part of the most massive centralization of authority in the White House that has ever been undertaken." In his new position, Shultz quickly became Nixon's "foremost economic consultant," according to James M. Naughton of the *New York Times*. Another *New York Times* writer, Edwin L. Dale Jr., described Shultz as "ideologically a 'free market' man" who favored "such things as flexible exchange rates among currencies and the importance of the money supply as a determinant of economic activity—and against such things as wage and price controls." Shultz's ability to steadily accumulate power while avoiding creating enemies probably helped earn him his appointment as secretary of the treasury in 1972. This appointment was the first time in the history of the office that the post was held by an economist.

Upon his resignation from the Nixon administration in 1974, Shultz was not only unharmed by the Watergate scandal, but had "amassed powers ranging far beyond the duties of a Treasury Secretary. Many in Washington considered the then-53-year-old economist to be almost as powerful as Secretary of State Kissinger," according to *New York Times* correspondent R. W. Apple Jr. He was able to brief reporters on "such disparate subjects as unemployment compensation, trade legislation, devaluation, energy, the budget and minimum wage policy," thus illustrating the "breadth of his responsibility." Apple reported that Shultz's reason for leaving was "because there was 'a tendency to stay too long' in government service." A *New York Times* editorial on the occasion of his resignation hailed Shultz as "a symbol of basic decency in a White House circle shot through with chicanery, intrigue and betrayal of official duty."

After leaving the Nixon administration, Shultz returned to teaching at Stanford University and assumed the presidency of Bechtel Corporation, an international construction company whose projects include the San Francisco and Washington, D.C., subway systems, an industrial metropolis in Saudi Arabia, and more than eighty nuclear power plants around the world. Some members of congress voiced reservations about Shultz's business connections at his confirmation hearings for his appointment as secretary of state in 1982, but his testimony suggested that his work with Bechtel would enable him to bring many assets to his position, including a hands-on knowledge of the international marketplace and good personal relationships

with many world leaders. During his tenure as secretary of state, Shultz became known as a team player on whom President Reagan relied. One high-ranking official was quoted in a 1993 *Newsweek* article as saying: "If Reagan could do it, he'd have George as his vice president."

Among the highlights of Shultz's tenure as secretary of state was "the most dramatic improvement in Soviet-American relations in 40 years," as Ray Moseley reported in the *Chicago Tribune*. Some of his other notable accomplishments included the negotiation of a peace agreement designed to bring independence to the African nation of Namibia, winning concessions from Palestine Liberation Organization (P.L.O.) chair Yasser Arafat that enabled the United States to open a dialogue with the P.L.O., and defending shipping lanes in the Persian Gulf by sending U.S. warships there. He was often the proponent of the use of force and took a hard line against terrorist threats. Yet another enduring legacy Shultz left behind at the State Department was a series of "new regulations regarding the use of polygraphs . . . carefully drawn to protect the rights of employees," according to Don Oberdorfer in the *Washington Post*. *New York Times Magazine* contributor Ronald Steel wrote that Shultz "declared he would resign [as secretary of state] 'the minute in this Government I am told that I'm not trusted,' " thereby getting Reagan to back down from his plan to administer lie-detector tests to officials to prevent news leaks.

Just as Shultz left the Nixon administration unaffected by scandal, so too did he avoid dishonor in the Reagan era, despite the Iran-contra affair that besmirched so many reputations during Reagan's presidency. Steel wrote that during that time, Shultz was "hailed as a paragon of common sense in a gaggle of crazed ideologues and Indiana Jones-style buccaneers. In the sleazy labyrinth of the Iran-contra affair, Shultz has been dubbed Mr. Integrity." Yet Steel did pose the question: "Did Shultz know little 'in detail' about the 1986 arms sale to Teheran because he was deceived, or because he chose not to know?"

Shultz is the author of many nonfiction books, some based directly on his government service. In 1977, he and Kenneth W. Dam coauthored a book that drew on his experience in the Nixon administration. As its title implies, *Economic Policy beyond the Headlines* focuses on economic policy, though Charles Mohr wrote in the *New York Times* that "much of it dwells on Mr. Shultz's more general views about government, policymakers and the nature of United States institutions." Mohr also reported that the book seemed free of "partisanship" and "signs of a Shultz ego. . . . By the standards of most other memoirists . . . Mr. Shultz is most self-effacing." Readers will find that Shultz "believes in the concept of masterly inaction," or "waiting for the lagged effects of actions already initiated to work their way through the market process." This is the reason why "perhaps the two most important words [Shultz] spoke in six years of Government service were: 'Do nothing.' "

In 1993, Shultz published *Turmoil and Triumph: My Years as Secretary of State,* a nearly 1200-page memoir written as part of a two-book contract with Scribner's—a contract that earned the former secretary of state more than two million dollars, according to *Washington Post* contributor David Streitfeld. *Turmoil and Triumph* held the greatest general interest of any of Shultz's publications, as it provided "a firsthand description of what he calls 'life . . . in the cockpit of the free world,' " according to Elaine Sciolino in the *New York Times Book Review.*

The Reagan White House was widely rumored to be rife with backbiting and feuding between its key players, and Shultz's book confirms this. *Newsweek* reviewer Russell Watson stated that the memoirs "describe the Reagan administration as a collection of squabbling warlords, many of them ignorant, dishonest, or blinded by ideology." While admitting that Reagan had "a poor grasp of detail and sometimes an even weaker grip on the truth," Shultz defended his former employer as a man who rose above "the duplicities and mistakes of his advisers" and who was the principal engineer of the U.S. victory in the Cold War. Despite Shultz's support of and praise for Reagan, however, Watson found the book damning to the former president. "The clear implication of Shultz's account is that Reagan . . . lied about Iran-contra—to himself, as well as to the American people. He kept denying he had traded arms for hostages when his administration deliberately did exactly that." Then-Vice President George Bush was also plainly exposed as a liar in Shultz's memoir, according to Watson.

Turmoil and Triumph was praised by *Chicago Tribune Books* reviewer Terry Atlas as "a detailed and troubling account of foreign policy-making during the Reagan years" in which the author "sets out his personal account of history and settles a few scores." Atlas likens the book to a "modern-day version of St. George and the Dragon—with Shultz as the one valiant knight doing battle against a beast of an administration that he fears would destroy his leader and abort a historic opportunity to bring about a safer world." The memoir also revealed the private side of Shultz, which was normally "as well-concealed in public as the Princeton tiger—a memento of his college years—that was said to be tattooed on his behind. He had a doggedness, an utter confidence in his own judgment, and, in the end, a readiness to battle for his ideas." Sciolino judged *Turmoil and Triumph* to be "the most balanced of all the Reagan-era confessions, falling somewhere between Caspar W. Weinberger's panegyric to Mr. Reagan and David A. Stockman's scathing attack. . . . It is also the most comprehensive."

BIOGRAPHICAL/CRITICAL SOURCES:

PERIODICALS

Chicago Tribune, December 25, 1988.
Chicago Tribune Books, May 2, 1993, pp. 3-4.
Los Angeles Times, August 9, 1988.
New York Review of Books, June 10, 1993, pp. 53-58.
New York Times, January 11, 1969, pp. 1, 13; June 12, 1970, pp. 1, 20; May 31, 1971, p. 7; May 21, 1972 pp. 1, 5; March 15, 1974, pp. 1, 13, 32; July 13, 1982, p. 104.
New York Times Book Review, May 16, 1993, pp. 3, 33.
New York Times Magazine, August 23, 1970, pp. 24, 70-72; January 11, 1987, pp. 17-25.
Newsweek, July 5, 1982, pp. 20-21; February 7, 1983, pp. 26-29; May 31, 1993, p. 55.
Time, July 5, 1982, p. 15.
Washington Post, February 3, 1989; March 19, 1989; July 12, 1989.*

*   *   *

SIEGEL, Bernie S(hepard)   1932-

PERSONAL: Born October 14, 1932, in New York, NY; son of Simon B. (a television executive) and Rose (a homemaker; maiden name, Papish) Siegel; married Barbara H. Stern (a teacher, editor and writer), July 11, 1954; children: Jonathan, Jeffrey, Stephen, Carolyn, Keith. *Education:* Colgate University, B.A., 1953; Cornell University, M.D., 1957. *Religion:* Jewish.

ADDRESSES: Home—Woodbridge, CT; and East Orleans, MA. *Office*—61 Ox Bow Ln., Woodbridge, CT 06525.

CAREER: Surgical Associates, New Haven, CT, practitioner of pediatric and general surgery, 1961-89. Founder and director of Exceptional Cancer Patients (ECP; therapy and healing program).

MEMBER: American Holistic Medical Association (president elect, 1988), American Cancer Society, Association for Humanistic Psychology, Association for Transpersonal Psychology, Phi Beta Kappa, Alpha Omega Alpha.

WRITINGS:

Love, Medicine, and Miracles, Harper (New York City), 1986.
Peace, Love and Healing, HarperCollins, 1989.
How to Live between Office Visits, HarperCollins, 1993.

Contributor of articles to newspapers and magazines.

WORK IN PROGRESS: Bible II—Conversations with God.

SIDELIGHTS: Bernie S. Siegel is a Connecticut surgeon who founded Exceptional Cancer Patients (ECP), a support group whose members participate in the healing process. By sharing their fear and anger with each other, members undergo a form of mind-body therapy which, according to Siegel, aids in the healing process. "Getting well is not the only goal," he writes. "Even more important is learning to live without fear, to be at peace with life and ultimately death." Joan Borysenko, writing in her *Los Angeles Times Book Review* critique of *Love, Medicine, and Miracles,* concludes that "Siegel's message distills down to one that the head may question, but in which the heart delights, 'The plain truth is: Love heals.' "

BIOGRAPHICAL/CRITICAL SOURCES:

PERIODICALS

Chicago Tribune, November 1, 1987.
Los Angeles Times Book Review, May 18, 1986; August 31, 1986.

*   *   *

SIMMONS, J(oseph) Edgar (Jr.)   1921-1979

PERSONAL: Born May 28, 1921, in Natchez, MS; son of Joseph Edgar and Hazel Dorothy (Clark) Simmons; married Kathleen Floyd, January 28, 1954; children: Joseph Edgar III (Jes), Edward Floyd. *Education:* Attended Copiah-Lincoln Junior College, 1939-41; Columbia University, B.S., 1947, M.A., 1948; Sorbonne, University of Paris, additional study in modern literature, 1953-54.

CAREER: DePauw University, Greencastle, IN, instructor in English, 1948-50; *Irish Press,* Dublin, Ireland, columnist, 1954-55; College of William and Mary, Williamsburg, VA, assistant professor of English, 1955-57; *New Orleans Times Picayune,* editorial writer, summer, 1956; *Natchez Times,* Natchez, MS, columnist, telegraph editor, editor, and managing editor, 1957-59; Southern Illinois University, Carbondale, lecturer in English, 1963-64; Mississippi College, Clinton, assistant professor of English, 1964-66; University of Texas at El Paso, assistant professor of creative writing, 1966-70; freelance writer, 1971-79. Past member of board of directors, Hinds County (MS) Mental Health Association. *Military service:* U.S. Army Air Forces, 1942-45.

AWARDS, HONORS: Bellamann Award for Poetry, 1964; Texas Institute of Letters Award, 1968, for *Driving to Biloxi;* elected to Literary Hall of Fame, Copiah-Lincoln Junior College (Wesson, MS), 1983.

WRITINGS:

Pocahantas, and Other Poems, Virginia Gazette, 1957.

Driving to Biloxi (poetry), Louisiana State University Press (Baton Rouge), 1968.

Contributor to *New Directions in Prose and Poetry,* edited by James Laughlin, New Directions, 1966; *Southern Writing in the Sixties,* edited by J. W. Corrington and Mary C. Williams, Louisiana State University Press, 1967; *Red Clay Reader 4,* edited by C. Whisnant, Southern Review, 1967; *Poems Southwest,* edited by A. Wilber Stevens, Prescott College Press, 1968; *New Directions,* Volume 20, 1968; *Doors into Poetry,* edited by Chad Walsh, Prentice-Hall (Englewood Cliffs, NJ), 1969; *New Southern Poets,* edited by Guy Owen, University of North Carolina Press (Chapel Hill), 1975; *Traveling America with Today's Poets,* edited by David Kherdian, Macmillan (New York City), 1977; *Contemporary Southern Poetry,* edited by Owen and M. Williams, Louisiana State University Press, 1979; *An Anthology of Mississippi Writers,* edited by Noel E. Polk and James R. Scafidel, University Press of Mississippi (Jackson), 1979; and *Osiris at the Roller Derby,* foreword by James Dickey, Cedarshouse Press, 1983. Contributor to periodicals, including *Yale Review, Nation, New Republic, Harper's, New York Times Book Review, Commonweal,* and *Prairie Schooner.*

SIDELIGHTS: J. Edgar Simmons's three-year sojourn in Europe in the 1950s included visits to "the homes and the haunts of the poets" in England and Ireland. He once told *CA* that numerous individuals influenced his life and poetry: Carl Jung (in particular, his principle of "individuation"), John Crowe Ransom, Alfred North Whitehead, Paul Valery, Ortega y Gasset, the existentialists, the moderns in aesthetics, Ernst Cassirer, Jacques Maritain, Erich Neumann, Wallace Stevens, and James Dickey.*

[Date of death provided by son, Jes Simmons.]

*   *   *

SIMON, Herbert A(lexander)   1916-

PERSONAL: Born June 15, 1916, in Milwaukee, WI; son of Arthur (an electrical engineer) and Edna (a pianist; maiden name, Merkel) Simon; married Dorothea Isobel Pye (an educational psychologist), December 25, 1937; children: Katherine Simon Frank, Peter Arthur, Barbara Simon Bender. *Education:* University of Chicago, B.A., 1936, Ph.D., 1943. *Politics:* Democrat. *Religion:* Unitarian. *Avocational interests:* Painting, playing the piano, walking, traveling, learning foreign languages.

ADDRESSES: Home—5818 Northumberland St., Pittsburgh, PA 15217. *Office*—Department of Psychology, Carnegie-Mellon University, Pittsburgh, PA 15213.

CAREER: International City Managers' Association, Chicago, IL, staff member and assistant editor of *Public*

Management and *Municipal Year Book,* 1936-39; University of California, Bureau of Public Administration, Berkeley, director of administrative measurement studies, 1939-42; Illinois Institute of Technology, Chicago, 1942-49, began as assistant professor, became professor of political science, 1947-49, chair of department of political and social science, 1946-49; Carnegie Institute of Technology (now Carnegie-Mellon University), Pittsburgh, PA, professor of administration, 1949-62, professor of administration and psychology, 1962-65, Richard King Mellon University Professor of Computer Science and Psychology, 1965—, chair of department of industrial management, 1949-59, associate dean of Graduate School of Industrial Administration, 1957-73.

Ford Distinguished Visiting Professor, New York University, 1960; distinguished lecturer, Princeton University, Northwestern University, Massachusetts Institute of Technology, Harvard University, University of Michigan, University of California, Berkeley, Bocconi University (Milan, Italy), and Stanford University; honorary professor, Tianjian University, 1980, Beijing University, 1986, and Institute of Psychology of the Chinese Academy of Sciences, 1986. Acting director of Management Engineering Branch and consultant, U.S. Economic Cooperation Administration, 1948; chair of board of directors, Social Science Research Council, 1961-65; chair, Division of Behavioral Sciences, National Research Council, 1967-69; member, President's Science Advisory Committee, 1968-72; trustee, Carnegie-Mellon University, 1972-92, Buhl Science Center, Pittsburgh, 1985-86, and Carnegie Institute of Pittsburgh, 1987—. Lecturer and national speaker. Consultant to several agencies and organizations, including Cowles Commission for Research on Economics, 1947-60, and Research and National Development (RAND) Corp., 1952-70.

MEMBER: Chinese Academy of Sciences, Yugoslav Academy of Sciences, Econometric Society (fellow), American Association for the Advancement of Science (fellow), American Academy of Arts and Sciences (fellow), American Economic Association (distinguished fellow), American Psychological Association (fellow), American Psychological Society (William James Fellow), Association for Computing Machinery (fellow), American Sociological Association (fellow), National Academy of Sciences (member of council, 1978-81, 1983-86), Institute of Management Sciences (vice president, 1954), American Philosophical Society, American Political Science Association, American Association of University Professors, Operations Research Society of America, Psychonomic Society, Phi Beta Kappa, Sigma Xi, University Club (Pittsburgh), Cosmos Club (Washington, DC).

AWARDS, HONORS: Administrator's Award, American College of Hospital Administrators, 1958; Distinguished

Scientific Contributions Award, 1969, and Gold Medal Award in Psychology, 1988, both from American Psychological Association; Turing Award (co-recipient with research collaborator Allen Newell), Association for Computing Machinery, 1975; Nobel Prize in Economics, 1978; James Madison Award, American Political Science Association, 1984; National Medal of Science, 1986, for work in the behavioral sciences; John Von Neumann Theory Prize, Operations Research Society of America and Institute of Management Science, 1988; Lifetime Contribution Award, 1993; Research Excellence Award, International Joint Conference on Artificial Intelligence, 1995; Dwight Waldo Award, American Society for Public Administration, 1995.

D.Sc., Yale University, 1963, Case Institute of Technology (now Case Western Reserve University), 1963, Marquette University, 1981, Columbia University, 1983, Gustavus Adolphus University, 1984, Duquesne University, 1988, Illinois Institute of Technology, 1988, Michigan Institute of Technology, 1988, and Carnegie-Mellon University, 1990; LL.D., University of Chicago, 1964, McGill University, 1971, University of Michigan, 1978, University of Pittsburgh, 1979, Universite Paul-Valery (Montpelier), 1984, and Harvard University, 1990; Fil.Dr., Lund University, 1967; Dr.Econ.Sci., Erasmus University (Rotterdam), 1974; Dr.Polit.Sci., University of Padua, 1988, Dr. Psychol., University of Rome, 1993.

WRITINGS:

(With C. E. Ridley) *Measuring Municipal Activities,* International City Managers' Association (Chicago, IL, and Washington, DC), 1938, 2nd edition, 1943.

(With W. R. Divine, W. W. Cooper, and M. Chernin) *Determining Work Loads for Professional Staff in a Public Welfare Agency,* Bureau of Public Administration, University of California (Berkeley), 1941.

Fiscal Aspects of Metropolitan Consolidation, Bureau of Public Administration, University of California, 1943.

(With R. W. Shephard and F. W. Sharp) *Fire Losses and Fire Risks,* Bureau of Public Administration, University of California, 1943.

(With others) *Technique of Municipal Administration,* 3rd edition, International City Managers' Association, 1947.

Administrative Behavior, Macmillan (New York City), 1947, 3rd edition, Free Press (New York City), 1976.

(Editor) *Local Planning Administration,* revised edition, International City Managers' Association, 1948.

(With Donald W. Smithburg and Victor A. Thompson) *Public Administration,* Knopf (New York City), 1950, reprinted with new introduction, Transaction Books (New Brunswick, NJ), 1991.

(With others) *Fundamental Research in Administration,* Carnegie Institute of Technology Press (Pittsburgh, PA), 1953.

(With C. Kozmetsky, H. Guetzkow, and G. Tyndall) *Centralization vs. Decentralization in Organizing the Controller's Department,* Controllership Foundation, 1954.

Models of Man, Wiley (New York City), 1958, reprinted as *Models of Man, Social and Rational: Mathematical Essays on Rational Human Behavior in a Social Setting,* Garland Publishing (New York City), 1987.

(With James G. March) *Organizations,* Wiley, 1958, 2nd edition (with Guetzkow), Blackwell (Cambridge, MA), 1993.

(With C. C. Holt, F. Modigliani, and J. Muth) *Planning Production, Inventories, and Work Force,* Prentice-Hall (Englewood Cliffs, NJ), 1960.

The New Science of Management Decision, Harper (New York City), 1960, revised edition, Prentice-Hall, 1977.

(Author of foreword) Harold Borko, editor, *Computer Applications in the Behavioral Sciences,* Prentice-Hall, 1962.

(Author of foreword) Timothy W. Costello and Sheldon S. Zalkind, *Psychology in Administration: A Research Orientation,* Prentice-Hall, 1963.

The Shape of Automation, Harper, 1965.

The Sciences of the Artificial, MIT Press (Cambridge, MA), 1969, 2nd edition, 1981.

(With Allen Newell) *Human Problem Solving,* Prentice-Hall, 1972.

(Editor and contributor with L. Siklossy) *Representation and Meaning: Experiments with Information Processing,* Prentice-Hall, 1972.

Models of Discovery, and Other Topics in the Methods of Science, D. Reidel (Dordrecht, Netherlands), 1978, Kluwer Academic (Hingham, MA), 1979.

Models of Thought, Yale University Press (New Haven, CT), Volume 1, 1979, Volume 2, 1989.

Models of Bounded Rationality, and Other Topics in Economics, two volumes, MIT Press, 1982.

Reason in Human Affairs, Stanford University Press (Stanford, CA), 1983.

(With K. Anders Ericsson) *Protocol Analysis: Verbal Reports as Data,* MIT Press, 1984, revised edition, 1993.

(With Patrick Langley, Gary L. Bradshaw, and Jan M. Zytkow) *Scientific Discovery: Computational Explorations of the Creative Processes,* MIT Press, 1987.

Models of My Life (autobiography), Basic Books (New York City), 1991.

(Editor with Ricardon Viale) Massimo Edigi and Robin Marris, *Economics, Bounded Rationality, and the Cognitive Revolution,* E. Elgar Publishing Co. (Brookfield, VT), 1992.

Also author, with Y. Ijiri, of *Skew Distributions and the Sizes of Business Firms,* 1977, and, with A. Ando and F. Fisher, of *Essays on the Structure of Social Science Models.* Contributor to numerous books, including *Research Frontiers in Politics and Government,* Brookings Institution (Washington, DC), 1955; *Management Organization and the Computer,* edited by Schultz and Whisler, Free Press of Glencoe (New York City), 1960; *Computer Augmentation of Human Reasoning,* edited by M. A. Sass and W. D. Wilkinson, Spartan Books, 1965; *Formal Representation of Human Judgment,* edited by Kleinmuntz, Wiley, 1968; and *Visual Information Processing,* edited by W. R. Close, Academic Press, 1973. Also contributor to published symposia, yearbooks, and conference proceedings. Contributor of more than eight hundred papers to periodicals, including *Public Management, British Journal of Psychology, Science, Management Science, Hospital Administration, Naval War College Review, Artificial Intelligence, Philosophy of Science,* and *Connaissance de l'Homme.*

SIDELIGHTS: "As much as any one person, Herbert A. Simon has shaped the intellectual agenda of the human and social sciences in the second half of the 20th century," asserts Sherry Turkle in the *New York Times Book Review.* A pioneer in the field of artificial intelligence (the use of computer programs to solve problems by simulating thinking), Simon won the 1978 Nobel Prize in Economics for research he conducted during the 1940s and 1950s on the decision-making process within organizations. "Because he has managed to blend genius with personal openness and graciousness, Simon's influence resonates across all the social sciences," writes Peter Gorner in the *Chicago Tribune.* In addition to economics and computer science, the Nobel laureate's other areas of specialization include psychology, political science, and applied mathematics.

Simon's Nobel Prize-winning work in economics involved examining the motivations behind the decision-making processes of business professionals. In his research, Simon discovered that rules of formal logic don't generally apply to human decision-making. As outlined in such books as *Administrative Behavior* and *Organizations,* Simon's findings, which include the necessary consideration of psychological factors that earlier economists had typically ignored, place him at odds with traditional economists. While classical economists believe that humans always act to maximize profits, Simon's research revealed that business executives, confronted with myriad choices and a limited amount of accurate information on which to base decisions, most often reject the risky, yet potentially more profitable solution and opt instead for a safer alternative which will produce acceptable, if not spectacular, results—a theory he describes as "bounded rationality." As Gorner explains in the *Chicago Tribune,* "The businessman, thus, makes decisions from a simple picture of the situation that takes into account just a few factors that he regards as most relevant and crucial. It is impossible to learn enough information to aim for maximum profits, and be able to automatically adjust to changing circumstances, as the classical economists describe business behavior. Instead, 'Administrative Man,' as Simon calls him, does the best he can and tries for 'satisfactory' profits, with sometimes unpredictable results." Gorner adds, "This idea of human beings as creatures striving to be rational while equipped with limited brainpower in a chaotic world of limited information is vintage Simon." Within his theory of bounded rationality, Simon defines this conduct as "satisficing"—that is, behavior that considers only those solutions that will satisfy reasonable goals with as few complications as possible.

Prior to his tenure at Carnegie Institute of Technology (now known as Carnegie-Mellon University) in 1949, Simon spent several years using applied mathematics in the field of public administration. His work in economics led him into numerous areas of study, particularly little-known fields still in their infancy. Constance Holden comments in *Psychology Today* that Simon "was involved in the intellectual ferment that surrounded the beginnings of disciplines such as operations research, management science, game theory, statistical decision theory and the field of cybernetics."

Since the mid-1950s, however, Simon has devoted less time to economic theory and more time to the creation of artificial intelligence through computer technology. By programming a computer to simulate human reasoning and record the steps it takes to reach a particular decision, Simon and his research partner Allen Newell believe they can not only gain insights into the thought process itself but also teach people to think more logically, quickly, and efficiently. "The birth date of AI [artificial intelligence] and cognitive simulation could well be set in 1955, when Simon and Newell developed the first AI computer program, called Logic Theorist," claims Holden, adding, "With this program, and later with one called General Problem Solver, Newell and Simon were able to show that computers could do something that looked like independent thinking: making judgments, millisecond by millisecond, about what data are relevant and which rules to follow." In the *New York Times Book Review*, Turkle reports Simon's initial reaction to the breakthrough magnitude of that first computer program which proved mathematical theorems by simulating logical thought: "Mr. Simon celebrated the achievement by walking into class in January [1956] and announcing to his students, 'Over the Christmas holiday, Al Newell and I invented a thinking machine.'" Simon's subsequent research and developments—including programming computers to play chess, distinguish between geometrical shapes, and even create

abstract art designs—have kept him on the cutting edge in the field of artificial intelligence.

In Simon's autobiography, *Models of My Life,* "artificial intelligence appears not only as a technical discipline but also, like psychoanalysis, as a structure for self-reflection," observes Turkle in the *New York Times Book Review.* She continues that Simon "sees himself as a pioneer, inventor and missionary, whose job is to present artificial intelligence in as sharp and clear a form as possible. . . . Artificial intelligence is the expression of Herbert Simon the economist and Herbert Simon the man." He applies the same measurement tools to the examination of his life as he does to his research, concludes Turkle: "In his autobiography, he explores the meaning of intimate experiences through the formal propositions that might hold them together."

But Simon has not concentrated solely on research in the decision-making process and artificial intelligence. He has taught graduate level courses in psychology, for example, and in 1977 he took over a freshman history course simply because he wanted to learn about the French Revolution. Yet as Simon indicates to *New York Times* reporter Jonathan Williams, "The fact that I've been involved in a number of disciplines results from the fact that decision making is pretty central to psychology, economics, political science and administration. . . . All this business about my wandering here and there isn't true. I've been working on the same problem all my life." His accomplishments in these disciplines, as well as his leisure time interest in such activities as learning foreign languages, playing the piano, sketching, and painting, make him unusual in this age of specialization—"a thinker of true Nobel Prize dimensions," describes Donald Michie in the *Times Literary Supplement.* As Gorner remarks in the *Chicago Tribune,* "In the view of economist Richard Cyert, the president of Carnegie-Mellon: 'He is the one man in the world who comes closest to the idea of Aristotle or a Renaissance man.'"

Simon told *CA:* "My research career has been devoted to understanding human decision-making and problem-solving processes. The pursuit of this goal has led me into the fields of political science, economics, cognitive psychology, computer science, and philosophy of science, among others."

BIOGRAPHICAL/CRITICAL SOURCES:

BOOKS

Baars, Bernard J., *The Cognitive Revolution in Psychology,* Guilford (New York City), 1985.

Klahr, David, and Kenneth Kotovsky, editors, *Complex Information Processing: The Impact of Herbert A. Simon,* Lawrence Erlbaum (Hillsdale, NJ), 1989.

Lindzey, Gardner, editor, *A History of Psychology in Autobiography,* Volume 7, W. H. Freeman (New York City), 1980.

McCorduck, Pamela, *Machines Who Think,* W. H. Freeman, 1979.

Notable 20th-Century Scientists, Gale (Detroit, MI), 1995.

Simon, Herbert A., *Administrative Behavior,* Macmillan (New York City), 1947, 3rd edition, Free Press (New York City), 1976.

Simon, Herbert A., *Models of My Life,* Basic Books (New York City), 1991.

PERIODICALS

Business Week, December 5, 1970.
Chicago Tribune, October 27, 1986.
Newsweek, October 30, 1978.
New York Times, November 26, 1978.
New York Times Book Review, March 17, 1991, pp. 1, 28-29; June 9, 1991, p. 36.
People, January 15, 1979.
Psychology Today, October, 1986, pp. 55-60.
Saturday Evening Post, May 4, 1968.
Time, October 30, 1978.
Times Literary Supplement, August 22, 1980.

—*Sketch by Michaela Swart Wilson*

*   *   *

SINGER, J(oel) David   1925-

PERSONAL: Born December 7, 1925, in Brooklyn, NY; son of Morris L. (a businessman) and Anne (Newman) Singer; married Sara Eleanor Green, June 22, 1957 (divorced, 1979); children: Kathryn Louise, Eleanor Anne. *Education:* Duke University, B.A., 1946; New York University, Ph.D., 1956.

ADDRESSES: Home—1042 South Maple Rd., Ann Arbor, MI 48103. *Office*—Department of Political Science, University of Michigan, Ann Arbor, MI 49109.

CAREER: Employed at Ken Classics Manufacturing Co., New York City, 1946-51; Vassar College, Poughkeepsie, NY, instructor, 1955-57; University of Michigan, Ann Arbor, assistant professor of political science, 1958-60; U.S. Naval War College, Newport, RI, resident consultant, 1960; University of Michigan, senior scientist, Mental Health Research Institute, 1960-83, associate professor, 1964-65, professor of political science, 1965—, coordinator, world politics program, 1969-75, 1979-90. Visiting fellow, Harvard University, 1957-58; visiting professor, University of Oslo and Institute for Social Research, 1963-64, 1990, Carnegie Endowment for International Peace and Graduate Institute of International Studies (Geneva), 1967-68, ZUMA and University of Mannheim (West Germany), 1976, Graduate Institute of International Studies, Geneva, 1983-84, and Netherlands Institute for Advanced Study, 1984. Consultant to Institute for Defense Analyses, Bendix Systems Division, Historical Evaluation and Research Organization, and several U.S. departments and agencies. *Military service:* U.S. Navy, 1943-46, 1951-53.

MEMBER: International Political Science Association (chair, Conflict and Peace Research Committee, 1974-89), International Studies Association (president, 1985-86), International Society of Political Psychology, International Society for Research on Aggression, Social Science History Association, Peace Science Society (president, 1972-73), World Association for International Relations, International Peace Research Society, Consortium on Peace Research Education and Development, American Political Science Association (member of Helen Dwight Reid award committee, 1967; Woodrow Wilson award committee chair, chair nominating committee, 1970), American Association for the Advancement of Science, Federation of American Scientists (member of national council, 1991-95), Union of Concerned Scientists, Arms Control Association, Committee for National Security, American Committee on East-West Accord, SANE, World Federalist Association, American Initiatives Project (member of board of advisors), Center for War/Peace Studies (member of board of sponsors).

AWARDS, HONORS: Ford Foundation training grant, 1957-58; Fulbright Research Scholar, Institute of Social Research, Oslo, Norway, 1963-64; Carnegie research grant, 1963-67; National Science Foundation research grant, 1967-76, 1978-83, 1986-89, 1992-94; Guggenheim Foundation research grant, 1978-79; Phoenix Memorial research grant, 1981-82; honorary LL.D, Northwestern University, 1983; World Society Foundation research grant, 1986-88.

WRITINGS:

Financing International Organization: The United Nations Budget Process, Nijhoff, 1961.

Deterrence, Arms Control, and Disarmament: Toward a Synthesis in National Security Policy, Ohio State University Press (Columbus), 1962, second edition, University Press of America (Washington, DC), 1984.

(Editor and contributor) *Human Behavior in International Politics: Contributions from the Social-Psychological Sciences,* Rand McNally (Chicago), 1965.

(Editor and contributor) *Quantitative International Politics: Insights and Evidence,* Free Press (New York City), 1968.

(With Melvin Small) *The Wages of War, 1816-1965: A Statistical Handbook,* Wiley (New York City), 1972.

(With Susan Jones) *Beyond Conjecture in International Politics: Abstracts of Data-Based Research,* F. E. Peacock (Itasa, IL), 1972.

(With Dorothy LaBarr) *The Study of International Politics: A Guide to Sources for the Student, Teacher, and Researcher,* Clio Books (Santa Barbara), 1976.

The Correlates of War I: Research Origins and Rationale, Free Press, 1979.

(With Michael Wallace) *To Augur Well: Early Warning Indicators in World Politics,* Sage Publications (Beverly Hills), 1979.

Explaining War, Sage Publications, 1979.

The Correlates of War II: Testing Some Realpolitik Models, Free Press, 1980.

(With Small) *Resort to Arms: International and Civil War Data, 1816-1980,* Sage Publications, 1982.

(Editor with Richard Stoll) *Quantative Indicators in World Politics: Timely Assurance and Early Warning,* Praeger (New York City), 1984.

(Editor with Small) *International War: An Anthology,* Dorsey (Homewood, IL), 1989.

Models, Methods, and Progress in World Politics: A Peace Research Odyssey, Westview (Boulder), 1990.

(Editor with Paul F. Diehl) *Measuring the Correlates of War,* University of Michigan Press (Ann Arbor), 1990.

(With Brian H. Gibbs) *Empirical Knowledge on World Politics: A Summary of Quantative Research, 1970-1991* Greenwood (Westport, CO), 1993.

Contributor of articles to journals, annuals, and anthologies, including *The Nature of Human Conflict,* edited by Elton McNeil, Prentice-Hall, 1965; *Theory and Research on the Causes of War,* edited by Snyder and Pruitt, Prentice-Hall, 1969; *Social Psychology of Political Life,* edited by Kirkpatrick and Pettit, Duxbury, 1973; *Strategies against Violence,* edited by Israel Charny, Westview, 1978; *From National Development to Global Community,* edited by Merritt and Russett, Allen & Unwin, 1981. Coeditor of special issue of *Journal of Conflict Resolution,* March, 1960. Member of editorial or advisory board of many journals, including *Journal of Conflict Resolution,* 1959—, *Political Science Reviewer,* 1971—, *Conflict Management and Peace Studies,* 1978—, *Etudes Polemologiques,* 1978—, *Aggressive Behavior,* 1982—, *Peace Research,* 1984—, *International Interactions,* 1985—, *International Studies Quarterly,* 1989—.

WORK IN PROGRESS: *Under the Gun: Accounting for International War* and *U.S. Foreign Policy: Substance and Process.*

SIDELIGHTS: J. David Singer wrote *CA:* "In my teaching and research, a major premise is that applying scientific method to the analysis of international affairs will reduce our error rate in making policy and thus reduce the amount of human misery inflicted by misguided government policies in the U.S. and abroad."

*   *   *

SINGER, Milton Borah   1912-1994

PERSONAL: Born July 15, 1912, in Poland; immigrated to the United States in 1920, naturalized citizen, 1921; died of a heart attack, December 5, 1994, in Chicago, IL; son of Julius M. and Esther (Greenberg) Singer; married Helen Goldbaum, October 1, 1935. *Education:* University of Texas, Main (now University of Texas at Austin), B.A., 1934, M.A., 1936; University of Chicago, Ph.D., 1940.

CAREER: University of Chicago, Chicago, IL, member of faculty beginning in 1941, professor of social sciences, 1950-52, Paul Klapper Professor of Social Sciences, 1952-79, professor of anthropology, 1954-79, New Collegiate Division, Civilizational Studies, professor, 1965-72, Paul Klapper Professor of Social Sciences Emeritus, 1979-94, chair of social sciences staff, 1947-52, executive secretary of committee on Asian studies, 1955-67, and chair of committee, 1967-70, chair of civilization studies and member of governing board of New Collegiate Division, 1966-71, Robert Redfield project on the comparative study of civilizations, associate director, 1951-58, director, 1958-61, co-director of South Asia Language and Area Center, 1959-63. Center for Psychosocial Studies, Chicago, IL, consultant, 1979-89, research advisor, 1979-94. Visiting professor of social sciences at University of Puerto Rico, 1949; visiting professor and senior anthropologist at Institute of International Studies, University of California, Berkeley, 1956; fellow of Center for Advanced Studies in the Behavioral Sciences, Stanford, CA, 1957-58, 1965; fellow of American Institute of Indian Studies, 1964; visiting professor at University of Hawaii, 1967, and University of California, San Diego, 1971; distinguished lecturer, American Anthropological Association, 1978.

MEMBER: International Society for the Comparative Study of Civilization (honorary member), American Academy of Arts and Sciences (fellow), American Anthropological Association (fellow), American Institute of Indian Studies (vice president, 1961-64), Association for Asian Studies, Phi Beta Kappa.

AWARDS, HONORS: Quantrell Award for excellence in undergraduate teaching, University of Chicago, 1948; Silver Pen Award for learned publications from the Journal Fund, 1950; Distinguished Scholarship Award, Association for Asian Studies, 1984.

WRITINGS:

(Translator with wife, Helen Singer) A. Gratry, *Logic,* Open Court (LaSalle, IL), 1944.

(With Gerhart Piers) *Shame and Guilt: A Psychoanalytic and a Cultural Study,* W. W. Norton (New York City), 1953, 2nd edition, 1973.

When a Great Tradition Modernizes: An Anthropological Approach to Indian Civilization, Praeger (New York City), 1972.

Man's Glassy Essence: Explorations in Semiotic Anthropology, Indiana University Press (Bloomington, IN), 1984.

(Author of preface) C. Borden, editor, *Contemporary Indian Tradition,* Smithsonian Institution (Washington, DC), 1989.

Semiotics of Cities, Selves, and Cultures: Explorations in Semiotic Anthropology, Mouton de Gruyer (Berlin, Germany), 1991.

EDITOR

Introducing India in Liberal Education: Proceedings of a Conference Held at University of Chicago, May 17, 18, 1957, University of Chicago Press (Chicago, IL), 1957.

(And contributor) *Traditional India: Structure and Change,* American Folklore Society, 1959.

(And contributor) *Kishna: Myths, Rites, and Attitudes,* East-West Center Press (Honolulu, HI), 1966.

(With Bernard S. Cohn, and contributor) *Structure and Change in Indian Society,* Wenner-Gren Foundation for Anthropological Research, 1968.

(And contributor) *Entrepreneurship and Modernization of Occupational Cultures in South Asia,* Duke University Press (Durham, NC), 1973.

Nuclear Policy, Culture and History, Center for International Studies, University of Chicago, 1988.

OTHER

Coeditor of "Comparative Studies of Cultures and Civilizations" series, 1953-58. Contributor to scholarly journals, including *American Anthropologist, American Ethnologist, American Journal of Semiotics, Annals of the American Academy of Political and Social Science, Current Anthropology, Diogenes, Economic Development and Cultural Change, Ethics, Far Eastern Quarterly, History of Religions, Journal of Developing Societies, Journal of Social and Biological Structures,* and *Semiotica.*

WORK IN PROGRESS: "Cultural Change: A Convergence of Innovation and Tradition," in *Theories of Social Change,* edited by D. Bell, forthcoming from Russell-Sage.

BIOGRAPHICAL/CRITICAL SOURCES:

BOOKS

Lee, Benjamin, and Greg Urban, editors, *Semiotics, Self and Society* (festschrift), Mouton de Gruyter, 1989.

OBITUARIES:

PERIODICALS

New York Times, December 9, 1994, p. D20.*

*   *   *

SINGH, Baljit   1929-1980

PERSONAL: Surname rhymes with "ring"; born October 1, 1929, in Budaum, India; immigrated to United States, 1957; naturalized citizen, 1966; died, 1980; son of Sardar Baboo (an architect and teacher) and Kartar (Kaur) Singh; married Barbara Leona Hassler, August 11, 1962; children: Balkrishna and Balram (sons). *Education:* Agra University, B.A., 1951; Aligarh Muslim University, M.A. and Diploma in Foreign Affairs, 1953; University of Pennsylvania, additional study, 1957-58; University of Maryland, College Park, Ph.D., 1961. *Politics:* Democrat. *Religion:* Buddhist. *Avocational interests:* Tennis, reading, gardening, family activities.

ADDRESSES: Home—2400 Tulane Dr., Lansing, MI 48912. *Office*—College of Social Sciences, 205 Berkey Hall, Michigan State University, East Lansing, MI 48824.

CAREER: University of Baroda, Baroda, India, senior lecturer in political science, 1953-55; Indian School of International Studies, New Delhi, India, research fellow, 1955-57; Embassy of India, Washington, DC, research assistant, 1958; Michigan State University, East Lansing, assistant professor of political science, 1961-62; Wayne State University, Detroit, MI, assistant professor of political science, 1962-63; Michigan State University, assistant professor, 1963-65, associate professor, 1965-71, professor of political science, 1971-80, assistant dean, College of Social Sciences, 1967-80. University of Maryland, instructor in government and politics, summer, 1961; Oakland University, visiting professor, summer, 1963. *Military service:* Indian Army, National Cadet Corps, second lieutenant, 1953-55; Indian Army Reserves, 1955-57.

MEMBER: International Studies Association, American Political Science Association, Midwest Political Science Association, Michigan Academy of Science, Arts, and Letters (program chairman, history and political science section, 1966), Pi Sigma Alpha, Delta Phi Epsilon.

AWARDS, HONORS: Ford Foundation fellow at University of Pennsylvania, 1957-58, research grants, 1964, 1965-67, 1971; Asia Foundation travel and study fellow, 1961.

WRITINGS:

(With Ko-Wang Mei) *The Theory and Practice of Modern Guerrilla Warfare,* Asia Publishing House (New York City), 1971.

Indian Foreign Policy: An Analysis, Sindhu (Bombay), 1972, Asia Publishing House, 1975.

Political Stability and Continuity in the Indian States during the Nehru Era, 1947-1964, Asian Studies Center, Michigan State University (East Lansing), 1973.

(With Dhirendra K. Vajpeyi) *Government and Politics in India,* Apt Books (New York City), 1981.

(Editor) *Economics of Indian Education,* Meenakshi Prakashan (Meerut, India), 1983.

REFERENCE BOOKS

India: Government and Politics, Office of World Affairs, Continuing Education Service (East Lansing), 1964.

(With Harold S. Johnson) *International Politics: An Annotated Bibliography,* International Programs, Michigan State University (East Lansing), 1968.

(With Johnson) *International Organization: A Selected Bibliography,* Asian Studies Center, Michigan State University, 1969.

Also contributor to books, including *Political Essays,* edited by D. P. Rastogi, Review Publications, 1968; *Terrorism: Interdisciplinary Perspectives,* edited by Yonah Alexander and S. M. Finger, John Jay Press, 1977; *The Subcontinent in World Politics,* edited by Lawrence Ziring, Praeger, 1978, and *Self-Determination: National, Regional, and Global Dimensions,* edited by Yonah Alexander and Robert Friedlander, Westview, 1980. Also author of numerous monographs on India's political and foreign policy. Contributor of numerous articles, reviews, and bibliographies to professional journals. Appeared on over two dozen radio and television programs dealing with current international affairs and year-end review.

The complete library of Baljit Singh is housed at Albion College, Albion, MI, in the Baljit Singh Memorial Library.*

*   *   *

SKINNER, Knute (Rumsey) 1929-

PERSONAL: Born April 25, 1929, in St. Louis, MO; son of George Rumsey (a salesman) and Lidi (a civil servant; maiden name, Skjoldvig) Skinner; married Jean Pratt, November, 1953 (divorced October, 1954); married Linda Kuhn, March, 1961 (divorced September, 1977); married Edna Faye Kiel, March 25, 1978; children: Frank, Dunstan, Morgan. *Education:* Attended Culver-Stockton College, Canton, MO, 1947-49; Colorado State College (now University of Northern Colorado), A.B., 1951; Middlebury College, M.A., 1954; State University of Iowa (now University of Iowa), Ph.D., 1958.

ADDRESSES: Home—1007 Queen St., Bellingham, WA 98225; and Killaspuglonane, Lahinch, County Clare, Ireland (summer). *Office*—Department of English, Western Washington University, Bellingham, WA 98225.

CAREER: Boise Senior High School, Boise, Idaho, teacher of English, 1951-54; State University of Iowa (now University of Iowa), Iowa City, instructor in English, 1955-56, 1957-58, and 1960-61; Oklahoma College for Women (now University of Science and Arts of Oklahoma), Chickasha, assistant professor of English, 1961-62; Western Washington University, Bellingham, assistant professor, 1971-73, professor of English, 1973—. Poetry editor, Southern Illinois University Press, 1975-76; editor and publisher, *Bellingham Review* and Signpost Press, 1977—. Has given poetry readings at conferences, colleges, universities, and high schools throughout the United States and Ireland.

MEMBER: American Conference for Irish Studies, Washington Poets Association.

AWARDS, HONORS: Huntington Hartford Foundation fellowship, 1961; National Endowment for the Arts fellowship in creative writing, 1975; Millay Colony for the Arts fellowship, 1976.

WRITINGS:

POETRY

Stranger with a Watch, Golden Quill (Francestown, NH), 1965.

A Close Sky over Killaspuglonane, Dolmen Press (Dublin), 1968, 2nd edition, Burton International, 1975.

In Dinosaur Country, Pierian (Ann Arbor, MI), 1969.

The Sorcerers: A Laotian Tale, Goliards Press (Bellingham, WA), 1972.

Hearing of the Hard Times, Northwoods Press (Stafford, VA), 1981.

The Flame Room, Folly Press, 1983.

Selected Poems, Aquila Press (West Midlands, England), 1985.

Learning to Spell 'Zucchini,' Salmon Publishing, 1988.

The Bears and Other Poems, Salmon Publishing, 1991.

What Trudy Knows and Other Poems, Salmon Publishing, 1994.

Contributor of poems to numerous periodicals, including *Ohio Review, Colorado Quarterly, New Republic, New Letters, Mid-American Review,* and *Chicago Review;* contributor of short stories and reviews to *Limbo, Quartet, Midwest, Irish Press, Northwest Review,* and *Hibernia.* Guest editor, *Pyramid,* Number 13, 1973.

WORK IN PROGRESS: The Barrowed Lion and Other Poems.

SIDELIGHTS: Knute Skinner, who divides his time between homes in Bellingham, Washington, and rural Ireland, told *CA* that life in Ireland "exerts a strong influence on my work." He has recorded his poetry for the British Council, for poetry rooms at Harvard, Leeds, Hull and Durham universities, and for radio programs in the United States and Ireland. His poetry is also the subject of two videotapes, one made at the University of Wisconsin—La Crosse and the other at Triton College in Chicago, and of an educational television film made at the State University of New York College at Brockport.

*   *   *

SKUTCH, Alexander F(rank)   1904-

PERSONAL: Born May 20, 1904, in Baltimore, MD; son of Robert Frank (an antiquarian) and Rachel (maiden name, Frank) Skutch; married Pamela Lankester, April 27, 1950; children: Edwin (adopted). *Education:* Johns Hopkins University, A.B., 1925, Ph.D., 1928. *Politics:* None. *Religion:* "Not affiliated with any church."

ADDRESSES: Home—El Quizarra, San Isidro del General, Costa Rica.

CAREER: After receiving doctorate, went to Panama and Honduras on research fellowships from Johns Hopkins University, 1928-30; National Research Council fellow, 1930-31; Johns Hopkins University, Baltimore, MD, instructor in botany, 1931-32; naturalist working independently in Guatemala, 1932-34, Panama, 1935, Costa Rica, 1935—, and Venezuela, 1966; Museo Nacional de Costa Rica, San Jose, curator of plants, 1940; U.S. Department of Agriculture, botanist on rubber survey in Peru, Ecuador, and Colombia, 1940-41; University of Costa Rica, San Jose, professor of ornithology, 1964, 1979. Member of El Quizarra School Board, 1962.

MEMBER: American Ornithologists' Union (life fellow), British Ornithologists' Union (honorary member), Cooper Ornithological Society (honorary member), Wilson Ornithological Society, Asociacion Ornitologica del Plata (corresponding member), Asociacion Ornitologica de Costa Rica (honorary president).

AWARDS, HONORS: Guggenheim fellowship, 1946-47, 1952; Brewster Medal, American Ornithologists' Union, for writings in ornithology, 1950; Aquileo J. Echeverria Award from the government of Costa Rica, 1977, for *Aves de Costa Rica;* testimonial from the Costa Rican Ministry of Culture, Youth, and Sports, 1981, for "the investigation and protection of the flora and fauna of Costa Rica"; Arthur A. Allen Award, Cornell Laboratory of Ornithology, 1983, for "outstanding service to ornithology"; John Burroughs Memorial Association medal, 1983, for *A Naturalist on a Tropical Farm;* medal from the second Congreso Iberoamericano de Ornitologia, 1983; plaque from Coopeagri El General, 1987, for promoting conservation;

plaque from Editorial Costa, 1989, for contributions to Costa Rican culture; Hal Borland Award, *Audubon Magazine,* 1989 for "lasting contribution to the understanding, appreciation, and protection of nature through writing"; plaque from the Community of San Inidro de El General, 1990, for "constant search for equilibrium between man and nature"; plaque from the National Museum of Costa Rica, 1992, for "contributions to the knowledge of the Neotropical avifauna."

WRITINGS:

Life Histories of Central American Birds, illustrated by Don R. Eckelberry, Cooper Ornithological Society, Volume I, 1954, Volume II, 1960, Volume III, 1969.

The Quest of the Divine: An Inquiry into the Source and Goal of Morality and Religion, Meador, 1956.

Life Histories of Central American Highland Birds, Nuttall Ornithological Club (Cambridge, MA), 1967.

The Golden Core of Religion, Holt (New York City), 1970.

A Naturalist in Costa Rica, University of Florida Press, 1971, revised edition, 1992.

Studies of Tropical American Birds, Nuttall Ornithological Club, 1972.

The Life of the Hummingbird, illustrated by Arthur B. Singer, Crown (New York City), 1973.

Parent Birds and Their Young, University of Texas Press (Austin), 1976.

A Bird Watcher's Adventures in Tropical America, illustrated by Dana Gardner, University of Texas Press, 1977.

Aves de Costa Rica, photographs by John S. Dunning, Editorial Costa Rica, 1977.

The Imperative Call: A Naturalist's Quest in Temperate and Tropical America, University Presses of Florida, 1979.

A Naturalist on a Tropical Farm, illustrated by Gardner, University of California Press (Berkeley), 1980.

New Studies of Tropical American Birds, illustrated by Gardner, Nuttall Ornithological Club, 1981.

Birds of Tropical America, illustrated by Gardner, University of Texas Press, 1983.

Nature through Tropical Windows, illustrated by Gardner, University of California Press, 1983.

Life Ascending, University of Texas Press, 1985.

The Life of the Woodpecker, illustrated by Gardner, Cornell University Press (New York City), 1985.

Helpers at Birds' Nests: A Worldwide Survey of Cooperative Breeding and Related Behaviour, illustrated by Gardner, University of Iowa Press (Iowa City), 1987.

A Naturalist Amid Tropical Splendour, illustrated by Gardner, University of Iowa Press, 1987.

Life of the Tanager, illustrated by Gardner, Cornell University Press, 1989.

Birds Asleep, illustrated by John Schmitt, University of Texas Press, 1989.

(With F. Gary Stilen) *A Guide to the Birds of Costa Rica,* illustrated by Gardner, Cornell University Press, 1989.

Life of the Pigeon, illustrated by Gardner, Cornell University Press, 1991.

Origins of Nature's Beauty, illustrated by Gardner, University of Texas Press, 1992.

Contributor to *Smithsonian Institution Annual Report,* 1947. Contributor to *Auk, Ibis, Condor, Wilson Library Bulletin, Animal Kingdom, Nature,* and *Scientific Monthly.*

WORK IN PROGRESS: Continuing research on birds of Costa Rica.

SIDELIGHTS: Alexander F. Skutch is "the dean of neotropical ornithology" as James R. Karr describes him in *Library Journal.* For over fifty years, Skutch has studied the bird life in the Central American country of Costa Rica. Many of his books on the flora and fauna of the tropics combine narrative descriptions with philosophical speculations. In his book *Life Ascending,* a history of evolution, for example, Skutch suggests that through evolution the universe has deliberately created human beings. Robert Paustian, writing in the *Library Journal,* calls the book an "upbeat philosophical argument."

Skutch told *CA:* "I grew up on the outskirts of Baltimore, near fields and woods, and in a house with many books, especially the fine editions that my father loved . . . The private school that I attended was strong on English literature and composition but weak on nature study and science. After entering Johns Hopkins, I took as many scientific courses as I could crowd into my schedule, but I never lost my early interest in literature and writing. In my years as a wandering naturalist with few books to read, I filled rainy afternoons, after bringing my field notes up to date, with writing stories and essays.

"After receiving my Ph.D in botany, I went to Central America for research on the anatomy and physiology of the banana plant, from 1928 to 1930. Here I became deeply interested in the birds. Since little was known about their life histories, I decided that the best use I could make of whatever abilities I had was to study them in-depth. In the depression years no support for this was available, so I paid my way largely by collecting and selling botanical specimens, never birds. After doing this for about eight years, I bought a farm amid still-unspoiled rain forests, in a Costa Rican valley readily accessible only by air. After living alone for nine years, I married the daughter of an English naturalist long established in Costa Rica. We continue to dwell with our son close by a rushing mountain torrent and the tract of old forest that we have preserved.

"I have regarded it a duty to make available to others, in readable form, the results of my studies of nature. In these days when violence, in the human world and the wider animal kingdom, receives so much publicity, I have tried to draw attention to the gentler, more endearing aspects of nature: parental devotion, cooperative breeding in birds, mutual aid, and the reciprocally beneficial interactions of animals and plants. Apart from ornithology and botany, philosophy and religion have been my chief interests. I have tried to develop an optimistic, spiritually sustaining world view consistent with scientific knowledge, and to net an ethic firmly upon this foundation. With the exception of *The Quest of the Divine* and *Life Ascending,* my philosophic writings remain largely unpublished. I am greatly concerned about man's spoilation of nature, and believe that the only sound approach to conservation is through the stabilization of human population. I believe that religions' chief contribution to humanity has been teaching people to care—about their souls or character, their neighbors, and (chiefly by oriental religions) the living creatures around them. To know, appreciate, and preserve all the beautiful and wonderful things our planet contains is, in my opinion, the proper end of humans. A major purpose of my writing has been to promote appreciation of nature, gratitude for the privilege of living in a well-endowed body on a unique planet, and determination to keep it beautiful and fruitful."

BIOGRAPHICAL/CRITICAL SOURCES:

PERIODICALS

Christian Science Monitor, June 4, 1993, p. 10.
Kirkus Reviews, March 15, 1987, p. 462.
Library Journal, June 15, 1985, p. 1424; April 1, 1987, p. 156.
Sierra, September, 1987, p. 94.
Times Literary Supplement, August 14, 1987, p. 885.
Tribune Books (Chicago), December 6, 1987, p. 8.*

*   *   *

SLADE, Bernard
    See NEWBOUND, Bernard Slade

*   *   *

SMITH, Dwight L.   1918-

PERSONAL: Born April 11, 1918, in West Elkton, OH; son of Clarence S. (a minister) and Mary (Barnhart) Smith; married Jane DeLeon, May 5, 1955; children: Gregory B. *Education:* Indiana Central College (now University of Indianapolis), A.B., 1940; Indiana University, A.M., 1941, Ph.D., 1949. *Religion:* Presbyterian.

ADDRESSES: Home—6195 Fairfield Road #12, Oxford, OH 45056. *Office*—Department of History, Miami University, Oxford, OH 45056.

CAREER: Indiana Central College (now University of Indianapolis), Indianapolis, instructor in history, 1942-43; Ohio State University, Columbus, instructor in history, 1949-53; Miami University, Oxford, OH, assistant professor, 1953-56, associate professor, 1956-60, professor of history, 1960-84, professor emeritus, 1984—. Visiting instructor in history, Centre College of Kentucky, 1952; Carnegie Visiting Assistant Professor of History, Columbia University, 1954-55; visiting professor of history, Indiana University, 1962-63, University of Alberta, 1964, Colorado College, 1965, University of British Columbia, 1967, and University of New Mexico, 1968. Presbyterian Church, deacon, 1957-60, elder, 1961-66, 1978-83, 1991—, church historian, 1966-79. *Military service:* U.S. Army Air Corps, 1943-46; became staff sergeant.

MEMBER: American Historical Association, Association for Canadian Studies, Canadian Historical Association, Organization of American Historians, Association for the Bibliography of History (president, 1980-81), American-Indian Ethnohistoric Conference (president, 1955-56), Western History Association (member of council, 1982-85), Ohio Academy of History (president, 1978-79), Ohio Historical Society (research historian, 1950-51), Indiana Central College Alumni Association (member of board of directors, 1964-70; president, 1968-69), Oxford Museum Association (member of board of trustees, 1956-60; president, 1957-58), Friends of the Miami University Library Society (president, 1979-80).

AWARDS, HONORS: Newbery Library fellow, 1952, 1964; Miami University research fellow, 1957, 1959, 1982; Lilly Endowment fellow, 1962; Outstanding Educators of America award recipient, 1971; Institute of Environmental Sciences fellow, 1977; award of merit, American Bibliographical Center, 1980; Samuel Foster Haven fellow, American Antiquarian Society, 1982; Huntington Library fellow, 1983; distinguished service award, Ohio Academy of History, 1985; Litt.D., University of Indianapolis, 1987; distinguished alumnus award, University of Indianapolis, 1988; award of merit, Western History Association, 1993.

WRITINGS:

From Greene Ville to Fallen Timbers, Indiana Historical Society, 1952.
(Editor) *The Western Journals of John May,* Historical and Philosophical Society of Ohio, 1961.

(Editor with C. Gregory Crampton) *The Hoskaninni Papers,* University of Utah Press (Salt Lake City), 1961.
Down the Colorado, University of Oklahoma Press (Norman), 1965.
Western Life in the Stirrups, Caxton Club (Chicago), 1965.
The Photographer and the River, Stagecoach Press, 1967.
(Editor) *John D. Young and the Colorado Gold Rush,* Lakeside Press, 1969.
(Editor with Lloyd W. Garrison) *The American Political Process,* American Bibliographical Center-Clio Press (Santa Barbara, CA), 1972.
Afro-American History: A Bibliography, American Bibliographical Center-Clio Press, 1974, Volume II, 1981.
Indians of the United States and Canada: A Bibliography, American Bibliographical Center-Clio Press, 1974, Volume II, 1983.
Era of the American Revolution, American Bibliographical Center-Clio Press, 1975.
The American and Canadian West, American Bibliographical Center-Clio Press, 1979.
The History of Canada, American Bibliographical Center-Clio Press, 1983.
The War of 1812, Garland Publishing, 1985.
(With C. Gregory Crampton) *The Colorado River Survey,* Howe Brothers (Salt Lake City), 1987.
Survival on a Westward Trek, 1858-59, Ohio University Press (Athens, OH), 1989.

Contributor to many books and professional journals, including *Historical Abstracts* and *America: History and Life.* Book review editor, *Ethnohistory,* 1954-60; editor, *Old Northwest,* 1974-87.

*   *   *

SPINIFEX
See MARTIN, David

*   *   *

SPODEK, Bernard 1931-

PERSONAL: Born September 17, 1931, in Brooklyn, NY; son of David and Esther (Lebenbaum) Spodek; married Prudence Hoy, June 21, 1957; children: Esther Yinling, Jonathan Chou. *Education:* Brooklyn College (now Brooklyn College of the City University of New York), B.A., 1952; Columbia University, M.A., 1955, Ed.D., 1962.

ADDRESSES: Home—1123 West Charles St., Champaign, IL 61820. *Office*—301 Education, University of Illinois, 1310 South Sixth St., Champaign, IL 61820.

CAREER: Beth Hayeled School, New York City, early childhood teacher, 1952-56; elementary school teacher in

New York City public schools, 1956-57; Brooklyn College (now Brooklyn College of the City University of New York), Brooklyn, NY, laboratory school teacher, 1957-60; University of Wisconsin—Milwaukee, assistant professor of elementary education, 1961-65; University of Illinois at Urbana-Champaign, professor of early childhood education, 1965—.

MEMBER: Association for Childhood Education International, National Association for the Education of Young Children (secretary, 1964-68; president, 1976-78), American Educational Research Association, American Association of University Professors.

WRITINGS:

(With Helen Robison) *New Directions in the Kindergarten,* Teachers College Press (New York City), 1965.

(Editor) *Preparing Teachers of Disadvantaged Young Children,* National Association for the Education of Young Children (Washington, DC), 1966.

(With H. G. Morgan and H. J. Shane) *Motivation,* National Education Association (Washington, DC), 1968.

(With others) *Early Childhood Education Today,* Association for Supervision and Curriculum Development (Washington, DC), 1968.

(With others) *A Black Curriculum for Early Childhood Education,* University of Illinois at Urbana-Champaign, 1972, 2nd edition published as *A Black Studies Curriculum for Early Childhood Education,* ERIC Clearinghouse in Early Childhood Education (Urbana, IL), 1976.

Teaching in the Early Years, Prentice-Hall (Englewood Cliffs, NJ), 1972, 3rd edition, 1985.

Early Childhood Education, Prentice-Hall, 1973.

How Should Reading Fit into the Preschool Curriculum?, U. S. Government Printing Office (Washington, DC), 1980.

(With Olivia N. Saracho) *In Praise of Diversity: Perspectives on Multicultural Multilingual Early Childhood Education,* National Association for the Education of Young Children, 1982.

(With Saracho and Richard C. Lee) *Mainstreaming Young Children,* Wadsworth Publishing (Belmont, CA), 1984.

(With Saracho and M. D. Davis) *Foundations of Early Childhood Education,* Prentice-Hall, 1987, new edition, 1991.

Handbook of Research on the Education of Young Children, Macmillan (New York City), 1993.

(With Saracho) *Dealing with Individual Differences in the Early Childhood Classroom,* Longman (New York City), 1994.

(With Saracho) *Right from the Start: Educating Children Ages Three through Eight,* Allyn & Bacon (Boston), 1994.

EDITOR AND CONTRIBUTOR

(Editor with others) *Open Education,* National Association for the Education of Young Children, 1970.

Teacher Education: Of the Teacher, by the Teacher, for the Child, National Association for the Education of Young Children, 1974.

(Editor with Herbert J. Walberg) *Studies in Open Education,* Agathon Press (New York City), 1975.

(With Walberg, and author of introduction) *Early Childhood Education: Issues and Perspectives,* McCutchan (Berkeley, CA), 1977.

Teaching Practices: Reexamining Assumptions, National Association for the Education of Young Children, 1977.

Handbook of Research in Early Childhood Education, Free Press (New York City), 1982.

(Editor with N. Nir-Janiv and D. Steg) *International Perspectives on Early Childhood Education,* Plenum (New York City), 1982.

(With Saracho) *Understanding the Multicultural Experience in Early Childhood Education,* National Association for the Education of Young Children, 1983.

Today's Kindergarten: Exploring the Knowledge Base, Expanding the Curriculum, Teachers College Press, 1986.

(Editor with D. L. Peters and Saracho) *Professionalism and the Early Childhood Practitioner,* Teachers College Press, 1988, published as *Early Childhood Practitioners: Perspectives on Professionalism,* 1988.

(Editor with Saracho) *Yearbook in Early Childhood Education,* Teachers College Press, Volume 1: *Early Childhood Teacher Education,* 1990, Volume 2: *Issues in Early Childhood Curriculum,* 1991, Volume 3: *Issues in Early Child Care,* 1992, Volume 4: *Language and Literacy in Early Childhood Education,* 1993.

Educationally Appropriate Kindergarten Practices, National Education Association (Washington, DC), 1991.

OTHER

Contributor to numerous books, including *Early Childhood Education,* edited by Ira J. Gordon, National Society for the Study of Education (Chicago), 1972; *Cognitive Style and Early Education,* edited by Saracho, Gordon & Breach (New York City), 1990; and *Resources for Early Childhood,* revised edition, edited by H. N. Scheffler, Garland Publishing (New York City), 1994. Contributor to encyclopedias, including *International Encyclopedia of Education, Encyclopedia of Early Childhood Education, Encyclopedia of School Administration and Supervision,*

World Book Encyclopedia, and *Academic American Encyclopedia.* General editor, "Early Childhood Education" series, Prentice-Hall, 1971-79. Contributor to periodicals, including *International Journal of Early Childhood, International Journal of Educology, Early Child Development and Care, Elementary School Journal, Journal of Teacher Education, Educational Leadership,* and *Early Education and Development.* Guest editor, *Studies in Educational Evaluation,* 1982; book review editor, *Young Children,* 1972-74.

Some of Spodek's books have been translated into Japanese, Portuguese, German, and Hebrew.

*   *   *

SPRIGEL, Olivier
See AVICE, Claude (Pierre Marie)

*   *   *

STACHYS, Dimitris
See CONSTANTELOS, Demetrios J.

*   *   *

STORY, Jack Trevor   1917-1991

PERSONAL: Born March 20, 1917, in Hertfordshire, England; died December 5, 1991, in Milton Keynes, England; son of James (a house painter and cook) and Rhoda (Dyball) Story; children: Jacqueline, Christine, Peter, Jennifer, Caroline, Lee, Lindsay, Lorel. *Education:* Attended night school in radio and electronics for seven years. *Politics:* "Lenny Bruce and Orwellian." *Religion:* "Varies."

ADDRESSES: Agent—Dina Lom, 6A Maddox St., London W1, England.

CAREER: Writer, 1951-91.

WRITINGS:

The Trouble with Harry, T. V. Boardman, 1949, Macmillan (New York City), 1950.
Protection for a Lady, Laurie (London), 1950.
Green to Pagan Street, Harrap (London), 1952.
The Money Goes Round and Round, Redman, 1958.
Mix Me a Person (mystery), W. H. Allen (London), 1959, Macmillan, 1960.
Man Pinches Bottom, W. H. Allen, 1962.
Live Now, Pay Later, Secker & Warburg (London), 1963.
Something for Nothing, Secker & Warburg, 1963.
The Urban District Lover, Secker & Warburg, 1964.
Company of Bandits, Mayflower (London), 1965.

I Sit in Hanger Lane, Secker & Warburg, 1968.
Dishonourable Member, Secker & Warburg, 1969.
One Last Mad Embrace, Allison & Busby (London), 1970.
The Blonde and the Boodle, Howard Baker (London), 1970.
The Season of the Skylark, Howard Baker, 1970.
Hitler Needs You, Allison & Busby, 1971.
Little Dog's Day, Allison & Busby, 1971.
The Wind in the Snottygobble Tree, Allison & Busby, 1971.
Letters to an Intimate Stranger: A Year in the Life of Jack Trevor Story, Allison & Busby, 1972.
Crying Makes Your Nose Run, Bruce & Watson, 1973.
Story on Crime, Baker Press, 1975.
Morag's Flying Fortress, Hutchinson (London), 1976.
Up River, Duckworth (London), 1979, republished as *The Screwrape Lettuce,* Savoy Books, 1982.
Dwarf Goes to Oxford: One Girl in the Life of Jack Trevor, Leveret, 1986.
Albert Rides Again, Allison & Busby, 1990.

Also author of twenty Sexton Blake detective novels for Sexton Blake Library, 1951-61. Writer of film, television, and radio scripts, including the adaptation of his novel *Live Now, Pay Later* and the television script *Jack on the Box,* 1979. Author of column for the London *Guardian.* Contributor of short stories to magazines.

ADAPTATIONS: The Trouble with Harry was adapted for film under the direction of Alfred Hitchcock, 1955.

SIDELIGHTS: Author of a variety of works for print and film media, Jack Trevor Story was known especially for his humorous and eccentric fiction. His first published novel, *The Trouble with Harry,* was made into a successful motion picture under the direction of Alfred Hitchcock, and a trilogy beginning with *Live Now, Pay Later* remained in print almost thirty years. During the early 1970s he entertained readers of his London *Guardian* column with tales about his former girlfriend, Maggie.

Story once told *CA:* "Like a steam engine that burns steam, I am a self-generating writer. Stories either get in the way or give you some kind of dramatic target which you smack from time to time. After suffering a broken heart and three-stone weight loss I woke up one morning in 1973 with a line in my head: 'It was the kind of morning when everything rhymed.' It was the kind of line to start a book. My miseries were phasing out. One trouble: I had no book to write. Weeks later I get myself two good themes. 'American flyers during the war took off pissed [drunk]. It was not safe to be on the runway—they took girls aboard, f— over Hamburg.' That sounded like a story. My Flying Fortress gets shot down on such an orgy, crashes in what the crew believe to be occupied Belgium. In fact they have crossed the North Sea and are in England, a few miles from home base. They dismount a machine gun and wipe out a platoon of British Home Guards, believing them to be Germans, then steal a boat off a Suffolk beach and start back for Germany—thinking it's England. They get picked up by an enemy vessel and end the war in the cage. After the war, survivors go searching for their mistake. Good story? Right. With it I had my second theme. The captain, Alec Ranger, is now an electronics engineer who has been spying for NATO and has discovered that thalidomide and its horrors is really a genocidal remnant of Hitler's plans for the Jews. This has been brainwashed out of Alec's head when the story opens.

"When the reviews of *Morag's Flying Fortress* come out, such a dramatic and ingenious story has got to sell film rights for at least one hundred thousand dollars?" However, a reviewer for the *Sunday Telegraph* interpreted the story somewhat differently than Story had intended. The critic wrote: "When his great love Maggie ran away to Brussels, Jack Trevor Story lamented her on Saturdays in the *Guardian* for several years; it must have been terribly trying for her. *Morag's Flying Fortress* purports to be a spy story; Maggie, though still fled to Brussels, has become Sandra; the deserted lover has become an electronics engineer called Alec Ranger . . . this funny and likeable book, full of energy and rudeness and mistrust of the human race, is really a roundabout and complicated daydream of getting Maggie/Sandra back. Readers will wonder how she can resist such overtures."

Story commented that he believed the reviewer "missed the point." Similarly, he believed the point was missed with *The Wind in the Snottygobble Tree*. He explained that "the plot dealt with the kidnapping of the Pope in order to replace him with a Mafia man. When they get him—he is electrocuted through his own piss—they discover that he is already mafiosa; Lucky Luciano, no less. Another great movie, surely? Uh uh." Story was frustrated with reviewers who interpreted *The Wind in the Snottygobble Tree* as a book about a travel agent bored with his job who thus instigates a worldwide espionage organization with himself as boss. "The Pope was never mentioned in any review of the book," he added.

"In *Little Dog's Day,*" Story continued, "my chief protagonists are forced to escape from a tyrannised Big Brother society by hi-jacking an airliner and taking it to the only remaining free country in the world, Iceland." He wrote that a *Guardian* reviewer thought this book was about a man who, in searching for his lost poodle, played a trombone through the streets of the city. Story concluded that "this and these are the best sidelights I can shed upon myself as a writer; they say it all."

BIOGRAPHICAL/CRITICAL SOURCES:

PERIODICALS

Observer (London), June 24, 1979, p. 36.
Punch, November 27, 1968.
Sunday Telegraph, October 24, 1976.
Times (London), July 26, 1990.

OBITUARIES:

PERIODICALS

Times (London), December 10, 1991, p. 16.*

*   *   *

STUBBINGS, Hilda Uren
    See U'REN-STUBBINGS, Hilda

*   *   *

SWADOS, Elizabeth (A.)   1951-

PERSONAL: Born February 5, 1951, in Buffalo, NY; daughter of Robert Orville (a lawyer) and Sylvia (an actress and poet; maiden name, Maisel) Swados. *Education:* Bennington College, B.A., 1972. *Religion:* Jewish.

ADDRESSES: Home—112 Waverly Pl., New York, NY 10011. *Agent*—Sam Cohn, International Creative Management Co., 40 W. 57th St., New York, NY 10019-4001.

CAREER: Writer, composer, and director. Peter Brooks's International Theatre Group, France, Africa, and United States, composer and music director, 1972-73; Columbia Broadcasting System, Inc., composer "Camera Three" shows, 1973-74; La Mama Experimental Theatre Club, New York City, composer-in-residence, 1977—. Member of faculty, Carnegie-Mellon University, Pittsburgh, PA, 1974, Bard College, Annandale-on-Hudson, NY, 1976-77, Sarah Lawrence College, Bronxville, NY, 1976-77, and Bennington College, Bennington, VT. Performer at Mark Taper Forum, Los Angeles, CA, 1985, and *Jerusalem Oratorio,* Rome, 1985.

MEMBER: Broadcast Music, Inc.; Actors Equity Association.

AWARDS, HONORS: Obie Awards from *Village Voice,* 1972, for *Medea,* and 1977, for *Nightclub Cantata;* grants from Creative Artists Service Program, 1976, and for playwriting from New York State Arts Council, 1977—; Outer Critics Circle Award, 1977; Antoinette Perry (Tony) Award nominations for best musical, musical score, direction of a musical, choreography, and musical book, all 1978, all for *Runaways;* Guggenheim fellow.

WRITINGS:

The Girl with the Incredible Feeling (juvenile; also see below), Persea Books (New York City), 1976.

Runaways (also see below), Bantam (New York City), 1979.

Lullaby, Harper (New York City), 1980.

Sky Dance, Harper, 1980.

Leah and Lazar: A Novel, Summit Books (New York City), 1982.

Listening Out Loud: Becoming a Composer, Harper, 1988.

Inside Out: A Musical Adventure (juvenile), Little, Brown (Boston, MA), 1990.

The Four of Us: The Story of a Family, Farrar, Straus (New York City), 1991.

The Myth Man, Viking (New York City), 1994.

STAGE PRODUCTIONS

(Adapter, composer, director, and member of cast) *Nightclub Cantata* (revue), first produced Off-Broadway at Village Gate Theatre, January 9, 1977.

(Adapter with Andrei Serban, and composer) *Agamemnon* (play; adapted from the work by Aeschylus), first produced in Lenox, MA, at Lenox Arts Theatre, 1976; produced on Broadway at Vivian Beaumont Theatre, May 18, 1977.

(Adapter, composer, and director) *Wonderland in Concert,* first produced Off-Broadway at New York Shakespeare Festival Newman Theatre, 1978.

(Author, composer, and director) *Runaways* (revue), first produced Off-Broadway at Public Theatre Cabaret, March 9, 1978, produced on Broadway at Plymouth Theatre, May 6, 1978.

(Adapter and composer) *The Incredible Feeling Show* (also see below; adapted from Swados's *The Girl with the Incredible Feeling*), first produced in New York City at First All Children's Theatre, 1979.

(Adapter, composer, and director) *Dispatches* (adapted from the work by Michael Herr), first produced at Public Theatre Cabaret, 1979.

Lullaby and Goodnight (opera), first produced at Public Theatre Cabaret, August, 1980.

(Adapter, composer, and director) *Haggadah,* first produced Off-Broadway at New York Shakespeare Festival Luester Theatre, 1980.

The Beautiful Lady (musical), 1984.

(And composer) *Alice in Concert,* S. French (New York City), 1987.

(And composer) *The Red Sneaks,* S. French, 1991.

COMPOSER

Medea (adapted from the work by Euripides; also see below), first produced Off-Broadway at La Mama Experimental Theatre, 1969.

Elektra (adapted from the work by Euripides; also see below), first produced at La Mama Experimental Theatre, 1970.

The Trojan Women (adapted from the work by Euripides; also see below), first produced at La Mama Experimental Theatre, 1974.

Fragments of a Trilogy (contains *Medea, Elektra,* and *The Trojan Women*), first produced at La Mama Experimental Theatre, 1974.

The Good Women of Setzuan (adapted from the work by Bertholt Brecht), first produced at La Mama Experimental Theatre, February, 1975.

The Cherry Orchard (adapted from the work by Anton Chekhov), first produced in New Haven, CT, at Yale Theatre, 1977.

As You Like It (adapted from the work by William Shakespeare), first produced at La Mama Experimental Theatre, 1979.

Doonesbury: A Musical Comedy (adapted from the comic strip by Garry Trudeau), Holt (New York City), 1984.

(And director) *Swing,* produced at Brooklyn Academy of Music, 1987.

Also composer of music for films *Step by Step,* 1978, and *Sky Dance,* 1979, and for television, including Public Broadcasting Service (PBS) short story series, 1979, *A Year in the Life* (miniseries), 1987, and various specials for Columbia Broadcasting System, Inc. (CBS-TV) and National Broadcasting Co., Inc. (NBC-TV). Composer of *Rap Master Ronnie,* 1986.

OTHER

The Girl with the Incredible Feeling (screenplay), Phoenix Films, 1977.

The Incredible Feeling Show (television script), Children's Television Workshop, 1979.

Also adapter of *Works of Yehuda Amichi* and *Book of Jeremiah.*

SIDELIGHTS: The music of Elizabeth Swados goes beyond conventional classification because it combines elements of calypso, East Indian ragas, rock and roll, American Indian chants, ragtime, disco, Japanese theatre music, cabaret, and even birdcalls. "Miss Swados' music is undeniably dramatic, original, and effective," Edith Oliver remarked in the *New Yorker.* Alan Rich of *New York,* however, recalled his first encounter with Swados's music as not entirely pleasant: "I do remember every now and then picking up a snatch of something that sounded like bad Carl Orff (*very* bad, in other words) to texts that sounded something like gratch, grotch, pook. I left with the firm resolve that the mysteries of Ms. Swados's art . . . might be safer in other hands in the future." But Harold Clurman observed, "The Swados music . . . is for the most part bony rhythm, stark, strong, insistent, with here and there . . . a faintly plaintive touch which nevertheless reaches toward hope."

Swados's first major success came with *Nightclub Cantata,* a theater revue based on text by major poets, including Sylvia Plath, Pablo Neruda, Isabella Leitner, Muriel Rukeyser, and Nazim Hikmet. It was, according to *New York Times* critic Clive Barnes, "the most original and perhaps the most pleasurable form of nightclub entertainment I have encountered." While Martin Gottfried of the *New York Post* allowed that "*Nightclub Cantata* is more professional than most avant-garde and the skill of its production creates a magnetic interest of sorts," he complained that "it still plays like women's college art in the days before liberation." And Michael Feingold, in his review for the *Village Voice,* also found elements lacking: "If I have one criticism of her method, it is that it is too tight, too breakneck-paced, too clipped; it wants the looseness that, in a cabaret, allows for warmth and the revelation of personality—author's as well as performer's."

Swados addressed the dichotomy of her work—major poets in informal cabaret settings—in an interview with Jean Ross for *CA.* "There's a feeling that one should either be extremely 'cultural' or one should be entertainment oriented," she told Ross. "I feel the two can be combined. I will not sway from that. I absolutely believe that's the way the Renaissance theater was and that's the way the Greek theater was too. It was both culturally oriented and entertainment oriented. I think we've gotten so specialized, and both areas have suffered by it. The cultural area has gotten too elite, and the entertainment business has gotten really tacky."

Swados is best known for her Broadway hit show *Runaways.* In it, actors ranging in age from early teens to early twenties deliver songs and soliloquies on such problems as growing up, child abuse, neglect, divorce, "making it" on the streets, and becoming a child prostitute. "With *Runaways,* Swados steps right into the front line of popular American theatrical composers," assessed Mel Gussow of the *New York Times.* Concluding that the show was a "triumph," Gussow added that it was "buoyant entertainment, filled with the bright colors, language, and vivacity of the street," but at the same time was "an eloquent and mature vision, a musical that touches our hearts."

In his review of *Runaways,* Barnes hailed the show as "a statement of power, brilliance and honesty. Its impact lingers in the mind long after its music is forgotten. It shouts for the unhappy, and bruises with the bruised." But for Douglas Watt, it was "too eclectic a work and too concerned with artifice at the expense of dramatic verity to strike more than an occasional spark." Jack Kroll, on the other hand, agreed with Barnes: "An immensely affecting

show. To call it far and away the best musical of the season is to insult it. *Runaways* seizes your heart, plays with your pulse, dances exuberantly across the line that separates entertainment from involvement." Although Laura Shapiro of *Rolling Stone* commended *Runaways,* she was also troubled by it: "What is disconcerting about the show is the rows and rows of cheerful parents applauding the anguish of their children."

Swados herself had some qualms about the show. "I didn't know if I was putting on this show about exploiting children by exploiting children," she told Ross. "I didn't know if I was saying people use children to work out their own problems by using children to work out my own problems. But . . . the reason I chose to do it was that the situation of family life in the United States, and the situation of the child *in* family life, is at a desperate low. If there was a possibility to relay to parents and children in some way—whether it was to infuriate them, to delight them, to at least engage them, even to bore them—some way to get that across, I felt that it was worth the possible compromising of these nineteen kids." Swados explained to Ross that "I have a very strong, almost spiritual belief that as a human being I have a responsibility to my fellow human beings on this earth, particularly to the children of this earth, to interpret and work out this world, to understand it better, to fight for a higher quality of living. . . . It's more than having been given talent, which one should be incredibly grateful for, but I was given a real sense of mission almost."

Family life also plays an important role in Swados's more recent work. In the novel *Leah and Lazar* and the memoir *The Four of Us: The Story of a Family,* she explores the circumstances of her own childhood—the alcoholism and depression that drove her mother to commit suicide, her brother's descent into madness. "By seeking not to apportion blame or justify mistakes but to understand," wrote Ellin Stein in the *New York Times Book Review,* ". . . Ms. Swados has created an unsparing yet compassionate picture of the particular way in which this unhappy family was unhappy."

BIOGRAPHICAL/CRITICAL SOURCES:

BOOKS

Contemporary Literary Criticism, Volume 12, Gale, 1980.

PERIODICALS

Christian Science Monitor, April 25, 1979.
Horizon, May, 1977.
Kliatt, July, 1993, p. 28.
Los Angeles Times Book Review, November 13, 1988, p. 4; September 1, 1991, p. 6.
Nation, January 29, 1977.
New Republic, June 11, 1977; March 24, 1979, pp. 24-25.

Newsweek, March 27, 1978, pp. 74-75.

New York, January 31, 1977; May 30, 1977; March 27, 1978; May 7, 1979.

New York Daily News, March 10, 1978.

New Yorker, January 24, 1977; March 20, 1978.

New York Post, January 10, 1977; May 19, 1977; March 10, 1978.

New York Times, January 25, 1976; January 27, 1976; January 10, 1977, p. 29; May 19, 1977; March 10, 1978, p. C3; May 18, 1978; June 3, 1979.

New York Times Book Review, April 26, 1981, p. 71; May 9, 1982, p. 10; January 22, 1989, p. 10; September 24, 1989, p. 60; February 23, 1992, p. 17; April 25, 1993, p. 32.

New York Times Magazine, February 13, 1977; March 5, 1978.

Publishers Weekly, March 29, 1993, p. 50.

Rolling Stone, June 15, 1978, pp. 54-6.

Saturday Review, May, 1982, p. 61.

Time, May 30, 1977.

Village Voice, January 17, 1977, p. 83; March 12, 1979; April 30, 1979, pp. 88-89.

Vogue, July, 1978.*

T

TANIKAWA, Shuntaro 1931-

PERSONAL: Born December 15, 1931, in Tokyo, Japan; son of Tetsuzo (a professor) and Taki (Osada) Tanikawa; married Eriko Kishida (a poet), December 21, 1954 (divorced, 1956); married Tomoko Ookubo, February 27, 1957 (divorced, 1989); married Sano Yoko, 1991, children: Kensaku, Shino Tanikawa Oglesby. *Education:* Attended public schools in Tokyo and Kyoto, Japan.

ADDRESSES: Office—Narita-higashi 4-16-6, Suginami-ku, Tokyo 166, Japan.

CAREER: Writer, 1950—. Has participated in many reading tours and poetry festivals, including International Poetry Festival in Washington, DC, 1970, Poetry International '77 in Rotterdam, Netherlands, and A Festival of Japanese Poetry in New York, NY, 1985.

MEMBER: Japan Writers Association, Group KAI.

AWARDS, HONORS: Japan Disc Grand Prix from Japan Phonograph Record Association, 1962, for *Gekkasuimokukindonichi no uta;* Japan Translation Culture Prize from Japan Society of Translators, 1975, for *Maza Gusu no uta;* Yomiuri Literary Award from Yomiuri Press, 1983, for *Hibi no chizu;* Hanatsubaki Award from Shiseido Company, 1985, for *Yoshinashi uta;* Hagiwara Prize, 1993, for *To A Woman;* American Book Award, 1989, for *Floating the River in Melancholy.*

WRITINGS:

POETRY IN ENGLISH TRANSLATION

Rokujuni no sonetto, Tokyo Sogensha, 1953, translation by William I. Elliott and Kazuo Kawamura published as *62 Sonnets,* Prescott Street Press, 1992.

Tabi, Kyuryudo, 1970, translation by Elliott and Kawamura published as *With Silence My Companion,* Prescott Street Press, 1975.

Teigi, Shityosha, 1975, translation by Elliott and Kawamura published as *Definitions,* Prescott Street Press, 1992.

Yonaka ni daidokoro de boku wa kimi ni hanashi kaketakatta, Seidosha, 1975, translation by Elliott and Kawamura published as *At Midnight in the Kitchen I Just Wanted to Talk to You,* Prescott Street Press, 1980.

Kokakora ressun, Shityosha, 1980, translation by Elliott and Kawamura published as *Coca-Cola Lesson,* Prescott Street Press, 1986.

The Selected Poems of Shuntaro Tanikawa (anthology), translated by Harold Wright, North Point Press, 1983.

Yoshinashi uta, Seidosha, 1985, translation by Elliott and Kawamura published as *Songs of Nonsense,* Prescott Street Press, 1987.

Floating the River in Melancholy, translation by Elliott and Kawamura, Prescott Street Press, 1989.

Naked, translation by Elliott and Kawamura, Prescott Street Press, 1994.

POETRY IN JAPANESE

Nijuoku konen no kodoku (title means "Twenty Billion Light Years of Loneliness"), Tokyo Sogensha, 1952.

Ai ni tsuite (title means "Concerning Love"), Tokyo Sogensha, 1955.

Ehon (title means "Picture Book"), Matoba Shobo, 1956.

Anata ni (title means "To You"), Tokyo Sogensha, 1960.

21, Shityosha, 1964.

Rakusyu kyujukyu (title means "Lampoons"), Asahi Shinbunsha, 1964.

Sonohoka ni (title means "Something Else"), Shueisha, 1979.

Hibi no chizu (title means "Map of Days"), Shueisha, 1982.

Nihongo no katarogu (title means "Catalog of Japanese"), Shityosha, 1984.

FOR CHILDREN; IN JAPANESE

Nihongo no okeiko (title means "Japanese Lessons"), Rironsha, 1965.

Ken wa hettyara (title means "Ken Doesn't Mind"), Akane Syobo, 1965.

Koppu (title means "A Glass"), Hukuinkan Shoten, 1972.

Toki (title means "Time"), Hukuinkan Shoten, 1973.

Kotoba asobi uta (title means "Word Play"), Hukuinkan Shoten, 1973.

Watashi (title means "Me"), Hukuinkan Shoten, 1976.

Mokomoko (title means "Popping Up"), Bunken Shuppan, 1977.

Kore wa nomi no Piko (title means "This Is Pico, a Flea"), Sun Reed, 1979.

Obaatyan (title means "Grandma"), Barunsha, 1981.

Warabe uta (title means "Nursery Rhymes"), Shueisha, 1981.

Mimi wo sumasu (title means "Let Your Ears Perk Up"), Hukuinkan Shoten, 1982.

Dokin, Rironsha, 1983.

PLAYS; IN JAPANESE

Ke no shi (one-act play; title means "Death of K"), first produced in Tokyo at Bungaku-za, 1956.

Oshibai wa oshimai (three-act play; title means "The Play Is Over"), first produced in Tokyo at Gekidan Shiki, 1960.

Obake ringo (one-act play for children; title means "Monster Apple"; first produced in Tokyo at Sangyakunin-Gekizyo, 1979), Shinsuisha, 1982.

Dondokodon (one-act play for children; title means "Boom, Boom"), first produced in Tokyo at Engeki-Syudan En, 1983.

Itsudatte imadamon (one-act play for children; title means "Anytime Is Now"), first produced in Tokyo at Engeki-Syudan En, 1985.

SCREENPLAYS; IN JAPANESE

(With Kon Ichikawa, Natto Wada, and Yoshio Shirasaka) *Tokyo Orinpikku* (title means "Tokyo Olympiad"), Thirteenth Olympic Organizing Committee/Toho, 1965 (released in the United States by Pan-World Films, 1966).

Kyo (title means "Kyoto"), Ing. C. Olivetti & Co., S.P.A., 1967.

Ai hutatabi, Toho, 1971.

(Co-author) *Matatabi* (title means "The Outlaws"), ATC/Kon, 1973.

Hinotori (title means "Phoenix"), Toho, 1978.

TELEVISION SCRIPTS; IN JAPANESE

Heya (title means "A Room"), Nihon Educational Television, 1959.

Anata wa dare desyo (title means "Who Are You?"), Nihon Hoso Kyokai, 1961.

Matsuri (title means "Festival"), Hokkaido Broadcasting Co., 1962.

Party, Nihon Hoso Kyokai-Osaka, 1962.

Zyaane (title means "Ciao"), Nihon Hoso Kyokai, 1974.

RADIO SCRIPTS; IN JAPANESE

Girisha kara kita otohuyasan (title means "The Tohu Vendor From Greece"), Radio Kyusyu, 1956.

Toi gita toi kao (title means "Faraway Guitar, Faraway Face"), Radio Kyusyu, 1958.

Zyuendama (title means "A Ten-Yen Coin"), Nihon Hoso Kyokai, 1963.

Makiba no nakano ippon no ki (title means "A Tree in a Meadow"), Nihon Hoso Kyokai, 1964.

Hohoemi no imi suru mono (a German and Japanese co-production), Nihon Hoso Kyokai/Hessian Radio, 1973.

OTHER

Author of a Japanese translation of Mother Goose rhymes entitled *Maza Gusu no uta* and of song lyrics in Japanese. Translator into Japanese of Charles M. Schulz's "Peanuts" comic strip. Author of video programs, including *Video Letter with Shuzi Terayama,* 1983, *Video Sampler,* 1987, and *Songs without Words,* 1987.

SIDELIGHTS: Shuntaro Tanikawa has achieved a level of popularity in his native Japan not often accorded American poets in their lifetimes. While as a rule, according to Geoffrey O'Brien of the *Village Voice,* Japanese poets are much more likely to enjoy celebrity in Japan than are their American counterparts in the United States, Tanikawa's fame is noteworthy even in the context of his own culture. O'Brien pointed out, for instance, that Tanikawa "is published in leading newspapers and interviewed in the equivalents of *People* and *Cosmopolitan.* [His] poetry receives critical praise and the kind of lavish editions reserved in America for the long deceased—and even they have to fight for it."

Tanikawa began his career as a poet not long after Japan suffered defeat in World War II, a national failure that led some Japanese to question and reject traditional values. As a result Tanikawa found himself, according to Harvey Shapiro of the *New York Times,* alongside "the rest of us, with no usable past, no fixed future, living in a present we have difficulty figuring out," and the poet asserted himself, O'Brien suggested, as "an emblem of postwar optimism."

Having severed himself from the Japanese literary tradition, Tanikawa developed themes in his poetry that include what Shapiro identified as a preoccupation with the notion of the frontier, with being alone on the edge of boundlessness. And the postwar cultural vacuum in Japan left room for an influx of Western, and particularly American, images to supply Tanikawa's palette. O'Brien notes references in Tanikawa's poems to jazz trumpeter Miles Davis, cartoonist and amusement park baron Walt Disney, and frontier outlaw Billy the Kid.

Tanikawa told *CA:* "Although I think of myself primarily as a poet, I've been writing children's books, song lyrics, and scripts for television and movies, as well as a few plays. I've also translated Mother Goose rhymes and have been translating 'Peanuts' comics for more than ten years. I'm interested in visual media, such as private video and still photography, and I collect and repair vintage radios."

BIOGRAPHICAL/CRITICAL SOURCES:

PERIODICALS

New York Times, November 12, 1983.
Village Voice, February 28, 1984.
World Literature Today, summer, 1984.

*   *   *

TELLER, Neville   1931-
(Edmund Owen)

PERSONAL: Born June 10, 1931, in London, England; son of Hyman (a company director) and Sarah (Ephron) Teller; married Sheila Brown, October 20, 1958; children: Richard Henry Marshall, Adam James Grenville, Matthew David Alexander. *Education:* St. Edmund Hall, Oxford, B.A. (with honors), 1955, M.A., 1963.

ADDRESSES: Home—15 Ewhurst Close Cheam, Surrey, England. *Office*—Department of Health and Social Security, Alexander Fleming House, Elephant & Castle, London SE1, England. *Agent*—Lorna Vestey, 33 Dryburgh Rd., London SW15, England.

CAREER: Butterworth & Co. Ltd. (publisher), Sevenoaks, England, marketing manager, 1966-68; Granada Publishing Ltd., St. Albans, England, marketing director, 1968-69; *Times,* London, England, marketing coordinator, 1969-70; Department of Health and Social Security, London, civil servant, 1970-89; Cancer Relief Macmillan Fund, director of operations, 1989—. Freelance radio writer.

MEMBER: Society of Authors (broadcasting committee chairman).

WRITINGS:

Bluff Your Way in Marketing, Wolfe, 1966, 2nd revised edition, 1969.

EDITOR

Whodunit: Ten Tales of Crime and Detection, Edward Arnold (London), 1970.
(With Jane Cicely Saunders and D. H. Summers) *Hospice: The Living Idea,* Edward Arnold, 1981.
British Construction Profile, McMillan Martin, 1985.

EDITOR; "BRITISH ARCHITECTURAL DESIGN AWARD" SERIES

British Architectural Design Awards, 1983, Templegate (Woking, Surrey), 1984.
British Architectural Design Awards, 1984, McMillan Martin, 1985.
British Architectural Design Awards, 1985-86, McMillan Martin, 1986.

OTHER

Also adaptor, sometimes under pseudonym Edmund Owen, of works for radio dramatization, including *Party Going* by Henry Green, *The Serpent's Smile,* by Olga Hesky, *The Sword in the Stone* by T. H. White, *The Daughter of Time,* by Josephine Tey, and *Shadows of Doubt* by Palma Harcourt.

WORK IN PROGRESS: Abridgements for British Broadcasting Corporation radio and for audiobooks to be published by Penguin and Hodder Headline.

SIDELIGHTS: Neville Teller once told *CA:* "I have been a radio writer since 1956, mainly though not exclusively for the British Broadcasting Corp. I specialize in abridgement, adaptation, dramatization, and serialization for reading on the air. The number of programs I have scripted runs into the thousands. I have researched and scripted such literary and historical features as 'The Horror at Bly,' an investigation of Henry James's *The Turn of the Screw;* 'The Queen and the Kaiser,' a study of the relationship between Queen Victoria and her grandson; a fifteen-part abridgement of *The Franchise Affair* by Josephine Tey; and 'Dizzy and the Faery Queen,' a feature on Queen Victoria and Disraeli; and I have researched and written quiz and music programs for radio among many others.

"I have been fascinated by radio since boyhood—television and film have never held the same appeal. At university, as a committee member of the Oxford University Dramatic Society and secretary of the Experimental Theatre Club, I specialized in radio productions, and later moved very quickly into writing freelance for radio, while pursuing a career in marketing and general management.

"In 1970 I moved out of the business world into the civil service, but I have continued and gradually extended the scope of my radio work. The range of artistic and technical possibilities inherent in the sound medium for interesting, moving and communicating with people, as individuals and en masse at one and the same time, is a never-ending source of wonder and delight. The radio writer's intense satisfaction stems from blending the words, sounds, music, and technical devices on his palette to produce in the mind's eye of his listening audience and on their emotions a precisely calculated effect.

"I pity those benighted parts of the civilized world where radio has degenerated into a form of aural wallpaper, and where artistry and craftsmanship by writer, producers, and actors for radio has atrophied. *Floreat* the BBC!"

*   *   *

THUM, Marcella

PERSONAL: Born in St. Louis, MO; daughter of Frank and Louise (Holle) Thum. *Education:* Washington University, St. Louis, B.A., 1948; University of California, Berkeley, M.L.S., 1954; Webster College, M.A., 1977. *Politics:* Democrat. *Religion:* Protestant.

ADDRESSES: Home—6507 Gramond Dr., St. Louis, MO 63123. *Agent*—Eleanor Wood, 432 Park Ave. S., New York, NY 10016.

CAREER: Advertising copywriter in St. Louis, MO, 1948-49; U.S. Army, Public Information Office, civilian writer on Okinawa, Japan, 1949-50, with historical division in Heidelberg and Karlsruhe, Germany, 1951-53; U.S. Air Force, civilian librarian in Korea, at Scott Air Force Base, IL, and at Schofield Barracks and Hickam Air Force Base, HI, 1954-60; Affton Senior High School, Affton, MO, school librarian, 1962-67; Meramec Community College, Kirkwood, MO, reference librarian, 1968-79; Scott Air Force Base, IL, Airlift Operations School librarian, 1979-85.

MEMBER: Romance Writers of America, Missouri Writer's Guild, St. Louis Writer's Guild (president, 1967).

AWARDS, HONORS: Dodd, Mead Librarian and Teacher Prize Competition award and Edgar Award for best juvenile mystery, Mystery Writers of America, both 1964, both for *The Mystery at Crane's Landing;* Missouri Writer's Guild award, 1966, for *Treasure of Crazy Quilt Farm;* American Library Association notable children's book award, 1975, for *Exploring Black America: A History and Guide.*

WRITINGS:

The Mystery at Crane's Landing, Dodd (New York City), 1964.

Treasure of Crazy Quilt Farm, F. Watts (New York City), 1965.

Anne of the Sandwich Islands, Dodd, 1967.

Librarian with Wings, Dodd, 1967.

Secret of the Sunken Treasure, Dodd, 1969.

(With sister, Gladys Thum) *The Persuaders: Propaganda in War and Peace* (nonfiction), Atheneum (New York City), 1972.

Fernwood, Doubleday (New York City), 1973.

Persuasion and Propaganda, McDougal, Little (Evanston, IL), 1973.

Exploring Black America: A History and Guide (nonfiction), Atheneum, 1975.

Abbey Court, Doubleday, 1976.

Exploring Literary America: A History and Travel Guide, Atheneum, 1979.

The White Rose, Fawcett (New York City), 1980.

(With G. Thum) *Exploring Military America: A History and Travel Guide,* Atheneum, 1981.

Blazing Star, Fawcett, 1983.

Jasmine, Fawcett, 1984.

Wild Laurel, Fawcett, 1985.

(With G. Thum) *Airlift: Story of the Military Airlift Command,* Dodd, 1986.

Margarite, Fawcett, 1987.

Mistress of Paradise, Fawcett, 1988.

The Thorn Trees, Fawcett, 1991.

U.S.A. Guide to Black America: A Directory of Historic and Cultural Sites Relating to Black America, Hippocrene Books (New York City), 1992.

WORK IN PROGRESS: A mystery for young adults.

SIDELIGHTS: Marcella Thum decided early in her life that she wanted to be a writer. "But I knew I wasn't going to be a literary writer," she wrote *CA:* "I wanted to write for a wide audience and sell what I wrote." She sold her first story when she was eighteen, but sold her first book, *The Mystery at Crane's Landing,* published in 1964, while she was working as a high school librarian. The book won an Edgar Award given by the Mystery Writers of America. She has been writing—and selling—ever since.

For many years Thum combined writing with a full-time career as a librarian, a combination she feels gave her an advantage. "I enjoyed library work, and the two careers sort of supplement each other," Thum commented. "I knew what was being read—sometimes better than publishers did—and where the needs were, vacant spaces on the library book shelves."

Thum also reported that she never found it difficult to write in many different fields, ranging from young adult fiction to gothics and mysteries, historical romances, and nonfiction. "For one thing, I get bored writing in just one genre, and another thing, I feel that if you are a writer, you should be able to write in any field. Writing is writing, when you come down to it. Also, perhaps because I am a librarian, I feel very strongly about good solid research, no matter in what field you're writing. I insist on historical accuracy in my romance novels. Readers do know the difference."

Thum's first nonfiction book, *The Persuaders: Propaganda in War and Peace,* was written in collaboration with her sister, Gladys Thum. "From my work as a high school librarian, I knew that students needed more information on what propaganda is and how it operates, and that there was no book on the subject at the high school level. I am very proud of the book which covers all types of propaganda and is lavishly illustrated with photographs. The book was used as a supplemental textbook and received excellent reviews."

Another nonfiction book, *Exploring Black America: A History and Guide,* is a travel-history guide. "At the time the book was published in 1975, there was little material about black history for young people. My book not only told of black history but listed and described sites about black history that could be visited." Anitra Gordon noted in *School Library Journal:* "Many of the pages missing from America's history books are found in this . . . guide."

Thum noted: "I don't pretend writing and research are easy. People don't appreciate how hard it is. All my books were written under contract, with deadlines. Working all day as a librarian and writing nights and weekends was difficult. You have to put words on paper day after day after day no matter how tired you might feel. When you do get published—which is not easy—you hardly ever make a fortune. I tell young writers starting out that their chances of making a lot of money from writing are about as good as their winning the lottery! If you aren't really dedicated to being a writer, forget it! It's just not worth the time, the emotions you pour into it, the rejections. Still," she added, "I've been lucky that I loved both my careers, library work and writing."

BIOGRAPHICAL/CRITICAL SOURCES:

PERIODICALS

Booklist, May 1, 1975, p. 909; October 15, 1976, p. 303; July, 1986, p. 1617.
Choice, June, 1992, p. 1529.
Kirkus Reviews, October 15, 1967, p. 1284; May 1, 1975, p. 527; August 1, 1976, p. 858; May 1, 1979, p. 525.

Library Journal, April 15, 1967, p. 1754; May 15, 1969, p. 2124; December 15, 1976, p. 2598; February 1, 1992, p. 117.
New York Times Book Review, December 30, 1973, p. 19; May 31, 1992, p. 11.
Publishers Weekly, August 2, 1976, p. 110; March 11, 1983, p. 82; June 1, 1984, p. 62; January 16, 1987, p. 68.
School Library Journal, November, 1975, p. 94; November, 1982, p. 104.

* * *

TICKLE, P(hyllis) A(lexander) 1934-

PERSONAL: Born March 12, 1934, in Johnson City, TN; daughter of Philip Wade (an educator) and Katherine (Porter) Alexander; married Samuel Milton Tickle (a physician), June 17, 1955; children: Nora Katherine Cannon, Mary Gammon Clark, Laura Lee Goodman, John Crockett II, Philip Wade (deceased), Samuel Milton, Jr., Rebecca Rutledge. *Education:* Attended Shorter College, 1951-54; East Tennessee State University, B.A., 1955; Furman University, M.A., 1961. *Religion:* Episcopalian.

ADDRESSES: Home—3522 Lucy Road South, Lucy, TN 38053.

CAREER: Furman University, Greenville, SC, instructor in psychology, 1960-62; Southwestern at Memphis, Memphis, TN, instructor in English, 1962-65; Memphis Academy of Arts, Memphis, TN, teacher and dean of humanities, 1965-71; St. Luke's Press, founding editor and managing editor, 1975-83, senior editor, 1983—; director of trade publishing, Wimmer Companies, 1989-91; *Publishers Weekly,* New York City, religion editor, 1992—. Poetry co-ordinator for Cumberland Valley Writers' Conference, 1977-81; poet in residence, Brooks Memorial, 1977-87. Member of literary panel and artist-in-education panel, Tennessee Arts Commission; member of board of directors of Upward Bound at LeMoyne-Owen College, 1968-70, and Sunshine Day Care Center, 1970-71; member of board of trustees of Grace-St. Luke's Episcopal School, 1970-76; member of bishop's committee on abortion, 1987-91; vestry woman, St. Anne's Episcopalian Church, 1987-90, 1991-94; executive board, Tennessee Humanities Council, 1989-92.

MEMBER: Tennessee Humanities Council (member of executive board, 1987—), Tennessee Literary Arts Association (former vice-president for western Tennessee), Publishers Association of the South (president, 1984-85; member of executive board, 1985—), Committee of Small Magazine Editors and Publishers.

AWARDS, HONORS: Tickle's narrative poem "American Genesis" was selected by Tennessee's American Bicentennial Commission as a bicentennial poem for the state, 1976; individual fellowship in literature, Tennessee Arts Commission, 1984; Polly Bond Award, 1985.

WRITINGS:

An Introduction to the Patterns of Indo-European Speech, Memphis Academy of Arts, 1968.

Figs and Fury (a chancel play; produced in Memphis, TN at Grace-St. Luke Episcopal Church), St. Luke's Press, 1974, 2nd edition, 1976.

It's No Fun to Be Sick (juvenile), St. Luke's Press, 1976.

The Story of Two Johns (juvenile), St. Luke's Press, 1976.

On Beyond Koch, Brooks Memorial, 1980.

On Beyond Ais, Tennessee Arts Commission, 1982.

Puppeteers for Our Lady, St. Michael's Church, 1982.

The City Essays, Dixie Flyer Press, 1982.

What the Heart Already Knows, Upper Room, 1985.

Final Sanity, Upper Room, 1987.

Ordinary Times, Upper Room, 1988.

The Tickled Papers, Abingdon, 1989.

Discovering the Sacred: Spirituality in America, Crossroad Publishing, 1995.

My Father's Prayer: A Remembrance, Upper Room, 1995.

Their Old Familiar Carol Say, Black Oak Press, 1995

Columnist for *Dixie Flyer* and *Feminist Digest,* 1975-78, and for *Church News;* poetry editor, *Chaff,* 1978; member of editorial board, *Church News,* 1986—; secretary of the board, Raccoon Books, a tax-exempt sister house to St. Luke's Press. Contributor of poems to periodicals, including *Images, Nexus,* and *Velvet Wings.* Contributor of articles and reviews to magazines.

WORK IN PROGRESS: Editing *Homewards II,* University of Tennessee Press; a non-fiction work on religious books in the public library; a non-fiction work on heaven.

SIDELIGHTS: P. A. Tickle told *CA:* "I lecture a great deal and find this a most satisfying experience. I still think of myself as a poetess by trade, but having had seven children has also given me some kind of background for enjoying children's literature and I am finding that rewarding, along with my continuing work on religion. Spanish is my second language of choice and all things Mexican and/or Spanish are as natural to me as breathing.

"The women's movement comes at a time when being a wife, mother, and writer is no longer regarded as natural, but rather as a social statement or a private protest. Within the framework of all these factors, I find myself drawn more and more toward the ancients—to the works and values of Sappho and Catullus—to Cavafy and Rilke in our own time, and always, to Eliot."

TIEDT, Iris M(cClellan)   1928-

PERSONAL: Surname rhymes with "bead"; born February 3, 1928, in Dayton, OH; daughter of Raymond Hill (an engineer) and Ermalene (Swartzel) McClellan; married Sidney W. Tiedt (a college professor), September 17, 1949 (divorced, 1978); children: Pamela Lynne, Ryan Sidney. *Education:* Northwestern University, B.S., 1950; University of Orgeon, M.A., 1961; Stanford University, Ph.D., 1972. *Politics:* Democrat. *Avocational interests:* The arts, writing poetry and stories, designing original rugs, wordplay, swimming, skiing.

ADDRESSES: Home—1654 Fairorchard Ave., San Jose, CA 95125. *Office*—San Jose State University, San Jose, CA 95192.

CAREER: Language arts teacher in Chicago, IL, 1950-51, Kenai, AK, 1951-52, and Anchorage, AK, 1953-57; University of Oregon, Eugene, teaching fellow and supervisor of student teaching, 1959-61; Roosevelt Junior High School, Eugene, English teacher/librarian, 1961; University of Santa Clara, Santa Clara, CA, director of teacher education, 1968-72, director of graduate reading program, 1972-75; San Jose State University, San Jose, CA, director of South Bay Writing Project, 1977-87; Northern Kentucky University, chair of education department, 1987-89; Moorhead State University, Moorhead, MN, dean of education and regional services, 1989-94, dean emerita and educational consultant, 1994—.

MEMBER: American Association of University Women (life membership), National Council of Teachers of English, National Organization for Women, National Women's Political Caucus, Sierra Club (life membership), Stanford Alumni Association (life membership), California Association of Teachers of English, Pi Lambda Theta, Sigma Delta Pi.

WRITINGS:

Bulletin Board Captions, Contemporary Press, 1964, revised edition, 1975.

Opening Classrooms, National Council of Teachers of English (Urbana, IL), 1973.

New Ways with Individualization, National Council of Teachers of English, 1973.

Women and Girls, National Council of Teachers of English, 1973.

(Editor) *Drama in Your Classroom,* National Council of Teachers of English, 1974.

(Editor) *What's New in Reading,* National Council of Teachers of English, 1974.

Sexism in Education, General Learning Press, 1974.

Books/Literature/Children, Houghton (Burlington, MA), 1975, third edition published as *The Language Arts Handbook,* 1981.

Effective English (sixth grade textbook), Silver Burdett (Morristown, NJ), 1978.

Exploring Books with Children, Houghton Mifflin, 1979.

(With daughter, Pamela Tiedt) *Multicultural Teaching: A Handbook of Activities, Information, and Resources,* Allyn & Bacon (Boston, MA), 1979, 4th edition, 1995.

The Writing Process: Composition and Applied Grammar (tenth grade textbook), Allyn & Bacon, 1981.

(Contributor) R. Baird Shuman, editor, *English in the 80s: English,* National Education Association (Washington, DC), 1981.

Elements of English (tenth grade textbook), Allyn & Bacon, 1982., 1982.

(With Suzanne Bruemmer, Sheila Lane, Patricia Stelwagon, Kathleen Watanabe, and Mary Young Williams) *The Time Has Come. . . Teaching Writing in the K-8 Classroom,* Prentice-Hall (Englewood Cliffs, NJ), 1983.

The Language Arts Handbook, Prentice-Hall, 1983.

(With Nora Ho, Lisa Johnson, and Williams) *Lessons from a Writing Project,* three volumes, Volume 1: *Catching the Writing Express,* Volume 2: *Enjoying the Written Word,* Volume 3: *Learning to Use Written Language,* David Lake, 1987.

(With Jo Ellen Carlson, Bert Howard, and Watanabe) *Teaching Thinking in K-12 Classrooms,* Allyn & Bacon, 1989.

(With Ruth Gibbs, Martha Howard, Marylue Timpson, and Williams) *Reading, Thinking, and Writing: A Holistic Language and Literacy Program,* Allyn & Bacon, 1989.

Writing: From Topic to Evaluation, Allyn & Bacon, 1989.

WITH HUSBAND, SIDNEY W. TIEDT

Unrequired Reading: An Annotated Bibliography for Teachers and School Administrators, Oregon State University Press (Corvallis, OR), 1963, 2nd edition, 1967.

Creative Writing Ideas, Contemporary Press, 1963, revised edition, 1964.

Exploring Words, Contemporary Press, 1963, published as *Exciting Reading Activities,* 1975.

Imaginative Social Studies Activities for the Elementary School, Prentice-Hall, 1964.

Selected Free Materials, Contemporary Press, 1964.

Elementary Teacher's Complete Ideas Handbook, Prentice-Hall, 1965.

Contemporary English in the Elementary School, Prentice-Hall, 1967, 2nd edition, 1975.

(Compilers) *Readings on Contemporary English in the Elementary School,* Prentice-Hall, 1967.

Language Arts Activities for the Classroom, Allyn & Bacon, 1978, 2nd edition, 1987.

Language Arts Activities: A Handbook of Activities, Information, and Resources, Allyn & Bacon, 1987.

OTHER

Contributor to *Encyclopedia of English Studies and Language Arts,* National Council of Teachers of English, 1994. Co-editor, "Contemporary Classics" series, Contemporary Press. Author of syndicated column, "An Open Letter to Women," 1981—. Co-editor (with S. Tiedt), *The Elementary Teachers Ideas and Materials Workshop* (monthly newsletter), Prentice-Hall, 1963-72. Editor, *Elementary English,* later changed to *Language Arts,* National Council of Teachers of English, 1972-76, and *Reading Ideas* (newsletter), 1978-85. Contributor to professional journals, including *Childhood Education, Elementary English, Elementary School Journal, English Journal, Instructor, The Kappan,* and *Language Arts.*

SIDELIGHTS: Iris M. Tiedt told *CA:* "As an educator, I write because I want to have an impact on what is happening in the world today. I am concerned, for example, about the role of women in our society and the values imposed on girls from birth. I am also very much concerned about multicultural education and teaching that develops positive self-esteem, empathy, and equity for all students. Through such approaches to teaching from early childhood, we have a hope of achieving harmony throughout the world.

"I grew up with an 'I can' attitude, and I wonder why. I want to develop that kind of attitude for all young people as they work to achieve their fullest potential. Children need self-esteem in order to learn. It is we adults who injure that self-esteem when children are quite young, so it is we adults who must change our ways of relating to children. This is the kind of thing I write about.

"I learned to write by writing, and I did not begin seriously until I was thirty-five. I see writing as a wonderful form of therapy, and I recommend keeping journals and writing about experiences that may be painful. I also recommend sharing these writings as a way of letting emotions out and gaining support others.

"We need to learn much more about teaching writing in schools in order to encourage students to write effectively. We still have many misperceptions that get in the way of really communicating through writing. We tend to focus on error avoidance—grammar, spelling, and penmanship—and think we are teaching writing. Writing is communication. We need to begin with thinking and talking about ideas. Communicating these ideas will lead young people to write and to savor the excitement of turning out a well-stated argument or describing a peak experience in poetic form. Thus, they will engage in thinking and learn to interact with their peers as they deal with real issues.

"Teacher education programs must prepare future teachers to interact positively with all students. Students who come to school eager to learn, but they need to know someone cares about their well-being and will help them succeed from the very first day they enter a classroom. The classroom climate, the teacher's attitude, and the teacher's communication with each student may be more important than any specific subject taught. All teachers must learn to interact with their students at a personal level."

*   *   *

TOCH, Hans (Herbert) 1930-

PERSONAL: Born April 17, 1930, in Vienna, Austria; became United States citizen. *Education:* Attended high school in Havana, Cuba; Brooklyn College (now Brooklyn College of the City University of New York), B.A. (summa cum laude), 1952; Princeton University, Ph.D., 1955.

ADDRESSES: Office—School of Criminal Justice, State University of New York, Albany, NY 12222.

CAREER: Michigan State University, East Lansing, instructor, 1957-58, assistant professor, 1958-61, associate professor, 1961-66, professor of psychology, 1966-67; State University of New York at Albany, School of Criminal Justice, professor of psychology, 1968-86, distinguished professor, 1986—. Harvard University, department of social relations, visiting lecturer, 1965-66. Consultant to National Commission on the Causes and Prevention of Violence, 1968-69; member of Governor's Advisory Panel on Violent Juvenile Delinquents, 1975. *Military service:* U.S. Naval Reserve, enlisted on active duty (morale researcher), 1955-57; reserve officer, 1957-66.

MEMBER: American Psychological Association (fellow), American Society of Criminology (fellow), Phi Beta Kappa, Sigma Xi.

AWARDS, HONORS: James Theodore Walker fellowship, 1952-54; Fulbright senior research fellowship to Oslo, Norway, 1963-64; Hadley Cantril Memorial Award, 1976, for *Men in Crisis: Human Breakdowns in Prison.*

WRITINGS:

The Social Psychology of Social Movements, Bobbs-Merrill (Indianapolis), 1965.

Violent Men: An Inquiry into the Psychology of Violence, Aldine (Chicago), 1969, revised edition, American Psychological Association, 1992.

(With J. D. Grant and R. Galvin) *Agents of Change: A Study in Police Reform,* Schenkman (Cambridge), 1975.

Men in Crisis: Human Breakdowns in Prison, Aldine, 1975, revised as *Mosaic of Despair: Human Breakdowns in Prison,* American Psychological Association (Washington, DC), 1992.

Peacekeeping: Police, Prisons and Violence, Heath (Washington, DC), 1976, published as *Police, Prisons, and the Problem of Violence,* U.S. Government Printing Office (Washington, DC), 1977.

Living in Prison: The Ecology of Survival, Free Press, 1977, revised edition, American Psychological Association, 1992.

(With Grant) *Reforming Human Services: Change through Participation,* Sage Publications (Beverly Hills), 1982.

(With Grant and K. Adams) *Coping: Maladaptation in the Prison,* Transaction Books (New Brunswick), 1989.

(With K. Adams) *The Disturbed Violent Offender,* Yale University Press (New Haven), 1989, revised edition, American Psychological Association, in press.

(With Grant) *Police as Problem Solvers,* Plenum (New York), 1991.

EDITOR

(And contributor) *Legal and Criminal Psychology,* Holt (New York), 1961.

(With H. C. Smith and contributor with others) *Social Perception: The Development of Interpersonal Impressions,* Van Nostrand (Princeton), 1968.

(And contributor) *The Psychology of Crime and Criminal Justice,* Holt, 1979.

(And contributor) *Therapeutic Communities in Corrections,* Praeger (New York), 1980.

(With R. Johnson and contributor) *Pains of Imprisonment,* Sage Publications, 1982.

Also author of foreword for books, including *Culture and Crisis in Confinement,* by R. Johnson, Lexington Books, 1976; *Crime: A Spatial Perspective,* by D. E. Georges and K. Harries, Columbia University Press, 1980; and *Prison Sexual Aggression,* by D. Lockwood, Elsevier-North Holland, 1980. Contributor of chapters and articles to numerous books, including *The Dynamics of Aggression,* edited by E. I. Magaree and J. E. Hokanson, Harper, 1970; and *Correctional Officer,* edited by R. Ross, Butterworth (Ontario), 1981.

Also author of research reports for U.S. Naval Personnel Research Field Activity, San Diego, CA; editor of conference proceedings for School of Criminal Justice, New York University; author of column, "Ripples on Lake Success," *United Nations World,* 1949-50; book reviewer for government agencies. Contributor of book reviews and articles on communication, public opinion, criminology, psychology of religion, and experimental psychology to journals, including *American Journal of Psychology,*

American Behavioral Scientist, Criminology, Police, Humanist, Corrections Magazine, and *Journal of Criminal Justice.* Editor of *Journal of Research in Crime and Delinquency,* 1974; member of editorial boards of several journals.

WORK IN PROGRESS: Editor and contributor with W. A. Geller, *And Justice for All: A National Agenda for Understanding and Controlling Police Abuse of Force,* forthcoming from Police Executive Research Council.

SIDELIGHTS: Hans Toch once told *CA:* "[I feel that] academic writing has become needlessly stilted and full of private language and obscurantisms. . . . [I] also feel that social science must deal with real life situations without loss of respect for scientific rigor."

*   *   *

TOLLAND, W. R.
  See HEITZMANN, William Ray

*   *   *

TRAVIS, Dempsey J(erome)   1920-

PERSONAL: Born February 25, 1920, in Chicago, IL; son of Louis and Mittie (Strickland) Travis; married Moselynne Hardwick, September 17, 1949. *Education:* Roosevelt University, B.A., 1949; School of Mortgage Banking, Northwestern University, certificate, 1969. *Avocational interests:* Travel (Latin America, Africa, Europe, Soviet Union, China).

ADDRESSES: Office—Travis Realty Co., 840 East 87th St., Chicago, IL 60619-6242.

CAREER: Sivart Mortgage Corp., Chicago, IL, president, 1945-78; Travis Realty Co., Chicago, founder and president, 1949—; Dempsey J. Travis Securities and Investment Co., Chicago, president, 1960-76; and Urban Research Press (formerly Urban Research Institute), Chicago, president, 1969—; Unibanc Trust, director, 1976-87; mayor of Chicago's real estate review committee, chairperson; member of board of directors, Chicago World's Fair Committee, New Regal Theater, Chicago, and Museum of Broadcast Communications, 1985—; member of board of trustees, Garrett-Evangelical Seminary, Evanston, IL, 1980-89, Northwestern Memorial Hospitals, Chicago, and Chicago Historical Society, 1985—. *Military service:* U.S. Army, Ordnance Corps, 1942-46.

MEMBER: United Mortgage Bankers Association of America (founder and president, 1961-74); National As-

sociation of Real Estate Brokers (first vice-president, 1959-60); National Association for the Advancement of Colored People (NAACP; president of Chicago branch, 1959-60); Institute of Real Estate Management; Dearborn Real Estate Board, president, 1957-59, 1970-71; Society of Professional Journalists; Society of Midland Authors (president, 1988-90); Beta Gamma Sigma, Lambda Alpha, Economics Club, Forty Club of Chicago, Assembly Club (Chicago).

AWARDS, HONORS: Honorary Doctorate of Economics, Olive-Harvey College, 1974; honorary Doctorate of Business Administration, Daniel Hale Williams University, Chicago, 1976; honorary Doctorate of Humane Letters, Kennedy-King College, 1982; Society of Midland Authors Award, 1982; Chicago Art Deco Society Award, 1985.

WRITINGS:

Don't Stop Me Now (autobiography), Childrens Press (Chicago), 1970.
An Autobiography of Black Chicago, Urban Research Institute (Chicago), 1981.
An Autobiography of Black Jazz, Urban Research Institute, 1983.
An Autobiography of Black Politics, Urban Research Institute, 1987.
Real Estate Is the Gold in Your Future, Urban Research Press (Chicago), 1988.
Harold: The People's Mayor; An Authorized Biography of Mayor Harold Washington, Urban Research Press, 1989.
Racism: American Style, A Corporate Gift, Urban Research Press, 1991.
I Refuse to Learn to Fail: The Autobiography of Dempsey J. Travis, Urban Research Press, 1992.

Book review critic, *Chicago Sun-Times,* 1991. Contributor to *Ebony.* Financial editor, *Dollars and Sense.*

SIDELIGHTS: Dempsey J. Travis writes primarily about black Chicago history. His book *An Autobiography of Black Jazz* is "about Chicago jazz and also about Chicago entertainment, night life, race relations and much more," according to Toronto *Globe and Mail* contributor Jack Chambers. He dubs it "Dempsey J. Travis's opulent scrapbook," and asserts that "its wealth of anecdote, history, legend and lore will delight jazz fans a long way from Chicago." The Rev. Don Benedict calls Travis's *Racism: American Style, A Corporate Gift* a book which "reminds all Americans, black and white, that as we face the 21st century we are confronted with a persistent and growing racism that is threatening our very existence as a nation."

BIOGRAPHICAL/CRITICAL SOURCES:

BOOKS

Famous Blacks Give Success Secrets, Johnson Publishing (Chicago, IL), 1973.

Seder, John, and Berkeley Burrell, *Getting It Together: Black Businessmen in America,* Harcourt (San Diego, CA), 1971.

Travis, Dempsey J., *Don't Stop Me Now* (autobiography), Childrens Press, 1970.

Travis, Dempsey J., *I Refuse to Learn to Fail: The Autobiography of Dempsey J. Travis,* Urban Research Press, 1992.

PERIODICALS

Globe and Mail (Toronto), March 31, 1984.

Los Angeles Times Book Review, January 1, 1984.

Tribune Books (Chicago), December 28, 1986, section 14, p. 3; November 25, 1988; March 31, 1991.*

*   *   *

TURNER, George W(illiam) 1921-

PERSONAL: Born October 26, 1921, in Dannevirke, New Zealand; son of Albert George (a farmer) and Elinor Jessie (a dressmaker; maiden name, Anderson) Turner; married Beryl Horrobin (an academic), April 18, 1949; children: Anton Eric, Neil Thurstan. *Education:* University of New Zealand, M.A., 1948; University of London, Diploma in English Linguistic Studies, 1964.

ADDRESSES: Home—3 Marola Ave., Rostrevor, South Australia 5073.

CAREER: Teacher of science and agriculture at a high school in Dannevirke, New Zealand, 1944, and Auckland Teachers' College in Auckland, New Zealand, 1945; teacher of languages at Wellington College, Wellington, New Zealand, 1946; University of Canterbury, Canterbury, New Zealand, University Library, head of orders department, 1949-52; Canterbury Public Library, Canterbury, New Zealand, head of reference department, 1953-54; University of Canterbury, lecturer, 1955-64, senior lecturer in English, 1964; University of Adelaide, Adelaide, Australia, reader in English, 1965—, chair of department, 1975-77. Lecturer in Germany, Sweden, England, France, Yugoslavia, and Canada. *Military service:* Served in New Zealand Army, 1942.

MEMBER: Australia and New Zealand Association for Medieval and Renaissance Studies, Linguistic Society of Australia (honorary life member), Australian Universities Language and Literature Association, Academy of the Humanities (fellow).

WRITINGS:

The English Language in Australia and New Zealand, Longmans, Green (London), 1966, 2nd edition, 1972.

(Author of introduction) Joseph Furphy, *Ribgy's Romance,* Ribgy, 1972.

German for Librarians, Massey University, 1972.

Stylistics, Penguin (London), 1973.

(Editor) *Good Australian English and Good New Zealand English,* illustrations by Daphne Howie, A. H. & A. W. Reed (London), 1973.

Linguistics in Australia since 1958, Sydney University Press for the Australian Academy of the Humanities, 1976.

(Editor) *The Australian Pocket Oxford Dictionary,* 2nd edition, Oxford University Press (New York City), 1984.

(Editor) *The Australian Concise Oxford Dictionary,* Oxford University Press, 1987.

Contributor to Australian edition of *Oxford Paperback Dictionary* and to *The Cambridge History of the English Language,* Volume 5, Cambridge University Press (New York City), 1994. Editor with Frances Devlin Glass, P. R. Eaden, and Lois Hoffmann of annotated edition of Joseph Furphy's *Such Is a Life,* 1991.

SIDELIGHTS: George W. Turner told *CA:* "In my early years I worked in a cheese factory, as a builder's laborer and shop assistant, in a radio factory, and as a meter reader. I became interested in books and language early.

"My writing has owed much—really everything—to academic colleagues. My main books have been commissioned for series; unprompted, I, a New Zealand country boy, would not have had the temerity to write them.

"I have two opposite ambitions in writing. In one mood I would simply like to establish a fact, however minute, that was not known before. This ambition comes nearest to fulfillment in the work I do as a consultant for the *Oxford English Dictionary* (second supplement) checking entries for Australian and New Zealand words, in which it is sometimes possible to fill in the earlier history of a word with quotations of earlier date than those collected by previous informants. The opposite ambition is symoptic, a desire to break down barriers between academic subjects. Articles I have written link linguistics with science or logic, or journalism or history. Especially important in this connection is an ambition to heal the old feud between linguistic and literary study.

"My habit when writing a book is to plan the outline in about eight or ten chapters, setting aside a folder for each chapter and putting all quotations, ideas, and facts into the appropriate folder as they come to hand. The book then organizes itself around the material. Quotations and

illustrative examples often seem to come in very aptly this
way, because in fact they precede the connecting text they
illustrate.''

*   *   *

TWOHILL, Maggie
  See GABERMAN, Judie Angell

U

UNDERWOOD, Lewis Graham
See WAGNER, C(harles) Peter

*   *   *

U'REN, Hilda
See U'REN-STUBBINGS, Hilda

*   *   *

UREN, Hilda
See U'REN-STUBBINGS, Hilda

*   *   *

U'REN-STUBBINGS, Hilda 1914-
(Hilda Uren Stubbings, Hilda U'Ren, Hilda Uren)

PERSONAL: Born December 14, 1914, in Connor Downs, Cornwall, England; daughter of John Percival and Florence Mary (Williams) Uren; married George A. Stubbings, 1935; children: Robert George, Carl Herbert, Katharine Beatrice Mott, Suzanne Joyce Willis. *Education:* Stetson University, B.A., 1960, M.A. (American studies), 1962, M.A. (English), 1965; Florida State University, graduate study, 1963; Vanderbilt University, Ph.D., 1968; George Peabody College for Teachers, M.L.S., 1977. *Avocational interests:* Classical music.

ADDRESSES: Home and office—2500 E. Eighth St., Bloomington, IN 47408.

CAREER: Willamette University, Salem, OR, assistant professor of English, 1968-70; Portland State University,

Division of Continuing Education, Portland, OR, bibliographical consultant, 1974-76; Vanderbilt University, Nashville, TN, researcher in collections department, beginning 1976. Bibliographical consultant.

MEMBER: Institute of Cornish Studies, American Library Association, Association of College & Research Libraries, Beta Phi Mu, Gamma Theta Upsilon, Phi Beta Kappa.

WRITINGS:

UNDER NAME HILDA UREN STUBBINGS

(Compiler) *Renaissance Spain in Its Literary Relations with England and France: A Critical Bibliography,* Vanderbilt University Press (Nashville, TN), 1969.

The Magic Glass: The Individual and Society as Seen in the Gams of Herman Melville's Moby-Dick, Rubena Press (Bloomington, IN), 1992.

Blitzkrieg and Books: British and European Libraries as Casualties of World War II, Rubena Press, 1993.

Women in Retrospect: A Research Guide to Studies in English and Romantic Languages, Rubena Press, 1994.

Several articles have been published under variations of the author's name including Hilda U'Ren and Hilda Uren. Contributor to *Christian Science Monitor* and *An Baner Kerenwek* (St. Austell, Cornwall, England).

WORK IN PROGRESS: Annotated comparative bibliographies in Spanish and Celtic literature and in literary thematology; bibliography of scholarly works about women; informal essays on Cornwall and Cornish customs; a bibliography on medieval and Renaissance women.

SIDELIGHTS: Hilda U'Ren-Stubbings told *CA:* "Before I knew better, I thought that bibliography was a dry-as-dust discipline. But now I see that it has a mystique of its own that is seductive. It is an intensely social activity, paradoxically carried on in general solitude in the deep recesses of libraries. The social aspect can be expressed metaphorically: the compiler is a hostess at a grand feast to which guests of like mind have been invited. One of the hostess' pleasant roles is that of introducing newcomers into this convivial and august society. The guests already there, of course, are the scholars whose works are listed in the bibliography who are meeting these authors and their works for the first time. They have a great deal in common, so the party should be a big success. What hostess does not wish this for every party?

"My conversion to bibliography has led me, also, into a preoccupation with the history of books and libraries (and printing). These are a part of our lives we take so much for granted that bringing new perspectives on them to the general reader can offer much to both the reader and the author. In this perspective, too, the role of the publisher, who is often criticized for his crass commercialism, can be seen as indispensable to the preservation of our book heritage which is at once so fragile and yet so enduring."

V

VANDENBUSCHE, Duane (Lee) 1937-

PERSONAL: Born August 4, 1937, in Detroit, MI; son of George C. (a farmer) and Ruby (Briggs) Vandenbusche. *Education:* Northern Michigan College (now University), B.S., 1959; Oklahoma State University, M.A., 1960, Ed.D., 1964. *Politics:* Democrat. *Religion:* Roman Catholic. *Avocational interests:* Fishing, hiking, boating, tennis, skiing, golf, running, mountain biking.

ADDRESSES: Home—West of Gunnison, Gunnison, CO 81230. *Office*—Department of History, Western State College of Colorado, Gunnison, CO 81230.

CAREER: Western State College of Colorado, Gunnison, instructor, 1962-63, assistant professor, 1963-67, associate professor, 1967-73, professor of history, 1973—.

MEMBER: Western History Association, Rocky Mountain Social Science Association.

AWARDS, HONORS: National Association for State and Local History research grants, 1967 and 1970; Boettcher Foundation grant, 1978; named Professor of the Year by Western State College of Colorado, 1967-68 and 1986-87; named Cross-Country Coach of the Year by National Association of Intercollegiate Athletics, 1986; named Regional Coach of the Year in Cross Country by National College Athletic Association Division II, 1994.

WRITINGS:

Marble, Colorado: City of Stone, Golden Bell (Denver, CO), 1970.
Early Days in the Gunnison Country, B & B Publishing (Saugus, CA), 1974.
The Gunnison Country, privately printed, 1980.
(With Duane Smith) *A Land Alone: Colorado's Western Slope,* Pruett (Boulder, CO), 1981.

Also author, with Walter Borneman, of *The Lake City Railroad* (*Colorado Rail Annual,* Number 14), 1979. Also author of videos *Through the Mists of Time,* 1988, and *Crested Butte: Jewel of the Elk Mountains,* 1990. Contributor of articles to periodicals, including *Colorado* and *Journal of the West.*

*　　*　　*

VANSITTART, Peter 1920-

PERSONAL: Born August 27, 1920, in Bedford, England; son of Edward and Mignon (maiden name, Clemence) Vansittart. *Education:* Attended Haileybury College and Worcester College, Oxford.

ADDRESSES: Home—9 Upper Park Rd., Hampstead, London NW3, England. *Agent*—Anthony Shell Associates, 2/3 Morwell St., London WC1B 3AR, England.

CAREER: Novelist, 1942—. Director of Burgess Hill School, Hampstead, England, 1947-59.

MEMBER: Royal Society of Literature (fellow), Beefsteak Club.

AWARDS, HONORS: Society of Authors traveling scholarship, 1970; Arts Council Bursaries, 1981 and 1985; Eastern arts award, 1988; Worcester College, Oxford, honorary fellow, 1995.

WRITINGS:

I Am the World, Chatto & Windus (London), 1942.
Enemies, Chapman & Hall (London), 1947.
The Overseer, Chapman & Hall, 1948.
Broken Canes, Bodley Head (London), 1950.
A Verdict of Treason, Bodley Head, 1951.
A Little Madness, Bodley Head, 1953.
The Game and the Ground, Abelard (London), 1955.

Orders of Chivalry, Abelard, 1956.

The Tournament, Walker (New York City), 1958.

A Sort of Forgetting, Bodley Head, 1960.

Carolina, Ace Books (New York City), 1961.

Sources of Unrest, Bodley Head, 1962.

The Siege, Walker, 1963, published in England as *The Friends of God,* Macmillan (London), 1963.

The Lost Lands, Walker & Co., 1964.

The Dark Tower (juvenile), Macdonald (London), 1965.

The Shadow Land, Macdonald, 1967.

The Story Teller, P. Owen (London), 1968.

Green Knights, Black Angels: A Mosaic of History (juvenile), Macmillan (London), 1969.

Pastimes of a Red Summer, P. Owen, 1969.

Landlord, P. Owen, 1970.

Vladivostok (essay), Covent Garden Press (London), 1972.

Dictators (nonfiction), Studio Vista (London), 1973.

Worlds and Underworlds: Anglo-European History through the Centuries (nonfiction), P. Owen, 1974.

Quintet, P. Owen, 1976.

Flakes of History (nonfiction), Park Editions, 1978.

Lancelot, P. Owen, 1978.

The Death of Robin Hood, P. Owen, 1981.

(Editor) *Voices from the Great War,* G. Cape (London), 1981.

Three Six Seven, P. Owen, 1983.

(Editor) *John Masefield's Letters from the Front, 1915-1917,* J. Cape (London), 1984, Watts, 1985.

(Editor) *Voices 1870-1914,* F. Watts (New York City), 1985.

The Ancient Mariner and the Old Sailor: Delights and Uses of Words (nonfiction), CPS, 1985.

Paths from a White Horse: A Writer's Memoir (autobiography), Quartet (London), 1985.

Aspects of Feeling, P. Owen, 1986.

(Editor) *Happy and Glorious: An Anthology of Royalty,* Collins (London), 1988.

Parsifal, P. Owen, 1988.

(Editor) *Voices of the Revolution,* Collins, 1989.

The Wall, P. Owen, 1990.

A Choice of Murder, P. Owen, 1992.

London: A Literary Companion, John Murray (London), 1994.

A Safe Conduct, P. Owen, 1995.

In the Fifties, John Murray, 1995.

ADAPTATIONS: Voices from the Great War was adapted for stage.

SIDELIGHTS: British author Peter Vansittart has been categorized as an historical novelist, even though—as he admits himself—his many works do not necessarily fall comfortably into that category. A demanding writer whose prose has sometimes drawn comparisons to poetry, Vansittart uses historical situations as groundwork for re-

flections on the human condition, both in its unchanging aspects and in its mutability under the pressures of circumstance. "The writing of Peter Vansittart appeals to a specialised taste, one that relishes a view of history as a teeming, vivid, unruly fairground of experience, jostling with brilliant detail, and palpable immediacy, while on the other hand liking this material to be co-ordinated by a numinous formal and symbolic arrangement that imposes a deeper portentousness," notes Alan Hollinghurst in *New Statesman.* "The reader must relive the actuality of the past as a way of being educated in its relevance to the present." Vansittart's unconventional approach to historical fiction has won a following among critics—especially in the United Kingdom—who praise him especially for his avoidance of the tired cliches that often mar books of that genre.

In his many novels Vansittart employs an elaborate style replete with obscure images and allusions through which he recreates an historical period. According to Herbert Howarth in *Critique: Studies in Modern Fiction,* "Although Vansittart draws the line of a story, as a novelist must or forfeit his audience, he is not emotionally focussed there. He is focussed on the images thrown up as he reflects on his characters and their predicaments; the images become, indeed, more important than the inventions which precede their sparking; and especially the images which pose myths. He writes his novels as a poet assembles a poem." Likewise, *Listener* essayist Kenneth Graham observes: "With Peter Vansittart the question for the critic is always one of style. . . . This is no jungle but a magic wood, a language of dense thickets, fierce elisions and sudden metamorphoses, shot through with colour and heat, a game and a spectacle in itself but at the same time an illumination to the mind, a challenge to discovery, a comedy of illusion and identity."

Born into a middle class family almost constantly beset with money problems, Vansittart grew up fascinated by the power of words and writing. After leaving Worcester College, Oxford, he spent two decades teaching young children in an experimental school in Hampstead, England. He began his own work as a novelist while still serving as a teacher, and some of his best-known works—such as *Green Knights, Black Angels: A Mosaic of History*—seek to reach a juvenile audience. In a review of *Green Knights, Black Angels,* a *Times Literary Supplement* critic asks: "Who will read and re-read it? The dedicated adolescent historian who thrills to fresh aspects of his subject, and the adult who perhaps teaches history, art, civics, philology, literature, or religion and enjoys being given a shot in the arm. These will survive Mr. Vansittart's primary (and flattering) assumption that all of us can follow him anywhere—up and down the centuries, in and out of cultures, the world over—then read on and become first filled with amazement at the author's rich scholarship, then fascinated by his startling ability to draw illuminating conclusions from his evidence."

"Challenging" is an adjective that appears repeatedly in reviews of Vansittart's adult novels. His many fictional works, ranging in time from the pre-Christian era to the present day, are so dense, disjointed, metaphorical, ironic, aphoristic, and compressed that he shares almost nothing in common with writers ordinarily termed historical novelists. *Times Literary Supplement* contributor Philip Oakes contends that all of Vansittart's fiction is "marked by a zest for language, a leaping imagination and indifference to literary fashion . . . What interests him is the interior landscape and the myths and monsters with which it teems." The author has applied this singular approach to a myriad of historical eras and famous figures, from the ancient Greek general Timoleon to such literary heroes as Lancelot, Parsifal, and Robin Hood.

One of Vansittart's breakthrough achievements was *The Death of Robin Hood,* a four-part novel set in Sherwood Forest during various periods in English history. From a prologue based on life in the primeval wood, the story moves on to the era of King John, the Luddite rebellion of 1812, and modern times, when the forest is littered with ice cream cartons, tin cans, and discarded shoes. *British Book News* reviewer Ian Scott-Kilvert praises the author's work for its "style which combines wit with a highly imaginative use of language." A similar reaction is voiced by Michael Wharton in a *Spectator* piece about Vansittart's novel *Three Six Seven,* a book about the Roman occupation of Britain. Wharton calls *Three Six Seven* "a haunting, many-coloured dream of murderous splendor, and evocation of the past which no other historical novelist now writing in England could rival."

Vast popularity has eluded Vansittart. His novels have not been widely published in America, and he has not received any of the major literary citations or prizes. In the *Listener,* Neil Hepburn describes Vansittart's fiction as "very laborious, difficult reading—ultimately rewarding, but confusing in the babble of sensation that it stimulates in the undermind." The demanding nature of Vansittart's prose has found its champions, however. According to Martin Seymour-Smith in the *London Review of Books,* "the very least of his intentions is to give any kind of 'true' picture of the past. He is instead anxious to convey the manner in which the present is permeated by the past. . . . But it does prove very hard to place Vansittart in any tradition or group." London *Times* correspondent Allan Massie concludes of Vansittart: "His original, beautiful and audacious historical novels have hardly had the success they deserve. . . . Vansittart is wise about politics, history, the writing of historical novels, the sadness and joys of life."

In keeping with his particular style, Vansittart's autobiography, *Paths from a White Horse: A Writer's Memoir,* is more an exploration of the author's imaginative life than it is a conventional autobiography. Vansittart touches only briefly on his personal life in the book, preferring to offer anecdote and memory as well as musings on literature and history. This approach intrigues reviewer Philip Oakes, who concludes of the work: "[Vansittart's] memoir is quirky, impressionistic and light on details . . . but it wonderfully illuminates the machinery—odd, arcane and unstoppable—which makes the author tick." Vansittart's other nonfiction includes several well-received anthologies, including *Voices from the Great War* and *Voices of the Revolution.* In a review of the latter title, *Times Literary Supplement* contributor Gwynne Lewis notes: "Peter Vansittart [offers] a cacophony of individual responses to '1789,' ranging from the shrill notes of Marat and Marie-Antoinette to the basso profundo of Danton and Mirabeau. Although this book contains more than a mere collection of memorable remarks—there is a genuine attempt to relate the hundreds of extracts to the major themes of the [French] Revolution—it will doubtless be quarried for Revolutionary aphorisms."

Vansittart told *CA* that each of his books "really has its own motives, some contradictory, difficult to express. It is not important. One's yearning to communicate, from out of a very private life, has many interpretations, none of them lies, yet none wholly truthful. But by setting myself to explore different people, different relationships, in different layers of time, trying to fuse the apparently bizarre with the apparently commonplace, I keep myself in movement. For me, remote pasts, surviving in myth, dream, and a certain obstinant intractibility in human nature, remain very much a power in our contemporary world. Here is the basic theme of my novels, whether 'historical' or 'contemporary.' For me, the novel is a form certainly as poetic as most verse, and I try to make my own work a kind of poetry. On the whole I have succeeded more with fellow writers than with the reading public. I have had many failures. One of my own favorite books, *Harry,* may never be published. But Dorothy Parker described one novel as 'as glittering a work of satire as we have had for many long years, and I think that it is safe to say will not have again for many more.' "

BIOGRAPHICAL/CRITICAL SOURCES:

BOOKS

Contemporary Literary Criticism, Volume 42, Gale, 1987, pp. 389-401.

PERIODICALS

Books, May 13, 1962, p. 4.
British Book News, May, 1981, p. 312.

Christian Science Monitor, May 3, 1962, p. 7.

Critique: Studies in Modern Fiction, spring-summer, 1958, pp. 54-64.

Listener, October 2, 1969, p. 460; July 22, 1976, pp. 94-95.

London Review of Books, March 27, 1986, pp. 14-15.

New Statesman, September 19, 1969, pp. 384-85; January 30, 1981, p. 19.

New York Times Book Review, May 7, 1961, p. 31; July 16, 1989, p. 31.

Saturday Review, July 6, 1957, p. 10.

Spectator, January 2, 1971, p. 23; May 6, 1978, p. 28; February 19, 1983, pp. 21-22; August 3, 1985, p. 6; August 1, 1992, p. 27.

Times (London), February 26, 1981; August 8, 1985; August 18, 1988.

Times Educational Supplement, June 10, 1983, p. 26.

Times Literary Supplement, May 25, 1956, p. 309; March 21, 1958, p. 149; August 26, 1960, p. 541; October 8, 1964, p. 913; November 30, 1967, p. 1159; August 6, 1976, p. 975; August 2, 1985, p. 844; January 24, 1986, p. 81; September 9, 1988; January 26-February 1, 1990, p. 93; August 14, 1992.

*   *   *

VARE, Ethlie Ann 1953-
(Lee Riley)

PERSONAL: Born March 8, 1953, in Montreal, Quebec, Canada; immigrated to the United States, 1953, naturalized citizen, 1958; daughter of Ben (an artist) and Shirley (in business; maiden name, Marder; present name, Riley) Herman; married Barry C. Vare, June 5, 1975 (divorced, November, 1983); children: Russell Alexander. *Education:* University of California, Santa Barbara, B.A. (summa cum laude), 1972. *Politics:* Liberal. *Religion:* Jewish.

ADDRESSES: Home—Los Angeles, CA. *Office*—8306 Wilshire Blvd., Suite 6005, Beverly Hills, CA 90211. *Agent*—Madeleine Morel, 121 West 27th St., New York, NY 10001.

CAREER: Mountain Messenger, Nevada City, CA, associate editor, 1978-80; *Cycling U.S.A.,* Nevada City, associate editor, 1980-82; *Rock,* Los Angeles, CA, editor, 1983-86; author of syndicated column "Rock On," United Features, 1978-91; author of syndicated column "Dateline: Hollywood," Syndicated International Network, 1990—.

MEMBER: National Association of Progressive Radio Announcers (charter member), Los Angeles Women in Music (president, 1987-88).

AWARDS, HONORS: Maggie Award from Western Magazine Publishers, 1987, for editorial content of *Rock;*

Mothers of Invention from the Bra to the Bomb: Forgotten Women and Their Unforgettable Ideas named a Best Book for Young Adults, American Library Association; *Adventurous Spirit: The Ellen Swallow Richards Story* named a Top Title for New Adult Readers, Public Library Association.

WRITINGS:

(With Ed Ochs) *Stevie Nicks,* Ballantine (New York City), 1985.

(Under pseudonym Lee Riley) *Tom Cruise,* Pinnacle (New York City), 1985.

Ozzy Osbourne, Ballantine, 1986.

(Under pseudonym Lee Riley) *Patrick Duffy,* St. Martin's (New York City), 1988.

(With Greg Ptacek) *Mothers of Invention from the Bra to the Bomb: Forgotten Women and Their Unforgettable Ideas,* Morrow (New York City), 1988.

(Under pseudonym Lee Riley) *The Sheens,* St. Martin's, 1989.

Adventurous Spirit: The Ellen Swallow Richards Story, CarolRhoda (Minneapolis), 1992.

(With Ptacek) *Women Inventors and Their Discoveries,* Oliver Press (New York City), 1993.

Legend: Frank Sinatra and the American Dream, Berkley Publishing (New York City), 1995.

Contributor to *Pulse!, Billboard, New York Times, Wall Street Journal, Hollywood Reporter,* and other publications. American correspondent for the Australian magazine *Countdown;* Los Angeles regional editor for Australian magazine *Now,* 1990-91; Hollywood Bureau chief for New Zealand magazine *RTR Countdown,* 1991-94. Pop editor, *Goldmine,* 1983-85.

SIDELIGHTS: Ethlie Ann Vare told *CA:* "I am a rock 'n' roller who came to legitimate journalism to disprove the notion that 'rock writing' is oxymoronic. Feature journalism expanded into books when the subjects got too interesting to cover in twelve hundred words. My work is topical and accessible, and I don't consider 'pop' an insulting description of it. I write to enlighten and entertain.

"*Mothers of Invention* came about when my co-author and co-editor at *Rock* magazine, Greg Ptacek, and I were going over a stringer's article on music video pioneer Michael Nesmith. Nesmith, it seems, had inherited $25 million from his mother, Bette Nesmith Graham—royalties from her invention of Liquid Paper. Of course a woman invented Liquid Paper. How logical! But one never thinks of women as inventors. So the question became 'What else have women invented that we never learned about in school?' The answer was 'Everything from the bra to the bomb.' And it all started with rock and roll."

BIOGRAPHICAL/CRITICAL SOURCES:

PERIODICALS

Los Angeles Times Book Review, March 13, 1988.

*   *   *

VERDUIN, John R(ichard), Jr. 1931-

PERSONAL: Born July 6, 1931, in Muskegon, MI; son of John Richard (a salesman) and Dorothy (Eckman) Verduin; married Janet M. Falk, January 26, 1963; children: John Richard III, Susan E. *Education:* University of Albuquerque, B.S., 1954; Michigan State University, M.A., 1959, Ph.D., 1962. *Avocational interests:* Woodworking, gardening, golfing, and tennis.

ADDRESSES: Home—107 North Lark Ln., Carbondale, IL 62901. *Office*—Department of Educational Administration and Foundations, Southern Illinois University, Carbondale, IL 62901.

CAREER: Public school teacher in Muskegon, MI, 1954-56, and Greenville, MI, 1956-59; State University of New York College at Geneseo, assistant professor, 1962-64, associate professor of education, 1964-67; Southern Illinois University at Carbondale, associate professor, 1967-70, professor in department of educational administration and foundations, 1970—, assistant dean, 1967-73. State of Illinois Gifted program, member of advisory council, 1968—, chairman, 1973—. Special consultant to American Association of Colleges for Teacher Education, Washington, DC, 1966-67, and to American Speech-Language and Hearing Association, Rockville, MD, 1994—. *Military service:* U.S. Marine Corps, 1951.

MEMBER: Association for Supervision and Curriculum Development (chair of education commission), First United Methodist Church, Carbondale; Carbondale Model Cities committee and of Goals for Carbondale committee; American Educational Research Association, Illinois Adult and Continuing Education Association, Phi Delta Kappa, Kappa Delta Phi.

WRITINGS:

Cooperative Curriculum Improvement, Prentice-Hall (Englewood Cliffs, NJ), 1967.
Conceptual Models in Teacher Education, American Association of Colleges for Teacher Education (Washington, DC), 1967.
(Co-author) *Pre-Student Teaching Laboratory Experiences,* Kendall/Hunt (Dubuque, IA), 1970.
(Contributor) William Joyce, Robert Oana, and W. Robert Houston, editors, *Elementary Education in the Seventies,* Holt (New York City), 1970.

(Co-author) *Project Follow Through,* State of Illinois, 1971.
(Co-author) *Adults Teaching Adults: Principles and Strategies,* Learning Concepts, 1977.
(Contributor) James R. Gress and David Purpel, editors, *Curriculum: An Introduction to the Field,* McCutchan, 1978.
(Co-author) *The Adult Educator: A Handbook for Staff Development,* Gulf Publishing (Houston, TX), 1979.
Curriculum Building for Adult Learning, Southern Illinois University Press (Carbondale, IL), 1980.
(Co-author) *Adults and Their Leisure: The Need for Lifelong Learning,* C. C. Thomas (Springfield, IL), 1984.
(Co-author) *Differential Education of the Gifted: A Taxonomy of 32 Key Concepts,* Southern Illinois University Press, 1986.
(Co-author) *The Lifelong Learning Experience: An Introduction,* C. C. Thomas, 1986.
(Co-author) *Differentielle Erziehung Besonders Begabter: Ein Taxonomisher Ansatz,* Deutches Institut fur International Padatogische Forschung, 1989.
(Co-author) *Distance Education: The Foundation for Effective Practice,* Jossey-Bass (San Francisco, CA), 1991.
(Co-author) *Strategic Planning for Health Professionals,* Jones & Bartlett, 1995.

Also author of reports on educational research and projects for the State of Illinois. Contributor of articles to education journals.

WORK IN PROGRESS: Cooperative Knowledge Production.

*   *   *

VINCENT, William R. See HEITZMANN, William Ray

*   *   *

VIOLI, Paul 1944-

PERSONAL: Born July 20, 1944; son of Joseph T. and Irma (Francesconi) Violi; married Carol Ann Boylston (a teacher), June, 1969; children: Helen, Alexander. *Education:* Boston University, B.A., 1966. *Avocational interests:* Travel (West Africa, Europe, Asia).

ADDRESSES: Home—23 Cedar Ledges, Putnam Valley, NY 10579.

CAREER: Architectural Forum, New York City, managing editor, 1972-74. Adjunct professor at New York University.

AWARDS, HONORS: Poetry award, New York State Council on the Arts, 1978; Ingram Merrill Foundation Poetry Award, 1979; National Endowment for the Arts grant, 1980, 1986; New York Foundation for the Arts grant, 1987; Fund for Poetry grant, 1988, 1992.

WRITINGS:

POETRY

Automatic Transmissions, Swollen Magpie Press (Putnam Valley, NY), 1970.

Waterworks, Toothpaste Press (West Branch, IA), 1972.

In Baltic Circles, Kulchur Press (New York City), 1973.

Some Poems, Swollen Magpie Press (Putnam Valley, NY), 1976.

Harmatan: Poem, with illustrations by Paula North, Sun Press (New York City), 1977.

Splurge: Poems, Sun Press, 1981.

American Express, J.S.C. Publications (London), 1982.

Likewise, Hanging Loose Press (Brooklyn, NY), 1987.

The Curious Builder, Hanging Loose Press, 1993.

The Anamorphosis, Pataphysics Press (New York City), 1995.

BIOGRAPHICAL/CRITICAL SOURCES:

PERIODICALS

American Book Review, July-August, 1989.

Choice, October, 1993.

Cover, April, 1994.

Daltonian, March 4, 1988.

Exile, Volume 1, number 3, 1993.

Global Tapestry Journal, Number 20, 1989.

Harvard Review, May, 1993.

Home Planet News, Volume 6, number 6, 1989; Volume 9, number 2, 1994.

Illinois Issues, fall, 1989.

Midwest Book Review, summer, 1988.

Multicultural Review, Volume 2, number 4, 1993.

Newsday, December 19, 1982.

Poetry Project, Volume 129, 1988; Volume 152, 1993.

Poetry Review, Volume 83, number 4, 1993-94.

Reporter Dispatch, July 25, 1993.

Small Press, summer, 1993.

Sulfur, Volume 9, number 2, 1994.

Voice Literary Supplement, May, 1983.

Washington Post Book World, January 1, 1978.

Wide Skirt, January, 1988; June-September, 1993.

*   *   *

VONNEGUT, Kurt, Jr. 1922-

PERSONAL: Born November 11, 1922, in Indianapolis, IN; son of Kurt (an architect) and Edith (Lieber) Vonnegut; married Jane Marie Cox, September 1, 1945 (divorced, 1979); married Jill Krementz (a photographer), November, 1979; children: (first marriage) Mark, Edith, Nanette; (adopted deceased sister's children) James, Steven, and Kurt Adams; (second marriage) Lili (adopted). *Education:* Attended Cornell University, 1940-42, and Carnegie Institute of Technology (now Carnegie-Mellon University), 1943; attended University of Chicago, 1945-47, M.A., 1971. *Avocational interests:* Painting, wood carving, welded sculpture.

ADDRESSES: Home—New York, NY. *Attorney/Agent*—Donald C. Farber, Tanner, Propp & Farber, 99 Park Ave., 25th Floor, New York, NY 10016.

CAREER: Editor, *Cornell Daily Sun,* 1941-42; Chicago City News Bureau, Chicago, IL, police reporter, 1947; General Electric Co., Schenectady, NY, employed in public relations, 1947-50; freelance writer, 1950—. Teacher at Hopefield School, Sandwich, MA, 1965—; lecturer at University of Iowa Writers Workshop, 1965-67, and at Harvard University, 1970-71; Distinguished Professor of English Prose, City College of the City University of New York, 1973-74. Speaker, National Coalition against Censorship briefing for the Attorney General's Commission on Pornography hearing, 1986. *Military service:* U.S. Army, Infantry, 1942-45; was POW; received Purple Heart.

MEMBER: Authors League of America, PEN (American Center; vice-president, 1974—), National Institute of Arts and Letters, Delta Upsilon, Barnstable Yacht Club, Barnstable Comedy Club.

AWARDS, HONORS: Guggenheim fellow, Germany, 1967; National Institute of Arts and Letters grant, 1970; Litt.D., Hobart and William Smith Colleges, 1974; Literary Lion award, New York Public Library, 1981; Eugene V. Debs Award, Eugene V. Debs Foundation, 1981, for public service; Emmy Award for Outstanding Children's Program, National Academy of Television Arts and Sciences, 1985, for *Displaced Person;* Bronze Medallion, Guild Hall, 1986.

WRITINGS:

NOVELS

Player Piano, Scribner (New York City), 1952, published as *Utopia 14,* Bantam (New York City), 1954, published under original title with new preface, Holt (New York City), 1966.

The Sirens of Titan, Dell (New York City), 1959.

Mother Night, Gold Medal Books (New York City), 1961; hardcover edition, Harper (New York City), 1966.

Cat's Cradle, Holt, 1963.

God Bless You, Mr. Rosewater; or, Pearls before Swine, Holt, 1965.

Slaughterhouse Five; or, The Children's Crusade: A Duty-Dance with Death, by Kurt Vonnegut, Jr., a Fourth-Generation German-American Now Living in Easy Circumstances on Cape Cod (and Smoking Too Much) Who, as an American Infantry Scout Hors de Combat, as a Prisoner of War, Witnessed the Fire-Bombing of Dresden, Germany, the Florence of the Elbe, a Long Time Ago, and Survived to Tell the Tale: This Is a Novel Somewhat in the Telegraphic Schizophrenic Manner of Tales of the Planet Tralfamadore, Where the Flying Saucers Come From, Seymour Lawrence/Delacorte (New York City), 1969, twenty-fifth anniversary edition, 1994.

Breakfast of Champions; or, Goodbye Blue Monday, Seymour Lawrence/Delacorte, 1973.

Slapstick; or, Lonesome No More, Seymour Lawrence/Delacorte, 1976.

Jailbird, Seymour Lawrence/Delacorte, 1979.

Deadeye Dick, Seymour Lawrence/Delacorte, 1982.

Galapagos: A Novel, Seymour Lawrence/Delacorte, 1985.

Bluebeard, Delacorte (New York City), 1987.

Hocus Pocus, Putnam (New York City), 1990.

Timequake, Putnam, in press.

SHORT FICTION

Canary in a Cathouse, Fawcett (New York City), 1961.

Welcome to the Monkey House: A Collection of Short Works, Seymour Lawrence/Delacorte, 1968.

PLAYS

Penelope (produced on Cape Cod, Massachusetts, 1960), revised version published as *Happy Birthday, Wanda June* (produced Off-Broadway, 1970), Seymour Lawrence/Delacorte, 1971, revised edition, Samuel French (New York City), 1971.

Between Time and Timbuktu; or, Prometheus Five: A Space Fantasy (television play; produced on National Educational Television Network, 1972), Seymour Lawrence/Delacorte, 1972.

Miss Temptation, edited by David Coperman, Dramatic Publishing Company, 1993.

Also author of *Something Borrowed,* 1958; *The Very First Christmas Morning,* 1962; *EPICAC,* 1963; *My Name Is Everyone,* 1964; and *Fortitude,* 1968.

OTHER

Wampeters, Foma, and Grandfalloons: (Opinions) (essays), Seymour Lawrence/Delacorte, 1974.

(With Ivan Chermayeff) *Sun, Moon, Star* (juvenile), Harper, 1980.

Palm Sunday: An Autobiographical Collage, Seymour Lawrence/Delacorte, 1981.

(Contributor) *Bob and Ray: A Retrospective, June 15-July 10, 1982,* Museum of Broadcasting, 1982.

(Contributor) Block, W. E., and M. A. Walker, editors, *Discrimination, Affirmative Action, and Equal Opportunity: An Economic and Social Perspective,* Fraser Institute, 1982.

Nothing Is Lost Save Honor: Two Essays (contains "The Worst Addiction of Them All" and "Fates Worth Than Death: Lecture at St. John the Divine, New York City, May 23, 1982"), Toothpaste Press (West Branch, IA), 1984.

Fates Worse than Death: An Autobiographical Collage of the 1980s (autobiography), Putnam, 1991.

(Author of foreword) Leeds, Marc, *The Vonnegut Encyclopedia: An Authorized Compendium,* Greenwood Press (Westport, CT), 1995.

Contributor of fiction to numerous publications, including *Cornell Daily Sun, Cosmopolitan, Ladies' Home Journal, McCall's, Playboy,* and *Saturday Evening Post.*

ADAPTATIONS: Happy Birthday, Wanda June was adapted for film, Red Lion, 1971; *Slaughterhouse Five* was adapted for film, Universal, 1972; "Who Am I This Time" (short story) was adapted for film, Rubicon Films, 1982; *God Bless You, Mr. Rosewater* was adapted for the stage by Howard Ashman and produced by Vonnegut's daughter, Edith, 1979; *Slapstick* was adapted for film as *Slapstick of Another Kind,* Paul-Serendipity, 1984; "D. P." (short story) was adapted for television as *Displaced Person,* Hemisphere, 1985.

Many of author's works have been adapted as books on tape.

SIDELIGHTS: Now lauded as one of America's most respected novelists, Kurt Vonnegut Jr. was virtually ignored by critics at the beginning of his writing career. In *Literary Disruptions: The Making of a Post-Contemporary Fiction,* Jerome Klinkowitz observes that "Vonnegut's rise to eminence coincides precisely with the shift in taste which brought a whole new reading public—and eventually critical appreciation—to the works of Richard Brautigan, Donald Barthelme, Jerzy Kosinski, and others. Ten years and several books their elder, Vonnegut by his long exile underground was well prepared to be the senior member of the new disruptive group, and the first of its numbers to be seriously considered for the Nobel Prize. By 1973, when *Breakfast of Champions* appeared . . . , there was little doubt that a fiction widely scorned only six years before was now a dominant mode in serious contemporary literature."

While such early works as *Piano Player* and *The Sirens of Titan* were at first categorized as science fiction, Vonnegut's books go far beyond the realm of most pure SF. Ernest W. Ranly explains in *Commonweal:* "Vonnegut at times adds fantasy to his stories, whereas pure sci-fi permits only what is possible within a given scientific hypothesis. Vonnegut adds humor, a wild black humor, while most sci-fi is serious to the point of boredom. Vonnegut, generally, adds a distinctive sense and literary class. And, finally, Vonnegut seems pre-occupied with genuine human questions, about war, peace, technology, human happiness. He is even bitterly anti-machine, anti-technology, anti-science."

Kurt Vonnegut, Jr. author Peter J. Reed sees *Player Piano* as an important social commentary, yet finds that it is the most difficult of Vonnegut's novels to analyze: "Initially it may strike us as another socio-moral analysis of the present through the future in the tradition of *The Time Machine, Brave New World,* or *1984.* But then the resemblance shows shifts in the direction of the more immediate kinds of social criticism, like *Babbitt, Main Street,* or even *The Grapes of Wrath.* Furthermore, comic episodes become frequent, sometimes roughly in the social-satiric vein of Aldous Huxley or Evelyn Waugh, sometimes as pure slapstick, sometimes almost of the comic strip guffaw-inducing variety." Such satiric and humorous qualities are common to much of Vonnegut's work. Like many writers, he uses satire as a means of emphasizing serious points. However, Vonnegut has the ability to temper biting satire with warmth and concern for his characters and to direct much of the humor toward himself. The result is that Vonnegut, even when he is at his most critical and fatalistic, does not tend to alienate readers; we are able to identify with the writer because he is just as much the object of satire as the rest of society. As Reed concludes, "the attacks on social ills obviously grow out of a deep compassion, and we sense the gentleness of this writer who so often portrays violence."

The Sirens of Titan, the second of Vonnegut's "science fiction" novels, is considered the author's "seminal work" by reviewer G. K. Wolfe in the *Journal of Popular Culture.* "It is not possible to read *Sirens* as mere escapist fiction, for we are constantly drawn back to the individual human element and the harsh realities of meaningless cruelty and death, whether on Mars, Titan, Mercury, or Earth. Vonnegut suggests that these realities will follow man wherever he goes, whatever he does, not because of a failure in man's vision of himself (though this is certainly involved), but because, fortunately or unfortunately, they are a part of what makes him human." *Sirens* marks the introduction of several themes that continue throughout much of Vonnegut's later work: the futility of trying to change the world and, as a result, the necessity of change within the

individual; the fatality of searching for meaning outside of the self when the answer is really a part of human nature; and the elevation of the main character to new levels of understanding through his quest for meaning in human existence.

Mother Night, Vonnegut's third novel, is the story of an American playwright living in Germany at the outbreak of World War II, who is persuaded by the Allies to remain in Germany as a spy while posing as a radio propagandist. After the war he fades into obscurity in the United States until, with his wartime cover still intact, he is kidnapped by Israeli agents to stand trial for his crime. Michael Wood remarks in the *New York Review of Books,* "What is impressive about *Mother Night* is its extraordinary tone which allows Vonnegut to be very funny without being crass or unfeeling. . . . [*Mother Night*] is not an attempt to defeat an enemy by ridicule, but an attempt to contemplate horror by means of laughter, because laughter, of all our inappropriate responses to total, terminal horror, seems the least inappropriate, the least inhuman."

Mother Night is Vonnegut's first novel to be written with a first-person narrator, and is also the first in which technology and the future play no significant part. For this reason it is seen by many as a "transitional" novel between Vonnegut's early and later work. Perhaps most obvious, in comparison with the first two novels, *Mother Night* relies very little on time shifts, resulting in a more unified or "conventional" book. Reed describes it as "Vonnegut's most traditional novel in form. Paradoxically, perhaps, that also accounts for the relative weaknesses of the book. For *Mother Night* lacks some of the excitement and verve of *The Sirens of Titan,* for example, and it is sometimes less likely to carry its reader along than that earlier, more wandering fantasy."

If one single point must be chosen for the transition of Vonnegut from "cult figure" to "popular author" it would most probably be a statement by Graham Greene calling the author's 1963 novel *Cat's Cradle* "one of the three best novels of the year by one of the most able living writers." *Cat's Cradle* is as autobiographical as any of Vonnegut's work up to that point. The Hoenikker family of the novel closely parallels Vonnegut's own family, consisting of an elder son who is a scientist, a tall middle daughter, and a younger son who joins Delta Upsilon. The narrator is again a writer who, in this case, is working on a book called *The Day the World Ended,* about the bombing of Hiroshima. Since its publication, *Cat's Cradle* has consistently appeared on high school and college reading lists; Reed says that it might be the most widely-read of Vonnegut's novels among young people. He explains that "to 'the counter-culture' it should appeal as a book which counters almost every aspect of the culture of our society. To a generation which delights in the 'put on,' parody and artifice, often as the most meaningful expressions of deeply held convictions in a world which they see as prone to distortion, *Cat's Cradle*'s play with language, symbol and artifice should find accord."

God Bless You, Mr. Rosewater; or, Pearls before Swine introduces a theme that crops up repeatedly in the later novels and which is often considered to be the essence of all of Vonnegut's writing. It is expressed by the main character, Eliot Rosewater, in the motto "Goddamn it, you've got to be kind." John R. May comments in a *Twentieth Century Literature* review that it is the author's "most positive and humane work. . . . We may not be able, Vonnegut is saying, to undo the harm that has been done, but we can certainly love, simply because there are people, those who have been made useless by our past stupidity and greed, our previous crimes against our brothers. And if that seems insane, then the better the world for such folly." *Book Week* contributor Daniel Talbot writes: "It's a tribute to Kurt Vonnegut Jr. that he has covered such a large territory of human follies in so short a book. . . . The net effect is at once explosively funny and agonizing."

In *Slaughterhouse Five; Or the Children's Crusade,* Vonnegut finally delivers a complete treatise on the World War II bombing of Dresden. The main character, Billy Pilgrim, is a very young infantry scout who is captured in the Battle of the Bulge and quartered in a Dresden slaughterhouse where he and other prisoners are employed in the production of a vitamin supplement for pregnant women. During the February 13, 1945, firebombing by Allied aircraft, the prisoners take shelter in an underground meat locker. When they emerge, the city has been levelled and they are forced to dig corpses out of the rubble. The story of Billy Pilgrim is the story of Kurt Vonnegut who was captured and survived the firestorm in which 135,000 German civilians perished, more than the number of deaths in the bombings of Hiroshima and Nagasaki combined. Robert Scholes sums up the theme of *Slaughterhouse Five* in the *New York Times Book Review,* writing: "Be kind. Don't hurt. Death is coming for all of us anyway, and it is better to be Lot's wife looking back through salty eyes than the Deity that destroyed those cities of the plain in order to save them." The reviewer concludes that "*Slaughterhouse Five* is an extraordinary success. It is a book we need to read, and to reread."

The popularity of *Slaughterhouse Five* is due, in part, to its timeliness; it deals with many issues that were vital to the late sixties: war, ecology, overpopulation, and consumerism. Klinkowitz, writing in *Literary Subversions: New American Fiction and the Practice of Criticism,* sees larger reasons for the book's success: "Kurt Vonnegut's fiction of the 1960s is the popular artifact which may be the fairest example of American cultural change. . . . Shunned as distastefully low-brow . . . and insufficiently

commercial to suit the exploitative tastes of high-power publishers, Vonnegut's fiction limped along for years on the genuinely democratic basis of family magazine and pulp paperback circulation. Then in the late 1960s, as the culture as a whole exploded, Vonnegut was able to write and publish a novel, *Slaughterhouse Five,* which so perfectly caught America's transformative mood that its story and structure became best-selling metaphors for the new age."

Writing in *Critique,* Wayne D. McGinnis comments that in *Slaughterhouse Five,* Vonnegut "avoids framing his story in linear narration, choosing a circular structure. Such a view of the art of the novel has much to do with the protagonist . . . Billy Pilgrim, an optometrist who provides corrective lenses for Earthlings. For Pilgrim, who learns of a new view of life as he becomes 'unstuck in time,' the lenses are corrective metaphorically as well as physically. Quite early in the exploration of Billy's life the reader learns that 'frames are where the money is.' . . . Historical events like the bombing of Dresden are usually 'read' in the framework of moral and historical interpretation." McGinnis feels that the novel's cyclical nature is inextricably bound up with the themes of "time, death, and renewal," and goes on to say that "the most important function of 'so it goes' [a phrase that recurs at each death in the book] . . . , is its imparting a cyclical quality to the novel, both in form and content. Paradoxically, the expression of fatalism serves as a source of renewal, a situation typical of Vonnegut's works, for it enables the novel to go on despite—even because of—the proliferation of deaths."

After the publication of *Slaughterhouse Five,* Vonnegut entered a period of depression during which he vowed, at one point, never to write another novel. He concentrated, instead, on lecturing, teaching, and finishing a play, *Happy Birthday, Wanda June,* that he had begun several years earlier. The play, which ran Off-Broadway from October, 1970 to March, 1971, received mixed reviews. *Newsweek*'s Jack Kroll wrote that "almost every time an American novelist writes a play he shows up most of our thumb-tongued playwrights, who lack the melody of mind, the wit, dash and accuracy of Saul Bellow and Bruce Jay Friedman. And the same thing must be said of the writing in *Happy Birthday, Wanda June,* . . . Vonnegut's dialogue is not only fast and funny, with a palpable taste and crackle, but it also means something. And his comic sense is a superior one; *Wanda June* has as many laughs as anything by Neil Simon." On the other hand, in the *New Republic* Stanley Kauffmann called it "a disaster, full of callow wit, rheumatic invention, and dormitory profundity. . . . The height of its imagination is exemplified by a scene in Heaven between a golden-haired little girl and a Nazi Gauleiter in which they discuss the way Jesus plays shuffleboard."

Breakfast of Champions marked the end of Vonnegut's depression and a return to the novel; in honor of this event, Vonnegut subtitled the work, *Goodbye Blue Monday.* Nora Sayre writes in the *New York Times Book Review* that "in this novel Vonnegut is treating himself to a giant brain-flush, clearing his head by throwing out acquired ideas, and also liberating some of the characters from his previous books. Thus, he has celebrated his fiftieth birthday in the same spirit that made Tolstoy release his serfs and Thomas Jefferson free his slaves. Once again, we're back on the people-grid; major and minor personae from other novels resurface in this one, their lives ridiculously entangled. . . . This explosive meditation ranks with Vonnegut's best."

In *Breakfast of Champions,* as in most of Vonnegut's work, there are very clear autobiographical tendencies. In this novel, however, the author seems to be even more wrapped up in his characters than usual. He appears as Philboyd Sludge, the writer of the book which stars Dwayne Hoover, a Pontiac dealer (Vonnegut once ran a Saab dealership) who goes berserk after reading a novel by Kilgore Trout, who also represents Vonnegut. Toward the end of the book, Vonnegut arranges a meeting between himself and Trout, who Robert Merrill calls his "most famous creation," in which he casts the character loose forever; by this time the previously unsuccessful Trout has become rich and famous and is finally able to stand on his own.

With his next book, *Slapstick,* Vonnegut undertakes the theme that the wane of the extended family has caused loneliness for most Americans, and he proposes a system for providing everyone with such a family (hence the subtitle, *Lonesome No More*). In a *New Republic* review, Klinkowitz calls *Slapstick* a "deceptively short and simple book" which, he says, "returns to the greatest strength of this writer's art: the ability to project the big and little concerns of his own life into the field of imaginary action." Klinkowitz also believes that the novel represents something of a departure for Vonnegut in that it contains no old characters or familiar themes. *New York Times Book Review* contributor Roger Sale disagrees: "*Slapstick* opens with a typical Vonnegut cynicism about America having become a place of interchangeable parts, so that Indianapolis, which 'once had a way of speaking all its own,' now is 'just another someplace where automobiles live.' I can't speak about Indianapolis, but one thing I resist in Vonnegut's books is that they seem formulaic, made of interchangeable parts, though this is one quality which may endear him to others. Once Vonnegut finds what he takes to be a successful character, motif or phrase, he can't bear to give it up, and so he carries it around from novel to

novel. . . . The story in *Slapstick* is part *Cat's Cradle,* part *God Bless You, Mr. Rosewater,* part Kilgore Trout and part Thomas Pynchon."

Reviewing Vonnegut's next work, 1979's *Jailbird,* John Leonard of the *New York Times* says that in previous novels Vonnegut has told us "that he believed in the Bill of Rights, Robert's *Rules of Order* and the principles of Alcoholics Anonymous. In his new novel, *Jailbird*—his best in my opinion since *Mother Night* and *Cat's Cradle*—he adds another sacred document. It is the Sermon on the Mount." In this novel the main character, Walter F. Starbuck, is asked by Congressman Richard M. Nixon at a 1949 hearing why he has joined the Communist Party; Starbuck replies: "Why? The Sermon on the Mount, sir." "When you think about it," notes Leonard, "the Sermon on the Mount is a radical document, promising that the meek shall inherit the earth. Shall they, indeed? Mr. Vonnegut has his doubts."

Even though Leonard makes a point of identifying *Jailbird* as a "fable of evil and inadvertence," *New York Times Book Review* contributor Michael Wood criticizes Vonnegut for his inability to "see evil at all. He sees only weakness, and in these long, flattened perspectives, everything—Watergate, Auschwitz, Goering and yesterday's news—comes to belong simply to a blurred, generalized representation of damage and error. There is a real subject here, and it is one of Vonnegut's subjects: What are we to do when we cannot perceive the reality of evil, or distinguish it from other forms of human failure?"

Catastrophe comes more easily in 1982's *Deadeye Dick.* The title character's father saves the life of a starving artist, the young Hitler, when they are in school together; the narrator, Rudy Waltz, gains his cruel nickname at age twelve when a shot he fires from his father's rifle accidentally kills a pregnant woman; and later, a neutron bomb detonates, either by accident, or by the government's covert design, in Waltz's home town, killing everyone, but leaving the machines and buildings unharmed. Interspersed with these horrors are recipes, provided by Rudy, who has become a chef and co-partner with his brother in a restaurant in Haiti. Throughout, "the grand old Vonnegutian comedy of causelessness still holds center stage. . . . Why does the child of a gun safety specialist, using a rifle from his father's collection, emerge as a double murderer? A tough question. Why do human beings take satisfaction in creating a neutron bomb that destroys 'only' human beings, not their accoutrements? Another toughie. Why should grief-struck Rudy Waltz, headed for a presumably moving moment at his parents' graveside, allow his train of thought to light on a certain cookie, whereupon . . . instead of grief we're provided with a recipe for almond macaroons?," Benjamin DeMott asks in the *New York Times Book Review.*

If catastrophe comes more easily to man than courtesy and decency, man's large brain is to blame, Vonnegut asserts in his next novel. "*Galapagos* brings Vonnegut's lifelong belief in the imperfectibility of human nature to its logical conclusion," observes a London *Times* reviewer. The novel recounts the evolution of man over thousands of years. Narrated by the spectral remains of Vietnam vet Leon Trout, the story tells how a group of tourists are shipwrecked in the islands where Darwin formulated the notion of progressive adaptation; over time, their oversized brains diminish, sexual interests atrophy, and their hands become flippers, all to the benefit of the race and the ecosystem. "This will eliminate war, starvation, and nuclear terror—that is, many of the things Mr. Vonnegut likes to complain about in his novels," remarks *New York Times* reviewer Michiko Kakutani. But for all the seriousness of its message, the book contains sufficient humor to make it satisfying as "a well-crafted comic strip," Kakutani adds.

Though some reviewers find Vonnegut's jokes an easy target for criticism, Thomas M. Disch, writing in the *Times Literary Supplement*, sees in the humor a secondary purpose, "which is moral instruction. Indeed, the interest of the Vonnegut voice is not in what it reveals of the author but in the audience that it hypothesizes, an audience that must have the most basic facts of life explained to it in the simplest terms, an audience that will crack up at the sound of a fart, an audience that has the best of intentions even as it paves the road to hell, an audience of children who know they need to be scolded. Vonnegut is unusual among novelists who dramatize the conflict (ever recurring in his work) between fathers and sons in that his sympathies always lie on the sadder-but-wiser side of the generation gap. In an era that has institutionalized adolescent rebellion, here is a father for foundlings of all ages. Small wonder that he is so popular."

Although it takes place in the near future, the text of 1990's *Hocus Pocus*, like many Vonnegut novels, ranges freely through the much of the twentieth century. As Vonnegut's protagonist Eugene Debs Hartke describes it, America in 2001 is "a thoroughly looted bankrupt nation whose assets had been sold off to foreigners, a nation swamped by unchecked plagues and superstition and illiteracy and hypnotic TV." Like the central characters in *Mother Night* and *Slaughterhouse-Five*, Hartke is a man incarcerated. His story ranges from West Point to Vietnam (he is the last American soldier to leave), from his job as physics instructor at a college for dyslexics (he is dismissed for his pessimism) to his job at a prison run for profit by the Japanese. Hartke is unjustly accused of masterminding a prison break and ends up in jail himself. Along the way some familiar Vonnegut standbys—the Tralfamadorians from *Sirens of Titan*, the SF writer Kil-

gore Trout from *Breakfast of Champions*—turn up, and as in other novels, Vonnegut freely peppers the text with quotes from Bartlett's *Familiar Quotations*.

Jay McInerney, in the *New York Times Book Review*, believes that *Hocus Pocus* "is the most topical, realistic Vonnegut novel to date, and shows the struggles of an artist a little impatient with allegory and more than a little impatient with his own country." He states: "Vonnegut is working much closer to the ground in *Hocus Pocus* . . . it is the most richly detailed and textured of Mr. Vonnegut's renderings of this particular planet. Unlike many of his major characters, Hartke seems like a real person, and Scipio seems like a real town." However, according to John Skow in *Time*: "The body of Vonnegut's writing contains some of the most uncomfortably funny social satire in the English language. What is offered here is something else, a try at prophecy in the darkest and gloomiest biblical sense. As prophecy it is major or minor, right or wrong, the reader's choice. As literature it is minor Vonnegut."

While Vonnegut's fiction is couchedly candid in its reflection of his personal views on many subjects, his essays and other works of nonfiction are even more so. He has published several collections of essays, interviews, and speeches, including *Palm Sunday: An Autobiographical Collage* in 1981 and *Fates Worse than Death: An Autobiographical Collage of the 1980s*, a similar mix to *Palm Sunday*, published a decade later. In *Fates Worse than Death*, collected essays and speeches are interwoven with memoir and parenthetical commentary written especially for the volume. Subject matter ranges from the broadly political—Western imperialism and America's war-greed—to the painfully personal—Vonnegut's own prisoner-of-war experiences and bouts with mental illness. Douglas Anderson describes the collection in the *New York Times Book Review* as "scarily funny" and feels that "it offers a rare insight into an author who has customarily hidden his heart." In the *Times Literary Supplement*, James Woods concludes that the "more Vonnegut writes the more American he seems—a kind of de-solemnized Emerson, at once arguer, doubter, sermonizer and gossip."

In addition to novels, plays and nonfiction, Vonnegut has also published two volumes of stories. *Canary in a Cathouse* brought together about half of his shorter fiction, and was later expanded with additional stories as *Welcome to the Monkey House*. All of the work collected here was penned from the late 1940s to the mid-1960s and appeared in a wide range of national magazines, including *Playboy, Esquire, Cosmopolitan, Ladies Home Journal*, and *Fantasy and Science Fiction*. In his preface to *Welcome to the Monkey House* Vonnegut seems to dismiss these stories as commercial efforts, describing them as "samples of work I sold in order to finance the writing of novels," and adding, "Business is business."

Larry L. King, in the *New York Times Book Review*, states that "*Welcome to the Monkey House* fails to enhance Kurt Vonnegut's reputation. There are only brief glimpses of the hilarious, uproarious Vonnegut whose black-logic extensions of today's absurdities into an imagined society of tomorrow at once gives us something to laugh at and much to fear. . . . The rather pitiful state of magazine fiction is what one remembers most about this book." However, although Stanley Schatt, in his *Kurt Vonnegut, Jr.*, grants that Vonnegut "will probably be remembered for his novels and not for his short stories," he does believe that some of the stories are "certainly memorable."

Apart from judgments regarding its literary worth, Vonnegut's short fiction is of interest for the insights it can provide into his novels. Like his longer fiction, his stories tend to fall into two categories: contemporary tales reflecting Vonnegut's own experience, and those that can be clearly labeled as science fiction. As Schatt points out, variations on many of Vonnegut's recurrent themes can be found in his short stories, and a number of stories actually contain settings and characters that also appear in the novels. "EPICAC" is about the same super computer that controls society in *Player Piano*. Diane Moon Glompers appears as a character in both *God Bless You, Mr. Rosewater* and "Harrison Bergeron."

Vonnegut's work has been likened to that of numerous literary figures, including Charles Dickens, Jonathan Swift, George Orwell, Aldous Huxley, Richard Stern, Bruce Jay Friedman, Thomas Pynchon, Joseph Heller, and Donald Barthelme, to name only a few. Vonnegut himself stated that the two main themes of all his work were best expressed by his brother, who soon after the birth of his first child, wrote, "Here I am cleaning shit off of practically everything," and by his sister, whose last words were, "no pain." In an essay in *The Critic as Artist: Essays on Books, 1920-1970*, J. Michael Crichton calls this analysis "as true as anything a writer has said of his work." Crichton thinks that Vonnegut's novels "have attacked our deepest fears of automation and the bomb, our deepest political guilts, our fiercest hatreds and loves. Nobody else writes books on these subjects; they are inaccessible to normal novelistic approaches. But Vonnegut, armed with his schizophrenia, takes an absurd, distorted, wildly funny framework which is ultimately anaesthetic."

Vonnegut's status as a master of contemporary fiction is built only partly on the strength of his themes. Concludes Robert Group in the *Dictionary of Literary Biography*, "The contribution of Kurt Vonnegut Jr. to American literature is twofold: through his artistry (and persistence) he has helped to elevate the pulp genre of science fiction to the level of critical recognition; and through his philosophy he offers a mixture of wistful humanism and cynical existentialism that implies a way of dealing with modern realities completely different from that of most American writers. In the tradition of [Laurence] Sterne and [Henry] Fielding, he uses wit and wisdom to show that though man may live in a purposeless universe full of self-seeking manipulations, there is hope for something better. . . . Like Trout or Vonnegut one must cry out against absurdity, even if one is ignored. Vonnegut creates a vision so preposterous that indignation might provide the basis for change—while laughter allows one to cope with the moment."

BIOGRAPHICAL/CRITICAL SOURCES:

BOOKS

Bellamy, Joe David, editor, *The New Fiction: Interviews with Innovative American Writers*, University of Illinois Press (Chicago), 1974.

Broer, Lawrence R., editor, *Sanity Plea: Schizophrenia in the Novels of Kurt Vonnegut* (revised edition), University of Alabama Press (Tuscaloosa), 1994.

Bryant, Jerry H., *The Open Decision*, Free Press, 1970.

Chernuchin, Michael, editor, *Vonnegut Talks!*, Pylon Press (Forest Hills, NY), 1977.

Clareson, Thomas D., editor, *Voices for the Future: Essays on Major Science Fiction Writers*, Volume 1, Bowling Green University Popular Press (Bowling Green, OH), 1976.

Contemporary Literary Criticism, Gale (Detroit), Volume 1, 1973, Volume 2, 1974, Volume 3, 1975, Volume 4, 1975, Volume 5, 1976, Volume 8, 1978, Volume 12, 1980, Volume 22, 1982, Volume 60, 1986.

Dictionary of Literary Biography, Gale, Volume 2: *American Novelists since World War II*, 1978, Volume 8: *Twentieth Century American Science Fiction Writers, Part 2*, 1981.

Dictionary of Literary Biography Documentary Series, Volume 3, Gale, 1983.

Dictionary of Literary Biography Yearbook 1980, Gale, 1981.

Dillard, R. H. W., George Garrett, and John Rees Moore, editors, *The Sounder Few: Essays from the "Hollins Critic,"* University of Georgia Press (Athens), 1971.

Giannone, Richard, *Vonnegut: A Preface to His Novels*, Kennikat, 1977.

Goldsmith, David H., *Kurt Vonnegut: Fantasist of Fire and Ice*, Bowling Green University Popular Press, 1972.

Harris, Charles B., *Contemporary American Novelists of the Absurd*, College and University Press, 1971.

Harrison, Gilbert A., editor, *The Critic as Artist: Essays on Books, 1920-1970*, Liveright (New York City), 1972.

Hassan, Ihab, *Contemporary American Literature 1942-1972,* Ungar (New York City), 1973.

Hudgens, Betty Lenhardt, *Kurt Vonnegut, Jr.: A Checklist,* Gale, 1972.

Karl, Frederick R., *American Fictions: 1940-1980,* Harper, 1983.

Kazin, Alfred, *Bright Book of Life: American Novelists and Storytellers from Hemingway to Mailer,* Little, Brown (Boston), 1973.

Kennard, Jean E., *Number and Nightmare: Forms of Fantasy in Contemporary Fiction,* Shoe String (Hamden, CT), 1975.

Klinkowitz, Jerome, and John Somer, editors, *The Vonnegut Statement: Original Essays on the Life and Work of Kurt Vonnegut,* Delacorte (New York City), 1973.

Klinkowitz, Jerome, and Asa B. Pieratt, *Kurt Vonnegut, Jr.: A Descriptive Bibliography and Secondary Checklist,* Shoe String, 1974.

Klinkowitz, Jerome, *Literary Disruptions: The Making of a Post-Contemporary American Fiction,* University of Illinois Press, 1975.

Klinkowitz, Jerome, and Donald L. Lawler, editors, *Vonnegut in America: An Introduction to the Life and Work of Kurt Vonnegut,* Delacorte, 1977.

Klinkowitz, Jerome, *The American 1960s: Imaginative Acts in a Decade of Change,* Iowa State University Press (Ames), 1980.

Klinkowitz, Jerome, *Kurt Vonnegut,* Methuen (New York City), 1982.

Klinkowitz, Jerome, *Literary Subversions: New American Fiction and the Practice of Criticism,* Southern Illinois University Press (Carbondale), 1985.

Krementz, Jill, editor, *Happy Birthday, Kurt Vonnegut: A Festschrift for Kurt Vonnegut on His Sixtieth Birthday,* Delacorte, 1982.

Leeds, Marc, *The Vonnegut Encyclopedia: An Authorized Compendium,* Greenwood Press, 1995.

Lundquist, James, *Kurt Vonnegut,* Ungar, 1977.

Mayo, Clark, *Kurt Vonnegut: The Gospel from Outer Space, or Yes, We Have No Nirvanas,* Borgo Press (San Bernardino, CA), 1973.

Mustazza, Leonard, editor, *The Critical Response to Kurt Vonnegut,* Greenwood Press, 1994.

Olderman, Raymond M., *Beyond the Wasteland: A Study of the American Novel in the 1960s,* Yale University Press (New Haven, CT), 1973.

Platt, Charles, *Dream Makers: The Uncommon People Who Write Science Fiction,* Berkley Books, 1980.

Plimpton, George, editor, *Writers at Work: The Paris Review Interviews,* sixth series, Penguin (New York City), 1984.

Reed, Peter J., *Kurt Vonnegut, Jr.,* Warner Books, 1972.

Schatt, Stanley, *Kurt Vonnegut, Jr.,* Twayne (Boston), 1976.

Short, Robert, *Something to Believe In: Is Kurt Vonnegut Exorcist of Jesus Christ Superstar?,* Harper, 1976.

Tanner, Tony, *City of Words: American Fiction 1950-1970,* Harper, 1971.

Tilton, John W., *Cosmic Satire in the Contemporary Novel,* Bucknell University Press (Cranbury, NJ), 1977.

Wohlheim, Donald A., *The Universe Makers,* Harper, 1971.

PERIODICALS

Book Week, April 11, 1965.

Commonweal, September 16, 1966; June 6, 1969; November 27, 1970; May 7, 1971; December 7, 1973.

Critique: Studies in Modern Fiction, Volume 12, number 3, 1971; Volume 14, number 3, 1973; Volume 15, number 2, 1973; Volume 17, number 1, 1975; Volume 18, number 3, 1977; Volume 26, number 2, 1985.

Detroit News, June 18, 1972; September 16, 1979; October 3, 1982; November 10, 1985; January 5, 1986.

Esquire, June, 1968; September, 1970.

Extrapolation, December, 1973.

Film Comment, November/December, 1985.

Globe and Mail (Toronto), March 17, 1984; February 8, 1986; October 17, 1987.

Harper's, May, 1973; July, 1974.

Hollins Critic, October, 1980.

Horizon, October, 1980.

Hudson Review, autumn, 1969.

International Fiction Review, summer, 1980.

Journal of Popular Culture, spring, 1972; winter, 1973.

Library Journal, April 15, 1973.

Life, April 9, 1965; August 16, 1968; September 12, 1969; November 20, 1970.

London Magazine, July, 1981.

Los Angeles Times, February 7, 1983.

Los Angeles Times Book Review, September 23, 1979; October 31, 1982; March 3, 1984; April 18, 1984; September 29, 1985; September 2, 1990, pp. 1, 10.

Media & Methods, January, 1971.

Modern Fiction Studies, spring, 1973; summer, 1975; winter, 1980-81.

Nation, September 23, 1968; June 9, 1969; September 15, 1979; March 21, 1981; November 13, 1982.

National Observer, June 29, 1974.

National Review, September 28, 1973; November 26, 1976; November 23, 1979; December 10, 1982.

New Republic, August 18, 1952; October 8, 1966; April 26, 1969; November 7, 1970; June 12, 1971; May 12, 1973; September 28, 1973; June 1, 1974; July 5, 1974; September 25, 1976; November 26, 1976.

Newsletter of the Conference on Christianity and Literature, fall, 1972.

New Statesman, April 4, 1975; November 5, 1976.

Newsweek, August 19, 1968; March 3, 1969; April 14, 1969; October 19, 1970; December 20, 1971; May 14, 1973; October 1, 1979.

New York, December 13, 1971.

New Yorker, August 16, 1952; May 15, 1965; May 17, 1969; October 17, 1970; October 25, 1976; November 8, 1982.

New York Review of Books, July 2, 1970; May 31, 1973; November 25, 1976; November 22, 1979.

New York Times, August 19, 1968; September 13, 1969; October 6, 1970; October 18, 1970; May 27, 1971; May 13, 1973; October 3, 1975; September 7, 1979; September 24, 1979; October 15, 1979; March 27, 1981; November 5, 1982; February 4, 1983; February 17, 1983; September 25, 1985; January 27, 1987; April 4, 1987.

New York Times Book Review, June 2, 1963; April 25, 1965; August 6, 1967; September 1, 1968; April 6, 1969; February 4, 1973; May 13, 1973; October 3, 1976; September 9, 1979; March 15, 1981; October 17, 1982; October 6, 1985; October 18, 1987, p. 12; September 9, 1990, p. 12; September 15, 1991, p. 26; November 1, 1992, p. 32.

New York Times Magazine, January 24, 1971.

North American Review, December, 1985.

Novel: A Forum on Fiction, winter, 1975.

Observer, March 22, 1970; November 3, 1985; September 4, 1994, p. 17.

Observer Review, March 15, 1970.

Paris Review, spring, 1977.

Partisan Review, number 1, 1970; Volume 41, number 2, 1974.

People, October 19, 1987.

Progressive, August, 1981.

Publishers Weekly, October 25, 1985; January 31, 1986.

Punch, December 4, 1968.

Queen's Quarterly, spring, 1981.

Saturday Review, April 3, 1965; March 29, 1969; February 6, 1971; May 1, 1971; September 15, 1979.

South Atlantic Quarterly, winter, 1979.

Southwest Review, winter, 1971.

Spectator, November 9, 1968.

THOUGHT, March, 1981.

Time, August 30, 1968; April 11, 1969; June 29, 1970; June 3, 1974; October 25, 1976; September 10, 1979; October 25, 1982; October 21, 1985; September 28, 1987, p. 68; September 3, 1990, p. 73.

Times (London), July 8, 1981; February 17, 1983; May 17, 1986; May 30, 1987.

Times Literary Supplement, November 11, 1965; December 12, 1968; July 17, 1969; November 5, 1976; December 7, 1979; June 19, 1981; September 26, 1980; February 25, 1983; November 8, 1985; October 26, 1990, p. 1146; November 15, 1991, p. 8.

Tribune Books (Chicago), September 27, 1987, p. 1; August 19, 1990, p. 6; September 1, 1991, p. 4; November 24, 1991, p. 8; September 6, 1992, p. 2.

Twentieth Century Literature, January, 1972.

Village Voice, February 22, 1983.

Virginia Quarterly Review, summer, 1981.

Washington Post, October 12, 1970; May 13, 1973; May 15, 1981; February 2, 1982.

Washington Post Book World, March 8, 1981; October 17, 1982; September 22, 1985; October 4, 1987; August 19, 1990, pp. 1-2; October 21, 1990, p. 15.

Western Humanities Review, summer, 1974.

World, June 19, 1973.

World Literature Today, winter, 1981.

W-Z

WAGNER, C(harles) Peter 1930-
(Epafrodito, Lewis Graham Underwood)

PERSONAL: Born August 15, 1930, in New York, NY; son of C. Graham (a buyer) and Mary (Lewis) Wagner; married Doris Mueller (a missionary), October 15, 1950; children: Karen, Ruth, Rebecca. *Education:* Rutgers University, B.S., 1952; Fuller Theological Seminary, B.D., 1955, M.A., 1968; Princeton Theological Seminary, Th.M., 1962; University of Southern California, Ph.D., 1977.

ADDRESSES: Home—135 North Oakland Ave., Pasadena, CA 91101.

CAREER: Congregational clergyman, 1955—; Instituto Biblico del Oriente, San Jose, Bolivia, director, 1956-61; Instituto Biblico Emaus, Cochabamba, Bolivia, professor and director, 1962-71; Andes Evangelical Mission (now S.I.M. International), Cochabamba, associate director, 1964-71; Fuller Theological Seminary, Pasadena, CA, professor of church growth, 1971—. Coordinator, A.D. 2000 United Prayer Track, 1991 —.

MEMBER: Phi Beta Kappa.

WRITINGS:

(With Joseph S. McCullough) *The Condor of the Jungle,* Revell (Old Tappen, NJ), 1966.

Defeat of the Bird God, Zondervan (Grand Rapids, MI), 1967.

Latin American Theology, Eerdmans (Grand Rapids, MI), 1969.

The Protestant Movement in Bolivia, William Carey Library (Pasadena, CA), 1970.

(With Ralph Covell) *An Extension Seminary Primer,* William Carey Library, 1971.

A Turned-On Church in an Uptight World, Zondervan, 1971.

Frontiers in Missionary Strategy, Moody (Chicago, IL), 1972.

Look Out! The Pentecostals Are Coming, Creation House (Wheaton, IL), 1973.

Stop the World, I Want to Get On, Regal Books (Ventura, CA), 1974.

Your Church Can Grow: Seven Vital Signs of a Healthy Church, Regal Books, 1976.

Your Church and Church Growth (includes workbook and six cassette tapes), Fuller Evangelistic Association of Pasadena, 1976, revised edition published as *The Growing Church,* 1982.

Your Spiritual Gifts Can Help Your Church Grow, Regal Books, 1979.

Your Church Can Be Healthy, Abingdon (Nashville, TN), 1979.

Our Kind of People: The Ethical Dimensions of Church Growth in America, John Knox (Atlanta, GA), 1979.

(With Bob Waymire) *The Church Growth Survey Handbook,* Global Church Growth Bulletin, 1980.

Church Growth and the Whole Gospel, Harper (New York City), 1981.

Effective Body Building: Biblical Steps to Spiritual Growth, Here's Life Publishers (San Bernadino, CA), 1982.

On the Crest of the Wave: Becoming a World Christian, Regal Books, 1983.

Leading Your Church to Growth, Regal Books, 1984.

Spiritual Power and Church Growth, Creation House, 1986.

Strategies for Church Growth, Regal Books, 1987.

The Third Wave of the Holy Spirit, Servant Publications (Ann Arbor, MI), 1988.

How to Have a Healing Ministry in Any Church, Regal Books, 1988.

Church Planting for a Greater Harvest, Regal Books, 1990.

Warfare Prayer, Regal Books, 1992.

Prayer Shield, Regal Books, 1992.

Churches That Pray, Regal Books, 1993.
Spreading the Fire, Regal Books, 1994.

Contributor, sometimes under pseudonyms Epafrodito and Lewis Graham Underwood, to religious periodicals.

EDITOR

Church/Mission Tensions Today, Moody, 1972.
(With Edward R. Dayton) *Unreached Peoples '79,* David C. Cook (Elgin, IL), 1978.
(With Dayton) *Unreached Peoples '80,* David C. Cook, 1980.
(With Dayton) *Unreached Peoples '81,* David C. Cook, 1981.
(With Donald A. McGavran and James H. Montgomery) *Church Growth Bulletin: Third Consolidated Volume,* Global Church Growth Bulletin, 1982.
Church Growth: State of the Art, Tyndale (Wheaton, IL), 1986.
Signs and Wonders Today, Creation House, 1987.
(With F. Douglas Pennoyer) *Wrestling with Dark Angels,* Regal Books, 1990.
(With McGavran) *Understanding Church Growth,* 3rd edition, Eerdmans, 1990.
Engaging the Enemy, Regal Books, 1991.
Breaking Strongholds in Your City, Regal Books, 1993.

Former editor of *Vision Evangelica* (Cochabamba, Bolivia), *Pensamiento Cristiano* (Cordoba, Argentina), and *Andean Outlook.*

*   *   *

WALKER, Alice (Malsenior) 1944-

PERSONAL: Born February 9, 1944, in Eatonton, GA; daughter of Willie Lee and Minnie Tallulah (Grant) Walker; married Melvyn Rosenman Leventhal (a civil rights lawyer), March 17, 1967 (divorced, 1976); children: Rebecca Grant. *Education:* Attended Spelman College, 1961-63; Sarah Lawrence College, B.A., 1965.

ADDRESSES: Home—San Francisco, CA. *Office*—Harcourt Brace Jovanovich, 1250 Sixth Ave., San Diego, CA 92101.

CAREER: Writer. Wild Trees Press, Navarro, CA, co-founder and publisher, 1984-88. Has been a voter registration worker in Georgia, a worker in Head Start program in Mississippi, and on staff of New York City welfare department. Writer in residence and teacher of black studies at Jackson State College, 1968-69, and Tougaloo College, 1970-71; lecturer in literature, Wellesley College and University of Massachusetts—Boston, both 1972-73; distinguished writer in Afro-American studies department, University of California, Berkeley, spring, 1982; Fannie

Hurst Professor of Literature, Brandeis University, Waltham, MA, fall, 1982. Lecturer and reader of own poetry at universities and conferences. Member of board of trustees of Sarah Lawrence College. Consultant on black history to Friends of the Children of Mississippi, 1967. Co-producer of film documentary, *Warrior Marks,* directed by Pratibha Parmar with script and narration by Walker, 1993.

AWARDS, HONORS: Bread Loaf Writer's Conference scholar, 1966; first prize, *American Scholar* essay contest, 1967; Merrill writing fellowship, 1967; McDowell Colony fellowship, 1967, 1977-78; National Endowment for the Arts grant, 1969, 1977; Radcliffe Institute fellowship, 1971-73; Ph.D., Russell Sage College, 1972; National Book Award nomination and Lillian Smith Award from the Southern Regional Council, both 1973, both for *Revolutionary Petunias and Other Poems;* Richard and Hinda Rosenthal Foundation Award, American Academy and Institute of Arts and Letters, 1974, for *In Love and Trouble: Stories of Black Women;* Guggenheim fellowship, 1977-78; National Book Critics Circle Award nomination, 1982, and Pulitzer Prize and American Book Award, both 1983, all for *The Color Purple;* Best Books for Young Adults citation, American Library Association, 1984, for *In Search of Our Mother's Gardens: Womanist Prose;* D.H.L., University of Massachusetts, 1983; O. Henry Award, 1986, for "Kindred Spirits"; Langston Hughes Award, New York City College, 1989; California Governor's Arts Award, 1994.

WRITINGS:

POETRY

Once: Poems (also see below), Harcourt (New York City), 1968.
Five Poems, Broadside Press (Highland Park, MI), 1972.
Revolutionary Petunias and Other Poems (also see below), Harcourt, 1973.
Goodnight, Willie Lee, I'll See You in the Morning (also see below), Dial (New York City), 1979.
Horses Make a Landscape Look More Beautiful, Harcourt, 1984.
Alice Walker Boxed Set—Poetry: Good Night, Willie Lee, I'll See You in the Morning; Revolutionary Petunias and Other Poems; Once, Poems, Harcourt, 1985.
Her Blue Body Everything We Know: Earthling Poems, 1965-1990 Complete, Harcourt, 1991.

FICTION; NOVELS EXCEPT AS INDICATED

The Third Life of Grange Copeland, Harcourt, 1970.
In Love and Trouble: Stories of Black Women, Harcourt, 1973.
Meridian, Harcourt, 1976.

You Can't Keep a Good Woman Down (short stories), Harcourt, 1981.

The Color Purple, Harcourt, 1982.

Alice Walker Boxed Set—Fiction: The Third Life of Grange Copeland, You Can't Keep a Good Woman Down, and In Love and Trouble, Harcourt, 1985.

The Temple of My Familiar, Harcourt, 1989.

Possessing the Secret of Joy, Harcourt, 1992.

FOR CHILDREN

Langston Hughes: American Poet (biography), Crowell (New York City), 1973, revised edition, HarperCollins, in press.

To Hell with Dying, illustrations by Catherine Deeter, Harcourt, 1988.

Finding the Green Stone, Harcourt, 1991.

NONFICTION

In Search of Our Mothers' Gardens: Womanist Prose, Harcourt, 1983.

Living by the Word: Selected Writings, 1973-1987, Harcourt, 1988.

(With Pratibha Parmar) *Warrior Marks: Female Genital Mutilation and the Sexual Blinding of Women,* Harcourt, 1993.

OTHER

(Editor) *I Love Myself When I'm Laughing . . . and Then Again When I Am Looking Mean and Impressive: A Zora Neale Hurston Reader,* introduction by Mary Helen Washington, Feminist Press, 1979.

Contributor to anthologies, including *Voices of the Revolution,* edited by Helen Haynes, E. & J. Kaplan (Philadelphia), 1967; *The Best Short Stories by Negro Writers from 1899 to the Present: An Anthology,* edited by Langston Hughes, Little, Brown (Boston), 1967; *Afro-American Literature: An Introduction,* Harcourt, 1971; *Tales and Stories for Black Folks,* compiled by Toni Cade Bambara, Zenith Books (New York City), 1971; *Black Short Story Anthology,* compiled by Woodie King, New American Library (New York City), 1972; *The Poetry of Black America: An Anthology of the Twentieth Century,* compiled by Arnold Adoff, Harper (New York City), 1973; *A Rock against the Wind: Black Love Poems,* edited by Lindsay Patterson, Dodd (New York City), 1973; *We Be Word Sorcerers: Twenty-five Stories by Black Americans,* edited by Sonia Sanchez, Bantam (New York City), 1973; *Images of Women in Literature,* compiled by Mary Anne Ferguson, Houghton (Boston), 1973; *Best American Short Stories: 1973,* edited by Margaret Foley, Hart-Davis, 1973; *Best American Short Stories, 1974,* edited by M. Foley, Houghton, 1974; *Chants of Saints: A Gathering of Afro-American Literature, Art and Scholarship,* edited by Michael S. Harper and Robert B. Stepto, University of Il-

linois Press (Chicago), 1980; *Midnight Birds: Stories of Contemporary Black Women Authors,* edited by Mary Helen Washington, Anchor Press (New York City), 1980; *Double Stitch: Black Women Write about Mothers and Daughters,* edited by Maya Angelou, HarperCollins (New York City), 1993.

Contributor to periodicals, including *Negro Digest, Denver Quarterly, Harper's, Black World, Essence, Canadian Dimension,* and the *New York Times.* Contributing editor, *Southern Voices, Freedomways,* and *Ms.*

ADAPTATIONS: The Color Purple was made into a feature film directed by Steven Spielberg, Warner Bros., 1985.

SIDELIGHTS: "*The Color Purple,* Alice Walker's third [novel,] could be the kind of popular and literary event that transforms an intense reputation into a national one," according to Gloria Steinem of *Ms.* Judging from the critical enthusiasm for *The Color Purple,* Steinem's words have proved prophetic. Walker "has succeeded," as Andrea Ford notes in the *Detroit Free Press,* "in creating a jewel of a novel." Peter S. Prescott presents a similar opinion in a *Newsweek* review. "I want to say," he comments, "that *The Color Purple* is an American novel of permanent importance, that rare sort of book which (in Norman Mailer's felicitous phrase) amounts to 'a diversion in the fields of dread.'"

Jeanne Fox-Alston and Mel Watkins both feel that the appeal of *The Color Purple* is that the novel, as a synthesis of characters and themes found in Walker's earlier works, brings together the best of the author's literary production in one volume. Fox-Alston, in the *Chicago Tribune Book World,* remarks: "Celie, the main character in Walker's third . . . novel, *The Color Purple,* is an amalgam of all those women [characters in Walker's previous books]; she embodies both their desperation and, later, their faith." Watkins states in the *New York Times Book Review:* "Her previous books . . . have elicited praise for Miss Walker as a lavishly gifted writer. *The Color Purple,* while easily satisfying that claim, brings into sharper focus many of the diverse themes that threaded their way through her past work."

Walker's central characters are almost always black women; the themes of sexism and racism are predominant in her work, but her impact is felt across both racial and sexual boundaries. Walker, according to Steinem, "comes at universality through the path of an American black woman's experience. . . . She speaks the female experience more powerfully for being able to pursue it across boundaries of race and class." This universality is also noted by Fox-Alston, who remarks that Walker has a "reputation as a provocative writer who writes about blacks in particular, but all humanity in general."

However, many critics see a definite black and female focus in Walker's writings. For example, in her review of *The Color Purple,* Ford suggests that the novel transcends "culture and gender" lines but also refers to Walker's "unabashedly feminist viewpoint" and the novel's "black . . . texture." Walker does not deny this dual bias; the task of revealing the condition of the black woman is particularly important to her. Thadious M. Davis, in his *Dictionary of Literary Biography* essay, comments: "Walker writes best of the social and personal drama in the lives of familiar people who struggle for survival of self in hostile environments. She has expressed a special concern with 'exploring the oppressions, the insanities, the loyalties and the triumph of black women.' " Walker explains in a *Publishers Weekly* interview: "The black woman is one of America's greatest heroes. . . . Not enough credit has been given to the black woman who has been oppressed beyond recognition."

Walker's earlier books—novels, volumes of short stories, and poems—have not received the same degree of attention, but neither have they been ignored. Gloria Steinem points out that *Meridian,* Walker's second novel, "is often cited as the best novel of the civil rights movement, and is taught as part of some American history as well as literature courses." In *Everyday Use,* Barbara Christian finds the story "Everyday Use," first published in Walker's collection *In Love and Trouble: Stories of Black Women,* to be "pivotal" to all of Walker's work in its evocation of black sisterhood and black women's heritage of quilting. William Peden, writing in *The American Short Story: Continuity and Change, 1940-1975,* calls this same collection "a remarkable book," and Barbara Smith observes in *Ms.* that "this collection would be an extraordinary literary work, if its only virtue were the fact that the author sets out consciously to explore with honesty the texture and terror of black women's lives . . . the fact that Walker's perceptions, style, and artistry are also consistently high makes her work a treasure." Similarly, Mary Helen Washington remarks in a *Black World* review that "the stories in *In Love and Trouble . . .* constitute a painfully honest, searching examination of the experiences of thirteen black women."

Walker bases her description of black women on what Washington refers to as her "unique vision and philosophy of the Black woman." According to Barbara A. Bannon of *Publishers Weekly,* this philosophy stems from the "theme of the poor black man's oppression of his family and the unconscious reasons for it." Walker, in her interview with the same magazine, asserts: "The cruelty of the black man to his wife and family is one of the greatest [American] tragedies. It has mutilated the spirit and body of the black family and of most black mothers." Through her fiction, Walker describes this tragedy. For instance,

Smith notes: "Even as a black woman, I found the cumulative impact of these stories [contained *In Love and Trouble*] devastating. . . . Women love their men, but are neither loved nor understood in return. The affective relationships are [only] between mother and child or between black woman and black woman." David Guy's commentary on *The Color Purple* in the *Washington Post Book World* includes this evaluation: "Accepting themselves for what they are, the women [in the novel] are able to extricate themselves from oppression; they leave their men, find useful work to support themselves." Watkins further explains: "In *The Color Purple* the role of male domination in the frustration of black women's struggle for independence is clearly the focus."

Some reviewers criticize Walker's fiction for portraying an overly negative view of black men. Katha Pollitt, for example, in the *New York Times Book Review,* calls the stories in *You Can't Keep a Good Woman Down* "too partisan." The critic adds: "The black woman is always the most sympathetic character." Guy notes: "Some readers . . . will object to her overall perspective. Men in [*The Color Purple*] are generally pathetic, weak and stupid, when they are not heartlessly cruel, and the white race is universally bumbling and inept." Charles Larson, in his *Detroit News* review of *The Color Purple,* points out: "I wouldn't go as far as to say that all the male characters [in the novel] are villains, but the truth is fairly close to that." However, neither Guy nor Larson feel that this emphasis on women is a major fault in the novel. Guy, for example, while conceding that "white men . . . are invisible in Celie's world," observes: "This really is Celie's perspective, however—it is psychologically accurate to her—and Alice Walker might argue that it is only a neat inversion of the view that has prevailed in western culture for centuries." Larson also notes that by the end of the novel, "several of [Walker's] masculine characters have reformed."

This idea of reformation, this sense of hope even in despair, is at the core of Walker's vision, even though, as John F. Callahan states in *New Republic,* "There is often nothing but pain, violence, and death for black women [in her fiction]." In spite of the brutal effects of sexism and racism suffered by the characters of her short stories and novels, critics note what Art Seidenbaum of the *Los Angeles Times* calls Walker's sense of "affirmation . . . [that] overcomes her anger." This is particularly evident in *The Color Purple,* according to several reviewers. Ford, for example, asserts that the author's "polemics on . . . political and economic issues finally give way to what can only be described as a joyful celebration of human spirit—exulting, uplifting and eminently universal." Prescott discovers a similar progression in the novel. He writes: "[Walker's] story begins at about the point that most

Greek tragedies reserve for the climax, then . . . by immeasurable small steps . . . works its way toward acceptance, serenity and joy." Walker, according to Ray Anello, who quotes the author in *Newsweek*, agrees with this evaluation. Questioned about the novel's importance, Walker explains: "Let's hope people can hear Celie's voice. There are so many people like Celie who make it, who come out of nothing. People who triumph."

Davis refers to this idea as Walker's "vision of survival" and offers a summary of its significance in Walker's work. "At whatever cost, human beings have the capacity to live in spiritual health and beauty; they may be poor, black, and uneducated, but their inner selves can blossom." This vision, extended to all humanity, is evident in Walker's collection *Living by the Word: Selected Writings 1973-1987*. Although "her original interests centered on black women, and especially on the ways they were abused or underrated," *New York Times Book Review* contributor Noel Perrin believes that "now those interests encompass all creation." Judith Paterson similarly observes in *Tribune Books* that in *Living by the Word,* "Walker casts her abiding obsession with the oneness of the universe in a question: Do creativity, love and spiritual wholeness still have a chance of winning the human heart amid political forces bent on destroying the universe with poisonous chemicals and nuclear weapons?" Walker explores this question through journal entries and essays that deal with Native Americans, racism in China, a lonely horse, smoking, and response to the criticism leveled against both the novel and film version of *The Color Purple*. Many of these treatments are personal in approach, and Jill Nelson finds many of them trivial. Writing in the *Washington Post Book World,* Nelson comments that "*Living by the Word* is fraught with . . . reaches for commonality, analogy and universality. Most of the time all Walker achieves is banality." But Derrick Bell differs, noting in his *Los Angeles Times Book Review* critique that Walker "uses carefully crafted images that provide a universality to unique events." The critic further asserts that *Living by the Word* "is not only vintage Alice Walker: passionate, political, personal, and poetic, it also provides a panoramic view of a fine human being saving her soul through good deeds and extraordinary writing."

Harsh criticisms of Walker's work crested with the 1989 publication of her fourth novel, *The Temple of My Familiar.* The novel, featuring several of the characters of *The Color Purple,* reflects concerns hinted at in that novel and confronted directly in *Living by the Word:* racism, a reverence for nature, a search for spiritual truths, and the universality referred to by reviewers Nelson and Bell. But according to David Gates in his *Newsweek* review, the novel "is fatally ambitious. It encompasses 500,000 years, rewrites Genesis and the Beatitudes and weighs in with

mini-lectures on everything from Elvis (for) to nuclear waste (against)." David Nicholson of the *Washington Post Book World* feels that *The Temple of My Familiar* "is not a novel so much as it is an ill-fitting collection of speeches . . . a manifesto for the Fascism of the New Age. . . . There are no characters, only types representative of the world Walker lives in or wishes could be." In a similar vein, *Time*'s Paul Grey notes that "Walker's relentless adherence to her own sociopolitical agenda makes for frequently striking propaganda," but not for good fiction. Though generally disliked even by sympathetic critics, the novel has its defenders. Novelist J. M. Coetzee, writing in the *New York Times Book Review,* implores the reader to look upon the novel as a "fable of recovered origins, as an exploration of the inner lives of contemporary black Americans as these are penetrated by fabulous stories," and Bernard W. Bell, writing in the *Chicago Tribune,* feels that the novel is a "colorful quilt of many patches," and that its "stylized lovers, remembrances of things past, bold flights of fantasy and vision of a brave new world of cultural diversity and cosmic harmony challenge the reader's willingness to suspend disbelief."

A *Publisher's Weekly* reviewer of Walker's 1991 children's story *Finding the Green Stone* says that "the tone is ethereal and removed . . . while the writing style, especially the dialogue, is stiff and didactic." But for Walker's collected poems, *Her Blue Body Everything We Know: Earthling Poems, 1965-1990 Complete,* a *Publishers Weekly* reviewer has high praise, characterizing Walker as "composed, wry, unshaken by adversity," and suggesting that her "strong, beautiful voice" beckons us "to heal ourselves and the planet."

Critics are nearly unanimous in their praise of Walker's controversial fifth novel, *Possessing the Secret of Joy,* about the practice of female genital mutilation in certain African, Asian and Middle Eastern cultures. Writing in the *Los Angeles Times Book Review,* Tina McElroy Ansa says that taking on such a taboo subject shows Walker's depth and range and feels that her portrait of the suffering of Tashi—a character from *The Color Purple*—is "stunning." "The description of the excision itself and its aftereffect is graphic enough to make one gag," but is the work of a thoughtful, impassioned artist, rather than a sensationalist, notes Charles R. Larson in the *Washington Post Book World.* And Donna Haisty Winchell writes in her *Dictionary of Literary Biography* essay that *Possessing the Secret of Joy* is "much more concise, more controlled, and more successful as art" than *The Temple of My Familiar* and demonstrates an effective blend of "art and activism."

Walker's concerns about the international issue of female genital mutilation prompted her to further explore the issue, both on film and in the book *Warrior Marks: Female Genital Mutilation and the Sexual Blinding of Women,* co-authored with documentary film director Pratibha Parmar. According to *Publisher's Weekly, Warrior Marks* is a "forceful account" of how the two filmed a documentary on the ritual circumcision of African women.

BIOGRAPHICAL/CRITICAL SOURCES:

BOOKS

Bestsellers '89, Issue 4, Gale (Detroit), 1989.

Black Literature Criticism, Volume 1, Gale, 1992, pp. 1808-1829.

Christian, Barbara, editor, *Everyday Use,* Rutgers University Press (New Brunswick, NJ), 1994.

Contemporary Literary Criticism, Gale, Volume 5, 1976, Volume 6, 1976, Volume 9, 1978, Volume 19, 1981, Volume 27, 1984, Volume 46, 1988, Volume 58, 1990, pp. 402-17.

Dictionary of Literary Biography, Gale, Volume 6: *American Novelists since World War II,* second series, 1980, Volume 33: *Afro-American Fiction Writers after 1955,* 1984, Volume 143: *American Novelists since World War II,* third series, 1994, pp. 277-93.

Evans, Mari, editor, *Black Women Writers (1950-1980): A Critical Evaluation,* Anchor (New York City), 1984.

O'Brien, John, *Interviews with Black Writers,* Liveright (New York City), 1973.

Peden, William, *The American Short Story: Continuity and Change, 1940-1975,* 2nd revised and enlarged edition, Houghton, 1975.

Prenshaw, Peggy W., editor, *Women Writers of the Contemporary South,* University Press of Mississippi (Jackson), 1984.

Short Story Criticism, Volume 5, Gale, 1990, pp. 400-24.

PERIODICALS

American Scholar, winter, 1970-71; summer, 1973.
Ann Arbor News, October 3, 1982.
Atlantic, June, 1976.
Black Scholar, April, 1976.
Black World, September, 1973; October, 1974.
Chicago Tribune, December 20, 1985; April 23, 1989.
Chicago Tribune Book World, August 1, 1982; September 15, 1985.
Commonweal, April 29, 1977.
Critique, summer, 1994.
Detroit Free Press, August 8, 1982; July 10, 1988; January 4, 1989.
Detroit News, September 15, 1982; October 23, 1983; March 31, 1985.
Freedomways, winter, 1973.
Globe and Mail (Toronto), December 21, 1985.
Jet, February 10, 1986.
Los Angeles Times, April 29, 1981; June 8, 1983.

Los Angeles Times Book Review, August 8, 1982; May 29, 1988; May 21, 1989, p. 1; July 5, 1992, p. 4.
Ms., February, 1974; July, 1977; July, 1978; June, 1982; September, 1986.
Nation, November 12, 1973; December 17, 1983.
Negro Digest, September/October, 1968.
New Leader, January 25, 1971.
New Republic, September 14, 1974; December 21, 1974; May 29, 1989, pp. 28-29.
Newsweek, May 31, 1976; June 21, 1982; April 24, 1989, p. 74; June 8, 1992, pp. 56-57.
New Yorker, February 27, 1971; June 7, 1976.
New York Review of Books, January 29, 1987.
New York Times, December 18, 1985; January 5, 1986.
New York Times Book Review, March 17, 1974; May 23, 1976; May 29, 1977; December 30, 1979; May 24, 1981; July 25, 1982; April 7, 1985; June 5, 1988; April 30, 1989, p. 7; June 28, 1992, p. 11.
New York Times Magazine, January 8, 1984.
Oakland Tribune, November 11, 1984.
Observer (London), October 11, 1992, p. 61.
Parnassus: Poetry in Review, spring/summer, 1976.
Poetry, February, 1971; March, 1980.
Publishers Weekly, August 31, 1970; February 26, 1988; March 1, 1991, p. 64; October 25, 1991, p. 66; October 25, 1993, p. 49.
Saturday Review, August 22, 1970.
Southern Review, spring, 1973.
Time, May 1, 1989, p. 69.
Times Literary Supplement, August 19, 1977; June 18, 1982; July 20, 1984; September 27, 1985; April 15, 1988; September 22, 1989, p. 1023; October 9, 1992, p. 22.
Tribune Books (Chicago), July 17, 1988; April 23, 1989, p. 5; June 21, 1992, p. 3.
Washington Post, October 15, 1982; April 15, 1983; October 17, 1983.
Washington Post Book World, November 18, 1973; October 30, 1979; December 30, 1979; May 31, 1981; July 25, 1982; December 30, 1984; May 29, 1988; May 7, 1989, p. 3; July 5, 1992, p. 1; January 16, 1994, pp. 4-5.
World Literature Today, winter, 1985; winter, 1986.
Yale Review, autumn, 1976.*

*   *   *

WALKER, Dale L(ee) 1935-

PERSONAL: Born August 3, 1935, in Decatur, IL; son of Russell Dale (a career soldier) and Eileen M. (Guysinger) Walker; married Alice McCord, September 30, 1960; children: Dianne, Eric, Christopher, Michael, John. *Education:* Texas Western College (now University of Texas at

El Paso), B.A., 1962. *Politics:* Democrat. *Religion:* Protestant.

ADDRESSES: Home—800 Green Cove, El Paso, TX 79932.

CAREER: KTSM-TV, El Paso, TX, reporter, 1962-66; University of Texas at El Paso, director of News-Information Office, 1966-93; Texas Western Press, El Paso, TX, director, 1985-93; freelance writer, 1993—. *Military service:* U. S. Navy, 1955-59.

MEMBER: Western Writers of America (former president), Texas Institute of Letters.

AWARDS, HONORS: Special Spur Award, Western Writers of America, 1986, for five-year editorship of *The Roundup;* Spur Award, 1988, for best Western short nonfiction.

WRITINGS:

(With Richard O'Connor) *The Lost Revolutionary: A Biography of John Reed,* Harcourt (San Diego, CA), 1967.

C. L. Sonnichsen: Grassroots Historian, Texas Western Press (El Paso, TX), 1972.

The Alien Worlds of Jack London (monograph), Wolf House Books (Minneapolis), 1973.

(Editor) Howard A. Craig, *Sunward I've Climbed,* Texas Western Press, 1974.

Jack London, Sherlock Holmes, and Sir Arthur Conan Doyle (monograph), Alvin S. Fick, 1974.

Death Was the Black Horse: The Story of Rough Rider, Buckey O'Neill, Madrona Press (Austin, TX), 1975.

(Editor and author of introduction) *Curious Fragments: Jack London's Tales of Fantasy Fiction,* Kennikat (Port Washington, NY), 1975.

No Mentor but Myself: Jack London, the Writer's Writer, Kennikat, 1979.

Only the Clouds Remain: Ted Parsons of the Lafayette Escadrille, Alandale (Amsterdam, NY), 1980.

Jack London and Conan Doyle: A Literary Kinship, Gaslight (Bloomington, IL), 1981.

(Editor and author of introduction) *Will Henry's West,* Texas Western Press, 1984.

(Editor and author of introduction) *In a Far Country: Jack London's Western Tales,* Green Hill (Ottawa, IL), 1986.

Januarius McGahan: The Life and Campaigns of an American War Correspondent, 1844-1878, Ohio University Press (Athens, OH), 1988.

Mavericks: Ten Uncorralled Westerners, Golden West (San Marino, CA), 1989.

(Editor and author of introduction) *The Golden Spurs,* Tor Books (New York City), 1992.

Contributor to books, including *Wine of Wizardry,* by George Sterling, Pinion Press, 1962. *Passing Through,* edited by W. Burns Taylor and Richard Santelli, Santay Publishers, 1974; *The Reader's Encyclopedia of the American West,* edited by Howard Lamar, Crowell (New York City), 1977; *An American for Lafayette: The Diaries of E. C. C. Genet,* University of Virginia Press (Charlottesville, VA), 1981; *Uncommon Men and the Colorado Prairie,* by Nell Brown Propst, Caxton (Caldwell, ID), 1992; *The West That Was,* Wings Books (Houston, TX), 1993; *New Trails,* Doubleday (New York City), 1994; *In the Big Country,* by John Jakes, Bantam (New York City), 1993; *The Bride Wore Crimson,* by Brian Woolley, Texas Western Press, 1993; *The American West,* Grolier (Danbury, CT), 1995; *Legends of the Old West,* Publications International, 1995; and *Wild West Show,* Wings Books, 1995. Contributor to newspapers and magazines, including *Newsweek, Ellery Queen's Mystery Magazine, Modern Fiction Studies, Soldier of Fortune, Aviation Quarterly, Louis L'Amour Western Magaizine* and *Baker Street Journal.* Books editor, *El Paso Times,* 1979-85; editor, *Roundup,* 1980-85; columnist, *Rocky Mountain News,* 1989—.

WORK IN PROGRESS: Disputed Barricades, a work on Americans in the French Foreign Legion, 1914-1918.

SIDELIGHTS: Dale L. Walker told *CA:* "I have been writing professionally since 1960, my freelancing done after-hours while holding full time jobs in news work and university staff positions. I retired in 1993 and now write full time.

"Most of my work has been periodical nonfiction—magazine articles, reviews, criticism, literary and historical studies, and newspaper work. I have been published in 130 different periodicals, and my books have been, for the most part, outgrowths of the periodical work.

"My best work has been in biography—book-length works on the 19th century war correspondent Januarius MacGahan (which I regard as my best work), Rough Rider William O. 'Buckey' O'Neill, and the American radical writer John Reed (author of *Ten Days That Shook the World),* and hundreds of shorter, biographical pieces for magazines. I have published a great deal about Jack London, a life-long interest of mine and the greatest influence I've had as a writer—a book-length annotated bibliography, three edited collections of his stories, a book-length literary study.

"I write every day, a minimum of four hours, most often longer, and while I have never written much more than my signature in longhand, I began writing on an antique upright Royal, graduated to an IBM selectric (which I swore was the end of all technology) and presently use, indeed am wedded to, a word processor.

"The writers I admire are a strange mix: I regard the British novelist George MacDonald Fraser as the finest writer in the English language today; I greatly admire the Western historical novels by the late Will Henry (Henry Wilson Allen); I love the language of certain British military historians—Sir John Fortescue and Alexander Kinglake among them; I am in awe of the work of Melville and Cormac McCarthy; I love such mystery-thriller writers as Ed McBain, Lawrence Block, and the late John D. MacDonald, the fantasies of Jack Vance, many Western and other genre writers who are great stylists. I am, and have been most of my working life, absorbed by 19th-century military history.

"In 1994 I published my 2,000th work, an interview with popular novelist John Jakes in *Louis L'Amour's Western Magazine.*"

BIOGRAPHICAL/CRITICAL SOURCES:

PERIODICALS

Journalism History, winter, 1988, pp. 149-50.
Journalism Quarterly, summer, 1989, pp. 481-82.
Smithsonian, March, 1989.

*   *   *

WALLERSTEIN, Immanuel   1930-

PERSONAL: Born September 28, 1930, in New York, NY; son of Lazar and Sally (Guensberg) Wallerstein; married Beatrice Friedman, May 25, 1964; children: Katharine Ellen. *Education:* Columbia University, A.B., 1951, M.A., 1954, Ph.D., 1959; Oxford University, graduate study, 1955-56. *Religion:* Jewish.

ADDRESSES: Office—Department of Sociology, Binghamton University, Binghamton, NY 13902-6000.

CAREER: Columbia University, New York, NY, instructor, 1958-59, assistant professor, 1959-63, associate professor of sociology, 1963-71; McGill University, Montreal, Quebec, professor of sociology, 1971-76; Binghamton University, Binghamton, NY, distinguished professor of sociology and director of Fernand Braudel Center for the Study of Economies, Historical Systems, and Civilizations, 1976—. *Military service:* U. S. Army, 1951-53.

MEMBER: International Sociological Association (president, 1994-98), Gulbenkian Commission on the Restructuring of the Social Sciences (chair, 1993-95), International African Institute (member of executive council, 1978-84), Social Science Research Council (member of board of directors, 1980-86), African Studies Association (president, 1972-73), American Sociological Association (member of executive council, 1977-80).

WRITINGS:

Africa: The Politics of Independence, Random House (New York City), 1961.
The Road to Independence: Ghana and the Ivory Coast, Mouton (Hawthorne, NY), 1964.
Africa: The Politics of Unity, Random House, 1967.
University in Turmoil: The Politics of Change, Atheneum (New York City), 1969.
The Modern World-System, Academic Press (San Diego), Volume 1: *Capitalist Agriculture and the Origins of the European World Economy in the Sixteenth Century,* 1974, Volume 2: *Mercantilism and the Consolidation of the European World-Economy, 1600-1740,* 1980, Volume 3: *The Second Great Expansion of the Capitalist World-Economy, 1730-1840s,* 1989.
World Inequality, Black Rose Books (Montreal), 1975.
The Capitalist World-Economy, Cambridge University Press (New York City), 1979.
(With Terence K. Hopkins and others) *World-System Analysis: Theory and Methodology,* Sage Publications, 1982.
(With Samir Amin, Giovanni Arrighi, and Andre Gunder Frank) *Dynamics of Global Crisis,* Macmillan, 1982.
Historical Capitalism, Verso (London), 1983.
The Politics of the World Economy, Cambridge University Press, 1984.
Africa and the Modern World, Africa World Press (Trenton, NJ), 1986.
(With Giovanni Arrighi and Terrance K. Hopkins) *Antisystematic Movements,* Verso, 1989.
(With Samir Amin, Arrighi, and Andre Gunder Frank) *Transforming the Revolution: Social Movements and the World-System,* Monthly Review Press (New York City), 1990.
(With Etienne Balibar) *Race, Nation, Class: Ambiguous Identities,* Verso, 1991.
Geopolitics and Geoculture: Essays on the Changing World-System, Cambridge University Press, 1991.
Unthinking Social Science: The Limits of Nineteenth Century Paradigms, Polity Press (Cambridge), 1991.

EDITOR

Social Change: The Colonial Situation, Wiley (New York City), 1966.
(With Paul Starr) *The University Crisis: A Reader,* two volumes, Random House, 1970.
(With Peter C. Gutkind) *Political Economy of Contemporary Africa,* Sage Publications (Beverly Hills, CA), 1976.
(With Hopkins) *Processes of the World-System,* Sage Publications, 1980.
(With Aquino de Braganca) *The African Liberation Reader,* three volumes, Zed Press (London), 1982.

(With Riccardo Parboni) *L'Europa e l'economia politica del sistema-mondo,* Franco Angeli (Milan, Italy), 1987.

(With Sergio Vieira and William G. Martin) *How Fast the Wind? Southern Africa, 1975-2000,* Africa World Press, 1991.

(With Smith) *Creating and Transforming Households: The Constraints of the World-Economy,* Cambridge University Press, 1992.

(With Alfred Kleinknecht and Ernest Mandel) *New Findings in Long-Wave Research,* Macmillan, 1992.

Also editor of *Review* and *Political Economy of the World System Annuals.* Contributor to professional journals.

*   *   *

WATSON, David 1934-

PERSONAL: Born January 20, 1934, in Nashville, TN; son of Manly Arthur (a lawyer) and Faye (a teacher; maiden name, Givens) Watson; married Joyce Frank (a librarian, editor, and writer), September 14, 1957 (divorced); children: Daniel, Malia. *Education:* Vanderbilt University, B.A., 1959; Yale University, Ph.D., 1963.

ADDRESSES: Office—Department of Psychology, University of Hawaii, Honolulu, HI 96822.

CAREER: University of Toronto, Toronto, Ontario, assistant professor, 1963-66, associate professor of psychology, 1966-67; Pierce College, Athens, Greece, Fulbright lecturer, 1967-68; University of Hawaii, Honolulu, associate professor, 1968-72, professor of psychology, 1972—, chair of undergraduate studies, 1994—.

WRITINGS:

Self-Directed Behavior, Brooks/Cole (Monterey, CA), 1972; 6th edition, 1993.

Here's Psychology, Ginn (Lexington, MA), 1977.

Psychology: What It Is, How to Use It, Canfield Press, 1978.

Social Psychology: Science and Application, Scott, Foresman (Glenview, IL), 1984.

Psychology, Brooks/Cole, 1993.

WORK IN PROGRESS: Thinking About Psychology: Critical Thinking Activities for the Introductory Course.

SIDELIGHTS: David Watson told *CA:* "I want to give psychology away, to teach people how to use it in their daily lives."

WAYNE, Anderson
See DRESSER, Davis

*   *   *

WEBB, Pauline M(ary) 1927-

PERSONAL: Born June 28, 1927, in London, England; daughter of Leonard F. (a Methodist minister) and Daisy (Barnes) Webb. *Education:* King's College, London, B.A. (with honors), 1948; London Institute of Education, teaching diploma, 1949; Union Theological Seminary, S.T.M., 1965.

ADDRESSES: Home and Office—14 Paddocks Green, Salomon St., London NW9 8NH, England.

CAREER: Teacher and assistant mistress of grammar school in Twickenham, England, 1949-52; Methodist Missionary Society, London, England, youth officer, 1952-54, editor, 1954-64, director of lay training, 1967-73, executive secretary, 1973-79; British Broadcasting Corp. World Service, London, organizer of religious broadcasting, 1979-87. Became accredited local preacher of Methodist Church, 1953. Vice-president of Methodist Conference, 1965-66; member of World Methodist Executive Committee, 1966-74. Teacher at Adult Evening Institute of Westminster College of Commerce, 1952-54; member of Anglican-Methodist Negotiating Commission, 1965-68; World Council of Churches, vice-chairman of central committee, 1968-75, moderator of Assembly Preparation committee, 1981-83.

AWARDS, HONORS: Honorary doctorates, University of Brussels, 1985, University of Victoria, Toronto, 1986, University of Mt. St. Vincent, Nova Scotia, 1987.

WRITINGS:

Women of Our Company, Cargate, 1958.

Women of Our Time, Cargate, 1960.

Operation Healing: Stories of the Work of Medical Missions throughout the World, with Bible Links and Things to Do, Edinburgh House Press (London), 1964.

All God's Children, Oliphants, 1965.

Are We Yet Alive?: Addresses on the Mission of the Church in the Modern World, Epworth (London), 1966.

Agenda for the Churches, SCM Press (London), 1968.

(Contributor) Rupert E. Davies, editor, *We Believe in God,* Allen & Unwin (London), 1968.

Salvation Today, SCM Press, 1974.

(Contributor) David Haslam, editor, *Agenda for Prophets,* Bowerham Press, 1980.

Where Are the Women, Epworth, 1980.

Celebrating Friendship, SCM Press, 1986.

Labor in the World Social Structure, Sage Publications, 1983.

(With Joan Smith and Hans-Dieter Evans) *Households and the World Economy,* Sage Publications, 1984.

Evidence for the Power of Prayer, Mowbray (Oxford), 1987.

Candles for Advent, Collins (London), 1989.

(Co-editor) *Dictionary of the Ecumenical Movement,* World Council of Churches (London), 1993.

She Flies Beyond, World Council of Churches, 1994.

(Editor) *A Long Struggle,* World Council of Churches, 1994.

Also author of pageants *Kingdoms Ablaze,* 1958, *Set My People Free,* 1960, and *Bring Them to Me,* 1964, film scripts *Bright Diadem* (on southern India), *The Road to Dabou, New Life in Nigeria,* and *Beauty for Ashes,* and television scripts *Man on Fire, Let Loose in the World, A Women's Place?,* and *A Death Reported.*

SIDELIGHTS: Pauline M. Webb told *CA* that her primary concerns are "the mission and unity of the Church, the ministry of the laity, race relations, world poverty, and the contribution of women in Church and community."

"Most of my writing," Webb related, "is of the ephemeral kind—scripts for radio programmes or films. The topicality of such scripts makes them far less suitable for printed publication, but [I am] working on books of short meditations and prayers for inclusion in a book intended for private daily use."

Webb has traveled in Sri Lanka, India, Burma, Nigeria, Kenya, Zambia, the United States, the Caribbean, and most of western Europe.

*   *   *

WEBER, Bruce   1942-

PERSONAL: Born November 20, 1942, in Brooklyn, NY; son of Paul Karl (an educator) and Miriam (Goldstein) Weber; married Annette Katz (in sales), May 30, 1968; children: Allison Emma, Jonathan Russell. *Education:* University of Maryland, B.S., 1964; Pace University, M.B.A., 1968. *Politics:* Democrat. *Religion:* Jewish. *Avocational interests:* Sports, music.

ADDRESSES: Home—511 Marion Lane, Paramus, NJ 07652. *Office*—Scholastic Inc., 555 Broadway, New York, NY 10012-3999.

CAREER: University of Maryland, College Park, assistant director of sports information, 1962-64; *Scholastic Coach* magazine, New York City, editor, 1965-81; publisher, 1981—. New York City Board of Education, Brooklyn, NY, music teacher, 1968-72; *Scholastic Sports Academy* (television series), writer, 1981-84. Member of Paramus, NJ, Board of Education, 1978-87, president,

1981-83; Paramus Run, director, 1979—; Devonshire School Board of Governors, president, 1988-90; Athletic Institute, director, 1991-93.

MEMBER: Football Writers Association of America, American Football Coaches Association, National Soccer Coaches Association of America.

AWARDS, HONORS: Action for Children's Television award, 1982, for *Scholastic Sports Academy;* award from Sports in America, 1987, for work for Athletic Institute; honorary member, American Football Coaches Association, 1995.

WRITINGS:

JUVENILE

(With William Hongash) *Questions and Answers about Baseball,* Scholastic Book Services (New York), 1974.

The Funniest Moments in School, illustrated by Kevin Callaham, M. Evans (New York), 1974, reprinted as *School Is a Funny Place,* Scholastic Book Services, 1977.

Weird Moments in Sports, Scholastic Book Services, 1975.

The Pro Football Quiz Book, Scholastic Book Services, 1976.

All-Pro Basketball Stars, annual editions, Scholastic Book Services, 1976-81, Scholastic Inc., 1982-83.

All-Pro Baseball Stars, annual editions, Scholastic Book Services, 1976-81, Scholastic Inc., 1982-83.

Pro Basketball Reading Kit, Bowmar/Noble (Los Angeles), 1976.

The Dynamite Animal Hall of Fame, Scholastic Book Services, 1979.

The T.V. Olympic Program Guide, Scholastic Book Services, 1980.

More Weird Moments in Sports, Scholastic Inc., 1983.

Bruce Weber's Inside Pro Football, annual editions, Scholastic Inc., 1983-85.

Bruce Weber's Inside Baseball, annual editions, Scholastic Inc., 1984-85.

Sparky Anderson, edited by Michael E. Goodman, Crestwood (Mankato, MN), 1988.

The Indianapolis 500, Creative Education (Mankato, MN), 1990.

Mickey Mantle: Classic Sports Shots, Scholastic Inc., 1993.

Lou Gehrig: Classic Sports Shots, Scholastic Inc., 1993.

Jackie Robinson: Classic Sports Shots, Scholastic Inc., 1993.

Ted Williams: Classic Sports Shots, Scholastic Inc., 1993.

Babe Ruth: Classic Sports Shots, Scholastic Inc., 1993.

Willie Mays: Classic Sports Shots, Scholastic Inc., 1993.

Baseball Trivia and Fun Book, Scholastic Inc. 1993.

Pro-Football Megastars, 1993, Scholastic Inc., 1993.

Pro-Football Megastars, 1994, Scholastic Inc., 1994.

Pro-Basketball Megastars, 1994, Scholastic Inc., 1994.

Sport Shots: Barry Bonds, Scholastic Inc., 1994.
Baseball Megastars, 1994, Scholastic Inc., 1994.
Baseball Megastars, 1995, Scholastic Inc., 1995.
Pro-Basketball Megastars, 1995, Scholastic Inc., 1995.

Also author of sixty-five half-hour instructional programs for the USA Network television series *Scholastic Sports Academy,* 1981-84; contributor to *Modern Encyclopedia of Basketball,* edited by Zander Hollander, Doubleday, 1979, and *Evetec, The McGregor Solution,* Houghton-Mifflin, 1985. Columnist for *Junior Scholastic, Science World, Voice, Scope, Dynamite, Scholastic Math, Sprint,* and *Action.* Contributor to *Teen Age* and other magazines for young people and writer under a pseudonym.

SIDELIGHTS: Bruce Weber told *CA:* "The most amazing conflict in my life is my variety of interests. In college—and as a professional—I've managed to find time for all of them: writing, sports, and music.

"At University of Maryland, I was deeply involved in both the athletics and publications programs, while obtaining a degree in instrumental music education. And although I've written professionally since then, I also went through a period where I taught music.

"How have I managed to combine the two seemingly distant interests? My favorite response is 'I'm probably the only sportswriter in New York who can cover both the football game and the half-time show with equal facility.' My critics might debate my ability to do either well, but I'm more than willing to go one-on-one with any of them."

*   *   *

WECHMAN, Robert Joseph 1939-

PERSONAL: Born September 23, 1939, in New York, NY; son of David Samuel (a businessman) and Blanche (Udell) Wechman; married Stephanie Helene Kellman, June 18, 1967; children: Craig Samuel, Evan Mitchell, Darren Max. *Education:* Hunter College of the City University of New York, B.A., 1961; City College of the City University of New York, M.A., 1964; Columbia University, M.A., 1966; Syracuse University, Ph.D., 1970; University of Pennsylvania, postdoctoral study, 1973. *Avocational interests:* Good books, good music, interesting conversation, and sports.

ADDRESSES: Home—9 Verdin Dr., New City, NY 10956.

CAREER: Teacher of history, New York City, 1961-63; high school teacher of history and economics, Dobbs Ferry, NY, 1963-66; Elmira College, Elmira, NY, instructor in history and economics, 1966-70; Hartwick College, Oneonta, NY, assistant professor of history and coordinator of urban studies, 1970-74; Beavertown Mills, assistant

vice president, 1976-80, vice president, 1980-90; City University of New York, New York City, professor of economics and business, 1990—. Adjunct professor of social science and business administration at New School for Social Research, State University of New York, and Rockland Community College, 1974-80, State University of New York and Empire State College, 1974—, Bergen Community College, 1976-80, and Berkeley College, 1979; adjunct associate professor of marketing at Pace University, 1980-87; adjunct professor of economics and business administration at St. Thomas Aquinas College, 1981—, and Dominican College, summer, 1981; adjunct assistant professor of business management at the City University of New York, 1981. Visiting lecturer, State University of New York, Corning, summers, 1967, 1970—. President, Verdin Associates, Inc., 1982-85, and Robert J. Wechman Consulting, 1984—. Member of City of Oneonta board of ethics, 1971-74, Otsego County Bicentennial Commission, 1972-74, and Antipollution and Environmental Commission, Oneonta, 1972-74. Speech writer for political candidates. District leader, Republican Committee Rockland County, NY, 1978—. *Military service:* U. S. Army, 1959-60. U.S. Army Reserve, 1960-65.

MEMBER: American Association of University Professors, Council for Basic Education, University Centers for Rational Alternatives, Phi Alpha Theta, Delta Tau Kappa, Delta Phi Epsilon.

AWARDS, HONORS: Marcus Award for distinguished teaching, 1972; Outstanding Educators of America Award, 1972; Rockland County distinguished service award for contributions to education, 1992; New York State Senate certificate of merit for outstanding achievement in teaching, 1993; City University of New York Award for teaching service, 1993; Rockland County distinguished service award for excellence in the teaching of traditional American values, 1993; certificate of recognition for excellence in the teaching of economics, Foundation for Teaching of Economics, 1994.

WRITINGS:

(Editor) *Readings and Interpretations of Critical Issues in Modern American Life,* Associated Educational Services, 1968.
(Editor with Albert Ovedovitz) *The Crisis in Population,* Stipes (Champaign, IL), 1969.
Urban America: A Guide to the Literature, Stipes, 1971.
(With David M. Zielonka) *The Eager Immigrants,* Stipes, 1972.
The Economic Development of the Italian-American, Stipes, 1983.
Encountering Management, Stipes, 1987.
Essentials of American Business, Stipes, 1989.
Aspects of German Nationalism, Stipes, 1994.

Contributor of articles and reviews to journals.

*   *   *

WEISS, David,
  See HALIVNI, David Weiss

*   *   *

WEST, Morris L(anglo)   1916-
  (Michael East, Julian Morris)

PERSONAL: Born April 26, 1916, in Melbourne, Australia; son of Charles Langlo and Florence Guilfoyle (Hanlon) West; married Joyce Lawford, August 14, 1952; children: Christopher, Paul, Melanie, Michael. *Education:* Studied with Christian Brothers Order, 1933, leaving before final vows, 1939; University of Melbourne, Australia, B.A., 1937.

ADDRESSES: Home—P. O. Box 102, Avalon, New South Wales 2017, Australia.

CAREER: Teacher of modern languages and mathematics in New South Wales, Australia, and Tasmania, 1933-39; secretary to William Morris Hughes, former prime minister of Australia, 1943; managing director, Australasian Radio Productions, 1943-53; film and drama writer for Shell Co. and Australian Broadcasting Network, 1954—; commentator and writer, 1954—. Publicity manager, Murdoch Newspaper Chain, Melbourne, 1945-46; chairperson, National Book Council; chairperson, Council of the National Library of Australia. *Military service:* Australian Imperial Forces, 1939-43; became lieutenant.

MEMBER: Royal Society of Literature (fellow), Royal Prince Alfred Yacht Club (Sydney).

AWARDS, HONORS: William Heinemann Award of the Royal Society, 1959, National Brotherhood Award of the National Council of Christians and Jews, 1960, and James Tait Black Memorial Award, 1960, both for *The Devil's Advocate;* Bestsellers Paperback of the Year Award, 1965, for *The Shoes of the Fisherman;* Dag Hammarskjoeld International Prize; Pax Mundi, Diplomatic Academy of Peace, 1978; Universe Literary Prize, 1981, for *The Clowns of God;* D.Litt., University of Santa Clara, Mercy College (Dobbs Ferry, NY), and University of Western Sydney; invested as member of Order of Australia, 1985 Honours List; fellow, World Academy of Arts and Sciences.

WRITINGS:

(Under pseudonym Julian Morris) *Moon in My Pocket,* Australasian Publishing, 1945.
Gallows on the Sand (also see below), Angus & Robertson (London), 1956.

Kundu (also see below), Dell (New York City), 1956.
The Crooked Road, Morrow (New York City), 1957, published in England as *The Big Story,* Heinemann (London), 1957.
Children of the Shadows: The True Story of the Street Urchins of Naples, Doubleday (New York City), 1957, published in England as *Children of the Sun,* Heinemann, 1957, reprinted, Fontana, 1977.
Backlash, Morrow, 1958, published in England as *The Second Victory* (also see below), Heinemann, 1958, second edition, Hodder & Stoughton (London), 1985.
(Under pseudonym Michael East) *McCreary Moves In,* Heinemann, 1958, published as *The Concubine* (also see below), New English Library (London), 1967, reprinted under name Morris L. West under original title, Coronet Books, 1983.
The Devil's Advocate (also see below), Morrow, 1959.
(Under pseudonym Michael East) *The Naked Country* (also see below), Heinemann, 1960, reprinted, Coronet Books, 1983.
Daughter of Silence (novel; also see below), Morrow, 1961.
Daughter of Silence: A Dramatization of the Novel (play; produced on Broadway by Richard Halliday, 1961), Morrow, 1962.
The Shoes of the Fisherman (novel; also see below), Morrow, 1963, limited edition, Franklin Library, 1980.
The Ambassador, Morrow, 1965.
The Tower of Babel (Book-of-the-Month Club selection), Morrow, 1967.
The Heretic: A Play in Three Acts, Morrow, 1969.
(With Robert Francis) *Scandal in the Assembly: The Matrimonial Laws and Tribunals of the Roman Catholic Church, 1970,* Morrow, 1970.
Summer of the Red Wolf, Morrow, 1971.
The Salamander (also see below), Morrow, 1973.
Harlequin, Morrow, 1974.
The Navigator, Morrow, 1976.
Selected Works, Heinemann Octopus (London), 1977.
The Devil's Advocate [and] *The Second Victory* [and] *Daughter of Silence* [and] *The Salamander* [and] *The Shoes of the Fisherman,* Heinemann, 1977.
Proteus, limited first edition, Franklin Library, 1979, Morrow, 1979.
The Clowns of God (novel; also see below), Morrow, 1981.
A West Quartet: Four Novels of Intrigue and High Adventure (contains *The Naked Country, Gallows on the Sand, The Concubine,* and *Kundu*), Morrow, 1981.
The World Is Made of Glass (novel), Avon (New York City), 1983.
Cassidy, Doubleday, 1986.
Masterclass (novel), St. Martin's (New York City), 1988.
Lazarus (novel; also see below), Heinemann Octopus, 1990.
The Ringmaster, Heinemann Octopus, 1991.

The Lovers (novel), D. I. Fine (New York City), 1993.
Three Complete Novels (contains *The Shoes of the Fisherman, The Clowns of God,* and *Lazarus*), Wings Books (New York City), 1993.

Also author of play *The World Is Made of Glass,* 1984, adapted from his novel of the same name.

ADAPTATIONS: The Devil's Advocate, dramatized by Dore Schary, was produced by the Theatre Guild at the Billy Rose Theatre in 1961; *The Shoes of the Fisherman* was filmed by Metro-Goldwyn-Mayer (MGM) in 1968.

SIDELIGHTS: Since the mid-1950s, Australian novelist Morris L. West has written suspense novels that plunge the reader into political turmoil, world-wide governmental corruption, and the internal workings of the Catholic Church. West spent several years in a Roman Catholic monastery and worked for six months as the Vatican correspondent for the *London Daily Mail.* These experiences have contributed to a moral and ethical outlook on current events that permeates all his work. According to *New York Times Book Review* contributor Herbert Mitgang, "West is known for his theological thrillers that pose hard, frequently unanswerable questions about today's turbulent world—including the constraints on liberty imposed by democratic societies." Claims Diane Casselberry Manuel in the *Christian Science Monitor,* "At his best, author West is a skillful storyteller who knows how to build suspense into every twist of the plot." Having written over twenty novels, "Morris West invents stories as though the world were running out of them," comments Webster Schott in the *New York Times Book Review.*

Three of West's better known works—*The Devil's Advocate, The Shoes of the Fisherman,* and *The Clowns of God*—feature protagonists who are representatives of the Church. *The Devil's Advocate* concerns a dying Catholic priest who is sent to an Italian village to investigate the life of a proposed saint and who ends up learning an important lesson for his own life. According to *Renascence* contributor Arnold L. Goldsmith, *The Devil's Advocate* is "a richly textured, finely constructed story with all of the ingredients of a literary classic. . . . West is able to blend the personal with the local and the universal, giving us not only the memorable portrait of a deeply disturbed theologian, but also a wider view of the troubled soul of a church, a country, and the world."

In *The Shoes of the Fisherman,* a humble Ukrainian pope finds himself the central negotiator in an attempt to prevent the United States and the Soviet Union from starting World War III. During the negotiations, the pope must confront the Russian who once tortured him. The work, a popular and critical success, demonstrates West's concern with modern man's inability to communicate. "We're not using the same words. We don't understand each other. We are not selecting, we aren't balancing . . . simply because life is too risky, too tormenting. . . . I've been trying, therefore, to use what is a very old manner of story telling. To make this conflict of legitimate points of view clear, through the medium of the novel," West told Shari Steiner in a *Writer's Digest* interview. "In *The Shoes of the Fisherman,* the idea of the central character was a man who believed that he was—and publicly claimed to be—the Vicar of Christ," West continued. "Now, theoretically, this is the man who must look at the world through the eye of God, and try to make some sense out of its complexity. He was therefore a natural character medium through which this hopeless attempt had to be made."

Eighteen years later, West again used a pope as a central character, this time in *The Clowns of God.* Pope Gregory is forced by the Church to abdicate his seat when he receives a vision of the Second Coming of Christ and decides to communicate this apocalyptic message to the rest of the world. *The Clowns of God* shows the Church in a harsher light than did West's previous theological novels and reflects West's ambivalence with the institution as a governing unit. "West has great faith in the power of faith, but little tolerance for the bureaucratic wranglings that often seem to accompany organized religion," declares the *Christian Science Monitor*'s Manuel. The ambivalence may have originated in West's experiences with the Christian Brothers monastery where he studied for six years. Intending to become a priest, he left before taking his final vows. "My education with the Christian Brothers . . . was very strongly tinged with Jansenism, a restrictive, puritanical attitude to religion," West explained to Steiner in *Writer's Digest.* "This has probably produced in me an attitude of extreme tolerance and the desire to find out what the other man thinks first before we make any judgments."

The Clowns of God received mixed reviews. Walter Shapiro in the *Washington Post* dislikes West's description of Christ, who appears at the book's conclusion. Robert Kaftan writes in the *Christian Century* that "the characters become so many pieces to be manipulated to propel the story forward." He applauds the novel's setting, however, saying that West's "portrait of the world at the edge is chilling and disquieting." The *Wall Street Journal*'s Edmund Fuller admires West's premise: "As a melodrama it is tautly absorbing in its doomthreat genre. Yet the book far transcends that aspect, for Mr. West is an intelligent, thoughtful writer with knowledge of the ecclesiastical and theological issues that are the essence of his tale." And Richard A. Blake maintains in *America* that "West has succeeded . . . in raising the most significant questions of human survival in a very human and religious context."

West's third theological papal thriller, *Lazarus,* was published in 1990. A fictitious cleric, Ludovico Gadda, has schemed and manipulated his way into becoming Pope Leo XIV. As pontiff, however, Leo—committed to remorselessly eliminating any religious opposition—lacks the compassion and understanding characteristic of earlier popes; rather, his vision of the papacy encompasses strict observance of Catholic doctrine and inflexible interpretation of holy teachings. As his health deteriorates due to heart disease, he faces coronary bypass surgery and realizes he must modify his uncompromising ambition. Like the biblical Lazarus raised from the dead by Jesus, so Leo attains a measure of resurrection in both mind and body through his fight for his life, promising to restore the Church to its congregants and members. Complicating Leo's convalescence and execution of his papal responsibilities is the discovery of an assassination plot against him by a mid-Eastern terrorist organization, the Sword of Islam. The novel explores in depth Leo's private demons in addition to offering political and religious intrigue.

Don G. Campbell hails *Lazarus* in the *Los Angeles Times Book Review* as "an absorbing novel of a complex man," further remarking that "West's knowledge of the inner working of the Catholic Church is encyclopedic—the political infighting, the jealousies, the stresses and strains that abound in the Vatican." Campbell concludes that the book presents "an agonizing story of a man in torment, impossible to forget." Hans Knight notes in the *New York Times Book Review* that "the last of the Australian novelist's papal trilogy might be the most potent yet," adding that West "has once more proved himself a masterly mixer of homily and horror."

In an exception from his mystery thrillers, *The World Is Made of Glass* treats a psychological relationship rooted in pseudo-fact. Andrew Greeley comments in the *Detroit News* that "so sharp is the departure from earlier stories that one wonders if West . . . has not reached an important and extremely fruitful turning point in his career as a storyteller." The basis of this book is West's imaginative expansion of a brief entry in Carl Jung's diary in which he records meeting with a woman who, after refusing to give her name, asked him to hear a confession. The lady, according to West, is Magda Liliane Kardoss von Gamsfeld, a horse breeder, physician, and the illegitimate daughter of an English Duchess and a Hungarian nobleman. Raised by her father, Magda was seduced by him at sixteen, which started her on a path of lesbianism, sadomasochism, and finally, murder. She comes to Jung in a state of suicidal depression.

The story deviates from West's usual fare in that it contains only two characters, Jung and Magda, who relate the plot in monologue form. "Within the course of a single day Jung has become the recipient of confessions that it would probably take the average psychoanalyst weeks, months or even years to elicit from a patient," writes

Francis King in the *Spectator*. But Magda's confessions produce an unexpected reaction in the psychiatrist. "Jung himself is constantly and disturbingly aware of the parallel between his own situation, in which he is poised to attempt the symbolic murder of his beloved father-figure Freud, and that of this siren, who is guilty of real murder," King continues. Magda's honesty also leads Jung to more closely examine his broken marriage and affair with a former student, plus his suddenly remembered, unsavory memories from childhood. The impact of these memories and realizations forces him to acknowledge similarities in their perceptions of reality. Jung's disclosures and behaviors prompt Magda finally to question his sanity.

Detroit News contributor Greeley believes *The World Is Made of Glass* to be one of West's finest works. "Morris West has done for Carl Gustav Jung what D. M. Thomas did for Sigmund Freud—written a novel which brings Jung and his milieu alive. In the process he has produced a story which is very unlike most of his previous work. . . . Jung's chaotic personal life is vividly portrayed." *New York Times Book Review* contributor Philippe Van Rjndt says "Magda von Gamsfeld is Mr. West's most impressive creation." Patricia Olson comments in the *Christian Century* that while West is generally "known for his realistic narration, his sensitive character portrayal and his concern for modern religion, [he] has never before presented such melodrama, such passionate characters, or such a critique of conventional Christianity as he does here."

Some reviewers criticized the book's conclusion, in which the physician who initially sent Magda to Jung provides her with a solution by giving her a job as director of a refuge for fallen women. Mayo Mohs notes in *Time* that "the author kisses off this denouement in a scant few pages, barely hinting at the thoughts and feelings of the new Magda. Having built the novel on the spectacle of her corruption, West might have reflected a bit more on the drama of her return to grace." Beryl Lieff Benderly indicates in the *Washington Post* that "Magda functions not as a person but as a plot device to permit West's exploration of certain themes—the line between good and evil, the nature of guilt and obsession, the curative power of redemption. . . . But to touch deeply, a story about sin and redemption or madness and cure must involve real people in a palpable world, not made-to-order abstractions in a universe of concepts." Van Rjndt, however, finds Magda's new life believable: "For all the cruelty Magda inflicts and receives, her struggle towards redemption demands our respect and compels our fascination."

In 1993's *The Lovers*, Mike Cuthbert observes in the *Washington Post Book World*, West "returns to some of his favorite themes: power politics of the Roman Catholic

Church, the complexities of international politics and the successes and failures of powerful men." The novel chronicles the experiences of Irish-Australian Bryan de Courcy Cavanagh and Giulia Farnese, who first meet aboard the yacht of Giulia's American fiance, where Giulia is a guest and Bryan a crew member. Giulia is promised to the wealthy Lou Molloy; the Farnese-Molloy marriage has been arranged by both Giulia's family and Molloy, with each seeking to solidify political, religious, and financial ambitions. Cavanagh and Giulia fall in love on board the yacht, but are inevitably parted and do not meet again until forty years later. The action of the novel is "woven through a rich tapestry of intrigue, betrayal, suspense and murder," remarks Sybil Steinberg in *Publishers Weekly.* Cuthbert further describes the book as "a novel of sexual passion, Cold War politics, murder, betrayal and morals."

West primarily sees himself as a communicator, and his stories as vehicles for his messages. He told Steiner in *Writer's Digest* that he wants to be "the type of person who . . . causes other people to examine their lives . . . the kind of man who turns the world upside down and says, lookit, it looks different, doesn't it?"

BIOGRAPHICAL/CRITICAL SOURCES:

BOOKS

Contemporary Literary Criticism, Gale (Detroit), Volume 6, 1976, Volume 33, 1985.

PERIODICALS

America, August 29, 1981.
Atlantic, April, 1968.
Best Sellers, March 1, 1968; April 1, 1970; June 1, 1970.
Books and Bookmen, April, 1968; April, 1979; August, 1983.
Catholic World, September, 1961; February, 1962.
Chicago Tribune Book World, December 25, 1983.
Christian Century, May 20, 1981; October 12, 1983.
Christian Science Monitor, August 10, 1981.
Detroit News, July 10, 1983.
International Fiction Review, January, 1975.
Jewish Quarterly, autumn, 1968.
Life, February 23, 1968.
Look, August 1, 1961.
Los Angeles Times Book Review, February 18, 1979; July 17, 1983; October 19, 1986; April 15, 1990, p. 15.
Nation, December 16, 1961; May 17, 1965.
National Observer, March 11, 1968.
National Review, February 14, 1975.
Newsweek, December 11, 1961.
New Yorker, December 9, 1961.
New York Times, May 27, 1987.
New York Times Book Review, April 25, 1965; February 22, 1968; April 7, 1968; September 19, 1971; October

21, 1973; October 27, 1974; August 29, 1976; March 4, 1979; March 11, 1979; August 9, 1981; November 26, 1981; July 3, 1983; November 9, 1986; May 27, 1987; April 15, 1990, p. 14; March 31, 1991, p. 28; June 9, 1991, p. 12.
Observer (London), March 25, 1990, p. 66.
Observer Review, March 3, 1968.
Plays and Players, September, 1970.
Publishers Weekly, July 5, 1993, p. 60.
Punch, March 6, 1968.
Renascence, summer, 1962.
Reporter, January 4, 1962.
Saturday Review, April 24, 1965; February 24, 1968.
Spectator, March 8, 1968; October 5, 1974; July 23, 1983.
Stage, July 23, 1970.
Theatre Arts, February, 1962.
This Week, December 4, 1966.
Time, December 8, 1961; July 6, 1970; November 4, 1974; October 4, 1976; January 22, 1979; July 25, 1983; July 1, 1991, p. 71.
Times (London), May 6, 1965; July 14, 1983; February 5, 1987.
Times Literary Supplement, May 6, 1965; July 16, 1970; August 3, 1973.
Tribune Books (Chicago), June 16, 1991, p. 8.
Wall Street Journal, August 24, 1981.
Washington Post, June 8, 1981; July 8, 1983; November 15, 1986.
Washington Post Book World, October 3, 1993, p. 11.
Writer's Digest, February, 1971.

*   *   *

WESTGATE, John
See BLOOMFIELD, Anthony (John Westgate)

*   *   *

WHARMBY, Margot
(Alison Winn)

PERSONAL: Born in England; married Ewart Wharmby; children: David, Martin, Alison, Philip.

ADDRESSES: Home—Cherry Burton, 3 Powys Ave., Leicester, England.

WRITINGS:

UNDER PSEUDONYM ALISON WINN; JUVENILE

Roundabout, Hodder & Stoughton (London), 1961.
Swings and Things, illustrations by Jennie Corbett and Peggie Fortnum, Hodder & Stoughton, 1963, Rand McNally (Chicago, IL), 1965.
Helter Skelter, illustrations by Janina Ede, Hodder & Stoughton, 1966.

A First Cinderella, Hodder & Stoughton, 1966.

Aunt Isabella's Umbrella, illustrations by Gladys Ambrus, Hodder & Stoughton, 1976, Children's Press (Chicago, IL), 1977.

Charlie's Iron Horse, Hodder & Stoughton, 1979.

Patchwork Pieces, Hodder & Stoughton, 1980.

"Hello God," Word Books (Berkhamsted, England), 1984.

Me Till I'm Three, Word Books, 1989.

INTERPRETER OF ENGLISH TEXTS FROM SWEDISH; UNDER PSEUDONYM ALISON WINN; JUVENILE

Gunilla Wolde, "The Thomas Books" series, ten volumes, Hodder & Stoughton, 1971-75.

Ulf Loefgren, *Who Holds Up the Traffic?,* Hodder & Stoughton, 1973.

Loefgren, *One, Two, Three, Four,* Hodder & Stoughton, 1973.

Loefgren, *The Flying Orchestra,* Hodder & Stoughton, 1973.

Loefgren, *The Magic Kite,* Hodder & Stoughton, 1973.

Loefgren, *The Colour Trumpet,* Hodder & Stoughton, 1973.

Wolde, "The Emma Books" series, ten volumes, Hodder & Stoughton, 1975-77.

Loefgren, *Harlequin,* Hodder & Stoughton, 1978.

Babro Lindgren, *The Wild Baby,* Hodder & Stoughton, 1981.

Lindgren, *The Wild Baby's Boat Trip,* Hodder & Stoughton, 1983.

Also author of English text for *The Tale of Two Hands,* by Loefgren, and *The Wild Baby's Dog,* by Lindgren.

*　　　*　　　*

WHITE, James F(loyd) 1932-

PERSONAL: Born January 23, 1932, in Boston, MA; son of Edwin T. (an engineer) and Madeline (Rinker) White; children: Louise, Robert, Ellen, Laura, Martin. *Education:* Harvard University, A.B., 1953; Union Theological Seminary, B.D., 1956; attended Cambridge University, 1956-57; Duke University, Ph.D., 1960. *Religion:* United Methodist. *Avocational interests:* Travel, hiking, music, nature.

ADDRESSES: Home—17840 Ponader Dr., South Bend, IN 46635-1506. *Office*—Department of Theology, University of Notre Dame, Notre Dame, IN 46556.

CAREER: Ordained minister of California-Nevada Conference of the United Methodist Church, 1961; Ohio Wesleyan University, Delaware, instructor in religion, 1959-61; Southern Methodist University, Dallas, TX, assistant professor, 1961-65, associate professor, 1965-71, professor of Christian worship, 1971-83; University of

Notre Dame, Notre Dame, IN, professor of liturgy, 1983—.

MEMBER: North American Academy of Liturgy.

AWARDS, HONORS: Berakah Award from North American Academy of Liturgy, 1983.

WRITINGS:

The Cambridge Movement: The Ecclesiologists and the Gothic Revival, Cambridge University Press (New York City), 1962, revised edition, 1979.

Protestant Worship and Church Architecture: Theological and Historical Considerations, Oxford University Press (New York City), 1964.

Architecture at Southern Methodist University, Southern Methodist University Press (Dallas, TX), 1966.

The Worldliness of Worship, Oxford University Press, 1967.

New Forms of Worship, Abingdon (Nashville, TN), 1971.

(Editor) *Supplemental Worship Resources,* Abingdon, Volume I, 1972, Volume VI, 1979, Volume X, 1980.

Christian Worship in Transition, Abingdon, 1976.

Introduction to Christian Worship, Abingdon, 1980.

Sacraments as God's Self Giving, Abingdon, 1983.

John Wesley's Sunday Service, Abingdon, 1984.

(With Susan J. White) *Church Architecture,* Abingdon, 1988.

Protestant Worship, Westminster/John Knox, 1989.

Documents of Christian Worship, Westminster/John Knox, 1992.

A Brief History of Christian Worship, Abingdon, 1993.

Roman Catholic Worship, Paulist Press (Ramsey, NJ), 1995.

Contributor to religious journals. Former editor of *Union Seminary Quarterly Review.*

WORK IN PROGRESS: A book on the sacraments.

SIDELIGHTS: James F. White told *CA:* "Much of my work has revolved around giving guidance to the changes in Protestant worship since Vatican II. Through writing, speaking, training ministers, and now, at Notre Dame, training those who will teach worship courses, I have worked and continue to work for the reshaping of Christian worship in America."

*　　　*　　　*

WHONE, Herbert 1925-

PERSONAL: Born June 4, 1925, in Bingley, England; son of Bannister (a textile designer) and Nellie (Stead) Whone; married Helen Margery Reed; children: Adam, Nicholas, Katrina, Helena, Hannah. *Education:* Victoria University of Manchester, B. Mus. (with honors), 1949; Royal College of Music, A.R.M.C.M., 1949. *Avocational interests:* Art, photography, ancient religions.

ADDRESSES: Home—46 Duchy Rd., Harrogate, Yorkshire, England.

CAREER: Violinist with Royal Philharmonic Orchestra, London, England, 1950-51, and British Broadcasting Corporation Symphony Orchestra, London, 1952-56; Scottish National Orchestra, Glasgow, Scotland, deputy leader, 1957-65; Huddersfield Polytechnic, Huddersfield, England, teacher of violin, 1966-90. *Military service:* Royal Air Force, 1943-46.

WRITINGS:

The Simplicity of Playing the Violin (self-illustrated), Gollancz, 1972.
The Hidden Face of Music (self-illustrated), Gollancz, 1974, revised edition, Garden Studio, 1979.
The Essential West Riding: Its Character in Words and Pictures, E. P., 1975, revised edition, Smith-Settle, 1987.
The Integrated Violinist (self-illustrated), Gollancz, 1976.
Church, Monastery, Cathedral: A Guide to the Symbolism of the Christian Tradition (drawings by Denys Baker, based on sketches by Whone), Compton Russell, 1977, revised edition, Element, 1990.
Nursery Rhymes for Adult Children, Tallis, 1985.
Fountains Abbey, Smith-Settle, 1987.
Touch Wood: A Journey among Trees (photographs by Whone), Smith-Settle, 1990.

Also contributor of articles to *Strad.*

SIDELIGHTS: Herbert Whone told *CA:* "Music books indicate the connection of music, and learning of a stringed instrument in particular, with the *whole man*—not simply an analytical technique. In this sense the message breaks academic limits. *Hidden Face of Music* is the symbology of the role of music in man's life—its power on all levels. Everything is simple once the veils of error have been removed.

"I am at present painting and am open to the movement of the spirit. All activities abide by the same laws and all help each other."

*   *   *

WILDING, Michael   1942-

PERSONAL: Born January 5, 1942, in Worcester, England; son of Richard (an iron molder) and Dorothy Mary (Bull) Wilding. *Education:* Lincoln College, Oxford, B.A., 1963, M.A., 1967.

ADDRESSES: Office—Department of English, University of Sydney, Sydney, New South Wales 2006, Australia.

CAREER: Teacher at primary school in Spetchley, England, 1960; University of Sydney, Sydney, Australia, lecturer in English, 1962-66; University of Birmingham, Birmingham, England, assistant lecturer, 1967, lecturer in English, 1968; University of Sydney, senior lecturer, 1969-72, reader in English, 1972-92, professor, 1993—. Director of Wild & Woolley Ltd. (publishers), 1974-79. Visiting professor, University of California at Santa Barbara, 1987; external examiner, Department of English, University of Western Australia, 1994. Member of council of Literature Board of Australia, 1975-76; member of international advisory board, Fourth and Fifth International Milton Symposium; member of the committee, Sydney Festival Writers' Week; chair of the judging panel, NSW State Literary Awards, 1994.

AWARDS, HONORS: Senior fellowship from Literature Board of Australia, 1978; elected fellow of the Australian Academy of the Humanities, 1988; George Watson Visiting Fellow, University of Queensland, 1990.

WRITINGS:

FICTION

Aspects of the Dying Process (stories), University of Queensland Press, 1972.
Living Together (novel), University of Queensland Press, 1974.
The Short Story Embassy (novel), Wild & Woolley (Sydney, Australia), 1975.
The West Midland Underground (stories), University of Queensland Press, 1975.
Scenic Drive (novel), Wild & Woolley, 1976.
The Phallic Forest (stories), Wild & Woolley, 1978.
Pacific Highway (novel), Hale & Iremonger (Sydney, Australia), 1981.
Reading the Signs (stories), Hale & Iremonger, 1984.
The Paraguayan Experiment (novel), Penguin Books (Melbourne and Harmondsworth, Australia), 1985.
The Man of Slow Feeling: Selected Short Stories, Penguin Books, 1985.
Under Saturn (stories), Black Swan (Sydney, Australia), 1987.
Great Climate (stories), Faber & Faber (London, England), 1990.
Her Most Bizarre Sexual Experience (stories), W. W. Norton (New York City), 1991.
This Is for You, Angus & Robertson (Sydney, Australia), 1994.
Book of the Reading, Paper Bark Press (Sydney, Australia), 1994.

NONFICTION

Milton's "Paradise Lost," Sydney University Press (Sydney, Australia), 1969.

(With Michael Green and Richard Hoggart) *Cultural Policy in Great Britain,* United Nations Educational, Scientific and Cultural Organization (Paris, France), 1970.

Marcus Clarke, Oxford University Press (Melbourne, Australia), 1977.

Political Fictions (criticism), Routledge & Kegan Paul (London, England), 1980.

Dragon's Teeth: Literature in the English Revolution (criticism), Clarendon Press (Oxford, England), 1986.

The Radical Tradition: Lawson, Furphy, Stead, Foundation for Australian Literary Studies (Townsville, Australia), 1993.

Social Visions, Sydney Studies in Society & Culture (Sydney, Australia), 1993.

EDITOR

(With Charles Higham) *Australians Abroad,* F. W. Cheshire (Melbourne, Australia), 1967.

Henry James, *Three Tales,* Hicks Smith (Sydney, Australia), 1967.

Marvell: Modern Judgements, Macmillan (London, England), 1969, Aurora (Nashville, TN), 1970.

John Sheffield, *The Tragedy of Julius Caesar and Marcus Brutus,* Cornmarket (London, England), 1970.

(With Shirley Cass, Ros Cheney, and David Malouf) *We Took Their Orders and Are Dead: An Anti-War Anthology,* Ure Smith (Sydney, Australia), 1971.

The Portable Marcus Clarke, University of Queensland Press, 1976, 2nd edition, 1988.

(With Stephen Knight) *The Radical Reader,* Wild & Woolley, 1977.

The Tabloid Story Pocket Book, Wild & Woolley, 1978.

William Lane, *The Workingman's Paradise,* Sydney University Press, 1980.

Marcus Clarke, *Stories,* Hale & Iremonger, 1983.

(With Rudi Krausmann) *Airmail from Down Under,* Gangan (Vienna, Austria), 1990.

The Oxford Book of Australian Short Stories, Oxford (Oxford, England and New York City), 1994.

OTHER

Also author of *The Phallic Forest* (film), released by Sydney Filmmakers Co-op, 1972. General editor of *Asian & Pacific Writing,* twenty volumes, University of Queensland Press, 1972-82. Editor of *Isis,* 1962; co-editor of *Balcony: The Sydney Review,* 1965-66, *Tabloid Story,* 1972-75, and *Post-Modern Writing,* 1979-81. Australian editor of *Stand Magazine,* 1971—. Member of advisory board of *Australian Literary Studies, Literature & Aesthetics, Outrider, Science Fiction,* and *Ulitarra.*

SIDELIGHTS: Michael Wilding told *CA:* "I grew up in the English Midlands and arrived in Australia when I was twenty-one. My early stories recount both worlds, a sense of provincial restrictions and the notation of English society, and the excitement of Sydney in the 1960s, of the sun, warmth and sensuality. These early stories were realist in mode. But working on the principle of that new experiences require new forms, I was soon exploring various experimental modes. So sometimes the critical guides list me as a realist, and sometimes as a post-modernist. Much of the early fiction dealt with the world of bohemia, or what became known as the alternative. *Living Together* recounted it in traditional narrative terms, *The Short Story Embassy* in a much more open-ended, fragmented postmodern way. With *Pacific Highway* I explored spontaneity, writing without any detailed plan or preliminary notes about an alternative life style. I wanted to capture the freshness of immediate inspiration, the unrepressed utterance. I followed that with an historical novel about an actual alternative experiment in the 1890s, *The Paraguayan Experiment.* It tells the story of some Australian tradesunionists who after the defeat of the big shearers' strike set up a co-operative settlement in South America. Here spontaneity was superseded by lengthy research, the incorporation of historical data and documents, and the renewal of a narrative line; only by finding out what happened when could I figure out why things happened.

"My earlier explorations of the new sexual liberation of the 60s, in all its ambiguities and contradictions, in the books from *Aspects of the Dying Process* to *Scenic Drive* were followed by more political explorations, looking at the controls and taboos of contemporary society in *Reading the Signs, Under Saturn,* and *This is for You;* conspiracies, drugs and paranoia joined my themes. Sometimes I've favoured fables, fantasies and science-fiction modes to explore these themes, sometimes psychological realism, sometimes explorations of voice and idiom. over the years I've given a lot of readings, in Australia and overseas, and the experience of writing for performance, and of working with poets, has found its way into my fiction. *Book of the Reading* is a programme souvenir of frequently read pieces.

"The post-modern phase in the late sixties and early seventies was valuable. It liberated us from a tired, unadventurous, no longer effective realism. It allowed for disruptions and discontinuities, broke a lot of formal taboos, encouraged the awareness of the nature of literary structures and conventions, helped to exploit allusion and intertextuality, and allowed a richer set of possibilities in all respects. But these formal breakthroughs were ultimately only valuable if they enabled the writer to say something new, to bring a new vision to content. I came out of postmodernism with a new interest in the story, in narrative, and with a renewed concern to engage with content, with the world around me. Minimalism and self-referentialism seemed fresh and lively, uncluttered by all the social baggage, until you paused to wonder what you were saying in the end, after removing all that was social baggage. I had to stop and ask, where is the 'pure' writing taking me? It wasn't taking me where I wanted to be. So I re-engaged with narrative, re-engaged with society. I don't want at all to minimize the formal and aesthetic aspects of writing; but these emerge from an engagement with subject matter. Alongside my fiction I've written and edited several volumes of literary studies, on political fiction, Australian fiction, and the poetry of the seventeenth century; in these I've always been concerned to set the writing in its social, historical and political context."

BIOGRAPHICAL/CRITICAL SOURCES:

BOOKS

Anderson, Don, *Hot Copy: Reading & Writing Now,* Penguin, Ringwood, 1986.

Capone, Givoanna, editor, *European Perspectives: Contemporary Essays on Australian Literature,* University of Queensland Press, 1991.

Clancy, Laurie, *Readers' Guide to Australian Fiction,* Oxford University Press, 1992.

Dutton, Geoffrey, editor, *Literature of Australia,* revised edition, Penguin Books, 1976.

Daniel, Helen, editor, *The Good Reading Guide,* McPhee Gribble, 1989.

Gelder, Ken, Salzman, Paul, *The New Diversity: Australian Fiction 1970-88,* McPhee Gribble (Melbourne, Australia), 1989.

Goodwin, Ken, *A History of Australian Literature,* Macmillan, 1986.

Hamilton, K. G., editor, *Studies in the Recent Australian Novel,* University of Queensland Press, 1978.

Hergenhan, L. T., editor, *The New Literary History of Australia,* Penguin, Ringwood, 1988.

Kramer, L. J., editor, *The Oxford History of Australian Literature,* Oxford University Press, 1981.

Ousby, Ian, editor, *Cambridge Guide to Literature in English,* Cambridge University Press (Cambridge, MA), 1988.

Wilde, W. H., Andrews, Barry, and Hooten, Joy, editors, *The Oxford Companion to Australian Literature,* Oxford University Press, 1985, 2nd edition, 1994.

Wilkes, G. A., *The Stockyard and the Croquet Lawn: Literary Evidence for Australia's Cultural Development,* Edward Arnold (Melbourne, Australia), 1981.

PERIODICALS

Age Monthly Review (Melbourne), September, 1985.
Aspect, spring, 1975.
Caliban, Volume 14, 1977.
Cleo, June, 1975.
Overland, Number 96, 1984.
Southwest Review, spring, 1993.
Sydney Morning Herald, February 8, 1986.
Washington Post Book World, March 20, 1983.

*   *   *

WILKINSON, (John) Burke 1913-

PERSONAL: Born August 24, 1913, in New York, NY; son of Henry and Edith Lee (Burke) Wilkinson; married Frances Proctor, June 11, 1938; children: Eileen Burke, Charles Proctor. *Education:* Harvard University, B.A. (magna cum laude), 1935; Cambridge University, graduate study as Lionel Harvard scholar, 1935-36. *Politics:* Independent. *Religion:* Episcopalian.

ADDRESSES: Home—3210 Scott Pl. N.W., Washington, DC 20007. *Office*—1518 K St. N.W., Washington, DC 20005. *Agent*—Phyllis Jackson, International Famous Agency, 1301 Avenue of the Americas, New York, NY 10019.

CAREER: Lord & Thomas (advertising agency), New York City, copywriter, 1936-38; Reynal & Hitchcock (publishers), New York City, assistant advertising manager, 1938-39; Little, Brown & Co., Boston, MA, advertising manager, 1939-41; freelance writer, 1946-50, 1952-54; U.S. Department of State, Washington, DC, 1954-58, deputy assistant secretary for public affairs, 1956-58; Supreme Headquarters, Allied Powers, Europe (SHAPE), public affairs adviser, 1958-62; novelist and biographer, 1962—. Foreign Students Service Council, director; U.S. Lawn Tennis Hall of Fame, vice president and director, 1959-83. *Military service:* U.S. Naval Reserve, 1941-46, 1950-52; became commander; received Navy Commendation Ribbon for work in preparing for Normandy Invasion.

MEMBER: Authors Guild, National Press Club, International Lawn Tennis Club of United States (director), International Lawn Tennis Club of United Kingdom (honorary), International Lawn Tennis Club of France (honorary), Phi Beta Kappa, Tavern Club (Boston).

AWARDS, HONORS: Commendatore, Italian Order of Merit, for Italian sections of *By Sea and by Stealth;* selection as one of twelve best juvenile books of 1964, *New York Times Book Review,* for *The Helmet of Navarre.*

WRITINGS:

Proceed at Will (also see below), Little, Brown (Boston), 1948.
Run, Mongoose (also see below), Little, Brown, 1950.
Last Clear Chance (also see below), Little, Brown, 1954.
By Sea and by Stealth (nonfiction), Coward, 1956.

Night of the Short Knives (suspense novel), Scribner (New York City), 1964.

The Helmet of Navarre (juvenile; biography of Henri IV), Macmillan (New York City), 1965.

Cardinal in Armor: The Story of Richelieu and His Times (juvenile), Macmillan, 1966.

The Adventures of Geoffrey Mildmay: A Trilogy (contains *Proceed at Will, Run, Mongoose,* and *Last Clear Chance*), Luce (Bridgeport, CT), 1969.

(Editor) *Cry Spy!: True Stories of Twentieth Century Spies and Spy Catchers* (juvenile), Bradbury (Scarsdale, NY), 1969.

Young Louis XIV: The Early Years of the Sun King (juvenile), Macmillan, 1970.

Cry Sabotage! (juvenile; sequel to *Cry Spy!*), Bradbury, 1972.

Francis in All His Glory (juvenile; biography of Francis I), Farrar, Straus (New York City), 1972.

The Zeal of the Convert (biography of Anglo-Irish patriot Erskine Childers), Luce (Washington, DC), 1976.

Uncommon Clay: The Life and Works of Augustus Saint Gaudens, Harcourt (San Diego), 1985, published as *The Life and Works of Augustus Saint Gaudens,* Dover (New York City), 1992.

Contributor of articles and over two hundred reviews to *New York Times Book Review,* 1948-70, and *Christian Science Monitor,* 1970—.

ADAPTATIONS: English actor Michael York optioned *The Zeal of the Convert* as a possible follow-up to his 1979 starring role in Erskine Childers's *The Riddle of the Sands.*

SIDELIGHTS: Burke Wilkinson has published four French historical biographies for young people; the first of these biographies, *The Helmet of Navarre,* was selected by the *New York Times Book Review* as one of the twelve best juvenile books of 1964. John Ratte enumerated the virtues of *The Helmet of Navarre* and *Cardinal in Armor: The Story of Richelieu and His Times* for a *Book Week* review: "solid narrative structure, clarity and zest of language, sustained dramatic interest. But most distinctive are his confident grasp of the main lines of recent scholarly investigation, and his conviction that matters of social and cultural history, and even of historiographical fashion, can be thoroughly and unapologetically integrated into a narrative which remains engrossing and entertaining."

Wilkinson told *CA:* "Encouraged by the success of the first four biographies, which seemed to appeal to young and old, I decided in 1974 to do a life of Erskine Childers, the Anglo-Irish patriot and martyr who wrote *The Riddle of the Sands.* He was a World War I naval hero and later was executed during the troubles in Ireland for his total addiction to the cause of an Irish Republic. The research involved many trips to Ireland and the discovery of some untouched papers, concerning his trial and execution, in Dublin Castle. The biography, *The Zeal of the Convert,* came out rather quietly here in 1976. Colin Smythe Ltd. did a British-Irish edition two years later. The Irish reviews were rewarding."

BIOGRAPHICAL/CRITICAL SOURCES:

PERIODICALS

Book Week, February 26, 1967.
Christian Science Monitor, November 19, 1976.
Los Angeles Times Book Review, December 8, 1985, p. 12; December 22, 1985, p. 4.
New York Times, November 1, 1985.
New York Times Book Review, November 9, 1969; March 8, 1970; December 1, 1985, p. 23.
Washington Post, May 4, 1969; April 5, 1970.
Washington Post Book World, January 12, 1986, p. 11.

*   *   *

WILLIAMS, Heathcote 1941-

PERSONAL: Born November 15, 1941, in Helsby, Cheshire, England; son of Heathcote Williams.

ADDRESSES: Office—c/o Curtis Brown, 168 Regent St., London W1R 5TB, England. *Agent*—Judy Daish Associates, 83 Eastbourne Mews, London W2 6LQ, England.

CAREER: Writer. Associate editor, *Transatlantic Review,* London, England. Actor in films, including *The Tempest,* 1982, and *Little Dorrit,* 1987.

AWARDS, HONORS: Evening Standard Drama Award, and Obie Award, *Village Voice,* both 1970, for *AC/DC;* George Devine Award, 1970; John Whiting Award, 1971.

WRITINGS:

PLAYS

The Speakers, Hutchinson (London), 1964, Grove (New York City), 1967.

The Local Stigmatic (produced in Edinburgh, 1965), published in *Traverse Plays,* edited by Jim Haynes, Penguin, 1966, published in *AC/DC [and] The Local Stigmatic: Two Plays* (also see below), Viking (New York City), 1973.

AC/DC (produced on West End, 1970), published as *AC/DC [and] The Local Stigmatic: Two Plays,* Viking, 1973.

Remember the Truth Dentist, produced in London at Royal Court Theatre, 1974.

A Christmas Pantomime Play, produced in London, 1975.

Playpen, produced in London at Royal Court Theatre, 1977.

Hancock's Last Half Hour (produced in London, 1977), published in *Ten of the Best British Short Plays,* edited by Ed Berman, Interaction, 1977.

The Immortalist (produced in London, 1978), John Calder (London), 1978.

At It, produced in London, 1983.

SCREENPLAYS

(With others) *What the Dickens,* Channel Four, 1984.

The Local Stigmatic, Chal Productions, 1986.

Also author with Eddie Constantine and Vladimir Pucholt of *Malatesta,* 1969, *Crash,* 1980, *The Extraordinary Episodes of William Beckford, The Caliph of Fonthill,* BBC TV.

POETRY

Whale Nation, Harmony Books (New York City), 1988.

Falling for a Dolphin, Harmony Books, 1989.

Sacred Elephant, Harmony Books, 1989.

OTHER

Severe Joy, John Calder, 1979.

Autogeddon, Zweitausendeins, 1985, Arcade (New York City), 1991.

Contributor to periodicals, including *The Beast, CoEvolution Quarterly/Whole Earth Review, The Guardian,* and *New Statesman.*

SIDELIGHTS: A playwright and a poet, Heathcote Williams is known for presenting unusual or controversial material to his audiences. In the London *Times,* Adam Sweeting described Williams as an "anarchist playwright, squatter and pamphleteer with a penchant for nature's lost causes." Kimball King, writing in the *Dictionary of Literary Biography* in 1982, summed up the first phase of Williams' career by noting that the 1960s provided the perfect milieu for this writer's talents. "Williams's examination of Marshall McLuhan's theories relating to television and civilization, the effects of hallucinogenic drugs, and the panic over the sexual revolution tie his plays to a particular cultural era." In the late 1980s, Williams once again achieved notoriety and acclaim for a series of poetic reports about endangered species: *Whale Nation, Falling for a Dolphin,* and *Sacred Elephant.*

At a young age Williams became fascinated with the gathering of radicals and eccentrics who spoke from the soapbox at Speaker's Corner in London's Hyde Park. This interest led to his writing *The Speakers,* which captured the spirit of the corner by reporting in detail what four of these would-be orators said and did. He later turned the book into a play.

With his first play, *The Local Stigmatic,* Williams shocked audiences by using obscene language and extreme violence to depict the lives of two young men who partake of the seamier side of London, according to King. The two men take drugs, bet on greyhounds, and get kicked out of pubs for stirring up trouble. The central act of violence in this play is the senseless killing of a stranger met in a pub, and yet, in the final analysis, this savage beating was perhaps only a fantasy.

Williams's next play, the widely acclaimed *AC/DC,* used closed-circuit television sets on stage to dramatize the effect of sensory overload brought on by the media. The first act, "Alternating Current," takes place in a penny arcade, and the second act, "Direct Current," is set in a room plastered with glossy photographs of famous people and banked by television sets. "Williams's skillful use of monologues," explained King, "has become his dramatic trademark, with his monologuist serving as his spokesman, promulgating the same obsessive ideas: the need for men to search for cosmic energy, the possibility that genetic research can find ways of prolonging life, the value of sexual promiscuity."

In 1988, Williams published *Whale Nation,* a long poem accompanied by photographs and quotations about whales, which was a best-seller in England and has also been performed on stage. Peter Gorner, writing in *Tribune Books,* said that "*Whale Nation* offers an evocative tribute in pictures, drawings and words to the Leviathan; its ancient origins, songs and play, mating rituals and near-destruction by human greed." In the London *Times,* Robert Dawson Scott called the cumulative effect of Williams's catalogue of facts about whales mesmerizing. These facts, he noted, are "presented in a disarmingly matter-of-fact fashion. We learn of the whales' capacity for play without goals, for games of tag across great oceans, of their husbandry of plankton, the great factories of oxygen for the planet, their tender courtship, and much else besides."

In order to research and write *Falling for a Dolphin,* Williams spent six months in the freezing ocean off southwest Ireland and caught pneumonia. Sweeting wrote that like *Whale Nation, Sacred Elephant* "is a technical analysis of what makes these creatures extraordinary, as well as a study of their place in culture and mythology." Williams's animal poems stress people's kinship to members of the animal kingdom. Sweeting summed up their appeal this way: "Williams's line is simple. Even the humble chicken or the lowly sardine has a right to share the planet. If we deny it, we diminish our humanity."

BIOGRAPHICAL/CRITICAL SOURCES:

BOOKS

Dictionary of Literary Biography, Volume 13: *British Dramatists since World War II,* Gale (Detroit), 1982.

Findlater, Richard, editor, *At the Royal Court: Twenty-five Years of the English Stage Company,* Grove, 1981.

King, Kimball, *Twenty Modern British Playwrights, A Bibliography, 1956-1976,* Garland (New York City), 1977.

Taylor, John Russell, *The Second Wave: New British Drama for the Seventies,* Hill and Wang (New York City), 1971.

PERIODICALS

Cue, March 6, 1971.

Guardian, August 14, 1988; January 8, 1989; August 20, 1989.

Listener, August 18, 1988; August 3, 1989.

Los Angeles Times Book Review, September 11, 1988.

Nation, March 15, 1971.

New Statesman, August 5, 1988; September 13, 1991.

Newsweek, February 13, 1967.

New York Times Book Review, February 26, 1967.

Observer (London), July 31, 1988; November 20, 1988; August 6, 1989; April 8, 1990; April 15, 1990; July 22, 1990.

Plays and Players, January, 1971.

Spectator, August 6, 1988; December 7, 1991.

Times (London), May 24, 1988; June 2, 1989.

Times Literary Supplement, December 29, 1972.

Tribune Books, December 4, 1988.

Washington Post Book World, December 4, 1988.*

*   *   *

WILSON, Keith   1929-

PERSONAL: Born August 14, 1929, in Newport, Shropshire, England; immigrated to Canada, 1956, naturalized citizen, 1961; son of Maurice Bruce (a bank manager) and Winifred (Shaw) Wilson; married Dorothy Lee Robinson (a librarian), December 27, 1965; children: Eric, Ian. *Education:* University of Sheffield, B.A. (with honors), 1952, M.A., 1953, Diploma in Education, 1954; University of Manitoba, B.Ed., 1958, M.Ed., 1962; Michigan State University, Ph.D., 1967. *Avocational interests:* Walking ("when Winnipeg winters permit"); classical music; reading biographies, espionage thrillers and mysteries.

ADDRESSES:Home—571 Oak St., Winnipeg, Manitoba, Canada R3M 3P9.

CAREER: Teacher at high schools in Manitoba and New Zealand, 1954-55; Bridgewater Grammar School, En-

gland, head of history department, 1955-56; Melita Collegiate, Melita, Manitoba, assistant principal, 1956-58; Brandon College (now University), Brandon, Manitoba, librarian and instructor in Latin and the history of education, 1958-59; conducted research in London, England, 1959-60; University of Manitoba, Winnipeg, assistant professor, 1960-65, associate professor and chairman of department of educational foundations, 1966-70, professor of education, 1970-87, emeritus professor, 1988—, head of educational foundations department, 1970-74 and 1975-76, assistant academic dean, 1970-74, chairman of the faculty of education's undergraduate curriculum committee, graduate studies committee, and library committee. Consultant to the Canadian Studies Project committee of the Manitoba Department of Education, 1974-77.

AWARDS, HONORS: Named outstanding researcher of 1985 by the Winnipeg chapter of Phi Delta Kappa.

WRITINGS:

Life at Red River, 1830-1860, Ginn (Toronto), 1971.

(Editor with Elva Motheral) *The Poets' Record: Verses on Canadian History,* Peguis (Winnipeg), 1975.

Manitoba: Profile of a Province, Peguis, 1976.

(With J. B. Wyndels) *The Belgians in Manitoba,* Peguis, 1976.

George Simpson and the Hudson's Bay Company, Book Society of Canada (Agincourt), 1977.

(With A. S. Lussier) *Off and Running: Horse Racing in Manitoba,* Peguis, 1978.

Donald Smith and the Canadian Pacific Railway, Book Society of Canada, 1978.

Hugh John Macdonald, Peguis, 1980.

Fur Trade in Canada, Grolier (Toronto), 1980.

Charles William Gordon, Peguis, 1981.

Railways in Canada: The Iron Link, Grolier, 1982.

John A. Macdonald and Confederation, Book Society of Canada, 1983.

The Red River Settlement, Grolier, 1983.

Album of the Fur Trade in Canada, Grolier, 1983.

Charles Arkoll Boulton, Faculty of Education, University of Manitoba (Winnipeg), 1984.

(With A. D. Gregor) *The Development of Education in Manitoba,* Kendall/Hunt (Dubuque), 1984.

Amor de Cosmos, Faculty of Education, University of Manitoba, 1985.

Album of Western Settlement, Grolier, 1985.

Thomas Greenway, Faculty of Education, University of Manitoba, 1985.

Robert Terrill Rundle, Faculty of Education, University of Manitoba, 1986.

William Cyprian Pinkham, Faculty of Education, University of Manitoba, 1986.

Francis Evans Cornish, Faculty of Education, University of Manitoba, 1986.

William Carpenter Bompas, Faculty of Education, University of Manitoba, 1988.

William Nassau Kennedy, Faculty of Education, University of Manitoba, 1989.

John Alexander Douglas McCurdy, Faculty of Education, University of Manitoba, 1990.

John Pyne Pennefather, Faculty of Education, University of Manitoba, 1991.

William Orme McRobie, Faculty of Education, University of Manitoba, 1991.

Benjamin Wait, Faculty of Education, University of Manitoba, 1992.

Thomas Clarkson Scoble, Faculty of Education, University of Manitoba, 1993.

Also contributor to books, including *Options: Reform and Alternatives for Canadian Education,* edited by Terrence Morrison and Anthony Burton, Holt (Toronto), 1973. General coeditor of "Monographs in Education" series, Faculty of Education, University of Manitoba, 1979—. Contributor of articles to *Winnipeg Free Press, Horizon Canada,* and to professional journals, including *Manitoba Journal of Educational Research, History and Social Science Teacher,* and *Journal of the Midwest History of Education Society;* also editor of children's book series, including "We Built Canada," Book Society of Canada/Irwin Publishing, 1976—, "Manitobans in Profile," Peguis, 1980-81, and "Canadian Biographies," Faculty of Education, University of Manitoba, 1984—.

SIDELIGHTS: Keith Wilson commented to *CA:* "At the age of fourteen I read Arthur Bryant's biography of King Charles II, and I have been interested in history ever since—first medieval English history, then Canadian. I am especially fascinated by biography, and my main interest has been to write for schools and the general public and make them more aware of their own history. I have been delighted that several of my short biographies have elicited responses from their subjects' descendants who were tracing their family histories. As a result, I have had the pleasure not only of assisting these researchers but also of learning from them. Another pleasure has been to show the part that local people have played in both national and international events. Through biography, the world certainly has become much smaller."

*   *   *

WINN, Alison
   See WHARMBY, Margot

WOLNY, P.
  See JANECZKO, Paul B(ryan)

*   *   *

WOOLERY, George W(illiam)   1931-

PERSONAL: Born January 25, 1931, in Los Angeles, CA; son of George Calvin (an administrator of the Los Angeles Board of Education) and Leotia Pearl (a homemaker; maiden name, Sutton) Woolery. *Education:* University of Southern California, B.A., 1951; Annenberg School of Communications, Los Angeles, CA, M.A., 1976. *Religion:* Episcopalian. *Avocational interests:* Playing the organ, bagpipe and classical music, trivia games, contemporary western art, summers at Flathead Lake, MT, sailing and swimming.

ADDRESSES: Home—Orange, CA 92665. *Office*—P. O. Box 3804, Orange, CA 92665.

CAREER: Hancock Foundation, Los Angeles, CA, public relations assistant, 1949-51; KUSC-FM Radio, Los Angeles, publicity director, 1951; Playhouse Pictures, Hollywood, CA, director of public relations, 1956-63; public relations consultant, 1963-75; historian, writer, and consultant on film animation and American television, 1977—. Executive director of Association Analysts Ltd., 1975-80; member of board of directors of College Survey Bureau, Inc., 1975-81. Lecturer at Annenberg School of Communications, University of Southern California, and California State University, Fullerton, 1979—. Promoter of Columbia Pictures/United Productions of America Film Festivals, 1956; organizer of Screen Cartoonists Guild Film Festivals, 1959-61; co-organizer and publicity director of Hollywood Radio and Television Society International Broadcasting Awards, 1960-74. *Military service:* U.S. Air Force, intelligence officer for Far East Air Force and staff information services officer for Strategic Air Command, 1951-56. U.S. Air Force Reserve, 1956-59; became captain.

MEMBER: Hollywood Radio and Television Society (member of board of directors, 1962-64), Disabled American Veterans, Interfraternity Alumni Association of Southen California (president, 1969-70), General Alumni Association of the University of Southern California, Annenberg School Alumni Association, Trojan Club of Orange County, Tau Kappa Epsilon (member of grand council and board of directors, 1969-75), Alpha Epsilon Rho, Phi Kappa Phi, Blue Key, Masons, Elks.

AWARDS, HONORS: Grand Prytanis Award from Tau Kappa Epsilon, 1965, for producing film *Fraternity for Life;* Theater Library Association Award nomination for *Children's Television: The First Thirty-Five Years, 1946-*

1981 (part 1), 1984; University of California—Irving, Friends of the Library citation and book award for *Animated TV Specials,* 1990; Radiotelevisione Italiana citation for *Children's Television, Parts I and II,* 1991; named Teke Alumnus of the Year, Tau Kappa Epsilon Fraternity, 1993.

WRITINGS:

Children's Television: The First Thirty-five Years, 1946-1981, Scarecrow (Metuchen, NJ), Part 1: *Animated Cartoon Series,* 1983, Part 2: *Live, Film, and Tape Series,* 1985.
Animated Television Specials: The Complete Directory of the First Twenty-five Years, 1962-1987, Scarecrow, 1989.

Also author of "View from the Box," a television column in *Brentwood News,* 1959-61. Scriptwriter for television live action and animated films, including *The Wonderful World of Paul Bunyan,* 1967. Contributor to magazines, including *American Cinematographer, Film World, Woman's Day, Westways, Art Direction, Television/Radio Age, Animato, Animator,* and *TV E Ragazzi.*

WORK IN PROGRESS: Animated Feature Films: The Complete Directory Since Snow White, World's Greatest Cartoon Stars, The Complete Biographical Directory of Cartoon Stars, and *The Animated Cartoon Lover's Quiz Book;* television scripts.

SIDELIGHTS: George W. Woolery told *CA:* "Since television is a child's primer to the world around them and children's television their introduction to the most powerful communications medium of our time, I believe its history is of preeminent importance. Yet, despite the fact the subject continues to evoke powerful critical response from virtually every quarter, there has been scant documentation against which to judge the arguments leveled at its content. Because of this, I felt there was a need to review children' programming in depth, providing a chronological retrospective of the genre. Even though popular history is the last to be written and taken seriously, fact can best document what happened."

The author added: "My book *Animated Cartoon Series,* Part I of my history *Children's Television: The First Thirty-five Years, 1946-1981,* combined literate documentation and descriptive narrative in a readable style and elicited widespread comment." Woolery described himself as "an unabashed aficionado of animated cartoons, involved in a continuing study of the film genre, their creators, characters, and impact on visual communications and entertainment."

WOZNICKI, Andrew N(icholas) 1931-

PERSONAL: Born October 19, 1931, in Katowice, Poland; son of Stanislaw (a tailor) and Anna (Jednoszyniec) Woznicki. *Education:* Catholic University of Lublin, M.A., 1960; active participant in graduate seminars at Universite de Fribourg, l'Universite de Paris (Sorbonne) and Universite de Louvian, 1965-66; Pontifical Institute of Mediaeval Studies, Toronto, M.S.L., 1965; University of Toronto, Ph.D., 1967. *Avocational interests:* Mountain climbing, polar explorations, travel.

ADDRESSES: Office—Department of Philosophy, University of San Francisco, 2130 Fullerton St., San Francisco, CA 94117.

CAREER: Major Seminary, Poznan, Poland, assistant professor of philosophy, 1960-62; University of San Francisco, San Francisco, CA, assistant professor of philosophy, 1967-74, acting head of department, 1969-70, associate professor of philosophy, 1974-80, professor of philosophy, 1980—; Fleishhacker Professor, 1993. Chairperson, USF Celebration of International Copernicus Year, 1973, USF Bicentennial Committee, 1976, Fleishhacker Symposium, 1991. Reviewer of philosophical manuscripts for publication by University of California Press, Berkeley, CA, 1975; official observer on behalf of International Society for Metaphysics in philosophical dialogues with Marxists, 1976-79; co-organizer of international meeting of World Union of Catholic Philosophical Societies and Polish Catholic Philosophers under sponsorship of Cardinal Karol Wojtyla, Krakow, Poland, 1978; assistant mediator in establishing exchange program between Catholic University of America and Polish Catholic Philosophical Circles (headed by Cardinal Karol Wojtyla), 1978; Eastern European Committee at American Catholic Philosophical Association, active member, 1980-85; program chairperson, Annual of American Catholic Philosophical Association, 1986; Visiting scholar, College of St. Thomas, St. Paul, 1983; research fellow, Catholic University of Lublin (Poland), 1981-91; research fellow, Universidad de Piura (Peru), 1992; Universidad Catolica Andres Bello, Caracas (Venezuela), 1994. Producer of radio programs, "Polish Cultural Hour," 1969-71, and "Central European Hour," 1972-74, both for station KQED-FM, San Francisco. Member of board of directors, Association for Peace in Middle East, San Francisco, 1980-83.

MEMBER: International Society for Metaphysics, International Society for St. Thomas, International Society for Universalism, Polish Institute of Arts and Sciences, Association of American University Professors, American Catholic Philosophical Association, Polish American Congress.

AWARDS, HONORS: Michaelmass Scholarship, Pontifical Institute of Mediaevel Studies, Toronto, 1963-65;

Province of Ontario Fellowship, Toronto, 1965-67; KQED Public Radio Award, Bay Area Educational Television Association, San Francisco, 1970; American Council of Learned Societies travel grant, 1976; honorary member, Alpha Sigma Nu, 1980—; Distinguished Research Award, University of San Francisco, 1991.

WRITINGS:

Socio-Religious Principles of Migration Movements, Polish Research Institute in Canada (Toronto, Canada), 1968.

Teologia spoleczna ruchu mi gracyjnego, Towarzystwo Naukowe Polskiego Uniwersytetu Lubelskiego (Lublin, Poland), 1978.

A Christian Humanism: Karol Wojtyla's Existential Personalism, Mariel Publications (New Britain, CT), 1980.

Journey to the Unknown: Catholic Doctrine on Ethnicity and Migration, Golden Phoenix (San Francisco, CA), 1982.

The Dignity of Man as a Person: Essays on the Christian Humanism of His Holiness, John Paul II, Society of Christ Publications (San Francisco, CA), 1987.

Na skalach, przez lady i morza (title means "On the Rocks, Through the Land and Sea"), Glob (Szczecin, Poland), 1988.

W poszukiwaniu pierwotnego czowieka (title means "Searching for Primitive People"), Wysawnictwo Katolickiego Uniwersytetu Lubelskiego (Lublin, Poland), 1993.

EDITOR

(Executive editor) Stefan Mrozewski, *Triumphus Boni Super Malum pro Evangelio Sancti Luci* (folio album of 6 woodcuts on Gospel), University of San Francisco Press, 1976.

(Philosophical editor) Mieczyslaw Krapiec, *I—Man: An Outline of Philosophical Anthropology,* Mariel Publications, 1983, 2nd abridged edition, 1985.

(General editor and author of Volume 1) *Catholic Thoughts from Lublin,* Peter Lang (New York City), Volume 1: *Order and Being,* 1990, Volume 2: Albert Krapiec, *Metaphysics,* 1991, Volume 3: Zofia Zdybicka, *Philosophy and Religion,* 1991, Volume 4: Karol Wojtyla, *Person and Community,* 1993, Volume 5: Wojtyla, *Ethics and Morality,* 1995, Volume 6: Wojtyla, *Lectures from Lublin,* 1996, Volume 7: Krapiec, *Person and Natural Law,* 1993, Volume 8: Stefan Swiezawski, *St. Thomas Re-Interpreted,* 1994.

OTHER

(Film and text editor with Jules Zonn) *Poland: Christian Homeland of John Paul II* (short film), Don Bosco Films/Multimedia, 1979.

Author and editor of audio-visual program, "Copernicus: The Origins of Modern Science", consisting of 97 slides with narration, Department of Instructional Media, USF, San Francisco, 1973.

Also contributor of numerous articles to journals and periodicals in North America and Europe. Editor and publisher, *San Francisco Echo,* 1969-71; editor-in-chief of quarterly, *Migrant Echo,* 1972-81; member of editorial group, *Migration Today,* 1975; guest editor, special issue on "New Spirituality in California", *Dialogue and Humanism,* 1991; field editor, The Mellen Research University Press, San Francisco, 1991-92. Assistant director of International Center for Lublin (KUL) Translations, 1983—; editorial director, Catholic Scholars Press, San Francisco, 1993—.

WORK IN PROGRESS: Continuing philosophical inquiry into existential personalism which is theantropic in nature and diathetical in character.

SIDELIGHTS: Andrew N. Woznicki's *A Christian Humanism: Karol Wojtyla's Existential Personalism* was reprinted in Spanish-language translation as *Un Humanismo Cristiano: El personalismo existencial de Karol Wojtyla,* in Lima, Peru, by Vida y Espiritualidad, in 1988. Woznicki presented "Philosophical Forum", an audiovisual adaptation of *A Christian Humanism: Karol Wojtyla's Existential Personalism,* consisting of 8 half-hour segments, as well as participating in a panel discussion on the book *I-Man,* by Mieczyslaw Albert Krapiec, part of "The Human Person and the Personalizing Ego", a 1-semester, 3-unit course, both at The Family Consecration Institute, Kenosha, Wisconsin.

*   *   *

ZAWADSKY, Patience   1927-
(Patience Hartman; Becky Lynne, a pseudonym)

PERSONAL: Surname is pronounced "Za-wad-sky"; born March 30, 1927, in Trenton, NJ; daughter of William C. and Mabel (Leicht) Hartman; married John P. Zawadsky (chairman of philosophy department at University of Wisconsin—Stevens Point), September 8, 1948; children: John, Paul, Rebecca, Elizabeth. *Education:* Douglass College, Rutgers University, B.A., 1948. *Politics:* Democrat.

ADDRESSES: Home—3900 Jordan Ln., Stevens Point, WI 54481.

CAREER: WTNJ, Trenton, NJ, writer, producer, and actor for radio series, "Teen-Age," 1943-44; Harvard University, Cambridge, MA, research assistant and secretary,

1949-51; self-employed editor and researcher, Cambridge, 1951-54; Kilmer Job Corps, Edison, NJ, writing consultant, 1966; University of Wisconsin—Stevens Point, lecturer in English, 1967-72, 1980—. Freelance writer for magazines. President of Children's Art Program, Stevens Point, 1980-81.

MEMBER: International Society of Dramatists, Dramatists Guild, American Association of University Women, Wisconsin Children's Theatre Association (vice-president, 1979-80), Shoestring Children's Theater, Inc. (president, 1991-94), Phi Beta Kappa.

AWARDS, HONORS: Author's Award, New Jersey Association of English Teachers, 1968, for *The Mystery of the Old Musket;* plays selected for merit by Wisconsin Children's Theatre Association, 1976-78, 1980; musicals *Milady* and *The Dragon in the Closet* selected by the National Music Theater Network for inclusion in their catalogues, J. C. Penney Award, 1993.

WRITINGS:

(Co-author) *Datebook of Popularity,* Prentice-Hall (Englewood Cliffs, NJ), 1960.
(Co-author) *Are These the Wonderful Years?,* Abbey Press, 1965.
The Mystery of the Old Musket (juvenile), Putnam (New York City), 1968.
Welcome to Longfellow, Transition, 1969.
Stand-In for Murder, Transition, 1969.
Demon of Raven's Cliff, Belmont-Tower, 1971.
The Man in the Long Black Cape, Scholastic Book Services (New York City), 1972.
How Much Is That in Rubles?, University of Wisconsin—Stevens Point (Stevens Point, WI), 1973.
From Peacehaven to Peace Haven, University of Wisconsin—Stevens Point, 1974.
The Devil's Chapel, Perfection From Co., 1985.

MUSICALS

Heavens to Bacchus, first produced at Douglass College, Rutgers University, 1945.
Navy Blues, first produced at Douglass College, Rutgers University, 1946.
Rest upon the Wind, first produced at Douglass College, Rutgers University, 1948.
Hey, Mr. Time, first produced by University of Florida Sandspurs, 1949.
The Toys in the Haunted Castle (juvenile; first produced in 1977) I. E. Clark, 1979.

The Secret in the Toyroom (juvenile; produced nearly fifty times in Wisconsin), I. E. Clark, 1984.
Milady, showcased on Broadway by Roger Hendricks Simm, 1987.

Also author of juvenile musicals including *Goldilocks and the Three Bears: A Moral Musical,* 1973, *The Princess and the Frog,* 1974, *The Bunny with the Lopsided Ear,* 1975, *The Twelve Dancing Princesses,* 1976, *Kitty Cat Blue,* 1977, *The All New Jack,* 1979, *Captain Meano and the Magic Song,* 1979, *From Poland with Love,* 1980, *The New Cinderella,* 1981, *The Little Troll Who Wasn't,* 1981, *Sleeping Beauty,* 1982, *The Firebird (Chaybarashka),* 1982, *Beauty and the Beast,* 1984, *The Princess and the Pea,* 1984, *The Dragon in the Closet,* 1985, *The Backward Prince,* 1986, *The Birthday Suit,* 1987, *Cry Wolf,* 1988, *The Boy Who Stole the 4th of July,* 1989, *Puss and Boots,* 1991, *Hansel and Gretel,* 1993, *Rumplestiltskin,* 1994.

OTHER

Author of radio play, *Christmas Fantasy,* 1944; author of screenplays, *The Beach House,* and *The Second Coming of Charlie Beezle,* both 1987, both under option. Contributor, under pseudonym Becky Lynne, of approximately forty articles and stories to *Teen;* contributor to *Datebook* under name, Patience Hartman; also contributor to ten other teen and juvenile magazines. Contributor of verse to *Empire, Laugh Book, Life Today, Saturday Evening Post,* and *Soviet Life,* and of articles to numerous periodicals, including *Chatelaine, Coronet, Discovery, Family Digest, Ford Times, Ladies Home Journal,* and *Personal Romances.*

WORK IN PROGRESS: *The Ghost of Hemlock Island,* a book.

SIDELIGHTS: "After decades of writing books and articles for money," Patience Zawadsky once wrote, "I felt I had paid my dues. I returned to my first love, musical comedy—but this time, musical comedy for children. I found there is little or no money in children's theater. Those who act in it are looked down upon by other actors; those who write for it are looked down upon by other playwrights. But the children's laughter and applause, and sometimes tears, are more of a reward than any other form of writing has to offer. What a shame that America has so little regard, on television and in the theaters, for the enrichment of its children."